HUDSONs

# Historic Houses & Gardens

## Castles and Heritage Sites

**2007**

NT Cliveden, Buckinghamshire

**Foreword by Fiona Reynolds**

Twenty years ago Norman Hudson handed me a copy of the first ever *Hudson's*. We were both members of the National Trust's Thames and Chilterns regional committee at the time, and I greedily accepted the gift, delighted with how easy it made country house visiting.

What I hadn't appreciated was how indispensable *Hudson's* was to become. Indeed, it's incredible now to think that nothing like it existed before 1987, and interesting to speculate why.

What is truly remarkable is how the fortunes of country houses have changed. In the forties their future looked bleak, and many owners turned to the Trust as the only solution. By the eighties, however, the tide was turning. The Trust had shown how warmly people respond to the opportunity to visit, and our membership had soared to over 1 million. Changes in the tax regime made it easier for private owners to hold on to their family houses; while grants from public sources made public access a condition. Since then, therefore, many private owners have retained and opened their houses themselves, highly successfully and occasionally surprising even themselves in their enjoyment of visitors' pleasure.

Today country house visiting is even more popular, and as the Trust's membership tops 3.4 million there seems no end to the enjoyment it stimulates. And it is both deepening and widening. People are no longer grateful just for the chance to get inside the door; they are, as Alice would say, *'curiouser and curiouser'*; asking questions and seeking more than glimpses of what goes on behind the scenes and the processes of management and conservation. Their interest is also spilling out more and more into the garden, park and wider estate – they want to see how the whole estate worked then and works today; and in our increasingly crowded island the access this provides to the countryside is ever more precious.

*Hudson's* has both tracked and anticipated these trends. Each issue is fuller and more informative, and brings more delight to more people. May it long continue!

*Fiona Reynolds.*

Fiona Reynolds CBE
Director-General, National Trust

# HUDSON's

## From the editor

Public interest and support for the heritage including historic houses, castles and gardens has never been greater. A recent MORI poll showed more people interested in visiting heritage property than going to football matches.

Its appeal is multi-faceted and goes far deeper than an interest in architecture, design, works of art and an enjoyable day out in a beautiful place. It is as much the stories these places can tell. From them we can learn about ourselves, our past and derive inspiration. History and heritage is relevant to all our lives.

The 'History Matters – pass it on' campaign started last year by the National Trust, English Heritage, Historic Houses Association, Civic Trust, the Heritage Lottery Fund and others, is a positive celebration of history and coincides with the current debate about nationality and identity. A better understanding of our shared history helps us to solve the problems we face as a nation. If we are in touch with the past we can have confidence in the future. Government should be aware of this and should do more to ensure that this heritage survives.

Some of the best buildings in Britain are featured in this book. Nearly all of them have associated stories – sometimes many stories – of relevance to our lives today. There are links to all sections of our society. Many resident ethnic minorities have been surprised to discover how much of their past and heritage can also be discovered through these buildings. So go out and discover for yourselves. Look beyond the building. Find the story. Then you will be convinced that history really does matter. And when you are – pass it on.

*Norman Hudson*

Norman Hudson OBE

## Hudson's Historic Houses & Gardens

Publisher and Editor-in-Chief ...................................................................... Norman Hudson
Production Co-ordinator & Advertising .............................................................. Sue Wintersgill
Administration ...................................................................................... Jennie Carwithen
Senior Designer...................................................... Cameron Buxton (www.onecubed.co.uk)
Supporting Designer..........................................................................................Antony Gray
Maps............................................................................... Cameron Buxton/Antony Gray
Scanning & Pre-press ...................................................................... Spot-On Design & Print
Sales......................................................................................................... Fiona Rolt
Printed by ............................................................................................ Butler & Tanner
UK & European Distribution........................................................ Portfolio (tel 020 8997 9000)

**Published by:**
Norman Hudson & Company
High Wardington House
Upper Wardington
Banbury, Oxfordshire OX17 1SP

**Tel:** 01295 750750
**Fax:** 01295 750800
**E-mail:** enquiries@hudsonsguide.co.uk
**Web:** www.hudsonsguide.co.uk

**2007**

# Contents

**Foreword** — 2
by Fiona Reynolds CBE,
Director General of the National Trust

**Snowdrops** — 4-9

**"The Country House Explained"** – Trevor Yorke — 10-17

**Food for Thought** — 18-21
The National Trust

**Heelis** — 22
The National Trust's new offices

**Historic Chapels Trust** — 23

**Waddesdon Manor** — 24-29

**Historic Houses Association** — 30-31

**The Finest Manor Houses** — 32-35
Country Life

**Work & Play** — 36-37
Life on the Yorkshire
Country House Estate

**Bringing History to Life** — 38-41
English Heritage

**Churches Conservation Trust** — 42-43

**Scotland and the Sea** — 44-45
Historic Scotland

**Restoration House, Kent** — 46-49

**RHS Partner Gardens** — 50-52

**Broughton Castle, Oxfordshire** — 53

**Great Dixter, Sussex** — 54-57

**Saving the Overlooked** — 58-59
Landmark Trust

**Celebrating the Castles of the Welsh Princes** — 60-63
CADW

**20th Anniversary** — 64-65
Hudson's Historic Houses & Gardens

**England** — 66
Property listings in alphabetical
order, by County, within Regions

**Scotland** — 444
Property listings in alphabetical
order, by Region

**Wales** — 494
North Wales — 496
South Wales — 502

**Northern Ireland** — 512

**English Heritage Access Listings** — 519
Opening arrangements for properties
given repair grants by English Heritage

**Special Indexes** — 563

**Maps** — 595

**Main Index** — 617

Easton Walled Gardens, Lincolnshire

Even in February – the coldest, darkest and least hospitable month of the year – garden visiting is becoming increasingly popular. Snowdrops are the draw. Their sheer audacity to brave the conditions and the sight of their bright, wide, nodding heads in broad meandering drifts, gives them special appeal. They signal that Spring is around the corner and are spiritually uplifting.

# Snowdrops

The scientific name for snowdrop – Galanthus – means milk flower. There are hundreds of different kinds, some 19 wild species and over 600 distinct cultivars. Viewing them can, for some, become an obsession. Galanthophiles (the name for snowdrop addicts) will often stretch out on wet ground to examine the blooms in detail to try and identify which variety or hybrid it is. The green markings on the petals and the texture and colour of the strap-like foliage muddle even the most knowledgable.

In the wild, snowdrops are found from Spain to the Caucasus. Most are found in Turkey. During the Crimean War (1853-56) soldiers were so enchanted by snowdrops that they brought them back to Britain to plant in their gardens.

When is the best time to visit? In Britain the majority of snowdrops flower from mid-January to early March, although this varies according to the cultivars, weather and location. Although most of those gardens that open publicise specific Snowdrop Days or Weekends, it is prudent if travelling any distance, to check beforehand by telephone or on their website, that their white carpets are actually in flower. Many of the best gardens to visit are featured in Hudson's. While they appear in the relevant county section, some of the most notable and worth visiting specifically for snowdrops are highlighted on pages 8 and 9.

Pencarrow, Cornwall

Painswick Rococo Garden, Gloucestershire

Painswick Rococo Garden,
Gloucestershire

Welford Park, Berkshire

Easton Walled Gardens, Lincolnshire

# Where to find them

**Berkshire**
Welford Park, Welford, Newbury RG20 8HU
**Tel:** 01488 608691
www.welfordpark.co.uk

**Cambridgeshire**
Anglesey Abbey Gardens, Lode, Cambridge CB25 9EJ
**Tel:** 01223 810080
www.nationaltrust.org.uk/angleseyabbey

**Cornwall**
Lanhydrock, Bodmin PL30 5AD
**Tel:** 01208 265950
www.nationaltrust.org.uk

**Dorset**
Kingston Lacy, Wimborne Minster BH21 4EA
**Tel:** 01202 880402
www.nationaltrust.org.uk

**Gloucestershire**
Painswick Rococo Garden, Painswick GL6 6TH
**Tel:** 01452 813024
www.rococogarden.org.uk

Rodmarton Manor, Cirencester GL7 6PF
**Tel:** 01285 841253
www.rodmarton-manor.co.uk

**Hertfordshire**
Benington Lordship Gardens, Stevenage SG2 7BS
**Tel:** 01438 869668
www.beningtonlordship.co.uk

**Lincolnshire**
Easton Walled Gardens, Grantham NG33 5AP
**Tel:** 01476 530063
www.eastonwalledgardens.co.uk

**Nottinghamshire**
Hodsock Priory Garden, Worksop S81 0TY
**Tel:** 01909 591204
www.snowdrops.co.uk

Welford Park, Berkshire

...ton Walled Gardens, ...colnshire

Welford Park, Berkshire

© Royal Botanic Garden Edinburgh

**Norfolk**
Walsingham Abbey Grounds,
Little Walsingham NR22 6BP
**Tel:** 01328 82059

**Sussex**
Great Dixter House & Gardens,
Northiam, Rye TN31 6PH
**Tel:** 01797 252878
www.greatdixter.co.uk

**Wiltshire**
Lacock Abbey, Chippenham SN15 2LG
**Tel:** 01249 730459
www.nationaltrust.org.uk

Great Chalfield Manor, Melksham SN12 8NH
**Tel:** 01225 782239
www.nationaltrust.org.uk

**Yorkshire**
Fountains Abbey & Studley Royal,
Ripon HG4 3DY
**Tel:** 01765 608888
www.fountainsabbey.org.uk

**Northern Ireland**
Castle Ward, Downpatrick,
Co Down BT30 7LS
**Tel:** 028 4488 1204
www.ntni.org.uk

Mount Stewart, Newtownards,
Co Down BT22 2AD
**Tel:** 028 4278 8387
www.ntni.org.uk

**Websites can easily be accessed via the portal website www.hudsonsguide.co.uk**

# THE
# COUNTRY HOUSE EXPLAINED

### TREVOR YORKE

## *The Service Rooms*

(one of eleven chapters extracted from 'The Country House Explained')

It was one thing to excite guests with architectural magnificence and lavish decoration, but the country house owner would also have to satisfy their stomachs in order to leave them with a positive impression of his or her hospitality. Medieval lords are known to have spent anything from half to three-quarters of their entire income on food and drink, and even in Victorian mansions vast sums went on maintaining specialist staff and buildings in order to create an almost self sufficient conveyer belt of meals. The fittings and layout of most service rooms that survive in country houses today date from this latter period.

The status and mix of people who manned these rooms changed over the centuries and the strict hierarchical structure of discreet, black and white dressed servants who would never speak directly to their employer is a rather late development and far removed from earlier arrangements. As already mentioned, the medieval country house was not designed for external show but rather in line with internal function and its household was a community composed from some of almost the same status as the lord himself down to local peasants from the area he was visiting. They would eat and drink with him in his hall, fight with him in his battles and expect a certain degree of protection in return for their service.

The move by the owner of the house from the 14th and 15th century towards more privacy gradually broke up this communal household. By the 17th century there was less

emphasis on military skills for young aristocrats and they were no longer sent into a lord's service. At the same time, the lesser gentry set up their own households with a smaller number of staff. These servants were now of a lower, uniform status in a world of widening social division. They were expected to keep out of sight and were increasingly female although at first women were involved mainly in the preparation of food. It wasn't until the Victorian and Edwardian times that the structure of servants strictly adhering to rules and regulations, which we are familiar with from period dramas, reached its zenith. These servants now worked in a wider range of specialist rooms covering all aspects of food storage, production, cooking and serving, as well as the cleaning of utensils, linen and clothes. Fig 9.1 shows how these rooms could be arranged around a kitchen courtyard, with the arrows showing the route that food and drinks took from production to finally appearing as a meal in the dining room. This chapter looks at the role of these rooms and the features you may find in them today.

**Fig 9.16: Brodsworth Hall, South Yorkshire.**
*An old wooden octagonal game larder set in the shade of trees just behind the service block.*

Fig 9.1: *A possible arrangement of service rooms around a kitchen courtyard of a 19th century country house, with arrows showing the route that ingredients, food and then the finished meals took to reach the dining room. The Victorians were the first to plan the layout of the service rooms with a real understanding of ergonomics.*

*As you can see from the plan in fig 9.1, these service rooms were organised like a production line to take the raw ingredients produced on the estate in at one end and supply a wide variety of meals at the other. By the late 19th century though, food and domestic supplies were increasingly coming from a local wholesaler and hence there was less need for areas to process raw ingredients. After the First World War most country house owners found the huge kitchens and suites of service rooms far too large for their greatly reduced household, and thus converted a smaller room into a new compact kitchen. More recently the original service rooms have been used to house tea rooms and restaurants, but now with a growing interest in how the mechanics of a stately home operated behind the scenes they are being refitted and opened for view, allowing visitors to see the tasks the household staff had to perform and the conditions in which they worked.*

## ❧ THE KITCHEN

The most important room around which most of the other service rooms were arranged was the kitchen. Its internal arrangement and position within the confines of the country house were mainly dependent on a constant battle for fire safety and the removal of the odours produced in cooking. It was a smelly, noisy and dangerous place and not every lord therefore wanted it right next to his dining room!

The earliest kitchens in medieval houses, of which a few survive today, were constructed as separate buildings, timber framed or stone structures, often square in plan with pointed roofs and a louvre opening at the top. This was principally to reduce the fire risk to the main hall if the kitchen went up in flames, although there was the age old problem of the food becoming cold as it was transported. This was done in a procession, along a covered way, into the house via the kitchen passage, along the hall and into the lord's private chamber beyond. It is likely though that much of the cooking was still done on the hearth in the hall or on a stone or cobbled area outside the kitchen.

By the Tudor period the kitchen was usually part of the main house, typically one of the rooms around the courtyard or clustered with other service rooms on the other side of the passage from the hall. Walls might be lime-washed plaster, with floors of stone or brick covered in straw or rushes. Cooking would be done on spits in front of a hearth set in a wide fireplace, while there would be baking ovens with arched openings built into the wall and a charcoal stove on which delicate dishes like sauces could be simmered. There may have also been a separate boiling house with a large copper in which stews, stock and meats could be cooked. Although there would be a table for preparation other furniture was limited as there were fewer cooking utensils and implements to store.

Fig 9.3: *An imaginary 16th or 17th century kitchen. The fire (A) held within the metal firedogs cooks the food supported on cob irons (B) and the spit (C). A clockwork mechanism spins the wheel (D) at the end of the spit though at this date most were probably turned by young boys. The fat dripping from the joints is caught in a tray below (E), other food is heated in pots hanging from the rail (F) and spare spits are stored above the fire (G). In the corner is a baking oven (H) with the peels (flat wooden shovels) used to insert and extract the bread leaning against the wall.*
*An important feature which rarely survives today was the stove (I); most were replaced by ranges in the 19th century. Fuel was stored in the recesses below (J) while the gaps (K) above allowed air in to feed the charcoals held on round gridirons above (like a barbecue today). Pots were held above the heat on metal trivets or from a crane (L), allowing the food to be cooked gently. A feature of most country house kitchens which appears in all periods is the large central table (M) on which the meals were prepared.*

**Fig 9.4:** *A Victorian kitchen with a closed range built into an old fireplace on the left and an open range retained on the far wall, with a spit in front turned by a smoke jack (see fig 9.5). Note the tall ceiling with windows and vents, dressers storing the massive selection of pots, pans, utensils and moulds, and in the middle the table with slatted boards for the cooks to stand upon.*

In the 17th century the division that was opened up between the elite and service sides of the country house saw the kitchen increasingly moved into the basement to keep the servants out of sight of the family and guests above. Some had stone vaulted ceilings which helped reduce the fire risk, while ranges, raised iron firebaskets which held the increasingly available coal rather than wood, were popular. In later Palladian houses the kitchen was on the move again, this time out of the way in a separate pavilion or wing, although many of the male dominated areas like the butlers' and stewards' rooms and the precious beer and wine cellars remained below the main house. In the pavilion the kitchen could be two storeys high with other single storey service rooms around it and servants' bedchambers above them. Some still had large hearths, but most featured ever more elaborate roasting ranges with mechanical spits and hob areas to the sides. Walls were sometimes painted blue as the colour was believed to repel flies.

The huge kitchens with masses of strange and elaborate devices which feature on country house tours today are usually a product of the later 19th century. In the early Victorian period it became difficult to retain staff as many villagers went off to work in the factories, so the Lady of the House became increasingly involved in the running of the kitchen. This prompted them to improve the standards below stairs or, as in many new houses of the time, build better designed service courtyards to the rear or side of the house. New cast iron ranges, running water, better ventilation and numerous time-saving gadgets were designed to make life easier and more hygienic.

Walls were still lime-washed, white or yellow, while by the early 20th century glazed rectangular white wall tiles covered areas behind the sink and range and sometimes all around the room with virtually no grout between them, so as not to attract dirt and grease. The room was often tall with windows high up or in the ceiling with rods to open them and ventilate the room. Dressers stored the now massive assortment of utensils and pans, the *batterie de cuisine*. The Victorians loved jellies and numerous strangely shaped moulds for them are often found upon dressers. New technologies start to appear in the kitchen like steam cooking with boilers supplying pressurised steam to kettles containing food or to separate warming cupboards. The centre of the kitchen would be dominated by a large wooden table usually made of deal, for preparing the meals, with slatted boards around for servants to stand upon.

**Fig 9.5:** *A diagram of a roasting range and smoke jack. The sides (A) of the range were adjustable and controlled the size of the fire. The spit in front of it was turned by the smoke jack which was powered by smoke rising up the flue (B) spinning the fan (C) above, and turning the connecting shafts and gears (D) which, via a horizontal rod above the fireplace and a pulley at the end, spun the spit (E) below.*

**Fig 9.7:** *(A) shows a bain marie, a shallow sink filled with hot water designed to cook sauces or keep them warm. The copper pots within had tags on the handles to identify the contents. (B) is a warming trolley with metal lined doors and iron racks within. It was wheeled in front of the fire and the doors were opened, heating the crockery within and at the same time protecting the servants working behind from the immense heat that range emitted.*

① Fire lit within oven

② Charcoal removed

③ Bread sealed in oven

**Fig 9.10:** *The beehive shaped oven was first filled with wood, coal or a local fuel and heated up to temperature. The charcoal or ash was then removed and the bread put inside before the door was sealed for baking.*

# BAKEHOUSE

In larger houses separate rooms were provided for some types of cooking or preparation, and one was the bakehouse where bread, cakes and biscuits were produced. It was ideally in a separate block or at least as far from the house as possible so that the flour dust and oven odours would not penetrate indoors, and so deliveries of food stuffs and fuel were easier. The earliest ovens were brick beehive shaped with a small arched opening and may have taken a number of days to reach the correct temperature! (see fig 9.10). They proved better at baking, though, than the cast iron ovens that were introduced with 19th century ranges, and many survived into the 20th century. The room would also contain floorchests, benches with a trough for kneading the dough, and a sink for washing utensils like the peel, which was the wooden paddle used to lift the bread in and out of the oven.

# PASTRY

A few larger houses had a pastry which originally was where meat pies and pastries were made, although by the 19th century it was used for the production of confectionery, sweets and tarts. They are often found on the cool northern side of the service block, with the oven in an adjoining room. The room would contain shelves and pin racks, benches with marble tops for rolling pastry, and bins below for flour.

# STILLROOM

The name comes from its original role as where the 'stills' were kept for the production of perfumes, medicines, and cordial waters from flowers, herbs and spices. These usually separate stillhouses (due to the fire risk from the furnace used in the distilling process) were important in medieval and Tudor households and were usually run by the Lady of the House.

By the late 17th century the stillhouses were replaced by stillrooms in the new basements, and as the aristocracy would now never be seen there, the housekeeper took charge of the process and the still is often located next to her room. Polishes, waxes and soaps could be produced here but these, along with distilling, died out during the 18th century as it became easier to buy the products. By the 19th century the stillroom was mainly used for making preserves, pickles and desserts, for storing ingredients and for preparing light meals.

**Fig 9.11:** *The iron door and opening of a brick oven which could be found not only in a bakehouse but also in other rooms like the kitchen, scullery, pastry and stillroom.*

**Fig 9.12:** *A diagram showing 19th century distilling equipment which could be used to produce cordial waters. The furnace (A) heated up a mix of flower petals or herbs covered in liquid within the bottom of the still (B). The steam rose up and along the thin tube, condensing in the spiral within the worm tub (C) which was full of cold water.*

# ❀ DAIRY

The dairy was rare among the service rooms in that it could be lavishly designed and decorated. This was originally due to the involvement of the Lady of the House who up until the 19th century could often be found running its production of unadulterated milk, butter, cheese etc. Although it was usually part of the suite of service rooms it could also be a freestanding building or part of the estate farm, and to keep everything cool it would be preferable on the north or shaded side of the building.

By the late 18th century the Gentleman of the House became interested in all forms of agricultural improvement and the application of science to farm production, including the dairy. The rooms they built had white tiled walls, marble floors and shelves, and in some a central fountain to keep things cool in summer. Shallow pans and tubs were used to pour the milk into, skimmers then removed the cream that settled on top, and this was either stored in vases or churned in tubs to make butter and cheese. Heated pipes would help keep the temperature steady in winter at 50-55 degrees while there would usually be a cleaning area or a separate scullery next door for washing the utensils, pans and dishes. In some houses the dairy work was carried out in the scullery with the dairy itself just being used for storage, a role it played increasingly as during the 19th century more products were bought in from outside rather than made on site.

**Fig 9.13:** *A view showing how hygienic and yet ornamental some dairies had become by the late 18th and early 19th century. The fountain in the middle emitted a spray to help keep the temperature down, while skimming dishes, pans, vases and churns stand upon the low stone table around the perimeter.*

**Fig 9.14:** *One of the types of churn to be found in a dairy for turning cream into butter. A plunge churn had a vertical barrel with a plunger on top, while an up and over churn had the barrel spun on the opposite axis to the one shown here.*

**Fig 9.9:** *A 19th century knife polisher. Abrasive powder was poured in through a hole at the top, the knives were inserted into the slots next to it and when the handle was turned it rotated felt pads which with the powder polished the blades within.*

**Fig 9.15:** *A diagram of the basic brewing process. (1) Water is heated to just below boiling point in a large copper with a fire beneath the tank and a doorway below this from which to remove the ashes. (2) The water is poured into the mash tun and malt added to produce wort which is poured into the underback below. This mashing process would usually be performed a second and third time, producing progressively weaker brews. (3) The wort is pumped up into either the original copper or as in this example into a second one and is boiled up with hops. (4) The final mixture is run off into cooling trays and then into casks for storage.*

## BREWHOUSE

Another important production room was the brewhouse, for in the days before safe drinking water, beer was drunk at mealtimes including breakfast. The building or room was tall in order to accommodate the coppers, and was usually distinguished by louvre openings high up for ventilation. It would be positioned to provide as easy access as possible for the deliveries of malt and hops, and to the trap door and chute which led to the beer cellar under the house.

The beer produced was varied in strength depending on its intended use. Small or table beer was made from the weaker wort produced in the final third mash and was consumed as we would drink water and pop today, by everyone in the house. A medium strength brew called ale was made from the second mash while a strong ale or malt liquor was produced by adding extra malt into the first mash. This latter brew was usually for special occasions like the birth of an heir, when the ale was bottled and then stored until his coming of age celebrations when it was drunk! Brewing was best done in the colder months of the year from October to March, which was a problem as the weakest beer might only last a few weeks.

## SCULLERY

The word comes from the French *escuele*, meaning dish, which in turn was derived from the Latin word *scutella*, a salver, and hence is the room used for washing up plates and dishes. In the country house it was more versatile and a lot of the messy tasks like peeling, chopping and washing vegetables, preparing meat for roasting and gutting fish were done here. It is usually found next door to the kitchen.

In the typical 19th century scullery there would be sinks, preferably under the window so that those washing up had the best light in which to make sure there was no dirt left on the crockery, cutlery or utensils. In country houses you can find some shallow stone sinks, or wooden ones with exposed planks of teak or lined with lead, but usually by this date earthenware or china sinks were used with wooden draining boards to the sides and plate racks above. In the days before centrally heated water was available, a separate boiler or one built into a range was essential, while the latter could also be used for some cooking tasks. There would have also been a pump for cold water until a tank in a tower in the house or nearby enabled it to be supplied under pressure of gravity to taps emerging out of the wall above the sink.

## BUTTERY AND PANTRY

It was usual in medieval houses to have a buttery and pantry side by side at the opposite end of the hall from the dais and solar. The word buttery, which is derived from the same source as 'butt' or 'bottle', was where the casks of beer and other drinks were stored while they were being dispensed; long term storage would usually be in the cellar or outbuilding. The word pantry is derived from the Latin for bread, *panis*, and was originally where the grain and bread were kept. Both rooms were close to the hall so that these staple parts of the meal could be easily distributed.

The pantry was the responsibility of the pantler while the buttery was the responsibility of the butler! Although the latter's name survived the buttery itself faded from use, its role being taken over by the butler's pantry. This is not to be confused with the pantry which still appears in later houses, being used for the storage of dairy products and some cooked dishes as well as bread, although in Victorian houses it was often called the dry larder.

## LARDERS

The larder (from the Latin *lardum* meaning bacon) was originally an outbuilding where the raw meat was salted and stored. In the later country houses it could exist alongside the pantry, though increasingly by the 19th century there would be a number of larders for specific uses. The wet larder was the one where pieces of meat were prepared and stored (it was called a 'butchery' if whole carcases were brought in), the dry larder had a similar role to the pantry, while fish and bacon larders are self-explanatory. Game larders were often a separate round or octagonal structure where deer and birds were hung up, but by the late 19th century when shoots could bag thousands of game birds at a time, larger rooms were required, some with a primitive form of refrigeration.

The larder had to be cool and is often found on the north of the building, or if not it usually has overhanging eaves or plants shading its walls, while wet cloth might be thrown over the roof in the hottest of weather. Windows could be part or fully covered in gauze to permit a through draught but keep out insects. Around the whitewashed or tiled walls there would be slate, brick or marble shelves with hooks in the roof for hanging meat and perhaps an ice box for fish and cool dishes.

## CELLARS

The cellar was principally where wine and beer was stored, and due to their high value and the cool temperatures they required the best place for them was below the main house. They were convenient here for the owner of the house, and for the butler who could keep a close eye on the contents of the cellar and then store the drinks ready for serving in his pantry which was usually close by.

Cellars usually have a low vaulted ceiling (made up of brick or stone arches) and pillars, which helped take the load from the rooms above.

There may have been separate cellars for beer, with the barrels (originally with willow hoops, but later with iron ones) containing the servants' weak beer and the owner's stronger ale. The huge quantities of coal which 18th and 19th century houses consumed means that there may have been a large store for this in the basement as well. Trap doors are to be found on the outside giving access to the cellar for deliveries, including those from the brewhouse.

## SERVANTS' HALL

As the owner distanced himself from his household and they in turn became wage earning servants of a general, lower status, separate servants' halls were provided. This meant that the staff could eat their meals among the service rooms, out of sight of the lord and his guests and not cluttering up his splendid new marble and stone entrance hall! Sometimes called the common hall, these rooms were furnished with a long table and in some a little beer barrel on wheels which could run up and down it for the dispensing of drinks. The walls might have portraits as at Erddig, near Wrexham, where the Yorke family commissioned paintings of ten of their staff.

## UPPER SERVANT ROOMS

Although the senior servants would dine with the other staff, they would then retire to one of their private rooms. The butler's pantry was usually in the main house, close to the dining room so he could take charge of the serving of food, but also with convenient access to the cellars and main entrance. Within it could be found the containers of drink, table linen, crockery, cutlery and glasses which were in use, and perhaps a brick safe in which the more precious pieces would be stored. There would also be space, materials and often two sinks for cleaning these items and polishing the silver. As it served additionally as his office and living room, a table, chairs, wash-basin, fireplace and a bed could be found

crammed into what was often only a twelve by twelve foot room!

It was only really in the later 17th century that women started to take a significant role within the country house and the housekeeper first appears. Her accommodation was usually positioned near or between the service rooms where she could keep an eye on the staff, and with a door leading directly into the stillroom. The bulk of the crockery could be stored here, shelves later with glass fronts lined the walls or a separate china store would be close by, and she was also responsible for repairing and storing the table linen that was not in use at the time. Again as it was an office and sitting room there would be similar contents to those in the butler's pantry. Most houses would have had a steward who was responsible for the running of the estate, and he would usually have been provided with his own room, while the cook would generally use the housekeeper's room for office work.

## LAUNDRY

The early laundry or washroom usually had a large copper for boiling clothes and a pump to bring in water, while the washing in some cases was simply draped over hedges and lawns outside to dry. Later houses would often have two rooms. Firstly, a wet laundry where the washing took place, still with boilers providing hot water and a vent in the roof to let the steam out. The dry laundry was where the airing, ironing and folding was done and it would contain drying racks suspended from the ceiling, a range or stove on which the irons could be heated and a large table which would have been covered with sheeting when in use. The centre of the room was often dominated by a box mangle, a large flat-bed trough which when filled with stone pressed down onto a bed below and flattened partially dry linen in between (it was not used to wring water from freshly washed fabric).

This extract is one of 11 chapters from Trevor Yorke's book, *The Country House Explained* – using his own drawings, diagrams and photographs he explains in an easy-to-understand manner, the features to be seen on the tour of a country house.

*"Readers of this book will enjoy an extra dimension to their country house visits. It will add immeasurably to almost everyone's understanding and pleasure"* – Norman Hudson.

*The Country House Explained* is available from all good bookshops, price £9.95, ISBN 1 85306 793 8.

Other books in the same series include *The Victorian House Explained, The 1930s House Explained, Tracing the History of Villages, English Abbeys Explained, English Castles Explained* and *The Edwardian House Explained*.

Published by Countryside Books, 3 Catherine Road, Newbury, Berkshire (www.countrysidebooks.co.uk).

## THE NATIONAL TRUST

When you think of a day out with the National Trust, historic houses and beautifully tended gardens in stunning locations probably spring to mind. However you will experience much more than a feast for the eyes when you visit, as there is a tantalising treat for the taste buds on offer as well; right round the clock from lunchtime to take home treats.

# Food for thought

By Anthony Westover

### Out to lunch: fresh fruit and vegetables straight to your plate

The National Trust looks after more than 25 working and ornamental kitchen gardens in England, Wales and Northern Ireland. Here you can see regional and traditional varieties of fruit and vegetables grown as they would have been in the gardens' heyday when they would have supplied the house with fresh produce throughout the year.

Growing your own food, whether in your back garden or an allotment, is once again all the rage and we have all become more aware of the distance much of our food has travelled before it reaches us. An increasing number of National Trust restaurants are now supplied with the tastiest seasonal ingredients direct from their own kitchen gardens. The food on the plate has travelled metres rather than miles, guaranteeing its freshness and preserving its home grown taste.

Why not visit one of these glorious kitchen gardens and see the mouth-watering array of crops grown, find inspiration for your own garden and taste the produce for yourself over lunch in the restaurant?

Barrington Court in Somerset has a one acre kitchen garden that was established in the 1920s and has been in continuous use ever since. The garden produces a diverse crop, including rhubarb, mini sweetcorn and leeks. In Devon, Knightshayes Court has a unique Victorian walled kitchen garden that produces fruit, vegetables and cut flowers, while Wimpole Hall's walled garden in Cambridgeshire produces a wide range of vegetables including an amazing 60 varieties of tomato, and hosts seasonal events such as the Tomato Festival in August and Squash Week in September.

©NTPL/Paul Harris

Hughenden Manor, near High Wycombe, is the former home of Queen Victoria's favourite Prime Minister, Benjamin Disraeli, and has recently opened its Victorian kitchen garden to the public for the first time. Visitors to Clumber Park in Nottinghamshire will be able to see the progress of Clumber's developing garden as it is extended to occupy all of the four and a half acres of the original Kitchen Garden, where they currently grow more than 70 varieties of fruit and vegetables. Clumber's walled garden has one of the longest glasshouses owned by the National Trust. Not to be outdone Llanerchaeron in mid Wales has not one, but two restored walled gardens, dating back to the 18th century, which produce organic home-grown fruit, vegetables and herbs.

Several National Trust kitchen gardens are working to highlight seasonal produce, as part of its 'From Plot to Plate' project, which takes visitors on a journey of discovery, showing the importance of local and seasonal food and providing practical advice with quick and easy steps to produce tasty and healthy dishes. The programme of events enables children and adults to find out more about the history and distinctiveness of British food and the choices that we make when deciding what we eat. A great opportunity for young and old to learn more about our food, its production and preparation, while having plenty of hands-on fun along the way.

**Time for tea: great places to stop**

If you're out and about with family and friends, a stop at a Trust attraction is the perfect place to pause. Most have relaxing tearooms where you can enjoy a fine selection of home made cakes that are sure to satisfy. In fact 95% are baked on the premises, using local ingredients.

Why not try one of the nation's favourite cakes, as revealed by a recent survey conducted by the Trust. Maybe not surprisingly, chocolate came top of the list; it seems we just can't get

enough of it with 1 in 4 preferring it to any other cake. Carrot cake came in a very close second with good old-fashioned fruit cake hanging on to third place, fighting off competition from the more glamorous trio of coffee and walnut, Victoria sponge and lemon drizzle.

Luckily, National Trust tearooms offer a selection of cakes to cater for all tastes, so everyone's favourite is sure to be amongst them. There are hundreds of locations to choose from as well, but the following will certainly give you something to get your teeth into!

In the South West try Dyrham Park, a beautiful country house set in extensive parkland, which is currently undergoing restoration to return the gardens to their 18th-century formal design. Situated between Bath and Bristol, you would never believe you were just off the M4. Also easily accessible is Stourhead in Wiltshire, an outstanding example of the English landscape style. This splendid garden with classical temples set around the central lake provides a series of vistas, which change as the visitor moves around the paths and through the magnificent mature woodland with its extensive collection of exotic trees.

Further west, Lanhydrock is a real treat. One of the most captivating and complete late 19th-century houses in England, it's full of period atmosphere. There is also an adventure playground, with wobbly bridge, scramble nets and animal sculptures to keep the kids entertained.

If you're travelling in the south-east, and the M25 is getting you down, take a break at Chartwell instead. Bought by Sir Winston Churchill for its magnificent views over the Weald of Kent to Sussex, this was his home from 1924 until the end of his life. The rooms and gardens remain much as they were when he lived here, with personal mementoes strongly evoking his career and wide-ranging interests. If it's glamour and glitz you're after, Cliveden is well worth a visit. This spectacular estate overlooking the River Thames has a series of gardens, each with its own character, featuring topiary, statuary, water gardens, a formal parterre, Octagon temple, informal vistas, woodland and riverside walks. A tea stop here is certainly in a different league from the motorway services.

To the East, why not stretch your legs in the beautiful gardens of Anglesey Abbey, not far from the M11, which are home to one of the finest collections of historic statuary in the country. Inside the house, there is also the unique collection of the last occupant which includes paintings, furniture and silver plus one of the Trust's largest collections of clocks!

In the Midlands, Hanbury Hall is in a tranquil setting off the busy M5. This fascinating house has many features including an orangery, ice house, pavilions and even a working mushroom house. There is also a recreated 18th-century crown bowling green available to play on. Baddesley Clinton, a picturesque medieval moated manor house, is a great place to stop just outside Birmingham. Have tea in the Barn restaurant and then browse the secondhand bookshop – you never know what you might find. Hardwick Hall – just off the M1, is another gem. Like a huge glass lantern, Hardwick dominates the surrounding area; a magnificent statement of the wealth and authority of its original Elizabethan owner.

Also fascinating is Cragside, where the house re-opens in 2007, having been closed for restoration last year. There is also plenty to see in the dramatic garden that surrounds it, including one of the largest rock gardens in Europe, a vast woodland garden, as well as lakeside walks, an adventure play area and labyrinth. If travelling north of the border, make this your last stop before Scotland.

### Take away: farm shops and markets

Many National Trust houses and gardens are now holding regular farmers' and food markets. From the 'Garden of England' in Kent to the great estates in Wiltshire, the Trust is working to promote local and seasonal food to its visitors.

At Sissinghurst in Kent there is a regular market selling local organic meat, cider and seasonal fruit and vegetables. Stourhead's market usually has up to 20 stalls with produce available including bison and elk meat, game, speciality cheeses and organic bread. Stourhead also has its own farm shop selling produce from the farmers, jam makers, bakers and brewers who work on the land. Also in Wiltshire, Lacock Abbey has a monthly market with the majority of meat, vegetables, preserves and cakes coming from within a ten mile radius. Dunster Castle and Montacute House, both in Somerset, also have markets that are jam-packed with delicious food from the surrounding area, providing a delight for all the senses.

So wherever you find yourself around the country you can sample great food in fantastic surroundings, see how it's grown and even get to take some of it home.

For all National Trust Property opening times, entry prices and travel directions visit www.nationaltrust.org.uk, call 0870 458 4000 or see the entries in this guide.

©NTPL/Stephen Robson

©NTPL/David Levenson

©NTPL/Paul Harris

©NTPL/Ian Shaw

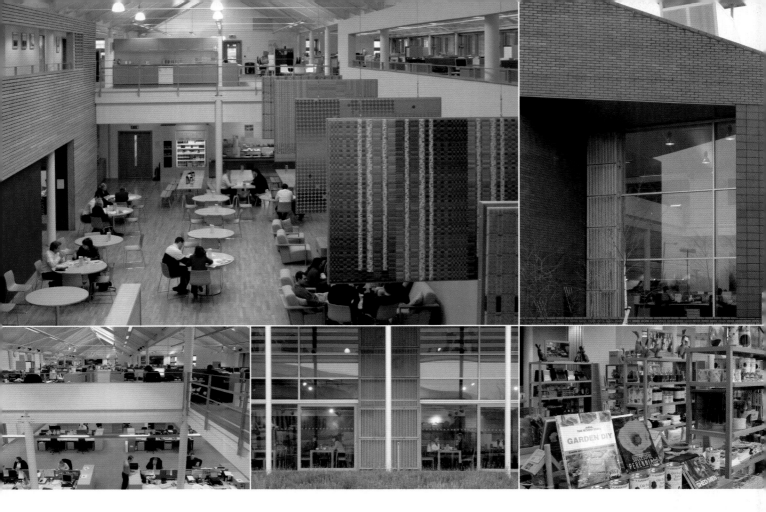

# Heelis
## The new offices of The National Trust

The National Trust's new central office building is named after one of Britain's best loved authors and one of the Trust's most famous benefactors – Heelis was the married name of Beatrix Potter.

On the site of a Victorian engineering foundry in Swindon, this striking and bold new building has been built to a very environmentally friendly sustainable design, being naturally lit and ventilated for most of the year. Timber from National Trust woodlands and wool from Herdwick sheep, grazed on NT farmlands, help to make it a unique environment and the 1,554 solar panels, mounted on the roof, generate electricity either for immediate use in the building or to be sold back to the National Grid.

The light and airy café serves traditional dishes made with fresh, local produce; in the summer dine 'al fresco' on the Colonnade, surrounded by Silver Birch, Lavender and Alliums. The café is also available as a venue for functions. The shop sells a wide range of gifts and National Trust products. The shop and café are open from 10am-4pm, Monday to Saturday and from 11am-4pm on Sundays and Bank Holidays.

There is a 'behind-the-scenes' tour of the office every Friday at 12.30pm (these tours are free but must be booked in advance on 01793 817400).

The National Trust, Heelis, Kemble Drive, Swindon SN2 2NA
**www.nationaltrust-org.uk**

## THE NATIONAL TRUST

# The Historic Chapels Trust
## Preserving places of worship in England

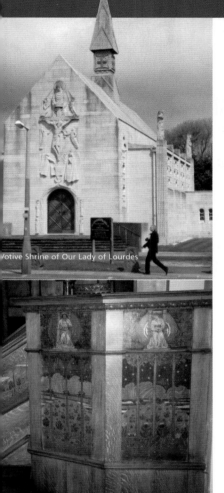

Votive Shrine of Our Lady of Lourdes

Pulpit, Wallasey Memorial Unitarian Church

St George's German Lutheran Church.

Salem Chapel

The Hisitoric Chapels Trust was established to take into ownership redundant chapels and other places of worship in England which are of outstanding architectural and historic interest – securing for public benefit their preservation, repair and regeneration.

Below are 14 of the chapels in the care of HCT which you can visit on application to the keyholder. Farfield and Coanwood are, experimentally, left open.

**Biddlestone RC Chapel,** Northumberland .....01665 574420, 01669 630270, 01669 620230

**Coanwood Friends Meeting House,** Northumberland ................................ 01434 321316

**Cote Baptist Chapel,** Oxfordshire ................................................................ 01993 850421

**Farfield Friends Meeting House,** West Yorkshire .......................................... 01756 710587

**The Dissenters' Chapel,** Kensal Green Cemetery, London ............................... 020 7602 0173

**Penrose Methodist Chapel,** St Ervan, Cornwall ......................................... 01841 540737

**Salem Chapel,** East Budleigh, Devon ............................................................. 01395 445236

**Shrine of Our Lady of Lourdes,** Blackpool, Lancashire .................................. 01253 302373

**St Benet's Chapel,** Netherton, Merseyside ..................................................... 0151 520 2600

**St George's German Lutheran Church,** Tower Hamlets, London ................. 020 7481 0533

**Todmorden Unitarian Church,** West Yorkshire ............................................... 01706 813255

**Wainsgate Baptist Church,** West Yorkshire .................................................... 01422 843315

**Wallasey Unitarian Church,** Merseyside ....................................................... 0151 639 9707

**Walpole Old Chapel,** Suffolk ......................................................................... 01986 798308

**For further information please visit our website: www.hct.org.uk or telephone: 020 7481 0533**

Historic Chapels Trust, St George's German Lutheran Church, 55 Alie Street, London E1 8EB
**Tel:** 020 7481 0533    **Fax:** 020 7488 3756    **E-mail:** chapels@hct.org.uk    **Web:** www.hct.org.uk
Company No. 2778395  Registered Charity No. 1017321

Cote Chapel

Biddlestone Chapel

2007 is an important year for Waddesdon Manor, marking as it does the 50th anniversary of the bequest of the house to the National Trust. Now as then, visitors are amazed at what confronts them on their first sight of the house. It stands on a hill, cloaked in trees which hide all but the prickling of towers and turrets.

By Pippa Shirley

# Waddesdon Manor

Approaching through open parkland, the drive begins to climb, with glimpses of an ornate building to one side and increasingly extensive views over the surrounding landscape on the other. Suddenly, an elaborate fountain heralds an arrival, but the vision on rounding the corner, an extravagant Renaissance château, is possibly one of the last things one would expect to find on a hill in Buckinghamshire.

The theatricality of this experience, with gardens to match, is thanks to the vision of its creator, Baron Ferdinand de Rothschild. Born in 1839 into the Viennese branch of the famous European banking family, he was the great grandson of Mayer Amschel Rothschild, who launched the family from roots in the Frankfurt ghetto to become the most influential financiers in the world by the end of the 19th century. Alongside their financial and economic operations, the family are perhaps most renowned as builders and collectors of spectacular proportions, and here Ferdinand followed very much in the family tradition. His father, Anselm, had instilled a love of collecting in him from a young age (later in life he

described how handling his father's precious collection as a small child had sent "*a thrill of delight through my small frame*"), and Waddesdon was partly conceived as a suitable setting to display his treasures. It was also, though, intended to entertain his friends and family in a setting of almost unimaginable luxury.

Ferdinand bought the Waddesdon estate from the Duke of Marlborough in 1874. The site had many advantages – it was close to London, and close to several of his relations who also had country houses in Buckinghamshire, but it retained a pleasing rural tranquillity, in Ferdinand's words, "*it had a bracing and salubrious air, pleasant scenery, excellent hunting and was untainted by factories and villadom*". He then had to set about transforming his acquisition, since there was no great house on the estate and the hill on which the Manor now stands was entirely bare. The summit had to be levelled, the drives excavated, water piped in from Aylesbury and the extensive grounds laid out and landscaped with mature trees, entailing the dismantling of telegraph wires to move them. The village was substantially rebuilt, an ornamental dairy added, and later an Aviary and Menagerie included. All in all, it was a Herculean task, but not at all unusual for someone of Ferdinand's background. Benjamin Disraeli is said to have commented after a visit to the site that the Almighty would have accomplished the creation of the world in less than seven days had he had the assistance of the Rothschilds.

Alongside this, the house itself was taking shape. Ferdinand employed a French architect, Gabriel-Hippolyte Destailleur, to realise his vision of a French Renaissance château, the style he had chosen as most suitable for his purpose, and a French landscape architect, Elie Lainé, to lay out the grounds. Destailleur achieved a remarkable synthesis of architectural quotations in the design of the Manor, drawing on sources as diverse as the châteaux of Blois and Chenonceaux and the Louvre. The interiors were equally historicising, but this time creating an 18th-century setting to set off the collection. Rooms were clad in 18th-century French carved panels salvaged from Parisian hotels and silks for walls, curtains and upholstery were specially woven in Lyon and Paris to 18th-century patterns. In Ferdinand's own words, his intention was to "*revive the decoration of the 18th-century in its purity, reconstructing…rooms out of old material, reproducing them as they had been during the reigns of the Louis*".

These glamorous interiors created an appropriate back-drop, not only for the superb collection, but for the fashionable guests who came to the Baron's famous house parties. The Manor was built for these "Saturday to Monday" parties, as they were known, and guests were either accommodated in the main bedroom suites or, if unaccompanied males, in the Bachelors' Wing, specifically designed by Destailleur for the purpose, and equipped with Smoking and Billiard Rooms. In 1889, Ferdinand's increasing social activity led him to extend the Manor, adding a Morning Room on the ground floor with bedrooms above. The house benefited from the latest technology and comforts, including electric light, draught-excluding windows and a lift.

The Visitors' Book reveals the range of Ferdinand's social circle. Apart from his family, a key figure was the Prince of Wales, the future Edward VII, whose passion for racing, hunting and shooting brought him into frequent contact with the Rothschilds, several of whom were his friends. His many visits to Waddesdon were also an opportunity to make political contacts. Ferdinand, who was elected Liberal MP for Aylesbury

in 1885, had a circle that included William Gladstone, Arthur Balfour and Lord Randolf Churchill. Literary and artistic figures included the novelist Henry James and the composer Arthur Sullivan of operatic fame. Royal visitors came to Waddesdon too, most famously Queen Victoria, who, intrigued by what she had heard about Ferdinand, invited herself to lunch in 1890. The Shah of Persia, who stayed during a state visit in 1889, was entertained by a magician, an 18th-century musical automaton in the form of an elephant, and Ferdinand's constant companion, his poodle Poupon, who performed tricks in one of the galleries.

No expense was spared to cater to guests' every need during these weekends. Ferdinand employed a French chef, Arthur Chategner, who had cooked for the Tsar of Russia. The wines were of the highest quality and fruit, vegetables and flowers were brought up from the huge range of glass houses. Visitors were encouraged to explore the immaculate gardens, the vividly planted Parterre, and admire the exotic birds in the Aviary. They viewed the estate and were taken to the ornamental Dairy to taste the milk. A highlight of any visit, however, was the opportunity to view new additions to the famous collection, "gimcracks" as their host disparagingly called them, which he delighted to show to his friends.

It is the fact that this collection remains largely intact at Waddesdon that makes it one of the only houses open to the public where the modern visitor gets a sense of how the Rothschilds lived and furnished their houses at the height of their influence. The combination of French furniture, textiles and porcelain with English 18th-century portraits, set off by damask-lined walls and delicate *boiseries* remains the most vivid expression of "*le goût Rothschild*", as it became known. In a family famed for its collectors, Ferdinand stands out as one of the most important. His first major purchase, bought before he had come into his inheritance, was a Sèvres porcelain ship vase (see p.25), supremely rare and valuable even at the time – so valuable, in fact, that he had to hide the cost from his uncles whom he feared would be appalled at his extravagance. The vase, made in 1767, is one of only ten surviving in the world. Two further examples are also at Waddesdon. This determination to buy only the best is evident throughout the collection, from the writing desk made for

**Above:** Accession No. 2409. Jean Latz; Long case clock Circa 1750. Waddesdon, The Rothschild Collection (The National Trust)

© The National Trust, Waddesdon Manor / Hugo Maertens

**Right:** The Aviary and its garden, painted and gilded in 2005 in a scheme based on 18th century German examples.

© The National Trust, Waddesdon Manor / Hugh Palmer

Queen Marie-Antoinette (the £6,000 that Ferdinand paid for it was commented on by the press) to the Savonnerie carpets made for the Long Gallery at the Louvre and the collection of 17th and 18th century rare books with their sumptuous bindings.

However, although Ferdinand was the inspiration behind the Manor, the house as the visitor sees it today is not the result of his vision alone. On his death in 1898, his sister, Alice de Rothschild inherited the house and the estate. She was already to hand, having bought the adjoining estate at the point that Ferdinand bought Waddesdon, so that she could act as his companion and hostess. After his death, she became fiercely protective of her brother's legacy, maintaining the house as he had done and introducing draconian measures to protect the contents. "Miss Alice's Rules" which required blinds to shut out the light when the house was not in use, covers to protect from dust and all handling to be done with both hands and in silence are still in essence in force today, and were later adopted as the basis for conservation by the National Trust as a whole. However, Alice was not merely a custodian. She was a formidable collector in her own right, and some of the most important furniture and porcelain in the house are her additions. She was also responsible for the collection of 16th and 17th century arms and armour, replacing that of her brother which had been bequeathed to the British Museum on his death. Another of her passions was the garden, both at Waddesdon and at her villa at Grasse in the South of France.

Alice, like Ferdinand, died childless in 1922, so had the task of identifying a suitable heir within the Rothschild family. Her choice fell upon her great-nephew James de Rothschild, from the French branch of the family, and his young English wife, Dorothy. James (unusually for a Rothschild), was not at all interested in collecting. His passions were racing and golf, and visitors to Waddesdon during these years were drawn mainly from these worlds, the family circle, and James's political contemporaries (he was a long-serving Liberal MP). Despite this, it was during his lifetime that the third great influx of objects took place. James's father, Baron Edmond, was, like Ferdinand, another passionate collector and after his death in 1934, a third of his collection arrived at Waddesdon including more superb Sèvres porcelain and over 2,000 18th-century European drawings. These had scarcely been assimilated into the collections when everything had to be packed up again on the outbreak of World War II. Although the Manor survived the War unscathed (it was the only time that children lived in the house, when it became a home for young evacuees from Croydon), the post-war world was a very different place for the owners of great historic houses. James had to decide on Waddesdon's future. He and Dorothy had no children, and so James began negotiations with the National Trust.

As a late 19th-century creation, there was keen debate within the Trust about whether to accept the Manor. The first assessment described it as "*undeniably hideous, but there is an awful impressiveness about its symmetry, the quality of the masonry and the finish of every detail…the Grounds are all concentrated on the hill and are very beautiful*". Happily, the quality of the collection proved decisive, combined with James's generous offer of an endowment to cover running costs, so when James died in 1957, the house, the immediate grounds and the majority of the contents passed to the National Trust. However, family involvement did not cease there. Dorothy remained at Waddesdon, overseeing every detail of the transfer and chairing the first Management Committee and, under her leadership, the house was readied for opening to the public. This involved difficult decisions, as the main rooms, designed to accommodate house parties of no more than 40, were prepared to receive thousands of visitors per year. Much of the 19th-century upholstered furniture was removed at this stage. In 1984, she instigated a major review of the fabric of the building, but before this could get properly off the ground, in 1988 Dorothy died.

The Red Drawing Room – a powerful expression of "le goût Rothschild"
© The National Trust, Waddesdon Manor / John Bigelow Taylor

The Blue Dining Room at Christmas
© The National Trust, Waddesdon Manor / Mike Fear

Stephen Cox; b.1946; Terra degli Etruschi
© 1999 The National Trust, Waddesdon Manor / Mike Fear

The enormous enterprise of what became known as the Centenary Restoration was carried out by her cousin and successor, Jacob, 4th Lord Rothschild, and involved a complete overhaul of the building both inside and out. Over four years, the collection was removed, floorboards taken up, a complete rewiring undertaken, new heating, security and fire detection systems installed, and areas of the house that had been made over to flats for staff in the early National Trust years reinstated as part of the public route. Nor was this renaissance limited to the house. During Lord Rothschild's tenure, the garden has been restored to its former high Victorian glory, and new features added. The Parterre and Aviary gardens are once more resplendent with carpet bedding, changed twice a year. The Dairy water garden has been restored and 19th-century paths have been uncovered and reinstated.

Today, the creative spirit, very much in the tradition of Baron Ferdinand, is as strong as ever. The restored Aviary glows in blue and gold, inspired by French and German Rococo examples. Contemporary sculpture has been added to the historic collection in the Gardens. New features have been created, most recently an installation of three huge vases set around a pool at Frog Fountain Steps. A Children's Play Area and Adventure Trail are in development. It also seems appropriate that a house famed for its culinary and entertaining flair should boast two restaurants and a full programme of public and private events which run all year round, including Christmas. It is also a place where the Rothschilds' equally famous connections with the world of great wines can be explored and enjoyed.

Inside the house, the Collection is alive and growing. Spectacular recent acquisitions include a silver dinner service made in the 1770s for King George III, a gilt-bronze table centrepiece, 24 feet long, given by Louis XVIII to his Sicilian ambassador, a spectacular modern chandelier made of broken ceramic plates and cutlery held frozen in mid-air on steel wires by the German designer Ingo Maurer commissioned specially for the house in 2004 and most recently a state portrait of Louis XVI in a magnificent contemporary frame, given to the French ambassador to London in 1783 which goes on display for the first time in 2007. This year is also the 50th anniversary of the bequest of the Manor to the National Trust, and in celebration of James's generosity, two new exhibitions explore his bequest.

Towards the end of his life, Baron Ferdinand fervently wished that the "*day be yet be distant when weeds will spread over the gardens, the terraces crumble into dust, the pictures and cabinets cross the Channel or the Atlantic and the melancholy cry of the night-jar sound from the deserted towers*". Happily, his fears have proved unfounded, and thanks to the care of four generations of the Rothschild family and the National Trust, the Manor continues to surprise and delight its many visitors.

*Pippa Shirley - Head of Collections*
*Waddesdon Manor, Waddesdon, Nr Aylesbury, Bucks HP18 0JH*

**visit hudsons guide online**

The Morning Room
© The National Trust, Waddesdon Manor / Andrew Peppard

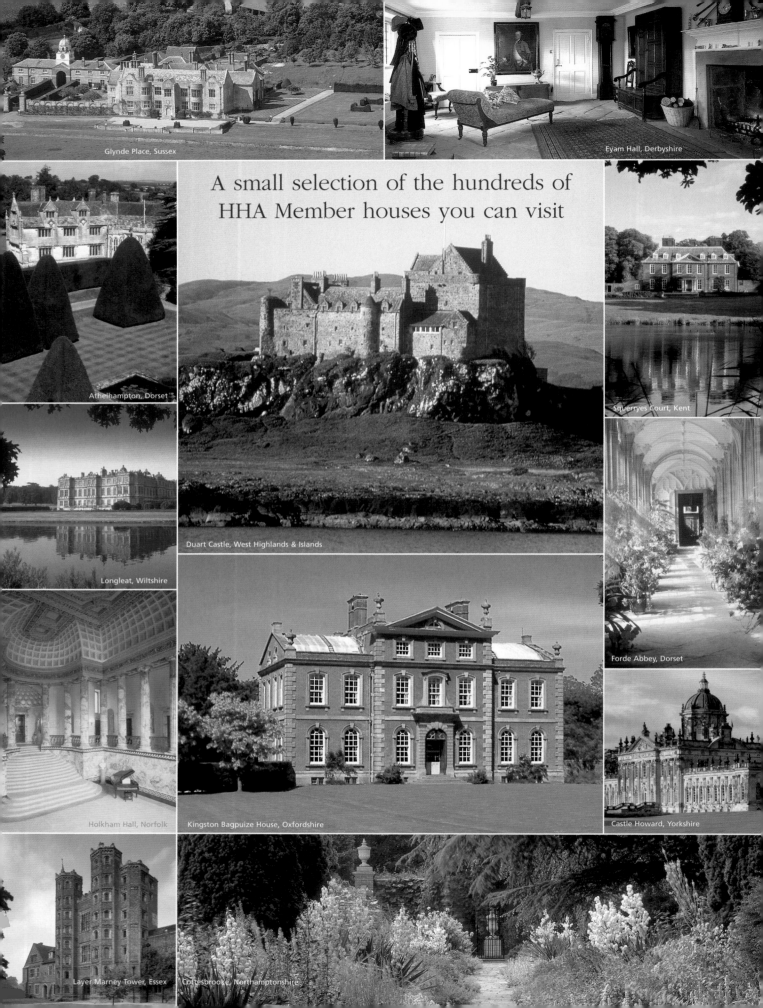

Glynde Place, Sussex

Eyam Hall, Derbyshire

A small selection of the hundreds of HHA Member houses you can visit

Athelhampton, Dorset

Squerryes Court, Kent

Longleat, Wiltshire

Duart Castle, West Highlands & Islands

Forde Abbey, Dorset

Holkham Hall, Norfolk

Kingston Bagpuize House, Oxfordshire

Castle Howard, Yorkshire

Layer Marney Tower, Essex

Cottesbrooke, Northamptonshire

# HISTORIC HOUSES ASSOCIATION

# Become a Friend of the HHA and visit nearly 300 privately owned houses and gardens FREE

Cottesbrooke, Northamptonshire

From just £35 for an annual membership, we offer free access to more houses than in the ownership of the National Trust and English Heritage combined.

**Friends Membership benefits include:-**
- Free entry to nearly 300 houses, parks and gardens
- 4 magazines a year
- Opportunities to join tours to see houses not usually open to the public

There is a fascinating diversity of properties to visit free with a Friends of the HHA card – from the great treasure houses such as Burghley and Woburn Abbey to intimate manor houses, such as Athelhampton and Owlpen. What makes these places so special is their individuality and the fact that they are generally still lived in – often by the same family that has owned them through centuries of British history. As well as the beautiful gardens which surround the houses, there are over 60 additional wonderful gardens to visit.

The subscription rate remains outstanding value for money. Individual Friend: £35. Double Friends living at the same address: £56 (each additional Friend living at same address, £17 – only available to holders of a Double Membership). If you wish to become a Friend of the HHA, then you can join, using your credit/debit card by calling 01462 896688 or simply fill in the form below.

You can also join online at **www.hha.org.uk**

Membership: Single £35, Double £56, £17 additional Friend at same address. Members of NADFAS, CLA and The Art Fund are offered special rates of £32 Individual and £53 Double (at same address).

---

## FRIENDS APPLICATION FORM    HHHG/07

PLEASE USE BLOCK CAPITALS   *DELETE AS APPROPRIATE

MR/MRS/MS or MR & MRS*       INITIALS ...............

SURNAME ........................................

ADDRESS ........................................

..................................................

..................................................

POST CODE ......................................

ADDITIONAL FRIENDS AT SAME ADDRESS

..................................................

I/We* are members of NADFAS / CLA / The Art Fund (please circle name of organisation to which you belong) our membership number is: ...............

☐ I/We* enclose remittance of £ ......... payable to the Historic Houses Association.

☐ I/We* have completed the direct debit adjacent.

*Please return to:*
**HHA, Friends Membership Dept, Heritage House, PO Box 21, Baldock, Hertfordshire SG7 5SH.**

Telephone: 01462 896688

---

## INSTRUCTION TO YOUR BANK TO PAY DIRECT DEBITS

Please complete Parts 1 to 5 to instruct your Bank to make payments directly from your account. Then return the form to: **Historic Houses Association, Membership Dept, Heritage House, PO Box 21, Baldock, Hertfordshire, SG7 5SH.**

**1.** Name and full postal address of your Bank

..................................................

..................................................

..................................................

Your Bank may decline to accept instructions to pay Direct Debits from some types of accounts.

**2.** Account holder name

..................................................

**3.** Account number  ☐☐☐☐☐☐☐☐

**4.** Bank sort code  ☐☐ ☐☐ ☐☐

Originator's identification No.  [9][3][0][5][8][7]

Originator's reference  [BACS OUTPUT]
(office use only)

 **DIRECT Debit**   Completion of the form above ensures that your subscription will be paid automatically on the date that it is due. You may cancel the order at any time. The Association guarantees that it will only use this authority to deduct annually from your account an amount equal to the annual subscription then current for your class of membership.

**5.** Your instructions to the Bank and signature.

■ I instruct you to pay Direct Debits for my annual subscription from my account at the request of the Historic Houses Association.

■ The amounts are variable and may be debited on various dates.

■ I understand that the Historic Houses Association may change the amounts and dates only after giving me prior notice of not less than 10 days.

■ Please cancel all previous Standing Order and Direct Debiting instructions in favour of the Historic Houses Association.

■ I will inform the Bank in writing if I wish to cancel this instruction.

■ I understand that if any Direct Debit is paid which breaks the terms of the instruction, the Bank will make a refund.

Signature(s)

..................................................

..................................................

Date: ...........................................

---

PHOTOCOPIES OF THIS FORM ARE ACCEPTABLE                    IF COMPLETING THE DIRECT DEBIT FORM, YOU MUST ALSO COMPLETE THE APPLICATION FORM.

# The Finest
# Manor House

Last year *Country Life*, the magazine founded by Edward Hudson in 1897, introduced an Award to be presented to the Nation's Finest Manor House. From its outset *Country Life* published remarkable photographs which made the weekly 'Country Homes & Gardens' articles a central feature. For over a century these have educated and influenced taste and provided inspiration for many of the changes and new developments in historic houses and gardens visited today.

*The Winner of the Nation's Finest Manor House – Mapperton, Dorset*

The aim of the Award was to celebrate a particular type of house – the manor house, and those who care for them. What constitutes a manor house? We may all have some idea in our mind but how, for the purpose of this Award, was it to be defined?

Historically a manor is a unit of land over which someone holding the manorial title – the Lord of the Manor – enjoyed right of service over tenants and the right to hold a Manorial Court. Dwelling houses of Lords of the Manor between the 12th and 17th centuries have some broadly familiar characteristics, of which for example, a Great Hall is one. But for the purpose of this Award it was decided to broaden the definition to include houses which were not technically manor houses but which were close in status and character, for example, the principal house in a village which might have been a large hunting lodge or farmhouse.

*Country Life* readers were invited to submit nominations for their favourite manor houses. They were asked to have regard to their historic and architectural merits, their settings, and to give consideration to those which played a role in their community, for example by hosting garden openings or fêtes. It was decided that the shortlist would include only houses that were still occupied. Houses kept solely as museums would not qualify, although this would not exclude houses owned, say by the National Trust, occupied by tenants.

Over 400 nominations were received. A shortlist of 16 was selected by a panel that included Nicholas Cooper, formerly of the Royal Commission on Historic Monuments and author of *Houses of the Gentry 1480-1680*; and Jeremy Musson, *Country Life's* Architectural Editor and author of *The English Manor House*. From this shortlist six would be selected to go forward to a national judging panel made up of Candida Lycett-Green (author of *The Perfect English Country House*), Lord Camoys (the owner of Stonor), Alexander Chancellor (columnist and former Editor of *The Spectator*), Clive Aslet (*Country Life's* Editor-at-Large) and Crispin Holborow (Head of the Country House Department at Savills, sponsors of the Award).

*Left, below and right: The winning manor house – Mapperton, Dorset*
Images © Gareth Rubin

As it happens, all the 16 houses shortlisted, bar one, feature in *Hudson's Historic Houses & Gardens*. The only exception was Brympton d'Evercy in Somerset, which used to be in *Hudson's* some years ago but is now no longer open to the public although is used for fund-raising events for the village church.

## The shortlist:

| | | |
|---|---|---|
| **Athelhampton** | Dorset | p 225 |
| **Brympton d'Evercy** | Somerset | – |
| **Cadhay** | Devon | p 214 |
| **Cothay** | Somerset | p 250 |
| **Doddington Hall** | Lincolnshire | p 320 |
| **Dorney Court** | Buckinghamshire | p 98 |
| **Eyam Hall** | Derbyshire | p 310 |
| **Godolphin** | Cornwall | p 203 |
| **Great Chalfield Manor** | Wiltshire | p 262 |
| **Kentwell Hall** | Suffolk | p 297 |
| **Levens Hall** | Cumbria | p 412 |
| **Mapperton** | Dorset | p 231 |
| **Markenfield Hall** | Yorkshire | p 391 |
| **Owlpen Manor** | Gloucestershire | p 242 |
| **Shipton Hall** | Shropshire | p 348 |
| **Tissington Hall** | Derbyshire | p 312 |

The judges found it extremely difficult to choose a winner from so distinguished a list, so much so that they asked to confer a Highly Commended status to the close runner-up – Dorney Court, Berkshire. The panel had great admiration for the way Mrs Palmer keeps the flag flying for a highly atmospheric and traditional manor house, home to the same family since the 1640s.

## The six finalists were:

| | |
|---|---|
| **Dorney Court** | Buckinghamshire |
| **Great Chalfield Manor** | Wiltshire |
| **Mapperton** | Dorset |
| **Markenfield Hall** | Yorkshire |
| **Owlpen Manor** | Gloucestershire |
| **Tissington Hall** | Derbyshire |

The winner, Mapperton owned by the Earl and Countess of Sandwich, is one of the oldest manor houses in Dorset, mentioned in the Domesday Book. It was largely built in the 1540s, incorporating an older house, with the main front being remodelled in the 17th century. One side was given a new contemporary look in the 18th century and in the early 20th century some of the interiors were amended to be more redolent of Tudor style.

What particularly appealed to the judges was the way in which the house related to the landscape and its very special atmosphere. It has the feel of a comfortable time-warp that has changed over time but is still comfortably occupied, as indeed it is, in the 21st century. In 1962 Arthur Oswald wrote, "*Mapperton has an extraordinary charm and beauty of a kind that drawing-board architecture is incapable of achieving*".

## Dorney Court (Highly Commended)

Hugely characterful, 15th and 16th century house with a magnificent Great Hall, family portraits, fine furniture, needlework and panelled rooms. Its location close to Windsor has made it a popular film location. Home of Mrs Peregrine Palmer.

## Great Chalfield Manor

Completed in 1480, the Manor and Gardens were restored early last century. The house, with its ancient church, moat and gatehouse, comprise one of the finest complete examples of a manorial complex. The house was restored (c1905-1911) by Major Fuller whose family (now Floyd) still live here although care of the house has now been handed over to the National Trust.

## Markenfield Hall

This little altered 14th century moated manor house, owned by the Grantley family since the 17th century, is a well-restored and well-loved home with outstanding rooms. The home of Lady Deidre Curteis, mother of the present Lord Grantley.

## Owlpen Manor

Set in a remote woodland valley setting, beside church and barns, this part-Tudor, part-Jacobean house with 16th and 17th century formal terraced gardens also has strong Cotswolds Arts and Crafts associations. Acquired by the Mander family in the 1970s, it remains a comfortable family home, but also with a restaurant in the old cider house.

## Tissington Hall

The home of Sir Richard FitzHerbert whose family have been here for over 500 years. The house stands as part of a group in a village in the Peak District National Park and is a popular wedding venue.

Will Pryce/Country Life Picture Library

© Skyscan

## Burton Constable

The Constable family have held lands in Yorkshire since the early 12th century and have been Lords of the East Riding coastal plain of Holderness since 1560. Their history is interwoven with the history of the region, touching the lives of local people through tenancy, employment, patronage and charity. The story of the Burton Constable estate is a fascinating one, encompassing tales of Gardeners and Groomsmen, Huntsmen and Hermits, 'Whippers-in' and Whales! It was the Burton Constable sperm whale that provided inspiration for Herman Melville's *Moby Dick*. The skeleton of this 58ft 'monster' will form a dramatic display in the Great Hall at Burton Constable – a must see for all visitors!

A trail guide to the estates of Burton Constable, Burton Agnes and Sledmere will be available FREE at each of these East Yorkshire houses.

## Temple Newsam

For 500 years Temple Newsam has been the centre of a thriving estate community. The great Tudor-Jacobean house, the birthplace of Lord Darnley, husband of Mary Queen of Scots, has supported the livelihood of countless domestic servants, estate employees, tenants, workers in the mines and forests and on the farms. Likewise much of the wealth of the owners (the Ingram family and their descendants) was largely based on the income from the 5,000 acre estate. The exhibition will explore this mutual dependency, looking at the lives of those involved as well as the changing appearance of a landscape which has now almost entirely vanished.

In 2007 the Yorkshire country houses of Brodsworth, Burton Agnes, Burton Constable, Harewood, Sledmere and Temple Newsam will be involved in a major project focussing on the country house estate. Visitors will be encouraged to consider not only the house and its family but also the wider estate and its community. Besides various exhibitions and visitor events, all the participating houses will offer an estate trail guide – free of charge – inviting visitors to explore the locality beyond the house, taking in parkland, farms, villages, churches, inns etc – each of which has an historic link to the country house.

# Work & Play
## Life on the Yorkshire Country House Estate

### Brodsworth Hall

Brodsworth Hall near Doncaster in South Yorkshire is a remarkable Victorian country house built in the 1860s. Its energetic owner, Charles Thellusson, also remodelled its gardens and parkland and invested in his estate, building many new farms and cottages. He and his family enjoyed the country life, particularly shooting, and this provided a livelihood for many workers in the gardens, woods and on the land. The exhibition looks at life on the estate for both the family and the workers from the 1860s to the present day. The period saw many changes, including the development of the Brodsworth Colliery and the mining village of Woodlands on the edge of the estate. The story of the estate and its people is brought to life in a new exhibition which includes an enormous 1890s map of the estate, many wonderful photographs and reminiscences which can be listened to. A leaflet guides visitors on a trail through the gardens and house, noting views of the estate, objects of interest and riveting stories, and there is also a lively programme of events, including talks, tours and costumed interpreters.

ENGLISH HERITAGE

*Days out worth talking about.*

With over 400 castles, monuments, gardens and historic houses, many brought to life by evocative and entertaining events, English Heritage offers you many wonderful days out. In 2007 there are new properties and exhibitions, along with action-packed events and activities, giving you more to see and do than ever before.

# Bringing History to Life

### Events in historic settings

There is no better way to find out about history than when it's brought to life before your eyes in the very places that helped shape it.

Events take place at English Heritage properties throughout the year. From big battle spectaculars and medieval jousts to theatre and family events, you're sure to find an English Heritage event of interest to you.

This year our events programme offers even more hands-on fun for families and children, including a children's history festival at Dover Castle and a Battle Abbey Boot Camp!

### FESTIVAL OF HISTORY: The event of the summer

If you visit only one event this summer, make this the one! Now in its fifth year, English Heritage's annual spectacular, The Festival of History, is the biggest of its kind in Europe. Over 1,000 top historical performers bring you 2,000 years of history, from the Roman Empire to the Swinging Sixties, for one

exciting weekend only on 11 and 12 August 2007. For further information and tickets, visit www.festivalofhistory.org.uk.

### 1066, re-told in a brand new exhibition

Discover what life was really like in England just before the conquest and find out about the realities of this, the bloodiest of battles, in a new state-of-the-art exhibition: "1066: The Battle for England". This exciting new interactive display is at the heart of a new purpose built visitor experience as of February 2007. A visit to the 1066 Battle of Hastings Abbey and Battlefield provides a full day out for all the family, whatever the weather.

You can also watch the most famous of battles unfold before your very eyes, as the Battle of Hastings is replayed on 13th and 14th October 2007.

### Open for the first time since the 1930s

There is now even more to see at Kenilworth Castle in the Midlands. Visit the Earl of Leicester's Gatehouse, open to the public only recently for the first time in decades. Explore a new exhibition charting the castle's 900-year history, including the royal love affair between the Earl of Leicester and Queen Elizabeth I, and browse the superb, award-winning, new shop or relax and unwind in the refurbished tea room.

### The Picture House exhibition

From May to September 2007, Belsay Hall Castle and Gardens, Northumberland hosts the Picture House Exhibition: a show guaranteed to fascinate and captivate visitors as 14 well-established artists use film, art, design and installation to interpret Belsay's beautiful setting.

### Unlocking doors

In Yorkshire, two new properties will be open to the public: Thornton Abbey and Gatehouse and St Peter's Church. The enormous gatehouse of Thornton Abbey is the finest surviving example of its kind and demonstrates the prosperity of the wealthiest Augustinian monasteries.

Whereas, the architectural and archaeological importance of St Peter's Church, with its history spanning a millennium, makes a fascinating visit. A new exhibition, Bones Alive!, opens in May and will reveal groundbreaking insights into our ancestors, from excavations dating back over 900 years.

### Rievaulx's birthday drinks

Finally, join us in celebrating the 875th anniversary of Rievaulx Abbey, to be marked with the launch of English Heritage's very own 'Brother Anthony' ale – just in time to toast the celebrations!

**For more information on visiting any English Heritage property or event, visit www.english-heritage.org.uk**

---

## Enjoy great days out throughout the year when you join English Heritage.

Enjoy great days out throughout the year when you join English Heritage. Membership gives you to free or reduced-price entry to our events as well as free entry to all our properties. And the benefits of membership don't end there. Members receive our award-winning quarterly magazine, Heritage Today. What's more, members can take children under 19 with them for free.*

Every penny from your membership makes a difference to our work in conserving England's historic environment. In return, we hope you'll gain a great deal of enjoyment from your membership.

Call 0870 333 1181 quoting HUDS2 to join today, or visit www.english-heritage.org.uk/membership to find out more.

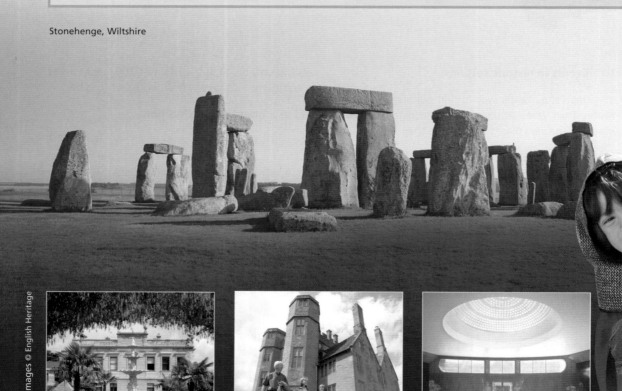

Stonehenge, Wiltshire

Images © English Heritage

Brodsworth Hall and Gardens, South Yorkshire

Kenilworth Castle, Warwickshire

Eltham Palace, London

*Membership allows free admission for you and up to six accompanying children within your family group.

**THE CHURCHES CONSERVATION TRUST**

# The Churches Conservation Trust

## Caring for England's historic churches for all to enjoy

The Churches Conservation Trust is the leading charity conserving England's most beautiful and historic churches which are no longer needed for regular worship. It promotes public enjoyment of these churches and encourages their use as an educational and community resource.

The Trust warmly welcomes visitors to more than 335 churches located throughout the length and breadth of England, and representing a microcosm of 1000 years of English history, art and architecture.

Now from as little as £30 a year you can join the Trust's Supporters and help to save these evocative symbols of our collective heritage for the nation. We receive only limited funding for our work to conserve these landmarks, and to open them to visitors and their local communities. Without help we cannot continue to save more churches in the future.

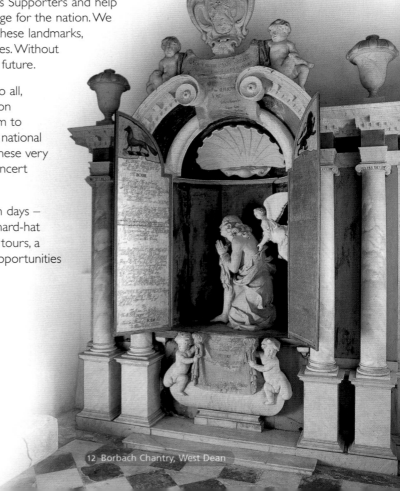

We work to make the churches in our care accessible to all, both physically and intellectually. Through formal education groups, informal workshops, talks and guidebooks we aim to help people of all ages to discover a unique part of our national history. We also seek to find appropriate new uses for these very special and individual buildings, and many are used as concert venues, exhibition spaces and meeting places.

Our Supporters enjoy exclusive Conservation in Action days – behind-the-scenes tours of work in progress including hard-hat days, a bi-annual newsletter, priority booking on church tours, a complimentary copy of the Trust's annual review and opportunities to volunteer and get actively involved with our work.

If you would like to find out more,
go to **www.visitchurches.org.uk**
or email **saveourchurches@tcct.org.uk**,
**quoting HH07** or call **020 7213 0673**.

The Churches Conservation Trust
1 West Smithfield, London EC1A 9EE

12 Borbach Chantry, West Dean

Registered Charity No. 258612     © 2006/7 CCT

4 St Mary, Barton Bendish

3 St George, Reforne, Portland

2 St Thomas, East Shefford

1 St Andrew, Hove

5 St Stephen Old Church, Fylingdales

6 All Saints, Harewood

7 All Saints, Aldwincle

8 St Peter, Satterleigh

9 All Saints, South Elmham

10 Holy Trinity, Halstead

11 St Gregory, Vale of Lune

# Scotland and the Sea

The oceans, and the sailors who crossed them throughout the millennia, did much to define the Scottish nation. This intimate connection with the sea is reflected in many of the castles and other properties in the care of Historic Scotland.

Some were bulwarks against invaders, others were the homes of powerful chiefs and one preserves the memory of the Scottish seamen who sailed the world in search of fame and fortune. The heritage and history of Scotland are closely linked with the seas that surround its long rugged coastline and the shores of its many islands.

Trinity House Maritime Museum, a little known gem in the ancient port of Leith, is dedicated to the seafarers who explored and opened up trade routes in every corner of the world. This impressive building, close to the docks where the Royal Yacht Britannia is now permanently berthed and open to the public as a museum, contains a remarkable array of maritime treasures. Among them are six portraits and a seascape secured for the nation by Historic Scotland in 2006 when they were purchased from the Incorporation of Masters and Mariners of Trinity House, Leith, a guild which dates back to 1380. Most notable among them is a portrait of Admiral Duncan, who became a national hero when he led the British fleet to victory against the Dutch at the Battle of Camperdown in 1797. The Incorporation commissioned Henry Raeburn to paint a portrait of the admiral following this critical action of the Napoleonic Wars.

Dumbarton Castle, high on a rock overlooking the Clyde estuary, also has Napoleonic connections having been considered as a place to imprison the French leader following his capture. Dumbarton Rock has been a vital strongpoint on the West Coast since prehistoric times and since 1230 the castle has been overseen by an unbroken succession of royal governors. The present incumbent Brigadier Donald Hardie, Lord Lieutenant of West Dunbartonshire, takes pride in the fact that while most of his predecessors were there to keep people out he is dedicated to bringing visitors in.

On the east coast is the attractive Broughty Castle, guardian of the Tay estuary, which is situated on the waterfront of the well-heeled town of Broughty Ferry at the edge of Dundee. To the south is Blackness Castle, which stands sentinel over the Forth estuary, and where the jetty has recently been opened for visitors arriving aboard yachts and cruisers.

Kisimul Castle's links with the sea are even more immediate as it dominates a small rocky islet in Castlebay, off the Isle of Barra, and can only be reached by a five-minute boat ride. The ancestral home of the MacNeals of Barra, this powerful, angular fortress enjoys one of the most dramatic settings of any Scottish castle.

A complete architectural contrast is the Castle of Rothesay, on Bute, a largely circular stronghold dating back to the early 13th century. At that time it was on the frontline of international politics, with many islands off the west coast being contested by the Scots and Norwegians. The castle was built at a key defensive point near the head of the island's best natural harbour. It was twice captured by the Norse, the second time by King Hakon IV in 1263, on the ill-fated campaign which resulted in the Scots claiming victory at the Battle of Largs and the Norwegian king dying on Orkney as he returned home. These days the castle has altogether more peaceful royal links. As recently as August 2006 His Royal Highness Prince Charles, known as the Duke of Rothesay while in Scotland, visited the castle to unveil a representation of the Cloth of Estate of James IV which now hangs in the great hall.

Restoration House, Rochester, Kent is so named because of the visit by Charles II who, on his 30th birthday in May 1660 and following his exile in France, spent a night there when travelling from Dover to London to be restored to the throne. Recent extensive work to revive the house makes its name doubly apt.

# Restoration House

More so then than with many other houses, the photograph accompanying the entry for Restoration House in *Hudson's* cannot convey the full extent of the intrigue, interest and enjoyment to be derived from a visit. Over the past 12 years Robert Tucker and Jonathan Wilmot, the owners, have adopted an archaeological approach to restoring this 38 roomed house. The exterior façades give only a hint of the puzzling complexity of the way the house appears to have developed.

It seems that originally the house was two separate medieval buildings, now forming the north and south wings. These were amalgamated, probably in the early 17th century, the infilling of the area between the two buildings creating the Great Hall and Great Chamber above with the whole subsequently enclosed in the red brickwork seen today.

In the process of structural repairs and restoring the house to as it might have been at the end of the 17th century, the owners have carefully peeled back layers to expose original work and to discover more about its history. It was clearly built in several phases and has undergone many alterations and schemes of decoration to meet new needs. So often has the interior been remodelled that there are several staircases inexplicably going in several directions. The current decoration contributes to the rather special atmosphere. The owners have amassed some fine pictures and a collection of furniture from varying periods, imaginatively brought together.

Uncovering traces of the past in the garden has been more difficult. Its renaissance is more a new interpretation than restoration. This has provided an opportunity for inspired recreation, design and planting providing a serene haven away from the hubbub of the surrounding city.

**Left, right & overleaf:** Various images of Restoration House and its garden giving some indication of its poetic beauty. For opening details see page 146.

48

# RHS
## Partner Gardens

Properties in Hudsons that offer free garden access at specified times to RHS Members

| GARDEN | FREE ACCESS DATES FOR 2007 |
| --- | --- |
| Abbotsbury Subtropical Gardens | Oct - Feb |
| Aberglasney Gardens | Jan-Mar |
| Arley Hall & Gardens | When open (Gardens only and not special event days) |
| Bedgebury National Pinetum | When open |
| Belvoir Castle | Apr-Jul, daily except Mon & Fri |
| Benington Lordship Gardens | 3-18 Feb and 17-22 June |
| Bicton Park Botanical Gardens | Jan-Feb & Nov (excl train rides) |
| Blenheim Palace Park & Gardens | 10 Feb - 25 May (excl. Easter) & 10 Sept – 9 Dec (Gardens only) |
| Bodnant Garden | When open |
| Branklyn Gardens | When open |
| Broadleas Gardens | When open |
| Burton Agnes Hall | When open |
| Cae Hir Gardens | When open |
| Caerhays Castle Garden | 13 Feb - 12 Mar |
| Cawdor Castle & Gardens | May - Jun & Sept - Oct (Gardens only) |
| Cholmondeley Castle Garden | June |
| Corsham Court Gardens | When open (Gardens only) |
| Cottesbrooke Hall & Gardens | When open (Gardens only) excl special event days |
| Coughton Court | Mar-Oct, Weds, Suns and Bank Holidays (Gardens only) |
| Dalemain | 1-30 Apr, 1-30 Sept and 10-28 Oct (Gardens only) |
| Docton Mill & Garden | Sats 1 Mar - 31 Oct inclusive |
| Doddington Hall | When open |
| The Dorothy Clive Garden | Jul - Aug |
| Drummond Castle | May, Sept and Oct |
| Duncombe Park | When open |
| Dunrobin Castle Gardens | When open |
| Dyffryn Gardens | 1 Apr -31 Oct (not special event days) |
| East Bergholt Place Garden | When open (except Sundays) |
| Elton Hall | May-Jul |
| Exbury Gardens | 17-31 Mar and Sept |
| Fairhaven Woodland & Water Garden | Feb - Apr & Oct |
| Floors Castle Gardens | When open (Gardens only) |
| Forde Abbey & Gardens | Oct - Feb (Gardens only) |
| Furzey Gardens | Mar - Oct |
| Glen Chantry | Apr-May, Aug and 1 Sept |
| Glenwhan Garden | Aug-Sept and 1-30 Oct by appointment |
| Goodnestone Park Gardens | Apr - May & Sept (Gardens only, not special event days) |
| Harewood House | 9 Feb - 30 Jun (Gardens only) |
| Harmony Garden | When open |
| Hatfield House & Gardens | When open (except major event days) |
| Hergest Croft | 2 Mar- 30 Apr and 1 Jul-28 Oct |
| Hestercombe Gardens | 1 Oct – 31 Mar inclusive |
| Hill of Tarvit Mansionhouse & Garden | When open (Gardens only) |
| Holker Hall & Gardens | Apr - Oct (Gardens only excl. special event days) |
| Houghton Hall | June (Gardens only) |

Doddington Hall

Wyken Hall, S.M Hansford

Kelmarsh Hall, Jonathan Harris

Royal Horticultural Society

| GARDEN | FREE ACCESS DATES FOR 2007 |
| --- | --- |
| Kellie Castle & Garden | When open |
| Kelmarsh Hall | When open |
| Kingston Maurward Garden | When open |
| Leith Hall and Garden | When open |
| Loseley Park | May & Sept (Garden only) except NGS days, 6 May & 2 Sept |
| Mannington Gardens | When open (Gardens only, not special event days) |
| Mapperton Gardens | When open |
| Muncaster Castle Garden | 1 Jul - 4 Nov |
| National Botanic Garden of Wales, The | Jan - Mar & Oct - Dec |
| Newby Hall & Gardens | Apr, May & Sept (not special event days) |
| Nymans Garden | When open |
| Painswick Rococo Garden | When open |
| Parcevall Hall Gardens | Apr - May |
| Penshurst Place & Gardens | Apr & Sept – Oct (Gardens only) |
| Picton Castle | Apr - Sept (Gardens only, not event days) |
| Plas Brondanw Gardens | When open |
| Portmeirion | When open |
| Raby Castle | When open (not special event days) |
| Ragley Hall | May-Sept, Thur-Fri, Jul-Aug, Thur-Sun |
| Renishaw Hall | When open |
| Ripley Castle | When open (not special event days) |
| Rode Hall | When open |
| Ryton Organic Gardens | When open |
| Sandringham | When open (Gardens only) |
| Sausmarez Manor | First week of every month when open |
| Scone Palace & Grounds | When open |
| Seaforde Gardens | Apr - Jun (Gardens only) |
| Sheffield Park Garden | When open |
| Syon Park | When open (Gardens only) |
| Tapeley Park | 8 Jun - 8 Jul |
| Tatton Park | When open (gardens only) |
| Thorp Perrow Arboretum | Mon - Fri (not BHs) when open |
| Threave Garden & Estate | Apr - May & Sept - Oct |
| Torosay Castle & Gardens | When open |
| Trebah Garden | Jan-Mar and Nov-Dec |
| Trewithen Gardens | Jul - Sept |
| Waddesdon Manor | Mar & Sept - Oct |
| Wartnaby Gardens | When open (excl 25 Feb, 29 Apr & 17 Jun) |
| Wentworth Castle Gardens | When open (not special event days) |
| West Dean | Jan-Mar and Nov-Dec (except special event days) |
| Westonbirt Arboretum | When open except 20-28 Aug and 1-31 Oct |
| Wilton House | When open |
| Wollerton Old Hall Garden | Apr - May & Sept |
| Wyken Hall Gardens | When open |
| Yalding Organic Gardens | 31 Mar -28 Oct, Weds-Suns |
| York Gate Garden | Apr - May and Sept |

The RHS, the UK's leading gardening charity

# Great Days Out
## At the RHS Flower Shows 2007

Royal
Horticultural
Society

Make 2007 the year you come along to one of the world class Royal Horticultural Society flower shows. Indulge your senses with inspirational new show gardens, fabulous floral displays and great gardening accessories.

Photo: Johnny Boylan

### RHS Spring Flower Show, Cardiff
20 – 22 April
Bute Park, Cardiff
Tickets: £8 - £10. To book tickets call 08700 66 77 99

### RHS Chelsea Flower Show
22 – 26 May (22 & 23 May, RHS members only)
The Royal Hospital, Chelsea, London
Tickets: £12.50 - £44 (All tickets must be booked in advance)

### Hampton Court Palace Flower Show
3 – 8 July (3 & 4 July, RHS members only)
Hampton Court Palace, East Molesey, Surrey
Tickets: £13 - £30

### RHS Flower Show at Tatton Park
18 – 22 July (18 July, RHS members only)
Tatton Park, nr Knutsford, Cheshire
Tickets: £17 - £23

To book tickets and for further information call
## 0870 842 2223 (except Cardiff)

or visit our website www.rhs.org.uk/flowershows
Groups rates available (except Chelsea), call 020 7014 8444

Ticket terms and conditions apply

Registered charity number: 222879

**The RHS, the UK's leading gardening charity**

# Broughton Castle

*"About the most beautiful castle in all England ...
for sheer loveliness of the combination of water,
woods and picturesque buildings."*

This generous tribute from historian Sir Charles Oman in 1898, was continued by the noted diarist James Lees-Milne in a 1989 entry "It is still the most romantic house imaginable. English to the core, as Henry James says. ... Perfection, what with moat, gatehouse, church, and gorgeous orange and buff stone". A more recent accolade came in 2003 in *England's Thousand Best Houses* by Sir Simon Jenkins. The author gives only twenty of the thousand houses five stars - and Broughton Castle is one of them.

Broughton has just celebrated its 700th anniversary, having been built by Sir John de Broughton in 1306. In 1448 it passed by marriage to the Fiennes family, Lords Saye & Sele, who still live there today.

The first edition of *Hudson's*, 20 years ago, featured Broughton Castle on the front cover – it remains one of the most delightful, interesting and charming houses to visit.

Broughton Castle, Banbury, Oxfordshire                         www.broughtoncastle.com

**Montage:** Christopher Lloyd in the Exotic Garden and The Sunken Garden in autumn behind

Images © Jonathan Buckley

The death of Christopher Lloyd last year has left many people wondering what the future holds for Great Dixter, the home and garden of a master plantsman and one of the world's great horticulturists. Under Christopher Lloyd's care and through his writings, it has become one of the most famous private gardens in Britain, known to garden enthusiasts the world over.

# Great Dixter and the Future

### By Charles Hind

To many people, the house is known more as the picturesque backdrop to the garden and less for its being largely designed by the greatest pre-War British architect, Sir Edwin Lutyens. Its great hall is the largest medieval, timber-framed hall in the country, restored and enlarged for Christopher's father 1910–12. Lutyens added a 16th century timber house moved from elsewhere and knitted the buildings together with service accommodation and bedrooms above. Despite a sale in 1994, the house retains most of the collections of furniture and other objects put together by the Lloyds early in the 20th century, with some notable modern additions by Christopher.

Christopher Lloyd always acknowledged that his career would have been quite different had he not had the good fortune to be born at Dixter and through a combination of accident (initially) and careful planning (later on), he was able to live there throughout his life, despite being the youngest of six children. He was born in 1921 and never married, so in the last few years before his death, his thoughts turned to finding some way to carry forward his vision for the estate.

The house and gardens first opened to the public in the early 1930s, raising funds for charity. In common with so many other country houses, this benevolent attitude had to give way to a more commercial approach in the 1950s. Christopher moved back to the house after military service and opened a commercial nursery selling many of the plants visitors could see in the gardens. The gardens featured regularly in *Country Life* from 1963, when Christopher was asked to contribute a series of weekly articles as a practical gardener – he never missed an issue in 42 years. The garden also featured in his many books and thousands of newspaper and other magazine articles, for all were deeply rooted in his practical approach to gardening and his personal experience. Since 1993, under the care of Head Gardener Fergus Garrett, the gardens have gone from strength to strength and an educational programme has been developing to pass on the skills of the immensely talented staff. This has already had a marked impact on the training and development of new gardeners but the intention is to make these skills more available to a non-professional audience as well.

Christopher Lloyd had a horror of the fossilisation that can attend the passing of houses and gardens into the care of such organisations as the National Trust. Although he lived in the house on his own, every room was used and its important collections of furniture were also there for use, not ornament. None of his dachshunds was ever shooed off a Georgian chair. To ensure continuity, Christopher set up the Great Dixter Charitable Trust in 2004 to take over in due course his share of the estate. The Trust thus had time to run in alongside him so its Trustees could be certain that they could carry out his wishes. Its first task is to raise more than £3 million to safeguard the gardens, the house and its contents, provide an endowment and to buy out the remaining family share. The trustees' intentions are to develop the existing educational side of the gardens, to keep house and gardens open and accessible to the public and under the Head Gardener Fergus Garrett, to continue the inspirational nature of the planting.

The estate is not large (only 57 acres) but it is more than the house and gardens presently seen by the visiting public. It includes ancient woodlands, meadows and ponds that have been consistently managed on a traditional basis. Coppicing the woodlands for example has provided pea sticks for plant supports and timber for fencing as well as wood to burn in the house's capacious inglenook fireplaces. Traditional methods have ensured that bird, animal and plant life has been preserved and encouraged. A Conservation Management Plan is being prepared. This will provide a detailed list of the heritage assets of the estate, ranging from the contents of the house to an assessment of the garden and its plant collections and the biodiversity of the woods and meadows. Armed with this information, the Trust will be able to assess priorities to ensure the proper maintenance and development of the estate.

To raise the £3 million plus needed to safeguard the future for Great Dixter, the Trust launched an appeal in 2006. The primary aim is to maintain, conserve and enhance the house and garden but the intention is also, if funds permit, to buy out the remaining Lloyd family interest in the estate. Some of the outbuildings will be converted to provide residential accommodation for students (of all ages) attending courses to learn how to garden the Dixter way. There will also be one-day workshops. A Friends organisation has been set up, and Friends get preferential access to the gardens when open, invitations to events and a quarterly newsletter.

The Trustees are confident that Great Dixter can continue to provide inspiration and enjoyment for gardeners and country house visitors alike. We owe it to Christopher Lloyd, whose enthusiasm and knowledge of plants and gardens was freely shared for so long. Future visitors will not be disappointed.

If you would like to help the Trust, email for information to friends@greatdixter.co.uk or telephone the Trust on 0870–922–2830.

*Charles Hind - Trustee, Great Dixter Charitable Trust*
*H.J. Heinz Curator of Drawings, Royal Institute of British Architects*

*Great Dixter House & Gardens,*
*Great Dixter, Northiam, Rye, East Sussex TN31 6PH*

| | |
|---|---|
| **Top left:** | The Porch and the Front Meadow. |
| **Top right:** | Lupins in the High Garden. |
| **Bottom:** | The Long Border in early June / © Jonathan Buckley. |
| **Below:** | Great Dixter from the south-west, showing the old part of the house on the left and the Benenden Wing on the right. |

# Saving the
# Overlooked

**The Landmark Trust was founded in 1965 to prevent the loss or irreversible alteration of small but worthwhile buildings, which were at the time overlooked by the conservation world.**

# The Landmark Trust

Landmark was based on the proposition, novel for its day, of restoring such buildings and then generating funds for their ongoing and costly maintenance by letting them for holidays, thus guaranteeing their future.

Without Landmark's help, many important buildings would have been lost for ever, buildings with no other use to justify their rescue and support their upkeep. Today, there are 184 Landmarks, a portfolio of national significance and a unique contribution to the protection of Britain's architectural heritage. They include follies, castles, towers and banqueting houses and range in age from the early 13th century to 1971. Anyone can stay in a Landmark, enriching their own lives by living for a time in a historic building, while knowing that every holiday spent in a Landmark helps ensure its survival.

Much has changed over the past forty years but the flow of buildings in need of rescue is as constant as ever. While the eventual letting income will pay for their ongoing maintenance, we must fundraise for the restoration, and sometimes acquisition of each building we accept into our care. Our restorations are guided by certain principles. We prefer to repair rather than renew and rather than commit to unseemly alterations, we trust to our visitors' sense of adventure and sometimes ask them to adapt to the building rather than the reverse. We support the use of traditional materials and craft skills and encourage training to ensure these techniques continue to survive.

Recent restorations have included The Grange, a Grade I listed house designed and lived in by architect and designer Augustus Pugin, Lengthsman's Cottage, a canal keeper's cottage on the South Stratford Canal and Keeper's Cottage, a gamekeeper's cottage in Bedfordshire. Our focus now moves to the rescue of another diverse selection of historic buildings.

Lengthsman's Cottage, Warwickshire

## Clavell Tower, Dorset

A folly built by a clergyman in 1830 on a lonely stretch of coastline in Dorset, today it stands just five metres from the edge of a crumbling cliff. The only way to save this well-loved local landmark is to dismantle it and re-erect it 25 metres back from the edge ensuring at least another 200 years of safety. Work began in September 2006. During the 18 month project students from a local college will be trained on site in stonemasonry.

## Glenmalloch Lodge, Dumfries and Galloway

Built in 1830 by the Countess of Galloway as a schoolhouse for the girls on her estate, Glenmalloch Lodge is a tiny, picturesque cottage within the policies of Cumloden House in Galloway. The remoteness of its exceptional setting led to its dereliction, stranded from modern services, but will also make it a wonderful place to stay. Gentle use as a Landmark will give it purpose, while leaving the lovely surroundings undisturbed.

## Queen Anne's Summerhouse, Bedfordshire

This folly, which stands on the Shuttleworth Estate in Bedfordshire, has a deceptive air of solidity. In reality, it is roofless, and its exceptionally finely jointed and rubbed brickwork is crumbling away. The summerhouse was probably built by Samuel Ongley, a wealthy linen draper who was knighted by Queen Anne in 1712. Our fundraising appeal has allowed us to erect an emergency roof to help the fabric dry out and delay further decay but we are left with a sizeable balance to raise before we can start work. It will be a challenge to today's bricklayers to match the standards of their predecessors.

For further details about the work of the Landmark Trust visit **www.landmarktrust.org.uk** or telephone **01628 825925**. The 22nd edition of the Landmark Trust Handbook, which contains details of all 184 buildings available for holidays, can be purchased for £11.50 (refundable on a booking).

With surviving remains of more than 470 earthwork and stone castles – roughly one to every sixteen square miles – Wales can truly claim to be 'a land of castles'. Most of them were built by Anglo-Norman Lords and are a lasting reminder of over 200 years of strife which followed the Norman Conquest.

Llywodraeth Cynulliad Cymru
Welsh Assembly Government

# Cadw
By Peter Humphries

## Celebrating the castles of the Welsh Princes

It was not only Anglo-Norman lords for the Welsh princes too were castle builders. The earliest record of a castle being built by a Welshman is at Cymer near Dolgellau in 1116, just fifty years after the Battle of Hastings. But although those sites formally recorded as being Welsh foundations number just ten out of well over 300 earthwork castles and twenty-two out of more than 150 stone castles in Wales, the actual numbers must have been very much greater.

### Protecting and Conserving

In recent years Cadw, the historic environment service of the Welsh Assembly Government, has carried out a comprehensive review of all sites in Wales which merit statutory protection – and now all the known castles of the Welsh princes are fully protected as scheduled ancient monuments.

But of those twenty-two stone castles referred to earlier, only ten contain substantial areas of original Welsh masonry. Eight of them – Castell y Bere, Criccieth, Dolbadarn, Dolwyddelan, Dolforwyn and Ewloe in north Wales, and Dinefwr and Dryslwyn in the south west – are in the direct care of Cadw. After extensive masonry consolidation work at Dinefwr in

recent years and major programmes of archaeological excavation and consolidation at Dryslwyn and Dolforwyn, all eight castles are now fully open to the public.

Of the two remaining Welsh stone castles, Dinas Brân, above Llangollen, is looked after by Denbighshire County Council and Caergwrle in the north-east is owned by the local community council. Over the last twenty years Cadw has provided more than £200,000 towards the conservation of these two sites and both are also now open to visitors.

### Discovering Buried Walls

Twenty years ago the only visible remains at Dryslwyn and Dolforwyn castles were small areas of standing masonry in the midst of grassy mounds. Cadw initiated major archaeological excavations at both sites led by archaeologists from Cardiff, Durham, Leeds and York universities. The results have been spectacular. Major defensive towers and complexes of buildings have emerged from the rubble, along with the great stone balls hurled at the castles from giant catapults by the English forces during their sieges at Dolforwyn in 1277 and Dryslwyn in 1287.

During this same period Clwyd County Council excavated the entire courtyard and gateway at Caergwrle Castle, and Cadw provided grant aid towards excavations by the Gwynedd Archaeological Trust at the Welsh princely court of Rhosyr on Anglesey. These, the first scientific excavations of Welsh castles and courts, have revolutionized our understanding of this aspect of Welsh history.

### Researching and Presenting

Our understanding of what these castles looked like and of how they were lived in over 700 years ago relies on careful analysis and research. As well as the results of archaeological excavation, detailed recording of the masonry is essential to identify hidden architectural features and to distinguish different building periods.

Valuable information can be provided also by archaeological fieldwork and by minute scrutiny of the early documentary evidence. Sometimes this can even lead to the discovery of sites which have lain unidentified for centuries past. An instance of this is the locating of some of the long-lost courts of the princes of Gwynedd, which have recently been rediscovered by the Gwynedd Archaeological Trust in a project grant-aided by Cadw to study princely courts and townships.

It is painstaking work like this which lies behind all the up-to-date interpretations presented by Cadw on site and in its guidebooks and other publications, and it underpins other recent academic books and articles on these Welsh princely sites.

### Castles of the Welsh princes: what to look for

There is little visible difference between earthwork castles built by the Welsh and those built by the Anglo Normans. Only at the end of the 12th century, when construction began in stone, can a clear distinction be seen between English and Welsh castle works.

Welsh castles tend to have simple plans of irregular shape and they are frequently sited on rocky outcrops in landlocked mountain passes. Natural defences are often supplemented by deep rock-cut ditches. Other common features are apsidal ('D' shaped) and rectangular towers, but these are rarely more than two storeys high. The curtain walls of Welsh castles tend to be relatively slight; they do not usually have large gatehouses and little provision was ever made for flanking fire between mural towers as would be normal in castles built by the English.

There are many possible reasons for these differences in design. The north Welsh were predominantly spearmen, not archers, and this would radically affect methods of defence. Lack of money and also of skilled labour, compared with that available to an English lord, would both be significant factors. But above all, the bonds of society were strong in Wales, whereas in England authority was maintained by force; thus the use and purpose of these castles would have been essentially different.

Dryslwyn Castle, Carmarthenshire before and after excavation.

© Cadw Crown Copyright

Dolwyddelan Castle, Gwynedd.

Dolforwyn Castle, Powys during excavation in 2005.

Castell y Bere, Gwynedd, perched on a rocky outcrop below Cader Idris.

Criccieth Castle, Gwynedd, as it may have appeared c1240.

## And where to see them

**Castell y Bere**, Gwynedd: the distinctive remains of a native Welsh castle probably begun by Prince Llywelyn ab Iorwerth ('the Great') around 1221. Near Llanfihangel y Pennant, off the B4405 6½ miles NE of Tywyn.

**Caergwrle Castle**, Flintshire: established by Dafydd, the brother of Llywelyn ap Gruffudd, in 1278. 4 miles N of Wrexham off the A541.

**Castell Dinas Brân**, Denbighshire: built by the Welsh rulers of Powys in a prominent and elevated position above Llangollen. Off the A539.

**Criccieth Castle**, Gwynedd: established by Prince Llywelyn ab Iorwerth ('the Great') in the 1230s. On a coastal bluff near Criccieth town centre.

**Dinefwr Castle**, Carmarthenshire: ancestral seat of the Welsh rulers of Deheubarth. 1½ miles W of Llandeilo off the A40.

**Dolbadarn Castle**, Gwynedd: probably built by Llywelyn ab Iorwerth ('the Great') early in the 13th century. ½ mile SE of Llanberis on the A4086

**Dolforwyn Castle**, Powys: begun by Llywelyn ap Gruffudd, prince of Gwynedd, in 1273. 3¾ miles NE of Newtown, signposted off the A483.

**Dolwyddelan Castle**, Gwynedd: established by Llywelyn ab Iorwerth ('the Great') around 1210. 1m (1.6km) W of Dolwyddelan, on the A470.

**Dryslwyn Castle**, Carmarthenshire: established in the 1220s by Rhys Grug of Deheubarth. 5 miles W of Llandeilo off the B4297.

**Ewloe**, Flintshire: probably built by Llywelyn ap Gruffudd ('the Last') after 1257. 1 mile NW of Ewloe, off the A55.

Cadw guidebooks for Castell y Bere, Criccieth, Dinefwr, Dolbadarn, Dolwyddelan, Dryslwyn and Ewloe castles are available from: Cadw, Plas Carew, Unit 5/7 Cefn Coed, Parc Nantgarw, Cardiff CF15 7QQ. Telephone 01443 33 6092/3

Full details of opening hours of all Cadw sites are available at www.cadw.wales.gov.uk

*Peter Humphries – Interpretation Manager, Cadw*

Dinefwr Castle, Carmarthenshire before and after conservation.

© Cadw. Crown Copyright

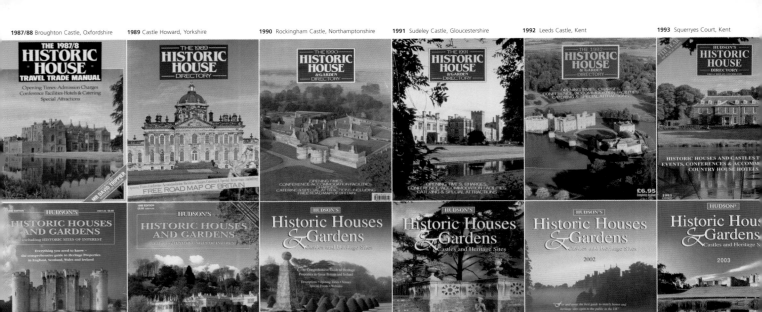

# 20th Anniversary
## of the best annual guide to UK Heritage sites

### By Norman Hudson

If visiting historic houses has lost some of its novelty, its appeal is undiminished. A recent MORI poll showed that more people in Britain were interested in history than in football – indeed more visit historic houses than go to football matches.

**20** years ago the first edition of *Hudson's* was produced to provide better information for the travel trade. Some of the great houses were well known, but few people knew of the hundreds of other open properties. While some are comparatively small, they nearly all have a story to tell, much to admire and can provide as much delight for visitors as the great 'treasure houses'.

The early 1950s was a difficult time for historic houses. Huge numbers were being pulled down. One 18 month period saw a house demolished at the rate of one every four days. The ravages of wartime occupation and lack of maintenance, perhaps the death of an heir, capital taxation, the absence of domestic labour-saving devices, all contributed to bleak prospects for these houses. But the growth in holiday and leisure time was bringing changes as was the increase in car ownership (2 million in 1950, over 30 million now). This gave people the independence to go where they wanted, when they wanted. Most people had Sundays off. There was no sport on Sunday. Shops were closed. There were few purpose-built attractions. This provided an opportunity for beleaguered historic house owners and for the National Trust also, whose country house scheme had gathered momentum during and after the War.

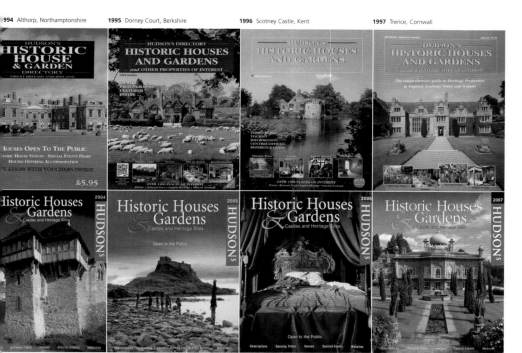

**2004** Stokesay Castle, Shropshire    **2005** Lindisfarne Castle, Northumberland    **2006** 18 Folgate Street, London    **2007** Sezincote, Gloucestershire

The future of such houses is in part dependent on the interest of coming generations and their willingness to help ensure their survival. That is why their increasing use as an educational resource is important. Visits by school parties have been greatly encouraged. History and an understanding of the past can be enhanced and made relevant by places and artefacts represent-ative of people and events that have helped shape how we live and what we are today.

Overall, historic houses are now in better condition, with higher standards of conservation and presentation than hitherto. But their continued upkeep and maintenance remains a chal-lenge. A majority of them are still lived in and occupied as family homes. They are not museums and therefore continue to evolve – this adds interest for visitors.

This book has also changed. It has grown from a black & white publication designed for the travel trade. It is now an established best-seller, often referred to as the 'bible' by all those with an interest in Britain's exceptional heritage of historic houses. However the greatest change in recent years has been in the use of the website, www.hudsonsguide.co.uk, one of the foremost portal sites to heritage property – but it is not quite so easily accessed on the move as a book, so the printed edition still has an important rôle.

Early pioneers led the way – the Duke of Bedford at Woburn Abbey, the Marquess of Bath at Longleat, and Lord Montagu at Beaulieu. They were learning a new business, often by trial-and-error. Other owners, including the National Trust, learned from them. They began to offer visitors light refreshment and souvenirs and these outlets have now developed into sophisticated restaurants and shops. Ancillary attractions have been added: special exhibitions, adventure playgrounds, plant centres and the currently popular sculpture trails.

Many of these buildings were designed initially to impress. Grand rooms to be used for entertaining, while everyday domestic life was often conducted in more modest style in another part of the building. With the growth of corporate entertainment in the 1970s, space provided a further commercial opportunity. Historic houses had room and oodles of style and could be used as venues for functions and events – in effect a rediscovery of some of their original purpose. Even the earliest edition of *Hudson's* included details of a house's capacity for such events and a special index.

Over the last 11 years, since it has been possible to conduct Civil weddings outside of the Registry Office, historic houses have become popular places in which to become married and hold post-wedding parties. The wedding index is now one of the most popular parts of the *Hudson's* website (www.hudsonsguide.co.uk).

*Then and Now: A spread from the first edition of Hudson's showing Hever Castle together with its updated page in this edition.*

**Above:** The Royal Observatory, Greenwich ©NMM
**Right:** The Chelsea Physic Garden

# London

*England's vibrant capital city contains not just the 'must-see' attractions such as Buckingham Palace and the Tower of London, but also many smaller and no less interesting properties. London's parks are the lungs of the city. From Regent's Park in the north to Battersea Park south of the river, via Hyde Park and St James's it is possible to walk for miles, hardly touching a pavement.*

The High Altar – St Paul's Cathedral

visit hudsons guide online

©English Heritage Photo Library/Nigel Corrie

■ **Owner**
English Heritage

■ **Contact**
House Manager
Apsley House
Hyde Park Corner
London W1J 7NT

**Tel:** 020 7499 5676
**Fax:** 020 7493 6576

■ **Location**
**MAP 20:L8**
**OS Ref. TQ284 799**

N. side of
Hyde Park Corner.

**Underground:**
Hyde Park Corner exit 1
Piccadilly Line.

**Bus:**
9,22, 148.

■ **Opening Times**
1 April–31 October
Tue–Sun & BHs
10am–5pm.
1 November–20 March
Tue–Sun, 10am–4pm.
Closed 24–26 Dec
& 1 Jan.

■ **Admission**
Adult                £5.30
Children             £2.70
Child (under 5yrs)   Free
Conc.                £4.00

Joint ticket with
Wellington Arch
(Wed–Sun):

Adult                £6.90
Children             £3.50
Child (under 5yrs)   Free
Conc.                £5.20
Family               £17.30

15% discount for groups
(11+) . Free for English
Heritage members and
for Overseas Visitor Pass
holders.

# APSLEY HOUSE ⌗

www.english-heritage.org.uk/visits

Apsley House (also known as No. 1 London) is the former residence of the first Duke of Wellington.

The Duke made Apsley House his London home after a dazzling military career culminating in his victory over Napoleon at Waterloo in 1815. Wellington enlarged the house (originally designed and built by Robert Adam between 1771–78) adding the magnificent Waterloo Gallery by Benjamin Dean Wyatt which holds many of the masterpieces from the Duke's extensive painting collection. It has been the London home of the Dukes of Wellington ever since.

The seventh Duke gave the house and contents to the Nation in 1947, with apartments retained for the family. With its collections of outstanding paintings, porcelain, silver, sculpture, furniture, medals and memorabilia largely intact and the family still in residence, Apsley House is the last great aristocratic town house in London.

©English Heritage Photo Library/Nigel Corrie

ℹ No photography in house.

🅰

♿ Partial.

🧍 By arrangement.

🎧 Free. English, French, Spanish & German.

🅿 In Park Lane.

🐕 Guide dogs only

✳

🛡

London – England

### ■ Owner
Official Residence of Her Majesty The Queen

### ■ Contact
Ticket Sales & Information Office
Buckingham Palace
London SW1A 1AA

**Tel:** 020 7766 7300
**Groups (15+):**
020 7766 7321
**Fax:** 020 7930 9625
**E-mail:** bookinginfo@royalcollection.org.uk

### ■ Location
**MAP 20:L8**
**OS Ref. TQ291 796**

Underground:
Green Park, Victoria,
St James's Park.

**Rail:** Victoria.

**Sightseeing tours**
A number of tour companies include a visit to Buckingham Palace in their sightseeing tours. Ask your concierge or hotel porter for details.

### ■ Opening Times
**The State Rooms**
August–September
Daily: 9.45am–6pm
(last admission 3.45pm).

Entry by timed ticket; pre-booking advised.

**The Queen's Gallery**
All year daily except 6 April & 25/26 December and between exhibitions.
10am–5.30pm
(last admission 4.30pm).
Entry by timed ticket.

Private Evening Tours are available to Groups (15+) contact 020 7766 7322.

**The Royal Mews**
March–October
Daily, except Fridays:
11am–4pm.
(last adm. 3.15pm)

### ■ Admission
For admission prices please visit www.royalcollection.org.uk or telephone 020 7766 7300.

As Buckingham Palace is a working royal palace, opening arrangements may change at short notice. Please check before planning a visit.

# BUCKINGHAM PALACE
## THE STATE ROOMS, THE QUEEN'S GALLERY, THE ROYAL MEWS
### www.royalcollection.org.uk

Buckingham Palace is the official London residence of Her Majesty The Queen and serves as both home and office. Its 19 State Rooms, which open for eight weeks a year, form the heart of the working palace. They are used extensively by The Queen and members of the Royal Family to receive and entertain their guests on State, ceremonial and official occasions. The State Rooms are lavishly furnished with some of the finest treasures from the Royal Collection – paintings by Rembrandt, Rubens, Van Dyck; sculpture by Canova; exquisite examples of Sèvres porcelain, and some of the most magnificent English and French furniture in the world. The garden walk offers superb views of the Garden Front of the Palace and the 19th-century lake.

Adjacent to Buckingham Palace are the Royal Mews and The Queen's Gallery. The Royal Mews is one of the finest working stables in existence and houses both the horse-drawn carriages and motor cars used for coronations, State visits, royal weddings and the State Opening of Parliament.

The Queen's Gallery hosts a programme of changing exhibitions of magnificent works of art from the Royal Collection. Exhibitions in 2007 include *Unfolding Pictures* (until 11 February 2007), *The Art of Italy in the Royal Collection, Renaissance and Baroque* (30 March 2007– 20 January 2008). For further information on these exhibitions, please visit the website, www.royalcollection.org.uk.

Royal Mews, The Royal Collection © 2007 HM Queen Elizabeth II

The Queen's Gallery Hallway, The Royal Collection © 2007 HM Queen Elizabeth II

The Royal Collection © 2007 HM Queen Elizabeth II

 No photography inside.

 Wheelchair users are required to pre-book.

 The Royal Mews.

 The State Rooms and some exhibitions.

 None.

 Guide dogs only.

© English Heritage Photo Library

# CHISWICK HOUSE ⌗

www.english-heritage.org.uk/visits

Chiswick House is internationally renowned as one of the first and finest English Palladian villas. Lord Burlington, who built the villa from 1725–1729, was inspired by the architecture and gardens of ancient Rome and this house is his masterpiece. His aim was to create a fit setting to show his friends his fine collection of art and his library. The opulent interior features gilded decoration, velvet walls and painted ceilings. The important 18th century gardens surrounding Chiswick House have, at every turn, something to surprise and delight the visitor from the magnificent cedar trees to the beautiful Italianate gardens with their cascade, statues, temples, urns and obelisks.

**Venue Hire and Hospitality**

English Heritage offers exclusive use of Chiswick House in the evenings and Saturday afternoons for dinners, receptions and weddings.

### Owner
English Heritage

### Contact
**Visits:**
House Manager
Chiswick House
Burlington Lane
London W4 2RP

**Tel:** 020 8995 0508

**Venue Hire and Hospitality:**
Hospitality Manager
**Tel:** 020 7973 3292

### Location
**MAP 19:C8**
**OS Ref: TQ210 775**

Burlington Lane
London W4.

**Rail:** ¼ mile NE of Chiswick Station.

**Tube:**
Turnham Green, ¾ mile

**Bus:** 190, E3.

### Opening Times
**Summer**
1 April–31 October
Wed–Sun & BHs,
10am–5pm.
Closes at 2pm on Sats.

**Winter**
1 November–20 March
2008. Pre-booked
appointments only.

### Admission
| | |
|---|---|
| Adult | £4.90 |
| Child (5–15yrs) | £2.10 |
| Conc | £3.20 |
| Family | £10.50 |

Groups (11+)
15% discount

© English Heritage Photo Library

© English Heritage Photo Library

ℹ WCs. Filming, plays, photographic shoots.

📷 Private & corporate hospitality.

♿ Please call in advance. WC.

☕ Café in grounds not managed by English Heritage.

🚶 Personal guided tours must be booked in advance.

🎧 Free audio tours in English, French & German.

🅿 Free if booked in advance. Tel: 020 7973 3485.

🐕 Guide dogs in grounds.

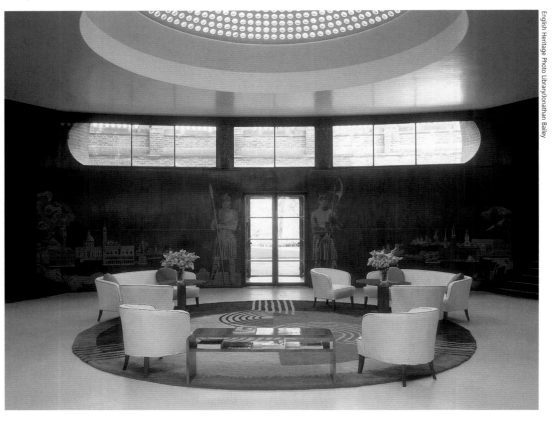

English Heritage Photo Library/Jonathan Bailey

### ■ Owner
English Heritage

### ■ Contact
Eltham Palace
Court Yard
Eltham
London SE9 5QE

**Visits**:
Property Secretary
**Tel:** 020 8294 2548

**Venue Hire and Hospitality**:
Hospitality Manager
**Tel:** 020 8294 2577

### ■ Location
**MAP 19:F8**
**OS Ref. TQ425 740**

M25/J3, then A20 towards Eltham. The Palace is signposted from A20 and from Eltham High Street.
A2 from Central London.

**Rail:** 20 mins from Victoria or London Bridge Stations to Eltham or Mottingham, then 15 min walk.

### ■ Opening Times
1 April–31 October
Sun–Wed
10am–5pm.

1 November–23 December
Sun–Wed
11am–4pm.

3 February–20 March
Sun–Wed
11am–4pm.

Closed 24 December–2 February.

Groups visits must be booked two weeks in advance.

### Venue Hire and Hospitality
English Heritage offers exclusive use of the Palace on Thu, Fri or Sat for daytime conferences, meetings and weddings and in the evenings for dinners, concerts and receptions.

### ■ Admission
**House and Garden**
| | |
|---|---|
| Adult | £7.90 |
| Child | £4.00 |
| Conc. | £5.90 |
| Family (2+3) | £19.80 |

**Garden only**
| | |
|---|---|
| Adult | £4.90 |
| Child | £2.50 |
| Conc. | £3.70 |

### Conference/Function
| ROOM | MAX CAPACITY |
|---|---|
| Great Hall | 300 standing 200 dining |
| Entrance Hall | 100 seated |
| Drawing Room | 120 standing 80 theatre-style |
| Dining Room | 80 standing 10 dining |

English Heritage Photo Library/Jonathan Bailey

# ELTHAM PALACE ⊞
www.english-heritage.org.uk/visits

The epitome of 1930s chic, Eltham Palace dramatically demonstrates the glamour and allure of the period.

Bathe in the light flooding from a spectacular glazed dome in the Entrance Hall as it highlights beautiful blackbeam veneer and figurative marquetry. It is a *tour de force* only rivalled by the adjacent Dining Room – where an Art Deco aluminium-leafed ceiling is a perfect complement to the bird's-eye maple walls. Step into Virginia Courtauld's magnificent gold-leaf and onyx bathroom and throughout the house discover lacquered, 'ocean liner' style veneered walls and built-in furniture.

A Chinese sliding screen is all that separates chic '30s Art Deco from the medieval Great Hall. You will find concealed electric lighting, centralised vacuum cleaning and a loud-speaker system that allowed music to waft around the house. Authentic interiors have been recreated by the finest contemporary craftsmen. Their appearance was painstakingly researched from archive photographs, documents and interviews with friends and relatives of the Courtaulds.

Outside you will find a delightful mixture of formal and informal gardens including a rose garden, pergola and loggia, all nestled around the extensive remains of the medieval palace.

New to the Palace: The Courtaulds' Home Movie, rare footage showing Eltham in its heyday.

| | | | |
|---|---|---|---|
|  | WCs. Filming, plays and photographic shoots. | 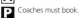 | Guided tours on request. |
| | | | Free. English, German & French. |
|  | Exclusive private and corporate hospitality. | | Coaches must book. |
| | WC. |  | |
| | |  | |

©English Heritage Photo Library/Paul Highnam

# KENWOOD HOUSE ▢

www.english-heritage.org.uk/visits

Kenwood, one of the treasures of London, is an idyllic country retreat close to the popular villages of Hampstead and Highgate.

The house was remodelled in the 1760s by Robert Adam, the fashionable neo-classical architect. The breathtaking library or 'Great Room' is one of his finest achievements.

Kenwood is famous for the internationally important collection of paintings bequeathed to the nation by Edward Guinness, 1st Earl of Iveagh. Some of the world's finest artists are represented by works such as a Rembrandt *Self Portrait*, Vermeer's *The Guitar Player*, *Mary,*

*Countess Howe* by Gainsborough and paintings by Turner, Reynolds and many others.

As if the house and its contents were not riches enough, Kenwood stands in 112 acres of landscaped grounds on the edge of Hampstead Heath, commanding a fine prospect towards central London. The meadow walks and ornamental lake of the park, designed by Humphry Repton, contrast with the wilder Heath below. The open air concerts held in the summer at Kenwood have become part of London life, combining the charms of music with the serenity of the lakeside setting.

■ **Owner**
English Heritage

■ **Contact**
Kenwood House
Hampstead Lane
London NW3 7JR

**Visits:**
The House Manager
**Tel:** 020 8348 1286

■ **Location**
**MAP 20:K1**
**OS Ref. TQ271 874**

M1/J2. Signed off A1, on leaving A1 turn right at junction with Bishop's Ave, turn left into Hampstead Lane. Visitor car park on left.

**Bus:** London Transport 210.

**Rail:** Hampstead Heath.

**Underground:**
Archway or Golders Green Northern Line then bus 210.

■ **Opening Times**
1 April–31 October,
Daily: 11am–5pm.

1 November–20 March
Daily: 11am–4pm.

Closed 24–26 December & 1 January.

**Venue Hire and Hospitality**
Events are available for up to 100 guests in the Service Wing. Please ring Company of Cooks on 020 8341 5384.

■ **Admission**
**House & Grounds**
Free. Donations welcome.

English Heritage Photo Library

English Heritage Photo Library

ℹ️ WCs. Concerts, exhibitions, filming. No photography in house.

🎁

🍽️ Exclusive private and corporate hospitality.

♿ Ground floor access. WC. Visitors can be dropped off in front of the House. Mobility vehicle provided for those who have difficulty with the walk from the car park to the House.

🍴 Available in the Brew House.

🚶 Available on request (in English). Please call for details.

🅿️ West Lodge car park (Pay & Display) on Hampstead Lane. Parking for the disabled.

🚌 Free when booked in advance on 020 7973 3485.

❄️

🙂

London – England

■ **Owner**
National Maritime Museum

■ **Contact**
**Groups:** Robin Scates
**Events:** Jo Rough
Park Row, Greenwich
London SE10 9NF

**Tel:** 020 8858 4422
**Fax:** 020 8312 6632

**Visit Bookings:**
**Tel:** 020 8312 6608
**Fax:** 020 8312 6522
**E-mail:**
bookings@nmm.ac.uk

**Functions:**
**Tel:** 020 8312 6693
**Fax:** 020 8312 6572

■ **Location**
**MAP 19:E7**
**OS Ref. TQ388 773**

Within Greenwich Park on the S bank of the Thames at Greenwich. Travel by river cruise or Docklands Light Railway (Cutty Sark station). M25 (S) via A2. From M25 (N) M11, A12 and Blackwall Tunnel.

■ **Opening Times**
Daily, 10am–5pm (later opening in summer). Last admission 30 mins prior. Varies at New Year and Marathon Day (22 April).

Closed 24–26 December.

Gallery talks and drama (see notices on arrival).

**Special Exhibitions**
Art for the Nation (from November 2006)

Lawrence Weiner (from March 2007)

Sailor Chic (from June 2007).

■ **Admission**
Free admission except for Planetarium shows.

© National Maritime Museum

# ROYAL OBSERVATORY, NATIONAL MARITIME MUSEUM & QUEEN'S HOUSE

www.nmm.ac.uk

The Royal Park at Greenwich provides a beautiful backdrop to the architectural landscape of Greenwich, now a World Heritage Site. The Tudor palace of Placentia, in which Henry VIII, Mary Tudor and Elizabeth I were born, is now covered by the 17th-century Old Royal Naval College with its Painted Hall and Chapel.

Illustrated above is Flamsteed House (Wren 1675), built to accommodate the first Astronomer Royal. It was restored for 2006 with new presentations of significant time-keepers, including those of John Harrison, and the story of Greenwich Mean Time. The Meridian Line, Longitude 0°, is marked in the courtyard as the base point for the calculation of the World's time zones and the 1833 timeball still drops punctually at 1 o'clock. New development is in progress for 2007 to add a new planetarium and modern astronomy displays.

The modern National Maritime Museum charts Britain's history of seafaring and empire. Nelson's uniform coat is on display and portraits and artefacts from various military and civil expeditions tell the human stories behind many great events. Contemporary themes are tackled including the ocean environment, slavery and travel at sea. Stained glass from the destroyed Baltic Exchange is in a separate memorial gallery. There are frequent events and talks for adults and children.

The Queen's House (Inigo Jones 1635) is significant as the first classical house in England. Introducing the Palladian style to England, it was called a 'House of Delights' by Henrietta Maria and was used for court entertainments and balls. The Great Hall, Orangery and 'Tulip' stairs provide an elegant setting for fine and contemporary art displays, occasional exhibitions and private functions.

### Conference/Function

| ROOM | SIZE | MAX CAPACITY |
|---|---|---|
| Queen's House | 40' x 40' | Dining 120 Standing 200 Conference 120 |
| Observatory, Octagon Rm | 25' x 25' | Dining 60 Standing 150 |
| NMM Upper Court | 140' x 70' | Dining 500 Standing 1000 |
| NMM Lecture Theatre | | Conference 120 |

© NMM

The Tulip Staircase, The Queen's House

| | |
|---|---|
| **i** | No photography. |
| 📷 | |
| 🍴 | Partial. WC. |
| ♿ | |
| ☕ | Licensed. |
| 🍴 | |
| 🏃 | |
| 🎧 | |
| **P** | Limited for coaches. |
| 🏛 | |
| | Guide dogs only. |
| 🔔 | |
| ❄ | |
| 🎭 | |

The Choir Stalls looking east towards the High Altar

# ST PAUL'S CATHEDRAL
www.stpauls.co.uk

St Paul's, with its world-famous Dome, is an iconic feature of the London skyline, but there is much more to Sir Christopher Wren's masterpiece than its impressive façade.

A spiritual focus for the nation since its first service in 1697, many important events have taken place within its walls, from State funerals of Lord Nelson, the Duke of Wellington and Sir Winston Churchill to the wedding of the Prince of Wales to Lady Diana Spencer and the Thanksgiving services for Her Majesty the Queen's Golden Jubilee and 80th Birthday.

The Cathedral is currently in the process of being restored and the results so far are breathtaking.

The West front, once blackened and damaged, now rises majestically at the top of Ludgate Hill and details previously hidden stand out crisp and proud. The interior has been transformed by state-of-the-art restoration techniques and the light that now floods the space, highlights the luminescent Portland stone and brings mosaics, carvings and sculpture to life. In the Dome, exquisite 18th century paintings by Sir James Thornhill, showing scenes from the life of St Paul, have been returned to their original beauty.

But of course, the pinnacle of any trip to St Paul's has to be the winding journey up the spiral staircase to the Whispering Gallery, to sample its unique audio effects before traveling up and out to the Stone and Golden Galleries, which afford a panoramic view of London that is second to none.

The High Altar

The West Front

 No photography, video or mobile phones.

 Partial.

 Licensed.

 None for cars, limited for coaches.

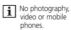 Guide dogs only.

## Owner
Dean & Chapter of St Paul's Cathedral

## Contact
The Chapter House
St Paul's Churchyard
London EC4M 8AD
**Tel:** 020 7246 8350
    020 7236 4128
**Fax:** 020 7248 3104
**E-mail:** chapter@stpaulscathedral.org.uk

## Location
**MAP 20:N7**
**OS Ref. TQ321 812**
Central London.

**Underground:**
St Paul's, Mansion House, Blackfriars, Bank.

**Rail:** Blackfriars, City Thameslink.

**Air:** London Airports.

## Opening Times
Mon–Sat, 8.30am–4.30pm, last admission 4pm.

Guided tours: Mon–Sat, 11am, 11.30am, 1.30pm & 2pm.

Tours of the Triforium: Mon & Tues, 11.30am & 2pm. Fri, 2pm.

All tours are subject to an additional charge.

**Cathedral Shop & Café:**
Mon–Sat, 9am–5pm.
Sun, 10am–5pm.

**Restaurant:**
Mon–Sat, 10am–5pm.
Sun, 12noon–5pm.

**Service Times**
Mon–Sat, 7.30am Mattins (Sat 8.30am) 8am Holy Communion (said), 12.30pm Holy Communion (said) 5pm Choral Evensong

Sun: 8am Holy Communion (said) 10.15am Choral Mattins & sermon, 11.30am Choral Eucharist & sermon, 3.15pm Choral Evensong & sermon 6pm Evening service

The Cathedral may be closed to tourists on certain days of the year. It is advisable to phone or check our website for up-to-date information.

## Admission
| | |
|---|---|
| Adult | £9.00 |
| Child | £3.50 |
| OAP/Student | £8.00 |
| Groups (10+) | |
| Adult | £8.00 |
| Child | £3.00 |
| OAP/Student | £7.00 |

## Conference/Function
| ROOM | MAX CAPACITY |
|---|---|
| Conference Suite | 100 (standing) |

■ **Owner**

Somerset House Trust

■ **Contact**

Director
Somerset House
Strand, London
WC2R 1LA

**Tel:** 020 7845 4600
**Fax:** 020 7836 7613
**E-mail:**
info@somerset-house.org.uk

■ **Location**

**MAP 20:N7**
**OS Ref. TQ308 809**

In the West End of London, overlooking the Thames, by Waterloo Bridge.

Entrances on Strand, Embankment and Waterloo Bridge.

**Underground:** Temple, Embankment, Charing Cross, Covent Garden.

■ **Opening Times**

**Somerset House**
Daily, 10am–6pm
Extended hours apply for the courtyard, river terrace and restaurants.

**Galleries**
Daily, 10am–6pm
(last admission 5.15pm).

Seasonal opening times apply 24–26 December and 1 January – check website for details

■ **Admission**

Entry to Somerset House is free

**Galleries**
One Collection:
Adult £5.00
Conc. £4.00

Two Collections:
Adult £8.00
Conc. £7.00

Three Collections:
Adult £12.00
Conc. £11.00

Galleries are free for under 18s, full-time UK students and registered unwaged.

©James Brittain

# SOMERSET HOUSE

www.somerset-house.org.uk

Home to: Courtauld Institute of Art Gallery www.courtauld.ac.uk, Gilbert Collection www.gilbert-collection.org.uk, and Hermitage Rooms www.hermitagerooms.org.uk.

Overlooking the Thames by Waterloo Bridge, Somerset House, now a unique part of the London cultural scene, is home to the world-famous collection of the Courtauld Institute of Art, including outstanding Impressionist and Post-Impressionist paintings; the dazzling gold, silver and micro-mosaics of the Gilbert Collection; and the Hermitage Rooms, showcasing objects from the State Hermitage Museum in St Petersburg.

In summer, linger and relax in the refreshing fountains, riverside terrace, cafés, and bars, or enjoy concerts, cinema, and dance performances in the majestic setting of the Edmond J. Safra Fountain Court. In winter, be captivated by London's most beautiful ice rink. Elegant spaces can also be hired for private events in a spectacular setting.

Sir William Chamber's 18th century architectural masterpiece has a proud history. Constructed to house learned societies and to provide purpose-built government offices – the Navy Board ran the operation of the British Navy during the Napoleonic Wars from Somerset House.

In 1990 the Courtauld Institute of Art moved to the north building on the Strand, joined by the Gilbert Collection and Hermitage Rooms in the south building in 2000. In this architecturally intriguing space are many grand rooms linked by impressive staircases.

You can enter Somerset House from the Strand under the striking arches, from Waterloo Bridge along the inviting River Terrace or from the Victoria Embankment, through what was originally the central Watergate to the Thames.

Hermitage Corridor

© The Samuel Courtauld Trust, Courtauld Institute of Art Gallery

A Bar at The Folies-Bergère – Manet

Licensed.

Licensed.

By arrangement.

None.

Guide dogs only.

# SPENCER HOUSE

www.spencerhouse.co.uk

Spencer House, built 1756–66 for the first Earl Spencer, an ancestor of Diana, Princess of Wales (1961–97), is London's finest surviving 18th century town house. The magnificent private palace has regained the full splendour of its late 18th century appearance, after a painstaking ten-year restoration programme.

Designed by John Vardy and James 'Athenian' Stuart, the nine State rooms are amongst the first neo-classical interiors in Europe. Vardy's Palm Room, with its spectacular screen of gilded palm trees and arched fronds, is a unique Palladian set-piece, while the elegant mural decorations of Stuart's Painted Room reflect the 18th century passion for classical Greece and Rome. Stuart's superb gilded furniture has been returned to its original location in the Painted Room by courtesy of the V&A and English Heritage. Visitors can also see a fine collection of 18th century paintings and furniture, specially assembled for the house, including five major Benjamin West paintings, graciously lent by Her Majesty The Queen.

The State rooms are open to the public for viewing on Sundays. They are also available on a limited number of occasions each year for private and corporate entertaining during the rest of the week.

i — No photography inside House or Garden.

House only, ramps and lifts. WC.

Obligatory. Comprehensive colour guidebook.

P — None.

---

### ■ Contact
Jane Rick
Director
Spencer House
27 St James's Place
London SW1A 1NR

**Tel:** 020 7514 1958
**Fax:** 020 7409 2952
**Info Line:**
020 7499 8620

### ■ Location
**MAP 20:L8**
**OS Ref. TQ293 803**

Central London:
off St James's Street,
overlooking
Green Park.

**Underground:**
Green Park.

### ■ Opening Times
All Year (except January & August) Suns,
10.30am–5.45pm.

Last tour 4.45pm.

Regular tours throughout the day. Maximum number on each tour is 20.

Mon mornings for pre-booked groups only.

Open for corporate hospitality except during January & August.

### ■ Admission
Adult             £9.00
Conc.*            £7.00

*Students, Friends of the V&A, Friends of the Tate, Friends of the Royal Academy and senior citizens (only on production of valid identification), children under 16. No children under 10 admitted. Group size: min 15–60.

Prices include guided tour.

**Specific Sundays**
The authentically restored garden of this 18th century London palace will be open to the public on specific Sundays during Spring and Summer.

For updated information telephone 020 7499 8620 or view www.spencerhouse.co.uk

### Conference/Function

| ROOM | MAX CAPACITY |
|---|---|
| Receptions | 400 |
| Lunches & Dinners | 130 |
| Board Meetings | 40 |
| Theatre-style Meetings | 100 |

### ■ Owner
The Duke of Northumberland

### ■ Contact
Estate Office
Syon House
Syon Park
Brentford
TW8 8JF

**Tel:** 020 8560 0882
**Fax:** 020 8568 0936
**E-mail:** info@
syonpark.co.uk

### ■ Location
**MAP 19:B8**
**OS Ref. TQ173 767**

Between Brentford and
Twickenham, off the A4,
A310 in SW London.

**Rail:** Kew Bridge or
Gunnersbury
Underground then
Bus 237 or 267.

**Air:** Heathrow 8m.

### ■ Opening Times
**Syon House**
21 March–28 October
Wed, Thur, Sun & BHs
11am–5pm
(open Good Fri &
Easter Sat).

Other times by
appointment for groups.

**Gardens only**
April–October
Daily, 10.30am–5pm
November–March
Sats & Suns, &
New Year's day,
10.30am–4pm or dusk,
whichever is earlier.

Last admissions House &
Gardens ¾ hr before
closing.

Please note from 2008
Syon House will be open
Tues, Weds & Suns.

### ■ Admission
**House and Gardens**
| | |
|---|---|
| Adult | £8.00 |
| Child | £4.00 |
| Conc. | £7.00 |
| Family (2+2) | £18.00 |

Group bookings (15–50)
| | |
|---|---|
| Adult | £7.50 |
| Conc. | £6.50 |
| School Group | £2.00 |

**Gardens & Great
Conservatory**
| | |
|---|---|
| Adult | £4.00 |
| Conc. | £2.50 |
| Family (2+2) | £9.00 |

Group bookings (15–50)
Price on application
(please telephone).

### Conference/Function

| ROOM | SIZE | MAX CAPACITY |
|---|---|---|
| Great Hall | 50' x 30' | 120 |
| Great Conservatory | 60' x 40' | 150 |
| Northumberland Room | 35' x 20' | 60 |
| Marquee | | 1000 |

# SYON PARK 🏛
www.syonpark.co.uk

Described by John Betjeman as the 'Grand Architectural Walk', Syon House and its 200-acre park is the London home of the Duke of Northumberland, whose family, the Percys, have lived here for 400 years.

Originally the site of a late medieval monastery, excavated by Channel 4's *Time Team*, Syon Park has a fascinating history. The present house has Tudor origins but contains some of Robert Adam's finest interiors, which were commissioned by the 1st Duke in the 1760s. The private apartments and State bedrooms are available to view. The house can be hired for filming and photo shoots subject to availability.

Within the 'Capability' Brown landscaped park are 40 acres of gardens which contain the spectacular Great Conservatory designed by Charles Fowler in the 1820s. The House and Great Conservatory are available for corporate and private hire.

The Northumberland Room in Syon House is an excellent venue for conferences, meetings, lunches and dinners (max 60). The State Apartments make a sumptuous setting for dinners, concerts, receptions, launches and wedding ceremonies (max 120). Marquees can be erected on the lawn adjacent to the house for balls and corporate events. The Great Conservatory is available for summer parties, launches, filming, photoshoots and wedding receptions (max 150).

ℹ No photography in house. Indoor adventure playground.

🏠

✿ Garden centre.

🍽 Partial.

♿ Partial.

🍴 By arrangement.

🏃 By arrangement.

🎧

🅿

🐕 Guide dogs only.

## 2 WILLOW ROAD

**HAMPSTEAD, LONDON NW3 1TH**

**Tel:** 020 7435 6166   **E-mail:** 2willowroad@nationaltrust.org.uk

**Owner:** The National Trust   **Contact:** The Custodian

The former home of Erno Goldfinger, designed and built by him in 1939. A three-storey brick and concrete rectangle, it is one of Britain's most important examples of modernist architecture and is filled with furniture also designed by Goldfinger. The interesting art collection includes works by Henry Moore and Max Ernst.

**Location:** MAP 20:J2, OS Ref. TQ270 858. Hampstead, London.

**Open:** 3–24 Mar, 3–31 Nov: Sats, 12 noon–5pm. 29 Mar–27 Oct: Thurs–Sat, 12 noon–5pm. Open Good Fri. Last admission 4.30pm. Tours: 12 noon, 1 & 2 pm. Unguided visits 3–5pm.

**Admission:** Adult £4.90, Child £2.50, Family £12.30. Joint ticket with Fenton House £7.20. Private groups are welcome throughout the year outside public afternoon opening times. Groups must be 5+, booking essential. Free to NT Members.

  Small ground floor area accessible. Filmed tour of whole house available.

## 7 HAMMERSMITH TERRACE – HOME OF EMERY WALKER

**7 Hammersmith Terrace, London W6 9TS**

**Tel:** 020 8741 4104   **E-mail:** admin@emerywalker.org.uk

**www.emerywalker.org.uk**

**Owner:** The Emery Walker Trust   **Contact:** Sue Bright

Emery Walker, friend and advisor to William Morris, lived in this riverside house for 30 years and it preserves the only authentic Arts and Crafts urban interior in Britain, with furniture, wallpapers, textiles and ceramics by Morris & Co, Philip Webb, William de Morgan, etc. Small, pretty garden.

**Location:** MAP 3:H1, OS Ref. TQ221 782. Between Chiswick Mall and South Black Lion Lane in Hammersmith, parallel with King Street (Buses 27, 190, 267, 391, H91). Underground: Stamford Brook or Ravenscourt Park (District Line, both 7 mins walk) or Hammersmith (Piccadilly Line, 15 mins walk). Very limited metered on-street parking.

**Open:** Apr–Jul & September: Guided tour. Please visit website for times, dates and booking arrangements. Admission strictly by pre-booked timed ticket.

**Admission:** Adult £10, Student £5. No children under 12yrs. Groups (max 8).

  No photography inside house. No WC. Refreshments available locally.

  Limited access to ground floor, no access to garden. Obligatory.

## 18 FOLGATE STREET

**Spitalfields, East London E1 6BX**

**Tel:** 020 7247 4013   **Fax:** 020 7377 5548   **www.dennissevershouse.co.uk**

**Owner:** Spitalfields Historic Buildings Trust   **Contact:** Mick Pedroli

A time capsule furnished and decorated to tell the story of the Jervis family, Huguenot silk weavers from 1724–1919.

**Location:** MAP 20:P6, OS Ref. TQ335 820. ½m NE of Liverpool St. Station. E of Bishopsgate (A10), just N of Spitalfields Market.

**Open:** "Silent Night" every Mon evening. Booking required. 1st & 3rd Sun each month: 2–5pm. Mons following these Suns 12 noon–2pm.

**Admission:** "Silent Night" Mons £12 (pm £5), Suns £8. Christmas prices may vary.

  Partial. Obligatory by private bookings.

## ALBERT MEMORIAL

**Princes Gate, Kensington Gore SW7 2AN**

**Tel:** Bookings – 020 7495 0916.  Enquiries – 020 7495 5504

An elaborate memorial by George Gilbert Scott to commemorate the Prince Consort.

**Location:** MAP 20:J8, OS Ref. TQ266 798. Victoria Station 1½m, South Kensington Tube ½m.

**Open:** All visits by booked guided tours; first Sun of the month Mar–Dec, 2pm & 3pm. Tours last 45 mins.

**Admission:** Adult £4.50, Conc £4. Booking advisable for groups of 10+.

## APSLEY HOUSE

*See page 69 for full page entry.*

Richard Lea-Hair/newsteam.co.uk/HRP

## THE BANQUETING HOUSE

**THE BANQUETING HOUSE, WHITEHALL, LONDON SW1A 2ER**

www.banqueting-house.org.uk

**Owner:** Historic Royal Palaces

**Contact:** General Enquiries: 0870 751 5178   Functions: 0870 751 5185 / 5186

This revolutionary building, the first in England to be designed in a Palladian style by Inigo Jones, was finished in 1622 for James I. Intended for the splendour and exuberance of court masques, the Banqueting House is probably most famous for the one real life drama: the execution of Charles I which took place here in 1649 to the "*dismal, universal groan*" of the crowd. One of Charles' last sights as he walked through the Banqueting House to his death was the magnificent ceiling, painted by Peter Paul Rubens in 1630–4.

**Location:** MAP 20:M8, OS Ref. TQ302 80, Underground: Westminster, Embankment and Charing Cross. Rail: Charing Cross.

**Open:** All Year, Mon–Sat, 10am–5pm. Last admission 4.30pm. Closed 24 Dec–1 Jan, Good Friday and other public holidays. NB. Liable to close at short notice for Government functions.

**Admission:** Enquiry line for admission prices: 0870 751 5178.

  Concerts. No photography inside.   Undercroft suitable. Video and audio guide. None.

Richard Lea-Hair/newsteam.co.uk/HRP

## BLEWCOAT SCHOOL 🌿

**23 Caxton Street, Westminster, London SW1H 0PY**

**Tel:** 020 7222 2877

**Owner:** The National Trust    **Contact:** Janet Bowden

Built in 1709 at the expense of William Green, a local brewer, to provide an education for poor children. Used as a school until 1926, it is now the NT London Gift Shop and Information Centre.

**Location:** MAP 20:L9, OS Ref. TQ295 794. Near the junction with Buckingham Gate.

**Open:** All year: Mon–Fri, 10am–5.30pm. Easter–Christmas: Thurs, 10am–7pm. 17 Nov–22 Dec: Sats, 10am–4pm. Closed BHs.

## BOSTON MANOR HOUSE

**Boston Manor Road, Brentford TW8 9JX**

**Tel:** 0845 456 2824    **E-mail:** info@cip.org.uk

**Owner:** Hounslow Cultural & Community Services    **Contact:** Victoria Northwood

A fine Jacobean house built in 1623

**Location:** MAP 19:B7, OS Ref. TQ168 784. 10 mins walk S of Boston Manor Station (Piccadilly Line) and 250yds N of Boston Manor Road junction with A4 Great West Road, Brentford.

**Open:** Apr–end Oct: Sat, Sun & BHs, 2.30–5pm. Due to structural works during 2007 please check times prior to your visit. Park open daily.

**Admission:** Free.

## BRUCE CASTLE MUSEUM

**Haringey Libraries, Archives & Museum Service, Lordship Lane, London N17 8NU**

**Tel:** 020 8808 8772    **Fax:** 020 8808 4118    **E-mail:** museum.services@haringey.gov.uk

**Owner:** London Borough of Haringey

A Tudor building. Sir Rowland Hill (inventor of the Penny Post) ran a progressive school at Bruce Castle from 1827.

**Location:** MAP 19:E6, OS Ref. TQ335 906. Corner of Bruce Grove (A10) and Lordship Lane, 600yds NW of Bruce Grove Station.

**Open:** All year: Wed–Sun & Summer BHs (except Good Fri), 1–5pm. Organised groups by appointment.

**Admission:** Free.

## BUCKINGHAM PALACE

*See page 70 for full page entry.*

## BURGH HOUSE

**New End Square, Hampstead, London NW3 1LT**

**Tel:** 020 7431 0144    **Buttery:** 020 7431 2516    **Fax:** 020 7435 8817

**E-mail:** burghhouse@talk21.com    **www.burghhouse.org.uk**

**Owner:** London Borough of Camden    **Contact:** Ms Helen Wilton

A Grade I listed building of 1703 in the heart of old Hampstead with original panelled rooms, "barley sugar" staircase banisters and a music room. Child-friendly, refurbished Hampstead Museum, permanent and changing exhibitions. Prize-winning terraced garden. Regular programme of concerts, art exhibitions, and meetings. Receptions, seminars and conferences. Rooms for hire. Special facilities for schools visits. Wedding receptions.

**Location:** MAP 20:J2, OS Ref. TQ266 859. New End Square, E of Hampstead underground station.

**Open:** All year: Wed–Sun, 12 noon–5pm. Sats by appointment only. BH Mons, 2–5pm. Closed Christmas fortnight, Good Fri & Easter Mon. Groups by arrangement. Buttery: Wed–Sun, 11am–5.30pm. BHs, 11am–4pm (later if required).

**Admission:** Free.

🔲 🔽 ♿ Ground floor & grounds. WC. ▣ Licensed buttery. 🍴 🎭 By arrangement. 🅿 None. ▦ By arrangement. 🐕 Guide dogs only. ▣ ✱

Queen's House, Greenwich

# CAPEL MANOR GARDENS

**BULLSMOOR LANE, ENFIELD EN1 4RQ**

www.capel.ac.uk

**Tel:** 08456 122122    **Fax:** 01992 717544

**Owner:** Capel Manor Charitable Organisation    **Contact:** Miss Julie Ryan

These extensive, richly planted gardens are delightful throughout the year offering inspiration, information and relaxation. The gardens include various themes - historical, modern, walled, rock, water, sensory and disabled and an Italianate Maze, Japanese Garden and 'Gardening Which?' demonstration and model gardens. Capel Manor is a College of Horticulture and runs a training scheme for professional gardeners originally devised in conjunction with the Historic Houses Association.

**Location:** MAP 19:E4, OS Ref. TQ344 997. Minutes from M25/J25. Tourist Board signs posted.

**Open:** Daily in summer: 10am–6pm. Last ticket 4.30pm. Check for winter times.

**Admission:** Adult £5, Child £2, Conc. £4, Family £12. Charges alter for special show weekends and winter months.

🔲 ♿ Grounds. WC. ▣ 🍴 🅿 🐕 In grounds, on leads. ✱ ▣

## CAREW MANOR DOVECOTE

**Church Road, Beddington SM6 7NH**

**Tel:** 020 8770 4781    **Fax:** 020 8770 4777    **E-mail:** sutton.museum@ukonline.co.uk

**www.sutton.gov.uk**

**Owner:** London Borough of Sutton    **Contact:** Ms V Murphy

An early 18th century octagonal brick dovecote with around 1200 nesting boxes and the original potence (circular ladder). Opened for tours with the adjacent late medieval Grade I listed Great Hall of Carew Manor.

**Location:** MAP 19:D9, OS Ref. TQ295 652. Just off A232 at entrance to Beddington Park.

**Open:** Tours: Suns only, 22 April, 20 May, 15 Jul & 23 Sept: 2 & 3.30pm.

**Admission:** Adult £4, Child £2.

## CARLYLE'S HOUSE 🌿

**24 Cheyne Row, Chelsea, London SW3 5HL**

**Tel:** 020 7352 7087    **Fax:** 020 7352 5108    **E-mail:** carlyleshouse@nationaltrust.org.uk

**Owner:** The National Trust    **Contact:** The Custodian

Atmospheric home of the writer Thomas Carlyle and his wife Jane from 1834–1881. There is a small walled garden and the surrounding streets are rich in literary and artistic associations.

**Location:** MAP 20:K10, OS Ref. TQ272 777. Off the King's Road and Oakley Street, or off Cheyne Walk between Albert Bridge and Battersea Bridge on Chelsea Embankment.

**Open:** 14 Mar–28 Oct: Wed–Fri (incl. Good Fri), 2–5pm; Sat, Sun & BH Mons, 11am–5pm. Last admission 4.30pm.

**Admission:** Adult £4.50, Child £2.30. Tel for groups visits and guided tours. Free to NT Members.

🎭 By arrangement for groups. ▣

## CHAPTER HOUSE ♯

**East Cloisters, Westminster Abbey, London SW1P 3PE**
**Tel:** 020 7654 4834   **www.westminster-abbey.org**
**Owner:** English Heritage   **Managed by:** Dean & Chapter of Westminster
The Chapter House, built by the Royal masons c1250 and faithfully restored in the 19th century, contains some of the finest medieval sculpture to be seen and spectacular wall paintings. The building is octagonal, with a central column, and still has its original floor of glazed tiles, which have been newly conserved. Its uses have varied and in the 14th century it was used as a meeting place for the Benedictine monks of the Abbey and as well as for Members of Parliament.
**Location:** MAP 20:M8, OS Ref. TQ301 795.
**Open:** All year: Daily, 10am–4pm. Liable to be closed at short notice on State & religious occasions. Closed Good Fri, 24–26 Dec & 1 Jan.
**Admission:** Integral part of tour of Westminster Abbey.

## CHELSEA PHYSIC GARDEN
### SWAN WALK (OFF ROYAL HOSPITAL ROAD), LONDON SW3 4HS
www.chelseaphysicgarden.co.uk

**Tel:** 020 7352 5646   **Fax:** 020 7376 3910
**E-mail:** enquiries@chelseaphysicgarden.co.uk
**Owner:** Chelsea Physic Garden Company
In the heart of London, hidden behind high walls beside the Thames and not far from the site of the world famous Chelsea Flower Show, there is a magical secret garden. Over 300 years old, it has been the scene of some of the most important developments in the history of horticulture, medicine and agriculture. Enjoy free guided tours with entertaining guides, delicious refreshments at the Garden's renowned tearoom, and browse the eclectic selection of garden-related gifts in the shop.
**Location:** MAP 20:L10, OS Ref. TQ277 778. Off Embankment between Chelsea & Albert Bridges. Underground Sloane Square/South Kensington. 239 Bus from Victoria and Clapham Junction to the Garden.
**Open:** 1 Apr–28 Oct: Weds 12 noon-dusk, Thurs & Fris 12 noon–5pm, Suns & BHs 12noon–6pm. Special winter openings: 3/4 Feb & 10/11 Feb 11am–3:30 pm. Chelsea Flower Show week 21–25 May incl.
**Admission:** Adult £7, Conc. £4, Carers for disabled: Free
☐ ☐ ☐ ☐ Partial. WCs. ☐ ☐ By arrangement. ☐ ☐ Guide dogs only. ☐

## CHISWICK HOUSE ♯
*See page 71 for full page entry.*

## CHURCH FARMHOUSE MUSEUM

**Greyhound Hill, London NW4 4JR**
**Tel:** 020 8203 0130   **E-mail:** gerrard.roots@barnet.gov.uk
**www.churchfarmhousemuseum.co.uk**
**Owner:** London Borough of Barnet   **Contact:** Gerrard Roots
The building is a Grade II* 1660s farmhouse with Victorian additions, in a small public garden. There are three 19th century furnished rooms – dining room (decorated for a Victorian Christmas each December), kitchen and laundry room. Exhibitions for 2007: *Toys*, *The 100th Anniversary of Hampstead Garden Suburb* and a local Black History exhibition.
**Location:** MAP 3:H1, OS Ref. TQ228 896. Greyhound Hill is a turning off the A41 (Watford Way) in Hendon. ½m from M1/J2.
**Open:** All year. Mon–Thurs, 10am–1pm & 2–5pm; Sat, 10am–1pm & 2–5.30pm; Sun, 2–5.30pm. Closed: 24–26 Dec & 1 Jan.
**Admission:** Free. Groups by appointment and restricted to no more than 30 people.
☐ Photography by permission. ☐ ☐ Unsuitable. ☐ By arrangement.
☐ Limited. No coaches. ☐ ☐ Guide dogs only. ☐

## COLLEGE OF ARMS

**Queen Victoria Street, London EC4V 4BT**
**Tel:** 020 7248 2762   **Fax:** 020 7248 6448   **E-mail:** enquiries@college-of-arms.gov.uk
**Owner:** Corp. of Kings, Heralds & Pursuivants of Arms   **Contact:** The Officer in Waiting
Mansion built in 1670s to house the English Officers of Arms and their records.
**Location:** MAP 20:O7, OS Ref. TQ320 810. On N side of Queen Victoria Street, S of St Paul's Cathedral.
**Open:** Earl Marshal's Court only; open all year (except BHs, State and special occasions) Mon–Fri, 10am–4pm. Group visits (up to 10) by arrangement only. Record Room: open for tours (groups of up to 20) by special arrangement in advance with the Officer in Waiting.
**Admission:** Free (groups by negotiation).

## EASTBURY MANOR HOUSE ✤

**Eastbury Square, Barking, Essex IG11 9SN**
**Tel:** 020 8724 1000   **Fax:** 020 8724 1003   **E-mail:** eastburyhouse@lbbd.gov.uk
**www.barking-dagenham.gov.uk**
**Owner:** The National Trust   **Contact:** Julie Packham
Eastbury Manor is a unique example of a medium sized Elizabethan Manor House with attractive grounds. Leased to the London Borough of Barking and Dagenham and used for a variety of events and arts and heritage activites. In addition Eastbury can be hired for business conferences, Civil wedding and Civil partnership ceremonies, and education days.
**Location:** MAP 19:F7, OS TQ457 838. In Eastbury Square off Ripple Road off A13, 10 mins S from Upney Station. Buses 287, 368 or 62.
**Open:** All year: Mons & Tues and 1st & 2nd Sat of the month, 10am–4pm.
**Admission:** Adult £2.50, Child 65p, Conc. £1.25, Family £5. Groups (15+) by arrangement: £2pp. Free to NT Members.
☐ ☐ ☐ ☐ ☐ In Eastbury Square. ☐ ☐ In grounds only. ☐ ☐ ☐

## ELTHAM PALACE ♯
*See page 72 for full page entry.*

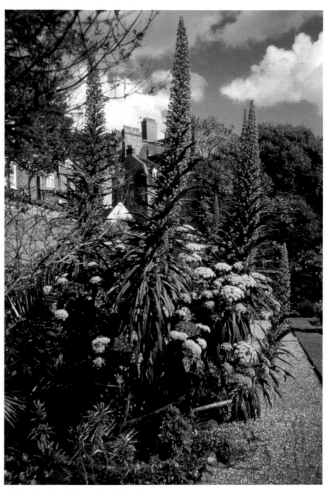

Echium in the Chelsea Physic Garden

NT Photographic Library/ Nadia MacKenzie

## FENTON HOUSE
### WINDMILL HILL, HAMPSTEAD, LONDON NW3 6RT

**Tel/Fax:** 020 7435 3471   **Infoline:** 01494 755563
**E-mail:** fentonhouse@nationaltrust.org.uk
**Owner:** The National Trust   **Contact:** The Custodian

A delightful late 17th century merchant's house, set among the winding streets of Old Hampstead. The charming interior contains an outstanding collection of Oriental and European porcelain, needlework and furniture. The Benton Fletcher Collection of beautiful early keyboard instruments is also housed at Fenton and the instruments are sometimes played by music scholars during opening hours. The walled garden has a formal lawn and walks, an orchard and vegetable garden and fine wrought-iron gates. Telephone for details of demonstrations and other events.

**Location:** MAP 20:J2, OS Ref. TQ262 860. Visitors' entrance on W side of Hampstead Grove. Hampstead Underground station 300 yds.
**Open:** 3–25 Mar: Sat & Sun, 2–5pm. 28 Mar–28 Oct: Wed–Fri, 2-5pm; Sat, Sun & BHs, 11am–5pm. Groups at other times by appointment.
**Admission:** Adult £5.20, Child £2.60, Family £12.50. Groups (15+) £4.30. Joint ticket with 2 Willow Road, £7.20. Garden only: Adult £2. Free to NT Members.
ℹ️ No picnics in grounds. ♿ Ground floor. Braille guide. 🎭 Demonstration tours.
🅿 None. ✳️ ♨ Send SAE for details.

## FORTY HALL
### FORTY HILL, ENFIELD, MIDDLESEX EN2 9HA
www.enfield.gov.uk/fortyhall

**Tel:** 020 8363 8196   **Fax:** 020 8367 9098   **E-mail:** forty.hall@enfield.gov.uk
**Contact:** London Borough of Enfield   **Contact:** Gavin Williams

This beautiful Grade I listed Jacobean House built in 1629 for Sir Nicholas Rainton, Lord Mayor of London, is a location for festivals, events and guided tours throughout the year. The 273-acre estate includes formal gardens, wildflower meadows and the site of Elsyng Palace, owned by Henry VIII and Elizabeth I.
**Location:** MAP 19:E5, OS Ref. TQ336 985. 1m from M25/J25, just off A10. Tourist Board sign posted.
**Open:** All year: Wed–Sun, 11am–4pm.
**Admission:** Free. Groups welcome.
📷 ♿ Partial. WCs. ♨ 🎭 By arrangement. 🅿 Ample for cars. Limited for coaches.
🐕 🐾 In grounds, on leads. ✳️ ♨

## THE FOUNDLING MUSEUM
**40 Brunswick Square, London WC1N 1AZ**
**Tel:** 020 7841 3600   **Fax:** 020 7841 3601
**Owner:** The Foundling Museum
Site of London's first home for abandoned children. Established in 1739. The museum charts the history of the Foundling Hospital and its residents until its closure in 1953.
**Location:** MAP 20:M6, OS Ref. TQ303 822. Underground: Russell Square.
**Open:** Tues–Sat, 10am–6pm; Sun, 12 noon–6pm.
**Admission:** Adult £5, Child up to 16yrs Free, Conc. £4. Special rates for groups & schools.

## BENJAMIN FRANKLIN HOUSE
**36 Craven Street, London WC2N 5NF**
**Tel:** 020 7930 6601 (Box Office)   **www.BenjaminFranklinHouse.org**
**Owner:** The Friends of Benjamin Franklin House   **Contact:** Dr Marcia Balisciano
Benjamin Franklin's only surviving residence. A dynamic museum and educational facility. The 'museum as theatre' Historical Experience takes visitors on a journey through three prime floors, blending live interpretation, leading-edge lighting, sound and visual projection to tell the rich story of Franklin in London in his own words.
**Location:** MAP 20:N7, OS Ref. TQ302 804. Nr Charing Cross Station.
**Open:** Jun–Sept: Wed–Mon 9.45am–5.15pm. Oct–May: Wed–Sun. All year Fris late nights 6.30 & 8pm (pre-book only).
**Admission:** Summer: Adult £9, Conc. £6. Winter: Adult £8, Conc. £5.
✳️

## FULHAM PALACE & MUSEUM
**Bishop's Avenue, Fulham, London SW6 6EA**
**Tel:** 020 7736 3233
**Owner:** London Borough of Hammersmith & Fulham & Fulham Palace Trust
Former home of the Bishops of London (Tudor with Georgian additions and Victorian Chapel). The gardens, famous in the 17th century, now contain specimen trees and a knot garden of herbs.
**Location:** MAP 20:I12, OS Ref. TQ240 761.
**Open:** Museum: From early Mar: Mons & Tues, 12 noon–5pm; Sats, 11am–2pm; Suns, 11.30am–3.30pm. Café: daily, 9am–5pm.
**Admission:** Palace & Gardens: Free.

## THE GEFFRYE MUSEUM

**Kingsland Road, London  E2 8EA**

**Tel:** 020 7739 9893   **Fax:** 020 7729 5647   **E-mail:** info@geffrye-museum.org.uk
**www.geffrye-museum.org.uk**
**Owner:** Independent Charitable Trust

The Geffrye presents the changing style of the English domestic interior from 1600 to the present day through a series of period rooms. The displays lead the visitor on a walk through time, from the 17th century with oak furniture and panelling, past the refined splendour of the Georgian period and the high style of the Victorians, to 20th century modernity. The museum's displays are complemented by a walled herb garden and a series of period gardens.

**Location:** MAP 20:P5, OS Ref. TQ335 833. 1m N of Liverpool St. Buses: 242, 149, 243, 67 & 394. Underground: Liverpool St. or Old St.

**Open:** Museum: Tue–Sat, 10am–5pm. Sun & BH Mon, 12 noon–5pm. Closed Mon (except BHs) Good Fri, 24 Dec–1 Jan. Gardens: Apr–Oct.

**Admission:** Free.

## GUNNERSBURY PARK & MUSEUM

**Gunnersbury Park, London  W3 8LQ**

**Tel:** 020 8992 1612   **Fax:** 020 8752 0686   **E-mail:** gp-museum@cip.org.uk
**Owner:** Hounslow and Ealing Councils   **Contact:** Lynn Acum

Built in 1802 and refurbished by Sydney Smirke for the Rothschild family.

**Location:** MAP 19:B7, OS Ref. TQ190 792. Acton Town Underground station. ¼m N of the junction of A4, M4 North Circular.

**Open:** Apr–Oct: daily: 11am–5pm. Nov–Mar: daily: 11am–4pm. Victorian kitchens summer weekends only. Closed Christmas Day & Boxing Day. Park: open dawn–dusk.

**Admission:** Free. Donations welcome.

Are you looking for unique
**Civil wedding** venues?
See our index on page 577

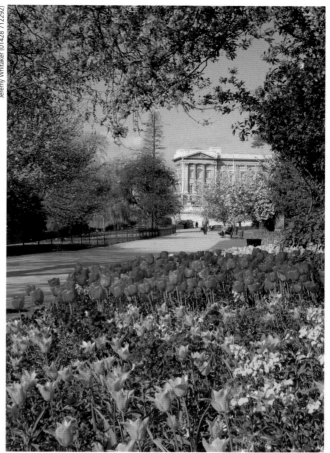
Jeremy Whitaker (01428 712292)

Buckingham Palace from St James Park

©NTPL/David Watson

©NTPL/David Archer

# HAM HOUSE & GARDEN ❧

## HAM, RICHMOND, SURREY  TW10 7RS

www.nationaltrust.org.uk/hamhouse

**Tel:** 020 8940 1950   **Fax:** 020 8439 8241   **E-mail:** hamhouse@nationaltrust.org.uk
**Owner:** The National Trust   **Contact:** The Property Manager

Ham House, set on the banks of the Thames near Richmond, is perhaps the most remarkable Stuart house in the country. Formerly the home of the influential Duke and Duchess of Lauderdale, Ham was a centre for Court intrigue throughout the 17th century. In its time, the house was at the forefront of fashion and retains much of its interior decoration from that period. Sumptuous textiles, furniture and paintings collected by the couple are shown in 26 rooms.

The garden is a remarkable survival of English formal gardening and is being gradually restored to its former glory. Statues of *Venus Marina* and *Mercury* have returned to the wilderness. The 18th century dairy, decorated with cast iron cows' legs supporting marble work surfaces, and hand-painted Wedgwood tiles, is now on view, as is the

17th century still house, used for distilling alcohol and perfumes.

Programme of events throughout the year, including open air theatre, guided tours, children's activities, recitals and Christmas specific events.

**Location:** MAP 19:B8, OS Ref. TQ172 732. 1½ m from Richmond and 2m from Kingston. On the S bank of the River Thames, W of A307 at Petersham.

**Open:** House: 31 Mar–28 Oct: Sat–Wed, 1–5pm. Gardens: All year, Sat–Wed, 11am–6pm or dusk if earlier. Closed 25/26 Dec & 1 Jan. Special Christmas openings for house, gardens, shop and café and Christmas lunches in December.

**Admission:** House & Garden: Adult £9, Child £5, Family £22. Garden only: Adult £3, Child £2, Family £7. Booked groups (15+): Adult £8, Child £4.50. Free to NT Members.
Partial. WC. Guide dogs.

© Matthew Hollow

## HANDEL HOUSE MUSEUM
### 25 BROOK STREET, LONDON W1K 4HB
www.handelhouse.org

**Tel:** 020 7495 1685 **Fax:** 020 7495 1759 **E-mail:** mail@handelhouse.org
**Owner:** The Handel House Trust Ltd **Contact:** Shuk Kwan Liu
Handel House Museum is located at 25 Brook Street, where the great baroque composer, George Frideric Handel lived for 36 years, and where he wrote such timeless masterpieces as Zadok the Priest, Messiah and Music for the Royal Fireworks. The elegantly refurbished interiors create the perfect setting for 18th century furniture and fine art, evoking the spirit of Georgian London. This landmark address is also brought to life by an inspiring programme of live music, events and activities for adults and families. The Thursday evening concerts every week are particularly popular, and you are recommended to book well in advance.
**Location:** MAP 20:K7, OS Ref. TQ286 809. Central London, between New Bond St and Grosvenor Square. Bond Street Tube.
**Open:** Tue–Sat, 10am–6pm (Thur until 8pm). Suns, 12 noon–6pm. Closed Mons. Groups by arrangement.
**Admission:** Adult £5, Child £2, Conc. £4.50. NACF cardholders Free.
ⓘ No inside photography. 🖼 🚻 ♿ 📷 By arrangement. ■ ❋ ♥

---

## HOGARTH'S HOUSE

**Hogarth Lane, Great West Road, Chiswick, London W4 2QN**
**Tel:** 020 8994 6757 **E-mail:** info@cip.org.uk **www.hounslow.info/hogarthshouse**
**Owner:** Hogarth House Foundation **Contact:** Victoria Northwood
This late 17th century house was the country home of William Hogarth, the famous painter, engraver, satirist and social reformer between 1749 and his death in 1764.
**Location:** MAP 19:D7, OS Ref. TQ213 778. 100 yds W of Hogarth roundabout on the Great West Road – junction of Burlington Lane. Car park in named spaces in Hogarth Business Centre behind house and Chiswick House grounds.
**Open:** Tue–Fri, 1–5pm (Nov–Mar: 1–4pm). Sat, Sun & BH Mons, 1–6pm (Nov–Mar: 1–5pm). Closed Mon (except BHs), Good Fri, Christmas Day, Boxing Day & Jan.
**Admission:** Free.
🖼 🅿 ❋

---

## HONEYWOOD HERITAGE CENTRE

**Honeywood Walk, Carshalton SM5 3NX**
**Tel:** 020 8770 4297 **Fax:** 020 8770 4297 **E-mail:** lbshoneywood@btconnect.com
**www.sutton.gov.uk/leisure/heritage/honeywood.htm**
**Owner:** London Borough of Sutton **Contact:** The Curator
A 17th century listed building next to the picturesque Carshalton Ponds, containing displays on many aspects of the history of the London Borough of Sutton plus a changing programme of exhibitions and events on a wide range of subjects. Attractive garden at rear.
**Location:** MAP 19:D9, OS Ref. TQ279 646. On A232 approximately 4m W of Croydon.
**Open:** Wed–Fri, 11am–5pm. Sat, Suns & BH Mons, 10am–5pm. Free admission to shop & tearooms.
**Admission:** Adult £1.30, Child 65p, under 5 Free. Groups by arrangement.
🖼 ♿ Ground floor. WC. ■ 📷 🅿 Limited. ■ 🐕 Guide dogs only. ❋ ♥

---

## JEWEL TOWER ⌗

**Abingdon Street, Westminster, London SW1P 3JX**
**Tel:** 020 7222 2219 **www.english-heritage.org.uk/visits**
**Owner:** English Heritage **Contact:** Visitor Operations Team
Built c1365 to house the personal treasure of Edward III. One of two surviving parts of the original Palace of Westminster. Now houses an exhibition on 'Parliament Past and Present'. The second floor now includes new illustrated panels, telling the story of this small but important building.
**Location:** MAP 20:M8, OS Ref. TQ302 794. Opposite S end of Houses of Parliament (Victoria Tower).
**Open:** 1 Apr–31 Oct: daily, 10am–5pm. 1 Nov–20 Mar: daily, 10am–4pm. Closed 24–26 Dec & 1 Jan.
**Admission:** Adult £2.90, Child £1.50, Conc. £2.20.
🖼 🚻 ❋ ♥

---

## DR JOHNSON'S HOUSE

**17 Gough Square, London EC4A 3DE**
**Tel:** 020 7353 3745 **E-mail:** curator@drjohnsonshouse.org
**Owner:** The Trustees
Fine 18th century house, once home to Dr Samuel Johnson, the celebrated literary figure, famous for his English dictionary.
**Location:** MAP 20:N7, OS Ref. TQ314 813. N of Fleet Street.
**Open:** Oct–Apr: Mon–Sat, 11am–5pm. May–Sept: Mon–Sat, 11am–5.30pm. Closed BHs.
**Admission:** Adult £4.50, Child £1.50 (under 10yrs Free), Conc. £3.50. Family £10. Groups: £3.50.

---

## KEATS HOUSE
### KEATS GROVE, HAMPSTEAD, LONDON NW3 2RR
www.cityoflondon.gov.uk/keats

**Tel:** 020 7435 2062 **Fax:** 020 7431 9293 **E-mail:** keatshouse@cityoflondon.gov.uk
**Owner:** City of London **Contact:** The Manager
This Grade I listed Regency house is where the poet John Keats lived from 1818 to 1820 with his friend Charles Brown. Here he wrote 'Ode to a Nightingale' and met and fell in love with Fanny Brawne. Suffering from tuberculosis, Keats left for Italy, where he died aged twenty-five.
**Location:** MAP 20:K3, OS Ref. TQ272 856. Hampstead, NW3. Nearest Underground: Belsize Park & Hampstead.
**Open:** All year: Tue–Sun & BHs, 1–5pm. Visits by appointment: Tue–Fri, 10am–12 noon. Please call to confirm times prior to visit.
**Admission:** Adult £3.50, Under 16s Free, Conc. £1.75.
🖼 ♿ Ground floor & garden. 🅿 None. ■ 🐕 Guide dogs only. ❋

---

See which properties offer **educational facilities** or **school visits** in our index on page 571

# KENSINGTON PALACE
## LONDON W8 4PX
www.kensington-palace.org.uk

**Tel:** Recorded Information: 0870 751 5170
Venue Hire and Corporate Hospitality: 0870 751 5184
All Other Enquiries: 0870 751 5176
**Owner:** Historic Royal Palaces

The feminine influence of generations of Royal women have shaped this stylish Palace and elegant gardens. The birthplace and childhood home of Queen Victoria, the Palace first became a royal residence for William and Mary in 1689. Mary felt 'shut in' at Whitehall and much preferred her new Kensington home, which was enlarged by Sir Christopher Wren. The famous Orangery was built in 1704 in by Queen Anne, and George II's wife, Queen Caroline, another keen gardener, added further improvements. Today, the Palace houses a stunning permanent display of fashionable and formal dresses, the Royal Ceremonial Dress Collection, which includes Queen Victoria's wedding dress and dresses worn by Diana, Princess of Wales.

**Location:** MAP 20:I8, OS Ref. TQ258 801 In Kensington Gardens. Underground: Queensway on Central Line, High Street Kensington on Circle & District Line.

**Open;** Mar–Oct: daily, 10am–6pm (last admission 5pm) Nov–Feb: daily, 10am–5pm (last admission 4pm) Closed 24–26 Dec.

**Admission:** Telephone Information Line for admission prices: 0870 751 5170. Advance Ticket Sales: 0870 751 5180 Group bookings 0870 751 7070. Quote Hudson's.

ℹ️ No photography indoors. 🅾️ 🆃 🆆 🍴 ♿ Partial. 🅿️ Nearby. ⬛ Please book, 0870 751 5192. 🐕 In grounds, on leads. Guide dogs only in Palace. ✳️

---

## KENWOOD HOUSE ⌗

*See page 73 for full page entry.*

---

## LSO ST LUKE'S UBS AND LSO MUSIC EDUCATION CENTRE
**161 Old Street, London EC1V 9NG**
**Tel:** 020 7490 3939   **Minicom:** 020 7490 8299   **Fax:** 020 7566 2881
**E-mail:** lsostlukes@lso.co.uk   **www.lso.co.uk/lsostlukes**
**Contact:** Alison Thompson, Centre Manager

Formerly St Luke's Church, a Grade I listed Hawksmoor church built in 1733. LSO St Luke's is the new home for the London Symphony Orchestra's music education and community programme, LSO Discovery. The church was derelict for 40 years, but has been rebuilt and opened in early 2003 with state-of-the-art facilities.

**Location:** MAP 20:O6, OS Ref. TQ325 824. On corner of Old Street and Helmet Row, 5mins walk from Old Street Station (Northern Line, National Rail).

**Open:** By appointment only. Contact the Centre Manager.

**Admission:** Free.

♿ 🆃 By arrangement. 🅿️ No cars, limited for coaches. ⬛ 🐕 Guide dogs only.

The Banqueting House

The White Tower, Tower of London

## LEIGHTON HOUSE MUSEUM

### 12 HOLLAND PARK ROAD, KENSINGTON, LONDON W14 8LZ

www.rbkc.gov.uk/leightonhousemusem

**Tel:** 020 7602 3316   **Fax:** 020 7371 2467
**E-mail:** museums@rbkc.gov.uk
**Owner:** Royal Borough of Kensington & Chelsea
**Contact:** Curator

Leighton House was the home of Frederic, Lord Leighton 1830–1896, painter and President of the Royal Academy, built between 1864–1879. It was a palace of art designed for entertaining and to provide a magnificent working space in the studio, with great north windows and a gilded apse. The Arab Hall is the centrepiece of the house, containing Leighton's collection of Islamic tiles, a gilt mosaic frieze and a fountain. Victorian paintings by Leighton, Millais and Burne-Jones are on display.

**Location:** MAP 20:I9, OS Ref. TQ247 793. Nearest underground: High Street Kensington (exit staircase turn left, take first right for Melbury Road after Commonwealth Institute. Leighton House is located in Holland Park Road, the first left. Bus: 9, 10, 27, 28, 33, 49, 328 (to Commonwealth Institute).

**Open:** Daily, except Tues, 11am–5.30pm. Also open Spring/Summer BHs. Guided tours on Wed & Thur, 2.30pm. Closed 25/26 Dec.

**Admission:** Adult £3, Conc £1. Family £6. Guided tours free on Weds & Thurs. Joint group guided tour with Linley Sambourne House £10pp.

ℹ️ No photography. 📷 🅣 ♿ Unsuitable.
🎟️ Wed & Thurs at 2.30pm. 🅿️ None.

## LINLEY SAMBOURNE HOUSE

### 18 STAFFORD TERRACE, LONDON W8 7BH

www.rbkc.gov.uk/linleysambournehouse

**Info:** 020 7602 3316 (ext 300 Mon–Fri) or 020 7938 1295 (Sats & Suns)
**Fax:** 020 7371 2467   **E-mail:** museums@rbkc.gov.uk
**Owner:** The Royal Borough of Kensington & Chelsea   **Contact:** Curatorial staff

Linley Sambourne House is the former home of the Punch cartoonist Edward Linley Sambourne and his family. Almost unchanged over the course of the last century, the house provides a unique insight into the life of an artistic middle-class family. The majority of the original decoration and furnishings remain in situ exactly as left by the Sambournes. All visits are by guided tour with special dramatic tours available and an introductory video. Larger groups can visit jointly with Leighton House Museum just 10 minutes walk away.

**Location:** MAP 20:I8, OS Ref. TQ252 794. Parallel to Kensington High St, between Phillimore Gardens & Argyll Rd. Bus: 9, 10, 27, 28, 31, 49, 52, 70 & C1. Underground: Kensington High St. Parking on Sun in nearby streets.

**Open:** Mid Mar–mid Dec: Sats & Suns; tours leaving 11.15am, 1pm, 2.15pm and 3.30pm. Pre-booking is advised. At other times for booked groups (10+), by appointment. Larger groups (12+) will be divided for tours of the House. Access for Group tours: Mon–Fri.

**Admission:** Adult £6, Child (under 18yrs) £1, Conc £4. Groups (12+): Min £72. Joint group (10+) guided tour with Leighton House Museum £10pp.

ℹ️ No photography. 📷 🎟️ Obligatory. 🅿️ None. ♿ Guide dogs only. ❄️

## LITTLE HOLLAND HOUSE

**40 Beeches Avenue, Carshalton SM5 3LW**
**Tel:** 020 8770 4781 **Fax:** 020 8770 4777
**E-mail:** valary.murphy@sutton.gov.uk
**www.sutton.gov.uk/leisure/heritage/lhh.htm**
**Owner:** London Borough of Sutton **Contact:** Ms V Murphy
The home of Frank Dickinson (1874–1961) artist, designer and craftsman, who dreamt of a house that would follow the philosophy and theories of William Morris and John Ruskin. Dickinson designed, built and furnished the house himself from 1902 onwards. The Grade II* listed interior features handmade furniture, metal work, carvings and paintings produced by Dickinson in the Arts and Crafts style.
**Location:** MAP 19:D9, OS Ref. TQ275 634. On B278 1m S of junction with A232.
**Open:** First Sun of each month & BH Suns & Mons (excluding Christmas & New Year), 1.30–5.30pm.
**Admission:** Free. Groups by arrangement, £4pp (includes talk and guided tour).
ⅈ No photography in house. ♿ Ground floor. 🎭 By arrangement. 🦮 Guide dogs only. ✸

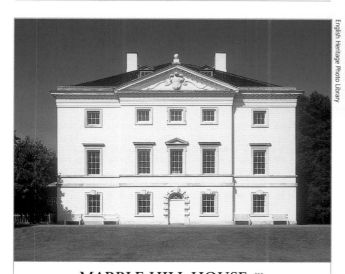

## MARBLE HILL HOUSE ♯

### RICHMOND ROAD, TWICKENHAM TW1 2NL

www.english-heritage.org.uk/visits

**Tel:** 020 8892 5115
**Owner:** English Heritage **Contact:** Visitor Operations Team
This beautiful villa beside the Thames was built in 1724–29 for Henrietta Howard, mistress of George II. Here she entertained many of the poets and wits of the Augustan age including Alexander Pope and later Horace Walpole. The perfect proportions of the villa were inspired by the work of the 16th century Italian architect, Palladio. Today this beautifully presented house contains an important collection of paintings and furniture, including some pieces commissioned for the villa when it was built. A recent installation recreates the Chinese wallpaper Henrietta Howard hung in the Dining Room in 1751. Summer concerts.
**Location:** MAP 19:B8, OS Ref. TQ174 736. A305, 600yds E of Orleans House.
**Open:** 1 Apr–31 Oct: Sat, 10am–2pm. Suns & BHs, 10am–5pm. Tours: Tues & Wed, 12 noon & 3pm. 1 Nov–20 Mar: by appointment only.
**Admission:** Adult £4.20, Child £2.10, Conc. £3.20, Family £10.50.
◻ ⊤ ♿ Ground floor. WC. 🎭 Summer only. 🅿 🦮 ▲ ⬇

## MORDEN HALL PARK ⚘

**Morden Hall Road, Morden SM4 5JD**
**Tel:** 020 8545 6850 **Fax:** 020 8417 8091
**E-mail:** mordenhallpark@nationaltrust.org.uk
**Owner:** The National Trust **Contact:** The Property Manager
Former deer park centred around historic snuff mills and rose garden featuring an extensive network of waterways, ancient hay meadows and wetlands. Workshops now house local craftworkers.
**Location:** MAP 19:D8, OS Ref. TQ261 684. Off A24 and A297 S of Wimbledon, N of Sutton.
**Open:** All year: daily. NT gift shop & Riverside Café: 10am–5pm (closed: 25/26 Dec & 1 Jan). Car park closes 6pm.
**Admission:** Free.

## WILLIAM MORRIS GALLERY

**Lloyd Park, Forest Road, Walthamstow, London E17 4PP**
**Tel:** 020 8527 3782 **Fax:** 020 8527 7070
**Owner:** London Borough of Waltham Forest **Contact:** The Keeper
**Location:** MAP 19:F6, OS Ref. SQ372 899. 15 mins walk from Walthamstow tube (Victoria line). 5–10 mins from M11/A406.
**Open:** Tue–Sat and first Sun each month, 10am–1pm and 2–5pm.
**Admission:** Free for all visitors but a charge is made for guided tours which must be booked in advance.

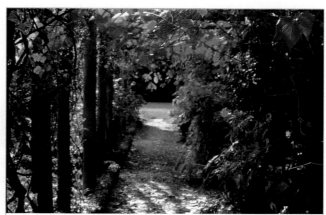

English Heritage Photo Library

## MYDDELTON HOUSE GARDENS

### BULLS CROSS, ENFIELD, MIDDLESEX EN2 9HG

www.leevalleypark.org.uk

**Tel:** 01992 702200
**Owner:** Lee Valley Regional Park Authority
Created by the famous plantsman and Fellow of the Royal Horticultural Society, E A Bowles, the gardens contain year round interest. From the January snowdrops, through the springtime flowering daffodils to the summer roses and beyond to the autumn crocus, there's always something in the gardens to interest the visitor. The gardens are an ideal place to draw, paint, photograph or picnic. Woodland walks. Carp lake. National Collection of award-winning Bearded Iris. Guided walks available.
**Location:** MAP 19:D4, OS Ref. TQ342 992. ¼m W of A10 via Turkey St. ¾m S M25/J25.
**Open:** Apr–Sept: Mon–Fri, 10am–4.30pm, Suns & BH Mons & NGS days, 12 noon–4pm. Oct–Mar: Mon–Fri, 10am–3pm. Last admission 30 mins before closing. Closed Christmas.
**Admission:** Adult £2.50, Conc. £1.90. Prices subject to change April 2007. Separate charge for guided walks.
◻ ⊞ ♿ Some paths. 🎭 🎭 Please ring 01992 709849. 🅿 🦮 Guide dogs only. ✸

## THE OCTAGON, ORLEANS HOUSE GALLERY

**Riverside, Twickenham, Middlesex TW1 3DJ**
**Tel:** 020 8831 6000 **Fax:** 020 8744 0501 **E-mail:** galleryinfo@richmond.gov.uk
**Owner:** London Borough of Richmond-upon-Thames **Contact:** The Curator
Outstanding example of baroque architecture by James Gibbs c1720. Art gallery.
**Location:** MAP 19:B8, OS Ref. TQ168 734. On N side of Riverside, 700yds E of Twickenham town centre, 400yds S of Richmond Road. Vehicle access via Orleans Rd only.
**Open:** Tue–Sat, 1–5.30pm, Sun & BHs, 2–5.30pm (Oct–Mar closes 4.30pm). Closed Mons. Garden: open daily, 9am–sunset.
**Admission:** Free.

© HRP 2007

Banqueting Suite, Kensington Palace

## OSTERLEY PARK AND HOUSE ❧
### JERSEY ROAD, ISLEWORTH, MIDDLESEX TW7 4RB
www.nationaltrust.org.uk/osterley/

**Tel:** 020 8232 5050  **Fax:** 020 8232 5080  **Infoline:** 01494 755566
**E-mail:** osterley@nationaltrust.org.uk
**Owner:** The National Trust  **Contact:** Visitor Services Manager

Osterley's four turrets look out across one of the last great 'Landscape' parks in suburban London, its trees and lakes an unexpected haven of green. Originally built in 1575, the mansion was transformed in the 18th century into an elegant villa by architect Robert Adam. The classical interior, designed for entertaining on a grand scale, still impresses with its specially made tapestries, furniture and plasterwork. The magnificent 16th century stables survive largely intact.

**Location:** MAP 19:B7, OS Ref. TQ146 780. Access via Thornbury Road on N side of A4.
**Open:** House: 14 Mar–28 Oct: Wed–Sun & BHs, 1–4.30pm. Garden: 14 Mar–28 Oct: Wed–Sun & BHs, 11am–5pm.Park: All year, daily. Winter (30 Oct 2006–24 Mar 2007 and 29 Oct 2007–23 Mar 2008), 8am–6pm, Summer (25 Mar–28 Oct), 8am–7.30pm.
**Admission:** House and Garden: Adult £7.50, Child £3.50, Family £20, Groups (15+) £6.50. Gardens: Adult £3, Child £1.50. Park: Free. Car Park: £3.50. Free to NT Members.
◻ ⊤ ⅃ Tel for details. ▪ **P** ▪ ▪ On leads in park. ▲ ✳ ▯

---

### PALACE OF WESTMINSTER
**London  SW1A 0AA**
**Tel:** 020 7219 3000 / 0870 906 3773  **Info:** 020 7219 4272
**Fax:** 020 7219 5839  **Contact:** Information Office
The first Palace of Westminster was erected on this site by Edward the Confessor in 1042 and the building was a royal residence until a devastating fire in 1512. After this, the palace became the two-chamber Parliament for government – the House of Lords  and the elected House of Commons. Following a further fire in 1834, the palace was rebuilt by Sir Charles Barry and decorated by A W Pugin.
**Location:** MAP 20:M8, OS Ref. TQ303 795. Central London, W bank of River Thames. 1km S of Trafalgar Square. Underground: Westminster.
**Open:** Aug–Sept (please ring for details). At other times by appointment. Please telephone Info line.
**Admission:** Adult £7, Child/Conc. £5 (under 4yrs Free).

---

### PITZHANGER MANOR-HOUSE
**Walpole Park, Mattock Lane, Ealing  W5 5EQ**
**Tel:** 020 8567 1227  **Fax:** 020 8567 0595
**E-mail:** pmgallery&house@ealing.gov.uk  **www.ealing.gov.uk/pmgalleryandhouse**
**Owner:** London Borough of Ealing  **Contact:** Anne Ninivin
Pitzhanger Manor House is a restored Georgian villa, once owned and designed by the architect Sir John Soane (1753 - 1837). Rooms in the house have been restored using Soane's highly individual ideas in design and decoration. Exhibitions of contemporary art are programmed year-round, sited in the adjacent Gallery and often also in the House.
**Location:** MAP 19:B7, OS Ref. TQ176 805. Ealing, London.
**Open:** All year: Tue–Fri, 1–5pm. Sat, 11am–5pm. Summer Sunday Openings, please ring for details. Closed Christmas, Easter, New Year and BHs.
**Admission:** Free.
⊤ ⅃ By arrangement. ◒ ▪ ▪ In grounds, on leads. ▲ ✳

---

### RED HOUSE ❧
**Red House Lane, Bexleyheath  DA6 8JF**
**Tel:** 020 8304 9878 (Booking line: Tues–Sat, 9.30am–1.30pm)
**Owner:** The National Trust
Commissioned by William Morris in 1859 and designed by Philip Webb, Red House is of enormous international significance in the history of domestic architecture and garden design. The garden was designed to "clothe" the house with a series of sub-divided areas that still clearly exist today. Inside, the house retains many of the original features and fixed items of furniture designed by Morris and Webb, as well as wall paintings and stained glass by Burne-Jones.
**Location:** MAP 19:G8, OS Ref. TQ48 1750. Off A221 Bexleyheath. Visitors will be advised on how to reach the property when booking. Nearest rail station Bexleyheath, 20 mins' walk.
**Open:** Feb–Dec: Wed–Sun, 11am–4.15pm. Last tour 3.30pm. Closed Christmas Day, Boxing Day, 1 Jan–14 Feb. Open Easter Sun, Good Fri, BH Mons. Admission by pre-booked guided tour only.
**Admission:** Adult £6.40, Child £3.20, Family £16. NT Members Free.
ⓘ No WC. ⅃ Ground floor only. ▪ Limited. **P** No parking on site. Parking at Danson Park (15 min walk). 90p parking charge at weekends and BHs. Disabled drivers can pre-book (limited parking).

---

### ROYAL OBSERVATORY NATIONAL MARITIME MUSEUM & QUEEN'S HOUSE
*See page 74 for full page entry.*

---

### ST GEORGE'S CATHEDRAL, SOUTHWARK
**Westminster Bridge Road, London  SE1 7HY**
**Tel:** 020 7928 5256  **Fax:** 020 7202 2189
**E-mail:** info@southwark-rc-cathedral.org.uk  **Contact:** Canon James Cronin
Neo-Gothic rebuilt Pugin Cathedral bombed during the last war and rebuilt by Romily Craze in 1958.
**Location:** MAP 20:N9, OS Ref. TQ315 794. Near Imperial War Museum. ½m SE of Waterloo Stn.
**Open:** 8am–6pm, every day, except BHs.
**Admission:** Free.

# ST JOHN'S GATE
## MUSEUM OF THE ORDER OF ST JOHN
### ST JOHN'S GATE, LONDON EC1M 4DA

www.sja.org.uk/museum

**Tel:** 020 7324 4074  **Fax:** 020 7336 0587  **E-mail:** museum@nhq.sja.org.uk
**Owner:** The Order of St John     **Contact:** Pamela Willis
Early 16 century Gatehouse (built 1504), Priory Church and Norman Crypt. The remarkable history of the Knights Hospitaller, dedicated to caring for the sick and dating back to the 11th century, is revealed in collections including furniture, paintings, armour, stained glass and other items. Notable associations with Shakespeare, Hogarth, Edward Cave, Dr Johnson, Dickens, David Garrick and many others. In Victorian times, St John Ambulance was founded here and a modern interactive gallery tells its story.
**Location:** MAP 20:N6, OS Ref. TQ317 821. St. John's Lane, Clerkenwell.  Nearest Underground: Farringdon.
**Open:** Mon–Fri: 10am–5pm. Sat: 10am–4pm. Closed BHs & Sat of BH weekend. Tours: Tue, Fri & Sat at 11am & 2.30pm. Reference Library: Open by appointment.
**Admission:** Museum Free. Tours of the building: £5, OAP £4 (donation).

◻ ♿ Ground floor. WC. 🅿 🖼 🐕 Guide dogs only. ❄          Reg. Charity No. 1077265

---

## ST PAUL'S CATHEDRAL                *See page 75 for full page entry.*

---

## SIR JOHN SOANE'S MUSEUM

**13 Lincoln's Inn Fields, London  WC2A 3BP**
**Tel:** 020 7405 2107   **Fax:** 020 7831 3957   **www.soane.org**
**Owner:** Trustees of Sir John Soane's Museum     **Contact:** Julie Brock
The celebrated architect Sir John Soane built this in 1812 as his own house. It now contains his collection of antiquities, sculpture and paintings.
**Location:** MAP 20:M6, OS Ref. TQ308 816. E of Kingsway, S of High Holborn.
**Open:** Tue–Sat, 10am–5pm. 6–9pm, first Tue of the month. Closed BHs & 24 Dec.
**Admission:** Free. Groups must book.

---

## SOMERSET HOUSE                *See page 76 for full page entry.*

---

Chelsea Physic Garden

# SOUTHSIDE HOUSE 🏛
### 3 WOODHAYES ROAD, WIMBLEDON, LONDON  SW19 4RJ

www.southsidehouse.com

**Tel:** 020 8946 7643   **E-mail:** info@southsidehouse.com
**Owner:** The Pennington-Mellor-Munthe Charity Trust     **Contact:** The Administrator
Described by connoisseurs as an unforgettable experience, Southside House provides an enchantingly eccentric backdrop to the lives and loves of generations of the Pennington Mellor Munthe families. Maintained in traditional style, without major refurbishment, and crowded with the family possessions of centuries, Southside offers a wealth of fascinating family stories.
Behind the long façade are the old rooms, still with much of the original furniture and a superb collection of art and historical objects. John Pennington-Mellor's daughter, Hilda, married Axel Munthe, the charismatic Swedish doctor and philanthropist. The preservation of the house was left to their youngest son who led a life of extraordinary adventure during the Second World War. Malcolm Munthe's surviving children continue to care for the property.
The gardens are as fascinating as the house, with a series of sculptural "rooms" linked by water and intriguing pathways.

**Location:** MAP 20:D8, OS Ref. TQ234 706. On S side of Wimbledon Common (B281), opposite Crooked Billet Inn.
**Open:** Easter Sun–30 Sept: Weds, Sats, Suns & BH Mons. Closed during Wimbledon fortnight in July. Guided tours on the hour 2, 3 & 4pm. Other times throughout the year by arrangement with the Administrator.
**Admission:** Adult £5, Child £2.50 (must be accompanied by an adult), OAP £4, Family £10.

ℹ No photography inside house. ♿ Unsuitable. 🅵 Obligatory. 🅿 Limited. 🖼
🐕 In grounds on leads. ♿

## SOUTHWARK CATHEDRAL

**London Bridge, London SE1 9DA**

**Tel:** 020 7367 6700    **Fax:** 020 7367 6730    **Visitors' Officer:** 020 7367 6734
**E-mail:** cathedral@southwark.anglican.org   **www.southwark.anglican.org/cathedral**
**Owner:** Church of England    **Contact:** Visitors' Officer

London's oldest gothic building and a place of worship for over 1,400 years, Southwark Cathedral has connections with Chaucer, Shakespeare, Dickens and John Harvard. Included in the new riverside Millennium buildings are: the Cathedral Shop, Refectory, and Archaeological Chamber.

**Location:** MAP 20:O8, OS Ref. TQ327 803. South side of London Bridge, near Shakespeare's Globe and Tate Modern.

**Open:** Daily: 8.30am–6pm. Weekday services: 8am, 12.30pm and 5.30pm. Sat services, 9am and 4pm. Sun services: 9am, 11am, 3pm & 6.30pm. Cathedral Shop: daily, 10am–6pm, Sun, 11am–5pm.

**Admission:** Recommended donation of £4 per person. Booked groups (min 10): Adult £4, Child £2, Conc. £3.50. Trade discounts available.

ℹ️ Indoor photography & video recording with permit. 🚫📷 🅣 🔊 Partial. WCs. 🖥️ 🍽️ Licensed. 🎭 By arrangement. 🔓 🅿️ None. 🖥️ 🦽 Guide dogs only. ❋ ♿

## SPENCER HOUSE

*See page 77 for full page entry.*

NT Photographic Library: Geoffrey Frosh

## STRAWBERRY HILL

### ST MARY'S, STRAWBERRY HILL, WALDEGRAVE ROAD, TWICKENHAM TW1 4SX

**Tel:** 0870 626 0402

**Owner:** Strawberry Hill Trust    **Contact:** The Administrator

Horace Walpole's little gothic castle is internationally known and admired as the first substantial building of the Gothic Revival. Featured by BBC 2's *Restoration* in 2004, it is now undergoing a major conservation programme. During 2007 the house will be open on Sunday afternoons for visitors to view the restoration process. Special group tours may also be booked on weekdays. During the 19th century Lady Waldegrave added a magnificent wing which is now owned by St Mary's College. This may be hired for weddings, corporate functions and conferences. Please telephone for details 020 8240 4044.

**Location:** MAP 19:B8, OS Ref. TQ158 722. Off A310 between Twickenham & Teddington.

**Open:** 1 Apr–31 Oct: Suns, 2–5pm. Group bookings & infomation: 0870 626 0402.

**Admission:** Adult £5.50. Group bookings and Special Tours by arrangement.

ℹ️ Conferences. 🚫📷 🖥️ 🎭 ✖️

## SUTTON HOUSE 🦌

### 2 & 4 HOMERTON HIGH STREET, HACKNEY, LONDON E9 6JQ

**Tel:** 020 8986 2264   **E-mail:** suttonhouse@nationaltrust.org.uk

**Owner:** The National Trust    **Contact:** The Custodian

A rare example of a Tudor red-brick house, built in 1535 by Sir Ralph Sadleir, Principal Secretary of State for Henry VIII, with 18th century alterations and later additions. Restoration revealed many 16th century details, even in rooms of later periods. Notable features include original linenfold panelling and 17th century wall paintings.

**Location:** MAP 20:P3, OS Ref. TQ352 851. At the corner of Isabella Road and Homerton High St.

**Open:** Historic rooms: 1 Feb–23 Dec: Thur–Sun, 12.30–4.30pm. Café, Shop & Art Gallery: 1 Feb–23 Dec: Thur–Sun, 12 noon–4.30pm. Open BH Mons, closed Good Fri.

**Admission:** Adult £2.70, Child 60p, Family £6. Group £2.20. Free to NT Members.

🚫📷 🔊 Ground floor only. WC. 🖥️ 🎭 🅿️ None. 🖥️ ▲ ❋ ♿

## SYON PARK 🏛️

*See page 78 for full page entry.*

## THE TOWER BRIDGE EXHIBITION

**Tower Bridge, London SE1 2UP**

**Tel:** 020 7940 3985    **Fax:** 020 7357 7935

**Owner:** Corporation of London    **Contact:** Emma Parlow

One of London's most unusual and exciting exhibitions is situated inside Tower Bridge. Enjoy spectacular views from the high level walkways.

**Location:** MAP 20:P8, OS Ref. TQ337 804. Adjacent to Tower of London, nearest Underground: Tower Hill.

**Open:** 1 Apr–30 Sep: 10am–5.30pm (last ticket). 1 Oct–31 Mar: 9.30am–5pm (last ticket). Closed 25 Dec.

**Admission:** Adult £5.50, Child £3, Conc. £4.25. (Prices may change April 2007.)

© English Heritage Photo Library

Kenwood House, Hampstead

© HRP 2007 / Stephen Pond/HRP/newstream.co.uk

© HRP 2007 / Stephen Pond/HRP/newstream.co.uk

# THE TOWER OF LONDON

## LONDON EC3N 4AB

www.tower-of-london.org.uk

**Contact: Recorded Information Line:** 0870 756 6060
**Venue Hire and Corporate Hospitality:** 0870 751 5183
**All Other Enquiries:** 0870 751 5177

**Owner:** Historic Royal Palaces

The ancient stones reverberate with dark secrets, priceless jewels glint in fortified vaults and pampered ravens strut the grounds. The Tower of London, founded by William the Conqueror in 1066–7, is one of the world's most famous fortresses, and Britain's most visited historic site. Despite a grim reputation for a place of torture and death, there are so many more stories to be told about the Tower. This powerful and enduring symbol of the Norman Conquest has been enjoyed as a royal palace, served as an armoury and, for a few years in the 1830s, even housed a zoo! An intriguing cast of characters have played their part: including the dastardly jewel-thief Colonel Blood, tragic Lady Jane Grey and maverick zoo keeper Albert Cops.

**Location:** MAP 20:P7, OS Ref. TQ336 806, Underground: Tower Hill on Circle/District Line. Docklands Light Railway: Tower Gateway Station. Rail: Fenchurch Street Station and London Bridge Station. Bus: 15, 25, 42, 78, 100, D1, RV1. Riverboat: From Charing Cross, Westminster or Greenwich to Tower Pier. London Eye to Tower of London Express.

**Open:** Summer: 1 Mar–31 Oct, Daily, Tues–Sat: 9am–6pm (last admission 5pm), Mons & Suns: 10am–6pm (last admission 5pm). Winter: 1 Nov–28 Feb, Tues–Sat: 9am–5pm, Mons & Suns: 10am–5pm (last admission 4pm). Closed 24–26 Dec and 1 Jan. Buildings close 30 minutes after last admission.

**Admission:** Telephone Information Line for admission prices: 0870 756 6060. Advance Ticket Sales: 0870 756 7070. Group bookings: 0870 751 7070. Quote Hudson's.
ℹ No photography in Jewel House. 🖼 ☎ 0870 751 5183. ♿ Partial. WC. ♨ 🍴
🎟 Yeoman Warder tours are free and leave front entrance every ½ hr. 🎧
🅿 None for cars. Coach parking nearby. ▣ To book 0870 751 5191.
🐕 Guide dogs only. ❀ ♥

© English Heritage Photo Library

Eltham Palace, Eltham

© English Heritage Photo Library

## WELLINGTON ARCH ⌗

### HYDE PARK CORNER, LONDON W1J 7JZ

www.english-heritage.org.uk/visits

**Tel:** 020 7930 2726   **Venue Hire and Hospitality:** 020 973 3292
**Owner:** English Heritage   **Contact:** Visitor Operations Team

Set in the heart of Royal London at Hyde Park Corner, Wellington Arch is a landmark for Londoners and visitors alike. George IV originally commissioned this massive monument as a grand outer entrance to Buckingham Palace. It was completed in 1830 by architect Decimus Burton, and moved to its present site in 1882.

Take a lift to the balconies just below the spectacular bronze sculpture, which tops the imposing monument, for glorious views over London's Royal Parks and the Houses of Parliament. The statue is the largest bronze sculpture in Europe, and depicts the angel of Peace descending on the chariot of war. Inside the Arch, three floors of exhibits tell its fascinating history.

**Location:** MAP 20:L8, OS Ref. TQ285 798. Hyde Park Corner Tube Station.
**Open:** 1 Apr–31 Oct: Wed–Sun & BHs, 10am–5pm (may close at short notice for functions, please call to check). 1 Nov–20 Mar: Wed–Sun, 10am–4pm. Closed 24–26 Dec & 1 Jan.
**Admission:** Adult £3.20, Child £1.60, Conc. £2.40. Groups (11+) 15% discount. Joint ticket available with Apsley House.
🔲 🇹 🛅 🛈 Mondays for groups only. ✳ 🛡

## THE 'WERNHER COLLECTION' AT RANGER'S HOUSE ⌗

**Chesterfield Walk, Blackheath, London SE10 8QX**
**Tel:** 020 8853 0035   www.english-heritage.org.uk
**Owner:** English Heritage   **Contact:** House Manager

This attractive red-brick villa built c1700 on the edge of Greenwich Park houses the 'Wernher Collection': the life-time collection of self-made millionaire, Julius Wernher. A superb display of fine and decorative arts with objects dating from 3BC to the 19th-century, and including a stunning array of Renaissance jewellery as well as paintings, sculpture, furniture, tapestries, enamels and ivories.

**Location:** MAP 4:I2, OS Ref. TQ388 768. N of Shooters Hill Road.
**Open:** 1 Apr–30 Sept: Sun–Wed, 10am–5pm. 1 Oct–20 Mar: by appointment only. Closed 22 Dec–29 Feb 2008.
**Admission:** Adult £5.50, Child £2.80, Conc. £4.10.
🛈 WC. 🔲 🛅 Limited, lift available. 🅿 🔳 🛅 Guide dogs only. 🛡

## WESTMINSTER CATHEDRAL

**Victoria, London SW1P 1QW**
**Tel:** 020 7798 9055   **Fax:** 020 7798 9090   www.westminstercathedral.org.uk
**Owner:** Diocese of Westminster   **Contact:** Revd Mgr Mark Langham

The Roman Catholic Cathedral of the Archbishop of Westminster. Spectacular building in the Byzantine style, designed by J F Bentley, opened in 1903, famous for its mosaics, marble and music. Westminster Cathedral celebrated the Centenary of its foundation in 1995.

**Location:** MAP 20:L9, OS Ref. TQ293 791. Off Victoria Street, between Victoria Station and Westminster Abbey.
**Open:** All year: 7am–7pm. Please telephone for times at Easter & Christmas.
**Admission:** Free. Lift charge: Adult £3. Child £1.50. Family (2+4) £7.
🔲 🛅 Ground floor. 🔳 🛅 Booking required. 🅿 None. 🔳 Worksheets & tours. 🛅 Guide dogs only. ✳

## WHITEHALL

**1 Malden Road, Cheam SM3 8QD**
**Tel/Fax:** 020 8643 1236   **E-mail:** whitehallcheam@btconnect.com
www.sutton.gov.uk/leisure/heritage/whitehall.htm
**Owner:** London Borough of Sutton   **Contact:** The Curator

A Tudor timber-framed house, c1500 with later additions, in the heart of Cheam Village conservation area. Displays on the history of the house and the people who lived here, plus nearby Nonsuch Palace, Cheam School and William Gilpin (Dr Syntax). Changing exhibition programme and special event days throughout the year. Attractive rear garden features medieval well from c1400.

**Location:** MAP 19:C9, OS Ref. TQ242 638. Approx. 2m S of A3 on A2043 just N of junction with A232.
**Open:** Wed–Fri, 2–5pm; Sat, 10am–5pm; Sun & BH Mons, 2–5pm.
**Admission:** Adult £1.30, Child (6-16yrs) 65p, under 5yrs Free. Groups by appt.
🔲 🛅 Ground floor. 🔳 🛅 🔲 🔳 🛅 Guide dogs only. ✳ 🛡

© James Brittain

18 Folgate Street – Master Bedroom

Coronation of the Virgin, Somerset House

**Above:** The Vyne ©NT Photographic Library
**Right:** Painshill Park ©Jerry Harpur

# South East

*Eight counties make up the this region. In each you can find world-famous properties such as Windsor Castle, Blenheim Palace and Leeds Castle – and lesser known treasures such as Belmont, Broughton Castle and Great Dixter House & Gardens that give a deeper insight into Britain's heritage and history both architectural and horticultural.*

Berkshire

Buckinghamshire

Hampshire

Kent

Oxfordshire

Surrey

Sussex

Isle of Wight

## Owner
The National Trust

## Contact
The Property Manager
Basildon Park
Lower Basildon
Reading
Berkshire  RG8 9NR

**Tel:** 0118 984 3040
**Fax:** 0118 976 7370
**E-mail:** basildonpark@
nationaltrust.org.uk

## Location
**MAP 3:E2**
**OS Ref. SU611 782**

2½ m NW of Pangbourne
on the west side of the
A329, 7m from M4/J12.

## Opening Times
**House**
21 Mar–28 Oct: daily
except Mon & Tue (open
BH Mons), 12 noon–5pm.

Property closes at 4pm
17–19 Aug.

**Park, Garden,
Woodland Walk &
Restaurant**
as house, 11am–5pm.

**Shop**
as house plus
31 Oct–16 Dec:
12 noon–4pm.

**Exhibition**
As house all year.

## *Admission
**House, Park & Garden:**
| | |
|---|---|
| Adult | £6.00 |
| Child | £3.00 |
| Family | £15.00 |

**Park & Garden only:**
| | |
|---|---|
| Adult | £3.00 |
| Child | £1.50 |
| Family | £8.00 |
| Groups (15+) by appointment | £4.20 |

Free to NT Members

All information correct at
time of going to print.

*includes a voluntary
donation but visitors can
choose to pay the standard
prices displayed at the
property and on the website.

# BASILDON PARK
### www.nationaltrust.org.uk/basildonpark

This beautiful Palladian mansion stars as Netherfield in the recent feature film adaptation of Jane Austen's classic novel *Pride and Prejudice*, and throughout 2007 you can see a fascinating exhibition which explains the enormous amount of work which went on behind the scenes at Basildon Park.

The beauty of Basildon Park is that it is here at all. At many times during its 220-year history it has faced decay, neglect and obliteration. After the Second World War, it seemed that it would go the way of many of England's great country houses and be pulled down.

Yet today Basildon's house and grounds are a fantastic example of how a passion for architecture, interiors and landscape, a personal attachment to a fine home and, most of all, perseverance through adversity, can make grand dreams a reality.

A striking Palladian house built between 1776 and 1783 by John Carr, Basildon Park was the home of Sir Francis Sykes, a man who had made his fortune in India. In the 19th century it was sold to the Liberal MP James Morrison, who completed some of the interiors left unfurnished by Sykes when his fortunes faltered.

From the early years of the 20th century, however, it remained variously empty or utilised for the war effort, during which time most of its contents and fittings were sold, damaged, dispersed or destroyed. By the early 1950s it seemed as if demolition was inevitable.

Its saviours were Lord and Lady Iliffe, who restored and refurnished the house to a grandeur that once seemed impossible. They in turn gave the house and grounds to the National Trust, to secure their future and to enable future generations to enjoy what was very nearly lost.

The house has rich interiors with fine plasterwork, pictures and furniture, and includes an unusual Octagon Room and a decorative Shell Room.

© Universal Studios

By appointment.
In grounds.
On leads, in grounds only.

*The Royal Collection © 2007 HM Queen Elizabeth II/Peter Packer*

# WINDSOR CASTLE
## ST GEORGE'S CHAPEL & FROGMORE HOUSE

www.royalcollection.org.uk

Whichever way you approach the town of Windsor, the view is dominated by the dramatic outline of Windsor Castle, the largest inhabited castle in the world and the oldest royal residence to have remained in continuous use by the monarchs of Britain. Today, along with Buckingham Palace and the Palace of Holyroodhouse in Edinburgh, it is one of the official residences of Her Majesty The Queen.

Windsor's rich history spans more than 900 years but, as a working royal palace, the Castle plays a large part in the official work of The Queen and members of the Royal Family today. The magnificent State Rooms are furnished with some of the finest works of art from the Royal Collection, including paintings by Rembrandt and drawings

by Leonardo da Vinci. Visitors should not miss the Castle Precinct Tours (which depart at regular intervals from the Admission Centre), Queen Mary's Dolls' House, a masterpiece in minature, and the last and largest suit of armour made for Henry VIII.

Within the precincts is St George's Chapel, one of the most beautiful ecclesiastical buildings in England, Ten monarchs are buried here, including Henry VIII with his favourite wife, Jane Seymour.

Frogmore House has been a favourite royal retreat for over 300 years. It is open to visitors on a limited number of days during the year. Guided pre-booked group visits are available throughout August and September. Please contact the Ticket Sales and Information Office for details.

St George's Chapel, Windsor Castle.

*Dennis Gilbert/The Royal Collection © 2007 HM Queen Elizabeth II*

Frogmore House.

*Christopher Simon Sykes/The Royal Collection © 2007 HM Queen Elizabeth II*

Grand Reception Room.

*The Royal Collection © 2007 HM Queen Elizabeth II/Mark Fiennes*

 No photography.

Audio Tours Windsor Castle.

 None.

Guide dogs only.

With the exception of Sundays, the Changing of the Guard takes place at 11am daily from April to the end of June and on alternate days at other times of the year.

---

### ■ Owner
Official Residence of Her Majesty The Queen

### ■ Contact
Ticket Sales & Information Office
Buckingham Palace
London  SW1A 1AA

**Tel:** 020 7766 7304
**Groups (15+):**
020 7766 7321
**Fax:** 020 7930 9625
**E-mail:** bookinginfo@ royalcollection.org.uk

### ■ Location
**MAP 3:G2**
**OS Ref. SU969 770**

M4/J6, M3/J3.
20m from central London.

**Rail:** Regular service from London Waterloo and London Paddington.

**Coach:** Victoria Coach Station – regular service.

**Sightseeing tours:**
Tour companies operate a daily service with collection from many London hotels. Ask your hotel concierge or porter for information.

### ■ Opening Times
March–October:
Daily except 6 Apr & 18 Jun: 9.45am–5.15pm
Last admission 4pm.

November–February:
Daily except 25/26 Dec, 9.45am–4.15pm.
Last admission 3pm.

The State Rooms are closed 8–19 Jan. (Reduced admission prices apply.)

**Opening arrangements may change at short notice. 24-hr info line 01753 831118.**

Private Evening Tours of the Castle for groups contact 020 7766 7322.

**St George's Chapel** is closed to visitors on Sundays as services are held throughout the day. Worshippers are welcome.

**Frogmore House & Mausoleum**
15–17 May and 25–27 Aug. Mausoleum only 23 May. For prices contact 020 7766 7305.

Private Tours of the house for pre-booked groups (15+) Aug & Sept. Contact 020 7766 7321.

### ■ Admission
For admission prices please contact our Ticket Sales and Information office

Groups (15+)
Discounts available.

All information correct at time of going to print.

## BASILDON PARK ✿

*See page 96 for full page entry.*

### DONNINGTON CASTLE ⊞

**Newbury, Berkshire**
**Tel:** 01424 775705   **www.english-heritage.org.uk/visits**
**Owner:** English Heritage   **Contact:** 1066 Battle Abbey
Built in the late 14th century, the twin towered gatehouse of this heroic castle survives amidst some impressive earthworks.
**Location:** MAP 3:D2, OS Ref. SU463 691. 1m N of Newbury off B4494.
**Open:** All year: Any reasonable time (exterior viewing only).
**Admission:** Free.
🚶 Steep slopes within grounds. 🅿 ⊠ On leads. ✺

## DORNEY COURT 🏠
**WINDSOR, BERKSHIRE  SL4 6QP**

www.dorneycourt.co.uk

**Tel:** 01628 604638   **E-mail:** palmer@dorneycourt.co.uk
**Owner/Contact:** Mrs Peregrine Palmer
Just a few miles from the heart of bustling Windsor lies "one of the finest Tudor Manor Houses in England", *Country Life*. Grade I listed with the added accolade of being of outstanding architectural and historical importance, the visitor can get a rare insight into the lifestyle of the squirearchy through 550 years, with the Palmer family, who still live there today, owning the house for 450 of these years. The house boasts a magnificent Great Hall, family portraits, oak and lacquer furniture, needlework and panelled rooms. A private tour on a 'non-open day' takes around 1½ hours, but when open to the public this is reduced to around 40 mins. The adjacent 13th century Church of St James, with Norman font and Tudor tower can also be visited, as well as the adjoining Plant Centre in our walled garden where light lunches and full English cream teas are served in a tranquil setting throughout the day. Highly Commended by Country Life - The Nation's Finest Manor House - 2006.
**Location:** MAP 3:G2, OS Ref. SU926 791. 5 mins off M4/J7, 10mins from Windsor, 2m W of Eton.
**Open:** May: BH Suns & Mons; Aug: daily except Sats, 1.30–4pm (last admission).
**Admission:** Adult: £6.50, Child (10yrs +) £4.50. Groups (10+): £6 when house is open to public. Private group rates at other times.
ℹ Film & photographic shoots. No stiletto heels. ⊞ Garden centre. ⊤
🚶 Garden centre. 🍽 ⓕ 🅿 🛏 ⊠ Guide dogs only. ✺

### ETON COLLEGE 🏠

**Windsor, Berkshire  SL4 6DW**
**Tel:** 01753 671177   **Fax:** 01753 671029   **www.etoncollege.com**
**E-mail:** r.hunkin@etoncollege.org.uk
**Owner:** Provost & Fellows   **Contact:** Rebecca Hunkin
Eton College, founded in 1440 by Henry VI, is one of the oldest and best known schools in the country. The original and subsequent historic buildings of the Foundation are a part of the heritage of the British Isles and visitors are invited to experience and share the beauty of the ancient precinct which includes the magnificent College Chapel, a masterpiece of the perpendicular style.
**Location:** MAP 3:G2, OS Ref. SU967 779. Off M4/J5. Access from Windsor by footbridge only. Vehicle access from Slough 2m N.
**Open:** Mar - early Oct: Times vary, please check with the Visits Office. Pre-booked groups welcome all year.
**Admission:** Ordinary admissions and daily guided tours during the season at 2.15pm and 3.15pm. Groups by appointment only. Rates vary according to type of tour.
🖼 ⊤ 🚶 Ground floor. WC. ⓕ 🅿 Limited. ⊠ Guide dogs only. ✺

*Savill Garden Visitor Centre*

## SAVILL GARDEN
**WINDSOR GREAT PARK, BERKSHIRE SL4 2HT**

www.theroyallandscape.co.uk

**Tel:** 01784 435544   **E-mail:** enquiries@theroyallandscape.co.uk
**Owner:** The Crown Estate   **Contact:** The Marketing Manager
World-renowned 35 acre woodland garden, providing a wealth of beauty and interest in all seasons. Spring is heralded by hosts of daffodils, masses of rhododendrons, azaleas, camellias, magnolias and much more. Roses, herbaceous borders and countless alpines are the great features of summer, and the leaf colours and fruits of autumn rival the other seasons with a great display.
**Location:** MAP 3:G2, OS Ref. SU977 706. Wick Lane, Englefield Green. Clearly signposted from Ascot, Bagshot, Egham and Windsor. Nearest station: Egham.
**Open:** Mar–Oct: 10am–6pm. Nov–Feb: 10am–4pm.
**Admission:** Adult £6.50, Child (6-16 yrs) £3.25, Conc. and Family tickets available. Groups (10+) £5.25.
ℹ Film & photographic shoots. 🖼 ⓕ Plant centre. ⊤ 🚶 Grounds. WC.
🍽 🍴 Licensed. ⓕ For groups, by appointment. 🅿 ⊠ Guide dogs only. ✺

## TAPLOW COURT 🏠
**BERRY HILL, TAPLOW, Nr MAIDENHEAD, BERKS  SL6 0ER**

www.sgi-uk.org

**Tel:** 01628 591230/209   **Fax:** 01628 773055
**Owner:** SGI-UK   **Contact:** Michael Yeadon
Set high above the Thames, affording spectacular views. Remodelled mid-19th century by William Burn. Earlier neo-Norman Hall. 18th century home of Earls of Orkney and more recently of Lord and Lady Desborough who entertained 'The Souls' here. Tranquil gardens and grounds. Anglo-Saxon burial mound. Permanent and temporary exhibitions.
**Location:** MAP 3:F1, OS Ref. SU907 822. M4/J7 off Bath Road towards Maidenhead. 6m off M40/J2.
**Open:** House & Grounds: 27 May–29 Jul & 9 Sept: Suns & BH Mons, 2–5.30pm. Groups at other times by appointment.
**Admission:** No charge. Free parking.
🖼 🚶 🍽 ⓕ 🛏 🅿 ⊠ Guide dogs only. ✺

## WINDSOR CASTLE, ST GEORGE'S CHAPEL & FROGMORE HOUSE

*See page 97 for full page entry.*

Savill Garden, Berkshire

# WELFORD PARK
## NEWBURY, BERKSHIRE  RG20 8HU

www.welfordpark.co.uk

**Tel:** 01488 608203 / 608691

**Owner/Contact:** Mr & Mrs J H L Puxley

A Queen Anne house with attractive gardens and grounds. Riverside walks. Wonderful snowdrops during February.

**Location:** MAP 3:C2, OS Ref: SU409 731. On Lambourn Valley Road. 6m NW of Newbury.

**Open:** 4 Jun–6 Jul: Mon–Sat, 11am to 5pm. Closed 16 Jun. Grounds open in Feb 11am–4pm. (closed Mon & Fri) for snowdrop woods and aconite riverbanks.

**Admission:** Booked House Tour: Adult £5, Children under 16yrs Free. Grounds free except when open in the aid of charities & in Feb. Grounds: Adults £4, Concs. £3. Tearoom serves home-made lunches and teas during Feb.

⌖ Grounds. ⬤ Home-made lunches & teas, must book in advance (except Feb). ⬛ On leads, in grounds. ⬛ Obligatory.

*giftaid it* This year, some properties will be operating the Gift Aid on Entry scheme at their admission points. Where the scheme is operating, visitors are offered a choice between paying the standard admission price or paying the 'Gift Aid Admission' which includes a voluntary donation of at least 10%. Gift Aid Admissions enable the charity to reclaim tax on the whole amount paid* - an extra 28% - potentially a very significant boost to property funds. Money raised from paying visitors in this way will go towards restoration projects at the property and will be very welcome. Where shown, the admission prices are inclusive of the 10% voluntary donation where properties are operating the Gift Aid on Entry scheme, but both the standard admission price and the Gift Aid Admission will be displayed at the property and on their website.

*Gift Aid donations must be supported by a valid Gift Aid declaration and a Gift Aid declaration can only cover donations made by an individual for him/herself or for him/herself and members of his/her family.

Dorney Court, Nr Windsor

### ■ Owner

Stowe House
Preservation Trust

### ■ Contact

Visitor Services Manager
Stowe School
Buckingham
MK18 5EH

**Tel:** 01280 818229
**Fax:** 01280 818186
House only
**E-mail:**
amcevoy@stowe.co.uk

### ■ Location

**MAP 7:C10**
**OS Ref. SP666 366**

From London, M1 to
Milton Keynes, 1½ hrs
or Banbury 1¼ hrs,
3m NW of Buckingham.

**Bus:** Buckingham 3m.

**Rail:** Milton Keynes 15m.

**Air:** Heathrow 50m.

### ■ Opening Times

**House:**
Easter & Summer
School Holidays.
Wed–Sun 12noon–5pm
(last admission 4pm),
Guided tour at 2pm &
also in term times, please
check website or
telephone for further
details.

### ■ *Admission

**House (including
optional tour)**
Adult              £4.00
Child (5–16yrs)    £2.50
Adult NT members  £3.00
Child NT members  £2.00
Family (2+3)      £12.00
  (NT members)    £10.00
Children under 5yrs  Free

Open to private groups
(15–60 persons), all year
round at discounted rates.
Please telephone 01280
818229 to pre-book.

Phase 3 of Restoration
will mean restricted
access, check website
(www.shpt.org) or 24hr
telephone line (01280
818166) for details, exact
opening times and prices.

Visit both The National
Trust Gardens & the
House. For Gardens
opening times telephone
01280 822850 or visit
www.nationaltrust.org.uk/
stowegardens

*includes a voluntary
donation but visitors can
choose to pay the standard
prices displayed at the
property and on the website.

### Conference/Function

| ROOM | MAX CAPACITY |
| --- | --- |
| ROXBURGH HALL | 460 |
| MUSIC ROOM | 100 |
| MARBLE HALL | 200 |
| STATE DINING RM | 160 |
| GARTER ROOM | 160 |

# STOWE HOUSE

www.shpt.org

Stowe owes its pre-eminence to the vision and wealth of two great owners. From 1715 to 1749 Viscount Cobham, one of Marlborough's Generals, continuously improved his estate, calling in the leading designers of the day to lay out the Gardens and commissioning several leading architects – Vanburgh, Gibbs, Kent and Leoni – to decorate them with garden temples. From 1750 to 1779 Earl Temple, his nephew and heir, continued to expand and embellish both House and Gardens. As the House and Gardens were expanded, and political and military intrigues followed, the family eventually fell into debt, resulting in two great sales – 1848 when all the contents were sold and 1922 when the contents and the estate were sold off separately. The House is now part of a major public

school, since 1923, and owned by Stowe House Preservation Trust, since 2000. Over the last four years, through the Trust, the House has under gone two phases of a six phase restoration – the North Front and Colonnades, the Central Pavilion and South Portico and the absolutely spectacular Marble Saloon, dating from the 1770s. Around the mansion is one of Britain's most magnificent and complete landscape gardens, taken over from the School by the National Trust in 1989. The Gardens have since undergone a huge, and continuing, restoration programme, and with the House restoration, Stowe is slowly being returned to its 18th century status on one of the most complete neo-classical estates in Europe.

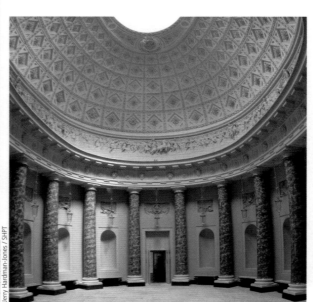

Jerry Hardman-Jones / SHPT

[i] Indoor swimming pool, sports hall, tennis court, squash courts, astroturf, parkland, cricket pitches and golf course. No photography in house.

International conferences, private functions, weddings, and prestige exhibitions. Catering on request.

Visitors may alight at entrance, tel. 01280 818229 for details. Allocated parking. WC. 'Batricars' available (from NT – tel. 01280 818825).

Morning coffee, lunch and afternoon tea available by pre-arrangement only,for up to 80.

For parties of 15–60 at additional cost. Tour time: house and garden 2½ - 4½ hrs, house only 1½ hrs.

[P] Ample.

In grounds on leads.

Civil Wedding Licence.

Available.

Please check website for 2007 events: www.stoweevents.co.uk

© The National Trust, Waddesdon Manor, photographer Hugh Palmer

# WADDESDON MANOR ✿

www.waddesdon.org.uk

Waddesdon Manor was built (1874–89) by Baron Ferdinand de Rothschild to display his outstanding collection of art treasures and to entertain the fashionable world. The 45 rooms on view combine the highest quality French furniture and decorative arts from the 18th century with magnificent portraits by Gainsborough and Reynolds, works by Dutch and Flemish Masters of the 17th century; Savonnerie carpets and Sèvres porcelain.

The Victorian gardens are considered some of the finest in Britain renowned for the colourful parterre, seasonal displays, statuary and fountains, walks and wonderful views across the Vale of Aylesbury. At the heart of the gardens lies the rococo-style aviary which houses a splendid collection of exotic birds and is well known for breeding

endangered species. The Wine Cellars, modelled on the private cellars at Château Lafite Rothschild, contain thousands of bottles of Rothschild wines dating back to 1868.

2007 is the 50th anniversary of the bequest of the Manor to the National Trust – an anniversary which acts as the focus of Waddesdon's annual displays.

Top quality food and wines are served throughout the day in the restaurants and the shops offer a superb range of gifts and wines, many of which are unique to Waddesdon. A full programme of events is organised throughout the year. Conveniently situated for London, Oxford and Milton Keynes, Waddesdon offers a memorable day out for all the family.

© The National Trust, Waddesdon Manor, photographer Mike Fear

ℹ️ No photography in house. NT members free. HHA Members free entry to grounds. RHS members free to grounds in Mar, Sept & Oct. Children welcomed under parental supervision in the House. Babies must be carried in a front-sling.

🛍️ Gift and Wine Shops.

🌿 Plant Sales

🍽️ Conferences, corporate hospitality.

♿ WCs.

☕ Licensed.

🍴 Licensed. Reservations can be made at the Manor Restaurant. Tel: 01296 653242

🚶 By arrangement.

🎧 Audio Tours

🅿️ Ample for coaches and cars.

🐕 Assistance dogs only.

🔔

🎪 Wine Tasting, Special Interest Days, Family Events. Please telephone 01296 653226 for details.

*includes a voluntary donation but visitors can choose to pay the standard prices displayed at the property and on the website.

## ■ Contact

Waddesdon
Nr Aylesbury
Buckinghamshire
HP18 0JH

**Tel:** (24-hour recorded info): 01296 653211
**Booking & Info:**
(Mon–Fri 10am–4pm): 01296 653226
**Fax:** 01296 653212
**E-mail:** waddesdonmanor @nationaltrust.org.uk

## ■ Location

**MAP 7:C11**
**OS Ref. SP740 169**

Between Aylesbury & Bicester, off A41.

**Rail:** Aylesbury 6m.

## ■ Opening Times

**Gardens, Aviary, Restaurants, Shops & Children's Playground**

6 Jan–18 Mar: Sats & Suns, 21 Mar–23 Dec & 27–31 Dec, Wed–Sun & BH Mons, 10am–5pm.

**House & Gardens, Wine Cellars, Aviary, Children's Playground, Shops & Restaurants**

21 Mar–28 Oct, Wed–Sun & BH Mons, 12noon–4pm (11am Sats & Suns). Last rec adm. 2.30pm.

**Bachelors' Wing**

21 Mar–28 Oct: Wed–Fri 12noon–4pm. Limited space, entry cannnot be guaranteed.

**Christmas Season (East Wing decorated for the festive season)**

14 Nov–23 Dec, Wed–Fri 12 noon–4pm. Sats & Suns 11am–4pm. Timed tickets to house avail. Booking fee £3 per transaction. Please call Booking Office.

## ■ *Admission

**House & Gardens, Wine Cellars, Aviary, Children's Playground, Shops & Restaurants**

Adult Wed–Fri £13.20
Sats, Suns & BHs £15.00
Child* Wed–Fri £9.35
Sats, Suns & BHs £11.00

Group rates available.

Christmas Season special rates apply.

**Gardens, Aviary, Children's Playground, Shops & Restaurants**

Adult Wed–Fri £5.50
Sats, Suns & BHs £7.00
Child* Wed–Fri £2.75
Sats, Suns & BHs £3.50

Group rates available.

6 Jan–18 Mar, Sats, Suns
Adult £5.50
Child £2.75

**Bachelors' Wing** £3.30

*Child (5–16 yrs).
Children under 5 Free.

## ASCOTT ⚘

**Wing, Leighton Buzzard, Buckinghamshire LU7 0PS**
**Tel:** 01296 688242 **Fax:** 01296 681904
**E-mail:** info@ascottestate.co.uk **www.ascottestate.co.uk**
**Owner:** The National Trust **Contact:** Resident Agent

Originally a half-timbered Jacobean farmhouse, Ascott was bought in 1876 by the de Rothschild family and considerably transformed and enlarged. It now houses a quite exceptional collection of fine paintings, Oriental porcelain and English and French furniture. The extensive gardens are a mixture of the formal and natural, containing specimen trees and shrubs, as well as an herbaceous walk, lily pond, Dutch garden and remarkable topiary sundial.

**Location:** MAP 7:D11, OS Ref. SP891 230. ½ m E of Wing, 2m SW of Leighton Buzzard, on A418.
**Open:** House & Garden: 27 Mar–29 Apr: daily except Mons, 2–6pm. 1 May–26 Jul: Tues–Thurs, 2–6pm. 31 Jul–14 Sept daily except Mons, 2–6pm. Last admission 5pm.
**Admission:** Adult £8, Child £4.50. Garden only: £4. Child £2. No reduction for groups which must book. NT members free (except NGS days) 7 May–27 Aug.
♿ Ground floor & grounds with assistance. 3 wheelchairs available. WCs.
🅿 220 metres. 🐕 In car park only, on leads.

## BOARSTALL DUCK DECOY ⚘

**Boarstall, Aylesbury, Buckinghamshire HP18 9UX**
**Tel:** 01844 237488 / 01280 822850 (Visitor Services Manager Mon–Fri)
**E-mail:** boarstallducdecoy@nationaltrust.org.uk
**Owner:** The National Trust **Contact:** Visitor Services Manager

A rare survival of a 17th century decoy in working order, set on a tree-fringed lake, with nature trail and exhibition hall.

**Location:** MAP 7:B11, OS Ref. SP624 151. Midway between Bicester and Thame, 2m W of Brill.
**Open:** 1 Apr–27 Aug: Sats & Suns, 10am–4pm; 4 Apr–22 Aug: Weds, 3.30–6.30pm; BH Mons 10am–4pm. Displays on Sats, Suns, & BH Mons: 11am & 3pm; Weds: 3.30pm. Bird walks and woodland talks occasionally, please telephone for details. Please telephone for winter opening details. Free to NT members.
**Admission:** Adult £2.50, Child £1.20. Family £6. Groups (6+) must book: £1.50.
♿ Partial. 📷 By arrangement. 🐕 In car park only, on leads.

## BOARSTALL TOWER ⚘

**Boarstall, Aylesbury, Buckinghamshire HP18 9UX**
**Tel:** 01280 822850 (Mon–Fri) **E-mail:** boarstalltower@nationaltrust.org.uk
**Owner:** The National Trust **Contact:** Visitor Services Manager

The stone gatehouse of a fortified house long since demolished. It dates from the 14th century, and was altered in the 16th and 17th centuries, but retains its crossloops for bows. The gardens are surrounded by a moat on three sides.

**Location:** MAP 7:B11, OS Ref. SP624 141. Midway between Bicester and Thame, 2m W of Brill.
**Open:** 4 Apr–31 Oct: Weds, 2–6pm. BH Sats: 11am–4pm & BH Mons: 2–6pm.
**Admission:** Adult £2.50, Child £1.20, Family £6. Free to NT members.
ℹ️ No WC. ♿ Ground floor & garden (steps to entrance). 🐕 In car park only.

## BUCKINGHAM CHANTRY CHAPEL ⚘

**Market Hill, Buckingham**
**Tel:** 01280 822850 (Mon–Fri) **Fax:** 01280 822437
**Owner:** The National Trust **Contact:** Buckingham Heritage Trust

Rebuilt in 1475 and retaining a fine Norman doorway. The chapel was restored by Gilbert Scott in 1875, at which time it was used as a Latin or Grammar School.

**Location:** MAP 7:B10, OS Ref. SP693 340. In narrow lane, NW of Market Hill.
**Open:** All year, Sats, 9am–1pm. Other times by appointment with the Buckingham Heritage Trust, c/o Old Gaol Museum, Market Hill, Buckingham MK18 1JX.
**Admission:** Free. Donations welcome.
ℹ️ No WCs. ♿ ❄

Who's offering **accommodation?**
See our index on page 575

# CHENIES MANOR HOUSE 🏛
## CHENIES, BUCKINGHAMSHIRE WD3 6ER
www.cheniesmanorhouse.co.uk

**Tel:** 01494 762888 **E-mail:** macleodmatthews@btinternet.com
**Owners:** Mrs E MacLeod Matthews & Mr C MacLeod Matthews
**Contact:** Susan Brock

Home of the MacLeod Matthews family, this 15th & 16th century Manor House with fortified tower is the original home of the Earls of Bedford. Visited by Henry VIII and Elizabeth I. She was a frequent visitor, first coming as an infant in 1534 and as Queen she visited on several occasions, once being for a six week period. The Bedford Mausoleum is in the adjacent church. The House contains tapestries and furniture mainly of the 16th and 17th centuries, hiding places, and a collection of antique dolls. Art Exhibitions are held throughout the season in the newly restored 16th century Pavilion with its unusual cellars. The Manor is surrounded by enchanting gardens, famed for the spring display of tulips, which have been featured in many publications and on television. From early June there is a succession of colour in the Tudor Sunken Garden, The White Garden, Herbaceous Borders and Fountain Court. The Physic Garden contains a wide selection of medicinal and culinary herbs. The Parterre has an ancient oak and complicated Yew Maze while the Kitchen Garden is in Victorian style with unusual vegetables and fruit. Attractive dried and fresh flower arrangements decorate the house.

**Location:** MAP 7:D12, OS Ref TQ016 984. N of A404 between Amersham & Rickmansworth. M25–Ext 18 3m
**Open:** 4th Apr–25th Oct: Wed & Thurs and BH Mon, 2–5pm. Last entry to House: 4.15pm.
**Admission:** House & Garden: Adult £5.50, Child £3, Garden only: Adult £4, Child £2, Groups (20+) by arrangement throughout the year (half price during Oct).
📷 🍴 🍽 🎁 🅿 🐕 ✕ ❄

🎭 9th Apr, 2–5pm Easter Fun for Children. 7th May, 2–5pm Tulip Festival. 28th May, 2–5pm Special entertainment. 15th Jul, 10am–5pm Plant and Garden Fair (The Manor House opens at 2pm). Rare and exceptional plants,topiary and trees from specialist nurseries. Gardening advice, sculpture, garden furniture. Lunch and refreshments. Children's entertainer. 27th Aug, 2–5pm Special entertainment.

## CHILTERN OPEN AIR MUSEUM

**Newland Park, Gorelands Lane, Chalfont St Giles, Buckinghamshire HP8 4AB**
**Tel:** 01494 871117 **Fax:** 01494 872774
**Owner:** Chiltern Open Air Museum Ltd **Contact:** Phil Holbrook
A museum of historic buildings showing their original uses including a blacksmith's forge, stables, barns etc.
**Location:** MAP 3:G1, OS Ref. TQ011 938. At Newland Park 1½ m E of Chalfont St Giles, 4½ m from Amersham. 3m from M25/J17.
**Open:** Apr–Oct: daily. Please telephone for details.
**Admission:** Adult £7, Child (5–16yrs) £4.50, Child under 5yrs Free, OAP £6, Family (2+2) £20.50. Groups discount available on request. 2006 prices.

© NT Photographic Library / Matthew Antrobus

Hughenden Manor, High Wycombe

# CLAYDON HOUSE ✹

### MIDDLE CLAYDON, Nr BUCKINGHAM MK18 2EY

**Tel:** 01296 730349 **Fax:** 01296 738511 **Infoline:** 01494 755561
**E-mail:** claydon@nationaltrust.org.uk
**Owner:** The National Trust **Contact:** The House and Premises Manager
A fine 18th century house with some of the most perfect rococo decoration in England. A series of great rooms have wood carvings in Chinese and Gothic styles, and tall windows look out over parkland and a lake. The house has relics of the exploits of the Verney family in the English Civil War and also on show is the bedroom of Florence Nightingale, a relative of the Verneys and a regular visitor to this tranquil place.
**Location:** MAP 7:C11, OS Ref. SP720 253. In Middle Claydon, 13m NW of Aylesbury, signposted from A413 and A41. 3½ m SW of Winslow.

**Open:** House & Grounds: 24 Mar–31 Oct: daily except Thur & Fri; House, 1–5pm, last admission 4.30pm. Restaurant (non-NT): 24 Mar–31 Oct, daily except Thur & Fri, 12 noon–5pm.
**Admission:** Adult £5.50, Child £2.70, Family £13. Groups: Adult £4.50 (50p extra for guided tour*). Private Gardens open same days as House. Adult £2.50, including National Trust Members. *Free to NT members.
🛈 No photography. No pushchairs. No backpacks. No large bags.
📷 Second-hand books, pottery & florist. 🚻 🚼 Ground floor only. WC. Braille guide. Photograph album. Ramp. 🦽 🛈 For groups only, by arrangement. 🅿 Limited for coaches. 🐕 In parkland only, on leads. 🛈 For details visit www.nationaltrust.org.uk.

Chenies Manor House, Chenies

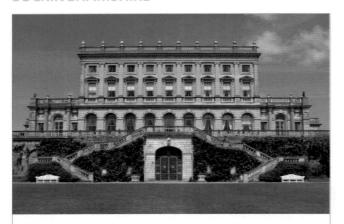

# CLIVEDEN ✤

## TAPLOW, MAIDENHEAD SL6 0JA

**Tel:** 01628 605069    **Infoline:** 01494 755562    **Fax:** 01628 669461
**E-mail:** cliveden@nationaltrust.org.uk

**Owner:** The National Trust    **Contact:** Property Manager

152 hectares of gardens and woodland. A water garden, 'secret' garden, herbaceous borders, topiary, a great formal parterre, and informal vistas provide endless variety. The garden statuary is one of the most important collections in the care of The National Trust and includes many Roman antiquities collected by 1st Viscount Astor. The Octagon Temple (Chapel) with its rich mosaic interior is open on certain days, as is part of the house (see below).

**Location:** MAP 3:F1, OS Ref. SU915 851. 3m N of Maidenhead, M4/J7 onto A4 or M40/J4 onto A404 to Marlow and follow signs. From London by train take Thames Train service from Paddington to Burnham (taxi rank and office adjacent to station).

**Open:** Estate & Garden: 14 Mar–28 Oct, daily, 11am–6pm; 29 Oct–23 Dec, daily, 11am–4pm. House (part) & Octagon Temple: 1 Apr–28 Oct: Thurs & Sun, 3–5.30pm. Admission to house by timed ticket, obtainable from information kiosk only. Woodlands: 1 Apr–28 Oct, daily, 11am–5.30pm; 29 Oct–23 Dec & 2 Jan–31 Mar, daily, 11am–4pm. Restaurant: 14 Mar–28 Oct, daily, 11am–5pm; 3 Nov–23 Dec, Sat & Sun, 11am–3pm. Shop: 14 Mar–28 Oct, daily, 12 noon–5.30pm; 29 Oct–23 Dec, daily, 12 noon–4pm. Some areas of formal garden may be roped off when ground conditions are bad.

**Admission:** Grounds: Adult £7.50 Child £3.70, Family £18.70, Groups (must book) £6.50 House: £1 extra, Child 50p extra.* Note: Mooring charge on Cliveden Reach. *Free to NT members.

🅿 🅑 Partial. WC. 🍽 Licensed. 🐕 Specified woodlands only. ✱ 🈳

## COWPER & NEWTON MUSEUM

Home of Olney's Heritage, Orchard Side, Market Place, Olney  MK46 4AJ
**Tel:** 01234 711516    **E-mail:** cnm@mkheritage.co.uk
**www.cowperandnewtonmuseum.org.uk**
**Owner:** Board of Trustees    **Contact:** Mrs S Whyte

Once the home of 18th century poet and letter writer William Cowper and now containing furniture, paintings and belongings of both Cowper and his ex-slave trader friend, Rev John Newton (author of "Amazing Grace"). Attractions include re-creations of a Victorian country kitchen and wash-house, two peaceful gardens and Cowper's restored summerhouse. Costume gallery, important collections of dinosaur bones and bobbin lace, and local history displays.

**Location:** MAP 7:D9, OS Ref. SP890 512. On A509, 6m N of Newport Pagnell, M1/J14.
**Open:** 1 Mar–23 Dec: Tue–Sat & BH Mons, 10.30am–4.30pm. Closed on Good Fri.
**Admission:** Adult £3, Conc. £2, Child/Students (with card) £1.50, Children under 12 yrs Free, Family £7.50, Garden only £1.

ⓘ No photography. 🅿 🅑 Gardens. 🇫 By arrangement. 🅿 🈳 Guide dogs only.

## FORD END WATERMILL

Station Road, Ivinghoe, Buckinghamshire
**Tel:** 01582 600391    **Contact:** David Lindsey

The Watermill, a listed building, was recorded in 1616 but is probably much older.

**Location:** MAP 7:D11, OS Ref. SP941 166. 600 metres from Ivinghoe Church along B488 (Station Road) to Leighton Buzzard.
**Open:** Easter Mon–end Sept: 2nd & 4th Suns of each month & BHs, 2.30–5.30pm. Milling between 3–5pm on BHs and the 2nd Sun in May (National Mills Day) and 4th Sun in Sept.
**Admission:** Adult £1.50, Child 50p (5–15yrs). Schools: Child 75p, Adults Free.

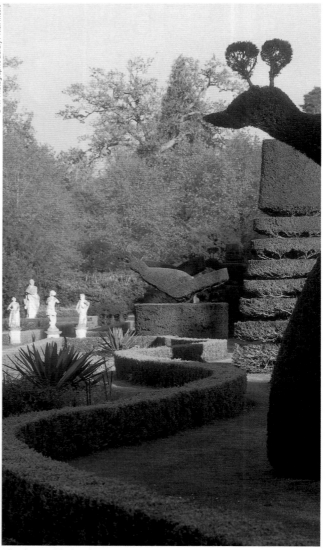

© NT Photographic Library / Nick Meers

Cliveden, Maidenhead

© NT Photographic Library / Matthew Antrobus

## HUGHENDEN MANOR 🌿

### HIGH WYCOMBE HP14 4LA

**Tel:** 01494 755573/ 755565 - Infoline  **Fax:** 01494 474284
**E-mail:** hughenden@nationaltrust.org.uk
**Owner:** The National Trust  **Contact:** The Property Manager
Home of Prime Minister Benjamin Disraeli from 1848–1881. The interior is a comfortable Victorian home and still holds many of Disraeli's pictures, books and furniture. The surrounding park and woodland have lovely walks, and the formal garden has been recreated in the spirit of Mary Anne Disraeli's colourful designs.
**Location:** MAP 3:F1, OS 165 Ref. SU866 955. 1½ m N of High Wycombe on the W side of the A4128.

**Open:** House: 3 Mar–28 Oct, 1–5pm (12 noon–1pm by guided tour only). Wed–Sun & BH Mon. Open Good Fri. On BHs and busy days entry is by timed ticket. Gardens open same days as house, 11am–5pm. Shop and Restaurant: open 11am–5pm also weekends 28 Oct–16 Dec, 11am–4pm. Park & Woodland: All year.
**Admission:** House & Garden: Adult £6.40, Child £3.20, Family £16. Groups: Adult £5.50. Garden only: Adult £2.60, Child £1.90. Park & Woodland Free. No groups at weekends or BHs. £1 off if arriving by public transport. Free to NT Members.
🔲 🔲 Ground floor only. WC. 🔲 🔲 For booked groups. 🔲 🔲 In grounds, on leads. Guide dogs in house & formal gardens. 🔲 🔲

---

## THE KING'S HEAD 🌿

**King's Head Passage, Market Square, Aylesbury, Buckinghamshire HP20 2RW**
**Tel:** 01296 381501  **Fax:** 01296 381502  **E-mail:** kingshead@nationaltrust.org.uk
**Owner:** The National Trust  **Contact:** The Custodian
This enchanting inn dates back to 1455 and remains a unique place to enjoy real ale or even a glass of Rothschild wine. It has many noteworthy architectural features including a medieval stained glass window, extensive timber framing and an ancient cobbled courtyard. Once a base for Oliver Cromwell it now houses a bookshop, coffee shop and visitor centre.
**Location:** MAP 7:C11, OS Ref. SP818 138. At NW corner of Aylesbury Market Square.
**Open:** All year: Mon–Sat, 10am–3pm and normal pub hours. Guided tours on Wed, Fri & Sat at 2pm.
**Admission:** Adult £2 (incl tour). NT members Free.
🔲 🔲 Partial. WC. 🔲 Licensed. 🔲 Obligatory. 🔲 None. 🔲 🔲 Guide dogs only. 🔲

---

## LONG CRENDON COURTHOUSE 🌿

**High St, Long Crendon, Buckinghamshire**
**Tel:** 01280 822850 (Mon–Fri)  **E-mail:** stowegarden@nationaltrust.org.uk
**www.nationaltrust.org.uk**
**Owner:** The National Trust  **Contact:** Visitor Services Manager
A fantastic opportunity to see very clearly a 15th century building. The exposed timber beams and early oak floorboards are a rare sight.
**Location:** MAP 7:B11, OS Ref. SP698 091. 3miles N of Thame.
**Open:** 1 Apr–30 Sept: Weds: 2–6pm. Sats, Suns & BH Mons, 11am–6pm.
**Admission:** Adult £1, Child 50p. Free to NT Members.

---

## JOHN MILTON'S COTTAGE

**21 Deanway, Chalfont St. Giles, Buckinghamshire  HP8 4JH**
**Tel:** 01494 872313  **E-mail:** info@miltonscottage.org  **www.miltonscottage.org**
**Owner:** Milton Cottage Trust  **Contact:** Mr E A Dawson
Grade I listed 16th century cottage where John Milton lived and completed 'Paradise Lost' and started 'Paradise Regained'. Four ground floor museum rooms contain important first editions of John Milton's 17th century poetry and prose works. Amongst many unique items on display is the portrait of John Milton by Sir Godfrey Kneller. Well stocked, attractive cottage garden, listed by English Heritage.
**Location:** MAP 3:G1, OS Ref. SU987 933. ½ m W of A413. 3m N of M40/J2. S side of street.
**Open:** 1 Mar–31 Oct: Tue–Sun, 10am–1pm & 2–6pm. Closed Mons (open BH Mons). Coach parking by prior arrangement only.
**Admission:** Adult £4, under 15s £2, Groups (20+) £3.
🔲 🔲 Ground floor. 🔲 Talk followed by free tour. 🔲 🔲

---

## NETHER WINCHENDON HOUSE 🏛

**Nether Winchendon, Nr Aylesbury, Buckinghamshire  HP18 ODY**
**Tel:** 01844 290101  **Fax:** 01844 290199  **www.netherwinchendonhouse.com**
**Owner/Contact:** Mr Robert Spencer Bernard
Medieval and Tudor manor house. Great Hall. Dining Room with fine 16th century frieze, ceiling and linenfold panelling. Fine furniture and family portraits. Home of Sir Francis Bernard Bt (d1779), the last British Governor of Massachussetts Bay. Continuous family occupation since mid-16th century. House altered in late 18th century in the Strawberry Hill Gothick style. Interesting garden (5 acres) and specimen trees.
**Location:** MAP 7:C11, OS Ref. SP734 121. 2m N of A418 equidistant between Thame & Aylesbury.
**Open:** 1–29 May & 27 Aug: 2.30–5.30pm (conducted tours only at ¼ to each hour). Groups at any time by prior written agreement (minimum charge £100, no concessions).
**Admission:** Adult £5, OAP £4 (no concession at weekends or BHs), Child (under 12yrs) £2. HHA members free (not on special groups).
🔲 Please tel in advance. WC. 🔲 By arrangement. 🔲 Obligatory. 🔲

Are you looking for unique
**Civil wedding** venues?
See our index on page 577

South East – England

## PITSTONE WINDMILL ✄

**Ivinghoe, Buckinghamshire**
**Tel:** 01442 851227   **Group organisers:** 01296 668223   **Fax:** 01442 850000
**E-mail:** pitstonemill@nationaltrust.org.uk
**Owner:** The National Trust
One of the oldest post mills in Britain; in view from Ivinghoe Beacon.
**Location: MAP 7:D11**, OS Ref. SP946 158. ½ m S of Ivinghoe, 3m NE of Tring.
Just W of B488.
**Open:** 3 Jun–26 Aug: Sun & BHs, 2.30–6pm.
**Admission:** Adult £1.20, Child 50p. Free to NT members.
ℹ No WC. ♿ Difficult access. 🅿

Waddesdon Manor, Nr Aylesbury

# STOWE LANDSCAPE GARDENS & PARK ✄
## Nr BUCKINGHAM MK18 5EH

www.nationaltrust.org.uk/stowegardens

**Tel:** 01280 822850   **Infoline:** 01494 755568   **Fax:** 01280 822437
**Group Visits:** 01280 822850   **E-mail:** stowegarden@nationaltrust.org.uk
**Owner:** The National Trust   **Contact:** The Property Manager

Discover one of Europe's most influential landscape gardens. Hidden amongst spectacular views and vast open spaces there are magical secret corners, hidden meanings, and over 40 monuments and temples waiting to be discovered. Visitors can also take a tour of Stowe House or explore the 750 acres of surrounding historic parkland, including the newly restored 250 acre Deer Park. Stowe is the perfect setting for a family picnic or those seeking peace and tranquility, with walks and trails for all to enjoy. With the changing seasons, continuing restoration and a calendar of events for all the family, each visit provides something new to discover. Recent restoration: completion of major work to the Corinthian Arch. Views not seen for over 200 years opened up with the restoration of the original 18th century Hermitage pathway. Recently completed work to the Central Pavilion, South Portico and Marble Saloon. Part of the ongoing restoration of the House.

**Location:** MAP 7:C10, OS Ref. SP665 366. Off A422 Buckingham – Banbury Rd. 3m NW of Buckingham.
**Open:** Gardens, Shop & Tearooms: 1 Mar–4 Nov, Wed–Sun; Gardens & Shop 10.30am–5.30pm, last admission 1½hrs before closing; Tearooms 10.30am–5pm. 10 Nov–24 Feb, Sat & Sun, Gardens & Shop 10.30am–4pm; Tearooms 10.30– 3.30 pm. Open BH Mons. Shop also open 7 Nov–21 Dec, 11am–3pm. May close in extreme weather conditions. House not NT. For house opening times 01280 818166.
**\*Admission:** Gardens: Adult £6.50, Child £3.30, Family £16.30. Free to NT Members. 15% discount for booked groups. House (inc. NT members): Phone 01280 818166. House admission payable at NT reception. *includes a voluntary donation but visitors can choose to pay the standard prices displayed at the property and on the website.

📷 ♿ Pre-booked self-drive powered chairs available. WC. 🍽 🔋 Free in gardens, 11am and 2pm most days. By arrangement for groups. 🎧 🔲 🐕 In grounds, on leads. 🅰 🌐 🛈 For details visit www.nationaltrust.org.uk/stowegardens.

**STOWE HOUSE** 🏛   *See page 100 for full page entry.*

**WADDESDON MANOR** ✄   *See page 101 for full page entry.*

See which properties offer **educational facilities** or **school visits** in our index on page 571

Stowe House, Buckingham

## WEST WYCOMBE PARK 🌿

**WEST WYCOMBE, HIGH WYCOMBE, BUCKINGHAMSHIRE HP14 3AJ**

**Tel:** 01494 513569

**Owner:** The National Trust  **Contact:** The Head Guide

A perfectly preserved rococo landscape garden, created in the mid-18th century by Sir Francis Dashwood, founder of the Dilettanti Society and the Hellfire Club. The house is among the most theatrical and Italianate in England, its façades formed as classical temples. The interior has Palmyrene ceilings and decoration, with pictures, furniture and sculpture dating from the time of Sir Francis.

**Location:** MAP 3:F1, OS Ref. SU828 947. At W end of West Wycombe S of the A40.

**Open:** House & Grounds: 3 Jun–30 Aug: daily except Fri & Sat, 2–6pm. Weekday entry by guided tour only every 20 mins (approx), last admission 5.15pm. Grounds only: 1 Apr–31 May: daily except Fri & Sat, 2–6pm.

**Admission:** House & Grounds: Adult £6, Child £3, Family £15. Groups £4.70. Grounds only: Adult £3, Child £1.50. Free to NT Members. Groups by arrangement. Note: The West Wycombe Caves and adjacent café are privately owned and NT members must pay admission fees.

🏛 Grounds partly suitable. 🎥 Obligatory on weekdays. 🐕 In car park only, on leads.

## WOTTON HOUSE

**Wotton Underwood, Aylesbury, Buckinghamshire HP18 0SB**

**Tel:** 01844 238363  **Fax:** 01844 238380  **E-mail:** david.gladstone@which.net

**Owner/Contact:** David Gladstone

The Capability Brown Pleasure Grounds at Wotton, currently undergoing restoration, are related to the Stowe gardens, both belonging to the Grenville family when Brown laid out the Wotton grounds between 1750 and 1767. A series of man-made features on the 3 mile circuit include bridges, follies and statues.

**Location:** MAP 7:B11, OS Ref. 468576, 216168. Either A41 turn off Kingswood, or M40/J7 via Thame. Rail: Haddenham & Thame 6m.

**Open:** 11 Apr–12 Sept: Weds only, 2–5pm. Also 7 Apr, 28 May, 7 Jul, 4 Aug, 1 Sept: 2–5pm.

**Admission:** Adult £5, Child Free, Conc. £3. Groups (max 25).

🎥 Obligatory. 🅿 Limited. 🚐

## WYCOMBE MUSEUM

**Priory Avenue, High Wycombe, Buckinghamshire HP13 6PX**

**Tel:** 01494 421895  **E-mail:** museum@wycombe.gov.uk

**Owner:** Wycombe District Council  **Contact:** John Sugg

Set in historic Castle Hill House and surrounded by peaceful and attractive gardens.

**Location:** MAP 3:F1, OS Ref. SU867 933. Signposted off the A404 High Wycombe/Amersham road. The Museum is about 5mins walk from the town centre and railway station.

**Open:** Mon–Sat, 10am–5pm. Open Suns, 2–5pm. Closed BHs.

**Admission:** Free.

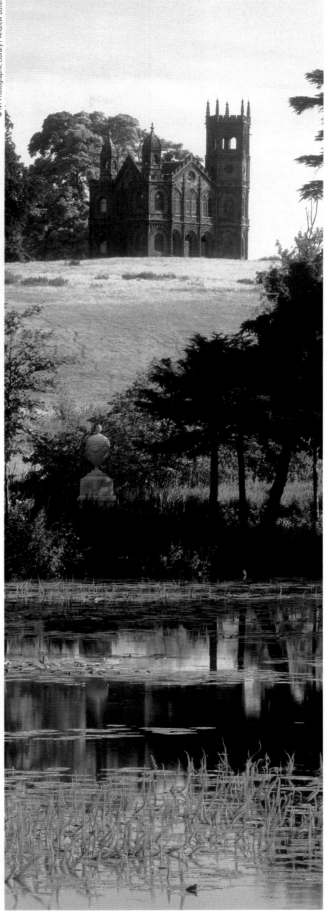

Gothic Temple, Stowe Landscape Gardens, Buckingham

### ■ Owner
Lord Montagu

### ■ Contact
John Montagu Building
Beaulieu
Brockenhurst
Hampshire SO42 7ZN

**Tel:** 01590 614769/87
**Fax:** 01590 612624
**E-mail:** conference@
beaulieu.co.uk

### ■ Location
**MAP 3:C6**
**OS Ref. SU387 025**

M27 to J2, A326, B3054
follow brown signs.

**Bus:** Local service within
the New Forest.

**Rail:** Stations at
Brockenhurst 7m away.

### ■ Opening Times
**Summer**
May–September
Daily, 10am–6pm.

**Winter**
October–April
Daily, 10am–5pm.

Closed Christmas Day.

### ■ Admission
All year

Individual rates upon
application.

Groups (15+)
Rates upon application.

### ■ Special Events
**Apr 29**
Boatjumble & Boatworld

**May 12/13**
Spring Motormart &
Autojumble

**June 23/24**
Motorcycle World

**Sept 8/9**
International Autojumble

**Oct 27**
Fireworks Spectacular

All enquiries should be
made to our Special
Events Booking Office
where advance tickets can
be purchased. The
contact telephone is
01590 612888.

### ■ Conference/Function

| ROOM | SIZE | MAX CAPACITY |
|---|---|---|
| Brabazon (x3) | 40' x 40' | 85 (x3) |
| Domus | 69' x 27' | 150 |
| Theatre | | 200 |
| Palace House | | 60 |
| Motor Museum | | 250 |

# BEAULIEU 🏛

## www.beaulieu.co.uk

The Beaulieu Estate has been owned by the same family since 1538 and is still the private home of the Montagus. Thomas Wriothesley, who later became the 1st Earl of Southampton, acquired the estate at the time of the Dissolution of the Monasteries when he was Lord Chancellor to Henry VIII.

Palace House, overlooking the Beaulieu River, was once the Great Gatehouse of Beaulieu Abbey with its monastic origins reflected in the fan vaulted ceilings of the 14th Century Dining Hall and Lower Drawing Room. The rooms are decorated with furnishings, portraits and treasures collected by past and present generations of the family. Visitors can enjoy the fine gardens or take a riverside walk around the Monks' Mill Pond.

Beaulieu Abbey was founded in 1204 when ing John gave the land to the Cistercians and although most of the buildings have now been destroyed, much of the beauty and interest remains. The former Monks' Refectory is now the local parish church and the Domus, which houses an exhibition and video presentation of monastic life, is home to beautiful wall hangings.

Beaulieu also houses the world famous National Motor Museum which traces the story of motoring from 1894 to the present day. 250 vehicles are on display including legendary world record breakers plus veteran, vintage and classic cars and motorcycles.

The modern Beaulieu is very much a family destination with many free and unlimited rides on a transportation theme to be enjoyed, including a mile long, high-level monorail and replica 1912 London open-topped bus.

# BEAULIEU ...

## Catering and Functions

Beaulieu also offers a comprehensive range of facilities for conferences, company days out, product launches, management training, corporate hospitality, promotions, film locations, exhibitions and outdoor events.

The National Motor Museum is a unique venue for drinks receptions, evening product launches and dinners or the perfect complement to a conference as a relaxing visit.

The charming 13th century Domus hall with its beautiful wooden beams, stone walls and magnificent wall hangings, is the perfect setting for weddings, conferences, dinners, buffets or themed evenings.

Palace House, the ancestral home of Lord Montagu is an exclusive setting for smaller dinners, buffets and receptions. With a welcoming log fire in the winter and the coolness of the courtyard fountain in the summer, it offers a relaxing yet truly 'stately' atmosphere to ensure a memorable experience for your guests whatever the time of year.

A purpose-built theatre, with tiered seating, can accommodate 200 people whilst additional meeting rooms can accommodate from 20 to 200 delegates. Bespoke marquees can also be erected in a charming parkland setting, for any event or occasion. With the nearby Beaulieu River offering waterborne activities and the Beaulieu Estate, with its purpose-built off road course, giving you the opportunity of indulging in a variety of country pursuits and outdoor management training, Beaulieu provides a unique venue for your conference and corporate hospitality needs.

**ℹ** Allow 3 hrs or more for visits. Last adm. 40 mins before closing. Helicopter landing point. When visiting Beaulieu arrangements can be made to view the Estate's vineyards. Visits, which can be arranged between Apr–Oct, must be pre-booked at least one week in advance with Beaulieu Estate Office.

**🏪** Palace House Shop and Kitchen Shop plus Main Reception Shop.

**♿** Disabled visitors may be dropped off outside Visitor Reception before parking. WC. Wheelchairs can be provided free of charge in Visitor Reception by prior booking.

**🍽** The Brabazon restaurant seats 250. Prices start at £18.95. Further details and menus from the Sales Office: 01590 614769.

**🚶** Attendants on duty. Guided tours by prior arrangement for groups.

**P** 1,500 cars and 30 coaches. During the season the busy period is from 11.30am to 1.30pm. Coach drivers should sign in at Information Desk. Free admission for coach drivers plus voucher which can be exchanged for food, drink and souvenirs.

**📷** Professional staff available to assist in planning of visits. Services include introductory talks, films, guided tours, rôle play and extended projects. In general, educational services incur no additional charges and publications are sold at cost. Information available from Education at Beaulieu, John Montagu Building, Beaulieu, Hants SO42 7ZN.

**🐕** In grounds, on leads only.
**❄**

### ■ Owner

Earl of Carnarvon

### ■ Contact

The Castle Office
Highclere Castle
Newbury
Berkshire RG20 9RN

**Tel:** 01635 253210
**Fax:** 01635 255315
**E-mail:** theoffice@
highclerecastle.co.uk

### ■ Location

**MAP 3:D3**
**OS Ref. SU445 587**

M4/J13–A34 south,
M3/J8–A303–A34 north.

**Air:** Heathrow M4
45 mins.

**Rail:** Paddington –
Newbury 45 mins.

**Taxi:** 4½m
07778 156392.

### ■ Opening Times

**Easter**
1–15 April,
Sunday–Thursday.

**May Bank Holidays**
6/7 May,
Sunday & Monday,

28/29 May,
Monday/Tuesday

**Summer**
1 July–30 August,
Sunday–Thursday

11am–4.30pm
(Gates open 10.30am)
last admission 3.30pm.

This information is correct
at the time of publication.
However it may be
subject to change so
please check in advance
of your visit.

### ■ Admission

| | |
|---|---|
| Adult | £7.50 |
| Child | £4.00 |
| Concession | £6.50 |
| Family (2+3/1+4) | £20.00 |

Free to members of HHA

**Grounds & Gardens**
Free of charge during
season.

**Groups** (20+)

| | |
|---|---|
| Adult | £6.50 |
| Child | £3.50 |
| Concession | £5.50 |

Private guided tours at
other times may be
arranged subject to
availability at a minimum
cost for up to 40 persons
of £600 plus VAT; each
additional person £15
plus VAT.

### Conference/Function

| ROOM | SIZE | MAX CAPACITY |
|---|---|---|
| Library | 43' x 21' | 140 |
| Saloon | 42' x 29' | 120 |
| Dining Rm | 37' x 18' | 70 |
| Library, Saloon, Drawing Rm, Music Rm, Smoking Rm | | 500 |

# HIGHCLERE CASTLE & GARDENS

www.highclerecastle.co.uk

Highclere Castle was designed by Charles Barry in the 1830s at the same time as he was building the Houses of Parliament. This soaring pinnacled mansion provided a perfect setting for the 4th Earl of Carnarvon, one of the great hosts of Queen Victoria's reign. The extravagant interiors range from church Gothic through Moorish flamboyance and Rococo Revival to the solid masculinity in the long Library. Old Master paintings mix with portraits by Van Dyck and 18th century painters. Napoleon's desk and chair, rescued from St Helena, sit with other 18th and 19th century furniture. The 5th Earl of Carnarvon, together with Howard Carter, discovered the tomb of Tutankhamun and the Castle houses a unique exhibition of some of his earlier discoveries. The 8th Earl and Countess take a very personal interest in the Castle and are often to be seen around their home, grounds and gardens.

### Gardens

The magnificent parkland, with its massive cedars, was designed by 'Capability' Brown. The walled gardens also date from an earlier house at Highclere, but the dark yew walks are entirely Victorian in character. The Secret Garden has a romance of its own with a beautiful curving lawn surrounded by densely planted herbaceous gardens, a place for romantics and poets.

ⓘ Conferences, exhibitions, filming, fairs, and concerts (cap. 8000). No photography in the house.

▣

☗ Receptions, dinners, corporate hospitality.

♿ Visitors may alight at the entrance. WC.

☕ Tearooms, licensed. Lunches for 20+ can be booked.

🅿 Ample.

📖 Egyptian Exhibition: £4 + VAT per child. 1 adult free per every 10 children, by prior arrangement – includes playgroups, Brownie packs, Guides etc. Nature walks, beautiful old follies, Secret Garden.

🐕 In grounds, on leads.

🔔

♿ Please visit website.

Buckingham House

Wymering Manor

### ■ Owner
Portsmouth Heritage

### ■ Contact
Mr Alan Dale

Buckingham House
High Street
Old Portsmouth  PO1 2LP

Wymering Manor
Old Wymering Lane
Cosham
Portsmouth  PO6 3NL

**Tel:** 023 9281 9699
**Mobile:** 0785 612 4267
**E-mail:** wymeringmanor
@yahoo.co.uk

### ■ Location
**MAP 3:E6**
**OS Refs:**
Buckingham House –
SZ634 994
Wymering Manor –
SU650 056

**Air:** Southampton.

**Rail:** Buckingham House
– Portsmouth & Southsea
or Portsmouth Harbour.
Wymering Manor –
Cosham.

### ■ Opening Times
Please contact property
for details.

### ■ Admission
Please contact property
for details.

# PORTSMOUTH HERITAGE
## BUCKINGHAM HOUSE & WYMERING MANOR
www.portsmouthheritage.co.uk

### Buckingham House
Dating back to around 1450, Buckingham House was the scene of the assassination of George Villiers, Duke of Buckingham in 1628. After years of decay, the house and adjoining property are being restored to create an Hotel and function venue. There are adjoining modern conference facilities to accommodate 280 – 500 delegates. 14 en-suite bedrooms plus two suites. Enclosed courtyard.

### Wymering Manor
The Manor of Wymering is listed in the Domesday Book and the House is reputed to be the oldest and most haunted building in the city. Important examples of Tudor timber framing in the structure and unusual period features span hundreds of years. After 50 years as a Youth Hostel the house is being restored to create some of the grand opulence which previous owners enjoyed. The house will have six en-suite bedrooms plus one suite, and an enclosed garden with direct access from all function rooms. Private car parking.

These unique lavishly presented properties will be available for exclusive hire, corporate events, conferences, filming, accommodation and dining from Spring 2008. Executive cars, sailing/motor yacht charter by arrangement.

Wymering Manor

Both properties.

Both properties.

Both properties.

Both properties.

Adjacent parking for 200 cars at Buckingham House. Private car parking at Wymering Manor.

Both properties.

Both properties.

Both properties.

Both properties.

€

### Conference/Function

| ROOM | SIZE | MAX CAPACITY |
|---|---|---|
| Buckingham House | | |
| Red Room | 7.5m x 4.3m | 50 |
| Wren Room | 8.7m x 4.3m | 100 |
| Tudor Room | 5m x 4.5m | 75 |
| Felton Room | 8m x 3.8m | 50 |
| Wymering Manor | | |
| Music Room | 11.6m x 5.2m | 100 |
| Dining Room | 6.3m x 5.3m | 50 |
| Drawing Room | 7.6m x 5.4m | 75 |

## JANE AUSTEN'S HOUSE
### CHAWTON, ALTON, HAMPSHIRE GU34 1SD

www.janeaustenmuseum.org.uk

**Tel:** 01420 83262  **E-mail:** enquiries@jahmusm.org.uk

**Owner:** Jane Austen Memorial Trust   **Contact:** Ann Channon

17th century house where Jane Austen wrote or revised her six great novels. Contains many items associated with her and her family, documents and letters, first editions of the novels, pictures, portraits and furniture. Pleasant garden, suitable for picnics, bakehouse with brick oven and wash tub, houses Jane's donkey carriage.

**Location:** MAP 3:E4, OS Ref. SU708 376. Just S of A31, 1m SW of Alton, signposted Chawton.

**Open:** Jan/Feb: Sats & Suns, 10.30am–4.30pm. Mar–end May: daily, 10.30am–4.30pm. June–Aug: daily, 10am–5pm. Sept–end Dec: daily, 10.30am–4.30pm. Closed 25/26 December.

**Admission:** Fee charged.

⬚ Bookshop. ⬚ Ground floor & grounds. WC. ⬚ Opposite house. ⬚ Opposite house. ⬚ Guide dogs only.⬚

Broadlands, Romsey

## AVINGTON PARK 🏛
### WINCHESTER, HAMPSHIRE SO21 1DB

www.avingtonpark.co.uk

**Tel:** 01962 779260   **E-mail:** enquiries@avingtonpark.co.uk

**Owner/Contact:** Mrs S L Bullen

Avington Park, where Charles II and George IV both stayed at various times, dates back to the 11th century. The house was enlarged in 1670 by the addition of two wings and a classical Portico surmounted by three statues. The State rooms are magnificently painted and lead onto the unique pair of conservatories flanking the South Lawn. The Georgian church, St. Mary's, is in the grounds.

Avington Park is a privately owned stately home and is a most prestigious venue in peaceful surroundings. It is perfect for any event from seminars, conferences and exhibitions to wedding ceremonies and receptions, dinner dances and private parties. The Conservatories and the Orangery make a delightful location for summer functions, whilst log fires offer a welcome during the winter. Excellent caterers provide for all types of occasion, ranging from breakfasts and light lunches to sumptuous dinners. All bookings at Avington are individually tailor-made and only exclusive use is offered. Several rooms are licensed for Civil wedding ceremonies and a delightful fully-equipped apartment is available for short stays.

**Location:** MAP 3:D4, OS Ref. SU534 324. 4m NE of Winchester ½m S of B3047 in Itchen Abbas.

**Open:** May–Sept: Suns & BH Mons plus Mons in Aug, 2.30–5.30pm. Last tour 5pm. Other times by arrangement, coach parties welcome by appointment all year.

**Admission:** Adult £4, Child £2.

ⓘ Conferences. ⬚ ⬚ Partial. WC. ⬚ ⬚ Obligatory. ⬚ ⬚ In grounds, on leads. Guide dogs only in house. ⬚ ⬚

## BASING HOUSE

**Redbridge Lane, Basing, Basingstoke RG24 7HB**
**Tel:** 01256 467294
**Owner:** Hampshire County Council    **Contact:** Alan Turton
Ruins, covering 10 acres, of huge Tudor palace. Recent recreation of Tudor formal garden.
**Location:** MAP 3:E3, OS Ref. SU665 526. 2m E from Basingstoke town centre. Signposted car parks are about 5 or 10 mins walk from entrance.
**Open:** Apr–Sept: Wed–Sun & BHs, 2–6pm.
**Admission:** Adult £2, Conc. £1.

## BEAULIEU 🏛

*See pages 108/109 for double page entry.*

## BISHOP'S WALTHAM PALACE ⌗

**Bishop's Waltham, Hampshire SO32 1DH**
**Tel:** 01489 892460    www.english-heritage.org.uk/visits
**Owner:** English Heritage    **Contact:** Visitor Operations Team
This medieval seat of the Bishops of Winchester once stood in an enormous park. Wooded grounds, the remains of the Great Hall and the three storey tower can still be seen. Dower House furnished as a 19th-century farmhouse.
**Location:** MAP 3:D5, OS Ref. SU552 173. In Bishop's Waltham, 5 miles NE from M27/J8.
**Open:** Grounds: 1 May–30 Sept: Sun–Fri, 10am–5pm. Farmhouse: by request. Guided tours: Aug, Suns, 11am.
**Admission:** Free.
ⓘ WCs. Exhibition. 📷 ♿ Grounds. 🅿 🚫 Grounds only, on leads. 🌳

## BREAMORE HOUSE & MUSEUM 🏛

### BREAMORE, FORDINGBRIDGE, HAMPSHIRE SP6 2DF

www.breamorehouse.com

**Tel:** 01725 512468    **Fax:** 01725 512858    **E-mail:** breamore@btinternet.com
**Owner/Contact:** Sir Edward Hulse Bt
Elizabethan manor with fine collections of pictures and furniture. Countryside Museum takes visitors back to the time when a village was self-sufficient.
**Location:** MAP 3:B5, OS Ref. SU152 191. W Off the A338, between Salisbury and Ringwood.
**Open:** Easter weekend; Apr: Tue & Sun; May–Sept: Tue/Wed, Thur, Sat/Sun & BHs. House: 2–5.30pm. Countryside Museum: 1–5.30pm. Last admission 4pm.
**Admission:** Combined ticket for house and museum: Adult £7, Child £5, OAP £6, Family £17.
📷 ♿ Ground floor & grounds. WC. 🚫 🚗

For **corporate hospitality**
at unique venues see the
index on page 567

© Lord Romsey

## BROADLANDS
### ROMSEY, HAMPSHIRE SO51 9ZD

www.broadlands.net

**Tel:** 01794 505010    **Event Enquiry Line:** 01794 505020    **Fax:** 01794 529755
**E-mail:** admin@broadlands.net
**Owner:** Lord & Lady Brabourne    **Contact:** Estate Manager
Broadlands, the home of Lord and Lady Brabourne by descent from Prime Minister Viscount Palmerston and The Earl Mountbatten of Burma, is open to the public by guided tour only. The Mountbatten Exhibition depicts the life and times of Lord and Lady Mountbatten. Limited tours, which include items normally available by appointment, are offered on certain days.
**Location:** MAP 3:C5, OS Ref. SU355 204. On A3090 at Romsey.
**Open/Admission:** Details of opening times and admission charges can be obtained from the website, or by telephone.
📱 ♿ Ground floor. WC. 📷 Obligatory. 🚫 Guide dogs only.

## CALSHOT CASTLE ⌗

**Calshot, Fawley, Hampshire SO45 1BR**
**Tel:** 02380 892023    www.english-heritage.org.uk/visits
**Owner:** English Heritage    **Contact:** Hampshire County Council
Henry VIII built this coastal fort in an excellent position, commanding the sea passage to Southampton. The fort houses an exhibition and recreated pre-World War I barrack room.
**Location:** MAP 3:D6, OS Ref. SU488 025. On spit 2 miles SE of Fawley off B3053.
**Open:** 31 Mar–31 Oct: daily, 10am–4pm.
**Admission:** Adult £2.50, Child £1.50, Conc. £1.80, Family £6.
ⓘ WCs. 📷 🅿 🚫

## ELING TIDE MILL

**The Toll Bridge, Eling, Totton, Southampton, Hampshire SO40 9HF**
**Tel:** 023 8086 9575    **E-mail:** info@elingtidemill.org.uk
**Owner:** Eling Tide Mill Trust Ltd & New Forest District Council
**Contact:** Mr David Blackwell-Eaton
**Location:** MAP 3:C5, OS Ref. SU365 126. 4m W of Southampton. ½m S of the A35.
**Open:** All year: Wed–Sun and BH Mons, 10am–4pm. Closed 25/26 Dec.
**Admission:** Adult £2.25, Child £1.25, OAP £1.75, Family £5.70. Discounts for pre-booked groups (10+).Prices may change, please telephone for details.

Highclere Castle & Gardens, Newbury

# EXBURY GARDENS & STEAM RAILWAY

### EXBURY, SOUTHAMPTON, HAMPSHIRE SO45 1AZ

www.exbury.co.uk

**Tel:** 023 8089 1203 **Fax:** 023 8089 9940

**Owner:** Edmund de Rothschild Esq **Contact:** Estate Office

HHA/Christie's *Garden of the Year* 2001. A spectacular 200-acre woodland garden showcasing the world famous Rothschild Collection of rhododendrons, azaleas and camellias. Enchanting river walks, ponds and cascades. Daffodil meadow, Rock and Heather Gardens, exotic plantings and herbaceous borders ensure year-round interest. The Steam Railway enchants visitors of all ages, passing through a Summer Garden, and featuring a bridge, tunnel, viaduct and causeway. Licensed for Civil weddings and a beautiful venue for marquee receptions and corporate events.

**Location:** MAP 3:D6, OS Ref. SU425 005. 11m SE of Totton (A35) via A326 & B3054 & minor road. In New Forest.

**Open:** 17 Mar–4 Nov: daily, 10am–5.30pm (dusk in Nov). Evening opening 14–18 May, last admission 8pm. Exbury 'Maize Maze' open during summer holidays. Separate admission.

**Admission:** High Season* 17 Mar–10 Jun: Adult £7.50, Child (3–15yrs) £1.50, OAP/Group £7, Family (2+3) £17.50; Railway +£3, Rover Ticket not available. Low Season (all other open times): Adult £6.50, Child (3–15yrs) £1.50, OAP/Group £6, Family (2+3) £15. Railway +£3, Rover Ticket £4. Child under 3yrs Free. Buggy tours +£3.50. *High Season visitors receive a free return voucher to see Autumn colours. RHS Members Free Mar & Sept.

Licensed. By arrangement. In grounds, on leads.

---

# FORT BROCKHURST

**Gunner's Way, Gosport, Hampshire PO12 4DS**

**Tel:** 02392 581059 **www.english-heritage.org.uk/visits**

**Owner:** English Heritage **Contact:** Visitor Operations Team

This 19th-century fort was built to protect Portsmouth. Today it houses a display of extraordinary objects found at sites across the region, including stonework, jewellery, textiles and furniture from various periods. Tours of the fort introduce the visitor to these hidden stores and will explain the exciting history of the site and the legend behind the ghostly activity in cell no. 3.

**Location:** MAP 3:E6, OS196, Ref. SU596 020. Off A32, in Gunner's Way, Elson on N side of Gosport.

**Open:** Heritage Open Days and Feb–Oct, 2nd Fri of each month for tours and handling sessions.

**Admission:** Please telephone for details.

WCs. Grounds and ground floor only. Dogs on leads (restricted areas).

---

# FURZEY GARDENS

**Minstead, Lyndhurst, Hampshire SO43 7GL**

**Tel:** 023 8081 2464 **Fax:** 023 8081 2297

**Owner:** Furzey Gardens Charitable Trust **Contact:** Maureen Cole

**Location:** MAP 3:C5, OS Ref. SU273 114. Minstead village ½m N of M27/A31 junction off A337 to Lyndhurst.

**Open:** Mar–Oct: daily. 1 Nov–17 Dec: Sats & Suns. Gardens only: 1 Nov–28 Feb: 10am–5pm.

**Admission:** Please contact property for prices.

For rare and unusual plants visit the **plant sales** index on page 564

---

# GILBERT WHITE'S HOUSE & THE OATES MUSEUM

### THE WAKES, HIGH STREET, SELBORNE, ALTON GU34 3JH

www.gilbertwhiteshouse.org.uk

**Tel:** 01420 511275 **E-mail:** info@gilbertwhiteshouse.org.uk

**Owner:** Oates Memorial Trust **Contact:** Duty Manager

Charming refurbished 18th century house, home of Rev Gilbert White, author of *The Natural History of Selborne*. Over 25 acres of garden and parkland with many plants of the Georgian era. Tea parlour with fare based on 18th century recipes and excellent gift shop. Exhibition on Captain Oates of Antarctic fame.

**Location:** MAP 3:E4, OS Ref. SU741 336. On W side of B3006, in village of Selborne 4m NW of the A3.

**Open:** 1 Jan–24 Dec: Tues–Sun & BHs (1 Apr–30 Sept, daily, 11am–5pm). Groups by arrangement.

**Admission:** Adult £6.50, Child Free (accompanied by Adult), OAP £5.50.

No photography in house. Partial. By arrangement. Guide dogs only.

---

Beaulieu, Brockenhurst

# GREAT HALL & QUEEN ELEANOR'S GARDEN
## WINCHESTER CASTLE, WINCHESTER  SO23 8PJ

www.hants.gov.uk/discover/places/great-hall.html

**Tel:** 01962 846476  **Fax:** for bookings 01962 841326
**Owner:** Hampshire County Council  **Contact:** Custodian
The only surviving part of Henry III's medieval castle at Winchester, this 13th century hall was the centre of court and government life. The Round Table closely associated with the legend of King Arthur has hung here for over 700 years. Queen Eleanor's garden is a faithful representation of the medieval garden visited by Kings and Queens of England.

**Location:** MAP 3:D4, OS Ref. SU477 295. Central Winchester. SE of Westgate archway.
**Open:** Mar–Oct daily, 10am–5pm. Nov–Feb: daily 10am–4pm. Closed 25/26 Dec and for Civic events only – see website for details.
**Admission:** Free. Donations appreciated towards the upkeep of the Great Hall.
� ⓘ By arrangement. ✱

# GUILDHALL GALLERY
## THE BROADWAY, WINCHESTER  SO23 9GH

www.winchester.gov.uk

**Tel:** 01962 848289 (gallery) 01962 848269 (office)  **Fax:** 01962 848299
**E-mail:** museums@winchester.gov.uk
**Owner:** Winchester City Council  **Contact:** Visitor Services Manager
A constantly changing programme of contemporary exhibitions including painting, sculpture, craft, photography and ceramics.
**Location:** MAP 3:D4, OS Ref. SU485 293. Winchester – city centre. Situated above the Tourist Office in Winchester's 19th century Guildhall.
**Open:** Apr–Oct: Mon–Sat, 10am–5pm; Sun, 12 noon–5pm. Nov–Mar: Tue–Sat, 10am–4pm; Sun, 12 noon–4pm.
**Admission:** Free.
⊠ ✱

### HIGHCLERE CASTLE 🏛
### & GARDENS

*See page 110 for full page entry.*

Exbury Gardens & Steam Railway, Southampton

NT Photographic Library: Stephen Robson

# HINTON AMPNER ❧

## BRAMDEAN, ALRESFORD, HAMPSHIRE  SO24 0LA

www.nationaltrust.org.uk

**Tel:** 01962 771305  **Fax:** 01962 793101  **E-mail:** hintonampner@nationaltrust.org.uk
**Owner:** The National Trust  **Contact:** The Property Manager

"I have learned during the past years what above all I want from a garden: this is tranquillity". So said Ralph Dutton, 8th and last Lord Sherborne, of his garden at Hinton Ampner. He created one of the great gardens of the 20th century, a masterpiece of design based upon the bones of a Victorian garden, in which he united a formal layout with varied and informal planting in pastel shades. It is a garden of all year round interest with scented plants and magnificent vistas over the park and surrounding countryside.

The garden forms the link between the woodland and parkland planting, which he began in 1930, and the house, which he remodelled into a small neo-Georgian manor house in 1936. He made further alterations when the house was reconstructed after a fire in 1960. Today it contains his very fine collection of English furniture, Italian paintings and hard-stones. Both his collection and every aspect of the decoration at Hinton Ampner reflects Ralph Dutton's sure eye and fine aesthetic judgement.

He placed the whole within the rolling Hampshire landscape that he loved and understood so well.

**Location:** MAP 3:E4, OS Ref. SU597 275. M3/J9 follow signs to Petersfield. On A272, 1m W of Bramdean village, 8m E of Winchester.

**Open:** House: 18 Mar–31 Oct: Tues, Weds & Suns also Sats in Aug, 1–5pm. Garden: 17 Mar–31 Oct, daily except Thur & Fri, 11am–5pm.

**Admission:** House & Garden: Adult £6.50, Child (5–16yrs) £3.25, Child (under 5yrs) Free. Garden only: Adult £5.50, Child (5-16yrs) £2.75, Child (under 5yrs) Free. Free to NT Members.

▢ ⬛ ⬛ 🅿 Limited for coaches. 🐕 Guide dogs only.

---

# HOUGHTON LODGE GARDENS 🏛

## STOCKBRIDGE, HAMPSHIRE, SO20 6LQ

www.houghtonlodge.co.uk

**Tel:** 01264 810502  **Fax:** 01264 810063  **E-mail:** info@houghtonlodge.co.uk
**Owner/Contact:** Captain M W Busk

A haven of peace above the tranquil beauty of the River Test. 12 acres of Grade II* Gardens with fine trees surround an enchanting and unique example of an 18th Century "Cottage Ornée". Chalk Cob walls enclose traditional Kitchen Garden with espaliers, herbs and heated greenhouses, hydroponicum and orchid collection. Gardens both formal and informal. 14 acres adjoining the garden provide an experience of the natural world with meadow walks through the peaceful and unspoiled surroundings of the River Test. Popular TV/Film location.

**Location:** MAP 3:C4, OS Ref. SU344 332. 1½m S of Stockbridge (A30) on minor road to Houghton village.

**Open:** 1 Mar–31 Oct, daily, 10am–5pm. Closed Wednesdays.

**Admission:** Adult £5, Children under 14 Free. Pre-booked groups welcome at special rates. House and Wednesdays by appointment.

🍴 ⬛ Self-service teas & coffees, home-made cakes. 🎭 By arrangement. 🅿
🐕 In grounds, on leads. 🔼

---

# HURST CASTLE ⌗

## Keyhaven, Lymington, Hampshire  SO41 0TP

**Tel:** 01590 642344  www.english-heritage.org.uk/visits

**Owner:** English Heritage  **Contact:** (Managed by) Hurst Castle Services

This was one of the most sophisticated fortresses built by Henry VIII, and later strengthened in the 19th and 20th centuries, to command the narrow entrance to the Solent. There is an exhibition in the castle, and two huge 38-ton guns form the fort's armaments.

**Location:** MAP 3:C7, OS196 Ref. SZ319 898. On Pebble Spit S of Keyhaven. Best approach by ferry from Keyhaven. 4 miles SW of Lymington.

**Open:** 1 Apr–31 Oct: daily, 10.30am–5.30pm. Café: open Apr–May weekends & Jun–Sept: daily.

**Admission:** Adult £3, Child £1.80, Conc. £2.80. EH Members free.

ℹ WCs. ♿ Unsuitable. ⬛ 🐕 Dogs on leads (restricted areas).

---

© English Heritage Photo Library / Jonathan Bailey

Hurst Castle, Lymington

© NT Photographic Library

## KING JOHN'S HOUSE
## & HERITAGE CENTRE
### CHURCH STREET, ROMSEY, HAMPSHIRE SO51 8BT
www.kingjohnshouse.org.uk

**Tel:** 01794 512200   **E-mail:** annerhc@aol.com
**Owner:** King John's House & Tudor Cottage Trust Ltd   **Contact:** Anne James
Three historic buildings on one site: Medieval King John's House, containing 14th-century graffiti and rare bone floor, Tudor Cottage complete with traditional tea room and Victorian Heritage Centre with recreated shop and parlour. Beautiful period gardens, special events/exhibitions and children's activities. Gift shop and Tourist Information Centre. Receptions and private/corporate functions.
**Location:** MAP 3:C5, OS Ref. SU353 212. M27/J3. Opposite Romsey Abbey, next to Post Office.
**Open:** Apr–Sept: Mon–Sat, 10am–4pm. Oct–Mar: Heritage Centre only. Limited opening on Sundays. Evenings also for pre-booked groups.
**Admission:** Adult £2.50, Child 50p, Conc. £2. Heritage Centre only: Adult £1.50, Child 50p, Conc. £1. Discounted group booking by appointment.
⬚ ⬚ ⬚ Partial. ⬚ ⬚ By arrangement.
⬚ Off Latimer St with direct access through King John's Garden.
⬚ ⬚ Guide dogs only. ⬚ ⬚

## MEDIEVAL MERCHANTS HOUSE ⬚

**58 French Street, Southampton, Hampshire SO1 0AT**
**Tel:** 02380 221503   www.english-heritage.org.uk/visits
**Owner:** English Heritage   **Contact:** Visitor Operations Team
The life of a prosperous merchant in the Middle Ages is vividly evoked in this recreated, faithfully restored 13th-century townhouse.
**Location:** MAP 3:D5, OS Ref. SU419 112. 58 French Street. ¼m S of Bargate off Castle Way. 150yds SE of Tudor House.
**Open:** 1 Apr–30 Sept: Fri–Sun & BHs, 12noon–6pm.
**Admission:** Adult £3.60, Child £1.80, Conc. £2.70. EH Members free.
⬚ ⬚ ⬚ ⬚

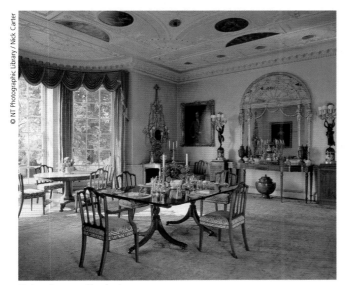

© NT Photographic Library / Nick Carter

Hinton Ampner, Alresford

## MOTTISFONT ABBEY & GARDEN ⬚
### MOTTISFONT, Nr ROMSEY, HAMPSHIRE SO51 0LP
www.nationaltrust.org.uk/mottisfontabbey

**Tel:** 01794 340757   **Fax:** 01794 341492   **Recorded Message:** 01794 341220
**E-mail:** mottisfontabbey@nationaltrust.org.uk
**Owner:** The National Trust   **Contact:** The Property Manager
The Abbey and Garden form the central point of an 809 ha estate including most of the village of Mottisfont, farmland and woods. A tributary of the River Test flows through the garden forming a superb and tranquil setting for a 12th century Augustinian priory which, after the Dissolution, became a house. It contains the spring or "font" from which the place name is derived. The magnificent trees, walled gardens and the National Collection of Old-fashioned Roses combine to provide interest throughout the seasons. The Abbey contains a drawing room decorated by Rex Whistler and the cellarium of the old Priory. In 1996 the Trust acquired Derek Hill's 20th century picture collection.
**Location:** MAP 3:C5, OS185 Ref. SU327 270. Signposted off A3057 Romsey to Stockbridge road, 4½m N of Romsey. Also signposted off B3084 Romsey to Broughton. Station: Dunbridge (U) ¾m.
**Open:** Garden: 3 Feb–18 Mar, 29 Oct–16 Dec, Sat–Sun, 11am–4pm.19 Mar–27 May, 3 Sept–28 Oct, Sat–Wed, 11am–5pm. 28 May–1 Jun, daily, 11am–5pm. 2 Jun–1 Jul, daily, 11am–8.30pm. 2 Jul–2 Sep, Sat–Thurs, 11am–5pm. House: 19 Mar–27 May, 3 Sept–28 Oct, Sat–Wed, 11am–5pm. 28 May–1 Jul, daily, 11am–5pm. 2 Jul–28 Oct, Sat–Wed, 11am–5pm. Shop / Café: As garden except in February when Shop is closed. Good Fri, 11am–5pm. Car park gates close at 6pm except in June. Access to some showrooms in the house may be limited on Sats due to weddings.
***Admission:** Adult £7.50, Child (5-18yrs) £3.80, Family £18.80. During June Rose Season: Adult £8.50. Group discount, rate on application. Free to NT Members.
*includes a voluntary donation but visitors can choose to pay the standard prices displayed at the property and on the website.
⬚ ⬚ Partial. ⬚ ⬚ Licensed. ⬚ ⬚ Guide dogs only. ⬚ ⬚

## NETLEY ABBEY ⬚

**Netley, Southampton, Hampshire**
**Tel:** 02392 378291   www.english-heritage.org.uk/visits
**Owner:** English Heritage   **Contact:** Portchester Castle
A peaceful and beautiful setting for the extensive ruins of this 13th-century Cistercian abbey converted in Tudor times for use as a house.
**Location:** MAP 3:D6, OS Ref. SU453 089. In Netley, 4 miles SE of Southampton, facing Southampton Water.
**Open:** 6 Apr–30 Sept: daily, 10am–6pm. 1 Oct–20 Mar 2008: Sats & Suns, 10am–3pm. Guided tours Sats 11am during Aug.
**Admission:** Free.
⬚ ⬚ ⬚ ⬚ Dogs on leads. ⬚

## NORTHINGTON GRANGE ⬚

**New Alresford, Hampshire**
**Tel:** 01424 775705   www.english-heritage.org.uk/visits
**Owner:** English Heritage   **Contact:** 1066 Battle Abbey
Northington Grange and its landscaped park as you see it today, formed the core of the house as designed by William Wilkins in 1809. It is one of the earliest Greek Revival houses in Europe.
**Location:** MAP 3:E4, OS 185, SU562 362. 4 miles N of New Alresford off B3046 along farm track – 550 metres.
**Open:** Grounds only: 1 Apr–31 Jul: daily, 10am–6pm. (3pm Jun & July). 1 Nov–20 Mar 2008: daily, 10am–4pm. Closed 24–26 Dec & 1 Jan.
**Admission:** Free.
⬚ Wheelchair access (with assistance). ⬚ ⬚ Dogs on leads.

## PORTCHESTER CASTLE

**Portsmouth, Hampshire PO16 9QW**
**Tel/Fax:** 02392 378291 **www.english-heritage.org.uk/visits**
**Owner:** English Heritage **Contact:** Visitor Operations Team
The rallying point of Henry V's expedition to Agincourt and the ruined palace of King Richard II. This grand castle has a history going back nearly 2,000 years and the most complete Roman walls in northern Europe. Exhibition telling the story of the castle and interactive audio tour.
**Location:** MAP 3:E6, OS196, Ref. SU625 046. On S side of Portchester off A27, M27/J11.
**Open:** 1 Apr–30 Sept: daily, 10am–6pm. 1 Oct–20 Mar 2008: daily, 10am–4pm. Closed 24–26 Dec & 1 Jan.
**Admission:** Adult £4, Child £2, Conc. £3. 15% discount for groups (11+). EH Members Free.
ⓘ WCs. Exhibition. ⬜ ⬜ Partial. ⬜ 🅿 ⬜ In grounds, on leads. ⬜

## PORTSMOUTH CATHEDRAL

**Portsmouth, Hampshire PO1 2HH**
**Tel:** 023 9282 3300 **Fax:** 023 9229 5480
**E-mail:** rosemary.fairfax@portsmouthcathedral.org.uk **Contact:** Rosemary Fairfax
Maritime Cathedral founded in 12th century and finally completed in 1991. A member of the ship's crew of Henry VIII's flagship *Mary Rose* is buried in Navy Aisle.
**Location:** MAP 3:E6, OS Ref. SZ633 994. 1½ m from end of M275. Follow signs to Historic Ship and Old Portsmouth.
**Open:** 7.45am–6pm all year. Sun service: 8am, 9.30am, 11am, 6pm. Weekday: 6pm (Choral on Tues and Fris in term time).
**Admission:** Donation appreciated.

## PORTSMOUTH HERITAGE BUCKINGHAM HOUSE & WYMERING MANOR

*See page 111 for full page entry.*

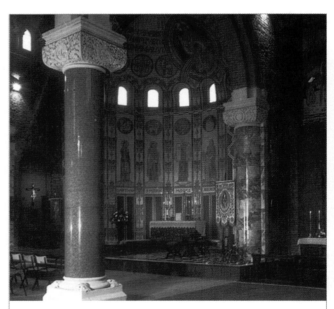

# ST AGATHA'S CHURCH
## MARKET WAY, PORTSMOUTH PO1 4AD

**Tel:** 02392 837050
**Owner:** St Agatha's Trust **Contact:** Fr J Maunder (Tel/Fax: 01329 230330)
A grand Italianate basilica of 1894 enriched with marble, granite and carved stone. The apse contains Britain's largest sgraffito mural, by Heywood Sumner c1901. Fine furnishings, untouched by Vatican II, by Randoll Blacking, Sir Ninian Comper, Sir Walter Tapper, Martin Travers, Norman Shaw and others. Described by Pevsner as containing *"one of Portsmouth's few major works of art"*.
**Location:** MAP 3:D3, OS Ref. SU640 006. On route for Historic Ships. Near Cascades Centre car park.
**Open:** All year, Sats, 10am–4pm. Suns, 10am–2pm (High Mass 11am). Jun–Aug, Weds, 10.30am–3pm. Other times by appointment – 01329 230330.
**Admission:** No charge.
ⓘ Available for hire – concerts, exhibitions & filming. Has featured in 'Casualty'. ⬜ ⬜ Partial. WCs. ⬜ ⬜ By arrangement. 🅿 Limited. ⬜ ⬜ ⬜

# SANDHAM MEMORIAL CHAPEL 💐
## BURGHCLERE, Nr NEWBURY, HAMPSHIRE RG20 9JT

**Tel/Fax:** 01635 278394 **E-mail:** sandham@nationaltrust.org.uk
**www.nationaltrust.org.uk/Sandham**
**Owner:** The National Trust **Contact:** The Custodian
This red brick chapel was built in the 1920s for the artist Stanley Spencer to fill with paintings inspired by his experiences of the First World War. Influenced by Giotto's Arena Chapel in Padua, Spencer took five years to complete what is arguably his finest achievement. The Chapel has gardens and an orchard at the front of the property, and views over to Watership Down. Pictures best viewed on a bright day as no artificial lighting.
**Location:** MAP 3:D3, OS Ref. SU463 608. 4m S of Newbury, ½m E of A34, W end of Burghclere.
**Open:** 3–25 Mar & 3–25 Nov: Sat & Sun, 11am–4pm. 1–23 Dec:, Sat & Sun, 11am–3pm. 28 Mar–28 Oct: Wed–Sun, 11am–5pm. Open BH Mons. Other times by appointment.
**Admission:** Adult £3.50, Child £1.75. NT Members free.
⬜ Portable ramp for entrance. ⬜ By arrangement. ⬜ ⬜ In grounds, on leads. ⬜

Sandham Memorial Chapel, Nr Newbury

**visit hudsons guide online**

# STRATFIELD SAYE HOUSE 🏠
### STRATFIELD SAYE, HAMPSHIRE  RG7 2BZ
www.stratfield-saye.co.uk

**Tel:** 01256 882882   **Fax:** 01256 881466

**Owner:** The Duke of Wellington     **Contact:** The Administrator

After the Duke of Wellington's victory against Napoleon at the Battle of Waterloo in 1815, the Duke chose Stratfield Saye as his country estate. The house provides a fascinating insight into how the 1st Duke lived and contains many of his possessions. It is still occupied by his descendents and is a family home rather than a museum. Over the last four years there has been an extensive programme of restoration and conservation. Of particular interest are many pieces of fine French furniture, porcelain and some rare examples of Print Rooms.

**Location:** MAP 3:E2, OS Ref. SU700 615. Equidistant from Reading (M4/J11) & Basingstoke (M3/J6) 1½m W of the A33.

**Open:** 5–10 Apr (Easter weekend) & 5–30 Jul: daily, 11.30am (Sats & Suns, 10.30am–3.30pm (last admission).

**Admission:** Weekends: Adult £8, Child £5, OAP/Student £7. Weekdays Adult £7, Child £4, OAP/Student £6. Groups by arrangement only.

🖼 ♿ WC. 🎧 ℹ Obligatory. 🅿 🐾 Guide dogs only.

# TITCHFIELD ABBEY ⚜
### Titchfield, Southampton, Hampshire PO15 5RA
**Tel:** 01329 842133   www.english-heritage.org.uk/visits

**Owner:** English Heritage     **Contact:** The Titchfield Abbey Association

Remains of a 13th-century abbey overshadowed by the grand Tudor gatehouse. Reputedly some of Shakespeare's plays were performed here for the first time. Under local management of Titchfield Abbey Society.

**Location:** MAP 3:D6, OS Ref. SU544 067. ½m N of Titchfield off A27.

**Open:** 6 Apr–30 Sept: daily, 10am–5pm. 1 Oct–20 Mar 2008 (closed 24–26 Dec & 1 Jan): daily, 10am–4pm. Guided tours Sats in Aug at 3pm.

**Admission:** Free.

♿ ℹ 🅿 🐾 Dogs on leads. ✠

The Vyne, Basingstoke

# THE VYNE 🌿
### SHERBORNE ST JOHN, BASINGSTOKE  RG24 9HL
www.nationaltrust.org.uk

**Tel:** 01256 883858  **Infoline:** 01256 881337  **Fax:** 01256 881720

**E-mail:** thevyne@nationaltrust.org.uk

**Owner:** The National Trust   **Contact:** The Property Manager

Built in the early 16th century for Lord Sandys, Henry VIII's Lord Chamberlain, the house acquired a classical portico in the mid-17th century (the first of its kind in England) and contains a fascinating Tudor chapel with Renaissance glass, a Palladian staircase and a wealth of old panelling and fine furniture. The attractive grounds feature herbaceous borders and a wild garden, with lawns, lakes and woodland walks. Weddings & Functions: Stone Gallery licensed for Civil weddings. Receptions and private/corporate functions in Walled Garden or Brewhouse restaurant.

**Location:** MAP 3:E3, OS Ref. SU639 576. 4m N of Basingstoke between Bramley & Sherborne St John.

**Open:** House: 24 Mar–28 Oct: Sat & Sun, 11am–5pm: Mon–Wed, 1–5pm. Grounds/Shop/Restaurant: 3 Feb–18 Mar: Sat & Sun; 24 Mar–28 Oct: Sat–Wed; 2 Feb–30 Mar 2008: Sat & Sun, 11am–5pm. Shop & Restaurant: 1 Nov–22 Dec, Thur–Sun, 11am–3pm. Open Good Fri: 11am–5pm (including House). Special opening for groups, by appointment only, 26 Mar–24 Oct: Mon, Tue & Wed, 11am–1pm.

**\*Admission:** House & Grounds: Adult £8, Child £4, Family £20. Groups £6.50. Grounds only: Adult £5, Child £2.50. Free to NT Members. \*includes a voluntary donation but visitors can choose to pay the standard prices displayed at the property and on the website.

ℹ No photography in house. 🖼 🎫 🍴 ♿ 🎧 ℹ 🏢 🅿 🐾 ⬆ ♿

*© Dean and Chapter, Winchester Cathedral*

# WINCHESTER CATHEDRAL
## 1 THE CLOSE, WINCHESTER  SO23 9LS

www.winchester-cathedral.org.uk

**Tel:** 01962 857225  **Fax:** 01962 857201  **E-mail:** visits@winchester-cathedral.org.uk
**Owner:** The Dean and Chapter  **Contact:** Group Visits Co-ordinator

Explore more than 1000 years of England's past. Walk in the footsteps of kings, saints, pilgrims, writers and artists in Europe's longest medieval Cathedral. Learn why Jane Austen was buried in the nave. See the Winchester Bible, the finest of all the great 12th-century manuscripts, illuminated in gold and lapis lazuli, and tour the crypt to find Antony Gormley's sculpture 'Sound II'.

**Location:** MAP 3:D4, OS Ref. SU483 293. Winchester city centre.
**Open:** Daily 8.30am–6pm. (5.30pm Sun). Times may vary for services and special events.
**Admission:** Adult £5, Conc. £4. Student/Schools £3. Conc. for booked groups.

🔲 🔲 🔲 🔲 Licensed. 🔲 🔲 🔲 🔲 In grounds, on leads. 🔲 🔲 See website for details.

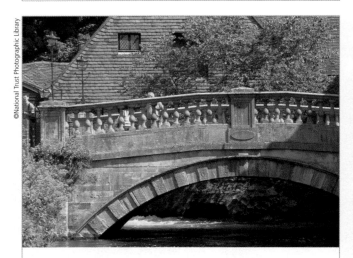

*©National Trust Photographic Library*

# WINCHESTER CITY MILL
## BRIDGE STREET, WINCHESTER

www.nationaltrust.org.uk/winchestercitymill

**Tel/Fax:** 01962 870057  **E-mail:** winchestercitymill@nationaltrust.org.uk
**Owner:** The National Trust  **Contact:** Anne Aldridge

Spanning the River Itchen and rebuilt in 1744 on an earlier medieval site, this corn mill has a chequered history. The machinery is completely restored making this building an unusual survivor of a working town mill. It has a delightful island garden and impressive mill races roaring through the building.

**Location:** MAP 3D:4, OS Ref. SU485 293. M3/J9 & 10. St Swithun's Bridge near King Alfred's statue. 15 min walk from station.
**Open:** 28 Feb–1 Apr, 16 Apr–27 May, 6 Jun–1 Jul, 12 Sept–21 Oct, 31 Oct–2 Dec, Wed–Sun; 17–25 Feb, 2–15 Apr, 28 May–3 Jun, 2 Jul–9 Sept, 22–28 Oct, 3–23 Dec, daily; 11am–5pm. Last entry 4.30pm. 1 Nov–23 Dec, 11am–4.30pm, last entry 4pm.
Admission: Adult £3.40, Child £1.70, Family £8.50. NT members Free.

🔲 🔲 Partial. 🔲 By arrangement. 🅿 Nearby public car park. 🔲 🔲

# WOLVESEY CASTLE ⌗
**College Street, Wolvesey, Winchester, Hampshire  SO23 8NB**
**Tel:** 02392 378291   www.english-heritage.org.uk/visits
**Owner:** English Heritage   **Contact:** Portchester Castle

The fortified palace of Wolvesey was the chief residence of the Bishops of Winchester and one of the greatest of all medieval buildings in England. Its extensive ruins still reflect the importance and immense wealth of the Bishops of Winchester, occupants of the richest seat in medieval England. Wolvesey Castle was frequently visited by medieval and Tudor monarchs and was the scene of the wedding feast of Philip of Spain and Mary Tudor in 1554.

**Location:** MAP 3:D4, OS Ref. SU484 291. ¾m SE of Winchester Cathedral, next to the Bishop's Palace; access from College Street.
**Open:** 6 Apr–30 Sept: daily, 10am–5pm. Guided tours: Aug, Suns, 2pm.
**Admission:** Free.

🔲 🔲 Grounds. 🔲 In grounds, on leads.

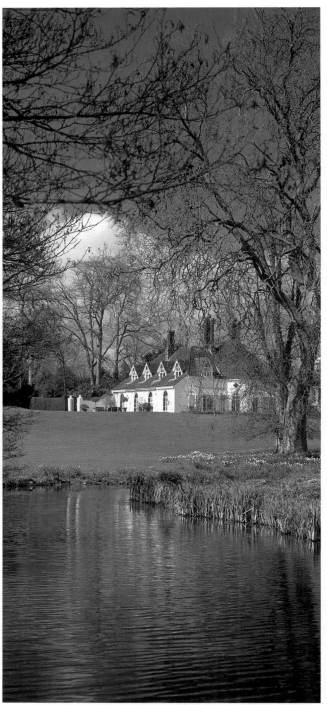

Houghton Lodge Gardens, Stockbridge

**visit hudsons guide online**

© Skyscan

Beaulieu, Brockenhurst

### Owner
Mr & Mrs D Kendrick

### Contact
Mrs M Kendrick
Boughton
Monchelsea Place
Boughton Monchelsea
Nr Maidstone
Kent ME17 4BU

**Tel:** 01622 743120
**E-mail:** mk@
boughtonplace.co.uk

### Location
**MAP 4:K3**
**OS Ref. TQ772 499**

On B2163, 5½ m from
M20/J8 or 4½ m from
Maidstone via A229.

### Opening Times
All year, except
24 Dec–4 Jan, by prior
arrangement only.

**House & Garden**
Not open to
individual visitors.

Group visits/ house tours:
(15–50),
Tues–Thur, 10am–4pm.

Private functions:
Mon–Fri, 9am–10pm.

Outdoor Event Site
365 days a year:
8am–11.30pm.

### Admission
**Gardens &**
**Guided House Tour**
Adult                    £5.50

**Venue Hire**
            Prices on application

**Day Delegate Rate**
                    From £40

### Special Events
**Open Air Theatre:**
**w/c July 9**
Taming of the Shrew

**w/c July 30** - production
to be confirmed.

Please telephone for
details.

# BOUGHTON MONCHELSEA PLACE
www.boughtonplace.co.uk

Boughton Monchelsea Place is a battlemented manor house dating from the 16th century, set in its own country estate just outside Maidstone, within easy reach of London and the channel ports. This Grade I listed building has always been privately owned and is still lived in as a family home.

From the lawns surrounding the property there are spectacular views over unspoilt Kent countryside, with the historic deer park in the foreground. A wicket gate leads from the grounds to the medieval church of St Peter, with its rose garden and ancient lych gate. At the rear of the house are to be found a pretty courtyard and walled gardens, while an extensive range of Tudor barns and outbuildings surround the old stableyard. Inside the house, rooms vary in character from Tudor through to Georgian Gothic; worthy of note are the fine Jacobean staircase and sundry examples of heraldic stained glass. Furnishings and paintings are mainly Victorian, with a few earlier pieces; the atmosphere is friendly and welcoming throughout.

The premises are licensed for Civil marriage and partnership ceremonies. In addition we welcome location work, group visits and all types of corporate, private and public functions, but please note times of availability. Use outside these hours is sometimes possible, subject to negotiation. All clients are guaranteed exclusive use of this prestigious venue.

### Conference/Function

| ROOM | SIZE | MAX CAPACITY |
|------|------|--------------|
| Entrance Hall | 25' x 19' | 50 Theatre |
| Dining Room | 31' x 19' | 50 Dining |
| Drawing Room | 28' x 19' | 40 Reception |
| Courtyard Room | 37' x 13' | 60 Theatre |

Film location.

By arrangement.

By arrangement.

By arrangement.

NTPL / Ian Shaw

# CHARTWELL 🌳

www.nationaltrust.org.uk/chartwell

The family home of Sir Winston Churchill from 1924 until the end of his life. He said of Chartwell, simply '*I love the place – a day away from Chartwell is a day wasted*'. With magnificent views over the Weald of Kent it is not difficult to see why.

The rooms are left as they were in Sir Winston & Lady Churchill's lifetime with daily papers, fresh flowers grown from the garden and his famous cigars. Photographs and books evoke his career, interests and happy family life. Museum and exhibition rooms contain displays, sound recordings and superb collections of memorabilia, including gifts, uniforms and family photographs, and give a unique insight into Sir Winston's political career and personal life.

The garden studio contains Sir Winston's easel and paintbox, as well as many of his paintings. Terraced and water gardens descend to the lake, the gardens also include a golden rose walk, planted by Sir Winston and Lady Churchill's children on the occasion of their golden wedding anniversary, and the Marlborough Pavilion decorated with frescoes depicting the battle of Blenheim. Visitors can see the garden walls that Churchill built with his own hands, as well as the pond stocked with the golden orfe he loved to feed.

The Mulberry Room at the restaurant can be booked for meetings, conferences, lunches and dinners. Please telephone for details.

NTPL / Andreas von Einsiedel

NTPL / Ian Shaw

ℹ️ Conference facilities.

🛍️

🍽️

♿ Partial. WC. Please telephone before visit.

🍴 Licensed.

🚶 By arrangement.

🅿️ In grounds, on leads.

🐕

## ◼ Owner
The National Trust

## ◼ Contact
The Property Manager
Chartwell
Westerham
Kent  TN16 1PS

**Tel:** 01732 866368
01732 868381
**Fax:** 01732 868193
**E-mail:** chartwell@
nationaltrust.org.uk

## ◼ Location
**MAP 19:F11**
**OS Ref. TQ455 515**

2m S of Westerham,
forking left off B2026.

**Bus:** 246 from Bromley
South, 401 from
Sevenoaks, Buses4U from
Oxted (All services
Suns & BHs only).
Please check times.

## ◼ Opening Times
17 March–1 July and
5 Sept–28 October
Wed–Sun & BHs

3 July–2 Sept
Tue–Sun & BHs
11am–5pm.

Last admission 4.15pm.

## ◼ *Admission
**House, Garden & Studio**
| | |
|---|---|
| Adult | £10.80 |
| Child | £5.40 |
| Family | £27.00 |

**Pre-booked groups**
(minimum 15)
| | |
|---|---|
| Adult | £9.00 |
| Child | £4.50 |

**Garden & Studio only**
| | |
|---|---|
| Adult | £5.40 |
| Child | £2.70 |
| Family | £13.50 |

*includes a voluntary
donation but visitors can
choose to pay the standard
prices displayed at the
property and on the website.

### Owner
The Denys Eyre Bower Bequest, Registered Charitable Trust

### Contact
Chiddingstone Castle
Edenbridge
Kent TN8 7AD

**Tel:** 01892 870347

**E-mail:**
info@chiddingstonecastle.org

### Location
**MAP 19:G12**
**OS Ref. TQ497 452**

10m from Tonbridge, Tunbridge Wells and Sevenoaks.
4m Edenbridge.
Accessible from A21 and M25/J5.

London 35m.

**Bus:** Enquiries: Tunbridge Wells TIC 01892 515675.

**Rail:** Tonbridge, Tunbridge Wells, Edenbridge then taxi. Penshurst then 2m walk.

**Air:** Gatwick 15m.

### Opening Times
Please refer to website.

### Admission
Please refer to website.

# CHIDDINGSTONE CASTLE

www.chiddingstonecastle.org

In 1803 Henry Streatfeild, Squire of Chiddingstone, intoxicated by the then current passion for medieval chivalry, embarked on the transformation of his ancient home into a fantasy castle. It would be the first major commission of young William Atkinson, which a contemporary guidebook predicted would be the '*fairest house*' in Kent. After five hectic years work ceased, leaving a random mix of old and new. The Establishment then was not impressed; today's visitors find the house enchanting.

In 1955 the now decrepit Castle was bought by the distinguished collector Denys Eyre Bower. He died in 1977, leaving his home and its rich collections to the Nation for the enjoyment of posterity. The place is now administered by a private Charitable Trust.

Chiddingstone Castle's fascinating array of Ancient Egyptian artefacts, Buddhist art, Japanese swords, armour and lacquer and a superb gathering of Royal Stuart portraits and mementoes celebrates twentieth-century collecting at its best.

The 35-acre landscaped park (a listed garden of Kent) is a haven for wildlife, providing idyllic walks.

Museum, weddings, business and private functions, scenic gardens and lake, picnics.

Available for special events. Wedding receptions.

Partial (grounds unsuitable). WC.

Ample for cars. Limited for coaches, please book.

We welcome visits from schools who wish to use the collections in connection with classroom work.

In grounds, on leads.

**visit hudsons guide online**

# CHIDDINGSTONE CASTLE ...

Samurai helmet and mask 18th Century -
part of the extensive collection of Japanese
arms and armour at Chiddingstone Castle.

### Owner
Cobham Hall School

### Contact
Mr N Powell
Bursar
Cobham Hall
Cobham
Kent  DA12 3BL

**Tel:** 01474 823371
**Fax:** 01474 825904
**E-mail:** windiates@
cobhamhall.com

### Location
**MAP 4:K2**
**OS Ref. TQ683 689**
Situated adjacent to the
A2/M2. ½m S of A2 4m
W of Strood. 8m E of
M25/J2 between
Gravesend & Rochester.

London 25m
Rochester 5m
Canterbury 30m

**Rail:** Meopham 3m
Gravesend 5m
Taxis at both stations.

**Air:** Gatwick 45 mins.
Heathrow 60 mins,
Stansted 50 mins.

### Opening Times
28 March.

1, 4, 6, 8/9, 11, 15, 18
April.

11, 15, 18, 22, 25, 29
July.

1, 5, 8, 12, 15, 19, 22,
26, 27, 29 August.

2 September.

**House & Shop**
2–5pm (5.30pm Shop).
Last tour at 4pm.

**Garden**
Closes at 6pm.

Dates could change,
please telephone to
confirm.

### Admission
| | |
|---|---|
| Adult | £4.50 |
| Child (4–14yrs.) | £3.50 |
| OAP | £3.50 |

**Gardens & Parkland**
Self-guided tour    £2.50

**Historical/Conservation
tour of Grounds**
(by arrangement)
Per person       £3.50

### Special Events
**April 1**
British Red Cross

**July 15**
Ellenor Foundation
Charity Walk

### Conference/Function
| ROOM | SIZE | MAX CAPACITY |
|---|---|---|
| Gilt Hall | 41' x 34' | 180 |
| Wyatt Dining Rm | 49' x 23' | 135 |
| Clifton Dining Rm | 24' x 23' | 75 |
| Activities Centre | 119' x 106' | 300 |

# COBHAM HALL
www.cobhamhall.com

Cobham Hall is now a leading Girls Boarding & Day School, and has been visited by several English monarchs from Elizabeth I to Edward VIII. Charles Dickens used regularly to walk through the grounds from his house in Higham to the Leather Bottle Public House in Cobham Village.

Cobham Hall is one of the largest, finest and most important houses in Kent, it is an outstanding beautiful red brick mansion in Elizabethan, Jacobean, Carolean and 18th century styles, it yields much interest to the students of art, architecture & history. The Elizabethan Wings were begun in 1584, whilst the central section, which contains the Gilt Hall, was wonderfully decorated by John Webb. Further rooms were decorated by James Wyatt in the 18th century.

In 1883 the Hon Ivo Bligh, later the 8th Earl of Darnley, led the victorious English cricket team against Australia bringing the Ashes home to Cobham.

### Gardens
The Park was landscaped for the 4th Earl by Humphry Repton, and is now gradually being restored. The Gothic Dairy, Aviary and the Pump House are all being restored. The gardens are beautiful at all times of the year but especially delightful in the spring when the spring flowers are out in full bloom.

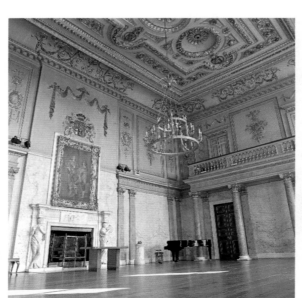

- Conferences, business or social functions, 150 acres of parkland for sports, corporate events, open air concerts, sports centre, indoor swimming pool, art studios, music wing, tennis courts, helicopter landing area. Filming and photography. No smoking.

- In-house catering team for private, corporate hospitality and wedding receptions. (cap. 100).

- House tour involves 2 staircases, ground floor access for w/chairs.

- Cream teas 2–5pm on open days. Other meals by arrangement.

- Obligatory guided tours; tour time 1½hrs. Garden tours arranged outside standard opening times.

- Ample. Pre-booked coach groups are welcome any time.

- Guide provided, Adult £4.50, Child / OAP £3.50.

- In grounds, on leads.

- 18 single and 18 double with bathroom. 22 single and 22 double without bathroom. Dormitory. Groups only.

# DANSON HOUSE
www.dansonhouse.com

Owner
Bexley Heritage Trust

Contact
Miss Sarah Fosker
Danson House
Danson Park
Bexleyheath
Kent  DA6 8HL

**Tel:** 020 8303 6699
**Fax:** 020 8304 6641
**E-mail:** sarah@
dansonhouse.com

Location
**MAP 19:G8**
**OS Ref. TQ475 768**

Signposted off the A2 and
A221 Danson Park, Bexley,
5 minutes London-bound
from M25 J/2.

**Rail:** Welling or
Bexleyheath (10 min walk).

**Bus:** B15 bus to Danson
Park.

Opening Times
21 March–4 November
Wed, Thur, Sun &
BH Mons, 11am–5pm.
Last entry 4.15pm.

Pre-booked group guided
tours year-round by
arrangement. Please
telephone 020 8298
6951.

Admission
Adult                        £5.00
Child (with Adult)      Free
OAP                        £4.50

The most significant building at risk in London in 1995, Robert Taylor's villa has undergone extensive restoration by English Heritage over a period of ten years. Restored to its former Georgian glory and open to the public for the first time in 35 years by Bexley Heritage Trust.

The house was built by wealthy merchant Sir John Boyd, for his young bride Catherine Chapone. The design and layout of the house reflect its original purpose, to be a country house dedicated to the entertainment and enjoyment of its inhabitants. The sumptuous interior decoration including the paintings and fireplaces tell stories that reveal the passion of Sir John for his wife and the love that they shared.

The route around the principal floor takes in the austere entrance hall that would have held Boyd's collection of sculpture – trophies from the Grand Tour – followed by the Dining Room that houses a complete cycle of wall paintings by Charles Pavillon. The Salon (pictured below) houses an original painting from the house, showing it with the wings that were demolished in 1805, that has been reframed to the original designs of Sir William Chambers, who made considerable changes to the house shortly after it was completed. The impressive Library is home to a George England organ built for the house in 1766, and still in working order.

The bedroom floor presents further period room displays and exhibitions relating to the history of the house and its inhabitants.

The principal floor is licensed for Civil wedding ceremonies and can accommodate up to 65 guests.

There is a programme of events and concerts throughout the year. Please telephone for details. Round off your visit with light lunches and home-made cakes in the newly-opened Breakfast Room.

© Bexley Heritage Trust/Jarrold Publishing

Two.

WCs.

Licenced.

By prior arrangement. Please telephone 020 8298 6951.

Limited for coaches.

## Owner
English Heritage

## Contact
Visitor Operations Team
Down House
Luxted Road
Downe
Kent  BR6 7JT

**Tel:** 01689 859119
**Fax:** 01689 862755

## Location
**MAP 19:F9**
**OS Ref. TQ431 611**

In Luxted Road, Downe,
off A21 near Biggin Hill.

**Rail:** From London
Victoria or Charing Cross.

**Bus:** Orpington
(& Bus R8) or Bromley
South (& Bus 146).
Buses R8 & 146
do not run on
Sundays or BHs.

## Opening Times
1 April–30 June &
1 September–31 October:
Wed–Sun & BHs,
11am–5pm.

1 July–31 August: daily
11am–5pm.

1 November–20 March
2008: Wed–Sun,
11am–5pm.

Closed:
17 December 2007–
29 February 2008

## Admission
| | |
|---|---|
| Adult | £7.20 |
| Child | £3.60 |
| Conc. | £5.40 |
| Family (2+3) | £18.00 |

EH Members Free.

Groups (11+)
15% discount

Tour leader and coach
driver have free entry.
1 extra place for every
20 additional people.

# THE HOME OF CHARLES DARWIN

www.english-heritage.org.uk/visits

A visit to Down House is a fascinating journey of discovery for all the family. This was the family home of Charles Darwin for over 40 years and now you can explore it to the full.

See the actual armchair in which Darwin wrote 'On the Origin of Species', which shocked and then revolutionised the way we think about the origins of mankind. His study is much the same as it was in his lifetime and is filled with belongings that give you an intimate glimpse into both his studies and everyday life.

At Down House you will discover both sides of Darwin – the great thinker and the family man. Explore the family rooms where the furnishings have been painstakingly restored. An audio tour narrated by Sir David Attenborough will bring the house to life and increase your understanding of Darwin's revolutionary theory. Upstairs you will find state-of-the-art interpretation of the scientific significance of the house – especially designed to inspire a younger audience.

Outside, take the Sandwalk which he paced daily in search of inspiration, then stroll in lovely gardens. Complete your day by sampling the delicious selection of home-made cakes in the tea room.

WCs.

Free.

Limited for coaches.

Guide dogs only.

English Heritage Photo Library

# DOVER CASTLE
## AND THE SECRET WARTIME TUNNELS
www.english-heritage.org.uk/visits

Journey deep into the White Cliffs of Dover and discover the top secret World War II tunnels. Through sight, sound and smells, relive the wartime drama of the underground hospital as a wounded Battle of Britain pilot is taken to the operating theatre in a bid to save his life. Discover how life would have been during the planning days of the Dunkirk evacuation and Operation Dynamo as you are led around the network of tunnels and casements housing the communications centre.

Above ground you can explore the magnificent medieval keep and inner bailey of King Henry II. Experience the exciting '1216 Siege' exhibition, and discover, through a dramatic light and sound presentation, how it must have felt to be a garrison soldier defending Dover Castle against the French King in 1216. See a reconstruction of the castle in preparation for a visit from Henry VIII and visit the hands-on exhibition explaining the travelling Tudor court.

Visit the evocative Princess of Wales' Royal Regiment Museum. There is also the Roman Lighthouse and Anglo-Saxon church to see as well as the intriguing 13th-century underground fortifications and medieval battlements. Enjoy magnificent views of the White Cliffs from Admiralty Lookout. The land train will help you around this huge site.

Throughout the summer there are many fun events taking place, bringing the castle alive through colourful enactments and living history.

English Heritage Photo Library

| | |
|---|---|
| **i** | WCs. |
| | Two. |
| **Y** | Exclusive private and corporate hire. Tel: 01034 209889. |
| | Lift for access to tunnels. Courtyard and grounds, some very steep slopes. |
| | 3 restaurants, hot and cold food and drinks. |
| | Tour of tunnels approx. every 20 mins, more at peak times when waits can occur. |
| **P** | Ample. |
| | Free visits available for schools. Education centre. Pre-booking essential. |

### Owner
English Heritage

### Contact
Visitor Operations Team
Dover Castle
Dover
Kent  CT16 1HU

**Tel:** 01304 211067
**Fax:** 01304 214739

**Venue Hire and Hospitality:**
Hospitality Manager
**Tel:** 01304 209889

### Location
**MAP 4:O4**
**OS Ref. TR326 416**

Easy access from A2 and M20. Well signed from Dover centre and east side of Dover.
2 hrs from central London.

**Rail:** London Charing Cross or Victoria 1½hrs.

**Bus:** 0870 6082608.

### Opening Times
**Summer**
1 April–30 September:
Daily, 10am–6pm
(August opens 9.30am).

October:
Daily, 10am–5pm.

**Winter**
1 November–31 January:
Thur–Mon, 1 February–20 March: daily, 10am–4pm.
(Closed 24–26 Dec & 1 Jan.)

NB. Keep closes at 5pm on days when events are booked.

### Admission
| | |
|---|---|
| Adult | £9.80 |
| Child | £4.90 |
| Conc. | £7.40 |
| Family (2+3) | £24.50 |

EH Members Free.

Groups: 15% discount for groups (11+). Free entry for tour leader and coach driver. One free place for every additional 20 paying.

### Venue Hire and Hospitality
English Heritage offers exclusive use of the Castle Keep or Tunnels in the evenings for receptions, dinners, product launches and themed banquets.

### Conference/Function
| ROOM | MAX CAPACITY |
|---|---|
| The Castle Keep | standing 120 dining 90 |
| Keep Yard Café | theatre-style 150 |
| Secret Wartime Tunnels | standing 120 dining 80 theatre-style 80 |
| Marquee on Palace Green | standing 400 dining 265 |

### ■ Owner
Groombridge Asset
Management

### ■ Contact
The Estate Office
Groombridge Place
Groombridge
Tunbridge Wells
Kent TN3 9QG

**Tel:** 01892 861444
**Fax:** 01892 863996
**E-mail:** office@
groombridge.co.uk

### ■ Location
**MAP 4:J4**
**OS Ref. TQ534 375**

Groombridge Place
Gardens are located on
the B2110 just off the
A264. 4m SW of
Tunbridge Wells and 9m E
of East Grinstead.

**Rail:** London Charing
Cross to Tunbridge Wells
55mins. (Taxis).

**Air:** Gatwick.

### ■ Opening Times
**Summer**
Gardens
31 March–3 November
Daily, 10am–5.30pm (or
dusk if earlier).

The house is not open
to visitors.

### ■ Admission
| | |
|---|---|
| Adult | £8.95 |
| Child* (3–12yrs) | £7.45 |
| Senior | £7.45 |
| Family (2+2) | £29.95 |
| Groups (12+) | |
| Adult | £7.25 |
| Child/School (3–12yrs) | |
| | £5.50 |
| Senior | £5.50/£6.25 |
| Student | £6.25 |
| Youth | £5.50 |

*Child under 3yrs Free.

### ■ Special Events
**April 6–9**
Easter Eggstravaganza.

**July 22**
Wings, Wheels and
Steam.

**August 5**
Hot Air Balloons and
Ferraris.

**October 26/27**
Halloween in the Spooky
Forest.

**November 3**
Spectacular Fireworks.

# GROOMBRIDGE PLACE GARDENS

www.groombridge.co.uk

There's magic and mystery, history and intrigue, romance and peace at this beautiful venue – which provides such an unusual combination of a traditional heritage garden with the excitement, challenge and contemporary landscaping of the ancient woodland – appealing to young and old alike.

First laid out in 1674 on a gentle, south-facing slope, the formal walled gardens are set against the romantic backdrop of a medieval moat, surrounding a classical Restoration manor house (not open to the public) and were designed as outside rooms. These award-winning gardens include magnificent herbaceous borders, the enchanting White Rose Garden with over 20 varieties of white roses, a Secret Garden with deep shade and cooling waters in a tiny hidden corner, Paradise Walk and Oriental Garden,

the Knot Garden and Nut Walk and the Drunken Garden with its crazy topiary. The gardens feature wonderful seasonal colour throughout spring, summer and autumn.

In complete contrast on a high hillside above the walled gardens and estate vineyard is the Enchanted Forest, where quirky and mysterious gardens have been developed in the ancient woodland by innovative designer, Ivan Hicks, to challenge the imagination. Children love the Dark Walk, Tree Fern Valley, Village of the Groms, the Serpent's Lair and the Mystic Pool, the Romany Camp, Double Spiral and the Giant Swings Walk. There are also Birds of Prey flying displays three times a day, a canal boat cruise to and from the Forest – plus a full programme of special events.

 Film location.

 Partial. WCs.

 Licensed.

 By arrangement.

 Limited for coaches.

 Guide dogs only.

■ **Owner**
Bexley Heritage Trust

■ **Contact**
Mrs Janet Hearn-Gillham
Hall Place & Gardens
Bourne Road
Bexley
Kent  DA5 1PQ

**Tel:** 01322 526574
**Fax:** 01322 522921
**E-mail:** jhearn-gillham
@btconnect.com

■ **Location**
**MAP 19:G8**
**OS Ref. TQ502 743**

On the A2 less than
5m from the M25/J2
(London bound).

■ **Opening Times**
1 April–31 October:
Mon–Sat, 10am–5pm;
Sun & BHs, 11am–5pm.
1 Nov–31 Mar: Tue–Sat,
10am–4.15pm.

■ **Admission**
Free. Charge made for
some Special Events.
Prearranged guided tours
(10+) £4.

# HALL PLACE & GARDENS

www.hallplaceandgardens.com

A fine Grade I listed country house built c1537 for Sir John Champneys, a wealthy merchant and former Lord Mayor of London, with a 17-century extension added by Sir Robert Austen.

Managed by Bexley Heritage Trust since 2000, this beautiful estate of 65 hectares stands on the banks of the River Cray at Bexley. Surrounding the house are award winning gardens with magnificent topiary, a herb garden, a secret garden, an Italianate garden, a grass maze and inspirational herbaceous borders. In the former walled gardens are a plant nursery, with plant sales, a sub-tropical plant house where you can see ripening bananas in mid-winter, and model display gardens. A recent addition is the Educational Enviromental Garden (wheelchair access), divided into Tudor Garden (looking at plants used for dyeing, medicine, beauty and cooking), meadow land, bug hunt ground and dipping pond. Beyond are recreational sports grounds and park land.

The house boasts a panelled Tudor Great Hall overlooked by a minstrel's gallery and various period rooms including a vaulted Long Gallery and splendid Drawing Room with a fine 17th-century plaster ceiling. There is a shop and numerous exhibitions, including an opportunity to purchase artists' work throughout the year. There is also an extensive programme of events, concerts and open-air theatre, both in the house and outside, including a special Christmas programme. Several rooms are available to hire for meetings and other events, including the Great Hall and Drawing Room, which are also licensed for Civil wedding ceremonies. Its close proximity to London makes Hall Place and Gardens an ideal location for photographic, film and television use.

The Education Team offer an extensive Education and Outreach Service for schools and adult groups and organised activities for the holidays.

 House, lift & WC.
 Licensed.
By arrangement (10+).
 Guide dogs only.

### ■ Owner
Hever Castle Ltd

### ■ Contact
Ann Watt
Hever Castle
Hever
Edenbridge
Kent  TN8 7NG

**Infoline:** 01732 865224
**Fax:** 01732 866796
**E-mail:**
mail@HeverCastle.co.uk

### ■ Location
**MAP 19:G12**
**OS Ref. TQ476 450**

Exit M25/J5 & J6
M23/J10, 1½m S of
B2027 at Bough Beech,
3m SE of Edenbridge.

**Rail:** Hever Station 1m
(no taxis), Edenbridge
Town 3m (taxis).

### ■ Opening Times
**Summer**
1 April–31 October
Daily
Grounds: 11am–6pm.
Castle: 12 noon–6pm.
Last admission 5pm.

**Winter**
Castle & Grounds:
March, Wed–Sun,
November, Thurs–Sun,
11am–3pm.
Castle only:
1–23 December,
Thurs–Sun,
12 noon–3pm.

### ■ Admission
**Castle & Gardens**
| | |
|---|---|
| Adult | £10.50 |
| Child (5–14 yrs) | £5.70 |
| OAP | £8.80 |
| Family (2+2) | £26.70 |

**Castle in December**
| | |
|---|---|
| Adult | £5.00 |
| Child (5–14 yrs) | £2.00 |

Groups (15+)
Available on request.

**Gardens only**
| | |
|---|---|
| Adult | £8.40 |
| Child (5–14yrs) | £5.40 |
| OAP | £7.20 |
| Family (2+2) | £22.20 |

**Christmas Shop
& Restaurant**
Free entry December

Groups (15+)
Available on request.

Pre-booked private guided
tours are available before
opening, during season.

### Conference/Function

| ROOM | SIZE | MAX CAPACITY |
|---|---|---|
| Dining Hall | 35' x 20' | 70 |
| Breakfast Rm | 22' x 15' | 12 |
| Sitting Rm | 24' x 20' | 20 |
| Pavilion | 96' x 40' | 250 |
| Moat Restaurant | 25' x 60' | 75 |

# HEVER CASTLE & GARDENS 🏛

www.hevercastle.co.uk

Hever Castle dates back to 1270, when the  gatehouse, outer walls and the inner moat were first built. 200 years later the Bullen (or Boleyn) family added the comfortable Tudor manor house constructed within the walls. This was the childhood home of Anne Boleyn, Henry VIII's second wife and mother of Elizabeth I. There are many items relating to the Tudors, including two books of hours (prayer books) signed and inscribed by Anne Boleyn. The Castle was later given to Henry VIII's fourth wife, Anne of Cleves.

In 1903, the estate was bought by the American millionaire William Waldorf Astor, who became a British subject and the first Lord Astor of Hever. He invested an immense amount of time, money and imagination in restoring the castle and grounds. Master craftsmen were employed and the castle was filled with a magnificent collection of furniture, tapestries and other works of art. 'From Castles to Country Houses' the Miniature Model Houses exhibition, a collection of 1/12 scale model houses, room views and gardens, depicts life in English Country Houses.

### Gardens
Between 1904–8 over 30 acres of formal gardens were laid out and planted, these have now matured into one of the most beautiful gardens in England. The unique Italian garden is a four acre walled garden containing a superb collection of statuary and sculpture. The award- winning gardens include the Rose garden and Tudor garden, a traditional yew maze and a 110 metre herbaceous border. A water maze has been added to the other water features in the gardens. The Sunday Walk Garden has a stream meandering through a mature woodland with borders filled with specimen plants.

ℹ Suitable for filming, conferences, corporate hospitality, weddings, product launches. Outdoor heated pool, tennis court  and billiard room. No photography in house.

🛍 Gift, garden & book.

🍽 250 seat restaurant available for functions wedding receptions, etc.

♿ Access to gardens, ground floor only (no ramps into castle), restaurants, gift shop, book shop and water maze. Wheelchairs available. WC.

🍴 Two licensed restaurants. Supper provided during open air theatre season. Pre-booked lunches and teas for groups.

🚶 Pre-booked tours in mornings. 1 Mar–23 Dec. Tour time 1 hr. Tours in French, German, Dutch, Italian and Spanish (min 20). Garden tours in English only (min 15).

🅿 Free admission and refreshment voucher for driver and courier. Please book, group rates for 15+.

👥 Welcome (min 15). Private guided tours available (min 20). 1:6 ratio (up to 8 year olds): 1:10 9yrs+. Free preparatory visits for teachers during opening hours. Please book.

🐕 In grounds, on leads.

✳ Tudor Village.

❄ Call infoline: 01732 865224.

### ■ Owner
The National Trust

### ■ Contact
The Property Manager
Ightham Mote
Mote Road
Ivy Hatch
Sevenoaks
Kent TN15 0NT

**Tel:** 01732 810378
**Info:** 01732 811145
**Fax:** 01732 811029
**E-mail:** ighthammote@
nationaltrust.org.uk

### ■ Location
**MAP 19:H11**
**OS Ref. TQ584 535**

6m E of Sevenoaks off
A25. 2½m S of Ightham
off A227.

### ■ Opening Times
4 March–28 October:
Daily except Tues & Sats.

**Gardens, Shop &
Restaurant**
10am–5.30pm
(last admission 5pm).

**House**
10.30am–5.30pm
(last admission 5pm).

**Restaurant & Shop**
winter opening times:
please call property.

### ■ *Admission
| | |
|---|---|
| Adult | £9.50 |
| Child | £4.75 |
| Family | £23.75 |
| Groups (booked) | |
| Adult | £7.50 |
| Child | £3.75 |

*includes a voluntary
donation but visitors can
choose to pay the standard
prices displayed at the
property and on the website.

# IGHTHAM MOTE

## www.nationaltrust.org.uk/ighthammote

Beautiful moated manor house covering nearly 700 years of history from medieval times to the 1960s. Discover the stories and characters associated with the house from the first owners in 1320 to Charles Henry Robinson, the American businessman who bequeathed Ightham Mote to the National Trust in 1985.

Following the completion of the largest conservation project ever undertaken by the National Trust on a house of this age and fragility, it is now possible to enjoy the most extensive visitor route open since Ightham Mote's acquisition by the Trust. This includes the refurbished Great Hall and Jacobean staircase, along with the Old Chapel, Crypt, Tudor Chapel with painted ceiling, Drawing Room with Jacobean

fireplace, frieze and 18th century hand-painted Chinese wallpaper, Victorian Billiards Room and the apartments of Mr Robinson. A special exhibition 'Conservation in Action' explains the project and gives insights into the techniques and skills used.

Extensive gardens with lakes and woodland walk. Surrounding 550 acre estate also provides many country walks including way-marked routes.

Free introductory talks, garden and tower tours. Varied events programme including children's events and lecture lunches through the season. Group and Educational Tours available, plus educational facility. For details please telephone: 01732 810378.

 Ground floor. WC.

 On leads, Estate only.

### ■ Owner
The National Trust

### ■ Contact
Property Manager
Knole
Sevenoaks
Kent  TN15 0RP

**Tel:** 01732 462100
**Info:** 01732 450608
**Fax:** 01732 465528
**E-mail:** knole@
nationaltrust.org.uk

### ■ Location
**MAP 19:H10**
**OS Ref. TQ532 543**

M25/J5. 25m SE of
London. Just off A225 at
S end of High Street,
Sevenoaks.

**Rail:** ½hr from London
Charing Cross to
Sevenoaks.

**Bus:** Arriva 402 Tunbridge
Wells–Bromley North.

### ■ Opening Times
**Great Hall, Shop &
Tearoom**
3/4 & 10/11 March,
11am–4pm.

**House**
17 March–28 October:
Wed–Sun & BH Mons,
12 noon–4pm.
Last admission 3.30pm.

Premium guided tours for
pre-booked groups while
house is closed to public,
Wed, Fri & Sat, plus Thurs
in Aug, 11am. Please
telephone for further
information.

**Garden**
Weds throughout the
season, 11am–4pm
(last admn. 3.30pm).

**Shop & Tearoom**
As House: 10.30am–5pm.

**Christmas Shop**
November–December:
Wed–Sun, 11am–4pm.

### ■ Admission
**House**
| | |
|---|---|
| Adult | £8.50 |
| Child | £4.25 |
| Family | £21.30 |

Groups (booked 15+)
| | |
|---|---|
| Adult | £6.60 |
| Child | £3.30 |
| Parking | £2.50 |

**Garden**
| | |
|---|---|
| Adult | £2.00 |
| Child | £1.00 |

NT members Free.

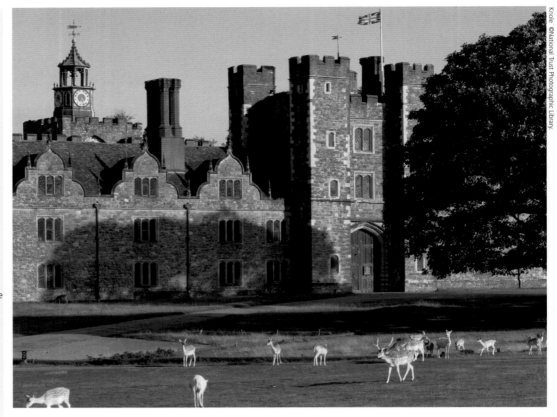

# KNOLE 🌳

www.nationaltrust.org.uk/knole

Knole's fascinating historic links with Kings, Queens and the nobility, as well as its literary links with Vita Sackville-West and her friend Virginia Woolfe, make this one of the most intriguing houses in England. Thirteen superb state-rooms are laid out much as they were in the 18th century to impress visitors by the wealth and status of the Sackville family, who continue to live at Knole. The house includes Royal Stuart furniture, paintings by Gainsborough, Van Dyck and Reynolds as well as many 17th century tapestries.

The house inspired Vita Sackville-West, who was born at Knole, to write her best-selling novel "*The Edwardians*" and was also the setting for Virginia Woolf's famous novel "*Orlando*"

Knole is set at the heart of the only remaining medieval deer park in Kent, where Sika and Fallow deer still roam freely amongst ancient oak, beech and chestnut trees, as they have since the days of Henry VIII.

Relax in the original "Brew House" with a cup of tea or enjoy a delicious lunch before browsing through the well-stocked shop full of local produce, exquisite gifts and its large collection of books, including those by Vita Sackville-West, her son Nigel Nicolson, and Virginia Woolf.

Visit on a Wednesday and enjoy a leisurely stroll through Lord Sackville's private garden. The garden provides the most beautiful view of the house and allows visitors to observe the outside of the Orangery and the Chapel. Witness the changing seasons in the garden from early spring through to the late autumn.

- 🏬 Full range of NT goods and souvenirs of Knole.
- ✻
- ♿ Wheelchair access to Green Court, Stone Court and Great Hall. WC. Virtual reality tour of upstairs showrooms.
- ☕ Serving morning coffee, lunch and teas. Also ice-creams and snacks in courtyard.
- 🚶 Guided tours for pre-booked groups, by arrangement. Short guides to the house available in French, Dutch & German.
- 🅿 Ample.
- 🏫 Welcome. Contact Education Officer.
- 🐕 Guide dogs only.
- ✳ Park open all year to pedestrians.
- 📺 Telephone for details.

**visit hudsons guide online**

# LEEDS CASTLE

www.leeds-castle.com

This "loveliest castle in the world", surrounded by 500 acres of magnificent parkland and gardens and set in the middle of a natural lake, is one of the country's finest historic properties. Leeds is also proud to be one of the Treasure Houses of England.

A Norman fortress and a royal palace to the mediaeval and Tudor Kings and Queens of England, the development of Leeds Castle continued well into the 20th century. The last private owner, the Hon Olive, Lady Baillie, bought the castle in 1926, restored the castle and furnished its beautiful interiors.

The castle has a fine collection of paintings, tapestries and antiques and is also home to an unusual dog collar museum. The park and grounds include the colourful and quintessentially English Culpeper Garden, the delightful Wood Garden, and the terraced Lady Baillie Garden with its views over the tranquil Great Water. The Aviary houses over 100 rare and endangered species from around the world and next to the Vineyard can be discovered the Maze with its secret underground grotto. Playgrounds delight younger visitors and falconry shows add more interest.

A highly popular and successful programme of special events is arranged throughout the year, details of which can be found on the website.

 **Owner**
Leeds Castle Foundation

**Contact**
Leeds Castle
Maidstone
Kent  ME17 1PL

**Tel:** 01622 765400
**Fax:** 01622 735616

**Location**
**MAP 4:L3**
**OS Ref. TQ835 533**

From London to A20/M20/J8, 40m, 1 hr. 7m E of Maidstone, ¼m S of A20.

**Rail:** Combined ticket with South Eastern Trains available, (train and admission). London–Bearsted.

**Coach:** Nat Express coach and admission from Victoria.

**Opening Times**
**Summer**
1 April–30 September Daily, 10am–5pm (last adm).

**Winter**
1 October–31 March Daily, 10am–3pm (last adm).

**Castle & Grounds**
Closed 3 November & 25 December. Please check before visiting for special closures.

Special private tours for pre-booked groups by appointment.

**Admission**
**Castle, Park & Gardens**
Individuals (valid 1 year)
Adult                £14.00
Child (4–15yrs)      £8.50
OAP/Student          £11.00

Group 15+
Adult                £10.50
Child (4–15yrs)      £7.00
OAP/Student          £10.00

Visitor with disabilities
(1 carer Free)       £11.00

Group 15+
Visitors with disabilities
(1 carer Free)       £10.00

A guidebook is published in English, French, Dutch, Spanish, Italian, Russian and Japanese.

 Residential conferences, exhibitions, sporting days, clay shooting off site, laser shooting, falconry, field archery, golf, croquet and heli-pad. Talks can be arranged for horticultural, viticultural, historical and cultural groups.

Corporate hospitality, large scale marquee events, wedding receptions, buffets and dinners.

Land train for elderly/disabled, wheelchairs, wheelchair lift, special rates. WC.

Restaurant, group lunch menus. Refreshment kiosks.

 Guides in rooms. French, Spanish, Dutch, German and Russian speaking guides.

For hire in English, French, Spanish, German and Japanese.

**P** Free parking.

Workshops, outside normal opening hours, private tours. Teacher's resource pack and worksheets.

€

**Conference/Function**

| ROOM | SIZE | MAX CAPACITY |
|------|------|--------------|
| Fairfax Hall | 19.8 x 6.7m | 200 |
| Gate Tower | 9.8 x 5.2m | 70 |
| Culpeper | 6.3 x 5.3m | 40 |
| Terrace | 8.9 x 15.4m | 100 |
| Castle Boardroom | 9.7 x 4.8m | 24 |
| Castle Dining Rm | 13.1 x 6.6m | 60 |

## Owner
Viscount De L'Isle

## Contact
Ian Scott
Penshurst Place
Penshurst
Nr Tonbridge
Kent TN11 8DG

**Tel:** 01892 870307
**Fax:** 01892 870866
**E-mail:** enquiries
@penshurstplace.com

## Location
**MAP 19:H12**
**OS Ref. TQ527 438**

From London M25/J5
then A21 to
Hildenborough, B2027
via Leigh; from Tunbridge
Wells A26, B2176.

Visitors entrance at SE
end of village,
S of the church.

**Bus:** Maidstone & District
231, 232, 233 from
Tunbridge Wells.

**Rail:** Charing Cross/
Waterloo–Hildenborough,
Tonbridge or Tunbridge
Wells; then bus or taxi.

## Opening Times
3–23 March:
Sats & Suns only.
24 March–28 October
Daily.

**House**
Daily, 12 noon–4pm.

**Grounds**
Daily, 10.30am–6pm.

**Shop**
Open all year.

**Winter**
Open to Groups by
appointment only
(see Guided Tours).

## Admission
**House & Gardens**
| | |
|---|---|
| Adult | £7.50 |
| Child* | £5.00 |
| Conc. | £7.00 |
| Family (2+2) | £21.00 |

**Groups (20+)**
| | |
|---|---|
| Adult | £7.00 |

**Garden only**
| | |
|---|---|
| Adult | £6.00 |
| Child* | £4.50 |
| Conc. | £5.50 |
| Family (2+2) | £18.00 |

**Garden Season Ticket**
| | |
|---|---|
| | £35.00 |

**House Tours**
(pre-booked)
| | |
|---|---|
| Adult | £7.50 |
| Child | £4.50 |

**Garden Tours**
(pre-booked)
| | |
|---|---|
| Adult | £8.50 |
| Child | £5.00 |

**House & Garden** £11.00

*Aged 5–16yrs;
under 5s Free.

## Conference/Function

| ROOM | SIZE | MAX CAPACITY |
|---|---|---|
| Sunderland Room | 45' x 18' | 100 |
| Barons' Hall | 64' x 39' | 250 |
| Buttery | 20' x 23' | 50 |

©David Sellman/Penshurst Place

# PENSHURST PLACE & GARDENS
www.penshurstplace.com

Penshurst Place is one of England's greatest family-owned stately homes with a history going back six and a half centuries.

In some ways time has stood still at Penshurst; the great House is still very much a medieval building with improvements and additions made over the centuries but without any substantial rebuilding. Its highlight is undoubtedly the medieval Barons' Hall, built in 1341, with its impressive 60ft-high chestnut-beamed roof.

A marvellous mix of paintings, tapestries and furniture from the 15th, 16th and 17th centuries can be seen throughout the House, including the helm carried in the state funeral procession to St Paul's Cathedral for the Elizabethan courtier and poet, Sir Philip Sidney, in 1587. This is now the family crest.

### Gardens
The Gardens, first laid out in the 14th century, have been developed over successive years by the Sidney family who first came to Penshurst in 1552. A twenty-year restoration and re-planting programme undertaken by the 1st Viscount De L'Isle has ensured that they retain their historic splendour. He is commemorated with a new Arboretum, planted in 1991. The gardens are divided by a mile of yew hedges into "rooms", each planted to give a succession of colour as the seasons change. There is also a Venture Playground, Woodland Trail, Toy Museum and a Gift Shop.

A variety of events in the park and grounds take place throughout the season.

**i** Adventure playground & parkland & riverside walks. Product launches, garden parties, photography, filming, fashion shows, receptions, archery, clay pigeon shooting, falconry, parkland for hire. Conference facilities. No photography in house.

Private banqueting, wedding receptions.

Limited. Virtual tour of first floor of house, garden leaflet guide. Disabled and elderly may alight at entrance. WC.

Licensed tearoom (waitress service can be booked by groups of 20+).

Mornings only by arrangement, lunch/dinner can be arranged. Out of season tours by appointment. Guided tours of the gardens and house.

**P** Ample. Double decker buses to park from village.

All year by appointment, discount rates, education room and packs.

Guide dogs only

# SQUERRYES COURT 🏛

www.squerryes.co.uk

Squerryes Court is a beautiful 17th century manor house which has been the Warde family home since 1731. It is surrounded by 10 acres of attractive and historic gardens which include a lake, restored parterres and an 18th century dovecote. Squerryes is 22 miles from London and easily accessible from the M25. There are lovely views and peaceful surroundings. Visitors from far and wide come to enjoy the atmosphere of a house which is still lived in as a family home.

There is a fine collection of Old Master paintings from the Italian, 17th century Dutch and 18th century English schools, furniture, porcelain and tapestries all acquired or commissioned by the family in the 18th century. General Wolfe of Quebec was a friend of the family and there are items connected with him in the Wolfe Room.

## Gardens

These were laid out in the formal style but were re-landscaped in the mid 18th century. Some of the original features in the 1719 Badeslade print survive. The family have restored the formal garden using this print as a guide. The garden is lovely all year round with bulbs, wild flowers and woodland walks, azaleas, summer flowering herbaceous borders and roses.

**ℹ** Suitable for conferences, product launches, filming, photography, outside events, garden parties. No photography in house. Picnics permitted in grounds.

Small.

**Y** Wedding receptions (marquee).

**♿** Limited access in house and garden. WCs.

**☕** Lunches and light refreshments on open days. Licenced.

**🚶** For pre-booked groups (max 55), small additional charge. Tour time 1 hr. Wine tasting groups by arrangement 45 mins–1 hr. Additional charge.

**P** Limited for coaches.

**🐕** On leads, in grounds.

## Owner
John St A Warde Esq

## Contact
Mrs P A White
Administrator
Squerryes Court
Westerham
Kent  TN16 1SJ

**Tel:** 01959 562345
**Fax:** 01959 565949
**E-mail:** enquiries
@squerryes.co.uk

## Location
**MAP 19:F11**
**OS Ref. TQ440 535**

10 min from M25/J5 or 6 off A25, ½m W from centre of Westerham

London 1–1½ hrs.

**Rail:** Oxted Station 4m. Sevenoaks 6m.

**Air:** Gatwick, 30 mins.

## Opening Times
**Summer**
1 April–30 September
Wed, Thu, Sun &
BH Mons. 1–5pm.
Last admission 4.30pm.

**Grounds**
11.30am–5pm

NB. Pre-booked groups welcome any day except Saturday.

**Winter**
October–31 March
Closed.

## Admission
**House & Garden**
| | |
|---|---|
| Adult | £6.50 |
| Child (under 16yrs) | £3.50 |
| Senior | £6.00 |
| Family (2+2) | £13.50 |

**Groups (20+)**
| | |
|---|---|
| Adult | £5.50 |
| Child (under 16yrs) | £3.50 |

**Wine Tasting**
| | |
|---|---|
| Adult | £7.50 |

**Garden only**
| | |
|---|---|
| Adult | £4.00 |
| Child (under 16yrs) | £2.00 |
| Senior | £3.50 |
| Family (2+2) | £8.00 |

**Groups (20+, booked)**
| | |
|---|---|
| Adult | £4.00 |
| Child (under 16yrs) | £2.00 |

## Conference/Function

| ROOM | SIZE | MAX CAPACITY |
|---|---|---|
| Hall | 32' x 32' | 60 |
| Old Library | 20' x 25' 6" | 40 |

## ■ Owner
Turkey Mill
Investments Ltd

## ■ Contact
Turkey Mill Events Ltd
The Events Office
Turkey Court
Turkey Mill
Ashford Road
Maidstone
Kent  ME14 5PP

**Tel:** 01622 765511
**Fax:** 01622 765522
**E-mail:** events@
turkeymill.co.uk

## ■ Location
**MAP 4:L3**
**OS Ref. TQ773 555**

Turkey Mill is located
1½m from M20/J7
(follow the signs).

The entrance is off
the A20 ½m east of
Maidstone Town Centre.

## ■ Admission
Available for privately
booked functions only.

The Orangery and
Grounds are available all
year round for private and
corporate events.

# TURKEY MILL
www.turkeymill.co.uk

Turkey Mill has a long and distinguished history. Originally a fulling mill, it was converted to papermaking at the end of the 17th century. Under the ownership of James Whatman, father and son, it became world famous. James Whatman pioneered the development of 'wove' paper, a superior quality white paper which was in great demand and the paper of choice for artists such as Thomas Gainsborough and J M W Turner. Whatman paper was used by William Blake for four of his illuminated books and by Queen Victoria for her personal correspondence. Napoleon wrote his long and detailed Will on Whatman paper only three weeks before his death in 1821, and George Washington used it for signing many State documents. In the 1930s Soviet leaders used the paper to publish their five-year plan for the future of the USSR while the Peace Treaty with Japan was signed on Whatman paper at the close of World War II.

Today Turkey Mill is a business park and home to more than 60 companies. Alongside the business park are nine acres of exquiste landscaped grounds and a lake through which runs the River Len. The focus of the gardens is the Orangery, completed in 2002, the perfect venue for wedding receptions, corporate functions, conferences and private parties.

The waterfall, lake, giant Wellingtonias and Blue Cedars create the perfect backdrop for filming, photography and product launches. The grounds are floodlit at dusk.

| | Film location. |
| | Private and corporate events. |
| | Licensed. |
| | 80 spaces weekdays. Unlimited weekends. |

## Conference/Function

| ROOM | SIZE | MAX CAPACITY |
|------|------|--------------|
| The Orangery | 82' x 30' | Dining 200 Dinner Dance 160 Theatre-style 200 (160 catered) Open block 38 |
| The Whatman Room | 23' x 19' | Theatre-style 40 (25 catered) Classroom-style 20 Open block 18 |

## BEDGEBURY NATIONAL PINETUM

**Goudhurst, Cranbrook, Kent  TN17 2SL**
**Tel:** 01580 211781   **Fax:** 01580 212423
**Owner:** Forestry Commission   **Contact:** Mrs Elspeth Hill
**Location:** MAP 4:K4, OS Ref. TQ714 337 (gate on B2079). 7m E of Tunbridge Wells on A21, turn N on B2079 for 1m.
**Open:** All year: daily, 8am–8pm, Sept & Apr closes 7pm, Oct & May closes 6pm, Nov & Mar closes 5pm..
**Admission:** Car parking £5 per car, £20 per minibus, Pay and Display.

## BOUGHTON MONCHELSEA PLACE   *See page 122 for full page entry.*

© English Heritage Photo Library

Dover Castle, Dover

# BELMONT HOUSE & GARDENS
## BELMONT PARK, THROWLEY, FAVERSHAM  ME13 0HH
www.belmont-house.org

**Tel:** 01795 890202   **Fax:** 01795 890042   **E-mail:** belmontadmin@btconnect.com
**Owner:** Harris (Belmont) Charity   **Contact:** Anne Partington-Omar

Belmont is an elegant 18th century house with views over the rolling Kentish North Downs. Its hidden gardens range from a Pinetum complete with grotto, a walled ornamental garden, a walled kitchen garden with Victorian greenhouse leading to a yew-lined walk to the family pets' graveyard.

Its very special collections echo its ownership by the Harris family since 1801 and include mementos of their travels and posts in India and Trinidad. The house was designed by Samuel Wyatt and includes many novel architectural details. In addition it has one of the most extensive collections of clocks in private hands in the country.

**Location:** MAP 4:M3, OS Ref. TQ986 564. 4½m SSW of Faversham, off A251.
**Open:** 31 Mar–30 Sept: Sats, Suns & BH Mons, 2–5pm (last tour 4pm). Group tours weekdays by appointment. Pre-booked specialist clock tours last Sat of month, Apr–Sept. Gardens: Daily 10am–6pm (or dusk if earlier).
**Admission:** House & Garden: Adult £6, Child £3, Conc. £5.50. Group tours (15+): Adult £5.50. Clock tours: £10. Garden only: Adult £3, Child £1, Conc. £3.
No photography in house. Partial. WC. Obligatory. Limited for coaches. In grounds on leads.

## CHART GUNPOWDER MILLS

**Chart Mills, Faversham, Kent ME13 7SE**
**Tel:** 01795 534542   **E-mail:** ticfaversham@btconnect.com
**Owner:** Swale Borough Council   **Contact:** Peter Garner
Oldest gunpowder mill in the world. Supplied gunpowder to Nelson for the Battle of Trafalgar, and Wellington at Waterloo.
**Location:** MAP 4:M3, OS Ref. TQ615 015. M2/J6. W of town centre, access from Stonebridge Way or South Road.
**Open:** Apr–Oct: Sat, Sun & BHs, 2–5pm, or by arrangement.
**Admission:** Free.

## CHARTWELL   *See page 123 for full page entry.*

## CHIDDINGSTONE CASTLE   *See pages 124/125 for double page entry.*

## COBHAM HALL   *See page 126 for full page entry.*

## DANSON HOUSE   *See page 127 for full page entry.*

## THE HOME OF CHARLES DARWIN   *See page 128 for full page entry.*

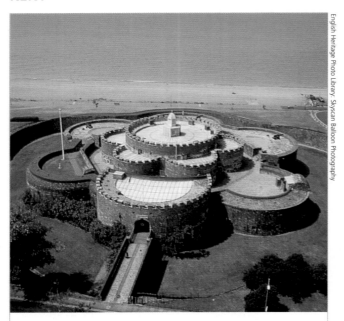

English Heritage Photo Library: Skyscan Balloon Photography

## DEAL CASTLE ⌗
### VICTORIA ROAD, DEAL, KENT CT14 7BA
www.english-heritage.org.uk/visits

**Tel:** 01304 372762 **Venue hire and Hospitality:** 01304 209889
**Owner:** English Heritage **Contact:** Visitor Operations Team
Crouching low and menacing, the huge, rounded bastions of this austere fort, built by Henry VIII, once carried 119 guns. A fascinating castle to explore, with long, dark passages, battlements and a huge basement. The interactive displays and exhibition give an interesting insight into the castle's history.
**Location:** MAP 4:O3, OS Ref. TR378 521. SE of Deal town centre.
**Open:** 1 Apr–30 Sept: daily, 10am–6pm (5pm Sats).
**Admission:** Adult £4, Child £2, Conc. £3. EH Members free.
ⓘ WCs. 🖾 🇹 Exclusive private & corporate hospitality. 🖺 Restricted. 🖾
🅿 Coach parking on main road. 🖼 Guide dogs only.

## DODDINGTON PLACE GARDENS 🏛
**Doddington, Nr Sittingbourne, Kent ME9 0BB**
**Tel:** 01795 886385
**Owner:** Mr & Mrs Richard Oldfield **Contact:** Mrs Richard Oldfield
10 acres of landscaped gardens in an area of outstanding natural beauty.
**Location:** MAP 4:L3, OS Ref. TQ944 575. 4m N from A20 at Lenham or 5m SW from A2 at Ospringe, W of Faversham.
**Open:** Easter Sun–24 Jun: Suns & BH Mons, 2–5pm.
**Admission:** Adult £4, Child £1. Groups (10+) £3.50.

## DOVER CASTLE AND THE ⌗ *See page 129 for full page entry.*
## SECRET WARTIME TUNNELS

## DYMCHURCH MARTELLO TOWER ⌗
**Dymchurch, Kent**
**Tel:** 01304 211067 **www.english-heritage.org.uk/visits**
**Owner:** English Heritage **Contact:** Dover Castle
Built as one of 74 such towers to counter the threat of invasion by Napoleon, Dymchurch is perhaps the best example in the country. Fully restored, you can climb to the roof which is dominated by an original 24-pounder gun complete with traversing carriage.
**Location:** MAP 4:M4, OS189, Ref. TR102 294. In Dymchurch, access from High Street.
**Open:** Aug BH & Heritage Open Days.
**Admission:** Free.
🖼

## EASTBRIDGE HOSPITAL OF ST THOMAS
**High Street, Canterbury, Kent CT1 2BD**
**Tel:** 01227 471688 **Fax:** 01227 781641 **E-mail:** eastbridge@freeuk.com
**www.eastbridgehospital.co.uk** **Contact:** The Warden
Medieval pilgrims' hospital with 12th century undercroft, refectory and chapel.
**Location:** OS189, Ref. TR148 579. S side of Canterbury High Street.
**Open:** MAP 4:N3, All year (except Good Fri, Christmas Day & 29 Dec): Mon–Sat, 10am–4.45pm. Includes Greyfriars Franciscan Chapel, House & Garden. Easter Mon–27 Sept: Mon–Sat, 2–4pm.
**Admission:** Adult £1, Child 50p, Conc. 75p.

© NT Photographic Library

Ightham Mote, Sevenoaks

NTPL / Jerry Harpur

## EMMETTS GARDEN ⚜
### IDE HILL, SEVENOAKS, KENT  TN14 6AY

www.nationaltrust.org.uk/emmetts

**Tel:** 01732 750367/868381 (Chartwell office)  **Info:** 01732 751509
**E-mail:** emmetts@nationaltrust.org.uk
**Owner:** The National Trust
**Contact:** The Property Manager (Chartwell & Emmetts Garden, Mapleton Road,
   Westerham, Kent  TN16 1PS)

Influenced by William Robinson, this charming and informal garden was laid out in the late 19th century, with many exotic and rare trees and shrubs from across the world. Wonderful views across the Weald of Kent – with the highest treetop in Kent. There are glorious shows of daffodils, bluebells, azaleas and rhododendrons, then acers and cornus in autumn, also a rose garden and rock garden.

**Location:** MAP 19:G11, OS Ref. TQ477 524. 1½m N of Ide Hill off B2042. M25/J5, then 4m.
**Open:** 17 Mar–3 Jun: Tue–Sun; 6 Jun–1 Jul: Wed–Sun, 4 Jul–28 Oct: Wed, Sat & Sun. Open BH Mons.
**Admission:** Adult £5.50 (£7.70 with Quebec House), Child £1, Family £12, Group Adult £4.50.

▢ ♿ Steep in places. WC. Buggy from car park to garden entrance. ▣
🐕 In grounds, on leads. ☞

## FINCHCOCKS
### GOUDHURST, KENT  TN17 1HH

www.finchcocks.co.uk

**Tel:** 01580 211702  **Fax:** 01580 211007  **E-mail:** katrina@finchcocks.co.uk
**Owner:** Mr Richard Burnett    **Contact:** Mrs Katrina Burnett

In 1970 Finchcocks was acquired by Richard Burnett, leading exponent of the early piano, and it now contains his magnificent collection of some eighty historical keyboard instruments: chamber organs, harpsichords, virginals, spinets and early pianos. About half of these are restored to full concert condition and are played whenever the house is open to the public. The house, with its high ceilings and oak panelling, provides the perfect setting for music performed on period instruments, and Finchcocks is now a music centre of international repute. Many musical events take place here.

There is a fascinating collection of pictures and prints, mainly on musical themes, and a special exhibition on the theme of the 18th century pleasure gardens, which includes costumes and tableaux.

Finchcocks is a fine Georgian baroque manor noted for its outstanding brickwork, with a dramatic front elevation attributed to Thomas Archer. The present house was built in 1725 for barrister Edward Bathurst. Despite having changed hands many times, it has undergone remarkably little alteration and retains most of its original features. The

beautiful grounds, with their extensive views over parkland and hop gardens, include the newly restored walled garden, which provides a dramatic setting for special events.
**Location:** MAP 4:K4, OS Ref. TQ701 366. 1m S of A262, 2m W of Goudhurst. 5m from Cranbrook, 10m from Tunbridge Wells, 45m from London (1½ hrs). Rail: Marden 6m (no taxi), Paddock Wood 8m (taxi), Tunbridge Wells 10m (taxi).
**Open:** Easter–30 Sept: Suns & BH Mons, plus Wed & Thurs in Aug, 2–6pm. Groups & indivduals: Apr–Dec, by appointment. Closed Jan–Mar.
**Admission:** Adult £8, Child £4, Student £5. Garden only: Adult £2.50, Child 50p. Group (25+): Charge dependent on numbers & programme.

ℹ Music events, conferences, seminars, promotions, archery, ballooning, filming, television. Instruments for hire. No videos in house, photography by permission only. ▢ ▤ ▤ Private and corporate entertaining, weddings. ♿ Limited. WC. Suitable for visually handicapped. ▣ ▥ Licensed. Picnics permitted in grounds. ▣ ▢ Musical tours/recitals. Tour time: 2½–4 hrs. 🅿 Pre-booked groups (25–100) welcome from Apr–Oct. ▣ Opportunity to play instruments. Can be linked to special projects & National Curriculum syllabus. ✖ ▣ Music a speciality. ☞

# THE FRIARS
## AYLESFORD, KENT ME20 7BX

www.thefriars.org.uk

**Tel:** 01622 717272  **Fax:** 01622 715575  **E-mail:** enquiry@thefriars.org.uk

**Owner:** Carmelite Charitable Trust  **Contact:** Pilgrimage and Tours Secretary

The Carmelites first arrived from Mount Carmel, Israel, in 1242. A number of medieval buildings remain, including two walks of the Cloisters and the Pilgrims' Hall. After the Dissolution of the Monasteries it became a private house, The Carmelites returned in 1949, restored the original buildings and built the present shrine dedicated to Our Lady. The Friars is a retreat and pilgrimage centre with some outstanding examples of religious modern art, including sculptures, stained glass and ceramics. A recently restored 17th century barn housing the tearooms and shop and a working pottery is open to the public.

**Location:** MAP 4:K3, OS Ref. TQ726 589. 3m NW of Maidstone. M20/J6 or M2/J3. Follow signs for Eccles and The Friars.

**Open:** Chapels & Grounds: all year, daily, 9am–5pm, (4pm winter). Shop, Tearooms & Pottery: all year, daily, Mon–Sat, 10am–5pm, Suns, 11am–5pm, (4pm winter).

**Admission:** No charge.

🛈 Retreat, conference centre & guesthouse. ⬜ ⬜ ⬜ WCs. ⬛ Licensed.
🅵 By arrangement. 🅿 🚍 ⬜ Guide dogs only. ⬜ ⬜ ⬜

---

## GOODNESTONE PARK GARDENS 🏛

**Goodnestone Park, Nr Wingham, Canterbury, Kent CT3 1PL**

**Tel/Fax:** 01304 840107  **E-mail:** fitzwalter@btinternet.com

**www.goodnestoneparkgardens.co.uk**

**Owner/Contact:** The Lady FitzWalter

The garden is approximately 14 acres, set in 18th century parkland. A new gravel garden was planted in 2003. There are many fine trees, a woodland area and a large walled garden with a collection of old-fashioned roses, clematis and herbaceous plants. Jane Austen was a frequent visitor, her brother Edward having married a daughter of the house.

**Location:** MAP 4:N3, OS Ref. TR254 544. 8m ESE of Canterbury, 1½m E of B2046, at S end of village. The B2046 runs from the A2 to Wingham, the gardens are signposted from this road.

**Open:** 18 Feb–28 Mar: Suns, 12 noon–5pm. 21 Mar–5 Oct: Wed–Fri, 11am–5pm. 24 Mar–29 Sept: Sats & Suns, 12 noon–5pm.

**Admission:** Adult £4.50, Child (6–16yrs) £1 (under 6 Free), OAP £4, Student £2.80, Groups (20+): Adult £4. Guided garden tours: £6.

⬜ ⬜ ⬛ 🅵 🚍

---

# GREAT COMP GARDEN
## COMP LANE, PLATT, BOROUGH GREEN, KENT TN15 8QS

www.greatcomp.co.uk

**Tel:** 01732 886154

**Owner:** Great Comp Charitable Trust  **Contact:** Mr W Dyson

A skilfully designed 7 acre garden surrounding a fine, early 17th century manor. A maze of winding paths leads visitors through areas of different character; romantic ruins and statuary, tranquil woodland, sweeping lawns and colourful, exotic borders. Magnolias and azaleas are very much a feature of the spring. Salvias, dahlias, cannas and heleniums add fiery colours throughout the summer and autumn months. An annual garden show is held in August.

**Location:** MAP 4:K3, OS Ref. TQ635 567. 2m E of Borough Green, B2016 off A20. First right at Comp crossroads. ½m on left.

**Open:** 1 Apr–31 Oct: daily, 11am–5pm.

**Admission:** Adult £4.50, Child £1. Groups (20+) £4, Annual ticket: Adult £13.50, OAP £9.

⬜ ⬜ ⬜ ⬛ Teas daily. 🍴 🅿 ⬜ Guide dogs only. ⬜

---

## THE GRANGE

**St Augustine's Road, Ramsgate, Kent CT11 9NY**

**Tel:** 01628 825925  **www.landmarktrust.org.uk**

**Owner/Contact:** The Landmark Trust

Augustus Pugin built this house in 1843–4 to live in with his family. It was at The Grange that Pugin produced the designs for the interiors of the House of Lords and the Mediaeval Court at the Great Exhibition but he reserved some of his finest and most characteristic flourishes for his own home. The Landmark Trust, a building preservation charity, has undertaken a major restoration of the building which will be available for holidays all year round. Full details of The Grange and 184 other historic and architecturally important buildings are featured in the Landmark Trust Handbook (£11.50 refundable against a booking).

**Location:** MAP 4:O2, OS Ref: TR3764

**Open:** Available for holidays for up to 8 people throughout the year. Parts of the ground floor will be open to the general public by appointment on Wednesday afternoons and there will be regular full Open Days. Contact the Landmark Trust for full details.

**Admission:** Wednesday afternoons & Open Days: Free.

🚍

**GROOMBRIDGE PLACE GARDENS**     *See page 130 for full page entry.*

**HALL PLACE & GARDENS**    *See page 131 for full page entry.*

**HEVER CASTLE**    *See page 132 for full page entry.*

## THE HISTORIC DOCKYARD, CHATHAM

**Chatham, Kent  ME4 4TZ**
**Infoline:** 01634 823807  **E-mail:** info@chdt.org.uk
**Owner/Contact:** Chatham Historic Dockyard Trust
An 80 acre site, in which the visitor can journey through 400 years of the history of Chatham and the Royal Navy, from its origins in the reign of Henry VII to the Falklands Crisis.
**Location:** MAP 4:K2, OS Ref. TQ759 690. Signposted from M2/J1,3&4. From M2/J1&4 follow A289 to the Medway Tunnel. From M2/J3 follow the signs to Chatham, A229 then A230 and A231 and the brown tourist signs.
**Open:** 11 Feb–29 Oct: daily, 10am–6pm (dusk if earlier). Nov: Sat & Sun only.
**Admission:** Adult £11.50, Child (5–15yrs) £6.50, Conc £9. Family (2+2) £29.50, Additional family child £5. Tickets valid for 12 months, terms and conditions apply.

Who's offering **accommodation?**
See our index on page 575

## HOLE PARK GARDENS
### ROLVENDEN, CRANBROOK, KENT  TN17 4JA
www.holepark.com

**Tel:** 01580 241344 / 241386  **Fax:** 01580 241882  **E-mail:** info@holepark.com
**Owner/Contact:** Edward Barham
A 15 acre garden with all year round interest, set in beautiful parkland with fine views. Trees, lawns and extensive yew hedges precisely cut are a feature. Walled garden with mixed borders, pools and water garden. Natural garden with bulbs, azaleas, rhododendrons and flowering shrubs. Bluebell walk and autumn colours a speciality.
**Location:** MAP 4:L4, OS Ref. TQ830 325. 1m W of Rolvenden on B2086 Cranbrook road.
**Open:** April–Oct: Wed & Thur. 1 April–1 July Suns. BH Mons: 9 April, 7 & 28 May. Suns: 30 Sept, 6, 30 & 20 Oct. All 2–6pm and by arrangement. Charity openings for the National Garden Scheme (NGS), telephone or visit the website.
**Admission:** Adult £4, Child 50p. Group visits with conducted tour of the gardens by the owner or head gardener a speciality. Please contact us for details.
🍴 Suns, BHs & by arrangement. 🅰 📷 🎦 By arrangement. 🅿 ♿ Car park only. 🐕

**IGHTHAM MOTE** 🦋    *See page 133 for full page entry.*

**KNOLE** 🦋    *See page 134 for full page entry.*

**LEEDS CASTLE & GARDENS**    *See page 135 for full page entry.*

## LESNES ABBEY

**Abbey Road, Abbey Wood, London  DA17 5DL**
**Tel:** 01322 526574
**Owner:** Bexley Council  **Contact:** Lynda Weaver
The Abbey was founded in 1178 by Richard de Lucy as penance for his involvement in events leading to the murder of Thomas à Becket. Today only the ruins remain.
**Location:** MAP 19:G7, OS Ref. TQ479 788. In public park on S side of Abbey Road (B213), 500yds E of Abbey Wood Station, ¾m N of A206 Woolwich–Erith Road.
**Open:** Any reasonable time.
**Admission:** Free.

## LULLINGSTONE CASTLE

**Lullingstone, Eynsford, Kent  DA4 0JA**
**Tel:** 01322 862114  **Fax:** 01322 862115  **E-mail:** info@lullingstonecastle.co.uk
**www.lullingstonecastle.co.uk**
**Owner/Contact:** Guy Hart Dyke Esq
Fine State rooms, family portraits and armour in beautiful grounds. The 15th century gatehouse was one of the first ever to be made of bricks. This is also the site for the World Garden of Plants and for Lullingstone's Parish Church of St Botolph.
**Location:** MAP 19:G9, OS Ref. TQ530 644. 1m S Eynsford W side of A225. 600yds S of Roman Villa.
**Open:** Apr–Sept: Fris & Sats, House 2–5pm, Gardens 12 noon–5pm; Suns & BHs, 2–6pm. Booked groups by arrangement. Closed Good Fri.
**Admission:** Adult £6, Child £3, OAP £5.50, Family £12.50, Groups (20+): £5 pp plus £40 for a dedicated guide (Weds & Thurs only).
ⓘ No interior photography. 📷 🍴 ♿ Partial. ☕ Teas at visitor centre, 1km.
🎦 By arrangement. 🅿 Limited for coaches. 🐕 Guide dogs only.

© English Heritage Photo Library

## LULLINGSTONE ROMAN VILLA ⌗
### LULLINGSTONE LANE, EYNSFORD, KENT  DA4 0JA
www.english-heritage.org.uk/visits

**Tel:** 01322 863467
**Owner:** English Heritage  **Contact:** Visitor Operations Team
Recognised as one of the most exciting archaeological finds of the century, the villa has splendid mosaic floors and one of the earliest private Christian chapels. Take the inclusive audio tour and discover how the prosperous Romans lived, worked and entertained themselves.
**Location:** MAP 19:G9, OS Ref. TQ529 651. ½m SW of Eynsford off A225, M25/J3. Follow A20 towards Brands Hatch. 600yds N of Castle.
**Open:** 1 Apr–30 Sept: daily, 10am–6pm. 1 Oct–30 Nov & 1 Feb–20 Mar 2008: daily, 10am–4pm. 1 Dec–31 Jan: Wed–Sun, 10am–4pm. Closed 24–26 Dec & 1 Jan.NB May be closed for part of 2007 for conservation works. Please call in advance of visit.
**Admission:** Adult £4, Child £2, Conc. £3. EH Members Free.
📷 ♿ Ground floor & grounds. WC. 📷 ❖ ✳ 🐕

Emmetts Garden, Sevenoaks

## MAISON DIEU

**Ospringe, Faversham, Kent**

**Tel:** 01795 534542   **www.english-heritage.org.uk/visits**

**Owner:** English Heritage   **Contact:** The Faversham Society

This forerunner of today's hospitals remains largely as it was in the 16th century with exposed beams and an overhanging upper storey.

**Location:** MAP 4:M3, OS Ref. TR002 608. In Ospringe on A2, ½m W of Faversham.

**Open:** 6 Apr–31 Oct: Sats & Suns, Good Fri & BHs, 2–5pm.

**Admission:** Adult £1, Child 50p, OAP 80p. EH Members Free. Subject to change.

WCs.

## MILTON CHANTRY

**New Tavern Fort Gardens, Gravesend, Kent**

**Tel:** 01474 321520   **www.english-heritage.org.uk/visits**

**Owner:** English Heritage   **Contact:** Gravesham Borough Council

A small 14th-century building which housed the chapel of the leper hospital and the chantry of the de Valence and Montechais families and later became a tavern.

**Location:** MAP 4:K2, OS Ref.TQ652 743. In New Tavern Fort Gardens ¼m E of Gravesend off A226.

**Open:** 1 Apr–30 Sept: Sats/Suns, Good Fri & BHs, 12 noon–5pm. Open by appointment outside these hours.

**Admission:** Free.

## MOUNT EPHRAIM GARDENS

**Hernhill, Faversham, Kent  ME13 9TX**

**Tel:** 01227 751496   **Fax:** 01227 750940

**www.mountephraimgardens.co.uk**

**Owner:** Mr & Mrs E S Dawes & Mrs M N Dawes   **Contact:** Mrs L Dawes

In these enchanting 10 acres, terraces of fragrant roses lead to a small lake and woodland area. A new grass maze, Japanese-style rock garden, arboretum and many beautiful mature trees are other highlights. Peaceful, unspoilt atmosphere set in Kentish orchards.

**Location:** MAP 4:M3, OS Ref.TR065 598. In Hernhill village, 1m from end of M2. Signed from A2 & A299.

**Open:** Easter–end Sept: Weds, Thurs, Sats, Suns & BH Mons only, 1–6pm. Groups Mar–end Oct, by arrangement.

**Admission:** Adult £4, Child £1. Groups: £3.50.

## NURSTEAD COURT

**Nurstead Church Lane, Meopham, Nr Gravesend, Kent  DA13 9AD**

**Tel:** 01474 812368 (guided tours); 01474 812121 (weddings & functions)

**Fax:** 01474 815133   **E-mail:** info@nursteadcourt.co.uk   **www.nursteadcourt.co.uk**

**Owner/Contact:** Mrs S Edmeades-Stearns

Nurstead Court is a Grade I listed manor house built in 1320 of timber-framed, crown-posted construction, set in extensive gardens and parkland. The additional front part of the house was built in 1825. Licensed weddings are now held in the house with receptions and other functions in the garden marquee.

**Location:** MAP 4:K2, OS Ref. TQ642 685. Nurstead Church Lane is just off the A227 N of Meopham, 3m from Gravesend.

**Open:** Sept: Wed & Thur & 3/4 Oct, 2–5pm. All year round by arrangement.

**Admission:** Adult £5, Child £2.50, OAP/Student £4. Group (max 54): £4.

Weddings & functions catered for.  Licensed.  WCs.  By arrangement.  Limited for coaches.  On leads, in grounds.

## OLD SOAR MANOR

**Plaxtol, Borough Green, Kent  TN15 0QX**

**Tel:** 01732 810378   **Info Line:** 01732 811145

**Owner:** The National Trust   **Contact:** The Property Manager

A solar chamber over a barrel-vaulted undercroft is all that remains of a late 13th century knight's dwelling of c1290 which stood until the 18th century.

**Location:** MAP 4:K3, OS Ref.TQ619 541. 1m E of Plaxtol.

**Open:** 6 Apr–28 Sept: daily except Fri, including BHs & Good Fri, 10am–6pm.

**Admission:** Free.

## OWLETTS

**The Street, Cobham, Gravesend, Kent  DA12 3AP**

**Tel:** 01372 453401   **Fax:** 01372 452023   **E-mail:** owletts@nationaltrust.org.uk

**Owner:** The National Trust   **Contact:** The Property Manager

Former home of the architect Sir Herbert Baker. Highlights include an impressive Carolean staircase, plasterwork ceiling and large kitchen garden.

**Location:** MAP 4:K2, OS Ref. TQ669 686. 1m south of A2 at west end of village. Limited car parking at property. Parking nearby in Cobham village.

**Open:** 31 Mar–27 Oct: Thur & Sat, 2–5.30pm

**Admission:** Adult £3, Child £1.50, Family £7.50. Not suitable for groups.

## PENSHURST PLACE & GARDENS   *See page 136 for full page entry.*

# QUEBEC HOUSE 🦋
## WESTERHAM, KENT TN16 1TD

**Tel:** 01732 868381 (Chartwell office)  **E-mail:** quebechouse@nationaltrust.org.uk
**Owner:** The National Trust  **Contact:** Chartwell Office

This Grade I listed gabled house is situated in the centre of the beautiful village of Westerham. Many features of significant architectural and historical interest reflect its 16th century origins as well as changes made in the 18th and 20th centuries.

Quebec House was the childhood home of General James Wolfe, and rooms contain family and military memorabilia, prints and portraits. The Tudor Coach House contains an exhibition about the Battle of Quebec (1759) and the part played there by Wolfe, who led the British forces to victory over the French.

**Location:** MAP 19:F10, OS Ref. TQ449 541. At E end of village, on N side of A25, facing junction with B2026, Edenbridge Road.
**Open:** 17 Mar–28 Oct: Wed–Sun & BH Mons 1–4.30pm.
**Admission:** Adult £3.90, Child £1.50, Family (2+3) £9.30. Group Adult £3.30. Joint ticket with Emmetts Garden £7.70.

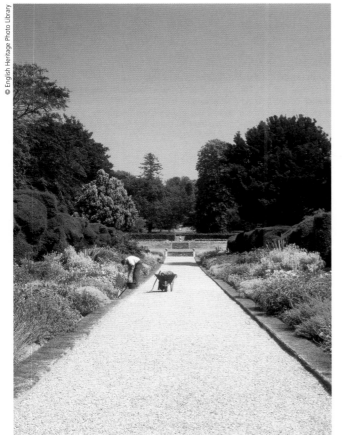
© English Heritage Photo Library

## QUEX MUSEUM, HOUSE & GARDENS & THE POWELL-COTTON COLLECTION

**Quex Park, Birchington, Kent  CT7 0BH**

**Tel:** 01843 842168  **E-mail:** pcmuseum@btconnect.com

**www.powell-cottonmuseum.co.uk**

**Owner:** Trustees of The Powell-Cotton Museum  **Contact:** Julia Walton, Director

World-class collections in a Regency/Victorian country residence. Walled gardens.
**Location:** MAP 4:N2, OS Ref. TR308 683. ½m from Birchington Church via Park Lane.
**Open:** Mid-March–end Oct, Sun–Thurs, 11am–5pm.
**Admission:** Summer: Adult £5, Child, OAP, Disabled & Carer £4, Student £3.50, Family (2+3) £14. Winter: Adult £3, Child, OAP, Disabled & Carer £2, Family (2+3) £10.

## RECULVER TOWERS & ROMAN FORT ⌗

**Reculver, Herne Bay, Kent**

**Tel:** 01227 740676  **www.english-heritage.org.uk/visits**

**Owner:** English Heritage  **Contact:** Reculver Country Park

This 12th-century landmark of twin towers has guided sailors into the Thames estuary for seven centuries. Includes walls of a Roman fort, which were erected nearly 2,000 years ago.

**Location:** MAP 4:N2, OS Ref. TR228 694. At Reculver 3m E of Herne Bay by the seashore.
**Open:** Any reasonable time. External viewing only.
**Admission:** Free.

ℹ️ WCs. ♿ Long slope up from car park. 🅿️ 🚌 Dogs on leads. ❄️

Are you looking for unique **Civil wedding** venues?
See our index on page 577

Walmer Castle & Gardens, Deal

David Winston, Period Piano Company

## RESTORATION HOUSE

**17–19 CROW LANE, ROCHESTER, KENT  ME1 1RF**

www.restorationhouse.co.uk

**Tel:** 01634 848520   **Fax:** 01634 880058
**E-mail:** robert.tucker@restorationhouse.co.uk
**Owner:** R Tucker & J Wilmot   **Contact:** Robert Tucker

Unique survival of an ancient city mansion deriving its name from the stay of Charles II on the eve of The Restoration. Beautiful interiors with exceptional early paintwork related to decorative scheme 'run up' for Charles' visit. The house also inspired Dickens to situate 'Miss Havisham' here.

'Interiors of rare historical resonance and poetry', *Country Life*. Fine English furniture and pictures (Mytens, Kneller, Dahl, Reynolds and several Gainsboroughs). Charming interlinked walled gardens of ingenious plan in a classic English style. A private gem. 'There is no finer pre-Civil war town house in England than this' – Simon Jenkins, *The Times*.

**Location:** MAP 4:K2, OS Ref, TQ744 683. Historic centre of Rochester, off High Street, opposite the Vines Park.
**Open:** 31 May–28 Sept: Thurs & Fris, plus Sat 3 Jun, 10am–5pm.
**Admission:** Adult £5.50 (includes 24 page illustrated guidebook), Child £2.75, Conc £4.50. Booked group (8+) tours: £6.50pp.
ℹ No stiletto heels. No photography in house. 🖼 Garden by appointment.
🍴 1st, 2nd & 4th Thurs in month & other days by arrangement.
🎓 By arrangement. 🅿 None. 🦮 Guide dogs only.

### RICHBOROUGH ROMAN FORT

**Richborough, Sandwich, Kent  CT13 9JW**
**Tel:** 01304 612013   www.english-heritage.org.uk/visits
**Owner:** English Heritage   **Contact:** Visitor Operations Team
This fort and township date back to the Roman landing in AD43. The fortified walls and the massive foundations of a triumphal arch which stood over 80 feet high still survive. The inclusive audio tour and the museum give an insight into life in Richborough's heyday as a busy township.
**Location:** MAP 4:O3, OS Ref. TR324 602. 1½m NW of Sandwich off A257.
**Open:** Fort: 1 Apr–30 Sept: daily, 10am–6pm. Amphitheatre: any reasonable time, access across grazed land from footpath, please telephone for details.
**Admission:** Gardens: Adult £4, Child £2, Conc. £3. EH Members Free.
ℹ Museum. 🔲 🖼 Ground floor. 🔲 🅿 🦮 Guide dogs only.

### RIVERHILL HOUSE

**Sevenoaks, Kent  TN15 0RR**
**Tel:** 01732 458802/452557   **Fax:** 01732 458802
**Owner:** The Rogers Family   **Contact:** Mrs Rogers
Small country house built in 1714.
**Location:** MAP 4:J3, OS Ref. TQ541 522. 2m S of Sevenoaks on E side of A225.
**Open:** Garden: 1 April–17 June: Suns & BH weekends, 11am–5pm.
House: 1 April–17 June, open only to pre-booked groups of adults (20+)
**Admission:** Adult £3, Child 50p. Pre-booked groups: £4.50.

### ROCHESTER CASTLE

**The Lodge, Rochester-upon-Medway, Medway  ME1 1SX**
**Tel:** 01634 402276   www.english-heritage.org.uk/visits
**Owner:** English Heritage (Managed by Medway Council)
**Contact:** Visitor Operations Team
Built in the 11th century. The keep is over 100 feet high and with walls 12 feet thick. Straegically placed astride the London Road, guarding an important crossing of the River Medway, this mighty fortress has a complex history of destruction and re-building.
**Location:** MAP 4:K2, OS Ref. TQ743 685. By Rochester Bridge. Follow A2 E from M2/J1 & M25/J2.
**Open:** 1 Apr–31 Oct: daily, 10am–6pm. 1 Nov–20 Mar 2008: daily, 10am–4pm. Closed 24–26 Dec & 1 Jan. Conservation works may be carried out in 2007/2008, please call in advance of visit.
**Admission:** Adult £4, Child/Conc £3, Family £11. EH Members Free.
ℹ WCs. 🔲 🔲 🦮 ❄ 🔲

### ROCHESTER CATHEDRAL

**Garth House, The Precinct, Rochester, Kent  ME1 1SX**
**Tel:** 01634 401301   **Fax:** 01634 401410   www.rochestercathedral.org
**E-mail:** visitsofficer@rochestercathedraluk.org
Rochester Cathedral has been a place of Christian worship since its foundation in 604AD. The present building is a blend of Norman and gothic architecture with a fine crypt and Romanesque façade. The first real fresco in an English Cathedral for 800 years is now on view to the public.
**Location:** MAP 4:K2, OS Ref. TQ742 686. Signed from M20/J6 & A2/M2/J3. Best access from M2/J3.
**Open:** All year: 8.30am–5pm. Visiting may be restricted during services.
**Admission:** Suggested donation. Adult £3. Guided groups: £4, please book on above number. For special out-of-season rates see website. Separate prices for schools.
ℹ Photography permit £1. 🔲 🖼 🔲 🎓 By arrangement. 🅿 🔲 🦮 ❄

### ROMAN PAINTED HOUSE

**New Street, Dover, Kent  CT17 9AJ**
**Tel:** 01304 203279
**Owner:** Dover Roman Painted House Trust   **Contact:** Mr B Philp
Discovered in 1970. Built around 200AD as a hotel for official travellers. Impressive wall paintings, central heating systems and the Roman fort wall built through the house.
**Location:** MAP 4:N4, OS Ref. TR318 414. Dover town centre. E of York St.
**Open:** Apr–Sept: 10am–5pm, except Mons. Suns 2–5pm.
**Admission:** Adult £2, Child/OAP 80p.

See which properties offer **educational facilities** or **school visits** in our index on page 571

## ST AUGUSTINE'S ABBEY ⌘

**Longport, Canterbury, Kent CT1 1TF**
**Tel:** 01227 767345  **www.english-heritage.org.uk/visits**
**Owner:** English Heritage  **Contact:** Visitor Operations Team

The abbey, founded by St Augustine in 598, is part of a World Heritage Site. Take the free interactive audio tour which gives a fascinating insight into the abbey's history and visit the museum displaying artefacts uncovered during archaeological excavations of the site.

**Location:** MAP 4:N3, OS Ref. TR154 578. In Canterbury ½m E of Cathedral Close.

**Open:** 1 Apr–30 Jun: Wed–Sun, 10am–5pm. Jul & Aug: daily, 10am–6pm. 1 Sept–20 Mar 2008: Suns, 11am–5pm. Mons for educational groups by request. Closed 24–26 Dec & 1 Jan.

**Admission:** Adult £4, Child £2, Conc. £3. 15% discount for groups (11+). EH Members Free.

▣ ⅙ Grounds. ⌕ Free. ℗ Nearby. ⅗ Guide dogs only. ✱

## ST JOHN'S COMMANDERY ⌘

**Densole, Swingfield, Kent**
**Tel:** 01304 211067  **www.english-heritage.org.uk/visits**
**Owner:** English Heritage  **Contact:** Dover Castle

A medieval chapel built by the Knights Hospitallers. It has a moulded plaster ceiling and a remarkable timber roof and was converted into a farmhouse in the 16th century.

**Location:** MAP 4:N4, OS Ref. TR232 440. 2m NE of Densole on minor road off A260.

**Open:** Any reasonable time for exterior viewing. Internal viewing by appointment only, please telephone 01304 211067.

**Admission:** Free.

⅗ ✱

For **corporate hospitality** at unique venues see the index on page 567

## ST JOHN'S JERUSALEM ⅗

**Sutton-at-Hone, Dartford, Kent  DA4 9HQ**
**Tel:** 01732 810378  **Fax:** 01732 811029  **E-mail:** stjohnsjerusalem@nationaltrust.org.uk
**Owner:** The National Trust  **Contact:** Property Manager

The site of a former Knights Hospitaller Commandery chapel. See the garden, moated by the River Darent, and look inside one of the rooms.

**Location:** MAP 4:J2, OS Ref. TQ557 701. 3m south of Dartford at Sutton-at-Hone, on east side of A225. Turn into entrance gate near Balmoral Road; parking at end of drive.

**Open:** 4 Apr–26 Sept: Weds, 2pm–6pm. 3 Oct–24 Oct: Weds, 2pm–4pm.

**Admission:** Adult £2, Child £1, Family £5.

Knole, Sevenoaks

# SCOTNEY CASTLE ⅗
## LAMBERHURST, TUNBRIDGE WELLS, KENT  TN3 8JN

www.nationaltrust.org.uk/scotneycastle

**Tel:** 01892 893868  **Fax:** 01892 890110  **E-mail:** scotneycastle@nationaltrust.org.uk
**Owner:** The National Trust  **Contact:** Property Manager

One of England's most romantic gardens designed by Edward Hussey in the picturesque style. Dramatic vistas from the terrace of the new Scotney Castle, built in the 1830s, lead down to the ruins of a 14th century moated castle. Rhododendrons, kalmia, azaleas and wisteria flower in profusion. Roses and clematis scramble over the remains of the Old Castle. In autumn the garden's glowing colours merge with the surrounding woodlands where there are many country walks to be explored all year round. New for 2007 will be the partial opening of the Scotney Mansion.

**Location:** MAP 4:K4, OS Ref. TQ688 353. Signed off A21 1m S of Lamberhurst village.

**Open:** Garden & Shop: 3–14 Mar, and 3 Nov–16 Dec, Sat & Sun. 17 Mar–28 Oct, Wed–Sun. 11am–5.30pm (or dusk if earlier) last admn. 1 hr before closing. Mansion: please telephone for details.

**Admission:** Garden & Mansion: Adult £7.70, Child £3.80, Family £19.30, Group Adult £6.50, Child £3.25. Garden only: Adult £5.80, Child £2.90, Family £14.30, Group (Wed–Fri) Adult £4.80, Child £2.40. NT members free.

▣ ⅌ ⅙ Grounds (but steep parts). ☐ ⅰ ℗ ⅗ ✱ ⅟

© NT Photographic Library / D Sellman

South East – England

© NT Photographic Library / Eric Crichton

# SISSINGHURST CASTLE GARDEN ✤
## SISSINGHURST, CRANBROOK, KENT TN17 2AB

www.nationaltrust.org.uk/sissinghurst

**Tel:** 01580 710700    **Infoline:** 01580 710701
**E-mail:** sissinghurst@nationaltrust.org.uk
**Owner:** The National Trust    **Contact:** The Administrator

One of the world's most celebrated gardens, the creation of Vita Sackville-West and her husband Sir Harold Nicolson. Developed around the surviving parts of an Elizabethan mansion with a central red-brick prospect tower, a series of small, enclosed compartments, intimate in scale and romantic in atmosphere, provide outstanding design and colour throughout the season. The study, where Vita worked, and library are also open to visitors.

**Location:** MAP 4:L4, OS Ref. TQ807 383. 2m NE of Cranbrook, 1m E of Sissinghurst village (A262).

**Open:** 17 Mar–28 Oct: Fri–Tues, including BHs & Good Fri, 11am–6.30pm; Sat, Sun, BHs & Good Fri, 10am–6.30pm. Last admission 1 hour before closing or dusk if earlier.

***Admission:** Adult £8.60, Child £4, Family (2+3) £22. NT members Free. *includes a voluntary donation but visitors can choose to pay the standard prices displayed at the property and on the website.

▢ ⊞ ⬙ WCs. ⬛ ⊞ Licensed. **P** Ample, £2 per car (NT Members free). Limited for coaches. ⬙ Grounds only, on leads. Guide dogs only in Garden.

© NT Photographic Library / David Sellham

# SMALLHYTHE PLACE ✤
## TENTERDEN, KENT TN30 7NG

www.nationaltrust.org.uk/smallhytheplace

**Tel:** 01580 762334    **Fax:** 01580 762334
**E-mail:** smallhytheplace@nationaltrust.org.uk
**Owner:** The National Trust    **Contact:** Assistant Property Manager

This early 16th century half-timbered house was home to Shakespearean actress Ellen Terry from 1899 to 1928. The house contains many personal and theatrical mementoes, including her lavish costumes. The grounds include the barn theatre and beautiful cottage garden. Many events take place in the grounds and the theatre.

**Location:** MAP 4:L4, OS Ref. TQ893 300. 2m S of Tenterden on E side of the Rye road B2082.

**Open:** 3–18 Mar: Sats & Suns. 24 Mar–28 Oct: daily except Thur & Fri (open Good Fri), 11am–5pm, last admission 4.30pm.

**Admission:** Adult £5, Child £2.50, Family £12.50. Group £3.90.

ℹ No photography in house. ⊞ ⬙ Ground floor only. **P** Limited. ⬙ On leads, in grounds. ⬛

# SOUTH FORELAND LIGHTHOUSE ✤
## THE FRONT, ST MARGARET'S BAY, Nr DOVER CT15 6HP

www.nationaltrust.org.uk/southforeland

**Tel:** 01304 852463    **Fax:** 01304 215484
**E-mail:** southforeland@nationaltrust.org.uk
**Owner:** The National Trust    **Contact:** Volunteer Co-ordinator

Distinctive and historical Victorian Lighthouse at St Margaret's Bay, part of the White Cliffs of Dover. Built to guide ships safely past Goodwin Sands, the lighthouse has the second highest light (above sea level) in the UK. Marconi and Faraday both used this lighthouse for their experimental work.

**Location:** MAP 4:O3, OS138 Ref. TR359 433. 2m walk from White Cliffs car park, 1m walk from St Margaret's Village, short walk from bus stop Diamond route 15.

**Open:** 30 Mar–29 Oct, Fri–Sun, 11am–5pm. Open daily during local school holidays.

**Admission:** Adult £4, Child £2, Family £10. NT Members free.

▢ Limited range of souvenirs. ⬙ In grounds only. ⬛

---

## SQUERRYES COURT ⊞
*See page 137 for full page entry.*

---

## STONEACRE ✤

**Otham, Maidstone, Kent ME15 8RS**
**Tel/Fax:** 01622 862157
**Owner:** The National Trust    **Contact:** The Tenant

A late 15th century yeoman's house, with great hall and crownpost, surrounded by harmonious garden, orchard and meadow.

**Location:** MAP 4:L3, OS Ref. TQ800 535. In narrow lane at N end of Otham village, 3m SE of Maidstone, 1m S of A20.

**Open:** 31 Mar–6 Oct: Sats & BH Mons, 11am–6pm (last admission 5pm).

**Admission:** Adult £3.50, Child £1.50, Family (2+3) £8.50. Groups £3.

---

## TEMPLE MANOR ⌗

**Strood, Rochester, Kent**
**Tel:** 01634 718743    **www.english-heritage.org.uk/visits**
**Owner:** English Heritage    **Contact:** Medway Council

The 13th-century manor house of the Knights Templar which mainly provided accommodation for members of the order travelling between London and the continent.

**Location:** MAP 4:K2, OS Ref. TQ733 686. In Strood (Rochester) off A228.

**Open:** 31 Mar–31 Oct: Sats & Suns, 11am–3pm. For group visits, please call 01634 843666.

**Admission:** Free.

⬙ Grounds only. **P** ⬙

For rare and unusual plants visit the **plant sales** index on page 564

**visit hudsons guide online**

## TONBRIDGE CASTLE

**Castle Street, Tonbridge, Kent TN9 1BG**
**Tel:** 01732 770929  **www.tonbridgecastle.org**
**Owner:** Tonbridge & Malling Borough Council  **Contact:** The Administrator
**Location:** MAP 19:H11, OS Ref. TQ588 466. 300 yds NW of the Medway Bridge at town centre.
**Open:** All year: Mon–Sat, 9am–4pm. Suns & BHs, 10.30am–4pm.
**Admission:** Gatehouse – Adult £5.30, Conc. £3.30. Family £15 (max 2 adults). Admission includes audio tour. Last tour 1 hour before closing.
🔲 ✳

## TURKEY MILL

*See page 138 for full page entry.*

## UPNOR CASTLE ♯

**Upnor, Kent**
**Tel:** 01634 718742  **www.english-heritage.org.uk/visits**
**Owner:** English Heritage  **Contact:** Medway Council
Well preserved 16th-century gun fort built to protect Queen Elizabeth I's warships. However in 1667 it failed to prevent the Dutch Navy which stormed up the Medway destroying half the English fleet.
**Location:** MAP 4:K2, OS Ref. TQ758 706. At Upnor, on unclassified road off A228. 2 miles NE of Strood.
**Open:** 1 Apr–30 Sept: daily 10am–6pm. Oct: daily, 10am–4pm.
**Admission:** Adult £4.50, Child/Conc £3.50, Family £12.50. EH Members Free.
ℹ WCs. 🅰 Grounds only. 🔲 🔲 🔲 On leads in restricted areas.

Many properties hold **special events** throughout the year
See the index on page 585

Scotney Castle, Lamberhurst

# WALMER CASTLE AND GARDENS ♯

## WALMER, DEAL, KENT CT14 7LJ

www.english-heritage.org.uk/visits

**Tel:** 01304 364288  **Venue Hire and Hospitality:** 01304 209889
**Owner:** English Heritage  **Contact:** Visitor Operations Team
A Tudor fort transformed into an elegant stately home. The residence of the Lords Warden of the Cinque Ports, who have included HM The Queen Mother, Sir Winston Churchill and the Duke of Wellington. Take the inclusive audio tour and see the Duke's rooms where he died over 150 years ago. Beautiful gardens including the Queen Mother's Garden, The Broadwalk with its famous yew tree hedge, Kitchen Garden & Moat Garden. Lunches and cream teas available in the delightful Lord Warden's tearooms.

**Location:** MAP 4:O3, OS Ref. TR378 501. S of Walmer on A258, M20/J13 or M2 to Deal.
**Open:** 1 Apr–30 Sept: daily, 10am–6pm (4pm Sats). Oct & 1–20 Mar 2008: Wed–Sun, 10am–4pm. Closed 13/14 & to 1pm 15 Jul when Lord Warden in residence.
**Admission:** Adult £6.30, Child £3.20, Conc. £4.70, Family £15.80. 15% discount for groups (11+). English Heritage members free.
ℹ WCs. 🔲 🔲 Private & corporate hire. 🅰 Grounds. 🔲 🔲 🅿 🔲 Guide dogs only. 🔲

South East - England

# WESTENHANGER CASTLE AND BARNS
## STONE STREET, WESTENHANGER, HYTHE, KENT CT21 4HX
www.westenhangercastle.co.uk

**Tel:** 01227 738223   **Fax:** 01227 738278   **E-mail:** graham.forge@btopenworld.com
**Owner:** G Forge Ltd   **Contact:** Graham Forge

Westenhanger Castle was once a magnificent residence of great importance owned by Henry VIII and Elizabeth I. What remains today are romantic ruins which tell the story of its illustrious past. The monument has undergone several phases of English Heritage-assisted restoration work and retains many features within the ruins of the curtain wall including Tudor fireplaces and a stunning dovecote with 420 nesting boxes. The medieval barn adjoins an earlier accommodation base court and was built extravagantly with a hammerbeam roof. It has four wagon porches and was built astride a tributary of the East Stour river.

**Location:** MAP 4:M4, OS Ref. TR123 372. Leave M20/J11 towards Hythe. Turn right to Westenhanger village and left before station.

**Open:** Tue–Thurs by prior arrangement.

**Admission:** Owner guided tours: Small groups £12pp. minimum. Groups (15–40) £6.50pp. Educational groups (schools and students): £3pp.

⊤ ⅃ ☞ Licensed. ⒡ Obligatory. ℙ Limited for coaches. ◼ ⊞ On leads, in grounds. ⌂ ❋ ⍿

# WHITE CLIFFS OF DOVER ⚘
## UPPER ROAD, LANGDON CLIFFS, Nr DOVER CT16 1HJ
www.nationaltrust.org.uk/whitecliffs

**Tel:** 01304 202756   **Fax:** 01304 215484
**E-mail:** whitecliffs@nationaltrust.org.uk
**Owner:** The National Trust   **Contact:** Visitor Services Manager

The Gateway to the White Cliffs is a Visitor Centre, Gift Shop and Coffee Shop with spectacular views across the English Channel. New interpretation gives visitors the opportunity to find out more about the formation of the cliffs, the importance of chalk grassland and the military history of the property.

**Location:** MAP 4:O3, OS138 Ref. TR336 422. Follow White Cliffs brown signs from roundabout 1 m NE of Dover at junction of A2/A258.

**Open:** All year, 1 Mar–31 Oct, 10am–5pm. 1 Nov–28 Feb, 11am–4pm.

**Admission:** Cars £2.50, Motorcycles & Blue Badge holders £1.50, Motor homes £3, Coaches £5, Season ticket £25. NT Members free.

⊡ ⅃ Visitor centre, toilets and car parks. ☞ ℙ ⊞ ❋ ⍿

## WILLESBOROUGH WINDMILL

### Mill Lane, Willesborough, Ashford, Kent TN24 0QG
**Tel:** 01233 661866

130 year old smock mill. Civil Wedding Licence.

**Location:** MAP 4:M4, OS Ref. TR031 421. Off A292 close to M20/J10. At E end of Ashford.

**Open:** Apr–end Sept; Sats, Suns & BH Mons, also Weds in Jul & Aug, 2–5pm or dusk if earlier.

**Admission:** Adult £3, Conc. £1.50. Groups 10% reduction by arrangement only.

© NT Photographic Library / Stephen Robson

Scotney Castle Gardens, Lamberhurst

**visit hudsons guide online**

# ARDINGTON HOUSE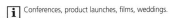

www.ardingtonhouse.com

### Owner
The Baring Family

### Contact
Nigel Baring
Ardington House
Wantage
Oxfordshire  OX12 8QA

**Tel:** 01235 821566
**Fax:** 01235 821151
**E-mail:** info@
ardingtonhouse.com

### Location
**MAP 3:D1**
**OS Ref. SU432 883**

12m S of Oxford,
12m N of Newbury,
2½ m E of Wantage.

### Opening Times
1 August–14 September,
daily **excluding
weekends and BHs**,
11am–2pm,
last entry at 1pm.

Guided tours at 12.30pm.

### Admission
**House & Gardens**
Adult          £5.00
Child          Free

Just a few miles south of Oxford stands the hauntingly beautiful Ardington House. Surrounded by well-kept lawns, terraced gardens, peaceful paddocks, parkland and its own romantic island this Baroque house is the private home of the Barings. You will find it in the attractive village of Ardington, close to the Ridgeway on the edge of the Berkshire Downs.

Built by the Strong brothers in 1720 with typical Georgian symmetry, the House is also famous for its Imperial Staircase. Leading from the Hall, the staircase is considered by experts to be one of the finest examples in Britain.

Away from the crowds and the hustle of the workplace Ardington House provides a private and secluded setting. The calm, exclusive use environment allows for weddings, offsite board meetings, conferences and workshops utilising the splendid gardens and grounds. There is a heated outdoor swimming pool, tennis court, croquet lawn and trout river. Close by is the ancient Ridgeway Path, a popular place for walking or mountain biking.

Ardington House is licensed to hold Civil wedding ceremonies. Receptions can range from drinks and intimate dining in the house, to a full dinner and dance reception using marquees in the grounds.

Poet Laureate Sir John Betjeman wrote of the homeliness and warmth of Ardington House, and the rooms have seen many special occasions and important visitors in the past with this tradition being continued. The astonishing mixture of history, warmth and style you'll find at Ardington truly does place it in a class of its own.

Conferences, product launches, films, weddings.

Lunches and teas by arrangement for groups.

By members of the family.

Free.

Guide dogs only.

## Conference/Function

| ROOM | MAX CAPACITY |
|---|---|
| **Imperial Hall** | |
| Theatre Style | 80 |
| U shape | 30 |
| Cabaret | 40 |
| **Oak Room** | |
| Theatre Style | 40 |
| U shape | 20 |
| Cabaret | 30 |
| **Music Room** | |
| Theatre Style | 40 |
| U shape | 20 |
| Cabaret | 30 |

South East – England

### Owner
The Duke of Marlborough

### Contact
Operations Director
Blenheim Palace
Woodstock  OX20 1PX

**Tel:** 08700 602080
**Fax:** 01993 810570
**E-mail:** operations@blenheimpalace.com

### Location
**MAP 7:A11**
**OS Ref. SP441 161**

From London, M40, A44 (1½ hrs), 8m NW of Oxford. London 63m Birmingham 54m.

**Air:** Heathrow 60m. Birmingham 50m.

**Coach:** From London (Victoria) to Oxford.

**Rail:** Oxford Station.

**Bus:** No.20 from Oxford Station, Gloucester Green & Cornmarket.

### Opening Times
10 February–28 October, daily.
31 October–9 December, Wed–Sun.

**Palace and formal Gardens**
10.30am–5.30pm (last admission 4.45pm).

**Park**
9am–6pm or dusk during autumn and winter months.

Open daily except for one day in June, November or December.

# BLENHEIM PALACE 🏛

www.blenheimpalace.com

The state rooms of Blenheim Palace hold many treasures, from world famous tapestries to furniture, paintings, porcelain, clocks and sculptures. An unusually large collection of family portraits by great masters graces the walls. These include Joshua Reynolds' painting of the 4th Duke and family, a John Singer Sargent of the 9th Duke and family including Consuelo Vanderbilt, and a huge Clostermann of John Churchill, the 1st Duke, with his family. The collection of Chippendale and Boulle furniture is 'second to none in a historic home'. See the restored terracotta statues to the front façade of the Palace.

The Palace, home of the 11th Duke of Marlborough and birthplace of Sir Winston Churchill, was built for John Churchill, 1st Duke of Marlborough by Sir John Vanbrugh between 1705 and 1722.

The original gardens were designed by Queen Anne's gardener Henry Wise, with later alterations by Lancelot "Capability" Brown which included the creation of Blenheim's most outstanding feature, the lake. The French architect, Archille Duchene created the Italian Garden and the beautiful Water Terraces. The newly restored Secret Garden lies to the east of the Palace.

The combination of house, gardens and park was recognised as uniquely important when Blenheim was listed as a World Heritage Site in 1987.

In Summer 2007 a fascinating new attraction opens in the heart of the Palace. "Blenheim Palace – the Untold Story" tells of dramatic events through 300 years of history at Blenheim, seen through the eyes of family servants.

The Pleasure Gardens area, which can be reached by miniature train, includes the Marlborough Maze, the Butterfly House and Adventure Playground, making it a great area for young children.

### Conference/Function

| ROOM | SIZE | MAX CAPACITY |
|------|------|-------------|
| Orangery | | 228 |
| Marlborough Room | | 80 |
| Saloon | 50' x 30' | 75 |
| Great Hall | | 150 |
| with Great Hall & Library | | 500 |
| Library | 180' x 30' | 300 |
| Oudenarde Room | | 20 |
| Ramillies Room | | 15 |
| Malplaquet Room | | 15 |

The Long Library

### Admission
Season Tickets available.

**Palace, Garden & Park**

*Main Season:*
10–17 Feb & 31 Mar–28 Oct
Adult       £16.00
Child*      £9.75
Conc.       £13.50
Family (2+2) £43.00

Groups (15+)
Adult       £11.70
Child*      £6.45
Conc.       £10.50

*Low Season:*
18 Feb–31 Mar, 31 Oct–10 Dec
Adult       £13.50
Child*      £7.50

Conc.       £11.00
Family (2+2) £36.00

Groups (15+)
Adult       £9.50
Child*      £5.50
Conc.       £8.50

**Park only**
10 Dec–mid Feb 2008
Adult       £3.00
Child*      £2.00

**Gardens & Park**
*Main Season:*
31 Mar–28 Oct
Adult       £9.30
Child*      £4.70
Conc.       £7.30
Family      £24.00

Groups (15+)
Adult       £6.50
Child*      £3.10
Conc.       £5.50

*Low Season:*
10 Feb–31 Mar, 31 Oct–10 Dec
Adult       £7.30
Child*      £2.60
Conc.       £5.20
Family      £17.50

Groups (15+)
Adult       £5.20
Child*      £1.90
Conc.       £4.15

*(5–16yrs)

Private tours by appointment only, prices on request.

ℹ Filming, product launches, activity days. No photography in house.

🏠 Four shops.

🍷 Corporate Hospitality includes weddings, receptions, dinners, meetings and corporate events.

♿ Car Park for disabled, adapted toilets, disabled lift into Palace.

🍴 3 cafés.

🍴 Group enquiries welcome (up to 150). Menus on request.

🚶 Guided tours except Sundays, BHs and extremely busy days.

**P** Unlimited for cars and coaches.

▦ Sandford Award holder since 1982. Teacher pre-visits welcome.

🐕 Dogs on leads in Park. Registered assistance dogs only in house and garden.

  Full programme.

**visit hudsons guide online**

**Owner**
Lord Saye & Sele

**Contact**
Mrs J Hummer
Broughton Castle
Broughton
Nr Banbury
Oxfordshire  OX15 5EB

**Tel:** 01295 276070
**E-mail:** info@broughton
castle.com

**Location**
**MAP 7:A10**
**OS Ref. SP418 382**

Broughton Castle is
2½m SW of Banbury
Cross on the B4035,
Shipston-on-Stour –
Banbury Road.
Easily accessible from
Stratford-on-Avon,
Warwick, Oxford, Burford
and the Cotswolds.
M40/J11.

**Rail:** From London/
Birmingham to Banbury.

**Opening Times**
**Summer**
Easter Sun & Mon
1 May–15 September
Weds & Suns, 2–5pm.

Also Thurs in July and
August and all BH Suns
& Mons, 2–5pm.

Groups welcome on
any day and at any time
throughout the year
by appointment.

**Admission**
Adult              £6.50
Child (5–15yrs)    £2.50
OAP/Student        £5.50

Groups (15–100)

Adult              £5.50
Child (5–15yrs)    £2.50
OAP/Student        £5.50

# BROUGHTON CASTLE 🏛

www.broughtoncastle.com

Broughton Castle is essentially a family home lived in by Lord and Lady Saye & Sele and their family.

The original medieval Manor House, of which much remains today, was built in about 1300 by Sir John de Broughton. It stands on an island site surrounded by a 3 acre moat. The Castle was greatly enlarged between 1550 and 1600, at which time it was embellished with magnificent plaster ceilings, splendid panelling and fine fireplaces.

In the 17th century William, 8th Lord Saye & Sele, played a leading role in national affairs. He opposed Charles I's efforts to rule without Parliament and Broughton became a secret meeting place for the King's opponents.

During the Civil War William raised a regiment and he and his four sons all fought at the nearby Battle of Edgehill. After the battle the Castle was besieged and captured.

Arms and armour from the Civil War and other periods are displayed in the Great Hall. Visitors may also see the gatehouse, gardens and park together with the nearby 14th century Church of St Mary, in which there are many family tombs, memorials and hatchments.

## Gardens

The garden area consists of mixed herbaceous and shrub borders containing many old roses. In addition, there is a formal walled garden with beds of roses surrounded by box hedging and lined by more mixed borders.

ℹ Photography allowed in house.

🛍

👶

♿ Partial.

☕ Teas on Open Days. Groups may book morning coffee, light lunches and afternoon teas.

🚶 Available for booked groups.

🅿 Limited.

🐕 Guide dogs only in house. On leads in grounds.

❄ Open all year for groups.

### ■ Owner
Lord & Lady Camoys

### ■ Contact
The Administrator -
Geoff Pitcher
Stonor Park
Henley-on-Thames
Oxfordshire  RG9 6HF

**Tel:** 01491 638587
**Fax:** 01491 639348
**E-mail:**
gpitcher@stonor.com

### ■ Location
**MAP 3:E1**
**OS Ref. SU743 893**

1 hr from London,
M4/J8/9. A4130 to
Henley-on-Thames.
On B480 NW of Henley.
A4130/B480 to Stonor.
Rail: Henley-on-Thames
Station 5m.

### ■ Opening Times
1st April–16th September
Sundays and BH Mondays
Also Wednesdays, July
and August only.

**Gardens**
1–5.30pm

**House, Tearoom,
Exhibition**
2–5.30pm
Private Groups (20+):
by arrangement
Tuesday–Thursday,
April–September

### ■ Admission
**House, Gardens,
Chapel, Exhibition**
| | |
|---|---|
| Adults | £7.00 |
| First Child (5–16) | £3.00 |
| 2 or more children (5–16) | Free |
| Under 5s | Free |

**Gardens**
| | |
|---|---|
| Adults | £3.50 |
| First Child (5–16) | £1.50 |
| 2 or more children (5–16) | Free |
| Under 5s | Free |

**Groups**
| | |
|---|---|
| Adults | £8.00 |
| Child (5–16) | £4.00 |

### ■ Special Events
**June 3**
VW Owners' Rally.

**August 4**
Classic Concert in the
Park.

**August 24–27**
Chilterns Craft Fair.

**September 12**
Evening Demonstration –
Historical Dress.

**September 21–23**
Stonor Flower Festival.

# STONOR 🏛
www.stonor.com

Family home of Lord and Lady Camoys and of generations of their family for over 800 years. Stonor, surrounded by deer park, and with a charming and old walled and terraced garden, sits in a beautiful wooded valley.

The House and Chapel date from the 12th century, with 14th and 18th century additions and changes. Rare furniture, artworks and family portraits feature strongly. Mass has been celebrated since medieval times in the Chapel, sited close by a pagan stone prayer circle.

St Edmund Campion sought refuge here during the Reformation and printed his famous pamphlet "Ten Reasons" here, in secret, on a press installed in the roof space. A small Exhibition celebrates his life and work.

Throughout 2007 there will also be a larger Exhibition entitled "Our American Ancestry". This relates to the Brown and Sherman families who were deeply involved in the founding and development of the State of Rhode Island. The Exhibition includes portraits, photographs, porcelain, glass, silver and sculptures, much of it commissioned and collected by them in Europe.

The gardens offer outstanding views of the Park and Valley. They are especially beautiful in May and June, and contain fine displays of daffodils, irises, peonies and roses.

ℹ️ No photography in house.

🛍️

🍸

♿ Unsuitable for physically disabled.

🍽️ Licensed.

🏃 For 20–60.

🅿️ 100yds away.

🐕 In Park on leads.

📋 See website or telephone for details.

## 26A EAST ST HELEN STREET

**Abingdon, Oxfordshire**

**Tel:** 01865 242918  **E-mail:** info@oxfordpreservation.org.uk

**www.oxfordpreservation.org.uk**

**Owner:** Oxford Preservation Trust    **Contact:** Ms Debbie Dance

One of best preserved examples of a 15th century dwelling in the area. Originally a Merchant's Hall House with later alterations, features include a remarkable domestic wall painting, an early oak ceiling, traceried windows and fireplaces.

**Location:** MAP 7:A12, OS Ref. SU497 969. 300 yards SSW of the market place and Town Hall.

**Open:** By prior appointment.

**Admission:** Free.

---

## ARDINGTON HOUSE 🏠

*See page 151 for full page entry.*

---

## ASHDOWN HOUSE 🌿

**Lambourn, Newbury  RG17 8RE**

**Tel:** 01793 762209    **E-mail:** ashdownhouse@nationaltrust.org.uk

**www.nationaltrust.org.uk**

**Owner:** The National Trust    **Contact:** Coleshill Estate Office

**Location:** MAP 3:C1, OS Ref. SU282 820. 3½m N of Lambourn, on W side of B4000.

**Open:** House & Garden: 4 Apr–31 Oct: Wed & Sat, 2–5pm. Admission by guided tour at 2.15, 3.15 & 4.15pm. Woodland: All year: daily except Fri, daylight hours.

**Admission:** House & garden: £2.50. Free to NT members. Woodland: Free.

---

## BLENHEIM PALACE 🏠

*See pages 152 for full page entry.*

---

## BROOK COTTAGE

**Well Lane, Alkerton, Nr Banbury  OX15 6NL**

**Tel:** 01295 670303/670590    **Fax:** 01295 730362

**Owner/Contact:** Mrs David Hodges

4 acre hillside garden. Roses, clematis, water gardens, colour co-ordinated borders, trees, shrubs.

**Location:** MAP 7:A10, OS Ref. SP378 428. 6m NW of Banbury, ½m off A422 Banbury to Stratford-upon-Avon road.

**Open:** Easter Mon–end Oct: Mon–Fri, 9am–6pm. Evenings, weekends and all group visits by appointment.

**Admission:** Adult £4, OAP £3, Child Free.

---

## BROUGHTON CASTLE 🏠

*See page 153 for full page entry.*

---

## BUSCOT OLD PARSONAGE 🌿

**Buscot, Faringdon, Oxfordshire  SN7 8DQ**

**Tel:** 01793 762209    **E-mail:** buscot@nationaltrust.org.uk

**Owner:** The National Trust    **Contact:** Coleshill Estate Office

An early 18th century house of Cotswold stone on the bank of the Thames with a small garden.

**Location:** MAP 6:P12, OS Ref. SU231 973. 2m from Lechlade, 4m N of Faringdon on A417.

**Open:** 4 Apr–31 Oct, Weds, 2–6pm by written appointment with tenant.

**Admission:** Adult £1.50, Child 70p, Family £3.70. Not suitable for groups. Free to NT members.

ℹ No WCs.  ♿ Partial.

NTPL / Thames and Chiltern

Part of the Harold Peto Water Garden

# BUSCOT PARK 🌿

### BUSCOT, FARINGDON, OXFORDSHIRE  SN7 8BU

www.buscotpark.com

**Tel:** Infoline 0845 345 3387 / Office 01367 240786  **Fax:** 01367 241794

**E-mail:** estbuscot@aol.com

**Owner:** The National Trust (Administered on their behalf by Lord Faringdon)

**Contact:** The Estate Office

The 18th century Palladian house contains the Faringdon Collection of fine paintings (including works by Murillo, Reynolds, Rossetti and the famous Briar Rose series by Burne-Jones) and furniture, with important pieces by Adam, Thomas Hope and others. The House is set in parkland, offering peaceful walks through water gardens and a well-stocked walled garden. A tearoom serves delicious home-made cream teas and cakes, and there is ample free parking.

**Location:** MAP 6:P12, OS Ref. SU239 973. Between Faringdon and Lechlade on A417.

**Open:** House & Grounds: 2 Apr–28 Sep: Wed–Fri, 2–6pm (last entry to house 5pm). Also open BH Mons & Good Fri and weekends 7/8 & 14/15 Apr; 5/6, 12/13, 26/27 May; 9/10, 23/24, Jun; 7/8 & 21/22 Jul; 11/12 & 25/26 Aug; 8/9 & 22/23 Sept. Grounds only: 2 Apr–28 Sep: Mon & Tues, 2–6pm. Tearoom: as House, 2.30–5.30pm.

**Admission:** House & Grounds: Adult £7, Child £3.50. Grounds only: Adult £5, Child £2.50. NT members Free. Groups must book in writing, or by fax or E-mail.  Booking required by disabled visitors wishing to use powered mobility vehicle.

ℹ No photography in house. 🎭 Fully equipped theatre. ♿ Partial, tel for details.
🍖 BBQ lunches for groups by arrangement. 🅿 Ample for cars, 2 coach spaces.
🐕 May be exercised in overflow car park only.

### CHASTLETON HOUSE

**Chastleton, nr Moreton-in-Marsh, Oxfordshire  GL56 0SU**
**Tel/Fax:** 01608 674355   **Infoline:** 01494 755560
**E-mail:** chastleton@nationaltrust.org.uk
**Owner:** The National Trust   **Contact:** The Custodian

One of England's finest and most complete Jacobean houses, dating from 1607. It is filled with a mixture of rare and everyday objects and the atmosphere of four hundred years of continuous occupation by one family. The gardens have a Jacobean layout and the rules of modern croquet were codified here.

**Location:** MAP 6:P10, OS Ref. SP248 291. 6m ENE of Stow-on-the-Wold. 1½ miles NW of A436. Approach only from A436 between the A44 (W of Chipping Norton) and Stow.
**Open:** 28 Mar–29 Sept: Wed–Sat, 1–5pm, last admission 4pm. 3–27 Oct: Wed–Sat, 1–4pm, last admission 3pm. Admission for all visitors (including NT members) by timed tickets booked in advance. Advanced bookings can be made until the day before your visit. Telephone 01608 674355.
**Admission:** Adult £7, Child £3.50, Family £17.50. Free to NT members.
⬇ Partial. 🅿 Coaches limited to 25 seat minibuses. 🦮 Guide dogs only.

### CHRIST CHURCH CATHEDRAL

**The Sacristy, The Cathedral, Oxford  OX1 1DP**
**Tel:** 01865 276154
**Contact:** Tony Fox

12th century Norman Church, formerly an Augustinian monastery, given Cathedral status in 16th century by Henry VIII. Private tours available.
**Location:** MAP 7:A12, OS Ref. SP515 059. Just S of city centre, off St Aldates. Entry via Meadow Gate visitors' entrance on S side of college.
**Open:** Mon–Sat: 9am–5pm. Suns: 1–5pm (last entry 4.30pm) closed Christmas Day. Services: weekdays 7.20am, 6pm. Suns: 8am, 10am, 11.15am & 6pm. Areas of the college (especially the Great Hall & Cathedral) are closed at various times during the year. Please telephone to check before visit.
**Admission:** Adult £4.50, Child under 5 Free, Conc. £3.50, Family £9.00.

### DEDDINGTON CASTLE

**Deddington, Oxfordshire**
**Tel:** 01424 775705   **www.english-heritage.org.uk/visits**
**Owner:** English Heritage   **Contact:** 1066 Battle Abbey

Extensive earthworks concealing the remains of a 12th century castle which was ruined as early as the 14th century.
**Location:** MAP 7:A10, OS Ref. SP471 316. S of B4031 on E side of Deddington, 17 miles N of Oxford on A423. 5 miles S of Banbury.
**Open:** Any reasonable time.
**Admission:** Free.
🦮 On leads. ✳

### DITCHLEY PARK

**Enstone, Oxfordshire  OX7 4ER**
**Tel:** 01608 677346   **www.ditchley.co.uk**
**Owner:** Ditchley Foundation   **Contact:** Brigadier Christopher Galloway

The most important house by James Gibbs, with magnificent interiors by William Kent and Henry Flitcroft. For three centuries the home of the Lee family, restored in the 1930s by Ronald and Nancy (Lancaster) Tree, it was frequently used at weekends by Sir Winston Churchill during World War II.
**Location:** MAP 7:A11, OS Ref. SP391 214. 2m NE from Charlbury. 13 miles NW of Oxford.
**Open:** Visits only by prior arrangement with the Bursar, weekdays preferred.
**Admission:** £6 per person (minimum charge £50).
🅵 🅿 ✳

Chastleton House, Nr Moreton-in-Marsh

### GREAT COXWELL BARN

**Great Coxwell, Faringdon, Oxfordshire**
**Tel:** 01793 762209   **E-mail:** greatcoxwellbarn@nationaltrust.org.uk
**Owner:** The National Trust   **Contact:** Coleshill Estate Office

A 13th century monastic barn, stone built with stone tiled roof, which has an interesting timber construction.
**Location:** MAP 3:C1, OS Ref. SU269 940. 2m SW of Faringdon between A420 and B4019.
**Open:** All year: daily at reasonable hours.
**Admission:** £1. Free to NT members.
✳

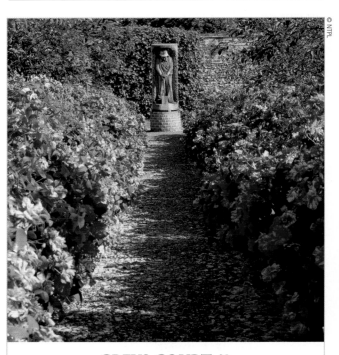

© NTPL

## GREYS COURT

### ROTHERFIELD GREYS, HENLEY-ON-THAMES, OXFORDSHIRE  RG9 4PG

**Infoline:** 01494 755564   **Tel:** 01491 628529
**E-mail:** greyscourt@nationaltrust.org.uk
**Owner:** The National Trust   **Contact:** The Custodian

Rebuilt in the 16th century and added to in the 17th, 18th and 19th centuries, the house is set amid the remains of the courtyard walls and towers of a 14th century fortified house. A Tudor donkey wheel, well-house and an ice house are still intact, and the garden contains Archbishop's Maze, inspired by Archbishop Runcie's enthronement speech in 1980.
**Location:** MAP 3:E1, OS Ref. SU725 834. 3m W of Henley-on-Thames, E of B481.
**Open:** House: 4 Apr–28 Sept: Wed–Fri, 2–5pm. Garden & Tearoom: 3 Apr–31 May, Tue–Sat. Jun, Tue–Sun & 3 Jul–29 Sept: Tue–Sat; 12 noon–5pm. All open BH Mons but closed Good Fri.
**Admission:** House & Garden: Adult £5.70, Child £2.90, Family £14.30. Garden only: £4.20, Child £2.10, Family £10.50. Coach parties must book in advance. Free to NT members.
⬇ Grounds partial. WCs. ▣ 🦮 In car park only, on leads. ▣ Contact Custodian.

### RICHARD JEFFERIES FARMHOUSE AND MUSEUM

**Marlborough Road, Coate  SN3 6AA**
**Tel:** 01793 783040   **E-mail:** R.Jefferies_Society@tiscali.co.uk
**Owner:** Swindon Borough Council

Dating from the early 18th century, the Museum was the home of Richard Jefferies who is cited by historians as an authority upon agriculture and rural life in Victorian England. The main house is a Grade II listed building.
**Location:** Adjacent to the Sun Inn on Marlborough Road A4259 close to Coate Water Country Park.
**Open:** 1st and 3rd Sundays from May to end Sept 2–5pm. 2nd Wed throughout the year. 10am–4pm. Open at other times by request.
**Admission:** Free

## KINGSTON BAGPUIZE HOUSE 🏛
### ABINGDON, OXFORDSHIRE  OX13 5AX
www.kingstonbagpuizehouse.org.uk

**Tel:** 01865 820259   **Fax:** 01865 821659   **E-mail:** virginiagrant@btinternet.com
**Owner/Contact:** Mrs Francis Grant

A family home, this beautiful house originally built in the 1660s was remodelled in the early 1700s in red brick with stone facings. It has a cantilevered staircase and panelled rooms with some good furniture and pictures. Set in mature parkland, the gardens, including shrub border and woodland garden, contain a notable collection of trees, shrubs, perennials and bulbs including snowdrops, planted for year round interest. A raised terrace walk leads to an 18th century panelled gazebo with views of the house and gardens, including a large herbaceous border and parkland. Licensed for Civil wedding ceremonies. Venue also available for wedding receptions, special events, corporate functions, product launches and filming. Facilities for small conferences.

**Location:** MAP 7:A12, OS Ref. SU408 981. In Kingston Bagpuize village, off A415 Abingdon to Witney road S of A415/A420 intersection. Abingdon 5m, Oxford 9m.
**Open:** House & Garden: 4/5, 18/19 Feb; 4/5 Mar; 1/2, 8–10 Apr; 6–8, 27–29 May; 3/4 Jun; 1/2, 15/16 Jul; 5/6, 26–28 Aug; 2/3, 16/17 Sept. New for 2007: Garden only; 1, 8, 15, 22 Feb ; 15 Mar; 19 Apr; 17 May; 21 Jun; 19 July; 16 Aug; 20 Sept. Gates open 2pm and close at 5.30pm. Last admission to house 4pm
**Admission:** House & Garden: Adult £5, Child (5–15) £2.50, (admission to house not recommended for children under 5yrs), Conc. £4.50. Gardens: £3 (child under 16yrs Free). Groups (20–80) by appointment throughout the year, prices on request.
ℹ No photography in house. ▣ Grounds. WC. ☞ Home-made cakes. Light meals for groups by appointment. 🅿 🎦 Obligatory 🔲 🔲 🔲 🔲

## MAPLEDURHAM HOUSE & WATERMILL
### MAPLEDURHAM, READING  RG4 7TR
www.mapledurham.co.uk

**Tel:** 01189 723350   **Fax:** 01189 724016   **E-mail:** enquiries@mapledurham.co.uk
**Owner:** The Mapledurham Trust     **Contact:** Mrs Lola Andrews

Late 16th century Elizabethan home of the Blount family. Original plaster ceilings, great oak staircase, fine collection of paintings and a private chapel in Strawberry Hill Gothick added in 1797. Interesting literary connections with Alexander Pope, Galsworthy's *Forsyte Saga* and Kenneth Grahame's *Wind in the Willows*. 15th century watermill fully restored producing flour and bran which is sold in the giftshop.
**Location:** MAP 3:E3, OS Ref. SU670 767. N of River Thames. 4m NW of Reading, 1½ m W of A4074.
**Open:** Easter–Sept: Sats, Suns & BHs, 2–5.30pm. Last admission 5pm. Midweek parties by arrangement only (Tue–Thur). Mapledurham Trust reserves the right to alter or amend opening times or prices without prior notification.
**Admission:** Please call 01189 723350 for details.
▣ Grounds. WCs. ☞ 🅿 🔲 Guide dogs only. 🔲 11 holiday cottages (all year). 🔲

## MILTON MANOR HOUSE
### MILTON, ABINGDON, OXFORDSHIRE  OX14 4EN

**Tel/Fax:** 01235 862321
**Owner:** Anthony Mockler-Barrett Esq     **Contact:** Alex Brakespear

Dreamily beautiful mellow brick house, traditionally designed by Inigo Jones. Celebrated Gothic library and Catholic chapel. Lived in by the family; pleasant relaxed and informal atmosphere. Park with fine old trees, stables, walled garden and woodland walk. Picnickers welcome.
**Location:** MAP 3:D1, OS Ref. SU485 924. Just off A34, village and house signposted, 9m S of Oxford, 15m N of Newbury. 3m from Abingdon and Didcot.
**Open:** Easter–Aug: BH Suns & Mons only, 27 May–10 Jun & 12–31 Aug: daily, 2–5pm. Guided tours of house: 2pm, 3pm & 4pm. For weddings/events etc. please write to the Administrator. Groups by arrangement throughout the year.
**Admission:** House & Gardens: Adult £5, Child £2.50. Garden only: Adult £3, Child £1.50. For group bookings only please telephone 01235 831287.
▣ Grounds. 🎦 Obligatory. 🅿 Free. 🔲 Guide dogs only. 🔲 🔲

## MINSTER LOVELL HALL & DOVECOTE ⌗

**Witney, Oxfordshire**
**Tel:** 01424 775705   **www.english-heritage.org.uk/visits**
**Owner:** English Heritage   **Contact:** 1066 Battle Abbey
The ruins of Lord Lovell's 15th century manor house stand in a lovely setting on the banks of the River Windrush.
**Location:** MAP 6:P11, OS Ref. SP324 114. Adjacent to Minster Lovell Church, ½mile NE of village. 3 miles W of Witney off A40.
**Open:** Any reasonable time. Dovecote – exterior only.
**Admission:** Free.
🐕 On leads. ✸

## PRIORY COTTAGES ✶

**1 Mill Street, Steventon, Abingdon, Oxfordshire  OX13 6SP**
**Tel:** 01793 762209
**Owner:** The National Trust   **Contact:** Coleshill Estate Office
Former monastic buildings, converted into two houses. South Cottage contains the Great Hall of the original priory.
**Location:** MAP 3:D1, OS Ref. SU466 914. 4m S of Abingdon, on B4017 off A34 at Abingdon West or Milton interchange on corner of The Causeway and Mill Street, entrance in Mill Street.
**Open:** The Great Hall in South Cottage only: 4 Apr–26 Sept: Wed, 2–6pm, by written appointment with the tenant.
**Admission:** Adult £1.40, Child 70p, Family £3.50. Free to NT members.

# ROUSHAM HOUSE
### Nr STEEPLE ASTON, BICESTER, OXFORDSHIRE  OX25 4QX
www.rousham.org

**Tel:** 01869 347110 / 07860 360407
**Owner/Contact:** Charles Cottrell-Dormer Esq
Rousham represents the first stage of English landscape design and remains almost as William Kent (1685–1748) left it. One of the few gardens of this date to have escaped alteration. Includes Venus' Vale, Townesend's Building, seven-arched Praeneste, Temple of the Mill and a sham ruin known as the 'Eyecatcher'. The house was built in 1635 by Sir Robert Dormer. Excellent location for fashion, advertising, photography etc.

**Location:** MAP 7:A10, OS Ref. SP477 242. E of A4260, 12m N of Oxford, S of B4030, 7m W of Bicester.
**Open:** Garden: All year: daily, 10am–4.30pm. House: Pre-booked groups, May–Sept.
**Admission:** Garden: £4. House: £4. No children under 15yrs.
♿ Partial. P 🐕 ✸

## RYCOTE CHAPEL ⌗

**Rycote, Oxfordshire**
**Tel:** 01844 210210   **www.english-heritage.org.uk/visits**
**Owner:** English Heritage   **Contact:** Mr Taylor - Rycote Building Charitable Foundation
A 15th century chapel with exquisitely carved and painted woodwork. It has many intriguing features, including two roofed pews and a musicians' gallery.
**Location:** MAP 7:B12, OS165 Ref. SP667 046. 3 miles SW of Thame, off A329. 1½ miles NE of M40/J7.
**Open:** 1 Apr–30 Sept: Fri–Sun & BHs, 2–6pm. Times may change at short notice, please telephone for details.
**Admission:** Adult £3.50, Child £1.50, Conc. £2.50. Subject to change.
P 🐕

## STONOR 📖

*See page 154 for full page entry.*

## SWALCLIFFE BARN

**Swalcliffe Village, Banbury, Oxfordshire**
**Tel:** 01295 788278   **Contact:** Jeffrey Demmar
15th century half cruck barn, houses agricultural and trade vehicles which are part of the Oxford County Museum Services Collection. Exhibition of 2500 years' of Swalcliffe history.
**Location:** MAP 7:A10, OS Ref. SP378 378. 6m W of Banbury Cross on B4035.
**Open:** Easter–end Oct: Suns & BHs, 2–5pm.
**Admission:** Free.

# THE COLLEGES OF OXFORD UNIVERSITY

**For further details contact:**
Oxford Information Centre,
15–16 Broad Street, Oxford OX1 3AS
Tel: +44 (0)1865 726871
Email: tic@oxford.gov.uk
Fax: +44 (0)1865 240261
www.visitoxford.org

**All Souls' College**
High Street
**Tel:** 01865 279379
**Founder:** Archbishop Henry Chichele 1438
**Open:** Mon–Fri, 2–4pm
(4.30pm in summer)

**Balliol College**
Broad Street
**Tel:** 01865 277777
**Founder:** John de Balliol 1263
**Open:** Daily, 2–5pm

**Brasenose College**
Radcliffe Square
**Tel:** 01865 277830
**Founder:** William Smythe,
Bishop of Lincoln 1509
**Open:** Daily, 10–11.30am (tour groups only) & 2–4pm (5pm in summer)

**Christ Church**
St. Aldates
**Tel:** 01865 286573
**Founder:** Cardinal Wolsey/Henry VIII 1546
**Open:** Mon–Sat, 9am–5.30pm;
Sun, 1–5.30pm (last adm 4.30pm)

**Corpus Christi College**
Merton Street
**Tel:** 01865 276700
**Founder:** Bishop Richard Fox 1517
**Open:** Daily, 1.30–4.30pm

**Exeter College**
Turl Street
**Tel:** 01865 279600
**Founder:** Bishop Stapleden of Exeter 1314
**Open:** Daily, Term time 2–5pm.

**Green College**
Woodstock Road
**Tel:** 01865 274770
**Founder:** Dr Cecil Green 1979
**Open:** By appointment only.

**Harris Manchester College**
Mansfield Road
**Tel:** 01865 271011
**Founder:** Lord Harris of Peckham 1996
**Open:** Chapel only: Mon–Fri,
8.30am–5.30pm. Sat, 9am–12 noon.

**Hertford College**
Catte Street
**Tel:** 01865 279400
**Founder:** TC Baring MP 1740
**Open:** Daily, 10am–noon & 2pm–dusk.

**Jesus College**
Turl Street
**Tel:** 01865 279700
**Founder:** Dr Hugh Price
(Queen Elizabeth I) 1571
**Open:** Daily, 2–4.30pm

**Keble College**
Parks Road
**Tel:** 01865 272727
**Founder:** Public money 1870
**Open:** Daily, 2–5pm

**Kellogg College**
Wellington Square
**Tel:** 01865 270383
**Founder:** Kellogg Foundation 1990
**Open:** Mon–Fri, 9am–5pm

**Lady Margaret Hall**
Norham Gardens
**Tel:** 01865 274300
**Founder:** Dame Elizabeth Wordsworth 1878
**Open:** Gardens: 10am–5pm

**Linacre College**
St Cross Road
**Tel:** 01865 271650
**Founder:** Oxford University 1962
**Open:** By appointment only.

**Lincoln College**
Turl Street
**Tel:** 01865 279800
**Founder:** Bishop Richard Fleming of Lincoln 1427
**Open:** Mon–Sat, 2–5pm; Sun, 11am–5pm

**Magdalen College**
High Street
**Tel:** 01865 276000
**Founder:** William of Waynefleete 1458
**Open:** Oct–Jun: 1- 6pm/dusk (whichever is the earlier) and Jul–Sept: 12 noon–6pm

**Mansfield College**
Mansfield Road
**Tel:** 01865 270999
**Founder:** Free Churches 1995
**Open:** Mon–Fri, 9am–5pm.

**Merton College**
Merton Street
**Tel:** 01865 276310
**Founder:** Walter de Merton 1264
**Open:** Mon–Fri, 2–4pm; Sat & Sun, 10am–4pm

**New College**
New College Lane
**Tel:** 01865 279555
**Founder:** William of Wykeham, Bishop of Winchester 1379
**Open:** Daily, 11am–5pm (summer); 2–4pm (winter)

**Nuffield College**
New Road
**Tel:** 01865 278500
**Founder:** William Morris (Lord Nuffield) 1937
**Open:** Daily, 9am–5pm.

**Oriel College**
Oriel Square
**Tel:** 01865 276555
**Founder:** Edward II/Adam de Brome 1326
**Open:** Daily, 1–4pm (by arrangement with TIC)

**Pembroke College**
St Aldates
**Tel:** 01865 276444
**Founder:** James I 1624
**Open:** By appointment only.

**The Queen's College**
High Street
**Tel:** 01865 279120
**Founder:** Robert de Eglesfield 1341
**Open:** By prior appointment through the Tourist Information Office.

**Somerville College**
Graduate House, Woodstock Road
**Tel:** 01865 270600
**Founder:** Association for the Education of Women 1879
**Open:** 2–5.30pm

**St. Anne's College**
56 Woodstock Road
**Tel:** 01865 274800
**Founder:** Association for the Education of Women 1878
**Open:** 9am–5pm

**St. Antony's College**
62 Woodstock Road
**Tel:** 01865 284700
**Founder:** M. Antonin Bess 1948
Open: By appointment only.

**St. Catherine's College**
Manor Road
**Tel:** 01865 271700
**Founder:** Oxford University 1964
**Open:** 9am–5pm

**St. Cross College**
Not open to the public.

**St. Edmund Hall**
Queens Lane
**Tel:** 01865 279000
**Founder:** St. Edmund Riche of Abingdon c.1278
**Open:** Daily, daylight hours.

**St. Hilda's College**
Cowley Place
**Tel:** 01865 276884
**Founder:** Miss Dorothea Beale 1893
**Open:** Daily, 2–5pm

**St. Hugh's College**
St. Margarets Road
**Tel:** 01865 274900
**Founder:** Dame Elizabeth Wordsworth 1886
**Open:** 10am–4pm

**St. John's College**
St. Giles
**Tel:** 01865 277300
**Founder:** Sir Thomas White 1555
**Open:** 1–5pm (or dusk)

**St. Peter's College**
New Inn Hall Street
**Tel:** 01865 278900
**Founder:** Rev. Christopher Charvasse 1928
**Open:** 10am–dusk

**Trinity College**
Broad Street
**Tel:** 01865 279900
**Founder:** Sir Thomas Pope 1554–5
**Open:** Mon–Fri 10am–noon and 2–4pm. Sat & Sun in term, 2–4pm; Sat & Sun in vacation 10am–noon and 2–4pm.

**University College**
High Street
**Tel:** 01865 276602
**Founder:** Archdeacon William of Durham 1249
**Open:** Contact College for details.

**Wadham College**
Parks Road
**Tel:** 01865 277900
**Founder:** Nicholas & Dorothy Wadham 1610
**Open:** Term time: daily, 1–4.15pm. Vacation: daily, 10.30–11.45am & 1–4.15pm.

**Wolfson College**
Linton Road
**Tel:** 01865 274100
**Founder:** Oxford University 1966
**Open:** Daylight hours.

**Worcester College**
Worcester Street
**Tel:** 01865 278300
**Founder:** Sir Thomas Cookes 1714
**Open:** Daily, 2–5pm.

Christchurch College, Oxford

This information is intended only as a guide. Times are subject to change due to functions, examinations, conferences, holidays, etc. You are advised to check in advance opening times and admission charges which may apply at some colleges, and at certain times of the year. Visitors wishing to gain admittance to the Colleges (meaning the Courts, not to the staircases and students' rooms) are advised to contact the Tourist Information Office. It should be noted that Halls normally close for lunch (12 noon–2pm) and many are not open during the afternoon. Chapels may be closed during services. Libraries are not normally open, and Gardens do not usually include the Fellows' garden. Visitors, and especially guided groups, should always call on the Porters Lodge first. Groups should always book in advance. Dogs, except guide dogs are not allowed in any colleges.

■ **Owner**
The National Trust

■ **Contact**
The Property Manager
Clandon Park &
Hatchlands Park
East Clandon
Guildford
Surrey GU4 7RT
**Tel:** 01483 222482
**Fax:** 01483 223176
**E-mail:** hatchlands@
nationaltrust.org.uk

■ **Location**
**MAP 19:A11**
**Clandon**
**OS Ref. TQ042 512**
At West Clandon
on the A247,
3m E of Guildford.

**Rail:** Clandon BR 1m.

**Hatchlands**
**OS Ref. TQ063 516**
E of East Clandon
on the A246 Guildford–
Leatherhead road.

**Rail:** Clandon BR
2½ m, Horsley 3m.

■ **Opening Times**
**Clandon – House**
18 March–28 October
Tue–Thur, Suns &
BH Mons, Good Fri
& Easter Sat
11am–4.30pm.

**Garden**
As house. 11am–5pm.

**Museum**
As house
12 noon–5pm.

**Hatchlands – House**
1 April–28 October
Tue–Thur,
Suns & BH Mon,
Fris in August.
2–5.30pm.

**Park Walks**
1 April–28 October:
Daily 11am–6pm.

■ ***Admission**
**Clandon**
House/Grounds  £7.20
Child  £3.60
Family  £18.00

Pre-booked Groups
Adult  £5.60

**Hatchlands**
House/Grounds  £6.60
Child  £3.30
Family  £17.00

Park Walks only  £3.30
Child  £1.70

Pre-booked Groups
Adult  £5.10

**Combined ticket**
Adult  £10.00
Child  £5.00
Family  £25.00

*includes a voluntary
donation but visitors can
choose to pay the standard
prices displayed at the
property and on the website.

■ **Conference/Function**

| ROOM | SIZE | MAX CAPACITY |
|---|---|---|
| Marble Hall Clandon Pk | 40' x 40' | 160 seated 200 standing |

# CLANDON PARK &
# HATCHLANDS PARK 🌿

www.nationaltrust.org.uk/clandonpark

Clandon Park & Hatchlands Park were built during the 18th century and are set amidst beautiful grounds. They are two of England's most outstanding country houses and are only five minutes' drive apart.

**Clandon Park** is a grand Palladian Mansion, built c1730 for the 2nd Lord Onslow by the Venetian architect Giacomo Leoni. Clandon's interior is the most complete of his work to survive and is notable for its magnificent two-storied, white Marble Hall.

The Onslows have been active in the country's political history, being the only family ever to have produced three Speakers of the House of Commons. The last of these, Arthur Onslow, held the post from 1727 for over 30 years. Activity was not restricted to England; at the end of the 19th century the 4th Earl of Onslow served as Governor of New Zealand, whereupon the Maori meeting house came to be in the gardens at Clandon Park.

There is also an intimate sunken Dutch garden, at its best in May and June and a stunning bulb field flowering in spring.

Displayed inside the house is a superb collection of 18th century furniture, textiles and one of the finest collections of porcelain, including Meissen *Commedia Dell' Arte* figures.

**Hatchlands Park** was built in 1756 for Admiral Boscawen, hero of the Battle of Louisburg, and contains the earliest recorded decorations in an English country house by Robert Adam, whose ceilings appropriately feature nautical motifs.

The rooms are hung with the Cobbe Collection of Old Master paintings and portraits. The house is also home to the Cobbe Collection of keyboard instruments, the world's largest group of early keyboard instruments owned or played by famous composers such as Purcell, JC Bach, Mozart, Liszt, Chopin, Mahler and Elgar.

Hatchlands is set in a beautiful 430-acre Repton park, with a variety of way-marked walks offering vistas of open parkland and idyllic views of the house. The woodlands are a haven for wildlife and there is a stunning Bluebell wood in May.

There are frequent concerts on the instruments on the collection (for more details please contact: The Cobbe Collection Trust, 01483 211474, www.cobbecollection.co.uk).

ℹ️ No photography.

🛍️ For Clandon weddings and receptions tel: 01483 222502.

♿ WCs. Hatchlands suitable. Clandon please tel for details.

🍴 Hatchlands: 01483 211120.

🍽️ Licensed. Clandon: 01483 222502.

🚶 Clandon – by arrangement.

🎒 Children's quizzes available.

🅿️ Hatchlands Parkland only.

🐕 Clandon only.

🔔 Tel: 01483 222482.

# THE COBBE COLLECTION AT HATCHLANDS ❧

www.cobbecollection.co.uk

The Cobbe Collections are set in sumptuous rooms designed by Robert Adam. The house, given to the National Trust with few contents, has been let to Mr & Mrs Alec Cobbe since 1987 and is lived in as a family home.

The resulting arrangement of pictures, furniture, *objéts d'art* and the celebrated collection of keyboards, spanning 400 years and formerly belonging to some of the greatest names of classical music, has been called 'one of the most beautiful musical museums in the world'. The family art collection, formed initially in the 18th century, includes pictures by Allori, Bernini, Guercino, Poussin, Van Dyck, Gainsborough, Zoffany and many others.

Recently identified pictures on view among the family portraits are the most youthful picture of Shakespeare's friend and patron, Henry Wriothesley, 3rd Earl of Southampton and what may be Southampton's portrait of Shakespeare himself.

The instruments in the collection, all in playing order, are used in lunchtime recitals on Wednesdays, master classes and evening concerts and tours from April to July and in October, giving an opportunity to hear the sounds of instruments played by Purcell, JC Bach, Mozart, Beethoven, Chopin, Liszt and Mahler.

■ **Owner**
The National Trust

■ **Contact**
Cobbe Collection Trust
Hatchlands Park
East Clandon
Guildford
Surrey GU4 7RT

**Tel:** 01483 211474
**E-mail:** enquiries@
cobbecollection.co.uk

■ **Location**
**MAP 19:A11**
**OS Ref. TQ063 516**
E of East Clandon, N of A246 Guildford to Leatherhead road.

■ **Opening Times**
**Hatchlands – House**
1 April–28 October
Tue–Thur,
Suns & BH Mons,
Fri in August.
2–5.30pm.

**Park Walks**
1 April–28 October:
Daily 11am–6pm.

■ **\*Admission**
**Hatchlands**
| | |
|---|---|
| House/Grounds | £6.60 |
| Child | £3.30 |
| Family | £17.00 |
| Park Walks only | £3.30 |
| Child | £1.70 |
| Pre-Booked Groups | |
| Adult | £5.10 |

**Combined ticket Clandon/Hatchlands**
| | |
|---|---|
| Adult | £10.00 |
| Child | £5.00 |
| Family | £25.00 |

\*includes a voluntary donation but visitors can choose to pay the standard prices displayed at the property and on the website.

 Suitable. WCs.

 Licensed. No booking required, except for groups, tel: 01483 222502.

 Children's quizzes.

 Dogs welcome in Parkland only.

01483 222482.

*Edward Elgar's inscription on the soundboard of the square piano by John Broadwood & Sons, London, 1844, with the names of some of the works he composed upon it. These include 'Sea Pictures', 'Caractacus' and 'The Dream of Gerontius'. (The piano is the property of the Royal Academy of Music, on permanent loan to the Cobbe Collection Trust.)*

## ■ Owner

Mr Michael
More-Molyneux

## ■ Contact

Sue Grant
Events Office
Loseley Park
Guildford
Surrey  GU3 1HS

**Tel:** 01483 304440
**Tel Events:**
01483 405119/120
**Fax:** 01483 302036
**E-mail:** enquiries
@loseley-park.com

## ■ Location

**MAP 3:G3**
**OS Ref. SU975 471**

30m SW of London, leave
A3 S of Guildford on to
B3000. Signposted.

**Bus:** 1¼m from House.

**Rail:** Farncombe 1½m,
Guildford 2m,
Godalming 3m.

**Air:** Heathrow 30m,
Gatwick 30m.

## ■ Opening Times

**Summer**
**Garden, Shop &**
**Tearoom**
May–September
Tues–Sun & BH Mons
in May & Aug,
11am–5pm.

**Loseley House**
(guided tours)
May–Aug
Tues–Thurs, Suns &
BH Mons in May & Aug,
1–5pm.

**Lunchtime Restaurant**
June–August: Tues–Thurs,
Sat, Sun.
12 noon–2.30pm.

**All Year (Private Hire)**
Tithe Barn, Chestnut
Lodge, House, Walled
Garden and Grounds. Civil
ceremonies and receptions.
Off-road 4x4 course.

## ■ Admission

**House & Gardens**
| | |
|---|---|
| Adult | £7.00 |
| Child (5–16yrs) | £3.50 |
| Conc. | £6.50 |
| Child (under 5yrs) | Free |
| Family (2 + 3) | £17.50 |

Booked Groups (10+)
| | |
|---|---|
| Adult | £6.00 |
| Child (5–16yrs) | £3.00 |
| Garden tours | £2.50pp |

**Garden & Grounds only**
| | |
|---|---|
| Adult | £4.00 |
| Child (5–16yrs) | £2.00 |
| Conc. | £3.50 |
| Family (2 + 3) | £10.00 |

Booked Groups (10+)
| | |
|---|---|
| Adult | £3.00 |
| Child (5–16yrs) | £1.50 |
| Garden tours | £2.50 pp |

## Conference/Function

| ROOM | SIZE | MAX CAPACITY |
|---|---|---|
| Tithe Barn | 100' x 18' | 180 |
| Marquee sites available | | 400 |
| Great Hall | 70' x 40' | 80 |
| Drawing Rm | 40' x 30' | 50 |
| Chestnut Ldg | 12.8' x 6.1' | 50 |

# LOSELEY PARK 🏛

www.loseley-park.com

Loseley Park, built in 1562 by Sir William More to entertain Queen Elizabeth I, is a fine example of Elizabethan architecture – its mellow stone brought from the ruins of Waverley Abbey now over 850 years old. The house is set amid magnificent parkland grazed by the Loseley Jersey herd. Many visitors comment on the very friendly atmosphere of the house. It is a country house, the family home of descendants of the builder.

Furniture has been acquired by the family and includes an early 16th century Wrangelschrank beautifully inlaid with many different woods, a Queen Anne cabinet, Georgian armchairs and settee, a Hepplewhite four-poster bed and King George IV's coronation chair. The King's bedroom has Oudenarde tapestry and a carpet commemorating James I's visit. Also many fine paintings and portraits of family members and a beautiful and unique chimney piece carved out of a single piece of chalk to a design by Holbein.

A Christian Cancer Help Centre meets twice monthly. Loseley Park is available for corporate and private hire, including Civil wedding ceremonies and receptions.

**Garden**

A magnificent Cedar of Lebanon presides over the front lawn. Parkland adjoins the lawn and a small lake adds to the beauty of Front Park. Walled Garden: Based on a Gertrude Jekyll design, the five gardens exist each with their own theme and character, making up the whole. These include the award-winning rose garden containing over 1,000 bushes, a magnificent vine walk, colourful fruit and flower garden and the serene white garden. Other features include an organic vegetable garden and moat walk. HDRA Seed Library plants.

ℹ️ Lakeside walk. Picnic area. Chapel. Hire of gardens and grounds for corporate and private events. All group visits to be booked in advance. Group garden tours available. Lectures on history of house and contents by arrangement.

🛒

🍴 Corporate and private hire for special functions, conferences, meetings, wedding receptions. Marquees for hire.

♿ May alight at entrance to property. Access to all areas except house first floor. WCs.

☕ Courtyard Tea Room.

🍴 Lunchtime restaurant.

🚶 House tour obligatory: 40 mins. Group Garden tours available.

🅿 150 cars, 6 coaches. Summer overflow car park.

🐕 Guide dogs only.

🔔

❄️

🎭 Tel for details.

# PAINSHILL PARK

### www.painshill.co.uk

A unique award winning restoration of England's 18th century heritage. Painshill Park is one of the most important parks in Europe. Within its 160 acres, its Hamilton Landscapes are a work of art that influenced the future of England's countryside and culture. Between 1738 and 1773 the Hon Charles Hamilton transformed barren heathland into a sequence of subtle and surprising vistas. Around the 14 acre serpentine lake, he assembled a series of carefully designed views known as the Hamilton Landscapes. The visitor moves from scene to scene; past the vineyard to an evergreen amphitheatre and on to the Gothic Temple, from the magical crystal grotto to a ruined Mausoleum, from a wild wood to the colourful flower beds that surround the site of the Temple of Bacchus. Following years of dereliction the Landscapes have been restored to their original pre-eminence, winning the Europa Nostra Medal for exemplary restoration. Available for corporate and private hire, location filming, wedding receptions, children's parties etc.

Full Educational Programme for all – Painshill Park's Discovery Centre offers a full programme of exciting activities for families, friends and all visitors to the park. School students can learn as they explore the Nature, Art, History and Science that is unique to this 18th century landscape. A programme of talks is available throughout the year or the Ambassador Speakers are available to visit groups. Group tours of 10+ can be arranged with optional guided tour (pre-booking is required).

**Discover American Roots at Painshill Park.** The American Roots Exhibition is a major horticultural exhibition recreating the 18th century exchange of plants between Europe and America. Over 250 years on, retrace the journey of these seeds from American wilds to English landscapes. Painshill Park has been awarded Full Collection Status for the John Bartram Heritage Plant Collection by the National Council for the Conservation of Plants and Gardens. This is the first award of its kind.

For more information please visit www.painshill.co.uk or telephone 01932 584286 for special events.

## Owner
Painshill Park Trust

## Contact
Visitor Manager
Painshill Park
Portsmouth Road
Cobham
Surrey  KT11 1JE

**Tel:** 01932 868113
**Fax:** 01932 868001
**E-mail:**
info@painshill.co.uk
education@painshill.co.uk

## Location
**MAP 19:B10**
**OS Ref. TQ099 605**

M25/J10 to London.
W of Cobham on A245.
Entrance 200 yds E of
A245/A307 roundabout.

## Opening Times
All year
March–October:
10.30am–6pm or dusk
(last entry 4.30pm),
November–February:
10.30am–4pm or dusk
(last entry 3pm)
Closed Christmas Day
and Boxing Day

## Admission
| | |
|---|---|
| Adult | £6.60 |
| Child (5–16) | £3.85 |
| under 5s Free, | |
| Conc. | £5.80 |
| Family (2 adults, | |
| 4 children) | £22.00 |

Season Tickets available

| | |
|---|---|
| Pre-booked | |
| groups (10+) | £5.80 |

(optional guided tour
£1.00 per person)

The Grotto is open on
Saturdays, Sundays
and BHs
11.30am–4.30pm in
summer and from
11.30am–3.30pm in
winter or by prior
appointment.

Marquee site.

Licensed.

By arrangement.

P

On leads,
restrictions apply.

## BOX HILL 🌿

**The Old Fort, Box Hill Road, Box Hill, Tadworth KT20 7LB**
**Tel:** 01306 885502 **Fax:** 01306 875030 **E-mail:** boxhill@nationaltrust.org.uk
**www.nationaltrust.org.uk/northdowns**
**Owner:** The National Trust **Contact:** Head Warden
An outstanding area of woodland and chalk downland with magnificent views across the weald. Long famous as a destination for naturalists and excursions from London.
**Location:** MAP 19:C11, OS Ref. TQ171 519. 1m N of Dorking, 1½m S of Leatherhead on A24.
**Open:** Shop, Information Centre and Servery: All year, daily (except 25/26 Dec & 1 Jan), 11–5pm or dusk.
**Admission:** Countryside: Free. Car/coach park £3, NT members Free.
✽

## CLANDON PARK & HATCHLANDS PARK 🌿

*See page 160 for full page entry.*

Titsey Place & Gardens, Oxted

NT Photographic Library

NTPL / John Bethell

## CLAREMONT LANDSCAPE GARDEN 🌿

### PORTSMOUTH ROAD, ESHER, SURREY KT10 9JG

www.nationaltrust.org.uk/claremont

**Tel:** 01372 467806 **Fax:** 01372 476420 **E-mail:** claremont@nationaltrust.org.uk
**Owner:** The National Trust **Contact:** The Property Manager
One of the earliest surviving English landscape gardens, restored to its former glory. Begun by Sir John Vanbrugh and Charles Bridgeman before 1720, the garden was extended and naturalised by William Kent. 'Capability' Brown also made improvements. Features include a lake, island with pavilion, grotto, turf amphitheatre, viewpoints and avenues.

**Location:** MAP 19:B9, OS Ref. TQ128 632. On S edge of Esher, on E side of A307 (no access from Esher bypass).
**Open:** Jan–end Mar, Nov–end Dec: daily except Mons: 10am–5pm or sunset if earlier. Apr–end Oct: daily: 10am–6pm. NB: 19 Jul: closes 4pm. Closed 25 Dec.
**Admission:** Adult £5.60, Child £2.80. Family (2+2) £14. Groups (15+), Adult £4.50, Child £2.25. £1 tearoom voucher given if arriving by public transport. Coach groups must book; no coach groups on Suns.
⬚ 🅰 Limited. WC. ◼ ▣ No dogs (Apr–Oct). ▣

## THE COBBE COLLECTION 🌿 AT HATCHLANDS

*See page 161 for full page entry*

## FARNHAM CASTLE

**Farnham, Surrey GU9 0AG**
**Tel:** 01252 721194 **Fax:** 01252 711283 **E-mail:** conf@farnhamcastle.com
**Owner:** The Church Commissioners **Contact:** Farnham Castle
Bishop's Palace built in Norman times by Henry of Blois. Tudor and Jacobean additions.
**Location:** MAP 3:F3, OS Ref. SU839 474. ½m N of Farnham town centre on A287.
**Open:** All year: Weds, 2–4pm except Christmas & New Year.
**Admission:** Adult £2.50, Child/Conc £1.50.

## FARNHAM CASTLE KEEP ⌗

**Castle Hill, Farnham, Surrey GU6 0AG**
**Tel:** 01252 713393 **www.english-heritage.org.uk/visits**
**Owner:** English Heritage **Contact:** Visitor Operations Team
Used as a fortified manor by the medieval Bishops of Winchester, this motte and bailey castle has been in continuous occupation since the 12th century. You can visit the large shell-keep enclosing a mound in which are massive foundations of a Norman tower.
**Location:** MAP 3:F3, OS Ref. SU839 474. ½m N of Farnham town centre on A287.
**Open:** 6–9 Apr, May BHs, 1 Jul–31 Aug: Fri–Sun, 1–5pm.
**Admission:** Adult £2.90, Child £1.50, Conc. £2.20. EH Members Free.
⬚ 🅰 Ground floor & grounds. 🅿 ▣ In grounds, on leads.

## GODDARDS

**Abinger Common, Dorking, Surrey  RH5 6TH**
**Tel:** 01628 825925  **www.landmarktrust.org.uk**
**Owner:** The Lutyens Trust, leased to The Landmark Trust  **Contact:** The Landmark Trust
Built by Sir Edwin Lutyens in 1898–1900 and enlarged by him in 1910. Garden by Gertrude Jekyll. Given to the Lutyens Trust in 1991 and now managed and maintained by the Landmark Trust, which let buildings for self-catering holidays. The whole house, apart from the library, is available for holidays. Full details of Goddards and 184 other historic buildings available for holidays are featured in The Landmark Handbook (price £11.50 refundable against booking).
**Location:** MAP 19:B12, OS Ref. TQ120 450. 4½ m SW of Dorking on the village green in Abinger Common. Signposted Abinger Common, Friday Street and Leith Hill from A25.
**Open:** Available for holidays for up to 12 people. Other visits strictly by appointment. Must be booked in advance, including parking, which is very limited. Visits booked for Weds afternoons from the Wed after Easter until the last Wed of Oct, between 2.30–5pm. Only those with pre-booked tickets will be admitted.
**Admission:** £3. Tickets available from Mrs Baker on 01306 730871, Mon–Fri, 9am & 6pm. Visitors will have access to part of the garden and house only.
🏠

© NT Photographic Library

Polesdon Lacey, Nr Dorking

## GREAT FOSTERS

**Stroude Road, Egham, Surrey  TW20 9UR**
**Tel:** 01784 433822  **Fax:** 01784 472455  **E-mail:** enquiries@greatfosters.co.uk
**www.greatfosters.co.uk**
**Owner:** The Sutcliffe family  **Contact:** Amanda Dougans
Grade II listed garden. Laid out in 1918 by W H Romaine-Walker in partnership with G H Jenkins, incorporating earlier features. The site covers 50 acres and is associated with a 16th century country house, reputed to be a former royal hunting lodge and converted into an hotel by the owners in 1931. The main formal garden is surrounded on three sides by a moat, thought to be of medieval origin, and is modelled on the pattern of a Persian carpet. The garden also includes an amphitheatre, lake and a sunken rose garden.
**Location:** MAP 3:G2, OS Ref. TQ015 694. M25 J/13, follow signs to Egham. Under motorway bridge, first left at roundabout (The Avenue). Left at the mini roundabout into Vicarage Rd. Right at next roundabout. Over M25, left into Stroude Rd. 500 yds on left.
**Open:** All year.
**Admission:** Free.
🚻 ♿ Partial. WC. 🍴 🍽 Licensed. 🅿 ♿ Guide dogs only. 🖼 🏠 ❄

## GUILDFORD HOUSE GALLERY

**155 High Street, Guildford, Surrey  GU1 3AJ**
**Tel/Fax:** 01483 444742 (Guildford Borough Council)  **www.guildfordhouse.co.uk**
**Owner/Contact:** Guildford Borough Council
A beautifully restored 17th century town house with a number of original features including a finely carved staircase, panelled rooms and decorative plaster ceilings. A varied temporary exhibition programme including paintings, photography and craft work. Exhibition and events leaflet available. Lecture and workshop programme. Details on application.
**Location:** MAP 3:G3, OS Ref. SU996 494. Central Guildford on High Street.
**Open:** All year, Tue–Sat, 10am–4.45pm.
**Admission:** Free.
🖼 🍴 🍽 🎨 Public car park nearby. 🅿 ♿ Guide dogs only. ❄ 🏴

©HRP 2007

# HAMPTON COURT PALACE

## HAMPTON COURT PALACE, SURREY  KT8 9AU

www.hrp.org.uk

**Tel:** Recorded info: 0870 752 7777  **All other enquiries:** 0870 751 5175
**Venue Hire and Corporate Hospitailty:** 0870 751 5182
**Owner/Contact:** Historic Royal Palaces
The flamboyant Henry VIII is most associated with this majestic Palace, which he extended and developed in grand style after acquiring it from Cardinal Wolsey in the 1520s. He lavished money on fabulous tapestries and paintings, housed and fed a huge court and pursued a succession of wives, political power and domination over Rome. The Tudor buildings which remain are among the most important in exisitence, but the elegance and romance of the Palace owes much to the elegant Baroque buildings commissioned by William and Mary at the end of the 17th century. The Palace is set in 60 acres of gardens, which include the famous Maze and awe-inspiring Great Vine.

**Location:** MAP 19:B9, OS Ref. TQ155 686. From M25/J15 and A312, or M25/J12 and A308, or M25/J10 and A307. Rail: From London Waterloo direct to Hampton Court (32 mins).
**Open:** Mar–Oct: Daily, 10am–6pm (last admission 5.15pm). Nov–Feb: Daily, 10am–4.30pm (last admission 3.45pm). Closed 24–26 Dec.
**Admission:** Telephone Information Line for admission prices: 0870 752 7777. Advance Ticket Sales:0870 753 7777. Group Bookings 0870 7517070, Quote Hudson's.
ℹ Information Centre. No photography indoors. 🖼 🚻
♿ Motorised buggies available at main entrance. WCs. 🍴 🍽 🎨 🖼
🅿 Ample for cars, coach parking nearby. 🍽 Rates on request 0870 7515190.
♿ In grounds, on leads. Guide dogs only in Palace. ❄ 🏴

## KEW GARDENS

**Kew, Richmond, Surrey TW9 3AB**
**Tel:** 020 8332 5655　**Fax:** 020 8332 5610　**E-mail:** info@kew.org　**www.kew.org**
**Contact:** Visitor Information

Kew Gardens is a World Heritage Site. It is a mixture of stunning vistas, magnificent glasshouses and beautiful landscapes beside the River Thames. This once Royal residence represents nearly 250 years of historical gardens and today its 300 acres are home to over 40,000 types of plants from rainforest to desert. There is always something to see … as the seasons change so does Kew.

**Location:** MAP 19:C7, OS Ref. TQ188 776. A307. Junc. A307 & A205 (1m Chiswick roundabout M4).

**Open:** All year: daily (except 24/25 Dec) from 9.30am. Closing time varies according to the season. Please telephone for further information.

**Admission:** Apr–Oct £11.75. 1 Nov–31 Mar £9.50. Concessions available. Child (under 17) Free. Discounts for groups (10+). School groups: Free. (2006 prices.)

🖹 🚻 ♿ 🏛 Licensed. **P** Limited. ▣ 🐕 Guide dogs only. 🔺 ❋

## KEW PALACE

**Kew Gardens, Kew, Richmond, Surrey TW9 3AB**
**Tel:** Group Bookings 020 8332 5648　**E-mail:** info@kew.org　**www:kew.org**
**Contact:** Visitor Information 020 8332 5655

Kew Palace and Queen Charlotte's Cottage. The most intimate of the five royal palaces, Kew was built as a private house but became a royal residence between 1728 and 1818. Both the palace and the nearby Queen Charlotte's cottage, built in 1770, are most closely associated with King George III and his family.

**Location:** MAP 19:C7, OS Ref. TQ188 776.193. A307. Junc A307 & A205 (1m Chiswick roundabout M4).

**Open:** 1 May–30 Sept: daily, 9.45am–5pm.

**Admission:** By joint ticket purchased through Kew Gardens.

## LEITH HILL 🌿

**Coldharbour, Surrey**
**Tel:** 01306 711777　**Fax:** 01306 712153　**www.nationaltrust.org.uk/northdowns**
**Owner:** The National Trust　**Contact:** Head Warden

The highest point in south-east England, crowned by an 18th century Gothic tower, from which there are magnificent views. The surrounding woodland contains ancient stands of hazel and oak, and there is a colourful display of rhododendrons in May–Jun.

**Location:** MAP 19:B12, OS Ref. TQ139 432. 1m SW of Coldharbour A29/B2126.

**Open:** Tower: 2 Mar–28 Oct: Fri–Sun, and Weds in Aug, 10am–5pm or dusk if earlier. 3 Nov–early Mar 2008: Sats & Suns, 10am–3.30pm. Open all BHs (closed 25 Dec). Wood & Estate: All year: daily.

**Admission:** Tower: £1, Child 50p. Rhododendron Wood: £2 per car. (2 circular nature trails with leaflet.)

ℹ️ No vehicular access to summit. ♿ Partial. ▣ When Tower open. 🅵 Guided walks. **P** Parking at foot of hill, ½m walk from Tower. 🐕 Not in picnic area or Tower. ❋

**LOSELEY PARK** 🏛　　*See page 162 for full page entry.*

## OAKHURST COTTAGE 🌿

### HAMBLEDON, GODALMING, SURREY GU8 4HF

**Tel:** 01483 208477　**E-mail:** oakhurstcottage@nationaltrust.org.uk
**Owner:** The National Trust　**Contact:** Winkworth Arboretum

A small 16th century timber-framed cottage, painted by both Helen Allingham and Myles Birket Foster, containing furniture and artefacts reflecting two or more centuries of continuing occupation. There is a delightful cottage garden and a small barn containing agricultural implements.

**Location:** MAP 3:G4, OS Ref. SU965 385. Hambledon, Surrey.

**Open:** 21 Mar–28 Oct: Weds, Thurs, Sats, Suns & BH Mons. Strictly by appointment, 2–5pm.

**Admission:** Adult £5, Child £3 (incl guided tour). No reduction for groups.

♿ Unsuitable. 🅵 Obligatory, by arrangement. **P** Limited. 🐕

**PAINSHILL PARK** 🏛　　*See page 163 for full page entry.*

© Jerry Harpur

Painshill Park, Cobham

# POLESDEN LACEY ❧

### GREAT BOOKHAM, Nr DORKING, SURREY  RH5 6BD

www.nationaltrust.org.uk/polesdenlacey

**Tel:** 01372 452048  **Infoline:** 01372 458203  **Fax:** 01372 452023
**E-mail:** polesdenlacey@nationaltrust.org.uk
**Owner:** The National Trust       **Contact:** The Property Manager
Originally an elegant 1820s Regency villa in a magnificent landscape setting. The house was remodelled after 1906 by the Hon Mrs Ronald Greville, a well-known Edwardian hostess. Her collection of fine paintings, furniture, porcelain and silver are still displayed in the reception rooms and galleries. Extensive grounds (1,400 acre estate), walled rose garden, lawns and landscaped walks.

**Location:** MAP 19:B11, OS Ref. TQ136 522. 5m NW of Dorking, 2m S of Great Bookham, off A246.
**Open:** House: 17 Mar–28 Oct: Wed–Sun, & BH Mons, 11am–5pm. Grounds: All year: daily, 11am–5pm, (closes 4pm 29 Oct–28 Feb 2008). Closed 24 Dec–2 Jan 2008.
**Admission:** House, Gardens, grounds and landscape walks: Adult £10.50, Child £5.20, Family £26.20, Groups £9. Gardens only: Adult £6.50, Child £3.20, Family £16.20, Groups (pre booked only): House £8.10, Gardens £5.

🖸 🖽 ♿ 🍴 Licensed. 🅿 Limited for coaches. 🐕 In grounds on leads.
✸ Grounds only. ♨ Tel: 01372 452048 for info.

# RHS GARDEN WISLEY

### Nr WOKING, SURREY  GU23 6QB

www.rhs.org.uk

**Tel:** 01483 224234  **Fax:** 01483 211750
**Owner/Contact:** The Royal Horticultural Society
A garden to enjoy all year round with something to see for everyone. Wisley provides the visitor with ideas and inspiration and the benefit of experience from experts. The Wisley Plant Centre with plants for sale, The Wisley Shop with books and gifts and for refreshments the Café, Restaurant and Coffee Shop.
**Location:** MAP 19:A10, OS Ref. TQ066 583. On A3 N of Guildford nr. M25 J/10. Brown Signs.

**Open:** All year: daily (except Christmas Day), Mon–Fri, 10am–6pm (4.30pm Nov–Feb). Sat & Sun, 9am–6pm (4.30pm Nov–Feb). Last entry 1 hr before closing.
**Admission:** RHS Members: Free. Adult £7.50, Child (6–16yrs) £2, Child (under 6) Free. Groups (10+): Adult £5.50, Child £1.60.

🖸 🖽 ♿ Wheelchairs available tel: 01483 211113 and special map. WC.
🖽 🍴 Licensed. 🎟 By arrangement. 🖸 🅿 🖼 🐕 Guide & Registered Support dogs only. ✸ ♨

## RAMSTER GARDENS

**Ramster, Chiddingfold, Surrey  GU8 4SN**
**Tel:** 01428 654167   **www.ramsterevents.com**
**Owner/Contact:** Mrs R Glaister
An idyllic, mature flowering shrub garden of 20 acres, with unusual and interesting plants. Spring colour changes from subtle daffodils and magnolias in April to the famous fiery display of rhododendrons, azaleas and bluebells in May, followed in June by the gentle pinks of climbing roses and cascades of primulas.
**Location:** MAP 3:G4, OS Ref. SU950 333. 1½ m S of Chiddingfold on A283.
**Open:** 6 Apr–24 Jun: daily. 10am–5pm.
**Admission:** Adult £5, Child (under 16) Free. Conc £4.50. Groups by arrangement.
⚑ ⅃ Partial. ⬛⬛ On leads. ⬛⬛ Embroidery Exhibition, 20 Apr–1 May.

## RUNNYMEDE ✄

**Egham, Surrey**
**Tel:** 01784 432891   **Fax:** 01784 479007   **E-mail:** runnymede@nationaltrust.org.uk
**www.nationaltrust.org.uk**
**Owner:** The National Trust   **Contact:** The Head Warden
Runnymede is an attractive area of riverside meadows, grassland and broadleaf woodland, rich in diversity of flora and fauna, and part-designated a Site of Special Scientific Interest. It was on this site, in 1215, that King John sealed Magna Carta.
**Location:** MAP 3:G2, OS Ref. TQ007 720. 2m W of Runnymede Bridge, on S side of A308, M25/J13.
**Open:** All year. Riverside Car park (grass): Apr–30 Sept: daily, 10am–7pm. Tearoom & car park (hard standing): daily, all year, 8.30am–5pm (later in Summer).
**Admission:** Fees payable for parking (NT members Free), fishing & mooring.
⬛ ⅃ Partial. ⬛ ⅋ P ⬛ ⬛

See all the properties that are **open all year** in the index on page 580

## TITSEY PLACE & GARDENS

**TITSEY PLACE, OXTED, SURREY  RH8 0SD**

www.titsey.org

**Tel:** 01273 715361   **Fax:** 01273 779783
**E-mail:** kate.moisson@struttandparker.co.uk
**Owner:** Trustees of the Titsey Foundation   **Contact:** Kate Moisson
Beautiful gardens incorporating formal lawns, rose garden, walled kitchen garden and 4 mile woodland walk and parkland. Titsey Place houses 4 stunning Canalettos and Porcelain Collection.
**Location:** MAP 19:F10, OS Ref. TQ406 553. 1 mile N of Limpsfield.
**Open:** mid May–end Sept: Weds & Suns, 1–5pm. Additionally Summer BHs. Gardens only Easter Mon.
**Admission:** House & Garden: Adult £6, Garden only £3.50. Child £1.
⅃ Partial. ⅋ Obligatory. P Limited for coaches. ⬛ Woods and park only.

NTPL / D Sellman

NTPL / D Sellman

## WINKWORTH ARBORETUM ✄

**HASCOMBE ROAD, GODALMING, SURREY  GU8 4AD**

www.nationaltrust.org.uk/winkwortharboretum

**Tel:** 01483 208477   **Fax:** 01483 208252
**E-mail:** winkwortharboretum@nationaltrust.org.uk
**Owner:** The National Trust   **Contact:** Head Arborist
Established in the 20th century, the hillside arboretum now contains over 1,000 different shrubs and trees, many of them rare. The most impressive displays are in spring for bluebells and azaleas, and in autumn for colour and wildlife. New wetland area with boardwalk and circular route. In the summer it is an ideal place for family visits and a picnic.

**Location:** MAP 3:G4, OS Ref. SU990 412. Near Hascombe, 2m SE of Godalming on E side of B2130.
**Open:** All year round: daily during daylight hours. May be closed due to high winds. Boathouse: Apr–Nov.
**Admission:** Adult £5, Child (5–16yrs) £2.50, Family (2+2) £12.50. Discounts for 15 or more.
⬛ ⅃ Limited. WC. ⬛ ⬛ In grounds, on leads. ⬛

# ARUNDEL CASTLE

www.arundelcastle.org

A thousand years of history is waiting to be discovered at Arundel Castle in West Sussex. Dating from the 11th century, the Castle is both ancient fortification and stately home of the Dukes of Norfolk and Earls of Arundel.

Set high on a hill, this magnificent castle commands stunning views across the River Arun and out to sea. Climb the Keep, explore the battlements, wander in the grounds and recently restored Victorian gardens and relax in the garden of the 14th century Fitzalan Chapel.

In the 17th century during the English Civil War the Castle suffered extensive damage. The process of structural restoration began in earnest in the 18th century and continued up until 1900. The Castle was one of the first private residences to have electricity and central heating and had its own fire engine, which is still on view today.

Inside the Castle over 20 sumptuously furnished rooms may be visited including the breathtaking Barons' Hall with 16th century furniture, the Armoury with its fine collection of armour and weapory, and the magnificent Gothic library entirely fitted out in carved Honduras mahogany. There are works of art by Van Dyck, Gainsborough, Canaletto and Mytens, tapestries, clocks, and personal possessions of Mary Queen of Scots including the gold rosary that she carried to her execution.

There are special events throughout the season, including outdoor concerts, jousting, and medieval re-enactments.

## Owner
Arundel Castle
Trustees Ltd

## Contact
Bryan McDonald
Head of Opening
Arundel Castle
Arundel
West Sussex  BN18 9AB

**Tel:** 01903 882173
**Fax:** 01903 884581
**E-mail:** info@
arundelcastle.org

## Location
**MAP 3:G6**
**OS Ref. TQ018 072**

Central Arundel, N of A27
Brighton 40 mins,
Worthing 15 mins,
Chichester 15 mins.
From London A3 or A24,
1½ hrs.
M25 motorway, 30m.

**Bus:** Bus stop 100 yds.

**Rail:** Station ½m.

**Air:** Gatwick 25m.

## Opening Times
31 March–28 October

Tuesday to Sunday
inclusive throughout the
season.

Closed on Mondays
(except Bank Holidays).

**Fitzalan Chapel,
Gardens & Grounds**
10am–5pm

**Restaurant**
10.30am – 4.30pm

**Gift Shop**
10.30am – 5pm

**Castle Keep**
11.00am – 4.30pm

**Main Castle Rooms**
12 noon – 5pm

Last entry 4pm

## Admission
**Summer**
| | |
|---|---|
| Adult | £12.00 |
| Child (5–16yrs) | £7.50 |
| Conc. | £9.50 |
| Family (2+5 max) | £32.00 |

Groups (20+)
| | |
|---|---|
| Adult | £10.00 |
| Child (5–16yrs) | £6.00 |
| Conc. | £8.00 |

Fitzalan Chapel, Castle
Keep Gardens & Grounds
£6.50

**Winter**
Closed.

No photography or video recording inside the Castle. Guidebooks in English, French & German.

Many areas accessible. Visitors may alight at the Castle gates. Free parking in the allocated areas in the town car park. Passenger buggy available. WCs.

Licensed restaurant in Castle seats 140. Special rates for booked groups. Self-service. Serves home-made food, morning coffee, lunch or afternoon tea.

Pre-booked groups only. Tour time 1½–2 hrs. Tours available in Japanese.

Ample in town car park. Coaches can park free in town coach park. Free admission and refreshment voucher for coach driver.

Items of particular interest include a Norman Motte & Keep, Armoury & Victorian bedrooms. Special rates for schoolchildren (aged 5–15) and teachers.

Registered Assistance Dogs only

For further information please visit our website, e-mail or telephone.

■ **Owner**
The National Trust

■ **Contact**
The Administrator
Bateman's
Burwash
Etchingham
East Sussex  TN19 7DS

**Tel:** 01435 882302
**Fax:** 01435 882811
**E-mail:** batemans@
nationaltrust.org.uk

■ **Location**
**MAP 4:K5**
**OS Ref. TQ671 238**

½ m S of Burwash
off A265.

**Rail:** Etchingham 3m,
then bus (twice daily).

**Air:** Gatwick 40m.

■ **Opening Times**
17 March–28 October:
Sat–Wed, Good Fri &
BH Mons, 11am–5pm.
Last admission 4.30pm.

■ ***Admission**
**House & Garden**

| | |
|---|---|
| Adult | £6.85 |
| Child | £3.45 |
| Family (2+3) | £17.10 |
| Groups | £5.30 |

*includes a voluntary
donation but visitors can
choose to pay the standard
prices displayed at the
property and on the website.

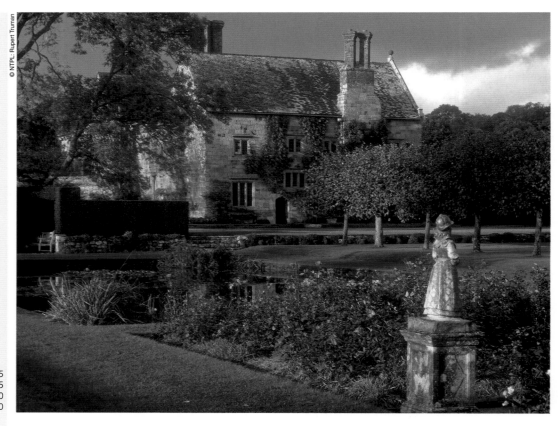

© NTPL: Rupert Truman

# BATEMAN'S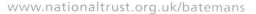

www.nationaltrust.org.uk/batemans

Built in 1634 and home to Rudyard Kipling for over 30 years, Bateman's lies in the richly wooded landscape of the Sussex Weald. Visit this Sussex sandstone manor house, built by a local ironmaster, where the famous writer lived from 1902 to 1936. See the rooms as they were in Kipling's day, including the study where the view inspired him to write some of his well-loved works including *Puck of Pook's Hill* and *Rewards and Fairies*. Find the mementoes of Kipling's time in India and illustrations from his famous Jungle Book tales of Mowgli, Baloo and Shere Khan.

Wander through the delightful Rose Garden with its pond and statues, with Mulberry and Herb gardens and discover the wild garden, through which flows the River Dudwell. Through the wild garden, you will find the Mill where you can watch corn being ground on most Saturday and Wednesday afternoons and one of the world's first water-driven turbines installed by Kipling to generate electricity for the house. In the garage, see a 1928 Rolls Royce, one of several owned by Kipling who was a keen early motorist.

Savour the peace and tranquillity of this beautiful  property which Kipling described as '*A good and peaceable place*' and of which he said '*we have loved it, ever since our first sight of it …*'.

There is a picnic glade next to the car park, or you can enjoy morning coffee, a delicious lunch or afternoon tea in the licensed tearoom where there is special emphasis on using local produce. The well-stocked gift shop offers the largest collection of Kipling books in the area.

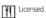 Ground floor & grounds. WC. Computerised virtual tour of upper floors.

 Licensed.

NTPL / Geoffrey Frosh

# BORDE HILL
## GARDEN, PARK & WOODLAND
www.bordehill.co.uk

The glorious heritage garden set in 200 acres of Grade II* parkland offers a wealth of inspiration and ideas for keen gardeners and dabblers alike and is the perfect backdrop for film locations and corporate or public functions.

Winner of the Historic Houses Association/Christie's 2004 'Garden of the Year', the garden is a plantsman's paradise, with rare trees and shrubs introduced by the great plant collectors in early 1900s, mainly from the Himalayas, Andes and Tasmania. This unique collection of trees extends to many woodland areas and includes native hardwoods and specimen trees. Created by Col. Stephenson Clarke in the 1890s, the Stephenson Clarke family continue to maintain his collection, which is of immense botanical and historical interest, with a rich variety of colour and breathtaking displays throughout the seasons.

Enjoy the distinctive formal 'garden rooms', including the sumptuous Rose Garden and the romantic Italian Garden. Find peace and tranquillity in the informal Azalea Ring and the Garden of Allah, and drama in the sub-tropical Round Dell. For children there is an exciting Pirates' Adventure Playground and lakeside walks to explore and picnic.

Guided tours of the garden can be organised for pre-booked groups as can tours of Borde Hill House at certain times. For more general lovers of the outdoors, Borde Hill hosts a wide variety of events including equestrian, countryside shows and open air concerts.

Borde Hill is easily accessible by road and rail. We would be happy to answer your queries, whether it is as a visitor, group booking or corporate enquiry. For more information on Borde Hill visit www.bordehill.co.uk

 Film location, product launches, corporate functions.

WC.

Licensed.

By arrangement.

 In grounds, on leads.

## ■ Owner
The Earl of March

## ■ Contact
Curator's PA
Goodwood House
Goodwood
Chichester
West Sussex  PO18 0PX

**Tel:** 01243 755048
01243 755042 (Weddings)
Recorded Info:
01243 755040
**Fax:** 01243 755005
**E-mail:** curator
@goodwood.co.uk
or weddings@
goodwood.co.uk

## ■ Location
**MAP 3:F6**
**OS Ref. SU888 088**

3½m NE of Chichester. A3
from London then A286 or
A285. M27/A27 from
Portsmouth or Brighton.

**Rail:** Chichester 3½m
Arundel 9m.

**Air:** Heathrow 1½ hrs
Gatwick ¾ hr.

## ■ Opening Times
**Summer**
25 March–8 October:
Most Sundays and
Mondays, 1–5pm.
(last entry 4pm.)
(Check Recorded Info.)

5–30 August,
Sundays–Thursdays, 1–5pm.

**Connoisseurs' Days**
12 & 25 April, 15 May,
20 September & 17 October

Special tours for booked
groups only.

**Closures**
Closed 6 & 27 May: 17/18,
24/25 June (Festival of
Speed), 1/2 August
(Raceweek), & 2 September
(Goodwood Revival). (Please
call Recorded Info 01243
755040 to check and for
occasional extra closures.)

## ■ Admission
**House**
| | |
|---|---|
| Adult | £8.00 |
| Young Person | |
| (12–18yrs) | £4.00 |
| Child (under 12yrs) | Free |
| Senior Citizen | £7.00 |
| Booked Groups (20–200) | |
| Open Day | £7.00 |
| Morning | £9.00 |
| Connoisseur | £9.50 |

## ■ Special Events
**June 22–24**
Festival of Speed*
**July 31–August 4**
Glorious Goodwood
Raceweek*
**August 31, Sept 1/2**
Goodwood Revival*

*Please visit our website for
up-to-date information.
www.goodwood.co.uk.

## Conference/Function

| ROOM | SIZE | MAX CAPACITY |
|---|---|---|
| Ballroom | 79' x 23' | 180 |
| 11 other rooms also available | | |

# GOODWOOD HOUSE 🏛

www.goodwood.co.uk

Goodwood is one of the finest sporting estates in the world. At its heart lies Goodwood House, the ancestral home of the Dukes of Richmond and Gordon, direct descendants of King Charles II. Today, it is still lived in by the present Duke's son and heir, the Earl of March and Kinrara, with his wife and young family. Their home is open to the public on at least 60 days a year.

To celebrate the tricentenary of the Act of Union between England and Scotland, in 2007 there will be a special exhibition at Goodwood House showing on open days in August and September. *Scotland in Sussex* will explain why the holder of the Dukedom of Gordon, by origin a Scottish title, lives in the south of England. Through paintings, watercolours, diaries, letters and *objets d'art* the story will emerge of how three great Scottish dynasties became linked: those of the Royal House of Stuart, of Lennox, and finally, of Gordon.

Set in the exquisitely decorated, gilded interiors of Goodwood House, the art collection is at museum level, with magnificent English paintings from the 17th and 18th centuries. These include famous horse paintings by George Stubbs, and views of London by Canaletto, the latter being especially topical because of the 2007 Canaletto exhibition at Dulwich in London. There is fine French furniture, Gobelins tapestries and Sèvres porcelain, also from the 18th century. Special works of art are regularly rotated and displayed. Arrangements to see books from the Goodwood libraries can be made by written application to the Curator (there is a special charge for these viewings).

Goodwood is not only a beautiful house to visit on an open day, with a relaxed and friendly atmosphere, but is also renowned for its entertaining. The House enjoys a reputation for excellence as a location for unforgettable weddings, parties and events. Goodwood's Home Farm, the largest organic lowland farm in England, provides food for the table in the various restaurants on the estate. With internationally renowned horseracing and motor sport events, the finest Downland golf course in the UK, our own aerodrome and hotel, Goodwood can offer an extraordinarily rich sporting experience.

5th Duke of Gordon by Sir Henry Raeburn

The Tapestry Drawing Room

ℹ️ Conference facilities. No photography. Highly trained guides. Shell House optional extra on Connoisseurs' Days or by Group Appointment, or written request.

🏬 Main shop at motor circuit.

🍸
☕
♿
🚻 Obligatory.

🅿️ Ample.

🍽

🐕 In grounds, on leads. Guide dogs only in house.

🔔 Civil Wedding Licence.

# LEONARDSLEE
# LAKES & GARDENS

www.leonardslee.com

Leonardslee represents one of the largest and most spectacular woodland gardens in England, in a most magnificent setting, only a few miles from the M23. The 240 acre (100 hectare) valley is world famous for its spring display of Azaleas and Rhododendrons flowering throughout the valley amongst the seven lakes, providing superb views and magnificent reflections.

2007 is the gardens centenary year; Leonardslee first opened to the public in 1907. The gardens have evolved over 200 years, and since 1889 have been maintained by the Loder family. The famous *Rhododendron loderi*, was raised by Sir Edmund Loder in 1901, and first flowered in 1907. The original plants can still be seen in the garden, and in May the fragrance of their huge blooms pervades the air throughout the valley. At this time the delightful Rock Garden is a kaleidoscope of colour. The many plantings of *Kalmias Cornus* and *Hydrangeas* bring colour to the valley over the summer months.

Ducks, geese and swans swim on the lakes, and huge carp can be seen basking under the surface. Wallabies, deer and other natural wildlife roam the parks. The wallabies have lived wild within the valley for over 100 years, and provide a useful environmentally-friendly mowing service.

For the centenary the famous one-twelfth scale miniature exhibition has been extended to include a market town and estate of 100 years ago. The Loder collection of Victorian Motor cars is one of the country's most impressive of this era, showing the development of the motor vehicle from 1890–1900.

### ■ Owner
The Loder Family

### ■ Contact
Tom Loder
Leonardslee Lakes &
Gardens
Lower Beeding
Horsham
West Sussex  RH13 6PP

**Tel:** 01403 891212
**Fax:** 01403 891305
**E-mail:** info@
leonardsleegardens.com

### ■ Location
**MAP 3:H4**
**OS Ref. TQ222 260**

M23 to Handcross then
B2110 (signposted
Cowfold) for 4m.
From London:
1 hr 15 mins.

**Rail:** Horsham
Station 4½ m.

**Bus:** No. 17 from
Horsham and Brighton.

### ■ Opening Times
**Summer**
1 April–31 October
Daily 9.30am–6pm
Last admission 4.30pm

**Winter**
1 November–31 March
Closed (facilities available
for private functions)

### ■ Admission
April, June–October
Adult                    £6.00

May (Mon–Fri)
Adult                    £8.00

May (Sats, Suns & BHs)
Adult                    £9.00
Child (any time)         £4.00

Coach Parties (20+)
April, June–October
Adult                    £5.00

May (Mon–Fri)
Adult                    £7.00

May (Sats, Suns & BHs)
Adult                    £8.00
Child (any time)         £3.50

### ■ Special Events
**May**
Azaleas and
Rhododendron
flowering season

**May 5–7**
Bonsai Weekend

**May 12/13**
Centenary Weekend

**June 30–July 1**
Vintage Engine Show

**July 14/15**
Model Boat Regatta

**Aug 18/19**
Model Boat Regatta

**October**
Autumn Colours

Splashes of colour in the rock garden

Miniature model estate "Behind the dolls house"

ℹ️ Photography – landscape & fashion, film location.

🍽 Restaurant available for private and corporate functions in the evenings and out of season.

♿ Unsuitable, due to natural valley slopes.

🍴 Restaurant/café. Morning coffee, lunches & teas.

🅿️ Ample. Average length of visit 3–5 hours.

### Conference/Function

| ROOM | MAX CAPACITY |
| --- | --- |
| Clock Tower | 100 |
| Garden Room | 30 |

## ■ Owner
Mr & Mrs
James A Sellick

## ■ Contact
Jenny Bigger
Pashley Manor
Ticehurst
Wadhurst
East Sussex  TN5 7HE

**Tel:** 01580 200888
**Fax:** 01580 200102
**E-mail:** info@
pashleymanorgardens
.com

## ■ Location
**MAP 4:K4**
**OS Ref. TQ707 291**

On B2099 between A21
and Ticehurst Village.

## ■ Opening Times
3 April–29 September:
Tues, Weds, Thurs, Sat &
BH Mons, 11am–5pm.

October: Garden only
Mon–Fri,10am–4pm.

## ■ Admission
| | |
|---|---|
| Adult | £6.50 |
| Children (6–16yrs) | £5.00 |
| Groups (20+) | £6.00 |

Coaches must book.
Please telephone for
details.

# PASHLEY MANOR GARDENS

www.pashleymanorgardens.com

A winner of HHA/Christie's Garden of the Year Award. The gardens offer a sumptuous blend of romantic landscaping, imaginative plantings and fine old trees, fountains, springs and large ponds. This is a quintessential English garden of a very individual character with exceptional views to the surrounding valleyed fields. Many eras of English history are reflected here, typifying the tradition of the English Country House and its garden.

The gardens first opened in 1992 and were brought to their present splendour with the assistance of the eminent landscape architect, Anthony du Gard Pasley. A number of different gardens have been created within the 11 acres allowing the visitor to travel from blazing colour to cool creams, greens and golds.

The gardens are always evolving and never static; it is hoped that they will be inspirational yet restful to the first-time visitor and will never disappoint those who return regularly. Pashley prides itself on its delicious food. During warm weather, visitors can enjoy their refreshments on the terrace overlooking the moat or in the Jubilee Courtyard. Home-made soups, ploughman's lunches with pickles and patés, fresh salad from the garden (whenever possible), home-made scones and delicious cakes, filter coffee, specialist teas and fine wines are served from the Garden Room café. The gift shop caters for every taste … from postcards and local honey to traditional hand-painted ceramics and tapestry cushions. A wide selection of plants and shrubs, many of which grow at Pashley, are available for purchase.

Permanent exhibition and sale of sculpture and botanical art.

Excellent location for wedding receptions. Pashley also caters for small corporate events and private parties.

Tulip Time

Gossiping Graces in the Park

 Partial.
 Licensed.
By arrangement.

 Guide dogs only.
Telephone for details.

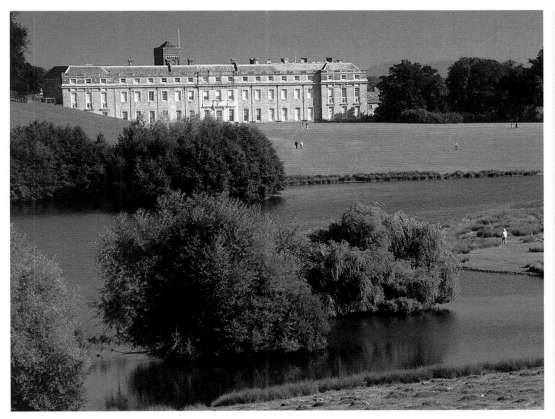

# PETWORTH HOUSE & PARK 🌿

www.nationaltrust.org.uk/petworth

Petworth House is one of the finest houses in the care of the National Trust and is home to an art collection that rivals many London galleries. Assembled by one family over 350 years, it includes works by Turner, Van Dyck, Titian, Claude, Gainsborough, Bosch, Reynolds and William Blake.

The state rooms contain sculpture, furniture and porcelain of the highest quality and are complemented by the old kitchens in the Servants' Quarters. The Carved Room contains some of Grinling Gibbons' finest limewood carvings.

Petworth House is also the home of Lord and Lady Egremont and extra family rooms are open on weekdays by kind permission of the family (not Bank Holidays).

Petworth Park is a 700 acre park landscaped by 'Capability' Brown and is open to the public all year free of charge. Spring and autumn are particularly breathtaking and the summer sunsets over the lake are spectacular.

©NTPL / Rupert Truman

## ■ Owner
The National Trust

## ■ Contact
The Administration Office
Petworth House
Petworth
West Sussex  GU28 0AE

**Tel:** 01798 342207
**Info:** 01798 343929
**Fax:** 01798 342963
**E-mail:** petworth@nationaltrust.org.uk

## ■ Location
**MAP 3:G5**
**OS Ref. SU976 218**

In the centre of Petworth town (approach roads A272/A283/A285) Car park signposted.

**Rail:** Pulborough 5¼m.

## ■ Opening Times
**House**
31 March–31October.
Daily except Thur & Fri, but open Good Fri, 11am–5pm.

Last admission to House 4.30pm.

Extra rooms shown on Mon–Wed (closed BH Mons).

**Pleasure Ground**
10–28 March for spring bulbs and events, 11am–4pm.

31 March–31 October. Saturday–Wednesday, 11am–6pm.

**Park**
All year: Daily, 8am–sunset.

**Shop & Restaurant**
10–28 March for Mothering Sunday lunches and events, 11am–4pm.

31 March–31 October. Saturday–Wednesday, 11am–5pm.

## ■ Admission
**House & Pleasure Ground**
Adult                          £9.00
Child (5–17yrs)          £4.50
Child (under 5yrs)      Free
Family (2+3)              £22.50

Groups (pre-booked 15+)
Adult                          £7.00

**Park Only**                Free
Parking charge for non-NT members.

**Pleasure Ground**
Adult                          £3.50
Child (5–17yrs)          £1.80

NT Members Free.

*includes a voluntary donation but visitors can choose to pay the standard prices displayed at the property and on the website.

ℹ Events & Exhibitions throughout the year. Baby feeding and changing facilities, highchairs. Pushchairs admitted in house but no prams, please. No photography or mobile phones in house.

🛍 Contact Retail & Catering Manager on 01798 344975.

♿ Car park is 800 yards from house; there is a vehicle available to take less able visitors to the House.

🍴 Licensed.

🚶 By arrangement with the Administration Office on variety of subjects.

🎧 Audio House Tours.

🅿 800 yards from house. Coach parties alight at Church Lodge entrance, coaches then park in NT car park. Coaches must book in advance.

🎒 Welcome. Must book. Teachers' pack available.

🐕 Assistance dogs only in House. Dogs in park only.

❄ 

🎭 Telephone for details.

### ■ Owner
Brighton & Hove
City Council

### ■ Contact
Visitor Services
The Royal Pavilion
Brighton
East Sussex  BN1 1EE

**Tel:** 01273 290900
**Fax:** 01273 292871
**email:** visitor.services
@brighton-hove.gov.uk

### ■ Location
**MAP 4:I6**

The Royal Pavilion is in
the centre of Brighton
easily reached by road
and rail. From London
M25, M23, A23 –
1 hr 30 mins.

**Rail:** Victoria to Brighton
station 50 mins.
15 mins walk from
Brighton station.

**Air:** Gatwick 20 mins.

### ■ Opening Times
**Summer**
April–September
Daily: 9.30am–5.45pm.
Last admission at 5pm.

**Winter**
October–March
Daily: 10am–5.15pm.
Last admission at 4.30pm.

Closed 24 (from 2.30pm),
25/26 December.

### ■ Admission
| | |
|---|---|
| Adult | £7.50 |
| Child | £5.00 |
| Conc. | £5.75 |

Groups (20+)
Adult          £6.50

Prices subject to change
in Spring 2007.

### ■ Special Events
Autumn, Winter
& Spring:
Children's Events.

Please telephone for
details of other events
throughout the year.

# THE ROYAL PAVILION
www.royalpavilion.org.uk

Universally acclaimed as one of the most exotically beautiful buildings in the British Isles, the Royal Pavilion is the former seaside residence of King George IV.

Originally a simple farmhouse, in 1787 architect Henry Holland created a neo-classical villa on the site. It was later transformed into its current Indian style by John Nash between 1815 and 1822. With interiors decorated in the Chinese style and an astonishingly exotic exterior, this Regency Palace is quite breathtaking.

Magnificent decorations and fantastic furnishings have been re-created in the recent extensive restoration programme. From the opulence of the main state rooms to the charm of the first floor bedroom suites, the Royal Pavilion is filled with astonishing colours and superb craftsmanship.

Witness the magnificence of the Music Room with its domed ceiling of gilded scallop-shaped shells and hand-knotted carpet, and promenade through the Chinese bamboo grove of the Long Gallery.

Lavish menus were created in the Great Kitchen, with its cast iron palm trees and dazzling collection of copperware, and then served in the dramatic setting of the Banqueting Room, lit by a huge crystal chandelier held by a silvered dragon.

Set in restored Regency gardens replanted to John Nash's elegant 1820s design, the Royal Pavilion is an unforgettable experience.

**i** Location filming and photography, including feature films, fashion shoots and corporate videos.

Gift shop with souvenirs unique to the Royal Pavilion.

Spectacular rooms available for prestigious corporate and private entertaining or wedding receptions.

Access to ground floor only. Tactile and signed tours can be booked in advance with Visitor Services Tel: 01273 292820/2.

Tearooms with a balcony providing sweeping views across the restored Regency gardens.

Tours in English, French and German and other languages by prior arrangement. General introduction and specialist tours provided.

Audio guides now available free with admission.

**P** Close to NCP car parks, town centre voucher parking. Coach drop-off point in Church Street, parking in Madeira Drive. Free entry for coach drivers.

Specialist tours relating to all levels of National Curriculum, must be booked in advance with Visitor Services. Slide lecture presentations by arrangement.

Civil Wedding Licence.

### Conference/Function

| ROOM | MAX CAPACITY |
|---|---|
| Banqueting Room | 200 |
| Great Kitchen | 90 |
| Music Rm | 180 |
| Queen Adelaide Suite | 100 |
| Small Adelaide | 40 |
| William IV | 80 |

# SAINT HILL MANOR

www.sainthillmanor.org.uk

Built 1792 by Gibbs Crawfurd. One of the finest Sussex sandstone buildings in existence and situated near the breathtaking Ashdown Forest. Subsequent owners included Edgar March Crookshank and the Maharajah of Jaipur. In 1959, Saint Hill Manor's final owner, acclaimed author and humanitarian L Ron Hubbard, acquired the Manor, where he lived for many years with his family. As a result of the work carried out under Mr Hubbard's direction, the Manor has been restored to its original beauty, including the uncovering of fine oak wood panelling, marble fireplaces and plasterwork ceilings.

Other outstanding features of this lovely house include an impressive library of Mr Hubbard's works, elegant winter garden, and delightful Monkey Mural painted in 1945 by Winston Churchill's nephew John Spencer Churchill. This 100-foot mural depicts many famous personalities as monkeys, including Winston Churchill. Also open to the public are 59 acres of landscaped gardens, lake and woodlands. Ideal for corporate functions and also available as a film location. Annual events include open-air theatre, arts festivals, classical and jazz concerts.

## Owner
Church of Scientology

## Contact
Mrs Liz Ostermann
Saint Hill Manor
Saint Hill Road
East Grinstead
West Sussex RH19 4JY

**Tel:** 01342 326711
**Fax:** 01342 317057
**E-mail:** info@ hubbardfoundation.co.uk

## Location
**MAP 4:I4**
**OS Ref. TQ383 359**

2m SW of East Grinstead. At Felbridge, turn off A22, down Imberhorne Lane and over crossroads into Saint Hill Road, 200 yds on right.

**Rail:** East Grinstead station.

**Air:** 15 mins drive from Gatwick airport.

## Opening Times
All year. Daily, 2–5pm, on the hour.

Groups welcome throughout the year.

## Admission Free

## Special Events
Open-air theatre, classical and jazz concerts, exhibitions and arts festivals.

This year's open air theatre will take place in June. Please telephone for details.

 Ground floor.
 Teas available.
Obligatory.

### ■ Owner

The National Trust

### ■ Contact

Jo Hopkins
Visitor Services &
Marketing Manager
Sheffield Park
East Sussex
TN22 3QX

**Tel:** 01825 790231
**Fax:** 01825 791264
**E-mail:** sheffieldpark@
nationaltrust.org.uk

### ■ Location

**MAP 4:15**

**OS Ref. TQ415 240**

Midway between East
Grinstead and Lewes, 5m
NW of Uckfield on E side
of A275.

### ■ Opening Times

6 January–25 February:
Sat & Sun,
10.30am–4pm.

27 February–29 April:
Tues–Sun,
10.30am–5.30pm.

1 May–3 June:
Daily,
10.30am–5.30pm.

5 June–30 September:
Tues–Sun,
10.30am–5.30pm.

1 October–4 November:
Daily,
10.30am–5.30pm.

6 November–
23 December, Tues–Sun
10.30am–4pm.

27–30 December:
Thurs–Sun,
10.30am–4pm.

5 January–2 March 2008:
Sat & Sun
10.30am–4pm.

Open BH Mons
April–August.

Last admission 1 hour
before closing or dusk if
earlier.

### ■ *Admission

| | |
|---|---|
| Adult | £7.00 |
| Child | £3.50 |
| Family | £17.50 |
| Groups (15+ prebooked) | |
| Adult | £5.40 |
| Child | £2.70 |
| Guided Tour | £2.00pp |

(inc. NT members)

NT, RHS Individual
Members and Great
British Heritage Pass
holders Free.

Joint Ticket available
with Bluebell Railway.

*includes a voluntary
donation but visitors can
choose to pay the standard
prices displayed at the
property and on the website.

©NTPL 2004/Lisa Barnard

# SHEFFIELD PARK GARDEN

## www.nationaltrust.org.uk/sheffieldpark

A magnificent 120 acre landscaped garden. The centrepiece of this internationally renowned, garden is the four lakes that mirror the unique planting and colour that each season brings. Displays of spring bulbs as the garden awakens, and a stunning exhibition of colour in May, of rhododendrons and the National Collection of Ghent Azaleas. Water lilies dress the lakes during the summer. Visitors to the garden during the summer months can enjoy a leisurely walk perhaps pausing to sit on a seat to enjoy the tranquil ambience. In the autumn the garden is transformed by trees planted specifically for their autumn colour including *Nyssa sylvatica*, *Amelanchier* and *Acer palmatum*. These and other fine specimen trees, particularly North American varieties, produce displays of gold, orange and crimson. *Gentiana sino-ornata* offers two borders of amazing 'Gentian Blue' colour during the autumn months. The garden is open throughout the year and has something for all, whether a quiet stroll or a family gathering, allowing the children to participate in the many activities offered. Special Events run throughout the year – please telephone for details.

Partial. WC.

(not NT).

By arrangement.

Assistance dogs only.

NTPL / Andrew Butler

## ALFRISTON CLERGY HOUSE �});
### THE TYE, ALFRISTON, POLEGATE, EAST SUSSEX BN26 5TL

**Tel:** 01323 870001   **Fax:** 01323 871318   **E-mail:** alfriston@nationaltrust.org.uk

**Owner:** The National Trust   **Contact:** The Property Manager

Step back into the Middle Ages with a visit to this 14th century thatched Wealden 'Hall House'. Trace the history of this building which in 1896 was the first to be acquired by the National Trust. Discover what is used to make the floor in the Great Hall and visit the excellent shop. Explore the delightful cottage garden and savour the idyllic setting beside Alfriston's parish church, with stunning views across the meandering River Cuckmere. An intriguing variety of shops, pubs and restaurants in Alfriston village make this a wonderful day out.

**Location:** MAP 4:J6, OS Ref. TQ521 029. 4m NE of Seaford, just E of B2108.

**Open:** 3–11 Mar: Sats & Suns, 11am–4pm. 17 Mar–28 Oct: daily except Tue & Fri, 10am–5pm. 29 Oct–16 Dec: daily except Tue & Fri, 11am–4pm.

**Admission:** Adult £3.60, Child £1.80, Family (2+3) £8.95. Pre-booked groups £3.10.

ℹ️ No WCs. 📷 🅿 Parking in village car parks.

## ANNE OF CLEVES HOUSE
### 52 SOUTHOVER HIGH STREET, LEWES, SUSSEX BN7 1JA

www.sussexpast.co.uk/anneofcleves

**Tel:** 01273 474610   **Fax:** 01273 486990   **E-mail:** anne@sussexpast.co.uk

**Owner:** Sussex Past   **Contact:** Stephen Watts

This 15th century timber-framed Wealden hall-house was given to Anne of Cleves as part of her divorce settlement from Henry VIII in 1541, and contains wide-ranging collections of Sussex interest including artefacts from the Lewes Priory, Sussex pottery and Weald ironwork. Furnished rooms give an impression of life in the 17th and 18th centuries. Replica costumes are available for dressing up.

**Location:** MAP 4:I5, OS198 Ref. TQ410 096. S of Lewes town centre, off A27/A275/A26.

**Open:** 1 Jan–28 Feb: Tue–Sat, 10am–5pm. 1 Mar–31 Oct: Tue–Sat, 10am–5pm; Sun, Mon & BHs, 11am–5pm. 1 Nov–31 Dec: Tue–Sat, 10am–5pm. Closed 24–26 Dec.

**Admission:** Adult £3.50, Child £1.60, Conc. £3, Family (2+2) £8 or (1+4) £6.50. Groups (15+): Adult £3, Child £1.45, Conc. £2.60. Combined ticket with Lewes Castle is also available.

📷 🎞 By arrangement. 🅿 Limited (on road). ▦ ▨ Guide dogs only. ▲ ❋ ♥

## ARUNDEL CASTLE   *See page 169 for full page entry.*

## ARUNDEL CATHEDRAL
**Parsons Hill, Arundel, Sussex  BN18 9AY**
**Tel:** 01903 882297   **Fax:** 01903 885335   **E-mail:** aruncath1@aol.com
**Contact:** Rev T Madeley
French Gothic Cathedral, church of the RC Diocese of Arundel and Brighton built by Henry, 15th Duke of Norfolk and opened 1873.
**Location:** MAP 3:G6, OS Ref. TQ015 072. Above junction of A27 and A284.
**Open:** Summer: 9am–6pm. Winter: 9am–dusk. Mon: Liturgy of the Word; Tues, Wed, Fri, Sat: Mass 10am; Thurs: Mass 8.30am (at Convent of Poor Clares, Crossbush); Sat: Vigil Mass 6.15pm (at Convent of Poor Clares, Crossbush); Sun: Masses 9.30am and 11.15am. Shop open in the summer, Mon–Fri, 10am–4pm and after services and on special occasions and otherwise on request.
**Admission:** Free.

## BATEMAN'S 🌱   *See page 170 for full page entry.*

Borde Hill Garden

# 1066 BATTLE OF HASTINGS ABBEY AND BATTLEFIELD ⌗

## BATTLE, SUSSEX TN33 0AD

www.english-heritage.org.uk/visits

**Tel:** 01424 773792   **Fax:** 01424 775059

**Owner:** English Heritage     **Contact:** Visitor Operations Team

Visit the site of the 1066 Battle of Hastings. An inclusive interactive audio tour will lead you around the battlefield and to the exact spot where Harold fell. Explore the magnificent abbey ruins and gatehouse and enjoy our new visitor centre with interactive dispalys and auditorium.

**Location:** MAP 4:K5, OS Ref. TQ749 157. Top of Battle High Street. Turn off A2100 to Battle.

**Open:** 1 Apr–30 Sept: daily, 10am–6pm. 1 Oct–20 Mar 2008: daily 10am–4pm. Closed 24–26 Dec & 1 Jan.

**Admission:** Adult £6.30, Child £3.20, Conc. £4.70, Family £15.80. 15% discount for groups (11+). English Heritage members Free.

ⓘ WCs. ⓐ ⓑ Ground floor & grounds. ● ⓟ Charge payable. ⓝ Inclusive. ⓜ In grounds, on leads. ⊞ ⓥ

---

## BAYHAM OLD ABBEY ⌗

**Lamberhurst, Sussex TN3 8DE**

**Tel/Fax:** 01892 890381   **www.english-heritage.org.uk/visits**

**Owner:** English Heritage     **Contact:** Visitor Operations Team

These riverside ruins are of a house of 'white' canons, founded c.1208 and preserved in the 18th century, when its surroundings were landscaped to create its delightful setting. Rooms in the Georgian dower house are also open to the public.

**Location:** MAP 4:K4, OS Ref. TQ651 366. 1¾m W of Lamberhurst off B2169.

**Open:** 1 Apr–30 Sept: daily, 10am–5pm.

**Admission:** Adult £3.60, Child £1.80, Conc. £2.70. English Heritage members Free.

ⓐ ⓑ Grounds. WC. ⓟ ⓜ In grounds, on leads.

---

## BIGNOR ROMAN VILLA

**Bignor Lane, Bignor, Nr Pulborough, West Sussex RH20 1PH**

**Tel/Fax:** 01798 869259   **E-mail:** t.r.tupper@farming.me.uk

**Owner:** Mr J R Tupper     **Contact:** John & Del Smith – Curators

One of the largest villas to be open to the public in Great Britain, with some of the finest mosaics all in situ and all under cover, including Medusa, Venus & Cupid Gladiators and Ganymede. Discovered in 1811 and open to the public since 1814. See the longest mosaic on display in Great Britain at 24 metres. Walk on original floors dating back to circa 350 AD. We have a small café and picnic area available.

**Location:** MAP 3:G5, OS Ref. SU987 146. 6m N of Arundel, 6m S of Pulborough A29. 7m S of Petworth A285.

**Open:** Mar & Apr: Tue–Sun & BHs, 10am–5pm; May & Oct: daily, 10am–5pm. Jun–Sept: daily, 10am–6pm.

**Admission:** Adult £4.50, Child £1.95, OAP £3.20. Groups (10+): Adult £3.60, Child £1.55, OAP £2.55. Guided tours (max 30 per tour) £19.50. Introductory talk £10 (one room only approx. 10 mins).

ⓐ ⓑ Partial. ● ⓕ By arrangement. ⓟ ⓜ ⓜ

Charleston, Nr Lewes

NT Photographic Library: D Sellman

# BODIAM CASTLE ❋
## BODIAM, Nr ROBERTSBRIDGE, EAST SUSSEX TN32 5UA
www.nationaltrust.org.uk/bodiamcastle

**Tel:** 01580 830436    **Fax:** 01580 830398
**E-mail:** bodiamcastle@nationaltrust.org.uk
**Owner:** The National Trust    **Contact:** The Property Manager
Built in 1385 to defend the surrounding countryside and as a comfortable dwelling for a rich nobleman, Bodiam Castle is one of the finest examples of medieval architecture. The virtual completeness of its exterior makes it popular with adults, children and film crews alike. Inside, although a ruin, floors have been replaced in some of the towers and visitors can climb the spiral staircase to enjoy superb views of the Rother Valley and local steam trains from the battlements. Discover more of its intriguing past in the new introductory film, and wander in the peacefully romantic Castle grounds.

**Location:** MAP 4:K5, OS Ref. TQ782 256. 3m S of Hawkhurst, 2m E of A21 Hurst Green.
**Open:** 1 Jan–9 Feb: Sats & Suns, 10.30am–4pm. 10 Feb–31 Oct: daily including Good Fri, Easter Sat & Sun, 10.30am–6pm. 3 Nov–17 Feb 2008: Sats & Suns, 10.30am–4pm. Last admission to Castle 1 hour before closing or dusk if earlier.
**\*Admission:** Adult £5, Child £2.50, Family (2+3) £12.50 Groups (15+) £3.90. Parking £2 per car. \*Includes a voluntary donation but visitors can choose to pay the standard prices displayed at the property and on the website.
🖸 🛆 Ground floor & grounds. 🍴 🅿 ▥ Teacher & student packs & education base. ❋ ♿

---

## BORDE HILL GARDEN, PARK & WOODLAND
*See page 171 for full page entry.*

## BOXGROVE PRIORY ♯
**Boxgrove, Chichester, Sussex**
**Tel:** 01424 775705   www.english-heritage.org.uk/visits
**Owner:** English Heritage    **Contact:** 1066 Battle Abbey
Remains of the Guest House, Chapter House and Church of this 12th-century priory, which was the cell of a French abbey until Richard II confirmed its independence in 1383.
**Location:** MAP 3:G6, OS Ref. SU909 076. N of Boxgrove, 4 miles E of Chichester on minor road N of A27.
**Open:** Any reasonable time.
**Admission:** Free.
🅿 🖾 ❋

## BRAMBER CASTLE ♯
**Bramber, Sussex**
**Tel:** 01424 775705   www.english-heritage.org.uk/visits
**Owner:** English Heritage    **Contact:** 1066 Battle Abbey
The remains of a Norman castle gatehouse, walls and earthworks in a splendid setting overlooking the Adur Valley.
**Location:** MAP 3:H5, OS Ref. TQ187 107. On W side of Bramber village NE of A283.
**Open:** Any reasonable time.
**Admission:** Free.
🅿 Limited. 🖾 On leads. ❋

## CAMBER CASTLE ♯
**Camber, Nr Rye, East Sussex TN31 7RS**
**Tel:** 01797 223862   www.english-heritage.org.uk/visits
**Owner:** English Heritage    **Contact:** Rye Harbour Nature Reserve
A fine example of one of many coastal fortresses built by Henry VIII to counter the threat of invasion during the 16th century. Monthly guided walks of Rye Nature Reserve including Camber Castle: telephone for details.
**Location:** MAP 4:L5, OS189, Ref. TQ922 185. Across fields off A259, 1 mile S of Rye off harbour road.
**Open:** 1 Jul–30 Sept: Sats & Suns, 2–5pm. Last admission 4.30pm. Opening times subject to change.
**Admission:** Adult £2, Child/Conc. £1. Accompanied children, Free. Friends of Rye Harbour Nature Reserve & EH Members Free. Prices subject to change.
🛆 Unsuitable. 🖾 By arrangement. 🅿 None. 🖾 Guide dogs only.

Goodwood House, Chichester

Who's offering **accommodation?**
See our index on page 575

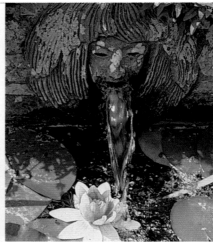

# CHARLESTON
### CHARLESTON, FIRLE, Nr LEWES, EAST SUSSEX BN8 6LL
www.charleston.org.uk

**Tel:** 01323 811265  **Fax:** 01323 811628  **E-mail:** info@charleston.org.uk
**Owner:** The Charleston Trust  **Contact:** Visitor Manager

When the artists Vanessa Bell and Duncan Grant moved to Charleston in 1916 they immediately began to transform the house with decorations. They painted the walls, doors, furniture and ceramics in their own unique and inspirational style and created original textiles. They also collected works of art by Renoir, Picasso, Matthew Smith, Sickert and Delacroix. Charleston became a meeting place for various members of the group of artists, writers and intellectuals known as Bloomsbury, which included the author, Virginia Woolf and the economist Maynard Keynes.

Guided tours of the house add a human touch and visitors can also explore the beautiful walled garden, with its mosaics, statues and ponds. Light refreshments are available in the Café and the Craft Council selected shop stocks a rich variety of ceramics, painted furniture, textiles, clothes and books

**Location:** MAP 4:J6, OS Ref. TQ490 069. 7m E of Lewes on A27 between Firle & Selmeston. Rail, bus, taxi & airport.

**Open:** Apr–Oct: Wed–Sun & BH Mons. Wed & Sat, 11.30am–6pm. Thurs & Fri, 2–6pm (Jul & Aug: 11.30am–6pm), guided tours. Sun & BH Mons, 2–6pm, unguided. (Last entry to the house 5pm.) "Sisters" Friday themed tour: (except in July and August). This 90 minute tour explores the lives of Vanessa Bell and Virginia Woolf and gives a rare opportunity to see the Kitchen and Bell's Studio.

**Admission:** House & Garden: Adult £6.50, Children £4.50, Disabled £4.50, Family £17.50, Conc £5.50, Wed–Thur only. Friday themed tour £7.50. Garden only: Adults £2.50, Children £1.50. Group bookings tel: 01323 811626 for rates and information.

ⓘ Filming & photography by arrangement. ⬚ ⊞ ⊤ ⑤ Partial. Access leaflet. WC. ⬛ ⑮ Obligatory, except Sun & BH Mons. Ⓟ ⬛ ⬛ Guide dogs only.

---

# CHICHESTER CATHEDRAL
### CHICHESTER, SUSSEX PO19 1PX
www.chichestercathedral.org.uk

**Tel:** 01243 782595  **Fax:** 01243 812499  **E-mail:** visitors@chichestercathedral.org.uk
**Contact:** Visitor Services Officer

In the heart of Chichester, this magnificent Cathedral has treasures ranging from medieval stone carvings to famous 20th century artworks. There is also a Treasury, regular exhibitions and free weekly lunchtime concerts. Guided tours daily and specialist tours are available (history, art, embroidery, stained glass, behind the scenes …). Superb new Cloisters Restaurant and Shop on site. The Cathedral does not charge for entry as we believe that this beautiful building should be available to all.

**Location:** MAP 3:F6, OS Ref. SU860 047. West Street, Chichester.

**Open:** Summer: 7.15am–7pm, Winter: 7.15am–6pm. Choral Evensong daily (except Wed) during term time.

**Admission:** Free entry. Donations greatly appreciated.

⬚ ⊤ Private functions and conferences. ⑤ ⊞ ⑮ ✤

---

## DENMANS GARDEN

**Denmans Lane, Fontwell, West Sussex BN18 0SU**
**Tel:** 01243 542808  **Fax:** 01243 544064  **E-mail:** denmans@denmans-garden.co.uk
**www.denmans-garden.co.uk**
**Owner:** John Brookes & Michael Neve  **Contact:** Mrs Claudia Murphy

Beautiful 4 acre garden designed for year round interest – through use of form, colour and texture – the home of John Brookes MBE, renowned garden designer and writer. Beautiful plant centre and Les Routiers award-winning fully licensed Garden Café (Café of the Year 2005 London & South East).

**Location:** MAP 3:G6, OS197 Ref. SZ947 070. Off the A27 (westbound) between Chichester (6m) and Arundel (5m).

**Open:** Daily. Garden: 9am–5pm (Nov–Feb, 9am–dusk). Plant centre: 9am–5pm. Café: 10am–5pm, and Fri & Sat evenings. Closed 24–26 Dec & 1 Jan.

**Admission:** Adult £4.25, Child (4–16) £2.50, OAP £3.80, Family (2+2) £12.50 & pre-booked groups (15+) £3.60.

⬚ ⊞ ⑤ WC. ⬛ Licensed. ⊞ Licensed. Group menus on request. Ⓟ ⬛ Guide dogs only. ✤

---

Parham House & Gardens, Storrington

Jeremy Whitaker

# FIRLE PLACE
## FIRLE, LEWES, EAST SUSSEX BN8 6LP

www.firleplace.co.uk

**Tel:** 01273 858307 (Enquiries)   **Events:** 01273 858567
**Fax:** 01273 858188   **Restaurant:** 01273 858307   **E-mail:** gage@firleplace.co.uk
**Owner:** The Rt Hon Viscount Gage

Firle Place is the home of the Gage family and has been for over 500 years. Set at the foot of the Sussex Downs within its own parkland, this unique house originally Tudor, was built of Caen stone, possibly from a monastery dissolved by Sir John Gage, friend of Henry VIII. Remodelled in the 18th century it is similar in appearance to that of a French château. The house contains a magnificent collection of Old Master paintings, fine English and European furniture and an impressive collection of Sèvres porcelain collected mainly by the 3rd Earl Cowper from Panshanger House, Hertfordshire.

**Events:** The Great Tudor Hall can, on occasion, be used for private dinners, with drinks on the Terrace or in the Billiard Room. A private tour of the house can be arranged. The paddock area is an ideal site for a marquee. The park can be used for larger events, using the house as a backdrop.

**Restaurant:** Enjoy the licensed restaurant and tea terrace with views over the garden for luncheon and cream teas.

**Location:** MAP 4:J6, OS Ref. TQ473 071. 4m S of Lewes on A27 Brighton / Eastbourne Road.

**Open:** Easter & BH Sun/Mon. Jun–Sept: Wed, Thur, Sun & BHs, 2–4.30pm. Dates and times subject to change without prior notice. Last admission 4.15pm.

**Admission:** Adult £6, Child £3, Conc. £5.50.

[i] No photography in house. ⬚ ⬚ ⬚ Ground floor & restaurant. ⬚ Licensed. ⬚ Tea Terrace. ⬚ Wed & Thur. P ⬚ In grounds on leads. ⬚

# FISHBOURNE ROMAN PALACE
## SALTHILL ROAD, FISHBOURNE, CHICHESTER, SUSSEX PO19 3QR

www.sussexpast.co.uk/fishbourne

**Tel:** 01243 785859   **Fax:** 01243 539266   **E-mail:** adminfish@sussexpast.co.uk
**Owner:** Sussex Past   **Contact:** David Rudkin

In the late first century AD, the Roman Palace was probably the largest domestic building in Britain. Today, the remains of its north wing, with many fine mosaic floors, can be seen inside a refurbished cover building. The story of this site is told through a new introductory programme using computer generated images, and in the museum using objects found in the excavations. Outside, the garden has been replanted to its original plan. 'Behind the Scenes' tours are given in the new Collections Discovery Centre, daily.

**Location:** MAP 3:F6, OS Ref. SU837 057. 1½m W of Chichester in Fishbourne village off A27/A259. 5 minutes walk from Fishbourne railway station.

**Open:** 22 Jan–15 Dec: daily. Jan/Feb, Nov/Dec: 10am–4pm. Mar–Jul & Sept/Oct: 10am–5pm. Aug: 10am–6pm. 16 Dec–21 Jan (excluding Christmas): Sats & Suns, 10am–4pm.

**Admission:** Adult £6.80, Child £3.60, Conc. £5.80, Family (2+2) £17.40, Registered disabled £5. Groups (20+): Adult £5.70, Child £3, Conc. £5.30.

⬚ ⬚ ⬚ ⬚ ⬚ By arrangement. P ⬚ ⬚ Guide dogs only. ✱ ⬚

# GLYNDE PLACE
## GLYNDE, Nr LEWES, EAST SUSSEX BN8 6SX

www.glyndeplace.com

**Tel/Fax:** 01273 858224   **E-mail:** info@glyndeplace.com
**Owners:** Viscount & Viscountess Hampden   **Contact:** Sue Tester

Glynde Place is a magnificent example of Elizabethan architecture commanding exceptionally fine views of the South Downs. Amongst the collections of 400 years of family living can be seen a fine collection of 17th and 18th century portraits of the Trevors, furniture, embroidery and silver.

**Location:** MAP 4:J5, OS Ref. TQ456 093. Sign posted off A27, 4m SE of Lewes at top of village. Rail: Glynde is on the London/Eastbourne and Brighton/Eastbourne mainline railway.

**Open:** May–Aug: Weds, Suns & BHs, 2–5pm (last admission to House 4.45pm). Garden & Tea Room: 12 noon–5pm. Private viewings by appointment.

**Admission:** House & Garden: Adult £6, Child (under 16yrs) £3. Garden: Adult £2, Child (under 16yrs) £1. Child under 12yrs Free. CPRE 2 for 1. Groups (25+) by appointment.

⬚ ⬚ ⬚ ⬚ ⬚ P Free. ⬚ Guide dogs only. ⬚

Jonathan Buckley

## GREAT DIXTER HOUSE & GARDENS

### NORTHIAM, RYE, EAST SUSSEX TN31 6PH

www.greatdixter.co.uk

**Tel:** 01797 252878   **Fax:** 01797 252879   **E-mail:** office@greatdixter.co.uk
**Owner:** Olivia Eller & The Great Dixter Charitable Trust   **Contact:** Perry Rodriguez
Great Dixter, built c1450 is the birthplace of the late Christopher Lloyd, gardening author. The house boasts the largest surviving timber-framed hall in the country. The gardens feature a variety of topiary, pools, wild meadow areas and the famous Long Border and Exotic Garden.
**Location:** MAP 4:L5, OS Ref. TQ817 251. Signposted off the A28 in Northiam.
**Open:** 1 April–28 Oct: Tue–Sun, 2–5pm. (May–Sept Gardens open 11am.)
**Admission:** House & Garden: Adult £7.50, Child £3. Gardens only: Adult £6, Child £2.50. Groups (25+) by appointment.
i No photography in House. Obligatory. P Limited for coaches. Guide dogs only.

## HAMMERWOOD PARK

### EAST GRINSTEAD, SUSSEX  RH19 3QE

www.hammerwoodpark.com

**Tel:** 01342 850594   **Fax:** 01342 850864   **E-mail:** latrobe@mistral.co.uk
**Owner/Contact:** David Pinnegar
Built in 1792 as an Apollo's hunting lodge by Benjamin Latrobe, architect of the Capitol and the White House, Washington DC. Owned by Led Zepplin in the 1970s, rescued from dereliction in 1982. Teas in the Organ Room; copy of the Parthenon frieze; and a derelict dining room still shocks the unwary. Guided tours (said by many to be the most interesting in Sussex) by the family.
**Location:** MAP 4:J4, OS Ref. TQ442 390. 3½ m E of East Grinstead on A264 to Tunbridge Wells, 1m W of Holtye.
**Open:** 1 June–end Sept: Wed, Sat & BH Mon, 2–5pm. Guided tour starts 2.05pm. Private groups: Easter–Jun. Coaches strictly by appointment. Small groups any time throughout the year by appointment.
**Admission:** House & Park: Adult £6, Child £2. Private viewing by arrangement.
i Conferences. Obligatory. In grounds. B&B. €

## GOODWOOD HOUSE

*See page 172 for full page entry.*

© NT Photographic Library / Bill Batten

Petworth House, Petworth

## HERSTMONCEUX CASTLE GARDENS

### HAILSHAM, SUSSEX  BN27 1RN

www.herstmonceux-castle.com

**Tel:** 01323 833816   **Fax:** 01323 834499   **E-mail:** c_dennett@isc.queensu.ac.uk
**Owner:** Queen's University, Canada   **Contact:** C Dennett
This breathtaking 15th century moated Castle is within 500 acres of parkland and gardens (including Elizabethan Garden) and is ideal for picnics and woodland walks. At Herstmonceux there is something for all the family. For information on our attractions or forthcoming events tel: 01323 834457.
**Location:** MAP 4:K5, OS Ref. TQ646 104. 2m S of Herstmonceux village (A271) by minor road. 10m WNW of Bexhill.
**Open:** 14 Apr–28 Oct (closed 4 Aug): daily, 10am–6pm (last adm. 5pm). Closes 5pm from Oct.
**Admission:** Grounds & Gardens: Adults £5, Child under 15yrs & Students £3 (child under 5 Free), Conc. £4, Family £13. Group rates/bookings available.
i Visitor Centre. Limited for Castle Tour. On leads.

David Sellman

## HIGH BEECHES WOODLAND & WATER GARDENS

**HIGH BEECHES, HANDCROSS, SUSSEX RH17 6HQ**

*www.highbeeches.com*

**Tel:** 01444 400589   **Fax:** 01444 401543   **E-mail:** gardens@highbeeches.com

**Owner:** High Beeches Gardens Conservation Trust (Reg. Charity)

**Contact:** Sarah Bray

Explore 25 acres of magically beautiful, peaceful woodland and water gardens. Daffodils, bluebells, azaleas, naturalised gentians, autumn colours. Rippling streams, enchanting vistas. Four acres of natural wildflower meadows. Rare plants. Marked trails. Recommended by Christopher Lloyd. Enjoy lunches and teas in the tearoom and tea lawn in restored Victorian farm building.

**Location:** MAP 4:I4, OS Ref. TQ275 308. S side of B2110. 1m NE of Handcross.

**Open:** 17 Mar–31 Oct: daily except Weds, 1–5pm (last adm. 4.30pm). Coaches/guided tours anytime, by appointment only.

**Admission:** Adult £5.50, Child (under 14yrs) Free. Concession for groups (30+). Guided tours for groups £10pp.

🚻 ♿ Partial. Tearoom fully accessible. 🍴 Licensed. 📷 By arrangement. 🅿 ✗ ♿

## LEWES CASTLE & BARBICAN HOUSE MUSEUM

**169 HIGH STREET, LEWES, SUSSEX BN7 1YE**

*www.sussexpast.co.uk/lewescastle*

**Tel:** 01273 486290   **Fax:** 01273 486990   **E-mail:** castle@sussexpast.co.uk

**Owner:** Sussex Past   **Contact:** Dr Sally White

Lewes's imposing Norman castle offers magnificent views across the town and surrounding downland. Barbican House, towered over by the Barbican Gate, is home to an interesting museum of local history and archaeology. A superb scale model of Victorian Lewes provides the centrepiece of a 25 minute audio-visual presentation telling the story of the county town of Sussex.

**Location:** MAP 4:I5, OS198 Ref. TQ412 101. Lewes town centre off A27/A26/A275.

**Open:** Daily (except Mons in Jan & 24–26 Dec). Tue–Sat: 10am–5.30pm; Sun, Mon & BHs, 11am–5.30pm. Castle closes at dusk in winter. Last admission 30 minutes prior to closing.

**Admission:** Adult £4.70, Child £2.40, Conc. £4.20. Family (2+2) £12.20 or (1+4) £9.50. Disabled/Carer £2.40. Groups (15+): Adult £4.20, Child £2, Conc. £3.60. Discounted joint ticket available with Anne of Cleves House.

🏠 ♿ Unsuitable. 📷 By arrangement. ▣ ✗ Guide dogs only. ❄ ♿

## HIGHDOWN GARDENS

**Littlehampton Road, Goring-by-Sea, Worthing, Sussex BN12 6PE**

**Tel:** 01903 501054

**Owner:** Worthing Borough Council   **Contact:** C Beardsley Esq

Unique gardens in disused chalk pit, begun in 1909.

**Location:** MAP 3:H6, OS Ref. TQ098 040. 3m WNW of Worthing on N side of A259, just W of the Goring roundabout.

**Open:** 1 Apr–30 Sept: Mon–Fri, 10am–6pm. W/ends & BHs, 10am–6pm. 1 Oct–30 Nov: Mon–Fri, 10am–4.30pm. 1 Dec–31 Jan: 10am–4pm. 1 Feb–31 Mar: Mon–Fri, 10am–4.30pm.

**Admission:** Free.

## LAMB HOUSE ⚜

**West Street, Rye, Sussex TN31 7ES**

**Tel:** 01580 762334   **Fax:** 01580 762334   **E-mail:** lambhouse@nationaltrust.org.uk

**Owner:** The National Trust

The beloved home of Henry James, where he wrote some of his best known novels including *The Wings of a Dove*. The house, with its pretty walled garden, has also been home to other literary names, including E F Benson and Rumer Godden.

**Location:** MAP 4:L5, OS Ref. TQ920 202. On West Street (facing west end of church).

**Open:** 22 Mar–27 Oct: Thurs & Sat, 2–6pm.

**Admission:** Adult £3.30, Child £1.70, Family £8.30. Group: £2.80.

## LEONARDSLEE LAKES & GARDENS

*See page 173 for full page entry.*

## MARLIPINS MUSEUM

**High Street, Shoreham-by-Sea, Sussex BN43 5DA**

**Tel:** 01273 462994 or 01323 441279   **E-mail:** marlipins@sussexpast.co.uk

*www.sussexpast.co.uk*

**Owner:** Sussex Past   **Contact:** Helen Poole

Shoreham's local and especially maritime history is explored at Marlipins, an important historic building of Norman origin.

**Location:** MAP 3:H6, OS198 Ref. TQ214 051. Shoreham town centre on A259, W of Brighton.

**Open:** 1 May–31 Oct: Tue–Sat, 10.30am–4.30pm.

**Admission:** Adult £2.50, Child £1.50, Conc. £2. Groups (15+): Adult £2, Child £1, Conc. £1.50.

© Patrick Lane

Lamb House, Rye

# MERRIMENTS GARDENS

### HAWKHURST ROAD, HURST GREEN, EAST SUSSEX TN19 7RA

www.merriments.co.uk

**Tel:** 01580 860666   **Fax:** 01580 860324   **E-mail:** info@merriments.co.uk

**Owner:** Family owned   **Contact:** Taryn Cook

Set in 4 acres of gently sloping Weald farmland, a naturalistic garden which never fails to delight. The garden is planted according to the prevailing conditions and many areas are planted only using plants suited for naturalising and colonising their environment. This natural approach to gardening harks back to the days of William Robinson and is growing in popularity, especially in Northern Europe. Most of the garden however is crammed with deep curved borders, colour themed and planted in the great tradition of English gardening. These borders use a rich mix of trees, shrubs, perennials, grasses and many unusual annuals which ensure an arresting display of colour, freshness and vitality in the garden right through to its closing in autumn.

**Location:** MAP 4:K5, OS198, Ref. TQ737 281. Signposted off A21 London–Hastings road, at Hurst Green.

**Open:** Apr–Sept: Mon–Sat, 10am–5pm, Suns, 10.30am–5pm.

**Admission:** Adult £4.50, Child £2. Groups (15+) by arrangement £4pp.

⬚ 🅴 ♿ 🖵 Licensed. 🍽 🎞 By arrangement. 🅿 🖮 In grounds, on leads.

# MICHELHAM PRIORY 🏛

### UPPER DICKER, HAILSHAM, SUSSEX BN27 3QS

www.sussexpast.co.uk/michelham

**Tel:** 01323 844224   **Fax:** 01323 844030   **E-mail:** adminmich@sussexpast.co.uk

**Owner:** Sussex Past   **Contact:** Chris Tuckett

Explore the Tudor mansion that evolved from the former Augustinian Priory, set on a tranquil island encircled by England's longest water-filled medieval moat. Beautiful grounds include physic, cloister and kitchen gardens, orchard, nature and sculpture trails, moat walk and rope museum. The watermill and forge are still working order. Telephone for special event details.

**Location:** MAP 4:J5, OS Ref. TQ557 093. 8m NW of Eastbourne off A22/A27. 2m W of Hailsham.

**Open:** 1 Mar–31 Oct: Tue–Sun & BH Mons & daily in Aug. Mar & Oct: 10.30am–4.30pm. Apr–Jul & Sept: 10.30am–5pm. Aug: 10.30am–5.30pm.

**Admission:** Adult £6, Child £3, Conc. £5, Family (2+2) £15.20, Registered disabled & carer £3 each. Groups (15+): Adult/Conc. £4.80, Child £2.80.

⬚ 🅴 🍴 🖵 💺 🍽 Licensed. 🎞 By arrangement. 🅿 Ample for cars & coaches. 🔳 🖮 Guide dogs only. 🅰 🖮

## MONK'S HOUSE 🦋

### Rodmell, Lewes BN7 3HF

**Tel:** 01323 870001 (Property Office)

**Owner:** The National Trust   **Contact:** Property Office

A small weather-boarded house, the home of Leonard and Virginia Woolf until Leonard's death in 1969.

**Location:** MAP 4:I6, OS Ref. TQ421 064. 4 m E of Lewes, off former A275 in Rodmell village, near church.

**Open:** 31 Mar–27 Oct: Weds & Sats, 2–5.30pm. Last admission 5pm. Groups by arrangement with tenant.

**Admission:** Adult £3.30, Child £1.65, Family £8.25.

## NYMANS GARDEN 🦋

### Handcross, nr Haywards Heath, RH17 6EB

**Tel:** 01444 400321   **Fax:** 01444 400253   **E-mail:** nymans@nationaltrust.org.uk

One of the great 20th century gardens, astonishing in its diversity and richness of its plant collection. Nymans Garden reflects the innovation of the Messel family who created it and the pioneering spirit of the plant hunters who supplied the garden with rare specimens.

**Location:** MAP 4:I4, On B2114 at Handcross, 4½m south of Crawley, just off London-Brighton M23/A23.

**Open:** Garden: 14 Feb–23 Dec: Weds–Sun, 11am–6pm (4pm 31 Oct–23 Dec). House: 21 Mar–28 Oct: Weds–Sun, 11.30am–5pm. Shop: 14 Feb–2 Dec: Weds–Sun, 11am–6pm. Christmas Shop: 3–24 Dec: daily, 11am–4pm. Restaurant: 14 Feb–23 Dec: Weds–Sun, 11am–5pm. Christmas Lunches 4–23 Dec Tues–Sun, 11am–4pm. Open BHs. Closed 25, 26, 29 & 30 Dec. Open 31 Dec.

**\*Admission:** Adult £7.70, Child £3.80, Family £19.20, Groups £6. *includes a voluntary donation but visitors can choose to pay the standard prices displayed at the property and on the website.

See which properties offer **educational facilities** or **school visits** in our index on page 571

## PALLANT HOUSE GALLERY

**9 North Pallant, Chichester, West Sussex. PO19 1TJ**
**Tel:** 01243 774557
**Owner:** Pallant House Gallery Trust    **Contact:** Reception
The Gallery of Modern Art in the South opened in 2006 with a contemporary wing alongside a Queen Anne townhouse and a contemporary extension showcasing the best of 20th century British Art.
**Location:** MAP 3:F6, OS Ref. SU861 047. City centre, SE of the Cross.
**Open:** Tue-Sat: 10am–5pm. Thur: 10am–8pm. Sun & BH Mons: 12.30–5pm
**Admission:** Adults £6.50, Children (6–15): £2, Students £3.50. Under 5s Free, Family (2 + 4): £15.

Arundel Castle, Arundel

## PARHAM HOUSE & GARDENS 🏠

### PARHAM PARK, STORRINGTON, Nr PULBOROUGH, WEST SUSSEX RH20 4HS

www.parhaminsussex.co.uk

**Tel:** 01903 742021   **Info Line:** 01903 744888   **Fax:** 01903 746557
**E-mail:** enquiries@parhaminsussex.co.uk
**Owner:** Parham Park Trust   **Contact:** Barbara Harwood
This stunning Elizabethan house, with its award-winning Gardens, is set in the heart of a medieval deer park, below the South Downs. Parham staff are renowned for the warm welcome they give to visitors, who come to see the light panelled rooms, from Great Hall to Long Gallery, filled with early paintings, furniture and needlework.
Much admired are the large bowls of informally-arranged flowers which have been grown in the walled garden with its huge herbaceous borders, greenhouse and herbiary. Light lunches and cream teas are served in the 16th century Big Kitchen and souvenirs

and gifts can be purchased from the shop. Plant sales area.
**Location:** MAP 3:G5, OS Ref. TQ060 143. Midway between Pulborough & Storrington on A283. Equidistant from A24 & A29.
**Open:** Easter Sun–end Sept: Wed, Thurs, Sun & BH Mon afternoons, also Tues & Fri afternoons in Aug.
**Admission:** Please contact property for details.
ℹ No photography in house. 🏠 🎫 ♿ Partial. 🍴 Licensed. 🎫 By arrangement 🏠
🅿 🚻 🐕 In grounds, on leads. 🎫 Special charges may apply. Please contact property for details. We regret that HHA passes are not valid for Special Event weekends. Annual Garden Weekend – 8/9 July.

## PASHLEY MANOR GARDENS 🌿    *See page 174 for full page entry.*

## PETWORTH COTTAGE MUSEUM

**346 High Street, Petworth, West Sussex  GU28 0AU**
**Tel:** 01798 342100   **E-mail:** stevensonguk@yahoo.co.uk
**Owner:** Petworth Cottage Trust    **Contact:** Curator
Step into a Leconfield Estate Cottage furnished as if it were 1910. Lighting is by gas, heating by coal-fired range. The scullery has a stone sink and a copper for the weekly wash.
**Location:** MAP 3:G5
**Open:** Apr–Oct: Wed–Sun & BH Mons, 2–4.30pm.
**Admission:** Adult £2.50, Child (under 14yrs) 50p. Group visits by arrangement.

## PETWORTH HOUSE & PARK 🌿    *See page 175 for full page entry.*

Stansted Park, Rowlands Castle

## PEVENSEY CASTLE ⌗

**Pevensey, Sussex BN24 5LE**

**Tel/Fax:** 01323 762604   www.english-heritage.org.uk/visits

**Owner:** English Heritage   **Contact:** Visitor Operations Team

Originally a 4th-century Roman fort, Pevensey was the place where William the Conqueror landed in 1066 and established his first stronghold. The Norman castle includes the remains of an unusual keep within the massive walls. An inclusive audio tour tells the story of the castle's 2,000 year history.

**Location:** MAP 4:K6, OS Ref. TQ645 048. In Pevensey off A259.

**Open:** 1 Apr–31 Oct: daily, 10am–6pm (Oct 4pm). 1 Nov–20 Mar 2008: Sats & Suns, 10am–4pm. Closed 24–26 Dec & 1 Jan. EH Members Free.

**Admission:** Adult £4, Child £2, Conc. £3. 15% discount for groups of 11+.

ℹ WC. 🖼 ♿ Grounds. 🐕 🎧 Inclusive. 🅿 🚌 In grounds, on leads. ✳

## PRESTON MANOR
### PRESTON DROVE, BRIGHTON, EAST SUSSEX BN1 6SD

www.prestonmanor.virtualmuseum.info

**Tel:** 01273 292770   **Fax:** 01273 292771   **Email:** museums@brighton-hove.gov.uk

**Owner:** Brighton & Hove City Council

A delightful Manor House which powerfully evokes the atmosphere of an Edwardian gentry home both 'upstairs' and 'downstairs'. Explore more than twenty rooms over four floors – from the servants' quarters, kitchens and butler's pantry in the basement to the attic bedrooms and nursery on the top floor. Plus charming walled gardens, pets' cemetery and 13th century parish church.

**Location:** MAP 4:I6, OS Ref. TQ303 064. 2m N of Brighton seafront on A23 London Road.

**Open:** Apr–Sept: Tues–Sat, 10am–5pm. Suns, 2–5pm. Oct–Mar: open for pre-booked groups, school visits & special events.

**Admission:** Adult £4, Child (under 16yrs) £2.30, Conc. £3.30. Family (2+4) £10.30 or (1+2) £6.30. Groups (up to 20) minimum charge £35, Groups (20+) £3.40 Tour leader & driver Free. Prices valid until 31 Mar 2007.

ℹ No photography. 🖼 Gift kiosk. 🍴 ♿ Unsuitable. 🎧 By arrangement. ▣ 🅿 For coaches and cars. 🚌 🎭 Spring, Summer & Autumn half-term. Easter & Summer. Children's activities all year round. Tel: 01273 292843 for details.

## THE PRIEST HOUSE
### NORTH LANE, WEST HOATHLY, SUSSEX RH19 4PP

www.sussexpast.co.uk/priest house

**Tel:** 01342 810479   **E-mail:** priest@sussexpast.co.uk

**Owner:** Sussex Past   **Contact:** Antony Smith

Standing in the beautiful surroundings of a traditional cottage garden on the edge of Ashdown Forest, The Priest House is an early 15th century timber-framed hall-house. In Elizabethan times it was modernised into a substantial yeoman's dwelling. Its furnished rooms now contain 17th and 18th century furniture, kitchen equipment, needlework and household items. A fragrant formal herb garden contains over 150 different herbs.

**Location:** MAP 4:J4, OS187 Ref. TQ362 325. In triangle formed by Crawley, East Grinstead and Haywards Heath, 4m off A22, 6m off M23.

**Open:** 1 Mar–31 Oct: Tue–Sat & BHs plus Mons during Aug: 10.30am–5.30pm; Sun, 12 noon–5.30pm.

**Admission:** Adult £2.90, Child £1.45, Conc. £2.60. Disabled/Carer £1.45, Groups (15+): Adult £2.60.

🖼 🍴 ♿ Partial. 🎧 By arrangement. 🅿 Limited (on street). ▣ 🚌 In grounds, on leads.

---

**THE ROYAL PAVILION**   *See page 176 for full page entry.*

---

**SAINT HILL MANOR**   *See page 177 for full page entry.*

---

For **corporate hospitality** at unique venues see the index on page 567

© Skyscan

Glynde Place, Nr Lewes

# ST MARY'S HOUSE & GARDENS 🏛
### BRAMBER, WEST SUSSEX BN44 3WE
www.stmarysbramber.co.uk

**Tel/Fax:** 01903 816205   **E-mail:** info@stmarysbramber.co.uk
**Owners:** Mr Peter Thorogood MBE and Mr Roger Linton MBE

This enchanting, medieval house is situated in the picturesque downland village of Bramber. The fine panelled interiors, including the unique Elizabethan 'Painted Room' with its intriguing *trompe l'oeil* murals, give an air of tranquillity and timelessness. Once the home of the real Algernon and Gwendolen brilliantly portrayed in Oscar Wilde's comedy, *The Importance of Being Earnest*, St Mary's has served as a location for a number of television series including the world-famous *Dr Who*. The formal gardens with amusing animal topiary include an exceptional example of the prehistoric 'Living Fossil' tree, *Gingko Biloba*, and a mysterious ivy-clad 'Monk's Walk'. In the Victorian 'Secret' Garden can be seen the fruit-wall and former potting shed (now housing the Rural Museum), Jubilee Rose Garden, Terracotta Garden and woodland walk. St Mary's features in Simon Jenkins' book *England's Thousand Best Houses*, and was highly commended in the Tourism ExSEllence Awards. The garden, becaue of its literary connections, was nominated by *The Independent* as one of "Britain's 50 Best Gardens to Visit". St Mary's is a house of fascination and mystery. Many thousands of visitors have admired its picturesque charm and enjoyed its atmosphere of friendliness and welcome, qualities which make it a visit to remember.

**Location:** MAP 3:H6, OS Ref. TQ189 105. Bramber village off A283. From London 56m via M23/A23 or A24. Bus from Shoreham to Steyning, alight St Mary's, Bramber.

**Open:** May–end Sept: Suns, Thurs & BH Mons, 2–6pm. Last entry 5pm. Groups at other times by arrangement.

**Admission:** House & Gardens: Adult £6. Child £3. Conc. £5.50. Groups (25+) £5.50.
ℹ No photography in house. Partial. Obligatory for groups (max 60). Visit time 2½hrs. 🅿 30 cars, 2 coaches.

# SACKVILLE COLLEGE
### HIGH STREET, EAST GRINSTEAD, WEST SUSSEX RH19 3BX
www.sackville-college.co.uk

**Tel:** 01342 326561   **E-mail:** sackvillecollege@yahoo.com
**Owner:** Board of Trustees   **Contact:** College Co-ordinator

Built in 1609 for Richard Sackville, Earl of Dorset, as an almshouse and overnight accommodation for the Sackville family. Feel the Jacobean period come alive in the enchanting quadrangle, the chapel, banqueting hall with fine hammerbeam roof and minstrel's gallery, the old common room and warden's study where "Good King Wenceslas" was composed. Chapel weddings by arrangement.

**Location:** MAP 4:I4, A22 to East Grinstead, College in High Street (town centre).
**Open:** 17 Jun–15 Sept: Wed–Sun, 2–5pm. Groups all year by arrangement.
**Admission:** Adult £3.50, Child £1. Groups: (10–60) no discount.
ℹ Large public car park adjacent to entrance. Partial. Obligatory. 🅿 Limited. Guide dogs only. By arrangement.

Goodwood House, Chichester

## SHEFFIELD PARK GARDEN 🌿 *See page 178 for full page entry.*

NTPL/ Rupert Trueman

Raymond Woodham

## STANDEN 🌿
### EAST GRINSTEAD, WEST SUSSEX RH19 4NE

www.nationaltrust.org.uk/standen

**Tel:** 01342 323029   **Fax:** 01342 316424   **E-mail:** standen@nationaltrust.org.uk
**Owner:** The National Trust   **Contact:** The Property Manager

Dating from the 1890s and containing original Morris & Co furnishings and decorations, Standen survives today as a remarkable testimony to the ideals of the Arts and Crafts Movement. The property was built as a family home by the influential architect Philip Webb and retains a warm, welcoming atmosphere. Details of Webb's designs can be found everywhere from the fireplaces to the original electric light fittings.

**Location:** MAP 4:I4, OS Ref. TQ389 356. 2m S of East Grinstead, signposted from B2110.

**Open:** House, Garden, Shop & Restaurant: 3–11 Mar: Sats & Suns, 11am–3pm. 17 Mar–28 Oct: Wed–Sun & BHs. 11am–4.30pm (last entry to house 4pm). Also Mons 16 Jul–2 Sept only. Garden, Shop & Restaurant: 3 Nov–16 Dec: Sats & Suns, 11am–3pm.

**Admission:** House & Garden: £7.50, Family £18.75. Garden only: £4.40. Joint ticket with same day entry to Nymans Garden £12.75, available Wed–Fri. Groups: £5.80, only if booked in advance.

🖸 🕸 🔲 🔄 Partial. WC. 🍽 Licensed. 🅿 🔲 🖪 In woods on leads, not in garden. 🖤

## STANSTED PARK 🏛
### STANSTED PARK, ROWLANDS CASTLE, HAMPSHIRE PO9 6DX

www.stanstedpark.co.uk

**Tel:** 023 9241 2265   **Fax:** 023 9241 3773   **E-mail:** enquiry@stanstedpark.co.uk
**Owner:** Stansted Park Foundation   **Contact:** House Administrator

'One of the South's most beautiful stately homes'. The State Rooms and fully restored Servants' Quarters of Stansted House give the visitor a fascinating insight into the social history of an English Country House in its heyday in Edwardian times.

**Location:** MAP 3:F5, OS Ref. SU761 103. Follow brown heritage signs from A3 Rowlands Castle or A27 Havant. Rail: Mainline station, Havant.

**Open:** House & Chapel: Easter Sun–24 Sept: 1–5pm (last entry 4pm). House & Chapel closed during events. Jul & Aug: Sun–Wed. Tea Room & Garden Centre open all year. Restricted access on Sats and during events. Stanstead Park Light Railway runs through Arboretum. 02392 413324 for timetable.

**Admission:** House, Grounds & Chapel: Adult £6, Child (5–15yrs) £3.50, Conc. £5, Family (2+3) £15. Groups/educational visits by arrangement.

🕸 🔲 Private & corporate hire. 🔄 🔲 🖪 By arrangement. 🅿 🔲 By arrangement. 🖪 Guide dogs only. 🔺🕸 Grounds. 🖤

St Mary's House, Bramber

## UPPARK 🌿
### SOUTH HARTING, PETERSFIELD GU31 5QR

www.nationaltrust.org.uk/uppark

**Tel:** 01730 825415   **Fax:** 01730 825873   **E-mail:** uppark@nationaltrust.org.uk
**Owner:** The National Trust   **Contact:** Administrator

Marvel at the historic elegance of Uppark – with fine, late-Georgian interiors and collections of paintings, ceramics and textiles, extensive basement rooms, famous dolls house, Regency garden (stunning views to the sea), children's activities, award-winning shop and restaurant – not to mention a fascinating Exhibition – there's everything for a perfect day out.

**Location:** MAP 3:F5, OS Ref 197 SU781 181. Between Petersfield & Chichester on B2146.

**Open:** 1 Apr–25 Oct: Sun–Thur; Grounds, Exhibition, Shop & Restaurant: 11.30am–5pm; House: 11.30am–4.30pm; rest of property: 11am–5pm (last entry 4pm). BH Suns, Mons & Good Fri. Print Room open 1st Mon of each month.

**Admission:** Adult £7.50, Child £3.75, Family £18, Groups (15+) must book: £6.50.

🖸 🕸 🔄 🅿 🖪 By arrangement. 🖤

South East – England

## WEALD & DOWNLAND OPEN AIR MUSEUM

**Singleton, Chichester, Sussex PO18 0EU**
**Tel:** 01243 811348    www.wealddown.co.uk

Over 45 original rescued historic buildings. Interiors and gardens through the ages. Plus traditional breed farm animals, all set in Sussex's beautiful South Downs.
**Location:** MAP 3:F5, OS Ref. SU876 127. 6m N of Chichester on A286. S of Singleton.
**Open:** Throughout the year, telephone or see website for details.
**Admission:** Adult £8.25, Child/Student £4.40, OAP £7.25. Family (2+3) £22.65. Group rates on request.

## WEST DEAN GARDENS

### WEST DEAN, CHICHESTER, WEST SUSSEX PO18 0QZ

www.westdean.org.uk

**Tel:** 01243 818210  **Fax:** 01243 811342  **E-mail:** gardens@westdean.org.uk
**Owner:** The Edward James Foundation  **Contact:** Jim Buckland, Gardens Manager

A place of tranquillity and beauty in the rolling South Downs all year round, West Dean features a restored walled kitchen garden with some of the finest Victorian glasshouses in the country. Rustic summerhouses, a 300ft Edwardian pergola, ornamental borders and a pond contrast with over 200 varieties of carefully trained fruit trees, rows of vegetables and exotic produce behind glass. For the more active, enjoy a circular walk through a 49-acre arboretum offers breathtaking views of the estate and its fine flint house and parkland setting.
**Location:** MAP 3:F5, OS Ref. SU863 128. SE of A286 Midhurst Road, 6m N of Chichester.
**Open:** Mar–Oct: daily, 10.30am–5pm (last adm 4.30pm). Nov–Feb: Wed–Sun, 10.30am–4pm.
**Admission:** Summer: Adult £6, Child £3, Family £15, Groups £5.50. Winter: Adult £3, Child £1.50, Family £7.50, Groups £2.75. Single Season £22.50. Family Season £50.

Licensed. P Limited for coaches. By arrangement. Guide dogs only.

## WILMINGTON PRIORY

**Wilmington, Nr Eastbourne, East Sussex BN26 5SW**
**Tel:** 01628 825925  www.landmarktrust.org.uk
**Owner:** Leased to the Landmark Trust by Sussex Archaeological Society
**Contact:** The Landmark Trust

Founded by the Benedictines in the 11th century, the surviving, much altered buildings date largely from the 14th century. Managed and maintained by the Landmark Trust, which lets buildings for self-catering holidays. Full details of Wilmington Priory and 184 other historic buildings available for holidays are featured in The Landmark Handbook (price £11.50 refundable against booking), from The Landmark Trust, Shottesbrooke, Maidenhead, Berkshire, SL6 3SW.
**Location:** MAP 3:F5, OS Ref. TQ543 042. 600yds S of A27. 6m NW of Eastbourne.
**Open:** Available for self-catering holidays for up to 6 people throughout the year. Grounds, Ruins, Porch & Crypt: on 30 days between Apr–Oct. Whole property including interiors on 8 of these days. Contact the Landmark Trust for detailss.
**Admission:** Free entry on open days.

© NT Photographic Library / Nadia MacKenzie

Uppark, Petersfield

www.hudsonsguide.co.uk

191

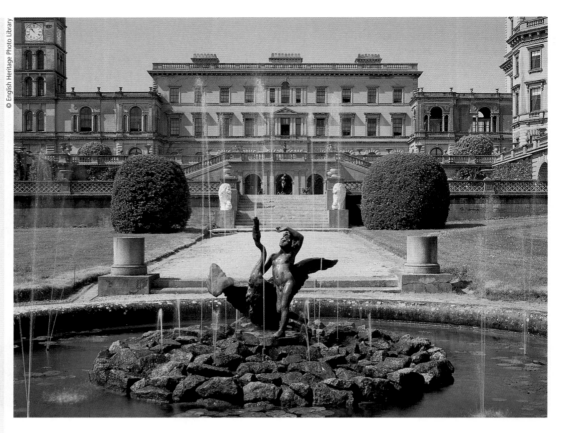

© English Heritage Photo Library

## Owner
English Heritage

## Contact
The House Administrator
Osborne House
Royal Apartments
East Cowes
Isle of Wight
PO32 6JX

**Tel:** 01983 200022
**Fax:** 01983 281380

Venue Hire and
Hospitality:
**Tel:** 01983 203055

## Location
**MAP 3:D6**
**OS Ref. SZ516 948**

1 mile SE of East Cowes.

**Ferry:** Isle of Wight
ferry terminals.

Red Funnel, East Cowes
1½ miles
Tel: 02380 334010.

Wightlink, Fishbourne
4 miles
Tel: 0870 582 7744

## Opening Times
**House**

1 April–30 September
Daily: 10am–5pm.
Last admission 4pm.

1–31 October
Daily: 10am–4pm.

1 Nov–20 March 2008,
Wed–Sun: 10am–4pm.
Guided tours only.
Last tour 2.30pm.
Christmas Tour Season:
10 November–6 January.
Pre-booking essential on
01983 200022.

Closed 24–26 December
& 1 January.

Closes early 20/21 &
27/28 July & 6 Aug for
special events.

## Admission
**House & Grounds**
| | |
|---|---|
| Adult | £9.80 |
| Child (5–15yrs) | £4.90 |
| Child under 5yrs | Free |
| Conc. | £7.40 |
| Family (2+3) | £24.50 |

**Grounds only**
| | |
|---|---|
| Adult | £5.90 |
| Child (5–15yrs) | £3.00 |
| Child under 5yrs | Free |
| Conc. | £4.40 |
| Family (2+3) | £14.80 |

Groups (11+) 15%
discount. Tour leader and
driver have free entry.
1 extra free place for
every additional 20
paying.

## Conference/Function

| ROOM | MAX CAPACITY |
|---|---|
| Durbar Hall | standing 80 seated 50 |
| Upper Terrace | standing 250 |
| Walled Gardens | standing 100 |
| Marquee | Large scale events possible |

# OSBORNE HOUSE

Osborne House was the peaceful, rural retreat of Queen Victoria, Prince Albert and their family; they spent some of their happiest times here.

Step inside and marvel at the richness of the State Apartments including the Durbar Room with its lavish Indian décor. The Queen died at the house in 1901 and many of the rooms have been preserved almost unaltered ever since. The nursery bedroom remains just as it was in the 1870s when Queen Victoria's first grandchildren came to stay. Children were a constant feature of life at Osborne (Victoria and Albert had nine). Don't miss the Swiss Cottage, a charming chalet in the grounds built for teaching the royal children domestic skills.

Enjoy the beautiful gardens with their stunning views over the Solent and the fruit and flower Victorian Walled Garden.

ℹ WCs. Suitable for filming, concerts, drama. No photography in the House. Children's play area.

🏠 Private and corporate hire.

♿ Wheelchairs available, access to house via ramp and first floor via lift. WC.

🍴 Hot drinks, light snacks & waiter service lunches in the stunning terrace restaurant.

🚶 Open from Nov–Mar for pre-booked guided tours only. These popular tours allow visitors to see the Royal Apartments and private rooms at a quieter time of the year, and in the company of one of our expert guides.

Ⓟ Ample.

📖 Visits free, please book. Education room available.

## APPULDURCOMBE HOUSE ⌗

**Wroxall, Shanklin, Isle of Wight**
**Tel:** 01983 852484   www.english-heritage.org.uk/visits
**Owner:** English Heritage    **Contact:** Mr & Mrs Owen
The bleached shell of a fine 18th-century Baroque style house standing in grounds landscaped by 'Capability' Brown. An exhibition displays prints and photographs depicting the history of the house.
**Location:** MAP 3:D7, OS Ref. SZ543 800. ½mile W of Wroxall off B3327.
**Open:** 1 Apr–30 Sept: daily, 10am–4pm. Last entry 1hr before closing.
**Admission:** House: Adult £3.25, Child £2.25, Conc. £3, Family £10. EH members Free.
🖬 🖾 🅿 Limited. 🖼 In grounds, on leads. 🖳 Tel. for details.

## BEMBRIDGE WINDMILL ⚘

**Correspondence to: NT Office, Strawberry Lane, Mottistone,**
**Isle of Wight PO30 4EA**
**Tel:** 01983 873945   www.nationaltrust.org.uk
**Owner:** The National Trust    **Contact:** The Custodian
Dating from around 1700, this is the only windmill to survive on the Island. Much of its original wooden machinery is still intact and there are spectacular views from the top.
**Location:** MAP 3:E7, OS Ref. SZ639 874. ½m S of Bembridge off B3395.
**Open:** 25 Mar–30 Jun & 1–28 Oct: daily except Sat; 1 Jul–30 Sept: daily, 10am–5pm. Open Easter Sat.
**Admission:** Adult £2.40, Child £1.20, Family £6. Free to NT members. All school groups are conducted by a NT guide; special charges apply.
🖬 🖳 🔧 By arrangement. 🅿 100 yds. 🔳 🖼 Guide dogs only.

## BRIGHSTONE SHOP & MUSEUM ⚘

**North St, Brighstone, Isle of Wight PO30 4AX**
**Tel:** 01983 740689
**Owner:** The National Trust    **Contact:** The Manager
The traditional cottages contain a National Trust shop and Village Museum (run by Brighstone Museum Trust) depicting village life in the late 19th century.
**Location:** MAP 3:D7, OS Ref. SZ428 828. North Street, Brighstone, just off B3399.
**Open:** 2 Jan–1 Apr: Mon–Sat, 10am–1pm. 2 Apr–25 May: Mon–Sat, 10am–4pm. 26 May–30 Sept: daily, 10am–5pm (Suns from 12 noon). 1 Oct–22 Dec: Mon–Sat, 10am–4pm. 24 Dec–1 Jan 2008: Mon, Fri, Sat, 10am–1pm.
**Admission:** Free.
🖾 Partial. 🏵

## CARISBROOKE CASTLE ⌗
### NEWPORT, ISLE OF WIGHT PO30 1XY

www.english-heritage.org.uk/visits

**Tel:** 01983 522107   **Fax:** 01983 528632
**Owner:** English Heritage    **Contact:** Visitor Operations Team
The island's royal fortress and prison of King Charles I before his execution in London in 1648. See the famous Carisbrooke donkeys treading the wheel in the Well House as donkeys would have done in the 18th century. Visit the on-site Carisbrooke Museum and enjoy an invigorating battlements walk.
**Location:** MAP 3:E7, OS196 Ref. SZ486 877. Off the B3401, 1¼ miles SW of Newport.
**Open:** 1 Apr–30 Sept: daily, 10am–5pm. 1 Oct–20 Mar 2008: daily, 10am–4pm. Closed 24–26 Dec & 1 Jan.
**Admission:** Adult £5.60, Child £2.80, Conc. £4.20, Family (2+3) £14. 15% discount for groups (11+). EH Members Free.
ℹ WCs. 🖬 🖾 🖳 🅿 🖼 In grounds, on leads. 🔳 🖳 Tel. for details.

## MORTON MANOR

**Brading, Isle of Wight PO36 0EP**
**Tel/Fax:** 01983 406168   **E-mail:** mortonmanor-iow@amserve.com
**Owner/Contact:** Mr J A J Trzebski
Refurbished in the Georgian period. Magnificent gardens, vineyard and maize maze.
**Location:** MAP 3:E7, OS Ref. SZ603 863 (approx.). ¼m W of A3055 in Brading.
**Open:** Easter–end Oct: daily except Sats, 10am–5.30pm. Last admission 4.30pm.
**Admission:** Adult £5, Child £2.50, Conc. £4.50, Group (10+) £4.

## MOTTISTONE MANOR GARDEN ⚘

**Mottistone, Isle of Wight PO30 4ED**
**Tel**: 01983 741302   www.nationaltrust.org.uk
**Owner:** The National Trust    **Contact:** The Gardener
This magical garden with colourful borders, shrub-filled banks and grassy terraces, is set in a sheltered valley with views to the sea and surrounds an Elizabethan manor house (tenanted). Family activity packs available plus delightful walks onto the Downs across the adjoining Mottistone Estate.
**Location:** MAP 3:D7, OS Ref. SZ406 838. 2m W of Brighstone on B3399.
**Open:** 25 Mar–28 Oct: Sun–Thur, 11am–5.30pm. House: Aug BH Mon only: 2–5.30pm. Guided tours for NT members on that day 10am–12 noon.
**Admission:** Garden: Adult £3.30, Child £1.70, Family £8.30. Free to NT members. Extra charges for house.
🖬 🖳 🖾 Limited access for wheelchair users. 🖳 🅿 🖼 In grounds, on leads.

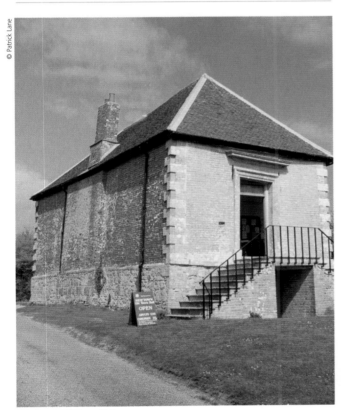

© Patrick Lane

Newtown Old Town Hall

For rare and unusual plants visit the **plant sales** index on page 564

© English Heritage Photo Library © Skyscan Balloon Photography

## NEEDLES OLD BATTERY

**West High Down, Totland, Isle of Wight  PO39 0JH**

**Tel:** 01983 754772   **www.nationaltrust.org.uk**

**Owner:** The National Trust   **Contact:** The Fort Manager

Built in 1862 following the threat of a French invasion, this spectacularly sited fort contains exhibitions about its involvement in both World Wars. Two original gun barrels are displayed on the parade ground and a tunnel leads to a searchlight emplacement perched above the Needles Rocks. Family activity packs available.

**Location:** MAP 3:C7, OS Ref. SZ300 848. Needles Headland W of Freshwater Bay & Alum Bay (B3322).

**Open:** 25 Mar–30 Jun, 1 Sept–28 Oct: Sat–Thur (open Good Fri); 1 Jul–31 Aug, daily, 10.30am–5pm. Tearoom also open: 13 Jan–18 Mar, 3 Nov–16 Dec, Sats & Suns; 11am–3pm. Closes in high winds; please telephone on day of visit to check.

**Admission:** Adult £4.20, Child £2.10, Family £10.50. Free to NT members. Special charges for guided tours.

⬚ ⬚ Partial. ⬚ ⬚ By appointment. ⬚ ⬚ In grounds, on leads.

## NEWTOWN OLD TOWN HALL ⬚

**Newtown, Isle of Wight**

**Tel:** 01983 531785   **www.nationaltrust.org.uk**

**Owner:** The National Trust   **Contact:** The Custodian

A charming 17th century building that was once the focal point of the 'rotten borough' of Newtown. Regular art exhibitions.

**Location:** MAP 3:D7, OS Ref. SZ424 905. Between Newport and Yarmouth, 1m N of A3054.

**Open:** 25 Mar–30 Jun, 1 Sept–24 Oct: Mon, Wed & Sun; 1 Jul–31 Aug: Sun–Thur, 2–5pm. Open Good Fri & Easter Sat.

**Admission:** Adult £1.90, Child 95p, Family £4.75.  Free to NT members.

⬚ Limited. ⬚ Guide dogs only.

## NUNWELL HOUSE & GARDENS

**Coach Lane, Brading, Isle of Wight  PO36 0JQ**

**Tel:** 01983 407240

**Owner:** Col & Mrs J A Aylmer   **Contact:** Mrs J A Aylmer

Nunwell has been a family home for five centuries and reflects much architectural and Island history. King Charles I spent his last night of freedom here. Jacobean and Georgian wings. Finely furnished rooms. Lovely setting with Channel views and five acres of tranquil gardens including walled garden. Family military collections.

**Location:** MAP 3:E7, OS Ref. SZ595 874. 1m NW of Brading. 3m S of Ryde signed off A3055.

**Open:** 27/28 May & 2 Jul–5 Sept: Mon–Wed, 1–5pm. House tours: 1.30, 2.30 & 3.30pm. Groups welcome by arrangement throughout the year.

**Admission:** Adult £5, Pair of Adults £9 (inc guide book), Child (under 10yrs) £1, OAP/Student £4. Garden only: Adult £2.50.

⬚ ⬚ Obligatory. ⬚ ⬚ Guide dogs only. ⬚

## OSBORNE HOUSE ⬚

*See page 192 for full page entry.*

## YARMOUTH CASTLE ⬚

**Quay Street, Yarmouth, Isle of Wight  PO41 0PB**

**Tel:** 01983 760678   **www.english-heritage.org.uk/visits**

**Owner:** English Heritage   **Contact:** Visitor Operations Team

This last addition to Henry VIII's coastal defences was completed in 1547 and is, unusually for its kind, square with a fine example of an angle bastion. It was garrisoned well into the 19th century. Fine views of the Solent and a new exhibition.

**Location:** MAP 3:C7, OS Ref. SZ354 898. In Yarmouth adjacent to car ferry terminal.

**Open:** 1 Apr–30 Sept: Sun–Thurs, 11am–4pm.

**Admission:** Adult £2.90, Child £1.50, Conc. £2.20. EH Members Free.

⬚ ⬚ Ground floor. ⬚ None. ⬚ In grounds, on leads.

Many properties hold **special events** throughout the year
See the index on page 585

Osborne House, East Cowes

© English Heritage Photo Library / Steve Cole

**visit hudsons guide online**

The Needles, Isle of Wight

**Above:** Chavenage
**Right:** Bourton House Garden

# South West

*The moorlands of Devon and Cornwall are among the most dramatic in Britain, contrasting with the unspoilt beaches. For keen gardeners, The Lost Gardens of Heligan contain over 200 acres of superb working Victorian gardens and pleasure grounds. The climate on the Scilly Isles means exotic and sub-tropical plants can be grown.*

Channel Islands

Cornwall

Devon

Dorset

Somerset

Wiltshire

Gloucestershire

South West – England

# THE ARTPARK AT SAUSMAREZ MANOR

www.artparks.co.uk

Dawn Benson 'Two's Company'

John Huggins 'Caprice'

Chris Manley 'Great Hornbill'

Nicola Godden 'Crouching Woman'

Jilly Sutton 'The Sleeper'

Graham Findlay 'Steelephant'

Lida Baas 'Henry VIII'

visit hudsons guide online

# SAUSMAREZ MANOR

www.sausmarezmanor.co.uk    www.artparks.co.uk

The home of the Seigneurs de Sausmarez since c1220 with a façade built at the bequest of the first Governor of New York.

An entrancing and entertaining half day encompassing something to interest everyone. The family have been explorers, inventors, diplomats, prelates, generals, admirals, privateers, politicians and governors etc, most of whom left their mark on the house, garden or the furniture.

The sub-tropical woodland garden is crammed with such exotics as banana trees, tree ferns, ginger, 300 plus camellias, lilies, myriads of bamboos, as well as the more commonplace hydrangeas, hostas etc. The RHS recommends the gardens to its own members.

The sculpture in the art park with its 200 or so pieces by artists from a dozen countries is the most comprehensive in Britain. The Magnolia Tree Art Gallery shows work by local and overseas artists and holds regular exhibitions. The pitch and put is a cruelly testing 500m 9 hole par 3. The Copper, Tin and Silversmith demonstrates his ancient skills in the large barn. The two lakes are a haven for ornamental wildfowl and some of the sculpture.

Sausmarez Manor is available for corporate hospitality functions and Civil weddings. It also offers guided tours, welcomes schools (has education programmes), and has a tearoom, café and gift shop.

There are concerts or plays on most Sunday afternoons in the summer and a Farmers' and Plantsmen's Market every other Saturday morning.

### ■ Owner
The Seigneur de Sausmarez

### ■ Contact
Peter de Sausmarez
Sausmarez Manor
Guernsey
Channel Islands
GY4 6SG
**Tel:** 01481 235571/235655
**Fax:** 01481 235572
**E-mail:** sausmarezmanor @cwgsy.net

### ■ Location
**Map 3:D10**
2m S of St Peter Port, clearly signposted.

### ■ Opening Times
The Grounds:
Easter–End Oct
Daily: 10am–5pm

Guided tours of House
Easter–End Oct.
Mon–Thurs:
10.30 & 11.30am.
Additional 2pm tour during high season.

### ■ Admission
There is no overall charge for admission.

| | |
|---|---|
| Sub Tropical Garden | £4.50 |
| Sculpture Trail | £4.50 |
| Pitch & Putt | £4.50 |
| Putting | £2.00 |
| House Tour | £6.50 |
| Ghost Tour | £10.00 |
| Train Rides | £2.00 |

Discounts for Children, Students, OAPs & Organised Groups.

Partial.

Guided tours of House Easter–Oct.

Two holiday flats are available see www.cottageguide.co.uk

€

### ■ Owner
The National Trust

### ■ Contact
Toby Fox
Property Manager
Cotehele
St Dominick
Saltash, Cornwall
PL12 6TA

**Tel:** 01579 351346
**Fax:** 01579 351222
**E-mail:**
cotehele@nationaltrust.
org.uk

### ■ Location
**MAP 1:H8**
**OS Ref. SX422 685**

1m SW of Calstock by
foot. 8m S of Tavistock,
4m E of Callington,
15m from Plymouth
via the Tamar bridge
at Saltash.

**Trains:** Limited service
from Plymouth to
Calstock (1¼m uphill).

**Boats:** Limited (tidal)
service from Plymouth to
Calstock Quay (Plymouth
Boat Cruises).
Tel: 01752 822797

**River ferry:** Privately
run from Calstock to
Cotehele Quay.
Tel: 01822 833331

**Buses:** Western National
(seasonal variations).
Tel: 01752 222666

### ■ Opening Times
**House & Restaurant**
17 Mar–4 Nov: Daily
except Fris (but open
Good Fri), 11am–4.30pm
Last admission 30 mins
before closing time.

**Mill**
17 Mar–4 Nov: Daily
except Fris (but open
Good Fri plus Fris in July &
August) 1–5.30pm (4pm
from 1 Oct).

**Garden**
All year: Daily,
10.30am–dusk.

### ■ Admission
**House, Garden & Mill**
| | |
|---|---|
| Adult | £8.40 |
| Family | £21.00 |
| 1-Adult Family | £12.60 |
| Pre-booked Groups | £7.40 |

**Garden & Mill only**
| | |
|---|---|
| Adult | £5.00 |
| Family | £12.50 |
| 1-Adult Family | £7.50 |

*Groups must book in
advance with the
Property Office.
No groups Suns or BHs.

NT members free.
You may join here.

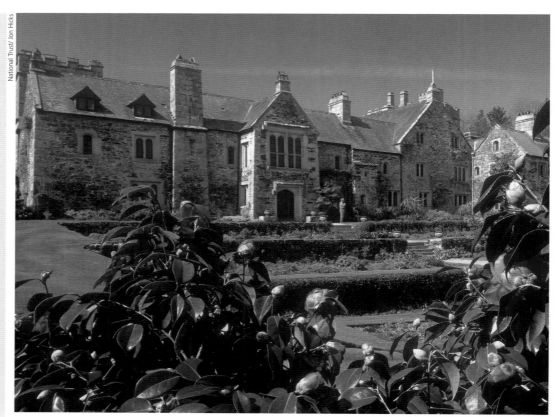

National Trust/ Jon Hicks

# COTEHELE
www.nationaltrust.org.uk

Cotehele, owned by the Edgcumbe family for nearly 600 years, is a fascinating and enchanting estate set on the steep wooded slopes of the River Tamar. Exploring Cotehele's many and various charms provides a full day out for the family and leaves everyone longing to return.

The steep valley garden contains exotic and tender plants which thrive in the mild climate. Remnants of an earlier age include a mediaeval stewpond and domed dovecote, a 15th-century chapel and 18th-century tower with fine views over the surrounding countryside. A series of more formal gardens, terraces, an orchard and a daffodil meadow surround Cotehele House.

One of the least altered medieval houses in the country, Cotehele is built in local granite, slate and sandstone. Inside the ancient rooms, unlit by electricity, is a fine collection of textiles, tapestries, armour and early dark oak furniture. The chapel contains the oldest working domestic clock in England, still in its original position.

A walk through the garden and along the river leads to the quay, a busy river port in Victorian times. The National Maritime Museum worked with the National Trust to set up a museum here which explains the vital role that the Tamar played in the local economy. As a living reminder, the restored Tamar sailing barge Shamrock (owned jointly by the Trust and the National Maritime Museum) is moored here.

A further walk through woodland along the Morden stream leads to the old estate corn mill which has been restored to working order.

This large estate with many footpaths offers a variety of woodland and countryside walks, opening up new views and hidden places. The Danescombe Valley, with its history of mining and milling, is of particular interest.

National Trust /Iynn Lintell

**ℹ** No photography or large bags in house. NPI National Heritage Award winners 1996 & 1999.

**🛍** National Trust shop.

**🍽** Available for up to 90 people.

**♿** 2 wheelchairs at Reception. Hall & kitchen accessible. Ramps at house, restaurant and shop. Most of garden is very steep with loose gravel. Riverside walks are flatter (from Cotehele Quay) & Edgcumbe Arms is accessible. WCs near house and at Quay. Parking near house & mill by arrangement.

**☕🍴** Barn restaurant daily (except Fri), 17 Mar–4 Nov, plus light refreshments from 17 Feb. Tel for details of pre-Christmas opening. At the Quay, Edgcumbe Arms offers light meals daily, 17 Mar–4 Nov. Both licensed.

**P** Near house and garden and at Cotehele Quay. No parking at mill.

**👥** Groups (15+) must book with Property Office and receive a coach route (limited to two per day). No groups Suns & BH weekends. Visitors to house limited to 80 at any one time. Please arrive early and be prepared to queue. Allow a full day to see estate.

**🐕**  Under control welcome only on woodland walks.

**❄**

The National Trust / Angelo Hornak

# LANHYDROCK 🌿

www.nationaltrust.org.uk

Lanhydrock is the grandest and most welcoming house in Cornwall, set in a glorious landscape of gardens, parkland and woods overlooking the valley of the River Fowey.

The house dates back to the 17th century but much of it had to be rebuilt after a disastrous fire in 1881 destroyed all but the entrance porch and the north wing, which includes the magnificent Long Gallery with its extraordinary plaster ceiling depicting scenes from the Old Testament. A total of 50 rooms are on show today and together they reflect the entire spectrum of life in a rich and splendid Victorian household, from the many servants' bedrooms and the fascinating complex of kitchens, sculleries and larders to the nursery suite where the Agar-Robartes children lived, learned and played, and the grandeur of the dining room with its table laid and ready.

Surrounding the house on all sides are gardens ranging from formal Victorian parterres to the wooded higher garden where magnificent displays of magnolias, rhododendrons and camellias climb the hillside to merge with the oak and beech woods all around. A famous avenue of ancient beech and sycamore trees, the original entrance drive to the house, runs from the pinnacled 17th-century gatehouse down towards the medieval bridge across the Fowey at Respryn.

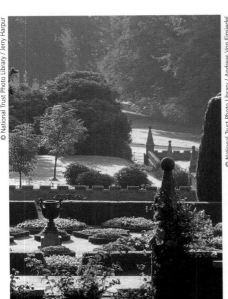

© National Trust Photo Library / Jerry Harpur

© National Trust Photo Library / Andreas Von Einsiedel

No photography in house.

By arrangement.

Suitable. Braille guide. WC.

Licensed restaurant

In park, on leads. Guide dogs only in house.

Limited for coaches.

## ◼ Owner
The National Trust

## ◼ Contact
Property Manager
Lanhydrock
Bodmin
Cornwall PL30 5AD

**Tel:** 01208 265950
**Fax:** 01208 265959
**E-mail:** lanhydrock@
nationaltrust.org.uk

## ◼ Location
**MAP 1:F8**
**OS Ref. SX085 636**

2½ m SE of Bodmin, follow signposts from either A30, A38 or B3268.

## ◼ Opening Times
**House:**
17 Mar–4 Nov: Daily except Mons
(but open BH Mons)
11am–5.30pm.
Oct: 11am–5pm.
Last admission ½ hr before closing.

**Garden:**
All year: Daily.
10am–6pm. Charge levied from
10 February–4 November.

**Refreshments:**
10 February–31 December (except 25/26 Dec): Daily. January–mid February:
Sats & Suns only.

**Plant Sales:**
10 February–31 March: Daily 11am–4pm
1 April–30 September: Daily 11am–5.30pm.
1 Oct–4 Nov: Daily 11am–5pm.

**Shop:** January–
9 February:
Sat & Sun, 11am–4pm.
10 February–16 March,
4 Nov–24 December &
27–31 December:
Daily, 11am–4pm.
17 March–30 September:
Daily 11am–5.30pm.
1 Oct–4 Nov: Daily
11am–5pm.

## ◼ *Admission
**House, Garden & Grounds**

| | |
|---|---|
| Adult | £9.40 |
| Family | £23.50 |
| 1-Adult Family | £14.10 |
| Groups | £8.00 |

**Garden & Grounds only** £5.30

*includes a voluntary donation but visitors can choose to pay the standard prices displayed at the property and on the website.

National Trust/ Peter Cade

# ANTONY HOUSE & GARDEN ✤ & ANTONY WOODLAND GARDEN

## TORPOINT, CORNWALL  PL11 2QA

www.nationaltrust.org.uk

**Antony House & Garden Tel:** 01752 812191
**Antony Woodland Garden Tel:** 01752 814210
**E-mail:** antony@nationaltrust.org.uk
**Antony House & Garden Owner:** The National Trust
**Antony Woodland Garden Owner:** Carew Pole Garden Trust

Superb 18th-century house on the Lynher estuary, grounds landscaped by Repton. Formal garden with sculptures & National Collection of day lilies; woodland garden with magnolias, rhododendrons & National Collection of Camellia japonica.

**Location:** MAP 1:H9, OS Ref. SX418 564. 5m W of Plymouth via Torpoint car ferry, 2m NW of Torpoint.

**Open:** House & Garden: 3 Apr–31 Oct: Tue–Thur & BH Mons. Also Suns in June, July & Aug: 1.30–5.30pm. Last adm. 4.45pm. Shop & Restaurant as house, 12.30–5.30pm. Woodland Garden (not NT) 1 Mar–31 Oct: daily except Mon & Fri (open BH Mons), 11am–5.30pm.

**Admission:** House & Garden: £5.80, Family £14.50, 1-Adult Family £8.70. Groups £4.90pp. NT Garden only: £3. Woodland Garden: Adult £4 (Free to NT members on days when the house is open). Woodland Garden season ticket: £20. Joint Gardens-only tickets: Adult £4.80. Groups £4. Under 16s Free.

⬜ ⬛ Braille guide. 🍴 🅿 ✖

## BURNCOOSE NURSERIES & GARDEN

**Gwennap, Redruth, Cornwall  TR16 6BJ**
**Tel:** 01209 860316  **Fax:** 01209 860011  **E-mail:** burncoose@eclipse.co.uk
**www.burncoose.co.uk**
**Owner/Contact:** C H Williams

The Nurseries are set in the 30 acre woodland gardens of Burncoose.

**Location:** MAP 1:D10, OS Ref. SW742 395. 2m SE of Redruth on main A393 Redruth to Falmouth road between the villages of Lanner and Ponsanooth.

**Open:** Mon–Sat: 9am–5pm, Suns, 11am–5pm. Gardens and Tearooms open all year (except Christmas Day).

**Admission:** Nurseries: Free. Gardens: Adult/Conc. £2. Child Free. Group conducted tours: £2.50 by arrangement.

⬜ ⬛ ⬛ Grounds. WCs. ⬛ ⬛ By arrangement. 🅿 ✖ In grounds, on leads. ⬛

© NT Photographic Library / Jerry Harpur

Lanhydrock – The Parterre

# BOCONNOC

## ESTATE OFFICE, BOCONNOC, LOSTWITHIEL, CORNWALL  PL22 0RG

www.boconnocenterprises.co.uk

**Tel:** 01208 872507  **Fax:** 01208 873836  **E-mail:** adgfortescue@btinternet.com
**Owner/Contact:** Anthony Fortescue Esq

Bought with the famous Pitt Diamond in 1717, Boconnoc remains one of Cornwall's best kept secrets. Home to three Prime Ministers, its unique combination of history, architecture, picturesque landscape and one of the great Cornish gardens created ideal film locations for Poldark and The Three Musketeers. King Charles I and the architect Sir John Soane played an influential part in Boconnoc's history. Groups visit the Boconnoc House restoration project, the gardens, church, Golden Jubilee lake walk, the Georgian Bath House and newly planted Pinetum. Ideal for private and corporate events, conferences, activities; weddings and receptions and holiday houses for long or short breaks.

**Location:** MAP 1:G8, OS Ref. 148 605. A38 Plymouth, Liskeard or from Bodmin to Dobwalls, then A390 to Middle Taphouse.

**Open:** House & Garden: 15, 22, 29 Apr & 6, 13, 20, 29 May: Suns: 2–5pm. Groups (15–255) by appointment all year.

**Admission:** House: £3, Garden £4.50. Child under 12yrs Free.

ⓘ ⬜ 🖼 Conferences. ⬛ Partial. ⬛ ⬛ By arrangement. 🅿 ⬛
✖ In grounds, on leads. 🛏 28 doubles, 1 single, 8 ensuite. ⬛ ⬛
⬛ 23–24 Mar: Tour of Cornwall Rally. 31 Mar/1 Apr: Cornwall Garden Society Spring Flower Show. 9/10 May: Spring Interiors Fair. 20 May: St John Ambulance Mini Marathon, all welcome to take part. 20–22 Jul: Boconnoc Steam Fair.

## CAERHAYS CASTLE & GARDEN 🏰
### CAERHAYS, GORRAN, ST AUSTELL, CORNWALL PL26 6LY
www.caerhays.co.uk

**Tel:** 01872 501310  **Fax:** 01872 501870  **E-mail:** estateoffice@caerhays.co.uk
**Owner:** F J Williams Esq    **Contact:** Cheryl Kufel
One of the very few Nash built castles still left standing – situated within approximately 60 acres of informal woodland gardens created by J C Williams, who sponsored plant hunting expeditions to China at the turn of the century. Noted for its camellias, magnolias, rhododendrons and oaks. English Heritage listing–Grade I: Outstanding.
**Location:** MAP 1:F9, OS Ref. SW972 415. S coast of Cornwall – between Mevagissey and Portloe. 9m SW of St Austell.
**Open:** House: 12 Mar–1 Jun: Mon–Fri only (including BHs), 12 noon–4pm, booking recommended. Gardens: 12 Feb–3 Jun: daily (including BHs), 10am–5pm (last admission 4pm).
**Admission:** House: £5.50. Gardens: £5.50. House & Gardens: £9.50. Guided group tours (15+) by Head Gardener, £6.50–by arrangement. Groups please contact Estate Office.
ℹ No photography in house. 🖼 🚻 Partial. WC. 🍴 Licensed. 🎟 By arrangement. 🅿 🐕 In grounds, on leads.

## CHYSAUSTER ANCIENT VILLAGE ⊞
**Nr Newmill, Penzance, Cornwall TR20 8XA**
**Tel:** 07831 757934  **E-mail:** customers@english-heritage.org.uk
www.english-heritage.org.uk/chysauster
**Owner:** English Heritage    **Contact:** Visitor Operations Team
On a windy hillside, overlooking the wild and spectacular coast, is this deserted Romano-Cornish village with a 'street' of eight well preserved houses, each comprising a number of rooms around an open court.
**Location:** MAP 1:C10, OS203 Ref. SW473 350. 2½m NW of Gulval off B3311.
**Open:** 1 Apr–30 Jun & Sept: daily, 10am–5pm. Jul & Aug: daily, 10am–6pm. 1–31 Oct: daily, 10am–4pm.
**Admission:** Adult £2.40, Child £1.20, Conc. £1.80. 15% discount for groups (11+).
ℹ WC. 🖼 🅿 No coaches. 🐕 On leads.

## COTEHELE 🌿            *See page 200 for full page entry.*

©National Trust Photographic Library/Hugh Palmer

## GLENDURGAN GARDEN 🌿
### MAWNAN SMITH, FALMOUTH, CORNWALL TR11 5JZ
www.nationaltrust.org.uk

**Tel:** 01326 250906 (opening hours) or 01872 862090  **Fax:** 01872 865808
**E-mail:** trelissick@nationaltrust.org.uk
**Owner:** The National Trust
A valley of great beauty with fine trees, shrubs and water gardens. The laurel maze is an unusual and popular feature. The garden runs down to the tiny village of Durgan and its beach on the Helford River. Replica Victorian school room, rebuilt in 2002 in traditional thatch and cob to replace the 1876 original.
**Location:** MAP 1:D10, OS Ref. SW772 277. 4m SW of Falmouth, ½m SW of Mawnan Smith, on road to Helford Passage. 1m E of Trebah Garden. Accessible by ferry from Helford.
**Open:** 10 Feb–3 Nov: Tue–Sat & BH Mons, 10.30am–5.30pm. Last admission 4.30pm. Closed Good Friday.
**Admission:** £5.20, Child £2.60, Family £13, 1-Adult Family £7.80. Booked groups: £4.40/£2.20.
🖼 🚻 Unsuitable. 🍴 🎟 By arrangement. 🅿 Limited for coaches. 🐕

## GODOLPHIN 🏰
### GODOLPHIN CROSS, HELSTON, CORNWALL TR13 9RE
www.godolphinhouse.com

**Tel/Fax:** 01736 763194  **E-mail:** info@godolphinhouse.com
**Owner:** Mrs L M P Schofield    **Contact:** Mrs Joanne Schofield
Unspoilt, Grade I mansion commenced in c1475 with early formal Side Garden (c1300 and c1500) set in beautiful, woodland surroundings. World Heritage Site. Home of Sidney,1st Earl, Lord High Treasurer to Queen Anne. Elizabethan stables with display of local, unrestored farm wagons, tea room, farm shop with local produce. Weddings, venue hire, events and exhibitions. Coaches welcome. For updates, visit our website.
**Location:** MAP 1:D10, OS Ref: SW602 318. On minor road from Godolphin Cross to Townshend. Some brown signs.
**Open:** 9 Apr–8 Jul: BH Mons, Wed, Thurs, Sun: 10am–4pm. 9 Jul–30 Sept: Mon–Fri, Sun: 10am–4pm.
**Admission:** House & Gardens: Adult £6. Child £1.50. Conc. £5. Gardens & Grounds: Adult £3. Children Free.
ℹ 🖼 🚻 🎟 By arrangement. 🅿 🐕

### GODOLPHIN BLOWINGHOUSE

**Blowinghouse Cottage, Godolphin Cross, Breage, Helston, Cornwall TR13 9RE**

**Tel:** 01736 763218    **E-mail:** brian.portch@ndirect.co.uk

**Owner/Contact:** Mr & Mrs B J Portch

The Blowinghouse dates from the 16th century and was built as part of the Godolphin family tin mining works. The tin ingots weighed in excess of three hundredweight and were stamped with a cat's head that was the Godophin Mine logo.

**Location:** MAP 1:D10, OS Ref. SW508 521, Situated in the Godolphin Woods-National Trust opposite entrance to the Godolphin Manor House.

**Open:** 12 & 19 Aug, 9.30am–4.30pm. Other times by appointment.

**Admission:** Free.

🚻 **P** Limited. ▣ 🐾 In grounds, on leads.

### THE JAPANESE GARDEN & BONSAI NURSERY

**St Mawgan, Nr Newquay, Cornwall TR8 4ET**

**Tel:** 01637 860116    **Fax:** 01637 860887    **E-mail:** rob@thebonsainursery.com

**Owner/Contact:** Mr & Mrs Hore

Authentic Japanese Garden set in 1½ acres.

**Location:** MAP 2:E8, OS Ref. SW873 660. Follow road signs from A3059 & B3276.

**Open:** Summer: Daily, 10am–6pm. Winter: 10am–5.30pm. Closed Christmas Day–New Year's Day.

**Admission:** Adult £3.50, Child £1.50. Groups (10+): £3.

### KEN CARO GARDENS

**Bicton, Nr Liskeard  PL14 5RF**

**Tel:** 01579 362446

**Owner/Contact:** Mr and Mrs K R Willcock

5 acre plantsman's garden with woods and picnic area.

**Location:** MAP 1:G8, OS Ref. SX313 692. 5m NE of of Liskeard. Follow brown sign off main A390 midway between Liskeard and Callington.

**Open:** 25 Feb–30 Sept: daily except Sats, 10am–6pm.

**Admission:** Adult £4, Child £1.

### LANHYDROCK 🌿

*See page 201 for full page entry.*

### LAUNCESTON CASTLE ♯

**Castle Lodge, Launceston, Cornwall  PL15 7DR**

**Tel:** 01566 772365    **Fax:** 01566 772396    **E-mail:** customers@english-heritage.org.uk

**www.english-heritage.org.uk/launceston**

**Owner:** English Heritage    **Contact:** Visitor Operations Team

Set on the motte of the original Norman castle and commanding the town and surrounding countryside. The shell keep and tower survive of this medieval castle which controlled the main route into Cornwall. An exhibition shows the early history.

**Location:** MAP 1:H7, OS201 Ref. SX330 846. In Launceston.

**Open:** 1 Apr–31 Oct: daily, 10am–5pm (6pm in Jul & Aug & 4pm in Oct).

**Admission:** Adult £2.40, Child £1.20, Conc. £1.80. 15% discount for groups (11+).

▣🚻 Grounds. **P** NCP adjacent. Limited. 🐾 In grounds, on leads.

### LAWRENCE HOUSE 🌿

**9 Castle Street, Launceston, Cornwall  PL15 8BA**

**Tel:** 01566 773277

**Owner:** The National Trust    **Contact:** The Property Manager

A Georgian house given to the Trust to help preserve the character of the street, and now leased to Launceston Town Council as a museum and civic centre.

**Location:** MAP 1:H7, OS Ref. SX330 848. Launceston.

**Open:** 18 Apr–29 Sept: daily, except Sat & Sun, 10.30am–4.30pm. Other times by appointment.

**Admission:** Free, but contributions welcome.

## THE LOST GARDENS OF HELIGAN
### PENTEWAN, ST AUSTELL, CORNWALL  PL26 6EN
www.heligan.com

**Tel:** 01726 845100    **Fax:** 01726 845101

**E-mail:** info@heligan.com    **Contact:** Lorna Tremayne

The award-winning restoration of Heligan's productive gardens is only one of many features which combine to create a destination with a breadth of interest around the year: Victorian pleasure grounds with spring flowering shrubs, summerhouses, pools and rockeries; a sub-tropical Jungle valley brimming with exotic foliage; woodland and farm walks through beautiful and sustainably managed Cornish countryside, and a pioneering project offering visitors a close-up view of native wildlife on site.

**Location:** MAP 1:F9, OS Ref. SX000 465. 5m SW of St Austell. 2m NW of Mevagissey. Take the B3273 to Mevagissey – follow tourist signs.

**Open:** Daily except 24 & 25 Dec: 10am–6pm (5pm Nov–Feb). Last admission 1½ hrs before closing.

**Admission:** Adult: £8.50. Child (5–16yrs) £5, OAP £7.50. Family £23.50. Groups by arrangement.

▢ 🎦 🚻 🍴 🎦 By arrangement. **P** ▣ 🐾 March–October ❄ ♨

## MOUNT EDGCUMBE HOUSE & COUNTRY PARK
### CREMYLL, TORPOINT, CORNWALL PL10 IHZ
www.mountedgcumbe.gov.uk

**Tel:** 01752 822236    **Fax:** 01752 822199    **E-mail:** mt.edgcumbe@plymouth.gov.uk

**Owner:** Cornwall County & Plymouth City Councils    **Contact:** Secretary

Former home of the Earls of Mount Edgcumbe. Miraculously the walls of the red stone Tudor House survived the bombs in 1941. Restored by the 6th Earl. Now beautifully furnished with family possessions. Set in historic 18th century gardens on the dramatic sea-girt Rame peninsula. Follies, forts; National camellia collection. Grade I listed gardens. Exhibitions and events.

**Location:** MAP 1:H9, OS Ref. SX452 527. 10m W of Plymouth via Torpoint.

**Open:** House & Earl's Garden: 1 Apr–30 Sept: Sun–Thur, 11am–4.30pm. Group bookings by arrangement. Country Park: All year, daily, 8am–dusk.

**Admission:** House & Earl's Garden: Adult £4.50, Child (5–15) £2.25, Conc. £3.50, Family (2+2 or 1+3) £10. Groups (10+): Adult £3.50, Child £2. Park: Free.

▢ 🎦 🎟 🚻 💺 🍴 Licensed. 🎦 By arrangement. **P** 🐾 In grounds, on leads.
▲ ❄ ♨

# PENCARROW 🏛

## BODMIN, CORNWALL PL30 3AG

www.pencarrow.co.uk

**Tel:** 01208 841369   **Fax:** 01208 841722   **E-mail:** pencarrow@.aol.com

**Owner:** Molesworth-St Aubyn family   **Contact:** Administrator

Still owned and lived in by the family. Georgian house and Grade II* listed gardens. Superb collection of pictures, furniture and porcelain. Marked walks through 50 acres of beautiful formal and woodland gardens, Victorian rockery, Italian garden, over 700 different varieties of rhododendrons, lake and ice house.

**Location:** MAP 1:F8, OS Ref. SX040 711. Between Bodmin and Wadebridge. 4m NW of Bodmin off A389 & B3266 at Washaway.

**Open:** 1 Apr–25 Oct: Sun–Thur, 11am–4pm (last tour). Gardens: 1 Mar–31 Oct: daily.

**Admission:** House & Garden: Adult £8, Child £4. Family £22. Garden only: Adult £4, Child £1. Groups (by arrangement): House & Garden: groups (20-30) £7, 31+ £6; Gardens only: groups (20-30) £3.50, 31+ £3. Discounts not normally available on Fri & Sat.

ℹ Craft centre, small children's play area, self-pick soft fruit. 🎨 🎭 By arrangement. ♿ 🍴 Licensed. 🏨 🎫 Obligatory. 🅿 🎪 ♿ Grounds only. 🔺 ❄ 🎗

# PINE LODGE GARDENS & NURSERY

Holmbush, St Austell, Cornwall  PL25 3RQ

**Tel:** 01726 73500   **Fax:** 01726 77370   **E-mail:** garden@pine-lodge.co.uk

**www.pine-lodge.co.uk**

**Owner/Contact:** Mr & Mrs R H J Clemo

30 acres with over 6,000 plants all labelled. Herbaceous and shrub borders. Many water features, pinetum, arboretum, Japanese garden, wild flower meadow, lake with waterfowl and black swans. Plant hunting expeditions every year to gather seeds for our nursery which contain very unusual plants, many rare. The gardens were given a Highly Commended Award by the Cornwall Tourist Board for 2002. Plenty of seats in the gardens. A new 3 acre Winter Garden is under construction.

**Location:** MAP 1:F9, OS Ref. SX044 527. Signposted on A390.

**Open:** Daily, 10am–6pm, last ticket 5pm.

**Admission:** Adult £5.50, Child £3.

ℹ WC. 🅿 🎫 ♿ 🖼 🎨 🅿 🎪 ❄

Boconnoc, Lostwithiel

© English Heritage Photo Library.  © Skyscan Balloon Photography

# PENDENNIS CASTLE �

## FALMOUTH, CORNWALL TR11 4LP

www.english-heritage.org.uk/pendennis

**Tel:** 01326 316594   **Fax:** 01326 319911   **E-mail:** customers@english-heritage.org.uk

**Venue and Hire Hospitality:** 01326 310106

**Owner:** English Heritage   **Contact:** Visitor Operations Team

Pendennis and its neighbour, St Mawes Castle, face each other across the mouth of the estuary of the River Fal. Built by Henry VIII in 16th century as protection against threat of attack and invasion from France. Extended and adapted over the years to meet the changing threats to national security from the French and Spanish and continued right through to World War II. It withstood five months of siege during the Civil War before becoming the penultimate Royalist Garrison to surrender on the mainland. Pendennis today stands as a landmark, with fine sea views and excellent site facilities including a hands-on discovery centre, exhibitions, a museum, guardhouse, shop and tearoom. Excellent special events venue.

**Location:** MAP 1:E10, OS Ref. SW824 318. On Pendennis Head.

**Open:** 1 Apr–30 Jun: daily, 10am–5pm (4pm Sats). Jul & Aug: daily, 10am–6pm (4pm Sats). Sept: daily 10am–5pm (4pm Sats), Oct/Nov–20 Mar: daily, 10am–4pm, (Nov–Mar, certain buildings by guided tour only, please telephone to check). Closed 24–26 Dec & 1 Jan. The Keep will close for 1hr at lunch on Sats when events are booked, please telephone to check.

**Admission:** Adult £5.40, Child £2.70, Conc. £4.10, Family £13.50. 15% discount for groups (11+).

ℹ WC. 🅿 🎫 ♿ Partial. 🖼 🅿 🎪 ♿ In grounds only. 🔺 ❄ 🎗 €

## PRIDEAUX PLACE
### PADSTOW, CORNWALL PL28 8RP
www.prideauxplace.co.uk

**Tel:** 01841 532411 **Fax:** 01841 532945 **E-mail:** office@prideauxplace.co.uk
**Owner/Contact:** Peter Prideaux-Brune Esq

Tucked away above the busy port of Padstow, the home of the Prideaux family for over 400 years, is surrounded by gardens and wooded grounds overlooking a deer park and the Camel estuary to the moors beyond. The house still retains its 'E' shape Elizabethan front and contains fine paintings and furniture. Now a major international film location, this family home is one of the brightest jewels in Cornwall's crown. The historic garden is undergoing major restoration work and offers some of the best views in the county. A cornucopia of Cornish history under one roof.

**Location:** MAP 1:E7, OS Ref. SW913 756. 5m from A39 Newquay/Wadebridge link road. Signposted by Historic House signs.

**Open:** Easter Sun–12 Apr, 13 May–4 Oct. Daily except Fris & Sats. Grounds & Tearoom: 12.30–5pm. House Tours: 1.30–4pm (last tour).

**Admission:** House & Grounds: Adult £7, Child £2. Grounds only: Adult £2, Child £1. Groups (15+) discounts apply.

By arrangement. Ground floor & grounds. Obligatory. By arrangement. In grounds, on leads.

---

## RESTORMEL CASTLE

**Lostwithiel, Cornwall PL22 0EE**
**Tel:** 01208 872687 **E-mail:** customers@english-heritage.org.uk
**www.english-heritage.org.uk/restormel**
**Owner:** English Heritage **Contact:** Visitor Operations Team

Perched on a high mound, surrounded by a deep moat, the huge circular keep of this splendid Norman castle survives in remarkably good condition. It is still possible to make out the ruins of Restormel's Keep Gate, Great Hall and even the kitchens and private rooms.

**Location:** MAP 1:F8, OS200 Ref. SX104 614. 1½m N of Lostwithiel off A390.

**Open:** 1 Apr–31 Oct: daily, 10am–5pm (6pm in Jul & Aug; 4pm in Oct).

**Admission:** Adult £2.40, Child £1.20, Conc. £1.80. 15% discount for groups (11+).

WC. Limited for coaches. In grounds, on leads.

---

## ST CATHERINE'S CASTLE

**Fowey, Cornwall**
**Tel:** 01326 310109
**Owner:** English Heritage **Contact:** Visitor Operations Administrator

A small fort built by Henry VIII to defend Fowey harbour, with fine views of the coastline and river estuary.

**Location:** MAP 1:F9, OS200 Ref. SX118 508. 1½m SW of Fowey along footpath off A3082.

**Open:** Any reasonable time, daylight only.

**Admission:** Free.

---

---

© English Heritage Photo Library

## ST MAWES CASTLE
### ST MAWES, CORNWALL TR2 3AA
www.english-heritage.org.uk/stmawes

**Tel/Fax:** 01326 270526 **Venue Hire and Hospitality:** 01326 310106
**E-mail:** customers@english-heritage.org.uk
**Owner:** English Heritage **Contact:** Visitor Operations Team

The pretty fishing village of St Mawes is home to this castle. On the opposite headland to Pendennis Castle, St Mawes shares the task of watching over the mouth of the River Fal as it has done since Henry VIII built it as a defence against the French. With three huge circular bastions shaped like clover leaves, St Mawes was designed to cover every possible angle of approach. It is the finest example of Tudor military architecture. The castle offers views of St Mawes' little boat-filled harbour, the passenger ferry tracking across the Fal, and the splendid coastline which featured in the *Poldark* TV series. Also the start of some delightful walks along the coastal path.

**Location:** MAP 1:E10, OS204 Ref. SW842 328. W of St Mawes on A3078.

**Open:** 1 Apr–30 Sept: Sun–Fri, 10am–5pm (6pm Jul & Aug); 1–31 Oct: daily 10am–4pm. 1 Nov–20 Mar: Fri–Mon, 10am–4pm. (May closes at 4pm on Suns & Fris for private events.) Closed 24–26 Dec & 1 Jan & 1–2pm in winter.

**Admission:** Adult £3.90, Child £2, Conc. £2.90. 15% discount for groups (11+).

Private & corporate hire. Grounds. WC. Limited. Grounds only.

---

## ST MICHAEL'S MOUNT 👓
### MARAZION, Nr PENZANCE, CORNWALL TR17 0HS

www.stmichaelsmount.co.uk          www.nationaltrust.org.uk

**Tel:** 01736 710507 (710265 tide information)   **Fax:** 01736 719930
**E-mail:** godolphin@manor-office.co.uk
**Owner:** The National Trust   **Contact:** The Manor Office

This beautiful island set in Mount's Bay has become an icon for Cornwall, and in turn there are magnificent views when you reach its summit. There the church and castle, whose origins date from the 12th century, have at various times acted as a Benedictine priory, a place of pilgrimage, a fortress, a mansion house and now a magnet for visitors from all over the world. Following the Civil War, the island was acquired by the St Aubyn family who still live in the castle today.

**Location:** MAP 1:C10, OS Ref. SW515 300. 4m E of Penzance. At Marazion there is access on foot over causeway at low tide. In the main season, the property is reached at high tide by a short evocative boat trip. Please note many paths are steep and cobbled.

**Open:** Castle: 1 Apr–2 Nov: Sun–Fri, 10.30am–4.45pm (last admission on the island). Nov–Mar: open when tide and weather favourable. Essential to telephone in advance. Garden (not NT): May & Jun: Weekdays only; Jul–Oct: Thur & Fri only, 10.30am–4.45pm. Church Service: Whitsun–end Sept (also Christmas Day, Good Fri & Easter Sun): Sun, 11.15am. All visits subject to weather and tides.

**Admission:** Adult £6.40, Child (under 17) £3.20, Family £16, 1-Adult Family £9.60. Booked groups £5.60. Gardens (not NT) £3.

⬜ 🚻 ▦ 🚻 ⏹ Tel for details. 🅿 On mainland (not NT.) 🐕 Not permitted in the castle or garden.

---

## TINTAGEL CASTLE ⬚
### TINTAGEL, CORNWALL PL34 0HE

www.english-heritage.org.uk/tintagel

**Tel/Fax:** 01840 770328   **E-mail:** customers@english-heritage.org.uk
**Owner:** English Heritage   **Contact:** Visitor Operations Team

The spectacular setting for the legendary castle of King Arthur on the wild and windswept Cornish coast. Clinging precariously to the edge of the cliff face are the extensive ruins of a medieval royal castle, built by Richard, Earl of Cornwall, younger brother of Henry III. Also used as a Cornish stronghold by subsequent Earls of Cornwall. Despite extensive excavations since the 1930s, Tintagel Castle remains one of the most spectacular and romantic spots in the entire British Isles. Destined to remain a place of mystery and romance, Tintagel will always jealously guard its marvellous secrets.

**Location:** MAP 1:F7, OS200 Ref. SX048 891. On Tintagel Head, ½m along uneven track from Tintagel.

**Open:** 1 Apr–31 Oct: daily, 10am–6pm (5pm in Oct). 1 Nov–20 Mar: daily, 10am–4pm. Closed 24–26 Dec & 1 Jan.

**Admission:** Adult £4.50, Child £2.30, Conc. £3.40. 15% discount for groups (11+).

ℹ️ WC. No vehicles. ⬜ ▦ 🐕 ❄ ▧

---

## SAUSMAREZ MANOR 🏠          *See pages 198/199 for double page entry.*

---

## TINTAGEL OLD POST OFFICE 👓
### Tintagel, Cornwall PL34 0DB

**Tel:** 01840 770024 or 01208 74281
**Owner:** The National Trust   **Contact:** The Custodian

One of the most characterful buildings in Cornwall, and a house of great antiquity, this small 14th-century yeoman farmhouse is full of charm and interest.

**Location:** MAP 1:F7, OS Ref. SX056 884. In the centre of Tintagel.

**Open:** 19 Mar–27 July & Sept: daily except Sats, 11am–5.30pm. 28 July–2 Sept: daily, 11am–5.30pm. 1–28 Oct daily except Sats, 11am–4pm. Last admission 30 mins before closing.

**Admission:** Adult £2.70, Child £1.35, Family £6.75, 1-Adult Family £4.05. Booked groups £2.40.

---

Trebah Garden, Nr Falmouth

St Michael's Mount, Nr Penzance – The Banqueting Hall

© Trebah Garden Trust

# TREBAH GARDEN

### MAWNAN SMITH, Nr FALMOUTH, CORNWALL TR11 5JZ

www.trebah-garden.co.uk

**Tel:** 01326 252200  **Fax:** 01326 250781  **E-mail:** mail@trebah-garden.co.uk

**Owner:** Trebah Garden Trust  **Contact:** V. Woodcroft

Steeply wooded 25 acre sub-tropical valley garden falls 200 feet from 18th century house to private beach on Helford River. Stream cascading over waterfalls through ponds full of Koi Carp and exotic water plants winds through 2 acres of blue and white hydrangeas and spills out over beach. Huge Australian tree ferns and palms mingle with shrubs of ever-changing colours and scent beneath over-arching canopy of 100 year old rhododendrons and magnolias. The striking Visitor Centre houses a garden shop, plant sales and stylish catering.

**Location:** MAP 1:D10, OS Ref. SW768 275. 4m SW of Falmouth, 1m SW of Mawnan Smith. Follow brown and white tourism signs from Treliever Cross roundabout at A39/A394 junction through Mawnan Smith to Trebah.

**Open:** All year: daily, 10.30am–5pm (last admission). Winter opening times may vary.

**Admission:** 1 Mar–31 Oct: Adult £6.50, Child (5–15yrs) £2. Disabled £3.25. Child under 5yrs Free, OAP £6. 1 Nov–28 Feb: Adult £3, Child (5–15yrs)/Disabled £1, Child under 5yrs Free, OAP £2.50. NT & RHS members: free entry 1 Nov–end Feb.

🗖 🖈 🖫 Partial. 🖭 🏨 🎏 By arrangement. 🅿 🖩 🖾 On leads. ❀

National Trust/ Tony Kent

# TRELISSICK GARDEN ❦

### FEOCK, TRURO, CORNWALL TR3 6QL

www.nationaltrust.org.uk

**Tel:** 01872 862090  **Fax:** 01872 865808  **E-mail:** trelissick@nationaltrust.org.uk

**Owner:** The National Trust  **Contact:** The Property Manager

A garden and estate of rare tranquil beauty with glorious maritime views over the Carrick Roads to Falmouth. The tender and exotic shrubs make this an attractive garden in all seasons. Extensive park and woodland walks beside the river. Art and Craft Gallery. Make your visit a really special day: travel to Trelissick by foot ferry from Truro, Falmouth and St Mawes by Fal River Links Partnerships Ferries, from April to September. Copeland Spode China on display in Trelissick House at 2pm on Thursdays, April to June, September and October, booking advisable 01872 864452.

**Location:** MAP 1:E10, OS Ref. SW837 396. 4m S of Truro on B3289 above King Harry Ferry.

**Open:** Garden, Shop, Restaurant, Gallery and Plant Sales: 29 Jan–10 Feb: Daily, 11am–4pm. 11 Feb–28 October: daily, 10.30am–5.30pm. 30 Oct–23 Dec: daily, 11am–4pm. 27–31 Dec: daily, 11am–4pm. Woodland Walks: All year: daily.

**\*Admission:** Adult £5.80, Family £14.50, 1-Adult Family £8.70. Pre-arranged groups £5.20pp. Car Park £3 (refunded on admission). Garden & Copeland Spode China: £9.20 (NT members £4). Discounted rate for winter visits.\*includes a voluntary donation but visitors can choose to pay the standard prices displayed at the property and on the website.

🗖 🖈 🝆 By arrangement. 🖫 🏨 🎏 By arrangement. 🅿 Limited for coaches.
🖾 In park on leads; only guide dogs in garden. ❀ 🖃

National Trust/ Giles Clotworthy

## TRENGWAINTON GARDEN ⚘
### PENZANCE, CORNWALL TR20 8RZ

www.nationaltrust.org.uk

**Tel:** 01736 363148   **Fax:** 01736 367762
**Owner:** The National Trust   **Contact:** David Milne – The Property Manager
Intimate and closely linked to the picturesque stream running through its valley, the garden leads up to a terrace and summer houses with splendid views across Mount's Bay to the Lizard. The walled gardens contain many rare and unusual species which are difficult to grow in the open anywhere else in the country.
**Location:** MAP 1:B10, OS Ref. SW445 315. 2m NW of Penzance, ½ m W of Heamoor on Penzance–Morvah road (B3312), ½ m off St. Just road (A3071).
**Open:** 11 Feb–4 Nov: Sun–Thur & Good Fri, 10am–5pm.
**Admission:** Adult £5.20, Child £2.60, Family £13, 1-Adult Family £7.80. Booked groups: £4.40.
▢ ⊞ ♿ Partial. ☕ Tea-house. 🐕 On leads (except in Tea-house garden).

National Trust/ Marcus Way

## TRERICE ⚘
### KESTLE MILL, Nr NEWQUAY, CORNWALL TR8 4PG

www.nationaltrust.org.uk

**Tel:** 01637 875404   **Fax:** 01637 879300   **E-mail:** trerice@nationaltrust.org.uk
**Owner:** The National Trust   **Contact:** David Milne – The Property Manager
Trerice is an architectural gem and something of a rarity – a small Elizabethan manor house hidden away in a web of narrow lanes and still somehow caught in the spirit of its age. An old Arundell house, it contains much fine furniture, ceramics, glasses and a wonderful clock collection. A small barn museum traces the development of the lawn mower. Several family activities.
**Location:** MAP 1:E8, OS Ref. SW841 585. 3m SE of Newquay via the A392 & A3058 (right at Kestle Mill). Or from A30–signs at Summercourt and Mitchell.
**Open:** 18 Mar–4 Nov: Daily except Sats, 11am–5pm. (Garden & tearoom 10.30am.)
**Admission:** Adult £6.40, Child £3.20, Family £16, 1-Adult Family £9.60. Pre-arranged groups £5.60. Garden only: Adult £2.20, Child £1.10, Family £3.30, 1-Adult Family £2.
▢ ⊞ ♿ Braille & taped guides. WC. ☕ Licensed. 🐕 Guide dogs only. ▣

## TREWITHEN 🏛
### GRAMPOUND ROAD, TRURO, CORNWALL TR2 4DD

www.trewithengardens.co.uk

**Tel:** 01726 883647   **Fax:** 01726 882301
**E-mail:** gardens@trewithen-estate.demon.co.uk
**Owner:** A M J Galsworthy   **Contact:** The Estate Office
Trewithen means 'house of the trees' and the name truly describes this fine early Georgian House in its splendid setting of wood and parkland. Country Life described the house as 'one of the outstanding West Country houses of the 18th century'. The gardens at Trewithen are outstanding and of international fame. It is now over 100 years since George Johnstone inherited and started developing the gardens which now contain a wide and rare collection of flowering shrubs. Some of the magnolias and rhododendron species in the garden are known throughout the world. They are one of two attractions in this county awarded three stars by Michelin. Viewing platforms and a Camera Obscura will be an additional interest to visitors.

**Location:** MAP 1:E9, OS Ref. SW914 476. S of A390 between Grampound and Probus villages. 7m WSW of St Austell.
**Open:** Gardens: 1 Mar–30 Sept: Mon–Sat, 10am–4.30pm. Suns in Mar–May only. House: Apr–Jul & Aug BH Mon, Mons & Tues, 2–4pm.
**Admission:** Mar–June: Adult £5 (groups 20+ £4.50), Child (5–15yrs) £1, Child under 5yrs Free. July–Sept: Adult £4.50 (groups 20+ £4), Child (5–15yrs) £1, Child under 5yrs Free.
ℹ No photography in house. ⊞ ♿ Partial. WC. ☕ 𝑓 By arrangement.
🅿 Limited for coaches. 🐕 In grounds, on leads.

## ■ Owner
Valerie Lister

## ■ Contact
Valerie Lister
Bicton Park
Botanical Gardens
East Budleigh
Budleigh Salterton
Devon
EX9 7BJ

**Tel:** 01395 568465
**Fax:** 01395 568374
**E-mail:** valerie@
bictongardens.co.uk

## ■ Location
**MAP 2:L7**
**OS Ref. SY074 856**

2m N of Budleigh
Salterton on B3178.

Follow the brown signs to
Bicton Park from M5/J30
at Exeter.

**Rail:** Exmouth 5mins,
Exeter St Davids 12m.

**Air:** Exeter Airport 5m.

## ■ Opening Times
**Summer**
10am–6pm.

**Winter**
10am–5pm.
Open all year except
Christmas Day &
Boxing Day.

## ■ Admission
| | |
|---|---|
| Adult | £6.95 |
| Child | £5.95 |
| Conc | £5.95 |
| Family (2+2) | £22.95 |

Groups (16-200)
| | |
|---|---|
| Adult | £4.95 |
| Child | £3.95 |
| Conc. | £3.95 |

Children under 3yrs Free

# BICTON PARK BOTANICAL GARDENS
www.bictongardens.co.uk

Spanning three centuries of horticultural history, Bicton Park Botanical Gardens are set in the picturesque Otter Valley, near the coastal town of Budleigh Salterton and 10 miles south of Exeter.

The 63 acre park's oldest ornamental area is the Italian Garden, created in the axial style of Versailles landscaper Andre le Notre, c1735. By that time formal designs were becoming unfashionable in England, which may explain why the garden was located out of view of the manor house. Today, the full grandeur of the Italian Garden can be seen from the spacious restaurant in the classically styled Orangery, built at the beginning of the 19th century.

Bicton's high-domed Palm House, one of the world's most beautiful garden buildings, was the first of many developments between 1820 and 1850. Others included an important collection of conifers in the Pinetum, now the subject of a rare species conservation project, and St Mary's Church, where Queen Victoria worshipped.

A large museum reflects changes in agriculture and rural life generally over the past 200 years. The Grade I listed gardens, which are open all year, also feature a narrow-gauge railway which meanders through the garden on its 1½ mile track. Gift shop, garden centre, children's inside and outdoor play areas.

| | | | |
|---|---|---|---|
| i | Children's inside & outdoor play areas. | ♈ | Licensed. |
| ⌂ | | 🧍 | By arrangement. |
| * | Garden Centre. | P | |
| Y | | 🛏 | In grounds, on leads. |
| ♿ | WCs. | ♨ | |
| 🍴 | Licensed. | ❄ | |

# CLOVELLY
www.clovelly.co.uk

From Elizabethan days until today, Clovelly Village has preserved its original atmosphere. The main traffic-free street, known as 'up-a-along' and 'down-a-long', tumbles its cobbled way down to the tiny harbour, which is protected by an ancient stone breakwater. It is a descent through flower-strewn cottages broken only by little passageways and winding lanes that lead off to offer the prospect of more picturesque treasures.

The New Inn, which is 400 years old, is halfway down the street, and another, the Red Lion, is right on the quayside. Both Inns have long histories and an atmosphere rarely found in the modern world. In addition you'll find the Visitor Centre, a range of gift shops, a café and an audio-visual theatre in which visitors are treated to a history of the village. Just below is the Stable Yard with a pottery and silk workshop. There are beautiful coastal and woodland walks.

Access is restricted to pedestrians only via the Visitor Centre with a Land Rover taxi service for those unable to walk.

### ■ Owner
Hon John Rous

### ■ Contact
Visitor Centre
Clovelly
Nr Bideford
N Devon  EX39 5TA

**Tel:** 01237 431781
**Fax:** 01237 431288

### ■ Location
**MAP 1:H5**
**OS Ref. SS248 319**

On A39 10 miles W of Bideford, 15 miles E of Bude. Turn off at 'Clovelly Cross' roundabout and follow signs to car park.

**Air:** Exeter & Plymouth Airport both 50 miles.

**Rail:** Barnstaple 19 miles.

**Bus:** from Bideford.

### ■ Opening Times
High season:
9am–6pm.

Low season:
10am–4.30pm.

### ■ Admission
The entrance fee covers parking and other facilities provided by Clovelly Estate, as well as admission to the audio-visual film, Fisherman's Cottage, and Kingsley Museum.

| | |
|---|---|
| Adult | £4.75 |
| Child (7–16yrs) | £3.25 |
| Child (under 7yrs) | Free |
| Family (2+2) | £14.00 |

| Group Rates (20+) | |
|---|---|
| Adult | £4.00 |
| Child | £3.00 |

Prices correct at time of going to press.

### ■ Special Events
**July 21/22**
Clovelly Maritime Festival.

| | |
|---|---|
| ℹ | Rubber soled, low heel shoes are recommended. |
| 🛍 | |
| ♿ | Partial. Around the Visitor Centre. |
| ☕ | Licensed. |
| 🍽 | Licensed. |
| 🅿 | |
| 🎦 | |
| 🐾 | On leads. |
| 🛏 | 18 double, 1 single, all en suite. |
| 🔔 | |
| ❄ | |

NTPL / David Garner

NTPL/Nadia MacKenzie

## A LA RONDE 🌿

### SUMMER LANE, EXMOUTH, DEVON  EX8 5BD

www.nationaltrust.org.uk

**Tel:** 01395 265514  **E-mail:** alaronde@nationaltrust.org.uk

**Owner:** The National Trust  **Contact:** Assistant Property Manager

A unique 16-sided house built on the instructions of two spinster cousins, Jane and Mary Parminter, on their return from a grand tour of Europe. Completed c1796, the house contains many 18th-century contents and collections brought back by the Parminters. The fascinating interior decoration includes a feather frieze and shell-encrusted gallery which, due to its fragility, can be viewed fully by remote control on closed circuit television.

**Location:** MAP 2:L7, OS Ref. SY004 834. 2m N of Exmouth on A376.

**Open:** 17 Mar–4 Nov: daily except Thurs & Fri, 11am–5pm. Last admission ½ hr before closing.

**Admission:** Adult £5.20, Child £2.60. Pre-booked Groups (15+) £4.40.

🔲 ⬛ ⬛ 🅿

## ARLINGTON COURT 🌿

### Nr BARNSTAPLE, NORTH DEVON EX31 4LP

www.nationaltrust.org.uk

**Tel:** 01271 850296  **Fax:** 01271 851108

**E-mail:** arlingtoncourt@nationaltrust.org.uk

**Owner:** The National Trust  **Contact:** Ana Chylak – Property Manager

Nestling in the thickly wooded valley of the River Yeo, stands the 3000-acre Arlington estate. It comprises a delightful and intimate Victorian house full of treasures including collections of model ships, pewter, shells, extensive informal gardens, a formal terraced Victorian garden, a restored walled garden and historic parkland with breathtaking woodland and lakeside walks. The stable block houses the National Trust's carriage collection and the working stables offer carriage rides around the gardens.

**Location:** MAP 2:I4, OS180 Ref. SS611 405. 7m NE of Barnstaple on A39.

**Open:** 18 Mar–28 Oct: daily except Sat (open BH weekend Sats), 10.30am–5pm. Last admission 4pm. Garden, shop, tearoom & Bat-cam also open Sats Jul & Aug, 10.30am–4pm. 1 Nov–Mar 2008: grounds open during daylight hours.

**Admission:** House, Garden & Carriage Collection: Adult £7.40, Child £3.70, Family £18.50, 1-Adult family £11.10. Group £6.30. Garden & Carriage Collection only: Adult £5.20, Child £2.60. Sats during July & Aug: Adult £2.80, Child £1.40.

🔲 ⬛ ♿  Ground floor & grounds. WC. 🍴 Licensed. 🅿 ⬛ Teachers' pack.
🐕 In grounds & carriage collection, on leads. ⬛ ❄ ⬛

## ANDERTON HOUSE

### Goodleigh, Devon  EX32 7NR

**Tel:** 01628 825925  **www.landmarktrust.org.uk**

**Owner/Contact:** The Landmark Trust

Anderton House is a Grade II* listed building of an exceptional modern design by Peter Aldington of Aldington and Craig. It was commissioned in 1969 as a family home and is highly evocative of its time, retaining the contemporary features and materials. Anderton House is cared for by The Landmark Trust, a building preservation charity who let it for holidays. Full details of Anderton House and 184 other historic and architecturally important buildings are featured in the Landmark Trust Handbook (price £11.50 refundable against a booking).

**Location:** MAP 2:I14, OS Ref. SS603 343. In village.

**Open:** Available for holidays for up to 5 people throughout the year. 2 Open Days a year. Other visits by appointment. Contact Landmark Trust for details.

**Admission:** Free on Open Days.

🏠

## BAYARD'S COVE FORT ♯

### Dartmouth, Devon

**Tel:** 01326 310109

**Owner:** English Heritage  **Contact:** Visitor Operations Administrator

Set among the picturesque gabled houses of Dartmouth, on the waterfront at the end of the quay, this is a small artillery fort built 1509–10 to defend the harbour entrance.

**Location:** MAP 2:K9, OS Ref. SX879 510. In Dartmouth, on riverfront 200 yds, S of South ferry.

**Open:** Any reasonable time, daylight hours.

**Admission:** Free.

🐕 ❄

## BERRY POMEROY CASTLE ♯

### Totnes, Devon  TQ9 6NJ

**Tel:** 01803 866618  **E-mail:** customers@english-heritage.org.uk

**www.english-heritage.org.uk/berrypomeroy**

**Owner:** The Duke of Somerset  **Contact:** Visitor Operations Team

A romantic late medieval castle, dramatically sited half-way up a wooded hillside, looking out over a deep ravine and stream. It is unusual in combining the remains of a large castle with a flamboyant courtier's mansion. Reputed to be one of the most haunted castles in the country.

**Location:** MAP 2:J8, OS202 Ref. SX839 623. 2½m E of Totnes off A385. Entrance gate ½m NE of Berry Pomeroy village, then ½m drive. Narrow approach, unsuitable for coaches.

**Open:** 1 Apr–31 Oct: daily, 10am–5pm (6pm in Jul & Aug; 4pm in Oct).

**Admission:** Adult £3.80, Child £1.90, Conc £2.90. 15% discount for groups (11+).

🔲 ♿  Ground floor & grounds. ⬛ Not EH. 🔲 🅿 No access for coaches. 🐕

## BICTON PARK
## BOTANICAL GARDENS

*See page 210 for full page entry.*

© NT Photographic Library / George Wright

Buckland Abbey, Yelverton

## BRADLEY MANOR ⚘

**Newton Abbot, Devon  TQ12 6BN**
**Tel:** 01803 843235   **E-mail:** bradley@nationaltrust.org.uk
**www.nationaltrust.org.uk**
**Owner:** The National Trust
A delightful small medieval manor house set in woodland and meadows. Still lived in and managed by the donor family.
**Location:** MAP 2:K8, OS Ref. SX848 709. On Totnes road A381. ¾ m SW of Newton Abbot.
**Open:** 3 Apr–27 Sept: Tue–Thur, 2–5 pm. Oct weekdays by appointment only. Last admission 4.30pm.
**Admission:** Adult £3.90, Child £1.95, no reduction for groups.
ℹ No WC. 🅿 From 1.30pm. Not suitable for coaches.

## BRANSCOMBE MANOR MILL, THE OLD BAKERY & FORGE ⚘

**Branscombe, Seaton, Devon  EX12 3DB**
**Tel:** Manor Mill – 01392 881691   Old Bakery – 01297 680333   Forge – 01297 680481
**www.nationaltrust.org.uk**
**Owner:** The National Trust   **Contact:** NT Devon Office
Manor Mill, still in working order and recently restored, is a water-powered mill which probably supplied the flour for the bakery. There are regular working demonstrations. The Old Bakery was, until 1987, the last traditional working bakery in Devon. The old baking equipment has been preserved in the baking room and the rest of the building is now a tearoom. Information display in the outbuildings. The Forge opens regularly and ironwork is on sale - please telephone to check opening times.
**Location:** MAP 2:M7, OS Ref. SY198 887. In Branscombe ½ m S off A3052 by steep, narrow lane.
**Open:** Manor Mill: 2 Apr–29 Oct: Suns, 2–5pm; also Weds in Jul & Aug. The Old Bakery: 31 Mar–30 Oct, Wed–Sun, 11am–5pm. The Forge Open all year round.
**Admission:** Adult £2.60, Child £1.30. Manor Mill only.
📷 🖵

## BUCKFAST ABBEY

**Buckfastleigh, Devon  TQ11 0EE**
**Tel:** 01364 645500   **Fax:** 01364 643891   **E-mail:** education@buckfast.org.uk
**Owner:** Buckfast Abbey Trust   **Contact:** The Warden
The original monastery at Buckfast was formed during the reign of King Cnut in 1018.
**Location:** MAP 2:J8, OS Ref. SX741 674. ½m from A38 Plymouth – Exeter route.
**Open:** Church & Grounds: All year: 9am–7pm.
**Admission:** Free.

Arlington Court, Nr Barnstaple

# BUCKLAND ABBEY ⚘
## YELVERTON, DEVON  PL20 6EY

www.nationaltrust.org.uk

**Tel:** 01822 853607   **Fax:** 01822 855448
**E-mail:** bucklandabbey@nationaltrust.org.uk
**Owner:** The National Trust   **Contact:** Jon Cummins – Visitor Services Manager
The spirit of Sir Francis Drake is rekindled at his home with exhibitions of his courageous adventures and achievements throughout the world. One of the Trust's most interesting historical buildings and originally a 13th century monastery, the abbey was transformed into a family residence before Sir Francis bought it in 1581. Fascinating decorated plaster ceiling in Tudor Drake Chamber. Outside there are monastic farm buildings, craft workshops and country walks. Introductory film presentation. Beautiful Elizabethan garden now open. Letterbox Trail through Great North Wood.

**Location:** MAP 2:I8, OS201 Ref. SX487 667. 6m S of Tavistock; 11m N of Plymouth off A386. Bus: 55/56 from Yelverton (except Sun).
**Open:** 17 Feb–11 Mar: Sats & Suns only, 12.30–5pm. 17 Mar–4 Nov: daily except Thurs, 10.30am–5.30pm (last adm. 4.45pm). 10 Nov–2 Dec: Sats & Suns only, 12.30 –5pm. 6–23 Dec: Thurs–Sun, 11am–5pm.
**Admission:** Abbey & Grounds: Adult £7.40, Child £3.70, Family £18.50, 1-Adult Family £11.50. Group (15+): Adult £6.30, Child £3.10. Grounds only: Adult £3.90, Child £1.90.
ℹ No photography in house. 📷 🖥 🗏 🔧 Ground floor & grounds. WC.
🖵 Licensed. 🍴 Licensed. 🎟 By arrangement. ▣ 🅿 🖰 Guide dogs only. ✳ 🖵

© NT Photographic Library / Andreas Von Einsiedel

NTPL / Alec MacKenzie

©NTPL/Lee Searle

© Lady Studley, Hartland Abbey

## CADHAY 🏠
### OTTERY ST MARY, DEVON EX11 1QT
www.cadhay.org.uk

**Tel:** 01404 812999

**Owner:** Mr R Thistlethwayte  **Contact:** Jo Holloway

Cadhay is approached by an avenue of lime-trees, and stands in an extensive garden, with herbaceous borders and yew hedges, with excellent views over the original medieval fish ponds. The main part of the house was built about 1550 by John Haydon who had married the de Cadhay heiress. He retained the Great Hall of an earlier house, of which the fine timber roof (about 1420–1460) can be seen. An Elizabethan Long Gallery was added by John's successor at the end of the 16th century, thereby forming a unique courtyard with statues of Sovereigns on each side, described by Sir Simon Jenkins as one of the 'Treasures of Devon'.

**Location:** MAP 2:L6, OS Ref. SY090 962. 1m NW of Ottery St Mary. From W take A30 and exit at Pattersons Cross, follow signs for Fairmile and then Cadhay. From E, exit at the Iron Bridge and follow signs as above.

**Open:** 26–28 May. May–July: Fris; August: Fris & BH Sat–Mon. Sept: Fris, 2–5.30pm. Last tour 4.30pm.

**Admission:** Guided tours: Adult £6, Child £2. Gardens: Adults £2, Child £1.

🚻 🔗 Ground floor & grounds. ● T 🎥 Obligatory. P 🔗 Guide dogs only. 🏠 🔺

Hartland Abbey, Bideford

David Cripps

©NTPL / John Such

## CASTLE DROGO 🌿
### DREWSTEIGNTON, EXETER EX6 6PB
www.nationaltrust.org.uk

**Tel:** 01647 433306  **Fax:** 01647 433186  **E-mail:** castledrogo@nationaltrust.org.uk

**Owner:** The National Trust  **Contact:** David Bailey, Property Manager

Extraordinary granite and oak castle, designed by Sir Edwin Lutyens, which combines the comforts of the 20th century with the grandeur of a Baronial castle. Elegant dining and drawing rooms and fascinating kitchen and scullery. Terraced formal garden with colourful herbaceous borders and rose beds. Panoramic views over Dartmoor and delightful walks in the dramatic Teign Gorge.

**Location:** MAP 2:J7, OS191 Ref. SX721 900. 5m S of A30 Exeter–Okehampton road.

**Open:** Castle: 3/4, 10/11 Mar, 11am–4pm. 17 Mar–4 Nov, daily except Tues, 11am–5pm (4pm 29 Oct–4 Nov). 1–23 Dec, Sats & Suns 12noon–4pm. Last admission ½ hr before closing. Garden, Shop & Tearoom: 3/4, 10/11 Mar, 10.30am–4.30pm. 17 Mar–4 Nov, daily 10.30am–5.30pm (4.30pm 29 Oct–4 Nov) 5 Nov–16 Dec, Fri–Sun, 11am–4pm.

**\*Admission:** House & Garden: Adult £7.40, Child £3.70, Family £18.50, 1-Adult Family £11.10. Group: £6.30. Garden only: Adult £4.75, Child £2.60, Group £4.05. \*includes a voluntary donation but visitors can choose to pay the standard prices displayed at the property and on the website.

🏠 🚻 🔗 2 rooms in castle & grounds. WCs. ● 🎥 By arrangement. 🐕 Guide dogs only in certain areas. 🔺

## CHAMBERCOMBE MANOR

**Ilfracombe, Devon  EX34 9RJ**

**Tel:** 01271 862624   **www.chambercombemanor.co.uk**

**Owner:** Chambercombe Trust   **Contact:** Angela Powell

Guided tours of Norman Manor House which is mentioned in Domesday Book. Hear the legend of Chambercombe and visit Haunted Room. Set in 16 acres of woodland and landscaped gardens. Lady Jane Tea Rooms offering light lunches and cream teas.

**Location:** MAP 2:I3, OS Ref. SS539 461. East of Ilfracombe between A399 and B3230, follow brown historic house signs. Private car park at end of Chambercombe Lane.

**Open:** Easter–end Oct: Mon–Fri, 10.30am–5pm; Sun, 2–5pm. Last tour 4.30pm.

**Admission:** Adult £6, Child/Conc. £4, Family £17, under 5s free. Group (max 50) discount - apply to Manor.

ⓘ No photography in house. 🅐 Partial. 🅑🅕 Obligatory. 🅟 Limited for coaches. 🅜🅚 On leads, in grounds.

## CLOVELLY

*See page 211 for full page entry.*

Clovelly, Nr Bideford

©National Trust Photographic Library

# COLETON FISHACRE HOUSE & GARDEN ✿

## BROWNSTONE ROAD, KINGSWEAR, DARTMOUTH  TQ6 0EQ

www.nationaltrust.org.uk

**Tel:** 01803 752466   **Fax:** 01803 753017

**E-mail:** coletonfishacre@nationaltrust.org.uk

**Owner:** The National Trust   **Contact:** Robyn Brown, Property Manager

A 9 hectare property set in a stream-fed valley within the spectacular scenery of the South Devon coast. The Lutyens-style house with art deco-influenced interior was built in the 1920s for Rupert and Lady Dorothy D'Oyly Carte who created the delightful garden, planted with a wide range of rare and exotic plants giving year round interest.

**Location:** MAP 2:K9, OS202 Ref. SX910 508. 3m E of Kingswear, follow brown tourist signs.

**Open:** House: 17 Mar–28 Oct: Weds–Suns & BH Mons, & Mons 23 Jul–20 Aug, 11am–4.30pm (last entry at 4pm). Garden & Tearoom: as House but 10.30am–5pm.

**Admission:** House & Garden: Adult £6.40, Child £3.20. Family £16, 1-Adult Family £9.60. Booked groups (15+): Adult £5.60, Child £2.85. Garden only: Adult £5.90, Child £3, Booked groups (15+) £5.

ⓘ No photography in house. 🅞🅕🅐 Limited access to grounds. WC. 🅑 🅟 Limited. Coaches must book. 🅚 Assistance dogs only in garden.

© NT Photographic Library / Stephen Robson

Knightshayes Court, Tiverton

## COMPTON CASTLE ❧

### MARLDON, PAIGNTON TQ3 1TA

www.nationaltrust.org.uk

**Tel:** 01803 843235  **E-mail:** compton@nationaltrust.org.uk

**Owner:** The National Trust    **Contact:** Carol Martin

Dramatic fortified manor house built by the Gilbert family between the 14th and 16th centuries. It has been the Gilberts' home for most of the last 600 years. Sir Humphrey Gilbert (1539-1583) was coloniser of Newfoundland and half-brother to Sir Walter Raleigh. There is a lovely rose garden and knot garden to complement the interior which includes great hall, solar, spiral staircases, old kitchen and chapel.

**Location:** MAP 2:K8, OS180 Ref. SX865 648. At Compton, 3m W of Torquay signed at Marldon. Coaches must approach from A381 Totnes Road at Ipplepen.

**Open:** 2 Apr–25 Oct: Mons, Weds & Thurs, 10am–1pm & 2–5pm; Last admission ½hr before closing.

**Admission:** Adult £3.90, Child £1.95. Pre-arranged Groups Adult £3.30, Child £1.70.

🖸 🕭 WC. 🖃 (not NT) Castle Barton 01803 873314. 🖹 By arrangement.
🅿 Outside Castle or in Castle Barton Car Park. Coaches by appointment only.

## CULVER HOUSE

### LONGDOWN, EXETER, DEVON EX6 7BD

www.culver.biz

**Tel:** 01392 811885   **Fax:** 01392 811817   **E-mail:** info@culver.biz

**Owner/Contact:** Charles Eden Esq

Culver was built in 1836, but redesigned by the great Victorian architect, Alfred Waterhouse in a mock Tudor style. The distinctive interior of the house makes it a favoured location for functions and Culver was featured in BBC1's 'Down to Earth' series in 2001. It has also been used by German and American filmcrews.

**Location:** MAP 2:J7, OS Ref. SX848 901. 5m W of Exeter on B3212.

**Open:** Not open to the public. Available for corporate hospitality.

**Admission:** Please telephone for booking details.

🖻

## CUSTOM HOUSE

**The Quay, Exeter EX2 4AN**

**Tel:** 01392 265169   **Fax:** 01392 265165   **E-mail:** michael.carson@exeter.gov.uk

**Owner:** Exeter City Council    **Contact:** Michael Carson

The Custom House, located on Exeter's historic Quayside, was constructed from 1680–1682. It is the earliest substantial brick building in Exeter and was used by HM Customs and Excise until 1989. The building has an impressive sweeping staircase and spectacular ornamental plaster ceilings.

**Location:** MAP 2:K6, OS Ref. SX919 921. Exeter's historic Quayside.

**Open:** 1 Apr–31 Oct: Guided tour programme, telephone 01392 265203. Other times by prior arrangement with Exeter City Council.

**Admission:** Free.

🕭 Partial. 🖹 Obligatory. 🔳 🖾 Guide dogs only.

## DARTMOUTH CASTLE ⌗

### CASTLE ROAD, DARTMOUTH, DEVON TQ6 0JN

www.english-heritage.org.uk/dartmouth

**Tel:** 01803 833588   **Fax:** 01803 834445

**E-mail:** customers@english-heritage.org.uk

**Owner:** English Heritage    **Contact:** Visitor Operations Team

This brilliantly positioned defensive castle juts out into the narrow entrance to the Dart estuary, with the sea lapping at its foot. When begun in 1480s it was one of the most advanced fortifications in England, and was the first castle designed specifically with artillery in mind. For nearly 500 years it kept its defences up-to-date in preparation for war. Today the castle is in a remarkably good state of repair, along with excellent exhibitions, the history of the castle comes to life. A picnic spot of exceptional beauty.

**Location:** MAP 2:K9, OS202 Ref. SX887 503. 1m SE of Dartmouth off B3205, narrow approach road.

**Open:** 1 Apr–31 Oct: daily, 10am–5pm (6pm in Jul & Aug; 4pm in Oct). 1 Nov–20 Mar: Sat & Sun, 10am–4pm. Closed 24–26 Dec & 1 Jan.

**Admission:** Adult £3.90, Child £2, Conc. £2.90. 15% discount for groups (11+).

🛈 WC. 🖸 🖃 🅿 Limited (charged, not EH). 🖾 🏵

Marker's Cottage, Exeter

## DOCTON MILL & GARDEN

**Spekes Valley, Hartland, Devon  EX39 6EA**
**Tel/Fax:** 01237 441369
**Owner/Contact:** John Borrett
Garden for all seasons in 8 acres of sheltered wooded valley, plus working mill.
**Location:** MAP 1:G5, OS Ref. SS235 226. 3m Hartland Quay. 15m N of Bude. 3m W of A39, 3m S of Hartland.
**Open:** 1 Mar–31 Oct: 10am–6pm.
**Admission:** Adult £4, Child (under 16 yrs) Free, OAP £3.75.

## DOWNES

**Crediton, Devon  EX17 3PL**
**Tel:** 01392 439046  **Fax:** 01392 426183
**Owner:** Trustees of the Downes Estate Settlement  **Contact:** Dianne Shirazian
Downes is a Palladian Mansion dating originally from 1692. As the former home of General Sir Redvers Buller, the house contains a large number of items relating to his military campaigns. The property is now predominantly a family home with elegant rooms hung with family portraits, and a striking main staircase.
**Location:** MAP 2:K6, OS Ref. SX852 997. Approx a mile from Crediton town centre.
**Open:** 9 Apr–3 July (and Aug BH Mon & Tues): Mons and Tues, guided tours 2.15 & 3.30pm. Open to groups (15+) at other times, Easter–3 July by prior appointment.
**Admission:** Adult £5, Child (5-16yrs) £2.50, Child (under 5yrs) Free, Groups (15+) £4.50. 🎦 Obligatory.

## THE ELIZABETHAN GARDENS

**Plymouth Barbican Assoc. Ltd, New St, The Barbican, Plymouth**
**Tel/Fax:** 01822 611027/612983  **E-mail:** amza36@dial.pipex.com
**Owner:** Plymouth Barbican Association Limited  **Contact:** Mr Tony Golding
Very small series of four enclosed gardens laid out in Elizabethan style in 1970.
**Location:** MAP 1:H8, OS Ref. SX477 544. 3 mins walk from Dartington Glass (a landmark building) on the Barbican.
**Open:** Mon–Sat, 9am–5pm. Closed Christmas.
**Admission:** Free.

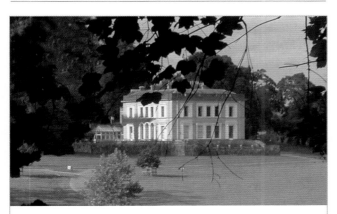

## ESCOT

### ESCOT PARK, OTTERY ST MARY, DEVON  EX11 1LU

www.escot-devon.co.uk

**Tel:** 01404 822188  **Fax:** 01404 822903  **E-mail:** info@escot-devon.co.uk
**Owner/Contact:** Mr J-M Kennaway
House: an idyllic setting for weddings, conferences and product launches. Gardens and Park: 25 acres of gardens set within 220 acres of 'Capability' Brown parkland. Conservation activities within the park include water meadows restoration, studies on water voles and bats, a resident beaver and even seahorses. The gardens are open to the public and feature a 4,000 beech-tree maze, wild boar, otters and birds of prey workshops and displays. Estate: 1200 privately owned acres of glorious East Devon – ideal as a film location, for musical festivals and other special events.
**Location:** MAP 2:L6, OS Ref. SY080 977 (gate). 9m E of Exeter on A30 at Fairmile.
**Open:** Gardens, Aquatic Centre, Restaurant & Gift Shop: open throughout the year as follows: Easter–31 Oct: daily, 10am–6pm. 1 Nov–Easter: daily, 10am–5pm except 25, 26 Dec.
**Admission:** Adult £5.50, Child £4, Child (under 3yrs) Free, OAP £4, Family (2+2) £16.50. Booked groups (10+): Adult £5, Child/Conc. £3.50. Reduced rates apply in winter months.
🎦 🚻 👤 Partial. 🍽 Licensed. 🍴 Licensed. 🎦 By arrangement. 🅿 🔲
🐕 In grounds, on leads. 🔺 ✳ ♨

## EXETER CATHEDRAL

**Exeter, Devon  EX1 1HS**
**Tel:** 01392 285983 (Visitors' Officer)  **Fax:** 01392 285986
**E-mail:** visitors@exeter-cathedral.org.uk
**Owner:** Dean & Chapter of Exeter  **Contact:** Visitors' Officer
Fine example of decorated gothic architecture. Longest unbroken stretch of gothic vaulting in the world.
**Location:** MAP 2:K6, OS Ref. SX921 925. Central to the City – between High Street and Southernhay. Groups may be set down in South Street.
**Open:** All year: Mon–Fri, 9.30am–6.30pm, Sats, 9am–5pm, Suns, 7.30am–6.30pm.
Admission: Donation requested of £3.50 per person. Charges apply to groups.

## FINCH FOUNDRY 🌰

**Sticklepath, Okehampton, Devon  EX20 2NW**
**Tel:** 01837 840046
**Owner:** The National Trust
19th-century water-powered forge, which produced agricultural and mining hand tools, holding regular demonstrations throughout the day.
**Location:** MAP 2:I6, OS Ref. SX641 940. 4m E of Okehampton off the A30.
**Open:** 17 Mar–28 Oct: Daily except Tue, 11am–5pm.
**Admission:** Adult £3.90, Child £1.95.
🎦 🍽 🅿 Not suitable for coaches. 🔲 🐕 Except tearoom.

## FURSDON HOUSE 🏛

**Cadbury, Nr Thorverton, Exeter, Devon  EX5 5JS**
**Tel:** 01392 860860  **Fax:** 01392 860126  **E-mail:** enquiries@fursdon.co.uk
**www.fursdon.co.uk**
**Owner:** Mr E D Fursdon  **Contact:** Mrs C Fursdon
The Fursdons have lived here since the 13th century and the house, which was greatly modified in the 18th century, is at the heart of a small farming estate within a wooded and hilly landscape. Family memorabilia is displayed including a letter to Grace Fursdon from King Charles during the Civil War and there are fine examples of costume and textiles. The garden to the south flows naturally into the parkland beyond; to the west it slopes up to a walled and terraced area with mixed borders, roses and herbs. There are two private wings of the house for self catering holiday accommodation.
**Location:** MAP 2:K6, OS Ref. SS922 046. 1½m S of A3072 between Tiverton & Crediton, 9m N of Exeter turning off A396 to Thorverton. Narrow lanes!
**Open:** House: Easter–end Aug, BH Suns & Mons. 30 May–26 Aug, Suns & Weds. Guided tours at 2.30 & 3.30pm. Garden: 2–5pm as house. Groups by prior arrangement only.
**Admission:** House and Garden: Adult £5, Child (under 10yrs) Free. Garden only: £2.50.
🎦 Conferences. No photography or video. 🚻 👤 Partial. 🍽 🎦 Obligatory. 🅿
🐕 Guide dogs only. 🏠 Self-catering.

## THE GARDEN HOUSE

**Buckland Monachorum, Yelverton, Devon  PL20 7LQ**
**Tel:** 01822 854769  **Fax:** 01822 855358  **E-mail:** office@thegardenhouse.org.uk
**www.thegardenhouse.org.uk**
**Owner:** The Fortescue Garden Trust  **Contact:** Julie Beesley
'Is this the best garden in Britain?' Sunday Express. Idyllic valley garden on the edge of Dartmoor offers year-round colour and interest. Centred on an enchanting walled garden surrounding the romantic ruins of a 16th century vicarage, also a modern garden planted in pioneering naturalistic style. 'You'd be mad to miss it' – Alan Titchmarsh.
**Location:** MAP 2:I8, OS Ref. SX490 682. Signposted W off A386 Plymouth – Tavistock Road, 10m N of Plymouth.
**Open:** 1 Mar–31 Oct: daily, 10.30am–5pm. Last admission 4.30pm.
**Admission:** Adult £5.50, Child (5–16) £2, Under 5s Free. Seniors £4.75, pre-booked groups (10+) £4.75. Prices subject to change.
🚻 👤 Partial. 🍽 🎦 🅿 🐕 Guide dogs only.

Knightshayes Court, Tiverton

## GREENWAY ⚜

**GREENWAY ROAD, GALMPTON, CHURSTON FERRERS, DEVON  TQ5 0ES**

www.nationaltrust.org.uk

**Tel:** 01803 842382  **Greenway Quay Ferry Services:** 01803 844010
**Riverlink ferry:** 01803 834488  **E-mail:** greenway@nationaltrust.org.uk
**Owner:** The National Trust  **Contact:** Carol Martin

A glorious woodland garden, held on the edge of wildness and set on the banks of the River Dart; Greenway is one of Devon's best kept secrets. Renowned for rare half-hardy trees and shrubs and underplanted with native wild flowers, this peaceful haven has magnificent views and some challenging paths. Travel by river ferry from Dartmouth, Totnes or Torquay for a perfect day out.

**Location:** MAP 2:K8, OS Ref. SX876 548.
**Open:** 7 Mar–13 Oct: Wed–Sat, 10.30am–5pm (last admission 4.30pm).
**Admission:** Booked groups & visitors arriving on foot or by ferry: Adult £4.40, Child £2.20. Others (by car): Adult £5.20, Child £2.60.

⬚ ⬚ ⬚ ⬚ Partial. WC. ⬚ Licensed. ⬚ Licensed. ⬚ By arrangement.
⬚ 1 midi size coach only. Groups must book. Please use river travel. ⬚

---

## HALDON BELVEDERE/LAWRENCE CASTLE

**Higher Ashton, Nr Dunchideock, Exeter, Devon  EX6 7QY**
**Tel/Fax:** 01392 833668  **E-mail:** enquiries@haldonbelvedere.co.uk
**www.haldonbelvedere.co.uk**
**Owner:** Devon Historic Building Trust  **Contact:** Ian Turner
18th century Grade II* listed triangular tower with circular turrets on each corner. Built in memory of Major General Stringer Lawrence, founder of the Indian Army. Restored in 1995 to illustrate the magnificence of its fine plasterwork, gothic windows, mahogany flooring and marble fireplaces. Breathtaking views of the surrounding Devon countryside.
**Location:** MAP 2:K7, OS Ref. SX875 861. 7m SW of Exeter. Exit A38 at Exeter racecourse for 2½m.
**Open:** Feb–Oct: Suns & BHs, 1.30–5.30pm.
**Admission:** Adult £2, Child Free.
⬚ ⬚ Unsuitable. ⬚ By arrangement. ⬚ ⬚ ⬚ In grounds, on leads. ⬚ ⬚

---

Fursdon House, Nr Thorverton

## HARTLAND ABBEY ⬚

**HARTLAND, Nr BIDEFORD, N DEVON  EX39 6DT**

www.hartlandabbey.com

**Tel:** 01237 441264/234 or 01884 860225  **Fax:** 01237 441264/01884 861134
**Owner:** Sir Hugh Stucley Bt  **Contact:** The Administrator
Founded as an Augustinian Monastery in a beautiful valley leading to the Atlantic coast a mile's walk away, the Abbey was given by Henry VIII in 1539 to the Sergeant of his Wine Cellar; it still remains a family home. Remodelled in the 18th and 19th centuries, stunning architecture, important paintings, furniture, porcelain, early photographs, documents from 1160 and family memorabilia collected over generations, fascinate visitors. Restored winding paths designed by Jekyll, through camellias, rhododendrons, the Bog Garden and Victorian Fernery make an enchanting walk to the 18th century Walled Gardens where herbaceous, tender and rare plants including *echium pininana* and vegetables thrive. Guinea fowl, peacocks, donkeys and black sheep. Access from Coastal Footpath. Rosamunde Pilcher film location. A romantic venue for weddings. Snowdrop Sunday 11 Feb, 12 noon–4pm.
**Location:** MAP 1:G5, OS Ref. SS240 249. 15m W of Bideford, 15m N of Bude off A39 between Hartland and Hartland Quay.
**Open:** House: 1 Apr–26 May: Wed/Thur, Sun & BHs. 28 May–30 Sept: Sun–Thurs, 2–5pm. Gardens & Grounds: 1 Apr–30 Sept: daily except Sats, 12.30–5.30pm.
**Admission:** House, Gardens & Grounds: Adult £8, Child (5–15ys) £2.50, Family £18. Groups (15+): £7, & (30+) £6.50. Gardens & Grounds only: Adult £4.50, Child (5–15ys) £1, Family £10.
⬚ ⬚ ⬚ Wedding receptions. ⬚ Partial. WC. ⬚ ⬚ By arrangement. ⬚
⬚ In grounds, on leads. ⬚ ⬚

---

## HEMERDON HOUSE ⬚

**Sparkwell, Plympton, Plymouth, Devon  PL7 5BZ**
**Tel:** Business hours 01822 610111; other times 01752 337350  **Fax:** 01752 331477
**E-mail:** jim.woollcombe@btopenworld.com
**Owner:** J H G Woollcombe Esq  **Contact:** Joseph E Hess
Late 18th century family house, rich in local history.
**Location:** MAP 2:I8, OS Ref. SX564 575. 3m E of Plympton off A38.
**Open:** 4–16 & 20–28 May; 6–13 Aug: 2–5.30pm. Last admission 5pm. Provisional dates, please telephone to confirm.
**Admission:** £4.50.
⬚ Ground floor. ⬚ Obligatory. ⬚

---

## HEMYOCK CASTLE

**Hemyock, Cullompton, Devon  EX15 3RJ**
**Tel:** 01823 680745
**Owner/Contact:** Mrs Sheppard
Former medieval moated castle, displays show site's history as fortified manor house, castle and farm.
**Location:** MAP 2:L6, OS Ref. ST135 134. M5/J26, Wellington then 5m S over the Blackdown Hills.
**Open:** BH Mons 2–5pm. Other times by appointment. Groups & private parties welcome.
**Admission:** Adult £1, Child 50p. Group rates available.

---

## HOUND TOR DESERTED MEDIEVAL VILLAGE ⬚

**Ashburton Road, Manaton, Dartmoor, Devon**
**Tel:** 01626 832093
**Owner:** English Heritage  **Contact:** Dartmoor National Park Authority
The remains of four bronze age to medieval dwellings.
**Location:** MAP 2:J7, OS191 Ref. SX746 788. 1½m S of Manaton off Ashburton road. 6m N of Ashburton.
**Open:** Any reasonable time, daylight only.
**Admission:** Free.
⬚ ⬚ ⬚

# KILLERTON HOUSE & GARDEN 🌿
## BROADCLYST, EXETER EX5 3LE
www.nationaltrust.org.uk

**Tel:** 01392 881345  **E-mail:** killerton@nationaltrust.org.uk
**Owner:** The National Trust  **Contact:** Denise Melhuish – Assistant Property Manager
The spectacular hillside garden is beautiful throughout the year with spring flowering bulbs and shrubs, colourful herbaceous borders and fine trees. The garden is surrounded by parkland and woods offering lovely walks. The house is furnished as a family home and includes a costume collection dating from the 18th century in a series of period rooms and a Victorian laundry. New costume exhibition for 2007 'Quilty Secrets' – wonderful quilted dresses, waistcoats and stunning accessories from the Killerton costume collection.

**Location:** MAP 2:K6, OS Ref. SS977 001. Off Exeter – Cullompton Rd (B3181). M5 N'bound J30, M5 S'bound J28.

**Open:** House: 14 Mar–4 Nov: daily except Tue (Oct also closed Mon); Aug: daily, 11am–5pm. Last entry ½ hour before closing. Garden: All year: daily, 10.30am–7pm or dusk.

**Admission:** House & Garden: Adult £7.40, Child £3.70, Family £18.50, 1-Adult Family £11.10. Group £6.30. Garden only: Adult £5.60, Child £2.80.

🖼️ 📷 📺 💻 ♿ 🍴 🅿️ 🚌  Guide dogs only in house. ♿

# KNIGHTSHAYES COURT 🌿
## BOLHAM, TIVERTON, DEVON EX16 7RQ
www.nationaltrust.org.uk

**Tel:** 01884 254665  **E-mail:** knightshayes@nationaltrust.org.uk
**Owner:** The National Trust  **Contact:** Penny Woollams – Property Manager
The striking Victorian gothic house is a rare survival of the work of William Burges with ornate patterns in many rooms. One of the finest gardens in Devon, mainly woodland and shrubs with something of interest throughout the seasons. Drifts of spring bulbs, summer flowering shrubs, pool garden and amusing animal topiary.
**Location:** MAP 2:K5, OS Ref. SS960 151. 2m N of Tiverton (A396) at Bolham.

**Open:** House: 17 Mar–4 Nov, daily except Fri (open Good Fri), 11am–5pm. Last adm. ½hr before closing. Garden, shop/plant centre & restaurant: 2–12 Mar: Fri–Mon, 11am–4pm; 17 Mar–4 Nov: daily, 11am–5pm. Shop & Restaurant also open Nov & Dec, tel. for details.

**Admission:** House & Garden: Adult £7.40, Child £3.70, Family £18.50, 1-Adult Family £11.10. Group £6.30. Garden only: Adult £5.90, Child £3. Group £5/£2.50.

🖼️ 📷 📺 ♿  Ground floor & grounds. WC. 🍴 🚌  On leads in park.

## LOUGHWOOD MEETING HOUSE

**Dalwood, Axminster, Devon EX13 7DU**
**Tel:** 01392 881691 **Fax:** 01392 881954
**Owner:** The National Trust **Contact:** National Trust Devon Office
Around 1653 the Baptist congregation of the nearby village of Kilmington constructed this simple thatched building dug into the hillside. It still contains the original box pews.
**Location:** MAP 2:M6, OS Ref. SY253993. 4m W of Axminster.
**Open:** All year, daily.
**Admission:** Free.
ⓘ Pushchairs and baby carriers admitted. Steep slope from the car park. Ground floor only. Very narrow country lanes. No parking for coaches.

## LYDFORD CASTLE & SAXON TOWN

**Lydford, Okehampton, Devon**
**Tel:** 01822 820320
**Owner:** English Heritage **Contact:** The National Trust
Standing above the lovely gorge of the River Lyd, this 12th century tower was notorious as a prison. The earthworks of the original Norman fort are to the south. A Saxon town once stood nearby and its layout is still discernible.
**Location:** MAP 2:I7, OS191 Castle Ref. SX510 848, Fort Ref. SX509 847. In Lydford off A386 8m SW of Okehampton.
**Open:** Any reasonable time, daylight hours.
**Admission:** Free.

## MARKER'S COTTAGE

**Broadclyst, Exeter, Devon EX5 3HR**
**Tel:** 01392 881345 (Killerton House for information)
**Owner:** The National Trust **Contact:** The Custodian
Thatched, medieval cob house containing a cross-passage screen decorated with a painting of St Andrew and his attributes.
**Location:** MAP 2:K6, OS Ref. SX985 973. ¼m E of B3181 in village of Broadclyst.
**Open:** 1 Apr–30 Oct: Sun–Tue, 2–5pm. Last entry ½ hour before closing.
**Admission:** Adult £2.60, Child £1.30. Joint ticket with Clyston Mill: Adult £4.20, Child £2.

## MARWOOD HILL

**Barnstaple, Devon EX31 4EB**
**Tel:** 01271 342528 **Contact:** Patricia Stout
20 acre garden with 3 small lakes. Extensive collection of camellias, bog garden. National collection of astilbes.
**Location:** MAP 2:I4, OS Ref. SS545 375. 4m N of Barnstaple. ½ m W of B3230. Signs off A361 Barnstaple – Braunton road.
**Open:** All year: 10am–5pm.
**Admission:** Adult £4, Child (under 12yrs) Free.

## MORWELLHAM QUAY

**Morwellham, Tavistock, Devon PL19 8JL**
**Tel:** 01822 832766 Fax: 01822 833808
**Owner:** The Morwellham & Tamar Valley Trust **Contact:** Anthony Power
Award-winning visitor centre at historic river port.
**Location:** MAP 1:H8, OS Ref. SX446 697. Off A390 about 15 mins drive from Tavistock, Devon. 5m SW of Tavistock. 3m S of A390 at Gulworthy.
**Open:** Summer: daily, 10am–5.30pm, last adm. 3.30pm. Winter: daily, 10am–4.30pm, last adm. 2.30pm.
**Admission:** Adult £8.90, Child £6, OAP £7.80, Family (2+2) £26. Group rate please apply for details. Usual concessions. Prices may be subject to change.

Cadhay, Ottery St Mary

## OKEHAMPTON CASTLE

**Okehampton, Devon EX20 1JB**
**Tel:** 01837 52844 **E-mail:** customers@english-heritage.org.uk
**www.english-heritage.org.uk/okehampton**
**Owner:** English Heritage **Contact:** Visitor Operations Team
The ruins of the largest castle in Devon stand above a river surrounded by splendid woodland. There is still plenty to see, including the Norman motte and the jagged remains of the Keep. There is a picnic area and lovely woodland walks.
**Location:** MAP 2:I6, OS Ref. SX584 942. 1m SW of Okehampton town centre off A30 bypass.
**Open:** 1 Apr–30 Sept: daily, 10am–5pm (6pm in July & Aug).
**Admission:** Adult £3, Child £1.50, Conc. £2.30. 15% discount for groups (11+).
Access difficult for ambulant disabilities. Grounds. WC.
In grounds, on leads.

## OLDWAY MANSION

**Paignton, Devon TQ3 2CR**
**Tel:** 01803 208979 **Fax:** 01803 207670
**Owner:** Torbay Council **Contact:** Facilities Management Officer – Stuart Left
Built by sewing machine entrepreneur I M Singer in the 1870s.
**Location:** MAP 2:K8, OS Ref. SX888 615. Off W side of A3022.
**Open:** All year: Mon–Sat, 9am–5pm (except Christmas & New Year). Easter–Oct: Suns, 2–5pm. Visitors should note that not all rooms will always be open, access depends on other activities.
**Admission:** Free.

© NTPL / Tony Murdoch

## OVERBECK'S

**SHARPITOR, SALCOMBE, SOUTH DEVON TQ8 8LW**
www.nationaltrust.org.uk

**Tel:** 01548 842893 **E-mail:** overbecks@nationaltrust.org.uk
**Owner:** The National Trust **Contact:** Property Manager
Elegant Edwardian house with diverse collections and luxuriant garden. The scientist Otto Overbeck lived here from 1928 to 1937 and the museum containing his collections of curios and nautical artefacts has an intimate atmosphere. Some of Overbeck's inventions are on show, including the intriguing 'rejuvenator' machine. The house is set in 2¾ ha (7acres) of beautiful exotic gardens with spectacular views over the Salcombe estuary. It enjoys a sheltered microclimate and so is home to many rare plants. There is also a secret room for children with dolls, tin soldiers, other toys and a ghost hunt.
**Location:** MAP 2:J10, OS Ref. SX728 374. 1½m SW of Salcombe. Signposted from Salcombe (single track lanes).
**Open:** House 18 Mar–15 Jul & 3–30 Sept, Sun–Fri & Easter Sat, 11am–5pm. 16 Jul–2 Sept, daily, 11am–5pm, 1–28 Oct, Sun–Thur, 11am–4.30pm. Tearoom open as house but 11.30am–4.15pm. Garden: All year (except Sats) summer: 10am–5.30pm, winter: 11am–4pm..
**Admission:** Adult £5.80, Child £2.90, Family £14.50, 1-Adult Family £8.70. Groups £5.20.
ⓘ No photography in house. Partial. By arrangement. Limited. Charge refunded on admission.

## POWDERHAM CASTLE 🏰
### KENTON, Nr EXETER, DEVON EX6 8JQ
www.powderham.co.uk

**Tel:** 01626 890243   **Fax:** 01626 890729   **E-mail:** castle@powderham.co.uk
**Owner:** The Earl of Devon     **Contact:** Mrs Clare Crawshaw – General Manager
Lying south of Exeter in a tranquil deer park adjacent to the Exe estuary. Built in 1391 by Sir Philip Courtenay, it has long been the family home of the Earl of Devon. Beautiful Rose Garden and spring walks through the Woodland Garden. Guided tours showcase the Castle's intriguing history, majestic interiors and fine collection of treasures. Victorian kitchen opening in 2007.
**Location:** MAP 2:K7, OS Ref. SX965 832. 6m SW of Exeter, 4m S M5/J30. Access from A379 in Kenton village.
**Open:** 4 Apr– 28 Oct: Sun–Fri, 10am–5.30pm (last guided tour 4.30pm).
**Admission:** Adult £7.95, Child (5–14yrs) £5.95, OAP £7.50, Family: £22.45. Groups (15+) special rates available.
ℹ️ Available for private hire all year round.📷 🎫 🅃 ♿ Partial. WC. 🍽 Licensed.
📷 Included. 1hr. 🅿 🎦 🐾 In part of grounds, on leads. ▲ ❄ ♅

## RHS GARDEN ROSEMOOR
### GREAT TORRINGTON, DEVON EX38 8PH
www.rhs.org.uk/rosemoor

**Tel:** 01805 624067   **Fax:** 01805 624717   **E-mail:** rosemooradmin@rhs.org.uk
**Owner/Contact:** The Royal Horticultural Society
A beautiful garden mixing new gardens with Lady Anne's original garden. Something for all interests and tastes whatever the season, from formal gardens to a lake and Arboretum. The Rosemoor Plant Centre stocks a variety of hardy plants, the shop has books and gifts and, for refreshments, there is a café and restaurant.
**Location:** MAP 2:I5, OS Ref. SS500 183. 1m S of Great Torrington on A3124.
**Open:** All year except Christmas Day; Apr–Sept: 10am–6pm. Oct–Mar: 10am–5pm.
**Admission:** Adult £6, Child (6–16yrs) £2, Child (under 6yrs) Free. Groups (10+) £5pp. Companion for disabled visitor Free. RHS member & 1 guest Free.
📷 🎫 ♿ 🖥 🍽 Licensed. 📷 By arrangement. 🅿 🐾 Guide dogs only. ❄ ♅

## PUSLINCH
### YEALMPTON, PLYMOUTH, DEVON PL8 2NN
**Tel:** 01752 880555   **Fax:** 01752 880909
**Owner/Contact:** Sebastian Fenwick
A perfect example of a medium sized early Georgian house in the Queen Anne tradition with fine contemporary interiors. Built in 1720 by the Yonge family.
**Location:** MAP 2:I9, OS Ref. SX570 509. Yealmpton.
**Open:** Groups only (min charge £30). All year, except Christmas & Boxing Day, by prior appointment only.
**Admission:** Adult £8.
ℹ️ No photography. 📷 Obligatory. 🅿 🐾 ❄

Powderham Castle

© NTPL/Rupert Truman

© NTPL/Joe Cornish

## SALTRAM ❧
### PLYMPTON, PLYMOUTH, DEVON PL7 1UH

www.nationaltrust.org.uk

**Tel:** 01752 333500 **Fax:** 01752 336474 **E-mail:** saltram@nationaltrust.org.uk

**Owner:** The National Trust **Contact:** Administrator

Saltram stands high above the River Plym in a rolling and wooded landscaped park that now provides precious green space on the outskirts of Plymouth. The house, with its magnificent decoration and original contents, was largely created between the 1740s and 1820s by three generations of the Parker family. It features some of Robert Adam's finest rooms, exquisite plasterwork ceilings, original Chinese wallpapers and an exceptional collection of paintings including many by Sir Joshua Reynolds and Angelica Kauffman. The garden is predominantly 19th-century and contains an orangery and several follies, as well as beautiful shrubberies and imposing specimen trees.

The shop and art gallery offer work for sale from contemporary local artists, and National Trust gifts. The Park Restaurant offers refreshments for its visitors. Corporate business and special functions are very welcome.

NB. A major project may necessitate the closure of some show rooms during the season. Please telephone for details.

**Location:** MAP 2:I9, OS Ref. SX520 557. From A38, exit 3 miles north of Plymouth City Centre at Marsh Mill's roundabout. Take Plympton exit; continue in right hand lane to third set of traffic lights then turn right onto Cott Hill. At the top of the hill turn right into Merafield Road then right again after 200 yards.

**Open:** House: 28 Mar–28 Oct: daily except Fris (open Good Fri), 12 noon–4.30pm. Last admission to house 3.45pm. Garden: Jan–21 Dec: daily except Fri (open Good Fri), 11am–4.30pm (4pm Nov–Mar). Gallery: 1 Mar–21 Dec: daily except Fri (open Good Fri), 11am–4.30pm (4pm Nov & Dec). Shop: 1–27 Mar, 11am–4pm, daily except Fri. 28 Mar–28 Oct, daily except Fri, 11am–5pm. 29 Oct–28 Jan, 11am–4pm, daily except Fri. Restaurant: 28 Mar–28 Oct: 11am–5pm daily. 29 Oct–28 Feb, 11am–4pm daily except Fri. For details of all out-of-season opening times, please telephone.

**Admission:** House & Garden: Adult £8.40, Child £4.20, Family £21, 1–Adult Family £12.60. Groups (15+): £7.10. Garden only: Adult £4.20, Child £2.10.

🏠 ♿ 🍴 ♿ WC. Braille guide. 🎧 🍴 Licensed. 🅰 🎧 🅿

🐕 On signed perimeter paths only, on leads. Guide dogs only in house & garden.
❄ 🎫

---

## SAND 🏛
### SIDBURY, SIDMOUTH EX10 0QN

www.sandsidbury.co.uk

**Tel:** 01395 597230 **E-mail:** info@sandsidbury.co.uk

**Contact:** Mrs Stella Huyshe-Shires

Sand is one of East Devon's hidden gems. The beautiful valley garden extends to 6 acres and is the setting for the lived-in house, the 15th century Hall House, and the 17th century Summer House. The family, under whose unbroken ownership the property has remained since 1560, provide guided house tours.

**Location:** MAP 2:L7, OS Ref. SY146 925. Well signed, 250 yards off A375 between Honiton and Sidmouth.

**Open:** House: BH Suns & Mons, 8/9 Apr, 6/7 May, 27/28 May & 26/27 Aug: 2–6pm. Garden: 1 Apr–2 Oct: Sun–Tues, 2–6pm. Last admission to house & garden 5pm. Groups by appointment throughout the year.

**Admission:** House & Garden: Adult £5, Child/Student £1. Garden only: Adult £3, accompanied Child (under 16) Free.

ℹ No photography in house. ♿ Partial. 🎧 🅰 Obligatory. 🅿
🐕 In grounds, on leads. ❄ 🎫 Tel. for details.

---

## SHUTE BARTON ❧

**Shute, Axminster, Devon EX13 7PT**

**Tel:** 01297 34692 (tenant) **www.nationaltrust.org.uk**

**Owner:** The National Trust

One of the most important surviving non-fortified manor houses of the Middle Ages.

**Location:** MAP 2:M6, OS Ref. SY253 974. 3m SW of Axminster, 2m N of Colyton, 1m S of A35.

**Open:** 4 Apr–30 Sept: Weds & Sats, 2–5.30pm. Last admission 5pm. 3–31 Oct: Weds & Sats, 2–5pm. Last admission 4.30pm.

**Admission:** Adult £2.70, Child £1.30. No group reductions.

---

## TAPELEY PARK & GARDENS

**Instow, Bideford, Devon EX39 4NT**

**Tel:** 01271 860897 **Fax:** 01271 342371

**Owner:** Tapeley Park Trust

Extensive gardens and park.

**Location:** MAP 1:H4, OS Ref. SS478 291. Between Bideford and Barnstaple near Instow. Follow brown tourist signs from the A39 onto B3233.

**Open:** Good Fri–end Oct: daily except Sats, 10am–5pm.

**Admission:** Adult £4, Child £2.50, OAP £3.50. Groups (5+): Adult £3.20, Child £2 (under 5s Free), OAP £2.80.

© 01271-378720

Clovelly, Nr Bideford

## TIVERTON CASTLE

**Tiverton, Devon EX16 6RP**

www.tivertoncastle.com

**Tel:** 01884 253200/255200 **Fax:** 01884 254200 **E-mail:** tiverton.castle@ukf.net

**Owner:** Mr and Mrs A K Gordon **Contact:** Mrs A Gordon

Celebrating 900 years since original construction, few buildings evoke such immediate feelings of history. Inside it looks like a fairytale castle, with romantic ruins, Norman towers and gatehouse, and later additions. Beautiful walled gardens, including working kitchen garden. Civil War Armoury – try some on – interesting furniture, pictures. Superb holiday apartments.

**Location:** MAP 2:K5, OS Ref. SS954 130. Just N of Tiverton town centre.

**Open:** Easter–end Oct: Sun, Thur, BH Mon, 2.30–5.30pm. Last admission 5pm. Open to groups (12+) by prior arrangement at any time.

**Admission:** Adult £4, Child (7–16yrs) £2, Child under 7 Free. Garden only: £1.50.

⬛ ⬛ Partial. 🅺 By arrangement. 🅿 ⬛ ⬛ ⬛ 4 Apartments. ❊

## TOTNES CASTLE ⬛

**Castle Street, Totnes, Devon TQ9 5NU**

**Tel/Fax:** 01803 864406 **E-mail:** customers@english-heritage.org.uk

www.english-heritage.org.uk/totnes

**Owner:** English Heritage **Contact:** Visitor Operations Team

By the North Gate of the hill town of Totnes you will find a superb motte and bailey castle, with splendid views across the roof tops and down to the River Dart. It is a symbol of lordly feudal life and a fine example of Norman fortification.

**Location:** MAP 2:J8, OS202 Ref. SX800 605. In Totnes, on hill overlooking the town. Access in Castle St off W end of High St.

**Open:** 1 Apr–31 Oct: daily 10am–5pm (6pm Jul–Aug, 4pm Oct). Closed 24–26 Dec & 1 Jan.

**Admission:** Adult £2.40, Child £1.20, Conc. £1.80. 15% discount for groups (11+).

⬛ ⬛ Unsuitable. 🅿 Charged parking 64 metres (70 yds). ⬛ In grounds, on leads.

© NT Photographic Library

Saltram, Plympton

Saltram, Plympton

## ■ Owner

The Hon
Mrs Townshend DL

## ■ Contact

Shop Manager
Abbotsbury
Weymouth
Dorset  DT3 4LA

**Tel:** 01305 871387
**E-mail:** info@abbotsbury-tourism.co.uk

## ■ Location

**MAP 2:N7**
**OS Ref. SY564 851**

Off A35 nr Dorchester, on
B3157 between
Weymouth & Bridport.

## ■ Opening Times

Mar–Nov: daily,
10am–6pm.

Winter: daily,
10am–4pm.
(Closed Christmas and
New Year.)

Last admission
1 hr before closing.

## ■ Admission

| | |
|---|---|
| Adult | £8.00 |
| Child | £5.00 |
| OAP | £7.50 |

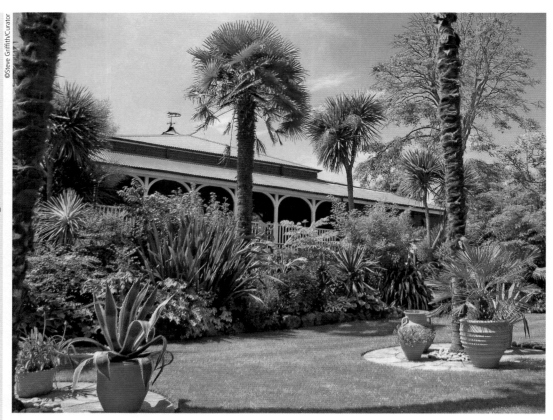

©Steve Griffith/Curator

# ABBOTSBURY SUBTROPICAL GARDENS 🏛

www.abbotsbury-tourism.co.uk          www.abbotsburyplantsales.co.uk

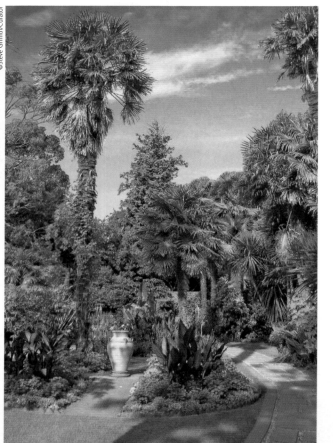

©Steve Griffith/Curator

Established in 1765 by the first Countess of Ilchester. Developed since then into a 20-acre Grade I listed, magnificent woodland valley garden.

World famous for its camellia groves, magnolias, rhododendron and hydrangea collections. In summer it is awash with colour.

Since the restoration after the great storm of 1990 many new and exotic plants have been introduced. The garden is now a mixture of formal and informal, with charming walled garden and spectacular woodland valley views.

Facilities include a Colonial Tea House for lunches, snacks and drinks, a plant centre and quality gift shop. Events such as Shakespeare and concerts are presented during the year. The floodlighting of the garden at the end of October should not be missed.

| | | | |
|---|---|---|---|
| 🛍 | | 🚶 | By arrangement. |
| ✱ | Plants also for sale online. | P | Free. |
| 🍽 | | 🐾 | |
| ♿ | Partial. | 🐕 | In grounds, on leads. |
| ☕ | Licensed. | ❄ | |
| 🍴 | | 🛡 | |

# ATHELHAMPTON HOUSE & GARDENS 🏛

### www.athelhampton.co.uk

The History of Athelhampton House near Dorchester goes back more than 500 years. The Great Hall was built by Sir William Martyn in around 1485.

One of Dorset's treasures, the fine 15th century manor house contains many finely furnished rooms including The Great Hall, Great Chamber, Dining Room, Bedrooms and Library. The second floor of the West Wing is now dedicated to an exhibition of paintings and sketches by the Russian artist Marevna (1892–1984). The collection of her works, painted mainly in the Cubist style, includes some painted whilst she lived at the house during the 1940s and 50s.

Far more than a museum, Athelhampton House captures the essence of a well-loved and lived-in family home, with wonderful panelled rooms and tapestries, fine pictures, furniture and china. The Great Hall with a medieval roof of curved brace timbers and an oriel window with fine heraldic glass is one of the finest examples of 15th century domestic architecture in the country.

The glorious award-winning, Grade I listed garden, dating from 1891, is full of vistas and gains much from the fountains and River Piddle flowing through it. The river board-walk has become a firm favourite with visitors and wildlife alike. The walled gardens include the world famous 30 ft high topiary yew pyramids, Ham Stone courts, fountains and collections of tulips, magnolias, roses, clematis and lilies in season. Also in the grounds can be found a 15th century Dovecote with a capacity for 1,200 birds, one of the earliest in Dorset, still housing around 50 doves.

The Coach House contains all the facilities required for the comfort of daily visitors including tea-room, gift shop and private rooms available for visiting groups. The House and Gardens can be opened by appointment for evening visits and dinners. Fridays and Saturdays are available for wedding ceremonies and/or receptions.

Great Hall

## Owner
Patrick Cooke Esq

## Contact
Owen Davies /
Tracy Winder
Athelhampton House
Dorchester  DT2 7LG

**Tel:** 01305 848363
**Fax:** 01305 848135
**E-mail:** enquiry@
athelhampton.co.uk

## Location
**MAP 2:P6**
**OS Ref. SY771 942**

Off A35 (T) at Puddletown
Northbrook junction, 5m E
of Dorchester.

**Rail:** Dorchester.

## Opening Times
March–October:
Daily (except Fri & Sat).

Closed throughout July 2007.

November–February:
Sun only.

10.30am–5pm/dusk.
Last admission 4.30pm.

Coach House Restaurant
open as house & gardens.
Carvery on Suns.
Please book.

All facilities at
Athelhampton are
available for private hire
outside our normal
opening hours.
We specialise in weddings
on Fridays and Saturdays
and dinners on any
evening. Please contact
Owen Davies, Manager.

Self catering cottage in the
grounds – see website or
telephone for details.

## Admission
**House & Gardens**
| | |
|---|---|
| Adult | £8.50 |
| Child (under 16) | Free |
| Student/Disabled | £6.00 |
| OAP | £8.00 |
| Groups (12+) | |
| Adult | £6.00* |

*£5.00 with pre-booked catering order.

## Special Events
**May 6**
NCCPG Plant Sale

**June 10–14**
Flower Festival

**August 5**
MG Car Club Rally

By arrangement.
Partial. WC.
Licensed.
Licensed.
By arrangement.
Guide dogs only.

## Conference/Function

| ROOM | SIZE | MAX CAPACITY |
|---|---|---|
| **Coach House\*** Long Hall | 13 x 6m | 100 |
| Conservatory* | 16 x 11m | 130 |
| **Main House\*** Great Hall | 12 x 8m | 70 |
| Great* Chamber | 10 x 6m | 40 |
| Garden Pavilions (2) | 3 x 3m | 6 |

*Licensed for Civil wedding ceremonies.

South West – England

■ **Contact**

Carolyn Clay
Forde Abbey
Chard
Somerset TA20 4LU

**Tel:** 01460 220231
**E-mail:**
info@fordeabbey.co.uk

■ **Location**

**MAP 2:N6**
**OS Ref. ST358 041**

Just off the B3167
4m SE of Chard.

■ **Opening Times**

**House**
1 April–31 October
Tue–Fri, Sun & BH Mons
12 noon–4pm.

**Gardens**
Daily all year:
10am–4.30pm.

■ **Admission**

For current admission
prices phone
01460 221290.

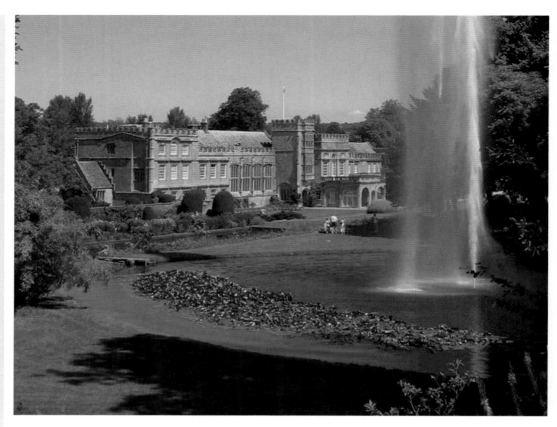

# FORDE ABBEY & GARDENS

www.fordeabbey.co.uk

Forde Abbey is a treasure in an area already known for its outstanding beauty. More than 900 years of history is encapsulated in this elegant former Cistercian monastery and its 30 acres of award-winning gardens. In the peaceful solitude of its secluded position it is possible to imagine just how it looked to many of its previous owners: monks going about their daily round of work and prayer, prosperous Parliamentary gentlemen discussing the Cavalier threat, gifted philosophers debating the imponderable, elegant Victorian ladies fanning themselves by the fireside and country gentlemen going about their work on the estate.

Set on the banks of the River Axe, this beautiful home contains many treasures including the Mortlake Tapestries, woven from cartoons painted for the Sistine Chapel by Raphael. The intricacy of their original design is matched by the story behind these particular tapestries involving Civil war, rebellion and loyalty rewarded.

The beautiful gardens that surround the house date from the early 18th century, although much work has been done by the present occupiers. Highlights of the garden include: carpets of springtime bulbs, a magnificent Bog Garden, Beech House, summer borders, a working kitchen garden and the remarkable Centenary Fountain – the highest powered fountain in England. The garden has been described by Alan Titchmarsh as *"one of the greatest gardens of the West Country"*.

The Undercroft Restaurant serving morning coffee, lunches and cream teas (using produce from the garden, estate and local suppliers), together with the unique gift shop, plant centre and pottery exhibition will complete a perfect day out.

[i] Available for wedding receptions. No photography in house.

Partial.

Licensed.

Licensed.

By arrangement.

[P]

On leads, in grounds.

# KINGSTON LACY

www.nationaltrust.org.uk

Kingston Lacy House lies at the heart of the 8,500 acre Bankes Estate. Opened to the public nearly twenty years ago, the 'secret estate' is still only slowly revealing itself. Lying a mile from Wimborne Minster and nine miles from the market town of Blandford Forum on the B3082, Kingston Lacy is the gateway to true, rural Dorset.

As the home of the Bankes family for 300 years, Kingston Lacy replaced the original family seat of Corfe Castle and is now presented by the National Trust as it was in its Edwardian heyday. This elegant country mansion contains an outstanding collection of fine works of art, including a Titian, two Rubens and a Velázquez, as well as an unique group of Egyptian artefacts. Set in 32 acres of formal gardens, which include one of only two Egyptian obelisks in the UK (the other being Cleopatra's Needle), the house is surrounded by hundreds of acres of park and woodland, crossed by way-marked walks and includes three child-friendly play areas.

In 2005 the restored Japanese Gardens opened for public viewing, part of a seven acre project funded by the Gordon Bulmer Charitable Trust, in the southern woodland shelter belt. In 2006 the magnificent Guido Reni detached fresco, "Separation of Night from Day", was remounted on the ceiling of the 18th century Library. The painting is unique and important, the only known example in England of the artist's fresco work, and a significant achievement of The Trust's conservation work at the property.

Events and activities occur throughout the year including concerts, outdoor theatre, walks, talks, a children's holiday club, and the fabulous 'Enchanted Garden' evenings in October.

  Garden only. Braille guide & Induction Loop system. WC. Less-abled access info: 01202 883402.

 Licensed.

By arrangement.

**P**

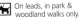 On leads, in park & woodland walks only.

Tel: 01202 883402.

## Owner
The National Trust

## Contact
The Property Manager
Kingston Lacy
Wimborne Minster
Dorset  BH21 4EA

**Tel:** 01202 883402 / 842913
(Sat & Sun 11am–5pm)
**Fax:** 01202 882402

**Restaurant:** 01202 889242

**E-mail:** kingstonlacy@nationaltrust.org.uk

## Location
**MAP 3:A6**
**OS Ref. ST980 019**

On B3082 – Blandford / Wimborne road, 1½m NW of Wimborne Minster.

**Rail:** Poole 8½m.

**Bus:** Wilts & Dorset 132/3, 182/3 from Bournemouth, Poole, alight Wimbourne Square 2½m.

## Opening Times
**House**
24 March–28 October
Wed–Sun, 11am–5pm.
Last admission 4pm.
(1hr to view the house thoroughly.)

**Garden & Park**
24 March–28 October, daily, 10.30am–6pm.
2 November–16 December, Fri–Sun, 10.30am–4pm.
2 February–18 March 2008, Sat & Sun, 10.30am–4pm.

**Shop & Restaurant**
18 March–29 October, daily, 10.30am–5.30pm.
2 November–16 December, Fri–Sun, 10.30am–4pm.
2 February–18 March, Sat & Sun,10.30am–4pm.

Timed entry tickets may be issued on BHs and some weekends.

## Admission
**House & Gardens**
| | |
|---|---|
| Adult | £10.00 |
| Child | £5.00 |
| Family | £25.00 |

Groups
| | |
|---|---|
| House & Gardens | £8.00 |
| Child (under 15yrs) | £4.00 |

**Park & Garden only**
| | |
|---|---|
| Adult | £5.00 |
| Child | £2.50 |
| Family | £12.50 |

## ABBOTSBURY SUBTROPICAL GARDENS 🏠

*See page 224 for full page entry.*

## ATHELHAMPTON HOUSE & GARDENS 🏠

*See page 225 for full page entry.*

### BROWNSEA ISLAND ❦

**Poole Harbour, Dorset  BH13 7EE**

**Tel:** 01202 707744  **Fax:** 01202 701635  **E-mail:** brownseaisland@nationaltrust.org.uk
www.nationaltrust.org.uk/brownsea

**Owner:** The National Trust    **Contact:** NT Office

Atmospheric island of heath and woodland with wide variety of wildlife. The island is dramatically located at the entrance to Poole harbour, offering spectacular views across to Studland and the Purbeck Hills. Its varied and colourful history includes use as a coastguard station, Victorian pottery, Edwardian country estate, daffodil farm, and as a decoy in the Second World War. In 1907 it was the site of Baden-Powell's experimental camp from which Scouting and Guiding evolved. Home to important populations of red squirrels and seabirds, the island provides a safe and relaxing place for walks and picnics, ideal for families to explore. 2007 sees the Centenary of Scouting – 100 years since the first experimental camp. There are events and celebrations planned throughout the year.

**Location:** MAP 3:A7, OS Ref. SZ032 878. In Poole Harbour. Boats run from Poole Quay and Sandbanks every 30 mins. There is also a service from Bournemouth and Swanage.

**Open:** 24 Mar–28 Oct: daily, 10am–5pm. Closed 1 Aug for special event.

**Admission:** Adult £4.70, Child: £2.30, Family (2+2) £11.70. 1 Adult Family £7. Groups: Adult £4, Child £2, Group visits outside normal hours £3.40.

🔲 🔲 Partial. 🔲 🔲 🔲 🔲

### CHETTLE HOUSE

**Chettle, Blandford Forum, Dorset  DT11 8DB**

**Tel:** 01258 830858

**Owner/Contact:** Mr & Mrs Peter Bourke

A fine Queen Anne manor house designed by Thomas Archer and a fine example of English baroque architecture. The house features a basement with the typical north-south passage set just off centre with barrel-vaulted ceilings and a magnificent oak staircase. Newly restored interiors. The house is set in 5 acres of peaceful gardens.

**Location:** MAP 3:A5, OS Ref. ST952 132. 6m NE of Blandford NW of A354.

**Open:** Easter–Oct: 1st Sun in each month. Other times by appointment. Group guided tours by appointment.

**Admission:** Adult £4, Child Free (under 16yrs).

🔲 Wedding receptions and special events. 🔲 Partial.🔲🔲 By appointment.  🔲

### CHURCH OF OUR LADY & ST IGNATIUS

**North Chideock, Bridport, Dorset DT6 6LF**

**Tel:** 01308 488348  **E-mail:** amyasmartelli40@hotmail.com

**Owner:** The Weld Family Trust    **Contact:** Mrs G Martelli

The Church, dedicated to Our Lady Queen of Martyrs and St Ignatius, was built on the site of an exisitng chapel-barn in 1872 by Charles Weld of Chideock Manor. He favoured the baroque style and oversaw much of the decoration himself. Several of the portraits of the 40 martyrs which surround the nave have been attributed to him. The Church is a shrine to Our Lady and has been a centre of Catholicism since penal times. A Museum of village life is on view in the adjoining cloister.

**Location:** MAP 2:N6, OS Ref. SY419 937. A35 from Bridport into Chideock. Right at St Giles' Church. Continue towards North Chideock for ½m. The Church is on the right.

**Open:** All year: 10am–4pm.

**Admission:** Donations welcome.

🔲 Moveable ramp in Church Porch. 🔲 Limited. 🔲 🔲

Corfe Castle, Wareham

### CLOUDS HILL ❦
#### WAREHAM, DORSET  BH20 7NQ

www.nationaltrust.org.uk

**Tel:** 01929 405616

**Owner:** The National Trust    **Contact:** The Custodian

A tiny isolated brick and tile cottage, bought in 1929 by T E Lawrence (Lawrence of Arabia) as a retreat. The austere rooms inside are much as he left them and reflect his complex personality and close links with the Middle East. An exhibition details Lawrence's extraordinary life.

**Location:** MAP 2:P6, OS Ref. SY824 909. 9m E of Dorchester, 1½m E of Waddock crossroads B3390.

**Open:** 22 Mar–28 Oct: Thurs–Sun & BH Mons, 12 noon–5pm or dusk if earlier; no electric light. Groups wishing to visit at other times must telephone in advance.

**Admission:** £4, no reduction for children or groups.

🔲 No WC. 🔲 Braille guide. 🔲 No coaches. 🔲 Small groups.

### CORFE CASTLE ❦
#### WAREHAM, DORSET  BH20 5EZ

www.nationaltrust.org.uk

**Tel:** 01929 481294  **Fax:** 01929 477067  **E-mail:** corfecastle@nationaltrust.org.uk

**Owner:** The National Trust    **Contact:** The Property Manager

One of Britain's most majestic ruins, the Castle controlled the gateway through the Purbeck Hills and had been an important stronghold since the time of William the Conqueror. Defended during the Civil War by the redoubtable Lady Bankes, the Castle fell to treachery from within and was substantially destroyed afterwards by the Parliamentarians. Many fine Norman and early English features remain. Visitor Centre at Castle View. Parts of Castle closed during 2007 for urgent conservation work. Please telephone property for details.

**Location:** MAP 3:A7, OS Ref. SY959 824. On A351 Wareham–Swanage Rd. NW of the village.

**Open:** All year: daily. Mar & Oct: 10am–5pm; Apr–Sept: 10am–6pm; Nov–Feb (Closed 25/26 Dec), 10am–4pm.

**Admission:** Adult £5.30, Child £2.70, Family (2+3) £13.30, (1+3) £8. Groups: Adult £4.60, Child £2.30.

🔲 🔲 Limited. Braille guide. WC. 🔲 🔲 🔲 🔲 🔲 On leads. 🔲 🔲

## DEANS COURT 🏛
### WIMBORNE, DORSET BH21 1EE

**Tel:** 01202 886116
**Owner:** Sir Michael & Lady Hanham  **Contact:** Wimborne Tourist Info Centre
13 peaceful acres. Specimen trees, lawns, borders, herb garden, long serpentine wall, kitchen and rose garden. Chemical-free produce usually for sale, also interesting herbaceous plants. Wholefood teas in garden or in Housekeeper's room (down steps).
**Location:** MAP 3:A6, OS Ref. SZ010 997. 2 mins walk S from centre of Wimborne Minster. Entrance signed from Deans Court Lane.
**Open:** 8/9 Apr, 6/7 & 27/28 May, 17 Jun, 26/27 Aug, 9 Sept: Suns, 2–6pm, BH Mons, 10am–6pm. House may be visited by prior written appointment, but not on garden open days.
**Admission:** Adult £3.50, Child under 16yrs Free, OAP £2.50. Groups by arrangement.
🍽 Garden produce sales.🔗 ▣ ℙ Free in Garden. 🐾 Guide dogs only.

## HARDY'S COTTAGE ✿
### HIGHER BOCKHAMPTON, DORCHESTER, DORSET DT2 8QJ
www.nationaltrust.org.uk

**Tel:** 01305 262366
**Owner/Contact:** The National Trust
A small cob and thatch cottage where the novelist and poet Thomas Hardy was born in 1840, and from where he would walk to school every day in Dorchester, six miles away. It was built by his great-grandfather and is little altered. Since the family left the interior has been furnished by the Trust (see also Max Gate). His early novels *Under the Green Wood Tree* and *Far From the Madding Crowd* were written here. Charming cottage garden.
**Location:** MAP 2:P6, OS Ref. SY728 925. 3m NE of Dorchester, ½m S of A35. 10 mins walk through the woods from car park.
**Open:** Please telephone 01297 561900 for opening arrangements.
**Admission:** Adult £3.50. No reduction for children.
ℹ No WC. ▣ 🔗 Partial. ℙ No coach parking. ▣ 🐾

---

## EDMONDSHAM HOUSE & GARDENS 🏛

**Cranborne, Wimborne, Dorset  BH21 5RE**
**Tel:** 01725 517207
**Owner/Contact:** Mrs Julia E Smith
Charming blend of Tudor and Georgian architecture with interesting contents. Organic walled garden, 6 acre garden with unusual trees and spring bulbs. 12th century church nearby.
**Location:** MAP 3:A5, OS Ref. SU062 116. Off B3081 between Cranborne and Verwood, NW from Ringwood 9m, Wimborne 9m.
**Open:** House & Gardens: All BH Mons & Weds in Apr & Oct 2–5pm. Gardens: Apr–Oct, Suns & Weds 2–5pm.
**Admission:** House & Garden: Adult £4, Child £1 (under 5yrs Free). Garden only: Adult £2, Child 50p. Garden Season Ticket (incl. children) £5. Groups by arrangement, teas for groups.
🍽 🔗 ▣ Pre-booked (max 50). 📷 Obligatory. 🐾 Car park only. 🔺 (max 50).

---

## FORDE ABBEY & GARDENS 🏛     *See page 226 for full page entry.*

---

Shaftesbury

Athelhampton House & Gardens – Great Hall, Dorchester

## HIGHCLIFFE CASTLE 🏛

**ROTHESAY DRIVE, HIGHCLIFFE-ON-SEA, CHRISTCHURCH  BH23 4LE**

www.highcliffecastle.co.uk

**Tel:** 01425 278807  **Fax:** 01425 280423  **E-mail:** enquiries@highcliffecastle.co.uk
**Owner:** Christchurch Borough Council  **Contact:** The Manager

Built in 1830 in the Romantic and Picturesque style of architecture for Lord Stuart de Rothesay using his unique collection of French medieval stonework and stained glass. Recently repaired externally, this Grade I listed building remains mostly unrepaired inside. Five State Rooms house a visitor centre, exhibitions, events and gift shop. Coastal grounds, village trail and nearby St Mark's church. Tearooms in the Claretian's Wing.

**Location:** MAP 3:B6, OS Ref. SZ200 930. Off the A337 Lymington Road, between Christchurch and Highcliffe-on-Sea.
**Open:** 1 Feb–23 Dec: daily, 11am–5pm. Grounds: All year: daily from 7am. Access for coaches. Tearooms closed Christmas Day.
**Admission:** Adult £2.20, Child Free. Group (10+) rates available. Guided tours of unrestored areas (may be unsuitable for people with mobility problems – please ring for details): Adult £3.50, Child Free. Grounds: Free.

⬜⬜♿ Partial. WC. ◻ 10am–5pm. 🎟 By arrangement. 🅿 Limited. Parking charge. ◼ By arrangement. 🐾 In grounds, on leads. ⬛✖♿

---

### HIGHER MELCOMBE

**Melcombe Bingham, Dorchester, Dorset  DT2 7PB**
**Tel:** 01258 880251
**Owner/Contact:** Mr M C Woodhouse

Consists of the surviving wing of a 16th century house with its attached domestic chapel. A fine plaster ceiling and linenfold panelling. Conducted tours by owner.

**Location:** MAP 2:P6, OS Ref. ST749 024. 1km W of Melcombe Bingham.
**Open:** May–Sept by appointment.
**Admission:** Adult £2 (takings go to charity).

♿ Unsuitable. 🎟 By written appointment only. 🅿 Limited. 🐾 Guide dogs only.

---

### KINGSTON LACY 🌿

*See page 227 for full page entry.*

*See page 227 for full page entry.*

Mapperton, Beaminster

Dave Penman

## KINGSTON MAURWARD GARDEN

**DORCHESTER, DORSET  DT2 8PY**

www.kmc.ac.uk/gardens

**Tel:** 01305 215003  **Fax:** 01305 215001  **E-mail:** events@kmc.ac.uk
**Contact:** Wendy Cunningham

Classical 18th century parkland setting, with majestic lawns sweeping down from the Grade I listed Georgian house to the lake. The Rainbow beds and beautiful herbaceous borders complement the series of 'rooms' within the formal Edwardian garden. National Collections of Penstemons and Salvias. Lakeside walks, animal park, shop, plant centre and refreshments.

**Location:** MAP 2:P7, OS Ref. SY713 911. 1m E of Dorchester. Roundabout off A35 by-pass.
**Open:** 4 Jan–21 Dec: daily, 10am–5.30pm or dusk if earlier.
**Admission:** Adult £5, Child £3 (under 3yrs Free), Family £15.50. Groups (10+): Adult £4.50. Guided tours (by arrangement) (12+): £5pp.

ℹ Conferences. ⬜♿⬜ Wedding receptions. ♿ Partial. ◻ Licensed. 🎟 By arrangement. 🅿◼🐾 Guide dogs only. ⬛✖♿

## KNOLL GARDENS & NURSERY

**Stapehill Road, Hampreston, Wimborne BH21 7ND**
**Tel:** 01202 873931 **Fax:** 01202 870842 **E-mail:** enquiries@knollgardens.co.uk
**Owner:** J & J Flude & N R Lucas **Contact:** Mr John Flude
Nationally acclaimed 6 acre gardens, with 6000+ named plants.
**Location:** MAP 3:B6, OS Ref. SU059 001. Between Wimborne & Ferndown. Exit A31 Canford Bottom roundabout, B3073 Hampreston. Signposted 1½m.
**Open:** 1 Feb–18 Dec: Wed–Sun, 10am–5pm or dusk if earlier. Closed Christmas & January.
**Admission:** Adult £4.50, Child (5–15yrs) £3, Conc £4. RHS Free. Groups: Adult £3.50, Family (2+2) £11.

# LULWORTH CASTLE & PARK

## WAREHAM, DORSET BH20 5QS

www.lulworth.com

**Tel:** 0845 4501054 **Fax:** 01929 400563 **E-mail:** office@lulworth.com
**Owner:** The Weld Estate
Surrounded by beautiful parkland this 17th century hunting lodge was destroyed by fire in 1929 and has been restored by English Heritage. Steeped in history the Castle has remained in the same family since 1641. Features include a gallery on the Weld family, reconstructed kitchen, dairy and laundry rooms and a wine cellar. The Chapel is reputed to be one of the finest pieces of architecture in Dorset and houses an exhibition on vestments and recusant silver.
**Location:** MAP 3:A7, OS Ref. SY853 822. In E Lulworth off B3070, 3m NE of Lulworth Cove.
**Open:** Castle & Park: All year (but closed 24/25 Dec & 7–20 Jan) Sun–Fri & Easter Sat: 10.30am–6pm (closes 4pm autumn/winter). Also open some Sats for Special Events.
**Admission:** Castle: Adult £7, Child (4–15yrs) £4 (under 4yrs Free), Conc. £6, Family (2+3) £21, Family (1+3) £14. 10% discount for groups of 10+. Prices may vary for special events including Summer Jousting Shows. Please see website or tel 0845 4501054 for details.
⬚ T ♿ Partial. WC. 🍴 Licensed. 🎦 By arrangement. ■ P 🐕 In grounds, on leads. 🏠 5 holiday cottages, tel: 01929 400100. ▲ ❄ 🎗 See website.

Durdle Door

# MAPPERTON 🏛

## BEAMINSTER, DORSET DT8 3NR

www.mapperton.com

**Tel:** 01308 862645 **Fax:** 01308 863348 **E-mail:** office@mapperton.com
**Owner/Contact:** The Earl & Countess of Sandwich
*'The Nation's Finest Manor House'* – *Country Life 2006*. Jacobean 1660s manor overlooking an Italianate upper garden with orangery, topiary and formal borders descending to fish ponds and shrub gardens. All Saints Church forms south wing opening to courtyard and stables. Area of Outstanding Natural Beauty with fine views of Dorset hills and woodlands.
**Location:** MAP 2:N6, OS Ref. SY503 997. 1m S of B3163, 2m NE of B3066, 2m SE Beaminster, 5m NE Bridport.
**Open:** House: 25 Jun–3 Aug: weekdays, plus 28 May & 27 Aug, 2–4.30pm, last admission 4pm. Other times by appointment. Garden & All Saints Church: 1 Mar–31 Oct: daily (exc. Sat) 11am–5pm. Café: Mar–Sept: daily (exc. Sat) 11am–5.30pm, for lunch and tea.
**Admission:** Gardens: Adult £4, Child (under 18yrs) £2, under 5yrs Free. House: £4. Group tours by appointment.
⬚ 🍴 ♿ Partial. 🍴 Licensed. 🍴 🎦 By arrangement. ■ P Limited for coaches. 🐕 Guide dogs only. ▲ 🎗

# MAX GATE 🌿

## ALINGTON AVENUE, DORCHESTER, DORSET DT1 2AA

www.thomas-hardy.connectfree.co.uk

**Tel:** 01305 262538 **E-mail:** maxgate@nationaltrust.org.uk
**Owner:** The National Trust **Contact:** The Tenant
Novelist and poet Thomas Hardy designed and lived in this house from 1885 until his death in 1928. Here he wrote *Tess of the d'Urbervilles*, *Jude the Obscure* and *The Mayor of Casterbridge*, as well as much of his poetry. The house contains several pieces of his furniture.
**Location:** MAP 2:P7, OS Ref. SY704 899. 1m E of Dorchester just N of the A352 to Wareham. From Dorchester follow A352 signs to the roundabout named Max Gate (at Jct. of A35 Dorchester bypass). Turn left and left again into cul-de-sac outside Max Gate.
**Open:** 26 Mar–30 Sept: Mons, Weds & Suns, 2–5pm. Only hall, dining, drawing rooms and garden open. Private visits, tours and seminars for schools, colleges and literary societies at other times by prior appointment with the tenants, Mr & Mrs Andrew Leah.
**Admission:** Adult £3, Child £1.50.
ℹ No WC. ♿ Partial. Braille guide. P ■ 🎗

## MILTON ABBEY CHURCH

**Milton Abbas, Blandford, Dorset DT11 0BZ**
**Tel:** 01258 880215
**Owner:** Diocese of Salisbury   **Contact:** Chris Fookes
Abbey church dating from 14th century.
**Location:** MAP 2:P6, OS Ref. ST798 024. 3½m N of A354. Between Dorchester/Blandford Road.
**Open:** Abbey Church: daily 10am–6pm. Groups by arrangement please.
**Admission:** By donation except Easter & mid-Jul–end Aug. Adult £2, Child Free.

## MINTERNE GARDENS

**Minterne Magna, Nr Dorchester, Dorset DT2 7AU**
**Tel:** 01300 341370   **Fax:** 01300 341747   **E-mail:** enquiries@minterne.co.uk
**www.minterne.co.uk**
**Owner/Contact:** The Hon Mr & Mrs Henry Digby
If you wish to wander peacefully through 20 wild woodland acres, where magnolias, rhododendrons, eucryphias, hydrangeas, water plants and water lilies provide a new vista at each turn, with small lakes and cascades landscaped in the 18th century, you will be welcome at Minterne, described by Simon Jenkins as 'a corner of paradise'. The home of the Churchill and Digby families for 350 years. The house, which contains magnificent Churchill tapestries and naval and other historical pictures, is open for organised groups only, which may be arranged by prior appointment.
**Location:** MAP 2:O6, OS Ref. ST660 042. On A352 Dorchester/Sherborne Rd, 2m N of Cerne Abbas.
**Open:** 1 Mar–31 Oct: daily, 10am–6pm.
**Admission:** Adult £4, accompanied children Free.
⊤ & Unsuitable. ⊞ In grounds on leads. ▲

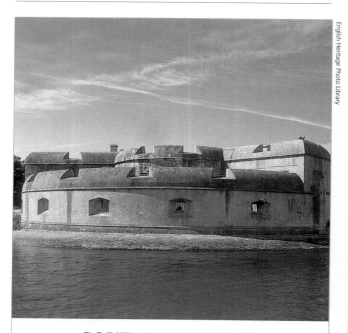

English Heritage Photo Library

## PORTLAND CASTLE ⊞

### CASTLETOWN, PORTLAND, WEYMOUTH, DORSET DT5 1AZ

www.english-heritage.org.uk/portland

**Tel:** 01305 820539   **Fax:** 01305 860853
**E-mail:** customers@english-heritage.org.uk
**Owner:** English Heritage   **Contact:** Visitor Operations Staff
Discover one of Henry VIII's finest coastal fortresses. Perfectly preserved in a waterfront location overlooking Portland harbour, it is a marvellous place to visit for all the family whatever the weather. Explore the Tudor kitchen and gun platform, see ghostly sculptured figures from the past, enjoy the superb battlement views or picnic on the lawn in front of the Captain's House. An excellent audio tour, included in the admission charge, brings the castle's history and characters to life. Visit the 'Contemporary Heritage' Garden.
**Location:** MAP 2:O7, OS Ref. SY684 743. Overlooking Portland harbour.
**Open:** 1 Apr–30 Jun & Sept: daily, 10am–5pm. 1 Jul–31 Aug: daily, 10am–6pm. 1–31 Oct: daily, 10am–4pm.
**Admission:** Adult £3.80, Child £1.90, Conc. £2.90. 15% discount for groups (11+).
▢⊤& Captain's House & ground floor. WCs. ▢ ▢ Ⓟ ▢ ▢ ▢

## SANDFORD ORCAS MANOR HOUSE

**Sandford Orcas, Sherborne, Dorset DT9 4SB**
**Tel:** 01963 220206
**Owner/Contact:** Sir Mervyn Medlycott Bt
Tudor manor house with gatehouse, fine panelling, furniture, pictures. Terraced gardens with topiary and herb garden. Personal conducted tour by owner.
**Location:** MAP 2:O5, OS Ref. ST623 210. 2½m N of Sherborne, Dorset 4m S of A303 at Sparkford. Entrance next to church.
**Open:** Easter Mon, 10am–5pm. May & Jul–Sept: Suns & Mons, 2–5pm.
**Admission:** Adult £4, Child £2. Groups (10+): Adult £3, Child £1.50.
& Unsuitable. ⓘ Obligatory. ⊞ In grounds, on leads.

Who's offering **accommodation?**
See our index on page 575

© NT Photographic Library / Christopher Hurst

Mary Bankes, Lady Jenkinson – Kingston Lacy Estate

© Ian Pollard

## SHERBORNE CASTLE 🏛
**SHERBORNE, DORSET DT9 5NR**
www.sherbornecastle.com

**Tel:** 01935 813182 **Fax:** 01935 816727 **E-mail:** enquiries@sherbornecastle.com
**Owner:** Mr & Mrs John Wingfield Digby **Contact:** Castle & Events Manager
Built by Sir Walter Raleigh in 1594, Sherborne Castle has been the home of the Digby family since 1617. Prince William of Orange was entertained here in 1688, and George III visited in 1789. Splendid interiors and collections of art, furniture and porcelain are on view in the Castle. Lancelot 'Capability' Brown created the lake in 1753 and gave Sherborne the very latest in landscape gardening, with magnificent vistas of the surrounding parklands. Today, some 30 acres of beautiful lakeside gardens and grounds are open for public viewing.

**Location:** MAP 2:O5, OS Ref. ST649 164. ¾m SE of Sherborne town centre. Follow brown signs from A30 or A352. ½m S of the Old Castle.
**Open:** Castle, Gardens, Shop & Tearoom: 1 Apr–31 Oct: daily except Mon & Fri (open BH Mons), 11am–4.30pm last admission. (Castle interior from 2pm Sats.) Groups (15+) by arrangement during normal opening hours.
**Admission:** Castle & Gardens: Adult £8.50, Child (0–15yrs) Free (max 4 per adult), OAP £8. Groups (15+): Adult/OAP £7.50, Child (0–15yrs) £3.50. Private views (15+): Adult/OAP £9.50, Child £4.50. Gardens only: Adult/OAP £4, Child (0–15yrs) Free (max 4 per adult), no concessions or group rates for gardens only.
⬛ Ⓣ ⬛ Partial. ⬛ Licensed. Ⓕ By arrangement. ⬛ ⬛ In grounds, on leads. ⬛ ⬛

## SHERBORNE OLD CASTLE ⚑
**Castleton, Sherborne, Dorset DT9 3SA**
**Tel/Fax:** 01935 812730 **E-mail:** customers@english-heritage.org.uk
**www.english-heritage.org.uk/sherborne**
**Owner:** English Heritage **Contact:** Visitor Operations Staff
The ruins of this early 12th century Castle are a testament to the 16 days it took Cromwell to capture it during the Civil War, after which it was abandoned. A gatehouse, some graceful arcading and decorative windows survive.
**Location:** MAP 2:O5, OS Ref. ST647 167. ½m E of Sherborne off B3145. ½m N of the 'new' 1594 Castle.
**Open:** 1 Apr–31 Oct: daily, 10am–5pm (6pm in Jul & Aug, 4pm in Oct).
**Admission:** Adult £2.40, Child £1.20, Conc. £1.80. 15% discount for groups of 11+.
⬛ ⬛ Grounds. ⬛ Limited for cars. No coach parking. ⬛ ⬛

## STOCK GAYLARD HOUSE
**Stock Gaylard, Sturminster Newton, Dorset DT10 2BG**
**Tel:** 01963 23215 **E-mail:** aclangmead@aol.com
**www.stockgaylard.com**
**Owner:** Mrs J Langmead **Contact:** Mrs J Langmead
A Georgian house overlooking an ancient deer park with the parish church of St Barnabas in the garden. The grounds and principal rooms of the house are open to the public for 28 days a year.
**Location:** MAP 2:P5, OS Ref. ST722 130. 1 mile S of the junction of the A357 and the A3030 at the Lydlinch Common.
**Open:** 22 Apr–1st May, 22–30 Jun & 22–30 Sept, 2–5pm. Access to the Park by arrangement, please telephone for information.
**Admission:** Adult £5, Child £2.

## WHITE MILL 🏚
**Sturminster Marshall, Nr Wimborne, Dorset BH21 4BX**
**Tel:** 01258 858051 **www.nationaltrust.org.uk**
**Owner:** The National Trust **Contact:** The Custodian
Rebuilt in 1776 on a site marked as a mill in the Domesday Book, this substantial corn mill was extensively repaired in 1994 and still retains its original elm and applewood machinery (now too fragile to be operative).
**Location:** MAP 3:A6, OS Ref. ST958 006. On River Stour ½m NE of Sturminster Marshall. From the B3082 Blandford to Wimborne Rd, take road to SW signposted Sturminster Marshall. Mill is 1m on right. Car park nearby.
**Open:** 24 Mar–28 Oct: Sats, Suns & BH Mons, 12 noon–5pm. Admission by guided tour only.
**Admission:** Adult £3, Child £2. Groups by arrangement.
ⓘ No WC. ⬛ Ground floor. Ⓕ Obligatory. ⬛ ⬛ Under close control in grounds and car park.

Kingston Maurward Gardens, Dorchester

# WOLFETON HOUSE 🏛

### Nr DORCHESTER, DORSET  DT2 9QN

**Tel:** 01305 263500   **Fax:** 01305 265090

**E-mail:** kthimbleby@wolfeton.freeserve.co.uk

**Owner:** Capt N T L L T Thimbleby     **Contact:** The Steward

A fine mediaeval and Elizabethan manor house lying in the water-meadows near the confluence of the rivers Cerne and Frome. It was much embellished around 1580 and has splendid plaster ceilings, fireplaces and panelling of that date. To be seen are the Great Hall, Stairs and Chamber, Parlour, Dining Room, Chapel and Cyder House. The mediaeval Gatehouse has two unmatched and older towers. There are good pictures and furniture.

**Location:** MAP 2:O6, OS Ref. SY678 921. 1½m from Dorchester on the A37 towards Yeovil. Indicated by Historic House signs.

**Open:** June–end Sept: Mons, Weds & Thurs, 2–5pm. Groups by appointment throughout the year.

**Admission:** £6.

⊤ By arrangement. 🔲 Ground floor. ☑ By arrangement. 🗷 By arrangement.
🅿 ✖ ❋

Brownsea Island, Poole Harbour

Forde Abbey, Nr Chard

# BERKELEY CASTLE 🏛

www.berkeley-castle.com

Not many can boast of having their private house celebrated by Shakespeare nor of having held it in the possession of their family for nearly 850 years, nor having a King of England murdered within its walls, nor of having welcomed at their table the local vicar and Castle Chaplain, John Trevisa (1342–1402), reputed as one of the earliest translators of the Bible, nor of having a breach battered by Oliver Cromwell, which to this day it is forbidden by law to repair even if it was wished to do so. But such is the story of Berkeley.

This beautiful and historic Castle, begun in 1117, still remains the home of the famous family who gave their name to numerous locations all over the world, notably Berkeley Square in London, Berkeley Hundred in Virginia and Berkeley University in California. Scene of the brutal murder of Edward II in 1327 (visitors can see his

cell and nearby the dungeon) and besieged by Cromwell's troops in 1645, the Castle is steeped in history but twenty-four generations of Berkeleys have gradually transformed a Norman fortress into the lovely home it is today.

The State Apartments contain magnificent collections of furniture, rare paintings by primarily English and Dutch masters, and tapestries. Part of the world-famous Berkeley silver is on display in the Dining Room. Many other rooms are equally interesting including the Great Hall upon which site the Barons of the West Country met in 1215 before going to Runnymede to force King John to put his seal to the Magna Carta.

The Castle is surrounded by lovely terraced Elizabethan Gardens with a lily pond, Elizabeth I's bowling green, and sweeping lawns.

 Fashion shows and filming. Butterfly House. No photography inside the Castle.

 Wedding receptions and corporate entertainment.

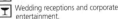 Visitors may alight in the Outer Bailey.

 Licensed. Serving lunches and home-made teas.

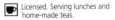 Free. Max. 120 people. Tour time: One hour. Evening groups by arrangement. Group visits must be booked.

**P** Cars 150yds from Castle, 15 coaches 250yds away. Free.

Welcome. General and social history and architecture.

**Owner**
Mr R J G Berkeley

**Contact**
The Custodian
Berkeley Castle
Gloucestershire
GL13 9BQ

**Tel:** 01453 810332
**Fax:** 01453 512995
**E-mail:** info@berkeley-castle.com

**Location**
MAP 6:M12
OS Ref. ST685 990

SE side of Berkeley village. Midway between Bristol & Gloucester, 2m W off the A38.

From motorway M5/J14 (5m) or J13 (9m).

**Opening Times**
April–September*
Tues–Sat & BH Mons, 11am–4pm,
Sun, 2–5pm.

October
Sundays only, 2–5pm.

The Butterfly House is closed in October.

Last admission 30 mins before closing.

* Except for weekends of 21/22 & 28/29 July: entry via the Joust Mediaeval Festival event only.

**Admission**
Global Ticket including Castle, Gardens & Butterfly House
Adult £7.50
Child (5–16yrs) £4.50
Child (under 5s) Free
OAP £6.00
Family (2+2) £21.00

Groups (25+ pre-booked)
Adult £7.00
Child (5-16yrs) £3.50
OAP £5.50

Gardens only
Adult £4.00
Child £2.00

Butterfly House
Adult £2.00
Child (5–16yrs) £1.00
School groups £0.80
Family (2+2) £5.00

**Conference/Function**

| ROOM | MAX CAPACITY |
|---|---|
| Great Hall | 150 |
| Long Drawing Rm | 100 |

### ■ Owner

Mr David Lowsley-Williams

### ■ Contact

D Lowsley-Williams
or Caroline
Lowsley-Williams
Chavenage
Tetbury
Gloucestershire
GL8 8XP

**Tel/Fax:** 01666 502329
**E-mail:** info@
chavenage.com

### ■ Location

**MAP 3:A1**
**OS Ref. ST872 952**

Less than 20m
from M4/J16/17 or 18.
1¾m NW of Tetbury
between the B4014 &
A4135. Signed from
Tetbury. Less than 15m
from M5/J13 or 14.
Signed from A46
(Stroud–Bath road)

**Rail:** Kemble Station 7m.

**Taxi:** SC Taxis
01666 504195.

**Air:** Bristol 35m.
Birmingham 70m.
Grass airstrip on farm.

### ■ Opening Times

**Summer**
May–September
Easter Sun, Mon
& BHs, 2–5pm.

Thurs & Suns 2–5pm.

NB. Will open on any day
and at other times by
prior arrangement for
groups.

**Winter**
October–March
By appointment only
for groups.

### ■ Admission

Tours are inclusive
in the following prices.

**Summer**
Adult          £6.00
Child (5–16 yrs)   £3.00

Concessions:
By prior arrangement,
concessions may be given
to groups of 40+ and also
to disabled and to
exceptional cases.

**Winter**
Groups only:
Rates by arrangement.

© Skyscan

# CHAVENAGE 🏛
## www.chavenage.com

Chavenage is a wonderful Elizabethan house of mellow grey Cotswold stone and tiles which contains much of interest for the discerning visitor.

The approach aspect of Chavenage is virtually as it was left by Edward Stephens in 1576. Only two families have owned Chavenage; the present owners since 1891 and the Stephens family before them. A Colonel Nathaniel Stephens, MP for Gloucestershire during the Civil War was cursed for supporting Cromwell, giving rise to legends of weird happenings at Chavenage since that time.

Inside Chavenage there are many interesting rooms housing tapestries, fine furniture, pictures and many relics of the Cromwellian period. Of particular note are the Main Hall, where a contemporary screen forms a minstrels' gallery and two tapestry rooms where it is said Cromwell was lodged.

Recently Chavenage has been used as a location for TV and film productions including a Hercule Poirot story *The Mysterious Affair at Styles*, many episodes of the sequel to *Are you Being Served* now called *Grace & Favour*, a Gotcha for *The Noel Edmonds' House Party*, episodes of *The House of Elliot* and *Casualty*, in 1997/98 *Berkeley Square* and *Cider with Rosie* and in 2002 the US series *Relic Hunter III*. In 2005 it was one of the homes Jeremy Musson visited in the BBC's *The Curious House Guest*.

Chavenage is especially suitable for those wishing an intimate, personal tour, usually conducted by the owner, or for groups wanting a change from large establishments. Meals for pre-arranged groups have proved hugely popular. It also provides a charming venue for small conferences and functions.

ℹ️ Clay pigeon shooting, archery, cross-bows, pistol shooting, ATV driving, small fashion shows, concerts, plays, seminars, filming, product launching, photography. No casual photography in house.

🍸 Corporate entertaining. In-house catering for drinks parties, dinners, wedding receptions. Telephone for details.

♿ Partial. WC.

☕ Lunches, teas, dinners and picnics by arrangement.

🚶 By owner. Large groups given a talk prior to viewing. Couriers/group leaders should arrange tour format prior to visit.

🅿️ Up to 100 cars. 2–3 coaches (by appointment). Coaches access from A46 (signposted) or from Tetbury via the B4014, enter the back gates for coach parking area.

🪑 Chairs can be arranged for lecturing.

🐕 In grounds on leads. Guide dogs only in house.

❄️

### Conference/Function

| ROOM | SIZE | MAX CAPACITY |
|------|------|--------------|
| Ballroom | 70' x 30' | 120 |
| Oak Room | 25 'x 20' | 30 |

# SUDELEY CASTLE GARDENS  & EXHIBITIONS

www.sudeleycastle.co.uk

Sitting proudly on the Cotswold escarpment, Sudeley Castle Gardens & Exhibitions not only celebrates its rich history but also explores the new. With many royal connections, it has played an important role in the turbulent and changing times of England's past. Sudeley is perhaps best known as the home of Queen Katherine Parr, who is entombed in St Mary's Church in the grounds.

Surrounding the Castle buildings and ruins are 14 acres of stunning award-winning gardens. Highlights include the Queen's Garden, famous for its double yew hedges and collection of English roses, the semi-Mediterranean planting of the Secret Garden, the intricate Tudor Knot Garden and the bold planting surrounding the Tithe Barn Ruins.

Family home to the Dent-Brocklehursts since the early 19th century, at which time an extensive and ambitious restoration programme was instigated, the family has remained devoted to the continued development of Sudeley. The Castle Apartments themselves are home to the three generations of the family, but at pre-arranged times on a Tuesday, Wednesday and Thursday are open to the public on an unmissable Connoisseur Tour (please call for further information).

The highly acclaimed Contemporary Art exhibition staged in the grounds returns for its third year. World-renowned artists will provide either specifically commissioned pieces or recent works reacting to the landscape and history of Sudeley.

Visitors can also enjoy The Pheasantry and varied exhibitions in the Long Room showcasing Sudeley's collection.

## Owner
Lady Ashcombe, Henry and Mollie Dent-Brocklehurst

## Contact
The Secretary
Sudeley Castle
Winchcombe
Gloucestershire
GL54 5JD

**Tel:** 01242 602308
**Fax:** 01242 602959
**E-mail:** enquiries@ sudeley.org.uk

## Location
**MAP 6:O10**
**OS Ref. SP032 277**

8m NE of Cheltenham, at Winchcombe off B4632.

From Bristol or Birmingham M5/J9. Take A46 then B4077 towards Stow-on-the-Wold.

**Bus:** Castleways to Winchcombe.

**Rail:** Cheltenham Station 8m.

**Air:** Birmingham or Bristol 45m.

## Opening Times
**Summer**
31 March–28 October: daily 10.30am–5.00pm

**Winter**
Groups by appointment.

## Admission
**Gardens & Exhibitions**

| | |
|---|---|
| Adults | £7.20 |
| Children (5–15yrs) | £4.20 |
| Conc. | £6.20 |

Group rates available.

**Castle Connoisseur Tours**
£15 per person – only available on Tuesdays, Wednesdays and Thursdays. Please call for timings.

Details may be subject to change – please ensure you telephone or visit our website for updated information.

- Photographs and filming by prior arrangement. Concerts, corporate events and conferences. Product launches and activity days. Sudeley reserves the right to close any area and to amend information as necessary.

- Corporate and private events, wedding receptions.

- Partial access to the grounds. WC.

- Licensed.

- Tours and talks by prior arrangement for groups and Connoisseur Tours of the Castle Apartments every Tuesday, Wednesday and Thursday.

- **P** 1,000 cars. Meal vouchers, free access for coach drivers.

- 13 holiday cottages for 2–5 occupants.

- Tel for details.

## Conference/Function

| ROOM | MAX CAPACITY |
|---|---|
| Chandos Hall | 60 |
| Banqueting Hall + Pavilion | 100 |
| Marquee | Unlimited |
| Long Room | 80 |
| Library | 50 |

South West – England

© M B Paice

## BATSFORD ARBORETUM

### MORETON-IN-MARSH, GLOUCESTERSHIRE GL56 9QB

www.batsarb.co.uk

**Tel:** 01386 701441   **Fax:** 01386 701829
**E-mail:** arboretum@batsfordfoundation.co.uk
**Owner:** The Batsford Foundation   **Contact:** Mr Chris Pilling
56 acres of magical walks alongside tumbling streams and flower fringed ponds. Make a wish with the giant Buddha (*The Japanese Buddha of 'Heroic size'* – see above) or visit the Hermit's Cave. From Snowdrop displays in Spring through to fiery Autumn colour. Peace and tranquillity, pure Cotswold magic!
**Location:** MAP 6:P10, OS Ref. SP180 338. 1 mile west of Moreton-in-Marsh on A44.
**Open:** All year, daily except Weds in Dec & Jan & Christmas Day.
**Admission:** Adult £6, Child (4–15 inc) £2. Conc. £5, Groups of 20 less 10%.
⬛🚻♿ Partial. ▣ Licensed. ⓘ By arrangement. 🅿 🔲 🐕 In grounds on leads. ❊

## BOURTON HOUSE GARDEN 🏛

### BOURTON-ON-THE-HILL GL56 9AE

www.bourtonhouse.com

**Tel:** 01386 700754   **Fax:** 01386 701081   **E-mail:** cd@bourtonhouse.com
**Owner/Contact:** Mr & Mrs Richard Paice
Exciting 3 acre garden surrounding a delightful 18th century Cotswold manor house and 16th century tithe barn. Featuring flamboyant borders, imaginative topiary, a unique shade house, a profusion of herbaceous and exotic plants and, not least, a myriad of magically planted pots. The mood is friendly and welcoming, the atmosphere tranquil yet inspiring. The garden … "positively fizzes with ideas". There are a further 7 of parkland where young trees progress apace. 'The Gallery' features contemporary art, craft and design in the tithe barn.
**Location:** MAP 6:P10, OS Ref. SP180 324. 1¾ m W of Moreton-in-Marsh on A44.
**Open:** 23 May–31 Aug: Wed–Fri; also 27/28 May & 26/27Aug (BH Sun & Mon). Sept–Oct: Thur & Fri. 10am–5pm.
**Admission:** Adult £5.50, Conc. £5, Child Free.
⬛🚻♿ Partial. ▣ⓘ By arrangement. 🅿 Limited for coaches. ❊

---

### BERKELEY CASTLE 🏛
*See page 235 for full page entry.*

### BLACKFRIARS PRIORY ⌗

**Ladybellegate Street, Gloucester**
**Tel:** 0117 9750700   **www.english-heritage.org.uk/visits**
**Owner:** English Heritage   **Contact:** The South West Regional Office
A small Dominican priory church converted into a rich merchant's house at the Dissolution. Most of the original 13th century church remains, including a rare scissor-braced roof.
**Location:** MAP 6:N11, OS Ref. SO830 186. In Ladybellegate St, Gloucester, off Southgate Street and Blackfriars Walk.
**Open:** Access by guided tour only (Jul & Aug: Suns 3pm). Heritage Open Days: (8/9 Sept only) Free: 12.30pm & 3pm. Please contact the South West Regional Office.
**Admission:** Adult £3.50, Child/EH members £3.
🅿 Nearby, not EH, charged. ❊

### CHAVENAGE 🏛
*See page 236 for full page entry.*

### CHEDWORTH ROMAN VILLA ⚜

**Yanworth, Nr Cheltenham, Gloucestershire GL54 3LJ**
**Tel:** 01242 890256   **Fax:** 01242 890909
**E-mail:** chedworth@nationaltrust.org.uk   **www.nationaltrust.org.uk**
**Owner:** The National Trust   **Contact:** The Property Manager
Discover one of the largest Romano-British sites in the country. Located within the beautiful Cotswolds scenery, a mile of walls survives along with several marvellous mosaics, two bathhouses, hypocausts, latrines and a water shrine. The site was first excavated in 1864 and retains a Victorian museum and atmosphere. A 15 minute introductory audio visual presentation is also available to visitors.
**Location:** MAP 6:O11, OS Ref. SP053 135. 3m NW of Fossebridge on Cirencester–Northleach road (A429) via Yanworth or from A436 via Withington. Coaches must approach from Fossebridge.
**Open:** 3 Mar–1 Apr: Tues–Sun, 11am–4pm. 3 Apr–28 Oct: Tues–Sun, 10am–5pm; 30 Oct–11 Nov: Tues–Sun, 10am–4pm. Open BH Mons. Shop open as Villa. Shop and reception close at above time.
**\*Admission:** Adult £6, Child £3.50, Family (2+3) £15.50. Booked group tours (max 30 per guide): Schools £25, others £50. \*includes a voluntary donation but visitors can choose to pay the standard prices displayed at the property and on the website.
⬛♿ Partial. WC. ⓘ By arrangement. 🅿 ⬛ Adult £1.50, Child free.
🔲 By arrangement. ❊ 🚻

---

For **corporate hospitality**
at unique venues see the
index on page 567

---

Sudeley Castle, Winchcombe

NT Photographic Library: Ian Shaw

## DYRHAM PARK ✤
### Nr BATH, GLOUCESTERSHIRE SN14 8ER

www.nationaltrust.org.uk

**Tel:** 01179 372501  **Fax:** 01179 371353  **E-mail:** dyrhampark@nationaltrust.org.uk
**Owner:** The National Trust  **Contact:** The Property Manager
Dyrham Park was built between 1691 and 1702 for William Blathwayt, William III's Secretary at War and Secretary of State. The rooms have changed little since they were furnished by Blathwayt and their contents are recorded in his housekeeper's inventory. Many fine textiles and paintings, as well as items of blue-and-white Delftware. Restored Victorian domestic rooms open, including kitchen, bells passage, bakehouse, larders, tenants' hall and Delft-tiled dairy.
**Location:** MAP 2:P2, OS Ref. ST743 757. 8m N of Bath, 12m E of Bristol. Approached from Bath–Stroud road (A46), 2m S of Tormarton interchange with M4/J18.
**Open:** House: 16 Mar–28 Oct, Fri–Tue: 12 noon–5pm, last entry 4pm. Garden, Shop & Tearoom: 16 Mar–30 Jun, Fri–Tues, 11am–5pm. 13 Jul–31 Aug, daily, 11am–5pm. 1 Sept–28 Oct, Fri–Tues , 11am–5pm; 3 Nov–1 Jan 2008, Sats & Suns 12noon–4pm. Plant Sales: 16 Mar–30 Sept, as shop; Park: all year, daily except Christmas Day.
**Admission:** Adult £9.60, Child £4.80, Family £23.90. Garden & Park only: Adult £3.80, Child £2, Family £8.50. Park only (on days when house & garden closed): Adult £2.50, Child £1.20, Family £5.60.
🔲 🚻 ♿ Partial. No electric wheelchairs admitted. �ై Dates as garden. 🍽 Licensed. 📷 Mons, 11.30am (max 20). 🏠 House. 🅿 ◼ 🐕 Only in dog-walking area. ❇ ♥

## FRAMPTON COURT
### FRAMPTON-ON-SEVERN, GLOUCESTERSHIRE GL2 7EU

www.framptoncourtestate.co.uk

**Tel:** 01452 740267  **Fax:** 01452 740698
**E-mail:** framptoncourt@framptoncourtestate.co.uk
**Owner:** Mr & Mrs Rollo Clifford  **Contact:** Jean Speed
Splendid Georgian family home of the Cliffords, who have lived in Frampton since the Norman Conquest. Built 1732, school of Vanbrugh, set in Grade I listed park and garden with fine views to extensive lake. Superb panelled interiors and period furniture. Also the famous 19th century "Frampton Flora" botanical watercolours. Principal bedrooms available for Bed and Breakfast.
Strawberry Hill Gothic Orangery with a Dutch ornamental canal is available for self catering holidays (tel: 01452 740698).
**Location:** MAP 6:M12, OS Ref. SO750 078. In Frampton, ¼ m SW of B4071, 3m NW of M5/J13.
**Open:** By arrangement for groups (10+).
**Admission:** House & Garden: £6.
ⓘ No photography in house. 🌸 Orangery walled garden. Pan Global Plants (tel: 01452 741641), rare plant nursery. 🍽 Small. ♿ Garden only. ◼📷 Obligatory. 🅿 Coaches limited. 🐕 In grounds, on leads. 🛏 B&B contact Gillian Keightley on 01452 740267. Orangery tel: 01452 740698. ❇

Frampton Court, Frampton-on-Severn

## FRAMPTON MANOR
**Frampton-on-Severn, Gloucestershire GL2 7EP**
**Tel:** 01452 740268  **Fax:** 01452 740698

**Owner:** Mr & Mrs Rollo Clifford  **Contact:** Mrs Rollo Clifford
Medieval/Elizabethan timber-framed manor house with walled garden. Reputed 12th century birthplace of 'Fair Rosamund' Clifford, mistress of King Henry II. Wool Barn c1560 and 16th century dovecote.
**Location:** MAP 6:M12, OS Ref. SO748 080. 3m M5/J13.
**Open:** House & Garden: open by appointment for groups (10+). Garden: 26 Apr–20 Jul: Thur & Fri, 2.30–5pm.
**Admission:** House, Garden & Wool Barn: £6. Garden only: £3. Wool Barn only £1.
ⓘ No photography inside. ◼ Tearoom for groups. 📷 Obligatory. 🅿 ♥

## GLOUCESTER CATHEDRAL
**Chapter Office, College Green, Gloucester GL1 2LR**
**Tel:** 01452 508211  **Fax:** 01452 300469
**E-mail:** lin@gloucestercathedral.org.uk  **www.gloucestercathedral.org.uk**
**Contact:** Mrs L Henderson
Daily worship and rich musical tradition continue in this abbey church founded 1300 years ago. It has a Norman nave with massive cylindrical pillars, a magnificent east window with medieval glass and glorious fan-vaulted cloisters. You can also find the tombs of King Edward II and Robert, Duke of Normandy.
**Location:** MAP 6:M11, OS Ref. SO832 188. Off Westgate Street in central Gloucester.
**Open:** Daily, 8am until after Evensong. Groups must book via the Chapter Office.
**Admission:** £3 donation requested.
🔲 🚻 ♿ Partial. WC. ◼ 📷 By arrangement. ◼ 🅿 None. 🐕 In grounds, on leads.

## HAILES ABBEY ⚑ ✤
**Nr Winchcombe, Cheltenham, Gloucestershire GL54 5PB**
**Tel/Fax:** 01242 602398  **E-mail:** customers@english-heritage.org.uk
**www.english-heritage.org.uk/hailes**
**Owner:** English Heritage & The National Trust  **Contact:** Visitor Operations Staff
Seventeen cloister arches and extensive excavated remains in lovely surroundings of an abbey founded by Richard, Earl of Cornwall, in 1246. There is a small museum and covered display area.
**Location:** MAP 6:O10, OS Ref. SP050 300. 2m NE of Winchcombe off B4632. ½m SE of B4632.
**Open:** 1 Apr–31 Oct: daily, 10am–5pm. (6pm in Jul & Aug, 4pm in Oct).
**Admission:** Adult £3.40, Child £1.70, Conc. £2.60.
🔲 🚻 ♿ Partial. WC. 🏠 🅿 🐕 In grounds, on leads. ♥

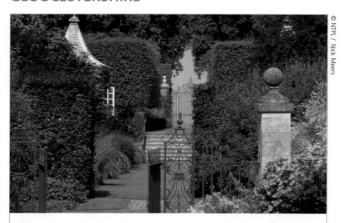

© NTPL / Nick Meers

## HIDCOTE MANOR GARDEN ❧
### HIDCOTE BARTRIM, Nr CHIPPING CAMPDEN, GLOUCESTERSHIRE GL55 6LR
www.nationaltrust.org.uk

**Tel:** 01386 438333   **Fax:** 01386 438817   **E-mail:** hidcote@nationaltrust.org.uk
**Owner:** The National Trust     **Contact:** Visitor Services Manager
One of the most delightful gardens in England, created in the early 20th century by the great horticulturist Major Lawrence Johnston; a series of small gardens within the whole, separated by walls and hedges of different species; famous for rare shrubs, trees, herbaceous borders, 'old' roses and interesting plant species.
**Location:** MAP 6:O9, OS Ref. SP176 429. 4m NE of Chipping Campden, 1m E of B4632 off B4081. At Mickleton ¼ m E of Kiftsgate Court. Coaches are not permitted through Chipping Campden High Street.
**Open:** 24 Mar–30 Sept: Sat–Wed, 10am–6pm. Also Fris Jul & August. 1 Oct–4 Nov: Sat–Wed, 10am–5pm. Last admission 1hr before closing. Open Good Fri.
**\*Admission:** Adult £8, Child £4, Family (2+3) £20. Groups (15+) Adult £7.20, Child £3.60. \*includes a voluntary donation but visitors can choose to pay the standard prices displayed at the property and on the website.
⌐ ⊡ 🄯 ⭒ Limited. WC. 🄯 ⯭ Licensed. 🄿 ▦ ⊠ ☞ Send SAE for details.

## HOLST BIRTHPLACE MUSEUM

4 Clarence Road, Pittville, Cheltenham GL52 2AY
**Tel:** 01242 524846   **E-mail:** holstmuseum@btconnect.com
www.holstmuseum.org.uk
**Owner:** Holst Birthplace Trust   **Contact:** Amelia Marriette – Curator
Birthplace of Gustav Holst (1874–1934), composer of The Planets, containing his piano and personal memorabilia. Holst's music is played. The museum is also a fine period house showing the 'upstairs – downstairs' way of life in Regency and Victorian times, including a working kitchen, elegant drawing room and charming nursery.
**Location:** MAP 6:N11, OS163 Ref. SO955 237. 5mins walk from town centre, opposite Pittville Gates.
**Open:** Mid Feb–mid Dec: Tue–Sat, 10am–4pm. Except for booked groups or guided tours who are welcome by appointment.
**Admission:** Adult £3.50, Child/Conc. £3, Family (2+3) £8. Groups pay same prices unless having a guided tour (6–15): Adult £4.50, Conc. £3.50. Special rates for school groups on request.
ⓘ Photography by prior permission only. ⌐ ⯭ 🄯 Partial. 🄵 By arrangement. 🄿 None. ▦ 🖳 Guide dogs only. ☎ Tel. for details.

## HORTON COURT ❧

Horton, Nr Chipping Sodbury, Bristol, South Gloucestershire BS37 6QR
**Tel:** 01179 372501   www.nationaltrust.org.uk
**Owner:** The National Trust   **Contact:** Dyrham Park
A Norman Hall and an exceptionally fine detached ambulatory are all that remain of what is probably the oldest rectory in England.
**Location:** MAP 2:P1, OS Ref. ST766 849. 3m NE of Chipping Sodbury, ¾ m N of Horton, 1m W of A46 (Bath-Stroud road).
**Open:** Easter Sat 7 Apr–20 Oct: Wed & Sat, 2–6pm. Other times by written appointment with tenant. Unsuitable for coach tours.
**Admission:** Adult £2.20, Child £1.10, Family (2+2) £5.60.
ⓘ No WC. 🄯 Partial. 🄿

Nigel Fisher

## KELMSCOTT MANOR 🏠
### KELMSCOTT, Nr LECHLADE, GLOUCESTERSHIRE GL7 3HJ
www.kelmscottmanor.co.uk

**Tel:** 01367 252486   **Fax:** 01367 253754   **E-mail:** admin@kelmscottmanor.co.uk
**Owner:** Society of Antiquaries of London   **Contact:** Jane Milne
Kelmscott Manor, a Grade I listed Tudor farmhouse adjacent to the River Thames, was William Morris' summer residence from 1871 until his death in 1896. Morris loved Kelmscott Manor, which seemed to have 'grown up out of the soil'. Its beautiful gardens with barns, dovecote, a meadow and stream provided a constant source of inspiration. The house, which is perhaps the most evocative of all the houses associated with Morris, contains an outstanding collection of the possessions and work of Morris, his family and associates, including furniture, original textiles, pictures, carpets and ceramics.
**Location:** MAP 6:P12, OS Ref. SU252 988. At SE end of the village, 2m due E of Lechlade, off the Lechlade – Faringdon Road.

**Open:** House & Garden: Weds, Apr–Sept, 11am–5pm (Ticket office open at 10.30am) Sats: 21 Apr, 19 May, 16 Jun, 7 & 21 Jul, 4 & 18 Aug, 15 Sept, 2–5pm (Ticket office open at 1.15pm). Last admission to the house 30 min prior to closing. No advance bookings on public open days. House has limited capacity; timed ticket system operates. Group Bookings: Thurs & Fri, must be booked in advance. Gardens: Jun–Sept, Thurs 2–5pm.
**Admission:** Adult £8.50, Child/Student £4.25. Gardens only: £2. Carer accompanying disabled person Free.
ⓘ No photography in house. ⌐ 🄯 Grounds. WCs. Parking on site.
🄯 Licensed. ⯭ Licensed. 🄵 By arrangement. 🄿 10 mins walk. Limited for coaches.
▦ 🖳 Guide dogs only. ☎ See website www.24hourmuseum.org.uk.

© NTPL/East Front

## NEWARK PARK ✿
### OZLEWORTH, WOTTON-UNDER-EDGE, GLOUCESTERSHIRE GL12 7PZ
www.nationaltrust.org.uk

**Tel/Fax:** 01453 842644   **Infoline:** 01793 817666
**E-mail:** newarkpark@nationaltrust.org.uk
**Owner:** The National Trust   **Contact:** Michael Claydon
A Tudor hunting lodge converted into a castellated country house by James Wyatt. An atmospheric house, set in spectacular countryside with outstanding views.
**Location:** MAP 2:P1, OS Ref172. ST786 934. 1½ m E of Wotton-under-Edge, 1¾ m S of Junction of A4135 & B4058, follow signs for Ozleworth, House signposted from main road.
**Open:** House & Garden: 4 Apr–31 May: Wed, Thurs & BH Mons; 2 Jun–31 Oct: Wed, Thur, Sat, Sun & BH Mons, 11am–5pm (last entry 4.30pm). Also open Easter: Good Fri–Mon, 11am–5pm.
**Admission:** Adult £5.30, Child £2.70, Family (2+3) £13.80. Groups by appointment. No reduction for groups.
ℹ No photography in house. 🗖 🖒 Partial. 𝕗 By arrangement. 🅿 ⬛
🐾 In grounds, on leads.

## KIFTSGATE COURT GARDENS 🏠
### CHIPPING CAMPDEN, GLOUCESTERSHIRE GL55 6LN
www.kiftsgate.co.uk

**Tel/Fax:** 01386 438777   **E-mail:** info@kiftsgate.co.uk
**Owner:** Mr and Mrs J G Chambers   **Contact:** Mr J G Chambers
Magnificently situated garden on the edge of the Cotswold escarpment with views towards the Malvern Hills. Many unusual shrubs and plants including tree peonies, abutilons, specie and old-fashioned roses. Winner HHA/Christie's Garden of the Year Award 2003.
**Location:** MAP 6:O9, OS Ref. SP173 430. 4m NE of Chipping Campden. ¼ m W of Hidcote Garden.
**Open:** Apr, Aug & Sept: Sun, Mon & Wed, 2–6pm. May, June & July: daily except Thurs & Fri, 12 noon–6pm. Coaches by appointment.
**Admission:** Adult: £5.50, Child £1.50. Groups (20+) £5.
🗖 🚻 ⬛ 🅿 🐾

## OLD CAMPDEN HOUSE

**Church St, Chipping Campden, Gloucestershire**
**Tel:** 01628 825925   **E-mail:** bookings@landmarktrust.org.uk
**www.landmarktrust.org.uk**
**Owner/Contact:** The Landmark Trust

The site of Old Campden House, a Scheduled Ancient Monument, is owned and managed by the Landmark Trust, a building preservation charity. The main house was burnt to the ground during the Civil War but other buildings remain. The East and West Banqueting Houses and Almonry have been restored and are let for holidays throughout the year. Full details of Landmark's 184 historic buildings are featured in the Landmark Trust Handbook (price £11.50 refundable against first booking).
**Location:** MAP 6:O10, OS Ref. SP156 394. Next to St James's Church in Church Street.
**Open:** Available for holidays for up to 6 people (East Banqueting House) and 4 people (West Banqueting House and Almonry). Site open 30 days per year, with buildings open on 8 of these days. Other visits by appointment. Contact the Landmark Trust for dates.
**Admission:** Free.
🐾 ⬛

© NT Photographic Library / Nadia MacKenzie

## LODGE PARK & SHERBORNE ESTATE 🍃
### ALDSWORTH, Nr CHELTENHAM, GLOUCESTERSHIRE GL54 3PP
www.nationaltrust.org.uk/lodgepark

**Tel:** 01451 844130   **Fax:** 01451 844131   **E-mail:** lodgepark@nationaltrust.org.uk
**Owner:** The National Trust   **Contact:** The Visitor Services Manager
Lodge Park is a rare example of a grandstand, situated on the picturesque Sherborne Estate in the Cotswolds, Lodge Park was created in 1634 by John 'Crump' Dutton. Inspired by his passion for gambling and banqueting, it is a unique survival of a Grandstand, Deer Course and Park. It was the home of Charles Dutton, 7th Lord Sherborne, until 1983 when he bequeathed his family's estate to The National Trust. The interior of the grandstand has been reconstructed to its original form and is the first project of its kind undertaken by the Trust that relies totally on archaeological evidence. The park behind was designed by Charles Bridgeman in 1725. The Sherborne Estate is 1650ha (4000 acres) of rolling Cotswold countryside with sweeping views down to the River Windrush. Much of the village of Sherborne is owned by the Trust, including the post office, shop, school and the social club. There are walks for all ages around the estate, which include the restored and working water meadows.
**Location:** MAP 6:O11, OS Ref. SP146 123. 3m E of Northleach, approach only from A40. Bus: Swanbrook 853 Oxford-Glouceste, 1m walk from bus stop.
**Open:** Grandstand & Deer Park: 16 Mar–28 Oct: Mon, Fri & Sun, 11am–4pm; Open Easter Saturday.
**Admission:** Adult £4.80, Child £2.70, Family £11.70. Estate: Free.
ℹ Video shows during the day. 🎫 Civil ceremonies only. 🖒 Partial. 🅿 ⬛
🐾 Dogs must be kept under close control. 🔺 ⬛

© NT Photographic Library / Nadia MacKenzie

Lodge Park, Nr Cheltenham

## OWLPEN MANOR
### Nr ULEY, GLOUCESTERSHIRE GL11 5BZ
www.owlpen.com

**Tel:** 01453 860261  **Fax:** 01453 860819  **Restaurant:** 01453 860816
**E-mail:** sales@owlpen.com

**Owner:** Sir Nicholas and Lady Mander  **Contact:** Jayne Simmons

Romantic Tudor manor house, 1450–1616, with Cotswold Arts & Crafts associations. Remote wooded valley setting, with 16th and 17th century formal terraced gardens and magnificent yews. Contains unique painted cloth wall hangings, family and Arts & Crafts collections. Mill (1726), Court House (1620); licensed restaurant in medieval Cyder House. Victorian church. *"Owlpen – ah, what a dream is there!"* – Vita Sackville-West.

**Location:** MAP 6:M12, OS Ref. ST801 984. 3m E of Dursley, 1m E of Uley, off B4066, by Old Crown pub.

**Open:** May–Sept: Tue, Thurs & Sun, 2–5pm. Restaurant 12 noon–5pm.

**Admission:** Adult £5.25, Child (4–14yrs) £2.25, Family (2+4) £14.50. Gardens & **Grounds:** Adult £3.25, Child £1.25. Group rates available.

⊤ & Unsuitable. 🍴 Licensed. 🅿 🖼 Holiday cottages, all seasons, sleep 2–9.

## PAINSWICK ROCOCO GARDEN
### PAINSWICK, GLOUCESTERSHIRE GL6 6TH
www.rococogarden.org.uk

**Tel:** 01452 813204  **Fax:** 01452 814888  **E-mail:** info@rococogarden.org.uk
**Owner:** Painswick Rococo Garden Trust  **Contact:** P R Moir

Unique 18th century garden restoration situated in a hidden 6 acre Cotswold combe. Charming contemporary buildings are juxtaposed with winding woodland walks and formal vistas. Famous for its early spring show of snowdrops. Anniversary maze.

**Location:** MAP 6:N11, OS Ref. SO864 106. ½ m NW of village of Painswick on B4073.

**Open:** 10 Jan–31 Oct: daily, 11am–5pm.

**Admission:** Adult £5, Child £2.50, OAP £4. Family (2+2) £13. Free introductory talk for pre-booked groups (20+).

📷 💱 & Partial. WC. 💻 Licensed. 🍴 🅿 🖼 🖼 In grounds, on leads. 🔺 ❋ 🔯

## RODMARTON MANOR
### CIRENCESTER, GLOUCESTERSHIRE GL7 6PF
www.rodmarton-manor.co.uk

**Tel:** 01285 841253  **Fax:** 01285 841298
**E-mail:** simon.biddulph@btinternet.com

**Owner:** Mr & Mrs Simon Biddulph  **Contact:** Simon Biddulph

A Cotswold Arts and Crafts house, one of the last great country houses to be built in the traditional way and containing beautiful furniture, ironwork, china and needlework specially made for the house. The large garden complements the house and contains many areas of great beauty and character including the magnificent herbaceous borders, topiary, roses, rockery and kitchen garden. Available as a film location and for small functions.

**Location:** MAP 6:N12, OS Ref. ST943 977. Off A433 between Cirencester and Tetbury.

**Open:** House & Garden: Easter Monday & May–Sept (Weds, Sats & BHs), 2–5pm (Not guided tours). Garden only, for snowdrops,: 11, 15 & 18 Feb: from 1.30pm. Groups please book. Individuals need not book. Guided tours of the house (last about 1hr) may be booked for groups (15+) at any time of year (minimum group charge of £105 applies). Groups (5+) may book guided or unguided tours of the garden at other times.

**Admission:** House & Garden: £7, Child (5–15yrs) £3.50. Garden only: £4, Child (5–15yrs) £1. Guided tour of Garden: Entry fee plus £40 per group.

ⓘ Colour guidebook & postcards on sale. Available for filming. No photography in house. WCs in garden. & Garden & ground floor. 💻 Most open days and groups by appointment. ☒ By arrangement. 🅿 🖼 🖼 Guide dogs only. ❋

**visit hudsons guide online**

## ST MARY'S CHURCH ⌗

**Kempley, Gloucestershire**

**Tel:** 0117 9750700   www.english-heritage.org.uk/visits

**Owner:** English Heritage   **Contact:** The South West Regional Office

A delightful Norman church with superb wall paintings from the 12th–14th centuries which were only discovered beneath whitewash in 1871.

**Location:** MAP 6:M10, OS Ref. SO670 313. On minor road. 1½m SE of Much Marcle, A449.

**Open:** 1 Mar–31 Oct: daily, 10am–6pm. Telephone for winter appointments

**Admission:** Free.

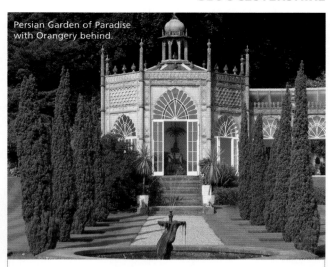

*Persian Garden of Paradise with Orangery behind.*

Dyrham Park, Nr Bath

## SEZINCOTE 🏛

**MORETON-IN-MARSH, GLOUCESTERSHIRE  GL56 9AW**

www.sezincote.co.uk

**Tel:** 01386 700444

**Owner:** Mr and Mrs D Peake   **Contact:** Mr E Peake

Exotic oriental water garden by Repton and Daniell. Large semi-circular orangery. House by S P Cockerell in Indian style was the inspiration for Brighton Pavilion.

**Location:** MAP 6:P10, OS Ref. SP183 324. 2½ m SW of Moreton-in-Marsh. Turn W along A44 to Broadway and left into gateway just before Bourton-on-the-Hill (opposite the gate to Batsford Park, then 1m drive.

**Open:** Garden: Thurs, Fris & BH Mons, 2–6pm (dusk if earlier) throughout the year except Dec. House: May, Jun, Jul & Sept, Thurs & Fris, 2.30–6pm. Groups by written appointment.

**Admission:** House & Garden: Adult £6 (no children in house). Garden: Adult £4, Child £1.50 (under 5yrs Free).

♿ Gravel paths. ⚑ Guide dogs only. ❄

## SNOWSHILL MANOR ❧

**SNOWSHILL, Nr BROADWAY, GLOUCESTERSHIRE  WR12 7JU**

www.nationaltrust.org.uk

**Tel:** 01386 852410   **Fax:** 01386 842822

**E-mail:** snowshillmanor@nationaltrust.org.uk

**Owner:** The National Trust   **Contact:** The Property Manager

Snowshill Manor contains Charles Paget Wade's extraordinary collection of craftsmanship and design, including musical instruments, clocks, toys, bicycles, weavers' and spinners' tools and Japanese armour. Each room has something to interest or inspire the visitor. Run on organic principles, the intimate garden is laid out as a series of outdoor rooms, with terraces and ponds, and wonderful views across the Cotswold countryside.

The Snowshill Costume Collection can be viewed by appointment only at Berrington Hall on Mondays and Tuesdays, please tel: 01568 613720.

**Location:** MAP 6:O10, OS Ref. SP096 339. 3m SW of Broadway, turning off the A44, by Broadway Green.

**Open:** House: 24 Mar–18 Oct: Wed–Sun & BH Mons, 12 noon–5pm. Last admission to the house 4.10pm. House is shown by timed ticket only. Garden: as House, 11am–5.30pm. Restaurant & Shop: as Garden, also 4 Nov–9 Dec, 12 noon–4pm.

**Admission:** House, Gardens, Shop & Restaurant: Adult £7.70, Child £3.90, Family £19.60. Garden, Shop & Restaurant only: Adult £4.20, Child £2.10, Family £10.60. Visitors arriving by bicycle or on foot offered a voucher redeemable at Snowshill NT shop or tearoom. Coach & School groups by written appointment only.

🔲 ♿ Partial. 🍴 Licensed. ▣ ⚑ ♿

## STANWAY HOUSE & WATER GARDEN 🏛
**STANWAY, CHELTENHAM, GLOS  GL54 5PQ**

www.stanwayfountain.co.uk

**Tel:** 01386 584528   **Fax:** 01386 584688   **E-mail:** stanwayhse@btconnect.com
**Owner:** Lord Neidpath   **Contact:** Debbie Lewis

"As perfect and pretty a Cotswold manor house as anyone is likely to see" (Fodor's Great Britain 1998 guidebook). Stanway's beautiful architecture, furniture, parkland and village are now complemented by the restored 18th century water garden and the magnificent fountain – 300 feet – making it the tallest garden fountain and gravity fountain in the world. Teas available. Beer for sale. Wedding reception venue.
**Location:** MAP 6:O10, OS Ref. SP061 323. N of Winchcombe, just off B4077.
**Open:** House & Garden: June–Aug: Tue & Thur, 2–5pm. Garden: July & Aug, Sats only, 2–5pm. Private tours by arrangement at other times.
**Admission:** Adult £6, Child £1.50, OAP £4.50. Garden only: Adult £4, Child £1, OAP £3.

ⓘ Film & photographic location. 🆃 Wedding receptions. 🖿🖿🖿 By arrangement. 🅿 🖿 In grounds on leads. ✳

---

**SUDELEY** 🏛                    *See page 237 for full page entry.*

---

## TYTHE BARN
**Tanhouse Farm, Churchend, Frampton-on-Severn, Gloucestershire  GL2 7EH**
**Tel:** 01452 741072   **E-mail:** tanhouse.farm@lineone.net
**Owner/Contact:** Michael Williams

Tythe Barn Grade II* c1650 recently restored in conjunction with English Heritage. Barn incorporating cow shed, the exceptional length and width of the timber framed structure upon a low stone plinth with box framing and undaubed wattle panels marks it out from other contemporary farm buildings.
**Location:** MAP 6:M12, OS Ref. SP014 206. Southern end of Frampton-on-Severn, close to church.
**Open:** By arrangement all year 10am–4pm.
**Admission:** Free.

♿ Partial. 🆃 By arrangement. 🅿 Limited. None for coaches. ✳

Bourton House Garden, Bourton-on-the-Hill

Westbury Court Garden, Westbury-on-Severn

## WHITTINGTON COURT

**Whittington, Cheltenham, Gloucestershire  GL54 4HF**
**Tel:** 01242 820556  **Fax:** 01242 820218
**Owner:** Mr & Mrs Jack Stringer     **Contact:** Mrs J Stringer
Elizabethan manor house. Family possessions including ceramics, antique and modern glass, fossils and fabrics.
**Location:** MAP 6:N11, OS Ref. SP014 206. 4m E of Cheltenham on N side of A40.
**Open:** 7–22 April & 11–27 Aug: 2–5pm.
**Admission:** Adult £4, Child £1, OAP £3.

# WESTBURY COURT GARDEN
### WESTBURY-ON-SEVERN, GLOUCESTERSHIRE GL14 1PD
www.nationaltrust.org.uk

**Tel:** 01452 760461   **E-mail:** westburycourt@nationaltrust.org.uk
**Owner:** The National Trust   **Contact:** The Head Gardener
A Dutch water garden with canals and yew hedges, laid out between 1696 and 1705; the earliest of its kind remaining in England. Restored in 1971 and planted with species dating from pre-1700 including apple, pear and plum trees.
**Location:** MAP 6:M11, OS Ref. SO718 138. 9m SW of Gloucester on A48.
**Open:** 7 Mar–30 Jun & 1 Sept–28 Oct: Wed–Sun, 10am–5pm. 1 Jul–31 Aug: daily, 10am–5pm. Open BH Mons. Other times of year by appointment.
***Admission:** Adult £4.25, Child £2.10, Family £11. *includes a voluntary donation but visitors can choose to pay the standard prices displayed at the property and on the website.
Grounds largely accessible. WCs.

Kiftsgate Court Gardens, Chipping Campden

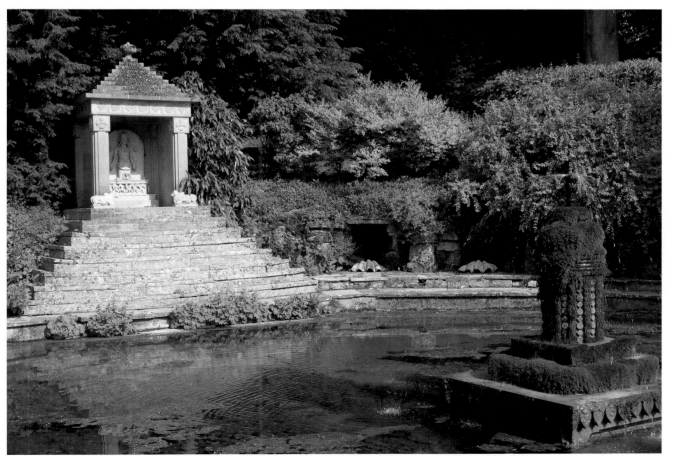
Temple to Surya, the Hindu God of the Sun, with Shivalinga Fountain and Pool – Sezincote,

### ■ Owner
The National Trust

### ■ Contact
**For Room Hire**
Mr Tom Deller
Room Hire Manager
Stall Street
Bath BA1 1LZ

**Tel:** 01225 477734
**Fax:** 01225 477476
**E-mail:** tom_deller@
bathnes.gov.uk

**Museum Enquiries**
**Tel:** 01225 477173
**Fax:** 01225 477743

### ■ Location
**MAP 2:P2**
**OS Ref. ST750 648**

Near centre of Bath,
10m from M4/J18.
Park & Ride or
public car park.

**Rail:** Great Western from
London Paddington
(regular service)
90 mins approx.

**Air:** Bristol airport
45 mins.

### ■ Opening Times
**All Year** January/February
& November/December:
11am–4pm. March–
October: 11am–5pm.

Closed 25 & 26 December
Last exit 1hr after closing.

**Special exhibitions**
'The Nureyev Style', until
25 Feb, 'Fashion and
Bath' until 31 Dec,
'Pockets of History' until
2 Sept, 'Pick of the
Bunch' 17 Jul–27 Aug.

### ■ Admission
**Assembly Rooms**     Free

**Museum of Costume**
| | |
|---|---|
| Adult | £6.75 |
| Child* (summer) | £4.75 |
| Conc. | £6.00 |
| Family (2+4) | £19.00 |

Groups (20+)
| | |
|---|---|
| Adult | £5.50 |
| Child* (summer) | £4.00 |
| Child* (winter) | £3.60 |

**Joint Saver Ticket with**
**Roman Baths**
| | |
|---|---|
| Adult | £13.50 |
| Child* | £8.00 |
| Conc. | £11.50 |
| Family (2+4) | £38.00 |

Groups (20+)
| | |
|---|---|
| Adult | £5.50 |
| Child* (summer) | £4.00 |
| Child* (winter) | £3.60 |

* Age 6–16yrs.
Child under 6yrs Free.

*©Bath & North East Somerset Council*

# MUSEUM OF COSTUME 🌿 & ASSEMBLY ROOMS

www.museumofcostume.co.uk

The Assembly Rooms in Bath are open to the public daily (free of charge) and are also popular for dinners, dances, concerts, conferences and Civil weddings. Originally known as the Upper Rooms, they were designed by John Wood the Younger and opened in 1771. The magnificent interior consists of a splendid Ball Room, Tea Room and Card Room, connected by two fine octagonal rooms. This plan was perfect for 'assemblies', evening entertainments popular in the 18th century, which included dancing, music, card-playing and tea drinking. They are now owned by The National Trust and managed by Bath & North East Somerset Council, which runs a full conference service.

The building also houses one of the largest and most comprehensive collections of fashionable dress in the world, the Museum of Costume. Its extensive displays cover the history of fashion from the late 16th century to the present day. Hand-held audioguides allow visitors to learn about the fashions on display while the lighting is kept to levels suitable for fragile garments. The 'Dress of the Year' collection traces significant moments in modern fashion history from 1963. For the serious student of fashion, the reference library and study facilities are available by appointment.

The museum shops sell publications and gifts associated with the history of costume and are open daily to all visitors.

| | |
|---|---|
| ℹ️ | Conference facilities. |
| 🏛️ | Extensive book & gift shops. |
| 🍸 | Corporate hospitality. Function facilities. |
| ♿ | Suitable. WC. |
| ☕ | |
| 🚶 | Hourly. Individual guided tours by arrangement. |
| 🎧 | English/Dutch/French/German/Italian/Japanese/Spanish. |
| 🅿️ | Charlotte Street car park. |
| 📖 | Teachers' pack. |
| 🐕 | Guide dogs only. |
| 🔔 | Civil Weddings/Receptions. |
| ❄️ | |

### Conference/Function

| ROOM | SIZE | MAX CAPACITY |
|---|---|---|
| Ballroom | 103' x 40' | 500/310 |
| Octagon | 47' x 47' | 120/120 |
| Tea Room | 58' x 40' | 260/170 |
| Card Room | 59' x 18' | 80/60 |

# THE ROMAN BATHS & PUMP ROOM

www.romanbaths.co.uk

The first stop for any visitor to Bath is the Roman Baths surrounding the hot springs where the city began and which are still its heart. Here you'll see one of the country's finest ancient monuments – the great Roman temple and bathing complex built almost 2,000 years ago. Discover the everyday life of the Roman spa and see ancient treasures from the Temple of Sulis Minerva. A host of new interpretive methods for adults and children bring these spectacular buildings vividly to life and help visitors to understand the extensive remains.

The Grand Pump Room, overlooking the Spring, is the social heart of Bath. The elegant interior of 1795 is something every visitor to Bath should see. You can enjoy a glass of spa water drawn from the fountain, perhaps as an appetiser to a traditional Pump Room tea, morning coffee or lunch. The Pump Room Trio and resident pianists provide live music daily. The Roman Baths shop sells publications and gifts related to the site.

In the evening, the Pump Room is available for banquets, dances and concerts. Nothing could be more magical than a meal on the terrace which overlooks the Great Bath, or a pre-dinner drinks reception by torchlight around the Great Bath itself.

## Owner
Bath & North East Somerset Council

## Contact
**For Room Hire**
Mr Tom Deller
Stall Street
Bath BA1 1LZ
**Tel:** 01225 477734
**Fax:** 01225 477476
**E-mail:** tom_deller@bathnes.gov.uk

**For visits to Roman Baths**
**Tel:** 01225 477785
**Fax:** 01225 477743

## Location
**MAP 2:P2**
**OS Ref. ST750 648**

Centre of Bath, 10m from M4/J18. Park & Ride recommended.

**Rail:** Great Western from London Paddington, half hourly service, 1 hr 17 mins duration.

## Opening Times
January–February: 9.30am–4.30pm.
March–June: 9am–5pm.
July–August: 9am–8pm.
September–October: 9am–5pm.
November–December: 9.30am–4.30pm.
Last exit 1 hour after closing.

Closed 25 & 26 December.

The Pump Room Trio plays 10am–12 noon Mon–Sat and 3–5pm Sunday. During the summer it also plays from 3–5pm, Mon–Sat. Resident pianists play at lunch-time.

## Admission
**Roman Baths**
| | |
|---|---|
| Adult | £10.25 |
| Child (6–16yrs) | £6.60 |
| Conc. | £8.75 |
| Family (2+4) | £29.00 |

Groups (20+)
| | |
|---|---|
| Adult | £7.50 |
| Child* (summer) | £4.80 |
| Child* (winter) | £4.50 |

**Joint Saver Ticket with Museum of Costume**
| | |
|---|---|
| Adult | £13.50 |
| Child* | £8.00 |
| Conc. | £11.50 |
| Family (2+4) | £38.00 |

Groups (20+)
| | |
|---|---|
| Adult | £9.20 |
| Child* (summer) | £5.80 |
| Child* (winter) | £5.00 |

*Age 6–16yrs.
Child under 6yrs Free.

i Award-winning guide book in English, French and German.

Extensive gift shop.

Comprehensive service for private and corporate entertainment. The Assembly Rooms, Guildhall, Victoria Art Gallery and Pump Room are all available for private hire, contact the Pump Room.

Free access to terrace. Restricted access to the Museum, special visits for disabled groups by appointment. People with special needs welcome, teaching sessions available.

Pump Room coffees, lunches and teas, no reservation needed. Music by Pump Room Trio or pianist.

Hourly. Private tours by appointment.

English, French, German, Italian, Japanese, Spanish, Dutch, Mandarin.

P City centre car parks available.

Teaching sessions available. Pre-booking necessary.

Civil Weddings in two private rooms with photographs around the Great Bath.

## Conference/Function

| ROOM | SIZE | MAX CAPACITY |
|---|---|---|
| Ballroom | 103' x 40' | 500/310 |
| Octagon | 47' x 47' | 120/120 |
| Tea Room | 58' x 40' | 260/170 |
| Card Room | 59' x 18' | 80/60 |

Rick Godley

© NT Photographic Library / Magnus Rew

# NO 1 ROYAL CRESCENT
## BATH  BA1 2LR

www.bath-preservation-trust.org.uk

**Tel:** 01225 428126   **Fax:** 01225 481850
**E-mail:** no1museum@bptrust.org.uk
**Owner:** Bath Preservation Trust   **Contact:** Victoria Barwell – Curator
Take a look inside a sumptuous piece of Bath's unmatched architectural heritage and revel in the opulence of grand Georgian life. The exquisitely restored and lavishly furnished house is the epitome of elegant 18th century living, and a unique museum shop completes the experience.
**Location:** MAP 2:P2, OS Ref. ST746 653. M4/J18. A46 to Bath. ¼m NW of city centre.
**Open:** Mid Feb–end Nov: Tues–Sun, 10.30am–5pm. BH Mons. Closes 4pm in Nov. Closed Good Fri. Last admission 30 mins before closing. Evening tours and other times by arrangement.
**Admission:** Adult £5, Child (5–16yrs) £2.50, Conc £3.50, Family £12. Groups: £3.
◻◻◻◻Unsuitable. ◻◻The Royal Crescent & Bath centre. ◻

Dunster Castle, Nr Minehead

# THE AMERICAN MUSEUM & GARDENS
## CLAVERTON MANOR, CLAVERTON HILL, BATH  BA2 7BD

www.americanmuseum.org

**Tel:** 01225 460503   **Fax:** 01225 469160   **E-mail:** info@americanmuseum.org
**Owner:** The Trustees of the American Museum in Britain   **Contact:** Julian Blades
Claverton Manor was built in 1820 by Jeffry Wyattville. In the late 1950s it became the home of the American Museum in Britain. Inside the Manor there are 18 period rooms which show the development of American decorative arts from the 1680s to the 1860s. In addition there are galleries devoted to Folk Art, Native American Art, and our large collection of quilts and other textiles. The extensive grounds contain a replica of part of the garden at Mount Vernon, George Washington's house in Virginia, and an

Arboretum of North American trees and shrubs. Light lunches and teas are available.
**Location:** MAP 2:P2, OS Ref. ST784 640. 2m SE of Bath city centre.
**Open:** 17 Mar–28 Oct: Tues–Sun (open BH Mons and Mons in Aug) 12noon–5pm. Last admission to museum 4pm. 24 Nov–16 Dec: Tues–Sun, 12–4.30pm.
**Admission:** Adult £7.50, Child £4.00, Conc. £6.50. Groups (15–70): Adult £6.
◻◻◻◻ Partial. WC. ◻ Licensed. ◻ By arrangement. ◻◻
◻ In grounds, on leads.◻

NTPL: Neil Campbell-Sharp

## BARRINGTON COURT ⚘
### BARRINGTON, ILMINSTER, SOMERSET TA19 0NQ
www.nationaltrust.org.uk

**Tel:** 01460 241938  **Info:** 01460 242614
**E-mail:** barringtoncourt@nationaltrust.org.uk
**Owner:** The National Trust   **Contact:** Visitor Services Manager

The enchanting formal garden, influenced by Gertrude Jekyll, is laid out in a series of walled rooms, including the White Garden, the Rose and Iris Garden and the Lily Garden. The working Kitchen Garden has espaliered apple, pear and plum trees trained along high stone walls. The Tudor manor house was restored in the 1920s by the Lyle family. It is let to Stuart Interiors as showrooms with antique furniture for sale, thereby offering NT visitors a different kind of visit.

**Location:** MAP 2:N5, OS Ref. ST395 181. In Barrington village, 5m NE of Ilminster, on B3168.

**Open:** House, Garden & Shop: 1–31 Mar & 1–30 Oct: daily except Weds, 11am–4.30pm. 1 Apr–30 Sept: daily except Weds, 11am–5pm. 1–16 Dec: Sats & Suns, 11am–4pm. Restaurant: 1 Apr–30 Sept (weekdays: lunches only, weekends: lunch & teas), 1–28 Mar & 1–30 Oct: daily except Weds, 11am–4pm. 29 Mar–30 Sept: Mon, Tues, Thurs & Fri, 12 noon–3pm. Sats & Suns, 12 noon–5pm. 1–16 Dec: Sat & Suns, 11am–4pm. Beagles café: 29 Mar–30 Sept: daily except Weds, 11am–5pm. 6–28 Oct: Sat & Suns, 11am–4pm. NB. Café may close in poor weather (Oct).

**\*Admission:** Adult £7, Child £3, Family (2+3) £17. Groups: £6. \*includes a voluntary donation but visitors can choose to pay the standard prices displayed at the property and on the website.

◻ ⊞ ⬛ Grounds. WC. ⑪ Licensed. ℗ ⬛ ⬛

**Who's offering accommodation?**
See our index on page 575

## BECKFORD'S TOWER & MUSEUM
**Lansdown Road, Bath BA1 9BH**
**Tel:** 01225 460705  **Fax:** 01225 481850  **E-mail:** beckford@bptrust.org.uk
**Owner:** Bath Preservation Trust   **Contact:** The Administrator
Built in 1827 for eccentric William Beckford and recently restored by Bath Preservation Trust. The tower is a striking feature of the Bath skyline.
**Location:** MAP 2:P2, OS Ref. ST735 676. Lansdown Road, 2m NNW of city centre.
**Open:** Easter weekend–end of Oct: Sats, Suns & BH Mons, 10.30am–5pm.
**Admission:** Adult £3, Child £1.50, Conc. £2, Family £8. BPT & NACF members: Free. Groups by arrangement.

## BREAN DOWN ⚘
**Brean, North Somerset**
**Tel:** 01934 844518  www.nationaltrust.org.uk
**Owner:** The National Trust   **Contact:** Property Manager
Brean Down, rich in wildlife and history, is one of the most striking landmarks of the Somerset coastline, extending 1½ m into the Bristol Channel. A Palmerston Fort built in 1865 and then re-armed in World War II, provides a unique insight into Brean's past.
**Location:** MAP 2:M3, OS Ref. ST290 590. Between Weston-super-Mare and Burnham-on-Sea about 8m from M5/J22. Rail: Highbridge 5m.
**Open:** All year.
**Admission:** Free.
ℹ The cliffs are extremely steep. Please stay on the main paths and wear suitable footwear. ◻ (Not NT.) ⬛ Partial. WC. ⬛ (Not NT.) Ⓕ Guided walks. ℗ ⬛ ⬛ On leads. ✳

## THE BUILDING OF BATH MUSEUM
**The Countess of Huntingdon's Chapel, The Vineyards, The Paragon, Bath BA1 5NA**
**Tel:** 01225 333895 / 01225 445473  **E-mail:** enquiries@bathmuseum.co.uk
**Owner:** Bath Preservation Trust   **Contact:** The Administrator
Discover the essence of life in Georgian Bath.
**Location:** MAP 2:P2, OS Ref. ST751 655. 5 mins walk from city centre. Bath M4/J18.
**Open:** 15 Feb–30 Nov: Tue–Sun & BH Mons, 10.30am–5pm (last adm. 4.30pm).
**Admission:** Adult £4, Child £2.50, Conc. £3. Groups: £3.

## THE CHALICE WELL & GARDENS
### CHILKWELL STREET, GLASTONBURY, SOMERSET BA6 8DD
www.chalicewell.org.uk

**Tel:** 01458 831154  **Fax:** 01458 835528  **E-mail:** info@chalicewell.org.uk
**Owner/Contact:** Chalice Well Trust
A jewel of a garden, nestling around one of Britain's oldest Holy Wells. Legend tells of the Well being visited by Joseph of Arimethea, bearing the Chalice of the Last Supper, and of King Arthur on his Grail Quest. Today, the beautifully landscaped grounds with the iron-rich waters are a haven of peace and tranquillity.
**Location:** MAP 2:N4, OS Ref. ST507 384. On the A361 Glastonbury - Shepton Mallet road, at the foot of Glastonbury Tor.
**Open:** All year: 1 Apr–31 Oct, 10am–5.30pm. 1 Nov–31 Mar, 10am–4pm.
**Admission:** Adult £3, Child £1.50, Conc. £2.50.
ℹ No smoking in gardens. ◻ ⬛ Ⓕ By arrangement.
℗ Limited. At nearby Rural Life Museum. ⬛ ⬛ Guide dogs only. ✳ ⬛

## CLEEVE ABBEY ⌗
**Washford, Nr Watchet, Somerset TA23 0PS**
**Tel:** 01984 640377  **Fax:** 01984 641348  **E-mail:** customers@english-heritage.org.uk
www.english-heritage.org.uk/cleeve
**Owner:** English Heritage   **Contact:** Visitor Operations Staff
There are few monastic sites where you will see such a complete set of cloister buildings, including the refectory with its magnificent timber roof. Built in the 13th century, this Cistercian abbey was saved from destruction at the Dissolution by being turned into a house and then a farm.
**Location:** MAP 2:L4, OS Ref. ST047 407. In Washford, ¼m S of A39.
**Open:** 1 Apr–30 Jun & Sept: daily, 10am–5pm. Jul & Aug: daily, 10am–6pm. Oct: daily, 10am–4pm.
**Admission:** Adult £3.50, Child £1.80, Conc. £2.60. 15% discount for groups (11+).
ℹ WC. ◻ ⬛ Partial. ℗ ⬛ In grounds, on leads. ⬛

## COLERIDGE COTTAGE 🌲

**35 Lime Street, Nether Stowey, Bridgwater, Somerset TA5 1NQ**
**Tel:** 01278 732662 **E-mail:** coleridgecottage@nationaltrust.org.uk
**Owner:** The National Trust **Contact:** The Custodian
The home of Samuel Taylor Coleridge for three years from 1797, with mementoes of the poet on display. It was here that he wrote *The Rime of the Ancient Mariner,* part of *Christabel, Frost at Midnight* and *Kubla Khan.*
**Location:** MAP 2:M4, OS Ref. ST191 399. At W end of Lime St, opposite the Ancient Mariner pub, 8m W of Bridgwater.
**Open:** 1 Apr–30 Sept: Thur–Sun, 2–5pm (open BH Mons).
**Admission:** Adult £3.90, Child £1.90, no reduction for groups, which must book.
ℹ No WC. ♿ Braille guide. 🅿 500yds (not NT). ✉

## COMBE SYDENHAM COUNTRY PARK 🏛

**Monksilver, Taunton, Somerset TA4 4JG**

**Tel:** 0800 7838572

**Owner:** Theed Estates **Contact:** John Burns

Built in 1580 on the site of a monastic settlement. Deer Park and woodland walks.

**Location:** MAP 2:L4, OS Ref. ST075 366. Monksilver.

**Open:** Country Park: Easter–end Sept. House: All year by appointment only.

**Admission:** Country Park & car park Free. House & Gardens £5pp. Tel for details.

Andrew Lawson

## COTHAY MANOR & GARDENS
### GREENHAM, WELLINGTON, SOMERSET TA21 0JR
www.cothaymanor.co.uk

**Tel:** 01823 672283 **Fax:** 01823 672345 **E-mail:** cothaymanor@btinternet.co.uk
**Owner/Contact:** Mr & Mrs Alastair Robb
The magical, romantic, gardens of Cothay surround what is said to be the most perfect example of a small classic medieval manor. Many garden rooms, each a garden in itself, are set off a 200yd yew walk. In addition there is a bog garden with azaleas, and drifts of primuli, fine trees, cottage garden, courtyards, and river walk. A plantsman's paradise. The manor is open to groups throughout the year.
**Location:** MAP 2:L5, OS Ref. ST085 212. From M5 W J/27, take A38 direction

Wellington. 3½m left towards Greenham. From N/J26 take A38 direction Exeter. 3½m right towards Greenham (1½m). On LH corner at bottom of hill turn right. Cothay 1m, always keeping left.
**Open:** Garden: Easter–Sept: Weds, Thurs, Suns, & BHs, 2–6pm. Groups: Daily all season by appointment. House: Groups (20+) by appointment throughout the year.
**Admission:** Garden: Adult £4.50, Child (under 12yrs) £2.50.
ℹ No photography in house. 🏛 Ⓣ ♿ 🍴 🅿 ✉

## CROWE HALL

**Widcombe Hill, Bath, Somerset BA2 6AR**
**Tel:** 01225 310322
**Owner/Contact:** John Barratt Esq
Ten acres of romantic hillside gardens. Victorian grotto, classical Bath villa with good 18th century furniture and paintings.
**Location:** MAP 2:P2, OS Ref. ST760 640. In Bath, 1m SE of city centre.
**Open:** Gardens only open 15 Apr, 13 May & 3 Jun, 2–6pm. House and Gardens by appointment.
**Admission:** House & Gardens: Adult £5. Gardens only: Adult £3, Child £1.

## DODINGTON HALL

**Nr Nether Stowey, Bridgwater, Somerset TA5 1LF**
**Tel:** 01278 741400
**Owner:** Lady Gass **Contact:** P Quinn (occupier)
Small Tudor manor house on the lower slopes of the Quantocks. Great Hall with oak roof. Semi-formal garden with roses and shrubs.
**Location:** MAP 2:L4, OS Ref. ST172 405. ½m from A39, 11m N of Bridgwater, 7m E of Williton.
**Open:** 1–11 Jun, 2–5pm.
**Admission:** Donations to charity.
ℹ No inside photography. ♿ Unsuitable. 🅿 Limited. No coach parking.

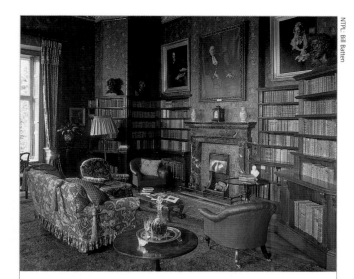

NTPL: Bill Batten

## DUNSTER CASTLE ✤
### DUNSTER, Nr MINEHEAD, SOMERSET TA24 6SL

www.nationaltrust.org.uk

**Tel**: 01643 821314  **Fax**: 01643 823000  **E-mail**: dunstercastle@nationaltrust.org.uk
**Owner:** The National Trust  **Contact:** The Property Manager

Dramatically sited on a wooded hill, a castle has existed here since at least Norman times. The 15th century gatehouse survives, and the present building was remodelled in 1868–72 by Antony Salvin for the Luttrell family, who lived here for 600 years. The fine oak staircase and plasterwork of the 17th century house he adapted can still be seen. There is a sheltered terrace to the south which is home to palms, sub-tropical plant species, and a varied collection of citrus. The terraced gardens also house the National Collection of strawberry trees (arbutus) and there is a pleasant riverside walk beside the River Avill.

**Location:** MAP 2:K4, OS Ref. SS995 435. In Dunster, 3m SE of Minehead.

**Open:** Castle: 23 Mar–25 Jul: daily except Thur, 11am–4pm; 27 Jul–2 Sept: daily except Thur, 11am–5pm; 3 Sept–31 Oct: daily except Thur, 11am–4pm. Garden & Park: 1–22 Mar & 1 Nov–31 Dec: daily (closed 25/26 Dec), 11am–4pm. 23 Mar–31 Oct: 10am–5pm daily. Varied events programme, please telephone for full details. Major roof repairs will be undertaken in 2007. Property open as normal. Access to one or two rooms may be restricted. Please telephone for details.

**Admission:** Castle, Garden & Park: Adult £7.80, Child £4, Family (2+3) £19. Groups (15+): £6.80. Garden & Park only: Adult £4.30, Child £2.20, Family £10.50.

⬛ 🅵 🅶 Braille guide. 🅵 Out of hours by arrangement. 🅿 £2. ▣
🐕 In park, on leads. 🎗 Tel for details (0870 2404068) or visit website.

---

## DUNSTER WORKING WATERMILL ✤

**Mill Lane, Dunster, Nr Minehead, Somerset TA24 6SW**
**Tel:** 01643 821759  **www.nationaltrust.org.uk**
**Owner:** The National Trust  **Contact:** The Tenant

Built on the site of a mill mentioned in the Domesday Survey of 1086. The mill is a private business and all visitors, including NT members, are asked to pay the admission charge.

**Location:** MAP 2:K4, OS Ref. SS995 435. On River Avill, beneath Castle Tor, approach via Mill Lane or Castle gardens on foot.

**Open:** 2 Apr–31 May & 1 Oct–6 Nov, daily except Fri; 1 Jul–30 Sept, daily; 11am–4.45pm.

**Admission:** Adult £2.85, Child £1.85, Senior Citizen £2.35, Family £7.

⬛ 🅶 Ground floor. ▣ 🅿

© NT Photographic Library / W H Rendell

Montacute House, Montacute

## ENGLISHCOMBE TITHE BARN

**Rectory Farmhouse, Englishcombe, Bath  BA2 9DU**
**Tel:** 01225 425073  **E-mail:** jennie.walker@ukonline.co.uk
**Owner/Contact:** Mrs Jennie Walker

An early 14th century cruck-framed Tithe Barn built by Bath Abbey.

**Location:** MAP 2:P2, OS172 Ref. ST716 628. Adjacent to Englishcombe Village Church. 1m SW of Bath.

**Open:** BHs, 2–6pm. Other times by appointment or please knock at house. Closed 1 Dec–7 Jan.

**Admission:** Free.

---

## FAIRFIELD

**Stogursey, Bridgwater, Somerset  TA5 1PU**
**Tel:** 01722 555131 / 01278 732251
**Owner:** Lady Gass  **Contact:** D W Barke FRICS

Elizabethan and medieval house. Occupied by the same family (Acland-Hoods and their ancestors) for over 800 years. Woodland garden. Views of Quantocks and the sea.

**Location:** MAP 2:L4, OS Ref. ST187 430. 11m W of Bridgwater, 8m E of Williton. From A39 Bridgwater/Minehead turn North. House 1m W of Stogursey.

**Open:** 25 Apr–28 May & 6 Jun–6 July: Wed–Fri and BHs. Guided house tours at 2.30 & 3.30pm. Groups at other times by arrangement. Garden open for NGS and other charities on dates advertised in Spring. Advisable to contact to confirm dates.

**Admission:** £4 in aid of Stogursey Church.

ℹ️ No inside photography. 🅶🅵 Obligatory. 🅿 No coach parking.
🐕 Guide dogs only.

---

## FARLEIGH HUNGERFORD CASTLE ⌗

**Farleigh Hungerford, Bath, Somerset  BA3 6RS**
**Tel/Fax:** 01225 754026  **E-mail:** customers@english-heritage.org.uk
**www.english-heritage.org.uk/farleighhungerford**
**Owner:** English Heritage  **Contact:** Visitor Operations Staff

Extensive ruins of 14th century castle with a splendid chapel containing wall paintings, stained glass and the fine tomb of Sir Thomas Hungerford, builder of the castle.

**Location:** MAP 2:P3, OS173, ST801 577. In Farleigh Hungerford 3½m W of Trowbridge on A366.

**Open:** 1 Apr–31 Oct: daily, 10am–5pm (6pm in Jul & Aug, 4pm in Oct). 1 Nov–20 Mar: Sats & Suns, 10am–4pm. Closed 24–26 Dec & 1 Jan.

**Admission:** Adult £3.50, Child £1.80, Conc. £2.60. 15% discount for groups of 11+.

ℹ️ WCs. ⬛ 🅶 Grounds, Ground Floor & Virtual Reality Tour. 🅿 🅞
🐕 Guide dogs only. ❋ ♿

---

## GATCOMBE COURT

**Flax Bourton, Somerset  BS48 3QT**
**Tel:** 01275 393141  **Fax:** 01275 394274
**Owner/Contact:** Mrs Charles Clarke

A Somerset manor house, dating from early 13th century, which has evolved over the centuries since. It is on the site of a large Roman village, traces of which are apparent. Rose and herb garden. Described in Simon Jenkins' book, *England's Thousand Best Houses.*

**Location:** MAP 2:N2, OS Ref. ST525 698. 5m W of Bristol, N of the A370, between the villages of Long Ashton and Flax Bourton. Close to Tyntesfield.

**Open:** May–July: for groups of 15–40 people by appointment.

🅶 Unsuitable. 🅵 By arrangement. ♿ 🅿 🐕 ❋

---

## THE GEORGIAN HOUSE

**7 Great George Street, Bristol, Somerset  BS1 5RR**
**Tel:** 0117 921 1362
**Owner:** City of Bristol Museums & Art Gallery  **Contact:** Karin Walton
**Location:** MAP 2:O2, OS172 ST582 730. Bristol.
**Open:** All year: Sat–Wed, 10am–5pm.
**Admission:** Free.

---

See all the properties that are **open all year** in the index on page 580

## GLASTONBURY ABBEY

**ABBEY GATEHOUSE, MAGDALENE STREET, GLASTONBURY BA6 9EL**

www.glastonburyabbey.com

**Tel:** 01458 832267 **Fax:** 01458 836117 **E-mail:** info@glastonburyabbey.com
**Owner:** Glastonbury Abbey Estate **Contact:** Francis Thyer

Magnificent ruined Abbey set in peaceful Somerset parkland. Explore 2,000 years of history and mystery at what was once England's largest and richest Abbey. Legendary burial place of King Arthur. In the summer: history brought to life with our Living History Characters. See website for events. Outdoor summer café.

**Location:** MAP 2:N4, OS Ref. ST499 388. 50 yds from the Market Cross, in the centre of Glastonbury. M5/J23, then A39.

**Open:** Daily (except Christmas Day), 9.30am–6pm or dusk if earlier. Jun, Jul & Aug: opens 9am. Dec, Jan & Feb: opens 10am.

**Admission:** Adult £4.50, Child (5–15 yrs) £3, Conc. £4, Family (2+2) £12.50. Groups (booked, 10+): Adult £4, Child £2.50.

⬚ ⬚ ⬚ Summer only. ⬚ ⬚ ⬚ ⬚ ⬚ ⬚ ⬚

---

## HALSWELL HOUSE

**HALSWELL PARK, GOATHURST, SOMERSET TA5 2DH**

www.halswell.co.uk

**Tel:** 0845 204 1066 **E-mail:** info@halswell.co.uk
**Owner:** Grahame Bond **Contact:** Mike Coles

Halswell is a Grade I listed William & Mary mansion house with 17 suites/ bedrooms and six principal reception rooms for exclusive use for weddings, corporate events or private parties.

Nestling at the foot of the Quantock Hills with far reaching views to the Bristol Channel and over to Wales, this beautiful house has been restored to its former glory and is resplendent with period furniture, grand paintings and original features.

**Location:** MAP 2:M4, OS Ref. ST253 337. 5m from M5/J24. 4m SW of Bridgwater.

**Open:** Grounds all year. House by appointment only except during open days.

**Admission:** No admission charges but donations to charity encouraged.

⬚ ⬚ Partial. ⬚ By arrangement. ⬚ None for coaches. ⬚ ⬚ In grounds on leads. ⬚ 17 double, all en-suite. ⬚ ⬚

---

### GLASTONBURY TOR ⬚

**Nr Glastonbury, Somerset**

**Tel:** 01985 843600 / 01934 844518

**Owner:** The National Trust **Contact:** The Regional Office

The dramatic and evocative Tor dominates the surrounding countryside and offers spectacular views over Somerset, Dorset and Wiltshire. At the summit of this very steep hill an excavation has revealed the plans of two superimposed churches of St Michael, of which only the 15th-century tower remains.

**Location:** MAP 2:N4, OS Ref. ST512 386. Signposted from Glastonbury town centre, from where seasonal park-and-ride (not NT) operates.

**Open:** All year.

**Admission:** Free.

⬚ Park & ride from town centre Apr–Sept. Also free at Rural Life Museum. Tel 01458 831197. ⬚ On leads only. ⬚

---

### GLASTONBURY TRIBUNAL ⬚

**Glastonbury High Street, Glastonbury, Somerset**

**Tel:** 01458 832954 **E-mail:** glastonbury.tic@ukonline.co.uk

**Owner:** English Heritage **Contact:** The TIC Manager

A well preserved medieval town house, reputedly once used as the courthouse of Glastonbury Abbey. Now houses Glastonbury Tourist Information Centre.

**Location:** MAP 2:N4, OS182 Ref. ST499 390. In Glastonbury High Street.

**Open:** 1 Apr–30 Sept: daily, 10am–5pm (Fri & Sat, 5.30pm). 1 Oct–20 Mar: daily, 10am–4pm (Fri & Sat, 4.30pm). Closed 25–26 Dec & 1 Jan.

**Admission:** TIC Free. Museum areas: Adult £2, Child/Conc £1.50. Senior £1.

⬚ Partial. ⬚ Charge. ⬚

---

See which properties offer **educational facilities** or **school visits** in our index on page 571

Cothay Manor & Gardens, Wellington

Andrew Lawson

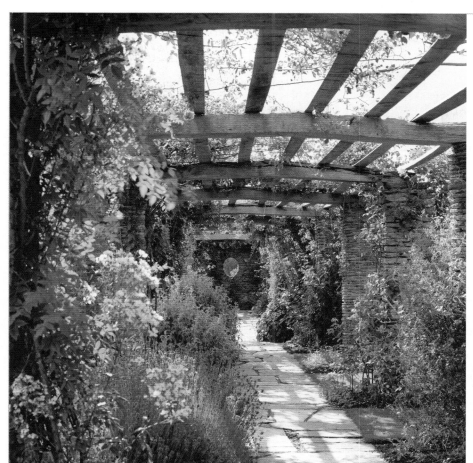

## HESTERCOMBE GARDENS
### CHEDDON FITZPAINE, TAUNTON, SOMERSET TA2 8LG

www.hestercombegardens.com

**Tel:** 01823 413923  **Fax:** 01823 413747
**E-mail:** info@hestercombegardens.com
**Owner:** Hestercombe Gardens Trust
**Contact:** The Gardens Office

Lose yourself in 40 acres of walks, streams and temples, vivid colours, formal terraces, woodlands, lakes, cascades and views that take your breath away. This is Hestercombe: a unique combination of three period gardens. The Georgian landscape garden was created in the 1750s by Copelstone Warre Bampfylde, whose vision was complemented by the addition of a Victorian terrace and shrubbery and the stunning Edwardian gardens designed by Sir Edwin Lutyens and Gertrude Jekyll. All once abandoned, now being faithfully restored to their former glory. Each garden has its own quality of tranquility, wonder and inspiration.

**Location:** MAP 2:M5, OS Ref. ST241 287. 4m NE from Taunton, 1m NW of Cheddon Fitzpaine.
**Open:** All year: daily, 10am–6pm (last admission 5pm). Groups & coach parties by arrangement.
**Admission:** Adult £6.95*, Conc. £6.50*, Student £3.50. Guided tour (20+): £8. *Prices include 2 children. Additional child £2.50.

▢ ▣ ⬛ Partial. WC. ◩ Licensed. ⑪ Licensed. ⚲ By arrangement. ⲡ Limited for coaches. ⛾ On short leads. ✲

## HOLBURNE MUSEUM OF ART
### Great Pulteney Street, Bath BA2 4DB

**Tel:** 01225 466669  **Fax:** 01225 333121
**Owner:** Trustees    **Contact:** Katie Jenkins

This jewel in Bath's crown houses the treasures collected by Sir William Holburne: superb English and continental silver, porcelain, majolica, glass and Renaissance bronzes, and paintings by Turner, Guardi and Stubbs.
**Location:** MAP 2:P2, OS Ref. ST431 545. Via A4 or A431, follow brown signs.
**Open:** Mid Jan–Dec, please telephone for details.
**Admission:** Varies with exhibitions – telephone for details.

## HOLNICOTE ESTATE ⛟
### Selworthy, Minehead, Somerset TA24 8TJ

**Tel:** 01643 862452  **Fax:** 01643 863011  **E-mail:** holnicote@nationaltrust.org.uk
**Owner:** The National Trust    **Contact:** The Estate Office

The Holnicote Estate covers 5042ha (12,500 acres) of Exmoor National Park. The Estate also covers 4 miles of coastline between Porlock Bay and Minehead. There are over 100 miles of footpaths to enjoy through the fields, woods, moors and villages.
**Location:** MAP 2:K3, OS Ref. SS920 469. Off A39 Minehead–Porlock, 3m W of Minehead. Station: Minehead 5m.
**Open:** Estate Office: All year: Mon–Fri, 8.30am–5pm.
**Admission:** Free.

▢ ⬛ ◩ (Not NT.) ⛾ ✲

## KENTSFORD
### Washford, Watchet, Somerset TA23 0JD

**Tel:** 01984 631307
**Owner:** Wyndham Estate    **Contact:** Mr R Dibble
**Location:** MAP 2:L4, OS Ref. ST058 426.
**Open:** House open only by appointment with Mr R Dibble. Gardens: 6 Mar–28 Aug: Tues & BHs.
**Admission:** House: £3, Gardens: Free.

⬛ Gardens only. ⲡ Limited. ⛾ In grounds, on leads. ✲

## KING JOHN'S HUNTING LODGE ⛟
### The Square, Axbridge, Somerset BS26 2AP

**Tel:** 01934 732012  **www.nationaltrust.org.uk**
**Owner/Contact:** The National Trust

An early Tudor merchant's house, extensively restored in 1971. Note: the property is run as a local history museum by Axbridge & District Museum Trust in co-operation with Sedgemoor District Council, County Museum's Service and Axbridge Archaeological & Local History Society.
**Location:** MAP 2:N3, OS Ref. ST431 545. In the Square, on corner of High Street, off A371.
**Open:** 1 Apr–30 Sept: Daily, 1–4pm.
**Admission:** Free. Donations welcome.

⬛ Ground floor. ⲡ ⛾ By arrangement.

Costumes from the Museum of Costume and Assembly Rooms, Bath.

### LOWER SEVERALLS

**Crewkerne, Somerset TA18 7NX**
**Tel:** 01460 73234   **E-mail:** mary@lowerseveralls.co.uk
**Owner:** Mrs Audrey Pring   **Contact:** Mary Pring
2½ acre garden, developed over the last 25 years including herb garden, mixed borders and island beds with innovative features, ie a giant living dogwood basket and a wadi.
**Location:** MAP 2:N5, OS Ref. ST457 112. 1½m NE of Crewkerne, between A30 & A356.
**Open:** Mar–Sept: Tue & Wed & Fri & Sat, 10am–5pm.
**Admission:** Adult £3.25, Child (under 16yrs) Free.

### LYTES CARY MANOR ❧

**Nr Charlton Mackrell, Somerset TA11 7HU**
**Tel:** 01458 224471 (property)   **E-mail:** lytescarymanor@nationaltrust.org.uk
**www.nationaltrust.org.uk**
**Owner:** The National Trust   **Contact:** Visitor Services Manager
The house with its 14th century chapel and 15th century Great Hall was much added to in the 16th century. In the 20th century it was rescued from dereliction by Sir Walter Jenner who refurnished the interiors in period style. At the same time the garden was laid out in a series of 'rooms' with many contrasts, topiary, mixed borders, and a herbal border based on the famous 16th century Lytes Herbal, which can be seen in the house. Several walks through the wider estate show many features typical of farmed lowland England, including ancient hedges, rare arable weeds and farmland birds. Parts of Lytes Cary Manor may be under repair.
**Location:** MAP 2:O5, OS Ref. ST529 269. 1m N of Ilchester bypass A303, signposted from Podimore roundabout at junction of A303. A37 take A372.
**Open:** 21 Mar–28 Oct: Wed & Fri–Sun, 11am–5pm. Closes dusk if earlier.
**Admission:** Adult £6, Child £3. Family £15. Garden only: Adult £4, Child £2.
⬚ Partial. Braille guide. ⬚ By arrangement. 🅿 Free. Small coaches only by arrangement. 🐕 On leads in car park & river walk only. ⬚ Tel 0870 4584000 or see website for details.

## MAUNSEL HOUSE
### NORTH NEWTON, Nr TAUNTON, SOMERSET TA7 0BU

www.maunselhouse.co.uk

**Tel:** 01278 661076   **Fax:** 01278 661074   **E-mail:** info@maunselhouse.co.uk
**Owner:** Sir Benjamin Slade   **Contact:** Alexa Plant
This imposing 13th century manor house offers the ideal location for wedding receptions, corporate events, private and garden parties, filming and family celebrations. The ancestral seat of the Slade family and home of the 7th baronet Sir Benjamin Slade, the house can boast such visitors as Geoffrey Chaucer, who wrote part of the *Canterbury Tales* whilst staying there. The beautiful grounds and spacious rooms provide both privacy and a unique atmosphere for any special event. Available for weekend/Christmas house parties, weddings, birthdays, dinner parties and conferences.
**Location:** MAP 2:M4, OS Ref. ST302 303. Bridgwater 4m, Bristol 20m, Taunton 7m, M5/J24, A38 to North Petherton. 2½m SE of A38 at North Petherton via North Newton.
**Open:** Coaches & groups welcome by appointment. Caravan rally field available.
⬚ Functions. ⬚ Partial. 🐕 In grounds, on leads. ⬚ ⬚ ⬚

### MILTON LODGE GARDENS 🏛

**Old Bristol Road, Wells, Somerset BA5 3AQ**
**Tel:** 01749 672168   **www.miltonlodgegardens.co.uk**
**Owner/Contact:** D Tudway Quilter Esq
"The great glory of the gardens of Milton Lodge are their position high up on the slopes of the Mendip Hills to the north of Wells … with broad panoramas of Wells Cathedral and the Vale of Avalon", (Lanning Roper). Charming, mature, Grade II listed terraced garden dating from 1909. Replanned 1962 with mixed shrubs, herbaceous plants, old fashioned roses and ground cover; numerous climbers; old established yew hedges. Fine trees in garden and in 7-acre arboretum across old Bristol Road.
**Location:** MAP 2:O3, OS Ref. ST549 470. ½m N of Wells from A39. N up Old Bristol Road. Free car park first gate on left.
**Open:** Garden & Arboretum: Easter–end Oct: Tues, Weds, Suns & BHs, 2–5pm. Parties & coaches by prior arrangement.
**Admission:** Adult £4, Children under 14 Free.
⬚ ⬚ ⬚ Unsuitable. ⬚ 🅿 🐕

NT Photographic Library: Rupert Truman

## MONTACUTE HOUSE ❧
### MONTACUTE, SOMERSET TA15 6XP

www.nationaltrust.org.uk

**Tel:** 01935 823289   **Fax:** 01935 826921   **E-mail:** montacute@nationaltrust.org.uk
**Owner:** The National Trust   **Contact:** The Property Manager
A glittering Elizabethan house, adorned with elegant chimneys, carved parapets and other Renaissance features, including contemporary plasterwork, chimney pieces and heraldic glass. The magnificent state rooms, including a long gallery which is the largest of its type in England, are full of fine 17th and 18th century furniture and Elizabethan and Jacobean portraits from the National Portrait Gallery.
**Location:** MAP 2:N5, OS Ref. ST499 172. In Montacute village, 4m W of Yeovil, on S side of A3088, 3m E of A303.
**Open:** House: 17 Mar–28 Oct: daily except Tue, 11am–5pm. Garden: 1 –16 Mar: 11am–4pm; 17 Mar–28 Oct: 11am–6pm, 29 Oct–29 Feb 2008: 11am–4pm.
**Admission:** House, Park & Garden: Adult £8.80, Child £4.40, Family £22. Groups (15+): Adult £8. Garden & Park only (17 Mar–29 Oct): Adult £5, Child £2.20. (1 Nov–29 Feb 2008): Adult £2.20, Child £1. Group organisers please book in writing to House Manager with a SAE.
⬚ ⬚ ⬚ Partial. Braille guide. WC. ⬚ ⬚ Licensed. Christmas lunches in Dec (must book). 🅿 🐕 In park, on leads. ⬚ ⬚

### MUCHELNEY ABBEY ⌗

**Muchelney, Langport, Somerset TA10 0DQ**
**Tel:** 01458 250664   **Fax:** 01458 253842   **E-mail:** customers@english-heritage.org.uk
**www.english-heritage.org.uk/muchelney**
**Owner:** English Heritage   **Contact:** Visitor Operations Staff
Well-preserved ruins of the cloisters, with windows carved in golden stone, and abbot's lodging of the Benedictine abbey, which survived by being used as a farmhouse after the Dissolution. Tactile displays and interactive video.
**Location:** MAP 2:N5, OS193 Ref. ST428 248. In Muchelney 2m S of Langport.
**Open:** 1 Apr–31 Oct: daily 10am–5pm (6pm in Jul & Aug, 4pm in Oct).
**Admission:** Adult £3.20, Child £1.60, Conc. £2.40. 15% discount for groups (11+).
⬚ WCs.⬚ ⬚ ⬚ Partial. 🅿 🐕 ⬚

### MUSEUM OF COSTUME ❧
### & ASSEMBLY ROOMS

*See page 246 for full page entry.*

## NUNNEY CASTLE ⚘

**Nunney, Somerset**
**Tel:** 0117 9750700   **E-mail:** customers@english-heritage.org.uk
**Owner:** English Heritage   **Contact:** Visitor Operations Staff
A small 14th century moated castle with a distinctly French style. Its unusual design consists of a central block with large towers at the angles.
**Location:** MAP 2:P3, OS183 Ref. ST737 457. In Nunney 3½m SW of Frome, 1m N of the A361.
**Open:** Any reasonable time.
**Admission:** Free.

## ORCHARD WYNDHAM

**Williton, Taunton, Somerset TA4 4HH**
**Tel:** 01984 632309   **Fax:** 01984 633526
**Owner:** Wyndham Estate   **Contact:** Wyndham Estate Office
English manor house. Family home for 700 years encapsulating continuous building and alteration from the 14th to the 20th century.
**Location:** MAP 2:L4, OS Ref. ST072 400. 1m from A39 at Williton.
**Open:** Telephone for details.
**Admission:** Telephone for details.
🚹 Obligatory & pre-booked. 🅿 Limited. No coach parking. 🐕 In grounds, on leads.

## PRIEST'S HOUSE 🌿

**Muchelney, Langport, Somerset TA10 0DQ**
**Tel:** 01458 253771 (Tenant)   www.nationaltrust.org.uk
**Owner:** The National Trust   **Contact:** The Administrator
A late medieval hall house with large gothic windows, originally the residence of priests serving the parish church across the road. Lived-in and recently repaired.
**Location:** MAP 2:N5, OS Ref. ST429 250. 1m S of Langport.
**Open:** 18 Mar–30 Sept: Sun & Mon, 2–5.30pm. Admission by guided tour. Last tour commences at 5pm.
**Admission:** Adult £3.20, Child £1.60. Not suitable for groups.
ℹ No WC. 🐕

©NTPL/ David Noton

# PRIOR PARK LANDSCAPE GARDEN 🌿
### RALPH ALLEN DRIVE, BATH BA2 5AH
www.nationaltrust.org.uk

**Tel:** 01225 833422   **E-mail:** priorpark@nationaltrust.org.uk
**Owner:** The National Trust   **Contact:** Visitor Services Manager
Beautiful and intimate 18th century landscape garden created by Bath entrepreneur Ralph Allen with advice from the poet Alexander Pope and 'Capability' Brown. Sweeping valley with magnificent views of the City of Bath, Palladian bridge and three lakes. The Wilderness Project, supported by the Heritage Lottery Fund, is the final phase of restoration of this sustainably managed garden. Access to the Bath Skyline Walk (NT) from the garden. Disabled parking only, telephone for a 'how to get there' leaflet. Prior Park College, a co-educational school, operates from the mansion (not NT).
**Location:** MAP 2:P2, OS Ref. ST760 633. Frequent bus service from City Centre. First 2, City Sightseeing Skyline open top tour bus. Pick up from railway station & Abbey. Tour bus half price to NT members.
**Open:** 3–25 Feb: Sat & Sun, 11am–dusk. 3 Mar–28 Oct: Wed–Mon, 11am–5.30pm or dusk if earlier. 30 Nov–25 Feb 2008: Sat & Sun, 11am–dusk. Last adm. 1 hr before closing. Closed 25/26 Dec & 1 Jan.
**Admission:** Adult: £4.80, Child £2.70, Family £12.20.
♿ Grounds. WC. Braille guide. Hearing Loop. 🍴 🚹 By arrangement.▣
🐕 Nov–Feb. ⊞ ▾ Tel for details (0870 458 4000) or visit website.

## ROBIN HOOD'S HUT

**Halswell, Goathurst, Somerset TA5 2EW**
**Tel:** 01628 825925   www.landmarktrust.org.uk
**Owner/Contact:** The Landmark Trust
Robin Hood's Hut is an 18th century garden building with two distinct faces. On one side it is a small rustic cottage, with thatched roof and bark clad door while on the other is an elegant pavilion complete with umbrello (or stone canopy). In the 1740s, Charles Kemeys Tynte began to transform the landscape around Halswell House into one of the finest Georgian gardens in the south west. He built several follies including in 1767 Robin Hood's Hut. It is cared for by The Landmark Trust, a building preservation charity who let it for holidays. Full details of Robin Hood's Hut and 184 other historic and architecturally important buildings are featured in the Landmark Trust Handbook (price £11.50 refundable against a booking).
**Location:** MAP 2:M4, OS Ref. ST255 333.
**Open:** Available for holidays for up to 2 people throughout the year. Other visits by appointment. Please contact the Landmark Trust for details.
**Admission:** Free.
▣ ⊞

## THE ROMAN BATHS & PUMP ROOM
*See page 247 for full page entry*

## STEMBRIDGE TOWER MILL 🌿

**High Ham, Somerset TA10 9DJ**
**Tel:** 01935 823289   www.nationaltrust.org.uk
**Owner:** The National Trust   **Contact:** The Administrator
The last thatched windmill in England, dating from 1822 and in use until 1910.
**Location:** MAP 2:N4, OS Ref. ST432 305. 2m N of Langport, ½m E of High Ham.
**Open:** BH Mons: 9 Apr, 28 May, 27 Aug, 12 noon–5pm.
**Admission:** Adult £2.70, Child £1.60. Arrangements may be made for school groups on 01935 827767.
ℹ No WC. 🅿 Limited. ▣ 🐕

## STOKE-SUB-HAMDON PRIORY 🌿

**North Street, Stoke-sub-Hamdon, Somerset TA4 6QP**
**Tel:** 01935 823289   www.nationaltrust.org.uk
**Owner/Contact:** The National Trust
A complex of buildings, begun in the 14th century for the priests of the chantry of St Nicholas, which is now destroyed. The Great Hall is open to visitors.
**Location:** MAP 2:N4, OS Ref. ST473 174. ½m S of A303. 2m W of Montacute between Yeovil and Ilminster.
**Open:** 17 Mar–28 Oct: daily, 10am–6pm or dusk if earlier. Not suitable for coaches.
**Admission:** Free.
ℹ No WC. 🅿 Limited. 🐕

## TINTINHULL GARDEN 🌿

**Farm Street, Tintinhull, Somerset BA22 9PZ**
**Tel:** 01935 823289   **E-mail:** tintinhull@nationaltrust.org.uk
www.nationaltrust.org.uk
**Owner:** The National Trust   **Contact:** The Head Gardener
A delightful formal garden, created in the 20th century around a 17th century manor house. Small pools, varied borders and secluded lawns are neatly enclosed within walls and clipped hedges and there is also an attractive kitchen garden.
**Location:** MAP 2:O5, OS Ref. ST503 198. 5m NW of Yeovil, ½m S of A303, on E outskirts of Tintinhull.
**Open:** 17 Mar–28 Oct: Wed–Sun (open BH Mon), 11am–5pm (Tearoom 11am–4.30pm).
***Admission:** Adult £5.30, Child £2.70, Family £13.30. No reduction for groups. *includes a voluntary donation but visitors can choose to pay the standard prices displayed at the property and on the website.
♿ Grounds. Braille guide. ▣ 🚹 By arrangement. 🅿 Limited. 🐕

## TREASURER'S HOUSE 🌿

**Martock, Somerset TA12 6JL**
**Tel:** 01935 825015   www.nationaltrust.org.uk
**Owner/Contact:** The National Trust
A small medieval house, recently refurbished by The Trust. The two-storey hall was completed in 1293 and the solar block is even earlier.
**Location:** MAP 2:N5, OS Ref. ST462 191. 1m NW of A303 between Ilminster and Ilchester.
**Open:** 18 Mar–30 Sept: Sun–Tue, 2–5pm. Only medieval hall, wall paintings and kitchen are shown.
**Admission:** Adult £3.20, Child £1.60. Not suitable for groups.
ℹ No WC. 🅿 Limited for cars. None for coaches & trailer caravans.

### TYNTESFIELD

**Wraxall, North Somerset  BS48 1NT**
**Tel:** 01275 461900  **E-mail:** tyntesfield@nationaltrust.org.uk
**Owner/Contact:** The National Trust
Situated on a ridge overlooking the beautiful Land Yeo Valley, Tyntesfield was inspired and remodelled by John Norton in c1864 for William Gibbs, a successful merchant. The mansion is an extraordinary Gothic Revival extravaganza and survives intact with an unrivalled collection of Victorian decorative arts, an insight into life below stairs and a sumptuously decorated private chapel. Its surrounding 200ha (500 acres) of land includes formal gardens and a wonderful walled kitchen garden. Tyntesfield was saved for the nation by the National Trust in June 2002 with funding from the National Heritage Memorial Fund, other heritage partners and a £3 million public appeal. The property is now one of the most exciting projects of the National Trust due to its innovative approach to giving access to the ongoing conservation. Visitors should expect to see building and conservation work in progress and access to parts of the estate will be restricted for health and safety reasons.
**Location:** MAP 2:N2, OS Ref. ST506 715. Off B3128.
**Open:** House, Chapel and Gardens: 17 Mar–4 Nov, Sat–Wed. House: 11am–5pm (last admission at 4pm by timed ticket). Chapel: 11am–5pm. Garden/Shop/Kiosk: 10.30am–5.30pm. Open Good Fri.
**\*Admission:** House, Chapel & Gardens: Adult £9.90, Child £5, Family £24.80. Gardens & Chapel only: Adult £5, Child £2.50, Family £12.50. Groups by appointment. *includes a voluntary donation but visitors can choose to pay the standard prices displayed at the property and on the website.

⬜ 🐾 ♿ Partial. 🅿️ 🅵 By arrangement. 🐾 🅿 🅺 ♿

### WELLS CATHEDRAL

**Cathedral Green, Wells, Somerset  BA5 2UE**
**Tel:** 01749 674483  **Fax:** 01749 832210
**Owner:** The Chapter of Wells  **Contact:** Mr John Roberts
Fine medieval Cathedral. The West Front with its splendid array of statuary, the Quire with colourful embroidery and stained glass, Chapter House and 1392 astronomical clock should not be missed.
**Location:** MAP 2:O3, OS Ref. ST552 458. In Wells, 20m S from both Bath & Bristol.
**Open:** Apr–Sept: 7am–7pm; Oct–Mar: 7am–6pm.
**Admission:** Suggested donation: Adult £5, Child/Student £2, OAP £3.50. Photo permit £2.

### THE WILLIAM HERSCHEL MUSEUM

**19 New King Street, Bath  BA1 2BL**
**Tel/Fax:** 01225 446865  **E-mail:** admin@herschelbpt.fsnet.co.uk
**Owner:** The Herschel House Trust  **Contact:** The Curator
Georgian town-house. Home to astronomer William Herschel and site of discovery of planet Uranus in 1781. Georgian garden. Audio tour. Star Vault Astronomy Auditorium.
**Location:** MAP 2:P2, OS Ref. ST750 648. Bath, Somerset.
**Open:** 1 Feb–15 Dec: daily except Weds, 1–5pm, Sats/Suns 11am–5pm. School visits and group bookings by arrangement.
**Admission:** Adult £3.50, Child £2, Full Time Student £2.50, OAP £3, Family £8.

The Roman Baths, Bath

# BOWOOD HOUSE & GARDENS

www.bowood.org

Bowood is the family home of the Marquis and Marchioness of Lansdowne. Begun c1720 for the Bridgeman family, the house was purchased by the 2nd Earl of Shelburne in 1754 and completed soon afterwards. Part of the house was demolished in 1955, leaving a perfectly proportioned Georgian home, over half of which is open to visitors. Robert Adam's magnificent Diocletian wing contains a splendid library, the laboratory where Joseph Priestley discovered oxygen gas in 1774, the orangery, now a picture gallery, the Chapel and a sculpture gallery in which some of the famous Lansdowne Marbles are displayed.

Among the family treasures shown in the numerous exhibition rooms are Georgian costumes, including Lord Byron's Albanian dress; Victoriana; Indiana (the 5th Marquess was Viceroy 1888–94); and superb collections of watercolours, miniatures and jewellery.

The House is set in one of the most beautiful parks in England. Over 2,000 acres of gardens and grounds were landscaped by 'Capability' Brown between 1762 and 1768, and are embellished with a Doric temple, a cascade, a pinetum and an arboretum. The Rhododendron Gardens are open for six weeks from late April to early June. All the walks have seats.

ℹ️ Receptions, film location, 2,000 acre park, 40 acre lake, 18-hole golf course and Country Club, open to all players holding a current handicap.

🛍️
♿ Visitors may alight at the House before parking. WCs.

🍴 Self-service snacks, teas etc.

🍽️ The Restaurant (waitress service, capacity 85). Groups that require lunch or tea should book in advance.

🧍 On request, groups can be given introductory talk, or for an extra charge, a guided tour. Tour time 1¼ hrs. Guide sheets in French, German, Dutch, Spanish & Japanese.

🅿️ 1,000 cars, unlimited for coaches, 400 yds from house. Allow 2–3 hrs to visit house, gardens and grounds.

📷 Special guide books. Picnic areas. Adventure playground.

🐕 Working assistance dogs only.

## Owner
The Marquis of Lansdowne

## Contact
The Administrator
Bowood House and Gardens
Calne
Wiltshire  SN11 0LZ

**Tel:** 01249 812102
**Fax:** 01249 821757
**E-mail:**
houseandgardens@
bowood.org

## Location
**MAP 3:A2**
**OS Ref. ST974 700**

From London M4/J17, off the A4 in Derry Hill village, midway between Calne and Chippenham. Swindon 17m, Bristol 26m, Bath 16m.

**Bus:** to the gate, 1½ m through park to House.

**Rail:** Chippenham Station 5m.

**Taxi:** AA Taxis, Chippenham 657777.

## Opening Times
House & Garden
31 March–31 October.
Daily, 11am–6pm.
Last admission 5pm (or 1hr earlier after the autumn clock change).

**Rhododendron Walks**
Off the A342 Chippenham to Devizes road, midway between Derry Hill and Sandy Lane.

Open daily for 6 weeks during the flowering season, usually from late April to early June, 11am–6pm.

We recommend visitors telephone or visit the website to check the progress of the flowering season.

## Admission
**House & Garden**

| | |
|---|---|
| Adult | £7.70 |
| Child (5–15yrs) | £5.20 |
| Child (2–4yrs) | £4.00 |
| Senior Citizen | £6.70 |
| Family (2+2) | £23.20 |

Groups (20+)

| | |
|---|---|
| Adult | £6.70 |
| Child (5–15yrs) | £4.20 |
| Child (2–4yrs) | £3.00 |
| Senior Citizen | £5.70 |

**Rhododendron Walks**

| | |
|---|---|
| Adult | £4.95 |
| Senior Citizen | £4.45 |

Season Tickets available, ask for details.

The charge for Rhododendron Walks is reduced by £1pp if combined on the same day with a visit to Bowood House & Gardens.

### ■ Owner
J Methuen-Campbell Esq

### ■ Contact
Corsham Court
Corsham
Wiltshire
SN13 0BZ

**Tel/Fax:** 01249 701610

### ■ Location
**MAP 3:A2**
**OS Ref. ST874 706**

Corsham Court is signposted from the A4, approx. 4m W of Chippenham. From Edinburgh, A1, M62, M6, M5, M4, 8 hrs. From London, M4, 2¼ hrs. From Chester, M6, M5, M4, 4 hrs.

**Motorway:** M4/J17 9m.

**Rail:** Chippenham Station 6m.

**Taxi:** 01249 715959.

### ■ Opening Times
**Summer**
20 March–30 September
Daily except Mons & Fris but including BH Mons
2–5.30pm
Last admission 5pm.

**Winter**
1 October–19 March
Weekends only
2–4.30pm
Last admission 4pm.

Closed December.

NB: Open throughout the year by appointment only for groups of 15+.

For further details and special viewings of the the collection, see our website.

### ■ Admission
**House & Garden**
| | |
|---|---|
| Adult | £6.50 |
| Child (5–15yrs) | £3.00 |
| OAP | £5.00 |

**Groups**
(includes 1 hr guided tour)
| | |
|---|---|
| Adult | £5.00 |

**Garden only**
| | |
|---|---|
| Adult | £2.50 |
| Child (5–15yrs) | £1.50 |
| OAP | £2.00 |

# CORSHAM COURT 🏛

www.corsham-court.co.uk

Corsham Court is an Elizabethan house of 1582 and was bought by Paul Methuen in the mid-18th century, to house a collection of 16th and 17th century Italian and Flemish master paintings and statuary. In the middle of the 19th century, the house was enlarged to receive a second collection, purchased in Florence, principally of fashionable Italian masters and stone-inlaid furniture.

Paul Methuen (1723–95) was a great-grandson of Paul Methuen of Bradford-on-Avon and cousin of John Methuen, ambassador and negotiator of the Methuen Treaty of 1703 with Portugal which permitted export of British woollens to Portugal and allowed a preferential 33⅓ percent duty discount on Portuguese wines, bringing about a major change in British drinking habits.

The architects involved in the alterations to the house and park were Lancelot 'Capability' Brown in the 1760s, John Nash in 1800 and Thomas Bellamy in 1845–9. Brown set the style by retaining the Elizabethan Stables and Riding School, but rebuilding the Gateway, retaining the gabled Elizabethan stone front and doubling the gabled wings at either end and inside, by designing the East Wing as Stateroom Picture Galleries. Nash's work has now largely disappeared, but Bellamy's stands fast, notably in the Hall and Staircase.

The State Rooms, including the Music Room and Dining Room, provide the setting for the outstanding collection of over 150 paintings, statuary, bronzes and furniture. The collection includes work by such names as Chippendale, the Adam brothers, Van Dyck, Reni, Rosa, Rubens, Lippi, Reynolds, Romney and a pianoforte by Clementi.

### Gardens
'Capability' Brown planned to include a lake, avenues and specimen trees such as the Oriental Plane now with a 200-yard perimeter. The gardens, designed not only by Brown but also by Repton, contain a ha-ha, herbaceous borders, secluded gardens, lawns, a rose garden, a lily pool, a stone bath house and the Bradford Porch.

| | |
|---|---|
| ℹ | Souvenir desk. No umbrellas, no photography. |
| ♿ | Visitors may alight at the entrance to the property, before parking in the allocated areas. |
| 🚶 | For up to 55. If requested the owner may meet the group. Tour time 1hr. |
| P | 120 yards from the house. Coaches may park in Church Square. Coach parties must book in advance. No camper vans, no caravans. |
| 🖼 | Available: rate negotiable. A guide will be provided. |
| 🐕 | Must be kept on leads in the garden. |

# LONGLEAT

www.longleat.co.uk

Set within 900 acres of 'Capability' Brown landscaped grounds, Longleat House is widely regarded as one of the best examples of high Elizabethan architecture in Britain and one of the most beautiful stately homes open to the public.

Visited by Elizabeth I in 1574, Longleat House was built by Sir John Thynne from 1568 and is the current home of the 7th Marquess of Bath, Alexander Thynn. Many treasures are included within. The fine collection of paintings ranges from English portraits dating from the 16th century to the present day, to Dutch landscapes and Italian Old Masters.

Inspired by various Italian palace interiors, including the Ducal Palace in Venice, the ceilings are renowned for their ornate paintings and abundance of gilt made by the firm of John Dibblee Crace in the 1870s and 1880s. The furniture collection includes English pieces from as early as the 16th century, 17th century chairs from the Coromandel coast of India, fine French furniture of the 17th and 18th centuries and a collection of major Italian pieces very unusual for an English country house.

The Murals in the private apartments in the West Wing have been painted by the present Marquess and are a fascinating and unique addition to the House. Incorporating a mixture of oil paints and sawdust, these private works of art offer a unique insight into Lord Bath's personality and beliefs. Mural Tours can be booked at the Front Desk of Longleat House on the day of your visit. They are subject to availability. Groups can enjoy a private tour of Longleat House or Gardens with a dedicated tour guide and a talk tailor-made to their interests, before enjoying a gourmet meal courtesy of the Longleat Banqueting Team.

Apart from the ancestral home, Longleat has a wonderland of attractions to suit all ages. Discover some of the world's most magnificent animals including lions, tigers and giraffe in the UK's original Safari Park; get lost in the Longleat Hedge Maze; voyage on the Safari Boats; journey on the Longleat Railway and much, much more!

## ■ Owner
Marquess of Bath

## ■ Contact
Longleat
Warminster
Wiltshire  BA12 7NW
**Tel:** 01985 844400
**Fax:** 01985 844885
**E-mail:** enquiries@
longleat.co.uk
www.longleat.co.uk

## ■ Location
**MAP 2:P4**
**OS Ref. ST809 430**
Just off the A36 between Bath–Salisbury (A362 Warminster–Frome). 2hrs from London following M3, A303, A36, A362 or M4/J18, A46, A36.
**Rail:** Warminster Station (5m) on the Cardiff/ Portsmouth line. Westbury Station (12m) on the Paddington/ Penzance line. Taxi rank at Warminster & Westbury Stations.
**Air:** Bristol 30m.

## ■ Opening Times
**House**
Open all year, daily (except Christmas Day). Easter–Sept: 10am–5.30pm. Guided tours available 10–11am. Rest of year: 11am–3pm. Guided tours only.
Guided tours may be subject to change – please tel. for up-to-date info.

**Safari Park**
17–25 Feb & 31 March– 4 Nov, daily. 3–25 March, Sats & Suns. 10am–4pm (5pm on weekends, BHs & State school holidays).

**Other attractions**
17–25 Feb & 31 March– 4 Nov, daily. 3–25 March, Sats & Suns. 11am–5.30pm.
Note: last admission times may be earlier in Feb, March, Oct & Nov.

## ■ Admission
**House & Grounds**
| | |
|---|---|
| Adult | £10.00 |
| Child (3–14yrs) | £6.00 |
| Senior (60yrs+) | £6.00 |

**Longleat Passport**
(see below)
| | |
|---|---|
| Adult | £20.00 |
| Child (3–14yrs) | £16.00 |
| Senior (60yrs+) | £16.00 |

**Groups (12+)**
| | |
|---|---|
| Adult | £14.00 |
| Child (3–14yrs) | £11.20 |
| Senior (60yrs+) | £11.20 |

*Longleat Passport includes:*
*Longleat House, Safari Park, Safari Boats, Longleat Hedge Maze, Pets Corner, Adventure Castle (including Blue Peter Maze)\*, Longleat Railway, Motion Simulator, Butterfly Garden, Postman Pat Village\*, Old Joe's Mine, Grounds & Gardens.*
*\*under 14yrs only*

| | |
|---|---|
| **i** | Rooms in Longleat House can be hired for conferences, gala dinners and product launches. Extensive parkland for company fun days, car launches, ride 'n' drive events, concerts, equestrian events, caravan rallies & fishing. Film location. |
| ⬛ | Wessex Pavilion (200 capacity). |
| ♿ | |
| ☕ | Cellar Café (capacity 80), licensed. Groups must book. From 3 course meals to cream teas, sandwiches & snacks. Traditional Wiltshire Fare. Not open all year. |

| | |
|---|---|
| 🧍 | Individuals & Groups (max 20; 15 for Murals). Booking essential. |
| **P** | Ample. |
| ⬛ | Welcome with 1 teacher free entry per 8 children. GNVQ talks and packs available on request. Booking essential. Education sheets. |
| 🐕 | In grounds, on leads. |
| 🔔 | Orangery. |
| ❄ | |
| 😊 | |

## Conference/Function

| ROOM | SIZE | MAX CAPACITY |
|---|---|---|
| Great Hall | 8 x 13m | 120 |
| Banqueting Suite | 2 x (7 x 10m) | 50 |
| Green Library | 7 x 13m | 70 |
| Wessex Pavilion | 13 x 12m | 200 |

©NTPL / Nick Meers

■ **Owner**

The National Trust

■ **Contact**

The Estate Office
Stourton
Nr Warminster
BA12 6QD

**Tel:** 01747 841152
**Fax:** 01747 842005
**E-mail:** stourhead@
nationaltrust.org.uk

■ **Location**
**MAP 2:P4**
**OS Ref. ST780 340**

At Stourton off the
B3092, 3m NW of A303
(Mere), 8m S of A361
(Frome).

**Rail:** Gillingham 6½m;
Bruton 7m.

**Bus:** South West Coaches
80 Frome to Stourhead
on Sat; First 58/0A.

■ **Opening Times**
**House**
17 Mar–28 Oct: Fri–Tue,
11.30am–4.30pm.

**Garden**
All year: daily,
9am–7pm or dusk if
earlier.

**King Alfred's Tower**
17 Mar–28 Oct: daily,
11.30am–4.30pm.
Last admission: 4pm.

**Restaurant**
All year, daily
(closed 25 December),
Mar & Oct: 10am–5pm;
Apr–Sept: 10am–5.30pm;
Nov–Feb: 10.30am–4pm.

**Shop & Plant Centre**
All year, daily,
(closed 25 December)
Mar & Oct: 10am–5pm;
Apr–Sept: 10am–6pm;
Nov–Feb: 10.30am–4pm.

■ **Admission**
**House & Garden**
Adult            £11.00
Child            £5.50
Family           £26.20
Groups (15+)     £10.50

**House OR Garden**
Adult            £6.60
Child            £3.60
Family           £15.80
Groups (15+)     £5.70

**King Alfred's Tower**
Adult            £2.40
Child            £1.30
Family           £5.70
Groups (15+)     £2.10

NB. Groups must book.

# STOURHEAD 🌿

www.nationaltrust.org.uk

Designed by Henry Hoare II and laid out between 1741 and 1780, Stourhead is an outstanding example of an English landscape garden. Follow the path around the lake to take in classical temples, the grotto and a series of unfolding vistas. The magnificent mature woodland contains a collection of exotic trees. The house, begun in 1721, contains furniture by the younger Chipppendale and many fine paintings. Alfred's Tower, an intriguing rectangular folly, is almost 50 metres high and affords breathtaking views over three counties.

Whitesheet Down is a nationally important archaeological site, with evidence of settlement from over 6,000 years ago, whilst also being a beautiful place for walking.

Also on the Estate: The Spread Eagle Inn, First View Art Gallery and Stourhead Farm Shop (all non-NT). New in 2007: View the beautifully restored Pope's Cabinet back on display in the house and see work in progress on the Gothic Cottage.

©NTPL / Nick Meers

 Wheelchair accessible. Designated parking. Transfer available in main season to house & garden entrances. Powered mobility vehicles, recommended route map available. WCs. Sensory trail.

Refreshment kiosk in Spread Eagle Courtyard during summer.

Licensed.

Group tours, by arrangement.

 1 Nov–18 Mar only; on short fixed leads. Not in the House or Alfred's Tower.

# WILTON HOUSE 🏛

www.wiltonhouse.com

Wilton House has been the ancestral home of the Earl of Pembroke and his family for 460 years. In 1544 Henry VIII gave the Abbey and lands of Wilton to Sir William Herbert who had married Anne Parr, sister of Katherine, sixth wife of King Henry.

The Clock Tower, in the centre of the east front, is reminiscent of this part of the Tudor building which survived a fire in 1647. Inigo Jones and John Webb were responsible for the rebuilding of the house in the Palladian style, whilst further alterations were made by James Wyatt from 1801.

The chief architectural features are the magnificent 17th century state apartments (including the famous Single and Double Cube rooms) and the 19th century cloisters.

The house contains one of the finest art collections in Europe, with over 230 original paintings on display, including works by Van Dyck, Rubens, Joshua Reynolds and Brueghel. Also on show are Greek and Italian statuary, a lock of Queen Elizabeth I's hair, Napoleon's despatch case, and Florence Nightingale's sash.

The Old Riding School houses a dynamic introductory film (narrated by Anna Massey), the reconstructed Tudor kitchen and the Estate's Victorian laundry. The house is set in magnificent landscaped parkland, bordered by the River Nadder which is the setting for the majestic Palladian Bridge. The 17th Earl of Pembroke was a keen gardener who created four new gardens after succeeding to the title in 1969 including the North Forecourt Garden, Old English Rose Garden, Water and Cloister Gardens.

| ℹ️ | Film location, fashion shows, product launches, equestrian events, garden parties, antiques fairs, concerts, vehicle rallies. No photography in house. French, German, Spanish, Italian, Japanese and Dutch information. |
| --- | --- |
| 🛍 | |
| 🌸 | |
| 🍽 | Exclusive banquets. |
| ♿ | Visitors may alight at the entrance. WCs. |
| 🍴 | Licensed. |
| 🚶 | By arrangement. £6. |
| 🅿️ | 200 cars and 12 coaches. Free coach parking. Group rates (min 15), meal vouchers, drivers' lounge. |
| 📖 | Teachers' handbook for National Curriculum. EFL students welcome. Free preparatory visit for group leaders. |
| 🐕 | Guide dogs only. |
| 🔔 | |

## ■ Owner

The Earl of Pembroke

## ■ Contact

The Estate Office
Wilton House
Wilton
Salisbury SP2 0BJ

**Tel:** 01722 746714
**Fax:** 01722 744447
**E-mail:** tourism@ wiltonhouse.com

## ■ Location

**MAP 3:B4**
**OS Ref. SU099 311**

3m W of Salisbury along the A36.

**Rail:** Salisbury Station 3m.

**Bus:** Every 10 mins from Salisbury, Mon–Sat.

**Taxi:** Sarum Taxi 01722 334477.

## ■ Opening Times
**Summer**

**House**
1–15 April
5 May– 31 August

**Gardens, Old Riding School, Exhibition**
1 April–30 September

Note: House, Old Riding School and Exhibitions closed on Saturdays except at BH weekends.

**Winter**
Closed except for private groups by prior arrangement.

## ■ Admission
**Summer**
**House, Grounds, ORS and Exhibitions**

| | |
| --- | --- |
| Adult | £12.00 |
| Child (5–15) | £6.50 |
| Concession | £9.75 |
| Family | £29.50 |
| Groups (15+) | |
| Adult | £10.00 |
| Child | £5.00 |
| Concession | £8.00 |
| Guided Tour | |
| Adult | £6.00 |
| Schoolchildren | £4.50 |
| **Grounds** | |
| Adult | £5.00 |
| Child (5–15) | £3.50 |
| Family | £15.00 |

**Membership**
From £20.00

## ■ Special Events

**March 2–4**
30th Annual Antiques Fair

**July 14**
BSO Fireworks Concert

## Conference/Function

| ROOM | SIZE | MAX CAPACITY |
| --- | --- | --- |
| Double cube | 60' x 30' | 150 |
| Exhibition Centre | 50' x 40' | 140 |
| Film Theatre | 34" x 20" | 67 |

# AVEBURY MANOR & GARDEN, AVEBURY STONE CIRCLE ❀ ⌗
## & ALEXANDER KEILLER MUSEUM
### AVEBURY, Nr MARLBOROUGH, WILTSHIRE SN8 1RF

**Tel:** 01672 539250 **E-mail:** avebury@nationaltrust.org.uk

**Owner:** The National Trust **Contact:** The Visitor Services Manager

**Avebury Manor & Garden:** A much-altered house of monastic origin, the present buildings date from the early 16th century, with notable Queen Anne alterations and Edwardian renovation by Col Jenner. The garden comprises tranquil 'rooms', featuring topiary and a succession of seasonal colour and contrast. The Manor House is occupied and furnished by private tenants, who open a part of it to visitors. Due to restricted space, guided tours are in operation. Tours run every 40 mins from 2pm, last tour 4.40pm. Following prolonged wet weather it may be necessary to close the house and garden.

**Avebury Stone Circle (above left):** One of Britain's finest, most impressive circles stands proud amidst the rolling Wiltshire landscape, steeped in 6,000 years of history.

**Alexander Keiller Museum Barn & Galleries:** The investigation of Avebury Stone Circle was largely the work of archaeologist and 'marmalade' millionaire Alexander Keiller in the 1930s. He put together one of the most important prehistoric archeological collections, which can be seen in the Stables Gallery. The 'Story of the Stones', the people who strove to reveal the true significance of Avebury's Stone Circle and the development of the Avebury landscape, are depicted through interactive displays in the spectacular 17th century thatched threshing barn.

**Location:** MAP 3:B2, OS Ref. SU101 701 (Avebury Manor). OS Ref. SU102 699 (Stone Circle). OS Ref. SU100 699 (Alexander Keiller Museum). 7m W of Marlborough, 1m N of the A4 on A4361 & B4003.

**Open: Avebury Manor & Stone Circle:** Any reasonable time. Usual facilities may not be available around summer solstice 20–22 Jun. **Alexander Keiller Museum Barn & Galleries** (above right): 1 Apr–31 Oct, daily, 10am–6pm; 1 Nov–20 Mar 2008; daily 10am–4pm.Closed 24–26 Dec. Barn Gallery may close in very cold temperatures.

**Admission: Avebury Manor:** House & Garden: Adult £4, Child £2. Garden only: Adult £3, Child £1.50. Stone Circle: Free. **Alexander Keiller Museum Barn & Galleries:** Adult £4.20, Child £2.10, Family (2+3) £10.50, Family (1+3) £7.50. Groups (15+): Adult £3.60, Child £1.80. Discount when arriving by public transport or cycle. EH members free to Museum Galleries.

▣ Keiller Museum & Shop. 🔊 Avebury Manor: ground floor with assistance & grounds; Avebury: ground floor fully accessible. WCs. Braille guide. ▣ Avebury, licensed. 🅿 £5 (pay & display) redeemable against Museum entry. ▣ 🐾 No dogs in house, guide dogs only in garden (Avebury Manor). On leads in Stone Circle. ❈ Stone Circle & Avebury Manor.

---

## BOWOOD HOUSE & GARDENS 🏛   *See page 257 for full page entry.*

---

## BRADFORD-ON-AVON TITHE BARN ⌗

**Bradford-on-Avon, Wiltshire**

**Tel:** 0117 975 0700   www.english-heritage.org.uk/visits

**Owner:** English Heritage   **Contact:** South West Regional Office

A magnificent medieval stone-built barn with a slate roof and wooden beamed interior.

**Location:** MAP 2:P2, OS Ref. ST824 604. ¼m S of town centre, off B3109.

**Open:** Daily, 10.30am–4pm. Closed 25 Dec.

**Admission:** Free.

🔊 🅿 Charged. ❈ ❈

---

## BROADLEAS GARDENS

**Devizes, Wiltshire SN10 5JQ**

**Tel:** 01380 722035

**Owner:** Broadleas Gardens Charitable Trust   **Contact:** Lady Anne Cowdray

10 acres full of interest, notably The Dell, where the sheltered site allows plantings of magnolias, camellias, rhododendrons and azaleas.

**Location:** MAP 3:A3, OS Ref. SU001 601. Signposted SW from town centre at S end of housing estate, (coaches must use this entrance) or 1m S of Devizes on W side of A360.

**Open:** Apr–Oct: Sun, Weds & Thurs, 2–6pm or by arrangement for groups.

**Admission:** Adult £5, Child (under 10yrs) £1.50, Groups (10+) £4.50.

---

## CORSHAM COURT 🏛   *See page 258 for full page entry.*

---

## GREAT CHALFIELD MANOR & GARDENS ❀

**Nr Melksham, Wiltshire SN12 8NH**

**Tel:** 01225 782239   www.nationaltrust.org.uk

**Owner:** The National Trust   **Contact:** The Tenant

Charming 15th century manor with Arts and Crafts gardens c1910. The manor sits between an upper moat, gatehouse and earlier parish church. Beautiful oriel windows and rooftop soldiers (c1480) adorn the house restored between 1905 and 1911 by Major R Fuller whose family live here and manage the property on behalf of the National Trust. Alfred Parsons designed the gardens, with walls, paths, terraces, gazebo and lily pond. There are large borders, lawn and roses surrounding a well. Grass paths offer romantic views across the spring fed fishpond which lies above the brook.

**Location:** MAP 3:A2, OS Ref. ST860 631. 3m SW of Melksham off B3107 via Broughton Gifford Common, sign for Atworth. Rail: Bradford-on-Avon 3m, Chippenham 10m.

**Open:** Apr–Oct: Tue–Thur, admission by guided tour only at 11.30am, 12.15, 2.15, 3 & 3.45pm, Sun 2–5pm only. The tours take 45 mins and numbers are limited to 25. Visitors arriving during a tour can visit the adjoining parish church and garden first. Note: Group visits are welcome on Fri & Sat (not BHs) by written arrangement with the tenant Mrs Robert Floyd, charge applies. Organisers of coach parties should allow 2 hrs because of limit on numbers in the house.

**Admission:** Adult £6, Child £3, Family (2+2) £15.30. Groups £5.40, Child £2.70. Garden only: Adult £4, Child £2.

🔊 Ground floor with assistance. Limited access to Garden. WC. 🎦 Obligatory. 🅿 Limited. ❈

---

© Skyscan. Taken from the book 'Historic Family Homes & Gardens from the Air'

## HAMPTWORTH LODGE 🏛

### HAMPTWORTH, LANDFORD, SALISBURY, WILTSHIRE SP5 2EA

www.hamptworthestate.co.uk

**Tel:** 01794 390700 **Fax:** 01794 390644 **E-mail:** nda@hamptworthestate.co.uk

**Contact:** Mr N D Anderson

Jacobean style manor house standing in mature deciduous woodland within the northern perimeter of the New Forest National Park. Grade II* with period furniture including clocks. The Great Hall has an unusual roof truss construction. There is a collection of prentice pieces and the Moffatt collection of contemporary copies. One room has late 17th century patterned wall hangings.

**Location:** MAP 3:C5, OS Ref. SU227 195. 10m SE of Salisbury on road linking Downton on A338. (Salisbury to Ringwood road) to Landford on A36 (Salisbury to Southampton road).

**Open:** House and Garden: 19 Mar–23 May, Mons (closed 9 April & 7 May), Tues & Weds. Private groups and coaches by prior appointment 1 Apr–31 Oct.

**Admission:** Adult £5, Child (under 11yrs) Free. Gardens £1.

♿ Ground floor & grounds. 📷 Obligatory.

## THE KING'S HOUSE

### Salisbury & South Wiltshire Museum, 65 The Close, Salisbury, Wiltshire SP1 2EN

**Tel:** 01722 332151 **Fax:** 01722 325611 **E-mail:** museum@salisburymuseum.org.uk

www.salisburymuseum.org.uk

**Owner:** Occupied by Salisbury & South Wiltshire Museum Trust

**Contact:** P R Saunders

Magnificent Grade 1 listed building, in the shadow of Salisbury Cathedral's glorious spire, which houses a museum with designated status for its archaeological collections. The museum also houses fine, Costume, Ceramics and local history galleries. Our fine art includes JMW Turner paintings. Also temporary exhibitions are held throughout the year.

**Location:** MAP 3:B4, OS Ref. SU141 295. In Salisbury Cathedral Close, W side, facing Cathedral.

**Open:** All year: Mon–Sat: 10am–5pm. Suns in Jul & Aug, 2–5pm.

**Admission:** Adult £5, Child £2, Conc. £3.50. Groups £3.50. Family (2+3) £11.

📷 ♿ Ground floor only. 📹 ❋

Larmer Tree Gardens, Salisbury

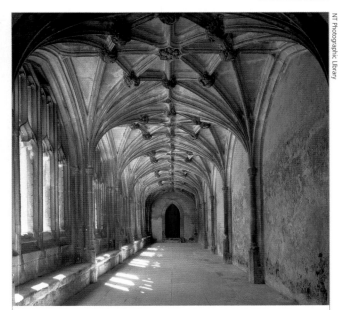

NT Photographic Library

## LACOCK ABBEY, FOX TALBOT MUSEUM & VILLAGE 🌿

### LACOCK, CHIPPENHAM, WILTSHIRE SN15 2LG

www.nationaltrust.org.uk

**Tel:** 01249 730459 (Visitor Reception) **Fax:** 01249 730501 (Estate Office)

**Owner:** The National Trust **Contact:** The Property Manager

Founded in 1232 and converted into a country house c1540, the fine medieval cloisters, sacristy, chapter house and monastic rooms of the abbey have survived largely intact. The handsome stable courtyard has half-timbered gables, a clockhouse, brewery and bakehouse. Victorian rose garden and a woodland garden boasting a fine display of spring flowers and magnificent trees. The Fox Talbot Museum commemorates William Fox Talbot, a previous resident of the Abbey and inventor of the modern photographic negative. The village has many limewashed half-timbered and stone houses, featured in the TV and film productions of *Pride & Prejudice*, *Moll Flanders*, *Emma* and the recent *Harry Potter* films.

**Location:** MAP 3:A2, OS Ref. ST919 684. In the village of Lacock, 3m N of Melksham, 3m S of Chippenham just E of A350.

**Open:** Museum, Cloisters & Garden: 24 Feb–28 Oct: daily, 11am–5.30pm (closed Good Fri). Only Museum open winter weekends (closed 22–30 Dec), 11am–4pm. Abbey: 24 Mar–28 Oct: Wed–Mon, 1–5.30pm (closed Tues & Good Fri).

**Admission: Abbey, Museum, Cloisters & Grounds:** Adult £8.30, Child £4.10, Family (2+2) £21.20. Groups: Adult £7.40, Child £3.70. **Museum, Cloisters & Grounds:** Adult £5.10, Child £2.50, Family (2+2) £12.90. Groups: Adult £4.60, Child £2.30. **Abbey, Cloisters & Grounds:** Adult £6.70, Child £3.40, Family (2+2) £17.10. Groups: Adult £6, Child £3. **Museum (winter):** Adult £3.60, Child £1.80, Family (2+2) £9.20. Groups: Adult £3.20, Child £1.60.

📷 ♿ Braille guides. 🎧 📷 By arrangement. 🅿 🍴 ❋ ❋ ♿

## LARMER TREE GARDENS

### Rushmore Estate, Tollard Royal, Salisbury, Wiltshire SP5 5PT

**Tel:** 01725 516228/516971 **Fax:** 01725 516321

**E-mail:** enquiries@larmertree.co.uk **www.larmertree.co.uk**

**Owner:** Pitt Rivers Trustees **Contact:** Gail Thomas

General Augustus Pitt Rivers created these extraordinary 11-acre pleasure grounds in 1880. They contain a unique collection of buildings including a Roman temple, open-air theatre, colonial style tea pavilion and Nepalese rooms. Beautifully laid out gardens with mature trees, laurel hedges, rides and stunning views of the Cranborne Chase. The gardens are well suited to weddings and corporate events.

**Location:** MAP 3:A5, OS Ref. ST943 169. 2m S Tollard Royal.

**Open:** Easter–last weekend in Sept: daily, 11am–4.30pm, closed Fri & Sat & Jul. Open other days, please check website for details.

**Admission:** Adult £3.75, Child £2.50 (under 5yrs Free), Conc. £3, Family (2+4) £12.50. Groups (15+) £3.

🍴 📹 Licensed for Sundays only. 📷 By arrangement. 🅿 🍴 By arrangement. ❋ ▲ ♿

## LONGLEAT 🏛

*See page 259 for full page entry.*

## LYDIARD PARK
### LYDIARD TREGOZE, SWINDON, WILTSHIRE SN5 3PA

www.lydiardpark.org.uk

**Tel:** 01793 770401  **Fax:** 01793 770968  **E-mail:** lydiardpark@swindon.gov.uk
**Owner:** Swindon Borough Council  **Contact:** The Keeper
Lydiard Park, ancestral home of the Bolingbrokes, is Swindon's treasure. Set in rolling lawns and woodland, this beautifully restored Georgian mansion contains the family's furnishings and portraits, exceptional plasterwork, rare 17th century window and room devoted to 18th century society artist Lady Diana Spencer. Exceptional monuments such as the 'Golden Cavalier' in adjacent church. The historic grounds of Lydiard Park are part of a major restoration project.
**Location:** MAP 3:B1, OS Ref. SU104 848. 4m W of Swindon, 1½ m N of M4/J16.
**Open:** House: Tues–Sun, 11am–5pm (4pm Nov–Feb). Grounds: all day, closing at dusk. Victorian Christmas decorations in December.
**Admission:** Adult £2.20, Child £1, Senior Citizen £2. Groups by appointment. Times and prices may change April 2007 – please telephone to confirm.
ⓘ No photography in house. 🄯 🔊 💻 Open all year, but groups must book.
🅵 By arrangement. 🄯 🅿 🄻 🚻 In grounds on leads. ❋ ♨ 🌂

## MOMPESSON HOUSE 🌼
### THE CLOSE, SALISBURY, WILTSHIRE SP1 2EL

www.nationaltrust.org.uk

**Tel:** 01722 335659  **Infoline:** 01722 420980  **Fax:** 01722 321559
**E-mail:** mompessonhouse@nationaltrust.org.uk
**Owner:** The National Trust  **Contact:** The Property Manager
An elegant and spacious 18th century house in the Cathedral Close. Featured in the award-winning film Sense and Sensibility and with magnificent plasterwork and a fine oak staircase. As well as pieces of good quality period furniture the house also contains the Turnbull collection of 18th century drinking glasses. Outside, the delightful walled garden has a pergola and traditional herbaceous borders.
**Location:** MAP 3:B4, OS Ref. SU142 297. On N side of Choristers' Green in Cathedral Close, near High Street Gate.
**Open:** 24 Mar–28 Oct: Sat–Wed, 11am–5pm. Last admission 4.30pm. Open Good Fri.
**Admission:** Adult £4.70, Child £2.30, Family (2+2) £11.70. Groups: £4.20. Garden only: £1. Reduced rate when arriving by public transport.
🄯 🔊 Ground floor & grounds. Braille guide. WC. 💻 🅵 By arrangement. 🄻 🚻

## THE MERCHANT'S HOUSE
### 132 HIGH STREET, MARLBOROUGH, WILTSHIRE SN8 1HN

www.merchantshouse.co.uk

**Tel/Fax:** 01672 511491  **E-mail:** manager@merchantshousetrust.co.uk
**Owner:** Marlborough Town Council  **Contact:** Michael Gray
Situated in Marlborough's world-famous High Street, The Merchant's House is one of the finest middle-class houses in England. Its well-preserved Panelled Chamber was completed in 1656. Both the Dining Room and Great Staircase display recently uncovered 17th century wall paintings which have aroused much expert interest. Leased to the Merchant's House (Marlborough) Trust.
**Location:** MAP 3:B2, OS Ref. SU188 691. N side of High Street, near Town Hall.
**Open:** Easter–end Sept: Fris & Sats, 11am–4pm. Booked groups at other times by appointment.
**Admission:** Adult £4, Child 50p. Booked groups (10–40): Adult £3, Child 50p.
ⓘ Photography only by arrangement. 🄯 🅵 🅿 Outside house, also in Hillier's Yard.
🚻 Guide dogs only. 🌂

## NEWHOUSE 🏛
### REDLYNCH, SALISBURY, WILTSHIRE SP5 2NX

**Tel:** 01725 510055  **Fax:** 01725 510284
**Owner:** George & June Jeffreys  **Contact:** Mrs Jeffreys
A brick, Jacobean 'Trinity' House, c1609, with two Georgian wings and a basically Georgian interior. Home of the Eyre family since 1633.
**Location:** MAP 3:B5, OS184, SU218 214. 9m S of Salisbury between A36 & A338.
**Open:** 1–30 Mar, 2–5 Apr, 9/10 Apr & 27 Aug: Mon–Fri, 2–5pm.
**Admission:** Adult £3.50, Child £2.50, Conc. £3.50. Groups (15+) Adult £3, Child £2.50, Conc. £3.
ⓘ No photography in house, except at weddings. 🄻 🅵 By arrangement.
🅿 Limited for coaches. 🚻 Guide dogs only. 🔺

Longleat, Warminster

## NORRINGTON MANOR

**Alvediston, Salisbury, Wiltshire SP5 5LL**

**Tel:** 01722 780367   **Fax:** 01722 780667

**Owner/Contact:** T Sykes

Built in 1377 it has been altered and added to in every century since, with the exception of the 18th century. Only the hall and the 'undercroft' remain of the original. It is currently a family home and the Sykes are only the third family to own it.

**Location:** MAP 3:A5, OS Ref. ST966 237. Signposted to N of Berwick St John and Alvediston road (half way between the two villages).

**Open:** By appointment in writing.

**Admission:** A donation to the local churches is asked for.

🚫 Unsuitable. 🅣 By arrangement. 🅟 Limited for cars, none for coaches. 🌣 ❄

## OLD WARDOUR CASTLE ⚏

### Nr TISBURY, WILTSHIRE SP3 6RR

www.english-heritage.org.uk/oldwardour

**Tel/Fax:** 01747 870487   **E-mail:** customers@english-heritage.org.uk

**Owner:** English Heritage   **Contact:** Visitor Operations Team

In a picture-book setting, the unusual hexagonal ruins of this 14th century castle stand on the edge of a beautiful lake, surrounded by landscaped grounds which include an elaborate rockwork grotto.

**Location:** MAP 3:A5, OS184, ST939 263. Off A30 2m SW of Tisbury.

**Open:** 1 Apr–31 Oct: daily, 10am–5pm (Jul & Aug, 6pm. Oct, 4pm). 1 Nov–20 Mar: Sats & Suns, 10am–4pm. Closed 24–26 Dec & 1 Jan.

**Admission:** Adult £3.40, Child £1.70, Conc. £2.60. Groups (11+): 15% discount.

ℹ WCs. 🅞 🚫 Grounds. 🅟 🌣 Grounds, on leads. 🔺 ❄ 🏷

## OLD SARUM ⚏

### CASTLE ROAD, SALISBURY, WILTSHIRE SP1 3SD

www.english-heritage.org.uk/oldsarum

**Tel:** 01722 335398 **Fax:** 01722 416037

**E-mail:** customers@english-heritage.org.uk

**Owner:** English Heritage   **Contact:** Visitor Operations Team

Built around 500BC by the Iron Age peoples, Old Sarum is the former site of the first cathedral and ancient city of Salisbury. A prehistoric hillfort in origin, Old Sarum was occupied by the Romans, the Saxons, and eventually the Normans who made it into one of their major strongholds, with a motte-and-bailey castle built at its centre. Old Sarum eventually grew into one of the most dramatic settlements in medieval England as castle, cathedral, bishop's palace and thriving township. When the new city we know as Salisbury was founded in the early 13th century the settlement faded away. With fine views of the surrounding countryside, Old Sarum is an excellent special events venue.

**Location:** MAP 3:B4, OS184, SU138 327. 2m N of Salisbury off A345.

**Open:** 1 Apr–30 Jun & Sept: daily, 10am–5pm. Jul & Aug: 9am–6pm. Oct: 10am–4pm. Nov–Feb: 11am–3pm (1–20 Mar, 10am–4pm). Closed 24–26 Dec & 1 Jan.

**Admission:** Adult £2.90, Child £1.50, Conc. £2.20. 15% discount for groups (11+).

ℹ WCs. 🅞 🚫 Grounds. 🅣 Jul/Aug. 🅟 🌣 Grounds, on leads. ❄ 🏷

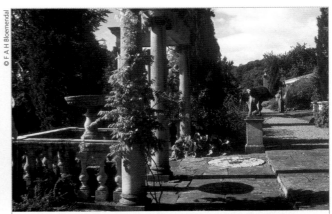

## THE PETO GARDEN AT IFORD MANOR 🏛

### BRADFORD-ON-AVON, WILTSHIRE BA15 2BA

www.ifordmanor.co.uk

**Tel:** 01225 863146   **Fax:** 01225 862364

**Owner/Contact:** Mrs E A J Cartwright-Hignett

This unique Grade I Italian-style garden is set on a romantic hillside beside the River Frome. Designed by the Edwardian architect Harold A Peto, who lived at Iford Manor from 1899–1933, the garden has terraces, a colonnade, cloister, casita, statuary, evergreen planting and magnificent rural views. Renowned for its tranquillity and peace, the Peto Garden won the 1998 HHA/Christie's *Garden of the Year* Award.

**Location:** MAP 2:P3, OS Ref. ST800 589. 7m SE of Bath via A36, signposted Iford. ½m SW of Bradford-on-Avon via Westwood on B3109.

**Open:** Apr & Oct: Suns only & Easter Mon, 2–5pm. May–Sept: Tue–Thur, Sats, Suns & BH Mons, 2–5pm. Children under 10yrs welcome weekdays only for safety reasons.

**Admission:** Adult £4.50, Conc, Students & Children £4. Groups (10+) welcome outside normal opening hours, by arrangment only, £5.

🚫 Partial. WCs. 🍴 Teas (May–Aug: Sats, Suns & BHs, 2.30–5pm).

🅣 By arrangement. 🅟 Limited for coaches. 🌣 On leads, in grounds.

© Steve Day

## SALISBURY CATHEDRAL
### 33 THE CLOSE, SALISBURY  SP1 2EJ
www.salisburycathedral.org.uk

**Tel:** 01722 555120  **Fax:** 01722 555116  **E-mail:** visitors@salcath.co.uk

**Owner:** The Dean & Chapter    **Contact:** Visitor Services

Salisbury Cathedral is a building of world importance. Set within the elegant splendour of the Cathedral Close. It is probably the finest medieval building in Britain. Built in one phase from 1220 to 1258. Britain's tallest spire (123m/404ft) was added a generation later. Discover nearly 800 years of history, the finest preserved Magna Carta (1215), Europe's oldest working clock and a unique 13th century frieze of bible stories in the beautiful Chapter House. Boy and girl choristers sing daily services which follow an historic tradition of worship. Explore the roof spaces on a tower tour, climbing 332 steps to the base of the spire, and marvel at the medieval craftsmanship and the magnificent views across Salisbury.

**Location:** MAP 3:B4, OS Ref. SU143 295. S of City. M3, A303, A30 from London or A36.

**Open:** All year: Sun, 7.15am–6.15pm. 1 Jan–10 Jun, 25 Aug–31 Dec: Mon–Sat, 7.15am–6.15pm. 11 Jun–24 Aug (excluding Sun): 7.15am–7.15pm.

**Admission:** Donation: Adult £5, Child £3, Conc. £4.25, Family (2+2) £12.

🖭 🗊 🔄 💺 Licensed. 🍴 🕮 By arrangement. 🅿 In city centre. ▣ 🐾 In grounds, on leads. ❋ ▼

---

**STOURHEAD** 🌿                    *See page 260 for full page entry.*

---

## STOURTON HOUSE FLOWER GARDEN
**Stourton, Warminster, Wiltshire  BA12 6QF**

**Tel:** 01747 840417

**Owner/Contact:** Mrs E Bullivant

Four acres of peaceful, romantic, plantsman's garden. Rare daffodils, camellias, rhododendrons, roses, hydrangeas and wild flowers.

**Location:** MAP 2:P4, OS Ref. ST780 340. A303, 2m NW of Mere next to Stourhead car park. Follow blue signs.

**Open:** Apr–end Nov: Weds, Thurs, Suns, and BH Mons, 11am–6pm. Plants & dried flowers for sale during the winter on weekdays. Groups any day.

**Admission:** Adult £3.50, Child 50p.

---

**WILTON HOUSE** 🏛                    *See page 261 for full page entry.*

---

© NT Photographic Library / Nick Meers

Stourhead, Stourton

## STONEHENGE ⊞
### AMESBURY, WILTSHIRE  SP4 7DE
www.english-heritage.org.uk/stonehenge

**Tel:** 0870 3331181 (Customer Services)

**Owner:** English Heritage

The mystical and awe-inspiring stone circle at Stonehenge is one of the most famous prehistoric monuments in the world, designated by UNESCO as a World Heritage Site. Stonehenge's orientation on the rising and setting sun has always been one of its most remarkable features. Whether this was simply because the builders came from a sun-worshipping culture, or because – as some scholars have believed – the circle and its banks were part of a huge astronomical calendar, remains a mystery. Visitors to Stonehenge can discover the history and legends which surround this unique stone circle, which began over 5,000 years ago, with a complimentary three part audio tour available in 9 languages (subject to availability).

**Location:** MAP 3:B4, OS Ref. SU123 422. 2m W of Amesbury on junction of A303 and A344/ A360.

**Open:** 16 Mar–31 May: daily 9.30am–6pm. 1 Jun–31 Aug: daily, 9am–7pm. 1 Sept–15 Oct: daily, 9.30am–6pm. 16 Oct–15 Mar: daily, 9.30am–4pm. Closed 24/25 Dec. Last recommended admission is ½ hr before advertised closing times and the site will be closed promptly 20 mins after the advertised closing times. Summer Solstice: 20–22 Jun, opening times may be amended.

**Admission:** Adult £6.30, Child £3.20, Conc £4.70, Family (2+3) £15.80. Groups (11+) 10% discount.

ℹ WCs. 🖭 🔄 💺 💺 🔄 🅿 ❋ ❋

Longleat, Warminster

**Above:** Helmingham Hall
**Right:** Wimpole Hall ©NT Photographic Library

# Eastern Region

*East Anglia has magical coastal areas ranging from The Wash in Norfolk down to the Essex marshes. The half timbered houses in Suffolk villages such as Lavenham contrast with the Norfolk flint found further north. Among the major properties that welcome visitors are Sandringham, the country home of HM The Queen, Woburn Abbey and Hatfield House; but off the beaten track find time for Copped Hall or The Manor, Hemingford Grey.*

Bedfordshire

Cambridgeshire

Essex

Hertfordshire

Norfolk

Suffolk

■ **Owner:**
The Duke and Duchess
of Bedford &
The Trustees of Bedford
Estates

■ **Contact**
William Lash
Woburn Abbey
Woburn
Bedfordshire  MK17 9WA

**Tel:** 01525 290333
**Fax:** 01525 290271
**E-mail:** admissions@
woburnabbey.co.uk

■ **Location**
**MAP 7:D10**
**OS Ref. SP965 325**

On A4012, midway
between M1/J13, 3m,
J14, 6m and the A5
(turn off at Hockliffe).
London approx. 1hr
by road (43m).

**Rail:** London Euston to
Leighton Buzzard,
Bletchley/Milton Keynes.
Kings Cross Thameslink
to Flitwick.

**Air:** Luton 14m.
Heathrow 39m.

■ **Opening Times**
**Woburn Abbey**
31 March–30 September:
daily, 11am–4pm (last
entry).

**Deer Park**
All year: Daily
10am–5pm.
(except 24–26 Dec).

**Antiques Centre**
All year: Daily
10am–5.30pm.
(except 24–26 Dec).

■ **Admission**
**Woburn Abbey**
(Prices incl. Private Apts)
Adult              £10.50
Child (5–15yrs)     £6.00
OAP                 £9.50
Group rates & family
tickets available.

**Car Park, Grounds &
Deer Park only** £2.00pp

Reduced rates apply
when Private Apartments
are in use by the family.

■ **Conference/Function**

| ROOM | SIZE | MAX CAPACITY |
|------|------|--------------|
| Sculpture Gallery | 128' x 24' | 300 250 (sit-down) |
| Lantern Rm | 44' x 21' | 60 |

# WOBURN ABBEY 🏛

www.discoverwoburn.co.uk

Set in a beautiful 3,000 acre deer park, Woburn Abbey has been the home of the Russell Family for nearly 400 years, and is now occupied by the 15th Duke of Bedford and his family.

The Abbey houses one of the most important private art collections in the world, including paintings by Gainsborough, Reynolds, Van Dyck, Cuyp, and Canaletto, 21 of whose views hang in the Venetian Room.

The tour of the Abbey covers three floors, including the vaults, with 18th Century French and English furniture, silver and a wide range of porcelain on display. Amongst the highlights is the Sèvres dinner service presented to the 4th Duke by Louis XV of France.

The Deer Park is home to ten species of deer, including the Père David, descended from the Imperial Herd of China, which was saved from extinction at Woburn and is now the largest breeding herd of this species in the world. In 1985 the 14th Duke gave 22 Père David deer to the People's Republic of China and the herd is now well established in its natural environment and numbers several hundred.

Woburn Abbey is also noted for its excellent and unique Antiques Centre with over 60 original 18th century shop fronts and show cases, and has an enviable reputation for its in-house catering. Woburn Abbey specialises in banqueting, conferences, receptions and company days; and the Sculpture Gallery overlooking the Private Gardens provides a splendid setting for weddings and wedding receptions.

2007 will see a number of events in the Park including the 27th de Havilland Moth Club Fly-In, Woburn Garden Show, Craft Fairs and a variety of musical and theatrical performances.

ⓘ Suitable for fashion shows, product launches and company 'days out'. Use of parkland and garden. No photography in House.

🏛 Conferences, exhibitions, banqueting, luncheons, dinners in the Sculpture Gallery, Lantern & Long Harness rooms.

☕ Group bookings in Sculpture Gallery. Flying Duchess Pavilion Coffee Shop.

🍴 Licensed.

🧍 £17.50, by arrangement, max 8. Tours in French, German & Italian available. Guide book available £5. Special interest tours can be arranged.

🅿 Please telephone for details.

🐕 In park on leads, and guide dogs in house.

## BROMHAM MILL & GALLERY

**Bridge End, Bromham, Bedfordshire  MK43 8LP**

**Tel:** 01234 824330  **E-mail:** bromham.mill@bedscc.gov.uk

**Owner:** Bedfordshire County Council

Working water mill on River Ouse. Flour milling and changing contemporary art & craft exhibitions.

**Location:** MAP 7:D9, OS Ref. TL010 506. Location beside the River Ouse bridge on N side of the former A428, 2½ m W of Bedford.

**Open:** Apr–Oct: Suns & BHs, 1–5pm. Other times for groups by arrangement.

**Admission:** Free. Group charges on application.

## BUSHMEAD PRIORY ⛪

**Colmworth, Bedford, Bedfordshire  MK44 2LD**

**Tel:** 01799 522842  **Regional Office:** 01223 582700

**Owner:** English Heritage   **Contact:** Visitor Operations Team

A rare survival of the medieval refectory of an Augustinian priory, with its original timber-framed roof almost intact and containing interesting wall paintings and stained glass.

**Location:** MAP 7:E9, OS Ref. TL115 607. On unclassified road near Colmworth; off B660, 2m S of Bolnhurst. 5m W of St. Neots (A1).

**Open:** 1 May–31 Aug. Pre-booked guided tours only, please call 01799 522842.

**Admission:** Adult £5 Child £2.50, Conc. £3.80.

🅿 ⌗

## CECIL HIGGINS ART GALLERY

### CASTLE LANE, BEDFORD  MK40 3RP

www.cecilhigginsartgallery.org

**Tel:** 01234 211222  **Fax:** 01234 327149  **E-mail:** chag@bedford.gov.uk

**Owner:** Bedford Borough Council & Trustees of Gallery   **Contact:** The Gallery

A recreation of an 1880s home, with superb examples of 19th century decorative arts. Room settings include items from the Handley-Read collection and the famous Gothic bedroom containing works by William Burges. Adjoining gallery housing renowned collections of watercolours, prints and drawings (exhibitions changed regularly), ceramics, glass and lace. Situated in pleasant gardens near the river embankment.

**Location:** MAP 7:E9, OS Ref. TL052 497. Centre of Bedford, just off The Embankment. E of High St.

**Open:** Tue–Sat, 11am–5pm (last admission 4.45pm). Sun & BH Mons, 2–5pm. Closed Mons, Good Fri, 25/26 Dec & 1 Jan.

**Admission:** Free.

ℹ Photography in house by arrangement. 📷 🎞 By arrangement. ♿
☕ Self-service coffee bar. 🎦 By arrangement. 🎭 🐕 Guide dogs only. ✳ ♻

## DE GREY MAUSOLEUM ⛪

**Flitton, Bedford, Bedfordshire**

**Tel:** 01525 860094 (Key-keeper)

**Owner:** English Heritage   **Contact:** Mrs Stimson

A remarkable treasure-house of sculpted tombs and monuments from the 16th to 19th centuries dedicated to the de Grey family of nearby Wrest Park.

**Location:** MAP 7:D10, OS Ref. TL059 359. Attached to the church on unclassified road 1½m W of A6 at Silsoe.

**Open:** Sats & Suns. Contact keyholder in advance: Mrs Stimson, 3 Highfield Rd, Flitton.

**Admission:** Free.

## HOUGHTON HOUSE ⛪

**Ampthill, Bedford, Bedfordshire**

**Tel:** 01223 582700 (Regional Office)

**Owner:** English Heritage   **Contact:** East of England Regional Office

The shell of a 17th century mansion with magnificent views, reputedly the inspiration for the 'House Beautiful' in John Bunyan's *Pilgrim's Progress*. Built around 1615 for Mary, Dowager Countess of Pembroke, in a mixture of Jacobean and Classical styles: the ground floors of two Italianate loggias survive, possibly the work of Inigo Jones. Houghton House has recently undergone major conservation work. The greatly enhanced condition of the house will also be shortly augmented with a new interpretation scheme for the site.

**Location:** MAP 7:E9, OS Ref. TL039 394. 1m NE of Ampthill off A421, 8m S of Bedford.

**Open:** Any reasonable time.

**Admission:** Free.

🅿 🎭 ✳

## MOGGERHANGER PARK

**Park Road, Moggerhanger, Bedfordshire  MK44 3RW**

**Tel:** 01767 641007  **Fax:** 01767 641515

**E-mail:** enquiries@moggerhangerpark.com  **www.moggerhangerpark.com**

**Owner:** Moggerhanger House Preservation Trust   **Contact:** Mrs Jenny Cooper

Outstanding Georgian Grade I listed Country House, recently restored in keeping with the original design of architect, Sir John Soane and set in 33 acres of parkland originally landscaped by Humphry Repton. Moggerhanger House has 3 executive conference suites and 2 function rooms, making an ideal venue for conferences, promotions and corporate entertainment.

**Location:** MAP 7:E9, OS Ref. TL048 475. On A603, 3m from A1 at Sandy, 6m from Bedford.

**Open:** House Tours: Jun–Sept: Grounds, Tearooms & Visitors' Centre: All year.

**Admission:** Please telephone 01767 641007.

ℹ No photography. No smoking. 📷 🎞 ♿ 🛍 Licensed. 🍴 Licensed.
🎦 By arrangement. 🅿 Limited for coaches. 🐕 In grounds, on leads. ✳

## SWISS GARDEN

**Old Warden Park, Bedfordshire**

**Tel:** 01767 627927  **www.shuttleworth.org**

**Operated By:** The Shuttleworth Trust

The Swiss Garden, Old Warden Park, Bedfordshire, created in the 1820s by Lord Ongley, is a late Regency garden and an outstanding example of the Swiss picturesque. The Swiss Cottage provides the main element for this unusual and atmospheric garden. It provides the principal aspect for a number of contrived vistas which lead the eye towards this attractive thatched structure. Interesting things to see in the garden are, a grotto and fernery, a thatched tree shelter, an Indian Pavilion, two ponds and many fine specimens of shrubs and conifers, plus some remarkable trees.

**Location:** MAP 7:E9, OS Ref. TL150 447. 1½m W of Biggleswade A1 roundabout, signposted from A1 and A600.

**Open:** Apr–Oct: 10am–5pm; Nov–Mar: 10am–4pm. Closed Christmas week.

**Admission:** Adult £5, Child Free, Conc. £4. Special rates for groups, tours & private hire.

🛍 ♿ 🎞 Catering. 🛍 Refreshments adjacent. 🅿 🎭 🏠 ✳

## TURVEY HOUSE 🏛

**Turvey, Bedfordshire  MK43 8EL**

**Tel/Fax:** 01234 881244  **E-mail:** danielhanbury@hotmail.com

**Owner:** Executors of Lady Hanbury   **Contact:** Daniel Hanbury

A neo-classical house set in picturesque parkland bordering the River Great Ouse. The principal rooms contain a fine collection of 18th and 19th century English and Continental furniture, pictures, porcelain, *objets d'art* and books. Walled Garden.

**Location:** MAP 7:D9, OS Ref. SP939528Between Bedford and Northampton on A428.

**Open:** 7/8, 10, 12/13, 22, 24, 26–28th May. 5, 7, 9/10 19, 21, 23/24 Jun. 3, 5, 7/8, 17, 19, 21/22 Jul. 26/27 Aug.

**Admission:** Adult £5, Child £3

ℹ No photography in house. ♿ Partial. 🎦 Obligatory.
🅿 Ample for cars, none for coaches. 🐕

Cecil Higgins Art Gallery, Bedford

## WREST PARK GARDENS⌗
### SILSOE, LUTON, BEDFORDSHIRE  MK45 4HS
www.english-heritage.org.uk/visits

**Tel:** 01525 860152

**Owner:** English Heritage    **Contact:** Visitor Operations Team

Over 90 acres of enchanting gardens originally laid out in the early 18th century, and inspired by the great gardens of Versailles and the Loire Valley in France. Marvel at the magnificent collection of stone and lead statuary, the Bath House and the vast Orangery, built by the Earl de Grey, and dream of days gone by. The gardens form a delightful backdrop to the house which is built in the style of an 18th century French château.

**Location:** MAP 7:E10, OS153, TL093 356. ¾ m E of Silsoe off A6, 10m S of Bedford.

**Open:** 1 Apr–30 Jun, Sept & Oct: Sat, Sun & BHs, 10am–6pm (5pm in Oct). Jul & Aug: Thur–Mon, 10am–6pm. Last admission 1hr before closing.

**Admission:** Adult £4.70, Child £2.40, Conc. £3.50. Family £11.80.

ⓘ WCs. Buggies available. ▣ ♿ ⌂ Ⓟ ⊞ On leads. ♨

*gift aid it* This year, some properties will be operating the Gift Aid on Entry scheme at their admission points. Where the scheme is operating, visitors are offered a choice between paying the standard admission price or paying the 'Gift Aid Admission' which includes a voluntary donation of at least 10%. Gift Aid Admissions enable the charity to reclaim tax on the whole amount paid* - an extra 28% - potentially a very significant boost to property funds.   Money raised from paying visitors in this way will go towards restoration projects at the property and will be very welcome. Where shown, the admission prices are inclusive of the 10% voluntary donation where properties are operating the Gift Aid on Entry scheme, but both the standard admission price and the Gift Aid Admission will be displayed at the property and on their website.

*Gift Aid donations must be supported by a valid Gift Aid declaration and a Gift Aid declaration can only cover donations made by an individual for him/herself or for him/herself and members of his/her family.

Woburn Abbey

# ANGLESEY ABBEY, GARDENS & LODE MILL

## LODE, CAMBRIDGE, CAMBRIDGESHIRE CB25 9EJ

www.nationaltrust.org.uk/angleseyabbey

**Tel:** 01223 810080 **Fax:** 01223 810088 **E-mail:** angleseyabbey@nationaltrust.org.uk
**Owner:** The National Trust **Contact:** The Property Manager

Dating from 1600, the house, built on the site of an Augustinian priory, contains the famous Fairhaven collection of paintings and furniture. Surrounded by an outstanding 100 acre garden and arboretum, with a wonderful display of hyacinths in spring, magnificent herbaceous borders, a dahlia garden in summer, winter garden and woodland path. A watermill in full working order is demonstrated on the first and third Saturday each month.

**Location:** MAP 7:G8, OS Ref. TL533 622. 6m NE of Cambridge on B1102, signs from A14.

**Open:** Summer: House & Mill: 21 Mar–28 Oct: Wed–Sun & BH Mons: 1–5pm. Garden, Shop, Plant Centre & Restaurant: 21 Mar–28 Oct: Wed–Sun & BH Mons; 10.30am–5.30pm. Winter: Winter Garden, Shop, Plant Centre & Restaurant: 31 Oct–23 Dec & 28 Dec–27 Feb 2008: Wed–Sun, 10.30am–4.30pm; Mill: Sat & Sun, 11am–3.30pm. Gardens & Mill also open Tues in school holidays. Groups must book, no groups on Suns & BHs.

**\*Admission:** Summer: House & Garden: Adult £8.40, Child £4.20. Groups: Adult £7.30, Child £3.65. Garden only: Adult £4.75, Child £2.40. Groups: Adult £4.40, Child £2.20. Winter (garden only): Adult £4, Child £2. Groups: Adult £3.50, Child £1.75.*includes a voluntary donation but visitors can choose to pay the standard prices displayed at the property and on the website.

Partial. Licensed.

---

©Nigel Luckhurst

# CAMBRIDGE UNIVERSITY BOTANIC GARDEN

## BATEMAN STREET, CAMBRIDGE CB2 1JF

www.botanic.cam.ac.uk

**Tel:** 01223 336265 **Fax:** 01223 336278 **E-mail:** enquiries@botanic.cam.ac.uk
**Owner:** University of Cambridge **Contact:** Enquiries Desk

This 40 acre oasis of listed heritage landscape showcases over 8000 species, including alpines from every continent in the Rock Garden, nine National Collections, the finest collection of trees in the Eastern Region, the historic Systematic Beds, the Dry Garden, the renowned Winter Garden and tropical forest in the Glasshouses.

**Location:** MAP 7:G9, OS Ref. TL453 573. ¾m S of Cambridge city centre; entrance on Bateman Street off A1309 (Trumpington Rd). 10mins walk from railway station.

**Open:** 3 Jan–24 Dec: daily, 10am–6pm; closes 5pm in Autumn & Spring and 4pm in winter. Closed over Christmas and New Year, please telephone for details.

**Admission:** Adult £3, Child (under 16yrs) Free, Conc. £2.50. Groups must book.

By arrangement. Street/Pay & Display. Schools must book. Guide dogs only.

---

## OLIVER CROMWELL'S HOUSE

**29 St Mary's Street, Ely, Cambridgeshire CB7 4HF**
**Tel:** 01353 662062 **Fax:** 01353 668518 **E-mail:** tic@eastcambs.gov.uk
**Owner:** East Cambridgeshire District Council

The former home of the Lord Protector.

**Location:** MAP 7:G7, OS Ref. TL538 803. N of Cambridge, ¼m W of Ely Cathedral.
**Open:** 1 Nov–31 Mar: Sun–Fri, 11am–4pm; Sats, 10am–5pm. 1 Apr–31 Oct: daily, 10am–5.30pm.
**Admission:** Adult £3.95, Child £2.70, Conc. £3.45, Family (2+3) £11 (prices subject to change April 2007).

---

## DENNY ABBEY & THE FARMLAND MUSEUM

**Ely Road, Chittering, Waterbeach, Cambridgeshire CB5 9TQ**
**Tel:** 01223 860489 **www.english-heritage.org.uk/visits**
**Owner:** English Heritage/Managed by the Farmland Museum Trust
**Contact:** Visitor Operations Team

What at first appears to be an attractive stone farmhouse is actually the remains of a 12th century Benedictine abbey which, at different times, also housed the Knights Templar and Franciscan nuns. Founded by the Countess of Pembroke. New family-friendly activities include hands-on interactives.

**Location:** MAP 7:G8, OS Ref. TL495 684. 6m N of Cambridge on the E side of the A10.
**Open:** 1 Apr–31 Oct: daily, 12 noon–5pm.
**Admission:** Abbey & Museum: Adult £4, Child £1.70, Child under 5 Free, Conc. £3, Family £10. Museum charge: EH Members/OVP £2.40.

Farmland musuem. WC. Weekends only. On leads.

---

## DOCWRA'S MANOR GARDEN

**Shepreth, Royston, Hertfordshire SG8 6PS**
**Tel:** 01763 261473 **Information:** 01763 260677
**Owner:** Mrs Faith Raven **Contact:** Peter Rocket

Extensive garden around building dating from the 18th century.

**Location:** MAP 7:F9, OS Ref. TL393 479. In Shepreth via A10 from Royston.
**Open:** All year: Weds & Fris, 10am–4pm & 1st Sun in month from Apr–Oct: 2–5pm.
**Admission:** £4.

# ELTON HALL
## Nr PETERBOROUGH PE8 6SH
www.eltonhall.com

**Tel:** 01832 280468 **Fax:** 01832 280584 **E-mail:** office@eltonhall.com

**Owner:** Sir William Proby Bt **Contact:** The Administrator

Elton Hall, the home of the Proby family for over 350 years is a fascinating mixture of styles. Every room contains treasures, magnificent furniture and fine paintings. The library is one of the finest in private hands and includes Henry VIII's prayer book. The beautiful gardens have been carefully restored, with the addition of a new gothic Orangery to celebrate the Millennium.

**Location:** MAP 7:E7, OS Ref. TL091 930. Close to A1 in the village of Elton, off A605 Peterborough - Oundle Road.

**Open:** 27/28 May; June: Weds. Jul & Aug: Wed, Thur, Sun & BH Mon, 2–5pm. Private groups by arrangement Apr–Sept.

**Admission:** House & Garden: £7.50, Conc. £6.50. Garden only: Adult £5, Conc. £4.50. Accompanied child under 16 Free.

No photography in house. Garden suitable. Obligatory. Guide dogs in gardens only.

# ELY CATHEDRAL

**The Chapter House, The College, Ely, Cambridgeshire CB7 4DL**

**Tel:** 01353 667735 ext.261 **Fax:** 01353 665658

**Contact:** Sally-Ann Ford (Visits & Tours Manager)

A wonderful example of Romanesque architecture. Octagon and Lady Chapel are of special interest. Superb medieval domestic buildings surround the Cathedral. Stained Glass Museum. Brass rubbing. Octagon and West Tower tours peak season.

**Location:** MAP 7:G7, OS Ref. TL541 803. Via A10, 15m N of Cambridge City centre.

**Open:** Summer: 7am–7pm. Winter: Mon–Sat, 7.30am–6pm, Suns and week after Christmas, 7.30am–5pm. Sun services: 8.15am, 10.30am and 3.45pm. Weekday services: 7.40am, 8am, and 5.30pm (Thurs only also 12.30pm).

**Admission:** Adult £5.20, Child Free, Conc. £4.50. Discounts for groups of 15+. Separate rates for school visits.

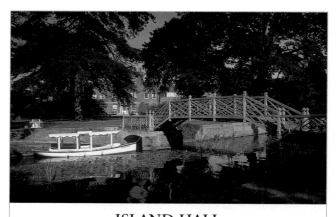

# ISLAND HALL
## GODMANCHESTER, CAMBRIDGESHIRE PE29 2BA
www.islandhall.com

**Tel:** 01480 459676 (Groups) 01206 573948 (Individuals via Invitation to View)

**E-mail:** cvp@cvpdesigns.com

**Owner:** Mr Christopher & Lady Linda Vane Percy **Contact:** Mr C Vane Percy

An important mid 18th century mansion of great charm, owned and restored by an award-winning interior designer. This family home has lovely Georgian rooms, with fine period detail, and interesting possessions relating to the owners' ancestors since their first occupation of the house in 1800. A tranquil riverside setting with formal gardens and ornamental island forming part of the grounds in an area of Best Landscape. Octavia Hill wrote *"This is the loveliest, dearest old house, I never was in such a one before."*

**Location:** MAP 7:F8, OS Ref. TL244 706. Centre of Godmanchester, Post Street next to free car park. 1m S of Huntingdon, 15m NW of Cambridge A14.

**Open:** Groups by arrangement: May–Jul & Sept. Individuals please call 01206 573948.

**Admission:** Groups: (40+) Adult £4.50, (10–40) Adult £5. Under 20 persons, min charge £100 per group (sorry but no children under 13yrs).

Home made teas.

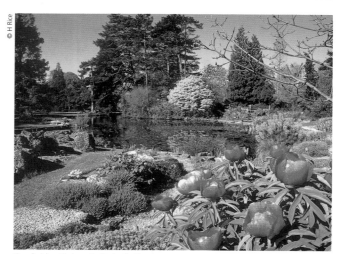

Cambridge University Botanic Garden

© H Rice

## KIMBOLTON CASTLE

**Kimbolton, Huntingdon, Cambridgeshire  PE28 0EA**
**Tel:** 01480 860505  **Fax:** 01480 861763
**www.kimbolton.cambs.sch.uk/castle_visits**
**Owner:** Governors of Kimbolton School    **Contact:** Mrs N Butler

A late Stuart house, an adaptation of a 13th century fortified manor house, with evidence of Tudor modifications. The seat of the Earls and Dukes of Manchester 1615–1950, now a school. Katharine of Aragon died in the Queen's Room – the setting for a scene in Shakespeare's Henry VIII. 18th century rebuilding by Vanbrugh and Hawksmoor; Gatehouse by Robert Adam; the Pellegrini mural paintings on the Staircase, in the Chapel and in the Boudoir are the best examples in England of this gifted Venetian decorator. New Heritage Room.

**Location:** MAP 7:E8, OS Ref. TL101 676. 7m NW of St Neots on B645.
**Open:** 4 Mar & 4 Nov, 1–4pm.
**Admission:** Adult £3.50, Child £2, OAP £2.50. Groups by arrangement throughout the year, including evenings.

🖻🔲 Unsuitable. 🔲🔳 By arrangement. 🅿🔲🔳 On leads in grounds. 🔺🔆

---

## LONGTHORPE TOWER ⌗

**Thorpe Rd, Longthorpe, Cambridgeshire  PE1 1HA**
**Tel:** 01799 522842    **www.english-heritage.org.uk/visits**
**Owner:** English Heritage    **Contact:** Visitor Operations Team

The finest example of 14th century domestic wall paintings in northern Europe showing a variety of secular and sacred objects, including the Wheel of Life, the Nativity and King David. The Tower, with the Great Chamber that contains the paintings, is part of a fortified manor house. Special exhibitions are held on the upper floor.

**Location:** MAP 7:E6, OS Ref. TL163 983. 2m W of Peterborough just off A47.
**Open:** 1 May–31 Aug: Pre-booked guided tours only, please call 01799 522842.
**Admission:** Adult £5, Child £2.50, Conc. £3.80.

ℹ️ No parking at site. 🔲🔳 By arrangement. 🔳

## THE MANOR, HEMINGFORD GREY

**HUNTINGDON, CAMBRIDGESHIRE  PE28 9BN**

www.greenknowe.co.uk

**Tel:** 01480 463134    **Fax:** 01480 465026    **E-mail:** diana_boston@hotmail.com
**Owner:** Mrs D S Boston    **Contact:** Diana Boston

Built about 1130, it is one of the oldest continuously inhabited houses in Britain. Made famous as 'Green Knowe' by the author Lucy Boston. Her patchwork collection is also shown. Four acre garden with topiary, old roses and herbaceous borders.

**Location:** MAP 7:F8, OS Ref. TL290 706. Off A14, 3m SE of Huntingdon. 12m NW of Cambridge. Access is by a small gate on the riverside footpath.
**Open:** House: All year (except May), to individuals or groups by prior arrangement. In May guided tours will be daily at 2pm (booking advisable). Garden: All year, daily, 11am–5pm (4pm in winter).
**Admission:** Adult £5, Child £1.50, OAP £4. Garden only: Adult £2, Child Free.

ℹ️ No photography in house. 🔲🔳🔲 Locally, by arrangement. 🔳 Obligatory.
🔲🅿 Disabled only. 🔳 In garden, on leads. 🔆

## PECKOVER HOUSE & GARDEN 🌿

**NORTH BRINK, WISBECH, CAMBRIDGESHIRE  PE13 1JR**

www.nationaltrust.org.uk

**Tel/Fax:** 01945 583463    **E-mail:** peckover@nationaltrust.org.uk
**Owner:** The National Trust    **Contact:** The Property Manager

A town house, built c1722 and renowned for its very fine plaster and wood rococo decoration. The outstanding 2 acre Victorian garden includes an orangery, summerhouses, roses, herbaceous borders, fernery, croquet lawn and Reed Barn Restaurant.

**Location:** MAP 7:G6, OS Ref. TF458 097. On N bank of River Nene, in Wisbech B1441.
**Open:** House, Garden, Shop & Restaurant: 17 Mar–28 Oct, Sat–Wed, 12 noon–5pm (House 1–4.30pm). Open Good Friday and 4/5 Jul for Wisbech Rose Fair.
**Admission:** Adult £5, Child £2.50, Family £12.50. Groups: £4.30.

🔲🔳🔲 Partial. 🔲🔳🅿 Signposted. 🔳🔲🔺🔳

---

## PETERBOROUGH CATHEDRAL

**Chapter Office, Minster Precincts, Peterborough  PE1 1XS**
**Tel:** 01733 355300  **Fax:** 01733 355316
**E-mail:** a.watson@peterborough-cathedral.org.uk
**www.peterborough-cathedral.org.uk**
**Contact:** Andrew Watson

'An undiscovered gem.' With magnificent Norman architecture a unique 13th century nave ceiling, the awe-inspiring West Front and burial places of two Queens to make your visit an unforgettable experience. Exhibitions tell the Cathedral's story. Tours by appointment, of the cathedral, tower, Deanery Garden or Precincts. Freshly prepared meals and snacks at Beckets Restaurant (advance bookings possible). Cathedral gift shop and Tourist Information Centre in Precincts. Business meeting facilities.

**Location:** MAP 7:E6, OS Ref. TL194 986. 4m E of A1, in City Centre.
**Open:** All year: Mon–Fri, 9am–6.30pm (restricted access after 5.30pm because of Evensong). Sat, 9am–5pm. Sun: services from 7.30am; visitors: 12 noon–5pm.
**Admission:** No fixed charge – donations are requested.

ℹ️ Visitors' Centre. 🔲🔳🔲 Mon–Sat. 🔳 By arrangement. 🅿 None. 🔲
🔳 Guide dogs only. 🔆

Kimbolton Castle, Huntingdon

© Patrick Lane

# WIMPOLE HALL & HOME FARM 🦋
## ARRINGTON, ROYSTON, CAMBRIDGESHIRE  SG8 0BW

www.nationaltrust.org.uk    www.wimpole.org

**Tel:** 01223 206000   **Fax:** 01223 207838   **E-mail:** wimpolehall@nationaltrust.org.uk
**Owner:** The National Trust    **Contact:** The Property Manager

Wimpole is a magnificent country house built in 18th century style with a colourful history of owners. The Hall is set in restored formal gardens with parterres and a walled garden. Home Farm is a working farm and is the largest rare breeds centre in East Anglia.

**Location:** MAP 7:F9, OS154. TL336 510. 8m SW of Cambridge (A603), 6m N of Royston (A1198).

**Open:** Hall: 17 Mar–31 Oct: Sat–Wed (open Good Fri & BH Mon); Aug: Sat–Thur (open BH Mons); 4, 11, 18 & 25 Nov, Suns only; 1–5pm, BH Mon, 11am–5pm, closes 4pm after 31 Oct. Garden: as Farm. Park: dawn–dusk. Farm: 17 Mar –31 Oct: Sat–Wed (open Good Fri & BH Mon); Aug: Sat–Thur & BH Mon; Nov–Mar 2008: Sat & Sun (open Feb half-term week); 17 Mar–31 Oct: 10.30am–5pm; 4 Nov–Mar 2008, 11am–4pm.

**\*Admission:** Hall: Adult £8, Child £4.40. Joint ticket with Home Farm: Adult £12, Child £6.50, Family £31. Garden: £3.30. Group rates (not Suns or BH Mons). Farm: Adult £6.60, Child (3yrs & up) £4.40. Discount for NT members (not Suns or BH Mons). *includes a voluntary donation but visitors can choose to pay the standard prices displayed at the property and on the website.

◻ ⬚ ⬚ ⬚ Partial. ⬚ ⬚ Licensed. ⬚ By arrangement. **P** Limited for coaches. ⬚ ⬚ In park, on leads. ⬚ ⬚ ⬚ Tel for details.

Wimpole Hall, Royston

# UNIVERSITY OF CAMBRIDGE

For further details contact:
Cambridge Tourism, The Old Library,
Wheeler Street, Cambridge CB2 3QB.
Tel: +44 (0)1223 464132
Infoline: 0906 5862526
Fax: +44 (0)1223 457549

**Christ's College**
St Andrew's Street,
Cambridge CB2 3BU
**Tel:** 01223 334900
**Website:** www.christs.cam.ac.uk/admissn
**Founder:** Lady Margaret Beaufort
**Founded:** 1505

**Churchill College**
Madingley Road, Cambridge CB3 0DS
**Tel:** 01223 336000
**Website:** www.chu.cam.ac.uk
**Founded:** 1960

**Clare College**
Trinity Lane, Cambridge CB2 1TL
Tel: 01223 333200
Website: www.clare.cam.ac.uk
Founded: 1326

**Clare Hall**
Herschel Road, Cambridge CB3 9AL
**Tel:** 01223 332360
**Website:** www.clarehall.cam.ac.uk
**Founded:** 1965

**Corpus Christi College**
King's Parade, Cambridge CB2 1RH
**Tel:** 01223 338000
**Website:** www.corpus.cam.ac.uk
**Founded:** 1352

**Darwin College**
Silver Street, Cambridge CB3 9EU
**Tel:** 01223 335660
**Website:** www.dar.cam.ac.uk
**Founded:** 1964

**Downing College**
Regent Street, Cambridge CB2 1DQ
**Tel:** 01223 334800
**Website:** www.dow.cam.ac.uk
**Founded:** 1800

**Emmanuel College**
St Andrew's Street, Cambridge CB2 3AP
**Tel:** 01223 334200
**Website:** www.emma.cam.ac.uk
**Founded:** 1584

**Fitzwilliam College**
Huntingdon Road, Cambridge CB3 0DG
**Tel:** 01223 332000
**Website:** www.fitz.cam.ac.uk
**Founded:** 1966

**Girton College**
Huntingdon Road, Cambridge CB3 0JG
**Tel:** 01223 338999
**Website:** www.girton.cam.ac.uk
**Founded:** 1869

**Gonville & Caius College**
Trinity Street, Cambridge CB2 1TA
**Tel:** 01223 332400
**Website:** www.cai.cam.ac.uk
**Founded:** 1348

**Homerton College**
Hills Road, Cambridge CB2 2PH
**Tel:** 01223 507111
**Website:** www.homerton.cam.ac.uk
**Founded:** 1976

**Hughes Hall**
Wollaston Road, Cambridge CB1 2EW
**Tel:** 01223 334897
**Website:** www.hughes.cam.ac.uk
**Founded:** 1885

**Jesus College**
Jesus Lane, Cambridge CB5 8BL
**Tel:** 01223 339339
**Website:** www.jesus.cam.ac.uk
**Founded:** 1496

**King's College**
King's Parade, Cambridge CB2 1ST
**Tel:** 01223 331100
**Website:** www.kings.cam.ac.uk
**Founded:** 1441

**Lucy Cavendish College**
Lady Margaret Road, Cambs CB3 0BU
**Tel:** 01223 332190
**Website:** www.lucy-cav.cam.ac.uk
**Founded:** 1965

**Magdalene College**
Magdalene Street, Cambridge CB3 0AG
**Tel:** 01223 332100
**Website:** www.magd.cam.ac.uk
**Founded:** 1428

**New Hall**
Huntingdon Road, Cambridge CB3 0DF
**Tel:** 01223 762100
**Website:** www.newhall.cam.ac.uk
**Founded:** 1954

**Newnham College**
Grange Road, Cambridge CB3 9DF
**Tel:** 01223 335700
**Website:** www.newn.cam.ac.uk
**Founded:** 1871

**Pembroke College**
Trumpington Street, Cambs CB2 1RF
**Tel:** 01223 338100
**Website:** www.pem.cam.ac.uk
**Founded:** 1347

**Peterhouse**
Trumpington Street, Cambs CB2 1RD
**Tel:** 01223 338200
**Website:** www.pet.cam.ac.uk
**Founder:** The Bishop of Ely
**Founded:** 1284

**Queens' College**
Silver Street, Cambridge CB3 9ET
**Tel:** 01223 335511
**Website:** www.quns.cam.ac.uk
**Founder:** Margaret of Anjou,
Elizabeth Woodville
**Founded:** 1448

**Ridley Hall**
Ridley Hall Road, Cambridge CB3 9HG
**Tel:** 01223 741080
**Website:** www.ridley.cam.ac.uk
**Founded:** 1879

**Robinson College**
Grange Road, Cambridge CB3 9AN
**Tel:** 01223 339100
**Website:** www.robinson.cam.ac.uk
**Founded:** 1979

**St Catherine's College**
King's Parade, Cambs CB2 1RL
**Tel:** 01223 338300
**Website:** www.caths.cam.ac.uk
**Founded:** 1473

**St Edmund's College**
Mount Pleasant, Cambridge CB3 0BN
**Tel:** 01223 336086
**Website:** www.st-edmunds.cam.ac.uk
**Founded:** 1896

**St John's College**
St John's Street, Cambridge CB2 1TP
**Tel:** 01223 338600
**Website:** www.joh.cam.ac.uk
**Founded:** 1511

**Selwyn College**
Grange Road, Cambridge CB3 9DQ
**Tel:** 01223 335846
**Website:** www.sel.cam.ac.uk
**Founded:** 1882

**Sidney Sussex College**
Sidney Street, Cambridge CB2 3HU
**Tel:** 01223 338800
**Website:** www.sid.cam.ac.uk
**Founded:** 1596

**Trinity College**
Trinity Street, Cambridge CB2 1TQ
**Tel:** 01223 338400
**Website:** www.trin.cam.ac.uk
**Founded:** 1546

**Trinity Hall**
Trinity Lane, Cambridge CB2 1TJ
**Tel:** 01223 332500
**Website:** www.trinhall.cam.ac.uk
**Founded:** 1350

**Wesley House**
Jesus Lane, Cambridge CB5 8BJ
**Tel:** 01223 350127 / 367980
**Website:** www.wesley.cam.ac.uk

**Wescott House**
Jesus Lane, Cambridge CB5 8BP
**Tel:** 01223 741000
**Website:** www.ely.anglican.org/westcott

**Westminster & Cheshunt**
Madingley Road Cambridge CB3 0AA
**Tel:** 01223 741084
**Website:** www.westminstercollege.co.uk

**Wolfson College**
Grange Road, Cambridge CB3 9BB
**Tel:** 01223 335900
**Website:** www.wolfson.cam.ac.uk
**Founded:** 1965

Visitors wishing to gain admittance to the Colleges (meaning the Courts, not to the staircases & students' rooms) are advised to contact the Tourist Office for further information. It should be noted that Halls normally close for lunch (12–2pm) and many are not open during the afternoon. Chapels may be closed during services. Libraries are not normally open, and Gardens do not usually include the Fellows' garden. Visitors, and especially guided groups, should always call on the Porters Lodge first.

■ **Owner**
English Heritage

■ **Contact**
Visitor Operations Team
Audley End House
Audley End
Saffron Walden
Essex CB11 4JF

**Tel:** 01799 522842
**Fax:** 01799 521276

Venue Hire and
Hospitality:
**Tel:** 01799 529403

■ **Location**
**MAP 7:G10**
**OS Ref. TL525 382**

1m W of Saffron Walden
on B1383,
M11/J8 & J10.

**Rail:** Audley End 1¼ m.

■ **Opening Times\***
**House**
March & October, Sat &
Sun: 10am–4pm (Sat
closes 3pm) Behind-the-
Scenes Tours only.

April–June &
September\*,
(Guided Historical Tours
only), and Jul–Aug,
Wed–Sun, 11am–5pm
(Sats closes 3pm).

Last admission 1 hr
before closing.

\*At certain times of the
year access to the house
is by 'Behind-The-Scenes'
& Guided Historical Tours
only. Some rooms will
not be open throughout
the season. Please call
for details.

In some rooms, light
levels are reduced to
preserve vulnerable
textiles and other
collections. House may
have to close at 4.30pm
when events are booked.

**Gardens**
March & October, Sats &
Suns, 10am–5pm.

April–end September:
Wed–Sun & BHs,
10am–6pm.

■ **Admission**
**House & Grounds**
| | |
|---|---|
| Adult | £9.20 |
| Child (5–15yrs) | £4.60 |
| Child (under 5yrs) | Free |
| Conc. | £6.90 |
| Family (2+3) | £23.00 |

**Grounds only**
| | |
|---|---|
| Adult | £5.00 |
| Child (5–15yrs) | £2.50 |
| Child (under 5yrs) | Free |
| Concessions | £3.80 |
| Family (2+3) | £12.50 |

**Groups**
(11+) 15% discount.

■ **Conference/Function**

| ROOM | MAX CAPACITY |
|---|---|
| Grounds | Large scale events possible |

# AUDLEY END HOUSE & GARDENS ▦

www.english-heritage.org.uk/visits

Audley End was a palace in all but name. Built by Thomas Howard, Earl of Suffolk, to entertain King James I. The King may have had his suspicions, for he never stayed there; in 1618 Howard was imprisoned and fined for embezzlement.

Charles II bought the property in 1668 for £50,000, but within a generation the house was gradually demolished, and by the 1750s it was about the size you see today. There are still over 30 magnificent rooms to see, each with period furnishings.

The house and its gardens, including a 19th century parterre and rose garden, are surrounded by an enchanting 18th century landscaped park laid out by 'Capability' Brown.

Visitors can also visit the working organic walled garden and purchase produce from its shop. Extending to nearly 10 acres the garden includes a 170ft long, five-bay vine house, built in 1802.

ℹ️ Open air concerts and other events. WCs.

🛍️ Private and corporate hire.

♿ Ground floor and grounds.

☕ Restaurant (max 50).

🍴 By arrangement for groups.

🅿️ Coaches to book in advance. Free entry for coach drivers and tour guides. One additional place for every extra 20 people.

📖 School visits free if booked in advance. Contact the Administrator or tel 01223 582700 for bookings.

🐕 On leads only.

## BOURNE MILL

**Bourne Road, Colchester, Essex  CO2 8RT**
**Tel:** 01206 572422  www.nationaltrust.org.uk
**Owner:** The National Trust  **Contact:** The Custodian
Originally a fishing lodge built in 1591. It was later converted into a mill with a 4 acre mill pond. Much of the machinery, including the waterwheel, is intact.
**Location:** MAP 8:J11, OS Ref. TM006 238. 1m S of Colchester centre, in Bourne Road, off the Mersea Road B1025.
**Open:** June, Suns 2–5pm. July–August: Tues, Suns (& BH Mons), 2–5pm.
**Admission:** Adult £2.50, Child £1. No reduction for groups.
Guide dogs only.

## BRENTWOOD CATHEDRAL
### INGRAVE ROAD, BRENTWOOD, ESSEX  CM15 8AT

**Tel:** 01277 232266  **E-mail:** bishop@dioceseofbrentwood.org
**Owner:** Diocese of Brentwood  **Contact:** Rt Rev Thomas McMahon
The new (1991) Roman Catholic classical Cathedral Church of St Mary and St Helen incorporates part of the original Victorian church. Designed by distinguished classical architect Quinlan Terry with roundels by Raphael Maklouf. Architecturally, the inspiration is early Italian Renaissance crossed with the English Baroque of Christopher Wren. The north elevation consists of nine bays each divided by Doric pilasters. This is broken by a huge half-circular portico. The Kentish ragstone walls have a natural rustic look, which contrasts with the smooth Portland stone of the capitals and column bases. Inside is an arcade of Tuscan arches with central altar with the lantern above.
**Location:** MAP 4:J1, OS Ref. TQ596 938. A12 & M25/J28. Centre of Brentwood, opposite Brentwood School.
**Open:** All year, daily.
**Admission:** Free.
Limited. None for coaches.

## CHELMSFORD CATHEDRAL

**New Street, Chelmsford, Essex  CM1 1TY**
**Tel:** 01245 294489  **E-mail:** office@chelmsfordcathedral.org.uk
**Contact:** Mrs Bobby Harrington
15th century building became a Cathedral in 1914. Extended in 1920s, major refurbishment in 1980s and in 2000 with contemporary works of distinction and splendid new organs in 1994 and 1996.
**Location:** MAP 7:H12, OS Ref. TL708 070. In Chelmsford.
**Open:** Daily: 8am–5.30pm. Sun services: 8am, 9.30am, 11.15am and 6pm. Weekday services: 8.15am and 5.15pm daily. Holy Communion: Wed, 12.35pm & Thur, 10am. Tours by prior arrangement.
**Admission:** No charge but donation invited.

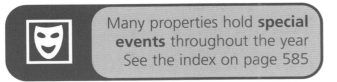
Many properties hold **special events** throughout the year
See the index on page 585

## COGGESHALL GRANGE BARN

**Grange Hill, Coggeshall, Colchester, Essex  CO6 1RE**
**Tel:** 01376 562226  www.nationaltrust.org.uk
**Owner:** The National Trust  **Contact:** The Custodian
One of the oldest surviving timber-framed barns in Europe, dating from around 1240, and originally part of a Cistercian Monastery. It was restored in the 1980s by the Coggeshall Grange Barn Trust, Braintree District Council and Essex County Council. Features a small collection of farm carts and wagons.
**Location:** MAP 8:I11, OS Ref. TL848 223. Signposted off A120 Coggeshall bypass. West side of the road southwards to Kelvedon.
**Open:** 1 Apr–14 Oct: Tues, Thurs, Suns & BH Mons, 2–5pm.
**Admission:** Adult £2.50, Child £1. Joint ticket with Paycocke's: Adult £4, Child £2.
Coaches must book.  Guide dogs only.

## COLCHESTER CASTLE MUSEUM

**14 Ryegate Road, Colchester, Essex  CO1 1YG**
**Tel:** 01206 282939  **Fax:** 01206 282925
**Owner:** Colchester Borough Council  **Contact:** Museum Resource Centre
The largest Norman Castle Keep in Europe with fine archaeological collections on show. Hands-on & interactive display brings history to life.
**Location:** MAP 8:J11, OS Ref. TL999 253. In Colchester town centre, off A12.
**Open:** All year: Mon–Sat, 10am–5pm, also Suns, 11am–5pm.
**Admission:** Adult £4.90, Child (5–15yrs)/Conc. £3.10. Child under 5yrs Free. Saver ticket: £13. Prices may increase from April 2007.

©Sylvia Keith

## COPPED HALL
### CROWN HILL, EPPING, ESSEX  CM16 5HH

www.coppedhalltrust.org.uk

**Tel:** 020 7267 1679  **Fax:** 020 7482 0557  **E-mail:** Coxalan1@aol.com
**Owner:** The Copped Hall Trust  **Contact:** Alan Cox
Shell of 18th century Palladian mansion under restoration. Situated on ridge overlooking excellent landscaped park. Ancillary buildings including stables and small racquets court. Former elaborate gardens being rescued from abandonment. Large early 18th century walled garden – adjacent to site of 16th century mansion where 'A Midsummer Night's Dream' was first performed. Ideal film location.
**Location:** MAP 7:G12, OS Ref. TL433 016. 4m SW of Epping, N of M25.
**Open:** By appointment only for groups (20+) and events. Special open days.
**Admission:** Gardens £3. Part of Mansion and Stables £3, Child under 14yrs Free.
Partial.  Obligatory.  In grounds on leads. Concerts/plays.

## FEERINGBURY MANOR

**Coggeshall Road, Feering, Colchester, Essex  CO5 9RB**
**Tel:** 01376 561946
**Owner/Contact:** Mrs Giles Coode-Adams
**Location:** MAP 8:I11, OS Ref. TL864 215. 1¼m N of A12 between Feering & Coggeshall.
**Open:** From 1st Thur in Apr to last Fri in Jul: Thur & Fri only, 8am–4pm.
**Admission:** Adult £3, Child Free. In aid of National Gardens Scheme.

Rona Cox

## GARDENS OF EASTON LODGE 🏛

**WARWICK HOUSE, EASTON LODGE, LITTLE EASTON, GT DUNMOW  CM6 2BB**

www.eastonlodge.co.uk

**Tel/Fax:** 01371 876979  **E-mail:** enquiries@eastonlodge.co.uk

**Owner/Contact:** Mr Brian Creasey

Beautiful gardens set in 23 acres. Horticultural associations from the 16th century to date. Visit the Italian gardens, currently undergoing restoration, designed by Harold Peto for 'Daisy' Countess of Warwick (Edward VII's mistress). In the dovecote, study the history of the house, garden and owners over 400 years. A peaceful and atmospheric haven! Millennium Project: Living yew and box sundial and Shakespeare border.

**Location:** MAP 7:H11, OS Ref. TL593 240. 4m NW of Great Dunmow, off the B184 Dunmow to Thaxted road.

**Open:** Feb/Mar (snowdrops): daily. Easter–31 Oct: Fri–Sun & BHs, 12 noon–6pm or dusk if earlier. Groups at other times by appointment.

**Admission:** Adult £4.20, Child (3–12yrs) £1.70, Conc. £3.80. Group (20+): £3.80. Schools (20+) £1.70 per child, 1 teacher free per 10 children.

ℹ Exhibition & Study Centre in Dovecote. 🏛 Ⓣ ♿ Partial. WC. Picnics. 🎦 By arrangement. Ⓟ Limited for coaches. 🐕 In grounds on leads. ❋ 🐾 €

---

## HYLANDS HOUSE

**HYLANDS PARK, LONDON ROAD, CHELMSFORD  CM2 8WQ**

www.chelmsford.gov.uk/hylands

**Tel:** 01245 605500   **Fax:** 01245 496804

**Owner:** Chelmsford Borough Council   **Contact:** Nicki Jones

This beautiful Grade II* listed villa, with its neo-classical exterior, is set in 570 acres of historic landscaped parkland, including formal gardens. Following five phases of restoration, visitors can now enjoy spectacular rooms throughout the completed House. The Library, Drawing Room and Saloon, which re-opened in 1999, have been restored to their early Victorian period. The Entrance Hall was restored to its Georgian origins in the 1995 restoration. April 2003 saw the opening of the West Wing, which includes the magnificent Victorian Banqueting Room and the Georgian Small Dining Room, as well as the original cellars, circa 1730. In September 2005, the final phase of restoration to the upper floors was completed, including the Victorian Grand Staircase and Repton Room, which offers stunning views over the park. Exhibition boards detail the history of the House, and guide books are available. The House hosts events and workshops throughout the year, and guided tours can be booked.

**Location:** MAP 7:H12, OS Ref. TL681 054. 2m SW of Chelmsford. Signposted on A414 (formerly A1016) from J15 near Chelmsford.

**Open:** All year: Suns, Mons & BHs, 11am–6pm (Oct–Apr: Mons, 11am–4pm). Closed 25 Dec.

**Admission:** Adult £3.40, accompanied children under 16 Free. Conc. £2.40. Groups: £3.60pp or £90 (whichever greater).

ℹ No photography in house. 🖼 🏛 Ⓣ ♿ 🎦 Sun & Mon. 🎦 By arrangement. Ⓟ Limited for coaches. 🐕 In grounds. Guide dogs only in house. 🔔 ❋ 🐾

---

## HARWICH REDOUBT FORT

**Main Road, Harwich, Essex**

**Tel/Fax:** 01255 503429   **E-mail:** info@harwich-society.co.uk

www.harwich-society.co.uk

**Owner:** The Harwich Society   **Contact:** Mr A Rutter

180ft diameter circular fort built in 1808 to defend the port against Napoleonic invasion. Being restored by Harwich Society and part is a museum. Eleven guns on battlements.

**Location:** MAP 8:K10, OS Ref. TM262 322. Rear of 29 Main Road.

**Open:** 1 May–31 Aug: daily, 10am–4pm. Sept–Apr: Suns only, 10am–4pm. Groups by appointment at any time.

**Admission:** Adult £2, Child Free (no unaccompanied children).

❋ €

---

© English Heritage Photo Library / Pat Payne

Audley End House & Gardens, Saffron Walden

---

## INGATESTONE HALL 🏛

**HALL LANE, INGATESTONE, ESSEX  CM4 9NR**

**Tel:** 01277 353010   **Fax:** 01245 248979

**Owner:** The Lord Petre   **Contact:** The Administrator

16th century mansion, set in 11 acres of grounds (formal garden and wild walk), built by Sir William Petre, Secretary of State to four Tudor monarchs, which has remained in the hands of his family ever since. The two Priests' hiding places can be seen, as well as the furniture, portraits and family memorabilia accumulated over the centuries.

**Location:** MAP 7:H12, OS Ref. TQ653 986. Off A12 between Brentwood & Chelmsford. Take Station Lane at London end of Ingatestone High Street, cross level-crossing and continue for ½ m to SE.

**Open:** 7 Apr–30 Sept: Sats, Suns & BH Mons. Aug: Wed–Fri, 1–6pm.

**Admission:** Adult £4, Child £2 (under 5yrs Free), Conc. £3.50. 50p per head discount for groups (20+).

ℹ No photography in house. 🖼 🏛 Ⓣ ♿ Partial. 🎦 By arrangement. Ⓟ 🐕 Guide dogs only. 🐾

# LAYER MARNEY TOWER

### Nr COLCHESTER, ESSEX CO5 9US

www.layermarneytower.co.uk

**Tel/Fax:** 01206 330784 **E-mail:** info@layermarneytower.co.uk
**Owner/Contact:** Mr Nicholas Charrington
Built in the reign of Henry VIII, the tallest Tudor gatehouse in Great Britain. Lord Henry Marney clearly intended to rival Wolsey's building at Hampton Court, but he died before his masterpiece was finished. His son John died two years later, in 1525, and building work stopped. Layer Marney Tower has some of the finest terracotta work in the country, most probably executed by Flemish craftsmen trained by Italian masters. The terracotta is used on the battlements, windows, and most lavishly of all, on the tombs of Henry and John Marney. Visitors may climb the Tower, passing through the History Room, and enjoy the marvellous views of the Essex countryside. There are fine outbuildings, including the Long Gallery with its magnificent oak roof and the medieval barn which now houses some of the Home Farm's collection of Rare Breed farm animals. Function rooms available for receptions, conferences and corporate days.
**Location:** MAP 8:J11, OS Ref. TL929 175. 7m SW of Colchester, signed off B1022.
**Open:** 1 Apr–30 Sept: Sun–Thur, 12 noon (11am on BHs)–5pm. Group visits/guided tours throughout the year by arrangement.
**Admission:** Adult £4, Child £2.50, Family £12. Groups (15+): Adult £3.75, Child £2.25. Guided tours (pre-booked) £5, min. charge £125. Schools by arrangement.
Partial. WC. By arrangement. In grounds, on leads. 1 double, 2 single. On BHs.

# MARKS HALL GARDENS AND ARBORETUM

### COGGESHALL, ESSEX CO6 1TG

www.markshall.org.uk

**Tel:** 01376 563796
**Owner:** The Thomas Philips Price Trust **Contact:** Julia Fosker
Five individual gardens and a double long border, combining contemporary and traditional landscaping and planting, form the newly redesigned Walled Garden at Marks Hall. This unique garden is open on one side to a lake – on the opposite bank the Millennium Walk is designed to be at its best during the shortest days of the year. There is much to see in this Arboretum and Garden of over 100 acres on every day of the year.
**Location:** MAP 8:I11, OS168 Ref. TQ840 252. Off B1024, 1½ m N of Coggeshall.
**Open:** Apr–Oct: Tues–Sun & BH Mons, 10.30am–5pm. Winter weekends, 10.30am–dusk.
**Admission:** Adult £3, Child £1, Groups (10+): £2.
Partial. WC. By arrangement.

## MISTLEY TOWERS

**Colchester, Essex**
**Tel:** 01206 393884 / 01223 582700 (Regional Office)
**Owner:** English Heritage **Contact:** The Keykeeper (Mistley Quay Workshops)
The remains of one of only two churches designed by the great architect Robert Adam. Built in 1776. It was unusual in having towers at both the east and west ends.
**Location:** MAP 8:K10, OS Ref. TM116 320. On B1352, 1½m E of A137 at Lawford, 9m E of Colchester.
**Open:** Key available from Mistley Quay Workshops, 01206 393884.
**Admission:** Free.
Grounds only. Restricted areas.

# SIR ALFRED MUNNINGS ART MUSEUM

### CASTLE HOUSE, CASTLE HILL, DEDHAM, ESSEX CO7 6AZ

www.siralfredmunnings.co.uk

**Tel:** 01206 322127 **Fax:** 01206 322127
**Owner:** Castle House Trust **Contact:** The Administrator
In 1959 Castle House was set up as an art museum and memorial to Sir Alfred Munnings. The house is a mixture of Tudor and Georgian periods restored and with original Munnings' furniture. Over 200 of Munnings' works are exhibited, representing his life's work. The house stands in spacious grounds with well maintained gardens. Visitors may also view his original studio where his working materials are displayed.
**Location:** MAP 8:K10, OS Ref. TM060 328. Approximately ¾m from the village centre on the corner of East Lane.
**Open:** Easter Sun–7 Oct. Sun, Wed & BH Mon. Also Thurs & Sats in Aug.
**Admission:** Adult £4, Child £1, Conc. £3.
Partial. WC. In grounds, on leads.

## PAYCOCKE'S

**West Street, Coggeshall, Colchester, Essex CO6 1NS**
**Tel:** 01376 561305 www.nationaltrust.org.uk
**Owner:** The National Trust **Contact:** The Tenant
A merchant's house, dating from about 1500, with unusually rich panelling and wood carving. A display of lace, for which Coggeshall was famous, is on show. Delightful cottage garden.
**Location:** MAP 8:I11, OS Ref. TL848 225. Signposted off A120.
**Open:** 1 Apr–14 Oct: Tues, Thurs, Suns & BH Mons, 2–5pm.
**Admission:** Adult £3, Child £1.50. Groups (10+) by prior arrangement, no reduction for groups. Joint ticket with Coggeshall Grange Barn: Adult £4, Child £2.
Access to ground floor and garden. NT's at the Coggeshall Grange Barn.

See all the properties that are **open all year** in the index on page 580

## PRIOR'S HALL BARN ⚏

**Widdington, Newport, Essex**

**Tel:** 01233 582700 (Regional Office)

**Owner:** English Heritage    **Contact:** East of England Regional Office

One of the finest surviving medieval barns in south-east England and representative of the group of aisled barns centred on north-west Essex.

**Location:** MAP 7:G10, OS Ref. TL538 319. In Widdington, on unclassified road 2m SE of Newport, off B1383.

**Open:** 1 Apr–30 Sept: Sats & Suns, 10am–6pm.

**Admission:** Free.

## RHS GARDEN HYDE HALL

### BUCKHATCH LANE, RETTENDON, CHELMSFORD, ESSEX  CM3 8ET

www.rhs.org.uk

**Tel:** 01245 400256    **Fax:** 01245 402100    **E-mail:** hydehall@rhs.org.uk

**Owner:** The Royal Horticultural Society    **Contact:** Reception

A visit to the 360-acre estate at Hyde Hall is unforgettable in any season. The developed area, in excess of 24 acres, demonstrates an eclectic range of inspirational horticultural styles. Highlights include the spectacular Dry Garden, colour-themed Herbaceous Borders, Australian Garden, Garden for Wildlife and Queen Mother's Garden.

**Location:** MAP 8:I12, OS Ref. TQ782 995. SE of Chelmsford, signposted from A130.

**Open:** All year, daily (except Christmas Day) from 10am. Closing time varies between 4pm and 6pm. Last entry 1hr before closing. Please contact us for details.

**Admission:** Adult £5, Child (6–16yrs) £1.50, Companion/Carer of disabled person Free. RHS member and one guest Free. Pre-booked Groups (10+): £4.

⌂ ⓣ 🅿 Partial 🄳 Licensed ⓣ Licensed. 🅿 Limited for coaches ▣ 🐕 Guide dogs only. ❋

## SALING HALL GARDEN

**Great Saling, Braintree, Essex  CM7 5DT**

**Tel:** 01371 850 243    **Fax:** 01371 850 274

**Owner/Contact:** Hugh Johnson Esq

Twelve acres including a walled garden dated 1698. Water garden and landscaped arboretum.

**Location:** MAP 7:H11, OS Ref. TL700 258. 6m NW of Braintree, 2m N of B1256.

**Open:** May, Jun & Jul: Weds, 2–5pm.

**Admission:** Adult £3, Child Free.

## TILBURY FORT ⚏

**No. 2 Office Block, The Fort, Tilbury, Essex  RM18 7NR**

**Tel:** 01375 858489    www.english-heritage.org.uk

**Owner:** English Heritage    **Contact:** Visitor Operations Team

The best and largest example of 17th century military engineering in England, commanding the Thames. Learn more about the fascinating history of Tilbury Fort with a new interpretation scheme in the North East Bastion magazine passages. See new graphic panels and displays, new reproduction lamps and two fully restored charging stations.

There is also an interactive oral history programme to provide every visitor with a fascinating new insight to Tilbury.

**Location:** MAP 4:K2, OS Ref. TQ651 754. ½m E of Tilbury off A126. Near Port of Tilbury.

**Open:** 1 Apr–31 Oct: daily, 10am–5pm. 1 Nov–20 Mar: Thur–Mon, 10am–4pm. Closed 24–26 Dec & 1 Jan.

**Admission:** Adult £3.50, Child £1.80, Under 5s Free. Conc. £2.60, Family £8.80. EH Members/OVP Free.

ⓘ WCs. ⌂ ♿ Grounds only. ⌂ 🅿 ▣ 🐕 On leads. ❋ ♿

## WALTHAM ABBEY GATEHOUSE & BRIDGE ⚏

**Waltham Abbey, Essex**

**Tel:** 01992 702200 / 01223 582700 (Regional Office)

**Owner:** English Heritage    **Contact:** East of England Regional Office (01223 582700)

The late 14th century abbey gatehouse, part of the north range of the cloister and the medieval 'Harold's Bridge' of one of the great monastic foundations of the Middle Ages.

**Location:** MAP 7:G12, OS Ref. TL381 008. In Waltham Abbey off A112. Just NE of the Abbey church.

**Open:** Any reasonable time.

**Admission:** Free.

♿ Sensory trail guide. 🐕 On leads. ❋

For rare and unusual plants visit the **plant sales** index on page 564

Hylands House, Chelmsford

The South Front

# HATFIELD HOUSE

www.hatfield-house.co.uk

Visit this stunning Jacobean house within an extensive Park. Home of the 7th Marquess of Salisbury and the Cecil family for 400 years, the house is steeped in Elizabethan and Victorian political history. Hatfield House has a fine collection of pictures, tapestries, furnishings and historic armour.

Delightful formal gardens, dating from 1611 when Robert Cecil employed John Tradescant the Elder to collect plants for the new scheme. The West garden includes scented garden, herb garden and knot garden. The adjoining wilderness areas are at their best in spring with masses of naturalised daffodils. The East garden's elegant parterres, topiary and rare plants are a delight for the gardening enthusiast and for those wishing to spend a quiet time in idyllic surroundings.

Within the gardens stands the surviving wing of The Royal Palace of Hatfield where Elizabeth I spent much of her childhood and held her first Council of State in November 1558. An oak tree marks the place where the young Princess Elizabeth first heard of her accession to the throne. Visitors can enjoy walking in the 1,000 acres of park with woodland trails plus picnic areas and a children's play park.

Knot Garden of the Elizabethan Old Palace

Elizabeth I, The Rainbow Portrait – by kind permission of Lord Salisbury

ℹ️ No photography in house. National Collection of model soldiers, 5m of marked trails, children's play area.

🍷 Weddings, functions: tel 01707 287080. Banquets held in the Old Palace: tel 01707 262055.

♿ WCs. Parking next to house. Lift.

🍴 Seats 150. Pre-booked lunch and tea for groups 20+. Tel: 01707 262030.

🚶 Wed–Fri only. Group tours available in French, German, Italian, Spanish or Japanese by prior arrangement.

🅿️ Ample. Hardstanding for coaches.

📚 Resource books, play area & nature trails. Living History days throughout the school year: tel 01707 287042. KS2 & 3 groups not permitted in house.

🐕 In grounds, on leads.

## Owner
The 7th Marquess of Salisbury

## Contact
Director – Visitors & Events
Hatfield House
Hatfield
Hertfordshire AL9 5NQ
**Tel:** 01707 287010
**Fax:** 01707 287033
**E-mail:** visitors@ hatfield-house.co.uk

## Location
**MAP 7:F11**
**OS Ref. TL 237 084**
21m N of London, M25/ J23 7m, A1(M)/J4, 2m.
**Bus:** Local services from St Albans and Hertford.
**Rail:** From Kings Cross every 30 mins. Station is opposite entrance to Park.
**Air:** Luton (30 mins). Stansted (45 mins).

## Opening Times
7 April–end September
**House**
Wed–Sun & BHs.
12 noon–4pm. Guided tours Wed–Fri (not Aug).
**Park, West Garden, Restaurant & Shop**
Daily, 11am–5.30pm.
**East Garden**
Thurs only.
11am–5.30pm.

## Admission
**House, Park & West Garden**
| | |
|---|---|
| Adult | £9.00 |
| Child (5–15yrs) | £4.50 |
| OAP | £8.50 |
| Family (2+4) | £25.00 |

Groups (20+)
| | |
|---|---|
| Adult | £8.00 |

**Park & West Garden**
| | |
|---|---|
| Adult | £5.00 |
| Child | £4.00 |

**Park only**
| | |
|---|---|
| Adult | £2.50 |
| Child (5–15yrs) | £1.50 |

**East Garden**
(Thursdays)   £3.50 extra

House tour   £5 extra
RHS members free entry to Park & West Garden daily during open season, except during special events.

## Special Events
**May 10–13**
Living Crafts.
**June 16/17**
Rose Weekend.
**July 21**
Battle Proms Concert.
**Aug 3–5**
Art in Clay.
**Aug 17–19**
Hatfield House Country Show.
Please see website for details of events programme.

## Conference/Function

| ROOM | SIZE | MAX CAPACITY |
|---|---|---|
| The Old Palace | 112' x 33' | 280 |
| Riding School Conference Centre | 100' x 40' | 140 |

■ **Owner**

The Hon Henry Lytton Cobbold

■ **Contact**

The Estate Office
Knebworth House
Knebworth
Hertfordshire SG3 6PY

**Tel:** 01438 812661
**Fax:** 01438 811908
**E-mail:** info@
knebworthhouse.com

■ **Location**

**MAP 7:E11**
**OS Ref. TL230 208**

Direct access off the
A1(M) J7 (Stevenage
South A602).
28m N of London.
15m N of M25/J23.

**Rail:** Stevenage Station
2m (from Kings Cross).

**Air:** Luton Airport 15m
Landing facilities.

**Taxi:** 01438 811122.

■ **Opening Times**

**House, Park & Gardens**
24/25 March, 21 April–20
May, 9–24 June & 8–30
September: Weekends
and BHs.

31 March–15 April,
26 May–3 June &
30 June–5 September:
Daily.

**Park, Playground &
Gardens**
11am–5.30pm.

**House**
12 noon–5pm
(last adm. 4.15pm).

■ **Admission**

**Including House**
| | |
|---|---|
| Adult | £9.00 |
| Child*/Conc | £8.50 |

Family Day Ticket
| | |
|---|---|
| (4 persons) | £31.00 |

Groups (20+)
| | |
|---|---|
| Adult | £8.00 |
| Child*/Conc | £7.50 |

**Excluding House**
| | |
|---|---|
| All Persons | £7.00 |
| Season Ticket | £32.00 |

Family Day Ticket
| | |
|---|---|
| (4 persons) | £24.00 |

Groups (20+)
| | |
|---|---|
| All persons | £6.00 |

House Supplements
| | |
|---|---|
| Adults | £2.00 |
| Child*/Conc | £1.50 |

*Under 4s Free.

■ **Conference/Function**

| ROOM | SIZE | MAX CAPACITY |
|---|---|---|
| Banqueting Hall | 26' x 41' | 80 |
| Dining Parlour | 21' x 38' | 50 |
| Library | 32' x 21' | 40 |
| Manor Barn | 70' x 25' | 250 |
| Lodge Barn | 75' x 30' | 150 |

# KNEBWORTH HOUSE 🏛

## www.knebworthhouse.com

Home of the Lytton family since 1490, and still a lived-in family house. Transformed in early Victorian times by Edward Bulwer-Lytton, the author, poet, dramatist and statesman, into the unique high gothic fantasy house of today, complete with turrets, griffins and gargoyles.

Historically home to Constance Lytton, the Suffragette, and her father, Robert Lytton, the Viceroy of India who proclaimed Queen Victoria Empress of India at the Great Delhi Durbar of 1877. Visited by Queen Elizabeth I, Charles Dickens and Sir Winston Churchill.

The interior contains various styles including the magnificent Jacobean Banqueting Hall, a unique example of the 17th century change in fashion from traditional English to Italian Palladian. The high gothic State Drawing Room by John Crace contrasts with the Regency elegance of Mrs Bulwer-Lytton's bedroom and the 20th century designs of Sir Edwin Lutyens in the Entrance Hall, Dining Parlour and Library.

25 acres of beautiful gardens, simplified by Lutyens, including pollarded lime avenues, formal rose garden, maze, Gertrude Jekyll herb garden and newly designed Walled Garden. 250 acres of gracious parkland, with herds of red and sika deer, includes children's giant adventure playground and miniature railway. New Dino Trail with 72 life-size dinosaurs set grazing through the Wilderness Walk within the Formal Gardens. World famous for its huge open-air rock concerts, and used as a film location for *Batman*, *The Shooting Party*, *Wilde*, *Jane Eyre* and *The Canterville Ghost*, amongst others.

ⓘ Suitable for fashion shows, air displays, archery, shooting, equestrian events, cricket pitch, garden parties, shows, rallies, filming, helicopter landing. No pushchairs, photography, smoking or drinking in House.

🛍

🍽 Indian Raj Evenings and Elizabethan Banquets with jousting. Full catering service.

♿ Partial. WCs. Parking. Ground floor accessible.

☕ Licensed tearoom. Special rates for advance bookings, menus on request.

🚶 Daily at 30 min intervals or at booked times including evenings. Tour time 1hr. Shorter tours by arrangement. Room Wardens on duty on busy weekends. Themed tours available.

🅿 Unlimited. Group visits must be booked in advance with Estate Office.

🏫 National Curriculum based school activity days.

🐕 Guide dogs only in House. Park, on leads.

💒 Licensed Garden Gazebo & Manor Barn.

🔔 Telephone for details.

## ASHRIDGE

**Ringshall, Berkhamsted, Hertfordshire HP4 1LX**
**Tel:** 01442 851227  **Fax:** 01442 850000  **E-mail:** ashridge@nationaltrust.org.uk
**Owner:** The National Trust  **Contact:** The Visitor Centre
The Ashridge Estate comprises over 1800ha of woodlands, commons and downland. At the northerly end of the Estate the Ivinghoe Hills are an outstanding area of chalk downland which supports a rich variety of plants and insects.
**Location:** MAP 7:D11 OS Ref. SP970 131. Between Northchurch & Ringshall, just off B4506.
**Open:** Visitor Centre & Shop: 17 Mar–16 Dec: daily, 12 noon–5pm. Monument: 17 Mar–28 Oct: Sats, Suns & BHs 12 noon–last admission 4.30pm. Tearoom: 18 Mar–10 Dec: Tues–Sun, 10am–5pm.
**Admission:** Monument: £1.40, Child 70p. Free to NT members.
ⓘ Visitor Centre. 🅿 🅰 Vehicles available. 🎥 🅿 Limited for coaches. 🎦 🐾 In grounds, on leads. ♿

## BENINGTON LORDSHIP GARDENS

**Stevenage, Hertfordshire SG2 7BS**
**Tel:** 01438 869668  **Fax:** 01438 869622  **E-mail:** rhbott@beningtonlordship.co.uk
**www.beningtonlordship.co.uk**
**Owner:** Mr R R A Bott  **Contact:** Mr or Mrs R R A Bott
7 acre garden overlooking lakes in a timeless setting. Features include Norman keep and moat, Queen Anne manor house, James Pulham folly, walled vegetable garden, grass tennis court and verandah. Renowned herbaceous borders and snowdrops in February. All location work welcome. Estate includes listed cottages, barns, buildings and airstrip.
**Location:** MAP 7:F11, OS Ref. TL296 236. In village of Benington next to the church. 4m E of Stevenage.
**Open:** Gardens only: Snowdrops: 3–25 Feb. Easter & Spring/Summer BH weekends. Suns, 2–5pm. Mons, 12 noon–5pm. Herbaceous Border week: 17–24 Jun, 2–5pm. By request all year, please telephone. Coaches must book.
**Admission:** Adult £3.50 (Suns in Feb £4.50), Child Free.
♿ Unsuitable. 🎥

## BERKHAMSTED CASTLE

**Berkhamsted, St Albans, Hertfordshire**
**Tel:** 01223 582700 (Regional Office)
**Owner:** English Heritage  **Contact:** East of England Regional Office
The extensive remains of a large 11th century motte and bailey castle which held a strategic position on the road to London.
**Location:** MAP 7:D12, OS Ref. SP996 083. Adjacent to Berkhamsted rail station.
**Open:** All year. Summer: daily, 10am–6pm; Winter: daily, 10am–4pm. Closed 25 Dec & 1 Jan.
**Admission:** Free.
🎥 ❄

## CATHEDRAL & ABBEY CHURCH OF ST ALBAN

**St Albans, Hertfordshire AL1 1BY**
**Tel:** 01727 860780  **Fax:** 01727 850944  **Contact:** Deputy Administrator
Abbey church of Benedictine Monastery founded 793AD commemorating Britain's first martyr.
**Location:** MAP 7:E12, OS Ref. TL145 071. Centre of St Albans.
**Open:** All year: 9am–5.45pm. Telephone for details of services, concerts and special events Mon–Sat, 11am–4pm.
**Admission:** Free of charge but donations welcomed.

## CROMER WINDMILL

**Ardeley, Stevenage, Hertfordshire SG2 7QA**
**Tel:** 01279 843301
**Owner:** Hertfordshire Building Preservation Trust  **Contact:** Cristina Harrison
17th century Post Windmill restored to working order.
**Location:** MAP 7:F10, OS Ref. TL305 286. 4m NE of Stevenage on B1037. 1m SW of Cottered.
**Open:** Mid-May–mid-Sept: Sun, 2nd & 4th Sat & BHs, 2.30–5pm.
**Admission:** Adult £2, Child 25p. Groups (10+) by arrangement: Adult £1, Child 25p.

Who's offering **accommodation?**
See our index on page 575

## FORGE MUSEUM & VICTORIAN COTTAGE GARDEN

**High Street, Much Hadham, Hertfordshire SG10 6BS**
**Tel/Fax:** 01279 843301  **E-mail:** cristinaharrison@btopenworld.com
**Owner:** The Hertfordshire Building Preservation Trust  **Contact:** The Curator
The garden reflects plants that would have been grown in 19th century.
**Location:** MAP 7:G11, OS Ref. TL428 195. Village centre.
**Open:** Fri, Sat, Sun & BHs, 11am–5pm (dusk in winter).
**Admission:** Adult £2, Child/Conc. 50p.

## GORHAMBURY

**St Albans, Hertfordshire AL3 6AH**
**Tel:** 01727 854051  **Fax:** 01727 843675
**Owner:** The Earl of Verulam  **Contact:** The Administrator
Late 18th century house by Sir Robert Taylor. Family portraits from 15th–21st centuries.
**Location:** MAP 7:E11, OS Ref. TL114 078. 2m W of St Albans. Access via private drive off A4147 at St Albans.
**Open:** May–Sept: Thurs, 2–5pm (last entry 4.15pm).
**Admission:** House & Gardens: Adult £6, Child £3, Conc £4. Visitors join guided tours. Special groups by arrangement (Thurs mornings preferred).
♿ Partial. 🎥 📷 Obligatory. 🅿

## HATFIELD HOUSE

*See page 283 for full page entry.*

## HERTFORD MUSEUM

**18 Bull Plain, Hertford SG14 1DT**
**Tel:** 01992 582686
**Owner:** Hertford Museums Trust  **Contact:** Helen Gurney
Local museum in 17th century house, altered by 18th century façade, with recreated Jacobean knot garden.
**Location:** MAP 7:F11, OS Ref. TL326 126. Town centre.
**Open:** Tue–Sat, 10am–5pm.
**Admission:** Free.

## KNEBWORTH HOUSE

*See page 284 for full page entry.*

## OLD GORHAMBURY HOUSE

**St Albans, Hertfordshire**
**Tel:** 01223 582700 (Regional Office)
**Owner:** English Heritage  **Contact:** East of England Regional Office
The decorated remains of this Elizabethan mansion, particularly the porch of the Great Hall, illustrate the impact of the Renaissance on English architecture.
**Location:** MAP 7:E11, OS Ref. TL110 077. On foot by permissive 2m path. By car, drive to Gorhambury Mansion and walk across the gardens.
**Open:** All year (except 1 Jun), any reasonable time.
**Admission:** Free.
🎥 ❄

## THE WALTER ROTHSCHILD ZOOLOGICAL MUSEUM

**Akeman Street, Tring, Hertfordshire HP23 6AP**
**Tel:** 020 7942 6171  **Fax:** 020 7942 6150
**Owner:** The Natural History Museum  **Contact:** General Organiser
The museum was opened to the public by Lord Rothschild in 1892. It houses his private natural history collection. Over 4,000 species of animal in a Victorian setting.
**Location:** MAP 7:D11, OS Ref. SP924 111. S end of Akeman Street, ¼m S of High Street.
**Open:** Mon–Sat, 10am–5pm, Suns, 2–5pm. Closed 24–26 Dec.
**Admission:** Free.

Benington Lordship Gardens, Stevenage

### ST PAULS WALDEN BURY

**Hitchin, Hertfordshire SG4 8BP**

**Tel/Fax:** 01438 871218   **E-mail:** spw@boweslyon.demon.co.uk

**Owner/Contact:** S and C Bowes Lyon

Formal woodland garden, covering about 60 acres, laid out 1730. Long rides lined with clipped beech hedges lead to temples, statues, lake and ponds, and to an outdoor theatre. Seasonal displays of snowdrops, daffodils, irises, magnolias, rhododendrons, woodland paeonies, lilies and shrub roses. Wild flower areas. Grade I listed.

**Location:** MAP 7:E11, OS Ref. TL186 216. 30m N of London. 5m S of Hitchin on B651.

**Open:** Suns: 22 April, 13 May & 3 June, 2–7pm. Other times by appointment.

**Admission:** Adult £3.50, Child 50p. Other times by appointment £6.

### SCOTT'S GROTTO

**Ware, Hertfordshire S912 9SQ**

**Tel:** 01920 464131

**Owner:** East Hertfordshire District Council    **Contact:** J Watson

One of the finest grottos in England built in the 1760s by Quaker Poet John Scott.

**Location:** MAP 7:F11, OS Ref. TL355 137. In Scotts Rd, S of the A119 Hertford Road.

**Open:** 1 Apr–30 Sept: Sat & BH Mon, 2–4.30pm. Also by appointment.

**Admission:** Suggested donation of £1 for adults. Children Free. Please bring a torch.

Ashridge, Berkhamstead

## WALKERN HALL

### STEVENAGE, HERTFORDSHIRE SG2 7JA

www.walkernhall.co.uk

**Tel:** 01438 869346   **E-mail:** info@walkernhall.co.uk

**Owner/Contact:** David de Boinville

Walkern Hall is an early 18th century country house surrounded by extensive gardens, set in the medieval hunting park of Walkern Manor. Very secluded and only thirty miles north of London. The garden has extensive lawns, magnificent trees and a large functional walled garden. Suitable for wedding receptions, functions, launches and locations.

**Location:** MAP 7:F10, OS Ref. TL300 249. Located ½ m SE of Walkern village.

**Open:** By appointment only. For events, functions, film & photography locations.

**Admission:** Prices on request. Telephone for information.

🖝 🖢 Grounds only. 🅿 🔲 Farm tours availble. 🐕 Guide dogs only. ❋ 🐾

NT Photographic Library/Matthew Antrobus

## SHAW'S CORNER 🌿

### AYOT ST LAWRENCE, WELWYN, HERTFORDSHIRE AL6 9BX

www.nationaltrust.org.uk

**Tel/Fax:** 01438 820307   **E-mail:** shawscorner@nationaltrust.org.uk

**Owner:** The National Trust    **Contact:** The Custodian

The fascinating home of playwright George Bernard Shaw until his death in 1950. The modest Edwardian villa contains many literary and personal relics, and the interior is still set out as it was in Shaw's lifetime. The garden, with its richly planted borders and views over the Hertfordshire countryside, contains the revolving summerhouse where Shaw retreated to write.

**Location:** MAP 7:E11, OS Ref. TL194 167. At SW end of village, 2m NE of

Wheathampstead, approximately 2m N from B653. A1(M)/J4, M1/J10.

**Open:** 17 Mar–28 Oct: Wed–Sun & BH Mons (open Good Fri), House: 1–5pm; Garden: 12 noon–5.30pm. Last admission to House & Garden 4.30pm. No large hand luggage inside house. Groups by prior appointment only.

**Admission:** Adult £4.50, Child £2.25, Family £11.25. Discounts for groups (15+).

ℹ️ WC. 🖢 🔲 Partial, ground floor, no WC. 🅿 🔲 🐕 Car park only.

🐾 Tel 01438 829221 for details.

John Worrall

# HOLKHAM HALL 🏛

www.holkham.co.uk

This elegant Palladian style mansion, based on designs by William Kent, was built between 1734 and 1764 by Thomas Coke, the 1st Earl of Leicester, and is home to his descendants. It reflects Coke's natural appreciation of classical art, developed during his Grand Tour. Built from local, yellow brick, with its pedimented portico, square corner towers and side wings, it has been little altered over the years, and has been described by Sir Nikolaus Pevsner as *"The most classically correct house in Britain"*.

"The Marble Hall" is a spectacular introduction to this vast and imposing house, with its 50ft pressed plaster dome ceiling and walls of English alabaster, not marble as its name implies. Stairs from the Hall lead to magnificent State rooms with superb collections of ancient statuary, original furniture, tapestries and paintings by Rubens, Van Dyck, Claude, Gaspar Poussin and Gainsborough.

On leaving the house, visitors enter the lavender-fringed Pottery Courtyard. Here the original stable block houses the Bygones Museum; a display of more than 4,000 items of domestic and agricultural memorabilia, ranging from working steam engines, vintage cars and tractors to gramophones, craft tools and kitchenware. In the adjacent former brew house and malt house, the History of Farming Exhibition highlights how a great Estate such as Holkham works and has evolved, explaining Coke of Norfolk's rôle in the great Agricultural Revolution of the 18th century.

In the same courtyard, the elegant Pottery Shop, once the former laundry for the Hall, offers a wide range of colourful and purposeful pottery manufactured on the Estate since 1951, along with a wide range of quality gifts and souvenirs. Opposite, the light and airy Stables Café tempts visitors with delicious, local produce for a light snack, lunch or afternoon tea and Holkham's own, home made, mouth-watering ice cream.

Set in a 3,000 acre park with herd of fallow deer and mile-long lake, visitors can explore the park and wildlife with designated walks and a nature trail, or enjoy boat trips on the lake in the summer months. Outside the north gates to the park, Holkham Village, with its internationally-acclaimed hotel, fascinating shops, gallery, tearooms and beach, famous for the closing scenes of *Shakespeare in Love* and National Nature Reserve, offers more to discover.

ℹ️ Grounds for shows, weddings, product launches, rallies and filming. Photography allowed in Hall. No smoking in the Hall.

🛍️ Pottery & Gift Shops. Gallery.

🍴 Hall & Grounds.

♿ Access to first floor in the Hall is suitable for most manual wheelchairs. Elsewhere, full disabled access.

☕ Stables Café & Marsh Larder Tearooms.

🍽️ Victoria Hotel. Licensed. Menus for pre-booked groups on request.

🎧 Acoustiguide £2.

🚶 Private guided tours of Hall are available by arrangement when the Hall is not open to the public. Please tel for details.

🅿️ Unlimited for cars, 12+ coaches. Parking, admission, refreshments free to coach drivers.

👥 Welcome. Areas of interest: Bygones Collection, History of Farming, three designated walks and a new Nature Trail.

🐕 No dogs in Hall, on leads in grounds.

❄️ Deer Park, except Christmas Day at no charge.

## Owner
The Earl of Leicester CBE

## Contact
Marketing Manager
Laurane Herrieven
Holkham Estate Office
Wells-next-the-Sea
Norfolk NR23 1AB

**Tel:** 01328 710227
**Fax:** 01328 711707
**E-mail:** l.herrieven@holkham.co.uk

## Location
**MAP 8:I4**
**OS Ref. TF885 428**

From London 120m
Norwich 35m
King's Lynn 30m.

**Rail:** Norwich Station 35m
King's Lynn Station 30m.

**Air:** Norwich Airport 32m.

## Opening Times
**Hall & Museum**
7–9 Apr, 5–7 May
12noon–5pm, last admission 4.30pm.

**Hall only**
8-24 May, Sunday to Thursday. Opening limited to two audio tours each day. First tour starts 1pm prompt, second tour starts 3pm prompt. Max 40 people each tour.

**Hall & Museum**
25 May–30 September, Sunday to Thursday, 12 noon–5pm, last admission 4.30pm (NB Open Spring & August BH Saturdays)

**Terraces**
29 May–30 September, Monday to Thursday, 1–4.45pm (NB Not BH Mondays).

The Libraries & Strangers' Wing form part of the private accommodation and are open at the family's discretion.

**The Stables Café & Pottery Shop:**
2–6 April, 10 April–4 May, 1–31 October, Sunday to Friday, 11am–4.30pm.
7–9 April & 5 May–30 September, Sunday to Friday, 10am–5.30pm)
(NB Open BH Saturdays).

## Admission
**Hall**
| | |
|---|---|
| Adult | £7.00 |
| Child (5–16yrs) | £3.50 |

**May Audio Tour**
| | |
|---|---|
| Adult | £9.00 |
| Child (5–16yrs) | £4.50 |

**Museum**
| | |
|---|---|
| Adult | £5.00 |
| Child (5–16yrs) | £2.50 |

**Hall & Museum**
| | |
|---|---|
| Adult | £10.00 |
| Child (5–16yrs) | £5.00 |
| Family (2+2) | £25.00 |

Acoustiguide Hire £2.00

Groups (20+)10% discount

Private Guided Tours £15.00

**Boat trips on the lake:**
| | |
|---|---|
| Adult | £3.00 |
| Child (5–16yrs) | £2.50 |

**Eastern – England**

## ■ Owner

H M The Queen

## ■ Contact

The Public Enterprises
Manager
The Estate Office
Sandringham
Norfolk  PE35 6EN

**Tel:** 01553 612908
**Fax:** 01485 541571
**E-mail:** visits@
sandringhamestate.co.uk

## ■ Location

**MAP 7:H5**
**OS Ref. TF695 287**

8m NE of King's Lynn on
B1440 off A148.

**Rail:** King's Lynn.

**Air:** Norwich.

## ■ Opening Times

**House, Museum &
Gardens**

7 April–late July &
early Aug–28 Oct.

## ■ Admission

**House, Museum
& Gardens**

| | |
|---|---|
| Adult | £9.00 |
| Child (5–15yrs) | £5.00 |
| Conc. | £7.00 |
| Family | £23.00 |

**Museum & Gardens**

| | |
|---|---|
| Adult | £6.00 |
| Child (5–15yrs) | £3.50 |
| Conc. | £5.00 |
| Family | £15.50 |

**Groups (20+):**

| | |
|---|---|
| Adult | £8.00 |
| Child (5–15yrs) | £4.00 |
| Conc. | £6.00 |

## Conference/Function

| ROOM | MAX CAPACITY |
|---|---|
| Restaurant | 200 |
| Tearoom | 60 |

By gracious permission of HM Queen Elizabeth II

# SANDRINGHAM

www.sandringhamestate.co.uk

Sandringham House is the charming country retreat of Her Majesty The Queen, hidden in the heart of 60 acres of beautiful wooded gardens. Still maintained in the style of Edward and Alexandra, Prince and Princess of Wales (later King Edward VII and Queen Alexandra), all the main ground floor rooms used by The Royal Family, full of their treasured ornaments, portraits and furniture, are open to the public.

More family possessions are displayed in the Museum housed in the old stables and coach houses, including vehicles ranging in date from the first car owned by a British monarch, a 1900 Daimler, to a half-scale Aston Martin used by Princes William and Harry. A display tells the mysterious tale of the Sandringham Company who fought and died at Gallipoli in 1915, and a photographic exhibition in the Museum shows the history of Sandringham House from 1870 to the present day.

The 60-acre gardens include the formal North Garden, the Stream Walk and Queen Alexandra's Summerhouse, perched above the lake; the formal planting of the Edwardian age has given way to great sweeping glades, bordered by splendid specimen trees and shrubs, to create an informal garden full of colour and interest throughout the year. Guided garden tours take place on Fridays and Saturdays. There are also 600 acres of the Country Park open to all, with tractor tours running daily; a free Land Train from within the entrance will carry passengers less able to walk through the gardens to the House and back.

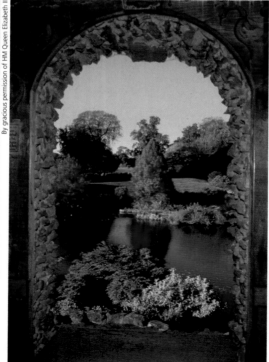

By gracious permission of HM Queen Elizabeth II

The view from Queen Alexandra's Nest

| | |
|---|---|
| ℹ | No photography in house. |
| | Licensed. |
| 🛍 | |
| | By arrangement. Private evening tours. |
| 🌱 | Plant Centre. |
| ⊥ | Visitor Centre only. |
| 🅿 | Ample. |
| ♿ | |
| | Guide dogs only. |
| 🍽 | Licensed. |

## BERNEY ARMS WINDMILL ⛨

**c/o 8 Manor Road, Southtown, Gt Yarmouth  NR31 0QA**
**Tel:** 01799 522842
**Owner:** English Heritage     **Contact:** Visitor Operations Team
A wonderfully situated marsh mill, one of the best and largest remaining in Norfolk, with seven floors, making it a landmark for miles around. It was in use until 1951.
**Location:** MAP 8 M:6, OS Ref. TG465 051. 3½m NE of Reedham on N bank of River Yare, 5m from Gt. Yarmouth. Accessible by boat from Yarmouth or by footpath from Halvergate (3½m).
**Open:** Closed for conservation. Telephone 01799 522842.

## BINHAM PRIORY ⛨

**Binham-on-Wells, Norfolk**
**Tel:** 01328 830362 / 01223 582700 (Regional Office)
**Owner:** English Heritage (Managed by Binham Parochial Church Council)
**Contact:** East of England Regional Office
Extensive remains of a Benedictine priory, of which the original nave of the church is still in use as the parish church, displaying a screen with medieval saints overpainted with Protestant texts.
**Location:** MAP 8:J4, OS Ref. TF982 399. ¼m NW of village of Binham-on-Wells, on road off B1388.
**Open:** Any reasonable time.
**Admission:** Free.
❄

## BIRCHAM WINDMILL

**Snettisham Road, Great Bircham, Norfolk  PE31 6SJ**
**Tel:** 01485 578393
**Owner/Contact:** Mr & Mrs S Chalmers
One of the last remaining complete windmills. Tearoom, bakery, windmill museum, gift shop, cycle hire, regular events and holiday cottage.
**Location:** MAP 8:I4, OS Ref. TF760 326. ½m W of Bircham. N of the road to Snettisham.
**Open:** Easter–end Sept: Daily 10am–5pm.
**Admission:** Adult £3.25, Child £2, OAP £3.

## BRADENHAM HALL GARDENS

**Bradenham, Thetford, Norfolk  IP25 7QP**
**Tel:** 01362 687279/243   **Fax:** 01362 687669   **E-mail:** info@bradenhamhall.co.uk
**www.bradenhamhall.co.uk**
**Owner:** Chris & Panda Allhusen     **Contact:** Chris Allhusen
A plant-lover's garden for all seasons. The house and garden walls are covered with unusual climbers. Flower gardens, formal rose gardens, paved garden, herbaceous and shrub borders. Arboretum of over 800 different trees, all labelled. Traditional walled kitchen gardens, mixed borders, and two glasshouses. Massed daffodils in spring.
**Location:** MAP 8:J6, OS Ref. TF921 099. Off A47, 6m of Swaffham. 3m W of E Dereham. S on Dale Road, then S 2m to Bradenham.
**Open:** Apr–Sept: 2nd & 4th Suns of each month, 2–5.30pm. Groups by appointment at other times.
**Admission:** Adult £4, Child Free. Group discounts available.
ℹ No commercial photography. House not open. 🖼 🚻 Partial. ☕
🎫 By arrangement. 🅿 Ample. Limited for coaches. 🐕 Guide dogs only.

## BURGH CASTLE ⛨

**Breydon Water, Great Yarmouth, Norfolk**
**Tel:** 01223 582700 (Regional Office)
**Owner:** English Heritage     **Contact:** East of England Regional Office
Impressive walls, with projecting bastions, of a Roman fort built in the late 3rd century as one of a chain to defend the coast against Saxon raiders.
**Location:** MAP 8:M6, OS Ref. TG475 046. At far W end of Breydon Water, on unclassified road 3m W of Great Yarmouth. SW of the church.
**Open:** Any reasonable time.
**Admission:** Free.
🐕 ❄

©National Trust Photographic Library

## BLICKLING HALL ❧

### BLICKLING, NORWICH, NORFOLK  NR11 6NF

www.nationaltrust.org.uk

**Tel:** 01263 738030   **Fax:** 01263 738035   **E-mail:** blickling@nationaltrust.org.uk
**Owner:** The National Trust     **Contact:** The Property Manager
Built in the early 17th century and one of England's great Jacobean houses. Blickling is famed for its spectacular long gallery, superb library and fine collections of furniture, pictures and tapestries.
**Location:** MAP 8:K5, OS133 Ref. TG178 286. 1½m NW of Aylsham on B1354. Signposted off A140 Norwich (15m) to Cromer.
**Open:** House: 17 Mar–30 Sept: Wed–Sun & BH Mons, 1–4.30pm (last admission, house closes at 5pm). 3–28 Oct: 1–3.30pm (last admission, house closes at 4pm).

Also open Mons during local school holidays. Garden: Same days as house, 10.15am–5.15pm. 1 Nov–end Mar 2008: Thurs–Sun, 11am–4pm. Park & Woods: daily, dawn–dusk.
**\*Admission:** Hall & Gardens: £8.50. Garden only: £5.50. Groups must book.
*includes a voluntary donation but visitors can choose to pay the standard prices displayed at the property and on the website.
ℹ Cycle hire available in Orchard, ring for details. 📷 Open as garden. 🖼 🚽
🚻 Mostly suitable. ☕ 🍴 Open as garden. Licensed. 🎫 By arrangement. 🅿 🔲
🐕 In park, on leads. ♿ ❄ 🎗

## CAISTER CASTLE CAR COLLECTION

**Caister-on-sea, Great Yarmouth, Norfolk NR30 5SN**

**Tel:** 01572 787251

**Owner/Contact:** Mr J Hill

Large collection of historic motor vehicles from 1893 to recent. Moated Castle built by Sir John Falstaff in 1432. Car park free.

**Location:** MAP 8:M6, OS Ref. TG502 122. Take A1064 out of Caister-on-sea towards Filby, turn left at the end of the dual carriageway.

**Open:** Mid May–End Sept: Sun–Fri (closed Sats), 10.30am–4pm.

**Admission:** Contact property for details.

ⓘ No photography. Ⓖ Partial. WCs. ▣ Ⓟ ⊠

## CASTLE ACRE PRIORY ⌗

**Stocks Green, Castle Acre, King's Lynn, Norfolk PE32 2XD**

**Tel:** 01760 755394   **www.english-heritage.org.uk/visits**

**Owner:** English Heritage   **Contact:** Visitor Operations Team

Explore the romantic ruins of this 12th century Cluniac priory, set in the picturesque village of Castle Acre. The impressive Norman façade, splendid prior's lodgings and chapel, and delightful recreated medieval herb garden should not be missed.

**Location:** MAP 8:I5, OS Ref. TF814 148. ¼m W of village of Castle Acre, 5m N of Swaffham.

**Open:** 1 Apr–30 Sept: daily, 10am–6pm. 1 Oct–20 Mar: Thur–Mon, 10am–4pm. Closed 24–26 Dec & 1 Jan. EH Members/OVP free.

**Admission:** Adult £4.70, Child £2.40, Conc. £3.50. Family £11.80.

▣ Ⓖ Ground floor & grounds. ⌂ Ⓟ ▣ ⊠ On leads. ❈ ☻

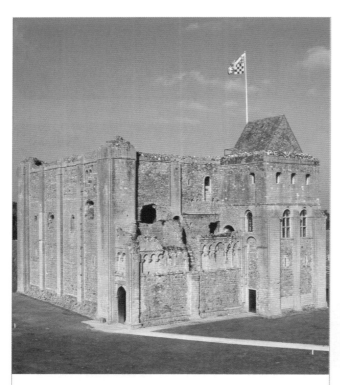

## CASTLE RISING CASTLE

### CASTLE RISING, KING'S LYNN, NORFOLK PE31 6AH

**Tel:** 01553 631330   **Fax:** 01553 631724

**Owner:** Lord Howard   **Contact:** The Custodian

Possibly the finest mid-12th century Keep left in England: it was built as a grand and elaborate palace. It was home to Queen Isabella, grandmother of the Black Prince. Still in surprisingly good condition, the Keep is surrounded by massive ramparts up to 120 feet high. Picnic area, adjacent tearoom. Free audio tour.

**Location:** MAP 7:H5, OS Ref. TF666 246. Located 4m NE of King's Lynn off A149.

**Open:** 1 Apr–1 Nov: daily, 10am–6pm. 2 Nov–31 Mar: Wed–Sun, 10am–4pm. Closed 24–26 Dec & 1 Jan.

**Admission:** Adult £3.85, Child £2.20, Conc. £3.10, Family £11.50. 15% discount for groups (11+). Prices include VAT.

ⓘ Picnic area. ▣ Ⓖ Grounds. WC. ▣ ⌂ Ⓟ ❈

Tom Mackie

## DRAGON HALL

### 115–123 KING STREET, NORWICH, NORFOLK NR1 1QE

www.dragonhall.org

**Tel:** 01603 663922   **E-mail:** info@dragonhall.org

**Owner:** The Norfolk & Norwich Heritage Trust

Magnificent medieval merchant's trading hall c1430 and one of Norwich's most important historic buildings. The Great Hall boasts a stunning crown post roof and intricately carved dragon. The vaulted undercroft is one of the finest in the city. Fascinating displays and interactive exhibits on three floors tell the story of this unique legacy of medieval life.

**Location:** MAP 8:K6, OS Ref. TG235 084. Riverside location, five minutes from city centre, ten minutes from railway station.

**Open:** 12 Feb–16 Dec: Daily 10am–5pm (Sun 11am–4pm). Last admission 4.15pm. Occasional closures for private events, esp Sats. Please tel to confirm open.

**Admission:** Adult £5, Child (5–16) £3. Child under 5yrs Free. Conc. £4.20, Family (2+3) £12. Pre-booked groups (10+) 10% discount.

▣ Ⓣ Ⓖ Except to cellars. ⓕ Groups only. ⌂ Free. ▣ ⊠ Guide dogs only. ▲ ❈ Except Jan. ☻

## FAIRHAVEN WOODLAND & WATER GARDEN

**School Road, South Walsham NR13 6DZ**

**Tel/Fax:** 01603 270449

**Owner:** The Fairhaven Garden Trust   **Contact:** George Debbage, Manager

Delightful natural woodland and water garden with private broad in the beautiful Norfolk Broads. 3 miles of scenic paths. Boat trips on our private broad: April–end October.

**Location:** MAP 8:L6, OS Ref. TG368 134. 9m NE of Norwich. Signed on A47 at junction with B1140.

**Open:** Daily (except 25 Dec), 10am–5pm, also May–Aug: Wed & Thurs evenings until 9pm.

**Admission:** Adult £4.50, Child £2 (under 5yrs Free), OAP £4. Group reductions.

Houghton Hall, King's Lynn

Image courtesy of: © The Marquess of Cholmondeley and Jarrold Publishing 1996.

The National Trust

# FELBRIGG HALL 🦋
### FELBRIGG, NORWICH, NORFOLK NR11 8PR
www.nationaltrust.org.uk

**Tel:** 01263 837444  **Fax:** 01263 837032  **E-mail:** felbrigg@nationaltrust.org.uk
**Owner:** The National Trust  **Contact:** The Property Manager

One of the finest 17th century country houses in East Anglia. The hall contains its original 18th century furniture and one of the largest collections of Grand Tour paintings by a single artist. The library is outstanding. The Walled Garden has been restored and features a series of pottager gardens, a working dovecote and the National Collection of Colchicums. The Park, through which there are way-marked walks, is well known for its magnificent and aged trees. There are also walks to the church and lake and through the 500 acres of woods.

**Location:** MAP 8:K4, OS133 Ref. TG193 394. Nr Felbrigg village, 2m SW of Cromer, entrance off B1436, signposted from A148 and A140.

**Open:** House: 17 Mar–28 Oct: daily except Thur & Fri, 1–5pm. (Open Good Fri.) Gardens: 17 Mar–28 Oct: daily except Thur & Fri (open Good Fri), 11am–5pm. Some additional opening, please telephone property for details.

**\*Admission:** House & Garden: Adult £7.50, Child £3.50, Family £18.50. Garden only: Adult £3.50, Child £1.50. Groups please telephone property to pre-book. *includes a voluntary donation but visitors can choose to pay the standard prices displayed at the property and on the website.

📷 01263 837040. 👶 🚻 01263 838237. ♿ Partial. 🍽 Licensed. 🏠 Licensed.
📷 By arrangement. Ⓟ 🐕 In grounds, on leads. 🛏 Tel 01263 837444 for details.

See which properties offer **educational facilities** or **school visits** in our index on page 571

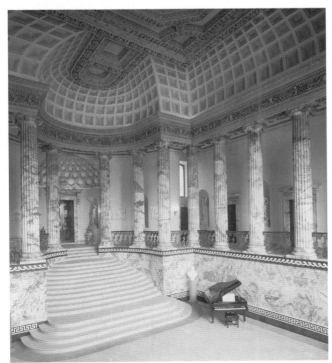

Holkham Hall, Wells-next-the-Sea

---

## GREAT YARMOUTH ROW HOUSES & GREYFRIARS' CLOISTERS ⌗
### South Quay, Great Yarmouth, Norfolk NR30 2RQ
**Tel:** 01493 857900

**Owner:** English Heritage  **Contact:** Visitor Operations Team

Two immaculately presented 17th century Row Houses, a type of building unique to Great Yarmouth. Row 111 House was almost destroyed by bombing in 1942/3 and contains items rescued from the rubble. Old Merchant's House boasts magnificent plaster-work ceilings and displays of local architectural fittings. Visitors can also visit Greyfriars' Cloisters, the remains of a 13th century friary of Franciscan 'grey friars', with wall paintings dating from c1300.

**Location:** MAP 8:M6, OS134, TG525 072. In Great Yarmouth, make for Historic South Quay, by riverside and dock, ½ m inland from beach. Follow signs to dock and south quay.

**Open:** 1 Apr–30 Sept: daily, 12 noon–5pm. Free guided tours of the Greyfriars' Cloisters on the first Wed on the month, tel for details.

**Admission:** Adult £3.50. Child £1.80, Conc. £2.60.

ℹ Museum. 📷 🐕

---

## GRIME'S GRAVES ⌗
### Lynford, Thetford, Norfolk IP26 5DE
**Tel:** 01842 810656

**Owner:** English Heritage  **Contact:** Visitor Operations Team

These remarkable Neolithic flint mines, unique in England, comprise over 300 pits and shafts. The visitor can descend some 30 feet by ladder into one excavated shaft, and look along the radiating galleries, from where the flint used for making axes and knives was extracted.

**Location:** MAP 8:I7, OS 144, TL818 898. 7m NW of Thetford off A134.

**Open:** Mar & Oct: Thur–Mon, 10am–5pm. 1 Apr–30 Sept: daily, 10am–6pm. Last visit to site 30 mins before close. No entry to the mines for children under 5 yrs. Closed 24 / 25 Dec and 1 Jan.

**Admission:** Adult £2.90, Child £1.50, Conc. £2.20, (Child under 5yrs free), Family £7.30. EH Members/OVP free.

📷 ♿ Exhibition area only. Ⓟ 🐕 Restricted areas. 🛏 Tel for details.

---

## HOLKHAM HALL 🏛    *See page 287 for full page entry.*

## HOUGHTON HALL 🏛
### HOUGHTON, KING'S LYNN, NORFOLK PE31 6UE
www.houghtonhall.com

**Tel:** 01485 528569  **Fax:** 01485 528167  **E-mail:** enquiries@houghtonhall.com
**Owner:** The Marquess of Cholmondeley  **Contact:** Susan Cleaver

Houghton Hall is one of the finest examples of Palladian architecture in England. Built in the 18th century by Sir Robert Walpole, Britain's first prime minister. Original designs by James Gibbs & Colen Campbell, interior decoration by William Kent. The House has been restored to its former grandeur, containing many of its original furnishings. The spectacular 5-acre walled garden is divided into areas devoted to fruit and vegetables, elegant herbaceous borders, and a formal rose garden with over 150 varieties – full of colour throughout the summer. The unique Model Soldier Collection contains over 20,000 models arranged in various battle formations. Contemporary Sculptures in the Park.

**Location:** MAP 8:I5, OS Ref. TF792 287. 13m E of King's Lynn, 10m W of Fakenham 1½m N of A148.

**Open:** Easter Sun–30 Sept: Weds, Thurs, Suns & BH Mons. House: 1.30–5pm (last admission 4.30pm). Park, Walled Garden, Soldier Museum, Restaurant & Gift Shop: 11am–5.30pm (last admission 5pm).

**Admission:** Adult £8, Child (5–16) £3, Family (2+2) £20. Excluding House: Adult £5, Child £2. Family (2+2) £12. Group (20+) discounts available, please tel for details.
ℹ️ 📷 👕 ♿ 🛍 Licensed. 🍴 Licensed. 🎦 By arrangement. 🅿 ▪
🐕 On leads, in grounds.

---

## HOVETON HALL GARDENS 🏛
**Wroxham, Norwich, Norfolk NR12 8RJ**

**Tel:** 01603 782798  **Fax:** 01603 784564  **E-mail:** info@hovetonhallgardens.co.uk
**Owner:** Mr & Mrs Andrew Buxton  **Contact:** Mrs Buxton

15 acres of rhododendrons, azaleas, woodland and lakeside walks, walled herbaceous and vegetable gardens. Traditional tearooms and plant sales. The Hall (which is not open to the public) was built 1809–1812. Designs attributed to Humphry Repton.

**Location:** MAP 8:L5, OS Ref. TG314 202. 8m N of Norwich. 1½m NNE of Wroxham on A1151. Follow brown tourist signs.

**Open:** 8 Apr–16 Sept: Apr, Sept, Sun & BH Mons only; May–Aug, Wed–Fri, Sun & BH Mons; 10.30am–5pm.

**Admission:** Adult £4.50, Child (5–14yrs) £2, Wheelchair user and carers £2.50pp. Season Ticket: Single £12, Family £24.
🐕

## KIMBERLEY HALL
### WYMONDHAM, NORFOLK NR18 0RT
www.kimberleyhall.co.uk

**Tel/Fax:** 01603 759447  **E-mail:** events@kimberleyhall.co.uk
**Owner/Contact:** R Buxton

Magnificent Queen Anne house built in 1712 by William Talman for Sir John Wodehouse, an ancestor of P G Wodehouse. Towers added after 1754 and wings connected to the main block by curved colonnades in 1835. Internal embellish-ments in 1770s include some very fine plasterwork by John Sanderson and a 'flying' spiral staircase beneath a coffered dome. The park, with its picturesque lake, ancient oak trees and walled gardens was laid out in 1762 by 'Capability' Brown.

**Location:** MAP 8:K6, OS Ref. TG091 048. 10m SW of Norwich, 3m from A11.

**Open:** House & Park not open to the public. Grounds, certain rooms and extensive cellars available for corporate hospitality and weddings (licensed for Civil ceremonies and partnerships) as well as product launches, film and fashion shoots. Tipis within walled garden available for hire.

**Admission:** Please telephone for details.
🍴 ♿ ▪

Felbrigg Hall, Norwich

## LETHERINGSETT WATERMILL

**Riverside Road, Letheringsett, Holt, Norfolk  NR25 7YD**
**Tel:** 01263 713153   **E-mail:** watermill@ic24.net
**Owner/Contact:** M D Thurlow
Water-powered mill producing wholewheat flour from locally grown wheat. Built in 1802.
**Location:** MAP 8:J4, OS Ref. TG062 387. Riverside Road, Letheringsett, Holt, Norfolk.
**Open:** Whitsun–Oct: Mon–Fri, 10am–5pm, Sat 9am–1pm. Working demonstration, Tue–Fri, 2–4.30pm. Open to visitors from midday on weekdays. Oct–Whitsun: Mon–Fri, 9am–4pm. Sat, 9am–1pm. Not open on Bank Holidays. Winter working demonstration times: ring for details.
**Admission:** Adult £2.50, Child £1.50. When demonstrating: Adult £3.50, Child £2.50, OAP £3, Family (2+2) £10.

# MANNINGTON GARDENS & COUNTRYSIDE

**MANNINGTON HALL, NORWICH  NR11 7BB**

www.manningtongardens.co.uk

**Tel:** 01263 584175   **Fax:** 01263 761214
**Owner:** The Lord & Lady Walpole     **Contact:** Lady Walpole
The gardens around this medieval moated manor house feature a wide variety of plants, trees and shrubs in many different settings. Throughout the gardens are thousands of roses especially classic varieties. The Heritage Rose and 20th Century Rose Gardens have roses in areas with designs reflecting their date of origin from the 15th century to the present day.
**Location:** MAP 8:K5, OS Ref. TG144 320. Signposted from Saxthorpe crossroads on the Norwich–Holt road B1149. 1½m W of Wolterton Hall.
**Open:** Gardens: May–Sept: Suns 12–5pm. Jun–Aug: Wed–Fri, 11am–5pm, and at other times by prior appointment. Walks: daily from 9am. Medieval Hall open by appointment. Grounds & Park open all year.
**Admission:** Adult £4, Child (under 16yrs) Free, Conc. £3. Groups by arrangement.
ⓘ ⬚ ⬚ ⬚ ⬚ Grounds. WCs. ⬚ Licensed. ⬚ By arrangement.
ⓟ £2 car park fee (walkers only). ⬚ ⬚ In park only. ⬚ Park. ⬚ €

## NORWICH CASTLE MUSEUM & ART GALLERY

**Norwich, Norfolk  NR1 3JU**
**Tel:** 01603 493625   **Fax:** 01603 493623   **E-mail:** museums@norfolk.gov.uk
Norman Castle Keep, housing displays of art, archaeology and natural history.
**Location:** MAP 8:K6, OS Ref. TG233 085. City centre.
**Open:** All year: Mon–Fri, 10.30am–4.30pm. Sat, 10am–5pm. Sun, 1–5pm. Closed 22–26 Dec & 1 Jan.
**Admission:** Adult £6.30, Child (4–16yrs) £4.60, Conc. £5.35. (2006 prices.)

# OXBURGH HALL & ESTATE ❧

**OXBOROUGH, KING'S LYNN, NORFOLK  PE33 9PS**

www.nationaltrust.org.uk

**Tel:** 01366 328258   **Fax:** 01366 328066   **E-mail:** oxburghhall@nationaltrust.org.uk
**Owner:** The National Trust     **Contact:** The Property Secretary
A moated manor house built in 1482 by the Bedingfeld family, who still live here. The rooms show the development from medieval austerity to Victorian comfort and include an accessible Priest's Hole and an outstanding display of embroidery by Mary Queen of Scots. The attractive gardens include a French parterre, kitchen garden and orchard and woodland walks.
**Location:** MAP 8:I6, OS143, TF742 012. At Oxborough, 7m SW of Swaffham on S side of Stoke Ferry road.
**Open: House:** 17 Mar–28 Oct, Sat–Wed, (Aug daily. Timed tours only Thurs/Fri) 1–5pm, closes 4pm Oct. **BH Mons & Good Fri**, 11am–5pm. **Gatehouse:** 6 Jan–11 Mar, Sat & Sun, timed tours only, 11am–4pm. **Garden:** 6 Jan–11 Mar & 3 Nov–23 Dec, Sat & Sun, 11am–4pm. 17 Mar–28 Oct, Sat–Wed, (Aug daily), 11am–5.30pm (closes 4.30pm Oct). **Shop, Restaurant, and/or Pantry:** as garden but closes 30mins earlier 17 Mar–28 Oct.
**\*Admission:** House & Garden: Adult £6.75, Child £3.50, Family £17, Group; Adult £5.75, Child £3. Garden & Estate only: Adult £3.50, Child £2. Gatehouse & Garden: Adult £5, Child £2.50, Family £15. Out of hours group: Members £6, Non-members £9. Groups must book with SAE to the Property Secretary. \*includes a voluntary donation but visitors can choose to pay the standard prices displayed at the property and on the website.
ⓘ ⬚ Licensed. ⬚ Partial. ⬚ By arrangement. ⬚ ⓟ ⬚ ⬚ Send SAE for details.

## RAVENINGHAM GARDENS
### RAVENINGHAM, NORWICH, NORFOLK NR14 6NS
www.raveningham.com

**Tel:** 01508 548152 **Fax:** 01508 548958
**E-mail:** info@raveningham.com
**Owner:** Sir Nicholas Bacon Bt **Contact:** Mrs Janet Woodard

Superb herbaceous borders, 18th century walled kitchen garden, Victorian glass-house, herb garden, Edwardian rose garden, contemporary sculptures, 14th century church and much more.

**Location:** MAP 8:L7, OS Ref. TM399 965. Between Norwich & Lowestoft off A146 then B1136/B1140.
**Open:** Easter–end Aug: Mon–Fri, 11am–4pm (no teas). BH Suns & Mons, 2–5pm.
**Admission:** Adult £4, Child (under 16yrs) Free, OAP £3. Groups by prior arrangement.
Teas only on Suns & BH Mons.

---

**SANDRINGHAM**                        *See page 288 for full page entry.*

---

## ST GEORGE'S GUILDHALL
**29 King Street, King's Lynn, Norfolk PE30 1HA**
**Tel:** 01553 765565   **www.west-norfolk.gov.uk**
**Owner:** The National Trust  **Contact:** The Administrator

The largest surviving English medieval guildhall. The building is now converted into a theatre and arthouse cinema. Many interesting features survive.

**Location:** MAP 7:H5, OS132, TF616 202. On W side of King Street close to the Tuesday Market Place.
**Open:** Mon–Fri, 10am–2pm. Closed; Sat & Sun, Good Fri, BHs & 24 Dec – 2 Jan. The Guildhall is not usually open on days when there are performances in the theatre. Please telephone box office 01553 764864 for details of opening dates and times.
**Admission:** Free.
Access to galleries. Licensed. Pay and Display

---

## SHERINGHAM PARK
**Upper Sheringham, Norfolk NR26 8TL**
**Tel:** 01263 820550 **E-mail:** sheringhampark@nationaltrust.org.uk
**www.nationaltrust.org.uk**
**Owner:** The National Trust  **Contact:** Visitor Centre

One of Humphry Repton's most outstanding achievements, the landscape park contains fine mature woodlands, and the large woodland garden is particularly famous for its spectacular show of rhododendrons and azaleas (mid May–June). There are stunning views of the coast and countryside from the viewing towers and many delightful waymarked walks. Programme of special events.

**Location:** MAP 8:K4, OS133, TG135 420. 2m SW of Sheringham, access for cars off A148 Cromer–Holt road; 5m W of Cromer, 6m E of Holt.
**Open:** Park open all year, daily, dawn–dusk.
**Admission:** Pay & Display: Cars £3.60 (NT members Free–display members' sticker in car). Coaches must book in advance.
Partial. WC. Easter–end Sept, daily. Sats/Suns all year.
Limited for coaches. In grounds, on leads.

---

## WALSINGHAM ABBEY GROUNDS & SHIREHALL MUSEUM
**Little Walsingham, Norfolk NR22 6BP**
**Tel:** 01328 820259 **Fax:** 01328 820098 **E-mail:** jackie@walsingham-estate.co.uk
**Owner:** Walsingham Estate Company **Contact:** Estate Office

Set in the picturesque medieval village of Little Walsingham, a place of pilgrimage since the 11th century, the grounds contain the remains of the famous Augustinian Priory with attractive gardens and river walks. The Shirehall Museum includes a Georgian magistrates' court and displays on the history of Walsingham.

**Location:** MAP 8:J4, OS Ref. TF934 367. B1105 N from Fakenham–5m.
**Open:** 17 Mar–28 Oct: daily, 10am–4.30pm. Also daily during snowdrop season (February) 10am–4pm. Abbey Grounds: many other times, please telephone for details.
**Admission:** Combined ticket: Adult £3, Conc. £2.
Partial. By arrangement. In grounds, on leads.

## WOLTERTON PARK
### NORWICH, NORFOLK NR11 7LY
www.manningtongardens.co.uk

**Tel:** 01263 584175 **Fax:** 01263 761214
**Owner:** The Lord and Lady Walpole **Contact:** The Lady Walpole

18th century Hall. Historic park with lake.

**Location:** MAP 8:K5, OS Ref. TG164 317. Situated near Erpingham village, signposted from Norwich–Cromer Rd A140.
**Open:** Park: daily from 9am. Hall: 13 Apr–26 Oct: Fridays, 2–5pm (last entry 4pm) and by appointment.
**Admission:** £5. £2 car park fee only for walkers. (Groups by application: from £4.)
Partial. WC. In park, on leads. Park.

Sandringham

## THE ANCIENT HOUSE

**Clare, Suffolk CO10 8NY**
**Tel:** 01628 825925  www.landmarktrust.org.uk
**Owner:** Leased to the Landmark Trust by Clare PC    **Contact:** The Landmark Trust
A 14th century house extended in the 15th and 17th centuries, decorated with high relief pargetting. Half of the building is managed by the Landmark Trust, which lets buildings for self-catering holidays. The other half of the house is run as a museum. Full details of The Ancient House and 184 other historic buildings available for holidays are featured in The Landmark Handbook (price £11.50 refundable against booking).
**Location:** MAP 8:I9, OS Ref. TL769 454. Village centre, on A1092 8m WNW of Sudbury.
**Open:** House: Available for holidays for up to to 2 people throughout the year. 7 Open Days a year and at other times by appointment. Contact the Landmark Trust for details. Museum: Easter & May–Sept: Thur, Fri & Sun, 2–5pm, Sat & BHs 11.30am–5pm.
**Admission:** Free on open days.

## EAST BERGHOLT PLACE GARDEN

**East Bergholt, Suffolk CO7 6UP**
**Tel/Fax:** 01206 299224    **E-mail:** sales@placeforplants.co.uk
**Owner:** Mr & Mrs R L C Eley    **Contact:** Sara Eley
Fifteen acres of garden and arboretum originally laid out at the beginning of the last century by the present owner's great-grandfather. A wonderful collection of fine trees and shrubs, many of which are rarely seen growing in East Anglia and originate from the famous plant hunter George Forrest. Particularly beautiful in the spring when the rhododendrons, magnolias and camellias are in flower.
**Location:** MAP 8:K10, OS Ref. TM084 343. 2m E of A12 on B1070, Manningtree Rd, on the edge of East Bergholt.
**Open:** Mar–Sept: daily, 10am–5pm. Closed Easter Sun.
**Admission:** Adult £3, Child Free. (Proceeds to garden up-keep.)
Specialist Plant Centre in the Victorian walled garden. By arrangement.

## BELCHAMP HALL
### BELCHAMP WALTER, SUDBURY, SUFFOLK CO10 7AT
www.belchamphall.com

**Tel:** 01787 881961  **Fax:** 01787 466778
**Owner/Contact:** Mr C F V Raymond
Superb Queen Anne house on a site belonging to the Raymond family since 1611. Historic portraits and period furniture. Suitable for corporate events and product launches, weddings in the church and receptions and as a film and television location. Gardens including a cherry avenue, follies, a sunken garden, walled garden and lake. Medieval church with 15th century wall paintings.
**Location:** MAP 8:I10, OS Ref. TL827 407. 5m SW of Sudbury, opposite Belchamp Walter Church.
**Open:** By appointment only: May–Sept: Tues and Thurs, 2.30–6pm.
**Admission:** Adult £10, Child £5. No reduction for groups.
No photography in house. Conference facilities. By arrangement.
Obligatory. Guide dogs only.

## EUSTON HALL
### ESTATE OFFICE, EUSTON, THETFORD, NORFOLK IP24 2QP
www.eustonhall.co.uk

**Tel:** 01842 766366  **Fax:** 01842 766764  **E-mail:** admin@euston-estate.co.uk
**Owner:** The Duke of Grafton    **Contact:** Mrs L Campbell
Euston Hall has been home to the Dukes of Grafton for over 300 years. It contains a collection of paintings of the Court of Charles II by Van Dyck and Lely, also "Mares and Foals" by George Stubbs. The gardens were laid out by the diarist John Evelyn and his walk through the Pleasure Grounds can still be enjoyed today. The park and river layout was designed by William Kent and is considered one of his greatest works. The project was completed by 'Capability' Brown. The 18th century watermill has been restored recently. The church is one of only four country churches built during the reign of Charles II.
**Location:** MAP 8:J8, OS Ref. TL897 786. 12m N of Bury St Edmunds, on A1088. 2m E of A134.
**Open:** 14 Jun–13 Sept: Thurs only. Also 24 Jun, 15 July & 2 Sept. 2.30–5pm.
**Admission:** Adult £6, Child £2, OAP £5. Groups (12+): £5pp.

## CHRISTCHURCH MANSION

**Christchurch Park, Ipswich, Suffolk IP4 2BE**
**Tel:** 01473 433554  **Fax:** 01473 433564
**Owner/Contact:** Ipswich Borough Council
A fine Tudor house set out as a museum.
**Location:** MAP 8:K9, OS Ref. TM165 450. Christchurch Park, near centre of Ipswich.
**Open:** All year: Tue–Sat, 10am–5pm (4pm in winter). Suns, 2.30–4pm. Also open BH Mons. Closed 24–26, 31 Dec/1 Jan & Good Fri.
**Admission:** Free.

## FLATFORD BRIDGE COTTAGE

**Flatford, East Bergholt, Colchester, Essex CO7 6OL**
**Tel:** 01206 298260  **Fax:** 01206 297212  www.nationaltrust.org.uk
**Owner:** The National Trust    **Contact:** The Property Manager
Just upstream from Flatford Mill, the restored thatched cottage houses a display about John Constable, several of whose paintings depict this property. Facilities include a tea garden, shop, boat hire, an Information Centre and countryside walks.
**Location:** MAP 8:J10, OS Ref. TM077 332. On N bank of Stour, 1m S of East Bergholt B1070.
**Open:** Mar & Apr: Wed–Sun, 11am–5pm. May–end Sept: daily, 10.30am–5.30pm. Oct: daily, 11am–4pm. Nov & Dec: Wed–Sun, 11am–3.30pm. Jan & Feb: Sats & Suns only, 11am–3.30pm. Closed Christmas & New Year.
**Admission:** Guided walks (when guide available) £2.50, accompanied child Free.
Tea garden & shop. WC. Charge applies. Guide dogs only.

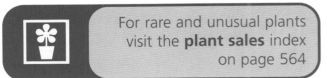

For rare and unusual plants visit the **plant sales** index on page 564

© English Heritage Photo Library

# FRAMLINGHAM CASTLE

### FRAMLINGHAM, SUFFOLK IP13 9BT

www.english-heritage.org.uk/visits

**Tel:** 01728 724189

**Owner:** English Heritage **Contact:** Visitor Operations Team

A magnificent 12th century castle which, from the outside, looks almost the same as when it was built. From the continuous curtain wall linking 13 towers, there are excellent panoramic views of Framlingham and the charming reed-fringed Mere. Throughout its colourful history the castle has been a fortress, an Elizabethan prison, a poor house and a school. The many alterations over the years have led to a pleasing mixture of historic styles. Entry also includes access to the LanmanTrust's Museum or local history.

**Location:** MAP 8:L8, OS Ref. TM287 637. In Framlingham on B1116. NE of town centre.

**Open:** 1 Apr–30 Sept: daily, 10am–6pm. 1 Oct–20 Mar: Thur–Mon, 10am–4pm. Closed 24–26 Dec & 1 Jan. May close early if an event is booked.Please call to check.

**Admission:** Adult £4.70, Child £2.40, Children under 5 Free. Conc. £3.50, Family £11.80. Members/OVP Free.

🖼 🔊 Ground floor & grounds. WCs. 🎧 **P** 📽 ❄ ⛨

---

# GAINSBOROUGH'S HOUSE

### 46 GAINSBOROUGH ST, SUDBURY, SUFFOLK CO10 2EU

www.gainsborough.org

**Tel:** 01787 372958 **Fax:** 01787 376991 **E-mail:** mail@gainsborough.org

**Owner:** Gainsborough's House Society **Contact:** Rosemary Woodward

Birthplace of Thomas Gainsborough RA (1727–88). Historic house dating back to the 16th century with attractive walled garden. The outstanding collection is shown together with 18th century furniture and displays more of Gainsborough's work than any other gallery. Varied programme of exhibitions on both historic British art and contemporary arts and crafts.

**Location:** MAP 8:I10, OS Ref. TL872 413. 46 Gainsborough St, Sudbury town centre.

**Open:** All year: Mon–Sat, 10am–5pm. Closed: Suns, Good Fri and Christmas to New Year.

**Admission:** Adult £4, Child/Student £1.50, Conc £3.20, Family Ticket £8.

ℹ No photography. 🖼 🔊 WCs. 📽 **P** None. 📽 ❄

---

## FRESTON TOWER

**Nr Ipswich, Suffolk IP9 1AD**

**Tel:** 01628 825925 **www.landmarktrust.org.uk**

**Owner/Contact:** The Landmark Trust

An Elizabethan six-storey tower overlooking the estuary of the River Orwell. The tower was built in 1578 by a wealthy Ipswich merchant called Thomas Gooding, perhaps to celebrate the recent grant of his coat of arms. Freston Tower is cared for by The Landmark Trust, a building preservation charity who let it for holidays. Full details of Freston Tower and 184 other historic and architecturally important buildings are featured in the Landmark Trust Handbook (price £11.50 refundable against a booking).

**Location:** MAP 8:K9, OS Ref. TM177 397.

**Open:** Available for holidays for up to 4 people throughout the year. Please contact the Landmark Trust for details. Open Days on 8 days a year. Other visits by appointment.

**Admission:** Free on Open Days.

📽

## HADLEIGH GUILDHALL

**Hadleigh, Suffolk IP7 5DT**

**Tel:** 01473 827752

**Owner:** Hadleigh Market Feoffment Charity **Contact:** Jane Haylock

Fine timber framed guildhall, one of the least known medieval buildings in Suffolk.

**Location:** MAP 8:J9, OS Ref. TM025 425. S side of churchyard.

**Open:** mid Jun–end Sept: Building: Thurs & Suns; Garden: Sun–Fri, 2–5pm.

**Admission:** Free. Donations welcome.

---

## HAUGHLEY PARK 🏛

**Stowmarket, Suffolk IP14 3JY**

**Tel:** 01359 240701 **www.haughleyparkbarn.co.uk**

**Owner/Contact:** Mr & Mrs Robert Williams

Mellow red brick manor house of 1620 set in gardens, park and woodland. Original five-gabled east front, north wing re-built in Georgian style, 1820. 6 acres of well tended gardens including walled kitchen garden. 17th century brick and timber barn restored as meeting rooms. Woodland walks with bluebells (special Sun opening), lily-of-the-valley (May), rhododendrons and azaleas.

**Location:** MAP 8:J8, OS Ref. TM005 618. 4m W of Stowmarket signed off A14.

**Open:** Garden only: May–Sept: Tues & last Sun in Apr & 1st Sun in May, 2–5.30pm. House visits and groups by appointment (even outside normal times). Barn bookable for tour lunches/teas, lectures, dinners, weddings etc (capacity 160).

**Admission:** House: £2. Garden: £3. Child under 16 Free.

ℹ Picnics allowed. 🍽 Bluebell Sun. 🔊 📽 Bluebell Sun. 🖼 By arrangement. **P** 📽 On leads only. 🔊 ❄

---

See all the properties that are **open all year** in the index on page 580

---

© Skyscan

Kentwell Hall & Gardens, Long Melford

## HELMINGHAM HALL GARDENS 🏛
### HELMINGHAM, SUFFOLK IP14 6EF

www.helmingham.com

**Tel:** 01473 890799   **Fax:** 01473 890776   **E-mail:** events@helmingham.com
**Owner:** The Lord & Lady Tollemache   **Contact:** Mrs Sarah Harris

The Tudor Hall, surrounded by its wide moat, is set in a 400 acre deer park. Two superb gardens, one surrounded by its own moat and walls extends to several acres and has wide herbaceous borders and an immaculate kitchen garden. The second enclosed within yew hedges, has a special rose garden with a herb and knot garden containing plants grown in England before 1750. Coach bookings welcome.

**Location:** MAP 8:K9, OS Ref. TM190 578. B1077, 9m N of Ipswich, 5m S of Debenham.
**Open:** Gardens only: 6 May–16 Sept: Suns & Weds, 2–6pm.
**Admission:** Adult £4.50, Child (5–15yrs) £2.50. Groups (30+) £4.

⬛🖼🚻♿ Grounds. WCs. 🖤 🅿 🖤 In grounds, on leads.
🖤 5 Aug: Festival of Classic & Sports Cars 10am–5pm, tel for details.
27 May: NCCPG Plant Sale 10am–4pm.

NT PL /Rupert Truman

## ICKWORTH HOUSE & PARK 🌿
### THE ROTUNDA, HORRINGER, BURY ST EDMUNDS IP29 5QE

www.nationaltrust.org.uk/ickworth

**Tel:** 01284 735270   **Fax:** 01284 735175   **E-mail:** ickworth@nationaltrust.org.uk
**Owner:** The National Trust   **Contact:** The Property Manager

One of the most unusual houses in East Anglia. The huge Rotunda of this 18th century Italianate house dominates the landscape. Inside are collections of Georgian silver, Regency furniture, Old Master paintings and family portraits.

**Location:** MAP 8:I9, OS155 Ref. TL816 611. In Horringer, 3m SW of Bury St Edmunds on W side of A143.
**Open:** House: 17 Mar–3 Nov: daily except Wed & Thur, 1–5pm, last admission 4.30pm (4pm in Oct). Garden: 2 Jan–16 Mar, daily, 11am–4pm. 17 Mar–4 Nov, daily, 10am–5pm. Park open all year dawn to dusk except Christmas Day.
**\*Admission:** Adult £7.50, Child £3, Family (2+2) £18 (subsequent children £1.55). Park & Garden only (includes access to shop & restaurant): Adult £3.50, Child £1, Family (2+2) £8 (subsequent children 45p). Group discounts on pre-booked visits, no group discounts on Suns & BH Mons. \*includes a voluntary donation but visitors can choose to pay the standard prices displayed at the property and on the website.

⬛🖼♿ Partial. 🖤 🍴 Licensed. 🖤 By arrangement. 🖤 🖤 In park, on leads. 🖤

## KENTWELL HALL & GARDENS 🏛
### LONG MELFORD, SUFFOLK CO10 9BA

www.kentwell.co.uk

**Tel:** 01787 310207   **Fax:** 01787 379318   **E-mail:** info@kentwell.co.uk
**Owner:** Patrick Phillips Esq   **Contact:** The Estate Office

A beautiful mellow redbrick Tudor Mansion, surrounded by a broad moat, with rare service building of c1500. Interior 'improved' by Thomas Hopper in 1820s. Still a lived-in family home. Famed for the long-time, long term, ongoing restoration works.

Gardens: Over 30 years endeavour has resulted in Gardens which are a joy in all seasons. Moats predominate with massed spring bulbs, extensive wild flowers; ancient fruit blossom and clipped yews to large Herb Garden and Potager. Woodland walks.

Re-Creations: Kentwell is renowned for its award-winning Re-Creations of Everyday Tudor Life. It also has occasional Re-Creations of WW2 Life. Re-Creations take place on selected weekends from April to September.

Corporate: Functions and company activity days, centred on Tudor-style activities including banquets as well as games and boats on the moat.

Schools: Half a million school children have now visited a Tudor Re-Creation, recognised by teachers to be an unequalled educational resource.

Filming: Much used for medieval and Tudor periods for its wide range of perfectly equipped locations inside and out and access to Kentwell's 700 Tudors as extras.

**Location:** MAP 8:I9, OS Ref. TL864 479. Off the A134. 4m N of Sudbury, 14m S of Bury St. Edmunds 1m NNW of Long Melford off A134.
**Open:** Feb–Oct. For full details see our website or e-mail info@kentwell.co.uk or telephone for leaflet.

ℹ️ No photography in house. ⬛ 🖤 Conferences, dinners, Tudor feasts for groups of 40 or more. Car rallies. ♿ 🖤 Home-made food. 🅿 🖤 🖤 🖤 Including themed ceremonies. 🖤 Open-air theatre, opera and concert season Jul–Aug.

### LANDGUARD FORT ⌗

**Felixstowe, Suffolk**
**Tel:** 07749 695523
**Owner:** English Heritage    **Contact:** Visitor Operations Team
(Managed by Languard Fort Trust)
Impressive 18th century fort with later additions built on a site originally fortified by Henry VIII and in use until after World War II. Existing guided tours and audio tours of the fort will be supplemented in 2007 by a DVD presentation of the site's history and by guided tours of the substantial outside batteries.
**Location:** MAP 8:L10, OS Ref. TM284 318. 1m S of Felixstowe town centre – follow brown tourist signs to Landguard Point and Nature Reserve from A14.
**Open:** 1 Apr–31 Oct: daily, 10am–6pm (5pm April, May & Oct). Last admission 1hr before closing. Telephone 07749 695523 for Battery & Group tour bookings.
**Admission:** Adult £3, Child £1, Conc. £2.50. Free entry for children under 5yrs and wheelchair users. No unaccompanied children.
◻ ◻ Ⓟ ◪ ◉ Contact David Morgan for details of tours of the outer batteries & charges for special events.

### LEISTON ABBEY ⌗

**Leiston, Suffolk**
**Tel:** 01223 582700 (Regional Office)
**Owner:** English Heritage    **Contact:** The East of England Regional Office
The remains of this abbey for Premonstratensian canons, including a restored chapel, are amongst the most extensive in Suffolk.
**Location:** MAP 8:M8, OS Ref. TM445 642. 1m N of Leiston off B1069.
**Open:** Any reasonable time.
**Admission:** Free.
◻ Ⓟ ◪ ◉

Who's offering **accommodation?**
See our index on page 575

### LAVENHAM: THE GUILDHALL OF CORPUS CHRISTI ✻

**THE MARKET PLACE, LAVENHAM, SUDBURY  CO10 9QZ**

www.nationaltrust.org.uk

**Tel:** 01787 247646  **E-mail:** lavenhamguildhall@nationaltrust.org.uk
**Owner:** The National Trust    **Contact:** The Property Manager
This splendid 16th century timber-framed building dominates the Market Place of the picturesque town of Lavenham with its many historic houses and wonderful church. Inside are exhibitions on local history, farming and industry, as well as the story of the medieval woollen cloth trade. There is also a walled garden with dye plants.
**Location:** MAP 8:J9, OS155, TL915 942. 6m NNE of Sudbury. Village centre. A1141 & B1071.
**Open:** 3 Mar–31 Oct: Tue–Sun, 11am–5pm. 1–25 Nov: Sats & Suns, 11am–4pm. Open BH Mon, closed Good Fri. Tearoom: 1 Nov–21 Dec: Thurs–Sun, 11am–4pm. Parts of the building may be closed occasionally for community use.
**Admission:** Adult £3.75, Accompanied Child £1.50. Family £9, Groups £3. School parties (by arrangement) £1 per child.
◻ ◻ Shop & tearoom. ◉

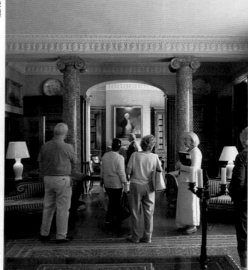

### MELFORD HALL ✻

**LONG MELFORD, SUDBURY, SUFFOLK  CO10 9AA**

www.nationaltrust.org.uk

**Tel/Fax:** 01787 379228  **Info:** 01787 376395
**E-mail:** melford@nationaltrust.org.uk
**Owner:** The National Trust    **Contact:** Stephen Bennett – Property Manager
Set in the unspoilt village of Long Melford, the house has changed little externally since 1578 when Queen Elizabeth I was entertained here, and retains its original panelled banqueting hall. It has been the home of the Hyde Parker family since 1786. There is a Regency Library, Victorian bedrooms, good collections of furniture and porcelain and a small display of items connected with Beatrix Potter, who was related to the family. The garden contains some spectacular specimen trees and a banqueting house, and there is an attractive walk through the park.

**Location:** MAP 8:I9, OS Ref. TL867 462. In Long Melford off A134, 14m S of Bury St Edmunds, 3m N of Sudbury.
**Open:** Apr: Sat & Sun only (also open 11–13 Apr). May–Sept: Wed–Sun. Oct: Sat & Sun only, 1.30–5pm. Last admission 4.30pm, BH Mons. Closed Good Friday.
**Admission:** Adult £5.50, Child (under 16yrs) £2.75, Family £13.75. Groups (15+): Adult £4.50, Child £2.25. Phone, e-mail or write with SAE to Property Manager.
ⓘ No photography in house. ◻ ◻ ◻ WC. ◉ Ⓟ
◪ In car park & park walk only, on leads. ◉ Tel info line for details.

## ORFORD CASTLE ⌗
### ORFORD, WOODBRIDGE, SUFFOLK IP12 2ND

www.english-heritage.org.uk/visits

**Tel:** 01394 450472

**Owner:** English Heritage    **Contact:** Visitor Operations Team

An enchanting royal castle built by Henry II for coastal defence in the 12th century. A magnificent keep survives almost intact with three immense towers offering beautiful views over Orford Ness and the surrounding countryside. New Orford Museum housed in the Castle

**Location:** MAP 8:M9, OS169, TM419 499. In Orford on B1084, 20m NE of Ipswich.

**Open:** 1 Apr–30 Sept: daily, 10am–6pm. 1 Oct–20 Mar: Thur–Mon, 10am–4pm. Closed 24–26 Dec & 1 Jan.

**Admission:** Adult £4.70, Child £2.40, Under 5s Free, Conc. £3.50, Family £11.80. Members/OVP Free.

## OTLEY HALL
### OTLEY, IPSWICH, SUFFOLK IP6 9PA

www.otleyhall.co.uk

**Tel:** 01473 890264    **Fax:** 01473 890803    **E-mail:** enquiries@otleyhall.co.uk

**Owner:** Dr Ian & Mrs Catherine Beaumont    **Contact:** Lucy Rudock

A stunning medieval Moated Hall (Grade I) frequently described as "one of England's loveliest houses". Noted for its richly carved beams, superb linenfold panelling and 16th century wall paintings, Otley Hall was once the home of the Gosnold family and is still a family home. Bartholomew Gosnold voyaged to the New World in 1602 and named Cape Cod and Martha's Vineyard, (an account of the voyage is believed to have inspired Shakespeare's Tempest). Gosnold returned in 1607 and founded the Jamestown colony, the first English-speaking settlement in the US. The unique 10 acre gardens include historically accurate Tudor re-creations designed by Sylvia Landsberg (author of The Medieval Garden).and were voted among the top 10 gardens to visit in Great Britain.

**Location:** MAP 8:K9, OS Ref. TM207 563. 7m N of Ipswich, off the B1079.

**Open:** BH Suns (6 & 27 May, 26 Aug), 1–5pm. Afternoon teas available. Groups and individuals welcome all year by appointment for private guided tours.

**Admission:** BHs: Adult £5, Child £2.50.

Partial. By arrangement.

Helmingham Hall

## ST EDMUNDSBURY CATHEDRAL

**Angel Hill, Bury St Edmunds, Suffolk IP33 1LS**

**Tel:** 01284 754933    **Fax:** 01284 768655    **E-mail:** cathedral@burycathedral.fsnet.co.uk
www.stedscathedral.co.uk

**Owner:** The Church of England    **Contact:** Sarah Friswell

The striking Millennium Tower, completed on 2005, is the crowning glory of St Edmundsbury Cathedral. Built from English limestone, brick and lime mortar, the 150ft Lantern Tower, along with new chapels, cloisters and North Transept, completes nearly fifty years of development in a style never likely to be repeated.

**Location:** MAP 8:I8, OS Ref. TL857 642. Bury St Edmunds town centre.

**Open:** All year: daily 8.30am–6pm.

**Admission:** Donation invited.

Partial. WC.

## SAXTEAD GREEN POST MILL ⌗

**Post Mill Bungalow, Saxtead Green, Woodbridge, Suffolk IP13 9QQ**

**Tel:** 01728 685789    www.english-heritage.org.uk/visits

**Owner:** English Heritage    **Contact:** Visitor Operations Team

The finest example of a Suffolk Post Mill. Still in working order, you can climb the wooden stairs to the various floors, full of fascinating mill machinery. Ceased production in 1947.

**Location:** MAP 8:L8, OS Ref. TM253 645. 2½ m NW of Framlingham on A1120.

**Open:** 1 Apr–29 Sept: Fri/Sat & BHs, 12 noon–5pm.

**Admission:** Adult £2.90, Child £1.50, Conc. £2.20.

Museum.

## SOMERLEYTON HALL & GARDENS
### SOMERLEYTON, LOWESTOFT, SUFFOLK NR32 5QQ

www.somerleyton.co.uk

**Tel:** 08712 224244 (office)   **Fax:** 01502 732143
**E-mail:** enquiries@somerleyton.co.uk
**Owner:** Hon Hugh Crossley   **Contact:** Cathy Hatt

Splendid early Victorian mansion built in Anglo-Italian style by John Thomas, with lavish architectural features, magnificent carved stonework and fine state rooms. Paintings by Landseer, Wright of Derby and Stanfield, wood carvings by Willcox of Warwick and Grinling Gibbons. Somerleyton's 12-acre gardens are justly renowned with beautiful borders, specimen trees and the 1846 yew hedge maze which ranks amongst the finest in the country. Special features include glasshouses by Paxton, 300ft pergola, walled garden, Vulliamy tower clock, Victorian ornamentation. Film location for BBC drama *The Lost Prince* (2002).

**Location:** MAP 8:M8, OS134 Ref. TM493 977. 5m NW of Lowestoft on B1074, 7m SW of Great Yarmouth off A143.

**Open:** 1 Apr–28 Oct: Thurs, Suns, & all BHs, also Tues & Weds in Jul & Aug. Gardens and Tearooms: 10am–5pm. Hall: 11.30am–4pm (guided tours only every half hour). Last tour 3.30pm.

**Admission:** Hall Tour & Gardens: Adult £8, Child (5-16yrs) £4, Conc. £7. Family £22. Groups: Adult £7, Child £3, Conc. £6. Gardens only: Adult £4.75, Child £2.75, Conc. £3.75. Groups: Adult £4, Child £2, Conc. £3. Season tickets available.

ℹ️ No photography in house. Receptions/functions/conferences/weddings. Obligatory.

---

## SOUTH ELMHAM HALL
### ST CROSS, HARLESTON, NORFOLK IP20 0PZ

www.southelmham.co.uk   www.batemansbarn.co.uk

**Tel:** 01986 782526   **Fax:** 01986 782203   **E-mail:** enquiries@southelmham.co.uk
**Owner/Contact:** John Sanderson

A Grade I listed medieval manor house set inside moated enclosure. Originally built by the Bishop of Norwich around 1270. Much altered in the 16th century. Self guided trail through former deer park to South Elmham Minster, a ruined Norman chapel with Saxon origins.

**Location:** MAP 8:L7, OS30 Ref. TM778 324. Between Harleston and Bungay from the A143 take the B1062.

**Open:** Minster, Walks (Café: 1 May–30 Sept: Thurs, Fris & BH Mons). 1 Oct–30 Apr: Suns only, 10am–5pm. Hall: Guided tours only: 1 May–30 Sept: Thurs, 2pm, Sun & BH Mons, 3pm.

**Admission:** House: Adult £6.50, Child £3. Groups (15-50): Adult £4.50, Child £2.50. Walks (free).

WC. Obligatory. In grounds, on leads.

---

## SUTTON HOO
### WOODBRIDGE, SUFFOLK IP12 3DJ

www.nationaltrust.org.uk/suttonhoo

**Tel:** 01394 389714   **Fax:** 01394 389702   **E-mail:** suttonhoo@nationaltrust.org.uk
**Owner:** The National Trust   **Contact:** The Property Secretary

Anglo-Saxon royal burial site where priceless treasure was discovered in a ship grave in 1939. Site includes an exhibition hall, restaurant, shop, site walks and the famous burial mounds. Exhibition Summer 2007: Anglo-Saxon Craftsmanship.

**Location:** MAP 8:L9, OS Ref. TM288 487. Off B1083 Woodbridge to Bawdsey road. Follow signs from A12. Train ½m Melton.

**Open:** Exhibition Hall, shop & restaurant: 17 Mar–1 Apr: Wed–Sun, 11am–5pm. 2–15 Apr: daily, 10.30am - 5pm. 16 Apr–1 Jul: Wed–Sun, 10.30am–5pm. 2 Jul–2 Sept: daily, 10.30am–5pm. 3 Sept–28 Oct: Wed–Sun, 11am–5pm. 29 Oct–26 Dec: Sat & Sun, 11am–4pm. Open BH Mons & daily during half terms.

**\*Admission:** Adult £5.90, Child £3. Family £15. Groups £4.50. Discount for visitors arriving by cycle or on foot. NT members free. *includes a voluntary donation but visitors can choose to pay the standard prices displayed at the property and on the website.

Licensed. 🍽️ Licensed. By arrangement. In grounds, on leads. Programme of events, tel for details.

## THE TIDE MILL

**Woodbridge, Suffolk IP12 4SR**
**Tel:** 01728 746959
**Contact:** Terina Booker
First recorded in 1170, now fully restored, machinery demonstrated at low tide. Ring for wheel turning times.
**Location:** MAP 8:L9, OS Ref. TM275 487. By riverside ¼m SE of Woodbridge town centre. 1¼m off A12.
**Open:** Easter & May–Sept: daily. Apr & Oct: Sats & Suns only, 11am–5pm.
**Admission:** Adult £2.50, Child Free, Conc. £1.50. (2006 prices.)

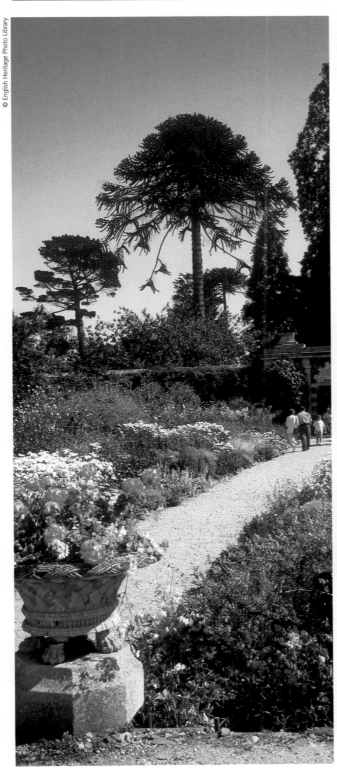

© English Heritage Photo Library

Somerleyton Hall & Gardens, Lowestoft

# WYKEN HALL GARDENS

### STANTON, BURY ST EDMUNDS, SUFFOLK IP31 2DW

www.wykenvineyards.co.uk

**Tel:** 01359 250287  **Fax:** 01359 253420
**Owner:** Sir Kenneth & Lady Carlisle    **Contact:** Mrs Storm Scott
The Elizabethan manor house is surrounded by a romantic, plant-lover's garden with maze, knot and herb garden and rose garden featuring old roses. A walk through ancient woodlands leads to Wyken Vineyards, winner of EVA Wine of the Year. In the 16th century barn, the Vineyard Restaurant serves our wines along with a varied menu from fresh local produce. It features in the Michelin and Good Food Guides.
**Location:** MAP 8:J8, OS Ref. TL963 717. 9m NE of Bury St. Edmunds 1m E of A143. Follow brown tourist signs to Wyken Vineyards from Ixworth.
**Open:** 5 Jan–24 Dec: daily, 10am–6pm. Garden: 1 Apr–1 Oct: daily except Sat, 2–6pm. Open for dinner from 7pm Fri & Sat (advisable to book).
**Admission:** Gardens: Adult £3, Child (under 12yrs) Free, Conc. £2.50. Groups by appointment.
⊡ 🏠 🖥 🍽 ㋤ Suitable. WC. 🍽 Licensed. 🅿 🚌 In grounds, on leads. ❄

# YAXLEY HALL

### EYE, SUFFOLK IP23 8BY

www.yaxleyhall.com

**Tel:** 01379 788869  **E-mail:** enquiries@yaxleyhall.net
**Owner:** Dominic Richards    **Contact:** Richard Orton
Yaxley Hall is an intimate country house located on the Suffolk/Norfolk borders. It is a private home, which the owner makes available on a limited basis throughout the year. The property has been the subject of a recent thorough refurbishment including the reinstatement of a large Gothick window.
**Location:** MAP 8:K8, OS Ref. TM 125 736. Half way between Ipswich & Norwich on the A140, located on the opposite side of the road to the village of Yaxley.
**Open:** By appointment for weddings and groups only: All year.
**Admission:** Contact property for details.
🍽 Licensed. 🚫 Obligatory. 🅿 Limited. 🔳 🚌 Guide dogs only. ▣ ❄

**Above:** Burghley House
**Right:** Belton House ©NT Photographic Library

# East Midlands

This is a part of Britain that is sadly often overlooked, but merits further investigation. Visit Rockingham Castle, with its dramatic views over five counties. Further north, Chatsworth and Haddon Hall are two very different examples of stately homes. Contrast them with the charming manor house of Eyam Hall and the stunning gardens of Coton Manor.

Derbyshire

Leicestershire & Rutland

Lincolnshire

Northamptonshire

Nottinghamshire

### ■ Owner
Trustees of the Chatsworth Settlement. Home of the Devonshire family

### ■ Contact
Mr Simon Seligman
Chatsworth
Bakewell
Derbyshire DE45 1PP

**Tel:** 01246 582204
01246 565300
**Fax:** 01246 583536
**E-mail:** visit@chatsworth.org

### ■ Location
**MAP 6:P2**
**OS Ref. SK260 703**

From London
3 hrs M1/J29,
signposted via
Chesterfield.

3m E of Bakewell,
off B6012,
10m W of Chesterfield.

**Rail:** Chesterfield Station, 11m.

**Bus:** Chesterfield – Baslow, 1½m.

### ■ Opening Times
14 March–23 December.
Daily: 11am–4.30pm.
The Park is open free throughout the year.

### ■ Admission
**House & Garden**
| | |
|---|---|
| Adult | £10.00 |
| Child | £3.50 |
| OAP/Student | £8.00 |
| Family | £25.00 |

**Pre-booked groups (12+)**
| | |
|---|---|
| Adult | £8.50 |
| OAP/Student | £7.00 |

**Garden only**
| | |
|---|---|
| Adult | £6.25 |
| Child | £2.75 |
| OAP/Student | £4.75 |
| Family | £15.00 |

**House, Garden & 11th Duke Exhibition**
| | |
|---|---|
| Adult | £11.75 |
| Child | £4.50 |
| OAP | £9.75 |
| Family | £28.50 |

**Groups**
| | |
|---|---|
| Adult | £10.25 |
| OAP/Student | £8.75 |

**Farmyard & Adventure Playground**
| | |
|---|---|
| All | £4.75 |
| Groups (5+) | £4.00 |
| OAP/School groups | £3.50 |
| Child under 3yrs | Free |

Family pass for all attractions £45.00

Rates differ during Christmas season (3 Nov–23 Dec).

### ■ Conference/Function

| ROOM | SIZE | MAX CAPACITY |
|---|---|---|
| Hartington Rm. | | 70 |
| Coffee Rm. | | 24 |

# CHATSWORTH
www.chatsworth.org

The great treasure house of Chatsworth was first built by Bess of Hardwick in 1552 and has been lived in by the Cavendish family, the Dukes of Devonshire, ever since. The House was rebuilt by the 1st Duke at the end of the 17th century, while the 6th Duke added a wing 130 years later. Visitors see the grandest rooms in the house, including the magnificent 17th century State Rooms. The Library, Great Dining Room and Sculpture Gallery reflect the taste of the 6th Duke, and the latter was used to great effect as Pemberley in the new Pride and Prejudice film. Among the treasures on view, there are painted ceilings by Verrio, Thornhill and Laguerre, tapestry, silk and leather wall hangings, furniture and decorative arts by the greatest British and European makers, classical and neo-classical sculpture, including four works by Antonio Canova and paintings by Rembrandt, Tintoretto, Veronese, Reynolds, Gainsborough, Landseer and Sargent. Visitors can also see an exhibition in eight rooms of the house, to celebrate the life and collecting of Andrew, the 11th Duke, including important 20th century works of art ranging from William Nicholson to Lucian Freud. Chatsworth has won many awards as the country's favourite stately home. From 3 November 13 rooms are open, richly decorated to celebrate Christmas.

### Garden
The 105 acre garden was created during three great eras in garden and landscape design. The 200 metre Cascade, the Willow Tree fountain and the Canal survive from the 1st Duke's formal garden. 'Capability' Brown landscaped the garden and park in the 1760s. The 6th Duke's gardener, Sir Joseph Paxton, built rockeries and designed a series of glasshouses. He also created the Emperor fountain, one of the tallest gravity-fed fountains in the world. More recent additions include the Rose, Cottage and Kitchen gardens, the Serpentine Hedge, the Maze, a new Sensory garden and contemporary sculpture.

Farmyard & Adventure Playground. Guide book translations.

Wheelchairs in part of the house, and welcome in garden (3 electric, 7 standard). WCs. Special leaflet.

Rooms available for conferences and private functions. Contact Head of Catering.

Restaurant (max 300); home-made food. Menus on request.

Private tours of house or Greenhouses and Behind the Scenes Days, by arrangement only (extra charges apply). Groups please pre-book.

In English.

Cars 100 yds, Coaches 25 yds from house.

Guided tours, packs, trails and school room. Free preliminary visit recommended.

# HADDON HALL 🏛

www.haddonhall.co.uk

Haddon Hall sits on a rocky outcrop above the River Wye close to the market town of Bakewell, looking much as is would have done in Tudor times. There has been a dwelling here since the 11th century but the house we see today dates mainly from the late 14th century with major additions in the following 200 years and some alterations in the early 17th century including the creation of the Long Gallery.

William the Conqueror's illegitimate son Peverel, and his descendants, held Haddon for 100 years before it passed to the Vernon family. In the late 16th century the estate passed through marriage to the Manners family, in whose possession it has remained ever since.

When the Dukedom of Rutland was conferred on the Manners family in 1703 they moved to Belvoir Castle, and Haddon was left deserted for 200 years. This was Haddon's saving grace as the Hall thus escaped the major architectural changes of the 18th and 19th centuries ready for the great restoration at the beginning of the 20th century by the 9th Duke of Rutland. Henry VIII's elder brother Arthur, who was a frequent guest of the Vernons, would be quite familiar with the house as it stands today.

Haddon Hall is a popular location for film and television productions. Recent films include *Pride & Prejudice* and the BBC dramatisation of *Jane Eyre*.

## Gardens

Magnificent terraced gardens with over 150 varieties of rose and clematis, many over 70 years old, provide colour and scent throughout the summer.

**ℹ** Haddon Hall is ideal as a film location due to its authentic and genuine architecture requiring little alteration. Suitable locations are also available on the Estate.

**♿** Unsuitable, steep approach, varying levels of house.

**☕🍽** Self-service, licensed (max 75). Home-made food.

**🚶** Special tours £10pp for groups of 15, 7 days' notice.

**P** Ample, 450 yds from house. £1 per car.

**▦** Tours of the house bring alive Haddon Hall of old. Costume room also available, very popular!

**🐕** Guide dogs only.

---

■ **Owner**
Lord Edward Manners

■ **Contact**
Janet O'Sullivan
Estate Office
Haddon Hall
Bakewell
Derbyshire DE45 1LA

**Tel:** 01629 812855
**Fax:** 01629 814379
**E-mail:** info@
haddonhall.co.uk

■ **Location**
**MAP 6:P2**
**OS Ref. SK234 663**

From London 3 hrs
Sheffield ½ hr
Manchester 1 hr
Haddon is on the
E side of A6 1½m
S of Bakewell.
M1/J30.

**Rail:** Chesterfield
Station, 12m.

**Bus:** Chesterfield
Bakewell.

■ **Opening Times**
**Summer**
Easter: 6–10 April
April & October:
Sat–Mon (inc 31 Mar).
May–September:
Daily, 12 noon–5pm
Last admission 4pm.

■ **Admission**
**Summer**
| | |
|---|---|
| Adult | £8.50 |
| Child (5–15yrs) | £4.50 |
| Conc | £7.50 |
| Family (2+3) | £22.00 |
| Regular Visitor Pass | £15.50 |

Groups (15+)
| | |
|---|---|
| Adult | £7.50 |
| Child (5–15yrs) | £3.50 |
| Conc | £6.50 |

■ **Owner**
The National Trust

■ **Contact**
Victoria Flanagan
Property Manager
Kedleston Hall
Derby  DE22 5JH

**Tel:** 01332 842191
**Fax:** 01332 844059
**Email:** kedlestonhall@
nationaltrust.org.uk

■ **Location**
**MAP 6:P4**
**OS ref. SK312 403**

5 miles NW of Derby,
signposted from the
roundabout where the
A38 crosses A52 Derby
ring road

■ **Opening Times**
**Hall**
10 March–31 October:
Sat–Wed (open Good Fri),
12 noon–4.30pm (last
entry to hall 4pm).

**Garden**
10 March–31 October:
Daily, 10am–6pm.

**Park**
10 March–31 October;
Daily, 10am–6pm.

1 November–7 March
2008: Daily, 10am–4pm.

Please note – occasional
day restrictions will apply
during December 2007 &
January 2008.

**Shop & Restaurant**
10 March–31 October:
Sat–Wed, 11am–5pm.

21 July–24 August: Thurs
& Fri,12 noon–4pm.

3 November–4 March
2008: Sat & Sun,
12 noon–4pm.

■ ***Admission**
**House & Garden**
Adult               £8.00
Child               £4.00
Family            £20.00

**Park & Garden**
Adult               £3.60
Child               £1.80
Family             £9.00

Winter admission for Park
only, £3.50 per vehicle.

*includes a voluntary
donation but visitors can
choose to pay the standard
prices displayed at the
property and on the website.

**Conference/Function**

| ROOM | SIZE | MAX CAPACITY |
|------|------|--------------|
| Caesars' Hall | 40' x 60' | 120 dining 150 reception 100 delegates theatre style |
| Saloon | | Civil Weddings only – seats 110 |
| Restaurant | | 90 dining split in 2 rooms |

# KEDLESTON HALL 🌳

www.nationaltrust.org.uk

Kedleston was built between 1759 and 1765 for the Curzon family who have lived in the area since the 12th century. The house boasts the most complete and least altered sequence of Robert Adam interiors in England, with the magnificent State rooms retaining much of their great collections of paintings and furniture. The Adam influence can also be seen across the 18th century pleasure grounds and 800 acre park. Since 1987 the National Trust has undertaken a programme of work to return these interiors to their original appearance so that visitors can re-live the experience of coming to see a 'palace of the arts'.

The Eastern Museum houses a remarkable collection by Lord Curzon when he was Viceroy of India (1899–1905).

Kedleston has a year wide programme of special events, please telephone for more details and to be sent an up-to-date programme or visit the website.

**New for 2007**
The Smoking Room on the ground floor of the hall has been set up as a 'rest and relaxation' room at the end of the hall tour to enable visitors to rest and enjoy a new 'virtual tour' of the the spectacular State Rooms. Kedleston is also available as a popular venue for corporate events and holds a licence for Civil wedding ceremonies in the Saloon on the State floor. Please ring the office on 01332 842191 to be sent an information pack.

Also available as a filming location.

Unfortunately no access to the State floor but visitors can access the ground floor rooms, which includes the Smoking Room where a virtual tour will enable visitors to experience the splendour of the State Rooms.

Must be booked in advance.

Dogs are permitted to all areas of the park apart from the Gardens and Long & Short Walk.

■ **Owner**
High Peak Borough Council

■ **Contact**
Administration
Pavilion Gardens
St John's Road
Buxton
Derbyshire  SK17 6XN

**Tel:** 01298 23114
**Fax:** 01298 27622
**E-mail:** paviliongardens@highpeak.gov.uk

■ **Location**
**MAP 6:O2**
**OS Ref. SK055 734**

Situated on the A6 in the Peak District, within easy reach of Manchester, Sheffield and the East Midlands.

**Rail:** Buxton station ½m.

■ **Opening Times**
Every day except Christmas Day.
Opens: 10am.

■ **Admission**
Free entry into building.
Charges vary for different events and fairs.

# PAVILION GARDENS

www.paviliongardens.co.uk

## Pavilion

With Grade II listed buildings dating from 1871 and 23 acres of beautiful Victorian landscaped gardens in the centre of Buxton on the River Wye, there are attractions to suit all tastes and ages.

The Pavilion hosts a range of fairs and events such as Antique, Book and Toy fairs to Classic Car Auctions, Tea Dances and Farmers' Markets.

There are facilities for conferences, seminars and meetings with a capacity to cater for up to 400 people with a full meal menu.

Visitors can also use the Restaurant, Café and Coffee Lounge or browse in the Food and Gift Shop, which specialises in locally produced goods.

## Gardens

Over the last 125 years, various changes have been made to the Gardens (they hosted the only Open Tennis Championships in the UK outside Wimbledon). The Gardens, originally designed by the eminent landscape gardener Edward Milner, have recently been restored to their original Victorian splendour, following a £4.5 million Heritage Lottery grant.

The bandstand is used on most summer Sundays, with brass bands playing from 2–4pm, when deckchairs are available on the terrace promenade.

There is also a colourful and relaxing Conservatory, housing an extensive range of flowers and plants, and which adjoins the renowned, Frank Matcham designed, Buxton Opera House.

Miniature train in gardens, crazy golf, adventure play areas.
Food & gift shops.
Civil weddings & wedding receptions, banquets, functions & conferences.
Partial.
Licensed.
Charge applies
In gardens on leads. Guide dogs only in Pavilion.

English Heritage Photo Library/Jonathan Bailey

## BOLSOVER CASTLE ⌗

### CASTLE STREET, BOLSOVER, DERBYSHIRE S44 6PR

www.english-heritage.org.uk/visits

**Tel:** 01246 822844

**Owner:** English Heritage **Contact:** Visitor Operations Team

An enchanting and romantic spectacle, situated high on a wooded hilltop dominating the surrounding landscape. Built on the site of a Norman castle, this is largely an early 17th century mansion. Most delightful is the 'Little Castle', with intricate carvings, panelling and wall painting. See the restored interiors of the Little Castle including the only remaining copies of Titian's Caesar Paintings, and the Venus Fountain and statuary. There is also an impressive 17th century indoor Riding House built by the Duke of Newcastle. Enjoy the Visitor and Discovery Centre. Exciting recent interpretation scheme includes Audio/Visual and scale model of Little Castle. Also contemporary Visitor Centre with information about Bolsover town's development. Picnickers are welcome. (Bolsover is now available for Civil weddings, receptions and corporate hospitality.)

**Location:** MAP 7:A2, OS120, SK471 707. Signposted from M1/J29, 6m from Mansfield. In Bolsover 6m E of Chesterfield on A632.

**Open:** Apr, Oct & Nov–20 Mar: Thur–Mon, 10am–5pm (Nov–Mar 4pm). May–30 Sept: daily, 10am–6pm. Closes 4pm Sats all year. Closed 24–26 Dec & 1 Jan. May close earlier for evening events.

**Admission:** Adult £6.80, Child £3.40, Conc. £5.10, Family £17. 15% discount for groups (11+).

◻ ▦ ♿ Grounds. WC. ☕ Airconditioned café. 📷 ⏺ Free with admission. 🅿 ▦ ✖ ▲ ❋ ♿

NT Photographic Library: Andreas von Einsiedel

## CALKE ABBEY ✶

### TICKNALL, DERBYSHIRE DE73 1LE

www.nationaltrust.org.uk

**Tel:** 01332 863822 **Fax:** 01332 865272 **E-mail:** calkeabbey@nationaltrust.org.uk

**Owner:** The National Trust **Contact:** The Property Manager

The house that time forgot, this baroque mansion, built 1701–3 for Sir John Harpur, is set in a landscaped park. Little restored, Calke is preserved by a programme of conservation as a graphic illustration of the English country house in decline; it contains the family's collection of natural history, a magnificent 18th century state bed and interiors that are virtually unchanged since the 1880s. Walled garden, pleasure grounds and orangery. Early 19th century Church. Historic parkland with Portland sheep and deer. Staunton Harold Church is nearby.

**Location:** MAP 7:A5, OS128, SK356 239. 10m S of Derby, on A514 at Ticknall between Swadlincote and Melbourne.

**Open:** House, Garden & Church: 17 Mar–28 Oct: Sat–Wed; House: 12.30–5pm (ticket office opens 11am). Closed 11 Aug for concert. Garden & Church: 11am–5pm. Park: most days until 8pm or dusk. Shop & Restaurant: 17 Mar–28 Oct: as house, 10.30am–5pm. (Shop & Restaurant open every day in Aug); 3–25 Nov & 5 Jan–9 Mar 2008: Sat & Sun, 11am–4pm; also 26 Nov–19 Dec: Sat–Wed, 11am–4pm.

**\*Admission:** All sites: Adult £8, Child £4, Family £20. Garden only: Adult £5, Child £2.50, Family £12.50. Discount for pre-booked groups. *includes a voluntary donation but visitors can choose to pay the standard prices displayed at the property and on the website.

◻ ♿ House. Braille guide. Wheelchairs. WCs. 🍴 Licensed. 📷 By arrangement. 🐕 In park, on leads only. ❋

## CARNFIELD HALL

**South Normanton, Nr Alfreton, Derbyshire  DE55 2BE**

**Tel:** 01773 520084

**Owner/Contact:** J B Cartland

Unspoilt Elizabethan manor house. Panelled rooms and two Jacobean staircases. Since 1502 home of the Revell, Wilmot, Radford and Cartland families. 300 years of fascinating contents. Old walled garden and deer park in course of restoration.

**Location:** MAP 7:A3, OS Ref. SK425 561. 1½m W of M1/J28 on B6019. Alfreton Station 5 mins walk.

**Open:** Groups (8–25) by appointment.

**Admission:** £5. Evening visits £7.

ℹ No photography in Hall. Park available for events. ▣ ⚑ ♿ Grounds.
☕ (Adjoining garden centre/café – in separate ownership.) ⚐ Obligatory.
🐕 In grounds, on leads only.

## CATTON HALL 🏠

**CATTON, WALTON-ON-TRENT, SOUTH DERBYSHIRE  DE12 8LN**

www.catton-hall.com

**Tel:** 01283 716311  **Fax:** 01283 712876  **E-mail:** kneilson@catton-hall.com

**Owner/Contact:** Robin & Katie Neilson

Catton, built in 1745, has been in the hands of the same family since 1405 and is still lived in by the Neilsons as their private home. This gives the house, with its original collection of 17th and 18th century portraits, pictures and antique furniture, a unique, relaxed and friendly atmosphere. With its spacious reception rooms, luxurious bedrooms and delicious food and wine, Catton is centrally located for residential or non-residential business meetings, product launches and team-building activities, as well as for accommodation for those visiting Birmingham, the NEC, the Belfry, the Potteries and Dukeries – or just for a weekend celebration of family and friends. The acres of parkland alongside the River Trent are ideal for all types of corporate and public events.

**Location:** MAP 6:P5, OS Ref. SK206 154. 2m E of A38 at Alrewas between Lichfield & Burton-on-Trent (8m from each). Birmingham NEC 20m.

**Open:** By prior arrangement all year for corporate hospitality, shooting parties, wedding receptions, private groups. Guided tours: 9 Apr–15 Oct. Mons only, 2pm (Groups 15+ by prior arrangement).

ℹ Conference facilities. ⊤ By arrangement. ♿ ⚐ By arrangement for groups.
🛏 4 x four posters, 5 twin, all en-suite. ♨

## CHATSWORTH

*See page 304 for full page entry.*

## ELVASTON CASTLE COUNTRY PARK

**Borrowash Road, Elvaston, Derbyshire  DE72 3EP**

**Tel:** 01332 571342  **Fax:** 01332 758751

**Owner:** Derbyshire County Council  **Contact:** The Park Manager

200 acre park landscaped in 19th century by William Barron. Walled garden.

**Location:** MAP 7:A4, OS Ref. SK407 330. 5m SE of Derby, 2m from A6 or A52.

**Open:** Please contact park for details.

**Admission:** Park and Gardens Free. Car park: Midweek £1, weekends/BHs £1.50, Coaches £10.

▣ ♿ Ground floor & grounds. WCs. ⚑ ⚐ By arrangement. 🅿 ▥
🐕 In grounds, under close control. ▲ ✳

© English Heritage Photo Library

Melbourne Hall & Gardens

# EYAM HALL 🏛
## EYAM, HOPE VALLEY, DERBYSHIRE  S32 5QW

www.eyamhall.com

**Tel:** 01433 631976  **Fax:** 01433 631603  **E-mail:** info@eyamhall.com
**Owner:** Mr R H V Wright  **Contact:** Mrs N Wright

A lively guided tour is a feature of this small but charming manor house in the famous plague village of Eyam. Eyam Hall has been the home of the Wright family since 1671 and it retains the intimate atmosphere of a much loved family home. The restoration of the beautiful walled garden is nearing completion. A working Craft Centre in the historic farmyard houses craftspeople, shops and a restaurant. Licensed for Civil wedding ceremonies, Eyam Hall is ideal for both intimate in-house and larger marquee receptions.

**Location:** MAP 6:P2, OS119, SK216 765. Approx 10m from Sheffield, Chesterfield and Buxton, Eyam is off the A623 between Chesterfield and Chapel-en-le-Frith. Eyam Hall is in the centre of the village past the church.

**Open:** House and Garden: Easter Week, 1 Jul–30 Aug: Wed, Thur, Sun & BH Mon, 12 noon–4pm. (Booked groups Easter to Oct.) Craft Centre: All year Tues–Sun.

**Admission:** Adult £6.25, Child £4, Conc. £5.75, Family: (2+4) £19. Group rates available. Craft Centre: Free. Car park: Free.

ℹ Craft Centre. ⬛⬛⬛ Partial. 🍽 Licensed. 📷 Obligatory. 🅿 ⬛
🐾 In grounds, on leads. Guide dogs only in house. ⬛✳⬛

HADDON HALL 🏛    *See page 305 for full page entry.*

## HARDSTOFT HERB GARDEN
**Hall View Cottage, Hardstoft, Chesterfield, Derbyshire  S45 8AH**
**Tel:** 01246 854268
**Owner:** Mr Stephen Raynor/L M Raynor  **Contact:** Mr Stephen Raynor
Consists of two display gardens with information boards and well labelled plants.
**Location:** MAP 7:A3, OS Ref. SK436 633. On B6039 between Holmewood & Tibshelf, 3m from J29 on M1.
**Open:** Gardens, Nursery & Tearoom: 15 Mar–15 Sept: Wed–Sun, 10am–5pm. Closed Mon & Tue except Easter and BHs when open throughout.
**Admission:** Adult £1, Child Free.

Eyam Hall

# HARDWICK HALL, GARDENS, PARK & STAINSBY MILL 🌾
## DOE LEA, CHESTERFIELD, DERBYSHIRE  S44 5QJ

www.nationaltrust.org.uk

**Tel:** 01246 850430  **Fax:** 01246 858424  **Shop/Restaurant:** 01246 858409
**E-mail:** hardwickhall@nationaltrust.org.uk
**Owner:** The National Trust  **Contact:** The Property Manager

**Hardwick Hall:** A late 16th century 'prodigy house' designed by Robert Smythson for Bess of Hardwick. The house contains outstanding contemporary furniture, tapestries and needlework including pieces identified in an inventory of 1601; a needlework exhibition is on permanent display. Walled courtyards enclose fine gardens, orchards and a herb garden. The country park contains Whiteface Woodland sheep and Longhorn cattle.

**Location:** MAP 7:A3, OS120, SK456 651. 7½m NW of Mansfield, 9½m SE of Chesterfield: approach from M1/J29 via A6175.

**Open:** Hall: 17 Mar–28 Oct: Wed, Thurs, Sat, Sun, BH Mon & Good Fri: 12 noon–4.30pm. Gardens: as Hall, Wed–Sun, 11am–5.30pm. Parkland: daily. Shop: As Hall, 11am–5pm. Restaurant: as Shop. Stone centre: as Hall, 11am–1pm, 2–4pm.

**Admission:** Hall & Garden: Adult £9, Child £4.50, Family £22.50. Garden only: Adult £4.50, Child £2.25, Family £11.25. Pre-booking for groups essential, discount for groups of 15+. Timed tickets on busy days. Admission price includes voluntary Gift Aid donation.

**Hardwick Estate – Stainsby Mill** is an 18th century water-powered corn mill in working order.

**Location:** MAP 7:A3, OS120, SK455 653. From M1/J29 take A6175, signposted to Clay Cross then first left and left again to Stainsby Mill.

**Open:** 17 Mar–28 Oct: Wed, Thur, Sat, Sun, BH Mons & Good Fri; 30 Jun–31 Aug: Wed–Sun & 1 Jan 2008, 11am–4.30pm.

**\*Admission:** Adult £3, Child £1.50, Family £7.50. No discounts for groups, suitable for school groups. For information send SAE to Property Manager at Hardwick Hall. \*includes a voluntary donation but visitors can choose to pay the standard prices displayed at the property and on the website.

⬛⬛ Garden, Hall: 3 display rooms only. 🍽 Licensed. ⬛🐾 In park, on leads.

Bolsover Castle

# HARDWICK OLD HALL ⌗
## DOE LEA, NR CHESTERFIELD, DERBYSHIRE S44 5QJ

www.english-heritage.org.uk/visits

**Tel:** 01246 850431

**Owner:** National Trust, managed by English Heritage

**Contact:** Visitor Operations Team

This large ruined house, finished in 1591, still displays Bess of Hardwick's innovative planning and interesting decorative plasterwork. New graphics panels will focus on the rich interiors Bess created. The views from the top floor over the country park and 'New' Hall are spectacular. Picnickers are welcome.

**Location:** MAP 7:A3, OS120, SK463 638. 7½m NW of Mansfield, 9½m SE of Chesterfield, off A6175, from M1/J29.

**Open:** 1 Apr–31 Oct: Wed, Thur, Sat & Sun, 10am–6pm, (5pm Oct).

**Admission:** Adult £3.90, Child £2, Conc. £2.90, Family £9.80. 15% discount for groups (11+). NT members free, but small charge at events.

🔲 📷 Free with admission. 🔲 🅿 🐕 On leads.

---

## KEDLESTON HALL 🦌     *See page 306 for full page entry.*

# MELBOURNE HALL & GARDENS 🏛
## MELBOURNE, DERBYSHIRE DE73 8EN

www.melbournehall.com

**Tel:** 01332 862502   **Fax:** 01332 862263

**Owner:** Lord & Lady Ralph Kerr    **Contact:** Mrs Gill Weston

This beautiful house of history, in its picturesque poolside setting, was once the home of Victorian Prime Minister William Lamb. The fine gardens, in the French formal style, contain Robert Bakewell's intricate wrought iron arbour and a fascinating yew tunnel. Upstairs rooms available to view by appointment.

**Location:** MAP 7:A5, OS Ref. SK389 249. 8m S of Derby. From London, exit M1/J24.

**Open:** Hall: Aug only (not first 3 Mons) 2–5pm. Last admission 4.15pm. Gardens: 1 Apr–30 Sept: Weds, Sats, Suns, BH Mons, 1.30–5.30pm. Additional open days possible in August, please telephone for details.

**Admission:** Hall: Adult £3.50, Child £2, OAP £3. Gardens: Adult £3.50, Child/OAP £2.50. Hall & Gardens: Adult £5.50, Child £3.50, OAP £4.50.

ℹ Crafts. No photography in house. 🔲 ♿ Partial. 🔲 📷 Obligatory in house.
🅿 Limited. No coach parking. 🐕 Guide dogs only.

---

## PAVILION GARDENS     *See page 307 for full page entry.*

---

### PEVERIL CASTLE ⌗

**Market Place, Castleton, Hope Valley S33 8WQ**

**Tel:** 01433 620613   www.english-heritage.org.uk/visits

**Owner:** English Heritage    **Contact:** Visitor Operations Team

There are breathtaking views of the Peak District from this castle, perched high above the pretty village of Castleton. The great square tower of Henry II stands almost to its original height. A walkway opens up new areas and views from the first floor of the Keep. Peveril Castle is one of the earliest Norman castles to be built in England. The new Peveril Castle Visitor Centre has displays which tell the story of Peveril as the focal point of the Royal Forest of the Peak as well as improved access and facilities. Picnickers are welcome.

**Location:** MAP 6:O2, OS110, SK150 827. S side of Castleton, 15m W of Sheffield on A6187.

**Open:** 1 Apr–31 Oct: daily, 10am–5pm (6pm May–Aug). 1 Nov–20 Mar: Thur–Mon, 10am–4pm. Closed 24–26 Dec & 1 Jan.

**Admission:** Adult £3.50, Child £1.80, Conc. £2.60, Family £8.80. 15% discount for groups (11+).

ℹ WCs 🔲 🔲 🐕 ❄ ♿

Hardwick Hall, Chesterfield

## RENISHAW HALL GARDENS 🏠
### SHEFFIELD, DERBYSHIRE S21 3WB
www.sitwell.co.uk

**Tel:** 01246 432310  **Fax:** 01246 430760  **E-mail:** info2@renishaw-hall.co.uk
**Owner:** Sir Reresby Sitwell Bt DL  **Contact:** The Administrator
Home of Sir Reresby and Lady Sitwell. Eight acres of Italian style formal gardens stand in 300 acres of mature parkland, encompassing statues, shaped yew hedges, herbaceous borders, a water garden and lakes. The Sitwell museum and art galleries are located in Georgian stables alongside craft workshops and Gallery café, furnished with contemporary art. Beautiful camellias and carpets of daffodils in April. New children's garden for 2007.
**Location:** MAP 7:A2, OS Ref. SK435 786. On A6135 3m from M1/J30, equidistant from Sheffield and Chesterfield.
**Open:** Mar–Oct: Thurs–Sun & BHs, 10.30am–4.30pm. Hall is not open to the general public, private groups (25+) only by prior arrangement. Hall tours may be booked.
**Admission:** Garden, Museum & Galleries: Adult £5, Conc. £4.20, Under 10s Free.
🖥 ⊞ ⊤ ♿ ⛑ 🎫 By arrangement. **P** 🚭 In grounds, on leads. ▣
🎗 Bluebell fortnight (26 Apr–13 May).

## SUTTON SCARSDALE HALL ⚜
**Chesterfield, Derbyshire**
**Tel:** 01604 735400 (Regional Office)  www.english-heritage.org.uk/visits
**Owner:** English Heritage  **Contact:** The East Midlands Regional Office
The dramatic hilltop shell of a great early 18th century baroque mansion.
**Location:** MAP 7:A2, OS Ref. SK441 690. Between Chesterfield & Bolsover, 1½m S of Arkwright Town.
**Open:** All year, daily: 10am–6pm (4pm winter). Closed 24–26 Dec & 1 Jan.
**Admission:** Free.
♿ **P** ❄

Renishaw Hall Gardens, Sheffield

Derbyshire Countryside Ltd

## TISSINGTON HALL 🏠
### ASHBOURNE, DERBYSHIRE DE6 1RA
www.tissington-hall.com

**Tel:** 01335 352200  **Fax:** 01335 352201  **E-mail:** tissington.hall@btinternet.com
**Owner/Contact:** Sir Richard FitzHerbert Bt
Home of the FitzHerbert family for over 500 years. The Hall stands in a superbly maintained estate village, and contains wonderful panelling and fine old masters. A 10 acre garden and arboretum. Schools very welcome. Award-winning Old Coach House Tearoom, open Apr–Oct daily; Nov–Mar, Thurs–Sun, 11am–5pm for coffees, lunch and tea.

**Location:** MAP 6:P3, OS Ref. SK175 524. 4m N of Ashbourne off A515 towards Buxton.
**Open:** 9–13 Apr, 28 May–1 Jun: daily. 24 Jul–24 Aug: Tue–Fri, 1.30–4pm.
**Admission:** Hall & Gardens: Adult £6.50, Child (10–16yrs) £3.50, Conc. £5, Gardens only: Adult £3, Child £1, Conc. £3.
ℹ No photography in house. ⊤ ♿ Partial. WCs at tearooms. ☕ Tearoom adjacent to Hall. 🎫 Obligatory. **P** Limited. ▣ 🚭 Guide dogs only. ▣ ❄ 🎗

# BELVOIR CASTLE

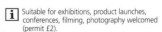

www.belvoircastle.com

Belvoir Castle, home of the Duke and Duchess of Rutland, commands a magnificent view over the Vale of Belvoir. The name Belvoir, meaning beautiful view, dates back to Norman times, when Robert de Todeni, Standard Bearer to William the Conqueror, built the first castle on this superb site. Destruction caused by two Civil Wars and by a catastrophic fire in 1816 have breached the continuity of Belvoir's history. The present building owes much to the inspiration and taste of Elizabeth, 5th Duchess of Rutland and was built after the fire.

Inside the Castle are notable art treasures including works by Poussin, Holbein, Rubens, and Reynolds, Gobelin and Mortlake tapestries, Chinese silks, furniture, fine porcelain and sculpture.

The Queen's Royal Lancers' Museum at Belvoir has a fascinating exhibition of the history of the Regiment, as well as a fine collection of weapons, uniforms and medals.

## Gardens

A remarkable survival of English garden history that are being sensitively restored to their former glory. The Spring Gardens, opened to all day visitors in 2005, contain a collection of Victorian daffodils planted sympathetically with primroses and bluebells, against a background of rhododendrons and azaleas. There are also rare specimen trees, many the largest of their type in the British Isles.

Belvoir Castle is available for exclusive hire as a film location and for conferences, weddings and special events. It is also possible to put on events in conjunction with the open season.

**☐ Owner**

Their Graces The Duke & Duchess of Rutland

**☐ Contact**

Mary McKinlay
Castle Opening Office
Belvoir Castle
Grantham
Leicestershire NG32 1PE

**Tel:** 01476 871003
**Fax:** 01476 871018
**E-mail:** info@
belvoircastle.com

**☐ Location**

**MAP 7:C4**
**OS Ref. SK820 337**

A1 from London 110m
Grantham Junction
York 100m. Leicester 30m
Grantham 7m.
Nottingham 20m.

**Air:** Nottingham
& Robin Hood Airports.
Helicopter Landing Pad.

**Rail:** Grantham Stn 7m

**Bus:** Melton Mowbray –
Vale of Belvoir via
Castle Car Park.

**Taxi:** Grantham Taxis
01476 563944 / 563988.

**☐ Opening Times**

**Summer**
3–12 April, daily.
May & June: daily except
Fris & Mons (open BH
Mons).
July & August: daily
except Fris.
September: Sats & Suns
11am–5pm.(Sats 4pm).

**Winter**
25 November–
2 December.
11am–5pm.
Last entry 4pm.

Groups welcome by
appointment.

**☐ Admission**

| | |
|---|---|
| Adult | £11.00 |
| Child (5–16yrs) | £6.00 |
| Conc. | £10.00 |
| Family (2+2/3) | £30.00 |

| Groups (15+) | |
|---|---|
| Adult | £8.40 |
| Child (5–16yrs) | £4.70 |
| Conc. | £7.35 |
| School | £4.70 |

**Grounds only**

| | |
|---|---|
| Adult/Conc. | £6.00 |
| Child (5–16yrs) | £2.00 |

Suitable for exhibitions, product launches, conferences, filming, photography welcomed (permit £2).

Banquets, private room available.

Ground floor and restaurant accessible. Please telephone for advice. WC.

Licensed. Groups catered for (100 max).

Tue–Thur, twice daily. Tour time: 1¼ hrs. Specialist picture and costume tours.

Ample. £1 per car at weekends. Coaches can take passengers to entrance by arrangement but should report to the main car park and ticket office on arrival.

Guided tours. Teacher's pack. Education room. Picnic area and adventure playground.

Guide dogs only.

Belvoir Castle is a day out for all the family and hosts different events every weekend from jousting to medieval re-enactments. Tel for details.

## Conference/Function

| ROOM | SIZE | MAX CAPACITY |
|---|---|---|
| State Dining Room | 52' x 31' | 130 |
| Regents Gallery | 131' x 16' | 220 |
| Old Kitchen | 45' x 22' | 100 |
| Ballroom | | 90 |
| Guards Room | | 175 |
| Stewards Restaurant | | 100 |

■ **Owner**

Mr Frederick de Lisle

■ **Owner**

Mr Frederick de Lisle

■ **Contact**

Mrs F de Lisle
Quenby Hall
Hungarton
Nr Leicester  LE7 9JF

**Tel/Fax:** 0116 2595224
**E-mail:** enquiries@
quenbyhall.co.uk

■ **Location**

**MAP 7:C6**
**OS Ref. SK702 065**

7m E of Leicester,
20 mins from M1/J21A,
40 mins A1.

**Air:** East Midlands
International 25 mins.

**Rail:** Market Harborough.

■ **Opening Times**

Not open to the public.
Available for exclusive hire
as a film location and for
conferences, weddings
and special events.

■ **Admission**

Please contact property
for details.

# QUENBY HALL

www.quenbyhall.co.uk

Quenby Hall lies seven miles east of Leicester and is a perfect and unspoiled example of a Jacobean country house. It was built by George Ashby in 1627. Amidst ancient cedars and beeches, it commands magnificent views of the countryside, in the secluded setting of 1400 acres of gardens, parkland and farm.

Stilton cheese was invented by the housekeeper at Quenby Hall. It was sold by her daughter who lived at the popular staging inn at Stilton, on the Great North Road: hence its name. The estate recommenced production of Quenby Stilton in 2005.

It is the private home of the de Lisle family and has been extensively restored, making it exceptionally warm and comfortable whilst remaining true to its Jacobean style, with beautiful panelling, plaster and stonework and other architectural features. It is not open to the public and is available for exclusive hire as a film location and for conferences, weddings and special events. The Old Dairy, with its old beams, stone floor and more 'country' ambience, is also available for hire.

Full exclusive use of the rooms can be made by groups numbering up to 150. Dinners can be held for up to 80 in the house with dancing in the old Dairy, or up to 300 in a marquee on the back lawn. Four beautiful ensuite bedrooms, two with four posters, available by special arrangement.

Banquets, private room available.

By arrangement.

Ample.

By arrangement.

# STANFORD HALL 🏛

www.stanfordhall.co.uk

Stanford has been the home of the Cave family, ancestors of the present owner, since 1430. In the 1690s, Sir Roger Cave commissioned the Smiths of Warwick to pull down the old Manor House and build the present Hall, which is an excellent example of their work and of the William and Mary period.

As well as over 5000 books, the handsome Library contains many interesting manuscripts, the oldest dating from 1150. The splendid pink and gold Ballroom has a fine coved ceiling with four *trompe l'oeil* shell corners. Throughout the house are portraits of the family and examples of furniture and objects which they collected over the

centuries. There is also a collection of Royal Stuart portraits, previously belonging to the Cardinal Duke of York, the last of the male Royal Stuarts. An unusual collection of family costumes is displayed in the Old Dining Room, which also houses some early Tudor portraits and a fine Empire chandelier.

The Hall and Stables are set in an attractive Park on the banks of Shakespeare's Avon. There is a walled Rose Garden behind the Stables. An early ha-ha separates the North Lawn from the mile-long North Avenue.

### Owner
Nicholas Fothergill Esq

### Contact
Tim Bowie
Stanford Hall
Lutterworth
Leicestershire
LE17 6DH

**Tel:** 01788 860250
**Fax:** 01788 860870
**E-mail:** s.maughan@
stanfordhall.co.uk

### Location
**MAP 7:B7**
**OS Ref. SP587 793**

M1/J18 6m,M1/J19 (from/to the N only) 2m, M6 exit/access at A14/M1(N)J 2m, A14 2m. Follow Historic House signs.

**Rail:** Rugby Stn 7½ m.

**Air:** Birmingham Airport 27m.

**Taxi:** Fone-A-Car. 01788 543333.

### Opening Times
Open on selected days in conjunction with park events.
Please see our website or telephone for details.

House open any day or evening (except Saturdays) for pre-booked groups.

### Admission
**House & Grounds**
| | |
|---|---|
| Adult | £6.00 |
| Child (5–15yrs) | £2.50 |

Private Group Tours (20+)
| | |
|---|---|
| Adult | £6.50 |
| Child (5–15yrs) | £2.50 |

**Grounds only**
| | |
|---|---|
| Adult | £3.50 |
| Child (5–15yrs) | £1.50 |

ℹ️ Craft centre (most Suns). Corporate days, clay pigeon shoots, filming, photography, small conferences. Parkland, helicopter landing area, lecture room, Blüthner piano. Caravan site.

🎁 

🍽 Lunches, dinners & wedding receptions.

♿ Visitors may alight at the entrance. WC.

☕ Teas, lunch & supper. Groups must book (70 max.)

🚶 Tour time: ¾ hr in groups of approx 25.

🅿️ 1,000 cars and 6–8 coaches. Free meals for coach drivers, coach parking on gravel in front of house.

🐕 In Park, on leads.

🛏 The Hall inc.4 x double ensuite bedrooms is available by special arrangement..

🎭 Concerts/Theatre in the Ballroom or Park.

### Conference/Function

| ROOM | SIZE | MAX CAPACITY |
|---|---|---|
| Ballroom | 39' x 26' | 100 |
| Old Dining Rm | 30' x 20' | 20 |
| Crocodile Room | 39' x 20' | 60 |

### ASHBY DE LA ZOUCH CASTLE ⌗

**South Street, Ashby de la Zouch, Leicestershire LE65 1BR**
**Tel:** 01530 413343 **www.english-heritage.org.uk/visits**
**Owner:** English Heritage **Contact:** Visitor Operations Team
The impressive ruins of this late medieval castle are dominated by a magnificent tower, over 80 feet high, which was split in two during the Civil War. Panoramic views. Explore the tunnel linking the kitchens to the Hastings Tower.
**Location:** MAP 7:A7, OS128, SK363 167. In Ashby de la Zouch, 12m S of Derby on A511. SE of town centre.
**Open:** 1 Apr–30 Jun: Thur–Mon, 10am–5pm. Jul & Aug: daily, 10am–6pm. 1 Sept–20 Mar: Thur–Mon, 10am–5pm (4pm Nov–Mar). Closed 24–26 Dec & 1 Jan.
**Admission:** Adult £3.50, Child £1.80, Conc. £2.60, Family £8.80. 15% discount for groups (11+).
ℹ WC. ▣ ⬖ Grounds. ▣ Free with admission. **P** Restricted. ▣ ▣ On leads. ❊ ⬛

### BELVOIR CASTLE ⛫

*See page 313 for full page entry.*

### BRADGATE PARK & SWITHLAND WOOD COUNTRY PARK

**Bradgate Park, Newtown Linford, Leics LE6 0HE**
**Tel:** 0116 2362713
**Owner:** Bradgate Park Trust **Contact:** M H Harrison
Includes the ruins of the brick medieval home of the Grey family and childhood home of Lady Jane Grey. Also has a medieval deer park.
**Location:** MAP 7:B6, OS Ref. SK534 102. 7m NW of Leicester, via Anstey & Newtown Linford. Country Park gates in Newtown Linford. 1¼ m walk to the ruins.
**Open:** All year during daylight hours.
**Admission:** No charge. Car parking charges.

### DONINGTON-LE-HEATH MANOR HOUSE

**Manor Road, Donington-le-Heath, Leicestershire LE67 2FW**
**Tel:** 01530 831259 / 0116 2658326
**Owner/Contact:** Leicestershire County Council
Medieval manor c1280 with 16th–17th century alterations.
**Location:** MAP 7:A6, OS Ref. SK421 126. ½ m SSW of Coalville. 4½ m W of M1/J22, by A511.
**Open:** Mar–Nov: daily, 11am–4pm. Dec–Feb: Sat & Sun only, 11am–4pm. (Plus occasional weekdays. Tel for details.)
**Admission:** Free.

### KIRBY MUXLOE CASTLE ⌗

**Kirby Muxloe, Leicestershire LE9 9MD**
**Tel:** 01162 386886 **www.english-heritage.org.uk/visits**
**Owner:** English Heritage **Contact:** East of England Regional Office (01223 528700)
Picturesque, moated, brick built castle begun in 1480 by William Lord Hastings. Recently reopened after extensive conservation work.
**Location:** MAP 7:B6, OS140, SK524 046. 4m W of Leicester off B5380.
**Open:** 1 Jul–31 Aug: Sats & Suns, 10am–5pm.
**Admission:** Adult £2.90, Child £1.50, Conc. £2.20.
▣ **P**

### LYDDINGTON BEDE HOUSE ⌗

**Blue Coat Lane, Lyddington, Uppingham, Rutland LE15 9LZ**
**Tel:** 01572 822438 **www.english-heritage.org.uk/visits**
**Owner:** English Heritage **Contact:** Visitor Operations Team
Located in this picturesque 'Cotswold' village of honey coloured stone cottages and public houses lies the splendid former 'palace' of the powerful medieval Bishops of Lincoln. In the 1600s the building was converted into an almshouse.
**Location:** MAP 7:D6, OS141, SP875 970. In Lyddington, 6m N of Corby, 1m E of A6003.
**Open:** 1 Apr–31 Oct: Thur–Mon, 10am–5pm.
**Admission:** Adult £3.30, Child £1.70, Conc. £2.50, Family £8.30. 15% group discount (11+).
ℹ Picnickers welcome. ▣ ⬖ Ground floor only. **P** ▣

See all the properties that are **open all year** in the index on page 580

### OAKHAM CASTLE

**Castle Lane (off Market Place), Oakham, Rutland LE15 6DF**
**Tel:** 01572 758440 **www.rutnet.co.uk/rcccastle**
**Owner:** Rutland County Council **Contact:** Rutland County Museum
Exceptionally fine Norman Great Hall of a late 12th century fortified manor house, with contemporary musician sculptures. Bailey earthworks and remains of earlier motte. The hall contains over 200 unique horseshoes forfeited by royalty and peers of the realm to the Lord of the Manor from Edward IV onwards.
**Location:** MAP 7:D6, OS Ref. SK862 088. Near town centre, E of the church. Off Market Place, Oakham.
**Open:** All year: Mon–Sat, 10.30am–1pm & 1.30–5pm; Sun, 2–4pm. Closed Good Fri, Christmas and New Year.
**Admission:** Free.
▣ ⬖ Great Hall. **P** For disabled, on request. ▣ ⬛ ❊

### QUENBY HALL ⛫

*See page 314 for full page entry.*

### STANFORD HALL ⛫

*See page 315 for full page entry.*

### STAUNTON HAROLD CHURCH ⚜

**Staunton Harold Church, Ashby-de-la-Zouch, Leicestershire**
**Tel:** 01332 863822 **Fax:** 01332 865272
One of the very few churches to be built during the Commonwealth, erected by Sir Robert Shirley, an ardent Royalist. The interior retains its original 17th century cushions and hangings and includes fine panelling and painted ceilings.
**Location:** MAP 7:A5, OS Ref. SK379 208. 5m NE of Ashby-de-la-Zouch, W of B587.
**Open:** 6 Jun–31 Aug: Wed–Sun, 1–4.30pm. 31 Mar–28 Oct: Sat & Sun, 1–4.30pm.
**Admission:** £1 donation.
⬖ Partial. ▣ At hall.

### WARTNABY GARDENS

**Melton Mowbray, Leicestershire LE14 3HY**
**Tel:** 01664 822549 **Fax:** 01664 822231 **www.wartnabygardenlabels.co.uk**
**Owner:** Lady King
This garden has delightful little gardens within it, including a white garden and a sunken garden. There are good herbaceous borders, climbers and old fashioned roses, and a series of pools, woodland walks with primulas, ferns and several varieties of Salix. There is an arboretum with a good collection of trees and shrub roses, and alongside the drive is a beech hedge in a Grecian pattern. Greenhouses, a fruit and vegetable garden with rose arches and cordon fruit.
**Location:** MAP 7:C5, OS Ref. SK709 228. 4m NW of Melton Mowbray. From A606 turn W in Ab Kettleby for Wartnaby.
**Open:** 3 Apr–31 Jul: Tues, 9.30am–12.30pm. Also Plant Fair, Suns: 25 Feb, 29 Apr & 17 Jun, 11am–4pm (Feb 3pm).
**Admission:** Adult £3, Child Free, RHS Members Free on Tuesdays.
⬗ On Plant Fair days. ⬖ ▣ ⟳ By arrangement. **P** Limited for coaches. ▣ In grounds on leads. ❊ ⬛

Stanford Hall, Lutterworth

**visit hudsons guide online**

# BURGHLEY HOUSE 🏛

www.burghley.co.uk

Burghley House, home of the Cecil family for over 400 years, was built as a country seat during the latter part of the 16th century by Sir William Cecil, later Lord Burghley, principal adviser and Lord Treasurer to Queen Elizabeth.

The House was completed in 1587 and there have been few alterations to the architecture since that date thus making Burghley one of the finest examples of late Elizabethan design in England. The interior was remodelled in the late 17th century by John, 5th Earl of Exeter who was a collector of fine art on a huge scale, establishing the immense collection of art treasures at Burghley. Burghley is truly a 'Treasure House', containing one of the largest private collections of Italian art, unique examples of Chinese and Japanese porcelain and superb items of 18th century furniture. The remodelling work of the 17th century means that examples of the work of the principal artists and craftsmen of the period are to be found at Burghley: Antonio Verrio, Grinling Gibbons and Louis Laguerre all made major contributions to the beautiful interiors.

## Park and Gardens

The house is set in a 300-acre deer park landscaped by 'Capability' Brown. A lake was created by him and delightful avenues of mature trees feature largely in his design. The park is home to a large herd of Fallow deer, established in the 16th century. Opening in 2007, the Gardens of Surprise incorporate the existing Contemporary Sculpture Garden, containing many specimen trees and shrubs, and the new Elizabethan Garden, over an acre of yew mazes, revolving Caesars' heads and spurting fountains. The private gardens around the house are open in April for the display of spring bulbs.

ℹ Suitable for a variety of events, large park, golf course, helicopter landing area, cricket pitch. No photography in house.

🛍 

♿ Visitors may alight at entrance. WC. Chair lift to Orangery Restaurant, house tour has two staircases one with chairlift.

☕ 

🍴 Restaurant/tearoom. Groups can book in advance.

🚶 Available.

🅿 Ample. Free refreshments for coach drivers.

▦ Welcome. Guide provided.

🐕 No dogs in house. In park on leads.

▲ Civil Wedding Licence.

🎭 

### ■ Owner

Burghley House Preservation Trust Ltd

### ■ Contact

The House Manager
Burghley House
Stamford
Lincolnshire  PE9 3JY

**Tel:** 01780 752451
**Fax:** 01780 480125
**E-mail:** burghley@ burghley.co.uk

### ■ Location

**MAP 7:E7**
**OS Ref. TF048 062**

Burghley House is 1m SE of Stamford. From London, A1 2hrs.

Visitors entrance is on B1443.

**Rail:** London – Peterborough 1hr (GNER). Stamford Station 1½m, regular service to Peterborough.

**Taxi:** Direct Line: 01780 481481.

### ■ Opening Times
**Summer**
31 March–28 October (closed 1 September) Daily (except Fridays) 11am–5pm (last admission 4.30pm).

**Winter**
**Orangery Restaurant**
3 January–31 March Wed–Sun, 11am–4pm.

**Gift Shop**
7 February–31 March Wed–Sun, 11am–4pm.

**South Gardens**
April: Daily, 11am–4pm.

**Park**
All year. Admission is free except on event days.

### ■ Admission
**House & Gardens**
Adult            £10.40
Child (5–15yrs)    £5.00
Conc.             £9.00
Family           £25.00

Groups (20+)
Adult             £8.70
School (up to 14yrs) £5.00

**Gardens of Surprise only**
Adult             £6.00
Child (5–15yrs)    £3.00
Conc.             £5.00
Family           £15.00

We are a charitable trust, by paying an extra 10% we can claim back the tax paid on this and use it for the benefit of the house and collections.

### Conference/Function

| ROOM | SIZE | MAX CAPACITY |
|------|------|--------------|
| Great Hall | 70' x 30' | 150 |
| Orangery | 100' x 20' | 120 |

### ■ Owner

Grimsthorpe and Drummond Castle Trust Ltd. A Registered Charity.

### ■ Contact

Ray Biggs
Grimsthorpe Estate Office
Grimsthorpe
Bourne, Lincolnshire
PE10 0LY

**Tel:** 01778 591205
**Fax:** 01778 591259
**E-mail:** ray@grimsthorpe.co.uk

### ■ Location

**MAP 7:D5**
**OS Ref. TF040 230**

4m NW of Bourne on A151, 8m E of Colsterworth roundabout off A1.

### ■ Opening Times

**Castle**
April–September: Suns, Thurs & BH Mons.

August: Sun–Thur. 1–4.30pm.

**Park & Gardens**
April & May:
Suns, Thurs & BH Mons.
June–September:
Sun–Thur.
11am–6pm (Gardens open 12 noon).

Groups: Apr–Sept: by arrangement. Also evening candlelight supper tours.

### ■ Admission

**Castle, Park & Garden**
| | |
|---|---|
| Adult | £8.00 |
| Child | £3.50 |
| Conc. | £7.00 |
| Family (2+2) | £18.50 |

**Park & Gardens**
| | |
|---|---|
| Adult | £3.50 |
| Child | £2.00 |
| Conc. | £3.00 |
| Family (2+2) | £9.00 |

Special charges may be made for special events. Group rates on application.

# GRIMSTHORPE CASTLE,  PARK & GARDENS

www.grimsthorpe.co.uk

Home of the Willoughby de Eresby family since 1516. Examples of 13th century architecture and building styles from the Tudor period. The dramatic 18th century North Front is Sir John Vanbrugh's last major work. State Rooms and picture galleries with magnificent contents including tapestries, furniture and paintings. Unusual collection of thrones, fabrics and objects from the old House of Lords, associated with the family's hereditary Office of Lord Great Chamberlain.

## The Grounds and Gardens

3,000 acre landscaped park with lakes, ancient woods, woodland walk with all-weather footpath, adventure playground, red deer herd. Family cycle trail. Park tours in a vehicle with the Ranger.

Unusual ornamental vegetable garden and orchard, created in the 1960s by the Countess of Ancaster and John Fowler. Intricate parterres lined with box hedges. Herbaceous border with yew topiary framing views across to the lake. Woodland garden.

Groups can explore the park from the comfort of their coach by booking a one-hour, escorted park tour, with opportunities to discover more about the site of the Cistercian Abbey, the ancient deer parks and extensive series of early tree-lined avenues.

| | |
|---|---|
| ℹ | No photography in house. |
| | |
| ☕ | Conferences (up to 40), inc catering. |
| ♿ | Partial. WC. |
| | Licensed. |
| | Obligatory except Suns. |
| P | Ample. |
| | In grounds, on leads. |
| | |

## AUBOURN HALL
### LINCOLN LN5 9DZ

**Tel:** 01522 788224   **Fax:** 01522 788199   **E-mail:** cnevile@ukonline.co.uk
**Owner:** Mr & Mrs Christopher Nevile   **Contact:** Ginny Lovell or Simon Moore
Early 17th century house by John Smithson. Important staircase and panelled rooms.
10 acre garden.
**Location:** MAP 7:D3, OS Ref. SK928 628. 6m SW of Lincoln. 2m SE of A46.
**Open:** House not open on a regular basis. Garden: Open for groups and tours all year
with head gardener, Simon Moore. Open to public May–July, please contact property
for details.
**Admission:** £4.

## BURGHLEY HOUSE  🏛          *See page 317 for full page entry.*

Grimsthorpe Castle

## AYSCOUGHFEE HALL MUSEUM & GARDENS
### CHURCHGATE, SPALDING, LINCOLNSHIRE PE11 2RA
www.ayscoughfee.org

**Tel:** 01775 764555   **E-mail:** museum@sholland.gov.uk
**Owner:** South Holland District Council   **Contact:** Museum Manager
Ayscoughfee Hall, a magnificent Grade II* listed building, of great architectural
importance, was built in the 1450s. The Hall is set in extensive landscaped grounds,
which include, amongst other impressive features, a memorial designed by
Edwin Lutyens. The building and gardens, combined, reflect the slendour of the
Medieval, Georgian and Victorian ages.
Ayscoughfee Hall Museum has now fully re-opened to the public following an extensive
restoration project, which has uncovered some very important and rare features. The
Museum explains the history of the Hall, and features the lives of the people who lived
there and in the surrounding Fens.
**Location:** MAP 7:F5, OS Ref. TF249 223. E bank of the River Welland, 5 mins walk
from Spalding town centre.
**Open:** Summer: Mon*–Fri, 10.30am–5pm (7pm Thurs). Sats & Suns, 9.30am–4pm.
Winter: 12 noon–5pm. Sats & Suns, 9.30am–4pm. (*BHs only).
**Admission:** Free.
🔲 🔳 🔳 🔳 🔳 By arrangement. 🅿 Limited for cars. 🔳 🔳 🔳

# BELTON HOUSE ✤
## GRANTHAM, LINCOLNSHIRE NG32 2LS
www.nationaltrust.org.uk

**Tel:** 01476 566116   **Fax:** 01476 579071   **E-mail:** belton@nationaltrust.org.uk
**Owner:** The National Trust   **Contact:** The Property Manager

Belton, considered by many to be the perfect English Country House, with stunning interiors, fine silver and furniture collections and the remnants of a collection of Old Masters. There are also huge garden scenes by Melchior d'Hondecoeter acquired by the last Earl. The 17th century saloon in the centre of the house is panelled and decorated with intricate limewood carvings of the Grinling Gibbons school. The virtually unaltered north-facing chapel has a baroque plaster ceiling by Edward Gouge. Built in 1685–88, Belton offers you a great day out whether you are looking for peace and tranquillity or lots to do. With magnificent formal gardens, Orangery, landscaped park with lakeside walk, woodland adventure playground and Bellmount Tower. Fine church with family monuments. Winners of "Excellence in Tourism" and Sandford Heritage Education awards 2002.

**Location:** MAP 7:D4, OS Ref. SK929 395. 3m NE of Grantham on A607. Signed off the A1.

**Open:** House: 17 Mar–28 Oct: Wed–Sun (open BH Mons), 12.30–5pm. Garden & Park: 17 Mar–31 Jul & 1 Sept–28 Oct: Wed–Sun, 11am–5.30pm. Aug: daily, 10.30am–5.30pm. 2 Nov–16 Dec: Fri–Sun, 12 noon–4pm. Adventure Playground: 17 Mar–31 Jul: Wed–Sun 11am–5.30pm. Aug: daily, 10.30am–5.30pm. 1 Sept–28 Oct: Wed–Sun, 11am–5.30pm. Shop & Restaurant: 17 Mar–31 Jul & 1 Sept–28 Oct: Wed–Sun, 11am–5pm. Aug: daily, 11am–5pm. 3 Nov–17 Dec: Fri–Sun, 12 noon–4pm. Property closed 14 July.

**\*Admission:** Adult £9, Child £5.50, Family £24. Discount for groups. Garden, Park & Playground: Adult £7, Child £4.50, Family £18.50. \*includes a voluntary donation but visitors can choose to pay the standard prices displayed at the property and on the website.

⬜ ♿ Partial. Please telephone for arrangements. 🍴 Licensed. 🅿 ■ ▲

# DODDINGTON HALL & GARDENS 🏛
## LINCOLN LN6 4RU
www.doddingtonhall.com

**Tel:** 01522 694308   **Fax:** 01522 682584   **E-mail:** info@doddingtonhall.com
**Owner:** Mr & Mrs J J C Birch   **Contact:** The Estate Office

Romantic Smythson mansion which stands today as it was built in 1595 with its mellow walled gardens and gatehouse. Never sold since it was built, Doddington is still very much a family home and its contents reflect over 400 years of unbroken family occupation. There is an elegant Georgian interior with fine collections of porcelain, paintings and textiles. The five acres of beautiful gardens contain a superb layout of box-edged parterres filled with bearded Iris in midsummer, sumptuous borders that provide colour in all seasons, and a wild garden with a marvellous succession of spring bulbs and flowering shrubs set amongst mature trees. Exclusive private group visits with guided tours a speciality. Please call the Estate Office to discuss your requirements. Award winning facilities for disabled visitors, include sensory tours of house and gardens for the Visually Impaired; free use of electric buggy and panaoramic tour of upper floors – please call for details. Free audioguides and children's activity trail.

Civil weddings and receptions at Doddington Hall and in The Littlehouse next door.
Newly resurrected working walled Kitchen Garden open for first time summer 2007.

Farm shop with kitchen garden and local produce plus café serving delicious, seasonal and freshly cooked teas and lunches. Open Tues-Sun from summer 2007.

**Location:** MAP 7:D2, OS Ref. SK900 710. 5m W of Lincoln on the B1190, signposted off the A46.

**Open:** Gardens only: 18 Feb–end April: Suns & Easter Mon, 1–5pm. House & Gardens: May–Sept inclusive: Weds, Suns & BH Mons, 1–5pm (gardens open 12 noon).

**Admission:** House & Gardens: Adult £5.60, Child £2.80, Family £15.90. Gardens only: Adult £3.90, Child £1.95. Family £10.50. 2 for 1 admission for disabled person and companion. Groups (20+): exclusive house-opening and private guided tour £7.10. Discount for pre-booked groups (20+) (self guided) on regular open days. Season tickets for gardens. RHS members Free.

ℹ No photography in Hall. No stilettos. ⬜ 🅃 ♿ Gardens & ground floor. WC. 🖢
🍴 Simple refreshments available until summer 2007 (but groups can pre-book meals), then full seasonal menu in new farm shop & café. 🅵 By arrangement.
🅰 Free. 🅿 ■ 🔲 Guide dogs only. ▲ 🔽

## EASTON WALLED GARDENS
### THE GARDEN OFFICE, EASTON, GRANTHAM, LINCOLNSHIRE NG33 5AP
www.eastonwalledgardens.co.uk

**Tel:** 01476 530063  **Fax:** 01476 530063  **E-mail:** info@eastonwalledgardens.co.uk
**Owner:** Sir Fred & Lady Cholmeley  **Contact:** Maggie Dickinson
President Franklin Roosevelt described these gardens as a *'Dream of Nirvana … almost too good to be true'*. 50 years later, the house was pulled down and the gardens abandoned. 100 years later see the ongoing revival of these magnificent gardens. Funded privately and with the support of visitors, this garden experience is like no other. Alongside the recovery of these 400 year old gardens are: fantastic snowdrops, David Austin Roses, Daffodil and Iris Collections, a cut flower garden, cottage garden and 80m of poppies. Teas and light lunches are served overlooking the garden. Groups can book out of hours if wished.
**Location:** MAP 7:D5, OS Ref. SK938 274. 1m from A1 (between Stamford and Grantham) N of the Colsterworth roundabout. Right onto B6403 and follow signs.
**Open:** 10–23 Feb for snowdrops: daily 11am–4pm; 1 April–28 Sept: BH Mons, Weds, Fris & Suns 11am–4pm. Sweet Pea Week 24–29 June: daily 11am–4pm.
**Admission:** Snowdrops Adult £4; Child Free. Apr–Sept Adult £4.50; Child 50p.
⊡ ⊞ ⊡ ⊡ Partial. WCs. ⊡ ⊡ By arrangement. P ⊡ ⊡ Guide dogs only. ⊡

## FULBECK MANOR
### Fulbeck, Grantham, Lincolnshire NG32 3JN
**Tel:** 01400 272231  **Fax:** 01400 273545  **E-mail:** fane@fulbeck.co.uk
**Owner/Contact:** Mr Julian Francis Fane
Built c1580. 400 years of Fane family portraits. Open by written appointment. Guided tours by owner approximately 1¼ hours. Tearooms at Craft Centre, 100 yards, for light lunches and teas.
**Location:** MAP 7:D3, OS Ref. SK947 505. 11m N of Grantham. 15m S of Lincoln on A607. Brown signs to Craft Centre & Tearooms and Stables.
**Open:** By written appointment.
**Admission:** Adult £6. Groups (10+) £5.
⊡ No photography. ⊡ Partial. WCs. ⊡ ⊡ ⊡ Obligatory. P Ample for cars. Limited for coaches. ⊡ Guide dogs only. ⊡

## GAINSBOROUGH OLD HALL ⊞
### Parnell Street, Gainsborough, Lincolnshire DN21 2NB
**Tel:** 01427 612669  www.english-heritage.org.uk/visits
**Owner:** English Heritage  **Contact:** Visitor Operations Team
A large medieval manor house with a magnificent Great Hall and suites of rooms. A collection of historic furniture and a re-created medieval kitchen are on display.
**Location:** MAP 7:C1, OS121, SK815 895. In centre of Gainsborough, opposite library.
**Open:** 1 Apr–31 Oct: Sun 1–4.30pm, Mon–Sat, 10am–5pm. 1 Nov–20 Mar: Mon–Sat 10am–5pm. Closed 24–26 & 31 Dec/1 Jan.
**Admission:** Adult £3.80, Child 5-15yrs £2.50, Child under 5yrs Free, Conc. £2.60, Family (2+3) £10.
⊡ WC. ⊡ ⊡ ⊡ ⊡

## GRIMSTHORPE CASTLE, ⊡
## PARK & GARDENS

*See page 318 for full page entry.*

## GUNBY HALL ⊗
### Gunby, Spilsby, Lincolnshire PE23 5SS
**Tel:** 01909 486411  **Fax:** 01909 486377  www.nationaltrust.org.uk
**Owner:** The National Trust  **Contact:** Regional Office
A red brick house with stone dressings, built in 1700 and extended in 1870s. Within the house, there is good early 18th century wainscoting and a fine oak staircase, also English furniture and portraits by Reynolds. Also of interest is the contemporary stable block, a walled kitchen and flower garden, sweeping lawns and borders and an exhibition of Field Marshal Sir Archibald Montgomery-Massingberd's memorabilia. Gunby was reputedly Tennyson's 'haunt of ancient peace'.
**Location:** MAP 7:G2, OS122, TF466 672. 2½ m NW of Burgh Le Marsh, 7m W of Skegness. On S side of A158 (access off roundabout).
**Open:** Open: House and Garden: Jun–Aug, Wed, 2–5pm. Garden only: May, Wed, 2–5pm; Jun–Aug, Tues & Thurs, 2–5pm. The garden is also open on Tues, Wed & Thurs in Apr and Sept and on Tues & Thurs in May, by written appointment only to Customer Services Department, East Midlands Regional Office, Clumber Park Stableyard, Worksop, Nottinghamshire. S80 3BE.
**Admission:** Adult £5, Child £2.50, Family £12.50. Garden only: £3.50, Child £2, Family £9.
⊡ Grounds. ⊡ In grounds, on leads.

## HECKINGTON WINDMILL
### Hale Road, Heckington, Sleaford, Lincolnshire NG34 9JW
**Tel:** 01529 461919  **Contact:** Derek James
Britain's last surviving eight sail windmill. Now in full working order.
**Location:** MAP 7:E4, OS Ref. TF145 437. W side of B1394, S side of Heckington village.
**Open:** Contact property for details.
**Admission:** Ground floor & Shop: Free. Mill: Adult £1.50, Child 75p.

## LEADENHAM HOUSE
### Leadenham House, Lincolnshire LN5 0PU
**Tel:** 01400 273256  **Fax:** 01400 272237
**Owner:** Mr P Reeve  **Contact:** Mr and Mrs P Reeve
Late eighteenth century house in park setting.
**Location:** MAP 7:D3, OS Ref. SK949 518. Entrance on A17 Leadenham bypass (between Newark and Sleaford).
**Open:** 1–4, 7–11, 14–18, 21–25, 27–31 May, 24–27 Sept & Spring & Aug BHs: all 2–5pm.
**Admission:** £3.50. Groups by prior arrangement only.
⊡ No photography. ⊡ ⊡

## LINCOLN CASTLE
### Castle Hill, Lincoln LN1 3AA
**Tel:** 01522 511068  **E-mail:** lincoln_castle@lincolnshire.gov.uk
**Contact:** The Manager
Built by William the Conqueror in 1068. Informative exhibition of the 1215 Magna Carta.
**Location:** MAP 7:D2, OS Ref. SK975 718. Opposite west front of Lincoln Cathedral.
**Open:** BST: Sats, 9.30am–5.30pm, Suns, 11am–5.30pm. GMT: Mon–Sat: 9.30am–4pm, Suns, 11am–4pm. Closed Christmas Day, Boxing Day & New Year's Day. Opening times are subject to change.
**Admission:** Adult £3.90, Child £2.25, Family (2+3) £11.20. Prices are subject to change.

## LINCOLN CATHEDRAL
### Lincoln LN2 1PZ
**Tel:** 01522 561600  **Fax:** 01522 511794  **Contact:** Communications Office
One of the finest medieval buildings in Europe.
**Location:** MAP 7:D2, OS Ref. SK978 718. At the centre of Uphill, Lincoln.
**Open:** All year: Summer, 7.15am–8pm. Winter, 7.15am–6pm. Sun closing 6pm in Summer & 5pm in Winter. Tours of the floor, roof & tower available. Pre-booked groups welcome.
**Admission:** £4, Child (5–16yrs) £1, Child (under 5s) Free, Conc. £3, Family £10. Optional guided tours & photography Free. No charge on Sun or for services.

For **corporate hospitality** at unique venues see the index on page 567

## LINCOLN MEDIEVAL BISHOPS' PALACE ⌗

**Minster Yard, Lincoln LN2 1PU**
**Tel:** 01522 527468   www.english-heritage.org.uk/visits
**Owner:** English Heritage   **Contact:** Visitor Operations Team

Constructed in the late 12th century, the medieval bishops' palace was once one of the most important buildings in England. Built on hillside terraces, it has views of the cathedral and the Roman, medieval and modern city. See a virtual tour of the Palace, explore the grounds and see the award winning Contemporary Heritage Garden and Vineyard (most northerly exposed vineyard in Europe).

**Location:** MAP 7:D2, OS121 Ref. SK981 717. S side of Lincoln Cathedral, in Lincoln.
**Open:** 1 Apr–31 Oct: daily, 10am–5pm (6pm Jul–Aug). 1 Nov–20 Mar: Thur–Mon, 10am–4pm. Closed 24–26 Dec & 1 Jan. Open daily for Lincoln Christmas Market.
**Admission:** Adult £3.90, Child £2, Conc. £2.90, Family £9.80. 15% discount for groups (11+).

🖼 🅿 Limited disability parking only. ▣ ▣ ▣

Patrick Lane

Gunby Hall, Spilsby

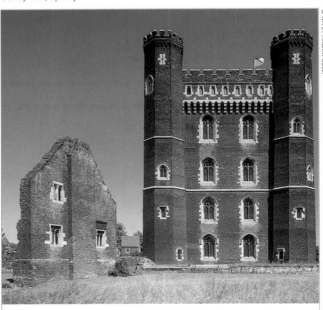

© NTPL / Andrew Butler

## TATTERSHALL CASTLE ⁕

**TATTERSHALL, LINCOLN LN4 4LR**

www.nationaltrust.org.uk

**Tel:** 01526 342543   **E-mail:** tattershallcastle@nationaltrust.org.uk
**Owner:** The National Trust   **Contact:** The Property Manager

A vast fortified tower built c1440 for Ralph Cromwell, Lord Treasurer of England. The Castle is an important example of an early brick building, with a tower containing state apartments, rescued from dereliction and restored by Lord Curzon 1911–14. Four great chambers, with ancillary rooms, contain late gothic fireplaces and brick vaulting. There are tapestries and information displays in turret rooms.

**Location:** MAP 7:E3, OS122 Ref. TF209 575. On S side of A153, 15m NE of Sleaford, 10m SW of Horncastle.
**Open:** 3–18 Mar & 3 Nov–9 Dec: Sat & Sun, 12 noon–4pm. 24 Mar–26 Sept: Sat–Wed, 11am–5.30pm. 29 Sept–31 Oct: Sat–Wed, 11am–4pm.
***Admission:** Adult £4.50, Child £2.30, Family £11.30. Group discounts. *includes a voluntary donation but visitors can choose to pay the standard prices displayed at the property and on the website.

♿ Ground floor. WC. 🅿 Free. 🚗 Car park only. 🛈

## MARSTON HALL

**Marston, Grantham NG32 2HQ**
**Tel/Fax:** 07812 356237   **E-mail:** johnthorold@aol.com
**Owner/Contact:** J R Thorold

The ancient home of the Thorold family. The building contains Norman, Plantaganet, Tudor and Georgian elements through to the modern day. Marston Hall is undergoing continuous restoration some of it which may be disruptive. Please telephone in advance of intended visits.

**Location:** MAP 7:D4, OS Ref. SK893 437. 5m N of Grantham and about 1m E of A1.
**Open:** 24–27 Feb, 24–27 Mar, 5–7 & 28 May, 7–15 Jul, 27 Aug & 15–18 Sept, 6–9 Oct, 1–6pm.
**Admission:** Adult £3.50, Child £1.50. Groups must book.

🛈 No photography.

## SIBSEY TRADER WINDMILL ⌗

**Sibsey, Boston, Lincolnshire PE22 0SY**
**Tel:** 01205 750036   www.english-heritage.org.uk/visits
**Owner:** English Heritage   **Contact:** The East Midlands Regional Office

An impressive old mill built in 1877, with its machinery and six sails still intact. Flour milled on the spot can be bought here. The award-winning tearoom sells produce made from the Mill's organic stoneground flour.

**Location:** MAP 7:F3, OS Ref. TF345 511. ½m W of village of Sibsey, off A16, 5m N of Boston.
**Open:** 1 Mar–31 Oct: Suns 11am–6pm. Sat, BHs, & Tues 1 May–30 Sept, 10am–6pm. 1 Nov–28 Mar: Sats only, 11am–5pm, Mill only. Closed 24–26 Dec & 1 Jan.
**Admission:** Adult £2, Child £1 (under 5yrs Free), Conc. £1.50. Members OUP Free.

🛈 WC. ♿ Exterior only. ▣ 🅿 ▣

© NTPL / Nick Meers

## WOOLSTHORPE MANOR ⁕

**23 NEWTON WAY, WOOLSTHORPE-BY-COLSTERWORTH, GRANTHAM NG33 5NR**

www.nationaltrust.org.uk

**Tel:** 01476 860338   **Fax:** 01476 862826
**E-mail:** woolsthorpemanor@nationaltrust.org.uk
**Owner:** The National Trust   **Contact:** The Property Manager

This small 17th century farmhouse was the birthplace and family home of Sir Isaac Newton. Some of his major work was formulated here, during the Plague years (1665–67); an early edition of the Principia is on display. The orchard has a descendant of the famous apple tree. Science Discovery Centre and exhibition of Sir Isaac Newton's work.

**Location:** MAP 7:D5, OS130 Ref. SK924 244. 7m S of Grantham, ½ m NW of Colsterworth, 1m W of A1.
**Open:** House & Science Discovery Centre: 3–25 Mar: Sat & Sun, 1–5pm; 28 Mar–30 Sept: Wed–Sun (open BH Mons & Good Fri), 1–5pm. 6–28 Oct: Sat & Sun, 1–5pm.
***Admission:** Adult £5, Child £2.50, Family £12.50, 1-Adult Family £7.50, no reduction for groups which must book in advance. Admission price includes voluntary Gift Aid donation.*includes a voluntary donation but visitors can choose to pay the standard prices displayed at the property and on the website.

♿ Ground floor. 🅿 Limited. 🚗 Car park only.

The Stable Block

# ALTHORP
www.althorp.com

The history of Althorp is the history of a family. The Spencers have lived and died here for nearly five centuries and twenty generations.

Since the death of Diana, Princess of Wales, Althorp has become known across the world, but before that tragic event, connoisseurs had heard of this most classic of English stately homes on account of the magnificence of its contents and the beauty of its setting.

Next to the mansion at Althorp lies the honey-coloured stable block, a truly breathtaking building which at one time accommodated up to 100 horses and 40 grooms. The stables are now the setting for the Exhibition celebrating the life of Diana, Princess of Wales and honouring her memory after her death. The freshness and modernity of the facilities are a unique tribute to a woman who captivated the world in her all-too-brief existence.

All visitors are invited to view the House, Exhibition and Grounds as well as the Island in the Round Oval where Diana, Princess of Wales is laid to rest.

■ **Owner**
The Earl Spencer

■ **Contact**
Althorp
Northampton  NN7 4HQ
**Tel:** 01604 770107
**Fax:** 01604 770042

Book online
www.althorp.com

**E-mail:** mail@althorp.com

■ **Location**
**MAP 7:C9**
**OS Ref. SP682 652**

From the M1/J16, 7m J18, 10m. Situated on A428 Northampton – Rugby. London on average 85 mins away.

**Rail:** 5m from Northampton station. 14m from Rugby station.

■ **Opening Times**
**Summer**
30 June–2 September, daily, 11am–5pm. (excluding 31 August.)

Last admission 4pm.

**Winter** Closed.

■ **Admission**
**House & Garden**
Contact for admission prices.

Groups
(by arrangement only)
tel 01604 772110
Adult                £10.50
Child* (5–17yrs)   £5.50
OAP                  £10.50
*under 5yrs Free.

Carers accompanying visitors with disabilities are admitted free.

Please check website for up to date information.

 Information leaflet issued to all ticket holders who book in advance. No indoor photography with still or video cameras.

Visitor Centre & ground floor of house accessible. WCs.

Café.

**P** Limited for coaches.

Guide dogs only.

The Picture Gallery

## ■ Owner

His Grace The Duke of Buccleuch & Queensberry KT

## ■ Contact

Charles Lister
The Living
Landscape Trust
Boughton House
Kettering
Northamptonshire
NN14 1BJ

**Tel:** 01536 515731
**Fax:** 01536 417255
**E-mail:**
llt@boughtonhouse.org.uk

## ■ Location

**MAP 7:D7**
**OS Ref. SP900 815**

3m N of Kettering on A43/J7 from A14. Signposted through Geddington.

## ■ Opening Times

**Summer**
**House**
1 August–1 September
Daily, 2–5pm.
Last entry 4pm.
Self guided tour normally in operation, entry by guided tour only on selected days – please contact for details.

**Grounds**
1 May–31 July,
daily, 12noon–5pm.
Closed Saturdays.

1 August–1 September,
daily, 12noon–5pm.

Opening of Adventure Play Area is subject to weather conditions for reasons of health and safety.

**Winter**
Daily by appointment throughout the year for educational groups – contact for details.

## ■ Admission

**Summer**
**House & Grounds**
Adult          £7.00
Child/Conc.    £6.00

**Grounds**
Adult          £1.50
Child/Conc.    £1.00

Wheelchair visitors Free. HHA Friends are admitted Free in August.

**Winter**
Group rates available – contact for further details.

## Conference/Function

| ROOM | MAX CAPACITY |
|---|---|
| Lecture | 100 |
| Seminar Rm | 25 |
| Conference facilities available in stable block adjacent to House | |

# BOUGHTON HOUSE 🏛

www.boughtonhouse.org.uk

Boughton House is the Northamptonshire home of the Dukes of Buccleuch and Queensberry and their Montagu ancestors since 1528. It is looked after by an educational charity, the Living Landscape Trust, established by the Duke in 1986. The Trust's purpose is to foster understanding of the House and its heritage and the surrounding Boughton Estate, with which it has always been intimately linked. Amongst its priorities are conservation of the extremely fragile structure and contents, and gradual restoration of the outstanding designed landscape.

Boughton has been described as 'at once palace, manor house, and village' – its transformation at the end of the 17th century earned it the title of "The English Versailles." The House contains an exceptionally rich art and furniture collection, as well as an early 18th century Designed Landscape which is currently under restoration.

For information on the group visits programme or education services, please contact The Living Landscape Trust.

Our website gives considerable information on Boughton House and the Living Landscape Trust, together with full details of our schools' educational facilities (Sandford Award winner 1988, 1993, 1998 and 2003).

*"I never desired anything so earnestly as to go to Boughton to see my Lord, the Good Company and learning in its full lustre."* Charles de Saint Evremond, the French soldier, poet and essayist writing in 1700 about the home of his good friend, Ralph Montagu.

ℹ Parkland available for film location and other events. Stableblock room contains 100 seats. No inside photography. No unaccompanied children. Browse our website for a 'virtual' tour of the house.

♿ Access to ground floor and all facilities. Virtual tour of first floor.

☕ Tearoom seats 80, groups must book. Licensed.

🚶 By arrangement.

Ⓟ

🏅 Heritage Education Trust Sandford Award winner 1988, 1993, 1998 & 2003. School groups Free.

🐕 No dogs in house and garden, welcome in Park on leads.

❋ By arrangement.

# DEENE PARK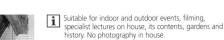

www.deenepark.com

A most interesting house, occupied and developed by the Brudenell family since 1514, from a mediaeval manor around a courtyard into a Tudor and Georgian mansion. Visitors see many rooms of different periods, providing an impressive yet intimate ambience of the family home of many generations. The most flamboyant member of the family to date was the 7th Earl of Cardigan, who led the charge of the Light Brigade at Balaklava and of whom there are many historic relics and pictures on view.

Mr Edmund Brudenell, the current owner, has taken considerable care in restoring the house after the Second World War. The gardens have also been improved during the last thirty years or so, with long, mixed borders of shrubs, old-fashioned roses and flowers, together with a parterre designed by David Hicks and long walks under fine old trees by the water. The car park beside the main lake is a good place for visitors to picnic.

**i** Suitable for indoor and outdoor events, filming, specialist lectures on house, its contents, gardens and history. No photography in house.

Including buffets, lunches and dinners.

Partial. Visitors may alight at the entrance, access to ground floor and garden. WC.

Special rates for groups, bookings can be made in advance, menus on request.

**¶** By arrangement.

Tours inclusive of admittance, tour time 90 mins. Owner will meet groups if requested.

**P** Unlimited for cars, space for 3 coaches 10 yds from house.

In car park only.

Residential conference facilities by arrangement.

## Owner
E Brudenell Esq

## Contact
The House Keeper
Deene Park
Corby
Northamptonshire
NN17 3EW

**Tel:** 01780 450278
or 01780 450223
**Fax:** 01780 450282
**E-mail:** admin@
deenepark.com

## Location
**MAP 7:D7**
**OS Ref. SP950 929**

6m NE of Corby off A43.
From London via M1/J15
then A43, or via A1, A14,
A43 – 2 hrs.

From Birmingham via M6,
A14, A43, 90 mins.

**Rail:** Kettering Station
20 mins.

## Opening Times
**Summer**
Open Suns & Mons of
Easter–August BH
weekends.
Also, June–August
Suns, 2–5pm

Open at all other times
by arrangement, including
pre-booked groups.

**Winter**
Gardens only
Suns 18 & 25 Feb:
11am–4pm for
snowdrops.
Refreshments available in
the Old Kitchen.

Otherwise House and
Gardens closed to casual
visitors. Open at all other
times by arrangement for
groups.

## Admission
**Public Open Days**
House & Gardens
Adult              £6.50
Child (10–14yrs)   £2.50
Conc.              £5.50

**Gardens only**
Adult              £4.00
Child (10–14yrs)   £1.50

Groups (20+)
by arrangement:
Weekdays           £5.50
            (Min £110)
Weekends & BHs     £6.00
            (Min £120)

*Child up to 10yrs free
with an accompanying
adult.

**Winter**
Groups visits only by prior
arrangement.

## Conference/Function

| ROOM | MAX CAPACITY |
|------|--------------|
| Great Hall | 150 |
| Tapestry Rm | 75 |
| East Room | 18 |

■ **Owner**
The Kelmarsh Trust

■ **Contact**
Administrator
Kelmarsh Hall
Kelmarsh
Northamptonshire
NN6 9LT

**Tel:** 01604 686543
**Fax:** 01604 686437
**E-mail:** enquiries@
kelmarsh.com

■ **Location**
**MAP 7:C7**
**OS Ref. SP736 795**

⅓ m N of A14-A508 jct.

**Rail & Bus:**
Mkt Harborough

■ **Opening Times**
**House and Garden**
Easter–end September.
BH Suns and Mons also
Thursdays: 3 May–27
September. 2–5pm.
Check our website for
additional events.

**Gardens**
Easter–end September.
BH Suns and Mons.
Tue–Thu & Sun. Check our
website to ensure the
gardens are not closed for
special events.

■ **Admission**
**House and Garden**
| | |
|---|---|
| Adult | £5.00 |
| Conc. | £4.50 |
| Child (5–12yrs) | £3.00 |

**Gardens**
| | |
|---|---|
| Adult | £4.00 |
| Conc. | £3.50 |
| Child (5–12yrs) | £2.50 |

■ **Special Events**
**February 11**
Snowdrop Sunday

**April 8/9**
Country Fair

**May 6/7**
Hardy Plant Fair

**June 8**
Elgar Concert

**June 15**
Hot Air Balloons & Jazz

**June 16/17**
Rolls Royce Enthusiasts
Annual Concours

**June 28**
RHS Garden Tour

**July 19–21**
Land Rover Enthusiasts
Annual Show

**August 11/12**
English Heritage "Festival
of History"

**August 19**
Cut Flower Day

# KELMARSH HALL
www.kelmarsh.com

Built in 1732 to a James Gibbs design, Kelmarsh Hall is surrounded by its working estate, grazed parkland and beautiful gardens. In 1928 Ronald and Nancy Tree rented the Palladian house from the Lancaster family and decorated the rooms in the manner that has become known as the English country house look. In the 1950s she returned to Kelmarsh as Nancy Lancaster and continued to develop her style both in the house and in the gardens. Additional schemes and designs by Geoffrey Jellicoe and Norah Lindsay have created a remarkable garden including a stunning triangular walled garden. The cutting garden in the walled garden is particularly beautiful from August onwards. Gifted to the Kelmarsh Trust by the Lancaster family the house, gardens and estate are now available for study, group and general visits.

Croome Court in Worcestershire was home to the Earls of Coventry until 1948. Due to the foresight of the family much of the furniture and chattels, together with their original bills of sale, were retained. From Easter 2007, thanks to the Croome Trustees, this fine collection of furniture, paintings and porcelain will be available for group visits. The cost of a guided tour of the Croome Collection is £7.50, by appointment only.

[i] No photography in house.

[*]

[Y] Conferences & functions

[&] Partial. WC.

Licensed.

[K] Obligatory.

[P]

In grounds, on leads.

[bell]

[*] For group visits.

# ROCKINGHAM CASTLE

www.rockinghamcastle.com

Rockingham Castle stands on the edge of an escarpment giving dramatic views over five counties and the Welland Valley below. Built by William the Conqueror, the Castle was a royal residence for 450 years. In the 16th century Henry VIII granted it to Edward Watson and for 450 years it has remained a family home. The predominantly Tudor building, within Norman walls, has architecture, furniture and works of art from practically every century including, unusually, a remarkable collection of 20th century pictures. Charles Dickens was a regular visitor to the Castle and based *Chesney Wolds* in *Bleak House* on Rockingham.

Surrounding the Castle are some 18 acres of gardens largely following the foot print of the medieval castle. The vast 400 year old "Elephant Hedge" dissects the formal 17th century terraced gardens. A circular yew hedge stands on the site of the mot and bailey and provides shelter for the Rose Garden. Surrounding the Rose Garden a three year project is underway to create a new garden with a series of new radial yew hedges and yew pillars providing vistas, walkways and seating within a series of garden 'rooms' that will contain deep borders of stunning herbaceous and shrub planting, each room being given a different character. Below the Castle is the beautiful 19th century Wild Garden replanted with advice from Kew Gardens during the early 1960s. Included in the gardens are many specimen trees and shrubs including the remarkable Handkerchief Tree.

## ■ Owner
James Saunders Watson

## ■ Contact
Andrew Norman
Operations Manager
Rockingham Castle
Market Harborough
Leicestershire
LE16 8TH
**Tel:** 01536 770240
**E-mail:** estateoffice@
rockinghamcastle.com

## ■ Location
**MAP 7:D7**
**OS Ref. SP867 913.**

1m N of Corby on A6003.
9m E of Market
Harborough. 14m SW of
Stamford on A427.

## ■ Opening Times
Easter (8 April)–end May:
Suns & BH Mons.

June–September:
Tues, Suns & BH Mon.

Grounds: 12 noon–5pm.

Castle opens at 1pm, last
entrance: 4.30pm.

## ■ Admission
**House & Grounds**
| | |
|---|---|
| Adult | £7.50 |
| Child (5–16yrs) | £4.50 |
| OAP | £6.50 |
| Family (2+2) | £19.50 |

Groups (20+) and school
parties can be
accommodated on most
days by arrangement.
| | |
|---|---|
| Adult (on open days) | £6.50 |
| Adult (private tour) | £8.50 |
| Child (5–16yrs) | £3.75 |
| Schoolchild* | £3.75 |

*1 Adult Free with every
15 children.

**Grounds only**
Including Gardens,
Salvin's Tower, Gift Shop
and Licensed Tea Room.

Adult or Child     £4.50
(Not available when
special events are held in
grounds.)

## ■ Special Events
**April 8/9**
Children's Easter Egg
Hunt & family fun quiz.

**June 10**
Medieval Jousting.

**August 26/27**
Vikings! Of Middle
England.

**November 19–23**
Victorian Christmas

| | |
|---|---|
| 🛈 | No photography in Castle. |
| 🛍 | |
| ⛾ | |
| ☕ | Licensed. |
| ♿ | Partial. WC. |
| 🚶 | By arrangement. |
| 🎧 | |
| 🅿 | |
| 🛏 | In grounds, on leads. |
| 🔔 | |

## ■ Owner

The Sulgrave Manor
Board

## ■ Contact

Sulgrave Manor
Manor Road
Sulgrave
Nr Banbury
Oxfordshire
OX17 2SD

**Tel:** 01295 760205
**Fax:** 01295 768056
**E-mail:**
enquiries@sulgravemanor
.org.uk

## ■ Location

**MAP 7:B9**
**OS152, SP561 457**

Off Banbury –
Northampton road 5m
from M40/J11. 15m from
M1/J15A.

## ■ Opening Times

1 April–28 October:
Sats & Suns, 12noon
–4pm (last entry).

1 May–31 October:
Tuesday–Thursday,
2–4pm (last entry).

Open for booked groups
on any day or evening
throughout the year
(except Jan).

Access to house may be
restricted during private
wedding ceremonies.

## ■ Admission

All visitors on non-event
days are taken round the
Manor House on regularly
organised guided tours.

# SULGRAVE MANOR

www.sulgravemanor.org.uk

A delightful 16th century Manor House that was the home of George Washington's ancestors. Today it presents a typical wealthy man's home and gardens of Elizabethan times. Restored with scholarly care and attention to detail that makes a visit both a pleasure and an education. The Manor contains wonderful Tudor to Georgian furniture and artefacts, displayed in their natural settings, and the largest UK collection of George Washington memorabilia demonstrating the British contribution to the origins of the USA. The gardens were designed in the formal style by Sir Reginald Blomfield. To the east is the knot-garden, in the centre of which has been placed a sundial dating from 1579. There are herbaceous borders, fine topiary work and an orchard underplanted with thousands of daffodils.

Sulgrave Manor is also home to The Herb Society who maintain the National Herb Garden and their Chelsea prize winning exhibit within the grounds. The Courtyard buildings house fine visitor/education/wedding and function facilities.

ℹ No photography in house.

♿ Partial.

Obligatory.

🅿

In grounds, on leads.

## Conference/Function

| ROOM | MAX CAPACITY |
|---|---|
| Courtyard Hall (seated) | 80 |
| Courtyard Hall (standing) | 110 |

## 78 DERNGATE
### 82 DERNGATE, NORTHAMPTON NN1 1UH

www.78derngate.org.uk

**Tel:** 01604 603407 **Fax:** 01604 603408 **E-mail:** info@78derngate.org.uk
**Owner:** 78 Derngate Northampton Trust **Contact:** House Manager
Charles Rennie Mackintosh, the renowned Scottish architect, artist and designer, transformed a typical terraced house into a startlingly modern home. It was his last major commission and his only work in England. Mackintosh's striking interiors have been painstakingly restored to their 1917 appearance.
**Location:** MAP 7:C9, OS Ref. SP759 603. In the heart of Northampton close to the rear of the Royal & Derngate Theatres. Follow Derngate out of the centre of town.
**Open:** 28 Mar–end Nov: Wed–Sun & BH Mons: 10.30am–3.30pm. Strictly pre-booked tours only. Group and school bookings are also available Tuesday afternoons and weekday evenings, as well as during normal opening hours.
**Admission:** Adult £5.50, Conc. £4.50. Family (2+2): £14. Groups (15+) £4pp.
ℹ No indoor photography. ⬚ ⬚ ⬚ Partial. ⬚ ⬚ Obligatory. ⬚ None. ⬚ ⬚ ⬚

---

**ALTHORP** *See page 323 for full page entry.*

**BOUGHTON HOUSE** 🏠 *See page 324 for full page entry.*

Deene Park, Corby

## CANONS ASHBY 🌿
### CANONS ASHBY, DAVENTRY, NORTHAMPTONSHIRE NN11 3SD

www.nationaltrust.org.uk

**Tel:** 01327 861900 **Fax:** 01327 861909 **E-mail:** canonsashby@nationaltrust.org.uk
**Owner:** The National Trust **Contact:** The Property Manager
Home of the Dryden family since the 16th century, this Elizabethan manor house was built c1550, added to in the 1590s, and altered in the 1630s and c1710; largely unaltered since. Within the house, Elizabethan wall paintings and outstanding Jacobean plasterwork are of particular interest. A formal garden includes terraces, walls and gate piers of 1710. There is also a medieval priory church and a 70 acre park.
**Location:** Map 7:B9, OS Ref. SP577 506. Access from M40/J11, or M1/J16. Signposted from A5 2m S of Weedon crossroads. Then 7m to SW.
**Open:** House: 17 Mar–30 Sept: Sat–Wed, 1–5.30pm, 1–9 Dec: Sats & Suns, 12 noon–4pm. Park & Church (as House): 11am–5.30pm (Oct–4 Nov, 11am–4.30pm). Gardens: 11am–5.30pm (1 Oct: 11am–4.30pm). Shop & Tearoom: 12 noon–5pm . (1 Oct–4 Nov, 12noon–4.30pm). Gardens, Shop, Tearoom, Park & Church: 10 Nov–16 Dec: Sats & Suns, 12 noon–4pm.
**Admission:** Adult £7, Child £3.50, Family £17.50. Garden only: £2.50. Discount for booked groups, contact Property Manager. *includes a voluntary donation but visitors can choose to pay the standard prices displayed at the property and on the website.
⬚ ⬚ Some steps. WC. ⬚ ⬚ In Home Paddock, on leads.

## COTON MANOR GARDEN
### GUILSBOROUGH, NORTHAMPTONSHIRE NN6 8RQ

www.cotonmanor.co.uk

**Tel:** 01604 740219 **Fax:** 01604 740838
**E-mail:** pasleytyler@cotonmanor.fsnet.co.uk
**Owner:** Ian & Susie Pasley-Tyler **Contact:** Sarah Ball
Traditional English garden laid out on different levels surrounding a 17th century stone manor house. Many herbaceous borders, with extensive range of plants, old yew and holly hedges, rose garden, water garden and fine lawns set in 10 acres. Also wild flower meadow and bluebell wood.
**Location:** Map 7:B8, OS Ref. SP675 716. 9m NW of Northampton, between A5199 (formerly A50) and A428.
**Open:** 1 Apr–29 Sept: Tue–Sat & BH weekends; also Suns Apr–May: 12 noon–5.30pm.
**Admission:** Adult £5, Child £2, Conc. £4.50. Groups: £4.50.
⬚ ⬚ ⬚ Grounds. WC. ⬚ ⬚ ⬚ By arrangement. ⬚ ⬚

# COTTESBROOKE HALL & GARDENS 🏠
## COTTESBROOKE, NORTHAMPTONSHIRE NN6 8PF
www.cottesbrookehall.co.uk

**Tel:** 01604 505808 **Fax:** 01604 505619 **E-mail:** enquiries@cottesbrooke.co.uk

**Owner:** Mr & Mrs A R Macdonald-Buchanan **Contact:** The Administrator

This magnificent Queen Anne house dating from 1702 is set in delightful rural Northamptonshire. Reputed to be the pattern for Jane Austen's *Mansfield Park*, the Hall's beauty is matched by the magnificence of the gardens and views and by the excellence of the picture, furniture and porcelain collections it houses. The Woolavington collection of sporting pictures at Cottesbrooke is possibly one of the finest of its type in Europe and includes paintings by Stubbs, Ben Marshall and many other artists renowned for works of this genre, from the mid 18th century to the present day. Portraits, bronzes, 18th century English and French furniture and fine porcelain are also among the treasures of Cottesbrooke Hall.

In the formal gardens huge 300-year-old cedars set off magnificent double herbaceous borders, pools and lily-ponds. In midsummer, visitors enjoy the splendid array of planters, a sight not to be missed. The Wild Garden is a short walk across the Park and is planted along the course of a stream with its small cascades and arched bridges. Winner of the HHA/Christie's *Garden of the Year* Award in 2000.

**Location:** MAP 7:B8, OS Ref. SP711 739. 10m N of Northampton near Creaton on A5199 (formerly A50). Signed from Junction 1 on the A14.

**Open:** 2 May–end of Sept. May & Jun: Wed & Thur, 2–5.30pm. Jul–Sept: Thur, 2–5.30pm. Open BH Mons (May–Sept), 2–5.30pm.

**Admission:** House & Gardens: Adult £7.50, Child £3.50, Conc £6. Gardens only: Adult £5, Child £2.50, Conc £4. RHS members receive free access to gardens. Group & private bookings by arrangement.

ⓘ No photography in house. Filming & outside events. 🌷 Unusual plants. 🍴 ♿ Gardens. WC. Parking. ☕ Home-made cakes. 🎫 Hall guided tours obligatory. 🅿 ⊠

---

## DEENE PARK 🏠

*See page 325 for full page entry.*

## DRAYTON HOUSE
**Lowick, Kettering NN14 3BB**
**Tel:** 01832 731779

**Owner:** The Stopford Sackville family **Contact:** Bruce Bailey

A large house dating from c1300 which has never been let or sold. Splendid Baroque architechture and furnishings. Unique embroidered State bed of c1700. The house came into the ownership of the Sackville family in 1770 and the Dining Room has superb plasterwork of that period.

**Location:** MAP 7:D7, OS Ref. SP963 799, Lowick village is on A6116, from A14 (J12).

**Open:** For groups by written appointment only, Easter–end Sept, Tue–Thur.

**Admission:** £10 per head, with a minimum charge of £120.

ⓘ No photography inside the house. ♿ Unsuitable. ☕ By arrangement.

## ELEANOR CROSS ⚏
**Geddington, Kettering, Northamptonshire**
**Tel:** 01604 735400 (Regional Office) **www.english-heritage.org.uk/visits**

**Owner:** English Heritage **Contact:** The East Midlands Regional Office

One of a series of famous crosses, of elegant sculpted design, erected by Edward I to mark the resting places of the body of his wife, Eleanor, when brought for burial from Harby in Nottinghamshire to Westminster Abbey in 1290. Picnickers are welcome.

**Location:** MAP 7:D7, OS Ref. SP896 830. In Geddington, off A43 between Kettering and Corby.

**Open:** Any reasonable time.

♿ ❋

---

See which properties offer **educational facilities** or **school visits** in our index on page 571

---

## HADDONSTONE SHOW GARDENS
**The Forge House, East Haddon, Northampton NN6 8DB**
**Tel:** 01604 770711 **Fax:** 01604 770027
**E-mail:** info@haddonstone.co.uk **www.haddonstone.co.uk**

**Owner:** Haddonstone Ltd **Contact:** Marketing Director

See Haddonstone's classic garden ornaments in the beautiful setting of the walled manor gardens – including urns, troughs, fountains, statuary, bird baths, sundials and balustrading. The garden is on different levels with shrub roses, conifers, clematis and climbers. The Jubilee garden features a pavilion, temple and Gothic grotto. An Orangery was opened in 2002.

**Location:** MAP 7:B8, OS Ref. SP667 682. 7m NW of Northampton off A428. Signposted.

**Open:** Mon–Fri, 9am–5.30pm. Closed weekends, BHs & Christmas period.

**Admission:** Free. Groups by appointment only. Not suitable for coach groups.

📷 ♿ 🎫 By arrangement. 🅿 Limited. 🐕 Guide dogs only.

Coton Manor Garden

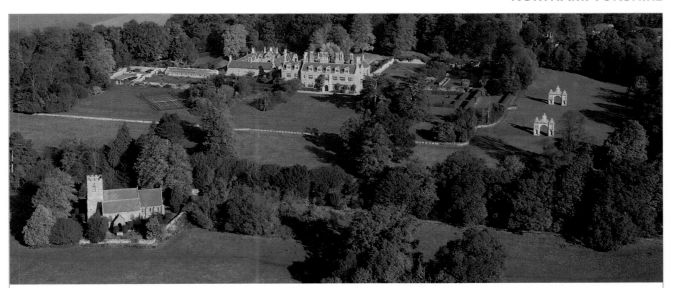

# HOLDENBY HOUSE 📷
## HOLDENBY, NORTHAMPTON NN6 8DJ

www.holdenby.com

**Tel:** 01604 770074 **Fax:** 01604 770962 **E-mail:** office@holdenby.com

**Owner:** James Lowther **Contact:** Commercial Manager

Once the largest private house in England and subsequently the palace and prison of King Charles I, Holdenby has a special atmosphere all of its own. Its elegant rooms and acres of gardens and parkland make it a magnificent venue for corporate events, dinners and meetings, as well as an ideal location for films and TV. Visitors to the gardens can enjoy fascinating flying displays of birds from our famous Falconry Centre, while couples continue to choose Holdenby as an enchanting venue for weddings. Holdenby is five times winner of the Sandford Award for Heritage Education.

**Location:** MAP 7:B8, OS Ref. SP693 681. M1/J15a. 7m NW of Northampton off A428 & A5199.

**Open:** Gardens & Falconry: May–Aug, Suns & BH Mons 1–5pm. Gardens only: Apr & Sep, Suns 1–5pm. House: 9 Apr & 28 May and by appointment.

**Admission:** (with Falconry Centre) Adult £5, Child £3.50, Conc. £4.50, Family (2+2) £15; (Gardens only) Adult £3, Child £2, Conc. £2.50, Family (2+2) £8. Different prices on event days. Groups must book.

ℹ Children's play area. 🅿🅸🆃🅰 Partial. WC. 🍽 Home made teas. (May–Aug). 🎦 By arrangement. 🅿 5 times Sandford Award Winner. 🐾 In grounds, on leads 🏠🅥 Victorian Easter – 8/9 Apr; Plant Fair – 27/28 May, 11am–6pm.

# KIRBY HALL ⚏
## DEENE, CORBY, NORTHAMPTONSHIRE NN17 3EN

www.english-heritage.org.uk/visits

**Tel:** 01536 203230

**Owner:** The Earl of Winchilsea & Nottingham (Managed by English Heritage)

**Contact:** Visitor Operations Team

Peaceful partial ruins of a large, stone-built Elizabethan mansion, begun in 1570 with 17th century alterations. The richly carved decoration is exceptional, full of amazing Renaissance detail. Fine gardens with topiary, home to peacocks. Jane Austen's *Mansfield Park* was filmed at Kirby Hall. Newly restored Elizabethan decorative schemes in the Great Hall, Billiard Room, Library and Best Bedchamber. Located in beautiful countryside close to both Rockingham Castle and Deene Park. Picnickers are welcome.

**Location:** MAP 7:D7 OS Ref. SP926 927. On unclassified road off A43, Corby to Stamford road, 4m NE of Corby. 2m W of Deene Park.

**Open:** 1 Apr–30 Jun: Thur–Mon, 10am–5pm. Jul & Aug: daily, 10am–6pm. 1 Sept–20 Mar: Thur–Mon, 10am–5pm (11am–3pm Nov–Mar). Closed 24–26 Dec & 1 Jan.

**Admission:** Adult £4.70, Child £2.40, Conc. £3.50, Family £11.80. 15% discount for groups (11+).

ℹ WC. 🅿🅰 Grounds, gardens & ground floor only. 🅿 Free with admission. 🅿🅸 🐾 Restricted areas. 🏠🅥

## LAMPORT HALL & GARDENS
### LAMPORT, NORTHAMPTONSHIRE NN6 9HD
www.lamporthall.co.uk

**Tel:** 01604 686272   **Fax:** 01604 686224   **E-mail:** admin@lamporthall.co.uk
**Owner:** Lamport Hall Trust   **Contact:** Executive Director
Home of the Isham family from 1560 to 1976. The 17th and 18th century façade is by John Webb and the Smiths of Warwick. The Hall contains an outstanding collection of furniture, china and paintings including portraits by Van Dyck, Kneller and Lely. The Library contains books dating back to the 16th century and the Cabinet Room houses rare Venetian cabinets. The first floor includes a replicated 17th century bedchamber and a photographic record of Sir Gyles Isham, a Hollywood actor, who initiated the restoration. The gardens owe much to the 10th Baronet who, in the mid 19th century, created the famous rockery.

**Location:** MAP 7:C8, OS Ref. SP759 745. Entrance on A508. 8m N of Northampton, 3m S of A14 J2. Bus: Limited Stagecoach from Northampton and Leicester.
**Open:** 8 Apr–14 Oct. Tours: Suns, 2.30 & 3.15pm; Mon–Fri in Aug, 2.30pm. Fair Days only 2.15pm non-guided tours. Group visits on other days by arrangement.
**Admission:** Adult £5.50, Child (5–16yrs) £2, OAP. £5. Groups (max 60): £5.50, min £150.

ⓘ No photography in house. ▣▣ Conferences & functions ⬧ Partial. WC.
▣ Licensed. 🛈 Obligatory other than Fair Days. 🅿 Cars free. Limited for coaches.
▣▣ In grounds, on leads. ▣▣▣ Telephone or visit website.

## LYVEDEN NEW BIELD ❦
### Nr OUNDLE, PETERBOROUGH PE8 5AT
www.nationaltrust.org.uk

**Tel:** 01832 205358   **Fax:** 01327 861909
**E-mail:** lyvedennewbield@nationaltrust.org.uk
**Owner:** The National Trust   **Contact:** The Property Manager
An incomplete Elizabethan garden house and moated garden. Begun in 1595 by Sir Thomas Tresham to symbolise his Catholic faith, Lyveden remains virtually unaltered since work stopped when Tresham died in 1605. Fascinating Elizabethan architectural detail; remains of one of the oldest garden layouts; set amongst beautiful open countryside.
**Location:** MAP 7:D7, OS141, SP983 853. 4m SW of Oundle via A427, 3m E of Brigstock, off Harley Way. Access by foot along a ½m farm track.
**Open:** House, Elizabethan water garden & visitor information room: 28 Mar–28 Oct: Wed–Sun (open BH Mons & Good Fri), 10.30am–5pm (Aug: daily); 3–25 Nov, & 2 Feb–24 Mar 2008, Sats & Suns, 10.30am–4pm. Groups by arrangement with Property Manager.
**\*Admission:** Adult £4, Child Free. \*includes a voluntary donation but visitors can choose to pay the standard prices displayed at the property and on the website.
🅿 Limited. ▣ On leads. ▣

### NORTHAMPTON CATHEDRAL
**Catholic Cathedral House, Primrose Hill, Northampton NN2 6AG**
**Tel:** 01604 714556   **Contact:** Father J Udris
Partly 19th century Pugin.
**Location:** MAP 7:C9 , OS Ref. SP753 617. ¾m N of town centre on A508.
**Open:** Apply at house: Services: Sat 7pm; Sun 8.30am, 10.30am & 5.15pm; weekday 9.30am & 7pm.
**Admission:** Guided visits by prior application.

### THE PREBENDAL MANOR
**Nassington, Peterborough PE8 6QG**
**Tel:** 01780 782575   **E-mail:** info@prebendal-manor.co.uk
**www.prebendal-manor.co.uk**
**Owner/Contact:** Mrs J Baile
Grade I listed, dating from the early 13th century, it retains many fine original medieval features and included in the visit are the 15th century dovecote, tithe barn museum and medieval fish ponds. Encompassing 6 acres are the largest 14th century re-created medieval gardens in Europe.
**Location:** MAP 7:E7, OS Ref. TL063 962. 6m N of Oundle, 9m W of Peterborough, 7m S of Stamford.
**Open:** Easter Mon & Suns in Apr, 2–5pm. May–Sept: Sun & Wed, & BH Mons, 2–5pm. Closed Christmas. Groups (20-50) outside normal times by arrangement.
**Admission:** Adult £5.50, Child £3, OAP £5. Groups (20–50) outside normal opening times by arrangement.
ⓘ No photography. ▣⬧ Partial. ▣ Home-made teas. 🅿 Limited. 🛈▣ Free.
▣ Guide dogs only.

### ROCKINGHAM CASTLE
*See page 327 for full page entry.*

❄ See all the properties that are **open all year** in the index on page 580

## RUSHTON TRIANGULAR LODGE

**Rushton, Kettering, Northamptonshire  NN14 1RP**
**Tel:** 01536 710761   **www.english-heritage.org.uk/visits**
**Owner:** English Heritage    **Contact:** Visitor Operations Team
This extraordinary building, completed in 1597, symbolises the Holy Trinity. It has three sides, 33 ft wide, three floors, trefoil windows and three triangular gables on each side. Picnickers are welcome.
**Location:** MAP 7:C7 OS141, SP830 831. 1m W of Rushton, on unclassified road 3m from Desborough on A6.
**Open:** 1 Apr–31 Oct: Thurs–Mon, 11am–4pm.
**Admission:** Adult £2.50, Child £1.30, Conc. £1.90.
⊡ 🅿 Nearby lay-by. ☒ Restricted areas.

## SOUTHWICK HALL

**Nr Oundle, Peterborough  PE8 5BL**
**Tel:** 01832 274064   **www.southwickhall.co.uk**
**Owner:** Christopher Capron    **Contact:** G Bucknill
A family home since 1300, retaining medieval building dating from 1300, with Tudor rebuilding and 18th century additions. Exhibitions: Victorian and Edwardian Life, collections of agricultural and carpentry tools and local archaeological finds.
**Location:** MAP 7:E7, OS152, TL022 921. 3m N of Oundle, 4m E of Bulwick.
**Open:** BH Suns & Mons: 8/9 Apr, 6/7 & 27/28 May and 26/27 Aug: 2–5pm. Last admission 4.30pm. Groups at other times by arrangement.
**Admission:** House & Grounds: Adult £5, Child £2.50.
🅶 Partial. WC. ☕ 🅿 By arrangement. 🅿 ☒ In grounds on leads.

## STOKE PARK PAVILIONS

**Stoke Bruerne, Towcester, Northamptonshire  NN12 7RZ**
**Tel:** 01604 862329 or 07768 230325
**Owner/Contact:** A S Chancellor Esq
The two Pavilions, dated c1630 and attributed to Inigo Jones, formed part of the first Palladian country house built in England by Sir Francis Crane. The central block, to which the Pavilions were linked by quadrant colonnades, was destroyed by fire in 1886. The grounds include extensive gardens and overlooks former parkland, now being restored.
**Location:** MAP 7:C10, OS Ref. SP740 488. 7m S of Northampton.
**Open:** Aug: daily, 3–6pm. Other times by appointment only.
**Admission:** Adult £3, Child £1.50.
🅶 Grounds. 🅿 Limited. ☒ In grounds, on leads.

## SULGRAVE MANOR

*See page 328 for full page entry.*

## WAKEFIELD LODGE

**Potterspury, Northamptonshire  NN12 7QX**
**Tel:** 01327 811395   **Fax:** 01327 811051
**Owner/Contact:** Mrs J Richmond-Watson
Georgian hunting lodge with deer park.
**Location:** MAP 7:C10, OS Ref. SP739 425. 4m S of Towcester on A5. Take signs to farm shop for directions.
**Open:** House: 18 Apr–31 May: Mon–Fri (closed BHs), 12 noon–4pm. Appointments by telephone. Access walk open Apr & May.
**Admission:** £5.
ⓘ No photography. ⊡ 🅶 Unsuitable. ☕ 🍴 🅿 Obligatory. 🅿 ☒ Guide dogs only.

Newstead Abbey, Nottinghamshire

## CARLTON HALL

**Carlton-on-Trent, Nottinghamshire NG23 6LP**
**Tel:** 01636 821421 **Fax:** 01636 821554
**Owner/Contact:** Lt Col & Mrs Vere-Laurie
Mid 18th century house by Joseph Pocklington of Newark. Stables attributed to Carr of York. Family home occupied by the same family since 1832.
**Location:** MAP 7:C3, OS Ref. SK799 640. 7m N of Newark off A1. Opposite the church.
**Open:** 1 Apr–30 Sept: Weds only, 2–5pm. Other dates and times by appointment.
Admission: Hall and Garden: £8. Groups (10+) £5pp.
Conferences. Unsuitable. Obligatory. In grounds, on leads. Guide dogs in house.

©National Trust Photographic Library/ Andrew Butler

## CLUMBER PARK

**CLUMBER PARK, WORKSOP, NOTTINGHAMSHIRE S80 3AZ**
www.nationaltrust.org.uk
**Tel:** 01909 476592 **Fax:** 01909 500721
**Owner:** The National Trust **Contact:** Property Manager
Historic parkland with peaceful woods, open heath and rolling farmland around a serpentine lake.
**Location:** MAP 7:B2, OS120 Ref SK626 746. 4½m SE of Worksop, 6½m SW of Retford, just off A1/A57 via A614. 11m from M1/J30.
**Open:** Park: All year except Concert Saturday in August & 25 Dec. Walled Kitchen Garden: 31 Mar–30 Sept: daily (open BH Mons), 10am–5pm (6pm on Sats & Suns). Shop, Restaurant & Plant Sales as Kitchen Garden & 1 Oct–30 Mar: daily 10am–4pm. Chapel: As Shop but closed 13 Jan–1 Apr 2008 for cleaning. Cycle Hire & Interpretation Centre as Shop but Oct–Mar weekends & school holidays only.
**Admission:** Pedestrians, Cyclists & Coaches: Free, Vehicle entry charge, £4.50 per vehicle. Walled Kitchen Garden: £2, Child Free.
Partial. Wheelchairs available. In grounds on leads.

## HODSOCK PRIORY GARDENS

**Blyth, Nr Worksop, Nottinghamshire S81 0TY**
**Tel:** 01909 591204 **Fax:** 01909 591578 **www.snowdrops.co.uk**
**Owner:** Sir Andrew & Lady Buchanan **Contact:** Kate Garton – 07860 329815
*"A magical sight you will never forget"*. Myriads of flowers in the 5-acre garden plus a half mile walk through the woodland with sheets of snowdrops. Banks of *hellebores*, carpets of pink *cyclamen*, ribbons of golden *aconites*, blue *irises*, the red, orange, green, black and white stems of *Acers*, *Cornus* and *Willows* and the heady fragrance of *sarcococca*. There is a clearly marked trail, with plenty of seats. Shortcuts are signed for those who prefer a shorter walk. See also snowdrop article in editorial section.
**Location:** MAP 7:B1, OS Ref. SK612 853. W of B6045 Worksop/Blyth road, 1m SW of Blyth, less than 2m from A1.
**Open:** 1 Feb–4 Mar: Daily, 10am–4pm (last entry).
**Admission:** Adult £4, accompanied Child (6–16yrs) £1.
Heritage shop.

Michael Penty

## HOLME PIERREPONT HALL

**HOLME PIERREPONT, Nr NOTTINGHAM NG12 2LD**
www.holmepierreponthall.com
**Tel:** 0115 933 2371
**Owner:** Mr & Mrs Robin Brackenbury **Contact:** Robert Brackenbury
This charming late medieval manor house is set in 30 acres of Park and Gardens with regional furniture and family portraits. The Ball Room, Drawing Room and Long Gallery are available to hire for functions on an exclusive basis. Filming welcome.
**Location:** MAP 7:B4, OS Ref. SK628 392. 5m ESE of central Nottingham. Follow signs to the National Water Sports Centre and continue for 1½m.
**Open:** 5 Feb–28 Mar, Mon–Wed; 18 Feb, 18 Mar, 1 & 15 Apr: 2–5pm. Corporate, private and wedding venue. Functions at other times by arrangement. Groups by appointment all year.
**Admission:** Adult £4.50, Child £1.50. Gardens only £2.50.
No photography or video recording in house when open to the public. Business and charity functions, wedding receptions, dinners, seminars and conferences. Please ring for details. In grounds on leads.

## D H LAWRENCE HERITAGE

**DURBAN HOUSE HERITAGE CENTRE, MANSFIELD ROAD, EASTWOOD, NOTTINGHAMSHIRE NG16 3DZ**
www.broxtowe.gov.uk
**Tel:** 01773 717353 **Fax:** 01773 713509 **E-mail:** culture@broxtowe.gov.uk
**Owner:** Broxtowe Borough Council **Contact:** Sally Nightingale
Durban House and the D H Lawrence Birthplace Museum bring to life the world of the famous novelist and artist D H Lawrence, author of Lady Chatterley's Lover. Discover more about the Victorian past of the writer's home town which inspired so much of his work.
**Location:** MAP 7:A4, OS Ref. SK466 469. M1/J26 take A610 towards Eastwood, follow brown tourism signs. Or M1/J27 take A608 through Brinsley towards Eastwood.
**Open:** Apr–Oct: 10am–5pm. Nov–Mar, 10am–4pm. Daily. Closed Christmas period please contact property for details.
**Admission:** Free, Mon–Fri. Sat/Sun & BHs charges apply. Single site: Adults £2, Conc £1.20, Family (2+2) £5.80. Joint ticket Adults £3.50, Conc £1.80, Family (2+2) £8. Groups welcome. (2006 prices, subject to change.)
Partial. WCs. Licensed. Licensed. By arrangement. Limited. Guide dogs only.

## NEWARK TOWN HALL

**Market Place, Newark, Nottinghamshire NG24 1DU**
**Tel:** 01636 680333  **Fax:** 01636 680350
**Owner:** Newark Town Council    **Contact:** The Curator
A fine Georgian Grade I listed Town Hall containing a museum of the town's treasures. Disabled access – lift and WC.
**Location:** MAP 7:C3, OS Ref. SK570 395. Close to A46 and A1.
**Open:** All year: Mon–Fri, 11am–4pm. Sats, 12 noon–4pm. Closed BHs.
**Admission:** Free.

## NEWSTEAD ABBEY

**Newstead Abbey Park, Nottinghamshire NG15 8NA**
**Tel:** 01623 455900  **Fax:** 01623 455904  **www.newsteadabbey.org.uk**
**Owner:** Nottingham City Council    **Contact:** Gillian Crawley
Historic home of the poet, Lord Byron, set in extensive formal gardens and parkland of 300 acres. See Byron's private apartments, period rooms and the medieval cloisters. The West Front of the Priory Church was featured as part of the BBC's *Restoration* series.
**Location:** MAP 7:B3, OS Ref. SK540 639. 12m N of Nottingham 1m W of the A60 Mansfield Rd.
**Open:** House: 1 Apr–30 Sept: 12 noon–5pm, last adm. 4pm. Grounds: All year: 9am–6pm or dusk except for the last Friday in November and 25 Dec.
**Admission:** House & Grounds: Adult £6, Child £2.50, Conc. £4, Family (2+3) £16. Groups (10+) £4. Grounds only: Adult £3, Child £1.50, Conc. £2.50, Family £8.50. Groups (10+) £2.50. (Oct–Mar: Adult £3, Child £1.50, Conc. £2.50). May be subject to change for 2007.

## NOTTINGHAM CASTLE

**Nottingham NG1 6EL**
**Tel:** 0115 9153700  **Fax:** 0115 9153653  **E-mail:** castle@ncmg.org.uk
**Owner:** Nottingham City Council
17th century ducal mansion built on the site of the original medieval Castle, with spectacular views of the city. A vibrant museum and art gallery housing collections of paintings, silver, Wedgwood and armour, 15 centuries of Nottingham history plus exhibitions of contemporary and historical art. Tour the underground caves system.
**Location:** MAP 7:B4, OS Ref. SK569 395. Just SW of the city centre on hilltop.
**Open:** Daily, 10am–5pm (4pm during winter). Closed 24–26 Dec & 1 Jan.
**Admission:** Adult £3, Child/Conc. £1.50, Family (2+3) £7. (Prices likely to change in 2007.)
Caves. Tel for details.

## PAPPLEWICK HALL

**Papplewick, Nottinghamshire NG15 8FE**
**Tel:** 0115 963 3491
**Owner/Contact:** J R Godwin-Austen
A beautiful stone built classical house set in a park with woodland garden laid out in the 18th century. The house is notable for its very fine plasterwork and elegant staircase. Grade I listed.
**Location:** MAP 7:B3, OS Ref. SK548 518. Halfway between Nottingham & Mansfield, 3m E of M1/J27. A608 & A611 towards Hucknall. Then A6011 to Papplewick and B683 N for ½m.
**Open:** 1st, 3rd & 5th Wed in each month, 2–5pm, by appointment.
**Admission:** Adult £7. Groups (10+): £4.
No photography. Obligatory. Limited for coaches. In grounds on leads.

## RUFFORD ABBEY

**Ollerton, Nottinghamshire NG22 9DF**
**Tel:** 01623 822944  **www.english-heritage.org.uk/visits**
**Owner:** English Heritage    **Contact:** Nottinghamshire County Council
The remains of a 17th century country house; built on the foundations of a 12th century Cistercian Abbey, set in Rufford Country Park. Picnickers welcome.
**Location:** MAP 7:B3, OS120, SK645 646. 2m S of Ollerton off A614.
**Open:** All year daily, 10am–5pm. Jan–Feb, 10am–4pm. Closed 25 Dec.
**Admission:** Free – parking charge applies.
WC.

## THRUMPTON HALL
### THRUMPTON, NOTTINGHAM NG11 0AX
www.thrumptonhall.com

**Tel:** 01159 830410  **E-mail:** mirandaseymour@btinternet.com
**Owner:** Miranda Seymour    **Contact:** Lynn Priestley
Magnificent lakeside Jacobean house, built in 1607. Priest's hiding hole, carved Charles II staircase, panelled saloon, Byron memorabilia. Large lawns separated from landscaped park by ha-ha. Personal tours are led by family members. Dining room with capacity for 50 silver service or buffet for 100. Free access for coach drivers.
**Location:** MAP 7:A5, OS Ref. SK508 312. 7m S of Nottingham, 3m E M1/J24, 1m from A453.
**Open:** By appointment throughout the year. Groups of (20+) 10.30am–6pm.
**Admission:** Adult £7.50, Child £3.50.
Wedding receptions, conferences, events. Ground floor & grounds. WC. Unlimited. In grounds on leads.

## WINKBURN HALL

**Winkburn, Newark, Nottinghamshire NG22 8PQ**
**Tel:** 01636 636465  **Fax:** 01636 636717
**Owner/Contact:** Richard Craven-Smith-Milnes Esq
A fine William and Mary house.
**Location:** MAP 7:C3, OS Ref. SK711 584. 8m W of Newark 1m N of A617.
**Open:** Throughout the year by appointment only.
**Admission:** £5.75.

## WOLLATON HALL & PARK

**Wollaton, Nottingham NG8 2AE**
**Tel:** 0115 915 3900  **E-mail:** wollaton@ncmg.org.uk
**Owner:** Nottingham City Council    **Contact:** The Manager
A 16th century Grade I listed building designed by Robert Smythson set in a scenic 500-acre historic park, home to red and fallow deer. Natural History Museum, Industrial Museum and The Yard gallery with constantly changing exhibitions. Visitors have the choice of a variety of walks. Due to refurbishment, some areas may be closed, please call for details.
**Location:** MAP 7:B4, OS Ref. SK532 392. Wollaton Park, Nottingham. 3m W of city centre.
**Open:** Hall: Summer, 11am–5pm; Winter, 11am–4pm. Park: All year, 9am–dusk.
**Admission:** Weekdays Free. Weekends & BHs: Joint ticket for all museums: Adult £1.50, Child £1. Child under 5yrs Free. Family (2+3) £4. Grounds £2/car (free for disabled badge holders). Yard Gallery Free. Prices may change in 2007.

Holme Pierrepont Hall

**Above:** Upton House ©NT Photographic Library
**Right:** Dorothy Clive Garden

# West Midlands

Herefordshire

Shropshire

Staffordshire

Warwickshire

West Midlands

Worcestershire

*Shakespeare's birthplace of Stratford-upon-Avon justly receives thousands of visitors each year, but travel further west too, into the gloriously unspoilt counties of Herefordshire and Worcestershire. Surrounded by the Malvern Hills, the fairytale Eastnor Castle has something to interest all visitors, whilst Warwick Castle provides exciting living history to entertain all ages within its medieval walls.*

## ■ Owner

The National Trust

## ■ Contact

The Property Manager
Berrington Hall
Nr Leominster
Herefordshire
HR6 0DW

**Tel:** 01568 615721
**Fax:** 01568 613263

**Restaurant:**
01568 610134

**Shop:**
01568 610529

**Costume Curator:**
01568 613720

**E-mail:** berrington
@nationaltrust.org.uk

## ■ Location

**MAP 6:L8**

**OS137 SP510 637**

3m N of Leominster, 7m
S of Ludlow on
W side of A49.

**Rail:** Leominster 4m.

## ■ Opening Times

**House**
3–18 March: Sats &
Suns,19 March–
4 November: Sat–Wed
(open Good Fri). 1–5pm.
Last admission 4.30pm.

**Garden**
3–18 March: Sats &
Suns,19 March–
4 November: Sat–Wed,
1 December–
16 December: Sats &
Suns.11am–5pm (closes
4.30pm in Nov & Dec).

**Park Walk**
16 June–4 November:
Sat–Wed, (closed 4/5
August) 1–16 December:
Sats & Suns. 11am–5pm
(closes 4.30pm in Nov
& Dec).

**Shop & Restaurant**
As Garden.

## ■ *Admission

| | |
|---|---|
| Adult | £6.00 |
| Child (5–12yrs) | £3.00 |
| Family (2+3) | £15.00 |

**Groups (15–25)****
| | |
|---|---|
| Adult | £4.70 |

**Garden Ticket**
| | |
|---|---|
| Adult | £4.20 |
| Child | £2.10 |

**Joint Ticket**
| | |
|---|---|
| for Berrington &
Croft Castle | £9.00 |

**Groups must pre-
book. Two groups can
visit at a time.

*includes a voluntary
donation but visitors can
choose to pay the standard
prices displayed at the
property and on the
website..

©NTPL

# BERRINGTON HALL 🌿

www.nationaltrust.org.uk/berrington

Berrington Hall is the creation of Thomas Harley, the 3rd Earl of Oxford's remarkable son, who made a fortune from supplying pay and clothing to the British Army in America and became Lord Mayor of London in 1767 at the age of thirty-seven. The architect was the fashionable Henry Holland. The house is beautifully set above the wide valley of a tributary of the River Lugg, with views west and south to the Black Mountains and Brecon Beacons. This was the site chosen by 'Capability' Brown who created the lake with its artificial island. The rather plain neo-classical exterior with a central portico gives no clue to the lavishness of the interior. Plaster ceilings decorated in muted pastel colours adorn the principal rooms. Holland's masterpiece is the staircase hall rising to a central dome. The rooms are set off with a collection of French furniture, including pieces which belonged to the Comte de Flahault, natural son of Talleyrand, and Napoleon's step-daughter Hortense.

In the dining room, vast panoramic paintings of battles at sea, three of them by Thomas Luny, are a tribute to the distinguished Admiral Rodney.

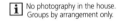 No photography in the house. Groups by arrangement only.

 2 single seater batricars for use outdoors; pre-booking essential. Audio tours for the visually impaired.

Licensed tearoom: open as house: 11am–5pm (4.30pm in Oct–Dec).

By arrangement only. Tour time: 1 hr.

Ample for cars. Parking for coaches limited; instructions given when booking is made.

Children's quizzes. Play area in walled garden.

Guide dogs only.

# EASTNOR CASTLE 🏛

www.eastnorcastle.com

In the style of a medieval Welsh-border fortress, Eastnor Castle was built in the early 19th century by John First Earl Somers and is a good example of the great Norman and Gothic revival in architecture of that time. The Castle is dramatically situated in a 5000 acre estate in the Malvern Hills and remains the family home of the Hervey-Bathursts, his direct descendants.

This fairytale home is as dramatic inside as it is outside. A vast, 60' high Hall leads to a series of State Rooms including a Gothic Drawing Room designed by Pugin, with its original furniture, and a Library in the style of the Italian Renaissance, with views across the Lake.

The Hervey-Bathursts have lovingly restored the interiors and many of the Castle's treasures which have been buried away in the cellars and attics since the Second World War – early Italian Fine Art, medieval armour, 17th century Venetian furniture, Flemish tapestries and paintings by Van Dyck, Reynolds, Romney and Watts and early photographs by Julia Margaret Cameron.

## Gardens

Castellated terraces descend to a 21 acre lake with a restored lakeside walk. The arboretum holds a famous collection of mature specimen trees. There are spectacular views of the Malvern hills across a 300 acre deer park, once part of a mediaeval chase and now designated a Site of Special Scientific Interest.

ℹ️ Tree trail, maze, assault course, off-road driving, clay-pigeon shooting, quad bikes, archery and falconry. Survival training, team building activity days. Product launches, fashion shows, concert, charity events, craft fairs, television and feature films. No photography in Castle.

🛍 

🍽 Wedding receptions. Catering for booked events.

♿ Wheelchair stairclimber to main State rooms. DVD tour of first floor rooms. Visitors may alight at the castle. Priority parking.

📷 

🚶 By arrangement.

🅿️ Ample 10–200 yds from castle. Coaches phone in advance to arrange parking & catering. Tea Room voucher for drivers/courier.

👥 Welcome. Guides available if required. Children's fun worksheets.

🐕 On leads in grounds.

🛏 Luxury accommodation within Castle for small groups (min. 10 guests). 1 single room, 11 double. Ensuite available.

🔔 

🎫 

## Owner

Mr J Hervey-Bathurst

## Contact

Simon Foster
Portcullis Office
Eastnor Castle
Nr Ledbury
Herefordshire HR8 1RL

**Tel:** 01531 633160
**Fax:** 01531 631776
**E-mail:** enquiries@ eastnorcastle.com

## Location

**MAP 6:M10**
**OS Ref. SO735 368**

2m SE of Ledbury on the A438 Tewkesbury road. Alternatively M50/J2 & from Ledbury take the A449/A438.

Tewkesbury 20 mins, Malvern 20 mins, Gloucester 25 mins, Hereford 25 mins, Worcester 30 mins, Cheltenham 30 mins, B'ham 1 hr, London 2¼ hrs.

**Taxi:** Richard James 07836 777196.

## Opening Times

Easter 5–9 April: Sundays and BH Mondays,
15 April–30 September,
16 July–31 August: daily (except Saturdays), 11am–4.30pm (last admission 4pm).

## Admission
### Summer

**Castle & Grounds**

| | |
|---|---|
| Adult | £7.50 |
| Child (5–15yrs) | £4.50 |
| OAP | £6.50 |
| Family (2+3) | £19.50 |

**Grounds only**

| | |
|---|---|
| Adult | £3.50 |
| Child (5–15yrs) | £1.50 |
| OAP | £2.50 |
| Family (2+3) | £8.50 |

**Groups (20+)**

| | |
|---|---|
| Guided | £9.50 |
| Freeflow | £6.00 |
| Schools | £5.00 |

### Privilege Pass

Valid for 1 year and includes all Castle special events

| | |
|---|---|
| Adult | £22.50 |
| Child (5–15yrs) | £13.50 |
| OAP | £19.50 |
| Family (2+3) | £58.50 |

## Special Events

See website for further details.

## Conference/Function

| ROOM | SIZE | MAX CAPACITY |
|---|---|---|
| Great Hall | 16 x 8m | 150 |
| Dining Rm | 11 x 7m | 80 |
| Gothic Rm | 11 x 7m | 80 |
| Octagon Rm | 9 x 9m | 50 |

## ABBEY DORE COURT GARDEN

**Abbey Dore, Herefordshire HR2 0AD**
**Tel/Fax:** 01981 240419
**Owner/Contact:** Mrs C L Ward

A peaceful 6 acre plant and bird lovers' garden with many contrasting areas. These include formal purple, gold and silver borders, an interesting walled garden, many herbaceous borders and a river walk leading to a further 5 acre meadow with unusual trees. Small nursery of herbaceous perennials.

**Location:** MAP 6:K10, OS Ref. SO387 309. 3 m W of A465 midway between Hereford and Abergavenny.

**Open:** Apr–Sept: Sat, Sun, Tue, Thur & BH Mons, 11am–5.30pm. Other times by appointment.

**Admission:** Adult £3.50, Child 50p.

## BERRINGTON HALL 🌿

*See page 338 for full page entry.*

## BROCKHAMPTON ESTATE 🌿

**Bringsty, Bromyard WR6 5TB**
**Tel:** 01885 488099/482077 **www.nationaltrust.org.uk/brockhampton**
**Owner:** The National Trust **Contact:** The Property Manager

Wood and parkland estate with waymarked walks including Lower Brockhampton, a 14th century moated manor house with timber framed gatehouse.

**Location:** MAP 6:L9, OS Ref. SO682 546. 2 m E of Bromyard on A44.

**Open:** House: 3 Mar–1 Apr: Sats & Suns, 12 noon–4pm; 4 Apr–30 Sept: Wed–Sun & BHs, 12 noon–5pm; 3–28 Oct: Wed–Sun, 12 noon–4pm. Estate woodland walks: All year: daily during daylight hours.

**\*Admission:** Whole Estate: Adult £5, Child £2.50, Family £12.50. Lwr Brockhampton only: Adult £4.50, Child £2.50. Park only: Adult £2, Child Free. \*includes a voluntary donation but visitors can choose to pay the standard prices displayed at the property and on the website.

🔲 Partial. 🔲🔲 Dogs in woodland walks, on leads. 🔲 🔲 Tel for details

## CROFT CASTLE & PARKLAND 🌿

**Leominster, Herefordshire HR6 9PW**
**Tel:** 01568 780246 **E-mail:** croftcastle@nationaltrust.org.uk
**www.nationaltrust.org.uk**
**Owner:** The National Trust **Contact:** The Property Manager

Home of the Croft family since Domesday. Walls and corner towers date from 14th and 15th centuries, interior mainly 18th century.

**Location:** MAP 6:K8, OS Ref. SO455 655. 5m NW of Leominster, 9m SW of Ludlow, approach from B4362.

**Open:** House: 3 Mar–1 Apr: Sats & Suns,1–5pm; 4 Apr–30 Sept: Wed–Sun, 1–5pm; 3 Oct–4 Nov: Wed–Sun, 1–4pm; 1– 16 Dec, Sats & Suns 12noon–4pm. Taster tours in House, Sats & Suns, 11am–1pm. Gardens, Tearoom & Shop as House. Park: All year.

**\*Admission:** House & Garden: Adult £6, Child £3, Family £15, Group (15+) £4.70, outside normal hours £10. Garden only: Adult £4, Child £2. Car park £3 (£2 reimbursement on entry, NT members Free). \*includes a voluntary donation but visitors can choose to pay the standard prices displayed at the property and on the website. Gift Aid is not included in group prices.

🔲🔲🔲🔲🔲 🅿

## EASTNOR CASTLE 🏰

*See page 339 for full page entry.*

Croft Castle, Leominster

# HELLENS 🏰
## MUCH MARCLE, LEDBURY, HEREFORDSHIRE HR8 2LY

**Tel:** 01531 660504
**Owner:** Pennington-Mellor-Munthe Charity Trust **Contact:** The Administrator

Built as a monastery and then a stone fortress in 1292 by Mortimer, Earl of March, with Tudor, Jacobean and Stuart additions and lived in ever since by descendants of the original builder. Visited by the Black Prince, Bloody Mary and the 'family ghost'. Family paintings, relics and heirlooms from the Civil War and possessions of the Audleys, Walwyns and Whartons as well as Anne Boleyn. Also beautiful 17th century woodwork carved by the 'King's Carpenter', John Abel. All those historical stories incorporated into guided tours, revealing the loves and lives of those who lived and died here. Goods and chattels virtually unchanged.

**Location:** MAP 6:M10, OS Ref. SO661 332. Off A449 at Much Marcle. Ledbury 4m, Ross-on-Wye 4m.

**Open:** 8 Apr–30 Sept: Wed, Thur, Sun & BH Mons. Guided tours only at 2pm, 3pm & 4pm. Other times by arrangement with the Administrator throughout the year.

**Admission:** Adult £5, Child £2.50, OAP £4, Family £10.

ℹ No photography inside house. 🔲 🔲 Partial. 🎬 Obligatory. 🅿
🔲 In grounds, on leads. 🔲

## HEREFORD CATHEDRAL

**Mappa Mundi and Chained Library Exhibition.**
**Hereford HR1 2NG**
**Tel:** 01432 374202  **Fax:** 01432 374220  **E-mail:** visits@herefordcathedral.org
**Contact:** The Visits Manager  **www: herefordcathedral.org**
Built on a place of worship used since Saxon times, Hereford Cathedral contains some of the finest examples of architecture from Norman times to the present day. The Mappa Mundi & Chained Library Exhibition houses the spectacular medieval map of the world and the Cathedral's unique Chained Library.
**Location:** MAP 6:L10, OS Ref. SO510 398. Hereford city centre on A49.
**Open:** Cathedral: Daily, 7.30am–Evensong. Exhibition: Easter–Oct: Mon–Sat, 10am–4.30pm, Sun, 11am–3.30pm; Nov–Easter: Mon–Sat, 10am–3.30pm.
**Admission:** Admission only for Mappa Mundi and Chained Library Exhibition: Adult £4.50, Child under 5yrs Free, OAP/Student/Unemployed £3.50. Family (2+3) £10.

## HERGEST COURT

**c/o Hergest Estate Office, Kington HR5 3EG**
**Tel:** 01544 230160  **Fax:** 01544 232031  **E-mail:** gardens@hergest.co.uk
**Owner/Contact:** W L Banks
The ancient home of the Vaughans of Hergest, dating from the 13th century.
**Location:** MAP 6:J9, OS Ref. SO283 554. 1m W of Kington on unclassified road to Brilley.
**Open:** Strictly by appointment only through Estate Office.
**Admission:** Adult £5, Child £1.50. Groups: Adult £3.50, Child £1.
⌖ Unsuitable. **P** Limited. ⌖ Guide dogs only. ⌖

## HERGEST CROFT GARDENS 🏛
### KINGTON, HEREFORDSHIRE HR5 3EG

www.hergest.co.uk

**Tel:** 01544 230160  **Fax:** 01544 232031  **E-mail:** gardens@hergest.co.uk
**Owner:** W L Banks  **Contact:** Mrs Melanie Lloyd
From spring bulbs to autumn colour, Hergest Croft is a garden for all seasons. Four distinct gardens with over 4,000 rare shrubs and trees including 60 Champions are sure to delight everyone. Rhododendrons in Park Wood and Azaleas in the Azalea Garden are spectacular in spring. The large Kitchen Garden contains long colourful herbaceous borders, the Rose Garden, Spring Borders and unusual vegetables. Autumn colour is superb.
**Location:** MAP 6:J9, OS Ref. SO281 565. On W side of Kington. ½ m off A44, left at Rhayader end of bypass. Turn right and the car park is ½ m on right. Signposted from bypass.
**Open:** Mar: Sats & Suns. 1 Apr–28 Oct: daily, 12noon–5.30pm. Season tickets and groups by arrangement throughout the year. Winter by appointment.
**Admission:** Adult £5.50, Child (under 16yrs) Free. Pre-booked groups (20+) £4.50. Season ticket £20.
⌖ ⌖ Rare plants. ⌖ Partial. WCs. ⌖ ⌖ By arrangement **P**
⌖ In grounds, on leads. ⌖ ⌖ Tel for details.

## LANGSTONE COURT

**Llangarron, Ross on Wye, Herefordshire  HR9 6NR**
**Tel:** 01989 770254
**Owner/Contact:** R M C Jones Esq
Mostly late 17th century house with older parts. Interesting staircases, panelling and ceilings.
**Location:** MAP 6:L11, OS Ref. SO534 221. Ross on Wye 5m, Llangarron 1m.
**Open:** 20 May–31 Aug: Wed & Thur, 11am–2.30pm, also spring & summer BHs.
**Admission:** Free.

## LONGTOWN CASTLE ⌗

**Abbey Dore, Herefordshire**
**Tel:** 01926 852078
**Owner:** English Heritage  **Contact:** Visitor Operations Administrative Assistant
An unusual cylindrical keep, perched atop a large earthen motte, built c1200, with walls 15ft thick. There are magnificent views of the nearby Black Mountains.
**Location:** MAP 6:K10, OS161 Ref. SO321 291. 4m WSW of Abbey Dore.
**Open:** Any reasonable time.
**Admission:** Free.
⌖ ⌖

## OLD SUFTON

**Mordiford, Hereford HR1 4EJ**
**Tel:** 01432 870268/850328  **Fax:** 01432 850381  **E-mail:** jameshereford@aol.com
**Owner:** Trustees of Sufton Heritage Trust  **Contact:** Mr & Mrs J N Hereford
A 16th century manor house which was altered and remodelled in the 18th and 19th centuries and again in this century. The original home of the Hereford family (see Sufton Court) who have held the manor since the 12th century.
**Location:** MAP 6:L10, OS Ref. SO575 384. Mordiford, off B4224 Mordiford–Dormington road.
**Open:** By written appointment to Sufton Court or by fax.
**Admission:** Adult £3, Child 50p.
⌖ Partial. ⌖ Obligatory. **P** ⌖ Small school groups. No special facilities. ⌖ ⌖

## ROTHERWAS CHAPEL ⌗

**Hereford**
**Tel:** 01926 852078
**Owner:** English Heritage  **Contact:** Visitor Operations Administrative Assistant
This Roman Catholic chapel, dating from the 14th and 16th centuries, is testament to the past grandeur of the Bodenham family and features an interesting mid-Victorian side chapel and High Altar.
**Location:** MAP 6:L10, OS149 Ref. SO536 383. 1½m SE of Hereford 500yds N of B4399.
**Open:** Any reasonable time. Keykeeper at nearby filling station.
**Admission:** Free.
⌖ **P** ⌖ ⌖

## SUFTON COURT 🏛

**Mordiford, Hereford HR1 4LU**
**Tel:** 01432 870268/850328  **Fax:** 01432 850381  **E-mail:** jameshereford@aol.com
**Owner:** J N Hereford  **Contact:** Mr & Mrs J N Hereford
Sufton Court is a small Palladian mansion house. Built in 1788 by James Wyatt for James Hereford. The park was laid out by Humphrey Repton whose 'red book' still survives. The house stands above the rivers Wye and Lugg giving impressive views towards the mountains of Wales.
**Location:** MAP 6:L10, OS Ref. SO574 379. Mordiford, off B4224 on Mordiford–Dormington road.
**Open:** 15–28 May & 14–27 Aug: 2–5pm. Guided tours: 2, 3 and 4pm.
**Admission:** Adult £5, Child 50p.
⌖ ⌖ Obligatory. **P** Only small coaches. ⌖ Small school groups. No special facilities.
⌖ In grounds, on leads.

See which properties offer **educational facilities** or **school visits** in our index on page 571

### ■ Owner
Mr & Mrs F Fisher

### ■ Contact
Mrs Ann E Fisher
Oakley Hall
Market Drayton
Shropshire  TF9 4AG

**Tel:** 07799 114802
**Fax:** 01630 653282

### ■ Location
**MAP 6:M4**
**OS Ref. SJ701 367**

From London 3hrs:
M1, M6/J14, then A5013
to Eccleshall, turn right
at T-junction, 200 yards,
then left onto B5026.
Mucklestone is 1¾ m
from Loggerheads on
B5026. 3m NE of Market
Drayton N of the A53,
1½ m W of Mucklestone,
off B5145.

### ■ Opening Times
**All Year**
Not open to the public.
The house is available all
year round for private or
corporate events.

### ■ Admission
Please telephone for
details.

# OAKLEY HALL

Oakley Hall is situated in magnificent countryside on the boundary of Shropshire and Staffordshire. The present Hall is a fine example of a Queen Anne mansion house and was built on the site of an older dwelling mentioned in the Domesday Survey of 1085. Oakley Hall was the home of the Chetwode family until it was finally sold in 1919.

### Gardens
Set in 100 acres of rolling parkland, the Hall commands superb views over the surrounding countryside and the gardens include wild areas in addition to the more formal parts.

Oakley Hall is a privately owned family house and since it is not open to the general public it provides a perfect location for exclusive private or corporate functions. The main hall can accommodate 100 people comfortably and has excellent acoustics for concerts. Four double bedrooms are available for those attending functions. The secluded location and unspoilt landscape make Oakley an ideal setting for filming and photography.

The surrounding countryside is rich in historical associations. St Mary's Church at Mucklestone, in which parish the Hall stands, was erected in the 13th century and it was from the tower of this Church that Queen Margaret of Anjou observed the Battle of Blore Heath in 1459. This was a brilliant victory for the Yorkist faction in the Wars of the Roses and the blacksmith at Mucklestone was reputed to have shod the Queen's horse back to front in order to disguise her escape.

**i** Concerts, conferences (see left for rooms available). Fashion shows, product launches, seminars, clay pigeon shooting, garden parties and filming. Grand piano, hard tennis court, croquet lawn, horse riding. No stiletto heels.

Wedding receptions, buffets, lunches and dinners can be arranged for large or small groups, using high quality local caterers.

Visitors may alight at the entrance to the Hall, before parking in allocated areas. WCs.

By prior arrangement groups will be met and entertained by members of the Fisher family.

**P** 100 cars, 100 yds from the Hall.

4 double with baths.

### Conference/Function

| ROOM | SIZE | MAX CAPACITY |
|------|------|--------------|
| Hall | 50' x 30' | 100 |
| Dining Rm | 40' x 27' | 60 |
| Ballroom | 40' x 27' | 60 |

Tapestry Room

# WESTON PARK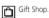

www.weston-park.com

Weston Park is a magnificent Stately Home and Parkland situated on the Staffordshire/Shropshire border. The former home of the Earls of Bradford, the Park is now held in trust for the nation by The Weston Park Foundation.

Built in 1671 by Lady Elizabeth Wilbraham, this warm and welcoming house boasts a superb collection of paintings, including work by Van Dyck, Gainsborough and Stubbs, furniture and *objéts d'art*, providing continued interest and enjoyment for all of its visitors.

Step outside to enjoy the 1,000 acres of glorious Parkland, take one of a variety of woodland and wildlife walks, all landscaped by the legendary 'Capability' Brown in the 18th century. Then browse through the Gift Shop before relaxing in The Stables Coffee Bar and Restaurant.

With the exciting Woodland Adventure Playground, Yew Hedge Maze, Orchard and Deer Park, as well as the Miniature Railway, there is so much for children to do.

Weston Park has a long-standing reputation for staging outstanding events. The exciting and varied programme of entertainment includes Music Festivals, Model Air Shows and Game Fairs.

South Side of the House

Formal Gardens

ℹ️ House available on an exclusive use basis. Conferences, product launches, outdoor concerts and events, filming location. Helipad and airstrip. Sporting activities organised for private groups eg. clay pigeon shooting, archery, hovercrafts, rally driving. Interior photography by prior arrangement only.

🏠 Gift Shop.

🍴 Full event organisation service. Residential parties, special dinners, wedding receptions. Dine and stay arrangements in the house on selected dates.

♿ House and part of the grounds. WCs.

☕ Licensed.

🍴 The Stables Bar and Restaurant provide meals and snacks. Licensed.

🚶 By arrangement.

🅿️ Ample 100 yds away. Private booked groups may park vehicles at front door.

📖 Award-winning educational programme available during all academic terms. Private themed visits aligned with both National Curriculum and QCA targets.

🐕 In grounds, on leads.

🛏️ Weston Park offers 28 delightful bedrooms with bathrooms (24 doubles & 4 singles) 17 en suite.

🔔

🎭

### ■ Owner
The Weston Park Foundation

### ■ Contact
Kate Thomas
Weston Park
Weston-under-Lizard
Nr Shifnal
Shropshire  TF11 8LE

**Tel:** 01952 852100
**Fax:** 01952 850430
**E-mail:** enquiries@weston-park.com

### ■ Location
**MAP 6:N6**
**OS Ref. SJ808 107**

Birmingham 40 mins. Manchester 1 hr. Motorway access M6/J12 or M54/J3 and via the M6 Toll road J11A. House situated on A5 at Weston-under-Lizard.

**Rail:** Nearest Railway Stations:Wolverhampton, Stafford or Telford.

**Air:** Birmingham, West Midlands, Manchester.

### ■ Opening Times
Easter Saturday, weekends and Bank Holidays until 2nd September and most days during July and August.

### ■ Admission
**House, Park & Gardens**
| | |
|---|---|
| Adult | £7.50 |
| Child (3–14yrs) | £5.00 |
| OAP | £6.00 |
| Family (2+3 or 1+4) | £18.00 |

Groups
| | |
|---|---|
| Adult | £5.50 |
| Child (3–14yrs) | £4.50 |
| OAP | £4.50 |

**Park & Gardens**
| | |
|---|---|
| Adult | £4.50 |
| Child (3–14yrs) | £2.50 |
| OAP | £3.50 |

Groups
| | |
|---|---|
| Adult | £3.50 |
| Child (3–14yrs) | £2.50 |
| OAP | £2.50 |

**Privilege Pass**
| | |
|---|---|
| Adult | £20.00 |
| Child (3–14yrs) | £15.00 |
| OAP | £18.00 |
| Family (2+3 or 1+4) | £55.00 |

NB. Visitors are advised to telephone to confirm opening times and admission prices.

### Conference/Function

| ROOM | SIZE | MAX CAPACITY |
|---|---|---|
| Dining Rm | 52' x 23' | 90 |
| Orangery | 56'1" x 22'4" | 120 |
| Music Rm | 55' x 17' | 60 |
| The Hayloft | 32' x 22' | 40 |
| Doncaster | 49' x 18'7" | 80 |

## ACTON BURNELL CASTLE

**Acton Burnell, Shrewsbury, Shropshire**

**Tel:** 01926 852078

**Owner:** English Heritage   **Contact:** Visitor Operations Administrative Assistant

The warm red sandstone shell of a fortified 13th century manor house.

**Location:** MAP 6:L6, OS126, SJ534 019. In Acton Burnell, on unclassified road 8m S of Shrewsbury.

**Open:** Any reasonable time.

**Admission:** Free.

Many properties hold **special events** throughout the year See the index on page 585

See the index on page 585

*gift aid it* This year, some properties will be operating the Gift Aid on Entry scheme at their admission points. Where the scheme is operating, visitors are offered a choice between paying the standard admission price or paying the 'Gift Aid Admission' which includes a voluntary donation of at least 10%. Gift Aid Admissions enable the charity to reclaim tax on the whole amount paid* - an extra 28% - potentially a very significant boost to property funds. Money raised from paying visitors in this way will go towards restoration projects at the property and will be very welcome. Where shown, the admission prices are inclusive of the 10% voluntary donation where properties are operating the Gift Aid on Entry scheme, but both the standard admission price and the Gift Aid Admission will be displayed at the property and on their website.

*Gift Aid donations must be supported by a valid Gift Aid declaration and a Gift Aid declaration can only cover donations made by an individual for him/herself or for him/herself and members of his/her family.

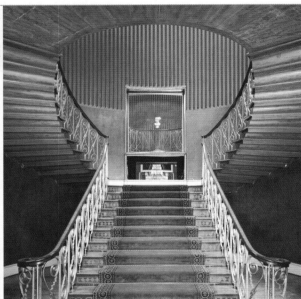

NTPL / Richard Bifield

NTPL / James Mortimer

## ATTINGHAM PARK ✤

### SHREWSBURY, SHROPSHIRE SY4 4TP

**Infoline:** 01743 708123   **Tel:** 01743 708162   **Fax:** 01743 708175

**Owner:** The National Trust   **Contact:** The Property Manager

Late 18th century house, sitting in 500 acres of wonderful parkland. Built for the 1st Lord Berwick, the Georgian house contains some beautiful Italian furniture and a large silver collection. Lord Berwick, and subsequently his two elder sons, had a passion for art and music and this is seen in the Picture Gallery with fine paintings and a Samuel Green organ, which is occasionally played for visitors' enjoyment during the season. Woodland walks along the River Tern and through the Deer Park take in picturesque views of the Wrekin and Shropshire Hills. Costumed guided tours of the House are on offer every day the house is open. Events planned for 2007 include Easter Egg Trail, Spring Plant Fair, Food Fayre and Apple Weekend.

**Location:** MAP 6:L6, OS127, SJ837 083. 4m SE of Shrewsbury on N side of B4380 in Atcham village.

**Open:** 3 Mar–30 Oct (weekends only 3–25 Mar): daily (closed Wed & Thur), 1–5pm, last admission to house 4.30pm. Timed Taster tours only 12 noon–1pm.

**Admission:** House & Grounds: Adult £7, Child £3.50, Family £17.50. Booked groups (15+): Adult £5.50, Child £2.75. Grounds only: Adult £4, Child £2. Family £10. Admission price includes voluntary Gift Aid donation. Gift Aid is not included in Group prices.

ⓘ No photography in house. 🅾 ♿ 🍴 Licensed. 🐾 By arrangement. 🅿 🚌 🐕 In grounds on leads. ✳ ♿

## BENTHALL HALL ✤

**Benthall, Nr Broseley, Shropshire TF12 5RX**

**Tel:** 01952 882159

**Owner:** The National Trust   **Contact:** The Custodian

A 16th century stone house with mullioned windows and moulded brick chimneys.

**Location:** MAP 6:M6, OS Ref. SJ658 025. 1m NW of Broseley (B4375), 4m NE of Much Wenlock, 1m SW of Ironbridge.

**Open:** House & Garden: 3 Apr–27 Jun: Tues & Weds; 1 Jul–30 Sept: Tues, Weds & Suns, 2–5.30pm. Open BH Suns & Mons.

**\*Admission:** House & Garden: Adult: £4.80, Child: £2.40. Garden: Adults £3, Child £1.50. Groups outside normal times £6 (NT members £3). *includes a voluntary donation but visitors can choose to pay the standard prices displayed at the property and on the website.

♿ Partial. Ground floor. WC. 🐾 By arrangement. 🅿 Limited.

Hodnet Hall Gardens, Market Drayton

## BOSCOBEL HOUSE & THE ROYAL OAK ⌗
### BISHOP'S WOOD, BREWOOD, SHROPSHIRE ST19 9AR

www.english-heritage.org.uk/boscobel

**Tel:** 01902 850244

**Owner:** English Heritage    **Contact:** Visitor Operations Team

This 17th century hunting lodge was destined to play a part in Charles II's escape from the Roundheads. A descendant of the Royal Oak, which sheltered the fugitive future King from Cromwell's troops after the Battle of Worcester in 1651, still stands in the fields near Boscobel House. The timber-framed house where the King slept in a tiny 'sacred hole' has been fully restored and furnished in Victorian period and there are panelled rooms and secret hiding places. There is an exhibition in the house as well as the farmyard and smithy.

**Location:** MAP 6:N6, OS127, SJ838 082. On unclassified road between A41 & A5. 8m NW of Wolverhampton.

**Open:** 1 Apr–31 Oct: Wed–Sun & BH Mons, 10am–5pm. Last entry 1hr before closing.

**Admission:** Adult £4.90, Child £2.50, Conc. £3.70, Family £12.30. Grounds only: Adult £2.40, Child £1.20, Conc. £1.80.

▣ ⬚ Grounds. WC. ⬛ ⬚ Obligatory. 🅿 ▣ ⬚ ⬚

---

## BUILDWAS ABBEY ⌗

**Iron Bridge, Telford, Shropshire TF8 7BW**

**Tel:** 01952 433274   www.english-heritage.org.uk/buildwas

**Owner:** English Heritage    **Contact:** Visitor Operations Team

Extensive remains of a Cistercian abbey built in 1135, set beside the River Severn against a backdrop of wooded grounds. The remains include the church which is almost complete except for the roof.

**Location:** MAP 6:M6, OS127, SJ643 043. On S bank of River Severn on A4169, 2m W of Ironbridge.

**Open:** 1 Apr–30 Sept: Wed–Sun & BH Mons, 10am–5pm.

**Admission:** Adult £2.90, Child £1.50, Conc. £2.20.

▣ ⬚ 🅿 ⬚

---

## CLUN CASTLE ⌗

**Clun, Ludlow, Shropshire**

**Tel:** 01926 852078

**Owner:** English Heritage    **Contact:** Visitor Operations Administrative Assistant

Remains of a four-storey keep and other buildings of this border castle are set in outstanding countryside, near the Welsh border. Built in the 11th century.

**Location:** MAP 6:J7, OS137, SO299 809. In Clun, off A488, 18m W of Ludlow. 9m W of Craven Arms.

**Open:** Any reasonable time.

**Admission:** Free.

⬚ ⬚

## COLEHAM PUMPING STATION

**Longden Coleham, Shrewsbury, Shropshire SY3 7DN**

**Tel:** 01743 361196    **Fax:** 01743 358411

**E-mail:** museums@shrewsbury.gov.uk    www.shrewsburymuseums.com

**Owner:** Shrewsbury & Atcham Borough Council    **Contact:** Mary White

Two Renshaw beam engines of 1901 now restored to steam by members of Shrewsbury Steam Trust.

**Location:** MAP 6:L6, OS Ref. SJ497 122. Shrewsbury town centre, near the River Severn.

**Open:** 22 Apr, 27 May, 24 Jun, 29 Jul, 8/9 Sept, 28 Oct, 10am–4pm. Plus occasional other days. Details: 01743 361196.

**Admission:** Adult £1, Child 50p, Student £1.

⬚ Partial. ⬚ By arrangement. 🅿 No parking. ⬛ ⬚ Guide dogs only.

---

## COMBERMERE ABBEY

**Whitchurch, Shropshire SY13 4AJ**

**Tel:** 01948 662880    **Fax:** 01948 871604

**E-mail:** estate@combermereabbey.co.uk    www.combermereabbey.co.uk

**Owner:** Mrs S Callander Beckett    **Contact:** Administrator

Combermere Abbey, originally a Cistercian monastery, remodelled as a Tudor manor house and in 1820 as a Gothic house, sits in a magnificent 1000 acre parkland designed by Webb, in front of a large natural mere. The Walled Gardens have been restored and a unique Fruit Tree Maze created. Tours can now include the gardens. Excellent accommodation is available on the Estate.

**Location:** MAP 6:L4, OS Ref. SJ590 440. 5m E of Whitchurch, off A530. Manchester, Liverpool and Birmingham airports 1hr.

**Open:** 10 Apr–8 Jun: Tues, Weds & Thurs only for tours, 12 noon, 2 & 4pm. Advance bookings necessary. Group visits (20–60) by arrangement. Available for corporate hospitality, meetings, location shoots, wedding and naming ceremonies. Please look at What's On/Abbey section on website for full events schedule.

**Admission:** On open days: Adult £5, Child (under 15yrs) £3. Group tours: £7.50–£10 per person inclusive of refreshments.

ⓘ No photography. ⬚ ⬚ Unsuitable. ⬛ By arrangement. ⬚ By arrangement. 🅿 Limited. ⬚ ⬚ ⬚ For groups. ⬚

---

## COUND HALL

**Cound, Shropshire SY5 6AH**

**Tel:** 01743 761721    **Fax:** 01743 761722

**Owner:** Mr & Mrs D R Waller    **Contact:** Mrs J Stephens

Queen Anne red brick Hall.

**Location:** MAP 6:L6, OS Ref. SJ560 053.

**Open:** 9–13 July: 10am–4pm.

**Admission:** Adult £4.50, Child £2.30, Conc. £3.40, Family £11.30.

ⓘ No photography. 🅿 Limited. ⬚

Attingham Park, Shrewsbury

Michael Caldwell

## DUDMASTON ❧

### QUATT, BRIDGNORTH, SHROPSHIRE WV15 6QN

**Tel:** 01746 780866   **Fax:** 01746 780744   **E-mail:** dudmaston@nationaltrust.org.uk
**Owner:** The National Trust   **Contact:** The House & Visitor Services Manager
Late 17th century manor house. Contains furniture and china, Dutch flower paintings, watercolours, botanical art and modern pictures and sculpture, family and natural history. 9 acres of lakeside gardens and Dingle walk. Two estate walks 5½m and 3½m starting from Hampton Loade car park.
**Location:** MAP 6:M7, OS Ref. SO748 888. 4m SE of Bridgnorth on A442.
**Open:** House & Garden: 1 Apr–30 Sept, Tues, Weds, Suns & BH Mons, 2–5.30pm.
Last admission to house 5pm. Garden: Mon–Wed, Suns & BH Mons, 12 noon–6pm.
**Admission:** House & Garden: Adult £5.80, Child £2.90, Family £14.50, Group £4.50.
Garden only: Adult £4.60, Child £2.30, Family £11.50, Group £3.60. Free tours Mon afternoons (except BHs). Admission price includes voluntary Gift Aid donation.
ⓘ Countryside walks. ⬛⬛⬛⬛ In parkland and estate, on leads, not garden.

## HAUGHMOND ABBEY ⌗

**Upton Magna, Uffington, Shrewsbury, Shropshire SY4 4RW**
**Tel:** 01743 709661   www.english-heritage.org.uk/haughmond
**Owner:** English Heritage   **Contact:** Visitor Operations Team
Extensive remains of a 12th century Augustinian abbey, including the Chapter House which retains its late medieval timber ceiling, and including some fine medieval sculpture.
**Location:** MAP 6:L5, OS126, SJ542 152. 3m NE of Shrewsbury off B5062.
**Open:** 1 Apr–30 Sept: Sun–Wed & BH Mons, 10am–5pm.
**Admission:** Adult £2.90, Child £1.50, Conc. £2.20.
⬛⬛⬛⬛

## HAWKSTONE HALL & GARDENS

**Marchamley, Shrewsbury SY4 5LG**
**Tel:** 01630 685242   **Fax:** 01630 685565
**Owner:** The Redemptorists   **Contact:** Guest Mistress
Grade I Georgian mansion and restored gardens set in spacious parkland.
**Location:** MAP 6:L5, OS Ref. SJ581 299. Entrance 1m N of Hodnet near A442.
**Open:** 14–31 Aug, 1–5pm.
**Admission:** Adult £5, Child £1.50. Group & Family concessions.

© English Heritage Photo Library

Boscobel House & The Royal Oak, Brewood

## HODNET HALL GARDENS 🏛

**Hodnet, Market Drayton, Shropshire TF9 3NN**
**Tel:** 01630 685786   **Fax:** 01630 685853
**E-mail:** secretary@heber-percy.freeserve.co.uk   www.hodnethallgardens.org
**Owner:** Mr and the Hon Mrs A Heber-Percy   **Contact:** Mrs M Revie
The 60+ acres are renowned as amongst the finest in the country. Forest trees provide a wonderful backdrop for formal gardens planted to give delight during every season, with extensive woodland walks amongst wild flowers and unusual flowering shrubs along the banks of a chain of ornamental pools.
**Location:** MAP 6:L5, OS Ref. SJ613 286. 12m NE of Shrewsbury on A53; M6/J15, M54/J3.
**Open:** 8/9 Apr; 7, 13–20, 27/28 May, 3, 10 & 24 Jun; 22 Jul; 26/27 Aug; 16 Sept.
12 noon–5pm. Group bookings by appointment.
**Admission:** £4 per person.
🚆 For groups. ⬛ ⬛ Educational package linked to Key stages I & 2 of National Curriculum. ⬛ On leads.

## IRON BRIDGE ⌗

**Ironbridge, Shropshire**
**Tel:** 0121 625 6820
**Owner:** English Heritage   **Contact:** Regional Head Office
The world's first iron bridge and Britain's best known industrial monument. Cast in Coalbrookdale by local ironmaster, Abraham Darby, it was erected across the River Severn in 1779. Iron Bridge is a World Heritage Site. Visit the recently refurbished Toll House on the Bridge, with interpretation displays.
**Location:** MAP 6:M6, OS127, SJ672 034. In Ironbridge, adjacent to A4169.
**Open:** Any reasonable time.
**Admission:** Free.
⬛

## LANGLEY CHAPEL ⌗

**Acton Burnell, Shrewsbury, Shropshire**
**Tel:** 0121 625 6820 (Regional Office)
**Owner:** English Heritage   **Contact:** The West Midlands Regional Office
A delightful medieval chapel, standing alone in a field, with a complete set of early 17th century wooden fittings and furniture.
**Location:** MAP 6:L6, OS126, SJ538 001. 1½m S of Acton Burnell, on unclassified road 4m E of the A49, 9½m S of Shrewsbury.
**Open:** 1 Mar–31 Oct: daily, 10am–5pm; 1 Nov–29 Feb 2008: daily, 10am–4pm.
**Admission:** Free.
⬛ ⬛

## LILLESHALL ABBEY ⌗

**Oakengates, Shropshire**
**Tel:** 01926 852078
**Owner:** English Heritage   **Contact:** Visitor Operations Administrative Assistant
Extensive ruins of an abbey of Augustinian canons including remains of the 12th and 13th century church and the cloister buildings. Surrounded by green lawns and ancient yew trees.
**Location:** MAP 6:M6, OS127, SJ738 142. On unclassified road off the A518, 4m N of Oakengates.
**Open:** 1 Apr–30 Sept: daily, 10am–5pm.
**Admission:** Free.
⬛

## LONGNER HALL 🏛

**Uffington, Shrewsbury, Shropshire SY4 4TG**
**Tel:** 01743 709215
**Owner:** Mr R L Burton   **Contact:** Mrs R L Burton
Designed by John Nash in 1803, Longner Hall is a Tudor Gothic style house set in a park landscaped by Humphry Repton. The home of one family for over 700 years. Longner's principal rooms are adorned with plaster fan vaulting and stained glass.
**Location:** MAP 6:L6, OS Ref. SJ529 110. 4m SE of Shrewsbury on Uffington road, ¼m off B4380, Atcham.
**Open:** Apr–Sept: Tues & BH Mons, 2–5pm. Tours at 2pm & 3.30pm. Groups at any time by arrangement.
**Admission:** Adult £5, Child/OAP £3.
ⓘ No photography in house. ⬛ ⬛ Partial. ⬛ By arrangement for groups.
🎦 Obligatory. ⬛ Limited for coaches. ⬛ By arrangement. ⬛ Guide dogs only. ⬛

## LUDLOW CASTLE
### CASTLE SQUARE, LUDLOW, SHROPSHIRE  SY8 1AY
www.ludlowcastle.com

**Tel:** 01584 873355   **E-mail:** hduce@ludlowcastle.plus.com
**Owner:** The Earl of Powis & The Trustees of the Powis Estates
**Contact:** Helen J Duce (Custodian)
This magnificent ruin, the heart of Ludlow, a medieval market town, dates from 1086. Extended over the centuries to a fortified Royal Palace and seat of the government for the Council of Wales and the Marches; privately owned by the Earls of Powis since 1811. Castle House, newly renovated, is also open to the public. The Castle Tea Rooms and The 1086 Restaurant serve fresh locally-sourced foods. The Beacon Rooms are available for corporate events, exhibitions and Civil weddings. Three self-catering holiday apartments (each for four persons), finished to the highest standards, are the ideal accommodation for a stay in Ludlow. Tel: 01584 873355/874465 for more details.
**Location:** MAP 6:L8, OS Ref. SO509 745. Shrewsbury 28m, Hereford 26m. A49 centre of Ludlow.
**Open:** Jan: weekends only, 10am–4pm, Feb–Mar & Oct–Dec: 10am–4pm. Apr–Jul & Sept: 10am–5pm. Aug: 10am–7pm. Last adm. 30mins before closing. Closed 25 Dec.
**Admission:** Adult £4, Child £2, Conc. £3.50, Family £11. 10% reduction for groups (10+).
⬚ ⬚ ⬚ Partial. WCs ⬚ Licensed. ⬚ Licensed. ⬚ By arrangement. ⬚ ⬚ None. ⬚ ⬚ In grounds on leads. ⬚ ⬚ ⬚

## MAWLEY HALL
### CLEOBURY MORTIMER DY14 8PN
www.mawley.com

**Tel:** 020 7495 6702  **Fax:** 020 7409 1810  **E-mail:** administration@mawley.com
**Owner:** R Galliers-Pratt Esq    **Contact:** Mrs R Sharp
Built in 1730 and attributed to Francis Smith of Warwick, Mawley is set in 18th century landscaped parkland with extensive gardens and walks down to the River Rea. Magnificent plasterwork and a fine collection of English and Continental furniture and porcelain.
**Location:** MAP 6:L8, OS137, SO688 753. 1m N of Cleobury Mortimer on the A4117 and 7m W of Bewdley.
**Open:** 16 Apr–19 Jul: Mons & Thurs, 3–5pm and throughout the year by appointment.
**Admission:** Adult £8, Child/OAP £5. Outside set opening dates and times all visitors £8.
⬚ By arrangement. ⬚ ⬚ ⬚ In grounds, on leads. ⬚

### MORETON CORBET CASTLE ⬚

**Moreton Corbet, Shrewsbury, Shropshire**
**Tel:** 01926 852078
**Owner:** English Heritage    **Contact:** Visitor Operations Administrative Assistant
A ruined medieval castle with the substantial remains of a splendid Elizabethan mansion, captured in 1644 from Charles I's supporters by Parliamentary forces.
**Location:** MAP 6:L5, OS126, SJ561 231. In Moreton Corbet off B5063, 7m NE of Shrewsbury.
**Open:** Any reasonable time.
Admission: Free.
⬚ ⬚ ⬚ ⬚

### MORVILLE HALL ⬚

**Bridgnorth, Shropshire WV16 5NB**
**Tel:** 01746 780838
**Owner:** The National Trust    **Contact:** Dr & Mrs C Douglas
An Elizabethan house of mellow stone, converted in the 18th century and set in attractive gardens.
**Location:** MAP 6:M7, OS Ref. SO668 940. Morville, on A458 3m W of Bridgnorth.
**Open:** By written appointment only with the tenants.
**Admission:** £3.50. NT members Free.

### OAKLEY HALL

*See page 342 for full page entry.*

**For corporate hospitality** at unique venues see the index on page 567

## PREEN MANOR GARDENS

**Church Preen, Church Stretton, Shropshire SY6 7LQ**
**Tel:** 01694 771207
**Owner/Contact:** Mrs P Trevor-Jones
Six acre garden on site of Cluniac monastery, with walled, terraced, wild, water, kitchen and chess gardens. 12th century monastic church.
**Location:** MAP 6:L6, OS Ref. SO544 981. 10m SSE of Shrewsbury. 7m NE of Church Stretton, 6m SW of Much Wenlock.
**Open:** 30 Apr & 1 Oct: 2–5pm. 28 Jun & 27 Jul: 2–6pm. Groups by arrangement in Jun & Jul.
**Admission:** Adult £3.50, Child 50p.

## SHIPTON HALL 🏠

**Much Wenlock, Shropshire TF13 6JZ**
**Tel:** 01746 785225 **Fax:** 01746 785125
**Owner:** Mr J N R Bishop **Contact:** Mrs M J Bishop
Built around 1587 by Richard Lutwyche who gave the house to his daughter Elizabeth on her marriage to Thomas Mytton. Shipton remained in the Mytton family for the next 300 years. The house has been described as *an exquisite specimen of Elizabethan architecture set in a quaint old fashioned garden, the whole forming a picture which as regards both form and colour, satisfies the artistic sense of even the most fastidious'*. The Georgian additions by Thomas F Pritchard include some elegant rococo interior decorations. There is some noteworthy Tudor and Jacobean panelling. Family home. In addition to the house visitors are welcome to explore the gardens, the dovecote and the parish church which dates back to Saxon times.
**Location:** MAP 6:L7, OS Ref. SO563 918. 7m SW of Much Wenlock on B4378. 10m W of Bridgnorth.
**Open:** Easter–end Sept: Thurs, 2.30–5.30pm. Also Suns and Mons of BH, 2.30–5.30pm. Groups of 20+ at any time of day or year by prior arrangement.
**Admission:** Adult £4.50, Child (under 14yrs) £2. 10% Discount for groups (20+).
🔲 Unsuitable. 🔲 By arrangement for groups (20+). 🔲 Obligatory. 🔲 Guide dogs only.

## SHREWSBURY ABBEY

**Shrewsbury, Shropshire SY2 6BS**
**Tel:** 01743 232723 **Fax:** 01743 240172
**Contact:** Gillian Keates
Benedictine Abbey founded in 1083, tomb of Roger de Montgomerie and remains of tomb of St Winefride, 7th century Welsh saint. The Abbey was part of the monastery and has also been a parish church since the 12th century.
**Location:** MAP 6:L6, OS Ref. SJ499 125. Signposted from Shrewsbury bypass (A5 and A49). 500yds E of town centre, across English Bridge.
**Open:** All year. Summer: 10am–4.30pm. Winter: 10.30am–3pm.
**Admission:** Donation. For guided tours, please contact Abbey.

## SHREWSBURY CASTLE & THE SHROPSHIRE REGIMENTAL MUSEUM

**Castle Street, Shrewsbury SY1 2AT**
**Tel:** 01743 358516 **Fax:** 01743 358411 **E-mail:** museums@shrewsbury.gov.uk
**www.shrewsburymuseums.com**
**Owner:** Shrewsbury & Atcham Borough Council **Contact:** Mary White
Norman Castle with 18th century work by Thomas Telford. Free admission to attractive floral grounds. The main hall houses The Shropshire Regimental Museum and displays on the history of the castle. Open-air theatre, music and events throughout the summer.
**Location:** MAP 6:L6, OS Ref. SJ495 128. Town centre, adjacent BR and bus stations.
**Open:** Main building & Museum: late May BH–mid Sept: Mon–Sat, 10am–5pm; Suns, 10am–4pm. Winter: Please call for details. Grounds: Mon–Sat, 10am–5pm & Suns as above.
**Admission:** Museum: Adult £2.50, OAP £1.25, Shrewsbury residents, under 18s, Students & members of the regiments Free. Grounds: Free. (2006 prices.)
ℹ️ No photography. 🔲 Partial. 🅿 None. 🔲 Guide dogs only. 🔲🔲

## SHREWSBURY MUSEUM & ART GALLERY

**Barker Street, Shrewsbury, Shropshire SY1 1QH**
**Tel:** 01743 361196 **Fax:** 01743 358411
**E-mail:** museums@shrewsbury.gov.uk **www.shrewsburymuseums.com**
**Owner:** Shrewsbury and Atcham Borough Council **Contact:** Mary White
Shrewsbury Museum & Art Gallery will be closed to the public in 2007. Please note that it will continue to be the headquarters of Shrewsbury Museums Service and all contact details remain as before. Visit www.shrewsburymuseums.com for details of events, exhibitions and educational opportunities and www.darwincountry.org for access to pictures, ceramics, archaeology and other parts of the museum collections.

©English Heritage Photo Library

## STOKESAY CASTLE ⊞
### Nr CRAVEN ARMS, SHROPSHIRE SY7 9AH
www.english-heritage.org.uk/stokesay

**Tel:** 01588 672544
**Owner:** English Heritage **Contact:** Visitor Operations Team
This perfectly preserved example of a 13th century fortified manor house gives us a glimpse of the life and ambitions of a rich medieval merchant. Lawrence of Ludlow built this country house to impress the landed gentry. The magnificent Great Hall, almost untouched since medieval times, was used for feasting. The family's private quarters were in the bright, comfortable solar on the first floor. From the outside the castle forms a picturesque grouping of castle, parish church and timber-framed Jacobean gatehouse set in the rolling Shropshire countryside.
**Location:** MAP 6:K7, OS148, SO446 787. 7m NW of Ludlow off A49. 1m S of Craven Arms off A49.
**Open:** Apr, Sept & Oct: Wed–Sun, 10am–5pm. May & Jun: daily, 10am–5pm. Jul & Aug: daily, 10am–6pm. 1 Nov–20 Mar 2008: Thur–Sun, 10am–4pm. Closed 24–26 Dec & 1 Jan. Open BH Mons.
**Admission:** Adult £4.90, Child £2.50, Conc. £3.70, Family £12.30. 15% discount for groups (11+).
🔲 🔲 Great Hall & gardens. WC. 🔲🔲🅿🔲🔲🔲

NTPL / Richard Bifield

## SUNNYCROFT ⚜
### 200 HOLYHEAD ROAD, WELLINGTON, TELFORD, SHROPSHIRE TF1 2DR

**Tel:** 01952 242884
**Owner:** The National Trust **Contact:** The Custodian
Late Victorian gentleman's suburban villa. The grounds amount to a 'mini-estate', with pigsties, stables, kitchen garden, orchards, conservatory, flower garden and superb Wellingtonia avenue.
**Location:** MAP 6:M6, OS Ref. SJ652 109. M54 exit 7, follow B5061 towards Wellington.
**Open:** House & Garden: 23 Mar–28 Oct: Mons, Fris & Suns. 1–5pm. Plus Good Fri and BH Mons.
***Admission:** House & Garden: Adult £5.50, Child £2.75, Family £13.50. Garden only: Adult £3.50, Child £1.75, Family £8.75. Groups at other times £13 (NT Members £10). *includes a voluntary donation but visitors can choose to pay the standard prices displayed at the property and on the website.
🔲 Ground Floor, Adapted WC. 🔲 By arrangement. 🅿

## WENLOCK GUILDHALL

**Much Wenlock, Shropshire  TF13 6AE**
**Tel:** 01952 727509
**Owner/Contact:** Much Wenlock Town Council
16th century half-timbered building has an open-arcade market area.
**Location:** MAP 6:L6, OS Ref. SJ624 000. In centre of Much Wenlock, next to the church.
**Open:** 1 Apr–31 Oct: Mon–Sat, 10.30am–1pm & 2–4pm. Suns: 2–4pm.
**Admission:** Adult 50p, Child Free.

## WENLOCK PRIORY ⚏

**Much Wenlock, Shropshire  TF13 6HS**
**Tel:** 01952 727466   www.english-heritage.org.uk/wenlock
**Owner:** English Heritage    **Contact:** Visitor Operations Team
A prosperous, powerful priory at its peak in the Middle Ages. A great deal of the structure still survives in the form of high, romantic ruined walls and it is the resting place of St Milburga the first Abbess. A monastery was first founded at Wenlock in the 7th century, and little more is known of the site until the time of the Norman Conquest when it became a Cluniac monastery. These majestic ruins of the priory church are set in green lawns and topiary, and there are substantial remains of the early 13th century church and Norman Chapter House.
**Location:** MAP 6:L6, OS127, SJ625 001. In Much Wenlock.
**Open:** Apr, Sept & Oct: Wed–Sun, 10am–5pm. 1 May–31 Aug: daily, 10am–5pm. 1 Nov–20 Mar 2008: Thur–Sun, 10am–4pm. Closed 24–26 Dec & 1 Jan. Open BH Mons.
**Admission:** Adult £3.40, Child £1.70, Conc. £2.60.
ℹ WC. ▢ ▢ **P** ▣ ✲ ▣

## WESTON PARK 🏛

*See page 343 for full page entry.*

## WOLLERTON OLD HALL GARDEN

**Wollerton, Market Drayton, Shropshire  TF9 3NA**
**Tel:** 01630 685760   **Fax:** 01630 685583
**Owner:** Mr & Mrs J D Jenkins    **Contact:** Mrs Di Oakes
Four acre plantsman's garden created around a 16th century house (not open).
**Location:** MAP 6:L5, OS Ref. SJ623 296. 14m NE of Shrewsbury off A53 between Hodnet and Market Drayton.
**Open:** Easter Good Fri–end Sept: Fris, Suns & BHs, 12 noon–5pm. Groups (25+) by appointment at other times.
**Admission:** Adult £4.50, Child £1.

## WROXETER ROMAN CITY ⚏

**Wroxeter, Shrewsbury, Shropshire  SY5 6PH**
**Tel:** 01743 761330   www.english-heritage.org.uk/wroxeter
**Owner:** English Heritage    **Contact:** Visitor Operations Team
The part-excavated centre of the fourth largest city in Roman Britain, originally home to some 6,000 men and several hundred houses. Impressive remains of the 2nd century municipal baths. There is a site museum in which many finds are displayed, including those from recent work by Birmingham Field Archaeological Unit.
**Location:** MAP 6:L6, OS126, SJ565 087. At Wroxeter, 5m E of Shrewsbury, on B4380.
**Open:** 1 Mar–31 Oct: daily, 10am–5pm. 1 Nov–29 Feb: Wed–Sun, 10am–4pm. Closed 24–26 Dec & 1 Jan.
**Admission:** Adult £4.10, Child £2.10, Conc. £3.10, Family £10.30.
ℹ WC. ▢ ▢ ▢ **P** ▣ ▣ ✲

© English Heritage Photo Library

Stokesay Castle, Craven Arms

## THE ANCIENT HIGH HOUSE

**Greengate Street, Stafford ST16 2JA**
**Tel:** 01785 619131 **Fax:** 01785 619132 **E-mail:** ahh@staffordbc.gov.uk
**www.staffordbc.gov.uk/heritage**
**Owner:** Stafford Borough Council **Contact:** Mark Hartwell

Over four hundred years of history are waiting to be discovered within the walls of Stafford's Ancient High House – England's largest timber-framed town house and one of the finest Tudor buildings in the country. Now fully restored, the superb period room settings reflect its fascinating story.

**Location:** MAP 6:N5, OS Ref. SJ922 232. Town centre.
**Open:** All year: Tues–Sat, 10am–4pm.
**Admission:** Free. Check for events, charges may apply.

⬚ ♿ Unsuitable. ✎ By arrangement. ■ School tours by arrangement. ⚐ Guide dogs only. ✳ ♨

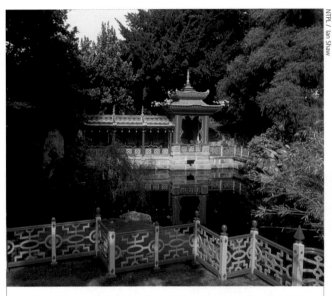

## BIDDULPH GRANGE GARDEN ❧

### GRANGE ROAD, BIDDULPH, STOKE-ON-TRENT ST8 7SD

**Tel:** 01782 517999 **Fax:** 01782 510624
**Owner:** The National Trust **Contact:** The Garden Office
**E-mail:** biddulphgrange@nationaltrust.org.uk

A rare and exciting survival of a High Victorian garden, restored by the National Trust. The garden is divided into a series of themed gardens within a garden, with a Chinese temple, Egyptian court, pinetum, dahlia walk, glen and many other settings. Difficult uneven levels, unsuitable for wheelchairs.

**Location:** MAP 6:N3, OS Ref. SJ891 592. E of A527, 3½m SE of Congleton, 8m N of Stoke-on-Trent.
**Open:** 17 Mar–28 Oct: Wed–Sun & BH Mons, 11.30am–5.30pm or dusk.
3 Nov–16 Dec: Sats & Suns, 11am–3pm.
**\*Admission:** Adult £6, Child £3, Family (2+3) £14. Groups £4.50. Guided tours £8.50. Nov & Dec: Adult £2.30, Child £1.10, Family £5.50. Voucher to visit Little Moreton Hall at a reduced fee when purchasing Adult ticket.*includes a voluntary donation but visitors can choose to pay the standard prices displayed at the property and on the website. Gift Aid is not included in group prices.

⬚ ✎ ♿ Unsuitable for wheelchairs and people with mobility problems. ■ ⚐ In car park, on leads. ♨

## CASTERNE HALL 🏛

**Ilam Nr Ashbourne, Derbyshire DE6 2BA**
**Tel:** 01335 310489 **E-mail:** mail@casterne.co.uk **www.casterne.co.uk**
**Owner/Contact:** Charles & Susannah Hurt
Small manor house in beautiful location.

**Location:** MAP 6:O3, OS Ref. SK123 523. Take first turning on left N of Ilam and continue past 'Casterne Farms only' sign.
**Open:** 1 May–11 Jun (closed 7 & 28 May): weekdays only. Tours on the hour: 2, 3, & 4pm.
**Admission:** £4.

♿ Partial. ✎ Obligatory. ■ ■♿€

NTPL / Ian Shaw

## CHILLINGTON HALL 🏛

### CODSALL WOOD, WOLVERHAMPTON, STAFFORDSHIRE WV8 1RE

www.chillingtonhall.co.uk

**Tel:** 01902 850236 **Fax:** 01902 850768 **E-mail:** mrsplod@chillingtonhall.co.uk
**Owner/Contact:** Mr & Mrs J W Giffard

Home of the Giffards since 1178. Built during 18th century by Francis Smith of Warwick and John Soane. Park designed by 'Capability' Brown. Smith's Staircase, Soane's Saloon and the Pool (a lake of 70 acres) are splendid examples of the days of the Georgian landowner.

**Location:** MAP 6:N6, OS Ref. SJ864 067. 2m S of Brewood off A449. 4m NW of M54/J2.
**Open:** House: BH Suns & Mons (Easter, May & Aug) & July Suns. Aug, Wed–Fri & Suns, 2–5pm. Grounds: as House, also Suns Easter–end May.
**Admission:** Adult £4, Child £2. Grounds only: half price.

♿ Partial. ✎ Obligatory. 🅿 ⚐ In grounds, on leads. €

## THE DOROTHY CLIVE GARDEN

**Willoughbridge, Market Drayton, Shropshire TF9 4EU**
**Tel:** 01630 647237 **Fax:** 01630 647902 **E-mail:** info@dorothyclivegarden.co.uk
**www.dorothyclivegarden.co.uk**
**Owner:** Willoughbridge Garden Trust **Contact:** Garden Office

The Dorothy Clive Garden accommodates a wide range of choice and unusual plants providing year round interest. Features include a quarry with spectacular waterfall, flower borders, a scree and water garden. Tearoom serving home-baked hot and cold snacks throughout the day.

**Location:** MAP 6:M4, OS Ref. SJ753 400. A51, 2m S of Woore, 3m from Bridgemere.
**Open:** 31 Mar–28 Oct: daily, 10am–5.30pm.
**Admission:** Adult £4.50, Child (11–16yrs) £1, (under 11yrs Free), OAP £3.80. Pre-booked Groups (20+) £3.80.

♿ ■ 🅿 ⚐ In grounds on leads.

## ERASMUS DARWIN HOUSE 🏛

**Beacon Street, Lichfield, Staffordshire WA13 7AD**
**www.erasmusdarwin.org**
**Tel:** 01543 306260 **E-mail:** enquiries@erasmusdarwin.org
**Owner:** The Erasmus Darwin Foundation **Contact:** Alison Wallis

Grandfather of Charles Darwin and a founder member of the Lunar Society, Erasmus Darwin (1731–1802) was a leading doctor, scientist, inventor and poet. This elegant Georgian house was his home and contains an exhibition of his life, theories, and inventions. There is also an 18th century herb garden.

**Location:** MAP 6:P5, OS Ref. SK115 098. Situated at the West end of Lichfield Cathedral Close.
**Open:** All year. Please telephone for detail and check our website.
**Admission:** Adult £2.50, Child/Conc. £2, Family £6. Groups (10–50) £2.

⬚ ✎ ⼁ ♿ ✎ By arrangement. ⬚ 🅿 Disabled only. ■ ⚐ Guide dogs only. ✳

## THE HEATH HOUSE

**Tean, Stoke-on-Trent, Staffordshire ST10 4HA**
**Tel:** 01538 722212 / 01386 792110
**E-mail:** philips@heathhouse1.freeserve.co.uk  **www.theheathhouse.co.uk**
**Owner/Contact:** Mr John Philips

The Heath House is an early Victorian mansion designed and built 1836 - 1840 in the Tudor style for John Burton Philips. The collection of paintings is a rare survival and has remained undisturbed since its acquisition. It is still a Philips family home. Large attractive formal garden.

**Location:** MAP 6:O4, OS Ref. SK030 392. A522 off A50 at Uttoxeter 5m W, at Lower Tean turn right.

**Open:** 26–30 May; 1–8 Jun; 23 Jul–5 Aug, 2–5pm. Please telephone in advance to confirm opening times.

**Admission:** £5. No Conc. No reductions for groups.

ℹ️ No photography or video recording. 🅰️ 🎥 Obligatory. 🅿️
🐕 In grounds, on leads. 🔲

## IZAAK WALTON'S COTTAGE

**Worston Lane, Shallowford, Nr Stafford ST15 0PA**
**Tel/Fax:** 01785 760278
**E-mail:** heritage@staffordbc.gov.uk  **www.staffordbc.gov.uk/heritage**
**Owner:** Stafford Borough Council  **Contact:** Mark Hartwell

Stafford's rural heritage is embodied in the charming 17th century cottage owned by the celebrated author of *The Compleat Angler*. Izaak Walton's Cottage gives a fascinating insight into the history of angling and the life of a writer whose work remains 'a unique celebration of the English countryside.'

**Location:** MAP 6:N5, OS Ref. SJ876 293. M6/J14, A5013 towards Eccleshall, signposted on A5013.

**Open:** May–Aug: Sat & Sun, 1–5pm.

**Admission:** Free. Check for events, charges may apply.

📷 🅰️ Partial. WCs. 🔲 🅿️ Limited for cars. 🐕 Guide dogs only. 🔲

**Who's offering accommodation?**
See our index on page 575

The Ancient High House, Stafford

## MOSELEY OLD HALL 🌿
### FORDHOUSES, WOLVERHAMPTON WV10 7HY

**Tel:** 01902 782808  **E-mail:** moseleyoldhall@nationaltrust.org.uk
**Owner:** The National Trust  **Contact:** The Property Manager

An Elizabethan timber-framed house encased in brick in 1870; with original interiors. Charles II hid here after the Battle of Worcester. The bed in which he slept is on view as well as the hiding place he used. An exhibition retells the story of the King's dramatic escape from Cromwell's troops, and there are optional, free guided tours. The garden has been reconstructed in 17th century style with formal box parterre, only 17th century plants are grown. The property is a Sandford Education Award Winner.

**Location:** MAP 6:N6, OS Ref. SJ932 044. 4m N of Wolverhampton between A449 and A460.

**Open:** 3 Mar–31 Oct: Sats, Suns, Weds, BH Mons & following Tues, (excluding Tues 8 May), 12 noon–5pm, BH Mons 11am–5pm. 4 Nov–16 Dec: Suns, 12–4pm (guided tours only). 25 Nov–16 Dec: Christmas activites. Last admission to the house 30 minutes before closing. Shop, Tearoom & Garden: Open 12 noon.

**Admission:** Adult £5.80, Child £2.90, Family £14.50. Groups (15+) £4.80pp (Weds £4.50). Private visits in closing times £7pp (Min £114). NT members free with valid membership card.

📷 🚻 🅰️ Ground floor & grounds. WC. 🔲 Tearoom in 18th century barn. 🎥 🅿️ ▪️
🐕 On leads. 🔲 ♿

## SANDON HALL
### SANDON, STAFFORDSHIRE ST18 OBZ

www.sandonhall.co.uk

**Tel/Fax:** 01889 508004   **E-mail:** info@sandonhall.co.uk

**Owner:** The Earl of Harrowby   **Contact:** Michael Bosson

Ancestral seat of the Earls of Harrowby, conveniently located in the heart of Staffordshire. Set amidst 400 acres of glorious parkland, Sandon, for all its grandeur and elegance, is first and foremost a home. The family museum incorporates several of the State Rooms. In June 2006 a superb extension to the delightful Victorian Conservatory was opened, adding a permanent bar and full facilities for the disabled. The 50 acre landscaped gardens feature magnificent trees and are especially beautiful in May and autumn.

**Location:** MAP 6:N5, OS Ref. SJ957 287. 5m NE of Stafford on the A51, between Stone and Lichfield, easy access from M6/J14.

**Open:** All year for events, functions and for pre-booked visits to the museum and gardens. Evening tours by special arrangement.

**Admission:** Museum: Adult £4, Child £3, OAP £3.50. Gardens: Adult £1.50, Child £1, OAP £1. NB. Max group size 22 or 45 if combined Museum and Gardens.

⬛ ♿ 🍴 Licensed. 🎫 Obligatory. 🅿 Limited for coaches.
🐕 In grounds, on leads. ⬛ ✳ ♿

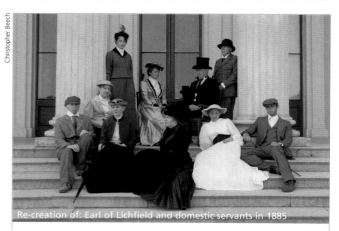

Re-creation of: Earl of Lichfield and domestic servants in 1885

Christopher Beech

## SHUGBOROUGH ESTATE 🌿
### MILFORD, STAFFORD ST17 OXB

www.shugborough.org.uk

**Tel:** 01889 881388   **Fax:** 01889 881323

**E-mail:** shugborough.promotions@staffordshire.gov.uk

**Owner:** The National Trust   **Contact:** Sales and Marketing Office

With evocative sounds, real smells and the true taste of a complete working historic estate, immerse yourself in a world of days gone by in a variety of sensory experiences that bring your visit to life. With its magnificent 18th century Mansion House, authentic Servants' Quarters and Georgian park farm with rare breeds, Shugborough provides a full day out with living costumed characters ready to share a powerful set of stories from the past.

**Location:** MAP 6:N5, OS Ref. SJ992 225. 10mins from M6/J13 on A513 Stafford/Lichfield Rd.

**Open:** 16 Mar–26 Oct. Daily 11am–5pm. Tearooms open 11am–4.30pm.

**Admission:** Adults £10, Child £6, Conc. £8, Family £25, Group Rate £7. Parking £4. (National Trust Members consult handbook.)

ℹ 📷 ⬛ ♿ 🍴 🎫 🎁 🅿 Limited for coaches. ⬛ 🐕 On leads. ⬛ ♿

## STAFFORD CASTLE & VISITOR CENTRE
Newport Road, Stafford ST16 1DJ

**Tel/Fax:** 01785 257698   **E-mail:** heritage@staffordbc.gov.uk

**www.staffordbc.gov.uk/heritage**

**Owner:** Stafford Borough Council   **Contact:** Mark Hartwell

Stafford Castle has dominated the Stafford landscape for over 900 years. William the Conqueror first built Stafford Castle as a fortress to subdue the local populace. The visitor centre – built in the style of a Norman guardhouse – features an audio-visual area that brings its turbulent past to life.

**Location:** MAP 6:N5, OS Ref. SJ904 220. On N side of A518, 1½m WSW of town centre.

**Open:** Apr–Oct: Tue–Sun, 10am–5pm (open BHs). Nov–Mar: Sat & Sun, 10am–4pm.

**Admission:** Free (admission charges may apply for events).

🎫 By arrangement. ✳

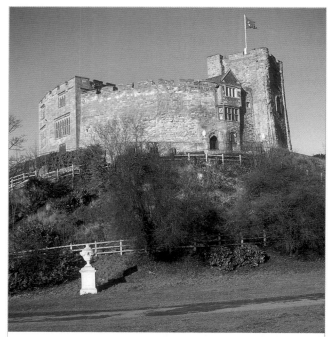

## TAMWORTH CASTLE
### THE HOLLOWAY, TAMWORTH, STAFFORDSHIRE B79 7NA

www.tamworthcastle.co.uk

**Tel:** 01827 709626 (during opening hours)

**Tel:** 01827 709629 (24 hr message board)   **E-mail:** heritage@tamworth.gov.uk

**Owner:** Tamworth Borough Council   **Contact:** Louise Troman

Dramatic Norman shell-keep castle with 15 rooms spanning 800 years of history. Battlemented wall-walks, passage within the courtyard walls and dungeon. Two exhibitions and lots of hands-on activities for children. Reputedly haunted by two female ghosts! Set in town centre park with floral terraces, adventure playgrounds and riverside walks.

**Location:** MAP 6:P6, OS Ref. SK206 038. Town centre off A51.

**Open:** Apr–Oct; Tues–Sun, Nov–Mar; Thurs - Sun, 12 noon–5.15pm. Last admission 4.30pm

**Admission:** Adult £4.95, Child £2.95, Conc £3.95, Family (2+2) £13. (Prices change in Oct 2007.)

🍴 ⬛ ⬛ ✳ ♿

Shugborough Estate, Milford

# TRENTHAM GARDENS
### STONE ROAD, TRENTHAM, STAFFORDSHIRE ST4 8AX
www.trentham.co.uk

**Tel:** 01782 646646  **Fax:** 01782 644536  **E-mail:** shamilton@trentham.co.uk
**Owner:** St. Modwen Properties   **Contact:** Steve Hamilton

Described as the largest contemporary planting scheme in Europe. Utilising top designers Tom Stuart-Smith and Piet Oudolf, this is an iconic restoration, bringing such an important historic garden back to life with vast new plantings with in excess of 120,000 perennials and 200,000 spring bulbs, which will provide interest throughout the year.

The 10 acre Italian Gardens, planted by Tom Stuart-Smith are now fully restored and the new plantings are well established. The new 7 acre Eastern Pleasure Garden, designed by Piet Oudolf, will be open for Easter 2007. Model Show Gardens, Children's activities, woodland walks and "Barfuss" Britain's first barefoot walking park ensure that the gardens provide lots of interest for everyone.

**Location:** MAP 6:N4, OS Ref. SJ864 408. 5 minute drive M6/J15. 45 minutes from Birmingham, Manchester, Liverpool & Nottingham.

**Open:** Apr–Sept; daily, 10am–6pm. Oct–Mar; daily, 10am–4pm. The Italian Gardens are open every day except Christmas Day.

**Admission:** Apr–Sept; Adult £6.50, Child £.5.50, Conc £6, Family (2+3) £22, Groups (12+) from £5, Schools £2.50. Oct–Mar; Adult £5, Child £3.50, Conc £4.50, Family (2+3) £14, Groups (12+) from £4, Schools £1.50

⬚ ⬚ ⬚ ⬚ ⬚ ⬚ Licensed. ⬚ By arrangement. ⬚ ⬚ ⬚ ⬚ Guide dogs only. ⬚ ⬚

---

## WALL ROMAN SITE (LETOCETUM)
**Watling Street, Nr Lichfield, Staffordshire WS14 0AW**
**Tel:** 0121 625 6820   www.english-heritage.org.uk/wall
**Owner:** English Heritage   **Contact:** Regional Head Office

The remains of a staging post alongside Watling Street. Foundations of an Inn and a Bath House can be seen and there is a display of finds in the site museum.

**Location:** MAP 6:O6, OS139, SK098 066. Off A5 at Wall, nr Lichfield.

**Open:** Museum by appointment only. Please telephone for details.

**Admission:** Free.

⬚ ⬚

Trentham Gardens, Trentham

# WHITMORE HALL
### WHITMORE, NEWCASTLE-UNDER-LYME ST5 5HW

**Tel:** 01782 680478 **Fax:** 01782 680906

**Owner:** Mr Guy Cavenagh-Mainwaring   **Contact:** Mr Michael Cavenagh-Thornhill

Whitmore Hall is a Grade I listed building, designated as a house of outstanding architectural and historical interest, and is a fine example of a small Carolinian manor house (1676), although parts of the hall date back to a much earlier period. The hall has beautifully proportioned light rooms, curving staircase and landing. There are some good family portraits to be seen with a continuous line, from 1624 to the present day. It has been the family seat, for over 900 years, of the Cavenagh-Mainwarings who are direct descendants of the original Norman owners. The interior of the hall has recently been refurbished and is in fine condition. The grounds include a beautiful home park with a lime avenue leading to the house, as well as landscaped gardens encompassing an early Victorian summer house. One of the outstanding features of Whitmore is the extremely rare example of a late Elizabethan stable block, the ground floor is part cobbled and has nine oak-carved stalls.

**Location:** MAP 6:M4, OS Ref. SJ811 413. On A53 Newcastle–Market Drayton Road, 3m from M6/J15.

**Open:** 1 May–31 Aug: Tues, Weds, 2–5pm (last tour 4.30pm).

**Admission:** Adult £4, Child 50p.

⬚ Ground floor & grounds.

⬚ Afternoon teas for booked groups (15+), May–Aug. ⬚ ⬚ ⬚

### ■ Owner
The Viscount Daventry

### ■ Contact
Miss Brenda Newell
Arbury Hall
Nuneaton
Warwickshire  CV10 7PT

**Tel:** 024 7638 2804
**Fax:** 024 7664 1147
**E-mail:** brenda.newell@
arburyhall.net

### ■ Location
**MAP 7:A7**
**OS Ref. SP335 893**

London, M1, M6/J3
(A444 to Nuneaton),
2m SW of Nuneaton.
1m W of A444.

Chester A51, A34, M6
(from J14 to J3), 2½ hrs.
Nuneaton 10 mins.

London 2 hrs,
Birmingham ½ hr,
Coventry 20 mins.

**Bus:** Nuneaton 3m.

**Rail:** Nuneaton
Station 3m.

**Air:** Birmingham
International 17m.

### ■ Opening Times
**All year**
Tues, Weds & Thurs only,
for corporate events.

Pre-booked visits to the
Hall and Gardens for
groups of 25+ on Tues,
Weds & Thurs (until 4pm)
from Easter to the end of
September.

Hall & Gardens open
2–5pm on BH weekends
only (Suns & Mons)
Easter–September.

### ■ Admission
**Summer**
**Hall & Gardens**
| | |
|---|---|
| Adult | £6.50 |
| Child (up to 14 yrs.) | £4.50 |
| Family (2+2) | £18.00 |

**Gardens Only**
| | |
|---|---|
| Adult | £5.00 |
| Child (up to 14 yrs.) | £3.50 |

**Groups (25+)**
| | |
|---|---|
| Adult | £6.50 |

### Conference/Function

| ROOM | SIZE | MAX CAPACITY |
|---|---|---|
| Dining Room | 35' x 28' | 120 |
| Saloon | 35' x 30' | 70 |
| Long Gallery | 48' x 11' | 40 |
| Stables Tearooms | 31' x 18' | 80 |

# ARBURY HALL

Arbury Hall has been the seat of the Newdegate family for over 400 years and is the ancestral home of Viscount Daventry. This Tudor/Elizabethan House was gothicised by Sir Roger Newdegate in the 18th century and is regarded as the 'Gothic Gem' of the Midlands. The Hall contains a fine collection of both oriental and Chelsea porcelain, portraits by Lely, Reynolds, Devis and Romney and furniture by Chippendale and Hepplewhite. The principal rooms, with their soaring fan vaulted ceilings and plunging pendants and filigree tracery, stand as a most breathtaking and complete example of early Gothic Revival architecture and provide a unique and fascinating venue for corporate entertaining, product launches, receptions, fashion shoots and activity days. Exclusive use of this historic Hall, its gardens and parkland is offered to clients. The Hall stands in the middle of beautiful parkland with landscaped gardens of rolling lawns, lakes and winding wooded walks. Spring flowers are profuse and in June rhododendrons, azaleas and giant wisteria provide a beautiful environment for the visitor.

George Eliot, the novelist, was born on the estate and Arbury Hall and Sir Roger Newdegate were immortalised in her book 'Scenes of Clerical Life'.

ℹ️ Corporate hospitality, film location, small conferences, product launches and promotions, marquee functions, clay pigeon shooting, archery and other sporting activities, grand piano in Saloon, helicopter landing site. No cameras or video recorders indoors.

🛒 

🍽️ Exclusive lunches and dinners for corporate parties in dining room, max. 50, buffets 120.

♿ Visitors may alight at the Hall's main entrance. Parking in allocated areas. Ramp access to main hall.

By arrangement for groups.

Obligatory. Tour time: 1hr.

🅿️ 200 cars and 3 coaches 250 yards from house. Follow tourist signs. Approach map available for coach drivers.

Welcome, must book. School room available.

In gardens on leads. Guide dogs only in house.

❄️

# BADDESLEY CLINTON

www.nationaltrust.org.uk

Enjoy a day at Baddesley Clinton, the medieval moated manor house with hidden secrets! One of the most enchanting properties owned by the National Trust, Baddesley Clinton has seen little change since 1633 when Henry Ferrers 'the Antiquary' died. He was Squire at Baddesley for almost seventy years and remodelled the house over a long period of time, introducing much of the panelling and chimney pieces. Henry was proud of his ancestry and began the tradition at Baddesley of armorial glass, which has continued until the present day. Henry let the house in the 1590s when it became a refuge for Jesuit priests, and hiding places, called 'priest's holes', created for their concealment, survive from this era.

Pictures painted by Rebecca, wife of Marmion Edward Ferrers, remain to show how the romantic character of Baddesley was enjoyed in the late 19th century when the family also re-created a sumptuously furnished Chapel.

The garden, which surrounds the house, incorporates many features including stewponds; a small lake (the 'Great Pool'); a walled garden with thatched summer house, and a lakeside walk with nature trail and wildflower meadow. Make a day of it! Complementary opening times and substantial discounts on joint ticket prices make a combined visit to Baddesley Clinton and Packwood House even more attractive, especially since both properties are only two miles apart.

Partial. WC.

Licensed.

By arrangement.

Guide dogs only.

## ■ Owner
The National Trust

## ■ Contact
The Estate Office
Baddesley Clinton Hall
Rising Lane
Baddesley Clinton
Knowle
Solihull  B93 0DQ

**Tel:** 01564 783294
**Fax:** 01564 782706
**E-mail:** baddesleyclinton@
nationaltrust.org.uk

## ■ Location
**MAP 6:P8**
**OS Ref. SP199 715**

¾ m W of A4141
Warwick/Birmingham
road at Chadwick End.

## ■ Opening Times
**House**
28 February–4 November:
Wed–Sun, Good Friday
& BH Mons.

February, March, April,
October & November:
1.30–5pm;

May–end September:
1.30–5.30pm.

**Grounds**
28 February–
16 December: Wed–Sun,
Good Friday & BH Mons.

February, March, April,
October & 1–4 Nov:
12 noon–5pm;

May–end September:
12 noon–5.30pm;

7 November–
16 December:
12 noon–4pm.

## ■ *Admission
| | |
|---|---|
| Adult | £8.00 |
| Child | £4.00 |
| Family | £20.00 |
| Groups | £6.20 |
| Guided tours (out of hours) | £13.60 |

**Grounds only**
| | |
|---|---|
| Adult | £4.00 |
| Child | £2.00 |

**Combined Ticket with Packwood House**
| | |
|---|---|
| Adult | £11.25 |
| Child | £5.60 |
| Family | £28.00 |
| Groups | £8.70 |

**Gardens only**
| | |
|---|---|
| Adult | £6.00 |
| Child | £3.00 |

*includes a voluntary
donation but visitors can
choose to pay the standard
prices displayed at the
property and on the website.

**West Midlands – England**

## ■ Owner

The National Trust

## ■ Contact

The Estate Office
Packwood House
Lapworth
Solihull  B94 6AT

**Tel:** 01564 783294
**Fax:** 01564 782706
**E-mail:** packwood@
nationaltrust.org.uk

## ■ Location

**MAP 6:O8**
**OS Ref. SP174 722**

2m E of Hockley Heath
(on A3400), 11m SE of
central Birmingham.

## ■ Opening Times

**House**
28 February–4 November:
Wed–Sun, Good Friday &
BH Mons:
12 noon–4.30pm.

**Garden**
28 February–4 November:
Wed–Sun, Good Friday
& BH Mons;

February, March, April,
October & November:
11am–4.30pm;

May–end September:
11am–5.30pm.

**Park & Woodland Walks**
All year: daily.

## ■ *Admission

| | |
|---|---|
| Adult | £7.00 |
| Child | £3.50 |
| Family | £17.50 |
| Groups | £5.40 |
| Guided tours (out of hours) | £12.00 |

**Garden only**
| | |
|---|---|
| Adult | £4.00 |
| Child | £2.00 |

**Combined Ticket with Baddesley Clinton**
| | |
|---|---|
| Adult | £11.25 |
| Child | £5.60 |
| Family | £28.00 |
| Groups | £8.70 |

**Gardens only**
| | |
|---|---|
| Adult | £6.00 |
| Child | £3.00 |

*includes a voluntary donation but visitors can choose to pay the standard prices displayed at the property and on the website. This does not apply to group prices.

# PACKWOOD HOUSE

www.nationaltrust.org.uk

Packwood lies in the pleasantly wooded Forest of Arden and was, for many years, the home of the Fetherstons, who allowed Cromwell's General, Henry Ireton, to stay overnight before the Battle of Edgehill in 1642. There is also a tradition that Charles II was given refreshment at Packwood after his defeat at Worcester in 1651. Many of Packwood's interiors were designed in the 1920s and 30s in idealised Elizabethan or Jacobean styles for Graham Baron Ash. They offer a wonderful insight into the taste, rich decoration and way of life of a wealthy connoisseur in the period between the wars. Packwood still retains the intimate atmosphere of a real home, with lavishly furnished rooms containing French and Flemish tapestries and fine 17th & 18th century furniture. The oak panelled bedrooms with their sumptuous four-poster beds give you a glimpse of what it was like to

stay the night as Baron Ash's guest. Queen Mary, another regal guest who took refreshment here, visited in August 1927. Look out for several reminders of that historic visit throughout the house.

The house is surrounded by its own delightful, tranquil grounds. A large flower garden complete with long terraced herbaceous borders, enclosed by red brick walls with a gazebo in each corner, is a blend of the traditional country house garden and the Carolean Garden of the Fetherstons. The famous 17th century Yew Garden is traditionally said to represent 'The Sermon on the Mount' and is a highly unusual and attractive feature. Make a day of it! Complementary opening times and substantial discounts on joint ticket prices make a combined visit to Packwood House and Baddesley Clinton even more attractive, especially since both properties are only two miles apart.

 Partial. WC.
 By arrangement.
 Guide dogs only.
 Parkland only.

# RAGLEY HALL & GARDENS

www.ragleyhall.com

Ragley Hall, the family home of the Marquess and Marchioness of Hertford, was designed by Robert Hooke, the inventive genius, in 1680 and is one of the earliest and loveliest of England's great Palladian Houses. The perfect symmetry of the architecture of Ragley remains unchanged save for the spectacular portico by Wyatt added in 1780.

The majestic Great Hall, soaring two storeys high, is adorned with some of England's finest and most exquisite baroque plasterwork by James Gibbs, dated 1750.

Ragley houses a superb collection of 18th century and earlier paintings, china, and furniture and wonderful ceilings decorated with Grisaille panels and insets by Angelica Kauffman.

A most striking feature of Ragley is the breathtaking mural "The Temptation" by Graham Rust in the south staircase hall, that was painted between 1969 and 1983.

Ragley is a working estate with more than 6000 acres of land. The house is set in 400 acres of picturesque parkland landscaped by Lancelot 'Capability' Brown and 27 acres of fascinating gardens including the enchanting rose garden, richly planted borders and mature woodland.

Near to the Hall the working stables, designed by James Gibbs in 1751, house a collection of carriages dating back to 1760 and equestrian equipment.

For children there is an exciting woodland adventure playground, 3D maze and an extensive lakeside play and picnic area, and for walkers the delightful woodland walk.

**i** Product launches, dinners and activity days, film and photographic location, park, lake and picnic area, marquee. No photography or video in the house.

Wedding ceremonies and receptions, private and corporate entertainment, conferences and seminars.

Visitors may alight at entrance. Parking in allocated areas. WCs. Lifts. Coffee House & Restaurant on ground floor. Electric scooter for visiting the gardens may be available. Please enquire.

Tearoom in the Park and Hooke's Coffee-House & Restaurant. Groups please book.

By arrangement.

**P** Coach drivers admitted free and receive info pack and voucher. Please advise of group visits.

Teachers' packs and work modules available. Adventure Wood and Woodland Walk.

In grounds, on leads.

## Owner
The Marquess of Hertford

## Contact
Richard Webb
Events Manager
Ragley Hall, Alcester
Warwickshire B49 5NJ

**Tel:** 01789 762090
**Fax:** 01789 764791
**E-mail:** richardwebb@ragleyhall.com

## Location
**MAP 6:O9**
**OS Ref. SP073 555**

Off A46/A435 1m SW of Alcester. From London 100m, M40 via Oxford and Stratford-on-Avon.

**Rail:** Evesham Station 9m.

**Air:** Birmingham International 20m.

**Taxi:** 007 Taxi 01789 414007

## Opening Times
**House & State Rooms**
22 March–30 September:
Thur–Sun & BH Mons
11am–4pm,
(Sat 11am–1pm).

**Gardens, Park, Adventure Wood & Jerwood Sculpture Park**
22 March–30 September:
Thur–Sun & BH Mons
10am–6pm,
(last admission 4.30pm).

Daily during School Holidays :
29 March–15 April,
24 May–3 June &
19 July–2 September.

**Winter:**
October 2007–
March 2008: Closed.

## Admission
**House, Garden, Park, Adventure Playground & Jerwood Sculpture Park incl.**

| | |
|---|---|
| Adult | £8.00 |
| Child (5–16yrs) | £4.50 |
| Conc. | £6.50 |
| Family (2+4) | £25.00 |

Groups
| | |
|---|---|
| Adult/Conc. | £6.00 |
| Child | £4.00 |

Season Tickets:
| | |
|---|---|
| Family(2+4) | £85.00 |
| Individual | £30.00 |

## Conference/Function

| ROOM | SIZE | MAX CAPACITY |
|---|---|---|
| Great Hall | 70' x 40' | 150 |
| Red Saloon | 30' x 40' | 40 |
| Hertford | 45' x 22' | 60 |
| Seymour | 25' x 23' | 30 |

### ■ Owner

The Shakespeare
Birthplace Trust

### ■ Contact

The Shakespeare
Birthplace Trust
Henley Street
Stratford-upon-Avon
CV37 6QW
**Tel:** 01789 204016
(General enquiries)
**Tel:** 01789
201806/201836
(Group Visits)
01789 201808
(Special/Evening Visits).
**Fax:** 01789 263138
**E-mail:** info@
shakespeare.org.uk
groups@
shakespeare.org.uk

### ■ Location

**MAP 6:P9**
**OS Refs:**
**Birthplace – SP201 552**
**New Place – SP201 548**
**Hall's Croft – SP200 546**
**Hathaway's – SP185 547**
**Arden's – SP166 582**

**Rail:** Direct service from
London (Marylebone)
2 hrs from London
45 mins from
Birmingham by car.
4m from M40/J15
and well signed from
all approaches.

### ■ Opening Times

**Mid Season:**
Apr–May & Sept–Oct.
**Birthplace &
Mary Arden's House**
Mon–Sun: 10am–5pm.
**Hall's Croft & Nash's
House & New Place**
11am–5pm.
**Anne Hathaway's**
Mon–Sat: 9.30am–5pm.
Suns: 10am–5pm.
**Summer Season:**
Jun–Aug.
**Birthplace &
Anne Hathaway's**
Mon–Sat: 9am–5pm.
Suns: 9.30am–5pm.
**Hall's Croft & Nash's
House & New Place**
Mon–Sat: 9.30am–5pm.
Suns: 10am–5pm.
**Mary Arden's House**
9.30am–5pm.
**Winter Season:**
Nov–Mar.
**Birthplace & Anne
Hathaway's House**
Mon–Sat: 10am–4pm.
Suns: 10.30am–4pm.
(Anne Hathaway's
10am–4pm)
**Hall's Croft &
Nash's House**
11am–4pm.
Closed 23–26 Dec.
All times are for
admission to last entry.

### ■ Admission

Multiple house tickets for
all five houses and the
three in-town houses and
single house tickets are
available. Please telephone
01789 204016 for further
information or visit
www.shakespseare.org.uk

Shakespeare's Birthplace

Anne Hathaway's Cottage

Hall's Croft

# THE SHAKESPEARE HOUSES

www.shakespeare.org.uk

**Step Back In To Elizabethan England At The Shakespeare Houses, Stratford-Upon-Avon**

The Shakespeare Houses are five beautiful historic houses and gardens all linked with William Shakespeare and his family. Each have a unique story to tell and together they provide a unique experience of the dramatist's life and times. In Spring 2007 period interpreters wearing replica clothing will be recreating the Elizabethan pace of life and sights, smells and lost skills of Shakespeare's time at Shakespeare's Birthplace and Mary Arden's House.

**In Town: Shakespeare's Birthplace** – this is the childhood home of William Shakespeare. During your visit the housewife or her maid will introduce the family rooms Shakespeare would have known as a boy and in the glover's workshop a glover and his journeyman will be stretching, cutting and sewing leather to make bags, points, purses, gloves and sword hangers just as the young William would have watched his father doing all those years ago.

**Nash's House and New Place** – New Place was the home which Shakespeare purchased in 1597 with his London earnings and where he died in 1616. The original house was sadly demolished but is now preserved as a beautiful garden. The adjacent Nash's House was owned by Shakespeare's granddaughter and the interior of the property reflects the style in which New Place would have been furnished. Admission includes entry to the Complete Works of Shakespeare Exhibition a new and exciting exhibition telling the

remarkable story of Shakespeare's Complete Works one of the best-loved and influential books in the English language.

**Hall's Croft** – This is an elegant 17th century house which belonged to Shakespeare's daughter Susannah and her eminent husband, Doctor John Hall. As well as Doctor Hall's consulting room, the house contains many elegant rooms with exquisite furnishings and paintings.

**Out of Town: Anne Hathaway's Cottage** – situated in the village of Shottery 1 mile from the centre of Stratford. This was the childhood home of Shakespeare's wife and remained occupied by the Hathaway family until 1899. The beautiful thatched farmhouse contains many rare items of family furniture and the house itself is set in stunning grounds with quintessential English cottage garden, orchard, sculpture garden, romantic willow cabin and maze.

**Mary Arden's House** – located in the village of Wilmcote 3 miles from the centre of Stratford, this was the childhood home of Shakespeare's mother.

Step back into the 1570's and experience a normal working day with a farming household from Shakespeare's time from the lighting of the fires, preparation of food, washing, soap and candle making to the feeding of livestock, milking cows, fetching water from the well and the cultivation of vegetables.

Glovers' Workshop at Birthplace

**i** City Sightseeing guided bus tour service connecting the town houses with Anne Hathaway's Cottage and Mary Arden's House. No photography inside houses.

Gifts are available at all five Shakespeare properties.

Available, tel for details.

WCs. Naturally difficult levels but much to enjoy at Mary Arden's House, ground floor & gardens accessible. Virtual reality tour at Shakespeare's Birthplace & Anne Hathaway's Cottage. The gardens at Nash's House and New Place are also easily accessible.

Available on site or close by.

By special arrangement.

**P** The Trust provides a free coach terminal for delivery and pick-up of groups, maximum stay 30 mins at Shakespeare's Birthplace. Parking at Anne Hathaway's Cottage and Mary Arden's House.

Available for all houses. For information 01789 201804.

Guide dogs only.

Hall's Croft

# STONELEIGH ABBEY

www.stoneleighabbey.org

Stoneleigh Abbey was founded in the reign of Henry II and after the Dissolution was granted to the Duke of Suffolk. The estate then passed into the ownership of the Leigh family who remained for 400 years. The estate is now managed by a charitable trust.

Visitors will experience a wealth of architectural styles spanning more than 800 years: the magnificent State rooms and chapel of the 18th century Baroque West Wing contain original pieces of furniture including a set of library chairs made by William Gomm in 1763; a medieval Gatehouse; the Gothic Revival-style Regency Stables. Jane Austen was a distant relative of the Leigh family and in her description of 'Sotherton' in *Mansfield Park* she recalls her stay at Stoneleigh

Abbey. Parts of *Northanger Abbey* also use Stoneleigh for inspiration.

The River Avon flows through the estate's 690 acres of grounds and parkland which displays the influences of Humphry Repton and other major landscape architects. In June 1858 Queen Victoria and Prince Albert visited Stoneleigh Abbey – during their stay Queen Victoria planted an oak tree. In 2003 HRH Prince Charles visited Stoneleigh to mark the completion of the restoration of the Abbey and during his visit he also planted an English oak tree.

Stoneleigh Abbey has been the subject of a major restoration programme funded by the Heritage Lottery Fund, English Heritage and the European Regional Development Fund.

## ■ Owner
Stoneleigh Abbey Ltd

## ■ Contact
Enquiry Office
Stoneleigh Abbey
Kenilworth
Warwickshire  CV8 2LF

**Tel:** 01926 858535
**Fax:** 01926 850724
**E-mail:** enquire
@stoneleighabbey.org

## ■ Location
**MAP 6:P8**
**OS Ref. SP318 712**

Off A46/B4115,
2m W of Kenilworth.
From London 100m,
M40 to Warwick.

**Rail:** Coventry station 5m,
Leamington Spa
station 5m.

**Air:** Birmingham
International 20m.

## ■ Opening Times
Good Fri–end October

Tue–Thur, Suns & BHs:
House tours at
11am, 1pm & 3pm.

Grounds: 10am–5pm.

## ■ Admission
**House Tour & Grounds**

| | |
|---|---|
| Adult | £6.50 |

1 Child Free with
each adult

| | |
|---|---|
| Additional Child | £3.00 |
| OAP | £5.00 |

Discounts for Groups
(20+).

| | |
|---|---|
| **Jane Austen Tour** | £6.50 |
| **Grounds only** | £3.00 |
| Parking | Free |

Groups are welcome
during the published
opening times or at other
times by arrangement.
Please telephone.

 Available for public and commercial hire.

 House only. WCs.

 Obligatory.

 Schools welcome.

 In grounds, on leads.

### Conference/Function

| ROOM | SIZE | MAX CAPACITY |
|---|---|---|
| Saloon | 14 x 9m | 100 |
| Gilt Hall | 7 x 7m | 60 |
| Servants' Hall | 14 x 8m | 100 |
| Riding School | 12 x 33m | 490 |
| Conservatory | 19 x 6m | 100 |

■ **Owner**

The National Trust

■ **Contact**

The Visitor Services
Manager
Upton House
Banbury
Oxfordshire OX15 6HT

**Tel:** 01295 670266
**Fax:** 01295 671144
**E-mail:** uptonhouse
@nationaltrust.org.uk

■ **Location**

**MAP 7:A9**
**OS Ref. SP371 461**

On A422, 7m NW
of Banbury. 12m SE of
Stratford-upon-Avon

**Rail:** Banbury
Station, 7m.

■ **Opening Times**

**Spring & Summer**
3 March–31 October
House: Sat–Wed
including BH Mons &
Good Fri: 12 noon–5pm
(last admission to house
4.30pm).

Garden, Restaurant &
Shop:
Sat–Wed & BHs:
(daily in August)
11am–5pm.

**Winter**
Garden, Restaurant, Shop
& House (ground floor):
3 November–
16 December, Sats &
Suns, 12 noon–4pm.

■ ***Admission**

**House & Garden**
Adult                £8.00
Child                £4.00
Family              £20.00
Groups (15+)     £6.20

**Garden only**
Adult                £4.80
Child                £2.40
Groups (15+)     £3.70

**House & Garden**
3 Nov–16 Dec
Adult                £4.00
Child                £2.00

*includes a voluntary
donation but visitors can
choose to pay the standard
prices displayed at the
property and on the website.
This does not apply to group
prices.

■ **Special Events**

**All Year**
Art tours, historical
re-enactments, concerts
and other events, please
send SAE or telephone.

'Picture in Focus' and
'Porcelain in Focus'
displays for 2007.

# UPTON HOUSE & GARDENS

www.nationaltrust.org.uk

Upton House stands less than a mile to the south of the battlefield of Edgehill and there has been a house on this site since the Middle Ages. The present house was built at the end of the 17th century and remodelled 1927–29 for the 2nd Viscount Bearsted.

He was a great collector of paintings, china and many other valuable works of art, and adapted the building to display them. The paintings include works by El Greco, Bruegel, Bosch, Canaletto, Guardi, Hogarth and Stubbs. The rooms provide an admirable setting for the china collection which includes Chelsea figures and superb examples of beautifully decorated Sèvres porcelain. The set of 17th century Brussels tapestries depict the Holy Roman Emperor Maximilian I's boar and stag hunts.

Artists and Shell Exhibition of Paintings and Posters commissioned by Shell for use in its publicity 1921–1949, while the 2nd Viscount Bearsted was chairman of the company, founded by his father.

### Garden

The outstanding garden is of interest throughout the season with terraces descending into a deep valley from the main lawn. There are herbaceous borders, the national collection of asters, over an acre of kitchen garden, a water garden laid out in the 1930s and pools stocked with ornamental fish.

An 80-seat licensed restaurant in the grounds serves full lunches and afternoon teas. It is available for hire throughout the year for dinners, conferences and functions by arrangement.

 Children's Trail. No indoor photography.

 Ground floor. Wheelchairs available. Virtual tour. WC. Motorised buggy to/from reception/lower garden on request.

Licensed. Self-service.

Tour time 1½–2hrs. Groups (15+) must pre-book. Evening tours by written appointment (no reduction).

 350 yds from House.

 In car park, on leads.

# WARWICK CASTLE

www.warwick-castle.com

Bursting to the towers with tales of treachery and torture, passion and power and above all fascinating people, times and events, Warwick Castle is so much more than simply a castle. Experience preparations for battle, feel the weight of a sword and get a solider's eye view from beneath a battle helmet, see lavishly decorated State Rooms, watch as a household prepares for a Victorian party and discover how electricity was generated over 100 years ago to light up the castle.

With 60 acres of landscaped grounds and gardens, there is plenty to see outside as well as in. Wander around the beautiful Peacock Garden and enter the 18th century Conservatory, filled with an array of exotic plants. There is also the Victorian Rose Garden to explore.

See the world's largest Trebuchet, a mighty siege machine similar to a catapult, measuring 18 metres high, weighing in at 22 tonnes and capable of shooting missiles up to 300 metres.

Throughout the year there is a programme of fantastic special events including opportunities to see the trebuchet in action. Visit www.warwick-castle.com for further information.

■ **Contact**
Warwick Castle
Warwick CV34 4QU
**Tel:** 0870 442 2000
**Fax:** 0870 442 2394
**E-mail:**
customer.information
@warwick-castle.com

■ **Location**
**MAP 6:P8**
**OS Ref. SP284 648**

2m from M40/J15.
Birmingham 35 mins
Leeds 2 hrs 5 mins
London, 1 hr 30 mins
Vehicle entrance from
A429 ½ m SW of town
centre.

**Rail:** Intercity from
London Euston to
Coventry. Direct service
from Marylebone &
Paddington to Warwick.

■ **Opening Times**
All year, daily,
except 25 December
10am–6pm
(closes 5pm during
October–March).

■ **Admission**
| | |
|---|---|
| Adult | from £13.95 |
| Child | from £8.95 |
| Student | from £10.75 |
| OAP | from £9.95 |
| Family (2+2) | from £38.00 |

Groups (15+)
| | |
|---|---|
| Adult | from £11.15 |
| Child | from £7.15 |
| Student | from £8.60 |
| OAP | from £7.95 |

Please visit
www.warwick-castle.com
for further information.

Admission prices are
subject to change
without prior notice.

ℹ️ Corporate events, receptions, Kingmaker's Feasts and Highwayman's Suppers. Guide books available in English, French, German, Japanese and Spanish.

🛍️ Three shops.

♿ Partial. WCs. Parking spaces in Stables Car Park. Telephone for details.

☕ Licensed. Ranging from cream teas to three-course hot meals. During the summer there is an open air barbecue and refreshment pavilion in the grounds (weather permitting).

🍽️ Licensed.

🚶 For groups (pre-booked). Guides in most rooms.

🅿️ Limited. A charge is made for car parking. Free coach parking, free admission and refreshment voucher for coach driver.

🏛️ Ideal location, being a superb example of military architecture dating back to the Norman Conquest and with elegant interiors up to Victorian times. Group rates apply. To qualify for group rates, groups must book in advance. Education packs available.

🐕 Registered assistance dogs only.

❄️

🎭

## Conference/Function

| ROOM | SIZE | MAX CAPACITY |
|---|---|---|
| Great Hall | 61' x 34' | 130 |
| State Dining Room | 40' x 25' | 30 |
| Undercroft | 46' x 26' | 120 |
| Coach House | 44' x 19' | 80 |
| Marquees | | 2000 |

NT Photographic Library

NT Severn SWT / D Sellman

## CHARLECOTE PARK ❧
### WARWICK CV35 9ER
www.nationaltrust.org.uk

**Tel:** 01789 470277 **Fax:** 01789 470544 **Events (info & booking):** 07788 658495
**E-mail:** charlecote.park@nationaltrust.org.uk
**Owner:** The National Trust

Owned by the Lucy family since 1247, Sir Thomas Lucy built the house in 1558. Now, much altered, it is shown as it would have been a century ago, complete with Victorian kitchen, brewhouse and family carriages in the coach house. A DVD of Victorian life can be viewed. The formal gardens and informal parkland lie to the north and west of the house. Jacob Sheep were brought to Charlecote in 1756 by Sir Thomas Lucy. It is reputed that William Shakespeare was apprehended for poaching c1583 and Sir Thomas Lucy is said to be the basis of Justice Shallow in Shakespeare's *'Merry Wives of Windsor'*.

**Location:** MAP 6:P9, OS151, SP263 564. 1m W of Wellesbourne, 5m E of Stratford-upon-Avon.

**Open:** Please telephone or see our website for opening times, dates, and details of regular events and activities.

**\*Admission:** NT members and those joining at Charlecote Park: Free. Adult £7.90, Child (5-16yrs) £4, Family £19. Garden & Grounds only: Adult £4, Child £2. *includes a voluntary donation but visitors can choose to pay the standard prices displayed at the property and on the website.

ⓘ Children's play area. 🅾 🆃 🛉 🆔 Licensed. 🅵 For booked groups.
🅿 Limited for coaches. ▣ By arrangement. 🦮 On leads, in car park only. ⏻

---

**ARBURY HALL** 🏛      *See page 354 for full page entry.*

**BADDESLEY CLINTON** ❧      *See page 355 for full page entry.*

Coughton Court Gardens, Alcester

## COMPTON VERNEY
### COMPTON VERNEY, WARWICKSHIRE CV35 9HZ
www.comptonverney.org.uk

**Tel:** 01926 645500 **Fax:** 01926 645501 **E-mail:** info@comptonverney.org.uk
**Owner:** Compton Verney House Trust    **Contact:** Ticketing Desk

Set in a restored 18th century Robert Adam mansion, Compton Verney offers a unique art gallery experience. Surrounded by 120 acres of 'Capability' Brown landscape, the gallery houses a diverse permanent collection, complemented by changing exhibitions, events and workshops. Call for details.

**Location:** MAP 7:A9, OS Ref. SP312 529. 7m E of Stratford-upon-Avon, 10 mins from M40/J12, on B4086 between Wellesbourne and Kineton.

**Open:** 24 Mar–9 Dec: Tues–Sun & BH Mons, 10am–5pm. Last entry to Gallery 4.30pm. Groups welcome, please book in advance.

**Admission:** Adult £7, Child (5–16yrs) £2, Conc. £6, Student £4, Family £16. Groups (15+): Adult £6.30, Conc. £5.40, group rate with tour, Adult £11, Conc. £10.

ⓘ No photography in the Gallery. 🅾 🆃 🛉 Licensed. 🍴 Licensed.
🅵 By arrangement. 🅿 Ample. ▣ 🦮 Assistance dogs only. ✳ ⏻

West Midlands – England

©NTPL/Robert Morris

# COUGHTON COURT ✣
## ALCESTER, WARWICKSHIRE  B49 5JA

www.nationaltrust.org.uk

**Tel:** 01789 400777  **Fax:** 01789 765544  **Visitor Information:** 01789 762435
**E-mail:** coughtoncourt@nationaltrust.org.uk
**Contact:** The National Trust

Coughton Court is one of England's finest Tudor houses. Home of the Throckmorton family since 1409, the house boasts fine collections of furniture, porcelain and family portraits and a fascinating exhibition of the Gunpowder Plot of 1605, with which the house has strong connections.

The family has created and developed the spectacular gardens over the past 12 years (see below for garden highlights).

**Location:** MAP 6:09, OS Ref. SP080 604, Located on A435, 2m N of Alcester, 8m NW of Stratford-upon-Avon, 18m from Birmingham City Centre.

**Open:** House: 1 Apr–1 Jul; Wed–Sun, 11.30am–5pm. 3 Jul–2 Sept; Tues–Sun, 11.30am–5pm. 5–30 Sept; Wed–Sun, 11.30am–5pm. 6–28 Oct; Sats & Suns, 11.30am–5pm. Closed Good Fri, 16 Jun & 14 Jul. Gardens, Plant Sales, Restaurant & Shop: As house, 11am–5.30pm. Walled Garden: As house, 11.30am–4.45pm.

**\*Admission:** House & Garden:  Adult £9, Child (5-16) £4.50, Family £22.60, Groups (15+) £7. Gardens only: Adult £6.20, Child (5-16) £3.10, Family £15.80, Groups (15+) £4.90. Walled Garden: NT members £2.50 (included in admission price for non-members). \*includes a voluntary donation but visitors can choose to pay the standard prices displayed at the property and on the website.

ℹ️ Children's trail. No indoor photography. 🎁 🍴 Private dinners can be provided by prior arrangement in restaurant. ♿ Ground floor of house, gardens & restaurant. WC. 🍴 Licensed. Capacity: 70 inside, Covered Courtyard 50. 🎫 By arrangement. 🐕 On leads and only in car park. 🏵️

# COUGHTON COURT GARDENS 🏛️
## ALCESTER, WARWICKSHIRE  B49 5JA

www.coughtoncourt.co.uk

**Garden Tours:** 01789 762542  **Fax:** 01789 764369
**E-mail:** office@throckmortons.co.uk
**Contact:** Throckmorton family

The beautiful 25 acres of grounds include a walled garden, lake, riverside walk, knot garden, colour-themed gardens, daffodils and fruit collections. The rose labyrinth boasts spectacular displays of roses and received an **"Award of Garden Excellence" from the World Federation of Rose Societies – a first for the UK.** Plants for sale are grown by the Family.

**Location / Open / Admission:** see above.
🎁 ♿ 🐕

*Gardens and Plant Sales also weekends in March.*

©Coughton Court

©Coughton Court

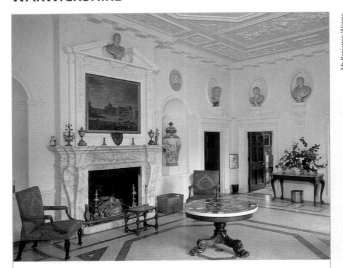

## FARNBOROUGH HALL ❧

### BANBURY, OXFORDSHIRE OX17 1DU

www.nationaltrust.org.uk

**Tel:** 01295 690002 (information line)

**Owner:** The National Trust

A classical stone house of the mid-18th century, the home of the Holbech family for 300 years. Collections include antiquities collected on the Grand Tour, whilst the interior plasterwork is some of the finest in the country. Superb Grade I listed grounds remain largely unchanged and include terraced walk with fine views, ornamented with temples.

**Location:** MAP 7:A9, OS151, SP430 490. 6m N of Banbury, ½ m W of A423.

**Open:** House, Garden & Terrace Walk: 7 Apr–29 Sept: Weds & Sats, 2–5.30pm. 6–7 May: Sun & Mon, 2–5.30pm. Last admission 5pm.

**Admission:** House, Garden & Terrace Walk: Adult £4.50, Child £2.25, Family £11.75. ♿ House & grounds, but steep terrace walk. 🐕 In grounds, on leads.

---

## THE HILLER GARDEN

**Dunnington Heath Farm, Alcester, Warwickshire B49 5PD**

**Tel:** 01789 491342  **Fax:** 01789 490439

**Owner:** A H Hiller & Son Ltd  **Contact:** Mr Jeff Soulsby

2 acre garden of unusual herbaceous plants and over 200 rose varieties.

**Location:** MAP 6:O9, OS Ref. SP066 539. 1½ m S of Ragley Hall on B4088 (formerly A435).

**Open:** All year: daily 10am–5pm.

**Admission:** Free.

---

Stoneleigh Abbey, Kenilworth

Honington Hall, Warwickshire

## HONINGTON HALL 🏛

### SHIPSTON-ON-STOUR, WARWICKSHIRE CV36 5AA

**Tel:** 01608 661434  **Fax:** 01608 663717

**Owner/Contact:** Benjamin Wiggin Esq

This fine Caroline manor house was built in the early 1680s for Henry Parker in mellow brickwork, stone quoins and window dressings. Modified in 1751 when an octagonal saloon was inserted. The interior was also lavishly restored around this time and contains exceptional mid-Georgian plasterwork. Set in 15 acres of grounds.

**Location:** MAP 6:P9, OS Ref. SP261 427. 10m S of Stratford-upon-Avon. 1½ m N of Shipston-on-Stour. Take A3400 towards Stratford, then signed right to Honington.

**Open:** Guided tours by appointment only.

**Admission:** Telephone for details.

🎦 Obligatory. 🐕

© English Heritage Photo Library

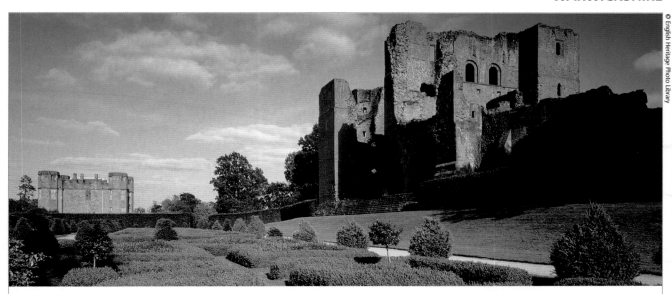

## KENILWORTH CASTLE ⊞
### KENILWORTH, WARWICKSHIRE CV8 1NE

www.english-heritage.org.uk/kenilworth

**Tel:** 01926 864152

**Owner:** English Heritage    **Contact:** Visitor Operations Team

Kenilworth is the largest castle ruin in England, the former stronghold of great Lords and Kings. Its massive walls of warm red stone tower over the peaceful Warwickshire landscape. The Earl of Leicester entertained Queen Elizabeth I with 'Princely Pleasures' during her 19 day visit. He built a new wing for the Queen to lodge in and organised all manner of lavish and costly festivities. The Great Hall, where Gloriana dined with her courtiers, still stands and John of Gaunt's Hall is second only in width and grandeur to Westminster Hall. Climb to the top of the tower beside the hall and you will be rewarded by fine views over the rolling wooded countryside. The stunning Elizabethan Gatehouse has reopened with restored interiors and brand new exhibitions that chart the Castle's turbulent 900 year history and tell the story of a very royal romance.

**Location:** MAP 6:P8, OS140, SP278 723. In Kenilworth, off A452, W end of town.

**Open:** 1 Apr–20 Mar: daily, 10am–5pm (4pm Nov–Feb & 6pm Jun–Aug). Closed 24–26 Dec & 1 Jan. Gatehouse may close early on Saturdays for private events. Tearoom: Apr–Oct.

**Admission:** Adult £6, Child £3, Conc. £4.50, Family £15. 15% discount for groups (11+).

ℹ️ WC. ⬚ 🖼 🔲 ♿ 🎧 **P** 🔲 🔳 🔺 ❀ ♨

## LORD LEYCESTER HOSPITAL
### HIGH STREET, WARWICK CV34 4BH

www.lordleycester.com

**Tel/Fax:** 01926 491422

**Owner:** The Governors    **Contact:** The Master

This magnificent range of 14th century half-timbered buildings was adapted into almshouses by Robert Dudley, Earl of Leycester, in 1571. The Hospital still provides homes for ex-servicemen and their wives. The Guildhall, Great Hall, Chapel, Brethren's Kitchen and galleried Courtyard are still in everyday use. The Queen's Own Hussars regimental museum is here. The historic Master's Garden, featured in BBC TV's *Gardener's World*, has been restored.

**Location:** OS Ref. 280 648. 1m N of M40/J15 on the A429 in town centre.

**Open:** All year: Tue–Sun & BHs (except Good Fri & 25 Dec), 10am–5pm (4pm in winter). Garden: Apr–Sept: 10am–4.30pm.

**Admission:** Adult £4.90, Child £3.90, Conc. £4.40. Garden only £2. 5% discount for adult groups (20+).

⬚ 🔲 🖼 ♿ Partial. 🖼 🔲 🔳 By arrangement. **P** Limited. 🔲 🔳 Guide dogs only. ❀

## MIDDLETON HALL

**Middleton, Tamworth, Staffordshire B78 2AE**

**Tel:** 01827 283095   **Fax:** 01827 285717   **E-mail:** middletonhall@btconnect.com

**Owner:** Middleton Hall Trust    **Contact:** Carol Sullivan

Hall (1285–1824). Former home of Hugh Willoughby (Tudor explorer), Francis Willughby and John Ray (17th century naturalists).

**Location:** MAP 6:P6, OS Ref. SP193 982. A4091, S of Tamworth.

**Open:** Easter–25 Sept: Suns, 2–5pm, BH Mons, 11am–5pm.

**Admission:** £2.50, OAP £1.50. BHs & Special Events: Adult £5, Child £1, OAP £3.50.

---

**PACKWOOD HOUSE** 🌼                *See page 356 for full page entry.*

---

**RAGLEY HALL & GARDENS** 🏛        *See page 357 for full page entry.*

---

**THE SHAKESPEARE HOUSES**          *See page 358 for full page entry.*

---

**STONELEIGH ABBEY**                *See page 359 for full page entry.*

---

**UPTON HOUSE & GARDENS** 🌼        *See page 360 for full page entry.*

---

**WARWICK CASTLE**                  *See page 361 for full page entry.*

---

Many properties hold **special events** throughout the year
See the index on page 585

## ■ Owner

Viscount Cobham

## ■ Contact

Mrs Joyce Purnell
Hagley Hall
Hagley
Worcestershire
DY9 9LG

**Tel:** 01562 882408
**Fax:** 01562 882632
**E-mail:** hagleyhall@
compuserve.com

## ■ Location

**MAP 6:N7**
**OS Ref. SO920 807**

Easily accessible from all
areas of the country.
¼m S of A456 at Hagley.

Close to the M42, M40,
M6 and only 5m from
M5/J3/J4.

Birmingham City
Centre 12m.

**Rail:** Railway Station and
the NEC 25 mins.

**Air:** Birmingham
International Airport
25 mins.

## ■ Opening Times

**House**

8 January–28 February,
daily, excluding Saturdays

Easter:
9–13 April

Whitsun:
27 May–1 June

August BH:
27–31August

2–5pm Guided tours.

Please telephone prior
to visit to ensure the
house is open.

Tea Room open during
House Opening

## ■ Admission

| | |
|---|---|
| Adult | £5.00 |
| Child (under 14 yrs) | £2.00 |
| Conc. | £2.50 |
| Student | £2.50 |

## Conference/Function

| ROOM | SIZE | MAX CAPACITY |
|---|---|---|
| Gallery | 85' x 17' | 120 |
| Crimson Rm | 23' x 31' | 40 |
| The Saloon | 34' x 27' | 70 |
| Westcote | 31' x 20' | 60 |

# HAGLEY HALL

www.hagleyhall.com

This elegant Palladian house, completed in 1760, contains some of the finest examples of Italian plasterwork. Hagley's rich rococo decoration is a remarkable tribute to the artistic achievement of great 18th century architects and designers. Hagley Hall was designed by Sanderson Miller and built for George, the First Lord Lyttelton, who was private secretary to The Prince of Wales in 1732, was made Lord of the Treasury in 1744 and Cofferer to the Royal Household in 1754. George was raised to the peerage in 1756 when he was created Baron of Frankley. The house is set in a 350-acre landscaped park and is the much loved, privately owned home of the 12th Viscount Cobham.

**i** Available on an exclusive basis for conferences, presentations, lunches, dinners, product launches, concerts, small wedding receptions, country sporting days, team-building activities, off-road driving and filming. Please telephone for details.

Visitors may alight at the entrance. No WC.

Teas available during opening times.

Obligatory. Please book parties in advance, guided tour of house time: 1hr. Colour guidebook.

**P** Unlimited for coaches and cars.

By arrangement.

Guide dogs only.

West Midlands – England

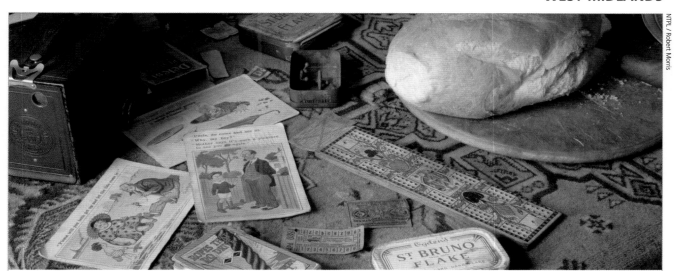

## BACK TO BACKS
### 55–63 HURST STREET, BIRMINGHAM  B5 4TE

www.nationaltrust.org.uk

**Tel:** 0121 666 7671 (Booking line open Tues–Fri, 10am–4pm)
**E-mail:** backtobacks@nationaltrust.org.uk
**Owner:** The National Trust    **Contact:** House & Visitor Services Manager
Take an exciting step back into Birmingham's industrial past by visiting the last remaining courtyard of Back to Back houses in Birmingham. Visitors are taken back in time to the start of the 1840s when Court 15 was both a home and workplace for its many inhabitants. Four houses have been restored to reflect the different time periods and lives of the pelpe who lived there. Experience the sights, sounds and smells of the 1930s sweetshop and see what life was like for George Saunders, a tailor from St Kitts, who came to live and work in Birmingham in the 1950s. The property is a Europa Nostra award winner.

**Location:** MAP 6:O7, OS Ref. SP071 861. In the centre of Birmingham next to the Hippodrome Theatre, within easy walking distance of bus and railway stations.
**Open:** 1 Feb–23 Dec, Tues–Sun, 10am–5pm. Admission is by timed ticket and guided tour only. Open BH Mons, closed following Tues. Please note: During term time property may be closed for use by school groups on Tues, Weds & Thurs mornings. Closed 1–7 September.
**\*Admission:** Adult £5, Child £2.50, Family £12.50. \*includes a voluntary donation but visitors can choose to pay the standard prices displayed at the property and on the website.
🅕 Obligatory. 🔲 🛈

---

## THE BIRMINGHAM BOTANICAL GARDENS AND GLASSHOUSES
### WESTBOURNE ROAD, EDGBASTON, BIRMINGHAM  B15 3TR

www.birminghambotanicalgardens.org.uk

**Tel:** 0121 454 1860    **Fax:** 0121 454 7835
**E-mail:** admin@birminghambotanicalgardens.org.uk
**Owner:** Birmingham Botanical & Horticultural Society    **Contact:** Mrs L Keen
Tropical, Mediterranean and Arid Glasshouses contain a wide range of exotic and economic flora. 15 acres of beautiful gardens with the finest collection of plants in the Midlands. Home of the National Bonsai Collection. Children's adventure playground, aviaries, gallery and sculpture trail.
**Location:** MAP 7:N7, OS Ref. SP048 855. 2m W of city centre. Follow signs to Edgbaston then brown tourist signs.
**Open:** Daily: 9am–Dusk (7pm latest except pre-booked groups). Suns opening time 10am. Closed Christmas Day.
**Admission:** Adult £6.10 (£6.40 on summer Suns & BHs), Conc. £3.60, Family £18 (£19 on summer Suns & BHs). Groups (10+): Adult £5, Conc. £3.20.
🔲 🅕 ♿ 🍴 Licensed. 🅿 🚻 Guide dogs only. 🅰 ❋ 🛈

---

## CASTLE BROMWICH HALL GARDENS
### Chester Road, Castle Bromwich, Birmingham  B36 9BT
**Tel/Fax:** 0121 749 4100   **E-mail:** admin@cbhgt.org.uk
**Owner:** Castle Bromwich Hall & Gardens Trust   **Contact:** Sue Brain
A unique example of 17th and 18th century formal garden design within a 10 acre walled area, comprising historic plants, vegetables, herbs and fruit, with a 19th century holly maze.
**Location:** MAP 7:O7, OS Ref. SP142 898. Off B4114, 4m E of Birmingham city centre, 1m from M6/J5 (exit northbound only). Southbound M6/J6 and follow A38 & A452.
**Open:** 1 Apr–30 Sept: Tue–Thurs, 11am–4.30pm, Café & Shop 1.30–4.15pm. Sats, Suns & BH Mon 1.30–5.30pm, Café & Shop close 5.15pm. Fris 11am–3.30pm, Café & Shop closed. 1 Oct–31 Mar 2008: Tue–Fri, 11.30am–3.30pm, Café & Shop closed.
**Admission:** Summer: Adult £3.50, Child 50p, Concs. £3. Includes printed tour guide. Guided tours normally available. Winter: Adults £3, Child 50p.

---

## COVENTRY CATHEDRAL
### 1 Hill Top, Coventry  CV1 5AB
**Tel:** 024 7652 1200   **Fax:** 024 7652 1220
**E-mail:** information@coventrycathedral.org.uk
**Owner:** Dean & Canons of Coventry Cathedral   **Contact:** The Visits Secretary
The remains of the medieval Cathedral, bombed in 1940, stand beside the new Cathedral by Basil Spence, consecrated in 1962. Modern works of art include a huge tapestry by Graham Sutherland, a stained glass window by John Piper and a bronze sculpture by Epstein. 'Reconciliation' statue by Josefina de Vasconcellos.
**Location:** MAP 7:P7, OS Ref. SP336 790. City centre.
**Open:** Cathedral: All year: 9am–5pm. Groups must book in advance.
**Admission:** Free – donations welcomed.

For rare and unusual plants visit the **plant sales** index on page 564

## HAGLEY HALL

*See page 366 for full page entry.*

### KINVER EDGE AND THE ROCKHOUSES

**Comer Road, Kinver, Nr Stourbridge, Staffordshire  DY7 6HU**

**Tel:** 01384 872553

**Owner:** The National Trust    **Contact:** The Custodian

The famous Holy Austin rockhouses, which were inhabited until the 1950s, have now been restored and are open to visitors at selected times.

**Location:** MAP 7:A8, OS Ref. SO836 836. 4m W of Stourbridge, 4m N of Kidderminster, 1½m W of A449.

**Open:** Kinver Edge: All year, daily: House grounds: 1 Apr–30 Sept; daily, 9am–7pm. 1 Oct–29 Feb 2008, daily, 9am–4pm. Upper Terrace; 4 Apr–29 Mar 2008, Wed, Sat & Sun, 2–4pm. Lower Rockhouses; 3 Mar–25 Nov, Sat & Sun, 2–4pm. Open BH Mons. Lower Rockhouses open for guided tours at other times (between Mar–Nov) by prior arrangement with the Custodian.

**Admission:** Adult £2, Child £1.

### SELLY MANOR

**MAPLE ROAD, BOURNVILLE, WEST MIDLANDS  B30 2AE**

www.bvt.org.uk/sellymanor

**Tel/Fax:** 0121 472 0199   **E-mail:** sellymanor@bvt.org.uk

**Owner:** Bournville Village Trust    **Contact:** Gillian Ellis

A beautiful half-timbered manor house in the heart of the famous Bournville village. The house has been lived in since the 14th century and was rescued from demolition by George Cadbury. It houses furniture dating back several centuries and is surrounded by a delightful typical Tudor garden.

**Location:** MAP 6:O7, OS Ref. SP045 814. N side of Sycamore Road, just E of Linden Road (A4040). 4m SSW of City Centre.

**Open:** All year: Tue–Fri, 10am–5pm. Apr–Sept: Sats, Suns & BHs, 2–5pm. Closed Mons.

**Admission:** Adult £3.50, Child £1.50, Conc. £2, Family £7.50.

Partial. WC. By arrangement. Limited. In grounds, on leads.

See all the properties that are **open all year** in the index on page 580

### WIGHTWICK MANOR

**WIGHTWICK BANK, WOLVERHAMPTON, WEST MIDLANDS  WV6 8EE**

**Tel:** 01902 761400   **Fax:** 01902 764663

**Owner:** The National Trust    **Contact:** The Property Manager

Begun in 1887, the house is a notable example of the influence of William Morris, with many original Morris wallpapers and fabrics. Also of interest are pre-Raphaelite pictures, Kempe glass and De Morgan ware. The 17 acre Victorian/Edwardian garden designed by Thomas Mawson has formal beds, pergola, yew hedges, topiary and terraces, woodland and two pools.

**Location:** MAP 6:N6, OS Ref. SO869 985. 3m W of Wolverhampton, up Wightwick Bank (A454), beside the Mermaid Inn.

**Open:** 1 Mar–22 Dec: Thur–Sat, 12.30–5pm (last entry 4.30pm). Admission by timed ticket. Guided groups through ground floor, freeflow upstairs (min. tour time approx. 1 hr). Also open BH Suns & Mons and Weds in Aug, 12.30–5pm (last entry 4.30pm) – ground floor only, no guided tours. Booked groups Tues & Weds. Garden: Wed–Sat, 11am–6pm; BH Suns & Mons, 11am–6pm.

**\*Admission:** Adult £7.50, Child £3.70. Garden only: £3.70, Child Free. *includes a voluntary donation but visitors can choose to pay the standard prices displayed at the property and on the website.

Ground floor & grounds. P 400 yds. In grounds, on leads.

Birmingham Botanical Gardens

## BROADWAY TOWER
### BROADWAY, WORCESTERSHIRE  WR12 7LB

www.broadwaytower.co.uk

**Tel:** 01386 852390  **Fax:** 01386 858038  **E-mail:** info@broadwaytower.co.uk
**Owner:** Broadway Tower Country Park Ltd  **Contact:** Annette Gorton
Broadway Tower is a unique historic building on top of the Cotswold ridge, having been built by the 6th Earl of Coventry in the late 1790s. Its architecture, the fascinating views as well as its exhibitions on famous owners and occupants (including William Morris) make the Tower a "must" for all visitors to the Cotswolds. The Tower is surrounded by 35 acres of parkland, picnic/ BBQ facilities. A complete family day out.
**Location:** MAP 6:O10, OS Ref. SP115 362. ½m SW of the A44 Evesham to Oxford Rd. 1½m E of Broadway.
**Open:** 1 Apr–31 Oct: daily, 10.30am–5pm. Nov–Mar: Sats & Suns (weather permitting), 11am–3pm.
**Admission:** Adult £3.80, Child £2.30, Conc. £3. Family (2+2) £10. Group rate on request.
🖻🖻 WC. 🖻🍴 🅿 🖻🖾 In grounds, on leads. 🏵

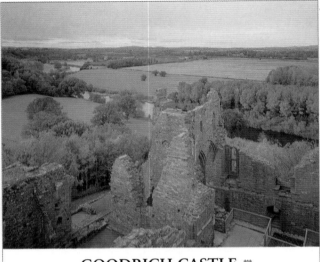

## GOODRICH CASTLE ♯
### ROSS-ON-WYE  HR9 6HY

www.english-heritage.org.uk/goodrich

**Tel:** 01600 890538
**Owner:** English Heritage  **Contact:** Visitor Operations Team
This magnificent red sandstone castle is remarkably complete with a 12th century keep and extensive remains from 13th & 14th centuries. From the battlements there are fine views over the Wye Valley to Symonds Yat. Marvel at the maze of small rooms and the 'murder holes'.
**Location:** MAP 6:L11, OS162 Ref. SO577 200. 5m S of Ross-on-Wye, off A40.
**Open:** 1 Apr–31 Oct: daily, 10am–5pm (Jun–Aug 6pm). 1 Nov–29 Feb: Wed–Sun, 10am–4pm. 1–20 Mar: daily, 10am–5pm. Closed 24–26 Dec & 1 Jan.
**Admission:** Adult £4.90, Child £2.50, Conc. £3.70, Family £12.30. 15% discount for groups (11+).
ℹ WC. 🖻🖻🅿🖾🏵🖻

## CROOME PARK 🍂
### ESTATE OFFICE, SEVERN STOKE, WORCESTERSHIRE  WR8 9JS

www.nationaltrust.org.uk

**Tel:** 01905 371006  **Fax:** 01905 371090  **E-mail:** croomepark@nationaltrust.org.uk
**Owner:** The National Trust  **Contact:** The Property Manager
Croome was 'Capability' Brown's first complete landscape, making his reputation and establishing a new parkland aesthetic which became universally adopted. The elegant park buildings are mostly by Robert Adam and James Wyatt. 2006 saw the completion of the first phase of restoration – a 10 year Heritage Lottery Funded programme that has replanted over 14 acres of shrubbery and thousands of trees, dredged the lake and river, reinstated miles of paths and restored elegant parkland buildings. Restoration work will continue throughout 2007.
**Location:** MAP 6:N9, OS150, SO878 448. 3m E of Severn Stoke and 4m W of Pershore.
**Open:** Park & Church: 2 Mar–29 Apr: Wed–Sun, 10am–5.30pm. 30 Apr–2 Sept: daily, 10am–5.30pm. 5 Sept–28 Oct: Wed–Sun, 10am–5.30pm. Nov & Dec: Weekends only, 10am–4pm. Open BH Mons. Last admission 30 min before park closes. Church open in association with The Churches Conservation Trust.
**\*Admission:** Adult £4.40, Child £2.20, Family £10.80. \*includes a voluntary donation but visitors can choose to pay the standard prices displayed at the property and on the website.
🖻🖻🖻🖻🅿🖾🖻

## THE GREYFRIARS 🍂
### WORCESTER  WR1 2LZ

www.nationaltrust.org.uk

**Tel:** 01905 23571  **E-mail:** greyfriars@nationaltrust.org.uk
**Owner:** The National Trust  **Contact:** The Custodian
Built about 1480 next to a Franciscan friary in the centre of medieval Worcester, this timber-framed house has 17th and late 18th century additions. It was rescued from demolition at the time of the Second World War and was carefully restored. The panelled rooms have noteworthy textiles and interesting furniture. An archway leads through to a delightful walled garden.
**Location:** MAP 6:N9, OS150, SO852 546. Friar Street, in centre of Worcester.
**Open:** 1 Mar–15 Dec: Wed–Sat (also Suns 1 Jul–26 Aug), 1–5pm. Open BH Mons.
**\*Admission:** Adult £4, Child £2, Family £10. Booked Groups (8+) £3.10. \*includes a voluntary donation but visitors can choose to pay the standard prices displayed at the property and on the website
🖻🖻🖻 Out of hours. 🖻🖻

## HANBURY HALL
### DROITWICH, WORCESTERSHIRE WR9 7EA
www.nationaltrust.org.uk

**Tel:** 01527 821214   **Fax:** 01527 821251   **E-mail:** hanburyhall@nationaltrust.org.uk
**Owner:** The National Trust   **Contact:** The Property Manager
Completed in 1701, this homely William & Mary-style house is famed for its fine painted ceilings and staircase, and has other fascinating features including an orangery, ice house, pavilions and working mushroom house. The stunning 8 hectare (20 acre) garden, recreated in keeping with the period of the house, is surrounded by 160 hectares (395 acres) of parkland, with beautiful views over the surrounding countryside.
**Location:** MAP 6:N8, OS150, SO943 637. 4½m E of Droitwich, 4m SE M5/J5.

**Open:** 3–18 Mar: Sat & Sun; 19 Mar–31 Oct: Sat–Wed, 11am–5.30pm (House 1–5pm). Park/Tearoom/Shop only: 3 Nov–16 Dec, Sat & Sun, 11am–4pm. Garden, Tearoom & Shop: daily, Jul–Aug.

**\*Admission:** House & Garden: Adult £6.80, Child £3.40, Family £17. Garden & Park only: Adult £4.50, Child £2.25, Family £11. Park only (Nov–Dec): Adult £2.70, Child £1.35, Family £6.75. *includes a voluntary donation but visitors can choose to pay the standard prices displayed at the property and on the website

⬚ 🚻 🍵 ♿ Partial. WC. 🐶 🎟 For pre-booked groups. 🅿 ♿ Guide dogs only. 🔺 🐶

## HARTLEBURY CASTLE
### HARTLEBURY, Nr KIDDERMINSTER DY11 7XZ

**Tel:** 01299 250416   **Fax:** 01299 251890   **E-mail:** museum@worcestershire.gov.uk
**Owner:** The Church Commissioners   **Contact:** The County Museum
Hartlebury Castle has been home to the Bishops of Worcester for over a thousand years. The principal State Rooms – the medieval Great Hall and the Saloon – contain period furniture, fine plasterwork and episcopal portraits. In the Castle's North Wing the Worcestershire County Museum brings the county's past to life through a wide variety of exhibitions and a regular events programme.
**Location:** MAP 6:N8, OS Ref. SO389 710. N side of B4193, 2m E of Stourport, 4m S of Kidderminster.
**Open:** 1 Feb–23 Dec: Tue–Fri, 10am–5pm. Sat, Sun & BHs, 11am–5pm. Closed Mons (except BHs) & Good Friday.
**Admission:** Adults £3, Conc. £1.50, Family (2+3) £8. Children under 5yrs Free. (2006 prices.)

⬚ ♿ 🐶 🎟 For pre-booked groups. 🅿 ⬛ ♿ Guide dogs only. 🐶

Little Malvern Court

## HARVINGTON HALL
### HARVINGTON, KIDDERMINSTER, WORCESTERSHIRE DY104LR
www.harvingtonhall.com

**Tel:** 01562 777846  **Fax:** 01562 777190
**E-mail:** harvingtonhall@btconnect.com
**Owner:** Roman Catholic Archdiocese of Birmingham  **Contact:** The Hall Manager
Harvington Hall is a moated, medieval and Elizabethan manor house. Many of the rooms still have their original Elizabethan wall paintings and the Hall contains the finest series of priest hides in the country. A full programme of events throughout the year including outdoor plays, craft fairs, living history weekends and a pilgrimage is available.

**Location:** MAP 6:N8, OS Ref. SO877 745. On minor road, ½ m NE of A450/A448 crossroads at Mustow Green. 3m SE of Kidderminster.
**Open:** Mar & Oct: Sats & Suns; Apr–Sept: Wed–Sun & BH Mons (closed Good Fri), 11.30am–5pm. Open throughout the year for pre-booked groups and schools. Occasionally the Hall may be closed for a private function.
**Admission:** Adult £5, Child £3.50, OAP £4.30, Family £14.50. Garden: £1.
⊡ Ⓣ Ⓖ Partial. Ⓟ Limited for coaches. ▨ ▧ Guide dogs only. ✳ ♨

---

### HAWFORD DOVECOTE ⅏
**Hawford, Worcestershire**
**Tel:** 01527 821214  **www.nationaltrust.org.uk**
**Owner:** The National Trust  **Contact:** Property Manager
A 16th century half-timbered dovecote.
**Location:** MAP 6:N9, OS Ref. SO846 607. 3m N of Worcester, ½m E of A449.
**Open:** 1 Apr–31 Oct: daily, 9am–6pm or sunset if earlier. Other times by prior appointment.
**Admission:** £1.

### LEIGH COURT BARN ⌗
**Worcester**
**Tel:** 01926 852078
**Owner:** English Heritage  **Contact:** Visitor Operations Administrative Assistant
Magnificent 14th century timber-framed barn built for the monks of Pershore Abbey. It is the largest of its kind in Britain.
**Location:** MAP 6:M9, OS150 Ref. SO783 535. 5m W of Worcester on unclassified road off A4103.
**Open:** 1 Apr–30 Sept: Thur–Sun & BH Mons, 10am–5pm.
**Admission:** Free.
▧

### LITTLE MALVERN COURT ⋔
**Nr Malvern, Worcestershire  WR14 4JN**
**Tel:** 01684 892988  **Fax:** 01684 893057
**Owner:** Trustees of the late T M Berington  **Contact:** Mrs T M Berington
Prior's Hall, associated rooms and cells, c1480, of former Benedictine Monastery. Formerly attached to, and forming part of the Little Malvern Priory Church which may also be visited. It has an oak-framed roof, 5-bay double-collared roof, with two tiers of cusped windbraces. Library. Collections of religious vestments, embroideries and paintings. Gardens: 10 acres of former monastic grounds with spring bulbs, blossom, old fashioned roses and shrubs. Access to Hall only by flight of steps.
**Location:** MAP 6:M9, OS Ref. SO769 403. 3m S of Great Malvern on Upton-on-Severn Road (A4104).
**Open:** 18 Apr–19 Jul: Weds & Thurs, 2.15–5pm. 25 Mar & 7 May for NGS: 2.15–5pm. Last admission 4.30pm.
**Admission:** House & Garden: Adult £5.50, Child £2, Garden only: Adult £4.50, Child £1. Groups must book, max 35.
Ⓖ Garden (partial). Ⓕ ▧

### MADRESFIELD COURT
**Madresfield, Malvern  WR13 5AU**
**Tel:** 01905 830680  **E-mail:** madrescourt@clara.co.uk
**Owner:** The Trustees of Madresfield Estate  **Contact:** Mrs Jane Facer
Elizabethan and Victorian house with medieval origins. Fine contents. Extensive gardens and arboretum.
**Location:** MAP 6:M9, OS Ref. SO809 474. 6m SW of Worcester. 1½ m SE of A449. 2m NE of Malvern.
**Open:** Guided tours: 11 Apr–26 Jul: mostly Wed & Thur, also Sats 21 Apr, 19 May & 14 Jul: 10.45am & 2.30pm. Numbers are restricted and prior booking, by telephone to Mrs Jane Facer, is strongly recommended to avoid disappointment.
**Admission:** £9.
Ⓕ Obligatory. ▧

Croome Park, Severn Stoke

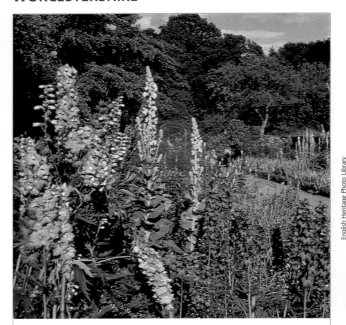

## SPETCHLEY PARK GARDENS

**SPETCHLEY PARK, WORCESTER  WR5 1RS**

www.spetchleygardens.co.uk

**Tel:** 01453 810303  **Fax:** 01453 511915  **E-mail:** hb@spetchleygardens.co.uk
**Owner:** Spetchley Gardens Charitable Trust  **Contact:** Mr R J Berkeley
This lovely 30 acre private garden contains a large collection of trees, shrubs and plants, many rare or unusual. A garden full of secrets, every corner reveals some new vista, some treasure of the plant world. The exuberant planting and the peaceful walks make this an oasis of beauty, peace and quiet. Deer Park close by.
**Location:** MAP 6:N9, OS Ref. SO895 540. 3m E of Worcester on A44. Leave M5/J6/J7.
**Open:** 21 Mar–30 Sept: Wed–Sun & BHs, 11am–6pm. Oct: Sats & Suns, 11am–4pm. (last admission 1hr before closing).
**Admission:** Adult £6, Child (under 16yrs) Free. Groups (25+): Adult £5.50. Adult Season Ticket £25.

## THE TUDOR HOUSE MUSEUM

**16 Church Street, Upton-on-Severn, Worcestershire  WR8 0HT**
**Tel:** 01684 592447
**Owner:** Mrs Lavender Beard  **Contact:** Mrs Wilkinson
Upton past and present, exhibits of local history.
**Location:** MAP 6:N10, OS Ref. SO852 406. Centre of Upton-on-Severn, 7m SE of Malvern by B4211.
**Open:** Apr–Oct: daily 2–5pm, inc BH. Winter: Suns only, 2–4pm. Groups by arrangement (out of hours if requested).
**Admission:** Adult £1, Conc. 50p, Family £2.

---

*giftaid it* This year, some properties will be operating the Gift Aid on Entry scheme at their admission points. Where the scheme is operating, visitors are offered a choice between paying the standard admission price or paying the 'Gift Aid Admission' which includes a voluntary donation of at least 10%. Gift Aid Admissions enable the charity to reclaim tax on the whole amount paid* - an extra 28% - potentially a very significant boost to property funds. Money raised from paying visitors in this way will go towards restoration projects at the property and will be very welcome.
Where shown, the admission prices are inclusive of the 10% voluntary donation where properties are operating the Gift Aid on Entry scheme, but both the standard admission price and the Gift Aid Admission will be displayed at the property and on their website.

*Gift Aid donations must be supported by a valid Gift Aid declaration and a Gift Aid declaration can only cover donations made by an individual for him/herself or for him/herself and members of his/her family.

---

## WICHENFORD DOVECOTE

**Wichenford, Worcestershire**
**Tel:** 01527 821214  **www.nationaltrust.org.uk**
**Owner:** The National Trust  **Contact:** Property Manager
A 17th century half-timbered black and white dovecote.
**Location:** MAP 6:M8, OS Ref. SO788 598. 5½ m NW of Worcester, N of B4204.
**Open:** 1 Apr–31 Oct: daily, 9am–6pm or sunset if earlier. Other times by appointment.
**Admission:** £1.

---

*English Heritage Photo Library*

## WITLEY COURT & GARDENS

**GREAT WITLEY, WORCESTER  WR6 6JT**

www.english-heritage.org.uk/witleycourt

**Tel:** 01299 896636
**Owner:** English Heritage  **Contact:** Visitor Operations Team
The spectacular ruins of a once great house. An earlier Jacobean manor house, converted in the 19th century into an Italianate mansion, with porticoes by John Nash. The adjoining church, by James Gibbs, has a remarkable 18th century baroque interior. The gardens, William Nesfield's 'Monster Work' were equally elaborate and contained immense fountains, which survive today. The largest is the Perseus and Andromeda Fountain which has been restored and now fires daily from April – October, contact the site for details and timings. The landscaped grounds, parterres, fountains and woodlands have recently been restored to their former glory. The Woodland Walks in the North Park include various species of tree and shrub acquired from all over the world.
**Location:** MAP 6:M8, OS150, SO769 649. 10m NW of Worcester off A443.
**Open:** 1 Apr–31 Oct: daily, 10am–5pm (Jun–Aug 6pm). 1 Nov–20 Mar: Wed–Sun, 10am–4pm (Mar 5pm). Closed 24–26 Dec & 1 Jan.
**Admission:** Adult £5.40, Child £2.70, OAP £4.10, Family £13.50. 15% discount for groups (11+).
i Visitor welcome point. Grounds. WC.
Tel for details.

Croome Park, Severn Stoke

**Above:** Whitby Abbey ©English Heritage Photo Library
**Right:** Beningbrough Hall

# Yorkshire & The Humber

*York contains reminders of its medieval origins but is as well known for its elegant Jacobean and Georgian architecture. Within easy reach are grand palaces such as Castle Howard and Harewood House, but there are also more modest gems to be seen such as Sion Hill Hall, and the gardens at RHS Harlow Carr are amongst the finest in Britain.*

# BRAMHAM PARK

www.bramhampark.co.uk

Bramham Park is the stunning family home of the Lane Fox family, who are direct descendants of Robert Benson, the founder of Bramham over 300 years ago. The gardens extend to some 66 acres and, with the Pleasure Grounds, extend to over 100 acres.

The focus at Bramham has always been the landscape (the house was merely built as a 'villa' from which to admire it). Inspiration for the design of the Garden at Bramham was French and formal, but the manner in which it was adapted to the national landscape is relaxed and entirely English. It is completely original and few other parks of this period survive; none on the scale and complexity of Bramham. It

is a rare and outstanding example of the formal style of the late 17th century and early 18th century.

Bramham is a garden of walks and vistas, architectural features and reflecting water. A broad vista stretches away at an angle from the house and a number of other *allées* have focal points – temples and vistas. This creates an experience of anticipation when walking around the grounds.

The house, gardens and surrounding parkland make an ideal venue for events, private dinners, corporate entertaining, product launches and filming.

 Grounds. WC.
Dogs on leads.

visit hudsons guide online

# BRODSWORTH HALL & GARDENS ⊞

www.english-heritage.org.uk/yorkshire

This once opulent Victorian Hall offers a fascinating insight into the changing fortunes of a previously wealthy Victorian family, with many original fixtures and fittings still in place.

The 15 acres of garden, a rare survival from the Victorian Age, have been replanted to their 1860s heyday. Against a backdrop of enchanting features like the summerhouse, pleasure grounds, fernery, pet cemetery and fountain centre-piece, the pathways wind through carpets of spring snowdrops, the dazzling laburnum arch, rainbows of period summer bedding and the seasonal delight of winter evergreens, all revealing the fashions and desires of the Victorian country gentry.

■ **Owner**
English Heritage

■ **Contact**
Visitor Operations Team
Brodsworth Hall
Brodsworth
Nr Doncaster
Yorkshire DN5 7XJ
**Tel:** 01302 724969
(infoline)
**Fax:** 01302 337165
**E-mail:** customers@
english-heritage.org.uk

■ **Location**
**MAP 11:B12**
**OS Ref. SE507 071**

In Brodsworth, 5m NW of Doncaster off A635. Use A1(M)/J37.

**Rail:** Doncaster.

■ **Opening Times**
**Summer**

**House**
3 April–30 September
Tue–Sun & BHs,
1–5pm.

October, Sats & Suns,
12 noon–4pm.

**Gardens & Tearoom**
1 April–31 October
Daily, 10am–5.30pm.

**Winter**

**Gardens, Tearoom, Shop & Servants' Wing**

1 November–20 March
Sats & Suns, 10am–4pm.

Closed 24–26 December
& 1 January.

Last admission ½ hr
before closing.

■ **Admission***
**House & Gardens**
Adult                £6.60
Child (5–15yrs)      £3.30
Child (under 5yrs)   Free
Conc.                £5.00

Groups (11+) 15%
discount

*Free admission for tour
leaders and coach drivers.

**Gardens only**
Adult                £4.60
Child (5–15yrs)      £2.30
Child (under 5yrs)   Free
Conc.                £3.50

ℹ️ Exhibitions about the family, the servants and the gardens. WCs.

♿ Most of house is accessible. WCs.

☕ Seating for 70.

🚶 Groups must book. Booked coach parties: 10am–1pm.

🅿️ 220 cars and 3 coaches. Free.

📖 Education Centre. Free if booked in advance.

### ■ Owner
Burton Constable
Foundation

### ■ Contact
Mrs Helen Dewson
Burton Constable
Skirlaugh
East Yorkshire
HU11 4LN

**Tel:** 01964 562400
**Fax:** 01964 563229
**Email:** helendewson
@btconnect.com

### ■ Location
**MAP 11:E10**
**OS Ref TA 193 369**

From Beverley (14 miles)
take A1035 Bridlington
road, turn right at White
Cross roundabout. A165
towards Hull, follow
Historic House signs from
Skirlaugh. From Hull (10
miles) follow A1033
towards Hedon, turn left
at Saltend roundabout,
follow sign to Preston and
Sproatley or A165
towards Bridlington,
follow Historic House
signs from Skirlaugh.

### ■ Opening Times
**Hall**
31 March–28 October:
Sat–Thur, 1–5pm.

**Grounds and Tearoom**
12.30–5pm.

Last admission 4pm.

### ■ Admission
**Hall & Grounds**
| | |
|---|---|
| Adult | £5.50 |
| Child | £2.50 |
| OAP | £5.00 |
| Family | £12.50 |
| Groups (15–60) | £4.50 |

Connoisseur Study Visits
prices on request.

**Grounds only**
| | |
|---|---|
| Adult | £1.50 |
| Child | 75p |

### ■ Special Events
**April 7–9**
Easter Egg Parkland Trail

**June 3**
Classic Car Rally

**July 8**
Open Air Theatre: Far
from the Madding Crowd.

**July 15**
Country Fair

**October 31**
Halloween Ghost Tours

# BURTON CONSTABLE HALL 🏛
www.burtonconstable.com

One of the most fascinating country houses to survive with its historic collections, Burton Constable Hall is a large Elizabethan mansion set in 300 acres of parkland with 30 rooms open to the public. The interiors of faded splendour are filled with fine furniture, paintings and sculpture, a library of 5,000 books and a remarkable 18th century 'Cabinet of Curiosities'. Occupied by the Constable family for over 400 years, the house still maintains the atmosphere of a home.

Outside there are pleasure grounds, a delightful 18th century Orangery ornamented with coadestone and a large stable block. The ancient deer park was landscaped by 'Capability' Brown in the 1770s and provides extensive parkland and lakeside walks.

**New for 2007**

• The on-going programme of conserving historic interiors means that there is something new to see in the house each year.

• The historic skeleton of a huge sperm whale that was erected in the park at Burton Constable in the early 19th century, and was the source of inspiration for Herman Melville's famous novel *Moby Dick*, will form a dramatic display in the Great Hall.

• New interpretation centre for the grounds, park and estate.

• Exhibition: *Work and Play: Life on the Yorkshire Country House Estate.*

• Parkland/Woodland trail with sculptural way-markers providing instructive fun for all the family.

  No photography in house. Free summer workshops: Art, Textiles & Creative Writing. Free of charge summer workshops: Art, Textiles and Creative Writing

 WC.

 In grounds on leads.

# CASTLE HOWARD

www.castlehoward.co.uk

In a dramatic setting between two lakes with extensive gardens and impressive fountains, this 18th century Palace was designed by Sir John Vanbrugh in 1699. Undoubtedly the finest private residence in Yorkshire, it was built for Charles Howard, 3rd Earl of Carlisle, whose descendants still live here.

With its painted and gilded dome reaching 80ft into the Yorkshire sky, this impressive house has collections of antique furniture, porcelain and sculpture, while its fabulous collection of paintings is dominated by the famous Holbein portraits of Henry VIII and the Duke of Norfolk.

Designed on a heroic scale covering 1,000 acres. The gardens include memorable sights such as the Temple of the Four Winds and the Mausoleum, the New River Bridge and the restored waterworks of the South Lake, Cascade, Waterfall and Prince of Wales Fountain. The walled garden has collections of old and modern roses.

Ray Wood, acknowledged by the Royal Botanic Collection, Kew, as a *"rare botanical jewel"* has a unique collection of rare trees, shrubs, rhododendrons, magnolias and azaleas.

ℹ️ Outdoor tours, events, concerts, theatre, exhibitions, adventure playground, plant centre, farm shop, chocolate shop, gift & book shops. Gift fairs, product launches, garden parties, firework displays, banqueting and other events. Suitable for helicopter landing. Used as a film location. No photography in the House unless prior permission is granted.

🛍️

❄️

🍷 Booked private parties and receptions, min. 25.

♿ Transport equipped for wheelchairs. Wheelchair lift in House to main floor. WCs.

🍽️ Four cafeterias (Stable Courtyard Café open all year).

🚶 Guides posted throughout House. Private tours and lectures by arrangement covering architecture, history, art, collections, House including tours of recently refurbished rooms.

🅿️ 400 cars, 20 coaches.

🎒 1:10 teacher/pupil ratio required. KS2&3 education pack. Special interest: architecture, art, history, wildlife, horticulture.

❄️

## Owner
The Hon Simon Howard

## Contact
Visitor Services
Castle Howard
York, North Yorks
YO60 7DA

**Tel:** 01653 648333
**Fax:** 01653 648529
**E-mail:** house@
castlehoward.co.uk

## Location
**MAP 11:C8**
**OS Ref. SE716 701**

Approaching from S, A64 to Malton, on entering Malton, take Castle Howard road via Coneysthorpe village.
Or from A64 following signs to Castle Howard via the Carrmire Gate
9' wide by 10' high.

York 15m (20 mins), A64.
From London: M1/J32, M18 to A1(M) to A64, York/Scarborough Road, 3½ hrs.

**Train:** London Kings Cross to York 1hr. 50 mins. York to Malton Station 30 mins.

**Bus:** Service and tour buses from York Station.

## Opening Times
**Summer**
House:
1 March–4 November
Daily, 11am–4pm
(last admission).

Gardens: All year, daily from 10am (except Christmas Day).

Stable Courtyard (gift shops, farm shop, chocolate shop, plant centre, café):
All year, daily, 10am–5pm, free admission.

Access to Pretty Wood Pyramid 1 July–31 August. Special tours to newly restored rooms in the house are available by arrangement.
For more information please contact Castle Howard Estate Office
on 01653 648444.

## Admission
**Summer**
**House & Garden**
| | |
|---|---|
| Adult | £10.00 |
| Child (4–16yrs) | £6.50 |
| Under 4yrs | Free |
| Conc. | £9.00 |

**Garden only**
| | |
|---|---|
| Adult | £7.50 |
| Child (4–16yrs) | £5.00 |
| Under 4yrs | Free |
| Conc. | £7.00 |

**Winter 5 Nov–29 Feb**
**Gardens**
| | |
|---|---|
| Adult | £4.00 |
| Child (4–16yrs) | £2.00 |
| Under 4yrs | Free |
| Conc. | £4.00 |

## Conference/Function

| ROOM | SIZE | MAX CAPACITY |
|---|---|---|
| Long Gallery | 197' x 24' | 280 |
| Grecian Hall | 40' x 40' | 160 |

©NTPL/Matthew Antrobus

### ■ Owner
The National Trust

### ■ Contact
The National Trust
Fountains Abbey
and Studley Royal
Ripon
North Yorkshire
HG4 3DY

**Tel:** 01765 608888
**Fax:** 01765 601002
**E-mail:** info@
fountainsabbey.org.uk

### ■ Location
**MAP 10:P8**
**OS Ref. SE275 700**

Abbey entrance:
4m W of Ripon off
B6265. 8m W of A1.

**Rail:** Harrogate 12m.

**Bus:** Regular
season service
tel: 0870 608 2608
for details.

### ■ Opening Times
March–October
Daily: 10am–5pm.

November–February
Daily: 10am–4pm.

Closed 24/25 December,
& Fridays from Nov–Jan.

Deer Park: All year,
daily during daylight
(closed 24/25 December).

### ■ Admission
| | |
|---|---|
| Adult | £7.50 |
| Child* (5–16yrs) | £4.00 |
| Family | £20.00 |

Groups (15+)
| | |
|---|---|
| Adult | £6.50 |
| Child* (5–16yrs) | £3.50 |

Groups (31+)
| | |
|---|---|
| Adult | £6.00 |
| Child* (5–16yrs) | £3.00 |

Group discount
applicable only with
prior booking.

Group visits and
disabled visitors, please
telephone in advance,
01765 643197.

*NT, EH Members &
Under 5s Free.

The Abbey is owned by
the National Trust and
maintained by English
Heritage. St Mary's
Church is owned by
English Heritage and
managed by the
National Trust.

# FOUNTAINS ABBEY & STUDLEY ROYAL
## www.fountainsabbey.org.uk

One of the most remarkable sites in Europe, sheltered in a secluded valley, Fountains Abbey and Studley Royal, a World Heritage Site, encompasses the spectacular remains of a 12th century Cistercian abbey with one of the finest surviving monastic watermills in Britain, an Elizabethan mansion, and one of the best surviving examples of a Georgian green water garden. Elegant ornamental lakes, avenues, temples and cascades provide a succession of unforgettable eye-catching vistas in an atmosphere of peace and tranquillity. St Mary's Church, built by William Burges in the 19th century, provides a dramatic focal point to the medieval deer park with over 500 deer. Exhibitions in Fountains Hall, Swanley Grange and the Mill.

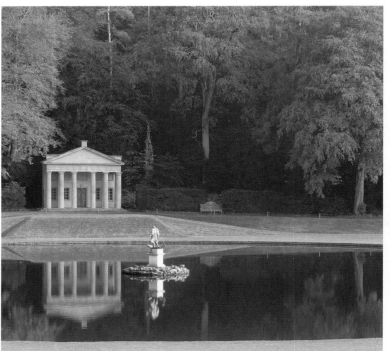

**i** Events held throughout the year. Exhibitions. Seminar facilities. Outdoor concerts, meetings, activity days, walks.

Two shops.

Dinners.

Free Batricars & wheelchairs, please book, tel. 01765 643185. 3-wheel Batricars not permitted due to terrain. Tours for visually impaired, please book. WC.

Groups please book, discounted rates. Licensed.

Licensed.

Free, but seasonal. Groups (please book on 01765 643197), please use Visitor Centre entrance.

Drivers must book groups.

In grounds, on leads.

Fountains Hall, an Elizabethan Mansion is an ideal setting for weddings. For details or a Wedding pack tel: 01765 643198.

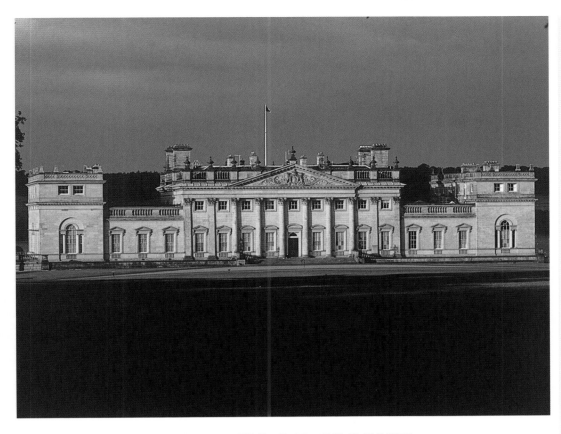

# HAREWOOD HOUSE

www.harewood.org

Harewood House is the magnificent Yorkshire home of the Queen's cousin, the Earl of Harewood. Nestling in 'Capability' Brown landscaped surrounds, Harewood is one of the great Treasure Houses of England and is renowned for its magnificent architecture and outstanding art collections. Designed by John Carr and completed in 1772, the House features exquisite interiors by Robert Adam, was furnished throughout by Thomas Chippendale, contains world-class art collections, including watercolours by J M W Turner, who stayed at Harewood under the patronage of Edward Lascelles; family portraits by Gainsborough and Sir Joshua Reynolds; and Renaissance masterpieces.

Steeped in history, Royal Family memorabilia recalls Lord Harewood's mother, HRH Princess Mary, the Princess Royal, who lived at Harewood from 1929 until her death in 1965. A permanent exhibition, 'Below stairs: Harewood's Hidden Collections', includes many items from throughout Princess Mary's life, as well as giving public access to previously unseen corridors and rooms, providing a fascinating glimpse into the hidden world of the servants' domain.

Harewood's stunning gardens enfold lakeside and woodland walks, a Rock Garden, Walled Garden and the restored Parterre Terrace. The Lakeside Bird Garden contains around 100 species of threatened and exotic birds as well as popular favourites, penguins and flamingos.

Throughout the season Harewood plays host to many special events, including concerts, craft festivals and car rallies, and features a programme of exhibitions within the House.

### ■ Owner
The Earl of Harewood

### ■ Contact
Harewood House Trust
Harewood
Leeds
West Yorkshire
LS17 9LG

**Tel:** 0113 2181010
**Fax:** 0113 2181002
**E-mail:** info@
harewood.org

### ■ Location
**MAP 10:P10**
**OS Ref. SE311 446**

A1 N or S to Wetherby. A659 via Collingham, Harewood is on A61 between Harrogate and Leeds. Easily reached from A1, M1, M62 and M18. Half an hour from York, 15 mins from centre of Leeds or Harrogate.

**Rail:** Leeds Station 7m.

**Bus:** No. 36 from Leeds or Harrogate.

### ■ Opening Times
**House**
16 March–28 October: Daily, 11am–4pm.

**Grounds**
9 February–16 December: Daily, 10am–6pm.

Please call for opening times of specific areas.

### ■ Admission
**All attractions***
Adult          £11.30
Child/Student    £6.50
OAP           £10.00
Family         £37.70

**Bird Garden, Grounds, & Adventure Playground**
Adult           £8.80
Child/Student    £5.90
OAP            £7.95
Family         £32.25

Groups (15+): please telephone for details.

*Prices are for Mon–Fri. Prices on weekends & BH Mons are slightly higher.

**i** Marquees can be accommodated, concerts and product launches. No photography in the House.

Ideal for corporate entertaining including drinks receptions, buffets and wedding receptions. Specific rooms available.

**&** Visitors may alight at entrance. Parking in allocated areas. Most facilities accessible. Wheelchair available at House and Bird Garden. WC. Special concessions apply to disabled groups. Some steep inclines.

Licensed.

 Licensed.

**P** Cars 400 yds from house. 50+ coaches 500 yds from house. Drivers to verify in advance.

Lectures by arrangement. Daily free talks.

Audio tour of house available.

Sandford Award for Education.

 Dogs on leads in grounds, guide dogs only in house.

### Conference/Function

| ROOM | MAX CAPACITY |
|---|---|
| State Dining Room | 32 |
| Gallery | 96 |
| Courtyard | 120 |

### ■ Owner
Mr Richard Compton

### ■ Contact
The Administrator
Newby Hall
Ripon
North Yorkshire
HG4 5AE

**Tel:** 01423 322583
Information Hotline:
0845 450 4068
**Fax:** 01423 324452
**E-mail:**
info@newbyhall.com

### ■ Location
**MAP 11:A8**
**OS Ref. SE348 675**

Midway between London
and Edinburgh, 4m W of
A1, towards Ripon. S of
Skelton 2m NW of (A1)
Boroughbridge.
4m SE of Ripon.

**Taxi:** Ripon Taxi Rank
01765 601283.

**Bus:** On Ripon–York
route.

### ■ Opening Times
**Summer**
**House***
1 April–1 October

April, May, June &
September:
Tues–Sun & BH Mons;
July–August: Daily
12 noon–5pm.
(The House will be closed
14/15 July.)
Last admission 4.30pm.
* Areas of the House can
be closed to the public
from time to time, please
check website for details.

**Garden**
Dates as House,
11am–5.30pm.
Last admission 5pm.

**Winter**
October–end March
Closed.

### ■ Admission
**House & Garden**
| | |
|---|---|
| Adult | £9.50 |
| Child/Disabled | £6.60 |
| OAP | £8.50 |

| | |
|---|---|
| Group (15+) | |
| Adult/Conc | £7.70 |
| Child/Disabled | £6.20 |

| | |
|---|---|
| Family (2+2) | £30.00 |
| Family (2+3) | £36.00 |

**Garden only**
| | |
|---|---|
| Adult | £7.00 |
| Child/Disabled | £5.50 |
| OAP | £6.00 |

| | |
|---|---|
| Group (15+) | |
| Adult | £6.00 |
| Child (4–16yrs) | £5.00 |

| | |
|---|---|
| Family (2+2) | £23.00 |
| Family (2+3) | £29.00 |

### ■ Conference/Function

| ROOM | SIZE | MAX CAPACITY |
|---|---|---|
| Grantham Room | 90' x 20' | 200 |

# NEWBY HALL & GARDENS
www.newbyhall.com

The home of Richard and Lucinda Compton, Newby Hall is one of England's renowned Adam houses. In the 1760s William Weddell, an ancestor of the Comptons, acquired a magnificent collection of Ancient Roman sculpture and Gobelins tapestries. He commissioned Robert Adam to alter the original Wren designed house and Thomas Chippendale to make furniture. The result is a perfect example of the Georgian 'Age of Elegance' with the atmosphere and ambience of a family home.

### Gardens
25 acres of stunning award-winning gardens contain rare and beautiful shrubs and plants, including the National collection of the Genus Cornus (Dogwoods). Newby's famous double herbaceous borders, framed by great bastions of yew hedges, make the perfect walkway to the River Ure. Formal gardens such as the Autumn and Rose Garden, the tranquillity of Sylvia's Garden and a tropical garden make Newby an inspiring and exciting place to explore. Walking through the curved pergolas leads to the Victorian rock garden, which is an enchanting magical space for all ages. The gardens feature an exciting children's adventure garden and miniature railway. From 1st June there is an annual exhibition of contemporary sculptures in the mature woodland.

**i** Suitable for filming and for special events, craft and country fairs, vehicle rallies etc, promotions and lectures. No indoor photography. Allow a full day for viewing house and gardens.

**Y** Wedding receptions & special functions.

**♿** 6 wheelchairs available. Access to ground floor of house and key areas in gardens. WC.

**✕ ¶** Garden restaurant, teas, hot and cold meals. Booked groups in Grantham Room. Menus/rates on request.

**P** Ample. Hard standing for coaches.

**▥** Welcome. Rates on request. Grantham Room for use as wet weather base subject to availability. Woodland discovery walk, adventure gardens and train rides on 10¼" gauge railway.

**🐕** Guide dogs only.

# RIPLEY CASTLE

www.ripleycastle.co.uk

Ripley Castle has been the home of the Ingilby family for twenty-six generations and Sir Thomas and Lady Ingilby together with their five children continue the tradition. The guided tours are amusing and informative, following the lives and loves of one family for over 670 years and how they have been affected by events in English history. The Old Tower dates from 1555 and houses splendid armour, books, panelling and a Priest's Secret Hiding Place, together with fine paintings, china, furnishings and chandeliers collected by the family over the centuries. The extensive Victorian Walled Gardens have been transformed and are a colourful delight through every season. In the Spring you can appreciate 150,000 flowering bulbs which create a blaze of colour through the woodland walks, and also the National Hyacinth Collection whose scent is breathtaking. The restored Hot Houses have an extensive tropical plant collection, and in the Kitchen Gardens you can see an extensive collection of rare vegetables from the Henry Doubleday Research Association.

Ripley village on the Castle's doorstep is a model estate village with individual charming shops, an art gallery, delicatessen and Farmyard Museum.

## Owner
Sir Thomas Ingilby Bt

## Contact
Tours: Jenny Carter
Meetings/Dinners:
Rachel Terry
Ripley Castle
Ripley, Harrogate
North Yorkshire
HG3 3AY

**Tel:** 01423 770152
**Fax:** 01423 771745
**E-mail:** enquiries@ ripleycastle.co.uk

## Location
**MAP 10:P9**
**OS Ref. SE283 605**

W edge of village. Just off A61, 3½ m N of Harrogate, 8m S of Ripon. M1 18m S, M62 20m S.
**Rail:** London–Leeds/York 2hrs. Leeds/York–Harrogate 30mins.
**Taxi:** Blueline taxis Harrogate (01423) 503037.

## Opening Times
**Castle**
Easter–end October: Daily.
November & March:
Tues, Thurs, Sat & Sun.
10.30am–3pm.
December–February:
Sats & Suns.
10.30am–3pm.

**Gardens**
All year, daily (except Christmas Day),
10am–5pm (winter 4.30pm).

## Admission
**All Year**
**Castle & Gardens**
| | |
|---|---|
| Adult | £7.00 |
| Child (5–16yrs) | £4.50 |
| Child under 5yrs | Free |
| OAP | £6.00 |

**Groups (25+)**
| | |
|---|---|
| Adult | £6.00 |
| Child (5–16yrs) | £4.00 |

**Gardens only**
| | |
|---|---|
| Adult | £4.50 |
| Child (5–16yrs) | £3.00 |
| OAP | £4.00 |

**Groups (25+)**
| | |
|---|---|
| Adult | £4.50 |
| Child (5–16yrs) | £2.50 |
| Child under 5yrs | Free |

## Special Events
**Jun 7–10**
Grand Summer Sale.

**Jun 12–Jul 1**
"Much Ado About Nothing".

**Jul 21**
Last Night of the Proms.

No photography inside Castle unless by prior written consent. Parkland for outdoor activities & concerts. Murder mystery weekends.

VIP lunches & dinners (max. 120): unlimited in marquees. Full catering service, wedding receptions, banquets, meetings and activity days.

5/7 rooms accessible. Gardens accessible (not Tropical Collection). WCs. Parking 50 yds.

The Castle Tearooms (seats 54) in Castle courtyard. Licensed. Pub lunches or dinner at hotel (100 yds). Groups must book.

Obligatory. Tour time 75 mins.

290 cars – 300 yds from Castle entrance. Coach park 50 yds. Free.

Welcome by arrangement, between 10.30am–7.30pm.

Guide dogs only.

Boar's Head Hotel (RAC★★★) 100 yds. Owned and managed by the estate.

## Conference/Function

| ROOM | SIZE | MAX CAPACITY |
|---|---|---|
| Morning Rm | 27' x 22' | 80 |
| Large Drawing Rm | 30' x 22' | 80 |
| Library | 31 x 19' | 70 |
| Tower Rm | 33' x 21' | 70 |
| Map Rm | 19' x 14' | 20 |
| Dining Rm | 23' x 19' | 20 |
| Long Gallery | 19' x 6.5' | 150 |
| Amcotts Suite | 10.2' x 6.6' 7.3' x 6' | 120 |

## Contact

Judith Parker
Skipton Castle
Skipton
North Yorkshire
BD23 1AW

**Tel:** 01756 792442
**Fax:** 01756 796100
**E-mail:** info@
skiptoncastle.co.uk

## Location

**MAP 10:O9**
**OS Ref. SD992 520**

In the centre of
Skipton, at the N end
of High Street.

Skipton is 20m W of
Harrogate on the A59
and 26m NW of
Leeds on A65.

**Rail:** Regular services
from Leeds & Bradford.

## Opening Times

**All year**
(closed 25 December)

Mon–Sat: 10am–6pm
Suns: 12 noon–6pm
(October–February 4pm).

## Admission

| | |
|---|---|
| Adult | £5.60 |
| Child (0–4yrs) | Free |
| Child (5–17yrs) | £3.00 |
| OAP | £5.00 |
| Student (with ID) | £5.00 |
| Family (2+3) | £16.90 |

Groups (15+)

| | |
|---|---|
| Adult | £4.60 |
| Child (0–17yrs) | £3.00 |

Includes illustrated tour
sheet in a choice of nine
languages, plus free
badge for children.

Groups welcome:
Guides available for
booked groups at no
extra charge.

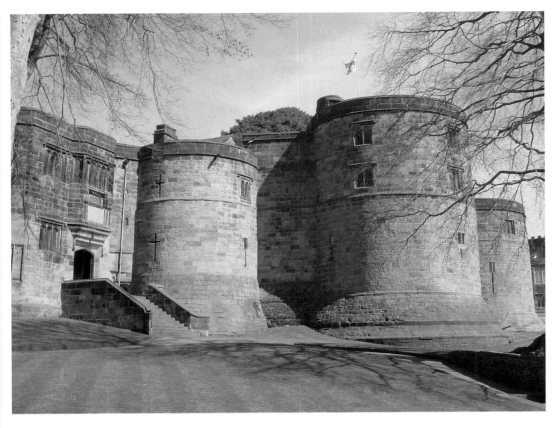

# SKIPTON CASTLE

www.skiptoncastle.co.uk

Guardian of the gateway to the Yorkshire Dales for over 900 years, this unique fortress is one of the most complete and well-preserved medieval castles in England. Standing on a 40-metre high crag, fully-roofed Skipton Castle was founded around 1090 by Robert de Romille, one of William the Conqueror's Barons, as a fortress in the dangerous northern reaches of the kingdom.

Owned by King Edward I and Edward II, from 1310 it became the stronghold of the Clifford Lords withstanding successive raids by marauding Scots. During the Civil War it was the last Royalist bastion in the North, yielding only after a three-year siege in 1645. 'Slighted' under the orders of Cromwell, the castle was skilfully restored by the redoubtable Lady Anne Clifford and today visitors can climb from the depths of the Dungeon to the top of the Watch Tower, and explore the Banqueting Hall, the Kitchens, the Bedchamber and even the Privy!

Every period has left its mark, from the Norman entrance and the

Medieval towers, to the beautiful Tudor courtyard with the great yew tree planted by Lady Anne in 1659. Here visitors can see the coat of arms of John Clifford, the infamous 'Bloody' Clifford of Shakespeare's Henry VI, who fought and died in the Wars of the Roses whereupon the castle was possessed by Richard III. Throughout the turbulent centuries of English history, the Clifford Lords fought at Bannockburn, at Agincourt and in the Wars of the Roses. The most famous of them all was George Clifford, 3rd Earl of Cumberland, Champion to Elizabeth I, Admiral against the Spanish Armada and conqueror of Puerto Rico in 1598.

In the castle grounds visitors can see the Tudor wing built as a royal wedding present for Lady Eleanor Brandon, niece of Henry VIII, the beautiful Shell Room decorated in the 1620s with shells and Jamaican coral and the ancient medieval chapel of St John the Evangelist. The Chapel Terrace, with its delightful picnic area, has fine views over the woods and Skipton's lively market town.

Unsuitable.

Tearoom. Indoor and outdoor picnic areas.

By arrangement.

**P** Large public coach and car park off nearby High Street. Coach drivers' rest room at Castle.

Welcome. Guides available. Teachers free.

In grounds on leads.

## ALDBOROUGH ROMAN SITE

**Main Street, Aldborough, Boroughbridge, North Yorkshire  YO51 9EP**
**Tel:** 01423 322768   **E-mail:** customers@english-heritage.org.uk
**www.english-heritage.org.uk/yorkshire**
**Owner:** English Heritage   **Contact:** Visitor Operations Team
Aldborough succeeded Stanwick as the tribal capital of Britian's largest Roman tribe, the Brigantes. Parts of the town's defences, now lying in the peaceful surroundings of a Victorian arboretum, are clearly visible, along with two spectacular mosaic pavements, still in their original position.
**Location:** MAP 11:A8, OS Ref. SE405 661. Close to Boroughbridge off A1.
**Open:** 1 Apr–30 Jun & Sept: Sats & Suns, 11am–5pm. Jul–Aug: Thur–Mon, 10am–5pm.
**Admission:** Adult £3, Child £1.50, Conc. £2.30. 15% discount for groups (11+).
ⓘ WC. ◻ ▣ ▣

## ASKE HALL

**Richmond, North Yorkshire  DL10 5HJ**
**Tel:** 01748 822000   **Fax:** 01748 826611   **E-mail:** office@aske.co.uk
**www.aske.co.uk**
**Owner:** The Marquess of Zetland   **Contact:** The Secretary
A good, predominantly Georgian collection of paintings, furniture and porcelain in house which has been the seat of the Dundas family since 1763.
**Location:** MAP 10:P6, OS Ref. NZ179 035. 4m SW of A1 at Scotch Corner, 2m from the A66, on the B6274.
**Open:** 25 Apr, 9 & 23 May, 6 & 20 June, 4 & 11 Jul, 30 Aug & 5 & 19 Sept. Tours at 10 & 11am & 12 noon. Booking advisable. Other times by arrangement.
**Admission:** House only: Adult £7.
Ⓕ Obligatory. Ⓟ Limited. ▣

## BAGSHAW MUSEUM

**Wilton Park, Batley, West Yorkshire  WF17 0AS**
**Tel:** 01924 326155   **Fax:** 01924 326164
**Owner:** Kirklees Cultural Services   **Contact:** Amanda Daley
A Victorian Gothic mansion set in Wilton Park.
**Location:** MAP10:P11, OS Ref. SE235 257. From M62/J27 follow A62 to Huddersfield. At Birstall, follow tourist signs.
**Open:** Mon–Fri, 11am–5pm. Sat & Sun, 12 noon–5pm. Pre-booked groups and school parties welcome. Closed for refurbishment from 3 July, re-opening scheduled for early 2008, please telephone for details.
**Admission:** Free.

## BENINGBROUGH HALL & GARDENS

**Beningbrough, North Yorkshire  YO30 1DD**
**Tel:** 01904 472027   **Fax:** 01904 472020   **E-mail:** beningbrough@nationaltrust.org.uk
**www.nationaltrust.org.uk**
**Owner:** The National Trust   **Contact:** Visitor Services Manager
Imposing 18th century house with new interpretation galleries with the National Portrait Gallery.
**Location:** MAP 11:B9, OS Ref. SE516 586. 8m NW of York, 3m W of Shipton, 2m SE of Linton-on-Ouse, follow signposted route.
**Open:** Grounds, Shop & Restaurant: 17 Mar–27 Jun & 1 Sep–28 Oct, Sat–Wed, 11am–5.30pm; 30 Jun–29 Aug, Fri–Wed, 11am–5.30pm; 3 Nov–16 Dec & 6 Jan–31 Mar, Sats & Suns, 11am–3.30pm. House: 17 Mar–27 Jun & 1 Sept–31 Oct, Sat–Wed; 30 Jun–29 Aug, Fri–Wed; 12 noon–5pm: Galleries only:3 Nov–16 Dec & 6 Jan–9 Mar 2008, Sats & Suns, 11am–3pm. Closed 22/23 & 29/30 Dec.
**Admission:** Summer: Adult £7.70, Child £3.90, Family £17.60. Groups: £6.50. Winter 07/08: Adult £5, Child £2.80, Family £11. Groups £4.
◻ ▣ ▣ Lift to all floors. WC. ▥ ◻ Ⓟ Reduced rates for groups (15+), not Suns or BHs. ▣ ▣ ▣

Nostell Priory, Wakefield

## BOLTON ABBEY
### SKIPTON, NORTH YORKSHIRE  BD23 6EX
www.boltonabbey.com

**Tel:** 01756 718009   **Fax:** 01756 710535   **E-mail:** tourism@boltonabbey.com
**Owner:** Chatsworth Settlement Trustees   **Contact:** Visitor Manager
Wordsworth, Turner and Landseer were inspired by this romantic and varied landscape. The Estate, centred around Bolton Priory (founded 1154), is the Yorkshire home of the Duke and Duchess of Devonshire and provides 80 miles of footpaths to enjoy some of the most spectacular landscape in England.
**Location:** MAP 10:O9, OS Ref. SE074 542. On B6160, N from the junction with A59 Skipton–Harrogate road, 23m from Leeds.
**Open:** All year.
**Admission:** £5 per car (occupants free).
◻ ▥ ▣ Licensed. ▥ Licensed. Ⓕ By arrangement. Ⓟ ▣ ▣ In grounds, on leads. ▣ Devonshire Arms Country House Hotel & Devonshire Fell Hotel nearby. ▣

## BOLTON CASTLE
### LEYBURN, NORTH YORKSHIRE  DL8 4ET
www.boltoncastle.co.uk

**Tel:** 01969 623981   **Fax:** 01969 623332   **E-mail:** info@boltoncastle.co.uk
**Owner/Contact:** Lord Bolton or Sarah Penty
A fine medieval castle which has dominated Wensleydale since 1379. The castle enjoys a wealth of history which includes connections with "the Pilgrimage of Grace" and Richard III. Mary Queen of Scots was imprisoned here for six months during 1568 and 1569 and the Royalists were besieged here during the Civil War. Enjoy the medieval gardens, maze and vineyard.
**Location:** MAP 10:O7, OS Ref. SE034 918. Approx 6m W of Leyburn. 1m NW of Redmire.
**Open:** Mar–Nov: daily, 10am–5pm. Please telephone for winter opening times.
**Admission:** Adult £5, Child/OAP. £3.50, Family £12.
◻ ▣ Wedding receptions. ▥ Partial. ▣ Ⓟ ▣ ▣ In grounds, on leads. ▣ ▣

© NT Photographic Library / Matthew Antrobus

## BRAMHAM PARK

*See page 376 for full page entry.*

## BROCKFIELD HALL

**Warthill, York YO19 5XJ**
**Tel:** 01904 489362  **Fax:** 01904 488982  **E-mail:** simon@brockfieldhall.co.uk
**www.brockfieldhall.co.uk**
**Owner:** Mr & Mrs Simon Wood  **Contact:** Simon Wood

A fine late Georgian house designed by Peter Atkinson, assistant to John Carr of York, for Benjamin Agar Esq. Begun in 1804, its outstanding feature is an oval entrance hall with a fine cantilevered stone staircase curving past an impressive Venetian window. It is the family home of Mr and Mrs Simon Wood. Mrs Wood is the daughter of the late Lord and of Lady Martin Fitzalan Howard. He was the brother of the 17th Duke of Norfolk and son of the late Baroness Beaumont of Carlton Towers, Selby. There are some interesting portraits of her old Roman Catholic family, the Stapletons, and some good English furniture. Permanent exhibition of paintings by Staithes Group Artists (by appointment outside August).
**Location:** MAP 11:C9, OS Ref. SE664 550. 5m E of York off A166 or A64.
**Open:** Aug: daily except Mons (open BH Mon), 1–4pm. Other times by appt.
**Admission:** Adult £5, Child £2.
ℹ No photography inside house. ♿ Partial. ⓘ By arrangement. 🅿
🐕 In grounds, on leads.

## BRODSWORTH HALL ⌗
## & GARDENS

*See page 377 for full page entry.*

Who's offering **accommodation?**
See our index on page 575.

## BRONTË PARSONAGE MUSEUM

**Church St, Haworth, Keighley, West Yorkshire BD22 8DR**
**Tel:** 01535 642323  **Fax:** 01535 647131  **E-mail:** bronte@bronte.org.uk
**www.bronte.info**
**Owner:** The Brontë Society  **Contact:** The Administrator

Haworth Parsonage, with its moorland setting, was home and inspiration to the Brontës, the world's most famous literary family. This homely Georgian house still retains the atmosphere of the Brontës' time, along with displays of personal treasures. Come and experience the tragic, romantic and fascinating lives of this remarkable family.
**Location:** MAP 10:O10, OS Ref. SE029 373. 8m W of Bradford, 3m S of Keighley.
**Open:** Apr–Sept: 10am–5pm, Oct–Mar: 11am–4.30pm. Daily except 2–31 Jan & 24–27 Dec 2007.
**Admission:** Adult £5, Child (5–16yrs) £2, Conc. £3.82, Family £12. Discounts for booked groups.
📷 ♿ Limited. ⬛ 🐕 Guide dogs only. ❉ ⬛

Hovingham Hall, York.

# BROUGHTON HALL

## SKIPTON, YORKSHIRE BD23 3AE

www.broughtonhall.co.uk

**Tel:** 01756 799608  **Fax:** 01756 700357
**E-mail:** tempest@broughtonhall.co.uk  **E-mail:** info@ruralsolutions.co.uk
**Owner:** The Tempest Family  **Contact:** The Estate Office

Stephen Tempest built Broughton Hall in 1597 and it was extended in the 18th and 19th centuries into the handsome and graceful form we see today. It is the private home of the Tempest family and is a Grade I listed building, the rooms containing fine Gillow furniture and interesting family portraits. Groups may visit for tours by prior arrangement. A 3,000 acre parkland setting and Italianate gardens which include a stunning conservatory, make Broughton Hall a desirable location for film makers and for corporate and promotional events, the owners being very experienced in successfully meeting the needs of such clients.

Nearby Estate buildings have been skilfully converted into the Broughton Hall Business Park. Here 45 companies employ over five hundred people in quality offices in unspoilt historic buildings and peaceful surroundings, thanks to the innovative approach of Rural Solutions, the rural regeneration specialists (01756 799955) who conceived and completed the project.
**Location:** MAP 10:N9, OS Ref. SD943 507. On A59, 3m W of Skipton midway between the Yorkshire and Lancashire centres. Good air and rail links.
**Open:** Tours by arrangement.
**Admission:** £8.
♿ ⓣ ⓘ By arrangement. 🅿 ❉

# BURTON AGNES HALL & GARDENS
## DRIFFIELD, EAST YORKSHIRE YO25 4NB
www.burton-agnes.com

**Tel:** 01262 490324 **Fax:** 01262 490513
**Owner:** Burton Agnes Hall Preservation Trust Ltd **Contact:** Mrs Susan Cunliffe-Lister
A lovely Elizabethan Hall containing treasures collected by the family over four centuries from the original carving and plasterwork to modern and Impressionist paintings. The Hall is surrounded by lawns and topiary yew. The award-winning gardens contain a maze, potager, jungle garden, campanula collection and colour gardens incorporating giant game boards. Children's corner.
**Location:** MAP 11:E9, OS Ref. TA103 633. Off A614 between Driffield and Bridlington.
**Open:** Gardens, shops & café: 3 Jan–1 Apr & 31 Oct–22 Dec, Thurs–Sun, 11am–4pm. Hall & Gardens: 1 Apr–31 Oct, daily 11am–5pm. For Christmas opening (Nov/Dec) & Snowdrop opening (Feb) details, please contact property.
**Admission:** Hall & Gardens: Adult £6, Child £3, OAP £5.50. Gardens only: Adult £3, Child £1.50, OAP £2.75. 10% reduction for groups of 30+.
Farm Shop. Ground floor & grounds. Café. Ice-cream parlour. P In grounds, on leads.

---

## BURTON CONSTABLE HALL
*See page 378 for full page entry.*

---

## BYLAND ABBEY
**Coxwold, Thirsk, North Yorkshire YO61 4BD**
**Tel:** 01347 868614 **E-mail:** customers@english-heritage.org.uk
**www.english-heritage.org.uk/yorkshire**
**Owner:** English Heritage **Contact:** Visitor Operations Team
This beautiful ruin was once one of the great northern monasteries, second only to Rievaulx and Fountains. Its design, a mixture of Romanesque and Gothic, proclaimed the arrival of a new architectural style, which Byland pioneered. The Abbey's splendid collection of medieval floor tiles is a testament to its earlier magnificence.
**Location:** MAP 11:B8, OS Ref. SE549 789. 2m S of A170 between Thirsk and Helmsley, NE of Coxwold village.
**Open:** 1 Apr–31 Jul & Sept: Thur–Mon (Aug: daily), 11am–6pm.
**Admission:** Adult £3.50, Child £1.80, Conc. £2.60. 15% discount for groups (11+).
WC. P Limited. On leads.

---

## CANNON HALL MUSEUM, PARK & GARDENS
Cawthorne, Barnsley, South Yorkshire S75 4AT
**Tel:** 01226 790270 **Fax:** 01226 792117 **E-mail:** cannonhall@barnsley.gov.uk
**www.barnsley.gov.uk**
**Owner:** Barnsley Metropolitan Borough Council **Contact:** The Museum Manager
Set in 70 acres of historic parkland and gardens, Cannon Hall now contains collections of fine furniture, old master paintings, stunning glassware and colourful pottery, much of which is displayed in period settings. Plus 'Charge', the Regimental museum of the 13th/18th Royal Hussars (QMO). Events and education programme and an ideal setting for conferences and Civil wedding ceremonies.
**Location:** MAP 10:P12, OS Ref. SE272 084. 6m NW of Barnsley of A635. M1/J38.
**Open:** Nov, Dec & Mar: Sun, 12 noon–4pm; closed Jan & Feb. Apr–Oct: Wed–Fri, 10.30am–5pm; Sat & Sun, 12 noon–5pm. Last admission 4.15pm for 5pm. Open all year for weddings, school visits and corporate hospitality.
**Admission:** Free except for some events. Charge for car parking.
Partial. WC. Weekends. P In grounds, on leads.

---

## CASTLE HOWARD
*See page 379 for full page entry.*

---

## CAWTHORNE VICTORIA JUBILEE MUSEUM
**Taylor Hill, Cawthorne, Barnsley, South Yorkshire S75 4HQ**
**Tel:** 01226 790545 / 790246
**Owner:** Cawthorne Village **Contact:** Mrs Mary Herbert
A quaint and eccentric collection in a half-timbered building. Museum has a ramp and toilet for disabled visitors. School visits welcome.
**Location:** MAP 10:P12, OS Ref. SE285 080. 4m W of Barnsley, just off the A635.
**Open:** Palm Sun–end Oct: Sats, Suns & BH Mons, 2–5pm. Groups by appointment throughout the year.
**Admission:** Adult 50p, Child 20p.

---

## CLIFFE CASTLE
**Keighley, West Yorkshire BD20 6LH**
**Tel:** 01535 618231
**Owner:** City of Bradford Metropolitan District Council **Contact:** Daru Rooke
Victorian manufacturer's house of 1878 with tall tower and garden. Now a museum.
**Location:** MAP 10:O10, OS Ref. SE057 422. ¾ m NW of Keighley off the A629.
**Open:** All year: Tues–Sat & BH Mons, 10am–5pm. Suns, 12 noon–5pm. Closed 25/26 Dec.
**Admission:** Free.

---

## CLIFFORD'S TOWER
**Tower Street, York YO1 9SA**
**Tel:** 01904 646940 **E-mail:** customers@english-heritage.org.uk
**www.english-heritage.org.uk/yorkshire**
**Owner:** English Heritage **Contact:** Visitor Operations Team
Visit this proud symbol of the might of our medieval kings – originally built by William the Conqueror to subdue the rebellious north, it was rebuilt by Henry III in the 13th century. Fantastic panoramic views of York and the surrounding countryside from the top of the Tower show why it played such a key role in the control of northern England.
**Location:** MAP 21, OS Ref. SE 605 515. York city centre.
**Open:** 1 Apr–30 Sept: daily, 10am–6pm; Oct: daily, 10am–5pm. 1 Nov–20 Mar 2008: daily, 10am–4pm. Closed 24–26 Dec & 1 Jan.
**Admission:** Adult £3, Child £1.50, Conc. £2.30. Family ticket £7.50. 15% discount available for groups (11+).
Unsuitable. P Charged.

---

## CONISBROUGH CASTLE
**Castle Hill, Conisbrough, South Yorkshire DN12 3BU**
**Tel:** 01709 863329 **E-mail:** customers@english-heritage.org.uk
**www.english-heritage.org.uk/yorkshire**
**Owner:** English Heritage **Contact:** The Administrator
The white, cylindrical keep of this 12th century castle is a spectacular structure. Built of magnesian limestone, it is the only example of its kind in England, and was one of the inspirations for Sir Walter Scott's "Ivanhoe". Managed by The Ivanhoe Trust.
**Location:** MAP 7:A1, OS Ref. SK515 989. 4½m SW of Doncaster.
**Open:** 1 Apr–30 Sept: daily, 10am–5pm (last admission 4.20pm). 1 Oct–20 Mar 2008: Thur–Mon, 10am–4pm (last admission 3.20pm). Closed 24–26 Dec & 1 Jan.
**Admission:** Adult £4, Child £2, Conc. £3, Family £10.
Limited access. P

---

*giftaid it* This year, some properties will be operating the Gift Aid on Entry scheme at their admission points. Where the scheme is operating, visitors are offered a choice between paying the standard admission price or paying the 'Gift Aid Admission' which includes a voluntary donation of at least 10%. Gift Aid Admissions enable the charity to reclaim tax on the whole amount paid* - an extra 28% - potentially a very significant boost to property funds. Money raised from paying visitors in this way will go towards restoration projects at the property and will be very welcome. Where shown, the admission prices are inclusive of the 10% voluntary donation where properties are operating the Gift Aid on Entry scheme, but both the standard admission price and the Gift Aid Admission will be displayed at the property and on their website.

*Gift Aid donations must be supported by a valid Gift Aid declaration and a Gift Aid declaration can only cover donations made by an individual for him/herself or for him/herself and members of his/her family.

## CONSTABLE BURTON HALL GARDENS 🏛

### LEYBURN, NORTH YORKSHIRE DL8 5LJ

www.constableburtongardens.co.uk

**Tel:** 01677 450428 **Fax:** 01677 450622

**Owner/Contact:** M C A Wyvill Esq

A delightful terraced woodland garden of lilies, ferns, hardy shrubs, roses and wild flowers, attached to a beautiful Palladian house designed by John Carr (not open). Garden trails and herbaceous borders. Stream garden with large architectural plants and reflection ponds. Impressive spring display of daffodils and tulips.

**Location:** MAP 10:P7, OS Ref. SE164 913. 3m E of Leyburn off the A684.

**Open:** Garden only: 24 Mar–15 Oct: daily, 9am–6pm.

**Admission:** Adult £3, Child (5–16yrs) 50p, OAP £2.50.

🚻 ♿ Partial, WC. 📷 Group tours of house & gardens by arrangement. 🅿 Limited for coaches. 🐕 In grounds, on leads. ♿

## CUSWORTH HALL & PARK

**Cusworth Lane, Doncaster, South Yorkshire DN5 7TU**

**Tel:** 01302 782342 **E-mail:** jackie.james@doncaster.gov.uk

**Owner:** Doncaster Metropolitan Borough Council **Contact:** Mr F Carpenter, Curator

A magnificent Grade I country house set in a landscaped parkland and built in 1740, with a chapel and other rooms designed by James Paine, the house is now the home of a museum showing the changing home, work and social conditions of the region over the last 250 years. Regular events and activities.

**Location:** MAP 10:P12, OS Ref. SE547 039. A1(M)/J37, then A635 and right into Cusworth Lane.

**Open:** The building will reopen in 2007 following extensive renovation. Please telephone for more information.

Burton Agnes Hall & Gardens, Driffield

Skyscan/William Cross

## DUNCOMBE PARK 🏛

### HELMSLEY, NORTH YORKSHIRE YO62 5EB

www.duncombepark.com

**Tel:** 01439 772625 **Fax:** 01439 771114 **E-mail:** liz@duncombepark.com

**Owner/Contact:** Lord & Lady Feversham

Lord and Lady Feversham's restored family home in the North York Moors National Park. Built on a virgin plateau overlooking Norman Castle and river valley, it is surrounded by 35 acres of beautiful 18th century landscaped gardens and 400 acres of parkland with national nature reserve and veteran trees.

**Location:** MAP 11:B7, OS Ref. SE604 830. Entrance just off Helmsley Market Square, signed off A170 Thirsk–Scarborough road.

**Open:** 6 May–28 Oct: Sun–Thur. House by guided tour only: 12.30, 1.30, 2.30 & 3.30pm. Gardens & Parkland Centre: 11am–5.30pm.

**Admission:** House & Gardens: Adult £7.25, Child (10–16yrs) £3.25, Conc. £5.50, Family (2+2) £15 Groups (15+): £5.25. Gardens & Parkland: Adult £4, Child (10–16yrs) £2, Conc £3.50. Groups (15+) £3. Parkland: Adult £2, Child (10–16yrs) £1. Season ticket: Adult £17.50, Family (2+2) £30.

ℹ Country walks, nature reserve, orienteering, conferences. 📷 🍴 Banqueting facilities. ♿ Partial. 🍴 Licensed. 📷 Obligatory. 🅿 🚌 🐕 In park on leads. ♿

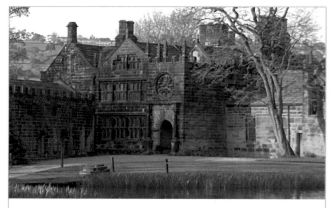

## EAST RIDDLESDEN HALL ✺

### BRADFORD ROAD, KEIGHLEY, WEST YORKSHIRE BD20 5EL

www.nationaltrust.org.uk

**Tel:** 01535 607075 **Fax:** 01535 691462

**E-mail:** eastriddlesden@nationaltrust.org.uk

**Owner:** The National Trust **Contact:** Visitor Services Manager

Homely 17th century merchant's house with beautiful embroideries and textiles, Yorkshire carved oak furniture and fine ceilings. Delightful garden with lavender and herbs. Also wild garden with old varieties of apple trees. Magnificent oak framed barn. Handling collection, children's play area. Costumed tours July and August. Events.

**Location:** MAP 10:O10, OS Ref. SE079 421. 1m NE of Keighley on S side of B6265 in Riddlesden. 50yds from Leeds/Liverpool Canal. Bus: Frequent services from Skipton, Bradford and Leeds. Railway station at Keighley 2m.

**Open:** 17 Mar–4 Nov: Tues, Wed, Sat & Sun (also Mons 2 Jul–25 Aug), 12 noon–5pm. Shop/Tearoom: 17 Mar–4 Nov: as house. 10 Nov–16 Dec, 12 noon–4pm. Also BHs & Good Fri.

**Admission:** Adult £4.50, Child £2.25, Family £10. Booked groups (15+): Adult £4, Child £2. £1 off when arriving by Keighley & District transport buses.

📷 🍴 ♿ Partial. 🍴 📷 By arrangement. 🚌 🅿 Limited for coaches, please book. 🐕 In grounds, on leads. ♿

# FAIRFAX HOUSE 🏛

**FAIRFAX HOUSE, CASTLEGATE, YORK  YO1 9RN**

www.fairfaxhouse.co.uk

**Tel:** 01904 655543  **Fax:** 01904 652262  **E-mail:** peterbrown@fairfaxhouse.co.uk
**Owner:** York Civic Trust  **Contact:** Mr Peter Brown

Fairfax House was acquired and fully restored by the York Civic Trust in 1983/84. The house, described as a classic architectural masterpiece of its age and certainly one of the finest townhouses in England, was saved from near collapse after considerable abuse and misuse this century, having been converted into a cinema and dance hall. The richly decorated interior with its plasterwork, wood and wrought-iron, is now the home for a unique collection of Georgian furniture, clocks, paintings and porcelain. The Noel Terry Collection, gift of a former treasurer of the York Civic Trust, has been described by Christie's as one of the finest private collections formed in the 20th century. It enhances and complements the house and helps to create that special 'lived-in' feeling, providing the basis for a series of set-piece period exhibitions which bring the house to life in a very tangible way.

**Location:** MAP 11:B9, OS Ref. SE605 515. In centre of York between Castle Museum and Jorvik Centre.
**Open:** 11 Feb–31 Dec, Mon–Thur: 11am –5pm. Fris: Guided tours only 11am and 2pm. Sats: 11am–5pm. Suns: 1.30–5pm. Last admission 4.30pm. Closed 1 Jan–10 Feb & 24–26 Dec.
**Admission:** Adult £5, Child Free with full paying adult, Conc. £4. Groups*: Adult £4, Child £1, Conc. £3.25 *Min payment 15 persons.
ℹ Suitable for filming. No photography in house. 📷 ⊤ Max. 28 seated. Groups up to 50. ♿ Partial. 🅸 🅿 ❄ 🅥

---

## FOUNTAINS ABBEY & STUDLEY ROYAL 🌿

*See page 380 for full page entry.*

---

## THE GEORGIAN THEATRE ROYAL

**Victoria Road, Richmond, North Yorkshire  DL10 4DW**
**Tel:** 01748 823710  **Box Office:** 01748 825252
**E-mail:** admin@georgiantheatreroyal.co.uk
**Owner:** Georgian Theatre Royal Trust  **Contact:** Judith Clark

The most complete Georgian playhouse in Britain. Built in 1788 by actor/manager, Samuel Butler and restored to its Georgian grandeur in 2003.
**Location:** MAP 10:P6, OS Ref. NZ174 013. 4m from the A1 (Scotch Corner) on the A6108.
**Open:** All year: Mon–Sat, 10am–7.30pm (5pm on non-performance nights, 4pm until curtain up on performance Suns). Guided tours: On the hour, 10am–4pm.
**Admission:** Donation £3.50. Child Free.

---

## HAREWOOD HOUSE

*See page 381 for full page entry.*

Markenfield Hall

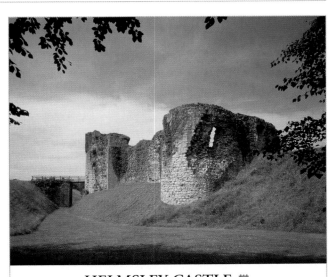

# HELMSLEY CASTLE ⊞

**CASTLEGATE, HELMSLEY, NORTH YORKSHIRE  YO62 5AB**

www.english-heritage.org.uk/yorkshire

**Tel:** 01439 770442  **E-mail:** customers@english-heritage.org.uk
**Owner:** English Heritage  **Contact:** Visitor Operations Team

Originally a medieval castle, a Tudor mansion was added in the 1600s, before Cromwell's men blew up the great keep, slicing it in half. The changing fortunes of the castle over 900 years are explored in an audio tour and interactive displays, including original artefacts excavated from the site.
**Location:** MAP 11:B7, OS Ref. SE611 836. In Helmsley town.
**Open:** 1 Apr–31 Oct: daily, 10am–6pm (Oct 5pm). 1 Nov–29 Feb 2008: Thur–Mon, 10am–4pm. Closed 24–26 Dec & 1 Jan.
**Admission:** Adult £4, Child £2, Conc £3, Family £10. 15% discount for groups (11+).
ℹ Tourist information located within Castle Visitor Centre. 📷 ♿ 🅟 🅿 Charged. 📷 ⊞ Dogs welcome on leads. ❄ 🅥

## HELMSLEY WALLED GARDEN

**Cleveland Way, Helmsley, North Yorkshire YO62 5AH**
**Tel/Fax:** 01439 771427
**Owner:** Helmsley Walled Garden Ltd **Contact:** Paul Radcliffe/Lindsay Tait
A 5 acre walled garden under restoration. Orchid house and vinery restored. Plant sales area and vegetarian café.
**Location:** MAP 11:B7, OS Ref. SE611 836. 25m N of York, 15m from Thirsk. In Helmsley follow signs to Cleveland Way.
**Open:** 1 Apr–31 Oct: daily, 10.30am–5pm. Nov–Mar: Sats/Suns, 12 noon–4pm.
**Admission:** Adult £4, Child Free, Conc. £3.

## HOVINGHAM HALL

**YORK, NORTH YORKSHIRE YO62 4LU**
www.hovingham.co.uk

**Tel:** 01653 628771 **Fax:** 01653 628668 **E-mail:** office@hovingham.co.uk
**Owner:** William Worsley **Contact:** Mrs Lamprey
This attractive Palladian family home, in its beautiful parkland setting, was designed and built by Thomas Worsley, Surveyor General to King George III. It is still lived in by his descendants and was the childhood home of Katharine Worsley, the Duchess of Kent. Hovingham Hall is unique in being entered through a huge riding school and features halls with vaulted ceilings and a beautiful collection of pictures and furniture. The house has attractive gardens with magnificent Yew hedges and the cricket ground in front of the house is reputed to be the oldest private cricket ground in England.
**Location:** MAP 11:C8, OS Ref. SE666 756. 18m N of York on Malton/Helmsley Road (B1257).
**Open:** 4 Jun–7 Jul except Suns. 1.15–4.30pm (last tour 3.30pm).
**Admission:** Adult £6, Conc. £5.50, Child £3. Gardens only: £3.50.
ⓘ No photography in house. 🚻 🅰 Partial. ■ 🎦 Obligatory. 🅿 Limited. 🦮 Guide dogs only.

## JERVAULX ABBEY

**Ripon, North Yorkshire HG4 4PH**
**Tel:** 01677 460226 / 460391
**Owner/Contact:** Mr I S Burdon
Extensive ruins of a former Cistercian abbey.
**Location:** MAP 10:P7, OS Ref. SE169 858. Beside the A6108 Ripon–Leyburn road, 5m SE of Leyburn and 5m NW of Masham.
**Open:** Daily during daylight hours. Tearoom: Mar–1 Nov (all home baking, staff permitting).
**Admission:** Adult £2, Child £1.50 in honesty box at Abbey entrance.

## KIPLIN HALL 🏛

**KIPLIN, Nr SCORTON, RICHMOND, NORTH YORKSHIRE DL10 6AT**
www.kiplinhall.co.uk www.herriotdaysout.com

**Tel/Fax:** 01748 818178 **E-mail:** info@kiplinhall.co.uk
**Owner:** Kiplin Hall Trustees **Contact:** The Administrator
A Grade I Listed Jacobean house built in 1620 by George Calvert, Secretary of State to James I, and founder of the State of Maryland, USA. Kiplin Hall is now furnished as a Victorian home with paintings and furniture collected over four centuries displayed in room settings. Visitors enjoy a uniquely relaxed tour of the Hall, freely wandering through the rooms and gardens. New exhibition for 2007: *'Between the Covers: 100 years of Kiplin family scrapbooks'.*
**Location:** MAP 11:A7, OS Ref. SE274 976. Signposted from Scorton–Northallerton road (B6271).
**Open:** Easter Fri & Sat, then Suns–Weds to 30 Sept, 2–5pm. Open at other times for group guided tours.
**Admission:** Adult £4.50, Child £2.50, Conc. £3.50. Family (2+3) £12.75. Groups (15–50) by arrangement.
🖼 🅰 Partial. ■ 🎦 By arrangement. 🅿 ■ 🦽 In grounds, on leads. Guide dogs only in house. 🔺 ♿

## KIRKHAM PRIORY ⌗

**Kirkham, Whitwell-on-the-Hill, North Yorkshire YO60 7JS**
**Tel:** 01653 618768 **E-mail:** customers@english-heritage.org.uk
www.english-heritage.org.uk/yorkshire
**Owner:** English Heritage **Contact:** Visitor Operations Team
The ruins of this Augustinian priory include a magnificent carved gatehouse, declaring to the world the Priory's association with the rich and powerful. However, the site also has more modern associations including a secret visit by the then Prime Minister Winston Churchill during the Second World War.
**Location:** MAP 11:C8, OS Ref. SE735 657. 5m SW of Malton on minor road off A64.
**Open:** 1 Apr–30 May & Sept: Thur–Mon, 10am–5pm. 1 Jun–31 Aug: daily, 10am–5pm. Oct: Sats & Suns, 10am–4pm.
**Admission:** Adult £3, Child £1.50, Conc. £2.30. 15% discount for groups (11+).
ⓘ WC. 🖼 🅰 🅿 Limited. ■ 🦽 On leads.

## KNARESBOROUGH CASTLE & MUSEUM

**Knaresborough, North Yorkshire HG5 8AS**
**Tel:** 01423 556188 **Fax:** 01423 556130
**Owner:** Duchy of Lancaster **Contact:** Ceryl Evans
Ruins of 14th century castle standing high above the town. Local history museum housed in Tudor Courthouse. Gallery devoted to the Civil War.
**Location:** MAP 11:A9, OS Ref. SE349 569. 5m E of Harrogate, off A59.
**Open:** Good Friday–1 Oct: daily, 10.30am–5pm.
**Admission:** Adult £2.50, Child £1.30, OAP £1.50, Family £6.50, Groups (10+) £2.

## LEDSTON HALL

**Hall Lane, Ledston, Castleford, West Yorkshire WF10 2BB**
**Tel:** 01423 523423 **Fax:** 01423 521373 **E-mail:** james.hare@carterjonas.co.uk
**Contact:** James Hare
17th century mansion with some earlier work.
**Location:** MAP 11:A11, OS Ref. SE437 289. 2m N of Castleford, off A656.
**Open:** Exterior only: May–Aug: Mon–Fri, 9am–4pm. Other days by appointment.
**Admission:** Free.

Brodsworth Hall & Gardens, Doncaster

**visit hudsons guide online**

## LINDLEY MURRAY SUMMERHOUSE

**The Mount School, Dalton Terrace, York YO24 4DD**
**Tel:** 01904 667500  www.mountschoolyork.co.uk
**Owner/Contact:** The Mount School
**Location:** MAP 21, OS Ref. SE593 510. Dalton Terrace, York.
**Open:** By prior arrangement: Mon–Fri, 9am–4.30pm all the year (apart from BHs).
**Admission:** Free.
⬒ 🅿 ♿ Guide dogs only. ✳

## LING BEECHES GARDEN

**Ling Lane, Scarcroft, Leeds, West Yorkshire LS14 3HX**
**Tel:** 0113 2892450
**Owner/Contact:** Mrs A Rakusen
A 2 acre woodland garden designed by the owner.
**Location:** MAP 11:A10, OS Ref. SE354 413. Off A58 midway between Leeds & Wetherby. At Scarcroft turn into Ling Lane, signed to Wike on brow of hill.
**Open:** By appointment, please telephone for details.
**Admission:** Adult £3, Child Free.

## LONGLEY OLD HALL

**Longley, Huddersfield, West Yorkshire HD5 8LB**
**Tel:** 01484 430852  **E-mail:** gallagher@longleyoldhall.co.uk
www.longleyoldhall.co.uk
**Owner:** Christine & Robin Gallagher  **Contact:** Christine Gallagher
This timber framed Grade II* manor house dates from the 14th century. It was owned by the Ramsden family, the former Lords of the Manors of Almondbury and Huddersfield, for over 400 years. It is included in Simon Jenkins' England's Thousand Best Houses.
**Location:** MAP 10:P11, OS Ref. SE154 150. 1½ m SE of Huddersfield towards Castle Hill, via Dog Kennel Bank.
**Open:** Easter and Summer BH weekends and 27–30 Dec for pre-booked guided tours. Group viewings by appointment (min 12 max 25 in winter and 50 in the summer; smaller groups by arrangement).
**Admission:** £6 for open days – £10 for groups.
🅾 ⬒ Unsuitable. 🎦 Obligatory. 🅿 Limited for coaches. ✳ ✳

## LOTHERTON HALL & GARDENS

### ABERFORD, LEEDS, WEST YORKSHIRE LS25 3EB

www.leeds.gov.uk/lothertonhall

**Tel:** 0113 2813259  **E-mail:** lotherton@leeds.gov.uk
**Owner:** Leeds City Council  **Contact:** The Supervisor
Charming Edwardian country home rich in collections of paintings, furniture, silver, china, costume and oriental art. Beautiful formal, wildflower and wooded grounds, red deer park and one of the country's most impressive and important collections of rare and endangered birds.
**Location:** MAP 11:B10, OS92, SE450 360. 2½ m E of M1/J47 on B1217 the Towton Road.
**Open:** 1 Apr–31 Oct: Tue–Sat, 10am–5pm, Suns, 1–5pm. 1 Nov–31 Dec & Mar: Tue–Sat, 10am–4pm, Sun, 12 noon–4pm. Last adm. ¾ hr before closing. Closed Jan & Feb. Open BH Mons.
**Admission:** Adult £3, Child £1, Conc/Groups: £1.50. Car parking: £3.50 per day or £15 per year (including one year free admission to house for driver). Coach parking £20 per day.
🅾 🍴 🎦 🅿 ▦ ✳ ✳

## MARKENFIELD HALL 🏛

**Nr Ripon, North Yorkshire HG4 3AD**
**Tel:** 01765 692303  **Fax:** 01765 607195
**E-mail:** info@markenfield.com  www.markenfield.com
**Owner:** Lady Deirdre Curteis  **Contact:** The Administrator
"This wonderfuly little-altered building is the most complete surviving example of the meduim-sized C14th country house in England" John Martin Robinson *The Architecture of Northern England*. Tucked privately away down a mile-long winding drive, Markenfield is one of the most astonishing and romantic of Yorkshire's medieval houses: fortified, completely moated, and still privately owned.
**Location:** MAP 10:P8, OS Ref. SE294 672. Access from W side of A61. 2½ miles S of the Ripon bypass.
**Open:** 29 Apr–12 May & 17–30 Jun: daily, 2–5pm. Groups all year round by appointment.
**Admission:** Adult £4, Conc £3. Booked groups (min charge £80).
🍴 🎦 🅿 🅰 ✳ ✳

## MIDDLEHAM CASTLE 🏛

**Castle Hill, Middleham, Leyburn, North Yorkshire DL8 4QR**
**Tel:** 01969 623899  **E-mail:** customers@english-heritage.org.uk
www.english-heritage.org.uk/yorkshire
**Owner:** English Heritage  **Contact:** Visitor Operations Team
This was the childhood and favourite home of Richard III, where he learnt the military skills and the courtly manners appropriate for a future king. The massive keep, one of the largest in England, was both a defensive building and a self-contained residence for the Lords of Middleham.
**Location:** MAP 10:O7, OS Ref. SE128 875. At Middleham, 2m S of Leyburn on A6108.
**Open:** 1 Apr–30 Sept: daily, 10am–6pm. 1 Oct–20 Mar 2008: Sat–Wed, 10am–4pm. Closed 24–26 Dec & 1 Jan.
**Admission:** Adult £3.50, Child £1.80, Conc. £2.60. 15% discount for groups (11+).
ℹ Exhibition. 🅾 ⬒ Partial. ✳ In grounds, on leads. ✳ ✳

## MOUNT GRACE PRIORY 🏛

**Staddlebridge, Nr Northallerton, North Yorkshire DL6 3JG**
**Tel:** 01609 883494  **E-mail:** customers@english-heritage.org.uk
www.english-heritage.org.uk/yorkshire
**Owner:** English Heritage  **Contact:** Visitor Operations Team
This 3-in-1 site is enchanting: the monastery ruins are the best-preserved of any in Britain; the manor-house is a rare building of the Commonwealth period; and the gardens, re-modelled in the Arts & Crafts style, are a haven for the famous 'Priory Stoats'.
**Location:** MAP11:A7, OS Ref. SE449 985. 12m N of Thirsk, 7m NE of Northallerton on A19.
**Open:** 1 Apr–30 Sept: Thur–Mon, 10am–6pm. 1 Oct–20 Mar 2008: Thur–Sun, 10am–4pm. Closed 24–26 Dec & 1 Jan.
**Admission:** Adult £4, Child £2, Conc. £3, Family £10. 15% discount for groups (11+). NT Members Free, except on event days.
ℹ WCs. 🅾 🍴 🅿 ▦ ✳ ✳ ✳

## NATIONAL CENTRE FOR EARLY MUSIC

**St Margaret's Church, Walmgate, York YO1 9TL**
**Tel:** 01904 632220  **Fax:** 01904 612631  **E-mail:** info@ncem.co.uk  www.ncem.co.uk
**Owner:** York Early Music Foundation  **Contact:** Mrs G Baldwin
The National Centre for Early Music is based in the medieval church of St Margaret's York. The church boasts a 12th century Romanesque doorway and a 17th century brick tower of considerable note. The Centre hosts concerts, music education activities, conferences, recordings and events.
**Location:** MAP 21, OS Ref. SE609 515. Inside Walmgate Bar, within the city walls, on the E side of the city.
**Open:** Mon–Fri, 10am–4pm. Also by appointment. Access is necessarily restricted when events are taking place.
**Admission:** Free, donations welcome.
⬒ 🎦 By arrangement. 🅿 Limited. No coaches. ✳ Guide dogs only. ▦ ✳ ✳

## NEWBY HALL & GARDENS 🏛
*See page 382 for full page entry.*

## NEWBURGH PRIORY
### COXWOLD, NORTH YORKSHIRE  YO61 4AS

**Tel:** 01347 868435

**Owner/Contact:** Sir George Wombwell Bt

Originally 1145 with major alterations in 1568 and 1720, it has been the home of the Earls of Fauconberg and of the Wombwell family since 1538. Tomb of Oliver Cromwell (3rd daughter Mary married Viscount Fauconberg) is in the house. Extensive grounds contain a water garden, walled garden, topiary yews and woodland walks.

**Location:** MAP 11:B8, OS Ref. SE541 764. 4m E of A19, 18m N of York, ½ m E of Coxwold.

**Open:** 1 Apr–27 Jun: Wed & Sun (open Easter Sun & Mon). House: 2.30–4.45pm. Garden: 2–6pm. Tours every ½ hour, take approximately 50mins. Booked groups by arrangement.

**Admission:** House & Grounds: Adult £5.50. Child £1.50. Gardens only: Adult £3, Child Free. Special tours of Private Apartment in addition to the above (Easter Sun & Mon and Weds & Suns 2 Apr–30 Apr) £5pp.

ℹ️ No photography in house. Ⓐ Partial. ☻ 🎞️ Obligatory. 🅿️ Limited for coaches. 🐕 In grounds, on leads. ▲

## NORTON CONYERS 🏛️
### Nr RIPON, NORTH YORKSHIRE  HG4 5EQ

**Tel/Fax:** 01765 640333  **E-mail:** norton.conyers@bronco.co.uk

**Owner:** Sir James and Lady Graham  **Contact:** Lady Graham

Visited by Charlotte Brontë in 1839, Norton Conyers is an original of 'Thornfield Hall' in 'Jane Eyre', and a family legend was an inspiration for the mad Mrs Rochester. House and garden have a friendly, quiet and unspoilt atmosphere. They have been in the Grahams' possession for 383 years. Family pictures, furniture, costumes and ceramics on display. 18th century walled garden near house, with Orangery and herbaceous borders. Small plants sales area specialising in unusual hardy plants. Pick your own fruit in season.

**Location:** MAP 11:A8, OS Ref. SF319 763. 4m N of Ripon. 3½ m from the A1.

**Open:** House: Closed for major structural repairs, due to re-open in June; please call for details. Garden: 8/9 Apr, 6/7 May; 27/28 May; 26/27 Aug. 3 Jun–30 Jul, Suns & Mons. 4–7 Jul, daily. All 2–5pm (last adm. 4.40pm). Groups by appointment.

**Admission:** House: Adult £5.50, Child (under 16yrs) Free, OAP £4. Garden: Admission is free; donations are welcome. A charge is made when the garden is open for charity. Groups by arrangement.

ℹ️ No interior photography. No high-heeled shoes. ☐ ℹ️ Ⓐ Partial. WC. ☻ Garden charity openings only. 🎞️ By arrangement. 🅿️ 🐕 Dogs, other than guide dogs, are not allowed in the house and must be on a lead in the grounds. 🐕

## NOSTELL PRIORY & PARKLANDS 🦌
### Doncaster Road, Wakefield, West Yorkshire  WF4 1QE
**Tel:** 01924 863892  **Fax:** 01924 866846  **E-mail:** nostellpriory@nationaltrust.org.uk
**www.nationaltrust.org.uk**

**Owner:** The National Trust  **Contact:** Visitor Services Manager

Set in over 350 acres of parkland, Nostell Priory is one of Yorkshire's jewels. It is an architectural treasure by James Pane with later additions by Robert Adam, and an internationally renowned Chippendale Collection.

**Location:** MAP 11:A11, OS Ref. SE403 175. 6m SE of Wakefield, off A638.

**Open:** Parklands open daily, dawn to dusk. Priory: 17 Feb–11 Mar, Sats & Suns, 12noon–4pm (pre-booked Conservation Tours). 17 Mar–4 Nov, Wed–Sun, 1–5pm (last admission 4.30pm). 7 Dec–16 Dec, 12 noon–4pm. Open BH. Gardens Shop & Stables Tearoom: 17 Feb–11 Mar & 7 Dec–16 Dec, 11am–4pm; 17 Mar–4 Nov, 11am–5.30pm.

**Admission:** Parkland: Free. House & Garden: Adult £7.20, Child £3.60, Family (2+4) £17.50. Garden only: Adult £4.40, Child £2. Groups (15+) £6.

ℹ️ Baby facilities. ☐ 🇹 Ⓐ Partial. WC. ☻ 🎞️ By arrangement. 🅿️ 🔲 🐕 In grounds, on leads. ▲ 🐕 Send SAE for details.

## NUNNINGTON HALL 🦌
### Nunnington, North Yorkshire  YO62 5UY
**Tel:** 01439 748283  **Fax:** 01439 748284
**Owner:** The National Trust  **Contact:** The Property Manager

17th century manor house with magnificent oak-panelled hall, nursery, haunted room, and attics, with their fascinating Carlisle collection of miniature rooms fully furnished to reflect different periods.

**Location:** MAP 11:C8, OS Ref. SE670 795. In Ryedale, 4½ m SE of Helmsley, 1½ m N of B1257.

**Open:** 17 Mar–4 Nov: Tues–Sun; Tearoom & Garden 12 noon–5pm, House & shop 1–5pm, (Jun, Jul & Aug closes 5.30). Last adm. 30 min before closing. Open BH Mons.

**\*Admission:** Adult £6, Child (under 17) £3, Family £15. Groups (15+) £5. National Trust Members Free. *includes a voluntary donation but visitors can choose to pay the standard prices displayed at the property and on the website.

☐ Ⓐ Ground floor and grounds. WC. ☻ 🐕 Guide dogs only. 🐕

## ORMESBY HALL 🦌
### Ladgate Lane, Ormesby, Middlesbrough  TS7 9AS
**Tel:** 01642 324188  **Fax:** 01642 300937  **E-mail:** ormesbyhall@nationaltrust.org.uk
**Owner:** The National Trust  **Contact:** Mr P Burton

A mid 18th century house with opulent decoration inside, including fine plasterwork by contemporary craftsmen.

**Location:** MAP 11:B6, OS Ref. NZ530 167. 3m SE of Middlesbrough.

**Open:** 17 Mar–4 Nov: Daily, 1.30–5pm. Tearoom: as House.

**Admission:** Adult £4.40, Child £2.80, Family £11.50. Groups £3.60pp. Grounds Free

☐ Ⓐ Ground floor & grounds. WC. ☻

## PARCEVALL HALL GARDENS
### Skyreholme, Skipton, North Yorkshire  BD23 6DE
**Tel:/Fax:** 01756 720311  **E-mail:** info@parcevallhallgardens.co.uk
**Owner:** Walsingham College (Yorkshire Properties) Ltd.
**Contact:** Phillip Nelson (Head Gardener)
**Location:** MAP 10:O8, OS Ref. SE068 613. E side of Upper Wharfedale, 1½ m NE of Appletreewick. 12m NNW of Ilkley by B6160 and via Burnsall.

**Open:** 1 Apr–31 Oct: 10am–6pm.

**Admission:** £5, Child 75p.

## PICKERING CASTLE ⚎
### Castlegate, Pickering, North Yorkshire  YO18 7AX
**Tel:** 01751 474989  **E-mail:** customers@english-heritage.org.uk
**www.english-heritage.org.uk/yorkshire**
**Owner:** English Heritage  **Contact:** Visitor Operations Team

An excellent example of a motte and bailey castle, built by William the Conqueror, with much of the original keep, towers and walls remaining, and offering superb views over North York Moors. It was used by a succession of medieval kings as a hunting lodge, holiday home and even stud farm.

**Location:** MAP 11:C7, OS Ref. SE800 845. In Pickering, 15m SW of Scarborough.

**Open:** 1 Apr–30 Sept: daily, 10am–6pm. Oct: Thur–Mon, 10am–5pm.

**Admission:** Adult £3, Child £1.50, Conc. £2.30, Family £7.50. 15% discount for groups (11+).

ℹ️ WCs. ☐ Ⓐ Partial. 🅿️ Limited. 🔲 🐕 In grounds, on leads. 🐕

## PLUMPTON ROCKS 🏠

**Plumpton, Knaresborough, North Yorkshire  HG5 8NA**
**Tel:** 01289 386360   **www.plumptonrocks.co.uk**
**Owner:** Edward de Plumpton Hunter   **Contact:** Robert de Plumpton Hunter
Grade II* listed garden extending to over 30 acres including an idyllic lake, dramatic millstone grit rock formation, romantic woodland walks winding through bluebells and rhododendrons. Declared by English Heritage to be of outstanding interest. Painted by Turner. Described by Queen Mary as '*Heaven on earth*'.
**Location:** MAP 11:A9, OS Ref. SE355 535. Midway between Harrogate and Wetherby on the A661, 1m SE of A661 junction with the Harrogate southern bypass.
**Open:** Mar–Oct: Sat, Sun & BHs, 11am–6pm.
**Admission:** Adult £2, Child/OAP £1. (Subject to change 2007.)
🚫 Unsuitable. 🅿 Limited for coaches. ⬛ ⬛ In grounds, on leads.

## RAF HOLMPTON - BUNKER TOURS

**RAF Holmpton, Rysome Lane, Withernsea, East Yorkshire  HU19 2QR**
**Tel:** 01964 630208 (24hr infoline)
**E-mail:** info@rafholmpton.com   **www.rafholmpton.com**
**Owner:** HIPPO/MOD   **Contact:** Peter Blake
Your chance to visit this vast Underground Headquarters some 100ft beneath the East Yorkshire Countryside. Fully guided tours, along with shows and displays, provide an insight into the Cold War history of this once secret place, still in operation today.
**Location:** MAP 11:G11, OS Ref. TA380 231. 19m from Hull, 3m S of Withernsea. (Follow the brown Bunker signs.)
**Open:** 17 Feb–1 Apr & 14 Sept–7 Oct: Fri–Sun. 6–22 Apr & 1 Jul–9 Sept: daily. 26 Apr–30 Jun: Thurs–Sun. 2pm. Tours depart at 2.30pm. Plus all BHs, Sat–Mon: 10.30 am. Tours depart 11am. Schools, groups, evening tours, other times by appointment.
**Admission:** Adult £5, Child £4, OAP. £4.50, Conc. £3, Family (2+3) £16.
ℹ Photography permitted. 📷 🚻 🚫 Partial. 🎦 ✖ Obligatory. 🅿 ⬛
⬛ In grounds on leads.

# RHS GARDEN HARLOW CARR
## CRAG LANE, HARROGATE, NORTH YORKSHIRE  HG3 1QB
### www.rhs.org.uk/harlowcarr

**Tel:** 01423 565418   **Fax:** 01423 530663   **E-mail:** harlowcarr@rhs.org.uk
**Owner:** Royal Horticultural Society   **Contact:** Allison Mitchell / Alison Allan
One of Yorkshire's most relaxing yet inspiring locations! Highlights of the beautiful 58 acre garden include contemporary herbaceous borders, Gardens through Time, streamside garden, alpines, scented and kitchen gardens, woodland and wildflower meadow, extensive Shop and Plant Centre, Betty's Café Tea Rooms and free parking. Events include outdoor theatre, festivals, workshops and children's activities.
**Location:** MAP 10:P9. OS Ref. SE285 543. 1½m W from town centre on B6162 Otley Road.
**Open:** Daily: 9.30am–6pm (4pm Nov–Feb). Last entry 1 hour before closing. Closed Christmas Day.
**Admission:** Adult £6, Child (6–16yrs) £2, Child (under 6yrs) Free. Groups (10+): £5. Groups must book in advance. RHS Members (+1 guest): Free.
ℹ Picnic area. 📷 🚻 🚫 Partial. WC. 🎦 Licensed. 🍴 Licensed. ✖ By arrangement.
🅿 ⬛ ⬛ Guide dogs only. ✱ 🎗

## RICHMOND CASTLE ⌗
### TOWER ST, RICHMOND, NORTH YORKSHIRE  DL10 4QW

www.english-heritage.org.uk/yorkshire

**Tel:** 01748 822493   **E-mail:** customers@english-heritage.org.uk
**Owner:** English Heritage   **Contact:** Visitor Operations Team
Built shortly after 1066 on a rocky promontory high above the River Swale, this is the best preserved castle of such scale and age in Britain. The magnificent Keep, with breathtaking views, is reputed to be the place where the legendary King Arthur sleeps. An exhibition and contemporary garden reflect the castle's military history from the 11th to 20th centuries.
**Location:** MAP 10:P6, OS Ref. NZ174 006. In Richmond.
**Open:** 1 Apr–30 Sept: daily, 10am–6pm. 1 Oct–20 Mar 2008: Thur–Mon, 10am–4pm. Closed 24–26 Dec & 1 Jan.
**Admission:** Adult £4, Child £2, Conc. £3. 15% discount for groups (11+).
ℹ Interactive exhibition. WCs. 📷 🚫 Partial. ⬛ ⬛ In grounds, on leads. ✱ 🎗

Sledmere House, Driffield

# RIEVAULX ABBEY ⌗
### RIEVAULX, Nr HELMSLEY, NORTH YORKSHIRE YO62 5LB
www.english-heritage.org.uk/yorkshire

**Tel:** 01439 798228   **E-mail:** customers@english-heritage.org.uk

**Owner:** English Heritage   **Contact:** Visitor Operations Team

Rievaulx was the first Cistercian Abbey to be founded in the North of England in the 12th century. Set in the Rye Valley, just a short drive from Helmsley, it is a place of beauty and calm. The atmospheric ruins were once home to the greatest spiritual writer of the Medieval Ages, St Aelred, who described it as *"everywhere peace, everywhere serenity, and a freedom from the tumult of the world"*. A special exhibition, "The Work of God and Man", looks at the commercial activities of the monks and shows how religion blended with business.

**Location:** MAP 11:B7, OS Ref. SE577 849. 2¼m W of Helmsley on minor road off B1257.

**Open:** 1 Apr–30 Sept: daily, 10am–6pm. 1 Oct–20 Mar 2008: Thur–Mon, 10am–4pm (5pm Oct). Closed 24–26 Dec & 1 Jan.

**Admission:** Adult £4.50, Child £2.30, Conc. £3.40. 15% discount for groups (11+).
ℹ WCs. 🔲 🚹 🚻 Partial. 🔳 🔘 🅿 ◼ 🔲 On leads. ✦ ⬛

---

## RIEVAULX TERRACE & TEMPLES
### Rievaulx, Helmsley, North Yorkshire YO62 5LJ
**Tel:** 01439 748283   **Fax:** 01439 748284

**Owner:** The National Trust   **Contact:** The Property Manager

A ½ m long grass-covered terrace and adjoining woodlands with vistas over Rievaulx Abbey and the Rye valley. There are two mid-18th century temples. Note: no access to the property Nov–end Mar.

**Location:** MAP 11:B7, OS Ref. SE579 848. 2½m NW of Helmsley on B1257. E of the Abbey.

**Open:** 17 Mar–30 Sept: Daily, 11am–6pm (5pm Oct–4 Nov). Last admission 1 hour before closing. Ionic Temple closed, 1-2pm.

**\*Admission:** Adult £4.40, Child (under 17yrs) £2.35, Family (2+3) £11. Groups (15+): £3.40. NT Members Free. *includes a voluntary donation but visitors can choose to pay the standard prices displayed at the property and on the website.
🔲 🔲 Grounds. Batricar available. 🔲 In grounds, on leads. ⬛

---

## RIPLEY CASTLE 🏠
*See page 383 for full page entry.*

---

## RIPON CATHEDRAL
### Ripon, North Yorkshire HG4 1QR
**Tel:** 01765 604108 (information on tours etc.)   **Contact:** Canon Keith Punshon

One of the oldest crypts in Europe (672). Marvellous choir stalls and misericords (500 years old). Almost every type of architecture. Treasury.

**Location:** MAP 10:P8, OS Ref. SE314 711. 5m W signposted off A1, 12m N of Harrogate.

**Open:** All year: 8am–6pm.

**Admission:** Donations: £3. Pre-booked guided tours available.

---

## ROCHE ABBEY ⌗
### Maltby, Rotherham, South Yorkshire S66 8NW
**Tel:** 01709 812739   **E-mail:** customers@english-heritage.org.uk
www.english-heritage.org.uk/yorkshire

**Owner:** English Heritage   **Contact:** Visitor Operations Team

Set in a beautiful, secluded valley landscaped by 'Capability' Brown in the 18th century, the early Gothic transepts of this 'miniature Fountains Abbey' still survive to their original height.

**Location:** MAP 7:B1, OS Ref. SK544 898. 1m S of Maltby off A634.

**Open:** 1 Apr–30 Sept: Thur–Mon, 10am–4pm.

**Admission:** Adult £3, Child £1.50, Conc. £2.30. 15% discount for groups (11+).
ℹ WCs. 🔲 🔲 Partial. 🅿 Limited. ◼ 🔲 In grounds, on leads.

---

## RYEDALE FOLK MUSEUM
### Hutton le Hole, York, North Yorkshire YO62 6UA
**Tel:** 01751 417367   **E-mail:** info@ryedalefolkmuseum.co.uk

**Owner:** The Crosland Foundation

13 historic buildings showing the lives of ordinary folk from earliest times to the present day.

**Location:** MAP 11:C7, OS Ref. SE705 902. Follow signs from Hutton le Hole. 3m N of Kirkbymoorside.

**Open:** 20 Jan–20 Dec: 10am–5.30pm (last adm. 4.30pm) or dusk during winter months.

**Admission:** Adult £4.50, Child £3, Conc. £4. Family (2+2) £12 (Season Ticket £25).

---

## ST PETER'S CHURCH & BONES ALIVE! EXHIBITION ⌗
### Beck Hill, Barton upon Humber DN18 5EX
**Tel:** 0870 333 1181   **E-mail:** customers@english-heritage.org.uk
www.english-heritage-org.uk

**Owner:** English Heritage   **Contact:** Customer Services

With a history spanning a millennium, St Peter's is both an architectural and archaeological treasure. The thousand-year architecture includes a working Anglo-Saxon bell-tower and some surprising gargoyles. A major new exhibition opening May 2007 includes the UK's largest resource for historic bone analysis from excavations of 2800 burials dating back over 900 years. This reveals groundbreaking new insights into the diseases, diet, medicine and beliefs of our ancestors, and the forgotten objects that lay with the dead for centuries – clues to human dreams and beliefs.

**Location:** MAP 11:E11, OS Ref TA03 3219. In Barton upon Humber town centre.

**Open:** 26 May–30 Sept, daily, 10am–5pm; Oct–20 Mar 2008, Sat–Mon, 10am–4pm. Closed 24-26 Dec & 1 Jan.

**Admission:** Adult £4, Child £2, Conc. £3.

---

©Tim Imrie-Tait/Country Life Picture Library

## SCAMPSTON HALL 🏛

### SCAMPSTON, MALTON, NORTH YORKSHIRE  YO17 8NG

www.scampston.co.uk

**Tel:** 01944 759111  **Fax:** 01944 758700  **E-mail:** info@scampston.co.uk
**Owner:** Sir Charles Legard Bt    **Contact:** The Administrator

Scampston is among the best examples of the English country house, set in 18th century 'Capability' Brown parkland. The Hall combines fine Regency architecture with a wealth of art treasures from earlier periods. Recently restored to its former glory, the house was voted *Country Life* "House of the Year" and was featured in 'Hidden Treasure Houses' on FIVE in 2006. Visitors are shown around this family home by the owner and other guides. Restaurant, disabled facilities and shop in the Walled Garden (see separate entry).

**Location:** MAP 11:D8, OS Ref. SE865 755. 4m E of Malton, off A64.
**Open:** 22 May–21 Jun: daily (closed Mons except BHs), 1.30–5pm (last adm. 4pm).
**Admission:** Adult £6, Child (12–16yrs) £3. Child (11yrs & under) Free. Combined Ticket for House and Walled Garden: Adult £9.50, Child (12–16yrs) £5. Groups by appointment. HHA Members & Friends free admission to house only.

🅵 🅿 ⌘

English Heritage Photo Library

## SCARBOROUGH CASTLE ⌗

### CASTLE ROAD, SCARBOROUGH, NORTH YORKSHIRE  YO11 1HY

www.english-heritage.org.uk/yorkshire

**Tel:** 01723 372451  **E-mail:** customers@english-heritage.org.uk
**Owner:** English Heritage    **Contact:** Visitor Operations Team

This 12th century castle conceals over 2,500 years of history encompassing the Roman army, Saxon monks, Viking invaders, Civil War besiegers and even First World War German naval guns. With wonderful views over the East Coast and a new exhibition giving further insight into the Castle's fascinating history, including artefacts excavated from the site.

**Location:** MAP 11:E7, OS Ref. TA050 893. Castle Road, E of town centre.
**Open:** 1 Apr–30 Sept: daily, 10am–6pm. 1 Oct–20 Mar 2008: Thur–Mon, 10am–4pm (5pm Oct). Closed 24–26 Dec & 1 Jan.
**Admission:** Adult £4, Child £2, Conc. £3, Family £10. 15% discount for groups (11+).

ℹ WCs. 📷 ♿ Partial. ☕ 🔊 Inclusive. 🔇 🔈 In grounds, on leads. ✱ ☗

## THE WALLED GARDEN
## AT SCAMPSTON

### SCAMPSTON HALL, MALTON, NORTH YORKSHIRE  YO17 8NG

www.scampston.co.uk

**Tel:** 01944 759111  **Fax:** 01944 758700  **E-mail:** info@scampston.co.uk
**Owner:** Sir Charles Legard Bt    **Contact:** The Administrator

A contemporary garden with striking perennial meadow planting, as well as traditional spring/autumn borders, created by internationally acclaimed designer and plantsman Piet Oudolf. Described in *The Times* as "a gem". "This garden will set standards for 21st century gardens for many years to come." *The Garden* November 2004. Excellent restaurant mentioned in *The Good Food Guide 2006*.

**Location:** MAP 11:D8, OS Ref. SE865 755. 4m E of Malton, off A64.
**Open:** 7 Apr–28 Oct: daily (closed Mons except BHs), 10am–5pm, last adm. 4.30pm.
**Admission:** Adult £5, Child (12–16yrs) £3, Senior £4.50. Child (11yrs & under) Free. Groups by arrangement. Combined Ticket for Walled Garden and House 22 May–21 Jun: Adult £9.50, Child (12–16yrs) £5. HHA Members & Friends free admission to house *only*.

🅵 🛇 ♿ ☕ 🍴 🅿 ⌘

## SHANDY HALL

### COXWOLD, NORTH YORKSHIRE  YO61 4AD

www.asterisk.org.uk

**Tel/Fax:** 01347 868465
**Owner:** The Laurence Sterne Trust    **Contact:** Mr P Wildgust

Here in 1760–1767 the witty and eccentric parson Laurence Sterne wrote Tristram Shandy and A Sentimental Journey. Shandy Hall was built as a timber-framed open-hall in the 15th century and added to by Sterne in the 18th. It houses the world's foremost collection of editions of Sterne's work, and is surrounded by a walled garden full of old-fashioned roses and cottage garden plants. Also an acre of wild garden in the adjoining old quarry. It is a lived-in house where you are sure of a personal welcome. May–Sept: exhibitions.

**Location:** MAP 11:B8, OS Ref. SE531 773. W end of Coxwold village, 4m E of A19 between Easingwold and Thirsk. 20m N of York.
**Open:** 1 May–30 Sept: Weds, 2–4.30pm. Suns, 2.30–4.30pm. Garden: 1 May–30 Sept: Sun–Fri, 11am–4.30pm. Other times by appointment.
**Admission:** Hall & Garden: Adult £4.50, Child £1.50. Garden only: Adult £2.50, Child £1.

ℹ No photography in house. 📷 ♿ Partial. ☕ In nearby village. 🅵 Obligatory.
🅿 ⌘

## SHIBDEN HALL

**Lister's Road, Halifax, West Yorkshire HX3 6XG**
**Tel:** 01422 352246   **Fax:** 01422 348440   **Email:** shibden.hall@calderdale.gov.uk
**www.calderdale.gov.uk**
**Owner:** Calderdale MBC   **Contact:** Valerie Stansfield
A half-timbered manor house, the home of Anne Lister, set in a landscaped park. Oak furniture, carriages and an array of objects make Shibden an intriguing place to visit.
**Location:** MAP 10:O11, OS Ref. SE106 257. 1½ m E of Halifax off A58.
**Open:** 1 Mar–30 Nov: Mon–Sat, 10am–5pm (last admission 4.30pm), Suns, 12 noon–5pm (last admission 4.30pm). Dec–Feb: Mon–Sat, 10am–4pm, Suns, 12 noon–4pm (last admission 3.30pm).
**Admission:** Adult £3.50, Child/Conc. £2.50, Family £10. Prices subject to change April 2007.
⬜ 🖼 ♿ Ground floor & grounds. 🖥 📷 By arrangement. 🅿 🔲 🐕 In grounds on leads.
❄

## SION HILL HALL 🏛

**KIRBY WISKE, THIRSK, NORTH YORKSHIRE YO7 4EU**
www.sionhillhall.co.uk

**Tel:** 01845 587206   **Fax:** 01845 587486   **E-mail:** sionhill@btconnect.com
**Owner:** H W Mawer Trust   **Contact:** R M Mallaby
Designed in 1912 by the renowned York architect Walter H Brierley, 'the Lutyens of the North', receiving an award from the Royal Institute of British Architects as being of 'outstanding architectural merit'. Sion Hill contains the H W Mawer collection of fine furniture, porcelain, paintings and clocks in superb settings.
**Location:** MAP 11:A7, OS Ref. SE373 844. 6m S of Northallerton off A167, signposted. 4m W of Thirsk, 6m E of A1 via A61.
**Open:** Jun–Sept: Weds only, 1–5pm, last entry 4pm. Also Easter Sun and all BH Mons. Guided tours during public opening times/Connoisseur tours at any time May–Oct by arrangement.
**Admission:** House: Adult £4.50, Child 12–16yrs, £2, Child under 12yrs £1, Conc. £4. Guided tours during public opening times: £5.75ea. Connoisseur Tours: £8.50. Grounds: £1.50.
♿ Partial. WC. 🖥 📷 🅿

---

**SKIPTON CASTLE**                    *See page 384 for full page entry.*

Burton Agnes Hall & Gardens, Driffield

---

## SLEDMERE HOUSE 🏛

**SLEDMERE, DRIFFIELD, EAST YORKSHIRE YO25 3XG**
www.sledmerehouse.com

**Tel:** 01377 236637   **Fax:** 01377 236560   **Email:** info@sledmerehouse.com
**Owner:** Sir Tatton Sykes Bt   **Contact:** The House Secretary
Nestling high on the Yorkshire Wolds, Sledmere House is the home of Sir Tatton Sykes, 8th Baronet. The present house was built in 1751 and enlarged by Sir Christopher Sykes, 2nd Baronet, in the 1780s. Sympathetically restored in the early 1900s after a disastrous fire, the house exudes 18th century elegance with each room containing decorative plasterwork by Joseph Rose Junior, and examples of the finest craftsmen of the period, including Chippendale, Hepplewhite and Sheraton. A tour of the house culminates in the magnificent Library which overlooks the 'Capability' Brown inspired landscaped park. Award–winning Garden including, Octagonal Walled Garden and Parterre, Wagoners' Military Museum, Children's Quiz, Picnic and Play Area, The Terrace Café and Gift Shop. Famous pipe organ played Wed & Sun, 1.30–3.30pm
**Location:** MAP 11:D9, OS Ref. SE931 648. Off the A166 between York & Bridlington. Half-hour scenic drive from York, Bridlington & Scarborough, 7 miles NW of Driffield.
**Open:** Easter: 6–9 Apr. 29 Apr–30 Sept, Tues–Thurs & Suns, also Fris Jun–Aug. BH Sats & Mons, 11am–4pm (last admission). Grounds, Shop & Café: 10am–5pm
**Admission:** House & Gardens: Adult £6, Child £2, Conc. £5.50. Groups (15+) £5. Gardens & Park: Adult £4, Child £1, RHS members £3 (Gardens & Grounds only).
ℹ No photography in house. ⬜ 🎁 🍴 ♿ 🖥 Licensed. 📷 By arrangement: Garden Tour & Park, Estate & Outbuildings Tour. Tel for arrangements. 🅿 🔲
🐕 In grounds on leads. Guide dogs in house. ▲

## STOCKELD PARK

**WETHERBY, NORTH YORKSHIRE LS22 4AW**
**Tel:** 01937 586101   **Fax:** 01937 580084
**Owner:** Mr and Mrs P G F Grant   **Contact:** Mrs L A Saunders
Stockeld is a beautifully proportioned Palladian villa designed by James Paine in 1763, featuring a magnificent cantilevered staircase in the central oval hall. The much loved home to the same family for 150 years, Stockeld houses a fine collection of 18th and 19th century furniture and paintings. The house is surrounded by stunning gardens of formal clipped hedges and topiary mixed with flowing herbaceous and shrub plantings. It is fringed by ancient woodland and set in over 100 acres of magnificent parkland in the midst of an extensive farming estate. A beautiful and fascinating house which is a popular location for filming and photography. Perfect parkland setting for exclusive outdoor activities.
**Location:** MAP 11:A9, OS Ref. SE376 497. York 12m, Harrogate 5m, Leeds 12m.
**Open:** Privately booked events only. Please contact the Estate Office: 01937 586101.
**Admission:** Prices on application.
♿ House only. 🐕

# SUTTON PARK

### SUTTON-ON-THE-FOREST, NORTH YORKSHIRE YO61 1DP

www.statelyhome.co.uk

**Tel:** 01347 810249/811239 **Fax:** 01347 811251 **E-mail:** suttonpark@fsbdial.co.uk
**Owner:** Sir Reginald & Lady Sheffield **Contact:** Administrator
The Yorkshire home of Sir Reginald and Lady Sheffield. Charming example of early Georgian architecture. Magnificent plasterwork by Cortese. Rich collection of 18th century furniture, paintings, porcelain, needlework, beadwork. All put together with great style to make a most inviting house. Award winning gardens attract enthusiasts from home and abroad. Silver Gilt Yorkshire in Bloom 2006.
**Location:** MAP 11:B9, OS Ref. SE583 646. 8m N of York on B1363 York–Helmsley Road.
**Open:** House: Apr–Sept: Wed, Sun & BHs, 1.30–5pm. Gardens: Apr–Sept: daily, 11am–5pm. Tearoom: Apr–end Sept: Wed–Sun, 11am–5pm. Private groups any other day by appointment. House open Oct–Mar for private parties (15+) only.
**Admission:** House & Garden: Adult £6, Child £3.50, Conc. £5. Coaches £5.50. Private Groups (15+): £6.50. Gardens only: Adult £3.50, Child £1, Conc. £2.50. Coaches £3. Caravans: £7 per unit per night. Electric hookup: £9 per unit per night.
[i] No photography. [T] Lunches & dinners in Dining Room. [&] Partial. WCs. [•] Home-baked fayre. [ƒ] Obligatory. [P] Limited for coaches.

# TEMPLE NEWSAM

### LEEDS LS15 0AE

www.leeds.gov.uk/templenewsam

**Tel:** 0113 2647321 **E-mail:** temple.newsam@leeds.gov.uk
**Owner:** Leeds City Council **Contact:** Denise Lawson
One of the great country houses of England, this Tudor-Jacobean mansion was the birthplace of Lord Darnley, husband of Mary Queen of Scots and home to the Ingram family for 300 years. Rich in newly restored interiors, paintings, furniture (including Chippendale), textiles, silver and ceramics; an ever-changing exhibitions programme, audio-tours, family activities and children's trails are also on offer along with one of the largest working rare breed farms in Europe. Temple Newsam sits within 1500 acres of grand and beautiful 'Capability' Brown parkland with formal and wooded gardens as well as national plant collections.
**Location:** MAP 10:P10, OS Ref. SE358 321. 5m E of city centre, off A63 Selby Road. M1/J46.
**Open:** 27 Mar–30 Oct: Tue–Sun and BHs, House: 10.30am–5pm, Farm: 10am–5pm. 31 Oct–26 Mar: Tue–Sun and BHs. House: 10.30am–4pm. Farm, 10am–4pm. Last admission ¾ hour before closing. Estate open free, dawn to dusk.
**Admission:** House only: Adult £3.50, Child £2.50, Family £9. House and Home Farm: Adult £5, Child £3.50, Family £14, special rates for educational groups. Parking £3.50 (car), £15 (coach), annual parking pass £10.
[□][T][&][•][ƒ][🌳][P][■][☒][♿]

## THORNTON ABBEY AND GATEHOUSE ⊞

**Ulceby DN39 6TU**
**Tel:** 0870 333 1181 **E-mail:** customers@english-heritage.org.uk
**www.english-heritage-org.uk**
**Owner:** English Heritage **Contact:** Customer Services
The enormous Gatehouse of Thornton Abbey is the finest surviving in Britain, its ornate facade trumpeting the prosperity of what was once one of the wealthiest Augustinian monasteries. But the Gatehouse has a darker side. Built and fortified in the nervous years following the Peasants' Revolt of 1381, it is thought to have protected the Abbey's treasures as well as the Abbot and his guests. A major restoration has opened locked doors and narrow passageways including the wall-walk. Now, for the first time, the Gatehouse will be opened to visitors in its entirety. In a new exhibition, explore the often turbulent lives of its former residents – and the wilder modern inhabitants of the Abbey ruins.
**Location:** MAP 11:E11, OS Ref TA117 188. 18m NE of Scunthorpe on a road N of A160. 7m SE of Humber Bridge, on a road E of A1077.
**Open:** 30 Jun–30 Sept: daily, 10am–5pm; 1 Oct–20 Mar, Fri–Sun, 10am–4pm. Closed 24–26 Dec & 1 Jan.
**Admission:** Adult £4, Child £2, Conc. £3.

## THORP PERROW ARBORETUM, WOODLAND GARDEN BIRDS OF PREY & MAMMAL CENTRE

**Bedale, North Yorkshire DL8 2PR**
**Tel/Fax:** 01677 425323 **E-mail:** enquiries@thorpperrow.com
**www.thorpperrow.com**
**Owner:** Sir John Ropner Bt **Contact:** Louise McNeill
85 acres of woodland walks. One of the largest collections of trees and shrubs in the north of England, including a 16th century spring wood and 19th century pinetum, and holds five National Collections – Ash, Lime, Walnut, Laburnum and Cotinus. The Falcons of Thorp Perrow is a captive breeding and conservation centre. Three flying demonstrations daily throughout the season. New for 2007 Mammal Centre.
**Location:** MAP 10:P7, OS Ref. SE258 851. Bedale–Ripon road, S of Bedale, 4m from Leeming Bar on A1.
**Open:** All year: dawn–dusk. Telephone for winter opening times.
**Admission:** Arboretum & Falcons: Adult £6.10, Child £3.30, OAP £4.80, Family (2+2) £18, (2+4) £24. Groups prices available.
[i] Picnic area. Children's playground. [□][■][&] Partial. WCs. [•] Licensed.
[ƒ] By arrangement. [P] Limited for coaches. [■][🐕] In grounds, on leads. [❋][♿]

## TREASURER'S HOUSE ⚜

**Minster Yard, York, North Yorkshire YO1 7JL**
**Tel:** 01904 624247 **Fax:** 01904 647372 **E-mail:** treasurershouse@nationaltrust.org.uk
**Owner:** The National Trust **Contact:** The Property Manager
Named after the Treasurer of York Minster and built over a Roman road, the house is not all that it seems! Nestled behind the Minster, the size and splendour and contents of the house are a constant surprise to visitors – as are the famous ghost stories. Free trails for children and free access to the National Trust tearoom.
**Location:** MAP 21, OS Ref. SE604 523. The N side of York Minster. Entrance on Chapter House St.
**Open:** 17 Mar–4 Nov: daily except Fri, 11am–4.30pm. 5–30 Nov: daily except Fri, 11am–3pm. (Tearoom, ghost cellar, partial access to show rooms via themed tours.)
**Admission:** Adult £5, Child £2.50, Family £12.50. Booked groups (15+): Adult £4.20, Child £2.10. House & Cellar: Adult £7, Child £4. Groups: Adult £6.20, Child £3.50.
[T][&] Partial. WC. [•] Licensed. [Ⅱ] Licensed. [P] None. [■][🐕] In grounds, on leads. [▲]

## WALCOT HALL

**Nr Alkborough, North Lincolnshire DN15 9JT**
**Tel:** 01724 720207 **Fax:** 01724 720226 **E-mail:** WalcotHallEstate@gmail.com
**www.WalcotHallEstate.com**
**Owner:** Mr & Mrs Anthony Lane-Roberts **Contact:** Lucinda
Grade II listed Georgian hall built in 1726 with canted bays at either end and an imposing doric portico. Originally the family seat of Goulton-Constables. Set in glorious parkland in the North Lincolnshire countryside with five acres of beautifully landscaped gardens.
**Location:** MAP 11:D11, OS Ref. SE872 872. 15 mins SW of Humber Bridge & 15 mins N of M181. 45 mins from Robin Hood & Doncaster international airports.
**Open:** Not open to the general public. Available for exclusive hire as a film location, corporate, weddings and special events.
[T][&] Partial. [P][▲][♿]

See which properties offer **educational facilities** or **school visits** in our index on page 571.

# WASSAND HALL
## SEATON, HULL, EAST YORKSHIRE HU11 5RJ
www.wassand.co.uk

**Tel:** 01964 534488　**Fax:** 01964 533334　**E-mail:** reorussel.wassand@tiscali.co.uk
**Owner/Contact:** R E O Russell – Resident Trustee
Fine Regency house 1815 by Thomas Cundy the Elder. Beautifully restored walled gardens, woodland walks, Parks and vistas over Hornsea Mere, part of the Estate since 1580. The Estate was purchased circa 1539 by Dame Joan Constable and has remained in the family to the present day, Mr Rupert Russell being the great nephew of the late Lady Strickland-Constable. The house contains a fine collection of 18/19th century paintings, English and Continental silver, furniture and porcelain. Wassand is very much a family home and retains a very friendly atmosphere. Homemade afternoon teas are served in the conservatory on Open Days.

**Location:** MAP 11:F9, OS Ref. TA174 460. On the B1244 Seaton–Hornsea road. Approximately 2m from Hornsea.
**Open:** 25–28 May; 7–11 & 22–26 Jun; 13/14 Jul; 3–6, 9–13 & 24–27 Aug: 2–5pm.
**Admission:** Hall, all grounds & walks: Adult £5, Child (11–15yrs) £3. Hall: Adult £3, Child (11–15yrs) £1.50. Grounds & Garden: Adult £3, Child (11–15yrs) £1.50. Child under 10yrs Free.

⟐ Limited. ⬛ ⟐ By arrangement. **P** Ample for cars, limited for coaches.
⬛ In grounds, on leads. ⬛ Victorian carriage rides on certain weekends.
15 Jul: Afternoon concert, 11 Aug: Music & Mirth Review evening.

---

## WENTWORTH CASTLE GARDENS

**Lowe Lane, Stainborough, Barnsley, South Yorkshire  S75 3ET**
**Tel:** 01226 776040　**Fax:** 01226 776042
**Owner:** Wentworth Castle Trust　**Contact:** Richard Evans – Heritage Director
This historic 18th century parkland estate features over 26 listed monuments and a magnificent 60-acre pleasure garden open on selected days from spring to autumn.
**Location:** MAP 10:P12, OS Ref. SE320 034. 5km W of Barnsley, M1/J36 via Birdwell & Rockley Lane then Lowe Lane.
**Open:** Gardens open on selected days while a programme of restoration takes place. Please telephone the gardens direct for details of opening times.
**Admission:** Garden: Adult £2.50, Conc. £2. Guided tours: Adult £3.50, Conc. £2.50.

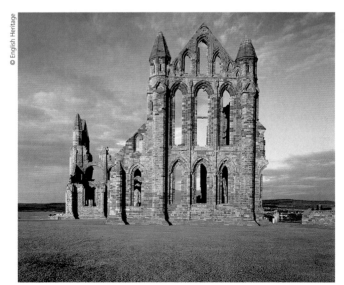

Whitby Abbey

# WHITBY ABBEY ⌗
## WHITBY, NORTH YORKSHIRE  YO22 4JT

www.english-heritage.org.uk/yorkshire

**Tel:** 01947 603568　**E-mail:** customers@english-heritage.org.uk
**Owner:** English Heritage　**Contact:** Visitor Operations Team
Since pre-history, successive generations have been drawn to this headland location. Founded by St Hilda in AD657, Whitby Abbey soon acquired great influence, before being ransacked by the invading Viking army. It was to be 200 years before the monastic tradition was revived, but yet again the Abbey was plundered, this time following the Dissolution. Following detailed archaeological investigation of the site, an interactive History Gallery recreates images of the Abbey over time and includes "Talking Heads" of personalities from the past.
**Location:** MAP 11:D6, OS Ref. NZ904 115. On cliff top E of Whitby.
**Open:** 1 Apr–31 Oct: daily, 10am–6pm (5pm in Oct). 1 Nov–20 Mar 2008: Thur–Mon, 10am–4pm. Closed 24–26 Dec & 1 Jan.
**Admission:** Adult £4.20, Child £2.10, Conc. £3.20, Family £10.50. 15% discounts for groups (11+).

ℹ WCs. ⟐ ⟐ Ground floor. ⬛ Managed by the YHA. ⟐ **P** Charged. ⬛
⬛ In grounds, on leads. ❋ ⬛

## WILBERFORCE HOUSE

**25 High Street, Hull, East Yorkshire HU1 1NQ**
**Tel:** 01482 613902 **Fax:** 01482 613710
**Owner:** Hull City Council **Contact:** S R Green
Birthplace of William Wilberforce – slavery abolitionist. Displays include costume gallery, the history of slavery, clocks and the Hull Silver Collection.
**Location:** MAP 11:E11, OS Ref. TA102 286. High Street, Hull.
**Open:** Currently closed for refurbishment. Open end March 2007.
**Admission:** Free.

## THE WORKHOUSE MUSEUM

**Allhallowgate, Ripon, North Yorkshire HG1 4LE**
**Tel:** 01765 690799 **Contact:** The Curator
"Vacancies for Vagrants: bath, 2 nights' bed and board; payment – stone breaking & wood chopping".
**Location:** MAP 10:P8, OS Ref. SE312 712 Close to Market Square.
**Open:** 1 Apr–31 Oct: daily except Weds, 1–4pm. During local school holidays open 11am–4pm. Groups anytime by appointment.
**Admission:** Adult £2.50, Child under 6yrs Free, Conc/Student £2. (Prices may change in 2007.)

## WORTLEY HALL

**Wortley, Sheffield, South Yorkshire S35 7DB**
**Tel:** 0114 2882100 **Fax:** 0114 2830695
**Owner:** Labour, Co-operative & Trade Union Movement **Contact:** Marc Mallender
15 acres of formal Italianate gardens surrounded by 11 acres of informal pleasure grounds.
**Location:** MAP 6:P1, OS Ref. SK313 995. 10kms S of Barnsley in Wortley on A629.
**Open:** Gardens: Mar–Oct, Wed–Fri. 3 Jun & 26 Aug: Specialist Plant Fairs.
**Admission:** Donation. Garden tours with Head Gardener for groups (15+) £2.

# YORK GATE GARDEN

**BACK CHURCH LANE, ADEL, LEEDS, WEST YORKSHIRE LS16 8DW**

www.perennial.org.uk/yorkgate.html

**Tel:** 0113 2678240
**Owner:** Perennial **Contact:** The Garden Co-ordinator
Inspirational one acre garden renowned for its outstanding design and exquisite detail. A series of smaller gardens, separated by hedges and stone walls, are linked by a succession of delightful vistas. One of many highlights is the famous herb garden with topiary.
**Location:** MAP 10:P10, OS Ref. 275 403. 2¼m SE of Bramhope. ½m E of A660.
**Open:** 8 Apr–30 Sept: Thur, Sun & BH Mons, 2–5pm. Also 21 & 27 Jun and 5 Jul, 6:30–9pm.
**Admission:** Adult £3.50, Child (16yrs & under) Free. Season Ticket £8.50.
Free access for RHS Members in Apr, May and Sept.
ⓘ Groups must book. 🍴 When available. ☕ Tea & Biscuits. 🅵 By arrangement.
🅿 Limited. 🐕 Guide dogs only.

## YORK MINSTER

**Deangate, York YO1 7HH**
**Tel:** 01904 557216 **Fax:** 01904 557218 **E-mail:** visitors@yorkminster.org
**Owner:** Dean and Chapter of York **Contact:** Stephen Hemming
Large gothic church housing the largest collection of medieval stained glass in England.
**Location:** MAP 21, OS Ref. SE603 522. Centre of York.
**Open:** All year: Mon–Sat, 9.30am–5pm, Sun: 12 noon–5pm.
**Admission:** Adult £5, Child (under 16yrs) Free, Conc. £4. Groups: Adult £4.50, Child (under 16yrs) Free, Conc. £3.50.

Who's offering **accommodation?**
See our index on page 575.

Burton Constable Hall, Skirlaugh

**Above:** Hutton-in-the-Forest
**Right:** Arley Hall

# North West

Cheshire

Cumbria

Lancashire

Merseyside

*Cheshire has two strikingly different faces; the East, more industrial and more rugged where it adjoins the Peak District National Park, and the West, the flatter 'Cheshire Plain', more densely farmed and with easily recognisable red brick buildings. On the edge of the Lake District is Levens Hall and to the west is Muncaster Castle and its fascinating Owl Centre. For children, a visit to the Beatrix Potter Gallery is a must.*

■ **Owner**

Mrs C J C Legh

■ **Contact**

**Corporate Enquiries:**
The Hunting Lodge
Adlington Hall
Macclesfield
Cheshire
SK10 4LF

**Tel:** 01625 827595
**Fax:** 01625 820797
**E-mail:** enquiries@
adlingtonhall.com

**Hall Tours:**
The Estate Office
Tel: 01625 829206

■ **Location**

**MAP 6:N2**
**OS Ref. SJ905 804**

5m N of
Macclesfield, A523,
13m S of Manchester.
London 178m.

**Rail:** Macclesfield
& Wilmslow
stations 5m.

**Air:** Manchester
Airport 8m.

■ **Opening Times**

**August**
Suns–Weds,
2–5pm.

(closed Sun 19th August).

■ **Admission**

**Hall & Gardens**
| | |
|---|---|
| Adult | £6.00 |
| Child | £3.00 |
| Student | £3.00 |
| Groups of 20+ | £5.50 |

# ADLINGTON HALL

www.adlingtonhall.com

Adlington Hall, the home of the Leghs of Adlington from 1315 to the present day, was built on the site of a Hunting Lodge which stood in the Forest of Macclesfield in 1040. Two oaks, part of the original building, remain with their roots in the ground and support the east end of the Great Hall, which was built between 1480 and 1505.

The Hall is a manor house, quadrangular in shape, and was once surrounded by a moat. Two sides of the Courtyard and the east wing were built in the typical 'Black and White' Cheshire style in 1581. The south front and west wing (containing the Drawing Room and Dining Room) were added between 1749 and 1757 and are built of red brick with a handsome stone portico with four Ionic columns on octagonal pedestals. Between the trees in the Great Hall stands an organ built

by 'Father' Bernard Smith (c1670-80). Handel subsequently played on this instrument and, now fully restored, it is the largest 17th century organ in the country.

**Gardens**

The gardens were landscaped in the style of 'Capability' Brown in the middle of the 18th century. Visitors may walk round the 'wilderness' area; among the follies to be seen are 'Temple to Diana', a 'Shell Cottage', Chinese bridge and T'ing house. There is a fine yew walk and a lime avenue planted in 1688. An old-fashioned rose garden and yew maze have recently been planted. In this continually evolving garden, the 'Father Tiber' water garden was created in 2002. The Hunting Lodge is part of the converted Georgian Mews, a first floor conference and banqueting suite.

| | Suitable for corporate events, product launches, business meetings, conferences, concerts, fashion shows, garden parties, rallies, clay-pigeon shooting, filming and weddings. |
|---|---|
| | The Great Hall and Dining Room are available for corporate entertaining. Catering can be arranged. |
| | Visitors may alight at entrance to Hall. WCs. |
| | By arrangement. |
| | For 100 cars and 4 coaches, 100 yds from Hall. |
| | By prior appointment. |

**Conference/Function**

| ROOM | SIZE | MAX CAPACITY |
|---|---|---|
| Great Hall | 11 x 8m | 80 |
| Dining Rm | 10.75 x 7m | 80 |
| Courtyard | 27 x 17m | 200 |
| Hunting Lodge | | 130 |

# ARLEY HALL & GARDENS

www.arleyhallandgardens.com

Owned by the same family for over 500 years, Arley is a delightful estate. The award-winning gardens, recently voted in the top 50 in Europe and in Britain's top 10, have been created gradually over 250 years with each generation of the family making its own contribution. The result is a garden of great atmosphere, interest and vitality, which blends strong elements of design from earlier centuries with modern ideas in both planting and design. Arley is, therefore, a wonderful example of the idea that the best gardens are living, changing works of art. Outstanding features are the renowned double herbaceous border (c1846), the Quercus Ilex and pleached Lime Avenues, Victorian Rootree, walled gardens, yew hedges and shrub rose collection. The family tradition continues today with the current Viscount Ashbrook, who over the last 30 years has created the less formal Grove and Woodland Walk, where 300 varieties of rhododendron grow amongst a collection of rare trees and shrubs in a delightful tranquil setting.

One of Cheshire's most charming stately homes, the Hall (Grade II*) was built by the present Viscount Ashbrook's great, great grandfather, Rowland Egerton-Warburton between 1832 and 1885 and is a fine example of the Victorian Jacobean style. Each room is given its own individual character by the elaborate plasterwork, wood panelling, family portraits and porcelain. From the grandeur of the Gallery to the intimacy of the Library the Hall exudes charm. The Emperor's Room was even home to Prince Louis Napoleon, later Napoleon III of France, in the winter of 1847–48.

Arley won the title of 2006 'Small Visitor Atraction of the Year' in the North West and is also a wonderful exclusive venue for weddings, corporate functions and private parties.

### Owner
Viscount & Viscountess Ashbrook

### Contact
Estate Secretary
Arley
Nr Northwich
Cheshire  CW9 6NA

**Tel:** 01565 777353
**Fax:** 01565 777465
**E-mail:** enquiries@ arleyhallandgardens .com

### Location
**MAP 6:M2**
**OS Ref. SJ675 809**

5m W Knutsford,
5m from M6/J19 & 20
and M56/J9 & 10.

### Opening Times
31 March–30 September & October weekends.

Gardens: Tuesday–Sunday & BHs,
11am–5pm.

Hall: Tues, Suns & BHs,
12noon–4.30pm.

### Admission
**Gardens, Grounds & Chapel:**
| | |
|---|---|
| Adult | £5.00 |
| Child (5–15yrs) | £2.00 |
| Concession | £4.50 |
| Family | £12.00 |

**Hall & Gardens**
| | |
|---|---|
| Adult | £7.50 |
| Child (5–15yrs) | £3.00 |
| Concession | £6.50 |
| Family | £18.50 |
| Individual Season ticket | £25.00 |
| Joint Season Ticket | £40.00 |
| Family Season Ticket (2+2) | £58.00 |

### Special Events
**April 6–9**
Easter with Winnie the Pooh

**May 26/27**
Arley Horse Trials & Country Fair

**June 23/24**
Arley Garden Festival

**July 14**
Concert on the Park

**July 19**
Romeo and Juliet

**August 9**
Little Women

**August 12–17**
Chhildren's Fun Week

**October 27–28**
Pumpkin and Halloween Festival

**December 1–10**
Christmas Floral Extravaganza

ℹ Suitable for weddings, corporate functions, product launches, conferences, filming, photography, concerts and fairs. Photography in Hall by permission only.

🏬 Open while the Garden is open.

🌷 Comprehensive set of menus available for entertaining in the Hall and Tudor Barn.

♿ Partial access to the Hall, full access to Gardens, WCs.

🍴 Licensed Tudor Barn Restaurant.

🚶 Welcomed by arrangement.

🅿

🚻

🐕 In the grounds on leads.

## ■ Owner

Mr & Mrs
Bromley-Davenport

## ■ Contact

Gwyneth Jones
Hall Manager
Capesthorne Hall
Siddington
Macclesfield
Cheshire  SK11 9JY

**Tel:** 01625 861221
**Fax:** 01625 861619
**E-mail:** info@
capesthorne.com

## ■ Location

**MAP 6:N2**
**OS Ref. SJ840 727**

5m W of Macclesfield.
30 mins S of Manchester
on A34.
Near M6, M63 and M62.

**Air:** Manchester
International 20 mins.

**Rail:** Macclesfield 5m
(2 hrs from London).

**Taxi:** 01625 533464.

## ■ Opening Times

**Summer**
April–Oct
Suns, Mons & BHs.

**Hall**
1.30–4pm.
Last admission 3.30pm.

**Gardens & Chapel**
12 noon–5pm.

Groups welcome by
appointment.

Caravan Park also open
Easter–end October.

Corporate enquiries:
March–December.

## ■ Admission

**Sundays & BHs only**
**Hall, Gardens & Chapel**
| | |
|---|---|
| Adult | £6.50 |
| Child (5–16yrs) | £3.00 |
| OAP | £5.50 |
| Family* | £15.00 |

*Parents and children
aged up to 16yrs in the
same car.

**Gardens & Chapel only**
| | |
|---|---|
| Adult | £4.00 |
| Child (5–16yrs) | £2.00 |
| OAP | £3.00 |

**Transfers from Gardens
& Chapel to Hall**
| | |
|---|---|
| Adult/OAP | £3.50 |
| Child (5–16yrs) | £1.50 |

**Mondays only: Hall,
Chapel & Gardens**
Car
| | |
|---|---|
| (up to 4 pass.) | £10.00 |
| Additional person | £2.50 |

Minibus
| | |
|---|---|
| (up to 12 pass) | £25.00 |

Coach
| | |
|---|---|
| (up to 50 pass) | £50.00 |

**Caravan Park**
| | |
|---|---|
| Up to 2 people | £16.00pn |
| Over 2 people | £20.00pn |

# CAPESTHORNE HALL 🏛

www.capesthorne.com

Capesthorne Hall, set in 100 acres of picturesque Cheshire parkland, has been touched by nearly 1,000 years of English history – Roman legions passed across it, titled Norman families hunted on it and, during the Civil War, a Royalist ancestress helped Charles II to escape after the Battle of Worcester. The Jacobean-style Hall has a fascinating collection of fine art, marble sculptures, furniture and tapestries. Originally designed by the Smiths of Warwick it was built between 1719 and 1732. It was altered by Blore in 1837 and partially rebuilt by Salvin in 1861 following a disastrous fire.

The present Squire is William Bromley-Davenport, Lord Lieutenant of Cheshire, whose ancestors have owned the estate since Domesday times when they were appointed custodians of the Royal Forest of Macclesfield.

In the grounds near the family Chapel the 18th century Italian Milanese Gates open onto the herbaceous borders and maples which line the beautiful lakeside gardens. But amid the natural spectacle and woodland walks, Capesthorne still offers glimpses of its man-made past … the remains of the Ice House, the Old Boat House and the curious Swallow Hole.

Facilities at the Hall can be hired for corporate occasions and family celebrations including Civil wedding ceremonies.

ℹ️ Available for corporate functions, meetings, product launches, promotions, exhibitions, presentations, seminars, activity days, Civil weddings and receptions, family celebrations, still photography, clay shooting, car rallies, garden parties, barbecues, concerts, antique, craft, country and game fairs. No photography in Hall.

🍽️ Catering can be provided for groups (full menus on request). Function rooms available for wedding receptions, corporate hospitality, meetings and other special events. 'The Butler's Pantry' serves tea, coffee and ices.

♿ Compacted paths, ramps. WCs.

🚶 For up to 50. Tours are by staff members or Hall Manager. Tour time 1 hr (approx).

🅿️ 100 cars/20 coaches on hard-standing and unlimited in park, 50 yds from house.

🐕 Guide dogs in Hall. Under control in Park.

**ADLINGTON HALL**   *See page 402 for full page entry.*

**ARLEY HALL AND GARDENS**   *See page 403 for full page entry.*

## BEESTON CASTLE ⚏

**Chapel Lane, Beeston, Tarporley, Cheshire  CW6 9TX**
**Tel:** 01829 260464   **E-mail:** customers@english-heritage.org.uk
**www.english-heritage.org.uk/beestoncastle**
**Owner:** English Heritage   **Contact:** Visitor Operations Team
Standing majestically on a sheer rocky crag, Beeston has perhaps the most stunning views of any castle in England. Its long history spans Bronze Age settlement to Iron Age hillfort, to impregnable royal fortress. This 4,000 year history is outlined in the "Castle of the Rock" exhibition.
**Location:** MAP 6:L3, OS Ref. SJ537 593. 11m SE of Chester on minor road off A49, or A41. 2m SW of Tarporley.
**Open:** 1 Apr–30 Sept: daily, 10am–6pm. 1 Oct–20 Mar: Thur–Mon, 10am–4pm. Closed 24–26 Dec & 1 Jan.
**Admission:** Adult £4, Child £2, Conc. £3. 15% discount for groups (11+).
ℹ Exhibition. WCs. ⬚ ♿ Unsuitable. 🅿 ■ ♿ In grounds on leads. ✳ ♨

**CAPESTHORNE HALL**   *See page 404 for full page entry.*

## CHESTER CATHEDRAL

**Werburgh Street, Chester, Cheshire**
**Tel:** 01244 500958   **Fax:** 01244 341110   **E-mail:** fry@chestercathedral.com
**Owner:** Church of England   **Contact:** Nicholas Fry
Medieval monastic complex.
**Location:** MAP 6:K2, OS Ref. SJ406 665. Chester city centre.
**Open:** Mon–Sat: 9am–5pm. Sun 1–5pm.
**Admission:** Adult £4, Child (5–16) £1.50, Senior Citizens/Groups £3, Family Ticket £10.

## CHESTER ROMAN AMPHITHEATRE ⚏

**Vicars Lane, Chester, Cheshire**
**Tel:** 01244 402466   **E-mail:** enquiries@chesteramphitheatre.co.uk
**www.chesteramphitheatre.co.uk**
**Owner:** Managed by English Heritage and Chester City Council
**Contact:** Chester City Council
The largest Roman amphitheatre in Britain, the site is in the process of being excavated. Work carried out over 2004/05 indicates that there were two stone-built amphitheatres, one very similar to those in Pompeii, emphasising the great importance of Chester during the Roman era.
**Location:** MAP 6:K2, OS Ref. SJ404 660. On Vicars Lane beyond Newgate, Chester.
**Open:** Any reasonable time.
**Admission:** Free.
♿ Partial ♿ On leads. ✳

# CHOLMONDELEY CASTLE GARDEN
## MALPAS, CHESHIRE  SY14 8AH

**Tel:** 01829 720383   **Fax:** 01829 720877   **E-mail:** penny@cholmondeleycastle.co.uk
**Owner:** The Marchioness of Cholmondeley   **Contact:** The Secretary
Extensive ornamental gardens dominated by romantic Gothic Castle built in 1801 of local sandstone. Visitors can enjoy the beautiful Temple Water Garden, Ruin Water Garden and memorial mosaic designed by Maggie Howarth. Rose garden and many mixed borders. Lakeside picnic area, children's play areas, rare breeds of farm animals, llamas, children's corner with rabbits, chickens and free flying aviary birds. Private chapel in the park.

**Location:** MAP 6:L3, OS Ref. SJ540 515. Off A41 Chester/Whitchurch Rd. & A49 Whitchurch/ Tarporley Road. 7m N of Whitchurch.
**Open:** 1 Apr–30 Sept, Wed, Thurs, Suns & BHs, 11.30am–5pm. Also opening for Autumn Tints Sun 7 and 21 Oct. Groups (25 +): Other days by prior arrangement at reduced rates. Castle not open to the public.
**Admission:** Adult £4, Child £2, no concessions.
⬚ 🏠 🍴 ♿ Limited. WCs. ♨ ♿ In grounds on leads only.

# DORFOLD HALL
## ACTON, Nr NANTWICH, CHESHIRE CW5 8LD

**Tel:** 01270 625245  **Fax:** 01270 628723

**Owner/Contact:** Richard Roundell

Jacobean country house built in 1616 for Ralph Wilbraham. Family home of Mr & Mrs Richard Roundell. Beautiful plaster ceilings and oak panelling. Attractive woodland gardens and summer herbaceous borders.

**Location:** MAP 6:L3, OS Ref. SJ634 525. 1m W of Nantwich on the A534 Nantwich–Wrexham road.

**Open:** Apr–Oct: Tue only and BH Mons, 2–5pm.

**Admission:** Adult £5, Child £3.

⚐ Obligatory. 🅿 Limited. Narrow gates with low arch prevent coaches. 🐕 In grounds on leads.

# GAWSWORTH HALL
## MACCLESFIELD, CHESHIRE SK11 9RN
www.gawsworthhall.com

**Tel:** 01260 223456  **Fax:** 01260 223469  **E-mail:** enquiries@gawsworthhall.com

**Owner:** Mr and Mrs T Richards  **Contact:** Mr T Richards

Fully lived-in Tudor half-timbered manor house with Tilting Ground. Former home of Mary Fitton, Maid of Honour at the Court of Queen Elizabeth I, and the supposed 'Dark Lady' of Shakespeare's sonnets. Pictures, sculpture and furniture. Open air theatre with covered grandstand – June, July and August, please telephone for details. Situated halfway between Macclesfield and Congleton in an idyllic setting close to the lovely medieval church.

**Location:** MAP 6:N2, OS Ref. SJ892 697. 3m S of Macclesfield on the A536 Congleton to Macclesfield road.

**Open:** Easter weekend then 5 May–23 Sept: Sun–Wed and for Special Events & BHs. Jul–Aug: daily, 2–5pm.

**Admission:** Adult £6, Child £3. Groups (20+): £5.

⬛ ⬛ 🅿 🐕 Guide dogs in garden only. ⬛ ⬛

## DUNHAM MASSEY

**Altrincham, Cheshire WA14 4SJ**

**Tel:** 0161 941 1025  **Fax:** 0161 929 7508

**E-mail:** dunhammassey@nationaltrust.org.uk  **www.nationaltrust.org.uk**

**Owner:** The National Trust  **Contact:** Property Manager

Originally an early Georgian house, Dunham Massey has sumptuous interiors with collections of walnut furniture, paintings and magnificent Huguenot silver. The richly planted garden contains waterside plantings, late flowering azaleas, an Orangery and Elizabethan mount. The surrounding deer park escaped the attentions of 18th century landscape gardeners and contains some notable specimen trees.

**Location:** MAP 6:M1, OS Ref. SJ735 874. 3m SW of Altrincham off A56. M6/J19. M56/J7. Station Altrincham (BR & Metro) 3m.

**Open:** House: 17 Mar–28 Oct: Sat–Wed, 12 noon–5pm (11am–5pm Good Fri, BH Sun & Mon). Garden: 17 Mar–28 Oct: daily, 11am–5.30pm. Last admission ½ hr before closing. Park open daily, all year.

**Admission:** House & Garden: Adult £7.50, Child £3.75, Family (2+3 max) £18.75. House or Garden: Adult £5, Child £2.50. Park entry: Car £4, Coach £10, Motorcycle £1. Groups should telephone for price details.

ⓘ No photography in house. ⬛ ⬛ ⬛ Partial. WC. Batricars. ⬛ Licensed. ⚐ Optional. No extra charge. 🅿 ⬛ 🐕 In grounds, on leads. ✳

## HARE HILL

**Over Alderley, Macclesfield, Cheshire SK10 4QB**

**Tel:** 01625 584412 (Countryside Office)

**www.nationaltrust.org.uk**

**Owner:** The National Trust  **Contact:** The Countryside Office

A woodland garden surrounding a walled garden with pergola, rhododendrons, hollies and hostas. Parkland.

**Location:** MAP 6:N2, OS Ref. SJ875 765. Between Alderley Edge and Macclesfield (B5087). Turn off N onto Prestbury Road, continue for ¾m.

**Open:** 31 Mar–6 May, 2 Jun–1 Nov: Wed, Thur, Sat, Sun 10am–5pm. 7 May–1 Jun: daily 10am–5pm.

**Admission:** Adult £3.20, Child £1.50. Car park fee £1.80 (refundable on entry to garden). Groups by written appointment c/o Garden Lodge at address above.

⬛ Gravel paths – strong companion advisable. 🐕 On leads in park.

## HOLMSTON HALL BARN

**Little Budworth, Tarporley, Cheshire CW6 9AY**

**Tel:** 01829 760366/07778 510287  **Fax:** 01829 760366

**Owner/Contact:** Mr Richard & Dr Yvonne Hopkins

Newly restored 15th century oak framed barn. Sandstone base and floors, with twelve exterior oak doors.

**Location:** MAP 6:L3, OS Ref. SJ607 626. Off A49. 2m from Eaton village.

**Open:** All year by appointment only.

**Admission:** Free.

✳

Patrick Lane

Dunham Massey, Altrincham

For **corporate hospitality** at unique venues see the index on page 567

## LITTLE MORETON HALL

**Congleton, Cheshire CW12 4SD**
**Tel:** 01260 272018   **www.nationaltrust.org.uk**
**Owner:** The National Trust   **Contact:** The Property Administrator
Begun in 1504 and completed 100 years later, Little Moreton Hall is regarded as the finest example of a timber-framed moated manor house in the country.
**Location:** MAP 6:N3, OS Ref. SJ833 589. 4m SW of Congleton on E side of A34.
**Open:** 3–18 Mar: Wed–Sun, 11.30am–4pm. 21 Mar–4 Nov: Wed–Sun & BH Mons, 11.30am–5pm. 10 Nov–16 Dec: Sats & Suns, 11.30am–4pm.
**Admission:** Adult £6, Child £3, Family £14. Groups: £5 (must book).
⬚ 🈳 ♿ Braille guide, wheelchair. WCs. 🖝 🍴 🎦 🅿 🐾 Car park only. 🐕

## LYME PARK

**Disley, Stockport, Cheshire SK12 2NX**
**Tel:** 01663 762023   **Fax:** 01663 765035   **www.nationaltrust.org.uk**
**Owner:** The National Trust   **Contact:** The Property Manager
Legh family home for 600 years. Part of the original Elizabethan house survives with 18th and 19th century additions by Giacomo Leoni and Lewis Wyatt. Mortlake tapestries, Grinling Gibbons carvings, unique collection of English clocks.
**Location:** MAP 6:N2, OS Ref. SJ965 825. Off the A6 at Disley. 6½m SE of Stockport. M60 J1.
**Open:** House: 23 Mar–30 Oct: Fri–Tue, 1–5pm (last adm 4.30pm) (BH Mons & Good Fri, 11am–5pm). Park: 1 Apr–31 Oct: daily, 8am–8.30pm; Nov–Mar: 8am–6pm. Gardens: 25 Mar–31 Oct: Fri–Tue, 11am–5pm; 4–24 Mar & 4 Nov–16 Dec: Sats & Suns only, 12noon–3pm.
**Admission:** House & Garden: £7. House only: £5.20. Garden only: £3.80. Park only: car £4.60 (refundable on purchase of adult House & Garden ticket), motorbike £2, coach £12, minibus £6. Booked coach groups Park admission Free. NT members Free.
ℹ No photography in house. ⬚ ♿ Partial. WC. 🖝 🍴 Licensed. 🎦 By arrangement. 🅿 🐾 In park, close control. Guide dogs only in house & garden. ❄

## NESS BOTANIC GARDENS

**Ness, Neston, Cheshire CH64 4AY**
**Tel:** 0151 353 0123   **Fax:** 0151 353 1004
**Owner:** University of Liverpool   **Contact:** Dr E J Sharples
New Visitor Centre opened in 2006. Leading garden in the North West for rhododendrons and azaleas.
**Location:** MAP 6:J2, OS Ref. SJ302 760 (village centre). Off A540. 10m NW of Chester. 1½m S of Neston.
**Open:** Mar–Oct: daily, 9.30am–5pm. Nov–Feb: 9.30am–4pm.
**Admission:** Adult £5, Conc £4.50, Child (under 18yrs) Free. 10% discount for groups. Please telephone for details.

## NETHER ALDERLEY MILL

**Congleton Rd, Nether Alderley, Macclesfield SK10 4TW**
**www.nationaltrust.org.uk**
**Tel:** 01625 527468 (Quarry Bank Mill Reception)
**E-mail:** netheralderleymill@nationaltrust.org.uk
**Owner:** The National Trust   **Contact:** Property Manager
15th century mill beside a tranquil millpond. Heavy framework, low beams and floors connected by wooden ladders, all set beneath an enormous sloping stone roof, help to create this wonderful corn mill.
**Location:** MAP 6:N2, OS Ref. SJ844 763. 1½m S of Alderley Edge, on E side of A34.
**Open:** 1 Apr–30 Oct: Thur, 1–5pm. Sun & BH Mons, 11am–5pm.
**Admission:** Adult £2.80, Child £1.50, Family £8.50. Groups by prior arrangement (max 20).
🎦 By arrangement. 🅿 Limited. Coaches must book. 🐾 By arrangement. ❄

Adlington Hall, Macclesfield

# NORTON PRIORY MUSEUM & GARDENS
### TUDOR ROAD, MANOR PARK, RUNCORN WA7 1SX
www.nortonpriory.org

**Tel:** 01928 569895   **E-mail:** info@nortonpriory.org
**Owner/Contact:** The Norton Priory Museum Trust
Discover the 800 year old priory range, excavated priory remains, museum gallery, the St Christopher statue – one of the great treasures of medieval Europe – exciting sculpture trail and award winning Walled Garden. Set in 38 acres of tranquil, woodland gardens, Norton Priory also has a coffee shop, retail area and temporary exhibitions gallery.
**Location:** MAP 6:K1, OS Ref. SJ545 835. 3m from M56/J11. 2m E of Runcorn.
**Open:** All year: daily, from 12 noon. Telephone for details.
**Admission:** Adult £4.75, Child/Conc. £3.45, Family £12.50. Groups £3.
⬚ 🈳 ♿ Wheelchairs, braille guide, audio tapes & WC. 🖝 🎦 By arrangement. 🅿 🐾 In grounds, on leads. ❄ 🐕

# PEOVER HALL 🏛
### OVER PEOVER, KNUTSFORD WA16 9HW
**Tel:** 01565 632358
**Owner:** Randle Brooks   **Contact:** I Shepherd
An Elizabethan house dating from 1585. Fine Carolean stables. Mainwaring Chapel, 18th century landscaped park. Large garden with topiary work, also walled and herb gardens.
**Location:** MAP 6:M2, OS Ref. SJ772 734. 4m S of Knutsford off A50 at Whipping Stocks Inn.
**Open:** Apr–Oct: House, Stables & Gardens: Mons except BHs, 2–5pm. Tours of the House at 2.30 & 3.30pm. Stables & Gardens only: Thur, 2–5pm.
**Admission:** House, Stables & Gardens: Adult £4.50, Child £3. Stables & Gardens only: Adult £3, Child £2.
🖝 Mondays only. 🎦 Obligatory. ❄

## QUARRY BANK MILL & STYAL ESTATE 🌿

**Styal, Wilmslow SK9 4LA**
**Tel:** 01625 527468   **Fax:** 01625 539267
**E-mail:** quarrybankmill@nationaltrust.org.uk   **www.nationaltrust.org.uk**
**Owner:** The National Trust   **Contact:** Visitor Services Manager
Unique Georgian Cotton Mill with working machinery, daily demonstrations and fascinating living history. See the steam engines and mighty watermill in action. Experience the grim conditions in the Apprentice House. Enjoy the beautiful 300 acre Styal Estate.

**Location:** MAP 6:N1, OS Ref. SJ835 835. 1½m N of Wilmslow off B5166. 2½m from M56/J5. Styal Shuttle Bus, Airport 2½m.
**Open:** Mill: 19 Mar–1 Oct: daily, 11am–5pm, last adm. 4pm. 2 Oct–28 Feb: Wed–Sun, 11am–4pm, last adm. 3pm. Apprentice House & Garden: 19 Mar–1 Oct, Tues–Sun; 2 Oct–28 Feb, Wed–Sun; 12.30–4.30pm term time, 11.30am–4.30pm, school holidays.
**Admission:** Mill only: Adult £6, Child £3.70, Family (2+3) £16. Mill & Apprentice House: Adult £9, Child £4.70, Family (2+3) £20, Group booking (15+) £7.50.
🖻 🖵 🛆 Partial. 🖼 🍴 Licensed. 🎦 By arrangement. 🅿 🖼 🖼 In grounds on leads.
🔺 ❀ ♨

Rode Hall

## RODE HALL 🏛
### CHURCH LANE, SCHOLAR GREEN, CHESHIRE ST7 3QP
www.rodehall.co.uk

**Tel:** 01270 873237   **Fax:** 01270 882962
**E-mail:** richard.wilbraham@btconnect.com
**Owner/Contact:** Sir Richard Baker Wilbraham Bt

The Wilbraham family have lived at Rode since 1669; the present house was constructed in two stages, the earlier two storey wing and stable block around 1705 and the main building was completed in 1752. Later alterations by Lewis Wyatt and Darcy Braddell were undertaken in 1812 and 1927 respectively. The house stands in a Repton landscape and the extensive gardens include a woodland garden, with a terraced rock garden and grotto, which has many species of rhododendrons, azaleas, hellebores and climbing roses following snowdrops and daffodils in the early spring. The formal rose garden was designed by W Nesfield in 1860 and there is a large walled kitchen garden which is at its best from the middle of June. The icehouse in the park has recently been restored.

**Location:** MAP 6:M3, OS Ref. SJ819 573. 5m SW of Congleton between the A34 and A50. Kidsgrove railway station 2m NW of Kidsgrove.
**Open:** 3 Apr–27 Sept: Weds & BHs and by appointment. Garden only: Tues & Thurs, 2–5pm. Snowdrop Walk: Feb daily (closed Mondays).
**Admission:** House, Garden & Kitchen Garden: Adult £5, Conc £4. Garden & Kitchen Garden: Adult £3, Concession £2.50. Snowdrop Walk: £3.
🎦 🖼 Home-made teas. 🖼 On leads.

## TABLEY HOUSE
### KNUTSFORD, CHESHIRE WA16 0HB
www.tableyhouse.co.uk

**Tel:** 01565 750151   **Fax:** 01565 653230   **E-mail:** inquiries@tableyhouse.co.uk
**Owner:** The University of Manchester   **Contact:** The Assistant Administrator
The finest Palladian House in the North West, Tabley a Grade I listing, was designed by John Carr of York for the Leicester family. Set in landscaped parkland it contains the first collection of English paintings, including works of art by Turner, Reynolds, Lawrence and Lely. Furniture by Chippendale, Bullock and Gillow and fascinating family memorabilia adorn the rooms. Interesting Tea Room and 17th century Chapel adjoin.

**Location:** MAP 6:M2, OS Ref. SJ725 777. M6/J19, A556 S on to A5033. 2m W of Knutsford.
**Open:** House: Apr–end Oct: Thurs–Suns & BHs, 2–5pm. Tea Room: All year, Thurs–Suns & BHs, 12noon–5pm. Closed 24 Dec 2007–9 Jan 2008.
**Admission:** Adult £4. Child/Student £1.50. Groups by arrangement.
🖻 🛆 Please telephone for easiest access. 🖼 🅿 🔺 Civil Wedding Licence plus Civil Naming Ceremonies & Re-affirmation of Vows. 🖼

# TATTON PARK 🌿
## KNUTSFORD, CHESHIRE WA16 6QN

www.tattonpark.org.uk

**Tel:** 01625 534400 **Info:** 01625 534435 **Fax:** 01625 534403
**Owner:** The National Trust (Managed by Cheshire County Council)

A stunning historic estate set in beautiful parkland. Over 1,000 acres of land are home to herds of red and fallow deer and provide the setting for the impressive Georgian Mansion designed by Wyatt. The Egerton family's collection of Gillow furniture, Baccarat glass, porcelain and paintings by Dutch and Italian artists are on display. The gardens extend over 50 acres and include Japanese, walled and formal gardens. The 1930s working farm includes rare breed animals and workshops. An extensive year-round events programme includes RHS Flower Show, picnic concerts and outdoor theatre.

**Location:** MAP 6:M2, OS Ref. SJ745 815. From M56/J7 follow signs. From M6/J19, signed on A56 & A50.

**Open:** High (24 Mar–30 Sep). Low (1 Oct–14 Mar 2008). Parkland: High, Daily 10am–7pm. Low, Tue–Sun 11am–5pm. Gardens: High, Tue–Sun, 10am–6pm. Low, 11am–4pm. Farm: High, Tue–Sun 12noon–5pm, Low, Sats & Suns 11am–4pm. Old Hall: High, Sats & Suns 12noon–5pm. Mansion: High, Tue–Sun 1–5pm. Last entry to Park and attractions 1 hour before closing. Special opening times for Mansion and Old Hall at Christmas and Half Term.

**Admission:** Per attraction: Adult £3.50, Child (4–15) £2, Family (2+3) £9. Discovery Saver Ticket (2 attractions) Adult £5, Child £3, Family £13.50 (NT members, see website/handbook). Park Entry: £4.20 per car (inc NT members). Coaches Free.
⬛ 🖼 🚻 Dinners, dances, weddings and conferences. ♿ Partial. WCs. ◼
🍴 Self-service. 🎦 By arrangement. 🅿 200–300 yds. Meal vouchers for coach drivers. ◼ Please book. 🐕 In grounds, on leads. ⬛ ❄ ♿

# WOODHEY CHAPEL
**Faddiley, Nr Nantwich, Cheshire CW5 8JH**
**Tel:** 01270 524215
**Owner:** The Trustees of Woodhey Chapel    **Contact:** Mr Robinson, The Curator
Small private chapel built in 1690, now restored.
**Location:** MAP 6:L3, OS Ref. SJ573 528. Proceeding W from Nantwich on A534, turn left 1m W of the Faddiley – Brindley villages onto narrow lane, keep ahead at next turn, at road end obtain key from farmhouse.
**Open:** Apr–Oct: Sats & BHs, 2–5pm, or apply for key at Woodhey Hall.
**Admission:** Donation box.

Lyme Park, Stockport

*giftaid it* This year, some properties will be operating the Gift Aid on Entry scheme at their admission points. Where the scheme is operating, visitors are offered a choice between paying the standard admission price or paying the 'Gift Aid Admission' which includes a voluntary donation of at least 10%. Gift Aid Admissions enable the charity to reclaim tax on the whole amount paid* - an extra 28% - potentially a very significant boost to property funds. Money raised from paying visitors in this way will go towards restoration projects at the property and will be very welcome.

Where shown, the admission prices are inclusive of the 10% voluntary donation where properties are operating the Gift Aid on Entry scheme, but both the standard admission price and the Gift Aid Admission will be displayed at the property and on their website.

*Gift Aid donations must be supported by a valid Gift Aid declaration and a Gift Aid declaration can only cover donations made by an individual for him/herself or for him/herself and members of his/her family.

Arley Hall & Gardens, Nr Northwich

## Owner
Lakeland Arts Trust

## Contact
Hannah Neale
Abbot Hall Art Gallery
Kendal
Cumbria  LA9 5AL

**Tel:** 01539 722464
**Fax:** 01539 722494
**E-mail:** info@
abbothall.org.uk

## Location
**MAP 10:L7**
**OS Ref. SD516 922**

10 mins from M6/J36.
Follow brown museum
signs to South Kendal.

**Rail:** Oxenholme.

**Air:** Manchester.

## Opening Times
16 January–22 December
Mon–Sat, 10.30am–5pm
(4pm, Jan–Mar, Nov/Dec.)
Closed Sun.

## Admission
Exhibition         £5.00
includes free entry
to collection. Gift Aid it
for £5.50.

Collection only    £4.00

All ages welcome.

# ABBOT HALL ART GALLERY

www.abbothall.org.uk

Abbot Hall is a jewel of a building in a beautiful setting on the banks of the River Kent, surrounded by a park and overlooked by the ruins of Kendal Castle. This is one of Britain's finest small art galleries and a wonderful place in which to see and enjoy changing exhibitions in the elegantly proportioned rooms of a Grade I Listed Georgian building. The collection includes works by Romney, Ruskin, Turner and Freud. The adjacent Museum of Lakeland Life is a popular family attraction with a Victorian street scene, farmhouse rooms, Arthur Ransome room and displays of Arts and Crafts Movement furniture and fabrics.

| | |
|---|---|
| **i** | No photography. No mobile phones. |
| | Bookshop. |
| | Chairlifts in split level galleries. WCs. |
| | Licensed. |
| | By arrangement. |
| **P** | Ample. |
| | Service dogs only. |
| | |

Pictures above, clockwise from top left: Peploe, Turner, Ruskin, A child enjoying the gallery, Schwitters, New Romney.

■ **Owner**
Lakeland Arts Trust

■ **Contact**
Sandy Kitchen
Blackwell
The Arts & Crafts House
Bowness on Windermere
Cumbria  LA23 3JT

**Tel:** 01539 446139
**Fax:** 01539 488486
**E-mail:** info@
blackwell.org.uk

■ **Location**
**MAP 10:K7**
**OS Ref. SD400 945**

1½ m S of Bowness just
off the A5074 on
the B5360.

**Rail:** Windermere.

**Air:** Manchester.

■ **Opening Times**
5 February–31 December
Daily, 10.30am–5pm,
(4pm, Feb/Mar, Nov/Dec.).

■ **Admission**
Adult                £5.45
Gift Aid it for £6.

All ages welcome.

# BLACKWELL –
# THE ARTS & CRAFTS HOUSE

www.blackwell.org.uk

Blackwell is a superb house situated in the Lake District. Completed in 1900, it sits in an elevated position overlooking Lake Windermere. Blackwell is the most important, and the largest, surviving early example of work by the architect Mackay Hugh Baillie Scott. Changing exhibitions of the highest quality applied arts and crafts can be seen in the setting of the Arts and Crafts Movement architecture itself.

In this treasure trove of 1890s Arts and Crafts design are fine examples of the decorative arts, drawn from natural forms. Lakeland birds and local wild flowers, trees and berries can be seen in the many original stained glass windows, pristine oak panelling and plasterwork. These rooms were designed for relaxation and everywhere you turn you will find inglenooks and places to sit and enjoy the views and garden terraces.

i No photography.
No mobile phones.

Ground floor & part
of 1st floor. WCs.

Licensed.

By arrangement.

P Free for cars, coaches
by appointment.

Service dogs only.

■ **Owner**

C H Bagot

■ **Contact**

Peter Milner
Levens Hall
Kendal
Cumbria  LA8 0PD

**Tel:** 01539 560321
**Fax:** 01539 560669
**E-mail:** houseopening@
levenshall.co.uk

■ **Location**

**MAP 10:L7**
**OS Ref. SD495 851**

5m S of Kendal on the
A6. Exit M6/J36.

**Rail:** Oxenholme 5m.

**Air:** Manchester.

■ **Opening Times**

**Summer**
1 April–11 October
Sun–Thur
(closed Fris & Sats).

House: 12 noon–4.30pm
Last admission 4pm.

Gardens, Plant Centre,
Gift Shop & Tearoom:
10am–5pm.

**Winter**
Closed.

■ **Admission**

**House & Gardens**
Adult               £9.50
Child               £4.50
Family (2+3*)      £24.00

Groups (20+)
Adult               £8.00
Child               £4.00

**Gardens**
Adult               £6.50
Child               £3.50
Family (2+3*)      £18.50

Groups (20+)
Adult               £6.00
Child               £3.00
*Additional children at
group rate.

**Evening Tours**
House tours for pre-
arranged groups (20+/
min charge £200)
Mon–Thur           £10.00

Gardens guided tour by
the Head Gardener or his
Assistant for pre-
arranged groups (20+/
min charge £150)
Mon–Thur            £7.50

**Morning Tours**
House tours starting
between 10–10.30am
for pre-arranged groups
(20+/min charge £180)
                    £9.00

No admission charge for
gift shop, tearoom and
plant centre.

# LEVENS HALL

www.levenshall.co.uk

Levens Hall is an Elizabethan mansion built around a 13th century pele tower. The much loved home of the Bagot family, visitors comment on the warm and friendly atmosphere. Fine panelling and plasterwork, period furniture, Cordova leather wall coverings, paintings by Rubens, Lely and Cuyp, the earliest English patchwork and Wellingtoniana combine with other beautiful objects to form a fascinating collection.

The world famous Topiary Gardens were laid out by Monsieur Beaumont from 1694 and his design has remained largely unchanged to this day. Over 90 individual pieces of topiary, some over nine metres high, massive beech hedges and colourful seasonal bedding provide a magnificent visual impact.

On Sundays and Bank Holidays 'Bertha', a full size Showman's Engine, is in steam. Delicious home-made lunches and teas are available, together with the award-winning Levens beer 'Morocco Ale', in the Bellingham Buttery.

 No indoor photography.

 Partial. WC. Electric buggy hire. DVD of interior.

 Licensed.

By arrangement.

Guide dogs only.

©Brian Sherwen

# MUNCASTER CASTLE 🏛
## GARDENS, OWL CENTRE & MEADOWVOLE MAZE
www.muncaster.co.uk

**Top Attraction (over 50,000 visitors) Cumbria Awards for Excellence 2006.**

Muncaster Castle, set in 77 acres of gardens with spectacular views of the Lakeland Fells, has been home to the Pennington family since at least 1208.

The Castle, complete with an impressive library, beautiful barrel-vaulted drawing room and exquisite dining room, is a treasure trove of paintings, silver, tapestries, and much more.

'Ghost tours' are possible by appointment, and up to 8 brave guests can book an overnight 'Ghost Sit' in the 'haunted' Tapestry Room.

The extensive, wild woodland gardens include glorious rhododendrons, camellias, azaleas, magnolias and many other interesting and rare trees and shrubs.

The World Owl Centre, HQ of the World Owl Trust, is home to one of the largest collections of these fascinating birds.

Most holiday and weekend evenings in winter (closed January), *Darkest Muncaster* transforms the gardens with hundreds of multi-coloured lights, as well as music, sound and other special effects.

In the MeadowVole Maze visitors young and old help Max MeadowVole safely find his way home through this innovative, indoor attraction, with a strong conservation message. *Muncaster Interactive* gives visitors access to computers with games and quizzes, as well as facts and figures on the Castle, gardens, owls and the surrounding area.

Muncaster is the perfect place to entertain in style and frequently hosts weddings, dinner parties and similar family celebrations or corporate events.

Accommodation is available in the 'Coachman's Quarters' in the gardens of the Castle and in two houses on the wider estate or in the newly refurbished Pennington Hotel in Ravenglass.

### Owner
Mrs Phyllida Gordon-Duff-Pennington

### Contact
Peter Frost-Pennington
Muncaster Castle
Ravenglass
Cumbria CA18 1RQ
**Tel:** 01229 717614
**Fax:** 01229 717010
**E-mail:** info@muncaster.co.uk

### Location
**MAP 10:J7**
**OS Ref. SD103 965**
On the A595 1m S of Ravenglass, 19m S of Whitehaven.
From London 6 hrs, Chester 2½ hrs, Edinburgh 3½ hrs, M6/J36, A590, A595 (from S). M6/J40, A66, A595 (from E). Carlisle, A595 (from N).
**Rail:** Ravenglass (on Barrow-in-Furness-Carlisle Line) 1½ m.
**Air:** Manchester 2½ hrs.

### Opening Times
**Castle**
11 February–4 November
Daily (closed Sat),
12 noon–5pm.
**Gardens & Owl Centre**
All year except January:
Daily, 10.30am–6pm
or dusk if earlier.
**'Meet the Birds'**
11 February–4 November
Daily at 2.30pm.
Watch the wild herons feeding during the 'Heron Happy Hour'. Daily at 4.30pm (3.30pm winter).
**Winter**
Castle closed. Open by appointment for groups.
**Darkest Muncaster**
A Winter Evening of Magic – see website for details.

### Admission
**Castle, Gardens, Owl Centre & MeadowVole Maze**
| | |
|---|---|
| Adult | £9.50 |
| Child (5–15yrs) | £6.50 |
| Under 5yrs | Free |
| Family (2+2) | £27.00 |
| Groups | |
| Adult | £8.00 |
| Child (5–15yrs) | £5.00 |

**Gardens, Owl Centre & MeadowVole Maze**
| | |
|---|---|
| Adult | £7.00 |
| Child (5–15yrs) | £5.00 |
| Under 5yrs | Free |
| Family (2+2) | £22.00 |
| Groups | |
| Adult | £6.00 |
| Child (5–15yrs) | £4.00 |

### Conference/Function
| ROOM | MAX CAPACITY |
|---|---|
| Drawing Room | 100 |
| Dining Room | 50 |
| Family Dining Rm | 60 |
| Great Hall | 100 |
| Old Laundry | 120 |
| Library | 48 |
| Guard Room | 30 |

©Brian Sherwen

ℹ Church. Garden parties, film location, clay pigeon shooting. No photography inside the Castle.

🛍 For wedding receptions, catering, & functions, tel: 01229 717614.

♿ By arrangement visitors can alight near Castle. Wheelchairs for loan. WCs. Audio tour tapes for partially sighted/those with learning difficulties. Allocated parking.

🍴 Creeping Kate's Kitchen (licensed) (max 80) – full menu. Groups can book: 01229 717614 to qualify for discounts.

🚶 Private tours with a personal guide (family member possible) can be arranged at additional fee. Ghost Sits our speciality.

🎧 Individual audio tour (40mins) included in price.

Ⓟ 500 cars 800 yds from House; coaches may park closer. Free.

📷 Guides available. Historical subjects, horticulture, conservation, owl tours.

🐕 In grounds, on leads.

## ABBOT HALL ART GALLERY

*See page 410 for full page entry.*

## ACORN BANK GARDEN & WATERMILL

**Temple Sowerby, Penrith, Cumbria CA10 1SP**
**Tel:** 01768 361893 **E-mail:** acornbank@nationaltrust.org.uk
**www.nationaltrust.org.uk**
**Owner:** The National Trust **Contact:** The Custodian
Seventeenth century walls enclose a herb garden with over 250 varieties of medicinal and culinary plants and orchards with traditional fruit trees surrounded by mixed borders. Beyond the walls, paths lead through woodland to a partially restored watermill. House not open.
**Location:** Gate: MAP 10:M5, OS Ref. NY612 281. Just N of Temple Sowerby, 6m E of Penrith on A66.
**Open:** 24 Mar–28 Oct: daily except Mon and Tue, 10am–5pm. Last admission 4.30pm. Tearoom: 11am–4.30pm.
**Admission:** Adult £3.40, Child £1.70, Family £8.50. Pre-arranged groups £2.85.
WCs. Woodland walks only.

## BEATRIX POTTER GALLERY

**Main Street, Hawkshead, Cumbria LA22 0NS**
**Tel:** 01539 436355 **Fax:** 01539 436187
**E-mail:** beatrixpottergallery@nationaltrust.org.uk **www.nationaltrust.org.uk**
**Owner:** The National Trust **Contact:** Ticket Office/House Steward
An annually changing exhibition of original watercolours and sketches by beloved children's author Beatrix Potter. *The Tale of Tom Kitten* features for his 100th birthday, along with displays on the forthcoming feature film "Miss Potter". The gallery was once the office of Beatrix Potter's husband, William Heelis. It is ideally matched with a visit to Beatrix Potter's house, Hill Top, two miles away. Quizzes for children.
**Location:** MAP 10:K7, OS Ref. SD352 982. 5m SSW of Ambleside. In the Square.
**Open:** 31 Mar–28 Oct: Sat–Wed and Good Fri plus Sats & Suns in Mar & Thurs in July–Aug, 10.30am–4.30pm. Last admission 4pm. Admission is by timed ticket (incl. NT members). Shop: daily.
**Admission:** Adult £3.80, Child £1.90, Family £9.50. No reduction for groups. Discount for Hill Top ticket holders (not groups). Group booking essential.
No photography inside. Assistance dogs only.

## BLACKWELL – THE ARTS & CRAFTS HOUSE

*See page 411 for full page entry.*

## BRANTWOOD

**Coniston, Cumbria LA21 8AD**
**Tel:** 01539 441396 **Fax:** 01539 441263 **E-mail:** enquiries@brantwood.org.uk
**www.brantwood.org.uk**
**Owner:** The Brantwood Trust
Brantwood, the former home of John Ruskin, is the most beautifully situated house in the Lake District. Explore Brantwood's estate and gardens or experience contemporary art in the Severn Studio. Brantwood's bookshop, the Jumping Jenny restaurant and Coach House Craft Gallery combine for a perfect day out.
**Location:** MAP 10:K7, OS Ref. SD313 959. 2½m from Coniston village on the E side of Coniston Water.
**Open:** Mid Mar–mid Nov: daily, 11am–5.30pm. Mid Nov–mid Mar: Wed–Sun, 11am–4.30pm.
**Admission:** Adult £5.95, Child £1.20, Student £4.50, Family (2+3) £11.95. Garden only: Adult £4, Family (2+3) £8.50. Groups: Adult £4.95, Child £1.20, Student £3.50. Garden only: £3.50.
No photography in the house. Licensed. Licensed. Licensed. By arrangement. Ample. Limited for coaches. in grounds, on leads.

## BROUGH CASTLE

**Brough, Cumbria**
**Tel:** 01228 591922
**Owner:** English Heritage **Contact:** Visitor Operations Manager
This ancient site dates back to Roman times. The 12th century keep replaced an earlier stronghold destroyed by the Scots in 1174.
**Location:** MAP 10:M6, OS Ref. NY791 141. 8m SE of Appleby S of A66. South part of the village.
**Open:** Any reasonable time.
**Admission:** Free.
On leads.

## BROUGHAM CASTLE

**Penrith, Cumbria CA10 2AA**
**Tel:** 01768 862488
**Owner:** English Heritage **Contact:** Visitor Operations Team
These impressive ruins on the banks of the River Eamont include an early 13th century keep and later buildings. You can climb to the top of the keep and survey the domain of its eccentric one-time owner Lady Anne Clifford. Exhibition about the Roman fort, medieval castle and Lady Anne Clifford.
**Location:** MAP 10:L5, OS Ref. NY537 290. 1½ m SE of Penrith, between A66 & B6262.
**Open:** 1 Apr–30 Sept: daily, 10am–5pm.
**Admission:** Adult £3, Child £1.50, Conc. £2.30. Family £7.50. 15% discount for groups (11+).
WCs. Grounds. Limited. In grounds, on leads.

© English Heritage Photo Library

# CARLISLE CASTLE

### CARLISLE, CUMBRIA CA3 8UR

**Tel:** 01228 591922
**Owner:** English Heritage **Contact:** Visitor Operations Team
This impressive medieval castle, where Mary Queen of Scots was once imprisoned, has a long and tortuous history of warfare and family feuds. A portcullis hangs menacingly over the gatehouse passage, there is a maze of passages and chambers, endless staircases to lofty towers and you can walk the high ramparts for stunning views. There is also a medieval manor house in miniature - a suite of medieval rooms furnished as they might have been when used by the castle's former constable. The castle includes the King's Own Royal Border Regimental Museum.
**Location:** MAP 10:K3, OS Ref. NY396 562. In Carlisle town, at N end of city centre.
**Open:** 1 Apr–30 Sept: daily, 9.30am–5pm. 1 Oct–20 Mar: daily, 10am–4pm. Closed 24–26 Dec & 1 Jan.
**Admission:** Adult £4.20, Child £2.10, Conc £3.20. 15% discount for groups (11+).
Partial, wheelchairs available. By arrangement. Disabled parking only. Dogs on leads.

## CARLISLE CATHEDRAL

**Carlisle, Cumbria CA3 8TZ**
**Tel:** 01228 548151 **Fax:** 01228 547049 **Contact:** Ms C Baines
Fine sandstone Cathedral, founded in 1122. Medieval stained glass.
**Location:** MAP 10:K3, OS Ref. NY399 559. Carlisle city centre, 2m from M6/J43.
**Open:** Mon–Sat: 7.40am–6.15pm, Suns, 7.40–5pm. Closes 4pm between Christmas Day & New Year. Sun services: 8am, 10.30am & 3pm. Weekday services: 8am, 5.30pm & a 12.30 service on Weds and Fris.
**Admission:** Donation.

## CONISHEAD PRIORY & BUDDHIST TEMPLE

**Ulverston, Cumbria LA12 9QQ**
**Tel:** 01229 584029 **Fax:** 01229 580080 **E-mail:** info@manjushri.org
**Owner:** Manjushri Kadampa Meditation Centre **Contact:** Geoffrey Roe
A Victorian gothic mansion. Special features include decorative ceilings, a vaulted great hall with fine stained glass and a 177 feet long cloister corridor.
**Location:** MAP 10:K8, OS Ref. SD305 757. 2m S of Ulverston on A5087 Coast Road.
**Open:** Easter–Oct: Sat, Sun & BHs, 2–5pm. Opening times sometimes vary, please telephone to confirm and for weekday details.
**Admission:** Free. Guided Tours: Adult £2.50, Conc. £2, Under 12yrs Free.

# DALEMAIN 🏛
## PENRITH, CUMBRIA CA11 0HB
www.dalemain.com

**Tel:** 017684 86450 **Fax:** 017684 86223 **E-mail:** admin@dalemain.com

**Owner:** Robert Hasell-McCosh Esq **Contact:** Jayne Pickles – General Manager

Dalemain is a fine mixture of mediaeval, Tudor and early Georgian architecture. The imposing Georgian façade strikes the visitor immediately but in the cobbled courtyard the atmosphere of the north country Tudor manor is secure. The present owner's family have lived at Dalemain since 1679 and have collected china, furniture and family portraits.

Delightful and fascinating 5 acre plantsman's gardens set against the picturesque splendour of the Lakeland Fells and Parkland. Richly planted herbaceous borders. Rose Walk with over 100 old-fashioned roses and ancient apple trees of named varieties. Magnificent Abies Cephalonica and Tulip Tree. Tudor Knot Garden. Wild Garden with profusion of flowering shrubs and wild flowers and in early summer the breathtaking display of blue Himalayan Poppies.

**Location:** MAP 10:L5, OS Ref. NY477 269. On A592 1m S of A66. 4m SW of Penrith. From London, M1, M6/J40: 5 hrs. From Edinburgh, A73, M74,M6/J40: 2½ hrs.

**Open:** Gardens & Tearoom: 4 Feb–29 Mar & 29 Oct–mid Dec:, Sun–Thur.11am–4pm. House, Gardens, Tearoom & Gift Shop: 1 Apr–28 Oct, 10.30am–5pm. House opens 11.15am for first guided tour. Free flow in afternoons. Groups (10+) please book.

**Admission:** House & Garden: Adult £6.50, Accompanied Child Free. Gardens only: Adult £4.50, Accompanied Child Free. Group prices on application.

ℹ No photography in house. Moorings available on Ullswater. 🖼 🚻 🅣 ♿ Visitors may drive into the Courtyard and alight near the gift shop. Electric scooter. WCs. 🍴 Licensed. Groups must book for lunches/high teas. 🎫 1hr tours. German and French translations. Garden tour for groups extra. 🅿 50 yds. 🐕 Guide dogs in house only. No dogs in garden, allowed in grounds. ♿

# DOVE COTTAGE
# & THE WORDSWORTH MUSEUM
## GRASMERE, CUMBRIA LA22 9SH

www.wordsworth.org.uk

**Tel:** 01539 435544 **Fax:** 01539 435748

**E-mail:** bookings@wordsworth.org.uk

**Owner:** The Wordsworth Trust **Contact:** Bookings Officer

Situated in the heart of the English Lake District, Dove Cottage is the beautifully preserved Grasmere home of England's finest poet William Wordsworth. Visitors are offered fascinating guided tours of his world-famous home. The award-winning Museum displays priceless Wordsworth manuscripts and memorabilia. Onsite tearooms and book and gift shop.

**Location:** MAP 10:K6, OS Ref. NY342 070. Immediately S of Grasmere village on A591. Main car/coach park next to Dove Cottage Tea Rooms and Restaurant.

**Open:** All year: daily, 9.30am–5.30pm (last admission 5pm). Closed 8 Jan–5 Feb.

**Admission:** Adult £5.50, Child £4.10, Family tickets available. Pre-arranged groups (10–60): Adult £5.10. Reciprocal discount ticket with Rydal Mount and Wordsworth House.

ℹ No photography. 🖼 ♿ Partial. WC. 🍴 🎫 Obligatory. 🅿 Limited. 🏠 🐕 Guide dogs only. ❋ ♿

©The Wordsworth Trust

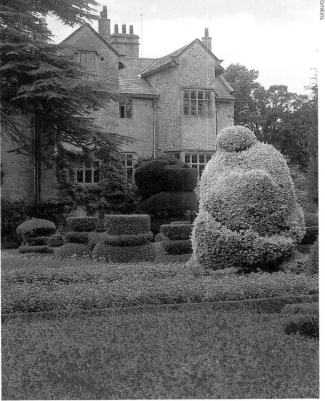

Nicola Stocken-Tomkins

Levens Hall, Kendal

## FELL FOOT PARK ⚘

**Newby Bridge, Cumbria  LA12 8NN**
**Tel:** 01539 531273  **Fax:** 01539 539926  **E-mail:** fellfootpark@nationaltrust.org.uk
**Owner:** The National Trust     **Contact:** Park Manager
Come and explore this lakeshore Victorian park on the edge of Windermere. A great place for the family, with boat hire, tearoom, play area, family activity sheets and wildlife room showing birds and bats who live around the park. Fantastic views of the Lakeland fells. Wonderful colour in spring.
**Location:** MAP 10:K7, OS Ref. SD381 869. S end of Lake Windermere on E shore, entrance from A592. Near Aquarium of the Lakes and Haverthwaite Steam Railway.
**Open:** Daily, 9am–5pm (except Christmas Day and Boxing Day).
**Admission:** Car park: 2hrs £3, 4hrs £5.50, all day £7. NT Members Free parking. Coaches by arrangement.
🔲 🔲 Partial. 🔲🔲 Charge. 🔲 On leads. 🔲🔲

## FURNESS ABBEY ⚜

**Barrow-in-Furness, Cumbria  LA13 0PS**
**Tel:** 01229 823420
**Owner:** English Heritage     **Contact:** Visitor Operations Staff
Hidden in a peaceful green valley are the beautiful red sandstone remains of the wealthy abbey founded in 1123 by Stephen, later King of England. This abbey first belonged to the Order of Savigny and later to the Cistercians. There is a museum and exhibition.
**Location:** MAP 10:J8, OS Ref. SD218 717. 1½m N of Barrow-in-Furness off A590.
**Open:** 1 Apr–30 Sept: daily, 10am–5pm. 1–31 Oct: Thur–Mon, 10am–4pm. 1 Nov–20 Mar: Thur–Sun, 10am–4pm. Closed 24–26 Dec & 1 Jan.
**Admission:** Adult £3.50, Child £1.80, Conc. £2.60. 15% discount for groups (11+).
ℹ️ WC. 🔲 🔲 Grounds. 🔲 Inclusive. 🔲 🔲 🔲 In grounds, on leads. 🔲🔲

## HARDKNOTT ROMAN FORT ⚜

**Ravenglass, Cumbria**
**Tel:** 0161 242 1400
**Owner:** English Heritage     **Contact:** The North West Regional Office
This fort, built between AD120 and 138, controlled the road from Ravenglass to Ambleside.
**Location:** MAP 10:J6, OS Ref. NY218 015. At the head of Eskdale. 9m NE of Ravenglass, at W end of Hardknott Pass.
**Open:** Any reasonable time. Access may be hazardous in winter.
**Admission:** Free.
🔲 🔲 On leads. 🔲

## HERON CORN MILL & MUSEUM OF PAPERMAKING

**Beetham Trust, Waterhouse Mills, Beetham, Milnthorpe  LA7 7AR**
**Tel:** 015395 65027  **Fax:** 015395 65033  **E-mail:** info@heronmill.org
**Owner:** Heron Corn Mill Beetham Trust     **Contact:** Audrey Steeley
A fascinating visitor attraction. An 18th century corn mill and museum of papermaking offers hand-made paper demonstrations and art workshops for visitors.
**Location:** MAP 10:L8, OS Ref. SD497 800. At Beetham. 1m S of Milnthorpe on the A6.
**Open:** Mar–Oct: daily except Mons (open BH Mons), 11am–5pm.
**Admission:** Adult £2, Child £1, OAP £1.50. Schools and groups welcome.

©National Trust Photographic Library/Geoffrey Frosh

## HILL TOP ⚘

**NEAR SAWREY, AMBLESIDE, CUMBRIA  LA22 0LF**
www.nationaltrust.org.uk

**Tel:** 01539 436269  **Fax:** 01539 436811  **E-mail:** hilltop@nationaltrust.org.uk
**Owner:** The National Trust     **Contact:** Ticket Office/Administrator
Beatrix Potter wrote and illustrated many of her famous children's stories in this little 17th century house, which contains her furniture and china. There is a traditional cottage garden attached. A selection of the original illustrations may be seen at the Beatrix Potter Gallery in Hawkshead. Shop specialises in Beatrix Potter items.
**Location:** MAP 10:K7, OS Ref. SD370 955. 2m S of Hawkshead, in hamlet of Near Sawrey, behind the Tower Bank Arms.
**Open:** 31 Mar–28 Oct: Sat–Wed & Good Fri, plus Thur in Jun, Jul & Aug, 10.30am–4.30pm. Garden & Shop: 31 Mar–23 Dec: Sats & Suns, 10am–4pm. Call for winter details. Admission by timed ticket (incl. NT members). Group booking essential.
**Admission:** Adult £5.40, Child £2.70, Family £13.50. No reduction for groups. Discount for Beatrix Potter Gallery ticket holders (not groups). Garden: Free on Thur & Fri.
ℹ️ No photography in house. 🔲 🔲 Partial. 🔲 None for coaches.
🔲 Assistance dogs only. 🔲

## HOLEHIRD GARDENS

**Patterdale Road, Windermere, Cumbria  LA23 1NP**
**Tel:** 01539 446008
**Owner:** Lakeland Horticultural Society     **Contact:** The Hon Secretary/Publicity Officer
Over 10 acres of hillside gardens overlooking Windermere, including a wide variety of plants, specimen trees and shrubs, extensive rock and heather gardens, a walled garden, alpine houses and herbaceous borders. The all year garden also is home to the national collections of Astilbe, Hydrangea and Polystichum ferns. Managed and maintained entirely by volunteers.
**Location:** MAP 10:K7, OS Ref. NY410 008. On A592, ¾m N of junction with A591. ½ m N of Windermere. 1m from Townend.
**Open:** All year: dawn till dusk. Groups strictly by arrangement. Reception: Apr–Oct, 10am–5pm.
**Admission:** Free. Donation appreciated (at least £3 suggested).

Acorn Bank Garden & Watermill, Penrith

## HOLKER HALL & GARDENS 🏛
### CARK-IN-CARTMEL, GRANGE-OVER-SANDS, CUMBRIA  LA11 7PL

www.holker-hall.co.uk

**Tel:** 01539 558328  **Fax:** 01539 558378  **E-mail:** publicopening@holker.co.uk
**Owner:** Lord Cavendish of Furness  **Contact:** Louise Jones

Holker Hall, home of Lord and Lady Cavendish, shows the confidence, spaciousness and prosperity of Victorian style on its grandest scale. Holker is very much a family home with visitors able to wander freely throughout the New Wing. The award-winning gardens include formal and woodland areas covering 25 acres. This inspiring garden includes a labyrinth, limestone cascade, fountain, the Sunken Garden, the Elliptical and Summer Gardens and many rare plants and shrubs.

**Location:** MAP 10:K8, OS Ref. SD359 773. Close to Morecambe Bay, 5m W of Grange-over- Sands by B5277. From Kendal, A6, A590, B5277, B5278: 16m. Motorway: M6/J36.

**Open:** Hall: 1 Apr–28 Oct: Sun–Fri, 12 noon–4pm. Gardens: 1 Apr–28 Oct: Sun–Fri, 10.30am–5.30pm. Food Hall/Courtyard Café/Gift Shop: daily, 10.30am–5.30pm.

**Admission:** Hall & Gardens: Adult £9.25, Child £5, Conc £8.50, Family £25. Gardens: Adult £5.95, Child £3, Conc £5.25, Family £15.50. Discount for groups.

ℹ No photography in house. 🅿 Holker Food Hall – produce from the estate.
🚻 🍽 ♿ Visitors alight at entrance. WCs. Licensed. 🎁 ⓕ By arrangement.
🅿 75 yds from Hall. 🐾 🐕 In grounds, on leads (not formal gardens).

## LANERCOST PRIORY ♯
### Brampton, Cumbria CA8 2HQ
**Tel:** 01697 73030
**Owner:** English Heritage  **Contact:** Visitor Operations Team

This Augustinian priory was founded c1166. The nave of the church, which is intact and in use as the local parish church, contrasts with the ruined chancel, transepts and priory buildings. Free audio tour.

**Location:** MAP 10:L3, OS Ref. NY556 637. 2m NE of Brampton. 1m N of Naworth Castle.

**Open:** 1 Apr–30 Sept: daily, 10am–5pm. 1–31 Oct: Thur–Mon, 10am–4pm. 3 Nov–16 Dec, Sats & Suns. 10am–4pm. Closed 24/25 Dec.

**Admission:** Adult £3, Child £1.50, Conc. £2.30, Family £7.50, Groups (11+): 15% discount.

📷 ♿ Ground floor. 🎧 Inclusive. 🅿 Limited. 🐾 🐕 🎈

## LEVENS HALL 🏛
*See page 412 for full page entry.*

## MIREHOUSE 🏛
### Keswick, Cumbria  CA12 4QE
**Tel:** 017687 72287  **E-mail:** info@mirehouse.com  **www.mirehouse.com**
**Owner:** James Fryer-Spedding  **Contact:** Janaki Spedding

Winner: Small Visitor Attraction of the Year 2006, Cumbria for Excellence Awards. Melvyn Bragg described Mirehouse as *'Manor from Heaven'*. Hunter Davies wrote *'Not to be missed'* and Simon Jenkins in *The Times* said *'It is the Lake District with its hand on its heart'*. Literary house linked with Tennyson and Wordsworth. Natural playgrounds and lakeside walk.

**Location:** MAP 10:J5, OS Ref. NY235 284. Beside A591, 3½ m N of Keswick. Good bus service.

**Open:** Apr–Oct: Gardens & Tearoom: daily, 10am–5.30pm. House: Suns & Weds (also Fris in Aug), 2–5pm (4.30pm last entry). Groups (20+) welcome by appointment.

**Admission:** House & Garden: Adult £4.80, Child £2.40, Family (2+4) £14.40. Gardens only: Adult £2.60, Child £1.30. Pre-booked 10% discount for groups (20+).

ℹ No photography in house. ♿ 🍽 ⓕ By arrangement. 🅿 Limited. 🐾
🐕 On leads only.

## HUTTON-IN-THE-FOREST 🏛
### PENRITH, CUMBRIA CA11 9TH

www.hutton-in-the-forest.co.uk

**Tel:** 017684 84449  **Fax:** 017684 84571  **E-mail:** info@hutton-in-the-forest.co.uk
**Owner:** Lord Inglewood  **Contact:** Edward Thompson

The home of Lord Inglewood's family since 1605. Built around a medieval pele tower with 17th, 18th and 19th century additions. Fine collections of furniture, paintings, ceramics and tapestries. Outstanding grounds with terraces, topiary, walled garden, dovecote and woodland walk through magnificent specimen trees.

**Location:** MAP 10:L5, OS Ref. NY460 358. 6m NW of Penrith & 2½ m from M6/J41 on B5305.

**Open:** 4–15 Apr & 2 May–30 Sept: Weds, Thurs, Suns & BH Mons, 12.30–4pm (last entry). Tearoom: As house: 11am–4.30pm. Gardens & Grounds: Apr–Oct, daily except Sats, 11am–5pm.

**Admission:** House, Gardens & Grounds: Adult £5.50, Child £3.50, Family £15. Gardens & Grounds: Adult £3.50, Child £1.

ℹ Picnic area. 🎁 Gift stall. 🍽 By arrangement. ♿ Partial. 🍽
ⓕ Obligatory (except Jul/Aug & BHs). 🅿 🐾 🐕 On leads. 🎈

## MUNCASTER CASTLE

*See page 413 for full page entry.*

### PENRITH CASTLE

**Penrith, Cumbria**
**Tel:** 0161 242 1400
**Owner:** English Heritage    **Contact:** The North West Regional Office
This 14th century castle, set in a park on the edge of the town, was built to defend Penrith against repeated attacks by Scottish raiders.
**Location:** MAP 10:L5, OS Ref. NY513 299. Opposite Penrith railway station. W of the town centre. Fully visible from the street.
**Open:** Park: All year, daily: 7.30am–9pm (closes 4.30pm winter).
**Admission:** Free.
i WC On leads.

Hill Top Garden, Ambleside

## RYDAL MOUNT & GARDENS
### RYDAL, CUMBRIA  LA22 9LU

www.rydalmount.co.uk

**Tel:** 01539 433002   **Fax:** 01539 431738   **E-mail:** info@rydalmount.co.uk
**Owner:** Rydal Mount Trustees    **Contact:** Peter & Marian Elkington
Home of William Wordsworth – England's finest poet. Nestling in the beautiful fells between Lake Windermere and Rydal Water, lies the 'most beloved home' of William Wordsworth from 1813–1850. Experience the splendid historic home of Wordsworth's descendants; Enjoy the beautiful terraced gardens landscaped by the poet; Feel the peaceful relaxed 'romantic' atmosphere; The freedom of wandering through this 'spot of more perfect and enjoyable beauty' as wrote Dr Thomas Arnold.
**Location:** MAP 10:K6, OS Ref. NY364 063. 1½m N of Ambleside on A591 Grasmere Road.
**Open:** Mar–Oct: daily, 9.30am–5pm. Nov–Feb (closed Jan): daily except Tues, 10am –4pm.
**Admission:** House & Garden: Adult £5, Child £2, Student £4, OAP £4.25, Family £12. Garden only: £2.50. Free parking. Reciprocal discount ticket with Dove Cottage & Wordsworth House (on full paying admission only).
i No inside photography. Partial. By arrangement. P Limited. In grounds, on leads. Guide dogs only in house.

## SIZERGH CASTLE & GARDEN
### SIZERGH, Nr KENDAL, CUMBRIA  LA8 8AE

www.nationaltrust.org.uk

**Tel/Fax:** 01539 560951   **E-mail:** sizergh@nationaltrust.org.uk
**Owner:** The National Trust    **Contact:** Property Administrator
Sizergh Castle is set in wonderful grounds with walks around the estate. The house has been lived in by the Strickland family for more than 750 years. The impressive 14th century tower was extended in Tudor times, with some of the finest Elizabethan carved overmantels in the country. Contents include good English and French furniture and portraits.
The castle is surrounded by a superb garden with two lakes, the National Trust's largest limestone rock garden, an outstanding National collection of hardy tree ferns – one of the largest in the UK with more than 200 varieties, a wild flower bank, a kitchen garden, orchard, wooded knoll and wetland area. This garden is particularly wonderful in spring and autumn. New café serving local seasonal produce – outdoor seating area and picnic area. Walks leaflet available in shop.
**Location:** MAP 10:L7, OS Ref. SD498 878. 3½m S of Kendal, NW of the A590 / A591 interchange.
**Open:** Castle: 1 Apr–28 Oct: daily except Fri & Sat, 1–5pm. Café, Garden & Shop: also open weekends in Mar, Nov & Dec, 10.30am–3.30pm.
**Admission:** House & Garden: Adult £6.70, Child £3.30, Family £16.70 (1+3) £10. Groups (15+): £5.70 by arrangement (not on BHs). Garden only: Adult £4.50, Child £2.20, Groups £3.80.
Partial. P Limited for coaches.

## STAGSHAW GARDEN ❀

**Ambleside, Cumbria LA22 0HE**

**Tel/Fax:** 015394 46027  **E-mail:** stagshaw@nationaltrust.org.uk

**Owner:** The National Trust

This woodland garden contains a fine collection of azaleas and rhododendrons, planted to give good blends of colour under thinned oaks on the hillside; also magnolias, camellias and embothriums. Adjacent to the woods are Skelghyll Woods which offer delightful walks and access to the fells beyond.

**Location:** MAP 10:K6, OS Ref. NY380 029. ½m S of Ambleside on A591. Ferry Waterhead ½m.

**Open:** 1 Apr–30 Jun: daily, 10am–6.30pm. Colours best Apr–Jun. Jul–end Oct: by appointment through the property office at St Catherines, Patterdale Road, Windermere LA23 1NH.

**Admission:** £2, by honesty box.

♿ Unsuitable. 🅿 Limited. ✉

## STOTT PARK BOBBIN MILL ♯

**Low Stott Park, Nr Newby Bridge, Cumbria LA12 8AX**

**Tel:** 01539 531087

**Owner:** English Heritage  **Contact:** Visitor Operations Team

When this working mill was built in 1835 it was typical of the many mills in the Lake District which grew up to supply the spinning and weaving industry in Lancashire but have since disappeared. A remarkable opportunity to see a demonstration of the machinery and techniques of the Industrial Revolution. Steam days: Tues–Thurs.

**Location:** MAP 10:K7, OS Ref. SD372 881. 1½m N of Newby Bridge off A590.

**Open:** 1 Apr–31 Oct: Mon–Fri, 10am–5pm (Steam days, Mon–Thurs). Last admission 1hr before closing.

**Admission:** Adult £4.20, Child £2.10, Conc. £3.20, Family £10.50. Groups: discount for groups (11+).

◧ ♿ Ground floor. WC. ⓕ Free. 🅿 🎦 ✉

## HELENA THOMPSON MUSEUM

**Park End Road, Workington, Cumbria CA14 4DE**

**Tel:** 01900 606155  **E-mail:** whghtm@hotmail.co.uk

**Owner:** Allerdale Borough Council  **Contact:** Museum Manager

The museum is housed in a fine listed mid-Georgian building. Displays include pottery, silver, glass, furniture and dress collection.

**Location:** MAP 10:I5, OS Ref. NY007 286. Corner of A66, Ramsey Brow & Park End Road.

**Open:** All year: Wed–Fri, 10am–4pm. Sat & Sun, 12 noon–4pm.

**Admission:** Free.

# TOWNEND ❀

### TROUTBECK, WINDERMERE, CUMBRIA LA23 1LB

www.nationaltrust.org.uk

**Tel:** 01539 432628  **E-mail:** townend@nationaltrust.org.uk

**Owner:** The National Trust  **Contact:** The Custodian

An exceptional relic of Lake District life during past centuries. Originally a 'statesman' (wealthy yeoman) farmer's house, built about 1626. Townend contains carved woodwork, books, papers, furniture and fascinating implements of the past which were accumulated by the Browne family who lived here from 1626 until 1943.

**Location:** MAP 10:K6, OS Ref. NY407 023. 3m SE of Ambleside at S end of Troutbeck village. 1m from Holehird, 3m N of Windermere.

**Open:** 31 Mar–28 Oct: Wed–Sun & BH Mons, 1–5pm or dusk if earlier. Last entry 4.30pm.

**Admission:** Adult £3.80, Child £1.90, Family £9.50. No reduction for groups which must be pre-booked.

♿ Unsuitable for wheelchairs. ✉ ♥

Mr & Mrs R Hasell-McCosh

## WORDSWORTH HOUSE ❀

**Main Street, Cockermouth, Cumbria CA13 9RX**

**Tel**: 01900 824805  **Opening Info:** 01900 820884  **Fax:** 01900 820883

**E-mail:** wordsworthhouse@nationaltrust.org.uk  **www.wordsworthhouse.org.uk**

**Owner:** The National Trust  **Contact:** The Custodian

This Georgian town house was the birthplace of William Wordsworth. Imaginatively presented as the home of the Wordsworth family in the 1770s, the house offers a lively and participative visit with costumed living history. The garden, with terraced walk overlooking the River Derwent, has been restored to its 18th century appearance with vegetables, herbs, fruit and flowers.

**Location:** MAP 10:J5, OS Ref. NY118 307. Main Street, Cockermouth.

**Open:** 27 Mar–27 Oct: Tues–Sat, open BHs Mons and Mons in Jul and Aug. 11am–4.30pm. Last entry 4pm. Shop: 26 Mar–23 Dec: Mon–Sat, 10am–5pm and Jan & Mar: Wed–Sat. 10am–4pm.

**Admission:** Adult £4.90, Child £2.60, Family £13.50. Pre-booked groups (15+): Adult £3.90, Child £1.60.

ⓘ No photography. ◧ ♿ Partial. WCs. ⓕ By arrangement only. 🎦 ✉ Guide dogs only.

Dalemain, Penrith

For rare and unusual plants visit the **plant sales** index on page 564

### ■ Owner

Richard Gillow
Reynolds Esq

### ■ Contact

Mrs C S Reynolds
Leighton Hall
Carnforth
Lancashire   LA5 9ST

**Tel:** 01524 734474
**Fax:** 01524 720357
**E-mail:** info@
leightonhall.co.uk

### ■ Location

**MAP 10:L8**
**OS Ref. SD494 744**

9m N of Lancaster,
10m S of Kendal,
3m N of Carnforth.
1½ m W of A6.
3m from M6/A6/J35,
signed from J35A.

**Rail:** Carnforth
Station 3m.

**Bus:** The Carnforth
Connect (line 1) bus from
Carnforth Railway Station
stops at the gates of
Leighton Hall
(info 01524 734311).

**Air:** Manchester
Airport 65m.

**Taxi:** Carnforth Radio
Taxis, 01524 732763.

### ■ Opening Times

**Summer**
May–September, Tue–Fri
(also BH Sun & Mon)
2–5pm.

August only: Tue–Fri & Sun
(also BH Mon)
12.30–5pm.

NB. Booked groups (25+)
at any time, all year by
arrangement.

**Winter**
1 October–30 April
Open to booked
groups (25+).

### ■ Admission

**Summer**
**House, Garden & Birds**
| | |
|---|---|
| Adult | £6.00 |
| Child (5-12yrs) | £4.00 |
| Student/OAP | £5.00 |
| Family (2+3) | £18.00 |
| Grounds & Birds | £3.75 |

**Groups (25+)**
| | |
|---|---|
| Adult | £4.50 |
| Child (5-12yrs) | £3.50 |
| Child under 5yrs, Free | |

**Grounds only**
| | |
|---|---|
| (after 4.30pm) Per person | £2.00 |

**Winter**
As above but groups by
appointment only.

Pre-booked Candlelit Tours
Nov–Jan.

Note: The owners reserve the
right to close or restrict access
to the house and grounds for
special events, or at any other
time without prior notice.

### ■ Conference/Function

| ROOM | SIZE | MAX CAPACITY |
|---|---|---|
| Music Room | 24' x 21'6" | 80 |
| Dining Rm | | 30 |
| Other | | 80 |

# LEIGHTON HALL 🏛

www.leightonhall.co.uk

Leighton Hall is one of the most beautifully sited houses in the British Isles, situated in a bowl of parkland, with the whole panorama of the Lakeland Fells rising behind. The Hall's neo-gothic façade was superimposed on an 18th century house, which, in turn, had been built on the ruins of the original medieval house. The present owner is descended from Adam d'Avranches who built the first house in 1246.

The whole house is, today, lived in by the Reynolds family whose emphasis is put on making visitors feel welcome in a family home.

Mr Reynolds is also descended from the founder of Gillow and Company of Lancaster. Connoisseurs of furniture will be particularly interested in the many 18th century Gillow pieces, some of which are unique. Fine pictures, clocks, silver and objéts d'art are also on display.

Leighton Hall is home to a varied collection of Birds of Prey. These birds are flown daily during opening hours, weather permitting.

### Gardens

The main garden has a continuous herbaceous border with rose covered walls, while the Walled Garden contains flowering shrubs, a herb garden, and an ornamental vegetable garden with a caterpillar maze. Beyond is the Woodland Walk where wild flowers abound from early spring.

ℹ No photography in house.

🎁 Unusual plants for sale.

🍸 Product launches, conferences, seminars, filming, garden parties. Outdoor events include: overland driving, archery and clay pigeon shooting. Wedding receptions, buffets, lunches and dinners.

♿ Partial. WC. Visitors may alight at the entrance to the Hall. Ground floor only.

☕ 🍽 Booking essential for group catering, menus on request.

🗝 Obligatory. By prior arrangement owner may meet groups. The 45 minute tour includes information on the property, its gardens and history. House and flying display tour time: 2 hrs.

🅿 Ample for cars and coaches.

🏫 School programme: all year round. Choice of Countryside Classroom, Victorian Leighton or Local History. Sandford Award for Heritage Education winner in 1983 and 1989.

🐕 In Park, on leads.

🏰 An unusual, but spectacular venue, Leighton Hall is a fairytale choice.

❄ For booked groups & functions.

😊 Visit website for details.

## BLACKBURN CATHEDRAL

**Cathedral Close, Blackburn, Lancashire  BB1 5AA**
**Tel:** 01254 503090  **Fax:** 01254 689666  **Contact:** Pauline Rowe
On an historic Saxon site in town centre. The 1826 Parish Church dedicated as the Cathedral in 1977 with new extensions to give a spacious and light interior.
**Location:** MAP 10:M11, OS Ref. SD684 280. 9m E of M6/J31, via A59 and A677. City centre.
**Open:** Daily, 9am–5pm. Sun services: at 8am, 9am, 10.30am and 4pm. Catering: Tues–Fri, 10am–2.30pm or Sat by arrangement.
**Admission:** Free. Donations invited.

## BROWSHOLME HALL 🏛

**Clitheroe, Lancashire  BB7 3DE**
**Tel:** 01254 827160  **E-mail:** rrp@browsholme.co.uk  **www.browsholme.co.uk**
**Owner/Contact:** Robert Parker
Built in 1507 by Edmund Parker, 2007 is the 500th Anniversary of Browsholme Hall the ancestral Home of the Parker Family. This remarkable Tudor Hall has a major collection of oak furniture and portraits, arms and armour, stained glass and many unusual antiquities from the Civil war to a fragment of a Zeppelin. Browsholme, pronounced 'Brusom', lies in the Forest of Bowland, and is set in unspoilt parkland in the style of Capability Brown. The façade still retains the ' H' shape of the original house with later Queen Anne and Regency additions when the house was refurbished by Thomas Lister Parker a noted antiquarian and patron of artists such as Turner and Northcote.
**Location:** MAP 10:M10, OS Ref. SD683 452. 5m NW of Clitheroe off B6243.
**Open:** 9 Apr, 26–29 May, 30 Jun–6 Jul, 11–31 Aug; Daily, 2–5pm except Mons (open BH Mons). Groups particularly welcome by appointment.
**Admission:** Adult £5, Child £1.50, OAP £4.50.

## GAWTHORPE HALL 🦋

**Padiham, Nr Burnley, Lancashire  BB12 8UA**
**Tel:** 01282 771004  **Fax:** 01282 776663  **E-mail:** gawthorpehall@nationaltrust.org.uk
**Owner:** The National Trust  **Contact:** Property Office
The house was built in 1600-05, and restored by Sir Charles Barry in the 1850s. Barry's designs have been re-created in the principal rooms. Gawthorpe was the home of the Shuttleworth family, and the Rachel Kay-Shuttleworth textile collections are on display in the house, private study by arrangement. Collection of portraits on loan from the National Portrait Gallery.
**Location:** MAP 10:N10, OS Ref. SD806 340. M65/J8. On E outskirts of Padiham, ¾ m to house on N of A671. Signed to Clitheroe, then signed from 2nd set of traffic lights.
**Open:** Hall & Tearoom: 1 Apr–28 Oct: daily except Mons & Fris, open Good Fri & BH Mons, 1–5pm. Last adm. 4.30pm. Garden: All year: daily, 10am–6pm.
**Admission:** Hall: Adult £4, Conc. £3, accompanied Child Free (prices may change). Garden: Free. Groups must book. Prices subject to confirmation in Mar 2007.
♿ Please ring in advance. 🖥 🏠 In grounds on leads. ❋

## HALL I'TH'WOOD

**off Green Way, off Crompton Way, Bolton  BL1 8UA**
**Tel:** 01204 332370
**Owner:** Bolton Metropolitan Borough Council  **Contact:** Liz Shaw
Late medieval manor house with 17/18th century furniture, paintings and decorative art.
**Location:** MAP 10:M12, OS Ref. SD724 116. 2m NNE of central Bolton. ¼ m N of A58 ring road between A666 and A676 crossroads.
**Open:** Apr–Oct: Wed–Sun, 11am–5pm. Nov–Mar: Sats & Suns, 11am–5pm.
**Admission:** Adult £2, Child/Conc. £1, Family £5.

Len Grant

# HEATON HALL

### HEATON PARK, PRESTWICH, MANCHESTER  M25 2SW

www.heatonpark.org.uk

**Tel:** 0161 773 1085  **Fax** 0161 798 0107  **E-mail:** heatonpark@manchester.gov.uk
**Owner:** Manchester City Council  **Contact:** Janet Kendall
Heaton Hall has been in public ownership since 1902 when the 5th Earl of Wilton sold it to the Manchester Corporation. The landscape surrounding the house was designed by William Emes and modified by John Webb and has recently been restored in partnership with the HLF, together with four of the park's historic buildings. The magnificent James Wyatt house was built for Sir Thomas Egerton in 1772, and is one of Manchester's most impressive and important buildings. The principal rooms have been beautifully restored and are used to display furniture, paintings and other decorative arts appropriate to the late 18th century.

**Location:** MAP 6:N1, OS Ref. SD833 044. NW Manchester, close to M60/J19. Main entrance off St Margaret's Road, off Bury Old Road – A665.
**Open:** House: 7 Apr–30 Sept, Weds–Sun & BH Mondays, 11am–5.30pm. Park: all year, daily, 8am–dusk.
**Admission:** Free.
ℹ No photography in house, no dogs in buildings. 📷 🎭 ♿ Partial. WCs. 🖥
🎦 By arrangement. 🅿 Ample for cars, but limited for coaches. 🏠
🐾 In grounds, on leads. 🛏 Double x 2. 🔺 ❋

©NTPL/Matthew Antrobus

# HOGHTON TOWER

**HOGHTON, PRESTON, LANCASHIRE PR5 0SH**

www.hoghtontower.co.uk

**Tel:** 01254 852986   **Fax:** 01254 852109   **E-mail:** mail@hoghtontower.co.uk

**Owner:** Sir Bernard de Hoghton Bt   **Contact:** Office

Hoghton Tower, home of 14th Baronet, is one of the most dramatic looking houses in northern England. Three houses have occupied the hill site since 1100 with the present house re-built by Thomas Hoghton between 1560–1565. Rich and varied historical events including the Knighting of the Loin 'Sirloin' by James I in 1617.

**Location:** MAP 10:L11, OS Ref. SD622 264. M65/J3. Midway between Preston & Blackburn on A675.

**Open:** Jul, Aug & Sept: Mon–Thur, 11am–4pm. Suns, 1–5pm. BH Suns & Mons excluding Christmas & New Year. Group visits by appointment all year.

**Admission:** Gardens & House tours: Adult £6, Child/Conc. £5, Family £18. Gardens, Shop & Tearoom only: £3. Children under 5yrs Free. Private tours by arrangement (25+) £6, OAP £5.

Conferences, wedding receptions. Unsuitable. Obligatory. P

# RUFFORD OLD HALL

**RUFFORD, Nr ORMSKIRK, LANCASHIRE L40 1SG**

www.nationaltrust.org.uk

**Tel:** 01704 821254   **Fax:** 01704 823813
**Email:** ruffordoldhall@nationaltrust.org.uk

**Owner:** The National Trust   **Contact:** The Property Manager

One of the finest 16th century buildings in Lancashire. The magnificent Great Hall contains an intricately carved movable screen and suits of armour, and is believed to have hosted Shakespeare. Collections of weapons, tapestries and oak furniture are found in the Carolean Wing and attractive gardens contain sculptures and topiary.

**Location:** MAP 10:L11, OS Ref. SD463 160. 7m N of Ormskirk, in Rufford village E of A59.

**Open:** 24 Mar–28 Oct: Mon–Wed, Sat, Sun. Also Garden, Shop & Restaurant 28 Oct–16 Dec: Wed–Sun, (also 10–18 Mar, Sats & Suns 12noon–4pm), free entry to visitors except for special events. Grounds, Shop & Restaurant: 11am–5pm. House: 1–5pm. Last adm. 4.30pm.

**Admission:** House & Garden: Adult £5.20, Child £2.60, Family £13. Garden only: Adult £3.50, Child £1.70. Booked groups (15+): Adult £3.30, Child £1.50.

No photography in house. Partial. Licensed. By arrangement. P Limited for coaches. In grounds, on leads.

---

## LEIGHTON HALL

*See page 420 for full page entry.*

## MANCHESTER CATHEDRAL

**Manchester M3 1SX**

**Tel:** 0161 833 2220   **Fax:** 0161 839 6218   **www.manchestercathedral.co.uk**

In addition to regular worship and daily offices, there are frequent professional concerts, day schools, organ recitals, guided tours and brass-rubbing. The cathedral contains a wealth of beautiful carvings and has the widest medieval nave in Britain.

**Location:** MAP 6:N1, OS Ref. SJ838 988. Manchester.

**Open:** Daily. Visitor Centre: Mon–Sat, 10am–4.30pm.

**Admission:** Donations welcome.

Visitor Centre.

## MARTHOLME

**Great Harwood, Blackburn, Lancashire BB6 7UJ**

**Tel:** 01254 886463

**Owner:** Mr & Mrs T H Codling   **Contact:** Miss P M Codling

Part of medieval manor house with 17th century additions and Elizabethan gatehouse.

**Location:** MAP 10:M10, OS Ref. SD753 338. 2m NE of Great Harwood off A680 to Whalley.

**Open:** 4 –13 & 25–28 May, 8–10 & 22–24 Jun, 24–28 Aug & 7–9 Sept. Tours at 2pm & 4pm.

**Admission:** £5. Groups welcome by appointment.

Obligatory.

## SAMLESBURY HALL

**Preston New Road, Samlesbury, Preston PR5 0UP**

**Tel:** 01254 812010   **Fax:** 01254 812174

**Owner:** Samlesbury Hall Trust   **Contact:** Mrs S Jones - Director

Built in 1325, the hall is an attractive black and white timbered manor house set in extensive grounds. Weddings & events welcome. Antiques & crafts all year.

**Location:** MAP 10:L11, OS Ref. SD623 305. N side of A677, 4m WNW of Blackburn.

**Open:** All year: daily except Sats: 11am–4.30pm.

**Admission:** Adult £3, Child £1. Free entry to Restaurant.

## SMITHILLS HALL HISTORIC HOUSE

**Smithills Dean Road, Bolton BL7 7NP**

**Tel:** 01204 332377   **E-mail:** office@smithills.org

**Owner:** Bolton Metropolitan Borough Council   **Contact:** Jeanette Rix

14th century manor house with Tudor panelling. Stuart furniture. Stained glass.

**Location:** MAP 10:M12, OS Ref. SD699 119. 2m NW of central Bolton, ½m N of A58 ringroad.

**Open:** Apr–Sept: Tue–Sat, 11am–5pm, Sun, 2–5pm. Last adm. 4.15pm. Closed Mon except BH Mons.

**Admission:** Adult £3, Conc. £1.75, Family (2+3) £7.75.

## TOWNELEY HALL ART GALLERY & MUSEUMS

**Burnley BB11 3RQ**

**Tel:** 01282 424213   **Fax:** 01282 436138   **www.towneleyhall.org.uk**

**Owner:** Burnley Borough Council   **Contact:** Miss Susan Bourne

House dates from the 14th century with 17th and 19th century modifications. Collections include oak furniture, 18th and 19th century paintings. There is a Museum of Local Crafts and Industries.

**Location:** MAP 10:N10, OS Ref. SD854 309. ½m SE of Burnley on E side of Todmorden Road (A671).

**Open:** All year: daily except Fris, 12 noon–5pm. Closed Christmas–New Year.

**Admission:** Small charge. Guided tours: Tues–Thur afternoons or as booked for groups.

WC.

For rare and unusual plants visit the **plant sales** index on page 564

## TURTON TOWER

**Tower Drive, Chapeltown Road, Turton  BL7 0HG**
**Tel:** 01204 852203    **Fax:** 01204 853759    **E-mail:** turtontower@mus.lancscc.gov.uk
**Owner:** The Trustees of Turton Tower (run by Lancashire County Museums Service)
**Contact:** Fiona Jenkins
Country house based on a medieval tower, extended in the 16th, 17th and 19th centuries.
**Location:** MAP 10:M11, OS Ref. SD733 153. On B6391, 4m N of Bolton.
**Open:** Mar, Apr & Nov, daily except Thurs & Fris, 12 noon–4pm. May–Sept, daily except Fris, 12 noon–5pm.
**Admission:** Adult £4, Child Free, Conc. £3.

## WARTON OLD RECTORY ⌗

**Warton, Carnforth, Lancashire**
**Tel:** 0161 242 1400
**Owner:** English Heritage    **Contact:** The North West Regional Office
A rare medieval stone house with remains of the hall, chambers and domestic offices.
**Location:** MAP 10:L8, OS Ref. SD499 723. At Warton, 1m N of Carnforth on minor road off A6.
**Open:** 1 Apr–30 Mar: daily, 10am–6pm. 1 Oct–20 Mar: daily 10am–4pm. Closed 24–26 Dec & 1 Jan.
**Admission:** Free.
🐕 On leads. ✷

Leighton Hall, Carnforth

## CROXTETH HALL & COUNTRY PARK

**Liverpool, Merseyside L12 0HB**

**Tel:** 0151 233 6910 **Fax:** 0151 228 2817

**Owner:** Liverpool City Council **Contact:** Mrs Irene Vickers

Ancestral home of the Molyneux family. 500 acres country park. Special events and attractions most weekends.

**Location:** MAP 6:K1, OS Ref. SJ408 943. 5m NE of Liverpool city centre.

**Open:** Parkland: daily throughout the year. Hall, Farm & Garden: Easter–Sept: daily, 10.30am–5pm. Telephone for exact dates.

**Admission:** Hall, Farm & Garden: Adult £4.50. Conc. £2.40 (subject to change from Easter 2007). Parkland: Free.

## LIVERPOOL CATHEDRAL

**Liverpool, Merseyside L1 7AZ**

**Tel:** 0151 709 6271 **Fax:** 0151 702 7292

**Owner:** The Dean and Chapter **Contact:** Eryl Parry

Sir Giles Gilbert Scott's greatest creation. Built last century from local sandstone with superb glass, stonework and major works of art, it is the largest cathedral in Britain.

**Location:** MAP 6:K1, OS Ref. SJ354 893. Central Liverpool, ½m S of Lime Street Station.

**Open:** All year: daily, 8am–6pm. Sun services: 8am, 10.30am, 3pm, 4pm. Weekdays: 8am & 5.30pm, also 12.05pm on Fri. Sats: 8am & 3pm.

**Admission:** Donation. Lift to Tower and Embroidery Exhibition: £4.25 (concessions available). Family Ticket (2+3) £10. New for 2007: 'The Great Space' panoramic film and audio tours £4.75 (concessions, family ticket and combination ticket to include tower available).

## LIVERPOOL METROPOLITAN CATHEDRAL OF CHRIST THE KING

**Liverpool, Merseyside L3 5TQ**

**Tel:** 0151 709 9222 **Fax:** 0151 708 7274 **E-mail:** enquiries@metcathedral.org.uk

**www.liverpoolmetrocathedral.org.uk**

**Owner:** Roman Catholic Archdiocese of Liverpool **Contact:** Canon Anthony O'Brien

Modern circular cathedral with spectacular glass by John Piper and numerous modern works of art. Extensive earlier crypt by Lutyens. Grade II* listed.

**Location:** MAP 6:K1, OS Ref. SJ356 903. Central Liverpool, ½m E of Lime Street Station.

**Open:** 8am–6pm (closes 5pm Suns in Winter). Sun services: 8.30am, 10am, 11am & 7pm. Weekday services: 8am, 12.15pm & 5.15pm. Sats, 9am & 6.30pm. Gift shop & **Restaurant:** Mon–Sat, 10am–5pm; Sun, 11am–4pm.

Admission: Donation.

🖾 🔄 Except crypt. WCs. 🍴 🎭 By arrangement. 🅿 Ample for cars. 🎪 🐕 Guide dogs only. ✳

## MEOLS HALL 🏛

**Churchtown, Southport, Merseyside PR9 7LZ**

**Tel:** 01704 228326 **Fax:** 01704 507185 **E-mail:** events@meolshall.com

**www.meolshall.com**

**Owner:** The Hesketh Family **Contact:** Pamela Whelan

17th century house with subsequent additions. Interesting collection of pictures and furniture. Tithe Barn available for wedding ceremonies and receptions all year.

**Location:** MAP 10:K11, OS Ref. SD365 184. 3m NE of Southport town centre in Churchtown. SE of A565.

**Open:** 14 Aug–14 Sept: daily, 2–5pm.

**Admission:** Adult £3, Child £1. Groups only (25+) £9 (inclusive of full afternoon tea).

🍴 Wedding ceremonies and receptions now available in the Tithe Barn.

🔄 🐕 🅿 🎪 🎭

## SPEKE HALL GARDEN & ESTATE 🍃

**The Walk, Liverpool L24 1XD**

**Tel:** 0151 427 7231 **Fax:** 0151 427 9860 **Info Line:** 08457 585702

**www.nationaltrust.org.uk**

**Owner:** The National Trust **Contact:** The Property Manager

One of the most famous half-timbered houses in the country.

**Location:** MAP 6:K1, OS Ref. SJ419 825. North bank of the Mersey, 6m SE of city centre. Follow signs for Liverpool John Lennon airport.

**Open:** House: 17 Mar–28 Oct: Daily except Mons & Tues (open BH Mons), 1–5pm; 3 Nov–2 Dec: Sats & Suns only, 1–4.30pm. Grounds: Daily, 11am–5.30pm. Check for winter opening.

**Admission:** Adult £6.70, Child £3.70, Family £20.50. Grounds only: Adult £4, Child £1.90, Family £11.

World H
LIVE

**Liver Building**
**1908-11 Listed Grade I**
The head offices of the Royal Liver Friendly Society were designed by Aubrey Thomas. It is notable as one of Britain's first multi-storey reinforced concrete framed buildings. The clock towers are mounted with copper Liver Birds which to many are the very identity of Liverpool.

**Cunard Building**
**1913-1916 Grade II\***
This substantial building was bu the offices of the Cunard Shippi Company to the designs of Willi Thicknesse. Its proportions give form of an Italian palazzo. The portraits of races from around th world symbolise the global oper of the company.

**Albert Dock Traffic Office**
**1846-7 Grade I**
This is one of a number of building designs by Hartley in collaboration with Philip Hardwick. It is built of brick with red sandstone dressings. The most remarkable feature is the cast iron Tuscan portico and frieze The building was restored by the Merseyside Development Corporation and re-opened as television studios.

**Stanley Dock Warehouse**
Stanley Dock opened in 1848, an between 1852-55 it was equippe import warehouses. The comple includes: The North Stanley Warehouse 1852-5 Grade II*, The Stanley Warehouse 1852-5 Grad The Stanley Dock Tobacco Ware The Hydraulic Tower 1852-55 Gr two entrances from Great Howa Street and two from Regent Roa

**Oriel Chambers**
**1864 Grade I**
Designed by Peter Ellis, the use of oriel windows was driven by a desire to provide good daylight. The oriels themselves are framed in the thinnest sections of iron. In its day, the building aroused much opposition. It is only recently that its futuristic qualities have become appreciated.

**St George's Hall**
**1840 – 55 Grade I**
A design competition for a new musical venue for Liverpool was and won by young architect Har Lonsdale Elmes. The Hall is built Grecian style externally with a R interior. It contains the lavish Gr Hall, with its Minton tiled floor a great organ, and the more intim Small Concert Room, much visit Charles Dickens. The Crown and courts at either end were introdu following a further competition. Hall will be fully open in April 20 following extensive refurbishme

**For further informatio**

UNESCO seeks to encourage the identification, protection and preservation of the cultural and natural heritage around the world that is considered to be of outstanding universal value to humanity. Sites that meet the strict criteria of eligibility established by UNESCO are inscribed onto the World Heritage List.

Liverpool – Maritime Mercantile City was nominated by the UK government as "The supreme example of a commercial port at the time of Britain's greatest global influence" and was inscribed as a World Heritage Site by UNESCO's World Heritage Committee in July 2004. The status is a great honour as it acknowledges that Liverpool's architectural and technological heritage is of international significance and should rank alongside Stonehenge, the Taj Mahal and the Pyramids of Egypt.

### of Liverpool Building
eted 1907   Grade II*
omed head office of the
ey Docks and Harbour Board
esigned by Briggs,
enholme and Thorneley
Features include cast iron
and gate piers decorated with
me symbols and lamp holders
form of naval monuments.

### George's Dock Tunnel Ventilation Building and Offices
1931-1934   Grade II
This stylized obelisk, reminiscent of ancient Egypt, was designed by Sir Basil Mott and J. A. Brodie, with Herbert J. Rowse, to serve the Mersey Road Tunnel. It has statues of Night and Day, symbols of the never-closing Mersey Tunnel and a black marble memorial to the workers who died in its construction.

### Memorial to Heroes of the Engine Room (Titanic Memorial)
Circa 1916   Grade II
The memorial was originally intended to be for the engineers who stayed at their posts on 15th April 1912 when the Titanic sank. Its dedication was broadened to include all maritime engine room fatalities incurred during the performance of duty. The figures are naturalistic, the detail of their work-clothes being carefully studied.

### Albert Dock Warehouses
Opened 1846/7   Grade I
Opened 1846-47 Albert Dock Warehouses form the largest group of Grade1 Listed Buildings in England. Jesse Hartley used well-established techniques adapted from textile mill methods. He introduced new solutions, such as the amazing stressed-skin iron roof. Raising of goods from the quaysides was performed with the first hydraulic cargo-handling installation in the world.

### s and Liverpool l Locks
48   Grade II
anal had been in partial use 1774 and was completed h to Leeds in 1816; a direct the docks was formed in The four locks were designed rtley, and are the only all- e canal locks in the country. rick viaduct carried the ool and Bury Railway.

### The Dock Wall
Its purpose was to control rather than prevent access from the town into the docks, and the monumental gateways with their heavy wooden gates sliding in iron guide rails effectively made the docks into a fortress-like stronghold. The design of the various gate piers demonstrates a fascinating progression from Foster's early classical style to Hartley's whimsical turrets.

### Liverpool Town Hall
Liverpool's finest Georgian building, is the result of three building campaigns. The original design was by John Wood of Bath, and was built in 1749-54. Additions and alterations were designed by James Wyatt and carried out by the elder John Foster in 1789-92. Following a fire of 1795, it was reconstructed the work continuing until 1820.

### India Building
1924-31   Grade II
This immense office block was built for the Blue Funnel Line and designed by Herbert J Rowse with Briggs, Wostenholme and Thorneley. It has stripped classical facades; Italian Renaissance detail is restricted to the top and bottom storeys. The building was badly damaged in the war, and restored under Rowse's supervision.

### Martins Building
1927-32   Grade II*
Originally Martin's Bank, designed by Rowse it is monumental and American influenced. The stylish top lit banking hall, with its Parisian jazz moderne fittings, survives well, as does the boardroom. Sculpture and carvings by Herbert Tyson Smith with Edmund Thompson and George Capstick celebrate maritime themes and commerce.

### am Brown Museum ibrary
0   Grade II*
ompletion of the magnificent all on St George's Plateau set tern for other civic projects acent land. The Liverpool vements Act was passed and a etition was opened in 1855 for museum and public library. MP William Brown donated and the street was renamed honour. The building is now to the internationally ant collections of World m Liverpool.

### The Walker Art Gallery
Opened 1877   Grade II*
It was designed by architects Sherlock and Vale and named after its principal benefactor, Alderman Andrew Barclay Walker, at that time Lord Mayor of Liverpool. A classical portico is the centerpiece of the exterior, which includes friezes of scenes from the city's history, and is surmounted by a personification of Liverpool.

### Bluecoat Chambers
Opened 1718   Grade I
Bluecoat Chambers was originally built as a charity school in 1717 in the Queen Anne style. The main entrance is round headed with a broken pediment above containing a cartouche of the arms of Liverpool. To the rear a landscaped garden provides a quiet environment, totally enclosed from the city. The building is closed for refurbishment for 2006 and will reopen in 2007. The Bluecoat Display Centre is still open to the public.

### The Bridewell
1861   Grade II
Located in the Duke Street area, the Bridewell, or Police Station, dates from c.1850. It is of brick with stone dressings and a slate roof. The building is of two storeys and three bays, with the centre bay projecting to form the base of a short tower. The Bridewell is now a public house and restaurant.

### The Royal Institution
1799   Grade II
The complex of buildings originally built for Thomas Parr is one of the earliest remaining residence/warehouse hybrids that were so characteristic of Duke Street following the construction of the Old Dock in 1715. It became the Royal Institution when it fell out of residential use in 1817, and it was incorporated by Royal Charter in 1822.

**Above:** Chipchase Castle
**Right:** Belsay Hall ©English Heritage Photo Library

# North East

*Rugged and Roman – the North East region of Britain offers the visitor a wealth of history going back to the Roman occupation. As well as visiting the magnificent fortress castles at Alnwick, Bamburgh and Chillingham, time should be set aside to explore properties such as Wallington, with its exceptional murals depicting Northumbrian history, and The Lady Waterford Murals at Ford, with its 1860 biblical murals.*

### ■ Owner

The Bowes Museum
Charitable Trust

### ■ Contact

Barnard Castle
Co. Durham
DL12 8NP

**Tel:** 01833 690606
**Fax:** 01833 637163
**E-mail:** info@
thebowesmuseum.org.uk

### ■ Location

**MAP 10:O6**
**OS Ref. NZ055 164**

¼ m E of Market Place in
Barnard Castle,
just off A66, between A1
at Scotch Corner & M6.

### ■ Opening Times

**All year**
Daily: 11am–5pm.

Closed 25/26 December
& 1 January.

### ■ Admission

| | |
|---|---|
| Adult | £7.00 |
| Child (under 16yrs) | Free |
| Conc. | £6.00 |
| Disabled carers | Free |
| Groups (15+) | |
| Adult | £6.00 |
| Conc. | £5.00 |

# THE BOWES MUSEUM

### www.thebowesmuseum.org.uk

Nestling in the historic market town of Barnard Castle, visitors' first sight of The Bowes Museum never ceases to amaze.

The founders, John Bowes and his wife Joséphine, were avid collectors of beautiful works of art; the foundation of the Museum a natural progression of their shared passion. The French-style château, completed in 1892, was designed specifically as a museum to house the 15,000 items acquired by the couple. Today, the designated collection includes some of the best examples of European fine and decorative art to be found in the UK, with works by Canaletto, El Greco and Goya. It also features the finest ceramics, furniture and textiles. One of the most enduring memories that visitors of all ages take away with them is that of the Silver Swan musical automaton, played every day to fascinated onlookers. The wonderful story of the Museum is recounted as you wander through its spellbinding galleries, with an audio guide and a variety of interactive materials to educate and entertain.

The quality of the permanent collections is enhanced by a rolling programme of exhibitions, due to a reciprocal loans programme with world-class galleries around the globe. Major shows for 2007 include *Fine and Fashionable: Lace from the Blackborne Collection*, until 29 April; and *Watercolours and Drawings from the Collection of Queen Elizabeth the Queen Mother*, 19 May until 2 September.

Open all year, the Museum has its own bistro, shop, beautiful parkland and landscaped gardens, making it a great day out for all.

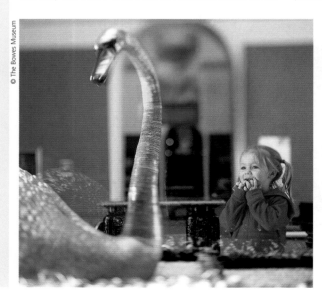

Palatial rooms and acres of parkland. Individual tailored packages for wedding or corporate function.

Access to most of the Museum including gift shop, café and WCs. Wheelchair facility is available. Signposted disabled parking and entrance.

Licensed.

By arrangement.

Ample.

In grounds. Guide dogs only in Museum.

# RABY CASTLE

www.rabycastle.com

The magnificent Raby Castle has been home to Lord Barnard's family since 1626, when it was purchased by his ancestor, Sir Henry Vane the Elder, the eminent Statesman and Politician. The Castle was built mainly in the 14th Century by the Nevill family on a site of an earlier Manor House. The Nevills continued to live at Raby until 1569, when after the failure of the Rising of the North, the Castle and its land were forfeited to the Crown.

Little now remains of the original mediaeval structure of the Barons Hall (below) where 700 knights met to plot The Rising of the North. Architect John Carr raised the floor level by 3 metres when constructing a carriageway below in the Entrance Hall and later William Burn extended the room by 17 metres over his elaborate

Octagon Drawing Room, creating the most impressive Hall. Today it houses a Meissen bird collection. Other Raby treasures also include fine furniture and artworks with paintings by Munnings, Reynolds, Van Dyck, Batoni, Teniers, Amigoni and Vernet.

There is a large Deer Park with two lakes and a beautiful walled garden with formal lawns, ancient yew hedges and ornamental pond. The 18th Century Stable block contains a horse-drawn carriage collection including the State Coach last used by the family for the Coronation of Edward VII in 1902. Parts of the Stables have been converted into a Gift Shop and Tearooms, where the former stalls have been incorporated to create an atmospheric setting.

© Heritage House Group Ltd.

 Film locations, product launches, corporate events, fairs & concerts. Raby Estates venison & game sold in tearooms. Soft fruit when in season. Lectures on Castle, its contents, gardens & history. No photography or video filming is permitted inside. Colour illustrated guidebook and DVD on sale. Christmas Shop in Stable Yard throughout December.

Partial. WC. Castle DVD viewing area.

Licensed.

By arrangement for groups (20+) or min charge. VIP & Standard Castle Tours available. Tour time 1½ hrs.

**P**

By arrangement (20+), weekday am. Primary & junior £3; Secondary £3.50.

Guide dogs welcome. All dogs welcome in Park on leads.

Varied programme throughout the summer.

### Owner
The Lord Barnard

### Contact
Clare Owen /
Catherine Turnbull
Raby Castle
Staindrop
Darlington
Co. Durham  DL2 3AH

**Tel:** 01833 660202
**Fax:** 01833 660169
**E-mail:** admin@
rabycastle.com

### Location
**MAP 10:O5**
**OS Ref. NZ129 218**

On A688, 1m N of Staindrop. 8m NE of Barnard Castle, 12m WNW of Darlington.

**Rail:** Darlington Station, 12m.

**Air:** Durham Tees Valley Airport, 20m.

### Opening Times
**Castle**
7–9 Apr, May, June & September, Sun–Wed. July & August: Daily except Sats. (Open BH Sats), 1–5pm.

**Park & Gardens**
As Castle, 11am–5.30pm.

### Admission
Castle, Park & Gardens
| | |
|---|---|
| Adult | £9.00 |
| Child (5–16yrs) | £4.00 |
| OAP/Student | £8.00 |
| Family (2+3) | £25.00 |

Groups (12+)
| | |
|---|---|
| Adult | £8.00 |
| Child (5–16yrs) | £3.00 |
| OAP/Student | £7.00 |

**Park & Gardens**
| | |
|---|---|
| Adult | £4.00 |
| Child (5–16yrs) | £2.50 |
| OAP/Student | £3.50 |
| Family (2+3) | £12.50 |

Groups (12+)
| | |
|---|---|
| Adult | £3.50 |
| Child (5–16yrs) | £2.50 |
| OAP/Student | £3.00 |

Season Tickets available.

**VIP Private Guided Tours***
 (incl. reception, tea/coffee in entrance hall) Easter–Sept, Mon–Fri mornings.
| | |
|---|---|
| 20+ | £12.00 |

**Standard Guided Tours***
(min group 20+).
Easter–Sept, Mon–Fri.
| | |
|---|---|
| Adult | £8.00 |
| OAP/Student | £7.00 |

*Please book in advance.

Free RHS access to Park & Gardens.

# AUCKLAND CASTLE 🏰

## BISHOP AUCKLAND, CO. DURHAM  DL14 7NR

www.auckland-castle.co.uk

**Tel:** 01388 601627    **Fax:** 01388 609323    **E-mail:** auckland.castle@zetnet.co.uk
**Owner:** Church Commissioners        **Contact:** The Manager

Principal country residence of the Bishops of Durham since Norman times and now the official residence of the present day Bishops. The Chapel, reputedly one of the largest private chapels in Europe, was originally the 12th century banquet hall.  Chapel and State Rooms including the Throne Room, Long Dining Room and King Charles Dining Room are open to the public. Access to the adjacent Bishop's Park with its 18th century Deer House.

**Location:** MAP 10:P5, OS Ref. NZ214 303. Bishop Auckland, N end of town centre.

**Open:** Easter Mon–30 Sept: Suns & Mons, 2–5pm. Jul & Aug: Suns, 2–5pm, Mons & Weds, 11am–5pm. Last admission 4.30pm. The management reserves the right to close the castle to visitors.

**Admission:** Adult £4, Child/Conc. £3. Child (up to 12yrs) Free. Special openings for groups (25+).

ℹ️ Exhibitions. No indoor photography. 📷 📶 Wedding receptions, functions.
♿ Wheelchair access to chapel, ground floor. WC. Stairwalker available for upstairs State Rooms by prior arrangement. 🅿️ 🚻 Guide dogs only.

---

## AUCKLAND CASTLE DEER HOUSE ⌗

**Bishop Auckland, Durham**
**Tel:** 0191 2691200
**Owner:** English Heritage        **Contact:** The Regional Office

A charming building erected in 1760 in the Park of the Bishops of Durham so that the deer could shelter and find food.

**Location:** MAP 10:P5, OS Ref. NZ216 304. In Bishop Auckland Park, just N of town centre on A68. About 500 yds N of the castle.

**Open:** Park: 1 Apr–30 Sept: daily, 10am–6pm 1 Oct–20 Mar: daily, 10am–4pm. Closed 24–26 Dec & 1 Jan.

**Admission:** Free.

🚶 On leads.

---

## BARNARD CASTLE ⌗

**Barnard Castle, Castle House, Durham  DL12 8PR**
**Tel:** 01833 638212
**Owner:** English Heritage        **Contact:** Visitor Operations Team

The substantial remains of this large castle stand on a rugged escarpment overlooking the River Tees. Parts of the 14th century Great Hall and the cylindrical 12th century tower, built by the Baliol family can still be seen. Sensory garden.

**Location:** MAP 10:O5, OS92, NZ049 165. In Barnard Castle.

**Open:** 1 Apr–30 Sept: daily, 10am–6pm. 1–31 Oct: daily, 10am–4pm. 1 Nov–20 Mar: Thur–Mon, 10am–4pm. Closed 24–26 Dec & 1 Jan.

**Admission:** Adult £4, Child £2, Conc. £3. 15% discount for groups (11+).

ℹ️ WCs in town. 📷 ♿ Grounds. 🚶 In grounds, on leads. ❄️ 🎫

---

## BINCHESTER ROMAN FORT

**Bishop Auckland, Co. Durham**
**Tel:** 01388 663089 / 0191 3834212 (outside opening hours)
**Owner:** Durham County Council        **Contact:** Deborah Anderson

Once the largest Roman fort in Co Durham, the heart of the site has been excavated.

**Location:** MAP 10:P5, OS92 Ref. NZ210 312. 1½ m N of Bishop Auckland, signposted from A690 Durham–Crook and from A688 Spennymoor–Bishop Auckland roads.

**Open:** Easter–30 Sept: daily, 11am–5pm.

**Admission:** Adult £2, Child/Conc. £1.

---

## THE BOWES MUSEUM

*See page 428 for full page entry.*

---

## CROOK HALL & GARDENS

**Sidegate, Durham  DH1 5SZ**
**Tel:** 0191 3848028
**Owner:** Keith & Maggie Bell        **Contact:** Mrs Maggie Bell

Medieval manor house set in rural landscape on the edge of Durham city.

**Location:** MAP 10:P4, OS Ref. NZ274 432. ½ m N of city centre.

**Open:** 28 May–10 Sept, Easter weekend & BHs: Wed–Sun, 11am–5pm.

**Admission:** Adult £4.50, Conc. £4, Family £14.

---

## DERWENTCOTE STEEL FURNACE ⌗

**Newcastle, Durham  NE39 1BA**
**Tel:** 0191 2691200 (Mon–Fri)
**Owner:** English Heritage        **Contact:** Regional Office

Built in the 18th century it is the earliest and most complete authentic steel making furnace to have survived.

**Location:** MAP 10:O3, OS Ref. NZ130 566. 10m SW of Newcastle N of the A694 between Rowland's Gill and Hamsterley.

**Open:** By arrangement.

**Admission:** Free.

🅿️ 🚶 On leads in restricted areas.

---

See all the properties that are **open all year** in the index on page 580

## DURHAM CASTLE

**Palace Green, Durham  DH1 3RW**
**Tel:** 0191 3343800  **Fax:** 0191 3343801  **Contact:** Mrs Julie Marshall
Durham Castle, founded in the 1070s, with the Cathedral is a World Heritage Site.
**Location:** MAP 10:P4, OS Ref. NZ274 424. City centre, adjacent to Cathedral.
**Open:** Mar–Sept: 10am–12 noon & 2–4.30pm. Oct–Mar: Mon, Wed, Sat & Sun 2–4pm.
**Admission:** Adult £5, OAP £2.50, Family (2+2) £10. Guide book £2.50.

## DURHAM CATHEDRAL

**Durham  DH1 3EH**
**Tel:** 0191 3864266  **Fax:** 0191 3864267  **E-mail:** enquiries@durhamcathedral.co.uk
**Contact:** Miss A Heywood
A World Heritage Site. Norman architecture. Burial place of St Cuthbert and the Venerable Bede.
**Location:** MAP 10:P4, OS Ref. NZ274 422. Durham city centre.
**Open:** June–Aug: 9.30am–8pm. Open only for worship and private prayer: All year: Mon–Sat, 7.30am–9.30am and Suns, 7.45am–12.30pm. The Cathedral is closed to visitors during evening recitals and concerts. Visitors welcome Mon–Sat, 9.30–5pm, Suns 12.30–3.30pm.
**Admission:** Cathedral: Request a donation of min. £4. Tower: Adult £2.50, Child (under 16) £1.50, Family £7. Monk's Dormitory: Adult £1, Child 30p, Family £2.10. AV: Adult £1.10, Child 30p, Family £2.

## EGGLESTONE ABBEY ⌗

**Durham**
**Tel:** 0191 2691200
**Owner:** English Heritage  **Contact:** The Regional Office
Picturesque remains of a 12th century abbey, located in a bend of the River Tees. Substantial parts of the church and abbey buildings remain.
**Location:** MAP 10:O6, OS Ref. NZ062 151. 1m S of Barnard Castle on minor road off B6277.
**Open:** Daily, 10am–6pm.
**Admission:** Free.
🅿 ⓘ  On leads.

## ESCOMB CHURCH

**Escomb, Bishop Auckland  DL14 7ST**
**Tel:** 01388 662265
**Owner:** Church of England  **Contact:** Mrs E Kitching
Saxon church dating from the 7th century built of stone from Binchester Roman Fort.
**Location:** MAP 10:P5, OS Ref. NZ189 302. 3m W of Bishop Auckland.
**Open:** Summer: 9am–8pm. Winter: 9am–4pm. Key available from 22 Saxon Green, Escomb.
**Admission:** Free.

## FINCHALE PRIORY ⌗

**Finchdale Priory, Brasside, Newton Hall  DH9 5SH**
**Tel:** 0191 269 1200/386 3828
**Owner:** English Heritage  **Contact:** Regional Office
These beautiful 13th century priory remains are located beside the curving River Wear.
**Location:** MAP 10:P4, OS Ref. NZ296 471. 3m NE of Durham.
**Open:** Telephone key keeper on 0191 386 3828.
**Admission:** Free.
ⓘ WC. 📷 ♿ (Not managed by EH.) 🅿 (charge) on S side of river. 🐕 On leads.

Finchale Priory

## RABY CASTLE 📖

*See page 429 for full page entry.*

## ROKEBY PARK

**BARNARD CASTLE, CO. DURHAM  DL12 9RZ**

www.rokebypark.com

**Tel:** 01609 748612  **E-mail:** admin@rokebypark.com
An original and effective variant of the Palladian formula, Rokeby was built by Sir Thomas Robinson c1730. It was acquired by JS Morritt in 1769, in whose family it has remained ever since. Paintings and period furniture are on display, together with a unique collection of needlework pictures by Ann Morritt (d1797) and an unusual "Print Room". Known as the setting for Sir Walter Scott's ballad "Rokeby", there is a beautiful walk to the banks of the River Greta.
**Location:** MAP 10:O6, OS Ref NZ 080 142. 3m SE of Barnard Castle, N of A66.
**Open:** 7 May. 28 May–4 Sept: Mons & Tues, 2–5pm (last admission 4.30pm). Groups (Max 60) by appointment on any day during open months.
**Admission:** Adult £6.50. Children under 16 Free. Over 60s £5.50. Students £4. Groups £5.50 on open days, by arrangement other days.
ⓘ No photography in house. ♿ Ground floor only, no WC. 📷 By arrangement. 🐕 In grounds on leads. 🅿

## THE WEARDALE MUSEUM & HIGH HOUSE CHAPEL

**Ireshopeburn, Co. Durham  DL13 1EY**
**Tel:** 01388 517433  **E-mail:** dtheatherington@ormail.co.uk
**Contact:** D T Heatherington
Small folk museum and historic chapel. Includes 1870 Weardale cottage room, John Wesley room and local history displays.
**Location:** MAP 10:N4, OS Ref. NZ872 385. Adjacent to 18th century Methodist Chapel.
**Open:** Easter & May–Sept: Wed–Sun & BH, 2–5pm. Aug: daily, 2–5pm.
**Admission:** Adult £1.50, Child 50p.

*giftaid it* This year, some properties will be operating the Gift Aid on Entry scheme at their admission points. Where the scheme is operating, visitors are offered a choice between paying the standard admission price or paying the 'Gift Aid Admission' which includes a voluntary donation of at least 10%. Gift Aid Admissions enable the charity to reclaim tax on the whole amount paid* - an extra 28% - potentially a very significant boost to property funds. Money raised from paying visitors in this way will go towards restoration projects at the property and will be very welcome. Where shown, the admission prices are inclusive of the 10% voluntary donation where properties are operating the Gift Aid on Entry scheme, but both the standard admission price and the Gift Aid Admission will be displayed at the property and on their website.

*Gift Aid donations must be supported by a valid Gift Aid declaration and a Gift Aid declaration can only cover donations made by an individual for him/herself or for him/herself and members of his/her family.

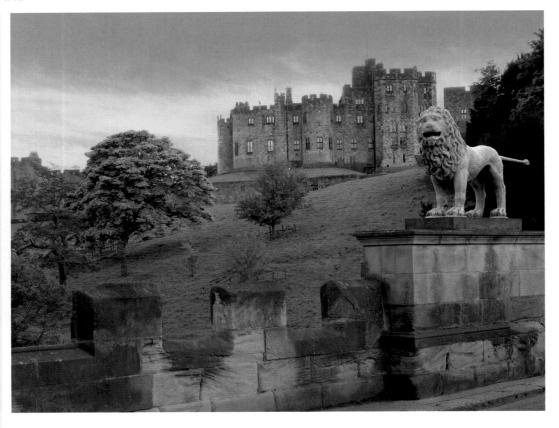

## Owner
His Grace the Duke of Northumberland

## Contact
Alnwick Castle
Estate Office
Alnwick
Northumberland
NE66 1NQ

**Tel:** 01665 510777
**Info:** 01665 511100
**Group bookings:**
01665 510777
**Fax:** 01665 510876
**E-mail:** enquiries@
alnwickcastle.com

## Location
**MAP 14:M11**
**OS Ref. NU187 135**

In Alnwick 1½ m
W of A1.
From London 6hrs,
Edinburgh 2hrs,
Chester 4hrs,
Newcastle 40mins
North Sea ferry
terminal 30mins.

**Bus:** From bus station
in Alnwick.

**Rail:** Alnmouth
Station 5m.
Kings Cross, London
3½hrs.

**Air:** Newcastle 40mins.

## Opening Times
2 April–28 October
Daily, 10am–5pm.
State Rooms open
at 11am (last adm. to
State Rooms 4.30pm).

## Admission
| | |
|---|---|
| Adult | £9.00 |
| Child (6–15yrs) | £4.00 |
| Child (under 5yrs) | Free |
| Conc. | £8.00 |

Booked Groups
(14+, tel 01665 510777)
| | |
|---|---|
| Adult | £6.50 |
| Child | £1.50 |
| Conc. | £6.00 |

Weekly & Season
Tickets available.

HHA members free
access to Castle only.

# ALNWICK CASTLE 🏛

www.alnwickcastle.com

Set in a stunning landscape designed by Capability Brown, Alnwick Castle was voted one of Britain's Finest Castles in 2003 and is the family home of the Duke of Northumberland.

Owned by his family since 1309, this beautiful castle originally built to defend England from the Scots now appeals to visitors of all ages from across the world.

Considered to be one of the finest castles in England, and known as the 'Windsor of the North', this has been the home of the Percy family for nearly 700 years. In the 1760s it was transformed from a fortification into a family home for the First Duke and Duchess. Today it is a tourist attraction of real significance, full of historical facts, fun and entertainment.

Visitors walking through the gates, set in massive stone walls, enter one of the most stunning castles in Europe. The Keep sits magnificently in the spacious grounds, with its medieval towers housing the castle's 14th century dungeon and the entrance to the remarkable State Rooms. New for 2007, the refurbished and restored dining room is worth a visit. Beautifully silked walls, a hand-woven carpet and intricate carved ceiling are among the delights. Important ceramics of the Meissen, Chelsea and Paris factories are impressively displayed in the china gallery.

Within the grounds are the museums and towers that tell the story of the Northumberland Fusiliers from 1674 to the present day, local archaeology of the area, the Percy Tenantry Volunteers and a new exhibition on siege craft.

Adding to the magic of this castle is an interactive and fun activity area where children can enter the exciting and enchanting world of knights and dragons. They can learn how to become a Knight or Lady of Alnwick then take the ultimate challenge to win their spurs by facing the monster which rules the kingdom in Dragon's Quest.

| | | |
|---|---|---|
| **i** Conference facilities. Fashion shows, fairs, filming, parkland for hire. No photography inside the castle. No unaccompanied children. | | Coffee, light lunches and teas. |
| | **P** | 500 cars and 12 coaches. |
| 🛍 | | Guidebook and worksheet, special rates for children and teachers. |
| ▼ Wedding receptions. | | Guide dogs only. |
| ♿ Unsuitable. | | |

## Conference/Function
| ROOM | SIZE | MAX CAPACITY |
|---|---|---|
| The Guest Hall | 100' x 30' | 250 |

# BAMBURGH CASTLE

www.bamburghcastle.com

Bamburgh Castle is the home of the Armstrong family. The earliest reference to Bamburgh shows the craggy citadel to have been a royal centre by AD 547. Recent archaeological excavation has revealed that the site has been occupied since prehistoric times.

The Norman Keep has been the stronghold for nearly nine centuries, but the remainder has twice been extensively restored, initially by Lord Crewe in the 1750s and subsequently by the 2nd Lord Armstrong at the beginning of the 20th century. This Castle was the first to succumb to artillery fire – that of Edward IV.

The public rooms contain many exhibits, including the loan collections of armour from The Board of Trustees, The Royal Armouries, Leeds, and other private sources, which complement the castle's armour. Porcelain, china, jade, furniture from many periods, oils, water-colours and a host of interesting items are all contained within one of the most important buildings of Britain's national heritage.

## Views

The views from the ramparts are unsurpassed and take in Holy Island, the Farne Islands, one of Northumberland's finest beaches and, landwards, the Cheviot Hills.

ℹ️ Filming. No photography in house.

📷 

♿ Limited access. WC.

☕ Tearooms for light refresh-ments. Groups can book.

🚶 By arrangement at any time, min charge out of hours £150.

🅿️ 100 cars, coaches park on tarmac drive at entrance.

🎓 Welcome. Guide provided if requested, educational pack.

🐕 Guide dogs only.

🔔

❄️

---

■ **Owner**

Trustees Lord Armstrong dec'd.

■ **Contact**

The Administrator
Bamburgh Castle
Bamburgh
Northumberland
NE69 7DF

**Tel:** 01668 214515
**Fax:** 01668 214060
**E-mail:** bamburghcastle @aol.com

■ **Location**
**MAP 14:M10**
**OS Ref. NU184 351**

42m N of Newcastle-upon-Tyne. 20m S of Berwick-upon-Tweed. 6m E of Belford by B1342 from A1 at Belford.

**Bus:** Bus service 200 yards.

**Rail:** Berwick-upon-Tweed 20m.

**Taxi:** J Swanston 01289 306124.

**Air:** Newcastle-upon-Tyne 45m.

■ **Opening Times**

10 March–31 October Daily, 11am–5pm. Last entry 4.30pm.

Tours by arrangement at any time.

■ **Admission**
**Summer**
| | |
|---|---|
| Adult | £6.50 |
| Child (6–15yrs) | £2.50 |
| OAP | £5.50 |

| Groups | |
|---|---|
| Adult | £4.50 |
| Child (6–15yrs) | £2.00 |
| OAP | £3.50 |

**Winter**
Group rates only quoted.

## ■ Owner

Sir Humphry Wakefield Bt

## ■ Contact

Administrator
Chillingham Castle
Northumberland
NE66 5NJ

**Tel:** 01668 215359
**Fax:** 01668 215463
**E-mail:** enquiries@
chillingham-castle.com

## ■ Location

**MAP 14:L11**
**OS Ref. NU062 258**

45m N of Newcastle
between A697 & A1.
2m S of B6348
at Chatton.
6m SE of Wooler.

**Rail:** Alnmouth
or Berwick.

## ■ Opening Times

**Summer**
Easter
1 May–30 September
Closed Sats, Castle,
1–5pm, Grounds, Garden
& Tearoom, 12 noon–5pm.

**Winter**
October–April: Groups &
Coach Tours any time by
appointment. All function
activities available.

## ■ Admission

**Summer**
| | |
|---|---|
| Adult | £6.75 |
| Child (under 16yrs) | £3.00 |
| Child (under 5yrs) | £1.00 |
| Conc. | £5.50 |
| | |
| Groups (10+) | |
| Per person | £6.00 |
| Guide | £25.00 |

# CHILLINGHAM CASTLE

www.chillingham-castle.com

Rated 4-star (amongst the top 100!) in Simon Jenkins' *England's Thousand Best Houses*. *The Independent*: First of *The 50 Best Castles in Britain & Ireland*.

This remarkable castle, the home of Sir Humphry Wakefield Bt, with its alarming dungeons has, as now and since the 1200s, been continuously owned by the family of the Earls Grey and their relations. You will see active restoration of complex masonry, metalwork and ornamental plaster as the great halls and state rooms are gradually brought back to life with tapestries, arms and armour as of old and even a torture chamber.

At first a 12th century stronghold, Chillingham became a fully fortified castle in the 14th century (see the original 1344 Licence to Crenellate). Wrapped in the nation's history it occupied a strategic position as a fortress during Northumberland's bloody border feuds,

often besieged and at many times enjoying the patronage of royal visitors. In Tudor days there were additions but the underlying medieval character has always been retained. The 18th and 19th centuries saw decorative extravagances including the lake, garden and grounds laid out by Sir Jeffrey Wyatville, fresh from his triumphs at Windsor Castle. These contrast with the prehistoric Wild Cattle in the park beyond (a separate tour).

## Gardens

With romantic grounds, the castle commands breathtaking views of the surrounding countryside. As you walk to the lake you will see, according to season, drifts of snowdrops, daffodils or bluebells and an astonishing display of rhododendrons. This emphasises the restrained formality of the Elizabethan topiary garden, with its intricately clipped hedges of box and yew. Lawns, the formal gardens and woodland walks are all fully open to the public.

## Conference/Function

| ROOM | MAX CAPACITY |
|---|---|
| King James I Room | |
| Great Hall | 100 |
| Minstrels' Hall | 60 |
| 2 x Drawing Room | |
| Museum | |
| Tea Room | 35 |
| Lower Gallery | |
| Upper Gallery | |

 Corporate entertainment, lunches, drinks, dinners, wedding ceremonies and receptions.

 Partial.

Booked meals for up to 100 people.

By arrangement.

**P** Avoid Lilburn route, coach parties welcome by prior arrangement. Limited for coaches.

 Self catering apartments.

# ESHOTT HALL

www.eshotthall.com

This elegant country house has a 17th century core, much refashioned in the 19th century to include sumptuous 18th century plasterwork in the drawing room done by the same Italian stuccatori who worked at Alnwick Castle. Its setting at the heart of a secluded estate is a haven of peace and tranquillity. Red squirrels can still be seen and wildlife abounds. Wooded walks lead to open countryside with views towards the Cheviot Hills straddling the Scottish Border. The location is advantageous, being close to the Northumberland coast with some of the best beaches in Britain, an array of spectacular castles, and yet only 20 minutes north of the rejuvenated cultural centre of Newcastle and the vibrant lifestyle of its quayside.

Whilst still the private home of Margaret and Ho Sanderson, the 6th generation of the family to live here, the house has been adapted to provide superb facilities for weddings, business use and comfortable accommodation.

The house is offered for exclusive use, or as a place to stay, or both. Margaret Sanderson's design talents are evident in each of the individually styled and beautifully furnished bedrooms, with comfortable king-size beds and en suite bathrooms. Her lifetime experience of exclusive catering ensures that the most discerning tastes are rewarded. Organic fruit and vegetables are harvested in the walled garden.

It is an exceptional location for weddings and events and one of comparatively few such houses offering accommodation.

## Owner
The Sanderson Family

## Contact
Margaret Sanderson
Eshott Hall
Morpeth
Northumberland
NE65 9EN

**Tel:** (01670) 787777
**Fax:** (01670) 787999
**E-mail:**
thehall@eshott.co.uk

## Location
**MAP 14:M12**

**OS Ref NZ203 978**

Almost equidistant between Morpeth and Alnwick, 1m E of the A1, 20m N of Newcastle-upon-Tyne.

Turn east off A1 trunk road about 6 miles north of Morpeth and 9 miles south of Alnwick at Eshott signpost. Unmarked Hall gates are approximately one mile down the country lane. Less than an hour's stunning coastal train journey from Edinburgh and about three hours from London, our local station, Alnmouth, is a taxi-ride away.

**Rail:** Newcastle 20m, Morpeth 8m, Alnmouth 5m.

**Air:** Newcastle International Airport ½hr drive.

**Bus:** Regular service.

## Opening Times
All year for accommodation, exclusive use and groups by appointment.

## Admission
The exclusive use of the house and grounds for events and activity days with no accommodation £1500.

**Accommodation rates:**

| | |
|---|---|
| Single with bath | £66.00 |
| Double with bath | £108.00 |
| Dinner | £27.50 |

ℹ️ Conferences, activity days, filming and photography, product launches, musical events, seminars, orienteering, training activity days, events, clay pigeon and game shooting, firework and laser shows, game and craft fairs, rope course. Non-smoking.

🍴 Exclusive dinners and weddings etc, prices and menus on request.

♿ Level access and WC for disabled visitors.

🅿️ Ample.

🐾 3 double with en suites, 3 twin with en suites.

🔔
❄️

Dining Room

Drawing Room

Library

Bedroom

## Conference/Function

| ROOM | SIZE | MAX CAPACITY |
|---|---|---|
| Reception hall | 15'6"x 39' | 50 |
| Drawing Room | 17'6"x 24'6" | 30 |
| Dining Room | 17'6"x 24'6" | 30 |
| Ballroom | 59'x 24'3" | 140 |
| Marquee | 120'x 40' | 500 |

## ALNWICK CASTLE

*See page 432 for full page entry.*

## AYDON CASTLE

**Corbridge, Northumberland  NE45 5PJ**
**Tel:** 01434 632450
**Owner:** English Heritage    **Contact:** Visitor Operations Team
One of the finest fortified manor houses in England, dating from the late 13th century. Its survival, intact, can be attributed to its conversion to a farmhouse in the 17th century.
**Location:** MAP 10:O3, OS Ref. NZ001 663. 1m NE of Corbridge, on minor road off B6321 or A68.
**Open:** 1 Apr–30 Sept: Thur–Mon, 10am–5pm.
**Admission:** Adult £3.50, Child £1.80, Conc. £2.60. 15% discount for groups (11+).
ⓘ WC. Ⓢ Ⓢ Ground floor & grounds. Ⓟ ▣ Ⓢ In grounds, on leads. Ⓢ

## BAMBURGH CASTLE

*See page 433 for full page entry.*

Aydon Castle

# BELSAY HALL, CASTLE & GARDENS
### BELSAY, Nr PONTELAND, NORTHUMBERLAND  NE20 0DX
www.english-heritage.org.uk/visits

**Tel:** 01661 881636  **Fax:** 01661 881043
**Owner:** English Heritage    **Contact:** Visitor Operations Team
Belsay is one of the most remarkable estates in Northumberland's border country. The buildings, set amidst 30 acres of magnificent landscaped gardens, have been occupied by the same family for nearly 600 years. The gardens, created largely in the 19th century, are a fascinating mix of the formal and the informal with terraced gardens, a rhododendron garden, magnolia garden, mature woodland and even a winter garden. The buildings comprise a 14th century castle, a manor house and Belsay Hall, an internationally famous mansion designed by Sir Charles Monck in the 19th

century in the style of classical buildings he had encountered during a tour of Greece.
**Location:** MAP 10:O2, OS87, NZ086 785. In Belsay 14m (22.4 km) NW of Newcastle on SW of A696. 7m NW of Ponteland. Nearest airport and station is Newcastle.
**Open:** 1 Apr–31 Oct: daily, 10am–5pm (4pm Oct). 1 Nov–20 Mar: Thur–Mon, 10am–4pm. Closed 24–26 Dec and 1 Jan.
**Admission:** Adult £6.10, Child £3.10, Conc. £4.60, Family £15.30. 15% discount for groups (11+).
Ⓢ Ⓢ Ⓣ Ⓢ Partial. WC. Ⓢ During summer & weekends Apr–Oct. Ⓟ ▣ Ⓢ In grounds, on leads. Ⓢ Ⓢ

## BERWICK BARRACKS

**The Parade, Berwick-upon-Tweed, Northumberland  TD15 1DG**
**Tel:** 01289 304493
**Owner:** English Heritage    **Contact:** Visitor Operations Team
Among the earliest purpose built barracks, these have changed very little since 1717. They house an exhibition 'By Beat of Drum', which recreates scenes such as the barrack room from the life of the British infantryman, the Museum of the King's Own Scottish Borderers and the Borough Museum with fine art, local history exhibition and other collections.
**Location:** MAP 14:L9, OS Ref. NU001 531. On the Parade, off Church Street, Berwick town centre.
**Open:** 1 Apr–30 Sept: daily, 10am–5pm. 1–31 Oct: daily, 10am–4pm. 1 Nov–20 Mar: telephone for details. Closed 24–26 Dec and 1 Jan.
**Admission:** Adult £3.40, Child £1.70, Conc. £2.60. 15% discount for groups (11+).
Ⓢ Ⓟ In town. ▣ Ⓢ In grounds, on leads. Ⓢ Ⓢ

## BERWICK RAMPARTS

**Berwick-upon-Tweed, Northumberland**
**Tel:** 0191 269 1200
**Owner:** English Heritage    **Contact:** The Regional Office
A remarkably complete system of town fortifications consisting of gateways, ramparts and projecting bastions built in the 16th century.
**Location:** MAP 14:L9, OS Ref. NT993 534. Surrounding Berwick town centre on N bank of River Tweed.
**Open:** Any reasonable time.
**Admission:** Free.
Ⓢ

© English Heritage Photo Library

## BRINKBURN PRIORY

**Long Framlington, Morpeth, Northumberland  NE65 8AR**
**Tel:** 01665 570628
**Owner:** English Heritage    **Contact:** Visitor Operations Staff
This late 12th century church is a fine example of early gothic architecture, almost perfectly preserved, and is set in a lovely spot beside the River Coquet.
**Location:** MAP 14:L12, OS Ref. NZ116 983. 4½ m SE of Rothbury off B6344 5m W of A1.
**Open:** 1 Apr–30 Sept: Thur–Mon, 10am–5pm.
**Admission:** Adult £2.90, Child £1.50, Conc. £2.20. 15% discount for groups (11+).
On leads.

## CAPHEATON HALL

**Newcastle-upon-Tyne  NE19 2AB**
**Tel/Fax:** 01830 530253
**Owner/Contact:** J Browne-Swinburne
Built for Sir John Swinburne in 1668 by Robert Trollope, an architect of great and original talent.
**Location:** MAP 10:O2, OS Ref. NZ038 805. 17m NW of Newcastle off A696.
**Open:** By written appointment only.

## CHERRYBURN – THOMAS BEWICK BIRTHPLACE

**Station Bank, Mickley, Stocksfield, Northumberland  NE43 7DD**
**Tel:** 01661 843276  www.nationaltrust.org.uk
**Owner:** The National Trust    **Contact:** The Administrator
Birthplace of Northumbria's greatest artist, wood engraver and naturalist, Thomas Bewick, b1753. The Museum explores his famous works. Farmyard animals, picnic area, garden.
**Location:** MAP 10:O3, OS Ref. NZ075 627. 11m W of Newcastle on A695 (400yds signed from Mickley Square). 1½m W of Prudhoe.
**Open:** 17 Mar–28 Oct: daily except Weds, 11am–5pm. Last admission 4.30pm. Booked groups, Mon–Fri, 10am–4pm.
**Admission:** Adult £4, Child £2, Child under 5yrs Free. Family £11.Groups (20+): £3.
Some steps. WC. Morning coffee for booked groups.

© English Heritage Photo Library.

## CHESTERS ROMAN FORT & MUSEUM

### CHOLLERFORD, Nr HEXHAM, NORTHUMBERLAND  NE46 3EU

**Tel:** 01434 681379
**Owner:** English Heritage    **Contact:** Visitor Operations Team
The best preserved example of a Roman cavalry fort in Britain, including remains of the bath house on the banks of the River North Tyne. The museum houses a fascinating collection of Roman sculpture and inscriptions.
**Location:** MAP 10:N2, OS87, NY913 701. ¼ m W of Chollerford on B6318.
**Open:** 1 Apr–30 Sept: daily, 9.30am–6pm. 1 Oct–20 Mar: daily, 10am–4pm. Closed 24–26 Dec and 1 Jan.
**Admission:** Adult £4.10, Child £2.10, Conc. £3.10. 15% discount for groups (11+).
Grounds. WC. Summer only. In grounds, on leads.

## CHILLINGHAM CASTLE

*See page 434 for full page entry.*

## CHIPCHASE CASTLE

**Wark, Hexham, Northumberland  NE48 3NT**
**Tel:** 01434 230203   **Fax:** 01434 230740
**Owner/Contact:** Mrs P J Torday
The castle overlooks the River North Tyne and is set in formal and informal gardens. One walled garden is used as a nursery specialising in unusual perennial plants.
**Location:** MAP 10:N2, OS Ref. NY882 758. 10m NW of Hexham via A6079 to Chollerton. 2m SE of Wark.
**Open:** Castle: 1–28 Jun: daily, 2–5pm. Tours by arrangement at other times. Castle Gardens & Nursery: Easter–31 Jul, Thur–Sun & BH Mons, 10am–5pm.
**Admission:** Castle £5, Garden £3, concessions available. Nursery Free.
Unsuitable. Obligatory.

## CORBRIDGE ROMAN TOWN

**Corbridge, Northumberland  NE45 5NT**
**Tel:** 01434 632349
**Owner:** English Heritage    **Contact:** Visitor Operations Team
A fascinating series of excavated remains, including foundations of granaries with a grain ventilation system. From artefacts found, which can be seen in the site museum, we know a large settlement developed around this supply depot.
**Location:** MAP 10:N3, OS Ref. NY983 649. ½m NW of Corbridge on minor road, signposted for Corbridge Roman Site.
**Open:** 1 Apr–30 Sept: daily, 10am–5.30pm. 1–31 Oct: daily, 10am–4pm. 1 Nov–20 Mar: Sat & Sun, 10am–4pm. Closed 24–26 Dec and 1 Jan.
**Admission:** Adult £4.10, Child £2.10, Conc. £3.10. 15% discount for groups (11+).
Partial. Inclusive. Limited for coaches. In grounds, on leads.

## CRAGSIDE

**Rothbury, Morpeth, Northumberland  NE65 7PX**
**Tel:** 01669 620150   **Fax:** 01669 620066   www.nationaltrust.org.uk
**Owner:** The National Trust    **Contact:** Property Manager
Revolutionary home of Lord Armstrong, Victorian inventor and landscape genius, Cragside sits on a rocky crag high above the Debdon Burn. Crammed with ingenious gadgets, it was the first house in the world lit electrically. Armstrong constructed 5 lakes, one of Europe's largest rock gardens and planted over 7 million trees and shrubs. Today, this magnificent estate can be explored on foot and by car and provides one of the last shelters for the endangered red squirrel. Children will love the tall trees, tumbling streams, adventure play areas and labyrinth.
**Location:** MAP 14:L12, OS Ref. NU073 022. ½m NE of Rothbury on B6341.
**Open:** House: 3 Apr–30 Sept, Tue–Sun & BH Mons, 1–5.30pm (last admission 4.30pm). 2 Oct–4 Nov 1–4.30pm (last admission 3.30pm). Gardens & Estate: 17 Mar–4 Nov, Tue–Sun & BH Mons, 10.30am–7pm (last admission 5pm). Gardens, Estate, Restaurant & Shop (House closed): 7 Nov–16 Dec, Wed–Sun, 11am–4pm (last admission 3pm).
**Admission:** House, Gardens & Estate: Adult £10.50, Child (5–17 yrs) £5, Family (2+3) £25. Groups (15+) £9. Estate & Gardens: Adult £7, Child (5–17 yrs) £3, Family (2+3) £17. Groups (15+) £5.50. Gardens, Estate, Restaurant & Shop (House closed): 7 Nov–16 Dec, Adult £3, Child (5–17 yrs) £1.50, Family (2+3) £7.50, Group (15+) £2.
Partial. In grounds, on leads.

## DUNSTANBURGH CASTLE

**c/o Grieves Garage, Embleton, Northumberland  NE66 3TT**
**Tel:** 01665 576231
**Owner:** The National Trust    **Guardian:** English Heritage
**Contact:** Visitor Operations Team
An easy, but bracing, coastal walk leads to the eerie skeleton of this wonderful 14th century castle sited on a basalt crag, rearing up more than 100 feet from the waves crashing on the rocks below. The surviving ruins include the large gatehouse, which later became the keep, and curtain walls.
**Location:** MAP 14:M11, OS75, NU257 219. 8m NE of Alnwick.
**Open:** 1 Apr–30 Sept: daily, 10am–5pm. 1–31 Oct, daily, 10am–4pm. 1 Nov–20 Mar: Thur–Mon, 10am–4pm.
**Admission:** Adult £2.90, Child £1.50, Conc. £2.20. 15% discount for groups (11+).
None. In grounds, on leads.

Who's offering **accommodation?**
See our index on page 575

## EDLINGHAM CASTLE

**Edlingham, Alnwick, Northumberland**

**Tel:** 0191 269 1200

**Owner:** English Heritage    **Contact:** The Regional Office

Set beside a splendid railway viaduct this complex ruin has defensive features spanning the 13th and 15th centuries.

**Location:** MAP 14:L11, OS Ref. NU116 092. At E end of Edlingham village, on minor road off B6341 6m SW of Alnwick.

**Open:** Any reasonable time.

**Admission:** Free.

In grounds, on leads.

## ETAL CASTLE

**Cornhill-on-Tweed, Northumberland  TD12 4TN**

**Tel:** 01890 820332

**Owner:** English Heritage    **Contact:** Visitor Operations Team

A 14th century castle located in the picturesque village of Etal. Award-winning exhibition about the castle, Border warfare and the Battle of Flodden.

**Location:** MAP 14:K10, OS75, NT925 393. In Etal village, 10m SW of Berwick.

**Open:** 1 Apr–30 Sept: daily, 11am–4pm.

**Admission:** Adult £3.50, Child £1.80, Conc. £2.60, Family £8.80. 15% discount for groups (11+).

WC in village. Partial. WC. Inclusive. In grounds, on leads.

## HERTERTON HOUSE GARDENS

**Hartington, Cambo, Morpeth, Northumberland  NE61 4BN**

**Tel:** 01670 774278

**Owner/Contact:** C J "Frank" Lawley

One acre of formal garden in stone walls around a 16th century farmhouse, including a small topiary garden, physic garden, flower garden, fancy garden and gazebo.

**Location:** MAP 10:N1, OS Ref. NZ022 881. 2m N of Cambo, just off B6342, Signposted (brown).

**Open:** 1 Apr–30 Sept: Mons, Weds, Fri–Sun, 1.30–5.30pm.

**Admission:** Adult £3, Child (5–15yrs) £1.20. Groups by arrangement.

Unsuitable. By arrangement. Limited for coaches. Guided tours for adult students only.

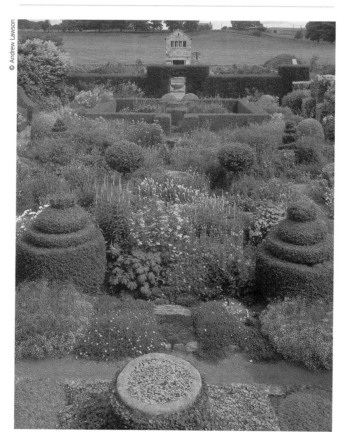

© Andrew Lawson

Herterton House Gardens

English Heritage Photo Library

## HOUSESTEADS ROMAN FORT

**Nr HAYDON BRIDGE, NORTHUMBERLAND  NE47 6NN**

**Tel:** 01434 344363

**Owner:** The National Trust    **Guardian:** English Heritage

**Contact:** Visitor Operations Team

Perched high on a ridge overlooking open moorland, this is the best known part of the Wall. The fort covers five acres and there are remains of many buildings, such as granaries, barrack blocks and gateways. A small exhibition displays altars, inscriptions and models.

**Location:** MAP 10:M3, OS Ref. NY790 687. 2m NE of Bardon Mill.

**Open:** 1 Apr–30 Sept: daily, 10am–6pm. 1 Oct–20 Mar: daily, 10am–4pm. Closed 24–26 Dec and 1 Jan.

**Admission:** Adult £4.10, Child £2.10, Conc. £3.10, Free entry to NT members.

Charge. In grounds, on leads.

## THE LADY WATERFORD HALL & MURALS

**Ford, Berwick-upon-Tweed  TD15 2QA**

**Tel:** 01890 820503    **Fax:** 01890 820384

**Owner:** Ford & Etal Estates    **Contact:** Dorien Irving

Commissioned in 1860 the walls of this beautiful building are decorated with beautiful murals depicting Bible stories.

**Location:** MAP 14:K10, OS Ref. NT945 374. On the B6354, 9m from Berwick-upon-Tweed, midway between Newcastle-upon-Tyne and Edinburgh, close to the A697.

**Open:** Apr–Oct: daily, 10.30am–12.30pm & 1.30–5.30pm. By arrangement with the caretaker during winter months. Note: the Hall may be closed on occasion for private functions. Please telephone prior to travelling.

**Admission:** Adult £2, Child 75p, Child (under 12yrs) Free, Conc. £1.50. Groups by arrangement. Prices subject to change.

## LINDISFARNE CASTLE

**Holy Island, Berwick-upon-Tweed, Northumberland  TD15 2SH**

**Tel:** 01289 389244   www.nationaltrust.org.uk

**Owner:** The National Trust    **Contact:** Property Manager

Built in 1550 to protect Holy Island harbour from attack, the castle was restored and converted into a private house for Edward Hudson by Sir Edwin Lutyens in 1903.

**Location:** MAP 14:L9, OS Ref. NU136 417. On Holy Island, ¾m E of village, 6m E of A1 across causeway. Usable at low tide.

**Open:** 17–25 Feb, 17 Mar–28 Oct, 27–30 Dec: daily (closed Mons except BHs). Times vary, please telephone for details.

**\*Admission:** Adult £5.80, Child £2.90, Family £14.50. Garden only: Adult £1, Child Free. Out of hours group tours (10+) by arrangement £6.50pp. \*includes a voluntary donation but visitors can choose to pay the standard prices displayed at the property and on the website.

NT Shop (in Main St). In grounds, on leads.

See which properties offer **educational facilities** or **school visits** in our index on page 571

Dunstanburgh Castle, Embleton

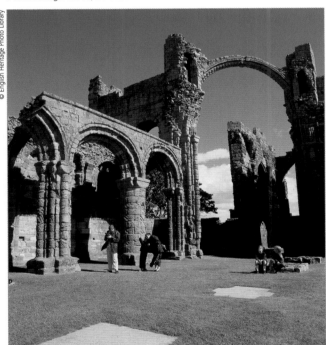

© English Heritage Photo Library

## LINDISFARNE PRIORY ⌗
### HOLY ISLAND, NORTHUMBERLAND TD15 2RX

**Tel:** 01289 389200

**Owner:** English Heritage    **Contact:** Visitor Operations Team

The site of one of the most important early centres of Christianity in Anglo-Saxon England. St Cuthbert converted pagan Northumbria, and miracles occurring at his shrine established this 11th century priory as a major pilgrimage centre. The evocative ruins, with the decorated 'rainbow' arch curving dramatically across the nave of the church, are still the destination of pilgrims today. The story of Lindisfarne is told in an exhibition which gives an impression of life for the monks, including a reconstruction of a monk's cell. The Priory can only be reached at low tide.

**Location:** MAP 14:L9, OS Ref. NU126 417. On Holy Island, check tide times.

**Open:** 1 Feb–20 Mar:daily 10am–4pm. 1 Apr–30 Sept: daily, 9.30am–5pm. Oct: daily, 9.30am–4pm. 1 Nov–31 Jan: Sat–Mon, 10am–2pm. Closed 24–26 Dec & 1 Jan.

**Admission:** Adult £3.90, Child £2, Conc. £2.90. 15% discount for groups (11+).

🖭 🖫 Partial. Disabled parking. **P** Charge. ▣ ▣ Restricted. ▣ ▣

### NORHAM CASTLE ⌗

**Norham, Northumberland  TD15 2JY**

**Tel:** 01289 304493

**Owner:** English Heritage    **Contact:** Visitor Operations Team

Set on a promontory in a curve of the River Tweed, this was one of the strongest of the Border castles, built c1160.

**Location:** MAP 14:K9, OS75, NT906 476. 6m SW of Berwick ,on minor road off B6470 (from A698).

**Open:** Admission is limited, please telephone for details.

**Admission:** Adult £2.90, Child £1.50, Conc. £2.20.

🖫 Partial. ▣ On leads.

### PRESTON TOWER 🏛

**Chathill, Northumberland  NE67 5DH**

**Tel:** 01665 589227

**Owner/Contact:** Major T Baker-Cresswell

The Tower was built by Sir Robert Harbottle in 1392 and is one of the few survivors of 78 pele towers listed in 1415. The tunnel vaulted rooms remain unaltered and provide a realistic picture of the grim way of life under the constant threat of "Border Reivers". Two rooms are furnished in contemporary style and there are displays of historic and local information. Visitors are welcome to walk in the grounds which contain a number of interesting trees and shrubs. A woodland walk to the natural spring from which water is now pumped up to the Tower for the house and cottages.

**Location:** MAP 14:M11, OS Ref. NU185 253. Follow Historic Property signs on A1 7m N of Alnwick.

**Open:** All year daily, 10am–6pm.

**Admission:** Adult £2, Child 50p, Conc. £1.50. Groups £1.

🖫 Grounds. ▣ ▣

### PRUDHOE CASTLE ⌗

**Prudhoe, Northumberland  NE42 6NA**

**Tel:** 01661 833459

**Owner:** English Heritage    **Contact:** Visitor Operations Team

Set on a wooded hillside overlooking the River Tyne are the extensive remains of this 12th century castle including a gatehouse, curtain wall and keep. Small exhibition and video presentation.

**Location:** MAP 10:O3, OS88 Ref. NZ091 634. In Prudhoe, on minor road off A695.

**Open:** 1 Apr–30 Sept: Thur–Mon, 10am–5pm.

**Admission:** Adult £3.50, Child £1.80, Conc. £2.60. 15% discount for groups (11+).

ℹ WC. 🖭 🖫 Partial. ▣ **P** ▣ ▣ In grounds, on leads. ▣

# SEATON DELAVAL HALL 🏛
### SEATON SLUICE, WHITLEY BAY, NORTHUMBERLAND NE26 4QR

**Tel:** 0191 237 1493/0191 237 0786   **E-mail:** lordhastings@onetel.net.uk

**Owner:** Lord Hastings     **Contact:** Mrs Mills

The home of Lord and Lady Hastings, half a mile from Seaton Sluice, is the last and most sensational mansion designed by Sir John Vanbrugh, builder of Blenheim Palace and Castle Howard. It was erected 1718–1728 and comprises a high turreted block flanked by arcaded wings which form a vast forecourt. The centre block was gutted by fire in 1822, but was partially restored in 1862 and again in 1959–1962 and 1999–2000. The remarkable staircases are a visual delight, and the two surviving rooms are filled with family pictures and photographs and royal seals spanning three centuries as well as various archives. This building is used frequently for concerts and charitable functions. The East Wing contains immense stables in ashlar stone of breathtaking proportions. Nearby are the Coach House with farm and passenger vehicles, fully documented, and the restored ice house with explanatory sketch and description. There are beautiful gardens described by gardening writers as '*a revelation and a delight*' and also as '*magical*' with herbaceous borders, rose garden, rhododendrons, azaleas, laburnum walk, statues, and a spectacular parterre by internationally famous Jim Russell, also a unique Norman Church.

**Location:** MAP 11:A2, OS Ref. NZ322 766. ½m from Seaton Sluice on A190, 3m from Whitley Bay.

**Open:** May & Aug BH Mons; Jun–Sept: Weds & Suns, 2–6pm.

**Admission:** Adult £4, Child £1, OAP £3.50, Student £2. Groups (20+): Adult £3, Child/Student £1.

⬛ ⬛ Partial. WC. ⬛ ⬛ Free. ⬛ ⬛ In grounds, on leads.

Charlotte Karsemeijer

# WALLINGTON 🦋
### CAMBO, MORPETH, NORTHUMBERLAND NE61 4AR

www.nationaltrust.org.uk

**Tel:** 01670 773600   **Fax:** 01670 774420   **E-mail:** wallington@nationaltrust.org.uk

**Owner:** The National Trust     **Contact:** The Estate Office

Dating from 1688, the much-loved home of the Trevelyan family contains magnificent rococco plasterwork, fine ceramics and a collection of dolls' houses. The Pre-Raphaelite Central Hall depicts floral wall paintings and a series of scenes of Northumbrian history by William Bell Scott.

There are extensive walks through a variety of lawns, shrubberies, lakes and woodland to the exuberant Walled Garden, which remain open throughout the year.

**Location:** MAP 10:O2, OS Ref. NZ030 843. Near Cambo, 6m NW of Belsay (A696).

**Open:** House: 17 Mar–4 Nov: daily, except Tues, 1–5.30pm (4.30pm from 3 Sept).

Restaurant & Shop: All year daily, (closed 24 Dec–4 Jan), 10.30am– 5.30 pm (3 Sept–15 Feb closes 4.30pm). 3 Sept–25 May closed Tues, 5 Nov–15 Feb closed Mon & Tues.. Last adm. 1 hr (House)/30 min (Restaurant) prior to closing. Walled garden: All year daily (except Christmas Day), 10am–7pm (closes 6pm in Oct & 4pm 1 Nov–31 Mar). Farm shop (outside turnstile): All year daily, 10.30am– 5pm (4pm 1 Nov–14 Mar), closed 25–27 Dec & 1/2 Jan.

**\*Admission:** House, garden & grounds: Adult £8.80, Child £4.40, Family £22, Groups £7.50. Garden & grounds only: Adult £6.05, Child £3.05, Family £15.40, Groups £5.20. *includes a voluntary donation but visitors can choose to pay the standard prices displayed at the property and on the website.

⬛ ⬛ ⬛ ⬛ Partial. ⬛ ⬛ By arrangement. ⬛ ⬛ ⬛ In grounds on leads. ⬛ ⬛ ⬛

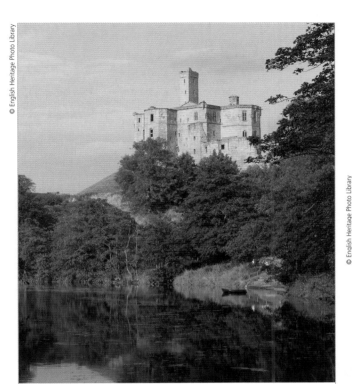

© English Heritage Photo Library

## WARKWORTH CASTLE ⌗

### WARKWORTH, ALNWICK, NORTHUMBERLAND NE65 0UJ

**Tel:** 01665 711423

**Owner:** English Heritage    **Contact:** Visitor Operations Team

The great towering keep of this 15th century castle, once the home of the mighty Percy family, dominates the town and River Coquet. Warkworth is one of the most outstanding examples of an aristocratic fortified residence. Upstream by boat from the castle lies Warkworth Hermitage, cutting into the rock of the river cliff (separate charge applies).

**Location:** MAP 14:M12, OS Ref. NU247 058. 7½m S of Alnwick on A1068.

**Open:** 1 Apr–30 Sept: daily, 10am–5pm. 1–31 Oct: daily, 10am–4pm. 1 Nov–20 Mar: Sat–Mon, 10am–4pm. Closed 24–26 Dec and 1 Jan.

**Admission:** Adult £3.50, Child £1.80, Conc. £2.60, Family £8.80. 15% discount for groups (11+).

ⓘ WC. ⬚ ⬚ Grounds. ⬚ Inclusive. ⯾ ⬚ ⬚ On leads. ⬚ ⬚

## WARKWORTH HERMITAGE ⌗

### Warkworth, Northumberland

**Tel:** 01665 711423

**Owner:** English Heritage    **Contact:** Visitor Operations Team

Upstream by boat from the castle this curious hermitage cuts into the rock of the river cliff.

**Location:** MAP 14:M12, OS Ref. NU242 060. 7½ m SE of Alnwick on A1068.

**Open:** 1 Apr–30 Sept: Weds, Suns & BHs, 11am–5pm.

**Admission:** Adult £2.50, Child £1.90, Conc. £1.90.

⬚ ⬚ Grounds. ⯾ At Castle. ⬚ ⬚ On leads.

© English Heritage Photo Library

Brinkburn Priory, Nr Rothbury

Seaton Delaval Hall, Whitley Bay

## ARBEIA ROMAN FORT

**Baring Street, South Shields, Tyne & Wear  NE33 2BB**
**Tel:** 0191 456 1369  **Fax:** 0191 427 6862
**Owner:** South Tyneside Metropolitan Borough Council  **Contact:** The Curator
**Managed by:** Tyne & Wear Museums
More than 1,500 years on, the remains at Arbeia represent the most extensively excavated example of a military supply base anywhere in the Roman Empire. Museum includes weapons, jewellery and tombstones.
**Location:** MAP 11:A3, OS Ref. NZ365 679. Near town centre and Metro Station.
**Open:** Easter–Sept: Mon–Sat: 10am–5.30pm, Suns, 1–5pm. Open BH Mons. Oct–Easter: daily except Suns, 10am–3.30pm. Closed 25/26 Dec, 1 Jan & Good Friday.
**Admission:** Free, except for Time Quest Gallery: Adult £1.50, Child/Conc. £1.

## BEDE'S WORLD MUSEUM

**Church Bank, Jarrow, Tyne & Wear  NE32 3DY**
**Tel:** 0191 489 2106  **Fax:** 0191 428 2361  **E-mail:** visitor.info@bedesworld.co.uk
**Managed by:** Bede's World  **Contact:** Visitor Services
Discover the world of the Venerable Bede, who lived and worked at the monastery of Wearmouth-Jarrow 1300 years ago.
**Location:** MAP 11:A3, OS Ref. NZ339 652. Just off A19, S end of Tyne Tunnel. 300yds N of St Paul's.
**Open:** Apr–Oct: Mon–Sat, 10am–5.30pm, Suns, 12 noon–5.30pm. Nov–Mar: Mon–Sat, 10am–4.30pm, Suns, 12 noon–4.30pm. Open BH Mons, closed Good Fri. Tel for Christmas opening times.
**Admission:** Adult £4.50, Child/Conc. £3, Family (2+2) £10. Groups by arrangement.

## BESSIE SURTEES HOUSE ⌗

**41–44 Sandhill, Newcastle, Tyne & Wear  NE1 3JF**
**Tel:** 0191 269 1200
**Owner:** English Heritage  **Contact:** Reception
Two 16th and 17th century merchants' houses stand on the quayside near the Tyne Bridge. One is a rare example of Jacobean domestic architecture. 3 rooms open.
**Location:** MAP 10:P3, OS Ref. NZ252 638. 41–44 Sandhill, Newcastle. Riverside. City centre.
**Open:** All year: Mon–Fri: 10am–4pm. Closed BHs & 24 Dec–3 Jan.
**Admission:** Free.
🛈 WC. ⬚ ⬛ ⬚ ❈

## GIBSIDE 🌿

**Nr Rowlands Gill, Burnopfield, Newcastle-upon-Tyne  NE16 6BG**
**Tel:** 01207 541820  **E-mail:** gibside@nationaltrust.org.uk  **www.nationaltrust.org.uk**
**Owner:** The National Trust  **Contact:** The Property Manager
Gibside is one of the finest 18th century designed landscapes in the north of England. The Chapel was built to James Paine's design soon after 1760. Outstanding example of Georgian architecture approached along a terrace with an oak avenue. Walk along the River Derwent through woodland.
**Location:** MAP 10:P3, OS Ref. NZ172 583. 6m SW of Gateshead, 20m NW of Durham. Entrance on B6314 between Burnopfield and Rowlands Gill.
**Open:** 5 Mar–28 Oct: daily, 10am–6pm. 29 Oct–23 Mar: daily, 10am–4pm.
**\*Admission:** Adult £5.50, Child £3.30, Family (2+4) £16.50, Family (1+3) £11. Booked groups £4.50. \*includes a voluntary donation but visitors can choose to pay the standard prices displayed at the property and on the website.
⬚ ⊤ ⬚ Partial. ⬛ 𝄞 By arrangement. 🅿 Limited for coaches. ⬛
🖼 On leads, in grounds. 🅰 ❈ ♥

## NEWCASTLE CASTLE KEEP

**Castle Keep, Castle Garth, Newcastle-upon-Tyne  NE1 1RQ**
**Tel:** 0191 232 7938
**Owner:** Newcastle City Council  **Contact:** Paul MacDonald
The Keep originally dominated the castle bailey. The 'new' castle was founded in 1080.
**Location:** MAP 10:P3, OS Ref. NZ251 638. City centre between St Nicholas church and the High Level bridge.
**Open:** All year: daily, 9.30am–5.30pm (4.30pm winter).
**Admission:** Adult £1.50, Child/Conc. 50p. Oct–Mar, special rates for groups (12+).

See all the properties that are **open all year** in the index on page 580

## ST PAUL'S MONASTERY ⌗

**Jarrow, Tyne & Wear**
**Tel:** 0191 489 7052
**Owner:** English Heritage  **Contact:** The Regional Office – 0191 269 1200
The home of the Venerable Bede in the 7th and 8th centuries, partly surviving as the chancel of the parish church. It has become one of the best understood Anglo-Saxon monastic sites.
**Location:** MAP 11:A3, OS Ref. NZ339 652. In Jarrow, on minor road N of A185. 300yds S of Bede's World.
**Open:** Any reasonable time.
**Admission:** Free.
⬚ ⬚ ⬚ 🅿 ⬛ ❈

## SEGEDUNUM ROMAN FORT, BATHS & MUSEUM

**Buddle Street, Wallsend, NE28 6HR**
**Tel:** 0191 236 9347  **Fax:** 0191 295 5858
Explore life on the Roman frontier as it was 1,800 years ago, at the most completely excavated fort on Hadrian's Wall. See reconstructions of a section of the Wall together with an impressive Roman military bath house building.
**Location:** MAP 11:A3, OS Ref. N2 301 660.
**Open:** 1 Apr–31 Oct: daily, 10am–5pm. 1 Nov–31 Mar: daily, 10am–3pm.
**Admission:** Adults £3.95, Child (16 and under) Free. Conc. £2.25. Groups: Adult £3.20, Conc. £1.80.

## SOUTER LIGHTHOUSE 🌿

**Coast Road, Whitburn, Sunderland, Tyne & Wear  SR6 7NH**
**Tel:** 0191 529 3161  **Fax:** 0191 529 0902  **E-mail:** souter@nationaltrust.org.uk
**www.nationaltrust.org.uk**
**Owner:** The National Trust  **Contact:** The Property Manager
Dramatic red and white lighthouse tower on rugged coast. Built in 1871, the first to be powered by alternating electric current.
**Location:** MAP 11:A3, OS Ref. NZ408 641. 2½m S of South Shields on A183. 5m N of Sunderland.
**Open:** 17 Mar–28 Oct: daily except Fri (open Good Fri), 11am–5pm. Last adm 4.30pm.
**\*Admission:** Adult £4.40, Child £2.80, Family £11.50. Booked Groups (10+): Adult £3.90, Child £2.20. NT members Free: membership available from shop. \*includes a voluntary donation but visitors can choose to pay the standard prices displayed at the property and on the website.
⬚ 🅰 ⊤ ⬚ Partial. WCs. ⬛ 🍴 𝄞 By arrangement. 🅿 ⬛ 🖼 In grounds, on leads.

## TYNEMOUTH PRIORY & CASTLE ⌗

**North Pier, Tynemouth, Tyne & Wear  NE30 4BZ**
**Tel:** 0191 257 1090
**Owner:** English Heritage  **Contact:** Visitor Operations Team
The castle walls and gatehouse enclose the substantial remains of a Benedictine priory founded c1090 on a Saxon monastic site. Their strategic importance has made the castle and priory the target for attack for many centuries. In World War I, coastal batteries in the castle defended the mouth of the Tyne. Gun Battery: Access limited, ask staff for details.
**Location:** MAP 11:A2, OS Ref. NZ373 694. In Tynemouth near North Pier.
**Open:** 1 Apr–30 Sept: daily, 10am–5pm. 1–31 Oct: daily, 10am–4pm. 1 Nov–20 Mar: Thur–Mon, 10am–4pm. Closed 24–26 Dec & 1 Jan.
**Admission:** Adult £3.50, Child £1.80, Conc. £2.60, Family £8.80. 15% discount for groups (11+).
⬚ ⊤ ⬚ Grounds. 𝄞 By arrangement. ⬛ 🖼 In grounds, on leads. ❈ ♥

## WASHINGTON OLD HALL 🌿

**The Avenue, Washington Village, Washington, Tyne & Wear  NE38 7LE**
**Tel:** 0191 416 6879  **Fax:** 0191 419 2065
**E-mail:** washington.oldhall@nationaltrust.org.uk  **www.nationaltrust.org.uk**
**Owner:** The National Trust  **Contact:** The Manager
Delightful 17th century house incorporating parts of the medieval home of George Washington's ancestors, their surname of "Washington" was taken from here. Furnished with Delftware, paintings and oak furniture. The knot and parterre gardens lead you to the tranquil wildflower nut orchard. This little gem is well worth a visit.
**Location:** MAP 11:A3, OS Ref. NZ312 566. In Washington on E side of The Avenue. 5m W of Sunderland (2m from A1), S of Tyne Tunnel, follow signs for Washington then A1231 - follow brown signs to Washington village. The Old Hall is on the avenue next to the church on the hill.
**Open:** House: 1 Apr–31 Oct: Sun–Wed, 11am–5pm. Garden: 1 Apr–31 Oct: 10am–5pm. Last admission 4.30pm. Open Good Fri & Easter Sat.
**\*Admission:** Adult £4.40, Child £2.80, Family £11.50. Booked groups (15+): Adult £3.90, Child £2.20. NT Membership available from reception. \*includes a voluntary donation but visitors can choose to pay the standard prices displayed at the property and on the website.
⬚ ⊤ Conferences. ⬚ Ground floor and grounds. ⬛ 𝄞 By arrangement. 🅿 Limited.
⬛ 🖼 In grounds, on leads. 🅰

Gibside Chapel and Avenue

**Above:** Mellerstain
**Right:** Edzell Castle & Gardens ©Historic Scotland

# Scotland

*First time visitors to Scotland can only scratch the surface of its cultural and social history. Edinburgh Castle is, of course, Scotland's most famous castle but there are so many others which merit a visit: fairytale Dunrobin on the east coast, Dunvegan on the Isle of Skye and Cawdor, home of the Thanes of Cawdor from the 14th century.*

Borders

South West Scotland

Edinburgh City,
Coast & Countryside

Greater Glasgow
& the Clyde Valley

Perthshire, Angus & Dundee
& The Kingdom of Fife

West Highlands & Islands,
Loch Lomond, Stirling
& Trossachs

Grampian Highlands,
Aberdeen &
The North East Coast

Highlands & Skye

Outer Islands, Western Isles,
Orkney & Shetland

'The Pink Boy' – Sir Joshua Reynolds

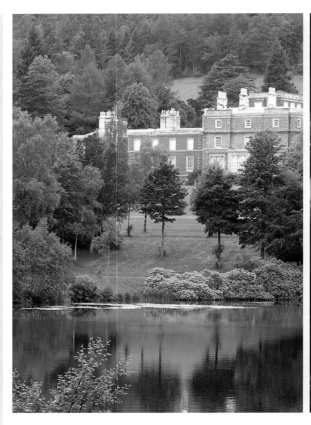

### ■ Owner
His Grace the Duke of Buccleuch & Queensberry KT

### ■ Contact
Buccleuch Heritage Trust
Bowhill House &
Country Park
Bowhill
Selkirk  TD7 5ET

**Tel:** 01750 22204
**Fax:** 01750 23893
**E-mail:** bht@
buccleuch.com

### ■ Location
**MAP 13:H10**
**OS Ref. NT426 278**

3m W of Selkirk off A708
Moffat Road,
A68 from Newcastle,
A7 from Carlisle
or Edinburgh.

**Bus:** 3m Selkirk.

**Taxi:** 01750 20354.

### ■ Opening Times
**House**
1–31 July:
Daily, 1–5pm.

Outwith stated times to
educational groups by
appointment.

**Country Park**
Easter, May–June:
Sats/Suns & BHs,
July–August: Daily,
10am–5pm.

### ■ Admission
**Summer**
House & Country Park
Adult          £7.00
Child (5–16yrs)  £3.00
OAP            £5.00
Groups         £5.00

**Country Park only**
Adults         £3.00
Child (under 5yrs) £2.00

Family tickets and group
tickets available.

# BOWHILL HOUSE & 🏛
# COUNTRY PARK

The Scottish Borders home of the Duke of Buccleuch and Queensberry KT, is at the centre of an extensive estate of hills and valleys where history and landscape combine to provide a unique experience, and christened "Sweet Bowhill" by Sir Walter Scott in his *Lay of the Last Minstrel*. Standing in ground that was once a part of the ancient Ettrick Forests, the attraction of Bowhill attaches not simply to the grandeur of the house but to what it contains. Paintings by masters such as Canaletto, Raeburn, Reynolds and Gainsborough line the walls of Bowhill's many fine rooms, while additional richness is provided by classic tapestries, French furniture, china and porcelain by Sèvres and Meissen, along with a fine collection of silverware,

In the courtyard, housed within a number of attractive buildings, you

will find a range of interesting things to see and enjoy including the James Hogg exhibition, which celebrates his life and work, and the Victorian Kitchen with its amazing collection of original Victorian cooking utensils that were a feature in the kitchens of the day. The courtyard also has a Visitor Centre giving estate and wildlife information, a licensed tearoom and a gift shop. Visit the exciting Adventure Playground.

Ranger-led walks through woodland, skirting lochs and rivers. Children's activities throughout the summer.

Bowhill Theatre has a full programme of music and drama throughout the year.

ⓘ Fashion shows, air displays, archery, clay pigeon shooting, equestrian events, charity garden parties, shows, rallies, filming, lecture theatre. House is open by appointment outside public hours to groups led by officials of a recognised museum, gallery or educational establishment. No photography inside house. No unaccompanied children.

🗑
❄
🍽 Inside caterers normally used but outside caterers considered.

♿ Visitors may alight at entrance. WC. Wheelchair visitors free.

☕ Groups can book in advance (special rates), menus on request. Licensed.

🚶 For groups. Tour time 1¼ hrs.

🅿 60 cars and 6 coaches within 50yds of house.

📖 Welcome. Projects in Bowhill House and Victorian kitchen, Education Officers (service provided free of charge), schoolroom, ranger-led nature walks, adventure playground. Heritage Education Trust Sandford Award winner '93, '98 & '04.

🐕 On leads.

❄

### Conference/Function

| ROOM | MAX CAPACITY |
|------|-------------|
| Bowhill Little Theatre | 72 |

Skyscan Photo Library

# FLOORS CASTLE 🏛

www.floorscastle.com

Floors Castle, home of the Duke and Duchess of Roxburghe, is situated in the heart of the Scottish Border Country. It is reputedly the largest inhabited castle in Scotland. Designed by William Adam, who was both masterbuilder and architect, for the first Duke of Roxburghe, building started in 1721.

It was the present Duke's great-great-grand-father James, the 6th Duke, who embellished the plain Adam features of the building. In about 1849 Playfair, letting his imagination and talent run riot, transformed the castle, creating a multitude of spires and domes.

The apartments now display the outstanding collection of French 17th and 18th century furniture, magnificent tapestries, Chinese and European porcelain and many other fine works of art. Many of the treasures in the castle today were collected by Duchess May, American wife of the 8th Duke.

The castle has been seen on cinema screens worldwide in the film Greystoke, as the home of Tarzan, the Earl of Greystoke.

## Gardens

The extensive parkland and gardens overlooking the River Tweed provide a variety of wooded walks. The garden centre and walled gardens contain splendid herbaceous borders and in the outer walled garden a parterre to commemorate the Millennium can be seen. An excellent children's playground and picnic area are very close to the castle.

Gala dinners, conferences, product launches, 4 x 4 driving, incentive groups, highland games and other promotional events. Extensive park, helicopter pad, fishing, clay pigeon and pheasant shooting.
No photography inside the castle.

Visitors may alight at the entrance. WC.

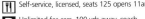

Self-service, licensed, seats 125 opens 11am.

**P** Unlimited for cars, 100 yds away, coach park 150 yds. Coaches can be driven to the entrance. Lunch or tea for coach drivers.

Welcome, guide provided. Playground facilities.

On leads, in grounds.

### Owner
His Grace the Duke of Roxburghe

### Contact
Sarah Macdonald
Sales & Events
Organiser
Roxburghe Estates Office
Kelso
Roxburghshire
Scotland  TD5 7SF

**Tel:** 01573 223333
**Fax:** 01573 226056
**E-mail:** smacdonald@ floorscastle.com

### Location
**MAP 14:J10**
**OS Ref. NT711 347**

From South A68, A698.

From North A68, A697/9 In Kelso follow signs.

**Bus:** Kelso Bus Station 1m.

**Rail:** Berwick 20m.

### Opening Times
**Summer**
Easter, then
1 May–28 October:
Daily: 11am–5pm.
Last admission 4.30pm.

**Winter**
November–March
Closed to the general public, available for events.

### Admission
**Summer**

| | |
|---|---|
| Adult | £6.50 |
| Child* (5–16yrs) | £3.50 |
| OAP/Student | £5.50 |
| Family | £16.00 |
| Groups (20+) | |
| Adult | £5.00 |
| Child* (5–16yrs) | £2.00 |
| OAP/Student | £4.50 |

*Under 5yrs Free.

### Special Events
**February 15**
Snowdrop Festival

**April 8**
Easter Eggstravaganza

**May 19/20**
Floors Castle Horse Trials

**July 7/8**
Gardeners' Festival

**August 26**
Massed Pipe Bands Day

**December 8/9**
Christmas Winter Wonderland

### Conference/Function

| ROOM | SIZE | MAX CAPACITY |
|---|---|---|
| Dining Rm | 18m x 7m | 150 |
| Ballroom | 21m x 8m | 150 |

## ■ Owner
The Lord Palmer

## ■ Contact
The Lord or Lady Palmer
Manderston
Duns
Berwickshire
Scotland  TD11 3PP

**Tel:** 01361 883450
Secretary: 01361 882636
**Fax:** 01361 882010
**E-mail:** palmer@
manderston.co.uk

## ■ Location
**MAP 14:K9**
**OS Ref. NT810 544**

From Edinburgh
47m, 1hr.
1½ m E of Duns on
A6105.

**Bus:** 400 yds.

**Rail:** Berwick
Station 12m.

**Taxi:** Chirnside 818216.

**Airport:** Edinburgh or
Newcastle both
60m or 80 mins.

## ■ Opening Times
**Summer**
Mid-May–end September
Thurs & Sun, 1.30–5pm
Last entry 4.15pm.
Gardens: 11.30am–dusk.

BH Mons, late May
& late August, 2–5pm.
Gardens open until dusk.

Groups welcome all year
by appointment.

**Winter**
September–May
Group visits welcome
by appointment.

## ■ Admission
**House & Grounds**
Adult            £8.00
Child (under 12yrs)  Free
Conc.            £8.00

Groups (20+)      £7.50
(£8.00 outside opening
days).

**Grounds only including
Stables & Marble Dairy**
                 £4.50

On days when the house
is closed to the public,
groups viewing by
appointment will have
personally conducted
tours. The Gift Shop will
be open. On these
occasions reduced party
rates (except for school
children) will not apply.
Group visits (20+) other
than open days are £6.50
(minimum £130).
Edwardian teas on open
days only.

## Conference/Function

| ROOM | SIZE | MAX CAPACITY |
|------|------|-------------|
| Dining Rm | 22' x 35' | 100 |
| Ballroom | 34' x 21' | 150 |
| Hall | 22' x 38' | 130 |
| Drawing Rm | 35' x 21' | 150 |

# MANDERSTON
www.manderston.co.uk

Manderston, together with its magnificent stables, stunning marble dairy and 56 acres of immaculate gardens, forms an ensemble which must be unique in Britain today.

The house was completely rebuilt between 1903 and 1905, with no expense spared. Visitors are able to see not only the sumptuous State rooms and bedrooms, decorated in the Adam manner, but also all the original domestic offices, in a truly 'upstairs downstairs' atmosphere. Manderston boasts a unique and recently restored silver staircase.

There is a special museum with a nostalgic display of valuable tins made by Huntly and Palmer from 1868 to the present day. Winner of the AA/NPI Bronze Award UK 1994.

## Gardens

Outside, the magnificence continues and the combination of formal gardens and picturesque landscapes is a major attraction unique amongst Scottish houses. The stables, still in use, have been described by *Horse and Hound* as 'probably the finest in all the wide world'.

Manderston has often been used as a film location, most recently it was the star of Channel 4's '*The Edwardian Country House*'.

ℹ️ Corporate & incentives venue. Ideal retreat: business groups, think-tank weekends. Fashion shows, air displays, archery, clay pigeon shooting, equestrian events, garden parties, shows, rallies, filming, product launches and marathons. Two airstrips for light aircraft, approx 5m, grand piano, billiard table, pheasant shoots, sea angling, salmon fishing, stabling, cricket pitch, tennis court, lake. Nearby: 18-hole golf course, indoor swimming pool, squash court. No photography in house.

Available. Buffets, lunches and dinners. Wedding receptions.

Special parking available outside the House.

Tearoom – home made lunches, teas, cakes and tray bakes. Can be booked in advance, menus on request.

Included. Available in French. Guides in rooms. If requested, the owner may meet groups. Tour time 1¼ hrs.

400 cars 125yds from house, 30 coaches 5yds from house. Appreciated if group fees are paid by one person.

Welcome. Guide can be provided. Biscuit Tin Museum of particular interest.

Grounds only, on leads.

6 twin, 4 double.

# TRAQUAIR

www.traquair.co.uk

Traquair, situated amidst beautiful scenery and close by the River Tweed, is the oldest inhabited house in Scotland - visited by twenty-seven kings. Originally a Royal hunting lodge, it was owned by the Scottish Crown until 1478 when it passed to a branch of the Royal Stuart family whose descendants still live in the house today. Nearly ten centuries of Scottish political and domestic life can be traced from the collection of treasures in the house. It is particularly rich in associations with the Catholic Church in Scotland, Mary Queen of Scots and the Jacobite Risings.

Visitors are invited to enjoy the house, extensive grounds, maze, craft workshops, 1745 Cottage Restaurant and the famous Traquair House Brewery housed in the eighteenth century wing and producing the world famous Traquair House Ales.

Traquair is a unique piece of living history welcoming visitors from all over the world, providing a magical and romantic setting for weddings, hosting a wide range of summer events and a superb venue for corporate groups. You can even stay at Traquair House. There are three spacious double bedrooms furnished with antique furniture, canopied beds, private bathrooms and central heating. They are all available on a bed and breakfast basis.

- ℹ️ No photography in house.
- 🍷 Exclusive lunches/dinners (max 30) in the Dining Room.
- ♿ Licensed, self-service.
- 🍴 Home cooked meals (max 50) at 1745 Cottage Restaurant.
- 📷 Apr & outside opening hours.
- 🚶 
- 🅿️ Coaches please book.
- 🐕 In grounds on leads.
- 🛏️ 3 en-suites. B&B.

## ■ Owner
Catherine Maxwell Stuart

## ■ Contact
Ms C Maxwell Stuart
Innerleithen
Peeblesshire EH44 6PW

**Tel:** 01896 830323
**Fax:** 01896 830639
**E-mail:** enquiries@
traquair.co.uk

## ■ Location
**MAP 13:H10**
**OS Ref. NY330 354**

On B709 near junction with A72. Edinburgh 1hr, Glasgow 1½ hrs, Carlisle 1½ hrs, Newcastle 1½ hrs.

## ■ Opening Times
6 Apr–31 October: daily, (Apr/May: 12 noon–5pm. June–August: 10.30am–5pm. October: 11am–4pm.)

November: weekends only, 11am–3pm.

Guided tours may be arranged outside normal opening hours. These can be conducted by an experienced guide or by the owner, Catherine Maxwell Stuart, 21st Lady of Traquair for an additional charge. Groups may also like to book a free introductory talk.

**Traquair Experiences**
Lunches, dinners, receptions, coffee and shortbread, ale tastings and ghost tours may all be arranged during opening hours.

## ■ Admission
**House & Grounds**

| | |
|---|---|
| Adult | £6.30 |
| Child | £3.40 |
| Senior | £5.70 |
| Family(2+3) | £17.70 |

Groups (20+)

| | |
|---|---|
| Adult | £5.60 |
| Child | £2.70 |
| Senior | £5.40 |

**Grounds only**

| | |
|---|---|
| Adult | £3.50 |
| Child | £2.50 |
| Guide book | £3.75 |

## ■ Special Events
**April 8**
Easter Egg Extravaganza
**May 26/27**
Medieval Fayre
**August 4/5**
Traquair Fair
**October 26–28**
Halloween Experience
**November 24/25**
Christmas Opening

## Conference/Function

| ROOM | SIZE | MAX CAPACITY |
|---|---|---|
| Dining Room | 33' x 16' | 34 seated |
| Drawing Rm | 27' x 24' | 50/60 receptions |

## ABBOTSFORD 🏛
### MELROSE, ROXBURGHSHIRE TD6 9BQ

www.scottsabbotsford.co.uk

**Tel:** 01896 752043    **Fax:** 01896 752916    **E-mail:** enquiries@scottsabbotsford.co.uk
**Contact:** Jacqui Wright
The Home of Sir Walter Scott. A wonderfully interesting house with fascinating collections. Garden, including walled garden, woodland walk, stunning grounds leading down to the River Tweed. Gift Shop. Tea Shop in grounds for light refreshments. Tours of the private apartments by arrangement.
**Location:** MAP 14:I10, OS Ref. NT508 343 35 mins S of Edinburgh. Melrose 3m, Galashiels 2m. On B6360.
**Open:** 19 Mar–31 Oct: Mon–Sat, 9.30am–5pm. Mar–May & Oct: Sun, 2–5pm. Jun–Sept: Sun, 9.30am–5pm. Other dates by arrangement.
**Admission:** Adult £6, Child £3, Groups £4.50
🖼 🖼 ⅈ By arrangement. 🅿 €

## AYTON CASTLE 🏛
### AYTON, EYEMOUTH, BERWICKSHIRE TD14 5RD

**Tel:** 018907 81212    **Fax:** 018907 81550
**Owner:** D I Liddell-Grainger of Ayton    **Contact:** The Curator
Built in 1846 by the Mitchell-Innes family and designed by the architect James Gillespie Graham. Over the last ten years it has been fully restored and is now a family home. It is a unique restoration project and the quality of the original and restored workmanship is outstanding. The castle stands on an escarpment surrounded by mature woodlands containing many interesting trees and has been a film-making venue due to this magnificent setting.
**Location:** MAP 14:K8, OS Ref. NT920 610. 7m N of Berwick-on-Tweed on Route A1.
**Open:** 14 May–10 Sept: by telephone appointment.
**Admission:** Adult £3, Child (under 15yrs) Free.
🍵 🖼 Partial. ⅈ Obligatory. 🅿 🖼 In grounds, on leads. ❄

---

## BOWHILL HOUSE & COUNTRY PARK 🏛

*See page 446 for full page entry*

---

## DAWYCK BOTANIC GARDEN
### Stobo, Peeblesshire EH45 9JU

**Tel:** 01721 760254    **Fax:** 01721 760214    **E-mail:** dawyck@rbge.org.uk
**Contact:** The Curator
Renowned historic arboretum. Amongst mature specimen trees – some over 40 metres tall – are a variety of flowering trees, shrubs and herbaceous plants. Explore the world's first Cryptogamic Sanctuary and Reserve for 'non-flowering' plants.
**Location:** MAP 13:G10, OS Ref. NT168 352. 8m SW of Peebles on B712.
**Open:** Feb–Nov: daily, 10am–6pm (closes 4pm Feb & Nov, 5pm Mar & Oct). Last admission 1 hr before closing.
**Admission:** Adult £3.50, Child £1, Conc. £3, Family £8. Group discounts & membership programme available.

---

## DRYBURGH ABBEY 🔔
### St Boswells, Melrose

**Tel:** 01835 822381
**Owner:** Historic Scotland    **Contact:** The Steward
Remarkably complete ruins of Dryburgh Abbey.
**Location:** MAP 14:I10, OS Ref. NT591 317. 5m SE of Melrose off B6356. 1½ m N of St Boswells.
**Open:** 1 Apr–30 Sept: daily, 9.30am–6.30pm, last ticket 6pm. 1 Oct–31 Mar: daily, 9.30am–4.30pm, last ticket 4pm.
**Admission:** Adult £4.50, Child £2.25, Conc. £3.50.
🖼 🖼 Partial. ⅈ By arrangement. 🅿 🖼 €

---

## DUNS CASTLE
### DUNS, BERWICKSHIRE TD11 3NW

www.dunscastle.co.uk

**Tel:** 01361 883211    **Fax:** 01361 882015    **E-mail:** aline_hay@lineone.net
**Owner:** Alexander Hay of Duns    **Contact:** Mrs Aline Hay
This historical 1320 pele tower has been home to the Hay family since 1696, and the current owners Alexander and Aline Hay offer it as a welcoming venue for individuals, groups and corporate guests to enjoy. This beautiful castle maintains high standards of comfort while retaining all the character of its rich period interiors. Wonderful lakeside and parkland setting.
**Location:** MAP 14:J9, OS Ref. NT777 544. 10m off A1. Rail: Berwick station 16m. Airports: Newcastle & Edinburgh, 1 hr.
**Open:** Available all year by reservation for individuals, groups, parties and companies for day visits or residential stays, on an exclusive use basis. Not open to the general public.
**Admission:** Rates for private and corporate visits, wedding receptions and filming on application.
🛏 4 x 4-poster, 4 x double, 3 x twin (all with bathrooms), 1 single plus 6 cottages in grounds. ❄

---

**For corporate hospitality** at unique venues see the index on page 567

## FERNIEHIRST CASTLE

**JEDBURGH, ROXBURGHSHIRE TD8 6NX**

**Tel:** 01835 862201
**Fax:** 01835 863992
**Owner:** The Ferniehirst Trust
**Contact:** Mrs J Fraser

Ferniehirst Castle – Scotland's Frontier Fortress. Ancestral home of the Kerr family. Restored (1984/1987) by the 12th Marquess of Lothian. Unrivalled 16th century Border architecture. Grand Apartment and Turret Library. A 16th century Chamber Oratory. The Kerr Chamber – Museum of Family History. A special tribute to Jedburgh's Protector to Mary Queen of Scots – Sir Thomas Kerr. Riverside walk by Jed Water. Archery Field opposite the Chapel where sheep of Viking origin still graze as they did four centuries ago.

**Location:**
MAP 14:J11, OS Ref. NT653 181. 2m S of Jedburgh on the A68.

**Open:** July: Tue–Sun, 11am–4pm. (Closed Mons.)

**Admission:** Adult £3.50, Child £1.50. Groups (max. 50) by prior arrangement (01835 862201).

⬜ ♿ Suitable. WCs.
ℹ Guided tours only, groups by arrangement.
🅿 Ample for cars and coaches.
🐕 In grounds, on leads.

---

## FLOORS CASTLE 🏛

*See page 447 for full page entry.*

## HALLIWELL'S HOUSE MUSEUM

**Halliwell's Close, Market Place, High Street, Selkirk**
**Tel:** 01750 20096   **Fax:** 01750 23282
**Owner:** Scottish Borders Council   **Contact:** Brian Appleby
Re-creation of buildings, formerly used as a house and ironmonger's shop.
**Location:** MAP 14:I10, OS Ref. NT472 286. In Selkirk town centre.
**Open:** Apr–Sept: Mon–Sat, 10am–5pm, Sun, 10am–12 noon. Jul & Aug: 10 am–1pm. Closed for Selkirk Common Riding. Please telephone in advance to confirm opening times.
**Admission:** Free.

## HERMITAGE CASTLE 🏛

**Liddesdale, Newcastleton**
**Tel:** 01387 376222
**Owner:** In the care of Historic Scotland   **Contact:** The Steward
Eerie fortress at the heart of the bloodiest events in the history of the Borders. Mary Queen of Scots made her famous ride here to visit her future husband.
**Location:** MAP 10:L1, OS Ref. NY497 961. In Liddesdale 5½m NE of Newcastleton, B6399.
**Open:** 1 Apr–30 Sept: daily, 9.30am–6.30pm, last ticket 6pm.
**Admission:** Adult £3.50, Child £2.80, Conc. £1.75.

⬜ 🍴 🅿 🐕 €

## THE HIRSEL GARDENS, COUNTRY PARK 🏛 & HOMESTEAD MUSEUM

**Coldstream, Berwickshire   TD12 4LP**
**Tel:** 01573 224144   **Fax:** 01573 226313   **E-mail:** rogerdodd@btconnect.com
**www.hirselcountrypark.co.uk**
**Owner:** Lord Home of the Hirsel   **Contact:** Roger G Dodd
Wonderful spring flowers and rhododendrons. Homestead museum and crafts centre. The Cottage Tearoom. Displays of estate life and adaptation to modern farming.
**Location:** MAP 14:K10, OS Ref. NT838 393. Immediately W of Coldstream off A697.
**Open:** All year during daylight hours.
**Admission:** £2.50 per car, coaches by appointment.

⬜ 🍴 ♿ WCs. 🅿 Limited for coaches. 🐕 In grounds, on leads. 🌼

Abbotsford, Melrose

For rare and unusual plants visit the **plant sales** index on page 564

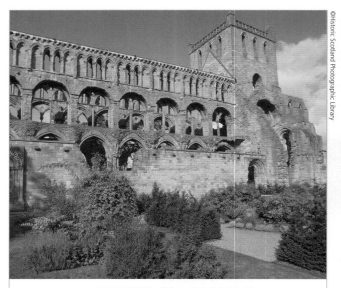

## JEDBURGH ABBEY
### 4/5 ABBEY BRIDGEND, JEDBURGH TD8 6JQ

**Tel:** 01835 863925

**Owner:** In the care of Historic Scotland **Contact:** The Steward

Founded by David I c1138 for Augustinian Canons. The church is mostly in the Romanesque and early Gothic styles and is remarkably complete. The award-winning visitor centre contains the priceless 12th century 'Jedburgh Comb' and other artefacts found during archaeological excavations.

**Location:** MAP 14:J11, OS Ref. NT650 205. In Jedburgh on the A68.

**Open:** Apr–Sept: daily, 9.30am–6.30pm. Oct–Mar: daily, 9.30am–4.30pm. Last ticket 30 mins before closing. 10% discount for groups (10+).

**Admission:** Adult £5, Child £2.50, Conc. £4.

Picnic area. Partial to visitor centre. WC. Free when booked. Guide dogs only.

## MELLERSTAIN HOUSE
### MELLERSTAIN, GORDON, BERWICKSHIRE TD3 6LG
www.mellerstain.com

**Tel:** 01573 410225 **Fax:** 01573 410636 **E-mail:** enquiries@mellerstain.com

**Owner:** The Earl of Haddington **Contact:** Rosemary Evans

One of Scotland's great Georgian houses and a unique example of the work of the Adam family; the two wings built in 1725 by William Adam, the large central block by his son, Robert 1770-78. Rooms contain fine plasterwork, colourful ceilings and marble fireplaces. The library is considered to be Robert Adam's finest creation. Many fine paintings and period furniture.

**Location:** MAP 14:J10, OS Ref. NT648 392. From Edinburgh A68 to Earlston, turn left 5m, signed.

**Open:** Easter weekend and 1 May–30 Sept: Suns, Weds & BH Mons. Oct: Suns only. House: 12.30–5pm. Last ticket 4.15pm. Groups any time by appointment. Tearoom, shop & gardens: 11.30am–5pm.

**Admission:** Adult £6, Child (under 16yrs) with adult Free. Groups (20+) £5.50 (outside normal hours £6.50). Grounds only: £3.50.

No photography or video cameras. Partial. Licensed. Licensed. By arrangement. In grounds, on leads. Guide dogs only in house.

---

### MANDERSTON

*See page 448 for full page entry.*

Paxton House, Berwick-upon-Tweed

## MELROSE ABBEY
### MELROSE, ROXBURGHSHIRE TD6 9LG

**Tel:** 01896 822562

**Owner:** Historic Scotland **Contact:** The Steward

The abbey was founded about 1136 by David I as a Cistercian abbey and at one time was probably the richest in Scotland. Richard II's English army largely destroyed it in 1385 but it was rebuilt and the surviving remains are mostly 14th century. Burial place of Robert the Bruce's heart. Local history displays.

**Location:** MAP 14:I10, OS Ref. NT549 342. In the centre of Melrose off the A68 or A7.

**Open:** Apr–Sept: daily, 9.30am–6.30pm. Oct–Mar: daily, 9.30am–4.30pm. Last ticket 30 mins before closing.

**Admission:** Adult £5, Child £2.50, Conc. £4. 10% discount for groups (10+).

Picnic area. Tape for visitors with learning difficulties. Pre-booked visits free. Guide dogs only.

## MERTOUN GARDENS

St Boswells, Melrose, Roxburghshire  TD6 0EA
**Tel:** 01835 823236   **Fax:** 01835 822474   **E-mail:** mertounestatefarms@farming.co.uk
**Owner:** His Grace the Duke of Sutherland      **Contact:** Angela Dodds/Susan Murdoch
26 acres of beautiful grounds. Walled garden and well-preserved circular dovecote.
**Location:** MAP 14:J10, OS Ref. NT617 318. Entrance off B6404 2m NE of St Boswells.
**Open:** Apr–Sept: Fri–Mon, 2–6pm. Last admission 5.30pm.
**Admission:** Adult £2.50, Child 50p, OAP £1.50. Groups by arrangement: 10% reduction.
By arrangement. P

## PAXTON HOUSE, GALLERY & COUNTRY PARK
### BERWICK-UPON-TWEED  TD15 1SZ
www.paxtonhouse.com

**Tel:** 01289 386291   **Fax:** 01289 386660   **E-mail:** info@paxtonhouse.com
**Owner:** The Paxton Trust    **Contact:** The Director
Award winning Palladian country house built 1758 to the design of John Adam. 12 period rooms contain the finest collections of Chippendale and Regency furniture. Magnificent picture gallery and restored Georgian kitchen. Enjoy the grounds and gardens, riverside and woodland walks, red squirrel and bird hides plus the salmon net fishing museum. Visit the shops, tearoom and our ever changing exhibition programme.
**Location:** MAP 14:K9, OS Ref. NT931 520. 3m off the A1 Berwick-upon-Tweed bypass on B6461.
**Open:** 1 Apr–31 Oct: House: 11am–5pm. Last house tour 4pm.
Grounds: 10am–sunset. Open to groups/schools all year by appointment.
**Admission:** Adult £6, Child £3. Groups (pre-arranged, 12+). Adult £5, Child £2.50. Grounds only: Adult £3, Child £1.50.
No photography. Conferences, weddings. Partial. Licensed. Obligatory. P In grounds, on leads.

## MONTEVIOT HOUSE GARDENS
### JEDBURGH, ROXBURGHSHIRE  TD8 6UQ

**Tel:** 01835 830380 (mornings only) / 01835 830704   **Fax:** 01835 830288
**Owner:** The Marquis of Lothian    **Contact:** The Administrator
The river garden planted with herbaceous shrub borders, has a beautiful view of the River Teviot. A semi-enclosed rose garden with a collection of hybrid teas, floribunda and shrub roses. The pinetum is full of unusual trees and nearby a water garden of islands is linked by bridges.
**Location:** MAP 14:J11, OS Ref. NT648 247. 3m N of Jedburgh. S side of B6400 (to Nisbet). 1m E of A68.
**Open:** House: 2–15 Jul: 12 noon–4.15pm. Garden: Apr–Oct: daily, 12 noon–5pm. Coach parties by prior arrangement.
**Admission:** House or Garden only: Adult £2.50. House & Garden: Adult £4.50. Under 16yrs Free.
Partial. Parking & WCs. By arrangement. P

## SMAILHOLM TOWER

Smailholm, Kelso
**Tel:** 01573 460365
**Owner:** In the care of Historic Scotland    **Contact:** The Steward
Set on a high rocky knoll this well preserved 16th century tower houses an exhibition of tapestries and costume dolls depicting characters from Sir Walter Scott's Minstrelsy of the Scottish Borders.
**Location:** MAP 14:J10, OS Ref. NT638 347. Nr Smailholm Village, 6m W of Kelso on B6937 then B6404.
**Open:** 1 Apr–30 Sept: daily, 9.30am–6.30pm. Oct: Sat–Wed, 9.30am–4.30pm. Nov–Mar: Sats & Suns only, 9.30am–4.30pm. Last tickets 30 mins before closing.
**Admission:** Adult £3.50, Child £1.75, Conc. £2.80.
P €

## OLD GALA HOUSE

Scott Crescent, Galashiels  TD1 3JS
**Tel:** 01750 20096   **Fax:** 01750 23282
**Owner:** Scottish Borders Council
Dating from 1583, the former house of the Lairds of Gala. Particularly memorable is the painted ceiling dated 1635.
**Location:** MAP 14:I10, OS Ref. NT492 357. S of town centre, signed from A7.
**Open:** Apr, May & Sept: Tue–Sat, 10am–4pm. Jun–Aug: Mon–Sat, 10am–4pm, Sun, 1–4pm. Oct: Tue–Fri, 1–4pm, Sat, 10am–4pm.
**Admission:** Free.

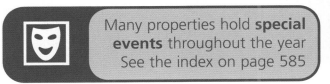

Many properties hold **special events** throughout the year
See the index on page 585

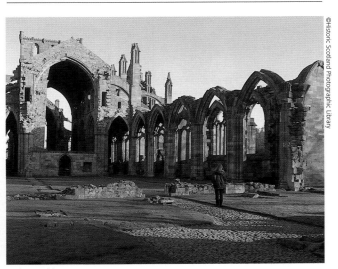

©Historic Scotland Photographic Library

Melrose Abbey

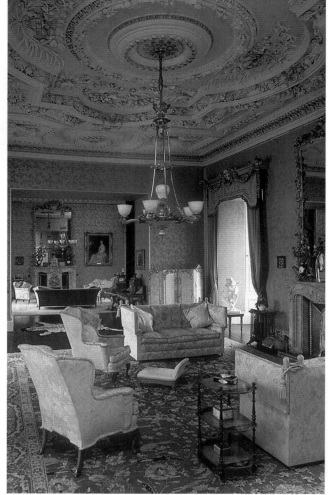

# THIRLESTANE CASTLE 🏛
## LAUDER, BERWICKSHIRE TD2 6RU
www.thirlestanecastle.co.uk

**Tel:** 01578 722430   **Fax:** 01578 722761   **E-mail:** admin@thirlestanecastle.co.uk
**Owner:** Thirlestane Castle Trust   **Contact:** Ian Garner

Thirlestane Castle was the ancient seat of the Earls and Duke of Lauderdale and is still home to the Maitlands.  Standing in beautiful Border countryside, Thirlestane has exquisite 17th century plasterwork ceilings, a fine portrait collection, historic toys, kitchens and country life exhibitions. Facilities include free parking, audio visual display, gift shop, café, adventure playground, and woodland picnic tables. Four star STB award; Registered Museum.The state rooms are available for banquets, dinners and receptions. Non-destructive events can be held in the grounds which overlook the Leader Valley and Lammermuir Hills.

**Location:** MAP 14:I9, OS Ref. NT540 473. Off A68 at Lauder, 28m S of Edinburgh.

**Open:** 6–9 Apr, 11 Apr–28 Jun: Sun, Wed & Thurs; 7 & 28 May, Jul & Aug: Sun–Thurs; 1–27 Sept Wed & Thurs; 10am–3pm (last admission). Special opening at other times can be arranged fro pre-booked groups with special rates. Minimum 20 people or £120.

**Admission:** Castle & Grounds: Adult £7, Child £5, Senior £6, Family (2+3) £20. Lauder Residents Seasonal Ticket £15. Groups (18+): Adult £4.50, Child £1.50. Grounds only: Adult £3, Child £1.50.

ℹ️ Woodland walk, children's adventure playground, country life display area.

📷 🚫 ♿ Unsuitable. 🍽 By arrangement. 🅿 🅿 🐕 In grounds, on leads.

Thirlestane Castle

---

# TRAQUAIR 🏛

*See page 449 for full page entry.*

---

The Library – Mellerstain

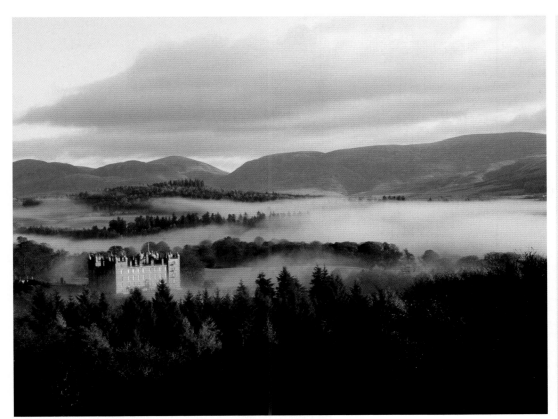

# DRUMLANRIG CASTLE 🏛

www.drumlanrig.com

Drumlanrig Castle, Gardens and Country Park, Dumfriesshire home of the Duke of Buccleuch and Queensberry KT was built between 1679 and 1691 by William Douglas, 1st Duke of Queensberry. Drumlanrig is rightly recognised as one of the first and most important buildings in the grand manner in Scottish domestic architecture. James Smith, who made the conversion from a 15th century castle, made a comparable transformation at Dalkeith a decade later.

The Castle, of local pink sandstone, offers superb views across Nithsdale. It houses a renowned art collection, cabinets made for Louis XIV's Versailles, relics of Bonnie Prince Charlie and a 300 year old silver chandelier.

The story of Sir James Douglas, killed in Spain while carrying out the last wish of Robert Bruce, pervades the Castle in the emblem of a winged heart. Douglas family historical exhibition. Other attractions include craft workshops, mountain bike trails and bike hire, Cycle Museum, working forge and adventure play area. The gardens, now being restored to the plan of 1738, include a plant centre and add to the overall effect. The fascination of Drumlanrig as a centre of art, beauty and history is complemented by its role in the Queensberry Estate, a model of dynamic and enlightened land management.

| | | |
|---|---|---|
| ℹ️ No photography inside the Castle. | | 🅿️ Adjacent to the Castle. |
| 📷 | | Children's quiz and worksheets. Ranger-led activities, including woodlands and forestry. Adventure playground. School groups welcome throughout the year by arrangement. |
| ♿ Suitable. WC. Please enquire about facilities before visit. | | |
| ☕ Licensed. | | 🐕 In grounds on leads. |
| 🍴 Snacks, lunches and teas during opening hours. | | ❄️ |
| 🚶 | | 🎭 |

## SOUTH WEST

### ■ Owner
His Grace the Duke of Buccleuch & Queensberry KT

### ■ Contact
Claire Oram
Drumlanrig Castle
Thornhill
Dumfriesshire
DG3 4AQ

**Tel:** 01848 331555
**Fax:** 01848 331682
**E-mail:** bre@
drumlanrigcastle.org.uk

### ■ Location
**MAP 13:E12**
**OS Ref. NX851 992**

18m N of Dumfries, 3m NW of Thornhill off A76. 16m from M74 at Elvanfoot. Approx. 1½ hrs by road from Edinburgh, Glasgow and Carlisle.

### ■ Opening Times
**Summer**
**Castle**
4 May–22 August: daily.
May & June:
12 noon–4pm (last tour).
July & August:
11am–4pm (last tour).

**Country Park, Gardens & Adventure Woodland**
31 March–30 September: daily, 11am–5pm.

**Winter**
By appointment only.

### ■ Admission*
**Castle and Country Park**
| | |
|---|---|
| Adult | £7.00 |
| Child (5–15yrs) | £3.00 |
| OAP/Student | £6.00 |
| Family (2+4) | £24.50 |
| Disabled in wheelchairs | Free |

| | |
|---|---|
| Pre-booked groups (20+) | |
| Adult | £5.00 |
| Child (5–15yrs) | £2.00 |

| | |
|---|---|
| Outside normal opening times | £8.00 |

**Country Park only**
| | |
|---|---|
| Adult | £4.00 |
| OAP | £3.50 |
| Child (5–15yrs) | £3.00 |
| Family (2+4) | £19.00 |
| Season Ticket | £25.00 |

*All visitors to the Castle must sign the visitor book as a condition of entry.

### Conference/Function
| ROOM | SIZE | MAX CAPACITY |
|---|---|---|
| Visitors' Centre | 6m x 13m | 50 |

## ARDWELL GARDENS

**Ardwell, Nr Stranraer, Dumfries and Galloway  DG9 9LY**
**Tel:** 01776 860227
**Owner:** Mr Francis Brewis    **Contact:** Mrs Terry Brewis
The gardens include a formal garden, wild garden and woodland.
**Location:** MAP 9:D4, OS Ref. NX102 455. A716 10m S of Stranraer.
**Open:** 1 Apr–30 Sept: daily, 10am–5pm.
**Admission:** Adult £3, Children under 14 free.

## AUCHINLECK HOUSE

**Ochiltree, Ayrshire**
**Tel:** 01628 825925   **Fax:** 01628 825417
**E-mail:** bookings@landmarktrust.org.uk   **www.landmarktrust.org.uk**
**Owner/Contact:** The Landmark Trust
One of the finest examples of an 18th century Scottish country house, the importance of which is further enhanced by its association with James Boswell, author of The Life of Samuel Johnson. The house has been restored by the Landmark Trust and is let for holidays for up to 13 people. Full details of staying at Auchinleck House and 184 other historic buildings are featured in the Landmark Trust Handbook (price £11.50 refundable against booking).
**Location:** MAP 13:C11, OS Ref. NS507 230. Ochiltree, Ayrshire.
**Open:** Available for holidays for up to 13 people throughout the year. Parts of the house will be open to the public Easter–Oct: Wed afternoons. Grounds: dawn–dusk in the Spring & Summer season. Contact the Landmark Trust for details.
**Admission:** By appointment only. Tickets £3 from 01628 825920.
⬛ In grounds, on leads. ⬛

## BARGANY GARDENS

**Girvan, Ayrshire  KA26 9QL**
**Tel:** 01465 871249   **Fax:** 01465 871282
**Owner/Contact:** Mr John Dalrymple Hamilton
Lily pond, rock garden and a fine collection of hard and softwood trees.
**Location:** MAP 9:E1, OS Ref. NX851 992. 18m N of Dumfries, 3m NW of Thornhill off A76. 16m from M74 at Elvanfoot.
**Open:** May: daily, 10am–5pm.
**Admission:** Adult £2, Child Free. Buses by arrangement.

## BRODICK CASTLE ♛

**Isle of Arran  KA27 8HY**
**Tel:** 0131 243 9300
**Owner:** The National Trust for Scotland
Castle built on the site of a Viking fortress with interesting contents.
**Location:** MAP 12:P10, OS Ref. NX684 509. Off A711 /A755, in Kirkcudbright, at 12 High St.

## BURNS' COTTAGE

**Alloway, Ayrshire  KA7 4PY**
**Tel:** 01292 441215   **Fax:** 01292 441750
**Contact:** J Manson
Thatched cottage, birthplace of Robert Burns in 1759, with adjacent museum.
**Location:** OS Ref. NS335 190. 2m SW of Ayr. Two separate sites, 600yds apart.
**Open:** Apr–Sept: daily, 10am–5.30pm. Oct–Mar: daily, 10am–5pm. Closed 25/26 Dec & 1/2 Jan.
**Admission:** Adult £4, Child/OAP £2.50, Family £9. Prices may change in Apr 2007.

Castle Kennedy Gardens, Stranraer

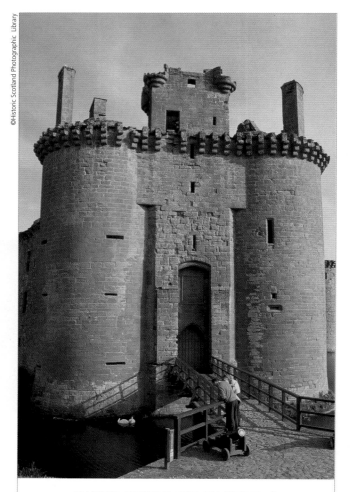
©Historic Scotland Photographic Library

## CAERLAVEROCK CASTLE ⬛

**GLENCAPLE, DUMFRIES  DG1 4RU**
**Tel:** 01387 770244
**Owner:** In the care of Historic Scotland    **Contact:** Valerie Bennett
One of the finest castles in Scotland on a triangular site surrounded by moats. Its most remarkable features are the twin-towered gatehouse and the Renaissance Nithsdale lodging. The site of two famous sieges. Exhibition with video presentation, children's park, replica siege engines and nature trail to site of earlier castle.
**Location:** MAP 10:I3, OS84 NY025 656. 8m S of Dumfries on the B725.
**Open:** Apr–Sept: daily, 9.30am–6.30pm; Oct–Mar: daily, 9.30am–4.30pm. Last ticket sold 30 mins before closing.
**Admission:** Adult £5, Child £2.50, Conc. £4. 10% discount for groups (10+).
ⓘ ⬛ ⬛ Partial. WCs. ⬛ ⬛ Limited for coaches. ⬛ Free if pre-booked.
⬛ In grounds, on leads. ⬛ €

## CARDONESS CASTLE ⬛

**Gatehouse of Fleet**
**Tel:** 01557 814427
**Owner:** In the care of Historic Scotland    **Contact:** The Steward
Well preserved ruin of a four storey tower house of 15th century standing on a rocky platform above the Water of Fleet. Ancient home of the McCullochs. Very fine fireplaces.
**Location:** MAP 9:G3, OS Ref. NX591 553. 1m SW of Gatehouse of Fleet, beside the A75.
**Open:** 1 Apr–30 Sept: daily, 9.30am–6.30pm. Last ticket 6pm. Oct: daily except Thurs & Fri; Nov–Mar: Sats & Suns only, 9.30am–4.30pm. Last ticket 4pm.
**Admission:** Adult £3.50, Child £1.75, Conc. £2.80.
⬛ ⬛ ⬛ ⬛ €

**For rare and unusual plants visit the plant sales index on page 564**

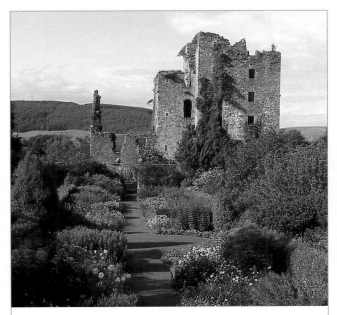

## CASTLE KENNEDY GARDENS
### STAIR ESTATES, REPHAD, STRANRAER, DUMFRIES AND GALLOWAY DG9 8BX
www.castlekennedygardens.co.uk

**Tel:** 01776 702024 / 01581 400225 (Gardens) **Fax:** 01776 706248
**E-mail:** info@castlekennedygardens.co.uk
**Owner/Contact:** The Earl of Stair
Originally laid out in 1734, the gardens are located between two natural lochs, and extend to 75 acres of landscaped terraces and avenues. With the romantic 16th century Castle Kennedy overlooking a walled garden, these gardens are famous for their woodland walks, fine specimen trees, rhododendrons and tender exotic plants.
**Location:** MAP 9:D3, OS Ref. NX109 610. 5m E of Stranraer on A75.
**Open:** 1 Apr–30 Sept: daily, 10am–5pm.
**Admission:** Adult £4, Child £1, OAP £3.
⬜ 🔲 🔲 Home baking.

## CRAIGDARROCH HOUSE
**Moniaive, Dumfriesshire DG3 4JB**
**Tel:** 01848 200202
**Owner/Contact:** Mrs Carin Sykes
**Location:** MAP 9:G1, OS Ref. NX741 909. S side of B729, 2m W of Moniaive, 19m WNW of Dumfries.
**Open:** Jul: daily, 2–4pm. Please note: no WCs.
**Admission:** £2.

## CRAIGIEBURN GARDEN
**Craigieburn House, Nr Moffat, Dumfriesshire DG10 9LF**
**Tel:** 01683 221250
**Owner/Contact:** Janet Wheatcroft
A plantsman's garden with a huge range of rare and unusual plants surrounded by natural woodland.
**Location:** MAP 13:G12, OS Ref. NT117 053. NW side of A708 to Yarrow & Selkirk, 2½m E of Moffat.
**Open:** 6 Apr–Oct: Wed–Sun (charges support Sherpa school in Nepal).
**Admission:** Adult £2.50, Child Free.

## CROSSRAGUEL ABBEY 🐚
**Maybole, Strathclyde**
**Tel:** 01655 883113
**Owner:** In the care of Historic Scotland    **Contact:** The Steward
Founded in the early 13th century by the Earl of Carrick. Remarkably complete remains include church, cloister, chapter house and much of the domestic premises.
**Location:** MAP 13:B11, OS Ref. NS275 083. 2m S of Maybole on the A77.
**Open:** 1 Apr–30 Sept: daily, 9.30am–6.30pm. Last ticket 6pm.
**Admission:** Adult £3.50, Child £1.75, Conc. £2.80.
⬜ ⬜ 🅿 ⬜ €

## CULZEAN CASTLE 🐱
**Maybole KA19 8LE**
**Tel:** 0131 243 9300
**Owner:** The National Trust for Scotland
Romantic 18th century Robert Adam clifftop mansion.
**Location:** MAP 13:B11, OS Ref. NS240 100. 12m SW of Ayr, on A719, 4m W of Maybole.

## DALGARVEN MILL MUSEUM
**Dalgarven, Dalry Road, Nr Kilwinning, Ayrshire KA13 6PL**
**Tel/Fax:** 01294 552448    **E-mail:** admin@dalgarvenmill.org.uk
**Owner:** Dalgarven Mill Trust    **Contact:** The Administrator
Museum of Ayrshire Country Life and Costume.
**Location:** MAP 13:B9, OS Ref. NS295 460. On A737 2m from Kilwinning.
**Open:** All year: Summer: Easter–end Oct: Tue–Sat, 10am–5pm, Suns, 11am–5pm. Winter: Tue–Fri, 10am–4pm, Sat 10am–5pm, Sun, 11am–5pm.
**Admission:** Charges. Groups (10+) must book.

## DEAN CASTLE COUNTRY PARK
**Dean Road, Kilmarnock, East Ayrshire KA3 1XB**
**Tel:** 01563 522702    **Fax:** 01563 572552
**Owner:** East Ayrshire Council    **Contact:** Andrew Scott-Martin
Set in 200 acres of Country Park. Visits to castle by guided tour only.
**Location:** MAP 13:C10, OS Ref. NS437 395. Off A77. 1¼m NNE of town centre.
**Open:** Country Park: All year: dawn–dusk. Please telephone 01563 578155 for Castle opening details.
**Admission:** Free (group charge on application).

## DRUMLANRIG CASTLE 🏰
*See page 455 for full page entry*

## DUNDRENNAN ABBEY 🐚
**Kirkcudbright**
**Tel:** 01557 500262
**Owner:** Historic Scotland    **Contact:** The Steward
Mary Queen of Scots spent her last night on Scottish soil in this 12th century Cistercian abbey founded by David I. The abbey stands in a small and secluded valley.
**Location:** MAP 9:G4, OS Ref. NX749 4750. 6½ m SE of Kirkcudbright on the A711.
**Open:** 1 Apr–30 Sept: daily, 9.30am–6.30pm. Last ticket 6pm. Oct: Sat–Wed; Nov–Mar: Sats & Suns only, 9.30am–4.30pm. Last ticket 4pm.
**Admission:** Adult £3, Child £1.50, Conc. £2.50.
⬜ ⬜ 🅿 ⬜ €

## GILNOCKIE TOWER
**Hollows, Canonbie, Dumfriesshire**
**Tel:** 01387 371876    **E-mail:** ted.armclan@btinternet.com
**Owner/Contact:** Edward Armstrong
16th century 5-storey tower house, on the west bank of the River Esk. A rare feature is the beacon grate perched on the roof. These were part of a signalling system to warn of an impending attack. See the view from the Tower top, learn how the reivers lived – walk upon the rich Armstrong Tartan Carpet and visit the 'First Foot' Moon Display.
**Location:** MAP 10:K2, OS Ref. NY383 787. 2m N of Canonbie on minor road E of A7 just N of Hollows.
**Open:** Summer months by guided tour at 2.30pm sharp (1 tour daily). Winter months open by appointment. Tours to be booked in advance by telephone.
**Admission:** Adult £5, Child (under 14yrs) £2.50.
🔲 Daily 2.30pm.

## GLENLUCE ABBEY 🐚
**Glenluce**
**Tel:** 01581 300541
**Owner/Contact:** In the care of Historic Scotland
A Cistercian abbey founded in 1190. Remains include a 16th century chapter house.
**Location:** MAP 9:D3, OS Ref. NX185 587. 2m NW of Glenluce village off the A75.
**Open:** 1 Apr–30 Sept: daily 9.30am–6.30pm. Last ticket 6pm. Oct: daily; Nov–Mar: Sats & Suns only, 9.30am–4.30pm. Last ticket 4pm.
**Admission:** Adult £3, Child £1.50, Conc. £2.50.
⬜ ⬜ 🅿 ⬜ ⬜ €

## GLENWHAN GARDENS
**Dunragit, Stranraer, Wigtownshire DG9 8PH**
**Tel/Fax:** 01581 400222    **Contact:** Tessa Knott
Beautiful 12 acre garden overlooking Luce Bay and the Mull of Galloway. Licensed tearoom, groups catered for.
**Location:** MAP 9:D3, OS Ref. NX150 580. N side of A75, 6m E of Stranraer.
**Open:** 1 Apr–30 Sept: daily, 10am–5pm or by appointment at other times.
**Admission:** Adult £4, Child £1.50, Conc. £3.50, Family £10. Honesty box runs until end of October.

## KELBURN CASTLE & COUNTRY CENTRE 🏠
### FAIRLIE, BY LARGS, AYRSHIRE KA29 0BE
www.kelburncountrycentre.com

Country Park and Castle tours: Earl of Glasgow
**Tel:** 01475 568685   **Fax:** 01475 568121   **E-mail:** admin@kelburncountrycentre.com
Functions in the Castle: Sue Nutsford-Mills
**Tel:** 01475 568204   **E-mail:** info@kelburncastle.com
**Owner:** The Earl of Glasgow

Kelburn is the home of the Earls of Glasgow and has been in the Boyle family for over 800 years. It is notable for its waterfalls, historic family gardens, romantic glen and unique trees, including two of the hundred most important in Scotland, and its outstanding views over the Firth of Clyde.

The Country Centre includes exhibitions, gift shop, licensed café, riding school, pottery workshop, falconry centre, full ranger service, stockade, new indoor playbarn, pet's corner and Scotland's most unusual attraction – The Secret Forest. The Castle is open for guided tours in July and August and available for weddings, conferences, dinner parties and other functions all the year round.

**Location:** MAP 13:B9, OS Ref NS210 580. A78 to Largs, 2m S of Largs.
**Open:** Country Centre: Easter–Oct: daily. Castle: July & Aug. Open by arrangement for groups at other times of the year.
**Admission:** Country Centre: Adult £7, Child/Conc. £4.50, Family £22. Groups (10+): **Adult:** £4.50, Conc. £3.50. Castle: £1.75 extra pp.

⬜🚻♿ Partial. 📷 🍴 Licensed. 🎭 July & August. By arrangement at other times of the year. 🅿 ⬛ 🐕 In grounds on leads. ❋

---

## LOGAN BOTANIC GARDEN
### Port Logan, Stranraer, Dumfries & Galloway DG9 9ND
**Tel:** 01776 860231   **Fax:** 01776 860333   **E-mail:** logan@rbge.org.uk
**Owner:** Royal Botanic Garden Edinburgh   **Contact:** The Curator

Scotland's most exotic garden. Take a trip to the south west of Scotland and experience the southern hemisphere!

**Location:** MAP 9:D4, OS Ref. NX097 430. 14m S of Stranraer on B7065, off A716.
**Open:** 1 Mar–31 Oct: daily, 10am–5pm (Apr–Sept: closes 6pm).
**Admission:** Adult £3.50, Child £1, Conc. £3, Family £8. Group discount and membership programme available.

---

## MACLELLAN'S CASTLE 🏛
### Kirkcudbright
**Tel:** 01557 331856
**Owner:** In the care of Historic Scotland   **Contact:** The Steward

Castellated mansion, built in 1577 using stone from an adjoining ruined monastery by the then provost. Elaborately planned with fine architectural details, it has been a ruin since 1752.

**Location:** MAP 9:G4, OS Ref. NX683 511. Centre of Kirkcudbright on the A711.
**Open:** 1 Apr–30 Sept: daily, 9.30am–6.30pm. Last ticket 6pm.
**Admission:** Adult £3.50, Child £1.75, Conc. £2.80.

⬜ ♿ Partial. ⬛ 🐕 €

©Ayrshire & Arran Tourist Board

Dean Castle Country Park, Kilmarnock

---

## NEW ABBEY CORN MILL 🏛
### New Abbey Village
**Tel:** 01387 850260
**Owner:** Historic Scotland   **Contact:** The Custodian

This carefully renovated 18th century water-powered oatmeal mill is in full working order and regular demonstrations are given for visitors in the summer.

**Location:** MAP 10:I3, OS Ref. NX962 663. 8m S of Dumfries on the A710. Close to Sweetheart Abbey.
**Open:** 1 Apr–30 Sept: daily, 9.30am–6.30pm. Last ticket 6pm. 1 Oct–31 Mar: Sat–Wed, 9.30am–4.30pm. Last ticket 4pm.
**Admission:** Adult £4, Child £2, Conc. £3.

⬜ ⬛ ❋ €

---

## RAMMERSCALES 🏠
### Lockerbie, Dumfriesshire DG11 1LD
**Tel:** 01387 810229   **Fax:** 01387 810940
**Owner/Contact:** Mr M A Bell Macdonald

Georgian house, with extensive library and fine views over Annandale.

**Location:** MAP 10:I2, OS Ref. NY080 780. W side of B7020, 3m S of Lochmoben.
**Open:** Last week in Jul, 1st three weeks in Aug: daily (excluding Sat), 2–5pm.
**Admission:** Adult £5, Conc. £2.50.

---

## SORN CASTLE 🏠
### Ayrshire KA5 6HR
**Tel:** 01290 551555
**Owner/Contact:** Mrs R G McIntyre

Dating from the 14th century, the Castle stands on a cliff overlooking the River Ayr, surrounded by wooded grounds. It has been enlarged throughout the centuries, most recently in 1908. Sorn contains many fine Scottish paintings and artifacts.

**Location:** MAP 13:C10, OS Ref. NS555 265. 4m E of Mauchline on B743.
**Open:** 14 Jul–11 Aug: daily, 2–4pm and by appointment.
**Admission:** Adult £4.

🎭 🐕

## STRANRAER CASTLE

**Stranraer, Galloway**
**Tel:** 01776 705088   **Fax:** 01776 705835
**Owner:** Dumfries & Galloway Council   **Contact:** John Picken
Also referred to as the Castle of St John. A much altered 16th century L-plan tower house, now a museum.
**Location:** MAP 9:D3, OS Ref. NX061 608. In Stranraer, towards centre, ¼m short of the harbour.
**Open:** Easter–mid Sept: Mon–Sat, 10am–1pm & 2–5pm.
**Admission:** Free.

## SWEETHEART ABBEY

**New Abbey Village**
**Tel:** 01387 850397
**Owner:** In the care of Historic Scotland   **Contact:** The Steward
Cistercian abbey founded in 1273 by Devorgilla, in memory of her husband John Balliol. A principal feature is the well-preserved precinct wall enclosing 30 acres.
**Location:** MAP 10:I3, OS Ref. NX965 663. In New Abbey Village, on A710 8m S of Dumfries.
**Open:** 1 Apr–30 Sept: daily, 9.30am–6.30pm. Last ticket 6pm. 1 Oct–31 Mar: Sat–Wed, 9.30am–4.30pm. Last ticket 4pm.
**Admission:** Adult £3, Child £1.50, Conc. £2.50.
P ❋ €

## THREAVE CASTLE

**Castle Douglas**
**Tel:** 07711 223101
**Owner:** The National Trust for Scotland   **Contact:** Historic Scotland
Built by Archibald the Grim in the late 14th century, early stronghold of the Black Douglases. Around its base is an artillery fortification built before 1455 when the castle was besieged by James II. Ring the bell and the custodian will come to ferry you over. Long walk to property. Owned by The National Trust for Scotland but under the guardianship of Historic Scotland.
**Location:** MAP 9:H3, OS Ref. NX739 623. 2m W of Castle Douglas on the A75.
**Open:** 1 Apr–30 Sept: daily, 9.30am–6.30pm. Last ticket 6pm.
**Admission:** Adult £4, Child £2, Conc. £3. Charges include ferry trip.

## WHITHORN PRIORY & MUSEUM

**Whithorn**
**Tel:** 01988 500508
**Owner:** In the care of Historic Scotland   **Contact:** The Project Manager
The site of the first Christian church in Scotland. Founded as 'Candida Casa' by St Ninian in the early 5th century it later became the cathedral church of Galloway. Visitors can now see the collection of early Christian carved crosses in a newly refurbished museum.
**Location:** MAP 9:F4, OS Ref. NX445 403. At Whithorn on the A746. 18m S of Newton Stewart.
**Open:** 21 Mar–31 Oct: daily, 10.30am–5pm.
**Admission:** Adult £3.50, Child £1.75, Conc. £2.50. Joint ticket gives entry to Priory, Priory Museum and 'The Story of Whithorn'.
▢ ⬚ ▣ P €

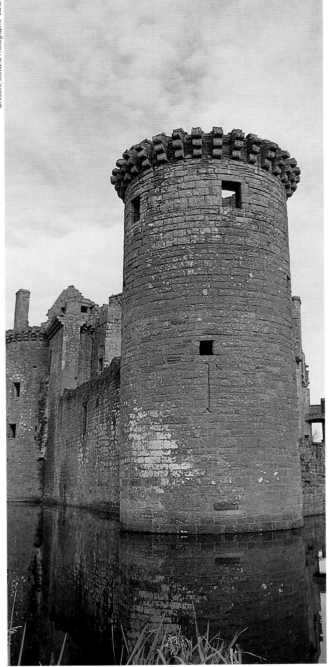

©Historic Scotland Photographic Library

Caerlaverock Castle, Dumfries

©Ayrshire & Arran Tourist Board

Ayrshire Coast – looking towards Arran

### ■ Owner
The Earl of Rosebery

### ■ Contact
The Administrator
Dalmeny House
South Queensferry
Edinburgh EH30 9TQ

**Tel:** 0131 331 1888
**Fax:** 0131 331 1788
**E-mail:** events@
dalmeny.co.uk

### ■ Location
**MAP 13:G8**
**OS Ref. NT167 779**

From Edinburgh A90,
B924, 7m N, A90 ½m.

On south shore
of Firth of Forth.

**Bus:** From St Andrew
Square to Chapel Gate
1m from House.

**Rail:** Dalmeny
station 3m.

**Taxi:** Call us Cabs
0131 331 3232.

### ■ Opening Times
**Summer**
July and August
Sun–Tue, 2–5.30pm.
Last admission 4.30pm.

**Winter**
Open at other times by
appointment only.

### ■ Admission
Summer
| | |
|---|---|
| Adult | £5.50 |
| Child (10–16yrs) | £3.50 |
| OAP | £4.50 |
| Student | £4.50 |
| Groups (20+) | £4.00 |

# DALMENY HOUSE

www.dalmeny.co.uk

Dalmeny House rejoices in one of the most beautiful and unspoilt settings in Great Britain, yet it is only seven miles from Scotland's capital, Edinburgh, fifteen minutes from Edinburgh airport and less than an hour's drive from Glasgow. It is an eminently suitable venue for group visits, business functions, meetings and special events, including product launches. Outdoor activities, such as off-road driving, can be arranged.

Dalmeny House, the family home of the Earls of Rosebery for over 300 years, boasts superb collections of porcelain and tapestries, fine paintings by Gainsborough, Raeburn, Reynolds and Lawrence, together with the exquisite Mentmore Rothschild collection of 18th century French furniture. There is also the Napoleonic collection, assembled by the 5th Earl of Rosebery, Prime Minister, historian and owner of three Derby winners.

The Hall, Library and Dining Room will lend a memorable sense of occasion to corporate receptions, luncheons and dinners. A wide range of entertainment can also be provided, from a clarsach player to a floodlit pipe band Beating the Retreat.

ℹ️ Fashion shows, product launches, archery, clay pigeon shooting, shows, filming, background photography, small meetings and special events. Lectures on House, contents and family history. Helicopter landing area.

🍽️ Conferences and functions, buffets, lunches, dinners.

♿ Partially suitable. Visitors may alight at entrance. WC.

☕ Teas, groups can book in advance.

🚶 Obligatory. Special interest tours can be arranged outside normal opening hours.

🅿️ 60 cars, 3 coaches. Parking for functions in front of house.

# HOPETOUN HOUSE

www.hopetounhouse.com

Hopetoun House is a unique gem of Europe's architectural heritage and undoubtedly 'Scotland's Finest Stately Home'. Situated on the shores of the Firth of Forth, it is one of the most splendid examples of the work of Scottish architects Sir William Bruce and William Adam. The interior of the house, with opulent gilding and classical motifs, reflects the aristocratic grandeur of the early 18th century, whilst its magnificent parkland has fine views across the Forth to the hills of Fife. The house is approached from the Royal Drive, used only by members of the Royal Family, notably King George IV in 1822 and Her Majesty Queen Elizabeth II in 1988.

Hopetoun is really two houses in one, the oldest part of the house was designed by Sir William Bruce and built between 1699 and 1707. It shows some of the finest examples in Scotland of carving, wainscotting and ceiling painting. In 1721 William Adam started enlarging the house by adding the magnificent façade, colonnades and grand State apartments which were the focus for social life and entertainment in the 18th century.

The house is set in 100 acres of rolling parkland including fine woodland walks, the red deer park, the spring garden with a profusion of wild flowers, and numerous picturesque picnic spots.

Hopetoun has been home of the Earls of Hopetoun, later created Marquesses of Linlithgow, since it was built in 1699 and in 1974 a charitable trust was created to preserve the house with its historic contents and surrounding landscape for the benefit of the public for all time.

**i** Private functions, special events, antiques fairs, concerts, Scottish gala evenings, conferences, wedding ceremonies and receptions, grand piano, helicopter landing. No smoking or flash photography in house.

Receptions, gala dinners.

Partial.

Licensed.

By arrangement.

**P** Close to the house for cars and coaches. Book if possible, allow 1–2hrs for visit (min).

Special tours of house and/or grounds for different age/ interest groups.

No dogs in house, on leads in grounds.

## ■ Owner
Hopetoun House
Preservation Trust

## ■ Contact
Mhairi MacDougall
Hopetoun House
South Queensferry
Edinburgh
West Lothian  EH30 9SL

**Tel:** 0131 331 2451
**Fax:** 0131 319 1885
**E-mail:** marketing@
hopetounhouse.com

## ■ Location
**MAP 13:F7**
**OS Ref. NT089 790**

2½m W of Forth Road
Bridge.

12m W of Edinburgh
(25 mins. drive).

34m E of Glasgow
(50 mins. drive).

## ■ Opening Times
**Summer**
6 April–30 September:
Daily, 10.30am–5pm.
Last admission 4pm.

**Winter**
By appointment only
for Groups (20+).

## ■ Admission
**House & Grounds**

| | |
|---|---|
| Adult | £8.00 |
| Child (5–16yrs)* | £4.25 |
| Conc/Student | £7.00 |
| Family (2+2) | £22.00 |
| Additional Child | £3.00 |
| Groups | £7.00 |

**Grounds only**

| | |
|---|---|
| Adult | £3.70 |
| Child (5–16yrs)* | £2.20 |
| Conc/Student | £3.20 |
| Family (2+2) | £10.00 |
| Groups | £3.20 |

**School Visits**

| | |
|---|---|
| Child | £5.50 |
| Teachers | Free |

*Under 5yrs Free.

Winter group rates on request.

Admission to Tearoom Free.

## ■ Special Events
**July 29**
Summer Fair

**November 23–25**
Christmas Fair

## Conference/Function

| ROOM | SIZE | MAX CAPACITY |
|---|---|---|
| Ballroom | 92' x 35' | 300 |
| Tapestry Rm | 37' x 24' | 100 |
| Red Drawing Rm | 44' x 24' | 100 |
| State Dining Rm | 39' x 23' | 20 |
| Stables | 92' x 22' | 200 |

Edinburgh City, Coast & Countryside

### ■ Owner
Official Residence of Her Majesty The Queen

### ■ Contact
Ticket Sales & Information Office Buckingham Palace London SW1A 1AA

**Tel:** 0131 556 5100
Groups (15+):
020 7766 7321
**Fax:** 020 7930 9625
**E-mail:** bookinginfo@
royalcollection.org.uk

### ■ Location
**MAP 21**
**OS Ref. NT269 739**

Central Edinburgh, end of Royal Mile.

### ■ Opening Times
**Palace of Holyroodhouse**
April–October:
Daily (closed 6 April and during Royal Visits), 9.30am–6pm.
Last admission 5pm.

November–March:
Daily (closed 25/26 December and during Royal Visits), 9.30am–4.30pm.
Last admission 3.30pm.

Opening times are subject to change at short notice. Please check before planning a visit.

Private tours of the Palace and The Queen's Gallery are available for pre-booked groups (15+).
Tel: 020 7766 7322.

**The Queen's Gallery**
Daily (closed 6 April, and between exhibitions, 25/26 December).
Opening times as Palace.

Each exhibition is priced separately. Timed admission may operate during peak periods.

### ■ Admission
For admission prices please call the Ticket Sales & Information Office.
Groups (15+) discounts available.

Information correct at time of going to print.

John Freeman/ The Royal Collection © 2007 HM Queen Elizabeth II

# PALACE OF HOLYROODHOUSE & THE QUEEN'S GALLERY

www.royalcollection.org.uk

The Palace of Holyroodhouse, the official residence in Scotland of Her Majesty The Queen, stands at the end of Edinburgh's Royal Mile against the spectacular backdrop of Arthur's Seat. This fine baroque palace is closely associated with Scotland's rich history. Today the Royal Apartments are used by The Queen for State ceremonies and official entertaining. They are finely decorated with magnificent works of art from the Royal Collection.

The Palace is perhaps best known as the home of Mary, Queen of Scots and was the setting for the many dramatic episodes in her short and turbulent reign. She witnessed the brutal murder of her secretary, Rizzio, by her jealous second husband, Lord Darnley, in her private apartments at Holyrood. Many of her personal belongings are on display in the Palace.

### The Queen's Gallery, Edinburgh
The Gallery provides purpose-built facilities and state-of-the-art environmental controls, which enable exhibitions of the most delicate works from the Royal Collection to be shown.

**Amazing Rare Things:** The Art of Natural History in the Age of Discovery. 2 March–16 September 2007.

**Bruegel to Rubens:** Flemish Painting in the Royal Collection. 28 September–6 April 2008.

See website for more details of exhibitions.

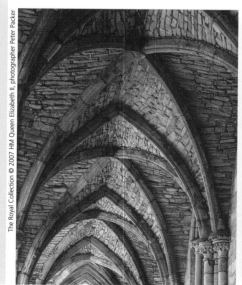

The Royal Collection © 2007 HM Queen Elizabeth II, photographer Peter Packer

The Royal Collection © 2007 HM Queen Elizabeth II, photographer Allan Forbes

 Please book in advance.

 Palace.

 Guide dogs only.

## AMISFIELD MAINS

**Nr Haddington, East Lothian EH41 3SA**
**Tel:** 01875 870201 **Fax:** 01875 870620
**Owner:** Wemyss and March Estates Management Co Ltd **Contact:** M Andrews
Georgian farmhouse with gothic barn and cottage.
**Location:** MAP 14:I8, OS Ref. NT526 755. Between Haddington and East Linton on A199.
**Open:** Exterior only: By appointment, Wemyss and March Estates Office, Longniddry, East Lothian EH32 0PY.
**Admission:** Please contact for details.

## ARNISTON HOUSE 🏠
### GOREBRIDGE, MIDLOTHIAN EH23 4RY
www.arniston-house.co.uk

**Tel/Fax:** 01875 830515 **E-mail:** arnistonhouse@btconnect.com
**Owner:** Mrs A Dundas-Bekker **Contact:** Miss H Dundas-Bekker
Magnificent William Adam mansion started in 1726. Fine plasterwork, Scottish portraiture, period furniture and other fascinating contents. Beautiful country setting beloved by Sir Walter Scott.
**Location:** MAP 13:H9, OS Ref. NT326 595. Off B6372, 1m from A7, Temple direction.
**Open:** Apr, May & Jun: Tue & Wed; 1 Jul–16 Sept: Tue, Wed & Sun, guided tours at 2pm & 3.30pm. Pre-arranged groups (10–50) accepted all year.
**Admission:** Adult £5, Child £2, Conc. £4.
ℹ️ No inside photography. 🚻 WC. 🎫 Obligatory. 🅿️ 🐕 In grounds, on leads. ✳️

Who's offering **accommodation?**
See our index on page 575

## BEANSTON

**Nr Haddington, East Lothian EH41 3SB**
**Tel:** 01875 870201 **Fax:** 01875 870620
**Owner:** Wemyss and March Estates Management Co Ltd **Contact:** M Andrews
Georgian farmhouse with Georgian orangery.
**Location:** MAP 14:I8, OS Ref. NT546 763. Between Haddington and East Linton on A199.
**Open:** Exterior only: By appointment, Wemyss and March Estates Office, Longniddry, East Lothian EH32 0PY.
**Admission:** Please contact for details.

## BLACKNESS CASTLE 🏠

**Blackness**
**Tel:** 01506 834807
**Owner:** In the care of Historic Scotland **Contact:** The Steward
One of Scotland's most important strongholds. Built in the 14th century and massively strengthened in the 16th century as an artillery fortress, it has been a royal castle and a prison armaments depot and film location for Hamlet. It was restored by the Office of Works in the 1920s. It stands on a promontory in the Firth of Forth.
**Location:** MAP 13:F7, OS Ref. NT055 803. 4m NE of Linlithgow on the Firth of Forth, off the A904.
**Open:** 1 Apr–30 Sept: daily, 9.30am–6.30pm. Last ticket 6pm. 1 Oct–31 Mar: daily, 9.30am–4.30pm. Last ticket 4pm. Closed Thur & Fri in winter.
**Admission:** Adult £4, Child £2, Conc. £3.
⬜ 📷 🅿️ 🐕 ✳️ €

## CRAIGMILLAR CASTLE 🏠

**Edinburgh**
**Tel:** 0131 661 4445
**Owner:** In the care of Historic Scotland **Contact:** The Steward
Mary, Queen of Scots fled to Craigmillar after the murder of Rizzio. This handsome structure with courtyard and gardens covers an area of one and a quarter acres. Built around an L-plan tower house of the early 15th century including a range of private rooms linked to the hall of the old tower.
**Location:** MAP 13:H8, OS Ref. NT285 710. 2½m SE of Edinburgh off the A68.
**Open:** 1 Apr–30 Sept: daily, 9.30am–6.30pm. Last ticket 6pm. 1 Oct–31 Mar: daily, 9.30am–4.30pm. Last ticket 4pm. Closed Thur & Fri in winter.
**Admission:** Adult £4, Child £2, Conc. £3.
⬜ 📷 🅿️ ✳️ €

## CRICHTON CASTLE 🏠

**Pathhead**
**Tel:** 01875 320017
**Owner:** In the care of Historic Scotland **Contact:** The Steward
A large and sophisticated castle with a spectacular façade of faceted stonework in an Italian style added by the Earl of Bothwell between 1581 and 1591 following a visit to Italy. Mary Queen of Scots attended a wedding here.
**Location:** MAP 13:H8, OS Ref. NT380 612. 2½m SSW of Pathhead off the A68.
**Open:** 1 Apr–30 Sept: daily, 9.30am–6.30pm, last ticket 6pm.
**Admission:** Adult £3.50, Child £1.75, Conc. £2.80.
🅿️ €

## DALMENY HOUSE

*See page 460 for full page entry.*

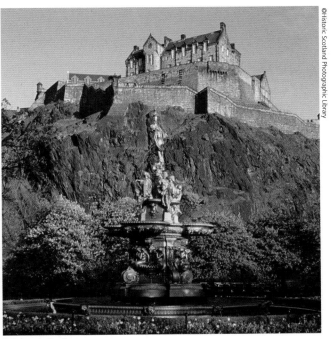

©Historic Scotland Photographic Library

Edinburgh Castle

©Historic Scotland Photographic Library

©Historic Scotland Photographic Library

## DIRLETON CASTLE & GARDEN

### DIRLETON, EAST LOTHIAN EH39 5ER

**Tel:** 01620 850330

**Owner:** In the care of Historic Scotland     **Contact:** The Steward

The oldest part of this romantic castle dates from the 13th century, when it was built by the De Vaux family. The renowned gardens, first laid out in the 16th century, now include a magnificent Arts and Crafts herbaceous border (the longest in the world) and a re-created Victorian Garden. In the picturesque village of Dirleton.

**Location:** MAP 14:I7, OS Ref. NT516 839. In Dirleton, 2m W of North Berwick on the A198.

**Open:** Apr–Sept: daily, 9.30am–6.30pm. Oct–Mar: daily, 9.30am–4.30pm. Last ticket 30 mins before closing.

**Admission:** Adult £4.50, Child £2.25, Conc. £3.50. 10% discount for groups (10+).

Partial. P Free if booked. €

## EDINBURGH CASTLE

### CASTLEHILL, EDINBURGH EH1 2NG

**Tel:** 0131 225 9846   **Fax:** 0131 220 4733

**Owner:** Historic Scotland     **Contact:** The Stewards

Scotland's most famous castle, dominating the capital's skyline and giving stunning views of the city and countryside. Home to the Scottish crown jewels, the Stone of Destiny and Mons Meg. Other highlights include St Margaret's Chapel, the Great Hall and the Scottish National War Memorial.

**Location:** MAP 21, OS Ref. NT252 736. At the top of the Royal Mile in Edinburgh.

**Open:** Apr–Sept: daily, 9.30am–6pm. Oct–Mar: daily, 9.30am–5pm. Last ticket 45 mins before closing.

**Admission:** Adult £11, Child £5.50, Conc. £9. Pre-booked school visits available Free, except May–Aug.

Private evening hire. Partial. WCs. Courtesy vehicle. Licensed. In 6 languages. P (except Jun–Oct). Guide dogs. €

## DUNGLASS COLLEGIATE CHURCH

**Cockburnspath**

**Tel:** 0131 668 8800

**Owner:** In the care of Historic Scotland

Founded in 1450 for a college of canons by Sir Alexander Hume. A handsome cross-shaped building with vaulted nave, choir and transepts.

**Location:** MAP 14:J8, OS67 NT766 718. 1m NW of Cockburnspath. SW of A1.

**Open:** All year.

**Admission:** Free.

## THE GEORGIAN HOUSE

**7 Charlotte Square, Edinburgh EH2 4DR**

**Tel:** 0131 243 9300

**Owner:** The National Trust for Scotland

A good example of the neo-classical 'palace front'. Three floors are furnished as they would have been around 1796. There is an array of china and silver, pictures and furniture, gadgets and utensils.

**Location:** MAP 21, OS Ref. NT247 738. In Charlotte Square.

## GLADSTONE'S LAND

**477b Lawnmarket, Royal Mile, Edinburgh EH1 2NT**

**Tel:** 0131 243 9300

**Owner:** The National Trust for Scotland

Gladstone's Land was the home of a prosperous Edinburgh merchant in the 17th century. Decorated and furnished to give visitors an impression of life in Edinburgh's Old Town some 300 years ago.

**Location:** MAP 21, OS Ref. NT255 736. In Edinburgh's Royal Mile, near the castle.

Many properties hold **special events** throughout the year See the index on page 585

Gosford House, Longniddry

## GOSFORD HOUSE 🏛
### LONGNIDDRY, EAST LOTHIAN EH32 0PX

**Tel:** 01875 870201   **Owner/Contact:** The Earl of Wemyss
Though the core of the house is Robert Adam, the family home is in the South Wing built by William Young in 1890. This contains the celebrated Marble Hall and a fine collection of paintings and works of art. The house is set in extensive policies with an 18th century Pleasure Garden and Ponds. Greylag geese and swans abound.
**Location:** MAP 14:I7, OS Ref. NT453 786. Off A198 2m NE of Longniddry.
**Open:** 15 Jun–10 Aug: Fri–Sun, 2–5pm.
**Admission:** Adult £6, Child £1.
🅿 ♿ In grounds, on leads.

### HAILES CASTLE 🏛

**East Linton**
**Tel:** 0131 668 8800
**Owner:** In the care of Historic Scotland
Beautifully-sited ruin incorporating a fortified manor of the 13th century. It was extended in the 14th and 15th centuries. There are two vaulted pit prisons.
**Location:** MAP 14:I8, OS Ref. NT575 758. 1½ m SW of East Linton. 4m E of Haddington. S of A1.
**Open:** All year.
**Admission:** Free.
🅿 ❋

### HARELAW FARMHOUSE

**Nr Longniddry, East Lothian  EH32 0PH**
**Tel:** 01875 870201   **Fax:** 01875 870620
**Owner:** Wemyss and March Estates Management Co Ltd     **Contact:** M Andrews
Early 19th century 2-storey farmhouse built as an integral part of the steading. Dovecote over entrance arch.
**Location:** MAP 14:I8, OS Ref. NT450 766. Between Longniddry and Drem on B1377.
**Open:** Exteriors only: By appointment, Wemyss and March Estates Office, Longniddry, East Lothian  EH32 0PY.
**Admission:** Please contact for details.

### HOPETOUN HOUSE 🏛          *See page 461 for full page entry.*

### HOUSE OF THE BINNS 👹

**Linlithgow, West Lothian  EH49 7NA**
**Tel:** 0131 243 9300
**Owner:** The National Trust for Scotland
17th century house, home of the Dalyells, one of Scotland's great families, since 1612.
**Location:** MAP 13:F7, OS Ref. NT051 786. Off A904, 15m W of Edinburgh. 3m E of Linlithgow.

## GREYWALLS 🏛
### MUIRFIELD, GULLANE, EAST LOTHIAN EH31 2EG

www.greywalls.co.uk

**Tel:** 01620 842144   **Fax:** 01620 842241   **E-mail:** hotel@greywalls.co.uk
**Owner:** Giles Weaver    **Contact:** Mrs Sue Prime
Stunning Edwardian Country House Hotel only 30 minutes from the centre of Edinburgh. Close to wonderful golf courses and beaches. Designed by Sir Edwin Lutyens with secluded walled gardens attributed to Gertrude Jekyll. Greywalls offers the delights of an award-winning menu and an excellent wine list in this charming and relaxed environment (non residents welcome).
**Location:** MAP 14:I7, OS Ref. NT490 835. Off A198, 5m W of North Berwick, 30 mins from Edinburgh.
**Open:** Mar–Dec inclusive.
🍴 ⑪ ♿

## LENNOXLOVE HOUSE 🏛
### HADDINGTON, EAST LOTHIAN EH41 4NZ

www.lennoxlove.com

**Tel:** 01620 823720   **Fax:** 01620 825112   **E-mail:** susanne-martin@lennoxlove.com
**Owner:** Lennoxlove House Ltd    **Contact:** Susanne Martin, General Manager
Service, Style and Seclusion. House to many of Scotland's finest artefacts, including the Death Mask of Mary, Queen of Scots, furniture and porcelain collected by the Douglas, Hamilton and Stewart families. Open to the public and available for events, the house lends itself perfectly to intimate parties offering 11 luxury suites for an overnight stay.
**Location:** MAP 14:I8, OS Ref. NT515 721. 18m E of Edinburgh, 1m S of Haddington.
**Open:** Jul–Oct: Tues, Thurs, & Suns, 3–5pm. Guided tours available.
🍴 🎦 ♿

Edinburgh City, Coast & Countryside

## LIBERTON HOUSE

**73 Liberton Drive, Edinburgh  EH16 6NP**
**Tel:** 0131 467 7777  **Fax:** 0131 467 7774  **E-mail:** mail@ngra.co.uk
**Owner/Contact:** Nicholas Groves-Raines
Built around 1600 for the Littles of Liberton, this harled L-plan house has been carefully restored by the current architect owner using original detailing and extensive restoration of the principal structure. Public access restricted to the Great Hall and Old Kitchen. The restored garden layout suggests the original and there is a late 17th century lectern doocot by the entrance drive.
**Location:** MAP 13:H8, OS Ref. NT267 694. 73 Liberton Drive, Edinburgh.
**Open:** 1 Mar–31 Oct: 10am–4.30pm, by prior appointment only.
**Admission:** Free.
&#91;&#93; Unsuitable. **P** Limited. &#91;&#93;

©Historic Scotland Photographic Library

# LINLITHGOW PALACE
### LINLITHGOW, WEST LOTHIAN  EH49 7AL

**Tel:** 01506 842896
**Owner:** Historic Scotland    **Contact:** The Steward
The magnificent remains of a great royal palace set in its own park and beside Linlithgow Loch. A favoured residence of the Stewart monarchs, James V and his daughter Mary, Queen of Scots were born here. Bonnie Prince Charlie stayed here during his bid to regain the British crown.
**Location:** MAP 13:F8, OS Ref. NT003 774. In the centre of Linlithgow off the M9.
**Open:** Apr–Sept: daily, 9.30am–6.30pm. Oct–Mar: Daily, 9.30am–4.30pm. Last ticket 30 mins before closing.
**Admission:** Adult £5, Child £2.50, Conc. £4. 10% discount for groups (10+).
&#91;i&#93; Picnic area. &#91;&#93; Private evening hire. &#91;&#93; Partial. &#91;&#93; Free if booked.
**P** Cars only. &#91;&#93; In grounds, on leads. &#91;&#93; €

See which properties offer **educational facilities** or **school visits** in our index on page 571

## NEWLISTON

**Kirkliston, West Lothian  EH29 9EB**
**Tel:** 0131 333 3231
**Owner/Contact:** Mrs Caroline Maclachlan
Late Robert Adam house. 18th century designed landscape, rhododendrons, azaleas and water features. On Sundays there is a ride-on steam model railway from 2–5pm.
**Location:** MAP 13:G8, OS Ref. NT110 735. 8m W of Edinburgh, 3m S of Forth Road Bridge, off B800.
**Open:** 2 May–3 Jun: Wed–Sun, 2–6pm. Also by appointment.
**Admission:** Adult £2, Conc. £1.
&#91;&#93; Grounds. &#91;&#93; In grounds, on leads. &#91;&#93;

## NIDDRY CASTLE

**By Winchburgh, West Lothian EH52 6RP**
**Tel:** 01506 891751
**Owner/Contact:** Richard Nairn
Niddry Castle is a late 15th/early 16th century L -plan tower built by George, 3rd Lord Seton. In 1676 it was sold to John Hope whose family lived there for around 30 years until Hopetoun House was built and the castle subsequently abandoned. It was ruined for almost 300 years until the mid-1980s when it was partially restored.
**Location:** MAP 13:F8, OS Ref. NT095 734. 1km S of Winchburgh, towards A89.
**Open:** 1 Sept–30 Sept; Sat & Sun, 1.30–4.30pm; Mon & Wed, 5–6pm; Tues & Fri, 3.30–5pm (except Tue 25 Sept). Limited access to interior pending restoration.
**Admission:** Adult £2, Child £1.
&#91;&#93; Unsuitable. **P** Limited. No coaches.  &#91;&#93; Guide dogs only.

## PALACE OF HOLYROODHOUSE & THE QUEEN'S GALLERY

*See page 462 for full page entry.*

## PRESTON MILL

**East Linton, East Lothian  EH40 3DS**
**Tel:** 0131 243 9300
**Owner:** The National Trust for Scotland    **Contact:** Property Manager
For centuries there has been a mill on this site and the present one operated commercially until 1957.
**Location:** MAP 14:I7, OS Ref. NT590 770. Off the A1, in East Linton, 23m E of Edinburgh.

## RED ROW

**Aberlady, East Lothian**
**Tel:** 01875 870201  **Fax:** 01875 870620
**Owner:** Wemyss & March Estates Management Co Ltd    **Contact:** M Andrews
Terraced Cottages.
**Location:** MAP 14:I7, OS Ref. NT464 798. Main Street, Aberlady, East Lothian.
**Open:** Exterior only. By appointment, Wemyss & March Estates Office, Longniddry, East Lothian  EH32 0PY.
**Admission:** Please contact for details.

## ROYAL BOTANIC GARDEN EDINBURGH

**20A Inverleith Row, Edinburgh  EH3 5LR**
**Tel:** 0131 552 7171  **Fax:** 0131 248 2901  **E-mail:** info@rbge.org.uk
**Contact:** Press Office
Scotland's premier garden. Discover the wonders of the plant kingdom in over 70 acres of beautifully landscaped grounds.
**Location:** MAP 21, OS Ref. NT249 751. Off A902, 1m N of city centre.
**Open:** Daily (except 25 Dec & 1 Jan): open 10am, closing: Nov–Feb: 4pm; Mar & Oct: 6pm; Apr–Sept: 7pm.
**Admission:** Free, with an admission charge on the Glasshouses.

## ST MARY'S EPISCOPAL CATHEDRAL

**Palmerston Place, Edinburgh  EH12 5AW**
**Tel:** 0131 225 6293  **Fax:** 0131 225 3181
**Contact:** Cathedral Secretary
Neo-gothic grandeur in the classical new town. Designed by G Gilbert Scott.
**Location:** MAP 21, OS Ref. NT241 735. 1/2 m W of west end of Princes Street.
**Open:** Mon–Fri, 7.30am–6pm; Sat & Sun, 7.30am–5pm. Sun services: 8am, 10.30am & 3.30pm. Services: Weekdays, 7.30am, 1.05pm & 5.30pm; Thurs, 11.30am, Sat, 7.30am.
**Admission:** Free.

## SCOTTISH NATIONAL PORTRAIT GALLERY

**1 Queen Street, Edinburgh  EH2 1JD**
**Tel:** 0131 624 6200
Unique visual history of Scotland.
**Location:** MAP 21, OS Ref. NT256 742. At E end of Queen Street, 300yds N of Princes Street.
**Open:** All year to permanent collection: daily, 10am–5pm (Thurs closes 7pm). Closed 25 & 26 Dec. Open 1 Jan, 12 noon–5pm.
**Admission:** Free

## TANTALLON CASTLE

### BY NORTH BERWICK, EAST LOTHIAN  EH39 5PN

**Tel:** 01620 892727

**Owner:** In the care of Historic Scotland    **Contact:** The Steward

Set on the edge of the cliffs, looking out to the Bass Rock, this formidable castle was a stronghold of the powerful Douglas family. The castle has earthwork defences and a massive 80-foot high 14th century curtain wall. Interpretive displays include a replica gun.

**Location:** MAP 14:I7, OS67 NT595 850. 3m E of North Berwick off the A198.

**Open:** Apr–Sept: daily, 9.30am–6.30pm. Last ticket 6pm. Oct–Mar: Sat–Wed, 9.30am–4.30pm. Last ticket 4pm.

**Admission:** Adult £4.50, Child £2.25, Conc. £3.50 10% discount for groups (11+).

ℹ️ Picnic area. 🅿 Partial. 🅿 Booked school visits free.
In grounds, on leads. €

## TRINITY HOUSE MARITIME MUSEUM

**99 Kirkgate, Edinburgh  EH6 6BJ**

**Tel:** 0131 5543289

**Owner:** Historic Scotland

**Contact:** The Monument Manager

Tucked away in a side street within a few minutes' walk from the Royal Yacht Britannia, this fine Georgian mansion contains a treasure trove of maritime art and artefacts. Among them are paintings by Henry Raeburn, including a specially commissioned portrait of Admiral Duncan, victor of the 1797 Battle of Camperdown. The site has been home to the Incorporation of Masters and Mariners of Trinity House, Leith, since the Middle Ages. Many of the artefacts were given to Trinity House by Leith sailors who travelled to the remotest parts of the world in centuries gone by.

**Location:** MAP 13:G8, OS Ref. NT269 760, Kirkgate, Leith, Edinburgh.

**Admission:** Adult £4, Child £2, Conc £3. Includes boat trip.

**Open:** Visits need to be prebooked by telephone.

🅿

Crichton Castle, Pathhead

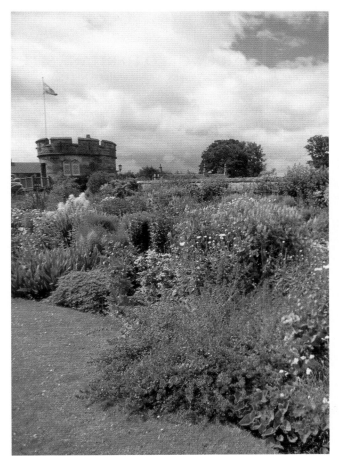

Dirleton Castle & Grounds

## BURRELL COLLECTION

**Pollok Country Park, 2060 Pollokshaws Road, Glasgow  G43 1AT**
**Tel:** 0141 287 2550  **Fax:** 0141 287 2597
**Owner:** Glasgow Museums
An internationally renowned, outstanding collection of art.
**Location:** MAP 13:C8, OS Ref. NS555 622. Glasgow 15 min drive.
**Open:** All year: Mon–Thur & Sats, 10am–5pm, Fri & Sun, 11am–5pm. Closed 25/26 Dec, 31 Dec (pm) & 1/2 Jan.
**Admission:** Free. Small charge may apply for temporary exhibitions.

## COLZIUM HOUSE & WALLED GARDEN

**Colzium-Lennox Estate, off Stirling Road, Kilsyth  G65 0RZ**
**Tel/Fax:** 01236 828156
**Owner:** North Lanarkshire Council    **Contact:** John Whittaker
A walled garden with an extensive collection of conifers, rare shrubs and trees, curling pond, picnic tables, woodland walks.
**Location:** MAP 13:D7, OS Ref. NS722 786. Off A803 Banknock to Kirkintilloch Road. ½m E of Kilsyth.
**Open:** Walled Garden: Apr–Sept: daily, 12noon–7pm; Oct–Mar: Sats & Suns, 12noon–4pm. House undergoing refurbishment.
**Admission:** Free.

## COREHOUSE 🏠

**Lanark ML11 9TQ**
**Tel:** 01555 663126
**Owner:** Colonel D A S Cranstoun of that Ilk TD    **Contact:** Estate Office
Designed by Sir Edward Blore and built in the 1820s, Corehouse is a pioneering example of the Tudor Architectural Revival in Scotland.
**Location:** MAP 13:E9, OS Ref. NS882 416. On S bank of the Clyde above the village of Kirkfieldbank.
**Open:** 1–23 May & 8–17 Sept: Sat–Wed. Guided tours: weekdays: 1.30 & 2.30pm, weekends: 2 & 3pm. Closed Thurs & Fri.
**Admission:** Adult £6, Child (under 14yrs)/OAP £3.
🚶 Obligatory.

## CRAIGNETHAN CASTLE 🏰

**Lanark, Strathclyde**
**Tel:** 01555 860364
**Owner:** Historic Scotland    **Contact:** The Steward
In a picturesque setting overlooking the River Nethan and defended by a wide and deep ditch with an unusual caponier, a stone vaulted artillery chamber, unique in Britain.
**Location:** MAP 13:E9, OS Ref. NS815 463. 5½m WNW of Lanark off the A72. ½m footpath to W.
**Open:** 1 Apr–30 Sept: daily, 9.30am–6.30pm. Oct: Sat–Wed; Nov–Mar: Sats & Suns only, 9.30am–4.30pm.
**Admission:** Adult £3.50, Child £1.75, Conc. £2.80.
ⓘ Picnic area. WC. 🖼 🅿 ✲ €

## GLASGOW CATHEDRAL 🏰

**Castle Street, Glasgow**
**Tel:** 0141 552 6891
**Owner:** Historic Scotland    **Contact:** The Steward
The only Scottish mainland medieval cathedral to have survived the Reformation complete. Built over the tomb of St Kentigern. Notable features in this splendid building are the elaborately vaulted crypt, the stone screen of the early 15th century and the unfinished Blackadder Aisle.
**Location:** MAP 13:D8, OS Ref. NS603 656. E end of city centre. In central Glasgow.
**Open:** 1 Apr–30 Sept: Mon–Sat, 9.30am–6pm, Sun, 1–5pm; 1 Oct–31 Mar: Mon–Sat, 9.30am–4pm, Sun 1–4pm.
**Admission:** Free.
🖼 ♿ Partial. 🚶 ✲ ✲ 🖱

---

Many properties hold **special events** throughout the year
See the index on page 585

---

## MOTHERWELL HERITAGE CENTRE

**High Road, Motherwell  ML1 3HU**
**Tel:** 01698 251000
**Owner:** North Lanarkshire Council    **Contact:** The Manager
VisitScotland 4-star attraction. Technopolois multi-media display tells the story of the area from the Romans, through the days of heavy industry, to the present time. Exhibition gallery, shop and tower viewing platform. A local studies and family history research room has census, newspaper and other databases on-line. Staff assistance available.
**Location:** MAP 13:E9, OS Ref. NS750 570. In High Road, 200yds N of A723 (Hamilton Road).
**Open:** All year, 10am–5pm. Sun, 12 noon–5pm (closed 25/26 Dec & 1/2 Jan).
**Admission:** Free.
🖼 ♿ 🅿 ✲ ✲

John Soury

# NEW LANARK WORLD HERITAGE SITE
### NEW LANARK MILLS, LANARK, S. LANARKSHIRE  ML11 9DB
www.newlanark.org

**Tel:** 01555 661345  **Fax:** 01555 665738  **E-mail:** visit@newlanark.org
**Owner:** New Lanark Conservation Trust    **Contact:** Rachael Love
Surrounded by native woodlands and close to the famous Falls of Clyde, this cotton mill village was founded in 1785 and became famous as the site of Robert Owen's radical reforms. Now beautifully restored as both a living community and attraction, the fascinating history of the village is interpreted in an award-winning Visitor Centre. Accommodation is available in the New Lanark Mill Hotel and Waterhouses, a stunning conversion from an original 18th century mill. New Lanark is now a World Heritage Site.
**Location:** MAP 13:E9, OS Ref. NS880 426. 1m S of Lanark.
**Open:** All year: daily, 10.30am–5pm (11am–5pm Sept–May). Closed 25 Dec & 1 Jan.
**Admission:** Visitor Centre: Adult £5.95, Child/Conc. £4.95. Groups: 1 free/10 booked.
ⓘ Conference facilities. 🖼 🍴 ♿ Partial. WC. Visitor Centre wheelchair friendly. ➤ 🍴 🚶 By arrangement. 🖼 🅿 5 min walk. 🔇 🐕 In grounds, on leads. 🛏 ✲ 🖱 €

## NEWARK CASTLE 🏰

**Port Glasgow,  Strathclyde**
**Tel:** 01475 741858
**Owner:** In the care of Historic Scotland    **Contact:** The Steward
The oldest part of the castle is a tower built soon after 1478 with a detached gatehouse, by George Maxwell. The main part was added in 1597–99 in a most elegant style. Enlarged in the 16th century by his descendent, the wicked Patrick Maxwell who murdered two of his neighbours.
**Location:** MAP 13:B8, OS Ref. NS329 744. In Port Glasgow on the A8.
**Open:** 1 Apr–30 Sept: daily, 9.30am–6.30pm. Last ticket 6pm.
**Admission:** Adult £3.50, Child £1.75, Conc. £2.80.
ⓘ WC. 🖼 🅿 €

**visit hudsons guide online**

## POLLOK HOUSE 🐾

**Pollok Country Park, Pollokshaws Road, Glasgow  G43 1AT**
**Tel:** 0131 243 9300
**Owner:** The National Trust for Scotland
The house contains an internationally famed collection of paintings as well as porcelain and furnishings appropriate to an Edwardian house.
**Location:** MAP 13:C8, OS Ref. NS550 616. In Pollok Country Park, off M77/J1, follow signs for Burrell Collection.

## ST MARY'S EPISCOPAL CATHEDRAL

**300 Great Western Road, Glasgow  G4 9JB**
**Tel:** 0141 339 6691   **Fax:** 0141 334 5669    **Contact:** The Office
Newly restored, fine Gothic Revival church by Sir George Gilbert Scott, with outstanding contemporary murals by Gwyneth Leech. Regular concerts and exhibitions.
**Location:** MAP 13:D8, OS Ref. NS578 669. ¼m after the Dumbarton A82 exit from M8 motorway.
**Open:** All year. Mon–Fri, 9.15–10am. Tue–Thur, 5.30–7.30pm. Sat, 9.30–10am. Sun services: 8.30am, 10am, 12 noon & 6.30pm.
**Admission:** Free

## SUMMERLEE HERITAGE PARK

**Heritage Way, Coatbridge, North Lanarkshire  ML5 1QD**
**Tel:** 01236 431261
**Owner:** North Lanarkshire Council   **Contact:** The Manager
VisitScotland 4-star attraction. 22 acres of industrial heritage based around the former 19th century Summerlee Ironworks and canal. Please note that, due to a major Heritage Lottery Fund supported redevelopment, the entire site will be closed during 2007. Reopening with new interactive displays and facilities in spring 2008.
**Location:** MAP 13:D8, OS Ref. NS729 655. 600yds NW of Coatbridge town centre.
**Open:** Closed until Spring 2008.

## THE TENEMENT HOUSE 🐾

**145 Buccleuch Street, Glasgow  G3 6QN**
**Tel:** 0131 243 9300
**Owner:** The National Trust for Scotland
A typical Victorian tenement flat of 1892, and time capsule of the first half of the 20th century.
**Location:** MAP 13:D8, OS Ref. NS583 662. Garnethill (three streets N of Sauchiehall Street, near Charing Cross), Glasgow.

## THE TOWER OF HALLBAR

**Braidwood Road, Braidwood, Lanarkshire w ML8 5RD**
**Tel:** 0845 090 0194   **Fax:** 0845 090 0174   **E-mail:** enquiries@vivat.org.uk
**www.vivat.org.uk**
**Owner:** The Vivat Trust    **Contact:** Miss Ellen Jordan
A 16th century defensive tower and Bothy set in ancient orchards and meadowland. Converted into self-catering holiday accommodation by The Vivat Trust and furnished and decorated in keeping with its history. Hallbar sleeps up to seven people, including facilities for a disabled person and their carer.
**Location:** MAP 13:E9, OS Ref. NS842 471. S side of B7056 between Crossford Bridge & Braidwood.
**Open:** All year: Sats, 2–3pm, by appointment. Also four open days a year.
**Admission:** Free.
⟡ Partial. ⟡ By arrangement. 🅟 Limited. ⟡ In grounds, on leads.
⟡ 3 single, 1 twin & 1 double. ✱

For **corporate hospitality** at unique venues see the index on page 567

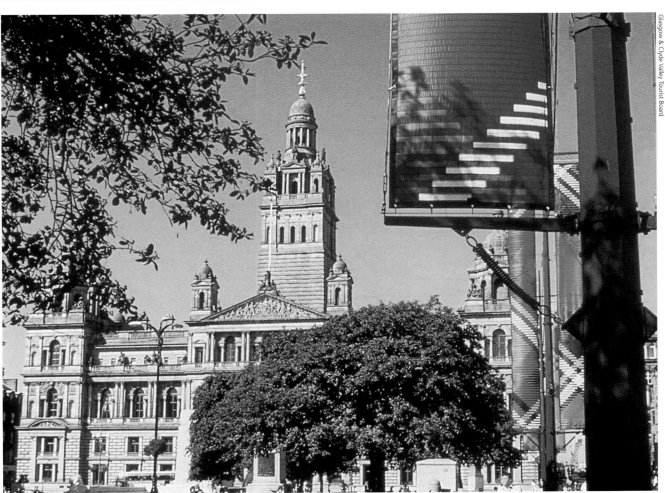

City Chambers, Glasgow

### ■ Owner
Blair Charitable Trust

### ■ Contact
Administration Office
Blair Castle
Blair Atholl
Pitlochry
Perthshire PH18 5TL

**Tel:** 01796 481207
**Fax:** 01796 481487
**E-mail:** office@
blair-castle.co.uk

### ■ Location
**MAP 13:E3**
**OS Ref. NN880 660**
From Edinburgh 80m,
M90 to Perth, A9,
follow signs for Blair
Castle, 1½ hrs.
Trunk Road A9 2m.

**Bus:** Bus stop 1m
in Blair Atholl.

**Train:** 1m, Blair Atholl
Euston-Inverness line.

**Taxi:** Elizabeth Yule,
01796 472290.

### ■ Opening Times
**Summer**
1 April–26 October
Daily, 9.30am–4.30pm
(Last admission).

**Winter**
Tuesday and Saturday
mornings and for groups
by arrangement.

### ■ Admission
**House & Grounds**
| | |
|---|---|
| Adult | £7.50 |
| Child (5–16yrs) | £4.70 |
| Senior | £6.50 |
| Student (with ID) | £6.20 |
| Family | £19.50 |
| Disabled | £2.50 |

**Groups\* (12+)**
(Please book)
| | |
|---|---|
| Adult | £5.80 |
| Child(5–16yrs) | £4.40 |
| Primary School | £3.40 |
| Senior/Student | £5.80 |
| Disabled | £2.20 |

**Grounds only**
(inc. Restaurant, Gift Shop
& WC)
| | |
|---|---|
| Adult | £2.50 |
| Child (5–16yrs) | £1.30 |
| Senior/Student | £2.50 |
| Family | £5.70 |
| Disabled | Free |
| Scooter Hire | £3.40 |

**Groups\* (12+)**
(Please book)
| | |
|---|---|
| Adult | £2.20 |
| Child (5–16yrs) | £1.20 |
| Primary School | £1.20 |
| Senior/Student | £2.20 |
| Disabled | Free |

\*Group rates only apply
when all tickets bought
by the Driver, Courier or
Group leader at one time.

### Conference/Function

| ROOM | SIZE | MAX CAPACITY |
|---|---|---|
| Ballroom | 88' x 36' | 400 or 220 dining |
| State Dining Room | 36' x 26' | 150 or 16–50 dining |
| Banvie Hall | 55' x 32' | 150 |

# BLAIR CASTLE
www.blair-castle.co.uk

Blair Castle has been the ancient home and fortress of the Earls and Dukes of Atholl for over 725 years. Its central location makes it easily accessible from all major Scottish centres in less than two hours.

The castle has known the splendour of Royal visitations, submitted to occupation by opposing forces on no less than four occasions, suffered siege and changed its architectural appearance to suit the taste of successive generations.

Today 30 rooms of infinite variety display fine furniture, paintings, arms, armour, china, costumes, lace and embroidery, and Jacobite relics. The Duke of Atholl has the unique distinction of having the only remaining private army in Europe – The Atholl Highlanders.

### Gardens
Blair Castle is set in extensive and beautiful grounds. Hercules Garden is a walled garden of some 9 acres, which has recently been restored. Diana's Grove is a two acre plantation, which includes some of the tallest trees in the UK. A picnic area and a deer park are readily accessible from the car park and castle.

ℹ️ Fashion shows, equestrian events, shows, rallies, filming, highland and charity balls, piping championships, grand piano, helicopter pad, cannon firing by Atholl Highlanders, resident piper, needlework displays. No smoking.

🛍️ 

🍷 Civil and religious weddings may be held in the castle and receptions for up to 220 guests can be held in the ballroom. Banquets, dinners and private functons are welcome.

♿ May alight at entrance. WC & wheelchair facilities. Limited mobility scooter available for hire.

🍴 Non-smoking. Seats up to 125. Private group lunches for up to 35 can be arranged in the Garry Room.

🎧 Audio visual presentation.

🧍 In English, German and French at no extra cost. Tour time 50mins. Illustrated guide books (English, German, French and Italian) £3.50.

🅿️ 200 cars, 20 coaches. Coach drivers/couriers free, plus free meal and shop voucher, information pack.

🌳 Nature walks, deer park, ranger service & pony trekking, children's play area.

🐎 Grounds only.

❄️

📋 Event programme available on application.

### ■ Owner
Grimsthorpe &
Drummond Castle Trust

### ■ Contact
The Caretaker
Drummond Castle
Gardens
Muthill
Crieff
Perthshire  PH7 4HZ

**Tel:** 01764 681433
**Fax:** 01764 681642
**E-mail:** thegardens@
drummondcastle.sol.co.uk

### ■ Location
**MAP 13:E5**
**OS Ref. NN844 181**

2m S of Crieff off the
A822.

### ■ Opening Times
Easter weekend & 1
May–31 October
Daily, 1–6pm.
Last admission 5pm.

### ■ Admission
| | |
|---|---|
| Adult | £4.00 |
| Child | £1.50 |
| Conc. | £3.00 |

Groups (20+)
10% discount.
Prices subject to change.

# DRUMMOND CASTLE GARDENS

www.drummondcastlegardens.co.uk

Scotland's most important formal gardens, among the finest in Europe. A mile of beech-lined avenue leads to a formidable ridge top tower house. The magnificent Italianate parterre is revealed from a viewpoint at the top of the terrace, celebrating the saltaire and family heraldry that surrounds the famous multiplex sundial by John Milne, master mason to Charles I. First laid out in the early 17th century by John Drummond, 2nd Earl of Perth and renewed in the early 1950s by Phyllis Astor, Countess of Ancaster. The gardens contain ancient yew hedges and two copper beech trees planted by Queen Victoria during her visit in 1842. Shrubberies are planted with many varieties of maple and other individual ornamental trees including purple-leaf oaks, whitebeam, weeping birch and a tulip tree, *Liriodendron tulipifera*. The tranquility of the gardens makes them the perfect setting to stroll amongst the well-manicured plantings or sit and absorb the atmosphere of this special place.

Partial. Viewing platform. WC.

By arrangement.

On leads.

### ■ Owner

The Earl of Strathmore & Kinghorne

### ■ Contact

Mr David Adams
Castle Administrator
Estates Office
Glamis
by Forfar
Angus  DD8 1RJ

**Tel:** 01307 840393
**Fax:** 01307 840733
**E-mail:** enquiries@ glamis-castle.co.uk

### ■ Location

**MAP 13:H4**
**OS Ref. NO386 480**

From Edinburgh M90, A94, 81m.
From Forfar A94, 6m.
From Glasgow 93m.
Motorway: M90.

**Rail:** Dundee Station 12m.

**Air:** Dundee Airport 12m.

**Taxi:** K Cabs 01575 573744.

### ■ Opening Times

March–December
Daily, 10am–6pm.
(November–December, 11am–5pm.)

Last admission 4.30pm.

Extended opening July–August.

Groups welcome. Out of hours visits can also be arranged.

### ■ Admission

**Castle & Grounds**

| | |
|---|---|
| Adult | £7.50 |
| Child (5–16yrs) | £4.30 |
| OAP/Student | £6.30 |
| Family | £21.50 |

Groups (20+)

| | |
|---|---|
| Adult | £6.40 |
| Child (5–16yrs) | £3.80 |
| OAP/Student | £5.70 |

Grounds only ticket available.

### Conference/Function

| ROOM | SIZE | MAX CAPACITY |
|---|---|---|
| Dining Rm | 84 sq.m | 90 |
| Restaurant | 140 sq.m | 100 |
| 16th century Kitchens | | 40 |

# GLAMIS CASTLE

www.glamis-castle.co.uk

Glamis Castle is the family home of the Earls of Strathmore and Kinghorne and has been a royal residence since 1372. It was the childhood home of Her Majesty Queen Elizabeth The Queen Mother, the birthplace of Her Royal Highness The Princess Margaret and the legendary setting of Shakespeare's play *Macbeth*. Although the Castle is open to visitors it remains a family home, lived in and loved by the Strathmore family.

The Castle, a five-storey 'L' shaped tower block, was originally a royal hunting lodge. It was remodelled in the 17th century and is built of pink sandstone. It contains the Great Hall, with its magnificent plasterwork ceiling dated 1621, a beautiful family Chapel constructed inside the Castle in 1688, an 18th century billiard room housing what is left of the extensive library once at Glamis, a 19th century dining room containing family portraits and the Royal Apartments which have been used by Her Majesty Queen Elizabeth The Queen Mother.

The Castle stands in an extensive park, landscaped towards the end of the 18th century, and contains the beautiful Italian Garden and the Pinetum which reflect the peace and serenity of the Castle and grounds.

**ℹ** Fashion shoots, archery, equestrian events, shows, rallies, filming, product launches, highland games, new shopping development, grand piano. Photography allowed during special events and private tours.

**🏬** Shopping pavilion.

**🍽** The State Rooms are available for grand dinners, lunches and wedding receptions.

**♿** Disabled visitors may alight at entrance. Those in wheelchairs will be unable to tour the castle but may visit the two exhibitions. WC.

**🍴** Morning coffees, light lunches, afternoon teas. Self-service, licensed restaurant.

**🚶** All visits are guided, tour time 50–60 mins. Tours leave every 10–15 mins. Tours in French, German, Italian and Spanish by appointment at no additional cost. Three exhibitions.

**P** 500 cars and 20 coaches 200 yds from castle. Coach drivers and couriers admitted free.

**🎓** One teacher free for every 10 children. Nature trail, family exhibition rooms, dolls' house, play park. Glamis Heritage Education Centre in Glamis village. Children's guide book. Children's Quest.

**🐕** In grounds, on leads.

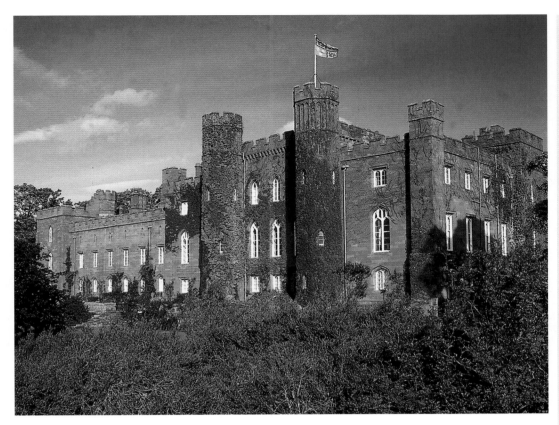

# SCONE PALACE & GROUNDS 🏛

www.scone-palace.co.uk

Scone Palace is the home of the Earl and Countess of Mansfield and is built on the site of an ancient abbey. 1500 years ago it was the capital of the Pictish kingdom and the centre of the ancient Celtic church. In the intervening years, it has been the seat of the parliaments and crowning place of kings, including Macbeth, Robert the Bruce and Charles II. The State Rooms house a superb collection of *objets d'art*, including items of Marie Antoinette, bought by the 2nd Earl of Mansfield. Notable works of art are also on display, including paintings by Sir David Wilkie, Sir Joshua Reynolds, and Johann Zoffany. The Library boasts one of Scotland's finest collections of porcelain, including Sèvres, Ludwigsburg and Meissen, whilst the unique 'Vernis Martin' *papier mâché* may be viewed in the Long Gallery.

## Gardens
The grounds of the Palace house magnificent collections of shrubs, with woodland walks through the pinetum containing David Douglas' original fir and the unique Murray Star Maze. There are Highland cattle and peacocks to admire and an adventure play area for children. The 100 acres of mature Policy Parks, flanked by the River Tay, are available for a variety of events, including corporate and private entertaining.

**ℹ** Receptions, fashion shows, war games, archery, clay pigeon shooting, equestrian events, garden parties, shows, rallies, filming, shooting, fishing, floodlit tattoos, product launches, highland games, parkland, cricket pitch, helicopter landing, croquet, racecourse, polo field, firework displays, adventure playground. No photography in state rooms.

**▣** Gift shop & food shop.

**🍷** Grand dinners in state rooms, buffets, receptions, wedding receptions, cocktail parties.

**♿** All state rooms on one level, wheelchair access to restaurants. Stairlift in gift shop.

**🍴** Licensed. Teas, lunches & dinners, can be booked, menus upon request, special rates for groups.

**🚶** By arrangement. Guides in rooms, tour time 45 mins. French and German guides available by appointment.

**🎧** Welcome.

**P** 300 cars and 15 coaches, groups please book, couriers and coach drivers free meal and admittance.

**🐕** In grounds on leads.

**❄** 

**♿** Please telephone for details.

## ■ Owner
The Earl of Mansfield

## ■ Contact
The Administrator
Scone Palace
Perth  PH2 6BD
**Tel:** 01738 552300
**Fax:** 01738 552588
**E-mail:** visits@
scone-palace.co.uk

## ■ Location
**MAP 13:G5**
**OS Ref. NO114 266**

From Edinburgh
Forth Bridge M90,
A93 1hr.

**Bus:** Regular buses
from Perth.

**Rail:** Perth Station 3m.

Motorway: M90 from
Edinburgh.

**Taxi:** 01738 636777.

## ■ Opening Times
**Summer**
1 April–31 October
Daily: 9.30am–6pm.

Last admission 5pm.

Evening tours by
appointment.

**Winter**
By appointment.

**Grounds only**
Fri, 11am–4pm.

## ■ Admission
**Summer**
**Palace & Grounds**
Adult                    £7.50
Child (under 16yrs) £4.50
Senior/Student     £6.50
Family                 £23.00

Groups (20+)
Adult                    £6.30
Child (5–16yrs)    £4.25
Senior/Student     £5.50

**Grounds only**
Adult                    £4.00
Child (5–16yrs)    £2.75
Senior/Student     £3.65

Under 5s Free
Private Tour £40
supplement.

**Winter**
On application.

## Conference/Function

| ROOM | SIZE | MAX CAPACITY |
|------|------|--------------|
| Long Gallery | 140' x 20' | 200 |
| Queen Victoria's Rm | 20' x 20' | 20 |
| Drawing Rm | 48' x 25' | 80 |

Perthshire, Angus & Dundee and The Kingdom of Fife

## ABERDOUR CASTLE

**Aberdour, Fife**

**Tel:** 01383 860519

**Owner:** In the care of Historic Scotland    **Contact:** The Steward

A 14th century castle built by the Douglas family. The gallery on the first floor gives an idea of how it was furnished at the time. The castle has a 14th century tower extended in the 16th and 17th centuries, a delightful walled garden and a circular dovecote.

**Location:** MAP 13:G7, OS Ref. NT193 854. In Aberdour 5m E of the Forth Bridge on the A921.

**Open:** 1 Apr–30 Sept: daily, 9.30am–6.30pm, last ticket 6pm. 1 Oct–31 Mar: daily, 9.30am–4.30pm, last ticket 4pm. Closed Thurs & Fri in winter.

**Admission:** Adult £4, Child £2, Conc. £3.

ℹ️ Picnic area. WCs. ♿ WC. 🖼 🅿 ❋ €

## ARBROATH ABBEY

**Arbroath, Tayside**

**Tel:** 01241 878756

**Owner:** In the care of Historic Scotland    **Contact:** The Steward

The substantial ruins of a Tironensian monastery, notably the gate house range and the abbot's house. Arbroath Abbey holds a very special place in Scottish history. Scotland's nobles swore their independence from England in the famous 'Declaration of Arbroath' in 1320. New visitor centre.

**Location:** MAP 14:J4, OS Ref. NO644 414. In Arbroath town centre on the A92.

**Open:** 1 Apr–30 Sept: daily 9.30am–6.30pm, last ticket 6pm. 1 Oct–31 Mar: daily, 9.30am–4.30 pm, last ticket 4pm.

**Admission:** Adult £4.50, Child £2.25, Conc. £3.50.

ℹ️ WCs. 📷 ♿ WC. 🅿 ❋ €

## BALCARRES

**Colinsburgh, Fife  KY9 1HL**

**Tel:** 01333 340520

**Owner:** Balcarres Trust    **Contact:** The Earl of Crawford

16th century tower house with 19th century additions by Burn and Bryce. Woodland and terraced gardens.

**Location:** MAP 14:I6, OS Ref. NO475 044. ½m N of Colinsburgh.

**Open:** Woodland & Gardens: 1–20 Feb & 2 Apr–23 Jun, 2–5pm. House not open except by written appointment and 9–28 Apr, excluding Sun.

**Admission:** Adult £6. Garden only: £3.

ℹ️ By arrangement.

## BALGONIE CASTLE

**Markinch, Fife  KY7 6HQ**

**Tel:** 01592 750119    **Fax:** 01592 753103    **E-mail:** sbalgonie@yahoo.co.uk

**Owner/Contact:** The Laird of Balgonie

14th century tower, additions to the building up to 1702. Still lived in by the family. 14th century chapel for weddings.

**Location:** MAP 13:H6, OS Ref. NO313 006. ½ m S of A911 Glenrothes–Leven road at Milton of Balgonie on to B921.

**Open:** All year: daily, 10am–5pm.

**Admission:** Adult £3, Child £1.50, OAP £2.

## BALHOUSIE CASTLE (BLACK WATCH MUSEUM)

**Hay Street, North Inch Park, Perth  PH1 5HR**

**Tel:** 0131 310 8530

**Owner:** MOD    **Contact:** Major Proctor

Regimental museum housed in the castle.

**Location:** MAP 13:G5, OS Ref. NO115 244. ½ m N of town centre, E of A9 road to Dunkeld.

**Open:** May–Sept: Mon–Sat, 10am–4.30pm. Oct–Apr: Mon–Fri, 10am–3.30pm. Closed 23 Dec–5 Jan & last Sat in Jun.

**Admission:** Free.

## BRANKLYN GARDEN

**Dundee Road, Perth  PH2 7BB**

**Tel:** 01738 625535

**Owner:** The National Trust for Scotland

Small garden with an impressive collection of rare and unusual plants.

**Location:** MAP 13:F5, OS Ref. NO125 225. On A85 at 116 Dundee Road, Perth.

## BLAIR CASTLE

*See page 470 for full page entry.*

## BRECHIN CASTLE

**Brechin, Angus  DD9 6SG**

**Tel:** 01356 624566    **E-mail:** fay@dalhousieestates.co.uk

**www.dalhousieestates.co.uk**

**Owner:** Dalhousie Estates    **Contact:** Fay Clark

Dating from 1711 the Castle contains many family pictures and artefacts. Beautiful gardens.

**Location:** MAP 14:J3, OS Ref. NO593 602. Off A90 on A935.

**Open:** 28 Jul–26 Aug: guided tours only, 2 & 3.15pm.

**Admission:** Adult £5. Child under 12yrs Free.

ℹ️ No photography. ♿ Unsuitable. 👥 Obligatory. ❋

## BROUGHTY CASTLE

**Broughty Ferry, Dundee  DD5 2TF**

**Tel:** 01382 436916

**Owner:** Historic Scotland    **Contact:** The Monument Manager

A delightful castle originating from the 15th century and spectacularly positioned overlooking the Tay estuary. It was adapted over the centuries to reflect advances in warfare and defence. The castle withstood many assaults, and still has the scars from cannon balls to prove the point. By the 18th century it had fallen into ruin but was restored to use in the 1860s as part of the Crimean War effort. The castle houses a museum with fascinating displays on changing life, times and people of Broughty Ferry and about its wildlife, which is run by Dundee City Council.

**Location:** MAP 14:F4, OS Ref. NO464 304. On the shores of the River Tay at Broughty Ferry, Dundee off the A930.

**Open:** Please telephone the site for details or visit http://www.dundeecity.gov.uk/broughtycastle/main.htm.

**Admission:** Please telephone the site for details.

🖼 🅿

## CASTLE CAMPBELL

**Dollar Glen, Central District**

**Tel:** 0131 243 9300

**Owner:** The National Trust for Scotland    **Contact:** Historic Scotland

Known as 'Castle Gloom' this spectacularly sited 15th century fortress was the lowland stronghold of the Campbells. Stunning views from the parapet walk.

**Location:** MAP 13:F6, OS Ref. NS961 993. At head of Dollar Glen, 10m E of Stirling on the A91.

❋

## CHARLETON HOUSE

**Colinsburgh, Leven, Fife  KY9 1HG**

**Tel:** 01333 340249  Fax: 01333 340583

**Location:** MAP 14:I6, OS Ref. NO464 036. Off A917. 1m NW of Colinsburgh. 3m NW of Elie.

**Open:** Sept: daily, 12 noon–3pm. Admission every ½hr with guided tours only.

**Admission:** £10.

👥 Obligatory.

## CORTACHY ESTATE

**Cortachy, Kirriemuir, Angus  DD8 4LX**

**Tel:** 01575 570108  **Fax:** 01575 540400

**E-mail:** office@airlieestates.com  **www.airlieestates.com**

**Owner:** Trustees of Airlie Estates    **Contact:** Estate Office

Countryside walks including access through woodlands to Airlie Monument on Tulloch Hill with spectacular views of the Angus Glens and Vale of Strathmore. Footpaths are waymarked and colour coded.

**Location:** MAP 13:H3, OS Ref. N0394 596. Off the B955 Glens Road from Kirriemuir.

**Open:** Woodland Walks: all year. Gardens: 6–9 Apr; 7 May & 14 May–3 Jun; 6 & 27 Aug: 10am–4pm, last admission 3.30pm. Castle not open.

**Admission:** Please contact estate office for details.

♿ Not suitable. 🅿 Limited. ❋ ❋

Who's offering **accommodation?**
See our index on page 575

**visit hudsons guide online**

## CULROSS PALACE

**Tel:** 0131 243 9300
**Owner:** The National Trust for Scotland     **Contact:** Property Manager
Relive the domestic life of the 16th and 17th centuries at this Royal Burgh fringed by the River Forth. Enjoy too the Palace, dating from 1597 and the medieval garden.
**Location:** MAP 13:F7, OS Ref. NS985 860. Off A985. 12m W of Forth Road Bridge and 4m E of Kincardine Bridge, Fife.

## DRUMMOND CASTLE GARDENS     *See page 471 for full page entry.*

## DUNFERMLINE ABBEY & PALACE

**Dunfermline, Fife**
**Tel:** 01383 739026
**Owner:** In the care of Historic Scotland     **Contact:** The Steward
The remains of the Benedictine abbey founded by Queen Margaret in the 11th century. The foundations of her church are under the 12th century Romanesque-style nave. Robert the Bruce was buried in the choir. Substantial parts of the abbey buildings remain, including the vast refectory.
**Location:** MAP 13:G7, OS Ref. NY090 873. In Dunfermline off the M90.
**Open:** 1 Apr–30 Sept: daily, 9.30am–6.30pm, last ticket 6pm. 1 Oct–31 Mar: Mon–Sat, 9.30am–4.30pm, Sun, 2–4.30pm, last ticket 4pm. Closed Thurs pm and Fri in winter.
**Admission:** Adult £3.50, Child £1.75, Conc. £2.80.

## DUNNINALD

**Montrose, Angus  DD10 9TD**
**Tel:** 01674 674842     **Fax:** 01674 674860     www.dunninald.com
**Owner/Contact:** J Stansfeld
This house, the third Dunninald built on the estate, was designed by James Gillespie Graham in the gothic Revival style, and was completed for Peter Arkley in 1824. It has a superb walled garden and is set in a planned landscape dating from 1740. It is a family home.
**Location:** MAP 14:J3, OS Ref. NO705 543 2m S of Montrose, between A92 and the sea.
**Open:** 28 Jun–29 Jul: Tue–Sun, 1–5pm. Garden: from 12.30pm.
**Admission:** Adult £5, Child (under 12) Free, Conc. £4. Garden only: £2.50.
No photography in house. Unsuitable. Obligatory. In grounds, on leads. €

## EDZELL CASTLE AND GARDEN

**Edzell, Angus**
**Tel:** 01356 648631
**Owner:** In the care of Historic Scotland     **Contact:** The Steward
The beautiful walled garden at Edzell is one of Scotland's unique sights, created by Sir David Lindsay in 1604. The 'Pleasance' is a delightful formal garden with walls decorated with sculptured stone panels, flower boxes and niches for nesting birds. The fine tower house, now ruined, dates from the last years of the 15th century. Mary, Queen of Scots held a council meeting in the castle in 1562 on her way north as her army marched against the Gordons.
**Location:** MAP 14:I2, OS Ref. NO585 691. At Edzell, 6m N of Brechin on B966. 1m W of village.
**Open:** 1 Apr–30 Sept: daily, 9.30am–6.30pm, last ticket 6pm. 1 Oct–31 Mar: daily, 9.30am–4.30pm, last ticket 4pm. Closed Thur and Fri in winter.
**Admission:** Adult £4.50, Child £2.25, Conc. £3.50.

## ELCHO CASTLE

**Perth**
**Tel:** 01738 639998
**Owner:** In the care of Historic Scotland     **Contact:** The Steward
This handsome and complete fortified mansion of 16th century date has four projecting towers. The original wrought-iron grilles to protect the windows are still in place.
**Location:** MAP 13:G5, OS Ref. NO164 211. On the Tay, 3m SE of Perth.
**Open:** 1 Apr–30 Sept: daily, 9.30am–6.30pm, last ticket 6pm.
**Admission:** Adult £3, Child £1.50, Conc. £2.50.

## FALKLAND PALACE

**Falkland  KY15 7BU**
**Tel:** 0131 243 9300
**Owner:** The National Trust for Scotland
Built between 1502 and 1541, the Palace is a good example of Renaissance architecture. Surrounded by gardens, laid out in the 1950s.
**Location:** MAP 13:G6, OS Ref. NO253 075. A912, 11m N of Kirkcaldy.

## GLAMIS CASTLE     *See page 472 for full page entry*

## GLENEAGLES

**Auchterarder, Perthshire  PH3 1PJ**
**Tel:** 01764 682388
**Owner:** Gleneagles 1996 Trust     **Contact:** J Martin Haldane of Gleneagles
Gleneagles has been the home of the Haldane family since the 12th century. The 18th century pavilion is open to the public by written appointment.
**Location:** MAP 13:F6, OS Ref. NS931 088. ¾m S of A9 on A823. 2½m S of Auchterarder.
**Open:** By written appointment only.

## HILL OF TARVIT MANSIONHOUSE

**Cupar, Fife  KY15 5PB**
**Tel:** 0131 243 9300
**Owner:** The National Trust for Scotland
House rebuilt in 1906 by Sir Robert Lorimer, the renowned Scottish architect, for a Dundee industrialist, Mr F B Sharp.
**Location:** MAP 13:F6, OS Ref. NO379 118. Off A916, 2½m S of Cupar, Fife.

## HOUSE OF DUN

**Montrose, Angus  DD10 9LQ**
**Tel:** 0131 243 9300
**Owner:** The National Trust for Scotland
Georgian house, overlooking the Montrose Basin, designed by William Adam and built in 1730 for David Erskine, Lord Dun.
**Location:** OS Ref. NO670 599. 3m W Montrose on A935.

## HUNTINGTOWER CASTLE

**Perth**
**Tel:** 01738 627231
**Owner:** In the care of Historic Scotland     **Contact:** The Steward
The splendid painted ceilings are especially noteworthy in this castle, once owned by the Ruthven family. Scene of a famous leap between two towers by a daughter of the house who was nearly caught in her lover's room. The two towers are still complete, one of 15th–16th century date, the other of 16th century origin. Now linked by a 17th century range.
**Location:** MAP 13:F5, OS Ref. NO084 252. 3m NW of Perth off the A85.
**Open:** 1 Apr–30 Sept: daily, 9.30am–6.30pm, last ticket 6pm. 1 Oct–31 Mar: daily, 9.30am–4.30pm, last ticket 4pm. Closed Thur & Fris in winter.
**Admission:** Adult £4, Child £2, Conc. £3.
By arrangement. €

## INCHCOLM ABBEY

**Inchcolm, Fife**
**Tel:** 01383 823332
**Owner:** In the care of Historic Scotland     **Contact:** The Steward
Known as the 'Iona of the East'. This is the best preserved group of monastic buildings in Scotland, founded in 1123. Includes a 13th century octagonal chapter house.
**Location:** MAP 13:H7, OS Ref. NT190 826. On Inchcolm in the Firth of Forth. Reached by ferry from South Queensferry (30 mins), or Newhaven (45 mins). Tel. 0131 331 5000 for times/charges.
**Open:** 1 Apr–30 Sept: daily, 9.30am–6.30pm, last ticket 6pm.
**Admission:** Adult £4.50, Child £2.25, Conc. £3.50. Additional charge for ferries.
Visitor Centre. €

## KELLIE CASTLE & GARDEN

**Pittenweem, Fife KY10 2RF**
**Tel:** 0131 243 9300
**Owner:** The National Trust for Scotland
Good example of domestic architecture in Lowland Scotland dates from the 14th century and was sympathetically restored by the Lorimer family in the late 19th century.
**Location:** MAP 14:I6, OS Ref. NO519 051. On B9171, 3m NW of Pittenweem, Fife.

## LOCHLEVEN CASTLE

**Loch Leven, Kinross**
**Tel:** 07778 040483
**Owner:** In the care of Historic Scotland    **Contact:** The Steward
Mary Queen of Scots endured nearly a year of imprisonment in this 14th century tower before her dramatic escape in May 1568. During the First War of Independence it was held by the English, stormed by Wallace and visited by Bruce.
**Location:** MAP 13:G6, OS Ref. NO138 018. On island in Loch Leven reached by ferry from Kinross off the M90.
**Open:** Last sailing 5.15pm. Open summer only.
**Admission:** Adult £4.50, Child £2.25, Conc. £3.50. Prices include ferry trip.
🖰 🅿 ▣ €

## MEGGINCH CASTLE GARDENS
### ERROL, PERTHSHIRE PH2 7SW

**Tel:** 01821 642222    **Email:** catherine.herdman@gmail.com
**Owner:** Mr Giles & The Hon Mrs Herdman
15th century castle, 1,000 year old yews, flowered parterre, double walled kitchen garden, topiary, astrological garden, pagoda dovecote in courtyard. Part used as a location for the film *Rob Roy*.
**Location:** MAP 13:G5, OS Ref. NO241 245. 8m E of Perth on A90.
**Open:** By appointment.
**Admission:** Contact property for details.
🖳 🔼 Partial. 🗲 By arrangement. 🅿 Limited for coaches. 🐾 In grounds, on leads.

## MONZIE CASTLE

**Crieff, Perthshire PH7 4HD**
**Tel:** 01764 653110
**Owner/Contact:** Mrs C M M Crichton
Built in 1791. Destroyed by fire in 1908 and rebuilt and furnished by Sir Robert Lorimer.
**Location:** MAP 13:E5, OS Ref. NN873 244. 2m NE of Crieff.
**Open:** 12 May–10 Jun: daily, 2–5pm. By appointment at other times.
**Admission:** Adult £5, Child £1. Group rates available, contact property for details.
❄

## ST ANDREWS CASTLE
### THE SCORES, ST ANDREWS KY16 9AR

**Tel:** 01334 477196
**Owner:** Historic Scotland    **Contact:** David Eaton
This was the castle of the bishops of St Andrews and has a fascinating mine and counter-mine, rare examples of medieval siege techniques. There is also a bottle dungeon hollowed out of solid rock. Cardinal Beaton was murdered here and John Knox was sent to the galleys when the ensuing siege was lifted.
**Location:** MAP 14:I5, OS Ref. NO513 169. In St Andrews on the A91.
**Open:** Apr–Sept: daily, 9.30am–6.30pm. Oct–Mar: daily, 9.30am–4.30pm. Last ticket 30 mins before closing.
**Admission:** Adult £5, Child £2.50, Conc. £4. 10% discount for groups (10+). Joint ticket with St Andrews Cathedral available.
ℹ Visitor centre. 🖰 🔼 Partial. WCs. 🗲 By arrangement. 🅿 On street. ▣ Free if booked. 🐾 Guide dogs. ❄ €

## ST ANDREWS CATHEDRAL

**St Andrews, Fife**
**Tel:** 01334 472563
**Owner:** Historic Scotland    **Contact:** Alison Sullivan
The remains still give a vivid impression of the scale of what was once the largest cathedral in Scotland along with the associated domestic ranges of the priory.
**Location:** MAP 14:I5, OS Ref: NO514 167. In St Andrews.
**Open:** 1 Apr–30 Sept: daily, 9.30am–6.30pm, last ticket 5.45pm. 1 Oct–31 Mar: daily, 9.30am–4.30pm, last ticket 3.45pm.
**Admission:** Adult £4, Child £2, Conc. £3. Joint entry ticket with St Andrews Castle available.
❄ €

## SCONE PALACE & GROUNDS    *See page 473 for full page entry.*

## STOBHALL

**Stobhall, Cargill, Perthshire PH2 6DR**
**Tel:** 01821 640332    www.stobhall.com
**Owner:** Viscount Strathallan
Original home of the Drummond chiefs from the 14th century. Romantic cluster of small-scale buildings around a courtyard in a magnificent situation overlooking the River Tay, surrounded by formal and woodland gardens. 17th century painted ceiling in Chapel depicts monarchs of Europe and North Africa on horse (or elephant) back.
**Location:** MAP 13:G4, OS Ref. NO132 343. 8m N of Perth on A93.
**Open:** 2 Jun–1 Jul: Tues–Sun, (closed Mons). Open by tour only. Tours at 2, 3 & 4pm of the Chapel, Drawing Room and Folly. Explore the garden at leisure after the tour. Library by prior appointment.
**Admission:** Adult £4, Child £2, Conc. £3. Large group visits must be booked.
🔼 Partial. Please see website or ring for details. 🗲 Obligatory.
🅿 Limited. Coaches please book.

## STRATHTYRUM HOUSE & GARDENS

**St Andrews, Fife**
**Tel:** 01334 473600  **E-mail:** info@strathtyrumhouse.com
**www.strathtyrumhouse.com**
**Owner:** The Strathtyrum Trust  **Contact:** Cheryl Hanlon
**Location:** MAP 14:I5, OS Ref: NO490 172. Entrance from the St Andrews/Guardbridge Road which is signposted when open.
**Open:** 7–11 May, 4–8 Jun, 2–6 Jul, 6–10 Aug and 3–7 Sept: 2–4pm. Guided tours at 2 & 3pm.
**Admission:** Adult £5, Child £2.50.
🎫 2pm and 3pm. 🅿 Free. 🐕 Guide dogs only.

Who's offering **accommodation?**
See our index on page 575

## TULLIBOLE CASTLE

**Crook of Devon, Kinross  KY13 0QN**
**Tel:** 01577 840236  **E-mail:** visit@tulbol.demon.co.uk
**www.tulbol.demon.co.uk/visit.htm**
**Owner:** Lord & Lady Moncreiff  **Contact:** Lord Moncreiff
Recognised as a classic example of the Scottish tower house. Completed in 1608, the Moncreiff family have lived here since 1747. The Castle is in a parkland setting with ornamental fishponds (moat), a roofless lectarn doocot, with a short walk to a 9th century graveyard and a ruined church.
**Location:** MAP 13:F6, OS Ref: NO540 888. Located on the B9097 1m E of Crook of Devon.
**Open:** Last week in Aug–30 Sept: Tue–Sun, 1–4pm. Admission every ½ hr with guided tours only.
**Admission:** Adult £3.50, Child/Conc. £2.50. Free as part of "Doors Open Day" (last weekend of Sept).
♿ Unsuitable. 🎫 Obligatory. 🅿 Ample for cars but limited for coaches. 🔲
🐕 Guide dogs only. 🛏 Twin x 1.

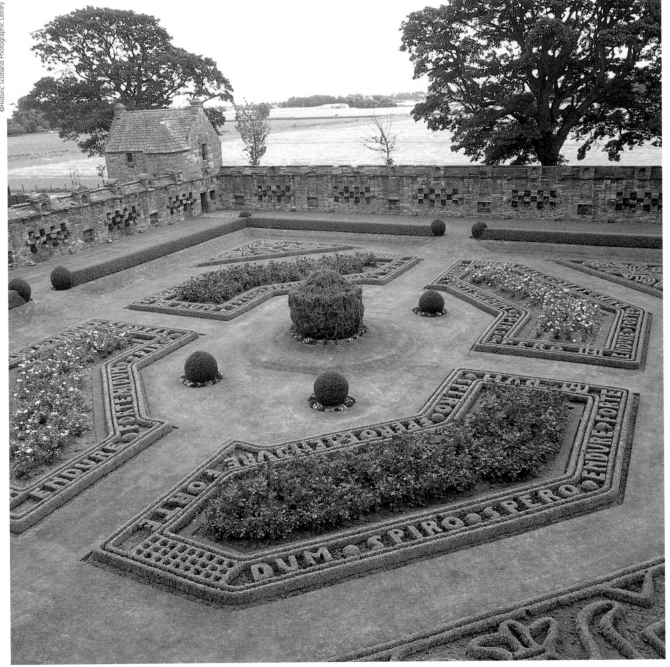

Edzell Castle & Garden

©Historic Scotland Photographic Library

### ■ Owner
Historic Scotland

### ■ Contact
The Steward
Argyll's Lodging
Castle Wynd
Stirling  FK8 1EJ

**Tel:** 01786 431319
**Fax:** 01786 448194

### ■ Location
**MAP 13:E7**
**OS Ref. NS793 938**

At the top and on
E side of Castle
Wynd in Stirling.
One way route from town
centre from Albert Street.

**Rail:** Stirling.

**Air:** Edinburgh or
Glasgow.

### ■ Opening Times
April–September
Daily, 9.30am–6pm.

October–March
Daily, 9.30am–5pm.

### ■ Admission
| | |
|---|---|
| Adult | £4.50 |
| Child* | £2.25 |
| Conc** | £3.50 |

\* up to 16 years.
  Under 5yrs free.

\*\* (60+ & unemployed)

Joint entry available.

# ARGYLL'S LODGING

This attractive townhouse, sitting at the foot of Stirling Castle, is decorated as it would have been during the 9th Earl of Argyll's occupation around 1680. Before coming into Historic Scotland's care the building was a youth hostel, but restoration revealed hidden secrets from the lodging's past. Perhaps the best of these was a section of 17th century *trompe l'oeil* panelling in the dining room, created by painter David McBeath.

Visitors to Argyll's Lodging might wonder at the highly decorated walls and rich materials and colours used but the restoration relied on a household inventory of 1680 found among the then Duchess's papers. But no matter how rich the decoration, it cannot match the colourful lives of Argyll Lodging's inhabitants.

The 9th Earl, Archibald Campbell, was sentenced to death for treason and imprisoned in Edinburgh Castle. However he escaped when his stepdaughter smuggled him out dressed as her page. Archibald escaped to Holland, but his stepdaughter was arrested and placed in public stocks – a major humiliation. He didn't cheat death a second time, however. Joining plots over the succession following Charles II's death, he was captured and beheaded in 1685.

An earlier inhabitant of Argyll's Lodging, Sir William Alexander, was tutor to James VI's son, Prince Henry and in 1621 he attempted to colonise Nova Scotia in Canada. Great wealth eluded him all his life, however, and he died a bankrupt in 1640, leading to the town council taking over the lodging and selling it to the Earl of Argyll in the 1660s.

**i** Interpretation scheme includes computer animations; joint ticket with Stirling Castle available.

Evening receptions/dinners.

Partial. No wheelchair access to upper floor.

**P** Ample parking for coaches and cars on Stirling Castle Esplanade.

Free pre-booked school visits scheme.

Guide dogs only.

### Conference/Function
| ROOM | SIZE | MAX CAPACITY |
|---|---|---|
| Laigh Hall | 11 x 6m | 60 for receptions |
| High Dining Room | 11 x 6m | 26 for dinner |
| Both rooms: 120 for receptions | | |

# INVERARAY CASTLE 🏛

www.inveraray-castle.com

The ancient Royal Burgh of Inveraray lies about 60 miles north west of Glasgow by Loch Fyne in an area of spectacular natural beauty. The ruggedness of the highland scenery combines with the sheltered tidal loch, beside which nestles the present Castle built between 1745 and 1790.

The Castle is home to the Duke of Argyll, Head of the Clan Campbell, whose family have lived in Inveraray since the early 15th century. Designed by Roger Morris and decorated by Robert Mylne, the fairytale exterior belies the grandeur of its gracious interior. The Clerk of Works, William Adam, father of Robert and John, did much of the laying out of the present Royal Burgh, which is an unrivalled example of an early planned town.

Visitors enter the famous Armoury Hall containing some 1,300 pieces including Brown Bess muskets, Lochaber axes, 18th century Scottish broadswords, and can see preserved swords from the Battle of Culloden. The fine State Dining Room and Tapestry Drawing Room contain magnificent French tapestries made especially for the Castle, fabulous examples of Scottish, English and French furniture and a wealth of other works of art. The unique collection of china, silver and family artifacts spans the generations which are identified by a magnificent genealogical display in the Clan Room.

## ■ Owner
Duke of Argyll

## ■ Contact
Argyll Estate Office
Inveraray Castle
Inveraray
Argyll  PA32 8XE

**Tel:** 01499 302203
**Fax:** 01499 302421
**E-mail:** enquiries@
inveraray-castle.com

## ■ Location
**MAP 13:A6**
**OS Ref. NN100 090**

From Edinburgh
2½–3hrs via Glasgow.

Just NE of Inveraray
on A83. W shore
of Loch Fyne.

Bus: Bus route stopping
point within ½m.

## ■ Opening Times
**Summer**
1 April–31 October:
Mon–Sat, 10am–5.45pm
Sun, 12 noon–5.45pm.
Last admission 5pm.

**Winter**
Closed.

## ■ Admission
**House only**
| | |
|---|---|
| Adult | £6.30 |
| Child (under 16yrs) | £4.10 |
| OAP/Student | £5.20 |
| Family (2+2) | £17.00 |

Groups (20+)
20% discount
Pre-booking available.

| | |
|---|---|
| ℹ | No photography. Guide books in French, Italian, Japanese and German translations. |
| 🛍 | |
| ♿ | Visitors may alight at the entrance. 2 wheelchair ramps to castle. All main public rooms suitable but two long flights of stairs to the smaller rooms upstairs. WCs. |
| ☕ | Seats up to 50. Licensed. Menus available on request. Groups book in advance. Tel: 01499 302112. |
| 🚶 | Available for up to 100 people at no additional cost. Groups please book. Tour time: 1 hr. |
| P | 100 cars. Separate coach park close to Castle |
| ▪ | £2.10 per child. A guide can be provided. Areas of interest include a nature walk. |
| 🐕 | In grounds, on leads. Guide dogs only inside Castle. |

## ANGUS'S GARDEN

**Barguillean, Taynuilt, Argyll, West Highlands PA35 1HY**
**Tel:** 01866 822335 **Fax:** 01866 822539
**Contact:** Sean Honeyman
Memorial garden of peace, tranquillity and reconciliation.
**Location:** MAP 12:P5, OS Ref. NM978 289. 4m SW on Glen Lonan road from A85.
**Open:** All year: daily, 9am–5pm (dusk during summer months).
**Admission:** Adult £2, Child Free.

## ARDENCRAIG GARDENS

**Ardencraig, Rothesay, Isle of Bute, West Highlands PA20 9BP**
**Tel:** 01700 505339 **Fax:** 01700 502492
**Owner:** Argyll and Bute Council **Contact:** Allan Macdonald
Walled garden, greenhouses, aviaries. Woodland walk from Rothesay 1 mile (Skippers Wood.)
**Location:** MAP 13:A8, OS Ref. NS105 645. 2m from Rothesay.
**Open:** May–Sept: Mon–Fri, 10am–3.30pm, Sat & Sun, 1–4.30pm.
**Admission:** Free.

## ARDKINGLAS ESTATE
### CAIRNDOW, ARGYLL PA26 8BH
www.ardkinglas.com

**Tel:** 01499 600261 **Fax:** 01499 600241 **E-mail:** info@ardkinglas.com
**Owner:** David Sumison **Contact:** Jean Maskell
Ardkinglas House, at the head of Loch Fyne, is the masterpiece of Robert Lorimer. Group visits can be made by prior arrangement and the house can be hired for private functions and is licensed for weddings and Civil ceremonies. The large lawns are suitable for marquees. The Woodland Garden has many champion trees.
**Location:** MAP 13:A6, OS Ref. NN175 104. Head of Loch Fyne, just off the A83 at Cairndow, 10m W of Arrochar. About 1hr from Glasgow.
**Open:** Woodland Garden & Woodland Trails: All year, dawn–dusk.
**Admission:** Garden – admission charge for adults.
⌂ Tree shop. 🔧 🚻 ♿ Partial. 📷 🍴 🎁 By arrangement. 🅿 Limited. 🐕 In grounds, on leads. ♿ €

## ARGYLL'S LODGING ♿

*See page 478 for full page entry.*

## BALLOCH CASTLE COUNTRY PARK

**Balloch, Dunbartonshire G83 8LX**
**Tel:** 01389 737000
**Contact:** West Dunbartonshire Council
A 200 acre country park on the banks of Loch Lomond.
**Location:** MAP 13:C7, OS Ref. NS390 830. SE shore of Loch Lomond, off A82 for Balloch or A811 for Stirling.
**Open:** All year: dawn–dusk.
**Admission:** Free.

## BENMORE BOTANIC GARDEN

**Dunoon, Argyll PA23 8QU**
**Tel:** 01369 706261 **Fax:** 01369 706369
**Contact:** The Curator
A botanical paradise. Enter the magnificent avenue of giant redwoods and follow trails through the Formal Garden and hillside woodlands with its spectacular outlook over the Holy Loch and the Eachaig Valley.
**Location:** MAP 13:A7, OS Ref. NS150 850. 7m N of Dunoon on A815.
**Open:** 1 Mar–31 Oct: daily, 10am–6pm. Closes 5pm in Mar & Oct.
**Admission:** Adult £3.50, Child £1, Conc. £3, Family £8. Group discounts available.

## BONAWE IRON FURNACE ♿

**Taynuilt, Argyll**
**Tel:** 01866 822432
**Owner:** In the care of Historic Scotland **Contact:** The Steward
Founded in 1753 by Cumbrian iron masters this is the most complete remaining charcoal fuelled ironworks in Britain. Displays show how iron was once made here.
**Location:** MAP 12:P4, OS Ref. NN005 310. By the village of Taynuilt off the A85.
**Open:** 1 Apr–30 Sept: daily, 9.30am–6.30pm, last ticket 6pm.
**Admission:** Adult £4, Child £2, Conc. £3.
⌂ 🎁 🅿 €

## CASTLE STALKER

**Portnacroish, Appin, Argyll PA38 4BA**
**Tel:** 01631 740306 **Fax:** 01631 740539 **www.castlestalker.com**
**Owner:** Mrs M Allward **Contact:** Messrs R & A Allward
Early 15th century tower house and ancient seat of the Stewarts of Appin. Picturesquely set on a rocky islet approx 400 yds off the mainland on the shore of Loch Linnhe. Reputed to have been used by James IV as a hunting lodge. Garrisoned by Government troops during the 1745 rising. Restored from a ruin by the late Lt Col Stewart Allward following acquisition in 1965 and now retained by his family.
**Location:** MAP 12:P3, OS Ref. NM930 480. Approx. 20m N of Oban on the A828. On islet ¼m offshore.
**Open:** 7–11 & 14–18 May, 20–24 & 27–31 Aug, 3–7 Sept. Telephone for appointments. Times variable depending on tides and weather.
**Admission:** Adult £8, Child £4.
ℹ Not suitable for coach parties. ♿ Unsuitable.

## DOUNE CASTLE ♿

**Doune**
**Tel:** 01786 841742
**Owner:** Earl of Moray (leased to Historic Scotland) **Contact:** The Steward
A formidable 14th century courtyard castle, built for the Regent Albany. The striking keep-gatehouse combines domestic quarters including the splendid Lord's Hall with its carved oak screen, musicians' gallery and double fireplace.
**Location:** MAP 13:D6, OS Ref. NN720 020. In Doune, 8m S of Callander on the A84.
**Open:** 1 Apr–30 Sept: daily, 9.30am–6.30pm. 1 Oct–31 Mar: Mon–Wed, Sat & Sun, 9.30am–4.30pm, last admission 30 mins before closing.
**Admission:** Adult £4, Child £2, Conc. £3.
⌂ 🅿 🚻 €

Kilchurn Castle, Argyll

**visit hudsons guide online**

## DUART CASTLE 🏛
### ISLE OF MULL, ARGYLL PA64 6AP
www.duartcastle.com

**Tel:** 01680 812309 or 01577 830311   **E-mail:** duartguide@btinternet.com

**Owner/Contact:** Sir Lachlan Maclean Bt

Duart is a fortress, one of a line of castles stretching from Dunollie in the east to Mingary in the north, all guarding the Sound of Mull. The earliest part of the Castle was built in the 12th century, the keep was added in 1360 by the 5th Chief Lachlan Lubanach and the most recent alterations were completed in 1673. The Macleans were staunchly loyal to the Stuarts. After the rising of 1745 they lost Duart and their lands were forfeited. Sir Fitzroy Maclean, 25th Chief, restored the Castle in 1910. Duart remains the family home of the Chief of the Clan Maclean.

**Location:** MAP 12:O4, OS Ref. NM750 350. Off A849 on the east point of the Isle of Mull.

**Open:** Apr: Sun–Thurs, 11am–4pm. 1 May–7 Oct: daily, 10.30am–5.30pm. Shop & Tearoom: 1 May–1 Oct.

**Admission:** Adult: £5, Child (3–14) £2.50, Conc. £4.50, Family (2+2) £12.50.

🔲 T 🔲 Unsuitable. 🔲 ✠ By arrangement. 🅿 🔲 In grounds, on leads.

---

## DUMBARTON CASTLE ⚐
### Dumbarton, Strathclyde

**Tel:** 01389 732167

**Owner:** Historic Scotland   **Contact:** The Steward

**Location:** MAP 13:C8, OS Ref. NS401 744. 600yds S of A84 at E end of Dumbarton.

**Open:** 1 Apr–30 Sept: daily, 9.30am–6.30pm, last ticket 5.45pm. 1 Oct–31 Mar: Sat–Wed, 9.30am–4.30pm, last ticket 3.45pm.

**Admission:** Adult £4, Child £2, Conc £3.

🔲 T 🔲 🅿 🔲 ✱ 🔲 €

---

## DUNBLANE CATHEDRAL ⚐
### Dunblane

**Tel:** 01786 823388

**Owner:** Historic Scotland   **Contact:** The Steward

One of Scotland's noblest medieval churches. The lower part of the tower is Romanesque but the larger part of the building is of the 13th century. It was restored in 1889–93 by Sir Rowand Anderson.

**Location:** MAP 13:E6, OS Ref. NN782 015. In Dunblane.

**Open:** All year: Mon–Sat, 9.30am–6pm, Sun 2–6pm. Closed daily 12.30–1.30pm.

**Admission:** Free.

✱

Iona Abbey

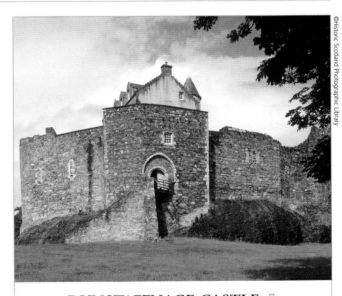

©Historic Scotland Photographic Library

## DUNSTAFFNAGE CASTLE ⚐
### BY OBAN, ARGYLL PA37 1PZ

**Tel:** 01631 562465

**Owner:** In the care of Historic Scotland   **Contact:** The Steward

A very fine 13th century castle built on a rock with a great curtain wall. The castle's colourful history stretches across the Wars of Independence to the 1745 rising. The castle was briefly the prison of Flora Macdonald. Marvellous views from the top of the curtain wall. Close by are the remains of a chapel with beautiful architectural detail.

**Location:** MAP 12:P4, OS49 NM882 344. 3½m NE of Oban off A85.

**Open:** Apr–Sept: daily, 9.30am–6.30pm, last ticket 30 mins before closing. Oct–Mar: daily, 9.30am–4.30pm. Closed Thurs & Fri.

**Admission:** Adult £3.50, Child £1.75, Conc. £2.80. 10% discount for groups (11+).

🔲 🔲 Partial. ✠ By arrangement. 🅿 🔲 Free pre-booked school visits.

🔲 In grounds, on leads. ✱ €

### THE HILL HOUSE

**Upper Colquhoun Street, Helensburgh  G84 9AJ**
**Tel:** 0131 243 9300
**Owner:** The National Trust for Scotland

Charles Rennie Mackintosh set this 20th century masterpiece high on a hillside overlooking the Firth of Clyde. Mackintosh also designed furniture, fittings and decorative schemes to complement the house.
**Location:** MAP 13:B7, OS Ref. NS300 820. Off B832, between A82 & A814, 23m NW of Glasgow.

### INCHMAHOME PRIORY

**Port of Menteith**
**Tel:** 01877 385294
**Owner:** In the care of Historic Scotland     **Contact:** The Steward

A beautifully situated Augustinian priory on an island in the Lake of Menteith founded in 1238 with much of the building surviving. The five year old Mary, Queen of Scots was sent here for safety in 1547.
**Location:** MAP 13:C6, OS Ref. NN574 005. On an island in Lake of Menteith. Reached by ferry from Port of Menteith, 4m E of Aberfoyle off A81.
**Open:** 1 Apr–30 Sept: daily, 9.30am–6.30pm, last ticket 6pm.
**Admission:** Adult £4.50, Child £2.25, Conc. £3.50. Charge includes ferry trip.
🖻 €

### INVERARAY CASTLE

*See page 479 for full page entry.*

### INVERARAY JAIL

**Church Square, Inveraray, Argyll  PA32 8TX**
**Tel:** 01499 302381     **Fax:** 01499 302195     **E-mail:** info@inverarayjail.co.uk
**www.inverarayjail.co.uk**
**Owner:** Visitor Centres Ltd     **Contact:** Gavin Dick

A living 19th century prison! Uniformed prisoners and warders, life-like figures, imaginative exhibitions, sounds, smells and trials in progress, bring the 1820 courtroom and former county prison back to life. See the 'In Prison Today' exhibition, an original 'Black Maria' and 'Katie' the cow. Don't forget to bring your camera!
**Location:** MAP 13 A:6, OS Ref. NN100 090. Church Square, Inveraray, Argyll.
**Open:** Apr–Oct: 9.30am–6pm, last admission 5pm. Nov–Mar: 10am–5pm, last admission 4pm.
**Admission:** Adult £6.50, Child £3.25, OAP £4.30, Family £17.80. Groups (10+): Adult £5.20, OAP £3.45.
🖻 🖳 Partial (FOC). 🔲 🖼 ✳

### IONA ABBEY & NUNNERY

**Iona, Argyll**
**Tel/Fax:** 01681 700512     **E-mail:** hs.ionaabbey@scotland.gov.uk
**www.historic-scotland.gov.uk**
**Owner:** In the care of Historic Scotland     **Contact:** The Steward

One of Scotland's most historic and venerated sites, Iona Abbey is a celebrated Christian centre and the burial place for many Scottish kings. The abbey and nunnery grounds house one of the most comprehensive collections of Christian carved stones in Scotland, dating from 600AD to the 1600s. Includes the Columba Centre, Fionnphort exhibition and giftshop.
**Location:** MAP 12:L5, OS Ref. NM270 240. Ferry service from Fionnphort, Mull.
**Open:** All year: daily.
**Admission:** Adult £4.50, Child (under 16yrs) £2.25, Conc. £3.50. Columba Centre, exhibition & giftshop: Free.
🖻 🖳 Partial. 🔲 🎫 🔲 🖼 In grounds. ✳ €

### KILCHURN CASTLE

**Loch Awe, Dalmally, Argyll**
**Tel:** 01786 431323
**Owner:** In the care of Historic Scotland     **Contact:** Neil Young

A square tower, built by Sir Colin Campbell of Glenorchy c1550, it was much enlarged in 1693 to give the building, now a ruin, its present picturesque outline. Spectacular views of Loch Awe.
**Location:** MAP 13:A5, OS Ref. NN133 276. At the NE end of Loch Awe, 2½ m W of Dalmally.
**Open:** Ferry service operates in the summer. Tel: 01838 200440 for times & prices.
**Admission:** Please telephone for details.

# MOUNT STUART
## ISLE OF BUTE  PA20 9LR
www.mountstuart.com

**Tel:** 01700 503877     **Fax:** 01700 505313     **E-mail:** contactus@mountstuart.com
**Owner:** Mount Stuart Trust     **Contact:** Donna Chisholm

Spectacular High Victorian gothic house, ancestral home of the Marquess of Bute. Splendid interiors, art collection and architectural detail. Set in 300 acres of stunning woodlands, mature Victorian pinetum, arboretum and exotic gardens.
**Location:** MAP 13:A9, OS Ref. NS100 600. SW coast of Scotland, 5m S of Rothesay. Local bus service to House, frequent ferry service from Wemyss Bay, Renfrewshire and Colintraive, Argyll.
**Open:** Easter & 1 May–30 Sept. Please telephone for detailed opening times.
**Admission:** Adult £7.50, Child £3.50, Conc. £6, Family £18. Groups (12+) discount available.
ℹ️ No photography. 🖻 🎫 🔲 🖳 🔲 Licensed. 🍽 Licensed. 🎫 Obligatory. 🅿 Ample.
🔲 🖼 Guide dogs only. 🎗 €

### ROTHESAY CASTLE

**Rothesay, Isle of Bute**
**Tel:** 01700 502691
**Owner:** In the care of Historic Scotland     **Contact:** The Steward

A favourite residence of the Stuart kings, this is a wonderful example of a 13th century circular castle of enclosure with 16th century forework containing the Great Hall. Attacked by Vikings in its earlier days.
**Location:** MAP 13:A8, OS Ref. NS088 646. In Rothesay, Isle of Bute. Ferry from Wemyss Bay on the A78.
**Open:** 1 Apr–30 Sept: daily, 9.30am–6.30pm, last ticket 6pm. 1 Oct–31 Mar: Sat–Wed, 9.30am–4.30pm, last ticket 4pm.
**Admission:** Adult £3.50, Child £1.50, Conc. £2.50.
🖻 🖳 Partial. 🖼 On leads. ✳ €

### ST BLANE'S CHURCH

**Kingarth, Isle of Bute**
**Tel:** 0131 668 8800
**Owner:** In the care of Historic Scotland

This 12th century Romanesque chapel stands on the site of a 12th century Celtic monastery.
**Location:** MAP 13:A9, OS Ref. NS090 570. At the S end of the Isle of Bute.
**Open:** All year: daily.
**Admission:** Free.
✳ €

See all the properties that are **open all year** in the index on page 580

**visit hudsons guide online**

©Historic Scotland Photographic Library

## TOROSAY CASTLE & GARDENS

### CRAIGNURE, ISLE OF MULL  PA65 6AY

www.torosay.com

**Tel:** 01680 812421   **Fax:** 01680 812470   **E-mail:** torosay@aol.com

**Owner/Contact:** Mr Chris James

Torosay Castle and Gardens set on the beautiful Island of Mull, was completed in 1858 by the eminent architect David Bryce in the Scottish baronial style, and is surrounded by 12 acres of spectacular gardens which offer a dramatic contrast between formal terraces, impressive statue walk and informal woodland, also rhododendron collection, alpine, walled, water and oriental gardens. The house offers family history, portraits, scrapbooks and antiques in an informal and relaxed atmosphere.

**Location:** MAP 12:O4, OS Ref. NM730 350. 1½m SE of Craignure by A849.

**Open:** House: 1 Apr–31 Oct: daily, 10.30am–5pm. Gardens: All year: daily, 9am–7pm or daylight hours in winter.

**Admission:** Adult £5.50, Child £3, Conc. £5, Family £15.

ℹ️ Children's adventure playground. ⬛ ⬛ Ⓣ ⬛ WC. ⬛ Ⓟ ⬛ Holiday cottages. ❄️ ♿ €

## STIRLING CASTLE ⬛

### CASTLE WYND, STIRLING  FK8 1EJ

**Tel:** 01786 450000   **Fax:** 01786 464678

**Owner:** Historic Scotland

Stirling Castle has played a key role in Scottish history, dominating the north–south and east–west routes through Scotland. The battles of Stirling Bridge and Bannockburn were fought in its shadow and Mary, Queen of Scots lived here as a child. Renaissance architecture, restored Great Hall and tapestry weaving.

**Location:** MAP 13:E7, OS Ref. NS790 941. At the top of Castle Wynd in Stirling.

**Open:** Apr–Sept: 9.30am–6pm. Oct–Mar: 9.30am–5pm. Last ticket 45 mins before closing.

**Admission:** Adult £8.50, Child £4.25, Conc. £6.50. 10% discount for groups (10+). Free booked school visits, except May–August.

ℹ️ Picnic area. Joint ticket with Argyll's Lodging. ⬛ Ⓣ Private hire. ♿ Partial. WC. ⬛ Licensed. ⬛ ⬛ Ⓟ ⬛ ⬛ Guide dogs only. ❄️ ♿ €

Stirling Castle

## ALTYRE ESTATE

**Altyre Estate, Forres, Moray IV36 2SH**

**Tel:** 01309 672265 **Fax:** 01309 672270 **E-mail:** agc@dialstart.net

**Contact:** Sir Alastair Gordon Cumming

Altyre Estate comprises architecturally interesting buildings including Italianate farm buildings, standing stones and access to areas of natural and ornithological interest. Altyre Estate may interest scientific groups, students, and the general public.

**Location:** MAP 16:P8, OS Ref. NJ028 552. Details given on appointment.

**Open:** Visitors are welcome by appointment on the first working day of Apr, May Jun, Jul & Aug.

**Admission:** Free.

## ARBUTHNOTT HOUSE

**Arbuthnott, Laurencekirk AB30 1PA**

**Tel:** 01561 361226 **E-mail:** keith@arbuthnott.co.uk **www.arbuthnott.co.uk**

**Owner:** The Viscount of Arbuthnot **Contact:** The Master of Arbuthnott

Arbuthnott family home for 800 years with formal 17th century walled garden on unusually steep south facing slope. Well maintained grass terraces, herbaceous borders, shrubs and greenhouses.

**Location:** MAP 14:K2, OS Ref. NO796 751. Off B967 between A90 and A92, 25m S of Aberdeen.

**Open:** House: 8/9 Apr, 27/28 May, 29/30 Jul, 5/6 & 26/27 Aug and by arrangement. Guided tours: 2–5pm. Garden: All year: 9am–5pm.

**Admission:** House: £4.50. Garden: £2.

⅃ Ground floor. ⓕ Obligatory. 🅿 ⊠ ✻

## BALFLUIG CASTLE

**Alford, Aberdeenshire AB33 8EJ**

**Tel:** 020 7624 3200

**Owner/Contact:** Mark Tennant of Balfluig

Small 16th century tower house in farmland, restored in 1967.

**Location:** OS Ref. NJ586 151. Alford, Aberdeenshire.

**Open:** Please write to M I Tennant Esq, 30 Abbey Gardens, London NW8 9AT. Occasionally let by the week for holidays. Graded *** by VisitScotland.

⅃ Unsuitable. ⊠ ⊞ 1 single, 4 double. ✻

## BALMORAL CASTLE (GROUNDS & EXHIBITIONS)

**Balmoral, Ballater, Aberdeenshire AB35 5TB**

**Tel:** 013397 42534 **Fax:** 013397 42034 **E-mail:** info@balmoralcastle.com **www.balmoralcastle.com**

**Owner:** Her Majesty The Queen **Contact:** Garry Marsden

Scottish home to The Royal Family. Ballroom, grounds and exhibitions, large café seating 120, quality gift shop. Excellent for coaches and groups. Holiday cottages, salmon fishing, Land Rover safaris and activity holidays.

**Location:** MAP 13:G1, OS Ref. NO256 951. Off A93 between Ballater and Braemar. 50m W of Aberdeen.

**Open:** 1 Apr–31 Jul: daily, 10am–5pm, last admission 4.30pm. Nov–20 Dec: Guided tours every Wed, 11am–2pm.

**Admission:** Adult £7, Child £1, OAP £6 (Audio tour included). Discounts for groups (20+).

▣ ▤ ⓕⒹ ▣

## BALVENIE CASTLE ⌂

**Dufftown**

**Tel:** 01340 820121

**Owner:** In the care of Historic Scotland **Contact:** The Steward

Picturesque ruins of 13th century moated stronghold originally owned by the Comyns. Visited by Edward I in 1304 and by Mary Queen of Scots in 1562. Occupied by Cumberland in 1746.

**Location:** MAP 17:B9, OS Ref. NJ326 408. At Dufftown on A941.

**Open:** 1 Apr–30 Sept: daily, 9.30am–6.30pm, last ticket 6pm.

**Admission:** Adult £3.50, Child £1.75, Conc. £2.80.

€

For rare and unusual plants visit the **plant sales** index on page 564

## BRODIE CASTLE ⚜

**Forres, Moray IV36 0TE**

**Tel:** 0131 243 9300

**Owner:** The National Trust for Scotland

The lime harled building is a typical 'Z' plan tower house with ornate corbelled battlements and bartizans, with 17th & 19th century additions.

**Location:** MAP 16:P8, OS Ref. NH980 577. Off A96 4½m W of Forres and 24m E of Inverness.

## CAIRNESS HOUSE
### LONMAY, FRASERBURGH, ABERDEENSHIRE AB43 8XP

www.cairnesshouse.com

**Tel/Fax:** 01346 582078 **E-mail:** info@cairnesshouse.com

**Owners:** Mr J Soriano-Ruiz / Mr K H Khairallah **Contact:** Property Manager

Cairness is Scotland's most extraordinary neoclassical house. Forgotten and neglected for decades, it is being brought back to life in a major restoration and now has one of the finest collections of furniture and paintings in the North East. The exquisite interiors include the earliest Egyptian room in Britain.

**Location:** MAP 17:F8, OS Ref. NK038 609. Off A90, 4m SE of Fraserburgh, ¼m W of B9033 about 2m S of St Comb's.

**Open:** 8 Apr–30 Sept: Mons, Weds, Fris & Suns 10am–4pm (last admission). Tours of house and restoration works every hour on the hour. Groups and special visits at all other times by prior appointment.

**Admission:** Adult £7, OAP/Student £6.

ⓘ No photography. No smoking. ⓕ Obligatory. 🅿 Limited. ⊠ ✻

## CASTLE FRASER & GARDEN ⚜

**Sauchen, Inverurie AB51 7LD**

**Tel:** 0131 243 9300

**Owner:** The National Trust for Scotland

Begun in 1575, the two low wings contribute to the scale and magnificence of the towers rising above them, combining to make this the largest and most elaborate of the Scottish castles built on the 'Z' plan.

**Location:** MAP 17:D11, OS Ref. NJ723 125. Off A944, 4m N of Dunecht & 16m W of Aberdeen.

## CORGARFF CASTLE ⌂

**Strathdon**

**Tel:** 013398 83635

**Owner:** In the care of Historic Scotland **Contact:** The Steward

A 16th century tower house converted into a barracks for Hanoverian troops in 1748.

**Location:** MAP 17:A11, OS Ref. NJ255 086. 8m W of Strathdon on A939. 14m NW of Ballater.

**Open:** 1 Apr–30 Sept: daily, 9.30am–6.30pm. 1 Oct–31 Mar: Sat & Sun, 9.30am–4.30pm. Last admission 30 mins before closing.

**Admission:** Adult £4.50, Child £2.25, Conc. £3.50.

✻ €

## CRAIG CASTLE

**Rhynie, Huntly, Aberdeenshire  AB54 4LP**
**Tel:** 01464 861705  **Fax:** 01464 861702
**Owner:** Mr A J Barlas  **Contact:** The Property Manager
The Castle is built round a courtyard and consists of a 16th century L-shaped Keep, a Georgian house (architect John Adam) and a 19th century addition (architect Archibald Simpson of Aberdeen). The Castle was a Gordon stronghold for 300 years. It has a very fine collection of coats-of-arms.
**Location:** MAP 17:C10, OS Ref. NJ472 259. 3m W of Rhynie and Lumsden on B9002.
**Open:** May–Sept: Wed & every 2nd weekend in each month, 2–5pm.
**Admission:** Adult £5, Child £1.
⊤ ⟐ Unsuitable. ⟨⟩ By arrangement. **P** Limited for coaches. ⟨⟩ Guide dogs only.

## CRAIGSTON CASTLE

**Turriff, Aberdeenshire  AB53 5PX**
**Tel:** 01888 551228/551640
**Owner:** William Pratesi Urquhart  **Contact:** Mrs Fiona Morrison
Built in 1607 by John Urquhart Tutor of Cromarty, Craigston bears the marks of a client's brief rather than an architect's whim, which seems to belong to that strange slightly Gothic world. Few changes have been made to its exterior in its 400 years. A sculpted balcony unique in Scottish architecture depicts a piper, two grinning knights and David and Goliath. The interior dates from the early 19th century. Remarkable carved oak panels of Scottish kings' biblical heroes, mounted in doors and shutters of the early 17th century. 18th century Craigston dinner service is on display until 2007 to mark the castle's 400th anniversary.
**Location:** MAP 17:D8, OS Ref. NJ762 550. On B9105, 4½m NE of Turriff.
**Open:** 30 Jun–8 Jul, 18–26 Aug, 8–16 Sept: daily, 11am–4pm.
**Admission:** Adult £6, Child £2, Conc. £4. Groups: Adult £5, Child/School £1.
⟐ Unsuitable. ⟨⟩ Obligatory. **P** ⟨⟩ In grounds on leads. ✳

## CRATHES CASTLE & GARDEN ♛

**Banchory  AB31 3QJ**
**Tel:** 0131 243 9300
**Owner:** The National Trust for Scotland
The building of the castle began in 1553 and took 40 years to complete. Just over 300 years later, Sir James and Lady Burnett began developing the walled garden.
**Location:** MAP 17:D12, OS Ref. NO733 969: On A93, 3m E of Banchory and 15m W of Aberdeen.

## CRUICKSHANK BOTANIC GARDEN

**St Machar Drive, Aberdeen  AB24 3UU**
**Tel:** 01224 272704  **Fax:** 01224 272703
**Owner:** University of Aberdeen  **Contact:** R B Rutherford
Extensive collection of shrubs, herbaceous and alpine plants and trees. Rock and water gardens.
**Location:** MAP 17:E11, OS Ref. NJ938 084. In old Aberdeen. Entrance in the Chanonry.
**Open:** All year: Mon–Fri, 9am–4.30pm. Also May–Sept: Sat & Sun, 2–5pm.
**Admission:** Free.

## DALLAS DHU DISTILLERY

**Forres**
**Tel:** 01309 676548
**Owner:** In the care of Historic Scotland  **Contact:** The Steward
A completely preserved time capsule of the distiller's craft. Wander at will through this fine old Victorian distillery then enjoy a dram. Visitor centre, shop and audio-visual theatre.
**Location:** MAP 16:P8, OS Ref. NJ035 566. 1m S of Forres off the A940.
**Open:** 1 Apr–30 Sept: daily, 9.30am–6.30pm, last ticket 6pm. 1 Oct–31 Mar: daily, 9.30am–4.30pm, last ticket 4pm. Closed Thurs and Fris in winter.
**Admission:** Adult £5, Child £2.50, Conc. £4.
ⓘ Visitor centre. WC. ⌂ ✳ €

Drum Castle, by Banchory

## DELGATIE CASTLE
### TURRIFF, ABERDEENSHIRE AB53 5TD
www.delgatiecastle.com

**Tel/Fax:** 01888 563479  **E-mail:** jjohnson@delgatie-castle.freeserve.co.uk
**Owner:** Delgatie Castle Trust  **Contact:** Mrs Joan Johnson
"Best Visitor Experience" Award Winner. Dating from 1030 the Castle is steeped in Scottish history yet still has the atmosphere of a lived in home. It has some of the finest painted ceilings in Scotland, Mary Queen of Scots' bed-chamber, armour, Victorian clothes, fine furniture and paintings are displayed. Widest turnpike stair of its kind in Scotland. Clan Hay Centre. 17th best place in Britain for afternoon tea.
**Location:** MAP 17:D9, OS Ref. NJ754 506. Off A947 Aberdeen to Banff Road.
**Open:** Daily, 10am–5pm. Closed Christmas & New Year weeks.
**Admission:** Adult £5, Child/Conc. £4, Family £14. Groups (10+): £4.
ⓘ No photography. ⌂ ⊤ ⟐ Ground floor. WC. ⟨⟩ Home-baking and lunches.
⟨⟩ By arrangement. **P** ▣ ⟨⟩ ✳ 6 x houses for self catering. ✳

## DRUM CASTLE & GARDEN ♛

**Drumoak, by Banchory  AB31 3EY**
**Tel:** 0131 243 9300
**Owner:** The National Trust for Scotland
Owned for 653 years by one family, the Irvines. The combination over the years of a 13th century square tower, a very fine Jacobean mansion house and the additions of the Victorian lairds make Drum Castle unique among Scottish castles.
**Location:** MAP 17:D12, OS Ref. NJ796 004. Off A93, 3m W of Peterculter and 10m W of Aberdeen.

## DRUMMUIR CASTLE

**Drummuir, by Keith, Banffshire  AB55 5JE**
**Tel:** 01542 810332  **Fax:** 01542 810302
**Owner:** The Gordon-Duff Family  **Contact:** Alison Noakes
Castellated Victorian Gothic-style castle built in 1847 by Admiral Duff. 60ft high lantern tower with fine plasterwork. Family portraits, interesting artefacts and other paintings.
**Location:** MAP 17:B9, OS Ref. NJ372 442. Midway between Keith (5m) and Dufftown, off the B9014.
**Open:** 1–30 Sept: tours 2–5pm.
**Admission:** Adult £2, Child £1.50. Pre-arranged groups: Adult £2, Child £1.50.
⟐ ⟨⟩ Obligatory. **P** ⟨⟩ In grounds on leads.

## DUFF HOUSE

**Banff  AB45 3SX**
**Tel:** 01261 818181  **Fax:** 01261 818900
**Contact:** The Manager
One of the most imposing and palatial houses in Scotland, with a strong classical façade and a grand staircase leading to the main entrance.
**Location:** MAP 17:D8, OS Ref. NJ691 634. Banff. 47m NW of Aberdeen on A947.
**Open:** Apr–Oct: daily, 11am–5pm. Nov–Mar: Thur–Sun, 11am–4pm.
**Admission:** Adult £5.50 Conc. £4.50, Family £14. Groups (10+): £4.50. Free admission to shop, tearoom, grounds & woodland walks. (Prices may change April 2007.)

## DUNNOTTAR CASTLE

**Dunnottar Castle Lodge, Stonehaven, Kincardineshire  AB39 2TL**
**Tel:** 01569 762173   **E-mail:** info@dunechtestates.co.uk
**www.dunechtestates.co.uk**    **Contact:** P McKenzie
Spectacular ruined cliff top fortress, home to the Earls Marischals of Scotland. The Crown Jewels of Scotland were hidden at this site, then smuggled away during the dark days of Cromwell's occupation.
**Location:** MAP 14:K1, OS Ref. NO881 839. Just off A92. 1½m SE of Stonehaven.
**Open:** Easter Mon–3rd week in Jun & 4th week in Sept–3rd week in Oct: Mon–Sat, 9am–6pm, Sun, 2–5pm. 4th week Oct–Easter Sun: Fri–Mon, 10.30am–sunset. Last ticket 30 mins before closing.
**Admission:** Adult £4, Child (under 16) £1. Groups (20+) 20% discount.

## ELGIN CATHEDRAL ⚶

**Elgin**
**Tel:** 01343 547171
**Owner:** Historic Scotland    **Contact:** The Steward
When entire this was perhaps the most beautiful of Scottish cathedrals, known as the Lantern of the North. 13th century, much modified after almost being destroyed in 1390 by Alexander Stewart, the infamous 'Wolf of Badenoch'. The octagonal chapterhouse is the finest in Scotland. You can see the bishop's home at Spynie Palace, 2m north of the town.
**Location:** MAP 17:A8, OS Ref. NJ223 630. In Elgin on the A96.
**Open:** 1 Apr–30 Sept: daily, 9.30am–6.30pm, last ticket 6pm. 1 Oct–31 Mar: daily, 9.30am–4.30pm, last ticket 4pm. Closed Thurs & Fris in winter.
**Admission:** Adult £4.50, Child £2.25, Conc. £3.50. Joint entry ticket available with Spynie Palace.
⌖ €

## FYVIE CASTLE ♔

**Turriff, Aberdeenshire  AB53 8JS**
**Tel:** 0131 243 9300
**Owner:** The National Trust for Scotland
The five towers of the castle bear witness to the five families who have owned it. Fyvie Castle has a fine wheel stair and a collection of arms and armour and paintings.
**Location:** MAP 17:D9, S Ref. NJ763 393. Off A947, 8m SE of Turriff, and 25m N of Aberdeen.

## HADDO HOUSE ♔

**Tarves, Ellon, Aberdeenshire  AB41 0ER**
**Tel:** 0131 243 9300
**Owner:** The National Trust for Scotland
Designed by William Adam in 1731 for William, 2nd Earl of Aberdeen. Much of the interior is 'Adam Revival' carried out about 1880 for John, 7th Earl and 1st Marquess of Aberdeen and his Countess, Ishbel.
**Location:** MAP 17:E10, OS Ref. NJ868 348. Off B999, 4m N of Pitmedden, 10m NW of Ellon.

## HUNTLY CASTLE ⚶

**Huntly**
**Tel:** 01466 793191
**Owner:** In the care of Historic Scotland    **Contact:** The Steward
Known also as Strathbogie Castle, this glorious ruin stands in a beautiful setting on the banks of the River Deveron. Famed for its fine heraldic sculpture and inscribed stone friezes.
**Location:** MAP 17:C9, OS Ref. NJ532 407. In Huntly on the A96. N side of the town.
**Open:** 1 Apr–30 Sept: daily, 9.30am–6.30pm, last ticket 6pm. 1 Oct–31 Mar: daily, 9.30am–4.30pm, last ticket 4pm. Closed Thurs & Fri in winter.
**Admission:** Adult £4.50, Child £2.25, Conc £3.50.
⌖ €

Tolquhon Castle, Aberdeenshire

©Historic Scotland Photographic Library

## KILDRUMMY CASTLE ⚶

**Alford, Aberdeenshire**
**Tel:** 01975 571331
**Owner:** In the care of Historic Scotland    **Contact:** The Steward
Though ruined, the best example in Scotland of a 13th century castle with a curtain wall, four round towers, hall and chapel of that date. The seat of the Earls of Mar, it was dismantled after the first Jacobite rising in 1715.
**Location:** MAP 17:C11, OS Ref. NJ455 164. 10m W of Alford on the A97. 16m SSW of Huntley.
**Open:** 1 Apr–30 Sept: daily, 9.30am–6.30pm, last ticket 6pm.
**Admission:** Adult £3.50, Child £1.75, Conc. £2.80.
ℹ WC. ⬚ ♿ WC 🅿 €

## KILDRUMMY CASTLE GARDEN

**Kildrummy, Aberdeenshire**
**Tel:** 01975 571203 / 563451    **Contact:** Alastair J Laing
Ancient quarry, shrub and alpine gardens renowned for their interest and variety. Water gardens below ruined castle.
**Location:** MAP 17:C11, OS Ref. NJ455 164. On A97 off A944 10m SW of Alford. 16m SSW of Huntly.
**Open:** Apr–Oct: daily, 10am–5pm.
**Admission:** Adult £3.50, Child Free.

## LEITH HALL ♔

**Huntly, Aberdeenshire  AB54 4NQ**
**Tel:** 0131 243 9300
**Owner:** The National Trust for Scotland    **Contact:** The Property Manager
This mansion house, built around a courtyard was the home of the Leith family for almost 300 years.
**Location:** MAP 17:C10, OS Ref. NJ541 298. B9002, 1m W of Kennethmont, 7m S of Huntley.

## LICKLEYHEAD CASTLE

**Auchleven, Insch, Aberdeenshire  AB52 6PN**
**Tel:** 01651 821276
**Owner:** The Leslie family    **Contact:** Mrs C Leslie
A beautifully restored Laird's Castle, Lickleyhead was built by the Leslies c1450 and extensively renovated in 1629 by John Forbes of Leslie, whose initials are carved above the entrance. It is an almost unspoilt example of the transformation from 'Chateau-fort' to 'Chateau-maison' and boasts many interesting architectural features.
**Location:** MAP 17:C10, OS Ref. NJ628 237. Auchleven is 2m S of Insch on B992. Twin pillars of castle entrance on left at foot of village.
**Open:** 1–4 & 8–17 May: daily. 2 & 9 Jun, Jul–Aug & 1 Sept: Sats. 12 noon–2pm.
**Admission:** Free.
♿ Unsuitable. 🅿 Limited. No coaches. 🐾 In grounds, on leads.

## PITMEDDEN GARDEN ♔

**Ellon, Aberdeenshire  AB41 0PD**
**Tel:** 0131 243 9300
**Owner:** The National Trust for Scotland
The centrepiece of this property is the Great Garden which was originally laid out in 1675 by Sir Alexander Seton, 1st Baronet of Pitmedden.
**Location:** MAP 17:E10, OS Ref. NJ885 280. On A920 1m W of Pitmedden village & 14m N of Aberdeen.

## PLUSCARDEN ABBEY

**Nr Elgin, Moray  IV30 8UA**
**Tel:** 01343 890257   **Fax:** 01343 890258   **E-mail:** monks@pluscardenabbey.org
**Contact:** Brother Michael
Valliscaulian, founded 1230.
**Location:** MAP 17:A8, OS Ref. NJ142 576. On minor road 6m SW of Elgin. Follow B9010 for first mile.
**Open:** All year: 4.45am–8.30pm. Shop: 8.30am–5pm.
**Admission:** Free.

## PROVOST SKENE'S HOUSE

**Guestrow, off Broad Street, Aberdeen  AB10 1AS**
**Tel:** 01224 641086  **Fax:** 01224 632133
**Owner:** Aberdeen City Council    **Contact:** Christine Rew
Built in the 16th century, Provost Skene's House is one of Aberdeen's few remaining examples of early burgh architecture. Splendid room settings include a suite of Georgian rooms, an Edwardian nursery, magnificent 17th century plaster ceilings and wood panelling. The house also features an intriguing series of religious paintings in the Painted Gallery and changing fashions in the Costume Gallery.
**Location:** MAP 17:E11, OS Ref. NJ943 064. Aberdeen city centre, off Broad Street.
**Open:** Mon–Sat, 10am–5pm, Suns 1–4pm.
**Admission:** Free.

## ST MACHAR'S CATHEDRAL TRANSEPTS

**Old Aberdeen**
**Tel:** 0131 668 8800
**Owner:** In the care of Historic Scotland
The nave and towers of the Cathedral remain in use as a church, and the ruined transepts are in care. In the south transept is the fine altar tomb of Bishop Dunbar (1514–32).
**Location:** MAP 17:E11, OS Ref. NJ939 088. In old Aberdeen. ½m N of King's College.
**Admission:** Free.

## SPYNIE PALACE

**Elgin**
**Tel:** 01343 546358
**Owner:** In the care of Historic Scotland    **Contact:** The Steward
Spynie Palace was the residence of the Bishops of Moray from the 14th century to 1686. The site is dominated by the massive tower built by Bishop David Stewart (1461–77) and affords spectacular views across Spynie Loch.
**Location:** MAP 17:A8, OS Ref. NJ231 659. 2m N of Elgin off the A941.
**Open:** 1 Apr–30 Sept: daily, 9.30am–6.30pm. 1 Oct–31 Mar: Sat & Sun, 9.30am–4.30pm. Last ticket 30 mins before closing.
**Admission:** Adult £3.50, Child £1.75, Conc. £2.80. Joint entry ticket with Elgin Cathedral: Adult £5, Child £2.10, Conc. £2.30.
Picnic area. WC. P €

## TOLQUHON CASTLE

**Aberdeenshire**
**Tel:** 01651 851286
Owner: In the care of Historic Scotland    **Contact:** The Steward
Tolquhon was built for the Forbes family. The early 15th century tower was enlarged between 1584 and 1589 with a large mansion around the courtyard. Noted for its highly ornamented gatehouse and pleasance.
**Location:** MAP 17:E10, OS Ref. NJ874 286. 15m N of Aberdeen on the A920. 6m N of Ellon.
**Open:** 1 Apr–30 Sept: daily, 9.30am–6.30pm. 1 Oct–31 Mar: Sat & Sun, 9.30am–4.30pm. Last ticket 30 mins before closing.
**Admission:** Adult £3.50, Child £1.75, Conc. £2.80.
Picnic area. WC. P €

## DAVID WELCH WINTER GARDENS – DUTHIE PARK

**Polmuir Road, Aberdeen, Grampian Highlands  AB11 7TH**
**Tel:** 01224 585310  **Fax:** 01224 210532  **E-mail:** wintergardens@aberdeencity.gov.uk
**www.aberdeencity.gov.uk**
**Owner:** Aberdeen City Council    **Contact:** Alan Findlay
One of Europe's largest indoor gardens with many rare and exotic plants on show from all around the world.
**Location:** MAP 17:E11, OS Ref. NJ97 044. Just N of River Dee, 1m S of city centre.
**Open:** All year: daily from 9.30pm.
**Admission:** Free.

See all the properties that are **open all year** in the index on page 580

Provost Skene's House

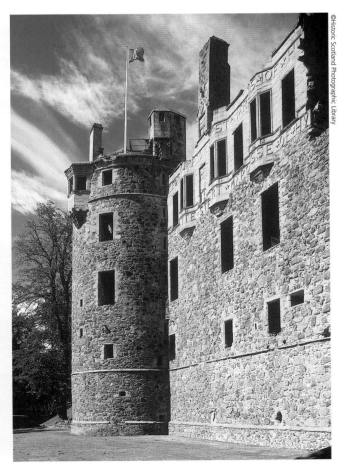

Huntly Castle

©Historic Scotland Photographic Library

### ■ Owner
The Dowager Countess Cawdor

### ■ Contact
The Administrator
David Broadfoot
Cawdor Castle
Nairn
Scotland  IV12 5RD

**Tel:** 01667 404401
**Fax:** 01667 404674
**E-mail:** info@
cawdorcastle.com

### ■ Location
**MAP 16:O9**
**OS Ref. NH850 500**

From Edinburgh
A9, 3½ hrs,
Inverness 20 mins,
Nairn 10 mins.
Main road: A9, 14m.

**Rail:** Nairn
Station 5m.

**Bus:** Inverness to Nairn
bus route 200 yds.

**Taxi:** Cawdor Taxis
01667 404315.

**Air:** Inverness
Airport 5m.

### ■ Opening Times
**Summer**
1 May–14 October
Daily: 10am–5.30pm.
Last admission 5pm.

**Winter**
October–April
Groups by appointment,
admission prices on
application.

**Auchindoune Garden**
May–July: Tue & Thurs,
10am–4.30pm.

Otherwise by
appointment.

### ■ Admission
**Summer**
**House & Garden**

| | |
|---|---|
| Adult | £7.30 |
| Child (5–15yrs) | £4.50 |
| OAP/Student | £6.30 |
| Family (2+5) | £23.50 |

**Groups (20+)**

| | |
|---|---|
| Adult | £6.30 |
| Child (5–15yrs) | £4.00 |
| OAP/Student | £6.30 |

**Garden only**

| | |
|---|---|
| Per person | £4.00 |

**RHS Access**
Free admission to gardens
May, June, September &
October.

### ■ Special Events
**June 9/10**
Special Gardens
Weekend: Guided tours
of Gardens / Garden
Festival.

**September 29**
Living Food at Cawdor
Castle – A celebration of
organic food.

### Conference/Function

| ROOM | SIZE | MAX CAPACITY |
|---|---|---|
| Cawdor Hall | | 40 |

# CAWDOR CASTLE
www.cawdorcastle.com

This splendid romantic castle, dating from the late 14th century, was built as a private fortress by the Thanes of Cawdor, and remains the home of the Cawdor family to this day. The ancient medieval tower was built around the legendary holly tree.

Although the house has evolved over 600 years, later additions, mainly of the 17th century, were all built in the Scottish vernacular style with slated roofs over walls and crow-stepped gables of mellow local stone. This style gives Cawdor a strong sense of unity, and the massive, severe exterior belies an intimate interior that gives the place a surprisingly personal, friendly atmosphere.

Good furniture, fine portraits and pictures, interesting objects and outstanding tapestries are arranged to please the family rather than to echo fashion or impress. Memories of Shakespeare's *Macbeth* give Cawdor an elusive, evocative quality that delights visitors.

### Gardens
The flower garden also has a family feel to it, where plants are chosen out of affection rather than affectation. This is a lovely spot between spring and late summer. The walled garden has been restored with a holly maze, paradise garden, knot garden and thistle garden. The wild garden beside its stream leads into beautiful trails through spectacular mature mixed woodland, in which paths are helpfully marked and colour-coded. The Tibetan garden and traditional Scottish vegetable garden are at the Dower House at Auchindoune.

| | |
|---|---|
| **i** | 9 hole golf course, putting green, golf clubs for hire, Conferences, whisky tasting, musical entertainments, specialised garden visits. No photography, video taping or tripods inside. |
| | Gift, book and wool shops. |
| | Lunches, sherry or champagne receptions. |
| | Visitors may alight at the entrance. WC. Only ground floor accessible. |
| | Licensed Buttery, May–Oct, groups should book. |
| | By arrangement. |
| **P** | 250 cars and 25 coaches. Two weeks' notice for group catering, coach drivers/couriers free. |
| | £3.70 per child. Room notes, quiz and answer sheet can be provided. |
| | Guide dogs only. |

# DUNVEGAN CASTLE

www.dunvegancastle.com

### ■ Owner
John Macleod of Macleod

### ■ Contact
The Administrator
Dunvegan Castle
Isle of Skye
Scotland  IV55 8WF

**Tel:** 01470 521206
**Fax:** 01470 521205
**Seal Tel:** 01470 521500
**E-mail:** info@
dunvegancastle.com

### ■ Location
**MAP 15:F9**
**OS Ref. NG250 480**

1m N of village. NW corner of Skye.

From Inverness A82 to Invermoriston, A887 to Kyle of Lochalsh 82m. From Fort William A82 to Invergarry, A87 to Kyle of Lochalsh 76m.

Kyle of Lochalsh to Dunvegan 45m via Skye Bridge (toll).

Ferry: To the Isle of Skye, 'roll-on, roll-off', 30 minute crossing.

**Rail:** Inverness to Kyle of Lochalsh 3–4 trains per day – 45m.

**Bus:** Portree 25m, Kyle of Lochalsh 45m.

### ■ Opening Times
**Summer**
20 March–31 October
Daily: 10am–5.30pm.
Last admission 5pm.

**Winter**
1 November–mid March
Daily: 11am–4pm.
Last admission 3.30pm.

Closed Christmas Day, Boxing Day, New Year's Day and 2 January.

### ■ Admission
**Summer**
**Castle & Gardens**

| | |
|---|---|
| Adult | £7.00 |
| Child (5–15yrs) | £4.00 |
| OAP/Student | £6.00 |
| Groups (10+) | £6.00 |

**Gardens only**

| | |
|---|---|
| Adult | £5.00 |
| Child (5–15yrs) | £3.00 |
| Senior/Student | £3.50 |

**Seal Boats**

| | |
|---|---|
| Adult | £6.00 |
| Child (5–12yrs) | £3.50 |
| Child (under 5yrs) | £1.50 |

**Winter**

| | |
|---|---|
| Adult | £5.00 |
| Child (5–15yrs) | £2.50 |
| Conc. | £3.50 |
| Groups (10+) | £3.50 |

(2006 prices.)

Dunvegan is unique. It is the only Great House in the Western Isles of Scotland to have retained its family and its roof. It is the oldest home in the whole of Scotland continuously inhabited by the same family – the Chiefs of the Clan Macleod. A Castle placed on a rock by the sea – the curtain wall is dated before 1200 AD – its superb location recalls the Norse Empire of the Vikings, the ancestors of the Chiefs.

Dunvegan's continuing importance as a custodian of the Clan spirit is epitomised by the famous Fairy Flag, whose origins are shrouded in mystery but whose ability to protect both Chief and Clan is unquestioned. To enter Dunvegan is to arrive at a place whose history combines with legend to make a living reality.

### Gardens
The gardens and grounds extend over some ten acres of woodland walks, peaceful formal lawns and a water garden dominated by two spectacular natural waterfalls. The temperate climate aids in producing a fine show of rhododendrons and azaleas, the chief glory of the garden in spring. One is always aware of the proximity of the sea and many garden walks finish at the Castle Jetty, from where traditional boats make regular trips to view the delightful Seal Colony.

The Library

The Dining Room

ℹ️ Boat trips to seal colony. Pedigree Highland cattle. No photography in Castle.

🛍️ Gift and craft shop.

♿ Visitors may alight at entrance. WC.

🍴 Licensed restaurant, (cap. 70) special rates for groups, menus upon request. Tel: 01470 521310. Open late peak season for evening meals.

🚶 By appointment in English or Gaelic at no extra charge. If requested owner may meet groups, tour time 45mins.

🅿️ 120 cars and 10 coaches. Do not attempt to take passengers to Castle Jetty (long walk). If possible please book. Seal boat trip dependent upon weather.

🎓 Welcome by arrangement. Guide available on request.

🐕 In grounds only, on lead. Guide Dogs allowed in Castle.

🛏️ 4 self-catering units, 3 of which sleep 6 and 1 of which sleeps 7.

❄️

### BALLINDALLOCH CASTLE

**Ballindalloch, Banffshire  AB37 9AX**
**Tel:** 01807 500205  **Fax:** 01807 500210  **E-mail:** enquiries@ballindallochcastle.co.uk
**www.ballindallochcastle.co.uk**
**Owner:** Mr & Mrs Oliver Russell    **Contact:** Mrs Clare Russell

Ballindalloch Castle is, first and foremost, a much-loved home, lived in by its original family, the MacPherson-Grants, since 1546. Filled with family memorabilia, including an important collection of 17th century Spanish paintings. Beautiful rock and rose gardens and river walks. The estate is home to the famous Aberdeen-Angus breed of cattle.

**Location:** MAP 17:A9, OS Ref. NJ178 366. 14 m NE of Grantown-on-Spey on A95. 22 m S of Elgin on A95.

**Open:** Good Fri–30 Sept: 10.30am–5pm. Closed Saturdays. Coaches outwith season by arrangement.

**Admission:** House & Grounds: Adult £7, Child (6–16) £3.50, Conc. £6, Family (2+3) £18, Groups (20+) Adult £5, Child £2.50, Season Ticket £18. Grounds only: Adult £3.50, Child (6–16) £2, Conc. £3, Season Ticket £9.

🏠📷 Ground floor and grounds only. WCs. 🎁🏠🅿️🚶 In grounds on leads. Dog walking area.

### CASTLE LEOD

**Strathpeffer  IV14 9AA**
**Tel/Fax:** 01997 421264   **E-mail:** cromartie@castle-leod.freeserve.co.uk
**Owner/Contact:** The Earl of Cromartie

Turreted 15th century tower house of rose-pink stone. Lived in by the Mackenzie family, chiefs of the clan, for 500 years and still very much a home where the family ensure a personal welcome. Magnificent setting below Ben Wyvis and amongst some of the finest trees in Scotland.

**Location:** MAP 16:M8, OS Ref. NH485 593. 1km E of Strathpeffer on the A834 Strathpeffer to Dingwall road.

**Open:** 26–29 Apr, 17–20 May, 7–10 Jun, 28 Jun–1 Jul, 29 Aug–2 Sept & 20–23 Sept: 2–5.30pm (last admission 4.45pm).

**Admission:** Adult £5, Child £2, OAP/Student £4.

ℹ️ No coaches. 🎁📷 Grounds only. WC. 🅵 By arrangement, all year. 🅿️ No coach parking. 🚶 Guide dogs only. 🎖️

## CASTLE OF MEY
### THURSO, CAITHNESS  KW14 8XH
www.castleofmey.org.uk

**Tel:** 01847 851473   **Fax:** 01847 851475   **E-mail:** castleofmey@totalise.co.uk
**Owner:** The Queen Elizabeth Castle of Mey Trust    **Contact:** James Murray

The home of The Queen Mother in Caithness and the only property in Britain that she owned. She bought the Castle in 1952, saved it from becoming a ruin and developed the gardens. It became her ideal holiday home because of the beautiful surroundings and the privacy she was always given. New purpose-built Visitors' Centre and an animal farm now open.

**Location:** MAP 17:B2, OS Ref. ND290 739. On A836 between Thurso and John O'Groats, just outside the village of Mey. 12m Thurso station, 18m Wick airport.

**Open:** 1 May–26 Jul & 8 Aug–30 Sept: daily, 10.30am–4pm.

**Admission:** Adult £7.50, Child (16yrs and under) £3, Conc. £6.50. Family £19. Booked groups (15+): £6.50. Gardens & grounds only: Adult £3, Conc. £2.50.

ℹ️ No photography in the Castle. 🏠🅵📷 Partial. WCs.🎁 🅵 By arrangement. 🅿️🚶🚶 In grounds, on leads.

### CASTLE OF OLD WICK 🏛️

**Wick**
**Tel:** 01667 460232
**Owner/Contact:** Historic Scotland

Essential work to safeguard the future of Scotland's best-preserved Norse castle has been completed. Visitors can now enjoy visiting this dramatically located castle once again. One of the oldest keeps in Scotland, the castle is a simple square keep of at least three storeys. In addition to the tower the site contains the low-lying ruins of other buildings. These have never been excavated and are largely covered by turf in order to protect them from damage.

**Location:** MAP 17:B3, OS Ref. ND368 487. 1m S of Wick on Shore Road, E of A9.

**Open:** All year.

**Admission:** Free.

✳️

### CAWDOR CASTLE 🏛️

*See page 488 for full page entry.*

### THE DOUNE OF ROTHIEMURCHUS 🏛️

**By Aviemore  PH22 1QH**
**Tel:** 01479 812345   **E-mail:** info@rothie.co.uk   **www.rothiemurchus.net**
**Owner:** J P Grant of Rothiemurchus    **Contact:** Rothiemurchus Visitor Centre

The family home of the Grants of Rothiemurchus was nearly lost as a ruin and has been under an ambitious repair programme since 1975. This exciting project may be visited on selected Mondays throughout the season and on other days by arrangement by email. Book with the Visitor Centre for a longer 2hr 'Highland Lady' tour which explores the haunts of Elizabeth Grant of Rothiemurchus, born 1797, author of Memoirs of a Highland Lady, who vividly described the Doune and its surroundings from the memories of her childhood.

**Location:** MAP 16:P11, OS Ref. NH900 100. 2m S of Aviemore on E bank of Spey river.

**Open:** House: selected Mons. Grounds: Apr–Aug: Mon, 10am–12.30pm & 2–4.30pm, also 1st Mon in the month during winter.

**Admission:** House only £1. Tour (booking essential, 4+) £10pp.

ℹ️ Visitor Centre. 🏠🅵 Obligatory. 🅿️ Limited. 🚶 In grounds, on leads.

## DUNROBIN CASTLE 🏛️
### GOLSPIE, SUTHERLAND  KW10 6SF
www.highlandescape.com

**Tel:** 01408 633177   **Fax:** 01408 634081   **E-mail:** info@dunrobincastle.net
**Owner:** The Sutherland Trust    **Contact:** Scott Morrison

Dates from the 13th century with additions in the 17th, 18th and 19th centuries. Wonderful furniture, paintings, library, ceremonial robes and memorabilia. Victorian museum in grounds with a fascinating collection including Pictish stones. Set in fine woodlands overlooking the sea. Magnificent formal gardens, one of few remaining French/Scottish formal parterres. Falconry display.

**Location:** MAP 16:O6, OS Ref. NC850 010. 50m N of Inverness on A9. 1m NE of Golspie.

**Open:** 1 Apr–15 Oct: Mon–Sat, 10.30am–4.30pm. Suns, 12 noon–4.30pm.
1 Jun–30 Sept: Mon–Sat, 10.30am–5.30pm, Suns, 12 noon–5.30pm (Jul & Aug: Suns, opens at 10.30am.)

**Admission:** Adult £7, Child £5, OAP/Student. £6, Family (2+2) £19. Booked groups: Adult £6, OAP. £5.50.

🏠🎁📷 Unsuitable for wheelchairs. 🎁 🍴🅵 By arrangement. 🅿️🚶

The Queen Elizabeth Castle of Mey Trust

**DUNVEGAN CASTLE** 🏛 *See page 489 for full page entry.*

### EILEAN DONAN CASTLE

**Dornie, Kyle of Lochalsh, Wester Ross IV40 8DX**
**Tel:** 01599 555202 **Fax:** 01599 555262 **E-mail:** info@donan.f9.co.uk
**www.eileandonancastle.com** **Contact:** David Win – Castle Keeper
**Location:** MAP 16:J10, OS Ref. NG880 260. On A87 8m E of Skye Bridge.
**Open:** Apr–Oct: 10am–5.30pm.
**Admission:** Adult £4.95, Conc. £3.95.

Ballindalloch Castle, Banffshire

©Historic Scotland Photographic Library

## FORT GEORGE 🏛
### ARDERSIER BY INVERNESS IV1 2TD

**Tel/Fax:** 01667 460232
**Owner:** In the care of Historic Scotland **Contact:** Brian Ford
Built following the Battle of Culloden to subdue the Highlands, Fort George never saw a shot fired in anger. One of the most outstanding artillery fortifications in Europe with reconstructed barrack room displays. The Queen's Own Highlanders' Museum.
**Location:** MAP 16:O6, OS Ref. NH762 567. 11m NE of Inverness off the A96 by Ardersier.
**Open:** Apr–Sept: daily, 9.30am–6.30pm. Oct–Mar: daily, 9.30am–4.30pm. Last ticket sold 45 mins before closing.
**Admission:** Adult £6.50, Child £3.25, Conc. £5. 10% discount for groups (11+).
ⓘ Picnic tables. 📷 🎭 Private evening hire. ♿ Wheelchairs available. WCs.
🍴 🏠 🅿 ▣ Free if pre-booked. 🐕 In grounds, on leads. ❋ 🎦 €

©Historic Scotland Photographic Library

## URQUHART CASTLE 🏛
### DRUMNADROCHIT, LOCH NESS

**Tel:** 01456 450551
**Owner:** In the care of Historic Scotland **Contact:** Euan Fraser
The remains of one of the largest castles in Scotland dominate a rocky promontory on Loch Ness. Most of the existing buildings date from the 16th century. New visitor centre with original artefacts, audio-visual presentation, shop and café.
**Location:** MAP 16:M10, OS Ref. NH531 286. On Loch Ness, 1½m S of Drumnadrochit on A82.
**Open:** 1 Apr–30 Sept: daily, 9.30am–6.30pm. Last ticket 5.45pm. 1 Oct–31 Mar: daily, 9.30am–4.30pm. Last ticket 3.45pm.
**Admission:** Adult £6.50, Child £3.25, Conc. £5.
📷 🎭 ♿ Partial. WCs. 🍴 🅿 🏠 ▣ Free if pre-booked. 🐕 Assistance dogs. ❋ €

Cawdor Castle, Nairn

## BALFOUR CASTLE

**Shapinsay, Orkney Islands  KW17 2DY**

**Tel:** 01856 711282   **Fax:** 01856 711283

**Owner/Contact:** Mrs Lidderdale

Built in 1848. Now a small private hotel specialising in house parties, weddings etc. A beautiful island escape.

**Location:** MAP 14, OS Ref. HY475 164 on Shapinsay Island, 3½m NNE of Kirkwall.

**Open:** May–Sept: Suns only, 2.15–5.30pm.

**Admission:** Admission includes boat fare, guided tour, gardens & afternoon tea. Bookings essential. Contact property for details.

## BISHOP'S & EARL'S PALACES

**Kirkwall, Orkney**

**Tel:** 01856 875461

**Owner:** In the care of Historic Scotland    **Contact:** The Steward

The Bishop's Palace is a 12th century hall-house with a round tower built by Bishop Reid in 1541–48. The adjacent Earl's Palace built in 1607 has been described as the most mature and accomplished piece of Renaissance architecture left in Scotland.

**Location:** MAP 14, Bishop's Palace: OS Ref. HY447 108. Earl's Palace: OS Ref. HY448 108. In Kirkwall on A960.

**Open:** 1 Apr–30 Sept: daily, 9.30am–6.30pm, last ticket 6pm.

**Admission:** Adult £3.50, Child £1.75, Conc. £2.80. Joint entry ticket available for all the Orkney monuments.

€

## BLACK HOUSE

**Arnol, Isle of Lewis**

**Tel:** 01851 710395

**Owner:** In the care of Historic Scotland    **Contact:** The Steward

A traditional Lewis thatched house, fully furnished, complete with attached barn, byre and stockyard. A peat fire burns in the open hearth. New visitor centre open and restored 1920s croft house.

**Location:** MAP 15, OS Ref. NB320 500. In Arnol village, 11m NW of Stornoway on A858.

**Open:** 1 Apr–30 Sept: Mon–Sat, 9.30am–6.30pm, last ticket 6pm. 1 Oct–31 Mar: Mon–Thur & Sat, 9.30am–4.30pm, last ticket 4pm.

**Admission:** Adult £3.50, Child £1.75, Conc. £2.80.

⊞ €

## BROCH OF GURNESS

**Aikerness, Orkney**

**Tel:** 01831 579478

**Owner:** In the care of Historic Scotland    **Contact:** The Steward

Protected by three lines of ditch and rampart, the base of the broch is surrounded by Iron Age buildings.

**Location:** MAP 14, OS Ref. HY383 268. At Aikerness, about 14m NW of Kirkwall on A966.

**Open:** 1 Apr–30 Sept: daily, 9.30am–6.30pm, last ticket 6pm.

**Admission:** Adult £4.50, Child £2.25, Conc. £3.50. Joint entry ticket available for all Orkney monuments.

€

## CARRICK HOUSE

**Carrick, Eday, Orkney  KW17 2AB**

**Tel:** 01857 622260

**Owner:** Mr & Mrs Joy    **Contact:** Mrs Rosemary Joy

17th century house built by John Stewart, Lord Kinclaven, Earl of Carrick younger brother of Patrick, 2nd Earl of Orkney in 1633. Scene of Pirate Gow's capture.

**Location:** MAP 14, OS Ref. NT227 773. N of island of Eday on minor roads W of B9063 just W of the shore of Calf Sound. Regular ferry service.

**Open:** Jun–Sept: occasional Suns by appointment only.

**Admission:** No fee. Donations to charity.

See which properties offer **educational facilities** or **school visits** in our index on page 571

## JARLSHOF PREHISTORIC & NORSE SETTLEMENT

**Shetland**

**Tel:** 01950 460112

**Owner:** In the care of Historic Scotland    **Contact:** The Steward

Over 3 acres of remains spanning 3,000 years from the Stone Age. Oval-shaped Bronze Age houses, Iron Age broch and wheel houses. Viking long houses, medieval farmstead and 16th century laird's house.

**Location:** MAP 17, OS Ref. HY401 096. At Sumburgh Head, 22m S of Lerwick on the A970.

**Open:** 1 Apr–30 Sept: daily, 9.30am–6.30pm. Last ticket 30mins before closing.

**Admission:** Adult £4.50, Child £2.25, Conc. £3.50.

€

## KISIMUL CASTLE

**Castlebay, Isle of Barra HS9 5UZ**

**Tel:** 01871 810313

**Owner:** In the care of Historic Scotland    **Contact:** The Monument Manager

The traditional seat of the chiefs of the clan Macneil, the castle stands on a rocky islet in a sea bay just off the island of Barra. It is the only significant surviving medieval castle in the Western Isles. Parts of Kisimul date back to the first half of the 1400s. The mighty curtain wall and strong tower helped fend off a series of attacks. It now makes a delightful place to visit and offers excellent views of the sea and the island.

**Location:** MAP 15 C:12. OS Ref. NL665 979. In Castlebay, Isle of Barra, five minute boat trip weather permitting.

**Open:** Summer only.

**Admission:** Adult £4.50, Child £2.25, Conc. £3.50. Includes boat trip.

▣ €

## MAESHOWE

**Orkney**

**Tel:** 01856 761606

**Owner:** In the care of Historic Scotland    **Contact:** The Steward

This world-famous tomb was built in Neolithic times, before 2700 BC. The large mound covers a stone-built passage and a burial chamber with cells in the walls. Runic inscriptions tell of how it was plundered of its treasures by Vikings.

**Location:** MAP 14, OS Ref. NY318 128. 9m W of Kirkwall on the A965.

**Open:** 1 Apr–30 Sept: daily, 9.30am–6.30pm. 1 Oct–31 Mar: daily, 9.30am–4.30pm.

**Admission:** Adult £5, Child £2.50, Conc. £4. Joint entry ticket for all Orkney monuments available. Timed ticketing in place – please telephone for details, and to book. Admission and shop at nearby Tormiston Mill.

▣ ♿ P Limited. ⊞ ⊞ €

## RING OF BRODGAR STONE CIRCLE & HENGE

**Stromness, Orkney**

**Tel:** 0131 668 8800

**Owner/Contact:** In the care of Historic Scotland

A magnificent circle of upright stones with an enclosing ditch spanned by causeways. Of late Neolithic date.

**Location:** MAP 14, OS Ref. HY294 134. 5m NE of Stromness.

**Open:** Any reasonable time.

**Admission:** Free.

⊞

©Historic Scotland Photographic Library

Ring of Brodgar Stone Circle & Henge, Orkney

## SKARA BRAE & SKAILL HOUSE 🏛

### SANDWICK, ORKNEY

**Tel:** 01856 841815

**Owner:** Historic Scotland/Major M R S Macrae     **Contact:** The Steward

Skara Brae is one of the best preserved groups of Stone Age houses in Western Europe. Built before the Pyramids, the houses contain stone furniture, hearths and drains. Visitor centre and replica house with joint admission with Skaill House – 17th century home of the laird who excavated Skara Brae.

**Location:** MAP 14, OS6 HY231 188. 19m NW of Kirkwall on the B9056.

**Open:** Apr–Sept: daily, 9.30am–6.30pm. Oct–Mar: daily, 9.30am–4.30pm. Last ticket 45 mins before closing.

**Admission:** Apr–Sept: Adult £6.50, Child £3.25, Conc. £5. Oct–Mar: Adult £5.50, Child £2.75, Conc. £4.50. 10% discount for groups (10+). Joint ticket with other Orkney sites available.

ℹ Visitor centre. 📷 ♿ Partial. WCs. 🍴 Licensed. 🅿
🏫 Free school visits when booked. 🐕 Guide dogs only. ✱ €

## TANKERNESS HOUSE

**Broad Street, Kirkwall, Orkney**

**Tel:** 01856 873535     **Fax:** 01856 871560

**Owner:** Orkney Islands Council     **Contact:** Steve Callaghan

A fine vernacular 16th century town house contains The Orkney Museum.

**Location:** MAP 14, OS Ref. HY446 109. In Kirkwall opposite W end of cathedral.

**Open:** Oct–Apr: Mon–Sat, 10.30am–12.30pm & 1.30–5pm. May–Sept: Mon–Sat, 10.30am–5pm. Gardens always open.

**Admission:** Free.

Skara Brae

Jarlshof Prehistoric and Norse Settlement

**Above:** Castell Coch   CADW Welsh Historic Monuments Crown Copyright
**Right:** Aberglasney Gardens

# Wales

North Wales

South Wales

*The traditional border between Wales and England is Offa's Dyke, built by King Offa between 757 and 796AD. North Wales is a holiday area attracting lovers of coast and countryside alike. To the west lies Snowdon, a popular destination for climbers and walkers. To the east is a gentler landscape of moorlands, valleys and the hills of the Welsh Borders. Further south, the Gower Peninsula was the first place in Britain to be designated an Area of Outstanding Natural Beauty.*

## ABERCONWY HOUSE �

**Castle Street, Conwy  LL32 8AY**

**Tel:** 01492 592246  **Fax:** 01492 564818

**Owner:** The National Trust

Dating from the 14th century, this is the only medieval merchant's house in Conwy to have survived the turbulent history of this walled town for nearly six centuries. Furnished rooms and an audio-visual presentation show daily life from different periods in its history.

**Location:** MAP 5:H2, OS Ref. SH781 777. At junction of Castle Street and High Street.

**Open:** 31 Mar–4 Nov: Wed–Mon, 11am–5pm. Last adm. 30 mins before close. Shop: 1 Mar–31 Dec: daily (closed 25/26 Dec), 10am–5pm (5.30pm 25 Mar–29 Oct). Jan–Feb 2007: Wed–Sun, 11am–5pm. Suns open at 11am.

**Admission:** Adult £3, Child £1.50, Family (2+2) £7.50. Pre-booked groups (15+) Adult £2.50, Child £1. National Trust members Free.

ⓘ No indoor photography. ⓐ All year. ⓕ By arrangement. ⓝ
ⓟ In town car parks only. ⓔ ⓗ Guide dogs only.

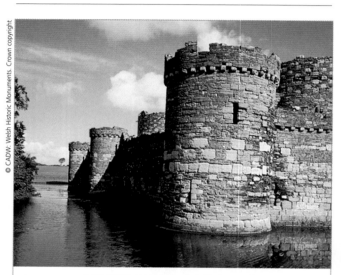

© CADW: Welsh Historic Monuments. Crown copyright

## BEAUMARIS CASTLE ✤

### BEAUMARIS, ANGLESEY LL58 8AP

www.cadw.wales.gov.uk

**Tel:** 01248 810361

**Owner:** In the care of Cadw  **Contact:** The Custodian

The most technically perfect medieval castle in Britain, standing midway between Caernarfon and Conwy, commanding the old ferry crossing to Anglesey. A World Heritage Listed Site.

**Location:** MAP 5:G2, OS Ref. SH608 762. 5m NE of Menai Bridge (A5) by A545. 7m from Bangor.

**Open:** 1 Apr–31 May & Oct: daily, 9.30am–5pm. 1 Jun–30 Sept: daily, 9.30am–6pm. 1 Nov–31 Mar: Mon–Sat, 9.30am–4pm, Suns 11am–4pm.

**Admission:** Adult £3.50, Child (under 16 yrs)/Conc. £3, Child under 5yrs Free, Family (2+3) £10.

ⓐ ⓖ ⓕ ⓟ ⓗ Guide dogs only. ✺

## BODELWYDDAN CASTLE

**Bodelwyddan, Denbighshire LL18 5YA**

**Tel:** 01745 584060  **Fax:** 01745 584563  **E-mail:** enquiries@bodelwyddan-castle.co.uk

**www.bodelwyddan-castle.co.uk**

**Owner:** Bodelwyddan Castle Trust  **Contact:** Kevin Mason

Set within 200 acres of historical parkland, Bodelwyddan Castle is the Welsh home of the National Portrait Gallery, displaying works from its 19th century collection. Complementary collection of sculpture and furniture in a period setting. Victorian games gallery. Temporary exhibitions and events.

**Location:** MAP 6:I2, OS Ref. SH999 749. Follow signs off A55 expressway. 2m W of St Asaph, opposite Marble Church.

**Open:** Easter–end Oct: daily except Fri: 10.30am–5pm. Nov–Easter: Thurs, Sats & Suns, 10.30am–4pm. Last admission 30 mins before close.

**Admission:** Adult £5, Child (5–16yrs) £2 (under 4yrs free), Conc. £4.50, Family (2+2) £12. Discounts for schools, groups & disabled. Season ticket available.

ⓐ ⓣ ⓖ Partial. WCs. ⓔ ⓕ By arrangement. ⓝ Free. ⓟ ⓔ ⓗ Guide dogs only.
ⓐ ✺ ⓥ

## BODNANT GARDEN ✷

**Tal-y-Cafn, Colwyn Bay  LL28 5RE**

**Tel:** 01492 650460  **Fax:** 01492 650448  **E-mail:** office@bodnantgarden.co.uk

**www.bodnantgarden.co.uk**

**Owner:** The National Trust

Bodnant Garden is one of the finest gardens in the country not only for its magnificent collections of rhododendrons, camellias and magnolias but also for its idyllic setting above the River Conwy with extensive views of the Snowdonia range.

**Location:** MAP 5:H2, OS Ref. SH801 723. 8 miles S of Llandudno and Colwyn Bay, off A470. Signposted from A55, exit at Junction 19.

**Open:** 10 Mar–4 Nov: daily, 10am–5pm (Tearoom from 11am). Plant Centre: Daily, 10am–5pm.

**Admission:** Adult £7, Child £3.50. Groups (20+): Adult £5.50, Child £3.25. RHS members free.

ⓐ ⓘ ⓖ Partial. WCs. ⓔ ⓟ ⓗ Guide dogs only.

## BODRHYDDAN 🏛

**Rhuddlan, Denbighshire LL18 5SB**

**Tel:** 01745 590414  **Fax:** 01745 590155  **E-mail:** bodrhyddan@hotmail.com

**www.bodrhyddan.co.uk**

**Owner/Contact:** Colonel The Lord Langford OBE DL

The home of Lord Langford and his family, Bodrhyddan is basically a 17th century house with 19th century additions by the famous architect, William Eden Nesfield, although traces of a 15th century semi-fortified Welsh farmhouse exist. The house has been in the hands of the same family since it was built over 500 years ago. There are notable pieces of armour, pictures, period furniture, a 3,000 year old mummy, a formal parterre, a woodland garden and attractive picnic areas. Bodrhyddan is a Grade I listing, making it one of few in Wales to remain in private hands.

**Location:** MAP 6:I2, OS Ref. SJ045 788. On the A5151 midway between Dyserth and Rhuddlan, 4m SE of Rhyl.

**Open:** Jun–Sept inclusive: Tues & Thurs, 2–5.30pm.

**Admission:** House & Gardens: Adult £5, Child £2.50 Gardens only: Adult £2, Child £1.
ⓖ Partial. ⓔ ⓕ Obligatory. ⓟ ⓐ

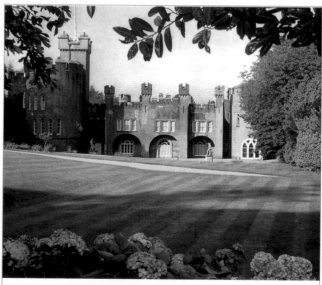

## BRYN BRAS CASTLE

### LLANRUG, CAERNARFON, GWYNEDD LL55 4RE

www.brynbrascastle.co.uk

**Tel/Fax:** 01286 870210  **E-mail:** holidays@brynbrascastle.co.uk

**Owner:** Mr & Mrs N E Gray-Parry  **Contact:** Marita Gray-Parry

Built in the Neo-Romanesque style in c1830, on an earlier structure, and probably designed by Thomas Hopper, it stands in the Snowdonian Range. The tranquil garden includes a hill-walk with fine views of Mt Snowdon, Anglesey and the sea. Bryn Bras, a much loved home, offers a delightful selection of apartments for holidays for twos within the Grade II* listed castle. Many local restaurants, inns.

**Location:** MAP 5:F3, OS Ref. SH543 625. ½m off A4086 at Llanrug, 4½m E of Caernarfon.

**Open:** Only by appointment.

**Admission:** By arrangement. No children please.

ⓧ ⓔ Self-catering apartments for twos within castle. ✺

CADW: Welsh Historic Monuments. Crown copyright

## CAERNARFON CASTLE ✠
### CASTLE DITCH, CAERNARFON LL55 2AY
www.cadw.wales.gov.uk

**Tel:** 01286 677617
**Owner:** In the care of Cadw    **Contact:** The Custodian
The most famous, and perhaps the most impressive castle in Wales. Taking nearly 50 years to build, it proved the costliest of Edward I's castles. A World Heritage Listed Site.
**Location:** MAP 5:F3, OS Ref. SH477 626. In Caernarfon, just W of town centre.
**Open:** 1 Apr–31 May & Oct: daily, 9.30am–5pm. 1 Jun–30 Sept: daily, 9.30am–6pm. 1 Nov–31 Mar: Mon–Sat, 9.30am–4pm, Suns 11am–4pm.
**Admission:** Adult £4.90, Child (under 16 yrs)/Conc. £4.50, Child under 5yrs Free, Family (2+3 all children under 16yrs) £15.
☐ ℗ ♿ Guide dogs only. ✳

Cadw: Welsh Historic Monuments. Crown Copyright

## CONWY CASTLE ✠
### CONWY  LL32 8AY
www.cadw.wales.gov.uk

**Tel:** 01492 592358
**Owner:** In the care of Cadw    **Contact:** The Custodian
Taken together the castle and town walls are the most impressive of the fortresses built by Edward I, and remain the finest and most impressive in Britain. A World Heritage Listed Site.
**Location:** MAP 5:H2, OS Ref. SH783 774. Conwy by A55 or B5106.
**Open:** 1 Apr–31 May & Oct: daily, 9.30am–5pm. 1 Jun–30 Sept: daily, 9.30am–6pm. 1 Nov–31 Mar: Mon–Sat, 9.30am–4pm, Suns 11am–4pm.
**Admission:** Adult £4.50, Child (under 16yrs)/Conc. £4, Child under 5yrs Free, Family (2+3) £14. Joint ticket for entry to Conwy Castle and Plas Mawr: Adult £6.50, Conc. £5.50, Family (2+3) £18.50. (Prices subject to review Mar 2007.)
☐ 🅵 By arrangement. ℗ ♿ Guide dogs only. ✳

## CHIRK CASTLE ⚜
### Chirk LL14 5AF
**Tel:** 01691 777701    **Fax:** 01691 774706    **E-mail:** chirkcastle@nationaltrust.org.uk
**Owner:** The National Trust
700 year old Chirk Castle, a magnificent marcher fortress, commands fine views over the surrounding countryside. Rectangular with a massive drum tower at each corner, the castle has beautiful formal gardens with clipped yews, roses and a variety of flowering shrubs. Voted best National Trust garden in 1999. The dramatic dungeon is a reminder of the castle's turbulent history, whilst later occupants have left elegant state rooms, furniture, tapestries and portraits. The castle was sold for five thousand pounds to Sir Thomas Myddelton in 1595, and his descendants continue to live in part of the castle today.
**Location:** MAP 6:J4, OS Ref. SJ275 388. 8m S of Wrexham off A483, 2m from Chirk village.
**Open:** Castle & Shop: 24 Mar–30 Sept, Wed–Sun & BH Mons (+Tues Jul–Aug), 12noon–5pm. 1 Oct–4 Nov, Weds–Sun, 12noon–4pm. Last admission ½hr before closing. Garden: as Castle, 10am–6pm (5pm in Oct), last admission 1hr before closing. Tearoom: as Castle, 10am–5pm (4pm in Oct). Shop: As Castle, 11am–5pm (4pm in Oct). Home Farm & Estate: as Garden.
**\*Admission:** House & Garden: Adult £7.40, Child £3.70, Family £18.50. Pre-booked groups (15+): Adult £6.40, Child £3.20. Garden only: Adults £4.80, Child £2.40, Family £12. Pre-booked groups: Adult £4, Child £2. *includes a voluntary donation but visitors can choose to pay the standard prices displayed at the property and on the website.
ℹ No indoor photography. ☐ 🍴 ♿ ✉ Licensed. 🅵 By arrangement. ℗ ▣ ♿ Guide dogs only. 🔼 ☗

## COCHWILLAN OLD HALL
### Talybont, Bangor, Gwynedd LL57 3AZ
**Tel:** 01248 355853
**Owner:** R C H Douglas Pennant    **Contact:** Miss M D Monteith
A fine example of medieval architecture with the present house dating from about 1450. It was probably built by William Gryffydd who fought for Henry VII at Bosworth. Once owned in the 17th century by John Williams who became Archbishop of York. The house was restored from a barn in 1971.
**Location:** MAP 5:G2, OS Ref. SH606 695. 3½m SE of Bangor. 1m SE of Talybont off A55.
**Open:** By appointment.
**Admission:** Please telephone for details.
✳

## CRICCIETH CASTLE ✠
### Castle Street, Criccieth, Gwynedd LL52 0DP
**Tel:** 01766 522227    www.cadw.wales.gov.uk
**Owner:** In the care of Cadw    **Contact:** The Custodian
Overlooking Cardigan Bay, Criccieth Castle is the most striking of the fortresses built by the native Welsh Princes. Its inner defences are dominated by a powerful twin-towered gatehouse.
**Location:** MAP 5:F4, OS Ref. SH500 378. A497 to Criccieth from Porthmadog or Pwllheli.
**Open:** 1 Apr–31 May & Oct : daily, 10am–5pm. 1 Nov–31 Mar: Fri & Sat, 9.30am–4pm, Suns, 11am–4pm. (Open and unstaffed with no admission charge at all other times.) Closed 24–26 Dec & 1 Jan.
**Admission:** Adult £2.90, Child (under 16yrs)/Conc. £2.50, Child under 5yrs Free, Family (2+3 all children under 16yrs) £8.30.
☐ ℗ ♿ Guide dogs only. ✳

Chirk Castle, Chirk – The Servants' Hall

## DENBIGH CASTLE ✤

**Denbigh, Clwyd**

**Tel:** 01745 813385   www.cadw.wales.gov.uk

**Owner:** In the care of Cadw   **Contact:** The Custodian

Crowning the summit of a prominent outcrop dominating the Vale of Clwyd, the principal feature of this spectacular site is the great gatehouse dating back to the 11th century. Some of the walls can still be walked by visitors.

**Location:** MAP 6:I2, OS Ref. SJ052 658. Denbigh via A525, A543 or B5382.

**Open:** 1 Apr–30 Sept: Mon–Fri, 10am–5.30pm, Sats & Suns, 9.30am–5.30pm. (Open and unstaffed at all other times with no admission charge.)

**Admission:** Castle: Adult £2.90, Child (under 16yrs)/Conc. £2.50, Child under 5 yrs Free, Family (2+3 all children under 16yrs) £8.30.

⬛ 🅿 🖼 Guide dogs only. ✱

## DOLBELYDR

**Trefnant, Denbighshire LL16 5AG**

**Tel:** 01628 825925   www.landmarktrust.org.uk

**Owner/Contact:** The Landmark Trust

A 16th century, Grade II* listed building, a fine example of a 16th century gentry house and has good claim to be the birthplace of the modern Welsh language. It was at Dolbelydr that Henry Salesbury wrote his Grammatica Britannica. Dolbelydr is cared for by The Landmark Trust, a building preservation charity who let it for holidays. Full details of Dolbelydr and 184 other historic and architecturally important buildings are featured in the Landmark Trust Handbook (£11.50 refundable against a booking).

**Location:** MAP 6:I2, OS Ref. SJ031 709.

**Open:** Available for holidays for max 6 people throughout the year. Open Days on 8 days throughout the year. Other visits by appointment. Contact the Landmark Trust for details.

**Admission:** Free on Open Days.

🖼

## DOLWYDDELAN CASTLE ✤

**Blaenau Ffestiniog, Gwynedd**

**Tel:** 01690 750366   www.cadw.wales.gov.uk

**Owner:** In the care of Cadw   **Contact:** The Custodian

Standing proudly on a ridge, this stern building remains remarkably intact and visitors cannot fail to be impressed with the great solitary square tower, built by Llewelyn the Great in the early 13th century.

**Location:** MAP 5:G3, OS Ref. SH722 522. A470(T) Blaenau Ffestiniog to Betws-y-Coed, 1m W of Dolwyddelan.

**Open:** All year: Mon–Sat, 10am–6pm (1 Oct–31 Mar, 4pm), Suns 11am–4pm.

**Admission:** Adult £2.50, Child (5–16yrs)/Conc. £2, Child under 5 yrs Free, Family (2+3 all children under 16yrs) £7. Children under 16 must be accompanied by an adult. Prices valid until 31 March 2008.

🅿 🖼 Guide dogs only. ✱

## ERDDIG 🍂

**Nr Wrexham LL13 0YT**

**Tel:** 01978 355314   **Fax:** 01978 313333   **Info Line:** 01978 315151

**Owner:** The National Trust

One of the most fascinating houses in Britain, not least because of the unusually close relationship that existed between the family of the house and their servants. The beautiful and evocative range of outbuildings includes kitchen, laundry, bakehouse, stables, sawmill, smithy and joiner's shop, while the stunning state rooms display most of their original 18th & 19th century furniture and furnishings, including some exquisite Chinese wallpaper.

**Location:** MAP 6:K3, OS Ref. SJ326 482. 2m S of Wrexham.

**Open:** House: 24 Mar–28 Oct: Sat–Wed (+Thur Jul–Aug), 12 noon–5pm (Mar/Apr & Oct closes 4pm). Garden: 24 Mar–4 Apr & Oct; Sat–Wed, 11am–5pm. 6 Apr–30 Jun & Sept; Sat–Wed, 11am–6pm. Jul & Aug; Sat–Thurs, 10am–6pm. 3 Nov–16 Dec, Sats & Suns, 11am–4pm. Restaurant & Shop/Plants: 24 Mar–4 Apr & 1–28 Oct, Sat–Wed, 11am–4.15pm. 6 Apr–30 Jun & Sept, Sat–Wed, 11am–5.15pm. Jul & Aug; Sat–Thurs, 11am–5.15pm. 3 Nov–16 Dec; Sats & Suns, 11am–4pm.

**\*Admission:** All-inclusive ticket: Adult £8.80, Child £4.40, Family (2+3) £22. Pre-booked group (15+) £7.50, Child £3.70. Garden: Adult £5.50, Child £2.75, Family £13.75. Groups, Adult £4.70, Child £2.35. NT members Free. *includes a voluntary donation but visitors can choose to pay the standard prices displayed at the property and on the website.

⬛ ⬛ ♿ Partial. WCs. 🍴 Licensed. 📷 AV presentation. 🅿 ⬛ 🖼 Guide dogs only.

Many properties hold **special events** throughout the year See the index on page 585

## FFERM

**Pontblyddyn, Mold, Flintshire**

**Tel:** 01352 770204

**Owner:** The Executors of the late Dr M Jones Mortimer

**Contact:** Miss Miranda Kaufmann

17th century farmhouse. Viewing is limited to 7 persons at any one time. Prior booking is recommended. No toilets or refreshments.

**Location:** MAP 6:J3, OS Ref. SJ279 603. Access from A541 in Pontblyddyn, 3½m SE of Mold.

**Open:** 2nd Wed in every month, 2–5pm. Pre-booking is recommended.

**Admission:** £4.

🖼 ✱

## GWYDIR CASTLE

### LLANRWST, GWYNEDD LL26 0PN

www.gwydircastle.co.uk

**Tel/Fax:** 01492 641687   **E-mail:** info@gwydircastle.co.uk

**Owner/Contact:** Mr & Mrs Welford

Gwydir Castle is situated in the beautiful Conwy Valley and is set within a Grade I listed, 10 acre garden. Built by the illustrious Wynn family c1500, Gwydir is a fine example of a Tudor courtyard house, incorporating re-used medieval material from the dissolved Abbey of Maenan. Further additions date from c1600 and c1828. The important 1640s panelled Dining Room has now been reinstated, following its repatriation from the New York Metropolitan Museum.

**Location:** MAP 5:H3, OS Ref. SH795 610. ½m W of Llanrwst on B5106.

**Open:** 1 Mar–31 Oct: daily, 10am–4pm. Closed Mons & Sats (except BH weekends). Limited openings at other times. Please telephone for details.

**Admission:** Adult £4, Child £2, OAP £3.50. Group discount 10%.

🍴 ♿ Partial. ⬛ By arrangement. 📷 By arrangement. 🅿 🖼 🛏 2 doubles. ▲

## HAFOD

**Hafod Estate Office, Pontrhydygroes, Ystrad-Meurig, Ceredigion  SY25 6DX**

**Tel:** 01974 282568   **Fax:** 01974 282579   **E-mail:** hafod.estate@forestry.gsi.gov.uk

www.hafod.org

**Owner:** Forestry Commission Wales   **Contact:** The Hafod Trust

Picturesque landscape, one of the most significant in Britain located in a remote valley and improved by Col Thomas Johnes 1780–1816. Ten miles of restored walks featuring cascades, bridges and wonderful views set in 500 acres of woodland and parkland. The epitome of the Picturesque and the Sublime.

**Location:** MAP 5:H7, OS Ref. SN768 736. 15 miles E of Aberystwyth near Devils Bridge, car park, off B4574.

**Open:** All year, daylight hours.

**Admission:** Free – guide book available at local shops or website.

♿ WC. 📷 By arrangement. 🅿 ⬛ 🖼 In grounds on leads. ✱

## HARLECH CASTLE ✤

**Harlech LL46 2YH**
**Tel:** 01766 780552    www.cadw.wales.gov.uk
**Owner:** In the care of Cadw    **Contact:** The Custodian
Set on a towering rock above Tremadog Bay, this seemingly impregnable fortress is the most dramatically sited of all the castles of Edward I. A World Heritage Listed Site.
**Location:** MAP 5:F4, OS Ref. SH581 312. Harlech, Gwynedd on A496 coast road.
**Open:** 1 Apr–31 May & Oct: daily, 9.30am–5pm. 1 Jun–30 Sept: daily, 9.30am–6pm. 1 Nov–31 Mar: Mon–Sat, 9.30am–4pm. Closed 24–26 Dec & 1 Jan.
**Admission:** Adult £3.50, Child (under 16yrs)/Conc. £3, Child under 5 yrs Free, Family (2+3 all children under 16yrs) £10. Children under 16 must be accompanied by an adult. Prices subject to review in March 2008.
◻ P ◻ Guide dogs only. ✳

## HARTSHEATH ⬜

**Pontblyddyn, Mold, Flintshire**
**Tel/Fax:** 01352 770204
**Owner:** The Executors of the late Dr M Jones Mortimer
**Contact:** Miss Miranda Kaufmann
18th and 19th century house set in parkland. Viewing is limited to 7 persons at any one time. Prior booking is recommended. No toilets or refreshments.
**Location:** MAP 6:J3, OS Ref. SJ287 602. Access from A5104, 3½m SE of Mold between Pontblyddyn and Penyffordd.
**Open:** 1st, 3rd & 5th Wed in every month, 2–5pm.
Admission: £4.
◻ ✳

## ISCOYD PARK

**Nr Whitchurch, Shropshire SY13 3AT**
**Owner/Contact:** Mr P C Godsal
18th century Grade II* listed redbrick house in park.
**Location:** MAP 6:L4, OS Ref. SJ504 421. 2m W of Whitchurch on A525.
**Open:** By written appointment only.
◻ ✳

## PENRHYN CASTLE ⬛

**Bangor LL57 4HN**
**Tel:** 01248 353084    **Infoline:** 01248 371337    **Fax:** 01248 371281
**Owner:** The National Trust
This dramatic neo-Norman fantasy castle sits between Snowdonia and the Menai Strait. Built by Thomas Hopper between 1820 and 1845 for the wealthy Pennant family, who made their fortune from Jamaican sugar and Welsh slate. The castle is crammed with fascinating things such as a 1-ton slate bed made for Queen Victoria.
**Location:** MAP 5:G2, OS Ref. SH602 720. 1m E of Bangor, at Llandygai (J11, A55).
**Open:** Castle: 31 Mar–4 Nov, daily (except Tues), 12 noon–5pm (11am Jul–Aug). Grounds & Tearoom: as Castle (10am Jul–Aug). Shop & Museums: 31 Mar–4 Nov, daily (except Tues), 11am–5pm.
**Admission:** Adult £8, Child £4, Family (2+2) £20. Pre-booked groups (15+) £6.50. Garden & Stableblock Exhibitions only: Adult £5.40, Child £2.70. Audio tour: £1 (including NT members). NT members Free.
◻ ◼ Licensed. ⬛ ◻ ◻ Guide dogs only. ◼

## PLAS BRONDANW GARDENS ⬜

**Plas Brondanw, Llanfrothen, Gwynedd LL48 6SW**
**Tel:** 01743 241181/07880 766741
**Owner:** Trustees of the Second Portmeirion Foundation.
Italianate gardens with topiary.
**Location:** MAP 5:G4, OS Ref. SH618 423. 3m N of Penrhyndeudraeth off A4085, on Croesor Road.
**Open:** All year: daily, 9.30am–5.30pm. Coaches accepted, please book.
**Admission:** Adult £3, Subsequent adult £2pp, Child Free if accompanied by an adult.

## PLAS MAWR ✤
### HIGH STREET, CONWY LL32 8EF
www.cadw.wales.gov.uk

**Tel:** 01492 580167
**Owner:** In the care of Cadw    **Contact:** The Custodian
The best preserved Elizabethan town house in Britain, the house reflects the status of its builder Robert Wynn. A fascinating and unique place allowing visitors to sample the lives of the Tudor gentry and their servants, Plas Mawr is famous for the quality and quantity of its decorative plasterwork.
**Location:** MAP 5:H2, OS Ref. SH781 776. Conwy by A55 or B5106 or A547.
**Open:** 1 Apr–31 May, Sept & Oct: Tues–Suns & BH Mons, 9.30am–5pm (4pm in Oct). 1 Jun–31 Aug: Tues–Suns & BH Mons, 9.30am–6pm.
**Admission:** Adult £4.90, Child (under 16yrs)/Conc. £4.50, Child under 5yrs Free, Family (2+3 all children under 16yrs) £15. Children under 16 must be accompanied by an adult. Joint ticket for entry to Conwy Castle and Plas Mawr: Adult £6.50, Conc. £5.50, Family (2+3) £18.50.
◻ P Limited. ◻ ◻ Guide dogs only.

## PLAS NEWYDD ⬛

**Llanfairpwll, Anglesey LL61 6DQ**
**Tel:** 01248 714795    **Infoline:** 01248 715272    **Fax:** 01248 713673
**Owner:** The National Trust
Set amidst breathtaking beautiful scenery and with spectacular views of Snowdonia. Fine spring garden and Australasian arboretum with an understorey of shrubs and wildflowers. Summer terrace, and, later, massed hydrangeas and Autumn colour. A woodland walk gives access to a marine walk on the Menai Strait. Rhododendron garden open April–early June only. Elegant 18th century house by James Wyatt, famous for its association with Rex Whistler whose largest painting is here. Military museum contains relics of 1st Marquess of Anglesey and Battle of Waterloo. A historic cruise, a boat trip on the Menai Strait operates from the property weather and tides permitting (additional charge). 5 seater buggy to rhododendron garden and woodland walk.
**Location:** MAP 5:F2, OS Ref. SH521 696. 2m S of Llanfairpwll and A5.
**Open:** 31 Mar–31 Oct: Sat–Wed & Good Fri. House: 12 noon–5pm. Garden: 11am–5.30pm. Last admission 4.30pm. Shop & Tearoom: 31 Mar–31 Oct, Sat–Wed, 10.30am–5.30pm, 3 Nov–16 Dec, 11am–4pm, Sats & Suns.
**Admission:** House & Garden: Adult £6.60, Child £3.30 (under 5yrs free), Family (2+3) £16.50. Groups (15+) £6. Garden only: Adult £4.60, Child £2.30. NT members Free.
ⓘ No indoor photography. ◻ ⬜ Partial. WCs. Minibus from car park to house. ◼ Licensed. ⬛ ⬜ By arrangement. P ◻ ◻ Guide dogs only. ◼

Plas Newydd, Anglesey

### PLAS YN RHIW

**Rhiw, Pwllheli LL53 8AB**
**Tel/Fax:** 01758 780219
**Owner:** The National Trust

A small manor house, with garden and woodlands, overlooking the west shore of Porth Neigwl (Hell's Mouth Bay) on the Llyn Peninsula. The house is part medieval, with Tudor and Georgian additions, and the ornamental gardens have flowering trees and shrubs, divided by box hedges and grass paths, rising behind to the snowdrop wood.

**Location:** MAP 5:D5, OS Ref. SH237 282. 16m SW of Pwllheli, 3m S of the B4413 to Aberdaron. No access for coaches.
**Open:** 5–30 Apr: Thur–Sun, 12noon–5pm. May & Jun; Thurs–Mon, 12noon–5pm. Jul & Aug; Wed–Mon, 12noon–5pm. Sept; Thurs–Mon, 12noon–5pm. 1–28 Oct; Thurs–Sun, 12noon–4pm.
**Admission:** Adult £3.40, Child £1.70, Family (2+3) £8.50. Groups: £2.80, Child £1.40. Gardens only: Adult £2.20, Child £1.10, Family (2+3) £5.50. Groups £1.70.
⊡ 🐾 ♿ Partial. WCs. 🎫 By arrangement. 🅿 Limited. 🐕 Guide dogs only.

### PORTMEIRION

**Portmeirion, Gwynedd LL48 6ET**
**Tel:** 01766 770000  **Fax:** 01766 771331  **E-mail:** info@portmeirion-village.com
**Owner:** The Portmeirion Foundation  **Contact:** Mr R Llywelyn
Built by Clough Williams-Ellis as an 'unashamedly romantic' village resort.
**Location:** MAP 5:F4, OS Ref. SH590 371. Off A487 at Minffordd between Penrhyndeudraeth and Porthmadog.
**Open:** All year: daily, 9.30am–5.30pm. Closed 25 Dec.
**Admission:** Adult £6.50, Child £3.50, OAP £5, Family (2+2) £16.

### POWIS CASTLE & GARDEN

**Nr Welshpool SY21 8RF**
**Tel:** 01938 551929  **Infoline:** 01938 551944  **Fax:** 01938 554336
**E-mail:** powiscastle@nationaltrust.org.uk
**Owner:** The National Trust  **Contact:** Visitor Services Manager

The world-famous garden, overhung with enormous clipped yew trees, shelters rare and tender plants in colourful herbaceous borders. Laid out under the influence of Italian and French styles, the garden retains its original lead statues and, an orangery on the terraces. Perched on a rock above the garden terraces, the medieval castle contains one of the finest collections of paintings and furniture in Wales.

**Location:** MAP 6:J6, OS Ref. SJ216 064. 1m W of Welshpool, car access on A483.
**Open:** Castle & Museum: 1 Apr–28 Oct; Thur–Mon, 1–5pm (Jul & Aug, Wed–Mon, 11am–5.30pm; 1–17 Sept, 11am–5pm; 20 Sept–28 Oct, 1–4pm). 3 Nov–16 Dec; Sats & Suns, 10am–3pm. Coach House, Shop & Restaurant: 1 Apr–31 Aug, 11am–5.30pm. Garden: 17–31 Mar; Sats & Suns, 11am–4.30pm. 1 Apr–28 Oct; Thur–Mon (+ Wed Jul–Aug), 11–6pm (20 Sept–28 Oct, 4.30pm). Last entry 45 mins before closing.
**\*Admission:** Castle & Garden: Adult £9.90, Child £4.95, Family (2+3) £24.75. Groups (15+ booked): £8.90. Garden only: Adult £6.90, Child £3.45, Family (2+3) £17.25. Groups (15+ booked): £5.90. No group rates on Suns or BHs. NT members & under 5s Free.*includes a voluntary donation but visitors can choose to pay the standard prices displayed at the property and on the website.
ℹ No indoor photography. ⊡ 🐾 ♿ Partial. 🍴 Licensed. 🎫 By arrangement. 🅿 Limited for coaches. 🐕 Guide dogs only.

### RHUDDLAN CASTLE ♣

**Castle Gate, Castle Street, Rhuddlan LL18 5AD**
**Tel:** 01745 590777  www.cadw.wales.gov.uk
**Owner:** In the care of Cadw  **Contact:** The Custodian
Guarding the ancient ford of the River Clwyd, Rhuddlan was the strongest of Edward I's castles in North-East Wales. Linked to the sea by an astonishing deep water channel nearly 3 miles long, it still proclaims the innovative genius of its architect.
**Location:** MAP 6:I2, OS Ref. SJ025 779. SW end of Rhuddlan via A525 or A547.
**Open:** 1 Apr–30 Sept: daily, 10am–5pm.
Admission: Adult £2.90, Child (under 16yrs)/Conc. £2.50, Child under 5 yrs Free, Family (2+3 all children under 16yrs) £7.75. Children under 16 must be accompanied by an adult. Prices subject to review March 2008.
⊡ 🅿 🐕 Guide dogs only.

Powis Castle, Nr Welshpool

### RUG CHAPEL & LLANGAR CHURCH ♣

**c/o Coronation Cottage, Rug, Corwen LL21 9BT**
**Tel:** 01490 412025  www.cadw.wales.gov.uk
**Owner:** In the care of Cadw  **Contact:** The Custodian
Prettily set in a wooded landscape, Rug Chapel's exterior gives little hint of the wonders within. Nearby the attractive medieval Llangar Church still retains its charming early Georgian furnishings.
**Location:** Rug Chapel: MAP 6:I4, OS Ref. SJ065 439. Off A494, 1m N of Corwen. Llangar Church: MAP 6:I4, OS Ref. SJ064 423. Off B4401, 1m S of Corwen (obtain key at Rug).
**Open:** **Rug** 1 Apr–30 Sept: Wed–Sun (but open BH Mons & Tues), 10am–5pm. **Llangar** 1 Apr–30 Sept: Wed–Sun (but open BH Mons & Tues). Access is arranged daily at 2pm through Custodian at Rug Chapel; please telephone 01490 412025 for details.
**Admission:** Adult £3.50, Child (under 16yrs)/Conc. £3, Child under 5 yrs Free, Family (2+3 all children under 16yrs) £10. Children under 16 must be accompanied by an adult. Prices subject to review March 2008.
🅿 🐕 Guide dogs only.

### ST ASAPH CATHEDRAL

**St Asaph, Denbighshire LL17 0RL**
**Tel:** 01745 583429  **Contact:** Chapter Office  www.stasaphcathedral.org.uk
The smallest ancient cathedral in Britain founded in 560AD. Memorial to Bishop William Morgan, translator of the Bible into Welsh. Wonderful stained glass windows and many interesting features. Venue for concerts and home of the annual North Wales International Music Festival.
**Location:** MAP 6:I2, OS Ref. SJ039 743. In St Asaph, S of A55.
**Open:** 9am–6pm. Sun services: 8am, 11am, 3.30pm. Morning Prayer: 9am.
🎫 By arrangement. ✳

### TOWER

**Nercwys, Mold, Flintshire CH7 4EW**
**Tel:** 01352 700220  **E-mail:** enquiries@towerwales.co.uk  www.towerwales.co.uk
**Owner/Contact:** Charles Wynne-Eyton
This Grade I listed building is steeped in Welsh history and bears witness to the continuous warfare of the time. A fascinating place to visit or for overnight stays.
**Location:** MAP 6:J3, OS Ref. SJ240 620. 1m S of Mold.
**Open:** 1–13 & 22–28 May & 4–12 & 27 Aug: 2–4.30pm. Groups also welcome at other times by appointment.
**Admission:** Adult £3, Child £2.
🖼

## TREWERN HALL

**Trewern, Welshpool, Powys SY21 8DT**

**Tel:** 01938 570243

**Owner:** Chapman Family     **Contact:** M Chapman

Trewern Hall is a Grade II* listed building standing in the Severn Valley. It has been described as *'one of the most handsome timber-framed houses surviving in the area'*. The porch contains a beam inscribed RF1610, though it seems likely that parts of the house are earlier. The property has been in the ownership of the Chapman family since 1918.

**Location:** MAP 6:J6 , OS Ref. SJ269 113. Off A458 Welshpool–Shrewsbury Road, 4m from Welshpool.

**Open:** Last week in Apr, 1–31 May: Mon–Fri, 2–5pm.

**Admission:** Adult £2, Child/Conc. £1.

🔲 Unsuitable. 🅿 Limited. None for coaches. 🔳

## TŶ MAWR WYBRNANT 🦌

**Penmachno, Betws-y-Coed, Conwy LL25 0HJ**

**Tel:** 01690 760213

**Owner:** The National Trust

Situated in the beautiful and secluded Wybrnant Valley, Tŷ Mawr was the birthplace of Bishop William Morgan, first translator of the entire Bible into Welsh. The house has been restored to its probable 16th-17th century appearance and houses a display of Welsh Bibles. A footpath leads from the house through woodland and the surrounding fields, which are traditionally managed.

**Location:** MAP 5:H3, OS Ref. SH770 524. From A5 3m S of Betws-y-Coed, take B4406 to Penmachno. House is 2½m NW of Penmachno by forest road.

**Open:** 5 Apr–30 Sept: daily, 10am–5pm, last adm 4.30pm. Winter: 10am–4pm, unstaffed with no admission charge.

**Admission:** Adult £2.50, Child £2, Child under 5 yrs Free, Family £7. Children under 16 must be accompanied by an adult.

🔲 Ground floor. 🅿 🔳 Guide dogs only.

## VALLE CRUCIS ABBEY ✤

**Llangollen, Clwyd**

**Tel:** 01978 860326   **www.cadw.wales.gov.uk**

**Owner:** In the care of Cadw     **Contact:** The Custodian

Set in a beautiful valley location, Valle Crucis Abbey is the best preserved medieval monastery in North Wales, enhanced by the only surviving monastic fish pond in Wales.

**Location:** MAP 6:J4, OS Ref. SJ205 442. B5103 from A5, 2m NW of Llangollen, or A542 from Ruthin.

**Open:** 1 Apr–30 Sept: daily, 10am–5pm. Last adm. 4.30pm. Unstaffed with no admission charge during winter, generally between 10am–4pm.

**Admission:** Adult £2.50, Child (under 16yrs)/Conc. £2, Child under 5 yrs Free, Family (2+3 all children under 16yrs) £7. Under 16s must be accompanied by an adult. Prices subject to review Mar 2008.

🔲 🅿 🔳 Guide dogs only. 🔳

## WERN ISAF

**Penmaen Park, Llanfairfechan LL33 0RN**

**Tel:** 01248 680437

**Owner/Contact:** Mrs P J Phillips

This Arts and Crafts house was built in 1900 by the architect H L North as his family home and it contains much of the original furniture and William Morris fabrics. It is situated in a woodland garden and is at its best in the Spring. It has extensive views over the Menai Straits and Conwy Bay. One of the most exceptional houses of its date and style in Wales.

**Location:** MAP 5:G2, OS Ref. SH685 75. Off A55 midway between Bangor and Conwy.

**Open:** 1–31 Mar: daily, except Tues, 1–4pm.

**Admission:** Free.

See which properties offer **educational facilities** or **school visits** in our index on page 571

Bodelwyddan Castle, Denbighshire

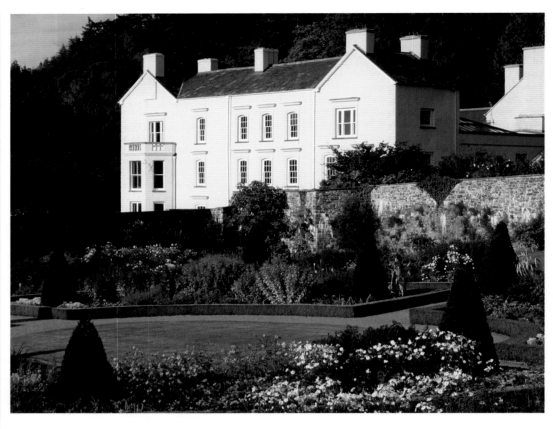

# ABERGLASNEY GARDENS

www.aberglasney.org

Aberglasney is one of the most remarkable garden restoration projects undertaken. When the property was purchased in 1995 the Mansion and gardens were so derelict and overgrown they were considered by most to be beyond restoration. It was not until the undergrowth was cleared, and extensive archaeological surveys undertaken, that the importance of this historical garden was realised. The parapet walkway, dating from 1600, is the only example that survives in the UK. The ten-acre garden is very diverse; it contains three walled gardens and stunning woodland areas planted with collections of many rare and unusual plants such as orchids, trilliums and meconopsis. There are many choice trees and shrubs, including over 50 different magnolias and a wide variety of roses. In 2006 a recently opened 'Winter Garden' built in the ruinous central courtyard of the mansion won an award for the Best Garden Design/Construction Project in the UK. This unique garden area displays a range of exotic sub-tropical plants.

Licensed.
Licensed.
Daily: 11.30am & 2.30pm.
Limited for coaches.
Guide dogs only.

## ABERCAMLAIS

**Brecon, Powys LD3 8EY**
**Tel:** 01874 636206 **Fax:** 01874 636964 **E-mail:** info@abercamlais.co.uk
**www.abercamlais.co.uk**
**Owner/Contact:** Mrs S Ballance
Splendid Grade I mansion dating from middle ages, altered extensively in early 18th century with 19th century additions, in extensive grounds beside the river Usk. Still in same family ownership and occupation since medieval times. Exceptional octagonal pigeon house, formerly a privy.
**Location:** MAP 6:I10, OS Ref. SN965 290. 5m W of Brecon on A40.
**Open:** Apr–Oct: by appointment.
**Admission:** Adult £5, Child Free.
i No photography in house. Obligatory. P

## ABERDULAIS FALLS

**Aberdulais, Vale of Neath SA10 8EU**
**Tel:** 01639 636674 **Fax:** 01639 645069
**Owner:** The National Trust **Contact:** The Property Warden
For over 300 years this famous waterfall has provided the energy to drive the wheels of industry, from the first manufacture of copper in 1584 to present day remains of the tinplate works. It has also been visited by famous artists such as J M W Turner in 1796. The site today houses a unique hydro-electrical scheme which has been developed to harness the waters of the Dulais river.
**Location:** MAP 5:G12, OS Ref. SS772 995. On A4109, 3m NE of Neath. 4m from M4/J43, then A465.
**Open:** 2 Apr–2 Nov, Mon–Fri, 10am–5pm. 31 Mar–4 Nov, Sats & Suns, 11am–6pm. 9 Nov–23 Dec, Fri–Sun, 11am–4pm. Winter Opening: 12 Jan–29 Feb 2008, Sats & Suns, 11am–4pm.
*****Admission:** Adult £4, Child £2, Family £10. Groups (15+): Adult £3, Child £1.50. Children must be accompanied by an adult. *includes a voluntary donation but visitors can choose to pay the standard prices displayed at the property and on the website.
Light refreshments (Summer only). P Limited.

## BLAENAVON IRONWORKS

**Nr Brecon Beacons National Park, Blaenavon, Gwent**
**Tel:** 01495 792615 **Winter Bookings:** 01633 648082 **www.cadw.wales.gov.uk**
**Owner:** In the care of Cadw **Contact:** The Custodian
The famous ironworks at Blaenavon were a milestone in the history of the Industrial Revolution. Visitors can view much of the ongoing conservation work as well as 'Stack Square' – a rare survival of housing built for pioneer ironworkers. Part of a World Heritage Site.
**Location:** MAP 6:J11, OS Ref. SO248 092. Via A4043 follow signs to Big Pit Mining Museum and Blaenavon Ironworks. Abergavenny 8m. Pontypool 8m. From car park, cross road, then path to entrance gate.
**Open:** 1 Apr–31 Oct: Mon–Fri, 9:30am–4:30pm. Sat & Suns, 10am–4.30pm. For other times, telephone Torfaen County Borough Council, 01633 648081.
**Admission:** Adult £2.50, Child (under 16 yrs)/Conc. £2, Child under 5yrs free, Family (2+3, all children under 16yrs) £7. Under 16's must be accompanied by an adult.
Partial. By arrangement. P Guide dogs only.

## CAE HIR GARDENS

**Cae Hir, Cribyn, Lampeter, Cardiganshire SA48 7NG**
**Tel:** 01570 470839
**Owner/Contact:** Mr W Akkermans
This transformed 19th century smallholding offers a succession of pleasant surprises and shows a quite different approach to gardening.
**Location:** MAP 5:F9, OS Ref. SN521 520. NW on A482 from Lampeter, after 5m turn S on B4337. Cae Hir is 2m on left.
**Open:** Open daily, 1–6pm.
**Admission:** Adult £4.50, Child 50p, OAP £4. Free to RHS members.

Caerphilly Castle

## CAERLEON ROMAN BATHS & AMPHITHEATRE

**High Street, Caerleon NP6 1AE**
**Tel:** 01633 422518 **www.cadw.wales.gov.uk**
**Owner:** In the care of Cadw **Contact:** The Custodian
Caerleon is the most varied and fascinating Roman site in Britain – incorporating fortress and baths, well-preserved amphitheatre and a row of barrack blocks, the only examples currently visible in Europe.
**Location:** MAP 2:N1, OS Ref. ST340 905. 4m ENE of Newport by B4596 to Caerleon, M4/J25 (westbound), M4/J26 (eastbound).
**Open:** 1 Apr–31 Oct: daily, 9.30am–5pm. Last admission 4.30pm. 1 Nov–31 Mar: Mon–Sat, 9.30am–5pm. Sun 11am–4pm.
**Admission:** Adult £2.90, Child (under 16 yrs)/Conc. £2.50, Child under 5yrs Free, Family (2+3, all children under 16yrs) £8.30. Under 16's must be accompanied by an adult. (Prices subject to review March 2008.)
P Guide dogs only.

## CAERPHILLY CASTLE

**Caerphilly CF8 1JL**
**Tel:** 029 2088 3143 **www.cadw.wales.gov.uk**
**Owner:** In the care of Cadw **Contact:** The Custodian
Often threatened, never taken, this vastly impressive castle is much the biggest in Wales. 'Red Gilbert' de Clare, Anglo-Norman Lord of Glamorgan, flooded a valley to create the 30 acre lake, setting his fortress on 3 artificial islands. Famous for its leaning tower, its fortifications are scarcely rivalled in Europe.
**Location:** MAP 2:L1, OS Ref. ST156 871. Centre of Caerphilly, A468 from Newport, A470, A469 from Cardiff.
**Open:** Summer 2007: 1 Apr–31 May, 9.30am-5pm; 1 June–30 Sept, 9.30am–6pm; daily. Winter 2007/08: Oct, daily, 9.30am–5pm; 1 Nov–31 Mar, Mon–Sat, 9.30am–4pm. Sun, 11am–4pm. Closed 24–26 Dec & 1 Jan.
**Admission:** Adults £3.50, Conc. £3, Family Ticket £10 (2 + 3, all children under 16 years). Children under 5 free. Under 16s must be accompanied by an adult.
P Limited. Guide dogs only.

## CALDICOT CASTLE & COUNTRY PARK

**Church Road, Caldicot, Monmouthshire NP26 4HU**
**Tel:** 01291 420241 **Fax:** 01291 435094
**E-mail:** caldicotcastle@monmouthshire.gov.uk **www.caldicotcastle.co.uk**
**Owner:** Monmouthshire County Council **Contact:** Castle Development Officer
Caldicot's magnificent castle is set in fifty acres of beautiful parkland. Founded by the Normans, developed in royal hands in the Middle Ages and restored as a Victorian home. Discover the Castle's past with an audio tour. Visitors can relax in tranquil gardens, explore medieval towers, discover children's activities and play giant chess.
**Location:** MAP 2:N1, OS Ref. ST487 887. From M4 take J23a and B4245 to Caldicot. From M48 take J2 and follow A48 & B4245. Castle signposted from B4245.
**Open:** Apr–Sept: daily, 11am–5pm. Please telephone for winter opening times.
Admission: Adult £3.75, Child/Conc £2.50. Groups (10–100): Adult £3, Child/Conc £2.
Partial. WCs. By arrangement. P Free for formal educational visits. In Castle, on leads.

## CARDIFF CASTLE

**Castle Street, Cardiff CF10 3RB**
**Tel:** 029 2087 8100 **Fax:** 029 2023 1417
**Owner:** City and County of Cardiff **Contact:** Booking Office
2000 years of history, including Roman Walls, Norman Keep and Victorian interiors.
**Location:** MAP 2:M1, OS Ref. ST181 765. Cardiff city centre, signposted from M4.
**Open:** 1 Mar–31 Oct: daily, 9.30am–6pm. Tours 10am–5pm, last entry 5pm; 1 Nov–28 Feb: daily, 9.30am–5pm. Tours 10am–4pm, last entry 4pm. Closed 25/26 Dec & 1 Jan.
**Admission:** Full Tour: Adult £6.95, Child £4.30, OAP £5.40. Grounds only: Adult £3.50, Child £2.20. OAP £2.70. Curator Tours: Adult/OAP £12. (2006 prices.)

## CARMARTHEN CASTLE

**Carmarthen, South Wales**
**Tel:** 0126 7224923 **E-mail:** clgriffiths@carmarthenshire.gov.uk
**Owner/Contact:** The Conservation Department, Carmarthenshire County Council
The fortress, originally founded by Henry I in 1109, witnessed several fierce battles, notably in the 15th century when the Welsh hero Owain Glyndwr burnt the town and took the castle from the English.
**Location:** MAP 5:E11, OS Ref. SN413 200. In the town centre.
**Open:** Throughout the year.
**Admission:** Free (guided tours while archaeologists continue to work at the site).

## CARREG CENNEN CASTLE ✠

**Tir-y-Castell Farm, Llandeilo**
**Tel:** 01558 822291   **www.cadw.wales.gov.uk**
**Owner:** In the care of Cadw    **Contact:** The Custodian
Spectacularly crowning a remote crag 300 feet above the River Cennen, the castle is unmatched as a wildly romantic fortress sought out by artists and visitors alike. The climb from Rare Breeds Farm is rewarded by breathtaking views and the chance to explore intriguing caves beneath.
**Location:** MAP 5:G11, OS Ref. SN668 190. Minor roads from A483(T) to Trapp village. 5m SE of A40 at Llandeilo.
**Open:** 1 Apr–31 Oct: daily, 9.30am–6.30pm. 1 Nov–31 Mar, daily, 9.30am–4pm. Closed 25 Dec.
**Admission:** Adult £3.50, Child (under 16 yrs)/Conc. £3, Child under 5yrs Free, Family (2+3, all children under 16yrs) £10. Under 16's must be accompanied by an adult.
◎ ☻ ⬚ ℙ ⬚ Guide dogs only. ✳

CADW: Welsh Historic Monuments. Crown Copyright

## CASTELL COCH ✠
### TONGWYNLAIS, CARDIFF  CF4 7JS
www.cadw.wales.gov.uk

**Tel:** 029 2081 0101
**Owner:** In the care of Cadw    **Contact:** The Custodian
A fairytale castle in the woods, Castell Coch embodies a glorious Victorian dream of the Middle Ages. Designed by William Burges as a country retreat for the 3rd Lord Bute, every room and furnishing is brilliantly eccentric, including paintings of Aesop's fables on the drawing room walls.
**Location:** MAP 2:L1, OS Ref. ST131 826. M4/J32, A470 then signposted. 5m NW of Cardiff city centre.
**Open:** 1 Apr–31 May & Oct: daily, 9.30am–5pm. 1 Jun–30 Sept: daily, 9.30am–6pm. Nov–Mar: Mon–Sat, 9.30am–4pm, Sun 11am–4pm.
**Admission:** Adult £3.50, Child (under 16 yrs)/Conc. £3, Child under 5yrs Free, Family (2+3, all children under 16yrs) £10. Under 16's must be accompanied by an adult.
◎ ♿ ☻ ⬚ ℙ ⬚ Guide dogs only. ▲ ✳

## CHEPSTOW CASTLE ✠

**Chepstow, Gwent**
**Tel:** 01291 624065   **www.cadw.wales.gov.uk**
**Owner:** In the care of Cadw    **Contact:** The Custodian
This mighty fortress has guarded the route from England to South Wales for more than nine centuries. So powerful was this castle that it continued in use until 1690, being finally adapted for cannon and musket after an epic Civil War siege. This huge, complex, grandiosely sited castle deserves a lengthy visit.
**Location:** MAP 2:O1, OS Ref. ST533 941. Chepstow via A466, B4235 or A48. 1½m N of M48/J22.
**Open:** 1 Apr–31 May & Oct: daily, 9.30am–5pm. 1 Jun–30 Sept: daily, 9.30am–6pm. 1 Nov–31 Mar: Mon–Sat, 9.30am–4pm, Sun 11am–4pm.
**Admission:** Adult £3.50, Child (under 16 yrs)/Conc. £3, Child under 5yrs Free, Family (2+3, all children under 16yrs) £10. Under 16s must be accompanied by an adult.
◎ ♿ Partial. ℙ ⬚ Guide dogs only. ✳

## CILGERRAN CASTLE ✠ ⚘

**Cardigan, Dyfed**
**Tel:** 01239 615007   **www.cadw.wales.gov.uk**
**Owner:** In the care of Cadw    **Contact:** The Custodian
Perched high up on a rugged spur above the River Teifi, Cilgerran Castle is one of the most spectacularly sited fortresses in Wales. It dates from the 11th–13th centuries.
**Location:** MAP 5:D10, OS Ref. SN195 431. Main roads to Cilgerran from A478 and A484. 3½m SSE of Cardigan.
**Open:** 1 Apr–30 Sept: daily, 9.30am–6pm. Oct: daily, 9.30am–5pm. 1 Nov–31 Mar: daily, 9.30am–4pm. Closed 24–26 Dec & 1 Jan.
**Admission:** Adult £2.90, Child (under 16 yrs)/Conc. £2.50, Child under 5yrs Free, Child under 5yrs free, Family (2+3, all children under 16yrs) £8.30. Under 16's must be accompanied by an adult.
◎ ℙ ⬚ Guide dogs only. ✳

## CLYNE GARDENS

**Mill Lane, Blackpill, Swansea  SA3 5BD**
**Tel:** 01792 401737   **E-mail:** botanics@swansea.gov.uk
**Owner:** City and County of Swansea    **Contact:** Steve Hopkins
50 acre spring garden, large rhododendron collection, 4 national collections, extensive bog garden, native woodland.
**Location:** MAP 2:I1, OS Ref. SS614 906. S side of Mill Lane, 500yds W of A4067 Mumbles Road, 3m SW of Swansea.
**Open:** All year.
**Admission:** Free.

## COLBY WOODLAND GARDEN ⚘

**Amroth, Narbeth, Pembrokeshire  SA67 8PP**
**Tel:** 01834 811885   **Fax:** 01834 831766
**Owner:** The National Trust
This 3½ ha (8 acre) garden has a fine display of colour in spring, with rhododendrons, magnolias, azaleas and camellias, underplanted with bluebells. Later highlights are the summer hydrangeas and autumn foliage. Open and wooded pathways through the valley offer lovely walks.
**Location:** MAP 5:D12, OS Ref. SN155 080. ½m inland from Amroth beside Carmarthen Bay. Signs from A477.
**Open:** 24 Mar–28 Oct: daily. Woodland Garden: 10am–5pm; Walled Garden: 11am–5pm.
**\*Admission:** Adult £4, Child £2, Family £10. Groups (15+): Adult £3.40, Child £1.70. *includes a voluntary donation but visitors can choose to pay the standard prices displayed at the property and on the website.
ℹ Gallery events. ◎ ☻

## CORNWALL HOUSE 🏛

**58 Monnow Street, Monmouth  NP25 3EN**
**Tel/Fax:** 01600 712031
**Owner/Contact:** Ms Jane Harvey
Town house, dating back to at least the 17th century. Red brick garden façade in Queen Anne style, dating from 1752. Street façade remodelled in Georgian style (date unknown). Many original features, including fine staircase. Delightful town garden with original walled kitchen garden.
**Location:** MAP 6:L11, OS Ref. SO506 127. Half way down main shopping street in Monmouth.
**Open:** 6–16 Apr, 5–7 May, 7–10 & 25–27 Aug, 8/9 & 15/16 Sept: 2–5pm.
**Admission:** Adult £4, Conc. £2.
♿ Grounds only. 🎫 Obligatory. ℙ Public car park nearby. ⬚ Guide dogs only. €

## CRESSELLY

**Kilgetty, Pembrokeshire  SA68 0SP**
**Fax:** 01646 687045   **E-mail:** hha@cresselly.org.uk   **www.cresselly.org.uk**
**Owner/Contact:** H D R Harrison-Allen Esq MFH
Home of the Allen family for 250 years. The house is of 1770 with matching wings of 1869 and contains good plasterwork and fittings of both periods. The Allens are of particular interest for their close association with the Wedgwood family of Etruria and a long tradition of foxhunting. Grade II listed holiday cottages nearby on river.
**Location:** MAP 5:C11, OS Ref. SN065 065. W of the A4075.
**Open:** Mon–Fri only. 11–15, 18–22, 25–29 Jun; 2–6, 9–13, 16–20 Jul: 10am–1pm. Guided tours only, on the hour. Coaches and at other times by arrangement.
**Admission:** Adult £4, no children under 12.
♿ Ground floor only. 🎫 Obligatory. ℙ Coaches by arrangement. ✳
⬚ Holiday cottages.

## CYFARTHFA CASTLE MUSEUM

**Brecon Road, Merthyr Tydfil, Mid Glamorgan  CF47 8RE**
**Tel/Fax:** 01685 723112  **E-mail:** museum@merthyr.gov.uk
**www.museums.merthyr.gov.uk**
**Owner:** Merthyr Tydfil County Borough Council   **Contact:** Scott Reid
Castle originates from 1824/1825, now a museum and school.
**Location:** MAP 6:I11, OS Ref. SO041 074. NE side of A470 to Brecon, ½m NW of town centre.
**Open:** 1 Apr–30 Sept: Mon–Sun, 10am–5.30pm. Winter: Tue–Fri, 10am–4pm, Sats & Suns, 12 noon–4pm. Closed between Christmas and New Year.
**Admission:** Free.

## DINEFWR ⚘

**Llandeilo  SA19 6RT**
**Tel:** 01558 650177   **Fax:** 01558 650707   **E-mail:** dolaucothi@nationaltrust.org.uk
**Owner:** The National Trust   **Contact:** The House Manager
Historic site with particular connections to the medieval Princes of Wales.
**Location:** MAP 5:G11, OS Ref. SN625 225. On outskirts of Llandeilo.
**Open:** House & Park: 17 Mar–28 Oct, Thurs–Mon, 11am–5pm. During the school holidays the park and house will be open daily.
**\*Admission:** House & Park: Adult £6, Child £3, Family £12.50. Groups (15+) £5.10. Park only: Adult £4, Child £2, Family £10. Groups: £3.40. *includes a voluntary donation but visitors can choose to pay the standard prices displayed at the property and on the website.
♿⬛🖼 By arrangement. 🅿 Limited for coaches. ⬛🖼 In grounds on leads.

CADW (Welsh Historic Monuments) Photo Library

Castell Coch, Cardiff – The Drawing Room

Dinefwr, Llandeilo

## DYFFRYN GARDENS AND ARBORETUM 🏛

### ST NICHOLAS, Nr CARDIFF  CF5 6SU

www.dyffryngardens.org.uk

**Tel:** 029 2059 3328   **Fax:** 029 2059 1966
**Owner:** Vale of Glamorgan Council   **Contact:** Ms G Donovan
Dyffryn Gardens is a beautiful Grade I registered Edwardian garden, set in the heart of the Vale of Glamorgan countryside. The 55-acre gardens are the result of a unique collaboration between the eminent landscape architect, Thomas Mawson, and the passionate plant collector, Reginald Cory. The garden includes great lawns, herbaceous borders, many individual themed garden 'rooms' and a well established Arboretum including 14 champion trees. The magnificent gardens have been undergoing extensive restoration work with assistance from the Heritage Lottery Fund, including a striking Visitor Centre and tearooms. Ongoing work includes the Walled Garden and new glasshouses, which are due for completion this summer.
**Location:** MAP 2:L2, OS Ref. ST095 723. 3m NW of Barry, J33/M4. 1½m S of St Nicholas on A48.
**Open:** All year from 1 Mar 2007. For details please telephone 029 2059 3328.
**Admission:** Adult £3.50, Child/Conc. £2.50. Discount for groups (15+). (2006 prices, telephone for details.)

⬛🖼♿⬛🖼🅿⬛🖼🖼❋⬛

© Skyscan

## FONMON CASTLE

### FONMON, BARRY, VALE OF GLAMORGAN CF62 3ZN

**Tel:** 01446 710206 **Fax:** 01446 711687 **E-mail:** Fonmon_Castle@msn.com
**Owner:** Sir Brooke Boothby Bt **Contact:** Anne Broadway
Occupied as a home since the 13th century, this medieval castle has the most stunning Georgian interiors and is surrounded by extensive gardens. Available for weddings, dinners, corporate entertainment and multi-activity days.
**Location:** MAP 2:L2, OS Ref. ST047 681. 15m W of Cardiff, 1m W of Cardiff airport.
**Open:** 1 Apr–30 Sept: Tue & Wed, 2–5pm (last tour 4pm). Other times by appointment. Groups: by appointment.
**Admission:** Adult £5, Child Free.
🛈 Conferences. 🖂 By arrangement (up to 120). ♿ WC. 🅿 🚍 Guide dogs only. 🔺❄

## THE JUDGE'S LODGING

### Broad Street, Presteigne, Powys LD8 2AD

**Tel:** 01544 260650 **Fax:** 01544 260652 **E-mail:** info@judgeslodging.org.uk
**www.judgeslodging.org.uk**
**Owner:** Powys County Council **Contact:** Gabrielle Rivers
Explore the fascinating world of the Victorian judges, their servants and felonious guests at this award-winning, totally hands-on historic house. From sumptuous judge's apartments to the gas-lit servants' quarters below, follow an 'eavesdropping' audio tour featuring actor Robert Hardy. Damp cells, vast courtroom and local history rooms included.
**Location:** MAP 6:K8, OS Ref. SO314 644. In town centre, off A44 and A4113. Easy reach from Herefordshire and mid-Wales.
**Open:** 1 Mar–31 Oct: daily, 10am–5pm. 1 Nov–22 Dec: Wed–Sun, 10am–4pm. Bookings by arrangement accepted all year.
**Admission:** Adult £5.25, Child £3.95, Conc. £4.75. Groups (10-80): Adult £4.75, Child/Conc. £4.25, Family £15.
🛈 🖂 Partial (access via lift). 🖂 By arrangement. 🅿 In town. 🖿 🚍 Guide dogs only. 🔺🌢

## KIDWELLY CASTLE ✚

### Kidwelly, West Glamorgan SA17 5BG

**Tel:** 01554 890104 **www.cadw.wales.gov.uk**
**Owner:** In the care of Cadw **Contact:** The Custodian
A chronicle in stone of medieval fortress technology this strong and splendid castle developed during more than three centuries of Anglo-Welsh warfare. The half-moon shape stems from the original 12th century stockaded fortress, defended by the River Gwendraeth on one side and a deep crescent-shaped ditch on the other.
**Location:** MAP 5:E12, OS Ref. SN409 070. Kidwelly via A484. Kidwelly Rail Station 1m.
**Open:** 1 Apr–31 May & Oct: daily, 9.30am–5pm. 1 Jun–30 Sept: daily, 9.30am–6pm. 1 Nov–31 Mar: Mon–Sat, 9.30am–4pm, Sun 11am–4pm. Closed 24–26 Dec & 1 Jan.
**Admission:** Adult £2.90, Child (under 16 yrs)/Conc. £2.50, Child under 5yrs Free, Family (2+3, all children under 16yrs) £8.30. Under 16's must be accompanied by an adult.
🛈 ♿ 🖂 By arrangement. 🛈 🅿 🚍 Guide dogs only. ❄

## LAMPHEY BISHOP'S PALACE ✚

### Lamphey, Dyfed SA71 5NT

**Tel:** 01646 672224 **www.cadw.wales.gov.uk**
**Owner:** In the care of Cadw **Contact:** The Custodian
Lamphey marks the place of the spectacular Bishop's Palace but it reached its height of greatness under Bishop Henry de Gower who raised the new Great Hall. Today the ruins of this comfortable retreat reflect the power enjoyed by the medieval bishops.
**Location:** MAP 5:C12, OS Ref. SN018 009. A4139 from Pembroke or Tenby. N of village (A4139).
**Open:** 1 Apr–31 Mar: daily, 10am–5pm (last admission 30 mins before closing). Closed at all other times.
**Admission:** Adult £2.90, Child (under 16 yrs)/Conc. £2.50, Child under 5yrs Free, Family (2+3, all children under 16yrs) £8.30. Under 16's must be accompanied by an adult.
🛈 🛈 🅿 🚍 Guide dogs only. ❄

## LAUGHARNE CASTLE ✚

### King Street, Laugharne SA33 4SA

**Tel:** 01994 427906 **www.cadw.wales.gov.uk**
**Owner:** In the care of Cadw **Contact:** The Custodian
Picturesque Laugharne Castle stands on a low ridge overlooking the wide Taf estuary, one of a string of fortresses controlling the ancient route along the South Wales coast.
**Location:** MAP 5:E11, OS Ref. SN303 107. 4m S of A48 at St Clears via A4066.
**Open:** 1 Apr–30 Sept: daily, 10am–5pm. The Monument is closed at all other times.
**Admission:** Adult £2.90, Child (under 16 yrs)/Conc. £2.50, Child under 5yrs Free, Family (2+3, all children under 16yrs) £8.30. Under 16's must be accompanied by an adult.
🛈 🅿 🚍 Guide dogs only.

## LLANCAIACH FAWR MANOR

### Nelson, Treharris CF46 6ER

**Tel:** 01443 412248 **Fax:** 01443 412688
**Owner:** Caerphilly County Borough Council **Contact:** The Administrator
Tudor fortified manor dating from 1530 with Stuart additions. Costumed guides.
**Location:** MAP 2:M1, OS Ref. ST114 967. S side of B4254, 1m N of A472 at Nelson, in the county borough of Caerphilly.
**Open:** All year: daily, 10am–5pm. Last admission 1hour before closing. Nov–Feb: closed Mons. Closed Christmas week.
**Admission:** Adult £4.95, Child £3.50, Conc. £3.75, Family £14.

## LLANERCHAERON 🌿

### Ciliau Aeron, Nr Aberaeron, Ceredigion SA48 8DG

**Tel:** 01545 570200
**Owner:** The National Trust
This rare example of a self-sufficient 18th-century Welsh minor gentry estate has survived virtually unaltered. The Villa, designed in the 1790s, is the most complete example of the early work of John Nash. It has its own service courtyard with dairy, laundry. brewery and salting house, and walled kitchen gardens produce fruit, vegetables, herbs and plants, all on sale in season. The Home Farm complex has an impressive range of traditional and atmospheric outbuildings and is now a working organic farm with Welsh Black Cattle, Llanwenog Sheep and rare Welsh Pigs. Visitors can see farming activities in progress, such as lambing, shearing and hay-making.
**Location:** MAP 5:F8, OS Ref. SN480 602. 2½ miles East of Aberaeron off A482 / 2½ mile foot/cycle track from Aberaeron to property along old railway track.
**Open:** House: 24 Mar–22 July & 5 Sep–28 Oct, Wed–Sun; 24 Jul–2 Sep, Tues–Sun; 11.30am–4pm. Farm/Garden as House but 11am–5pm.
**\*Admission:** Adult £6.40, Child £3.20, Family £16, Groups: Adult £5.50, Child £2.75.\*includes a voluntary donation but visitors can choose to pay the standard prices displayed at the property and on the website.

## LLANVIHANGEL COURT

### Nr Abergavenny, Monmouthshire NP7 8DH

**Tel:** 01873 890217 **Fax:** 01873 890380 **www.llanvihangel-court.co.uk**
**Owner/Contact:** Julia Johnson
A Grade I Tudor Manor. The home in the 17th century of the Arnolds who built the imposing terraces and stone steps leading up to the house. The interior has a fine hall, unusual yew staircase and many 17th century moulded plaster ceilings. Delightful grounds. Includes 17th century features, notably Grade I stables.
**Location:** MAP 6:K11, OS Ref. SO433 139. 4m N of Abergavenny on A465.
**Open:** 5–15 May & 4–27 Aug, daily 2.30–5.30pm. Last tour 5pm.
**Admission:** Entry and guide, Adult £4.00, Child/Conc. £2.50.
🛈 No inside photography. ♿ Partial. 🛈 🅿 Limited. 🚍 On leads. 🔺

# THE NATIONAL BOTANIC GARDEN OF WALES
## CARMARTHENSHIRE SA32 8HG

www.gardenofwales.org.uk

**Tel:** 01558 668768 **Fax:** 01558 668933 **E-mail:** info@gardenofwales.org.uk
**Owner:** The National Botanic Garden of Wales **Contact:** Helen Edwards
This first national botanic garden of the new millennium is developing into one of the most exciting and beautiful gardens in the UK. At the centre of 568 acres of Regency parkland is the largest single-span glasshouse in the world, housing endangered plants from mediterranean climates around the globe.

The sensitively restored Double Walled Garden is a major highlight, telling the story of plant evolution and plotting the family trees of these plants. There are many other outdoor themed gardens for the visitor to enjoy such as the award-winning Japanese Garden and the Apothecaries' Garden, exhibitions, multi-media theatre, water features, adventure playground, mini-farm, gift shop, restaurant and plant sales. For further information visit www.gardenofwales.org.uk.

**Location:** MAP 5:F11, OS159 Ref. SN518 175. ¼m from the A48 midway between Crosshands and Carmarthen. Clearly signposted from A48 and Carmarthen. Train & Bus in Carmarthen (7m).
**Open:** British Summer Time: 10am–6pm. British Winter Time: 10am–4.30pm. Closed Christmas Day.
**Admission:** Adult £8, Child £3, OAP/Students £6, Family (2+4) £17. Groups (10+): Adult £7, Child £2, OAP/Student £5.

⬚ ♿ 🍴 ♿ Free disability scooter hire, booking advisable. 🎦 Licensed. 🍴 Licensed. 🎨 By arrangement. 🅿 🐕 Guide dogs only. 🔺 ❄

## OXWICH CASTLE ♣

**c/o Oxwich Castle Farm, Oxwich SA3 1NG**
**Tel:** 01792 390359 **www.cadw.wales.gov.uk**
**Owner:** In the care of Cadw **Contact:** The Custodian
Beautifully sited in the lovely Gower peninsula, Oxwich Castle is a striking testament to the pride and ambitions of the Mansel dynasty of Welsh gentry.
**Location:** MAP 2:I1, OS159 Ref. SS497 864. A4118, 11m SW of Swansea, in Oxwich village.
**Open:** 1 Apr–30 Sept: daily, 10am–5pm. The Monument is closed at all other times.
**Admission:** Adult £2.50, Child (under 16 yrs)/Conc. £2, Child under 5yrs Free, Family (2+3, all children under 16yrs) £7. Under 16's must be accompanied by an adult.
⬚ 🅿 🐕 Guide dogs only.

# PEMBROKE CASTLE
## PEMBROKE SA71 4LA

www.pembrokecastle.co.uk

**Tel:** 01646 681510 **Fax:** 01646 622260 **E-mail:** info@pembrokecastle.co.uk
**Owner:** Trustees of Pembroke Castle **Contact:** Mr D Ramsden
Pembroke Castle is situated within minutes of beaches and the breathtaking scenery of the Pembrokeshire Coastal National Park. This early Norman fortress, birthplace of the first Tudor King, houses many fascinating displays and exhibitions. Enjoy a picnic in the beautifully kept grounds, or on the roof of St. Anne's Bastion and take in the views along the estuary. Events every weekend in July and August.
**Location:** MAP 5:C12, OS Ref. SM983 016. W end of the main street in Pembroke.
**Open:** All year. 1 Apr–Sept: daily, 9.30am–6pm. Mar & Oct: daily, 10am–5pm. Nov–Feb: daily, 10am–4pm. Closed 24–26 Dec & 1 Jan. Cafe closed Dec–Jan. Brass rubbing centre open Summer months and all year by arrangement.
**Admission:** Adult £3.50, Child/Conc. £2.50, Family (2+2) £10. Groups (20+): Adult £3, OAP/Student £2.

⬚ ♿ 🎦 Closed Dec & Jan. 🎨 End of May–Sept by arrangement. 🅿 🐕 In grounds on leads. ❄ ❄

Chepstow Castle, Gwent

# PICTON CASTLE
## HAVERFORDWEST, PEMBROKESHIRE  SA62 4AS

www.pictoncastle.co.uk

**Tel/Fax:** 01437 751326  **E-mail:** pct@pictoncastle.freeserve.co.uk
**Owner:** The Picton Castle Trust  **Contact:** Mr D Pryse Lloyd
Built in the 13th century by Sir John Wogan, his direct descendants still use the Castle as their family home. The medieval castle was modernised in the 1750s, above the undercroft and extended around 1790 with fine Georgian interiors. The 40 acres of woodland and walled gardens are part of The Royal Horticultural Society access scheme for beautiful gardens. There is a unique collection of rhododendrons and azaleas, mature trees, unusual shrubs, wild flowers, fern walk, fernery, maze, restored dewpond, a herb collection labelled with medicinal remedies and a children's nature trail. The Picton Gallery is used for nationally acclaimed exhibitions. Events include spring and autumn plant sales.
**Location:** MAP 5:C11, OS Ref. SN011 135. 4m E of Haverfordwest, just off A40.
**Open:** 1 Apr–30 Sept: daily except Mon (open BH Mons), 10.30am–5pm. Entrance to Castle by guided tours only, between 12 noon–4pm. Oct: Gardens only, daily, 10.30am–dusk.
**Admission:** Castle, Garden & Gallery: Adult £5.95, Child £3, OAP £5.75. Garden & Gallery: Adult £4.95, Child £2.50, OAP £4.75. Groups (20+): reduced prices by prior arrangement.
[i] No indoor photography. 🖼 🎁 🍵 ♿ 🍴 Licensed. 🎥 Obligatory. P
🐕 In grounds, on leads. 🔼 🔽

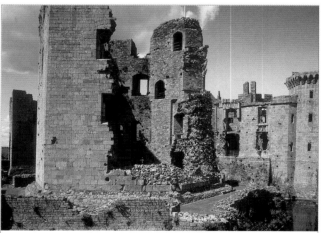

# RAGLAN CASTLE ♣
## RAGLAN NP5 2BT

www.cadw.wales.gov.uk

**Tel:** 01291 690228
**Owner:** In the care of Cadw  **Contact:** The Custodian
Undoubtedly the finest late medieval fortress-palace in Britain, it was begun in the 1430s by Sir William ap Thomas who built the mighty 'Yellow Tower'. His son William Lord Herbert added a palatial mansion defended by a gatehouse and many towered walls. The high quality is still obvious today.
**Location:** MAP 6:K12, OS Ref. SO415 084. Raglan, NE of Raglan village off A40 (eastbound) and signposted.
**Open:** 14 Apr–31 May & Oct: daily, 9.30am–5pm. 1 Jun–30 Sept: daily, 9.30am–6pm. 1 Nov–31 Mar: Mon–Sat, 9.30am–4pm, Sun 11am–4pm.
**Admission:** Adult £2.90, Child (under 16 yrs)/Conc. £2.50, Child under 5yrs Free, Family (2+3, all children under 16yrs) £8.30. Under 16's must be accompanied by an adult.
🖼 P 🐕 Guide dogs only. ✳

## ST DAVIDS BISHOP'S PALACE ♣

**St Davids, Pembrokeshire  SA62 6PE**
**Tel:** 01437 720517  www.cadw.wales.gov.uk
**Owner:** In the care of Cadw  **Contact:** The Custodian
The city of St Davids boasts not only one of Britain's finest cathedrals but also the most impressive medieval palace in Wales. Built in the elaborate 'decorated' style of gothic architecture, the palace is lavishly encrusted with fine carving.
**Location:** MAP 5:B11, OS Ref. SM750 254. A487 to St Davids, minor road past the Cathedral.
**Open:** 1 Apr–31 May & Oct: daily, 9.30am–5pm. 1 Jun–30 Sept: daily, 9.30am–6pm. 1 Nov–31 Mar: Mon–Sat, 9.30am–4pm, Sun 11am–4pm.
**Admission:** Adult £2.90, Child (under 16 yrs)/Conc. £2.50, Child under 5yrs Free, Family (2+3, all children under 16yrs) £8.30. Under 16's must be accompanied by an adult.
🖼 ♿ Partial. P 🐕 Guide dogs only. ✳

## ST DAVIDS CATHEDRAL

**St Davids, Pembrokeshire  SA62 6QW**
**Tel:** 01437 720691  **Fax:** 01437 721885
**Contact:** Mr R G Tarr
Over eight centuries old. Many unique and 'odd' features.
**Location:** MAP 5:B11, OS Ref. SM751 254. 5–10 mins walk from car/coach parks: signs for pedestrians.
**Open:** Daily: 8.30am–5.30pm. Sun: 12.30–5.30pm, may be closed for services in progress. Sun services: 8am, 9.30am, 11.15am & 6pm. Weekday services: 8am & 6pm. Weds extra service: 10am.
**Admission:** Donations. Guided tours (Adult £4, Child £1.20) must be booked.

## ST FAGANS: NATIONAL HISTORY MUSEUM

**St Fagans, Cardiff  CF5 6XB**
**Tel:** 029 2057 3500  **Fax:** 029 2057 3490
One of the world's best-loved open-air museums. Original buildings have been moved from all over Wales and re-erected at the Museum – these include a Victorian school, industrial ironworkers' cottages and a rural chapel. St Fagans Castle, an Elizabethan Manor House, also stands within the grounds.
**Location:** MAP 2:L2, OS Ref. ST118 772. 4m W of city centre, 1½ m N of A48, 2m S of M4/J33. Follow the brown signs (Museum of Welsh Life). Entrance drive is off A4232 (southbound only).
**Open:** All year: daily, 10am–5pm. Closed 24–26 Dec & 1 Jan.
**Admission:** Free.

## STRATA FLORIDA ABBEY ♣

**Ystrad Meurig, Pontrhydfendigaid  SY25 6BT**
**Tel:** 01974 831261  www.cadw.wales.gov.uk
**Owner:** In the care of Cadw  **Contact:** The Custodian
Remotely set in the green, kite-haunted Teifi Valley with the lonely Cambrian mountains as a backdrop, the ruined abbey has a wonderful doorway with Celtic spiral motifs and preserves a wealth of beautiful medieval tiles.
**Location:** MAP 5:H8, OS Ref. SN746 658. Minor road from Pontrhydfendigaid 14m SE of Aberystwyth by the B4340.
**Open:** 1 Apr–30 Sept: Wed–Sun, 10am–5pm. The Monument will be open and unstaffed on Mon & Tue (except BH Mons) between 1 Apr–30 Sept. Open at all other times generally between 10am–4pm, but unstaffed and with no admission charge.
**Admission:** Adult £2.90, Child (under 16 yrs)/Conc. £2.50, Child under 5yrs Free, Family (2+3, all children under 16yrs) £8.30. Under 16's must be accompanied by an adult.
🖼 ♿ P 🐕 Guide dogs only. ✳

Picton Castle, Haverfordwest

## TINTERN ABBEY ✤
### TINTERN NP6 6SE

www.cadw.wales.gov.uk

**Tel:** 01291 689251

**Owner:** In the care of Cadw    **Contact:** The Custodian

Tintern is the best preserved abbey in Wales and ranks among Britain's most beautiful historic sites. Elaborately decorated in 'gothic' architecture style this church stands almost complete to roof level. Turner sketched and painted here, while Wordsworth drew inspiration from the surroundings.

**Location:** MAP 6:L12, OS Ref. SO533 000. Tintern via A466, from M4/J23. Chepstow 6m.

**Open:** 1 Apr–31 May & Oct: daily, 9.30am–5pm. 1 Jun–30 Sept: daily, 9.30am–6pm. 1 Nov–31 Mar: Mon–Sat, 9.30am–4pm, Sun 11am–4pm.

**Admission:** Adult £3.50, Child (under 16 yrs)/Conc. £3, Child under 5yrs Free, Family (2+3, all children under 16yrs) £10. Under 16's must be accompanied by an adult.

⬚ ⬚ ⬚ **P** ⬚ Guide dogs only. ✷

## TREDEGAR HOUSE & PARK 🏛
### NEWPORT, SOUTH WALES NP1 9YW

**Tel:** 01633 815880    **Fax:** 01633 815895    **E-mail:** tredegar.house@newport.gov.uk

**Owner:** Newport City Council    **Contact:** The Manager

South Wales' finest country house, ancestral home of the Morgan family. Parts of a medieval house remain, but Tredegar owes its reputation to lavish rebuilding in the 17th century. Visitors have a lively and entertaining tour through 30 rooms, including glittering State Rooms and 'below stairs'. Set in 90 acres of parkland with formal gardens. Winner of Best Public Park and Garden in Great Britain 1997. Craft workshops.

**Location:** MAP 2:M1, OS Ref. ST290 852. M4/J28 signposted. From London 2½hrs, from Cardiff 20 mins. 2m SW of Newport town centre.

**Open:** Easter–Sept: Wed–Sun & BHs, 11.30am–4pm. Evening tours & groups by appointment. Oct–Mar: Groups only by appointment.

**Admission:** Adult £5.40, Child Free (when accompanied by paying adult), Conc. £3.95. Special discounts for Newport residents. (2006 prices.)

ⓘ Conferences. No photography in house. ⬚ ⬚ ⬚ Partial. WC. ⬚ ⬚ Obligatory. **P** ⬚ ⬚ In grounds, on leads. ⬚ ⬚

---

### TREBERFYDD

**Bwlch, Powys LD3 7PX**

**Tel:** 01874 730205    **E-mail:** david.raikes@btinternet.com    **www.treberfydd.net**

**Owner:** David Raikes

Treberfydd is a Victorian country house, built in the Gothic style in 1847–50. The house was designed by J L Pearson, and the garden and grounds by W A Nesfield.

**Location:** MAP 6:I10, From A40 in Bwlch take road to Llangors, after ¼m turn left, follow lane for 2m until white gates and Treberfydd sign.

**Open:** 1–27 Aug. Guided tours of the House: 2 & 4pm, telephone or e-mail to secure a place on a tour. Grounds: 2–6pm.

**Admission:** Adult £3 (inc. tour), Child (under 12yrs) Free. Grounds: £2.

⬚ Partial. ⬚ Obligatory. **P** Limited. None for coaches. ⬚ On leads, in grounds.

---

### TREOWEN 🏛

**Wonastow, Nr Monmouth NP25 4DL**

**Tel/Fax:** 01600 712031    **E-mail:** john.wheelock@virgin.net    **www.treowen.co.uk**

**Owner:** R A & J P Wheelock    **Contact:** John Wheelock

Early 17th century mansion built to double pile plan with magnificent well-stair to four storeys.

**Location:** MAP 6:L11, OS Ref. SO461 111. 3m WSW of Monmouth.

Open: May, Jun Aug & Sept: Fri, 10am–4pm. Also 24/25 Mar; 21/22 & 28/29 Apr; 15/16 & 22/23 Sept: 2–5pm. HHA Friends Free on Fri only.

**Admission:** £5 (£3 if appointment made). Groups by appointment only.

⬚ ⬚ Entire house let, self-catering. Sleeps 24+. ⬚

---

### TREBINSHWN

**Nr Brecon, Powys LD3 7PX**

**Tel:** 01874 730653    **Fax:** 01874 730843

**Owner/Contact:** R Watson

16th century mid-sized manor house. Extensively rebuilt 1780. Fine courtyard and walled garden.

**Location:** MAP 6:I10, OS Ref. SO136 242. 1½m NW of Bwlch.

**Open:** Easter–31 Aug: Mon–Tue, 10am–4.30pm.

**Admission:** Free.

**P**

---

### TRETOWER COURT & CASTLE ✤

**Tretower, Crickhowell NP8 2RF**

**Tel:** 01874 730279    **www.cadw.wales.gov.uk**

**Owner:** In the care of Cadw    **Contact:** The Custodian

A fine fortress and an outstanding medieval manor house, Tretower Court and Castle range around a galleried courtyard, now further enhanced by a beautiful recreated medieval garden.

**Location:** MAP 6:J11, OS Ref. SO187 212. Signposted in Tretower Village, off A479, 3m NW of Crickhowell.

**Open:** Mar & Oct: Tues–Sun, 10am–4pm (5pm, Apr–Sept). Both Monuments closed at all other times.

**Admission:** Adult £2.90, Child (under 16 yrs)/Conc. £2.50, Child under 5yrs Free, Family (2+3, all children under 16yrs) £8.30. Under 16's must be accompanied by an adult.

⬚ ⬚ **P** ⬚ Guide dogs only.

© NT Photographic Library
Andrew Butler

Colby Woodland Garden, Pembrokeshire

For rare and unusual plants visit the **plant sales** index on page 564

## TUDOR MERCHANT'S HOUSE

**Quay Hill, Tenby  SA70 7BX**
**Tel/Fax:** 01834 842279
**Owner:** The National Trust    **Contact:** The Custodian

A late 15th century town house, characteristic of the area at the time when Tenby was a thriving trading port. The house is furnished to recreate family life from the Tudor period onwards. There is access to the small herb garden.

**Location:** MAP 5:D12, OS Ref. SN135 004. Tenby. W of alley from NE corner of town centre square.
**Open:** 26 Mar–26 Oct: daily (closed Sats), 11am–5pm.
Admission: Adult £2.50, Child £1.20, Family £6.20. Groups: Adult £2, Child £1.
ℹ️ No indoor photography. 🅿️ No parking. ◼️ 🐕 Guide dogs only.

## TYTHEGSTON COURT

**Tythegston, Bridgend  CF32 0NE**
**E-mail:** cknight@tythegston.com    **www.tythegston.com**
**Owner/Contact:** C Knight
**Location:** MAP 2:K1, OS Ref. SS857 789. 2m E of Porthcawl on Glamorgan coast.
**Open:** By written appointment (no telephone calls please).
**Admission:** Adult £10, Child £2.50, Conc. £5.
🅃 ♿ Partial. 📷 Obligatory. 🅿️ Limited. No coaches. 🐕 Guide dogs only.

## USK CASTLE

**Usk, Monmouthshire  NP5 1SD**
**Tel:** 01291 672563   **E-mail:** info@uskcastle.co.uk   **www.uskcastle.com**
**Owner/Contact:** J H L Humphreys

Romantic, ruined castle overlooking the picturesque town of Usk. Inner and outer baileys, towers and earthwork defences. Surrounded by enchanting gardens (open under NGS) incorporating The Castle House, the former medieval gatehouse.

**Location:** MAP 6:K12, OS Ref. SO376 011. Up narrow lane off Monmouth road in Usk, opposite fire station.
**Open:** Castle ruins: daily, 11am–5pm. Groups by appointment. Gardens: private visits welcome & groups by arrangement. House: Jun & BHs: 2–5pm (closed 23/24 Jun), small groups & guided tours only.
**Admission:** Castle ruins: Adult £2, Child Free. Gardens: Adult £4. House: Adult £6, Child £3.
🅃 ♿ Partial. 📷 By arrangement. 🅿️ No coaches. ◼️ 🐕 In grounds, on leads. ✸

## WEOBLEY CASTLE ✤

**Weobley Castle Farm, Llanrhidian  SA3 1HB**
**Tel:** 01792 390012   **www.cadw.wales.gov.uk**
**Owner:** In the care of Cadw    **Contact:** The Custodian

Perched above the wild northern coast of the beautiful Gower peninsula, Weobley Castle was the home of the Knightly de Bere family. Its rooms include a fine hall and private chamber as well as numerous 'garderobes' or toilets and an early Tudor porch block.

**Location:** MAP 2:I1, OS Ref. SN477 928. B4271 or B4295 to Llanrhidian Village, then minor road for 1½m.
**Open:** 1 Apr–31 Oct: daily, 9.30am–6pm (5pm, Nov–Mar).
**Admission:** Adult £2.50, Child (under 16 yrs)/Conc. £2, Child under 5yrs Free, Family (2+3, all children under 16yrs) £7. Under 16's must be accompanied by an adult.
📷 🅿️ 🐕 Guide dogs only. ✸

## WHITE CASTLE ✤

**Llantillio Crossenny, Gwent**
**Tel:** 01600 780380   **www.cadw.wales.gov.uk**
**Owner:** In the care of Cadw    **Contact:** The Custodian

With its high walls and round towers reflected in the still waters of its moat, White Castle is the ideal medieval fortress. It was rebuilt in the mid-13th century by the future King Edward I to counter a threat from Prince Llywelyn the Last.

**Location:** MAP 6:K11, OS Ref. SO380 167. By minor road 2m NW from B4233 at A7 Llantilio Crossenny. 8m ENE of Abergavenny.
**Open:** 1 Apr–30 Sept: Wed–Sun, 10am–5pm. The Monument will be open and unstaffed on Mon & Tue (except BH Mons). Open at all other times generally between 10am–4pm, but unstaffed and with no admission charge.
**Admission:** Adult £2.50, Child (under 16 yrs)/Conc. £2, Child under 5yrs Free, Family (2+3, all children under 16yrs) £7. Under 16's must be accompanied by an adult.
📷 🅿️ 🐕 Guide dogs only. ✸

The Judge's Lodging, Presteigne

Castell Coch, Cardiff

**Above:** Mount Stewart ©NT Photographic Library
**Right:** Rowallane Garden ©NT Photographic Library

512

# Ireland

*Visitors come largely to enjoy the countryside and what it has to offer.
Fishing (both river and sea) and golf are two of the most popular
attractions. There are many heritage properties both in private ownership
and owned by the National Trust for Ireland that have fascinating
histories, among them Mount Stewart, once the home of Lord Castlereagh.*

## ANTRIM CASTLE GARDENS

**Randalstown Road, Antrim  BT41 4LH**
**Tel:** 028 9448 1338   **Fax:** 028 9448 1344   **E-mail:** clotworthyarts@antrim.gov.uk
**Owner:** Antrim Borough Council     **Contact:** Philip Magennis
Situated adjacent to Antrim Town, the Sixmilewater River and Lough Neagh's shore, these 17th century Anglo-Dutch water gardens are maintained in a manner authentic to the period. The gardens comprise of ornamental canals, round pond, ancient motte and a parterre garden planted with 17th century plants - many with culinary or medicinal uses. An interpretative display introducing the history of the gardens and the process of their restoration is located in the reception of Clotworthy Arts Centre.
**Location:** MAP 18:O3, OS Ref. J186 850. Outside Antrim town centre off A26 on A6.
**Open:** All year: Mon–Fri, 9.30am–9.30pm (dusk if earlier). Sats, 10am–5pm. Jul & Aug: also open Suns, 2–5pm.
**Admission:** Free. Charge for guided group tours (by arrangement only).

## ARDRESS HOUSE

**64 Ardress Road, Portadown, Co Armagh  BT62 1SQ**
**Tel** 028 8778 4753   **Fax:** 028 3885 1236   **E-mail:** ardress@nationaltrust.org.uk
**www.ntni.org.uk**
**Owner:** The National Trust     **Contact:** The Custodian
Nestled in the apple orchards of Armagh, Ardress is a 17th century house with elegant 18th century decoration. On display is the 1799 table made for the Speaker of the Irish Parliament upon which King George V signed the Constitution of Northern Ireland on 22 June 1921.
**Location:** MAP 18:N4, OS Ref. H912 561. On B28, 5m from Moy, 5m from Portadown, 3m from M1/J13.
**Open:** 17 Mar–30 Sept: Sats, Suns & BH/PHs, 2–6pm. My Lady's Mile: all year dawn–dusk.
***Admission:** House tour: Adult £4, Child £2, Family £10. Groups £3.10 (outside normal hours £5.10). *includes a voluntary donation but visitors can choose to pay the standard prices displayed at the property and on the website.
Ground floor. WC. Obligatory. On leads.

## THE ARGORY

**Moy, Dungannon, Co Tyrone  BT71 6NA**
**Tel:** 028 8778 4753   **Fax:** 028 8778 9598
**E-mail:** argory@nationaltrust.org.uk   **www.ntni.org.uk**
**Owner:** The National Trust     **Contact:** The Property Manager
The Argory was built in the 1820s on a hill and has wonderful views over the gardens and 320 acre wooded riverside estate. This former home of the McGeough-Bond family has a splendid stable yard with horse carriages, harness room, acetylene gas plant and laundry.
**Location:** MAP 18:N4, OS Ref. H871 577. On Derrycaw road, 4m from Moy, 3m from M1/J13 or J14 (coaches J13).
**Open:** House: Closed for conservation work until March 2008. Grounds: 1 Oct–30 Apr: daily, 10am–4pm; 1 May–30 Sept: daily, 10am–7pm (2–7pm on Event Days). Tearoom & Shop: 17 Mar–30 Jun & Sept: Sats/Suns & BH/PHs, (Jul & Aug: daily).
***Admission:** Car £3, Minibus £15, Coach £20, Motorcycle £1.50. *includes a voluntary donation but visitors can choose to pay the standard prices displayed at the property and on the website.
Ground floor. WC. Obligatory. On leads.

Main Hall, Mount Stewart

## BALLYWALTER PARK

**BALLYWALTER, NEWTOWNARDS, CO DOWN  BT22 2PP**
www.ballywalterpark.com

**Tel:** 028 4275 8264   **Fax:** 028 4275 8818   **E-mail:** enq@dunleath-estates.co.uk
**Owner:** The Lord and Lady Dunleath
**Contact:** Mrs Sharon Graham, The Estate Office
Ballywalter Park was built, in the Italianate Palazzo style, between 1846 and 1852 by Sir Charles Lanyon for the present owner's great, great, great, grandfather Andrew Mulholland. A single-storey Gentlemen's wing, comprising Billiard Room, Smoking Room and Conservatory, was added in 1870 for Andrew's son, John Mulholland, later 1st Baron Dunleath. Further Edwardian additions were made by W J Fennell. The house has a fine collection of original furniture and paintings, complemented by contemporary pieces added by the present owner. The house has undergone major conservation works over the past 20 years with the Billiard and Smoking Rooms being restored in 2003/4. Access to the Conservatory is likely to be restricted in 2007/8 due to major works being undertaken.
**Location:** MAP 18:P3, OS Ref. J610 723. Off A2 on unclassified road, 1 km S of Ballywalter village.
**Open:** By prior appointment only; please contact The Estate Office.
**Admission:** House or Gardens: £6. House & Gardens: £10. Groups (max 50): £6.
No photography indoors. Pick-your-own, Jun–Aug.
By prior arrangement. Obligatory. Tel for details. €

## BARONS COURT

**Newtownstewart, Omagh, Co Tyrone  BT78 4EZ**
**Tel:** 028 8166 1683   **Fax:** 028 8166 2059   **E-mail:** info@barons-court.com
**www.barons-court.com**
**Contact:** The Agent
The home of the Duke and Duchess of Abercorn, Barons Court was built between 1779 and 1782, and subsequently extensively remodelled by John Soane (1791), William and Richard Morrison (1819–1841), Sir Albert Richardson (1947–49) and David Hicks (1975–76).
**Location:** MAP 18:M3, OS Ref. H236 382. 5km SW of Newtownstewart.
**Open:** By appointment only.
**Admission:** Adult £6. Groups max. 50.
Partial. WCs. By arrangement. €

## CASTLE COOLE

**Enniskillen, Co Fermanagh  BT74 6JY**
**Tel:** 028 6632 2690   **Fax:** 028 6632 5665   **E-mail:** castlecoole@nationaltrust.org.uk
**www.ntni.org.uk**
**Owner:** The National Trust     **Contact:** The Property Manager
Surrounded by its stunning landscape park on the edge of Enniskillen, this majestic 18th century home of the Earls of Belmore, designed by James Wyatt, was created to impress. The surrounding wooded landscape park sloping down to Lough Coole is ideal for long walks.
**Location:** MAP 18:L4, OS Ref. H245 436. On A4, 1.5m from Enniskillen on A4, Belfast–Enniskillen road.
**Open:** House: 17–19 Mar, 1–6pm. 1 Apr–28 May: Sats, Suns & BH/PHs 1–6pm, (6–15 Apr: daily). Jun: daily (except Thurs), 1–6pm. Jul & Aug: daily 12 noon–6pm. Sept: Sats & Suns, 1–6pm. Grounds: 1 Apr–30 Sept, daily, 10am–8pm, 1 Oct–31 Mar: daily, 10am–4pm.
***Admission:** House Tour & Grounds: Adult £5, Child £2.20, Family £12.20. Groups: £3.90 (outside normal hours £5). *includes a voluntary donation but visitors can choose to pay the standard prices displayed at the property and on the website.
Partial. WC. In grounds, on leads.

## CASTLE WARD & STRANGFORD LOUGH WILDLIFE CENTRE

**Strangford, Downpatrick, Co Down BT30 7LS**
**Tel:** 028 4488 1204  **Fax:** 028 4488 1729  **E-mail:** castleward@nationaltrust.org.uk
**www.ntni.org.uk**
**Owner:** The National Trust  **Contact:** The Property Manager
Situated in a stunning location within an 820 acre walled demesne overlooking Strangford Lough, the lawns rise up to the unique 18th century house and its Gothic façade. This fascinating house features both Gothic and Classical styles of architectural treatment, internally and externally.
**Location:** MAP 18:P4, OS Ref. J573 498. On A25, 7m from Downpatrick and 1½m from Strangford.
**Open:** House: 17–19 Mar, 1 Apr–30 Jun: Sats, Suns & BH/PHs (6–15 Apr: daily); Jul & Aug: daily, Sept: Sats & Suns, 1–6pm. Grounds: All year: daily, 10am–4pm (8pm Apr–Sept).
**\*Admission:** Grounds, Wildlife Centre & House Tour: Adult £6.50, Child £3, Family £16. Groups: £6.50. Grounds & Wildlife Centre: Adult £4.50, Child £2, Family £10.50, Groups £3.10. \*includes a voluntary donation but visitors can choose to pay the standard prices displayed at the property and on the website.
Ground floor & grounds. Obligatory. In grounds, on leads. Caravan park, holiday cottages, basecamp.

## CROM

**Newtownbutler, Co Fermanagh BT92 8AP**
**Tel/Fax:** 028 6773 8118 (Visitor Centre) 028 6773 8174 (Estate)
**E-mail:** crom@nationaltrust.org.uk  **www.ntni.org.uk**
**Owner:** The National Trust  **Contact:** The Visitor Facilities Manager
Crom is one of Ireland's most important nature conservation areas. It is set in 770 hectares of romantic and tranquil islands, woodland and ruins on the shores of Upper Lough Erne.
**Location:** MAP 18:M4, OS Ref. H359 246. 3m from A34, well signposted from Newtownbutler. Jetty at Visitor Centre.
**Open:** Grounds: 17 Mar–1 Jun & Sept: daily, 10am–6pm; 2 Jun–31 Aug: daily, 10am–7pm. Visitor Centre: 17 Mar–29 Apr: Sats, Suns & BH/PHs, 10am–6pm (6–15 Apr: daily); 1 May–9 Sept: daily, 10am–6pm. 15–30 Sept: Sats & Suns, 10am–6pm.
**\*Admission:** Demesne & Visitor Centre: Car/Boat £5.50. Minibus £15, Coach £19, Motorcycle £2.20. \*includes a voluntary donation but visitors can choose to pay the standard prices displayed at the property and on the website.
7 x 4-star holiday cottages & play-area.

## THE CROWN BAR

**46 Great Victoria Street, Belfast BT2 7BA**
**Tel:** 028 9027 9901
Belfast has many watering holes but none quite like The Crown! Rich in colour and design, it is famous for its special atmosphere, gas lamps, cosy snugs, fine ales and wines, and delicious lunch-time cuisine. The most famous pub in Belfast and one of the finest high-Victorian gin palaces in the UK, with an ornate interior of brightly-coloured tiles, carvings and glass. Wonderfully atmospheric setting in which to down a pint.
**Location:** MAP 18:O3, OS Ref. J336 736. Central Belfast.
**Open:** Mon–Sat: 11.30am–11pm, Sun: 12.30–10pm.
**Admission:** Free.

© NT Photographic Library / Chris Hill

Drawing Room, The Argory

## DERRYMORE

**Bessbrook, Newry, Co Armagh BT35 7EF**
**Tel:** 028 8778 4753  **Fax:** 028 8778 9598  **E-mail:** derrymore@nationaltrust.org.uk
**www.ntni.org.uk**
**Owner:** The National Trust
An elegant late 18th century thatched cottage, built by Isaac Corry, who represented Newry in the Irish House of Commons. Park laid out in the style of 'Capability' Brown.
**Location:** MAP 18:O5, OS Ref. J059 276. On A25, 2m from Newry on road to Camlough.
**Open:** Grounds: May–Sep: daily, 10am–7pm. Oct–Apr: daily, 10am–4pm.
**\*Admission:** Treaty Room Tour: Adult £3.50, Child £1.70, Family £8.50. \*includes a voluntary donation but visitors can choose to pay the standard prices displayed at the property and on the website.
On leads.

## DIVIS & THE BLACK MOUNTAIN

**12 Divis Road, Hannahstown, Belfast BT17 0NG**
**Tel:** 028 9082 5434  **Fax:** 028 9082 5065  **E-mail:** divis@nationaltrust.org.uk
With spectacular panoramic views over Belfast, Divis and the Black Mountain is a haven for those seeking the wild countryside experience. On a clear day there are views of Strangford Lough, the Mournes and the Sperrins, as well as Scotland and Donegal.
**Location:** MAP 18:O3, OS Ref. J265 740. Access from Divis Road, off Upper Springfield Road. Signed from M1 Kennedy Way roundabout.
**Open:** All year.
**Admission:** Free

## FLORENCE COURT

**Enniskillen, Co Fermanagh BT92 1DB**
**Tel:** 028 6634 8249  **Fax:** 028 6634 8873  **E-mail:** florencecourt@nationaltrust.org.uk
**www.ntni.org.uk**
**Owner:** The National Trust  **Contact:** The Property Manager
Florence Court is a fine mid-18th century house and estate set against the stunning backdrop of the Cuilcagh Mountains. House tour includes service quarters popular with all ages. Beautiful walled garden and lots of walks in grounds.
**Location:** MAP 18:L4, OS Ref. H178 347. 8m SW of Enniskillen via A4 and then A32 to Swanlinbar.
**Open:** House: 17–19 Mar: 1 Apr–28 May: Sats, Suns & BH/PHs (6–15 Apr: daily). Jun: daily except Tues, 1–6pm; Jul & Aug: daily, 12 noon–6pm. Sept: Sats & Suns, 1–6pm. Grounds: All year, daily, 10am–4pm (8pm Apr–Sept).
**\*Admission:** House tour: Adult £5, Child £2.20, Family £12.20. Groups: £3.90 (outside normal hours £5). Grounds only: Car £3.50, Minibus £16.50, Coach £22. \*includes a voluntary donation but visitors can choose to pay the standard prices displayed at the property and on the website.
Ground floor. WC. Obligatory. In grounds, on leads. Holiday cottage.

## GIANT'S CAUSEWAY

**North Coast Office, 60 Causeway Road, Bushmills BT57 8SU**
**Tel:** 028 2073 1582 / 2972  **Fax:** 028 2073 2963
**E-mail:** giantscauseway@nationaltrust.org.uk
The Giant's Causeway, renowned for its polygonal columns of layered basalt, is the only World Heritage Site in Northern Ireland. Resulting from a volcanic eruption 60 million years ago, this is the focal point of a designated Area of Outstanding Natural Beauty and has attracted visitors for centuries. It harbours a wealth of local and natural history. Geology, flora and fauna of international importance. Beautiful coastal path extends 11 miles to the Carrick-a-Rede rope bridge with wonderful views and coastal scenery.
**Location:** MAP 18:O1, OS Ref. C952 452. Off A2 Bushmills to Ballintoy road.
**Open:** Stones & North Antrim Coastal Path: all year. NT Shop & Tea Room: all year but closed 25 & 26 December. For opening times please contact property directly.
**Admission:** Specialist guided tours: Adult £3.50 Child £2.25. Outside of hours: £4.50. Car park charge (inc NT members). \*includes a voluntary donation but visitors can choose to pay the standard prices displayed at the property and on the website.
Suitable for picnics. For groups (15+), must be booked. Charge. On leads

## GRAY'S PRINTING PRESS

**49 Main Street, Strabane, Co Tyrone BT82 8AU**
**Tel:** 028 7188 0055  **E-mail:** grays@nationaltrust.org.uk  **www.ntni.org.uk**
**Owner:** The National Trust  **Contact:** The Administrator
An icon of Strabane's 18th century reputation as Ireland's capital of publishing, a local museum with a fine collection of print presses. Fascinating guided tours, demonstrations and audio-visual displays.
**Location:** MAP 18:M2, OS Ref. H345 976. in the centre of Strabane.
**Open:** 7 Apr–26 May & 1–29 Sept: Sats, 2–5pm; 2–30 Jun: Tue–Sat, 2–5pm; 3 Jul–31 Aug: Tue–Sat, 11am–5pm.
**Admission:** Press Tour: Adult £3, Child £2, Family £8. Group £2.30 (outside normal hours £4). \*includes a voluntary donation but visitors can choose to pay the standard prices displayed at the property and on the website.

## HEZLETT HOUSE ✤

**107 Sea Road, Castlerock, Coleraine, Co Londonderry  BT51 4TW**

**Tel/Fax:** 028 8778 4753   **E-mail:** downhillcastle@nationaltrust.org.uk
**www.ntni.org.uk**

**Owner:** The National Trust   **Contact:** The Custodian

Charming 17th century thatched house with 19th century furnishings. One of only a few pre-18th century Irish buildings still surviving.

**Location:** MAP 18:N1, OS Ref. C773 356. 5m W of Coleraine on Coleraine–Downhill coast road, A2.

**Open:** Contact the property for visiting times..

**\*Admission:** House Tour: Adult £3, Child £2, Family £8. Groups £2.30. (£4 outside normal hours.) \*includes a voluntary donation but visitors can choose to pay the standard prices displayed at the property and on the website.
⬚ Ground floor. ⬚ Obligatory. ⬚⬚ In grounds, on leads.

## KILLYLEAGH CASTLE

**Killyleagh, Downpatrick, Co Down  BT30 9QA**

**Tel/Fax:** 028 4482 8261   **E-mail:** gatehouses@killyleagh.plus.com
**www.killyleaghcastle.com**

**Owner/Contact:** Mrs G Rowan-Hamilton

Oldest occupied castle in Ireland. Self-catering towers available to sleep 4–15. Swimming pool and tennis court available by arrangement. Access to garden.

**Location:** MAP 18:P4, OS Ref. J523 529. At the end of the High Street.

**Open:** By arrangement. Groups (30–50): by appointment.

**Admission:** Adult £3.50, Child £2. Groups: Adult £2.50, Child £1.50.
⬚ No photography in house. ⬚ Wedding receptions. ⬚ Unsuitable. ⬚ Obligatory.
⬚ ⬚ ⬚ ⬚

## MOUNT STEWART ✤

**Newtonards, Co Down  BT22 2AD**

**Tel:** 028 4278 8387   **Fax:** 028 4278 8569   **E-mail:** mountstewart@nationaltrust.org.uk

**Owner:** The National Trust   **Contact:** The Property Manager

Home of the Londonderry family since the early 18th century, Mount Stewart was Lord Castlereagh's house and played host to many prominent political figures. The magnificent gardens planted in the 1920s have made Mount Stewart famous and earned it a World Heritage Site nomination.

**Location:** MAP 18:P3, OS Ref. J556 703. On A20, 5m from Newtownards on the Portaferry road.

**Open:** House: 10 Mar–29 Apr: Sats, Suns & BH/PHs (6–15 Apr: daily), 12 noon–6pm; 2 May–30 Jun: daily (except Tues in May), 1–6pm (12 noon–6pm Sats & Suns); 1 Jul–30 Sept: daily 12 noon–6pm (except Tues in Sept); 6–28 Oct: Sats & Suns, 12 noon–6pm. Lakeside Gardens: All year, daily, 10am–sunset. Formal Gardens: 10–31 Mar: Sats, Suns & BH/PHs, 10am–4pm; 1 Apr–31 Oct: daily, 10am–8pm (6pm in Apr & Oct). Temple of the Winds: 1 Apr–28 Oct: Suns & BH/PHs, 2–5pm.

**\*Admission:** House Tour, Gardens & Temple of Winds: Adult £6.50, Child £3, Family £16. Group: £5 (outside normal hours £6.50). Gardens only: Adult £5, Child £2.50, Family £12.50. Group: £4. \*includes a voluntary donation but visitors can choose to pay the standard prices displayed at the property and on the website.
⬚ ⬚ ⬚ ⬚ ⬚ ⬚ Obligatory. ⬚ ⬚ ⬚ In grounds, on leads. ⬚ ⬚ Lakeside area. ⬚ €

## MUSSENDEN TEMPLE & DOWNHILL DEMESNE ✤

**North Coast Office, 60 Causeway Road, Bushmills  BT57 8SU**

**Tel/Fax:** 028 2073 1582   **E-mail:** downhilldemesne@nationaltrust.org.uk
**www.ntni.org.uk**

**Owner:** The National Trust

Set on a stunning and wild headland with fabulous views over Ireland's north coast is the landscaped demesne of Downhill.

**Location:** MAP 18:N1, OS Ref. C757 357. 1m W of Castlerock.

**Open:** Grounds: Dawn to dusk all year.

**Admission:** Contact property for admission rates.
⬚ ⬚ On leads. ⬚

© NT Photographic Library / Chris Hill

Florence Court

## PATTERSON'S SPADE MILL ✤

**751 Antrim Road, Templepatrick  BT39 0AP**

**Tel:** 028 9443 3619   **Fax:** 028 9443 9713   **E-mail:** pattersons@nationaltrust.org.uk

**Owner:** The National Trust

Listen to the hammers, smell the grit, feel the heat and witness the thrill of the only surviving water-driven spade mill in Ireland. Visitors can watch as red-hot billets of steel are removed from the forge and fashioned into spades using the mill's massive trip hammer.

**Location:** MAP 18:O3, OS Ref. J263 852. 2m NE of Templepatrick on A6. M2/J4.

**Open:** 17–19 & 24/25 Mar: 2–6pm; 1 Apr–28 May: Sats, Suns & BH/PHs (6–15 Apr: daily); 1 Jun–31 Aug: daily (except Tues), 2–6pm; Sept & 6–14 Oct: Sats & Suns, 2–6pm. Last admission 1 hour prior to closing.

**\*Admission:** Adult £4.30, Child £2.50, Family £11.10, Group £3.30, Group outside normal hours £5. \*includes a voluntary donation but visitors can choose to pay the standard prices displayed at the property and on the website.
⬚ Suitable for picnics. ⬚ ⬚ ⬚ ⬚ In grounds, on leads. ⬚

## ROWALLANE GARDEN ✤

**Saintfield, Ballynahinch, Co Down  BT24 7LH**

**Tel:** 028 9751 0721   **Fax:** 028 9751 1242   **E-mail:** rowallane@nationaltrust.org.uk
**www.ntni.org.uk**

**Owner:** The National Trust   **Contact:** Head Gardener

Rowallane is an enchanting garden enclosed within a demesne landscape of some 21 hectares, planted with an outstanding collection of trees, shrubs and other plants from many parts of the world, creating a beautiful display of form and colour throughout the year.

**Location:** MAP 18:P4, OS Ref. J405 585. On A7, 1m from Saintfield on road to Downpatrick.

**Open:** 14 Apr–16 Sept: daily, 10am–8pm; 17 Sept–11 Apr (2008): daily, 10am–4pm. Closed 25/26 Dec & 1 Jan.

**\*Admission:** Adult £4.50, Child £2, Family £11, Group £3.50. Group outside normal hours £5. \*includes a voluntary donation but visitors can choose to pay the standard prices displayed at the property and on the website.
⬚ Grounds. WC. ⬚ Apr–Aug. ⬚ In grounds, on leads. ⬚

## SEAFORDE GARDENS ⬚

**Seaforde, Co Down  BT30 8PG**

**Tel:** 028 44811 225   **Fax:** 028 44811 370   **E-mail:** plants@seafordegardens.com
**www.seafordegardens.com**

**Owner/Contact:** Patrick Forde

18th century walled garden and adjoining pleasure grounds, containing many rare and beautiful trees and shrubs; many of them tender. There are huge rhododendrons and the National Collection of Eucryphias. The oldest maze in Ireland is in the centre of the walled garden, which can be viewed from the Mogul Tower. The tropical butterfly house contains hundreds of beautiful highly coloured butterflies; also a collection of parrots, insects and reptiles. The nursery garden contains many interesting plants for sale.

**Location:** MAP 18:P4, OS Ref. J401 433. 20m S of Belfast on the main road to Newcastle.

**Open:** Easter–end Sept: Mon–Sat, 10am–5pm; Suns, 1–6pm. Gardens only: Oct–Mar: Mon–Fri, 10am–5pm.

**Admission:** Butterfly House or Gardens: Adult £3, Child £2. Groups (10+): Adult £2.40, Child £1.50. Butterfly House & Gardens: Adult £5.50, Child £3. Groups: Adult £4.50, Child £2.70, Family (2+2) £15. RHS members Free access: Apr–Jun.
⬚ ⬚ ⬚ ⬚ ⬚ ⬚ By arrangement. ⬚ ⬚ ⬚ ⬚ €

## SPRINGHILL HOUSE & COSTUME COLLECTION ✤

**20 Springhill Road, Moneymore, Co Londonderry  BT45 7NQ**

**Tel/Fax:** 028 8674 8210   **E-mail:** springhill@nationaltrust.org.uk   **www.ntni.org.uk**

**Owner:** The National Trust   **Contact:** The Property Manager

Described as 'one of the prettiest houses in Ulster'. A charming plantation house with portraits, furniture and decorative arts that bring to life the many generations of Lenox-Conynghams who lived here from 1680. The old laundry houses one of Springhill's most popular attractions, the Costume Collection with some exceptionally fine 18th to 20th century pieces.

**Location:** MAP 18:N3, OS Ref. H845 819. 1m from Moneymore on B18 to Coagh, 5m from Cookstown.

**Open:** 17 Mar–30 Jun: Sats, Suns & BH/PHs (6–15 Apr, daily); 1 Jul–31 Aug: daily; Sept: Sats & Suns, 2–6pm.

**\*Admission:** House & Costume Collection Tour: Adult £4.80, Child £2.50, Family £12.10. Group £3.70 (outside normal hours £5.50). \*includes a voluntary donation but visitors can choose to pay the standard prices displayed at the property and on the website.
⬚ ⬚ ⬚ Partial. WC. ⬚ ⬚ ⬚ ⬚ In grounds, on leads. ⬚

## TEMPLETOWN MAUSOLEUM

**Templepatrick, Antrim  BT39**

**Tel:** 028 9082 5870

The mausoleum or monumental tomb was erected in 1789 by the Hon Sarah Upton to the Rt Hon Arthur Upton and displays some of Robert Adam's best classical work which is chaste, crisp and elegant. Given to the National Trust in 1965 by William Henderson Smith and Sir Robin Kinahan, it stands in the graveyard of Castle Upton. Castle Upton is privately owned and not open to the public.

**Location:** MAP 18:P4, OS Ref. J225 855. At Templepatrick on the Belfast-Antrim Road.

**Open:** All year.

**Admission:** Free access. Please contact Belfast Properties Office for further information.

See all the properties that are **open all year** in the index on page 580

## WELLBROOK BEETLING MILL

**20 Wellbrook Road, Corkhill, Co. Tyrone  BT80 9RY**

**Tel:** 028 8674 8210/8675 1735   **E-mail:** wellbrook@nationaltrust.org.uk

**www.ntni.org.uk**

**Owner:** The National Trust   **Contact:** The Custodian

If you come to the mill when there is a flax pulling you will find a hive of industry and when the beetling engines are running their thunder fills the valley. There are hands-on demonstrations of the linen process, led by costumed guides, original hammer machinery, used to beat a sheen into the cloth, lovely walks and picnic opportunities by the Ballinderry River. A truly unique experience.

**Location:** MAP 18:N3, OS Ref. H750 792. 4m from Cookstown, following signs from A505 Cookstown–Omagh road.

**Open:** 17 Mar–30 Jun: Sats, Suns & BH/PHs (6–15 Apr, daily); 1 Jul–31 Aug: daily; Sept: Sats & Suns; 2–6pm.

**\*Admission:** Mill Tour: Adult £3.50, Child £2, Family £9. Group: £2.70 (outside normal hours £4.10).\*includes a voluntary donation but visitors can choose to pay the standard prices displayed at the property and on the website.

Florence Court

# Opening Arrangements
at properties grant-aided by English Heritage

ENGLISH HERITAGE

I am very pleased to introduce this year's list of opening arrangements at properties grant-aided by English Heritage. The extent of public access varies from one property to another. The size of the building or garden, their nature and function are all taken into account. Some buildings, such as town halls, museums or railway stations, are of course open regularly. For other properties, especially those which are family homes or work places, access may need to be arranged in a way that also recognises the vulnerability of the building or the needs of those who live or work in it. Usually this will mean opening by appointment or on an agreed number of days each year. This is made clear by each entry.

Some properties are open by written appointment only. In most cases you should still be able to make initial contact by telephone, but you will be asked to confirm your visit in writing. This is to confirm the seriousness of your interest just as you would for example when making a hotel booking. It also provides a form of identification, enabling owners to feel more confident about inviting strangers into their house.

Over half the properties are open free, but we give details of admission charges where appropriate. There is also a brief description of each property, information on parking and access for people with disabilities.

It has always been a condition of grant-aid from English Heritage that the public should have a right to see the buildings to whose repair they have contributed. We therefore welcome feedback from visitors on the quality of their visit to grant-aided properties. In particular, please let us know if you are unable to gain access to any of the buildings on the list on the days or at the times specified, or if you have difficulty in making an appointment to visit and do not receive a satisfactory explanation from the owner. Please contact English Heritage Customer Services at PO Box 569, Swindon SN2 2YP (telephone: 0870 3331181; e-mail: customers@english-heritage.org.uk).

Information about public access is also included on our website (www.english-heritage.org.uk). The website is updated regularly to include new properties, any subsequent changes that have been notified to us or any corrections. We suggest that you consult our website for up-to-date information before visiting. If long journeys or special requirements are involved, we strongly recommend that you telephone the properties in advance, even if no appointment is required.

Finally, may I use this introduction to thank all those owners with whom we work. Their support for the access arrangements has been hugely encouraging. That the public can enjoy a visit to a grant-aided property is not only good in itself, it demonstrates that the historic environment is in a very real sense a common wealth, part of the richness and diversity that makes the English landscape – both urban and rural – so special. It also illustrates how crucially important the private owner is in maintaining that quality and distinctiveness.

I very much hope you enjoy the sites and properties you find in this list – from the famous to the many lesser-known treasures. They are all worth a visit – I hope we have helped you to find, and enjoy, them.

*Neil Cossons.*

Sir Neil Cossons
Chairman

## BEDFORDSHIRE

### OLD WARDEN PARK

**Old Warden nr. Biggleswade, Bedfordshire SG18 9EA**

Built in 1872 by Joseph Shuttleworth in a Jacobean design by Henry Clutton. Still housing original Gillows furniture, oak panelling and carvings, and a collection of 18th century paintings. The park was laid out by landscape architect Edward Milner.

www.shuttleworth.org
**Grant Recipient:** The Shuttleworth Trust
**Access contact:** Ms Amanda McBrayne
**T:** 01767 627972   **F:** 01767 627976
**Open:** To the exterior of the building daily between May and September 9–5pm. Access to the interior by arrangement. Occasionally the site will be closed for private events, please call in advance: 01767 627972.
**Heritage Open Days:** No.
**P** Spaces: 15
**&** Partial. Ramps available. WC for the disabled. Guide Dogs allowed.
**£** Free, except on event days.

## BERKSHIRE

### BASILDON PARK

**Lower Basildon, Reading, Berkshire RG8 9NR**

Designed in the 18th century by Carr of York and set in parkland in the Thames Valley. Rich interiors with fine plasterwork. Small flower garden, pleasure ground and woodland walks.

www.nationaltrust.org.uk
**Grant Recipient:** The National Trust
**Access contact:** Property Manager
**T:** 01189 843040   **F:** 01189 767370
**E-mail:** basildonpark@nationaltrust.org.uk
**Open:** House: 21 March to 28 October: daily except Mondays and Tuesdays (but open pm Bank Holiday Mondays and Good Friday), 12–5pm. Park, garden and woodland walks: as house, 11–5pm. Property closes at 5pm on 17/18 & 19 August for concerts. 5–9 December: Wednesday, Thursday, Saturday and Sunday 12–4pm, Friday, 12–7pm.
**Heritage Open Days:** No.
**P** Car park 400 metres from property.
**&** Partial. Wheelchair access to ground floor and garden, ramp available. Stairs with handrail to other floors. WC for the disabled. Guide Dogs allowed.
**£** **Adult:** £6.00 (house), £3.00 (park & garden only). **Child:** £3.00 (house), £1.50 (park & garden only). **Other:** Family: £15.00 (house), £8 (park & garden only). Free to National Trust members.

### WELFORD PARK

**Welford, Newbury, Berkshire RG20 8HU**

Red brick country house c1652 and remodelled in 1702, when a third storey was added and the front façade was decorated with Ionic columns. Other alterations were made in the Victorian period.

www.welfordpark.co.uk
**Grant Recipient:** Mr J H L Puxley
**Access contact:** Mr J H L Puxley
**T:** 01488 608691   **F:** 01488 608853
**E-mail:** pamela@welfordpark.co.uk
**Open:** 4 June–6 July (except 16 June and Sundays): to the exterior only, 11am–5pm. Interior of house (4 principal rooms) by prior arrangement only.
**Heritage Open Days:** No.
**P** Spaces: 40. 80 more spaces within ½ mile walk.
**&** Full. No WC for the disabled. Guide Dogs allowed.
**£** **Adult:** £5.00 (for interior of house). Free entry to garden and grounds, except on occasional charity days.
**Child:** Free entry except on occasional charity days. **Other:** £5.00 (for interior of house). Free entry to garden and grounds, except on occasional charity days.

## BRISTOL

### 29 QUEEN SQUARE RAILINGS

**Bristol  BS1 4ND**

Fronted by repaired, grant-aided railings, 29 Queen Square is an early Georgian town house, 1709-11, listed Grade II*. One of the few surviving original houses in Queen Square which was laid out in 1699 and has claim to be the largest square in England.

**Grant Recipient:** The Queen Square Partnership
**Access contact:** Ms Kara Fitzhugh
**T:** 0117 975 0700
**E-mail:** southwest@english-heritage.org.uk
**Open:** Access to the exterior at all reasonable times to view the railings from the pavement.
**Heritage Open Days:** No.
**P** Paid parking in Queen Square and car park in The Grove (behind 29 Queen Square).
**&** Full. No WC for the disabled. Guide Dogs allowed.
**£** No.

### ARNOS VALE CEMETERY

**Bath Road, Bristol BS4 3EW**

Forty five acre burial grounds together with exterior of three Grade II* listed building and other listed structures. West Lodge also Grade II*, now fully restored.

www.arnosvale.org.uk
**Grant Recipient:** Arnos Vale Cemetery Trust & Bristol City Council
**Access contact:** Mr Richard Smith
**T:** 0117 971 9117   **F:** 0117 971 5505
**E-mail:** richard@arnosvale.org.uk
**Open:** Cemetery: March–September: Monday–Saturday, 9am–5pm, Sunday and Public Holidays, 10am–5pm; October to February: Monday–Saturday, 9am–4.30pm, Sunday and Public Holidays, 10am–4.30pm, or dusk whichever is earlier. West Lodge Visitor Centre: Monday–Friday (except Bank Holidays) same as Cemetery opening times; Saturday, 10am–1.00pm. Sundays and Bank Holidays: closed.
**Heritage Open Days:** Yes
**P** Spaces: 50. There may be reduced parking during 2007/8 due to major restoration works.
**&** Partial. Lower level Arcadian Garden area accessed from Bath Road. No WC for the disabled. Guide Dogs allowed.
**£** No.

### BRITISH EMPIRE AND COMMONWEALTH MUSEUM

**Clock Tower Yard, Temple Meads, Bristol BS1 6QH**

Museum housed in world's earliest surviving railway terminus, which was completed in 1840 and was originally part of the Great Western Railway designed by I.K. Brunel. Over 220ft long with timber and iron roof spans of 72ft, this Grade I listed building has been nominated as a World Heritage Site. Contains the Passenger shed and the adjoining former Engine and Carriage shed.

www.empiremuseum.co.uk
**Grant Recipient:** Empire Museum Ltd
**Access contact:** Mrs Anne Lineen
**T:** 0117 925 4980   **F:** 0117 925 4983
**E-mail:** anne.lineen@empiremuseum.co.uk
**Open:** Daily, 10am–5pm, except 25 and 26 December. Access to exterior is unrestricted.
**Heritage Open Days:** No.
**P** Spaces: 15. Additional parking in Station car park.
**&** Full. WC for the disabled. Guide Dogs allowed.
**£** **Adult:** £6.95 (subject to change). **Child:** £3.95 (subject to change). **Other:** £5.95 (subject to change). Free annual pass available on payment of admission.

### LORD MAYOR'S CHAPEL

**College Green, Bristol BS1 5TB**

13th century church with 16th century floor of Spanish tiles in the Poyntz Chapel and a collection of stained glass. The only church in England that is owned, maintained and run by a City Council.

**Grant Recipient:** Bristol City Council
**Access contact:** Mr Alan F Canterbury
**T:** 0117 922 2000/0117 929 4350   **F:** 0117 929 4350
**Open:** Wednesday–Saturday, 10am–12pm and 1–4pm. Sunday service 11am.
**Heritage Open Days:** Yes
**P** On-street parking and multi-storey car park behind Council House and Trenchard Street.
**&** No wheelchair access. No WC for the disabled. Guide Dogs allowed.
**£** No.

### ROYAL WEST OF ENGLAND ACADEMY

**Queen's Road, Clifton, Bristol BS8 1PX**

Bristol's first Art Gallery, founded in 1844, Grade II* listed and a registered museum. A fine interior housing five naturally lit art galleries, a new commercial gallery and a permanent fine art collection.

www.rwa.org.uk
**Grant Recipient:** Royal West of England Academy
**Access contact:** Mrs Dee Smart
**T:** 0117 9735129   **F:** 0117 9237874
**E-mail:** info@rwa.org.uk
**Open:** Monday–Saturday, 10am–5.30pm, Sunday, 2–5pm. Bank Holidays, 11am–4pm. Closed 25 December–3 January and Easter Day.
**Heritage Open Days:** Yes
**P** Parking for Disabled Badge Holders only (5 spaces).
**&** Partial. Wheelchair access to New Gallery on ground floor and Main Galleries accessible by lift. Fedden Gallery not accessible. WCs fitted with handrails. No WC for the disabled. Guide Dogs allowed.
**£** **Adult:** £3.00. **Child:** Free (under 16s). **Other:** £2.00 (students/senior citizens).

## BUCKINGHAMSHIRE

### CLIVEDEN MANSION & CLOCK TOWER

**Cliveden, Taplow, Maidenhead, Buckinghamshire SL6 0JA**

Built by Charles Barry in 1851, once lived in by Lady Astor now let as an hotel. Series of gardens, each with its own character, featuring roses, topiary, water gardens, a formal parterre, informal vistas, woodland and riverside walks.

www.nationaltrust.org.uk
**Grant Recipient:** The National Trust
**Access contact:** Property Manager
**T:** 01628 605069   **F:** 01628 669461
**E-mail:** cliveden@nationaltrust.org.uk
**Open:** House (main ground floor rooms) and Octagon Temple: 1 April–28 October, Thursday and Sunday, 3–5.30pm. Estate and garden: 14 March–23 December, daily, 11am–6pm (closes at 4pm from 29 October). Entire estate closed 16 June 2007.
**Heritage Open Days:** No.
**P** Spaces: 300. Woodlands car park: open all year, daily 11am–5.30pm (closes at 4pm November–March). Overflow car park with 1000 spaces available.
**&** Full. WC for the disabled. Guide Dogs allowed.
**£** **Adult:** £1.00 extra (house), £7.50 (grounds), £3.00 (woodlands). **Child:** 50p extra (house), £3.70 (grounds), £1.50 (woodlands). **Other:** £18.70 (family: grounds), £7.50 (family: woodlands). Free to NT members.

### HALL BARN GOTHIC TEMPLE

**Beaconsfield, Buckinghamshire HP9 2SG**

Garden building in existence by 1740 but possibly c1725 and by Colen Campbell. Gothic Revival style hexagonal-shaped garden building. Situated in landscaped garden, laid out in 1680s.

**Grant Recipient:** 5th Baron Burnham's Will Trust
**Access contact:** J A C Read
**T:** 01494 673 020
**Open:** By written application to Mrs Farncombe, Hall Barn, Windsor End, Beaconsfield, Buckinghamshire HP9 2SG.
**Heritage Open Days:** No.
**P** Spaces: 10
**&** Full. No WC for the disabled. Guide Dogs allowed.
**£** No.

### STOWE HOUSE

**Buckingham, Buckinghamshire MK18 5EH**

Mansion built in 1680 and greatly altered and enlarged in the 18th century, surrounded by important 18th century gardens which are owned by the National Trust (see entry for Stowe Landscape Gardens). House and gardens variously worked on by Vanbrugh, Gibbs, Kent and Leoni and is one of the most complete neo-classical houses in Europe. The House is now occupied by the Preservation Trust's tenant, Stowe School.

www.shpt.org
**Grant Recipient:** The Stowe House Preservation Trust
**Access contact:** Ms Anna McEvoy
**T:** 01280 818229 (Mon–Fri)   **F:** 01280 818186
**E-mail:** amcevoy@stowe.co.uk
**Open:** 12–18 February: 2pm tours only. 4–9, 11 -13, 15, 18–22 April, 28 May–1 June, 4 July–19 August: Wednesday–Sunday (closed Saturdays) and 22–24, 26 & 27 August, 24–28 October: 12 noon–5pm (last admission 4pm), tours at 2pm. Group visits for 2pm tours by arrangement throughout the year. Dates are subject to change. Please check opening arrangements before visiting (tel: 01280 818229 or 01280 818166 for 24 hour info line).
**Heritage Open Days:** No.

Spaces: 520. Free parking. 20 spaces adjacent to site, 500 spaces 500 yards away.
Full. WC for the disabled. Guide Dogs allowed.
**Adult:** £4.00. **Child:** £2.50.

## STOWE LANDSCAPE GARDENS

### Buckingham, Buckinghamshire MK18 5EH

Extensive and complex pleasure grounds and park around a country mansion. Begun late 17th century but substantially developed in the 18th and 19th centuries by, among others, Charles Bridgeman, Sir John Vanbrugh, James Gibbs, William Kent and Lancelot 'Capability' Brown (Brown was originally head gardener here before leaving to set up his landscape practice). The park and gardens contain over 30 buildings, many of great architectural importance. Stowe was supremely influential on the English landscape garden during the 18th century.
**www.nationaltrust.org.uk**
**Grant Recipient:** The National Trust
**Access contact:** Property Manager
**T:** 01280 822850   **F:** 01280 822437
**E-mail:** stowegarden@nationaltrust.org.uk
**Open:** 1 January–25 February and 10 November–31 December: Saturday and Sunday, 10.30am–4pm (last admission 3pm). 1 March–4 November: daily, except Monday and Tuesday, 10.30am–5.30pm ( last admission 4pm). Open Bank Holiday Mondays and closed 26 May. Contact property for Christmas opening arrangements.
**Heritage Open Days:** No.
Spaces: 100
Partial. Self-drive battery cars available. Uneven surfaces, map of accessible areas available. WC for the disabled. Guide Dogs allowed.
**Adult:** £6.50. **Child:** £3.30 **Other:** £16.30 (family). Free for National Trust members.

## WIDMERE FARM CHAPEL

### Widmere, nr. Marlow, Buckinghamshire SL7 3DF

Chapel attached to farmhouse, early 13th century with traces of 14th century windows and later alterations, listed Grade II*. 11th or 12th century crypt and medieval roof.
**Grant Recipient:** Mr G J White
**Access contact:** Mr G J White
**T:** 01628 484204
**Open:** Access by prior arrangement.
**Heritage Open Days:** No.
Spaces: 6
No wheelchair access. No WC for the disabled. No Guide Dogs allowed.
No.

# CAMBRIDGESHIRE

## BUCKDEN TOWERS

### High Street, Buckden, Cambridgeshire PE19 5TA

Former ecclesiastical palace set in 15 acres of gardens and parkland. Buildings include the Great Tower and the Inner Gatehouse (both constructed in the late 15th century) and the Victorian mansion. The grounds include an Elizabethan knot garden. Famous occupants include St Hugh of Lincoln (12th century) and Katherine of Aragon (1533-4).
**Grant Recipient:** The Claretian Missionaries
**Access contact:** Mr Michael Allwright
**T:** 01480 810344   **F:** 01480 811284
**E-mail:** buckden@claret.org.uk
**Open:** January–5 June: Guided tours by prior arrangement. Grounds open throughout the year.
**Heritage Open Days:** Yes
Spaces: 50
Full. WC for the disabled. Guide Dogs allowed.
No.

## ELTON HALL

### Elton, nr. Peterborough, Cambridgeshire PE8 6SH

Grade I historic building and country house. Late 15th century gatehouse and chapel built by Sapcote family. Main entrance façade built by Sir Thomas Proby in the 17th century and remodelled by Henry Ashton for 3rd Earl of Carysfort in the 19th century. South Garden façade built between 1789 and 1812 in Gothic style.
**www.eltonhall.com**
**Grant Recipient:** Sir William Proby Bt
**Access contact:** Sir William Proby Bt
**T:** 01832 280468   **F:** 01832 280584
**E-mail:** whp@eltonhall.com
**Open:** 28 May;  June: Wednesdays; July and August:

Wednesdays, Thursdays and Sundays plus August Bank Holiday Monday, 2–5pm. Private groups by arrangement April–October.
**Heritage Open Days:** No.
Spaces: 500. Parking 300 metres from the Hall.
Partial. Full wheelchair access to garden. Access to house is difficult. Please telephone 01832 280468. WC for the disabled. Guide Dogs allowed.
**Adult:** £7.50 (house), £5.00 (garden). **Child:** Free if accompanied by an adult. **Other:** Concessions £6.50 (house), £4.50 (garden).

## MADINGLEY POST MILL

### Mill Farm, Madingley Road, Coton, Cambridgeshire CB3 7PH

Historic post mill with machinery intact.
**Grant Recipient:** Mr Matthew Mortlock
**Access contact:** Mr Matthew Mortlock
**T:** 01954 211047   **F:** 01954 210752
**E-mail:** mattcb37ph@aol.com
**Open:** January–19 March: weekdays and Saturdays, 11am–4pm by prior telephone arrangement.
**Heritage Open Days:** No.
Spaces: 5. Parking available in car park of American Cemetery (next door).
Partial. Wheelchair access around base of Windmill only. No WC for the disabled. Guide Dogs allowed.
No.

## MINSTER PRECINCTS

### Peterborough Cathedral, Peterborough, Cambridgeshire PE1 1XS

The Minster Precincts incorporate many remains from the medieval monastery of which the Cathedral church was a part. These include the richly decorated 13th century arcades of the former infirmary, the originally 13th century Little Prior's Gate and the 15th century Table Hall.
**www.peterborough-cathedral.org.uk**
**Grant Recipient:** The Dean & Chapter of Peterborough Cathedral
**Access contact:** The Chapter of Peterborough Cathedral
**T:** 01733 355300   **F:** 01733 355316
**E-mail:** a.watson@peterborough-cathedral.org.uk
**Open:** All year, exterior only.
**Heritage Open Days:** Yes
Spaces: 2. Disabled parking only. City centre car parks (nearest 5 minute walk).
Full. WC for the disabled in Cathedral restaurant, Tourist Information Centre and Cathedral Education Centre. Guide Dogs allowed.
**Adult:** £3.50 (guided tour). **Other:** £2.50 (concession guided tour), £1.50 (school visit guided tour). Otherwise, donations welcome from Cathedral visitors.

## PRIOR CRAUDEN'S CHAPEL

### The College, Ely, Cambridgeshire CB7 4DL

Private chapel built by Prior Crauden in 1524-5 of Barnack stone ashlar with clunch carved interior, over a 13th century vaulted undercroft. Has windows in the "Decorated" style, octagonal entrance and tower with spiral staircase, richly carved interior and a 14th century mosaic tile floor.
**www.cathedral.ely.anglican.org**
**Grant Recipient:** The Dean & Chapter of Ely Cathedral
**Access contact:** Mrs Constance Heald
**T:** 01353 667735   **F:** 01353 665658
**E-mail:** chapter.clerk@cathedral.ely.anglican.org
**Open:** By prior written arrangement with The Chapter House, The College, Ely, Cambs CB7 4DL.
**Heritage Open Days:** No.
Parking in town centre car parks. Parking for the disabled in Cathedral car park by prior arrangement.
Partial. Wheelchair access to the undercroft only. WC for the disabled in Cathedral. Guide Dogs allowed.
No.

## QUEEN'S HALL

### The Gallery, Ely, Cambridgeshire CB7 4DL

Built by Prior Crauden c1330 of Carr stone rubble with Barnack, or similar, stone dressings and much brick patching. Has original undercroft with ribbed vaulting, 14th century pointed arched windows with curvilinear tracery and corbels carved in the shape of crouching figures. Reputedly constructed for entertaining Queen Philippa, wife of Edward III.
**Grant Recipient:** The Dean & Chapter of Ely Cathedral
**Access contact:** The Assistant Bursar

**T:** 01353 660700   **F:** 01353 662187
**E-mail:** NigelC@kings-ely.cambs.sch.uk
**Open:** By prior written arrangement with the Assistant Bursar, the King's School, Ely, Cambs CB7 4DN.
**Heritage Open Days:** No.
Spaces: 5. Parking in town centre car parks. Parking for the disabled in Cathedral car park by prior arrangement.
Partial. Wheelchair access to ground floor only. WC for the disabled in Cathedral. Guide Dogs allowed.
No.

## SIR JOHN JACOB'S ALMSHOUSE CHAPEL

### Church Street, Gamlingay, Cambridgeshire SG19 3JH

Built 1745 of Flemish bond red brick with plain tiled roof, in keeping with adjoining terrace of ten almshouses constructed 80 years before. Now used as parish council offices.
**Grant Recipient:** The Trustees of Sir John Jacob's Almshouses
**Access contact:** Mrs K Rayner and  Mrs L Bacon
**T:** 01767 650310   **F:** 01767 650310
**E-mail:** gamlingaypc@lineone.net
**Open:** January–10 July: The office is generally open on Monday, Wednesday and Friday between 9.15am and 3.00pm.
**Heritage Open Days:** Yes
On-street parking.
Full. WC for the disabled. Guide Dogs allowed.
No.

## SULEHAY HOUSE

### 32 Old Market, Wisbech, Cambridgeshire PE13 1NF

Grade II* town house, built 1723, with fine original staircase.
**Grant Recipient:** Cambridgeshire Historic Buildings Preservation Trust
**Access contact:** Richard Miers
**T:** 01945 461 873
**Open:** By prior arrangement.
**Heritage Open Days:** Yes
No.
No wheelchair access. No WC for the disabled. Guide Dogs allowed.
No.

## THE BLACK HOSTELRY

### The College, Ely, Cambridgeshire CB7 4DL

Built c1291-2 of Carr stone rubble with Barnack, or similar, stone dressings, upper storey is timber-framed and plastered on the south and east sides with stone on the west side. Has early 13th century undercroft with ribbed vaults, 13-14th century King Post roof, and 15th century red brick chimney and doorway. Constructed to accommodate visiting monks from other Benedictine monasteries.
**www.cathedral.ely.anglican.org**
**Grant Recipient:** The Dean & Chapter of Ely Cathedral
**Access contact:** Canon P M Sills
**T:** 01353 667735   **F:** 01353 665658
**Open:** By prior written arrangement with The Chapter House, The College, Ely, Cambs CB7 4DL.
**Heritage Open Days:** No.
Parking in town centre car parks. Parking for the disabled in Cathedral car park by prior arrangement.
Partial. Wheelchair access to rear entrance hall only. WC for the disabled in Cathedral. Guide Dogs allowed.
No.

## THE CHAPTER HOUSE

### The College, Ely, Cambridgeshire CB7 4DL

Originally part of the chapel of the Infirmary, now the remains of this house the Deanery and the Chapter Office. Contains part of the arch, ribbed vaulting and arcade of the 12th century chancel.
**www.cathedral.ely.anglican.org**
**Grant Recipient:** The Dean & Chapter of Ely Cathedral
**Access contact:** Mrs Constance Heald
**T:** 01353 667735   **F:** 01353 665658
**E-mail:** chapter.clerk@cathedral.ely.anglican.org
**Open:** By prior written arrangement with The Chapter House, The College, Ely, Cambs CB7 4DL.
**Heritage Open Days:** No.
Parking in town centre car parks. Parking for the disabled in Cathedral car park by prior arrangement.
Partial. Wheelchair access to ground floor only. WC for the disabled in Cathedral. Guide Dogs allowed.
No.

## THE MANOR

**Hemingford Grey, Huntingdon, Cambridgeshire PE28 9BN**

Built c1130 and one of the oldest continuously inhabited houses in Britain. Made famous as Green Knowe by the author Lucy Boston. Her patchwork collection is also shown. Four acre garden, laid out by Lucy Boston and surrounded by moat, with topiary, irises, old roses and herbaceous borders.
www.greenknowe.co.uk
**Grant Recipient:** Mrs Diana Boston
**Access contact:** Mrs Diana Boston
**T:** 01480 463134   **F:** 01480 465026
**E-mail:** diana_boston@hotmail.com
**Open:** House: all year (except May) to individuals or groups by prior arrangement. May: guided tours daily at 2pm (booking advisable). Garden: all year, daily, 11am–5pm (4pm in winter).
**Heritage Open Days:** No.
**P** Spaces: 2. Parking for the disabled only adjacent to property.
**&** Partial. Wheelchair access to garden and dining room only. WC for the disabled. Guide Dogs allowed.
**£** **Adult:** £5.00, £2.00 (garden only). **Child:** £1.50, free (garden only). **Other:** £4.00, £2.00 (garden only).

## THE OLD PALACE

**Sue Ryder Care, Palace Green, Ely, Cambridgeshire CB7 4EW**

Grade I listed building formerly a bishops palace opposite cathedral, with an Elizabethan promenading gallery, bishops chapel and monks' room. Two acre garden contains the oldest plane tree in Europe. Used as a neurological centre for the physically disabled.
www.suerydercare.org/theoldpalace
**Grant Recipient:** The Sue Ryder Care
**Access contact:** Mr Martin Russell
**T:** 01353 667686   **F:** 01353 669425
**E-mail:** martin.russell@suerydercareely.org.uk
**Open:** By prior arrangement for access to the Long Gallery and Chapel. Gardens: open during the Open Gardens Scheme May–June. Other events held throughout the year, contact Mr Russell for details.
**Heritage Open Days:** No.
**P** Nearest car park: St Mary's Street and Barton Road.
**&** Partial. Wheelchair access to garden and Long Gallery. WC for the disabled. Guide Dogs allowed.
**£** No. **Other:** Charge made on garden open days: adult £3.00, child 50p.

## THORPE HALL HOSPICE

**Sue Ryder Care, Longthorpe, Peterborough, Cambridgeshire PE3 6LW**

Built in the 1650s by Peter Mills for Oliver St John, Oliver Cromwell's Lord Chief Justice. Ground floor retains many original features.
**Grant Recipient:** Sue Ryder Care
**Access contact:** Hospice Manager
**T:** 01733 330060   **F:** 01733 269078
**E-mail:** thorpe.fundraising@suerydercare.org
**Open:** Access to the Hall by prior arrangement. Gardens: open all year.
**Heritage Open Days:** Yes
**P** Spaces: 150
**&** Full. WC for the disabled. Guide Dogs allowed.
**£** Donations welcome.

## CHESHIRE

### ADLINGTON HALL

**Mill Lane, Adlington, Macclesfield, Cheshire SK10 4LF**

Tudor/Elizabethan/Georgian manor house built around a Medieval hunting lodge. The Great Hall houses a 17th century organ, the most important of its type in the country, once played by Handel.
www.adlingtonhall.com
**Grant Recipient:** Mrs C J C Legh
**Access contact:** Mrs Camilla J C Legh
**T:** 01625 829 206   **F:** 01625 828 756
**E-mail:** camilla@adlingtonhall.com

**Open:** August: Sunday–Wednesday, 2–5pm (except 19 August). Open to groups on weekdays throughout the year by prior arrangement.
**Heritage Open Days:** No.
**P** Spaces: 100. Ample areas for parking at North front and East front.
**&** Partial. Wheelchair access to ground floor and some areas of gardens. WC for the disabled. Guide Dogs allowed.
**£** **Adult:** £6.00 (house & gardens), £2.00 (gardens only). **Child:** £3.00 (house & gardens), £1.00 (gardens only). **Other:** £5.50 (groups).

## BACHE HOUSE FARM

**Chester Road, Hurleston, Nantwich, Cheshire CW5 6BO**

A timber-framed house with slate roof dating from 17th century with an 18th century extension. The house is a four square house with two gables at the rear. The interior shows timbers in the house walls and an oak staircase.
**Grant Recipient:** Mr P R Posnett
**Access contact:** Mr P R Posnett
**T:** 01829 260251
**Open:** By prior arrangement at all reasonable times.
**Heritage Open Days:** No.
**P** Spaces: 10
**&** No wheelchair access. No WC for the disabled. No Guide Dogs allowed.
**£** No.

## BELMONT HALL

**Great Budworth, Northwich, Cheshire CW9 6HN**

Country house, built 1755, initial design by James Gibbs, with fine plasterwork interiors. Set in parkland. Now a private day school with family apartments in the East Wing. Also accessible is surrounding farmland, woods and medieval moat.
**Grant Recipient:** The Trustees of Belmont Hall
**Access contact:** Mr R C Leigh
**T:** 01606 891235   **F:** 01606 892349
**E-mail:** asmleigh@hotmail.com
**Open:** Guided tours during the school holidays and on weekends by prior arrangement with the Estate Manager, Belmont Hall, Great Budworth, Northwich, Cheshire CW9 6HN (tel: 01606 891235). Please note: the property and adjacent area are also open by way of a Countryside Stewardship Educational Access Agreement for schools as well as adult parties.
**Heritage Open Days:** No.
**P** Spaces: 100. Unlimited free parking on site.
**&** No wheelchair access. No WC for the disabled. Guide Dogs allowed.
**£** **Adult:** £5.00.

## BRAMALL HALL

**Bramall Park, Stockport, Cheshire SK7 3NX**

Black and white timber-framed manor house dating back to the 14th century, with several subsequent renovations (many during the Victorian period). Contains 14th century wall paintings, an Elizabethan plaster ceiling and Victorian kitchen and servants quarters.
www.bramallhall.org.uk
**Grant Recipient:** Stockport Metropolitan Borough Council
**Access contact:** Ms Caroline Egan
**T:** 0845 833 0974   **F:** 0161 486 6959
**E-mail:** bramall.hall@stockport.gov.uk
**Open:** 1 April–30 September: Sunday–Thursday 1–5pm, Friday–Saturday 1–4pm. Bank Holidays 11am–5pm. 1 October–1 January: Tuesday–Sunday 1–4pm. Last entry 1 hour before closing.
**Heritage Open Days:** No.
**P** Spaces: 60. Pay parking.
**&** Partial. Wheelchair access to ground floor only. WC for the disabled. Guide Dogs allowed.
**£** **Adult:** £3.95. **Child:** £3.00. **Other:** £3.00 (concessions).

## CAPESTHORNE HALL

**Macclesfield, Cheshire SK11 9JY**

Jacobean style hall with a collection of fine art, sculpture, furniture, tapestry and antiques from Europe, America and the Far East. The Hall dates from 1719 when it was originally designed by the Smith's of Warwick. Altered in 1837 by Blore and rebuilt by Salvin in 1861 following a disastrous fire.
www.capesthorne.com
**Grant Recipient:** Mr William Arthur Bromley-Davenport

**Access contact:** Mrs Gwyneth Jones
**T:** 01625 861221   **F:** 01625 861619
**E-mail:** info@capesthorne.com
**Open:** April–October: Sunday, Monday and Bank Holidays. Gardens and Chapel, 12 noon–5.00pm, Hall from 1.30–4pm (last admission 3.30pm). Parties on other days by arrangement.
**Heritage Open Days:** No.
**P** Spaces: 2000. 80 parking spaces in the car park and remainder in park.
**&** Partial. Wheelchair access to ground floor and butler's pantry. WC for the disabled. Guide Dogs allowed.
**£** **Adult:** £6.50 (Sundays & Bank Holidays), £4.00 (garden & chapel only). **Child:** £3.00 (5-18 yrs), £2.00 (garden & chapel only). **Other:** £5.50 (senior citizen), £3.00 (senior citizen: garden & chapel), £15 (family). Mon only: £10 (car: 4 people) £25 (minibus) £50 (coach).

## HIGHFIELDS

**Audlem, nr. Crewe, Cheshire CW3 0DT**

Small half-timbered manor house dating back to c1600.
**Grant Recipient:** Mr J B Baker
**Access contact:** Mrs Susan Baker
**T:** 01630 655479
**Open:** Guided tour of hall, drawing room, dining room, parlour, bedrooms and gardens by prior written arrangement.
**Heritage Open Days:** No.
**P** Spaces: 20
**&** Partial. Wheelchair access to ground floor only. WC for the disabled with assistance (down 2 steps). Guide Dogs allowed.
**£** **Adult:** £5.00. **Child:** £2.50. **Other:** £5.00.

## RODE HALL

**Church Lane, Scholar Green, Cheshire ST7 3QP**

Country house built early–mid 18th century, with later alterations. Set in a parkland designed by Repton. Home to the Wilbraham family since 1669.
www.rodehall.co.uk
**Grant Recipient:** Sir Richard Baker Wilbraham Bt
**Access contact:** Sir Richard Baker Wilbraham Bt
**T:** 01270 873237   **F:** 01270 882962
**E-mail:** richard.wilson@btconnect.com
**Open:** Hall and Gardens: 1 April–30 September, Wednesdays and Bank Holidays (closed Good Friday), 2–5pm. Gardens only: Tuesdays and Thursdays, 2–5pm. Snowdrop Walks: February, daily except Mondays, 12–4pm.
**Heritage Open Days:** No.
**P** Spaces: 200. Parking for the disabled available adjacent to entrance by arrangement.
**&** Partial. Wheelchair access with assistance to ground floor. WC for the disabled. Guide Dogs allowed.
**£** **Adult:** £5.00 (house & garden), £3.00 (garden only). **Child:** £4.00 over 12s (house & garden), £2.50 (garden only). **Other:** £4.00 (house & garden, senior citizens), £2.50 (garden only).

## ST CHAD'S CHURCH TOWER

**Wybunbury, Nantwich, Cheshire CW5 7NA**

Grade II* listed 15th or 16th century church tower, rest of Church demolished in 1977. 96ft high and containing six restored bells, spiral staircase, charity boards, monuments and affords panoramic views over the South Cheshire plain. Bells are rung every Thursday evening.
www.wybunburytower.org.uk
**Grant Recipient:** Wybunbury Tower Preservation Trust
**Access contact:** Mrs D Lockhart
**T:** 01270 841481
**Open:** Saturday 9 June 'Fig Pie Wakes' (local race and festival), 1–5pm. Heritage Open Days, 11am–4pm. At other times by prior arrangement with Mrs D Lockhart (tel: 01270 841481) or Mr John Colbert (tel: 01270 841158).
**Heritage Open Days:** Yes
**P** Spaces: 20
**&** Partial. Wheelchair access to ground floor only. No WC for the disabled. Guide Dogs allowed.
**£** **Adult:** £2.00. **Child:** £1.00.

## THE CAGE

**Lyme Park, Disley, Stockport, Cheshire SK12 2NX**

Early 18th century hunting tower within the 1400 acre medieval deer park of Lyme Park.
www.nationaltrust.org.uk
**Grant Recipient:** The National Trust
**Access contact:** Mr Philip Burt

T: 01663 762023   F: 01663 765035
**E-mail:** lymepark@nationaltrust.org.uk
**Open:** The Cage: April–October, second and fourth Saturday and Sunday of each month, 1–4pm. Hall: 23 March–30 October, daily except Wednesday and Thursday, 1–5pm. Garden: 23 March–30 October, daily, 11am–5pm. 1 November–17 December: weekends, 12–3pm. Park: 1 April– 14 October, daily, 8am–8.30pm. 15 October–31 March: daily, 8am–6pm.
**Heritage Open Days:** No.
**P** Spaces: 1000. Park entry £4.60 per car.
**&** Partial. Wheelchair access to garden, first floor of house, parts of park, shop and restaurant. WC for the disabled. Guide Dogs allowed.
**£** **Adult:** £1.00 (The Cage only), £7.50 (house & garden). **Child:** 50p (The Cage only), £3.75 (house & garden). **Other:** National Trust members free.

## CORNWALL

### CAERHAYS CASTLE & GARDENS

**Gorran, St Austell, Cornwall PL26 6LY**
Built by John Nash in 1808. Set in 60 acres of informal woodland gardens created by J C Williams, who sponsored plant hunting expeditions to China at the turn of the 19th century.
www.caerhays.co.uk
**Grant Recipient:** The Trustees of Charles Williams (Caerhays Estate)
**Access contact:** Mrs Cheryl Kufel
T: 01872 501144/501310   F: 01872 501870
**E-mail:** estateoffice@caerhays.co.uk
**Open:** House: 12 March–3 June (including Bank Holidays), Monday–Friday, 12–4pm. Conducted tours every 45 minutes. Gardens: 12 February–3 June, daily, 10am to 5pm (last entry 4pm).
**Heritage Open Days:** No.
**P** Spaces: 500
**&** Partial. Limited wheelchair access to gardens (area around castle). Access to ground floor of castle with assistance, please telephone 01872 501144 or 01872 501310 in advance to check. WC for the disabled. Guide Dogs allowed.
**£** **Adult:** £9.50 (garden & house), £5.50 (house tour only), £5.50 (gardens). **Child:** £3.50 (garden & house), £2.50 (house tour only), £2.50 (gardens). Under 5s free. **Other:** £5.00 (groups 15+, house tour), £6.50 (groups, garden tour), £4.00 (groups, garden without tour).

### COTEHELE

**St Dominick, Saltash, Cornwall PL12 6TA**
Cotehele, situated on the west bank of the River Tamar, was built mainly between 1485-1627. Home of the Edgcumbe family for centuries. Its granite and slatestone walls contain intimate chambers adorned with tapestries, original furniture and armour.
www.nationaltrust.org.uk
**Grant Recipient:** The National Trust
**Access contact:** Mr Toby Fox
T: 01579 351346   F: 01579 351222
**E-mail:** cotehele@nationaltrust.org.uk
**Open:** House and restaurant: 17 March–30 September daily except Friday (but open Good Friday), 11am–4pm. Mill: 17 March–30 June daily except Friday (but open Good Friday), 1–5.30pm. 1 July–31 August open daily. 1 September–30 September daily except Friday, 1–5.30pm. 1–31 October daily except Friday, 1–4.30pm. Garden: daily all year, 10.30am–dusk.
**Heritage Open Days:** No.
**P** Spaces: 100. Parking space available for pre-booked coaches.
**&** Partial. Wheelchair access to house (hall, kitchen and Edgcumbe Room only), garden, area around house, restaurant and shop. Ramps available. Woodland walks: some paths accessible. WC for the disabled. Guide Dogs allowed.
**£** **Adult:** £8.40 (house, garden & mill). £5.00 (garden & mill). **Child:** £4.20 (house, garden & mill), £2.50 (garden & mill). **Other:** Family: house, garden & mill: 1 adult £12.60, 2 adults £21.00. Family: garden & mill: 1 adult £7.40, 2 adults £12.50. £7.40 (pre-booked groups).

### CULLACOTT FARMHOUSE

**Werrington, Launceston, Cornwall PL15 8NH**
Grade I listed medieval hall house, built in the 1480s as a long house, and extended 1579. Contains wall paintings of fictive tapestry, Tudor arms, St James of Compostella and remains of representation of St George and the Dragon. Extensively restored 1995-7 but still retains many original features. Now used as holiday accommodation.
www.cullacottholidays.co.uk
**Grant Recipient:** Mr & Mrs J Cole
**Access contact:** J Cole
T: 01566 772631
**E-mail:** marycole@cullacottholidays.co.uk
**Open:** By prior arrangement.
**Heritage Open Days:** No.
**P** Spaces: 20
**&** Partial. Wheelchair access to Great Hall, through passage. WC for the disabled. Guide Dogs allowed.
**£** **Adult:** £2.50. **Child:** Free.

### GODOLPHIN HOUSE

**Godolphin Cross, Helston, Cornwall TR13 9RE**
Tudor-Stuart mansion of granite round a courtyard. For many generations seat of the Godolphin family who were courtiers from the 16th to the 18th century, the 1st Earl (who was born here) rose to be Queen Anne's Lord Treasurer. Has late Elizabethan stables with wagon collection and large medieval and other gardens.
www.godolphinhouse.com
**Grant Recipient:** Mrs L M P Schofield
**Access contact:** Mrs Joanne Schofield
T: 01736 763194   F: 01736 763194
**E-mail:** godo@euphony.net
**Open:** 9 April–8 July: Monday, Wednesday and Sunday, 11am–4pm. 9 July–31 October: Monday–Friday and Sundays, 11am–4pm. Open Bank Holidays. Groups all year by prior arrangement.
**Heritage Open Days:** No.
**P** Spaces: 100. Parking for 3 coaches.
**&** Partial. Wheelchair access to all of the house except one room, but no access to the stables and gardens may be difficult. WC for the disabled. Guide Dogs allowed.
**£** **Adult:** £6.00 (house and gardens). **Child:** £1.50 (5-15 years). **Other:** £3.00 (gardens only), £5.00 (senior citizens).

### PENCARROW

**Washaway Bodmin, North Cornwall, Cornwall PL30 3AG**
A Georgian house, completed in c1771, set in 50 acres of formal woodland gardens. Owned and lived in by the Molesworth-St Aubyn Family. Gardens include a sunken Italian Garden, Ice House, lake and many specimen trees.
www.pencarrow.co.uk
**Grant Recipient:** Trustees of Pencarrow House
**Access contact:** Mr James Reynolds
T: 01208 841 369   F: 01208 841 722
**E-mail:** pencarrow@aol.com
**Open:** Gardens: 1 March–31 October. House: 1 April–25 October.
**Heritage Open Days:** Yes
**P** Spaces: 120. Main car park is 50 yards from house, also overflow car park with 220 spaces.
**&** Partial. Wheelchair access to ground floor only. If visitor cannot walk upstairs, admission is free. Video recording of the upstairs tour is provided. WC for the disabled. Guide Dogs allowed.
**£** **Adult:** £8.00 (house & garden) £4.00 (garden only). **Child:** £4.00 (house & garden) £1.00 (garden only).

### PORTH-EN-ALLS LODGE

**Prussia Cove, St Hilary, Cornwall TR20 9BA**
Originally a chauffeur's lodge, built c1910-1914 and designed by Philip Tilden. It is built into the cliff and sits in close proximity to the main house. The Chauffeur's lodge is one of a number of historic houses on the Porth-en-Alls Estate.
www.prussiacove.com
**Grant Recipient:** Trustees of Porth-en-Alls Estate
**Access contact:** Mr P Tunstall-Behrens
T: 01736 762 014   F: 01736 762 014
**E-mail:** penapc@dial.pipex.com
**Open:** Available as self-catering holiday lets throughout the year. Members of the public may view the property by arrangement, but only if it is unoccupied at the time.
**Heritage Open Days:** No.
**P** Spaces: 50. Public car park approximately ½ mile from the Lodge, off the A394 (near Rosudgeon village).

**&** No wheelchair access. Wheelchair access to the lodge is very difficult. No WC for the disabled. Guide Dogs allowed.
**£** **Other:** Charges apply.

### TREGREHAN

**Par, Cornwall PL24 2SLJ**
Mid 19th century gardens and pleasure grounds designed by W A Nesfield together with significant 19th and 20th century plant collections. Concentrating on genera from warm temperate regions. An important green gene bank of known source plants. 1846 glasshouse range in walled garden. Set in 18th and 19th century parkland.
www.tregrehan.org
**Grant Recipient:** Mr T C Hudson
**Access contact:** Mr T C Hudson
T: 01726 814 389   F: 01726 814389
**E-mail:** greengene@tregrehan.org
**Open:** Mid March–end of May: Wednesday–Sunday and Bank Holidays, 10.30am–5pm. June–end August: Wednesdays only, 2–5pm.
**Heritage Open Days:** No.
**P** Spaces: 50
**&** Partial. Wheelchair access to 10 acres of garden. WC for the disabled. Guide Dogs allowed.
**£** **Adult:** £4.50. **Child:** Free.

### TRESCO ABBEY GARDENS

**Tresco Estate, Isles of Scilly, Cornwall TR24 0QQ**
25 acre garden with plants mainly from the Mediterranean region. Plant groups include protea, aloe from South Africa, succulents from Canary Isles and palms from Mexico. All grown outside all year round. Unique, frost-free climate.
www.tresco.co.uk
**Grant Recipient:** Tresco Estate
**Access contact:** Mr Michael Nelhams
T: 01720 424105
**E-mail:** mikenelhams@tresco.co.uk
**Open:** Daily, 10am–4pm.
**Heritage Open Days:** No.
**P** No.
**&** Partial. Wheelchair access to all garden areas but some gravel slopes which may be difficult. WC for the disabled. Guide Dogs allowed.
**£** **Adult:** £9.00. **Child:** £3.00. **Other:** £20.00 (family).

### TREVELVER FARMHOUSE

**St Minver, Wadebridge, Cornwall PL27 6RJ**
Remains of manor house now farmhouse. Dining room with 17th century painted panelling, a painted frieze and an over-mantle painted picture.
**Grant Recipient:** Mr Wills
**Access contact:** Miss Melanie Wills
T: 01208 816 982
**E-mail:** melanie@pawtondairy.com
**Open:** January–30 April: by prior arrangement with Melanie Wills at any reasonable time.
**Heritage Open Days:** No.
**P** Spaces: 4
**&** No wheelchair access. No WC for the disabled. No Guide Dogs allowed.
**£** No.

## CUMBRIA

### CROWN & NISI PRIUS COURT

**The Courts, English Street, Carlisle, Cumbria CA3 8NA**
Former Crown Court in Carlisle situated at southern entrance to the city. One of a pair of sandstone towers built in the early 19th century as replicas of the medieval bastion. The towers were built to house the civil and criminal courts, used until the 1980s.
**Grant Recipient:** Cumbria Crown Court
**Access contact:** Mr Mike Telfer
T: 01228 606116
**Open:** Guided Tours July and August Monday–Friday, 1.30pm and 3pm (excluding August Bank Holiday Monday).
**Heritage Open Days:** Yes
**P** Town centre car parks.
**&** Partial. Wheelchair access to Grand Jury Room, Court No.2 and Public Area Crown Court Room. WC for the disabled. Guide Dogs allowed.
**£** **Adult:** £3.00. **Child:** £2.00 (age 5-15). **Other:** £2.50.

## DIXON'S CHIMNEY

**Shaddongate, Carlisle, Cumbria CA2 5TZ**

270ft chimney, formerly part of Shaddongate Mill. Built in 1836 by Peter Dixon. At its original height of 306ft the chimney was the tallest cotton mill chimney to have been constructed. Structural problems meant that the decorative stone capping had to be removed in the 1950s.

**Grant Recipient:** Carlisle City Council
**Access contact:** Mr Peter Messenger
**T:** 01228 871195   **F:** 01228 817199
**E-mail:** PeterMe@carlisle-city.gov.uk
**Open:** Chimney can be viewed from Shaddongate and Junction Street.
**Heritage Open Days:** Yes
**P** No.
🔲 No wheelchair access. No WC for the disabled. No Guide Dogs allowed.
**£** No.

## DRAWDYKES CASTLE

**Brampton Old Road, Carlisle, Cumbria CA6 4QE**

Pele tower, probably 14th century, converted to house 1676 by William Thackery and John Aglionby. Original tower with Classical Revival facade. Grade II* listed.

**Grant Recipient:** Mr J M Milbourn
**Access contact:** Mr J M Milbourn
**T:** 01228 525 804
**Open:** By prior arrangement.
**Heritage Open Days:** No.
**P** No.
🔲 No wheelchair access. No WC for the disabled. No Guide Dogs allowed.
**£** No.

## KIRKBY HALL WALLPAINTINGS

**Kirkby-in-Furness, Cumbria LA17 7UX**

Chapel in west wing, accessible only from trap door in dairy passage. Wallpaintings in red ochre and black consisting of panels with stylised trees, animals and birds with texts above of the Lord's Prayer, Creed, Ten Commandments and Galations 5, 16-21 from the Great Bible of 1541.

**Grant Recipient:** Holker Estates Company Ltd
**Access contact:** Mr D P R Knight
**T:** 015395 58313   **F:** 015395 58966
**E-mail:** estateoffice@holker.co.uk
**Open:** By prior written arrangement with the Holker Estate Office, Cark-in-Cartmel, Grange-over-Sands, Cumbria LA11 7PH.
**Heritage Open Days:** No.
**P** Spaces: 3
🔲 No wheelchair access. No WC for the disabled. No Guide Dogs allowed.
**£** No.

## LEVENS HALL

**Kendal, Cumbria LA8 0PD**

Elizabethan house built around a 13th century pele tower, containing fine furniture, panelling, plasterwork and an art collection. The gardens, which include much topiary, were laid out in the late 17th century by Monsieur Beaumont for Colonel James Grahme and are of national importance.

**www.levenshall.co.uk**
**Grant Recipient:** Mr C H Bagot
**Access contact:** Mr PE Milner
**T:** 01539 560321   **F:** 01539 560669
**E-mail:** houseopening@levenshall.co.uk
**Open:** House: 1 April–11 October, Sunday–Thursday, 12 noon–5pm (last admission 4pm). Garden: as house, 10am–5pm. Admission prices are under review at time of publication, please check with Mr Milner at the Estate Office for current information.
**Heritage Open Days:** No.
**P** Spaces: 80
🔲 Partial. House unsuitable for wheelchair users due to stairs and narrow doorways but all other facilities (topiary garden, plant centre, gift shop, and tea room) are accessible. A DVD tour of the House is available in the Buttery during opening hours. A mobility buggy is available for hire. WC for the disabled. Guide Dogs allowed.
**£** **Adult:** £9.00 (house & garden) £6.00 (garden only). **Child:** £4.00 (house & garden) £3.00 (garden only).

## MUNCASTER CASTLE

**Ravenglass, Cumbria CA18 1RQ**

Large house incorporating medieval fortified tower, remodelled by Anthony Salvin for the 4th Lord Muncaster in 1862-66. Ancestral home of the Pennington family for 800 years containing a panelled Hall and octagonal library. Headquarters of the World Owl Trust. Woodland garden, Lakeland setting. World-famous rhododendrons, camelias and magnolias with a terrace walk along the edge of the Esk valley.

**www.muncaster.co.uk**
**Grant Recipient:** Mrs P R Gordon-Duff-Pennington
**Access contact:** Mrs Iona Frost-Pennington
**T:** 01229 717614   **F:** 01229 717010
**E-mail:** info@muncaster.co.uk
**Open:** Castle: 11 February–4 November, daily (except closed Saturday) ,12 noon–5pm (or dusk if earlier). Gardens, Owl Centre and Maze open throughout the year (closed January), 10.30am–6.30pm (or dusk if earlier). Refreshments available.
**Heritage Open Days:** No.
**P** Spaces: 150
🔲 Partial. Wheelchair access to ground floor of Castle only but other attractions and facilities accessible. The hilly nature of the site can create access difficulties so please ask for further information on arrival. WC for the disabled. Guide Dogs allowed.
**£** **Adult:** £9.50 (Castle, gardens, owls & maze), £6.00 (gardens, owls & maze). **Child:** £6.50 (Castle, gardens, owls & maze), £4.50 (gardens, owls & maze). Under 5s free. **Other:** £27.00 (family: Castle, gardens, owls & maze), £20.00 (family: gardens, owls & maze).

## ORTHWAITE HALL BARN

**Uldale, Wigton, Cumbria CA7 1HL**

Grade II* listed agricultural barn. Former house adjoining later Hall, probably late 16th or early 17th century, now used for storage and housing animals.

**Grant Recipient:** Mrs S Hope
**Access contact:** Mr Jonathan Hope
**T:** 016973 71344
**Open:** By prior telephone arrangement.
**Heritage Open Days:** No.
**P** Spaces: 3
🔲 No wheelchair access. No WC for the disabled. Guide Dogs allowed.
**£** No.

## PERCY HOUSE

**38-42 Market Place, Cockermouth, Cumbria CA13 9NG**

Built in 1598 by Henry Pery the 9th Earl of Northumberland. Many of the original features of the building still remain, including carved plaster ceiling, Percy coat of arms, Tudor fireplace, oak plank and muslin screen and flag stone and oak floors.

**www.percyhouse.co.uk**
**Grant Recipient:** Mr R E Banks
**Access contact:** Mr R E Banks
**T:** 01900 85643/ 07710 800973   **F:** 01900 85543
**E-mail:** banksrothersyke@aol.com
**Open:** Monday–Saturday, 10am–5pm.
**Heritage Open Days:** Yes
**P** Spaces: 150. On street parking in Market Place and public car park off Market Place.
🔲 Partial. Wheelchair access to ground floor only. WC for the disabled available in public toilets in nearby car park. Guide Dogs allowed.
**£** No.

## PRIOR SLEE GATEHOUSE

**Carlisle Cathedral, Carlisle, Cumbria CA3 8TZ**

Dated 1528, the Gatehouse would have replaced an earlier one. It has a large chamber over the gate, with two Tudor fireplaces. Graffiti carved in the stonework is believed to include merchants' marks. One of two integral lodges survives on the north-east side of the building. Now used as residential accommodation.

**Grant Recipient:** The Chapter of Carlisle Cathedral
**Access contact:** Mr T I S Burns
**T:** 01228 548151   **F:** 01228 547049
**E-mail:** office@carlislecathedral.org.uk
**Open:** January–2 October: By prior arrangement with Mr T I S Burns, The Chapter of Carlisle Cathedral, 7 The Abbey, Carlisle, Cumbria CA3 8TZ
**Heritage Open Days:** No.
**P** Parking in nearby City centre car parks. 2 parking

spaces for the disabled in Cathedral grounds.
🔲 No wheelchair access. WC for the disabled is nearby (approx. 200 yards). Guide Dogs allowed.
**£** No.

## PRIOR'S TOWER

**The Abbey, Carlisle, Cumbria CA3 8TZ**

This Grade I listed three storey pele tower type building was constructed c1500. It formed part of the Prior's Lodgings and until relatively recently was part of the Deanery. Of special interest is the magnificent ceiling of 45 hand-painted panels dating from c1510 and associated with Prior Senhouse.

**Grant Recipient:** The Chapter of Carlisle Cathedral
**Access contact:** Mr T I S Burns
**T:** 01228 548151   **F:** 01228 547049
**E-mail:** office@carlislecathedral.org.uk
**Open:** By prior arrangement with Mr T I S Burns, The Chapter of Carlisle Cathedral, 7 The Abbey, Carlisle, Cumbria CA3 8TZ.
**Heritage Open Days:** Yes
**P** Parking in nearby City centre car parks. 2 parking spaces for the disabled in Cathedral grounds.
🔲 No wheelchair access. WC for the disabled is nearby (approx. 100 yards). Guide Dogs allowed.
**£** No.

## SCALEBY CASTLE

**Scaleby, Carlisle, Cumbria CA6 4LN**

Medieval ruins of Scaleby Castle which is a Scheduled Ancient Monument.

**Grant Recipient:** Lord Henley
**Access contact:** Smiths Gore
**T:** 01228 527586   **F:** 01228 520802
**E-mail:** charles.baker@smithsgore.co.uk
**Open:** By prior written arrangement with the owner's agents Smiths Gore, 64 Warwick Road, Carlisle CA1 1DR
**Heritage Open Days:** No.
**P** Spaces: 10
🔲 Partial. All areas viewable but no wheelchair access to internal parts of the monument. No WC for the disabled. Guide Dogs allowed.
**£** No.

## SIZERGH CASTLE

**nr. Kendal, Cumbria LA8 8AE**

Sizergh Castle has been the home of the Strickland family for over 760 years. Its core is the 14th century tower, later extended and containing some fine Elizabethan carved wooden chimney-pieces and inlaid chamber. The Castle is surrounded by gardens, including a rock garden.

**www.nationaltrust.org.uk**
**Grant Recipient:** The National Trust
**Access contact:** Ms Fiona Clark, Property Manager
**T:** 01539 560 951
**E-mail:** sizergh@nationaltrust.org.uk
**Open:** Castle: 1 April–28 October, daily except Friday and Saturday, 1–5pm. Garden: 1 April–28 October, daily except Friday and Saturday, 11–5pm. Closed Good Friday. Great Barn: 1 April–28 October, daily except Friday and Saturday, 11am–5pm.
**Heritage Open Days:** No.
**P** Spaces: 130
🔲 Partial. Wheelchair access to Castle Lower Hall and garden gravel paths only. WC for the disabled. Guide Dogs allowed.
**£** **Adult:** £6.50, £4.30 (garden only). **Child:** £3.20, £2.10 (garden only). **Other:** £16.20 (family), £5.50 per person (pre-booked parties, minimum 15 persons, not Bank Holidays).

## SMARDALE GILL VIADUCT

**Kirkby Stephen, Cumbria**

Rail overbridge, built 1860-1 by Sir Thomas Bouch for the South Lancashire and Durham Union Railway. 550ft long with 14 arches spanning Scandal Beck at Smardale Gill, a National Nature Reserve. A well-preserved example of a large road bridge on this line.

**Grant Recipient:** The Trustees of the Northern Viaduct Trust
**Access contact:** Mr G J Biddle
**T:** 01539 560993
**Open:** All year, access by footpaths only from Newbiggin-on-Lune or Smardale. Path along former railway.
**Heritage Open Days:** No.
**P** Spaces: 8. Parking at Smardale.

Partial. Wheelchair access from Smardale only. No WC for the disabled. Guide Dogs allowed.
£ No.

## ST ANNE'S HOSPITAL

### Boroughgate, Appleby, Cumbria
17th century almshouses. There are 13 dwellings and a chapel set round a cobbled courtyard. Founded by Lady Anne Clifford in 1653.
**Grant Recipient:** The Trustees of St Anne's Hospital
**Access contact:** Lord Hothfield
**T:** 017683 51487    **F:** 017683 53259
**E-mail:** lulieant@aol.com
**Open:** All year: daily, 9am–5pm.
**Heritage Open Days:** No.
P Spaces: 50. On-street parking.
No wheelchair access. No WC for the disabled. Guide Dogs allowed.
£ No.

## WRAY CASTLE

### Low Wray, Ambleside, Cumbria
A large Gothic mock castle and arboretum. Built in the 1840s over looking the western shore of Lake Windermere.
www.nationaltrust.org.uk
**Grant Recipient:** The National Trust
**Access contact:** Property Manager
**T:** 015394 36269    **F:** 015394 36811
**E-mail:** hilltop@nationaltrust.org.uk
**Open:** Grounds: all year. Castle: (entrance hall, music room, drawing room and fern house) July and August: daily except Thursday and Friday, 2- 4pm. Dates of special open days to be confirmed. Building works may be taking place in 2007 which will affect access to the Castle. Please contact the Property Manager before visiting (tel: 015394 36269).
**Heritage Open Days:** Yes
P Spaces: 30
No wheelchair access. No WC for the disabled. Guide Dogs allowed.
£ Adult: £2.75. Child: £1.00. Other: National Trust members free.

# DERBYSHIRE

## ASSEMBLY ROOMS

### The Crescent, Buxton, Derbyshire SK17 6BH
The Crescent was designed by John Carr of York and built by the Fifth Duke of Devonshire between 1780-89. It provided hotels, lodgings and a suite of elaborately decorated Assembly Rooms. The front elevation of three storeys is dominated by Doric pilasters over a continuous rusticated ground floor arcade.
**Grant Recipient:** Derbyshire County Council
**Access contact:** Mr Allan Morrison
**T:** 01629 580 000 X3351    **F:** 01629 585 507
**E-mail:** allan.morrison@derbyshire.gov.uk
**Open:** Exterior accessible from public highway. No interior access until refurbishment works completed, other than special agreement. Renovation works are likely to be in progress during 2007.
**Heritage Open Days:** No.
P Spaces: 20. On-street pay and display parking available.
No wheelchair access. No WC for the disabled. No Guide Dogs allowed.
£ No.

## BARLBOROUGH HALL

### Barlborough, Chesterfield, Derbyshire S43 4TL
Built by Sir Francis Rhodes in the 1580s, the Hall is square in plan and stands on a high basement with a small internal courtyard to provide light. Contains Great Chamber, now a chapel, bearing a date of 1584 on the overmantel whilst the porch is dated 1583. Now a private school.
**Grant Recipient:** The Governors of Barlborough Hall School
**Access contact:** Mr C F A Bogie
**T:** 01246 435138    **F:** 01246 435090
**Open:** By prior arrangement only 29 March–11 April, 31 May–5 June, 4 July–3 September and most weekends throughout the year. External visits (without guide) any evening after 6pm or weekend.
**Heritage Open Days:** No.
P Spaces: 50

No wheelchair access. No WC for the disabled. Guide Dogs allowed.
£ No.

## BENNERLEY VIADUCT

### Erewash Valley, Ilkeston, Derbyshire
Disused railway viaduct over the Erewash valley, c1878-9, and approximately 500 yards long with 15 piers. It is one of two remaining wrought iron lattice-girder bridges in the British Isles.
**Grant Recipient:** Railway Paths Ltd
**Access contact:** Mr Simon Ballantine
**T:** 01548 550 331    **F:** 01548 550 331
**E-mail:** simonb@sustrans.org.uk
**Open:** There is access to the viaduct by a public footpath running underneath it, but the deck itself is inaccessible.
**Heritage Open Days:** No.
P No.
No wheelchair access. No WC for the disabled. No Guide Dogs allowed.
£ No.

## CALKE ABBEY

### Ticknall, Derbyshire DE73 1LE
Baroque mansion, built 1701-3 for Sir John Harpur and set in a landscaped park. Little restored, Calke is preserved by a programme of conservation as a graphic illustration of the English house in decline. It contains the natural history collection of the Harpur Crewe family, an 18th century state bed and interiors that are essentially unchanged since the 1880s.
www.nationaltrust.org.uk
**Grant Recipient:** The National Trust
**Access contact:** Property Manager
**T:** 01332 863822    **F:** 01332 865272
**E-mail:** calkeabbey@nationaltrust.org.uk
**Open:** House: 17 March–28 October: daily except Thursday and Friday, 12.30–5pm (ticket office opens at 11am). Garden and Church: 17 March–28 October: daily except Thursday and Friday, 11am–5pm; 5 July–7 September: daily, 11am–5pm. Park: most days until 8pm or dusk if earlier. Timed ticket system is in operation. All visitors (including NT members) require a ticket from the ticket office.
**Heritage Open Days:** No.
P Spaces: 75
Partial. Wheelchair access to ground floor of house, stables, shop and restaurant. Garden and park partly accessible. WC for the disabled. Guide Dogs allowed.
£ Adult: £8.00, £5.00 (garden only). Child: £4.00, £2.50 (garden only). Other: £20.00 (family) £12.50 (family: garden only). Admission price includes voluntary gift aid donation.

## CASTERNE HALL

### Ilam, Ashbourne, Derbyshire DE6 2BA
Casterne Hall is a Grade II* manor house. The house was rebuilt in 1730, with a classic Georgian front and incorporating a 17th century and medieval back. Home of the Hurt family since the 16th century.
www.casterne.co.uk
**Grant Recipient:** Mr Charles Hurt
**Access contact:** Mr Charles Hunt
**T:** 01335 310 489
**E-mail:** mail@casterne.co.uk
**Open:** 1 May–11 June: weekday afternoons. Tours at 2pm, 3pm and 4pm. Closed on 7 and 28 May.
**Heritage Open Days:** No.
P Spaces: 20
Partial. Wheelchair access to ground floor only. No WC for the disabled. Guide Dogs allowed.
£ Adult: £5.00.

## CATTON HALL

### Catton, Walton-on-Trent, Derbyshire DE12 8LN
Country house built c1741 by Smith of Warwick for Christopher Horton. Property owned by the same family since 1405. Contains an interesting collection of 17th and 18th century pictures, including Royal and Family portraits; also Byron and Napoleon memorabilia. Gardens, which run down to the River Trent, include a family chapel.
www.catton-hall.com
**Grant Recipient:** Mr R Neilson
**Access contact:** Mrs C Neilson
**T:** 01283 716311    **F:** 01283 712876
**E-mail:** kneilson@catton-hall.com
**Open:** 2 April–8 October: including tour of the house,

chapel and gardens every Monday at 2pm. Group tours (15 or more) at any time of year by prior arrangement.
**Heritage Open Days:** Yes
P Spaces: 200. Unlimited parking available.
Partial. Wheelchair access by separate entrance to all ground floor rooms. No WC for the disabled. Guide Dogs allowed.
£ Adult: £4.00. Other: £3.00 (concessions).

## CROMFORD MILL

### Mill Lane, Cromford, nr. Matlock, Derbyshire DE4 3RQ
Grade I listed mill complex established by Sir Richard Arkwright in 1771. The world's first successful water powered cotton spinning mill situated in the Derwent Valley Mills World Heritage Site. Currently being conserved by the Arkwright Society, an educational charity. The Mill is permanently home to five shops and a restaurant.
www.arkwrightsociety.org.uk
**Grant Recipient:** The Arkwright Society
**Access contact:** Mrs Sarah McLeod
**T:** 01629 823256    **F:** 01629 824297
**E-mail:** smcleod@arkwrightsociety.org.uk
**Open:** Daily 9am–5pm, closed on Christmas Day. Free entry to main site, charges for guided tours.
**Heritage Open Days:** No.
P Spaces: 100
Partial. Wheelchair access to shops, lavatories and restaurant. WC for the disabled. Guide Dogs allowed.
£ Adult: £2.00 (guided tour). Child: £1.50 (guided tour). Other: £1.50 (guided tour).

## DEVONSHIRE ROYAL HOSPITAL

### 1 Devonshire Road, Buxton, Derbyshire SK17 6LX
Originally built as stables to service the adjacent Crescent, converted to a hospital in 1859. Central feature is a large circular colonnade capped with a spectacular dome added, along with the clock tower, in 1880. Listed Grade II*. Converted to and opened as the University of Derby Buxton campus in 2006.
www.derby.ac.uk/buxton
**Grant Recipient:** University of Derby
**Access contact:** Professor David Davies, Dean
**T:** 01298 71100
**Open:** University working site open throughout the year during normal working hours.
**Heritage Open Days:** No.
P Spaces: 30. Access needs to be pre-arranged.
Full. WC for the disabled. Guide Dogs allowed.
£ No.

## HARDWICK HALL

### Doe Lea, Chesterfield, Derbyshire S44 5QJ
A late 16th century 'prodigy house' designed by Robert Smythson for Bess of Hardwick. Contains an outstanding collection of 16th century furniture, tapestries and needlework. Walled courtyards enclosed gardens, orchards and herb garden.
www.nationaltrust.org.uk
**Grant Recipient:** The National Trust
**Access contact:** Property Manager
**T:** 01246 850430    **F:** 01246 858424
**E-mail:** hardwickhall@nationaltrust.org.uk
**Open:** 17 March–28 October: daily except Monday, Tuesday and Friday (but open Bank Holiday Mondays and Good Friday),12 noon–4.30pm. Garden: Wednesday–Sunday, 11am–5.30pm. Parkland: daily 8am–6pm (closes at dusk in winter).
**Heritage Open Days:** No.
P Spaces: 200
Partial. WC for the disabled. Guide Dogs allowed.
£ Adult: £9.00, £4.50 (garden only). Child: £4.50, £2.25 (garden only). Other: £22.50 (family), £11.25 (garden only) Admission price includes voluntary gift aid donation.

## KEDLESTON HALL

### Derby, Derbyshire DE22 5JH
A classical Palladian mansion built 1759-65 for the Curzon family and little altered since. Robert Adam interior with state rooms retaining their collection of paintings and original furniture. The Eastern museum houses a range of objects collected by Lord Curzon when Viceroy of India (1899-1905). Set in 800 acres of parkland and 18th century pleasure ground, garden and woodland walks.
www.nationaltrust.org.uk
**Grant Recipient:** The National Trust
**Access contact:** Property Manager

T: 01332 842191    F: 01332 844059
E-mail: kedlestonhall@nationaltrust.org.uk
**Open:** House: 10 March–31 October: daily except Thursday and Friday, 12 noon–4.30pm. Garden: 10 March–31 October: daily, 10am–6pm. Park: all year (occasional day restrictions may apply in December and January 2008); 10 March–31 October, 10am–6pm;  1 November–7 March 2008, 10am–4pm.
**Heritage Open Days:** No.
P Spaces: 60. Winter admission for park only, parking charge of £2.70.
& Partial. Wheelchair access to ground floor of house via stair-climber, garden, restaurant and shop. WC for the disabled. Guide Dogs allowed.
£ **Adult:** £8.00, £3.60 (park & garden only). **Child:** £4.00, £1.80 (park & garden only). **Other:** £20.00 (family), £9.00 (park & garden only) Admission price includes voluntary gift aid donation.

### MASSON MILLS

**(Sir Richard Arkwright's), Derby Road, Matlock Bath, Derbyshire DE4 3PY**
Sir Richard Arkwright's 1783 showpiece Masson Mills are the finest surviving example of one of Arkwright's cotton mills. The "Masson Mill pattern" of design was an important influence in nascent British and American mill development. Museum with historic working textile machinery. Part of the Derwent Valley Mills World Heritage Site.
www.massonmills.co.uk
**Grant Recipient:** Mara Securities Ltd
**Access contact:** Museum Reception
T: 01629 581001    F: 01629 581001
**Open:** All year except Christmas Day and Easter Day: Monday–Friday, 10am–4pm, Saturday, 11am–5pm and Sunday, 11am–4pm.
**Heritage Open Days:** No.
P Spaces: 200
& Partial. Wheelchair access to most areas. WC for the disabled. No Guide Dogs allowed.
£ **Adult:** £2.50. **Child:** £1.50. **Other:** £2.00 (school groups £1.00 per child).

### NORTH LEES HALL

**Birley Lane, Outseats, Hathersage, Derbyshire S30 1BR**
Tower House built c1590 in the Peak District National Park and designed by the architect Robert Smythson. The Hall's tenants were the Eyre family. They were visited by Charlotte Bronte who is thought to have based Thornfield Hall on North Lees Hall.
www.vivat.org.uk
**Grant Recipient:** Ms The Vivat Trust
**Access contact:** Miss Lisa Simm
T: 0845 090 2212    F: 0845 090 0174
E-mail: enquiries@vivat.org.uk
**Open:** Heritage Open Days in September, 10am–4.30pm. At other times by prior arrangement with Miss Lisa Simm, The Vivat Trust, 70 Cowcross Street, London, EC1M 6EJ.
**Heritage Open Days:** Yes
P Spaces: 7
& Partial. Wheelchair access to ground floor rooms by arrangement. No WC for the disabled. Guide Dogs allowed.
£ No.

### SACHEVERELL-BATEMAN MAUSOLEUM

**Churchyard of St Matthew's Church, Church Lane, Morley, Derbyshire**
A Grade II* listed small rectangular mausoleum built in red sandstone designed in the Perpendicular Revival style by GF Bodley, in 1897. It contains a marble sarcophagus with a cut-glass cross incorporated in its lid, stained glass, a painted panelled roof and a framed memorial inscription written on vellum.
www.mausolea-monuments.org.uk
**Grant Recipient:** Mausolea & Monuments Trust
**Access contact:** Miss Sheila Randall
T: 0115 875 8393
E-mail: se.randall@ntlworld.com
**Open:** Open when events are taking place in the Church (advertised locally). At other times by prior arrangement with Miss Sheila Randall (116 Kenilworth Drive, Kirk Hallam, Ilkeston, Derbyshire DE7 4EW. Tel: 0115 875 8393).
**Heritage Open Days:** No.
P Spaces: 20

& Full. No WC for the disabled. Guide Dogs allowed.
£ No.

### ST ANN'S HOTEL

**The Crescent, Buxton, Derbyshire SK17 6BH**
The Crescent was designed by John Carr of York and built by the Fifth Duke of Devonshire between 1780-89. It provided hotels, lodgings and a suite of elaborately decorated Assembly Rooms. The front elevation of three storeys is dominated by Doric pilasters over a continuous rusticated ground floor arcade.
**Grant Recipient:** High Peak Borough Council
**Access contact:** Mr Richard Tuffrey
T: 01457 851653    F: 01457 860290
E-mail: richard.tuffrey@highpeak.gov.uk
**Open:** Exterior accessible from public highway. No interior access until refurbishment works completed.
**Heritage Open Days:** No.
P On-street parking available.
& No wheelchair access. No WC for the disabled. No Guide Dogs allowed.
£ No.

### SUDBURY HALL

**Sudbury, Ashbourne, Derbyshire DE6 5HT**
17th century house with rich interior decoration including wood carvings by Laguerre. The Great Staircase (c1676) with white-painted balustrade with luxuriantly carved foliage by Edward Pierce, is one of the finest staircases of its date in an English house. 19th century service wing houses the National Trust Museum of Childhood.
www.nationaltrust.org.uk
**Grant Recipient:** The National Trust
**Access contact:** Property Manager
T: 01283 585305    F: 01283 585139
E-mail: sudburyhall@nationaltrust.org.uk
**Open:** Hall: 10 March–28 October: Wednesday–Sunday (but open Bank Holiday Mondays), 1–5pm. Grounds: as House to 28 October, 10am–6pm. Museum closed during 2007.
**Heritage Open Days:** No.
P Spaces: 100. Car park is a short distance from the Hall; six-seater volunteer driven buggy available.
& Partial. Wheelchair access to lake, tea room and shop. Ground floor access to museum. Access to Hall difficult–please contact the Property Manager in advance. WC for the disabled. Guide Dogs allowed.
£ **Adult:** £6.30. **Child:** £3.00, under 3s free. **Other:** £15.00 (family). Admission price includes voluntary gift aid donation.

### TISSINGTON HALL

**Tissington, Ashbourne, Derbyshire DE6 1RA**
Grade II* listed Jacobean manor house altered in the 18th century and extended in the 20th. Contains fine furniture, pictures and interesting early 17th century panelling. Home of the FitzHerbert family for over 500 years.
www.tissington-hall.com
**Grant Recipient:** Sir Richard FitzHerbert Bt
**Access contact:** Sir Richard FitzHerbert Bt
T: 01335 352200    F: 01335 352201
E-mail: tisshall@dircon.co.uk
**Open:** 9 April–13 April, 28 May–1 June and 24 July–24 August inclusive: Tuesday–Friday, 1.30–4pm.
**Heritage Open Days:** Yes
P Spaces: 100
& Partial. Wheelchair access to gardens and various rooms. Guide Dogs: by arrangement. WC for the disabled.
£ **Adult:** £6.50 (house & garden), £3.00 (garden). **Child:** £3.50 age 10-16 (house & garden), £1.00 (garden) **Other:** £5.00 (house & garden), £3.00 (garden).

## DEVON

### 21 THE MINT

**Exeter, Devon EX4 3BL**
The refectory range of St Nicholas Priory, converted into a substantial town house in the Elizabethan period and later into tenements. Features include medieval arch-braced roof, traces of the Norman priory and later Elizabethan panelling. Recently restored, now dwellings and meeting room.
www.ehbt.org.uk
**Grant Recipient:** Exeter Historic Buildings Trust
**Access contact:** Ms Katharine Chant
T: 01392 436000 / 496653    F: 01392 496653

E-mail: enquiries@ehbt.org.uk
**Open:** Every Monday throughout the year, 2–4pm (except Bank Holidays). Also open Spring Bank Holiday, Festival of Exeter weekend in July and Heritage Open Days, 11am–4pm. Redcoat guided tour 'Catacomb and The Mint' starting from Cathedral Close, March–October every Wednesday and Friday, 2pm.
**Heritage Open Days:** Yes
P No.
& Partial. Wheelchair access to ground floor and courtyard garden only. No WC for the disabled. Guide Dogs allowed.
£ No.

### ANDERTON HOUSE/RIGG SIDE

**Goodleigh, North Devon, Devon**
Anderton House also known as Rigg Side. 1970-1 to the designs of Peter Aldington and John Craig for Mr and Mrs Anderton. The inspiration for its profile is taken from the longhouses of Devon. Timber frame, forming a two-row grid of double posts and beams with a tent roof, set half proud of concrete block walls and glazed clerestory and stained tiled gabled roof. Timber linings and ceilings internally, with tiled floors. Its sliding doors give views of the Devon countryside.
www.landmarktrust.org.uk
**Grant Recipient:** The Landmark Trust
**Access contact:** Mrs Victoria O'Keeffe
T: 01628 825920    F: 01628 825417
E-mail: vokeeffe@landmarktrust.org.uk
**Open:** The Landmark Trust is an independent charity, which rescues small buildings of historic or architectural importance from decay or unsympathetic improvement. Landmark's aim is to promote the enjoyment of these historic buildings by making them available to stay in for holidays. Anderton House can be rented by anyone, at all times of the year, for periods ranging from a weekend to three weeks. Bookings can be made by telephoning the Booking Office on 01628 825925. As the building is in full-time use for holiday accommodation, it is not normally open to the public. However the public can view the building by prior arrangement by telephoning the access contact (Victoria O'Keeffe on 01628 825920) to make an appointment. Potential visitors will be asked to write to confirm the details of their visit.
**Heritage Open Days:** Yes
P Parking at local playing fields.
& Partial. Wheelchair access to kitchen, bedrooms and dining room. No WC for the disabled. Guide Dogs allowed.
£ No.

### AYSHFORD CHAPEL

**Ayshford, Burlescombe, Devon**
Grade I listed private medieval chapel with a simple medieval screen. Distinctive stained glass of 1848 and 17th century monuments to the Ashford family.
www.friendsoffriendlesschurches.org.uk
**Grant Recipient:** Friends of Friendless Churches
**Access contact:** Mr & Mrs Kelland
T: 01884 820271
**Open:** At any reasonable time. Keyholder lives nearby.
**Heritage Open Days:** Yes
P Spaces: 2. On-street parking.
& Partial. Wheelchair access possible with assistance: access to church through field and up one step. No WC for the disabled. No Guide Dogs allowed.
£ No.

### BROOMHAM FARM

**King's Nympton, Devon EX37 9TS**
Late medieval Grade II* listed Devon long-house of stone and cob construction with thatched roof. Contains a smoking room. Currently undergoing renovation.
**Grant Recipient:** Mr  Clements
**Access contact:** Miss J Clements
T: 01769 572322
**Open:** By prior telephone arrangement.
**Heritage Open Days:** No.
P Spaces: 3
& No wheelchair access. No WC for the disabled. No Guide Dogs allowed.
£ No.

## COLDHARBOUR MILL

**Uffculme, Devon EX15 3EE**
Woollen mill built by Thomas Fox between 1797-1799. Grade II* listed building. Now a working textile mill museum with demonstrations of textile machinery. Exhibition gallery, picnic area, café, waterside walks and shop.
www.coldharbourmill.org.uk
**Grant Recipient:** The Coldharbour Mill Trust
**Access contact:** Coldharbour Mill
**T:** 01884 840960   **F:** 01884 840858
**E-mail:** info@coldharbourmill.org.uk
**Open:** Opening arrangements under review at time of publication, please contact the Mill for current information.
**Heritage Open Days:** No.
P Spaces: 100
Partial. Wheelchair access to the mill via lift. Café not accessible but planning to relocate. WC for the disabled. Guide Dogs allowed.
£ **Adult:** £6.25 (Mill tour), £1.50 (site only) **Child:** £2.95 (Mill tour), free (site only). **Other:** Mill tour: £17.00 (family), £5.75 (senior citizens), £5.50 (groups, per person).

## COOKWORTHY MUSEUM OF RURAL LIFE IN SOUTH DEVON

**The Old Grammar School, 108 Fore Street, Kingsbridge, Devon TQ7 1AW**
17th century schoolroom with 19th century annex in Tudor style. Original entrance arch. Now a local museum with Victorian kitchen, Edwardian pharmacy and walled garden.
www.devonmuseums.net
**Grant Recipient:** William Cookworthy Museum Society
**Access contact:** Miss Margaret Lorenz
**T:** 01548 853235
**E-mail:** wcookworthy@talk21.com
**Open:** 26 March–31 October: Monday–Saturday, 10.30am–5pm (October 10.30am–4pm). Pre-booked groups all year (contact Mr Clifford Peach at the Cookworthy Museum). Local History Resource Centre open throughout the year.
**Heritage Open Days:** No.
P Spaces: 100. Public car park on Fore Street, 100 metres from Museum.
Partial. Wheelchair access with assistance to Victorian kitchen and scullery, Farm Gallery, walled garden, shop and Local Heritage Resource Centre. Ground floor viewing gallery with 'Virtual Museum Tour' film. WC for the disabled. Guide Dogs allowed.
£ **Adult:** £2.00. **Child:** £1.00. **Other:** £1.50 (senior citizens), £5.00 (family).

## DARTINGTON HALL

**Dartington, Totnes, Devon TQ9 6EL**
Medieval mansion and courtyard built 1388-1399 by John Holland, Earl of Huntingdon and later Duke of Exeter, half brother to Richard II. Set in a landscaped garden and surrounded by a 1200 acre estate. The Champernowne family owned Dartington for 400 years before selling the estate to Leonard and Dorothy Elmhirst who founded the Dartington Hall Trust.
www.dartingtonhall.org.uk
**Grant Recipient:** The Dartington Hall Trust
**Access contact:** Mrs K Hockings
**T:** 01803 847002   **F:** 01803 847007
**E-mail:** trust@dartingtonhall.org.uk
**Open:** Throughout the year for courses, events and activities. The Hall, courtyard and gardens are accessible for external viewing all year. Access to the interior by prior arrangement. Coach parties by prior arrangement only.
**Heritage Open Days:** Yes
P Spaces: 250
Partial. Wheelchair access to Great Hall, courtyard and top garden paths. WC for the disabled. Guide Dogs allowed.
£ No. **Other:** Some activities have an entry fee.

## EXETER CUSTOM HOUSE

**The Quay, Exeter, Devon EX1 1NN**
Located on the historic quayside, the Custom House was constructed in 1680-1 and is the earliest purpose-built customs house in Britain. Contains many original fittings and three exceptionally ornamental plaster ceilings by John Abbot of Frithelstock (amongst the finest such work of this date in the south west).
www.exeter.gov.uk/visiting/attractions
**Grant Recipient:** Exeter City Council
**Access contact:** Tourism Promotion Officer
**T:** 01392 265204   **F:** 01392 265625
**E-mail:** tourismpr@exeter.gov.uk
**Open:** Guided tours from May–September: Thursdays & Saturdays, 2pm, subject to building works.
**Heritage Open Days:** Yes
P Spaces: 400. Cathedral and Quay car park (75 metres). 5 public spaces for the disabled in front of Custom House.
Partial. Wheelchair access to ground floor stair area only. WC for the disabled in car park. Guide Dogs allowed.
£ No.

## FINCH FOUNDRY

**Sticklepath, Okehampton, Devon EX20 2NW**
19th century water-powered forge, which produced agricultural and mining hand tools. Still in working order with regular demonstrations. The foundry has three water-wheels driving the huge tilt hammer and grindstone.
www.nationaltrust.org.uk
**Grant Recipient:** The National Trust
**Access contact:** Mr Roger Boney
**T:** 01837 840046   **F:** 01837 840809
**E-mail:** rboney@nationaltrust.org.uk
**Open:** 25 March–29 October: daily except Tuesday, 11am–5.30pm (last admission 5pm). Tea room/shop as Foundry.
**Heritage Open Days:** Yes
P Spaces: 50. Access to car park is narrow and unsuitable for coaches and wide vehicles.
Partial. Wheelchair access to museum and workshop is difficult, Foundry can be viewed through shop window. No WC for the disabled. Guide Dogs allowed.
£ **Adult:** £3.90. **Child:** £1.95.

## KILWORTHY FARM COW HOUSES & GRANARY

**Tavistock Hamlets, Devon PL9 0JN**
Kilworthy Farm was part of the Duke of Bedford's Devon estates. The farm buildings dated 1851 consist of three parallel ranges of cowhouses situated over an undercroft of granite construction. A two storey granary adjoins the cowhouses to the east and a stableyard of single storey buildings lies separately to the west. An unusually large and complete example of a planned farmyard covering all functions of the farm for dairy and arable. The cowhouses with underground dung pit are of exceptional interest.
**Grant Recipient:** Mesdames Coren, Dennis & Edworthy
**Access contact:** Mrs Sandra Vallance
**T:** 01822 614477/ 07792645589   **F:** 01822 614477
**Open:** 25 July–20 August: daily except Sunday and excluding Thursdays in August; Easter Saturday and Easter Monday; both May and the August Bank Holiday weekends. At other times by prior arrangement with Mr & Mrs A Vallance, 10am–5pm. Guided tour to start at 11am and 2pm and or by special arrangement.
**Heritage Open Days:** Yes
P Spaces: 4. Please ensure access for farm traffic is not obstructed.
Partial. Wheelchair access to the ground floor of the granary and the lengthwise walkways of the cowhouses. The undercroft is cobbled and the central passages are passable but rough. Guide dogs are welcome but as a working farm care is requested. No WC for the disabled.
£ **Adult:** £3.00 (to include information leaflet & guided tour). **Child:** £1.00 (under 10).

## LAWRENCE CASTLE HALDON BELVEDERE

**Higher Ashton, nr. Dunchideock, Exeter, Devon EX6 7QY**
Grade II* listed building built in 1788 as the centrepiece to a 11,600 acre estate. Stands 244 metres above sea level overlooking the cathedral city of Exeter, the Exe estuary and the surrounding countryside. Contains a spiral staircase and miniature ballroom.
www.haldonbelvedere.co.uk
**Grant Recipient:** Devon Historic Buildings Trust
**Access contact:** Mr Ian Turner
**T:** 01392 833668   **F:** 01392 833668
**E-mail:** turner@haldonbelvedere.co.uk
**Open:** February–28 October: Sundays and Bank Holidays, 1.30–5.30pm. At other times by prior arrangement. Grounds open all year.
**Heritage Open Days:** No.
P Spaces: 15. Parking for the disabled adjacent to building.
Partial. Wheelchair access to ground floor only. WC for the disabled. Guide Dogs allowed.
£ **Adult:** £2.00. **Child:** Free. **Other:** Free for wheelchair bound visitors.

## LYNTON TOWN HALL

**Lee Road, Lynton, Devon EX35 6HT**
Grade II* listed Town Hall. Cornerstone laid 1898, opened by the donor Sir George Newnes, 15 August 1900. Neo-Tudor design with Art Nouveau details. In use as Town Hall and community facility.
www.lyntonandlynmouth.org.uk/towncouncil
**Grant Recipient:** Lynton & Lynmouth Town Council
**Access contact:** Mr Dwyer
**T:** 01598 752384   **F:** 01598 752677
**E-mail:** ltc@northdevon.gov.uk
**Open:** Monday–Friday, 9.30–11.00am. Other times by arrangement.
**Heritage Open Days:** No.
P No.
Partial. No WC for the disabled. Guide Dogs allowed.
£ No.

## OLD QUAY HEAD

**The Quay, Ilfracombe, Devon EX34 9EQ**
Grade II* listed quay originally constructed early in the 16th century by William Bourchier, Lord Fitzwarren. The Quay was paved with stone in the 18th century and extended further in the 19th. This extension is marked by a commemorative stone plaque at its southern end. The Quay separates the inner harbour basin from the outer harbour.
**Grant Recipient:** North Devon District Council
**Access contact:** Lieutenant Commander R Lawson
**T:** 01271 862108   **F:** 01271 862 108
**E-mail:** harbour_master@northdevon.gov.uk
**Open:** At all times.
**Heritage Open Days:** No.
P Spaces: 144. Charges apply. Places for disabled available.
Full. WC for the disabled immediately adjacent to the Old Quay Head. Guide Dogs allowed.
£ No.

## SALEM CHAPEL

**East Budleigh, Budleigh Salterton, Devon EX9 7EF**
Dating from 1719, built as a Presbyterian Chapel which later became congregational. Three galleries and school room added later in 1836 when the façade was re-designed.
www.hct.org.uk
**Grant Recipient:** Historic Chapels Trust
**Access contact:** Mrs Kathy Moyle
**T:** 01395 445 236
**Open:** At any reasonable time by prior arrangement with the key holder, Kathy Moyle, 4 Collins Park, East Budleigh, Budleigh Salterton, Devon EX9 7EG. There will be occasional events during the summer. Please check the Historic Chapels Trust website or contact the key holder for further information.
**Heritage Open Days:** Yes
P Two parking spaces for the disabled, otherwise public parking close by.
Partial. Wheelchair access to ground floor only. WC for the disabled. Guide Dogs allowed.
£ Donations invited.

## SALTRAM HOUSE

**Plympton, Plymouth, Devon PL7 1UH**
A remarkable survival of a George II mansion, complete with its original contents and set in a landscaped park. Robert Adam worked here on two occasions to create the state rooms and produced what are claimed to be the finest such rooms in Devon. These show his development as a designer, from using the conventional Rococo, to the low-relief kind of Neo-Classical detail that became his hallmark and with which he broke new ground in interior design.
www.nationaltrust.org.uk
**Grant Recipient:** The National Trust
**Access contact:** Carol Murrin
**T:** 01752 333500   **F:** 01752 336474
**E-mail:** saltram@nationaltrust.org.uk
**Open:** House: 25 March–29 October daily except Friday (but open Good Friday), 12 noon–4.30pm. Garden: 1 March–29 October daily except Friday (but open Good Friday), 11am–4.30pm. 30 October–28 February daily except Friday, 11am–4pm.
**Heritage Open Days:** No.
P Spaces: 2500. Parking 500 metres from house, 30 marked spaces on tarmac, remainder on grass.

**&** Partial. Wheelchair access to ground floor. WC for the disabled. Guide Dogs allowed.
**£** **Adult:** £8.40 (house & garden), £4.20 (garden only). **Child:** £4.20 (house & garden), £2.10 (garden only). Under 5s Free. **Other:** £12.60 (family: 1 adult), £21.00 (family: 2 adults). £7.10 (groups 15+).

### SMEATON'S TOWER

**The Hoe, Plymouth, Devon PL1 2NZ**

Re-sited upper part of the former Eddystone Lighthouse. Built 1759 by John Smeaton, erected here on new base in 1882. Circular tapered tower of painted granite with octagonal lantern. When this lighthouse was first constructed it was considered to be an important technical achievement.

**www.plymouthmuseum.gov.uk**
**Grant Recipient:** Plymouth City Museum & Art Gallery
**Access contact:** Mr Mark Tosdevin
**T:** 01752 304386    **F:** 01752 256361
**E-mail:** enquiry@plymouth.gov.uk
**Open:** Easter–end October: Tuesday–Saturday, 10am–4pm. November–Easter: Tuesday–Saturday, 10am–3pm.
**Heritage Open Days:** Yes
**P** Spaces: 40. On-street parking.
**&** No wheelchair access. No WC for the disabled. No Guide Dogs allowed.
**£** **Adult:** £2.25 (provisional). **Child:** £1.25 (provisional).

### SOUTH MOLTON TOWN HALL AND PANNIER MARKET

**South Molton, Devon EX36 3AB**

Guild Hall, dating from 1743 and Grade I listed. Incorporates Court Room, Old Assembly Room and Mayors Parlour with Museum on ground floor. Adjacent to Pannier Market and New Assembly Room.
**Grant Recipient:** South Molton Town Council
**Access contact:** Mr Malcolm Gingell
**T:** 01769 572501    **F:** 01769 574008
**E-mail:** smtc@northdevon.gov.uk
**Open:** Museum open March–October: Monday, Tuesday, Thursday and Saturday. All other rooms used for meetings and functions as and when required. Constable Room rented by Devon County Council.
**Heritage Open Days:** No.
**P** Parking available in Pannier Market except Thursdays and Saturdays.
**&** Partial. Wheelchair access to all areas except Court Room, Mayors Parlour and Old Assembly Room. WC for the disabled. Guide Dogs allowed.
**£** No.

### UGBROOKE PARK

**Chudleigh, Devon TQ13 0AD**

House and chapel built c1200 and redesigned by Robert Adam in the 1760s for the 4th Lord Clifford. Chapel and library wing in Adam's characteristic castle style. Set in 'Capability' Brown landscaped park with lakes and 18th century Orangery. Home of the Lords Clifford of Chudleigh for 400 years.
**www.ugbrooke.co.uk**
**Grant Recipient:** Clifford Estate Company Ltd
**Access contact:** Lord Clifford
**T:** 01626 852179    **F:** 01626 853322
**E-mail:** cliffordestate@btconnect.com
**Open:** 8 July–13 September: Tuesday, Wednesday, Thursday, Sunday and August Bank Holiday Monday, 1–5.30pm. Group tours and private functions by prior arrangement.
**Heritage Open Days:** No.
**P** Spaces: 200
**&** Full. WC for the disabled. Guide Dogs allowed.
**£** **Adult:** £6.50 (house & garden), £4.00 (garden). **Child:** £3.00 (house & garden), £2.00 (garden) **Other:** £5.50 (senior citizens, house & garden).

## DORSET

### BLANDFORD FORUM TOWN HALL & CORN EXCHANGE

**Market Place, Blandford Forum, Dorset DT1 7PY**

The Town Hall built by the Bastard Brothers and completed in 1734, has a Portland stone façade. On the ground floor is a loggia with 3 semi-circular arches enclosed by iron gates. The former magistrates room and the mid 20th century Council Chamber sit at 1st floor level. Attached to the rear of the building is the Corn Exchange, built in 1858, with interesting elliptical roof-trusses.
**www.blandford-tc.co.uk**
**Grant Recipient:** Blandford Forum Town Council
**Access contact:** The Town Clerk
**T:** 01258 454500    **F:** 01258 454432
**E-mail:** admin@blandford-tc.co.uk
**Open:** Throughout the year for markets, civic functions and other events. At other times by prior telephone arrangement with The Town Clerk, Monday–Friday, 9.30am–12.30pm.
**Heritage Open Days:** No.
**P** Spaces: 20. On-street meter parking, except on market days on Thursdays and Saturdays. Other parking is available in the town.
**&** Partial. Wheelchair access to ground floor only. WC for the disabled. Guide Dogs allowed.
**£** No.

### HIGHCLIFFE CASTLE

**Rothesay Drive, Highcliffe-on-Sea, Christchurch, Dorset BH23 4LE**

Cliff-top mansion built in the 1830s by Charles Stuart. Constructed in the romantic, picturesque style, much of its stonework is medieval coming from France. Exterior has been restored, interior houses changing exhibitions and the 16th century stained glass Jesse window. Gift shop and tea rooms on site with 14 acre cliff-top park.
**www.highcliffecastle.co.uk**
**Grant Recipient:** Christchurch Borough Council
**Access contact:** Mr David Hopkins
**T:** 01425 278807    **F:** 01425 280423
**E-mail:** d.hopkins@christchurch.gov.uk
**Open:** 1 February–23 December: daily, 11 am–5pm. Also some evenings for special events. Tea Rooms open all year, 10am–late afternoon; grounds all year from 7am.
**Heritage Open Days:** Yes
**P** Spaces: 120. Charged parking in Council car park April–September (free October–March) with additional parking in Highcliffe Village (1 mile from Castle).
**&** There is currently no wheelchair access to the building but there are toilet facilities for the disabled at the site. Guide Dogs allowed.
**£** **Adult:** £2.20 (from 1 April 2007). **Child:** Free. **Other:** HHA/Season ticket holders free.

### THE CHANTRY

**128 South Street, Bridport, Dorset DT6 3PA**

14th or 15th century two-storey stone rubble house, originally situated on a promontory of the River Brit. At one time known as the "Prior's House", more probably the house of a chantry priest. Interesting internal details including fragments of 17th century domestic wall paintings.
**www.vivat.org.uk**
**Grant Recipient:** The Vivat Trust Ltd
**Access contact:** Miss Lisa Simm
**T:** 0845 090 2212    **F:** 0845 090 0174
**E-mail:** enquiries@vivat.org.uk
**Open:** January–4 June: by prior arrangement with The Vivat Trust (tel: 0845 090 2212, fax: 0845 090 0174, email: enquiries@vivat.co.uk).
**Heritage Open Days:** Yes
**P** Spaces: 1. Additional on-street parking.
**&** Partial. Wheelchair access with difficulty through back entrance to kitchen and sitting room on ground floor. No WC for the disabled. Guide Dogs allowed.
**£** No.

## DURHAM

### BARNARD CASTLE MARKET CROSS

**Barnard Castle, Durham DL12 8EL**

Two-storey building dating from 1747 with a colonnaded ground floor and enclosed upper storey. Two slate roofs crowned by a bell tower and gilded weather vane with two bullet holes from 1804. Formerly used as Town Hall, butter market, lock-up, Court room and fire station.
**Grant Recipient:** Teesdale District Council
**Access contact:** Mr James Usher
**T:** 01833 696209    **F:** 01833 637269
**E-mail:** j.usher@teesdale.gov.uk
**Open:** Colonnaded area (ground floor) is open to the public at all times. The first floor is only accessible through organised tours with keys available from Teesdale House, Galgate, Barnard Castle, Co. Durham DL12 8EL by prior arrangement.
**Heritage Open Days:** No.

**P** On-street parking.
**&** No wheelchair access. No WC for the disabled. No Guide Dogs allowed.
**£** No.

### CROXDALE HALL

**Durham DH6 5JP**

18th century re-casing of an earlier Tudor building, containing comfortably furnished mid-Georgian rooms with Rococo ceilings. There is also a private chapel in the north elevation, walled gardens, a quarter-of-a-mile long terrace, an orangery and lakes which date from the mid-18th century.
**Grant Recipient:** The Trustees of Captain GM Salvin's 1983 Settlement
**Access contact:** Mr W H T Salvin
**T:** 01833 690100    **F:** 01833 637004
**E-mail:** williamsalvin@whtsalvin@aol.com
**Open:** By prior arrangement on Tuesdays and Wednesdays from the first Tuesday in May to the second Wednesday in July, 10am–1pm.
**Heritage Open Days:** Yes
**P** Spaces: 20
**&** Partial. WC for the disabled. No Guide Dogs allowed.
**£** **Adult:** £7.50. **Child:** Free (under 16s).

### DURHAM CASTLE

**Palace Green, Durham DH1 3RW**

Dating from 1072, the Castle was the seat of the Prince Bishops until 1832. Together with the Cathedral, the Castle is a World Heritage site. It now houses University College, the Foundation College of Durham University, and is a conference, banqueting and holiday centre in vacations.
**www.durhamcastle.com**
**Grant Recipient:** University of Durham
**Access contact:** University of Durham
**T:** 0191 374 4682
**Open:** Easter–30 September: guided tours daily. At other times: Monday, Wednesday, and Saturday (afternoons only). Tours may not take place when the Castle is being used for functions.
**Heritage Open Days:** Yes
**P** Parking in city car parks.
**&** Partial. Wheelchair access to courtyard only. WC for the disabled inaccessible to wheelchairs. Guide Dogs allowed.
**£** **Adult:** £5.00, £4.50 (group rate 10+). **Child:** £3.50 (3-14), £3.00 (group rate 10+). **Other:** £3.50 (concessions), £12.00 (family).

### FORMER STOCKTON & DARLINGTON RAILWAY BOOKING OFFICE

**48 Bridge Road, Stockton-on-Tees, Durham TS18 3AX**

Original booking office of the Stockton and Darlington Railway. Cottage of plain brick with slate roof facing railway line. A bronze tablet on the gable ends "Martin 1825 the Stockton and Darlington Company booked first passenger, thus marking an epoch in the history of mankind". The first rail of the Railway was laid outside the building. Now used as an administration office and accommodation for single homeless men.
**Grant Recipient:** Stockton Church's Mission to the Single Homeless
**Access contact:** Mr Spencer Wiggins
**T:** 01642 800311    **F:** 01642 800311
**E-mail:** wiggins.s@ntlworld.com
**Open:** January–12 June: Monday–Friday, 9am–3pm.
**Heritage Open Days:** No.
**P** Spaces: 50. Parking on opposite side of the road.
**&** Partial. Wheelchair access to exterior of site. No WC for the disabled. Guide Dogs allowed.
**£** No.

### HAMSTEELS HALL

**Hamsteels Lane, Quebec, Durham DH7 9RS**

Early 18th century farmhouse with 19th century alterations. Panelled window shutters; ground-floor room with full early 18th century panelling; similar panelling and cupboards in first-floor room. Good quality dogleg stair with turned balusters.
**www.hamsteelshall.co.uk**
**Grant Recipient:** Mr G F Whitfield
**Access contact:** Mrs June Whitfield
**T:** 01207 520 388    **F:** 01207 520 388
**E-mail:** june@hamsteelshall.co.uk
**Open:** By prior arrangement.

**Heritage Open Days:** No.

🅿 Spaces: 8

♿ Partial. Wheelchair access to Dining Room and Front Parlour only. No WC for the disabled. No Guide Dogs allowed.

💲 No.

## LOW BUTTERBY FARMHOUSE

### Croxdale & Hett, Durham DH6 5JN

Stone built farmhouse constructed on medieval site incorporating elements of 17th, 18th and 19th century phases of development.

**Grant Recipient:** The Trustees of Captain GM Salvin's 1983 Settlement

**Access contact:** Mr W H T Salvin

**T:** 01833 690100  **F:** 01833 637004

**E-mail:** williamsalvin@whtsalvin@aol.com

**Open:** By prior written or telephone arrangement with Mr W H T Salvin, The Estate Office, Egglestone Abbey, Barnard Castle, Co. Durham DL12 9TN.

**Heritage Open Days:** Yes

🅿 Spaces: 2

♿ Partial. Limited wheelchair access with assistance (some changes in floor level). No WC for the disabled. No Guide Dogs allowed.

💲 No.

## RECTORY FARM BARN

### Hall Walks, Easington, Peterlee, Durham SR8 3BS

Barn, possibly 13th century with extensive alterations. May originally have been an oratory connected with Seaton Holme. Limestone rubble construction; first floor contains medieval windows. Purchased by Groundwork in 1997 and recently renovated. Listed Grade II*.

**Grant Recipient:** Groundwork East Durham

**Access contact:** Mr Peter Richards

**T:** 0191 5273333  **F:** 0191 5273665

**E-mail:** peter.richards@groundwork.org.uk

**Open:** Access to the exterior all year, Monday to Friday, 9am–5pm.

**Heritage Open Days:** Yes

🅿 Spaces: 10

♿ Full. WC for the disabled. Guide Dogs allowed.

💲 No.

## SHOTLEY HALL

### Shotley Bridge, Consett, Durham DH8 9TE

Grade II* listed building designed in 1862 by Edward Robson in a Gothic style. Exceptionally complete and unaltered interior with stained glass tiles and interior elements designed by Edward Burne-Jones and made by William Morris.

**Grant Recipient:** Mr Martell

**Access contact:** A Martell

**T:** 01207 582285

**E-mail:** lallamartell@reme.co.uk

**Open:** 1 May–1 June: daily except Sundays, 10am to 4pm. It is advisable to telephone the Hall before visiting. By prior appointment only at other times between 1 April and 30 September to scholars, researchers and enthusiasts of William Morris and Edward Burne-Jones.

**Heritage Open Days:** No.

🅿 Spaces: 5

♿ Partial. Wheelchair access to ground floor only. No WC for the disabled. Guide Dogs allowed.

💲 No.

## UNTHANK HALL

### Stanhope, Durham DL13 2PQ

Jacobean farmhouse dating from 1520s. Many original features still remain.

**Grant Recipient:** Alan Morton

**Access contact:** Mr Alan Morton

**T:** 01388 526025  **F:** 01388 527 390

**E-mail:** alanunthank@aol.com

**Open:** 9,16, 23 and 30 January, 6 and 13 February, 6, 13 and 20 March, 8, 15 and 22 May, 12, 19 and 26 June, 11, 18 and 25 September, 2, 9 and 16 October, 6, 13, 20 and 27 November, 4, 11 and 18 December: 10am–3pm.

**Heritage Open Days:** No.

🅿 Parking by river.

♿ No wheelchair access. No WC for the disabled. Guide Dogs allowed.

💲 No.

## ESSEX

## HARWICH REDOUBT FORT

### behind 29 Main Road, Harwich, Essex CO12 3LT

180ft diameter circular fort commanding the harbour entrance built in 1808 to defend the port against a Napoleonic invasion. Surrounded by a dry moat, there are 11 guns on the battlements. 18 casemates which originally sheltered 300 troops in siege conditions now house a series of small museums.

**www.harwich-society.co.uk**

**Grant Recipient:** The Harwich Society

**Access contact:** Mr A Rutter

**T:** 01255 503429  **F:** 01255 503429

**E-mail:** info@harrwich-society.com

**Open:** 1 May–31 August: daily, 10am–4pm. Rest of year: Sundays only, 10am–4pm.

**Heritage Open Days:** Yes

🅿 No.

♿ No wheelchair access. No WC for the disabled. Guide Dogs allowed.

💲 **Adult:** £2.00. **Child:** Accompanied children free. **Other:** £2.00.

## HYLANDS HOUSE

### Hylands Park, London Road, Widford, Chelmsford, Essex CM2 8WQ

Grade II* listed building, surrounded by 600 acres of landscaped parkland, partly designed by Humphry Repton. Built c1730, the original house was a red brick Queen Anne style mansion, subsequent owners set about enlarging the property, which produced a neo-classical style house. Internal inspection of the house reveals its Georgian and Victorian features.

**www.chelmsfordbc.gov.uk/hylands**

**Grant Recipient:** Chelmsford Borough Council

**Access contact:** Mrs Ceri Lowen

**T:** 01245 605 500  **F:** 01245 496804

**E-mail:** ceri.lowen@chelmsford.gov.uk

**Open:** Throughout the year: Sundays and Bank Holidays (except Christmas Day), 11am–6pm. April–end September: Mondays, 11am–6pm. October–end March: Mondays, 11am–4pm. Tea Room: Sundays throughout the year, 11am–4.30pm. April–end September: Mondays, 11am–4.30pm. October–end March: Mondays, 11am–3pm. Group visits by prior arrangement.

**Heritage Open Days:** Yes

🅿 Spaces: 84. 4 parking spaces for the disabled, coaches by arrangement. Please note that during construction work this will be reduced–with alternative parking nearby.

♿ Full. WC for the disabled. Guide Dogs allowed.

💲 **Adult:** £3.30. **Child:** Free (under 16). **Other:** £2.30.

## JOHN WEBB'S WINDMILL

### Fishmarket Street, Thaxted, Essex CM6 2PG

Brick tower mill built in 1804 consisting of five floors. Has been fully restored as a working mill. On two floors there is a museum of rural and domestic bygones. There is also a small picture gallery of early photographs of the mill and the surrounding countryside.

**Grant Recipient:** Thaxted Parish Council

**Access contact:** Mr L A Farren

**T:** 01371 830285  **F:** 01371 830285

**Open:** May–September: Saturday–Sunday and Bank Holidays, 2–6pm. Groups during weekdays by special arrangement. For further information please contact Mr L A Farren, Borough Hill, Bolford Street, Thaxted, Essex CM6 2PY.

**Heritage Open Days:** Yes

🅿 Spaces: 80. Public parking in Thaxted.

♿ Partial. Wheelchair access to ground floor only. WC for the disabled in public car park in Margaret Street. Guide Dogs allowed.

💲 Donations welcome.

## OLD FRIENDS MEETING HOUSE

### High Street, Stebbing, Essex CM6 3SG

The Stebbing Meeting House is the earliest Quaker meeting House in Essex. Built c1674 it is a particularly fine and complete example of an early Quaker meeting house and its historical importance is recognised by its Grade II* listing.

**Grant Recipient:** The Trustees of the Old Friends Meeting House

**Access contact:** Mr R T Guyer

**T:** 01799 530430

**E-mail:** clareguyer@aol.com

**Open:** By prior telephone or written arrangement with Mr R T Guyer, 43 Pilgrim Close, Great Chesterford, Saffron Walden, Essex CB10 1QG (tel: 01799 530430).

**Heritage Open Days:** Yes

🅿 Spaces: 10

♿ Partial. Wheelchair access to ground floor. WC for the disabled. Guide Dogs allowed.

💲 No.

## THE GREAT DUNMOW MALTINGS

### Mill Lane, Great Dunmow, Essex CM6 1BD

Grade II* maltings complex (listed as Boyes. Croft Maltings, White Street), early 16th century and later, timber-framed and plastered, part weatherboarding and brick. The building exhibits the entire floor malting process whilst the Great Dunmow Museum Society occupies the ground floor with displays of local history. The first floor is available for community use.

**www.greatdunmowmaltings.co.uk**

**Grant Recipient:** Great Dunmow Maltings Preservation Trust

**Access contact:** Mr David A Westcott

**T:** 01371 873958  **F:** 01371 873958

**E-mail:** david.westcott2@btinternet.com

**Open:** All year: Saturday, Sunday and Bank Holidays, 11am–4pm. Groups at any reasonable time by prior arrangement. Closed over Christmas/New Year holiday week.

**Heritage Open Days:** Yes

🅿 Spaces: 100. Public car park nearby (pay and display, free on Sundays and Bank Holidays).

♿ Full. WC for the disabled. Guide Dogs allowed.

💲 **Adult:** £1.00. **Child:** 50p. **Other:** 50p (senior citizens).

## VALENTINES MANSION

### Emerson Road, Ilford, Essex IG1 4XA

Valentines Mansion is a late 17th century house, largely Georgian in appearance with Regency additions. Of particular interest is the unusual curved early 19th century porte cochere. The exterior was extensively repaired and restored in 2000.

**www.valentinesmansion.org.uk**

**Grant Recipient:** London Borough of Redbridge

**Access contact:** Mr Nigel Burch

**T:** 020 8708 3619  **F:** 020 8708 3178

**E-mail:** nigel.burch@redbridge.gov.uk

**Open:** 19 May for annual May Fair and at other times by prior arrangement with Nigel Burch (Chief Leisure Officer, London Borough of Redbridge, Lynton House, 255/259 High Road, Ilford, Essex IG1 1NY. Tel:020 8708 3619). Mansion will be closed from July 2007 to end of 2008 for restoration work.

**London Open House:** Yes

🅿 On-street parking, Emerson Road, Tillotson Road, Bethell Avenue and Holcombe Road.

♿ Partial. Wheelchair access to ground floor only. No WC for the disabled. Guide Dogs allowed.

💲 No.

## GLOUCESTERSHIRE

## ACTON COURT

### Latteridge Road, Iron Acton, South Gloucestershire BS37 9TJ

Seat of the Poyntzes, an influential courtier family who occupied the house until 1680 when it was converted into a farm house. A Tudor range, constructed in 1535 to accommodate King Henry VIII and Queen Anne B oleyn survives along with part of the North range. The rooms are unfurnished but contain important traces of original decoration.

**www.actoncourt.com**

**Grant Recipient:** Rosehill Corporation

**Access contact:** Ms Lisa Kopper

**T:** 01454 228224  **F:** 01454 227256

**E-mail:** actonct@dircon.co.uk or info@actoncourt.com

**Open:** Guided tours and events 12 June–19 August. Closed Mondays. Pre-booking essential. Ring information line for details 01454 228 224.

**Heritage Open Days:** No.

🅿 Spaces: 40

♿ Partial. WC for the disabled. Guide Dogs allowed.

💲 **Adult:** £5.50. **Child:** £4.00. **Other:** £4.00 (senior citizens & the disabled), £100 (exclusive group tours maximum 25). Special events priced separately.

## CHASTLETON HOUSE

**Chastleton, Moreton-in-Marsh, Gloucestershire GL56 0SU**

Jacobean house filled with a mixture of rare and everyday objects, furniture and textiles collected since 1612. Continually occupied for 400 years by the same family. Emphasis lies on conservation rather than restoration.
**www.nationaltrust.org.uk**
**Grant Recipient:** The National Trust
**Access contact:** The Custodian
**T:** 01608 674355   **F:** 01608 674355
**E-mail:** chastleton@nationaltrust.org.uk
**Open:** 28 March–29 September: Wednesday–Saturday, 1–5pm (last admission 4pm). 3 October–27 October: Wednesday–Saturday, 1–4pm (last admission 3pm). Visitor numbers limited, pre-booking advised. Groups by written arrangement with the Custodian.
**Heritage Open Days:** No.
P Spaces: 50
 Partial. Wheelchair access to ground floor with assistance and parts of garden only. WC for the disabled. Guide Dogs allowed.
£ **Adult:** £7.00. **Child:** £3.50. **Other:** £17.50 (family), Private View £7.50 (£2.50 NT members).

## CHAVENAGE

**Tetbury, Gloucestershire GL8 8XP**

Elizabethan Manor House (c1576), contains tapestry rooms, furniture and relics from the Cromwellian Period. Has been the home of only two families since the time of Elizabeth I. Used as a location for television and film productions.
**www.chavenage.com**
**Grant Recipient:** Trustees of the Chavenage Settlement
**Access contact:** Miss Caroline Lowsley-Williams
**T:** 01666 502329   **F:** 01453 836778
**E-mail:** info@chavenage.com
**Open:** May–September: Thursday, Sunday and Bank Holidays plus Easter Sunday and Monday, 2–5pm. Groups at other times by prior arrangement.
**Heritage Open Days:** Yes
P Spaces: 40
 Partial. Wheelchair access to ground floor only. Parking for the disabled near front door. WC for the disabled. Guide Dogs allowed.
£ **Adult:** £6.00. **Child:** £3.00.

## DEER PARK

**Cirencester Park, Cirencester, Gloucestershire**

The Deer Park is part of a much larger landscaped area. It has recently been landscaped to remove concrete bases and roadways of World War II military hospitals, reinstating the original landscape designed in the 1700s by the First Earl and Alexander Pope.
**Grant Recipient:** Bathurst Estate
**Access contact:** Mr Allsop
**T:** 01285 653135   **F:** 01285 656291
**Open:** All year: daily, 8am–5pm.
**Heritage Open Days:** No.
P Car parking in the town and limited parking in Cecily Hill (short stay).
 Partial. Wheelchair access available but may be uneven due to unsurfaced tracks which may be rough or wet. Guide dogs should be accompanied due to farm hazards. WC for the disabled in the town. Guide Dogs allowed.
£ No.

## DYRHAM PARK

**Dyrham, nr. Bath, Gloucestershire SN14 8ER**

17th century house set within an ancient deer park, woodlands and formal garden. The house was furnished in the Dutch style and still has many original contents including paintings, ceramics, furniture and 17th century tapestries. The Victorian domestic rooms include the kitchen, larder, bakehouse, dairy and tenants hall.
**www.nationaltrust.org.uk**
**Grant Recipient:** The National Trust
**Access contact:** Visitor Services Manager
**T:** 01179 372501   **F:** 01179 371353
**E-mail:** dyrhampark@nationaltrust.org.uk
**Open:** House: 17 March–28 October, daily except Wednesday and Thursday, 12 noon–5pm (last admission to house 4pm). Garden: as for house 11am–4pm or dusk if earlier. Park: all year (closed 25 December) 11am–5pm or dusk if earlier. Bank Holiday Mondays and Good Friday 11am–5pm.
**Heritage Open Days:** Yes

P Spaces: 250. Free shuttle bus from car park to house.
 Partial. Wheelchair access to all but four upstairs rooms. A photograph album of these rooms is available. WC for the disabled. Guide Dogs allowed.
£ **Adult:** £9.60 (House, park & garden), £3.80 (park & garden), £2.50 (garden only). **Child:** £4.80 (House, park & garden), £2.00 (park & garden), £1.20 (garden only). **Other:** Family: £23.90 (House, park & garden), £8.50 (park & garden), £5.60 (garden only).

## EBLEY MILL

**Westward Road, Stroud, Gloucestershire GL5 4UB**

19th century riverside textile mill, now restored and converted into offices occupied by Stroud District Council. Has Gothic-style clock tower and block designed by George Bodley.
**www.stroud.gov.uk**
**Grant Recipient:** Stroud District Council
**Access contact:** Mr M Hammond
**T:** 01453 754 447   **F:** 01453 754 947
**E-mail:** mike.hammond@stroud.gov.uk
**Open:** Monday–Thursday, 8.45am–5pm; Fridays, 8.45am–4.30pm. Closed Bank Holidays. Tours by prior arrangement.
**Heritage Open Days:** Yes
P Spaces: 30
 Full. WC for the disabled. Guide Dogs allowed.
£ No.

## ELMORE COURT ENTRANCE GATES

**Elmore, Gloucestershire GL2 3NT**

Early 18th century carriage and pedestrian gateway, with 19th century flanking walls. By William Edney, blacksmith of Bristol for Sir John Guise at Rendcomb. Gateway was removed from Rendcomb and re-erected here in early 19th century.
**Grant Recipient:** Trustees of the Elmore Court Estate
**Access contact:** Trustees of the Elmore Court Estate
**T:** 01452 720293
**Open:** Visible at all times from public highway.
**Heritage Open Days:** No.
P Spaces: 5. Off-road parking on forecourt in front of gates.
 Full. No WC for the disabled. Guide Dogs allowed.
£ No.

## FRAMPTON MANOR BARN

**(The Wool Barn, Manor Farm), The Green, Frampton-on-Severn, Gloucestershire GL2 7EP**

Grade I listed timber framed barn built c1560. Re-used worked stones in ashlar plinth wall were found during repair works.
**www.framptoncourtestate.co.uk**
**Grant Recipient:** Mr P R H Clifford
**Access contact:** Mr P R H Clifford
**T:** 01452 740698   **F:** 01452 740698
**E-mail:** clifford@framptoncourt.wanadoo.co.uk
**Open:** During normal office hours (8.30am–4.30pm Monday–Friday). Other times by arrangement.
**Heritage Open Days:** No.
P Spaces: 30
 Full. WC for the disabled. Guide Dogs allowed.
£ **Adult:** £1.00. **Child:** Free (special rates for school parties). **Other:** Free.

## NEWARK PARK

**Ozleworth, Wotton-under-Edge, Gloucestershire GL12 7PZ**

Tudor hunting lodge built c1550 for one of Henry VIII's courtiers, Sir Nicholas Poyntz (who married into the equally wealthy Berkeley family), reputedly with stone from the destroyed Kingswood Abbey. Enlarged in early 17th century and then remodelled into a castellated country house by James Wyatt in the late 18th century. Retains many original features and is located on the edge of a 40ft cliff with outstanding views of the surrounding countryside.
**www.nationaltrust.org.uk**
**Grant Recipient:** The National Trust
**Access contact:** Visitor Services Manager
**T:** 01453 842644   **F:** 01453 842644
**E-mail:** newarkpark@nationaltrust.org.uk
**Open:** 4 April–31 May: Wednesday and Thursday, 11am–5pm. 2 June–29 October: Wednesday, Thursday, Saturday and Sunday, 11am–5pm. Open Bank Holiday

Mondays, Good Friday, and Easter Saturday and Sunday, 11am–5pm.
**Heritage Open Days:** Yes
P Spaces: 10
 No wheelchair access. No WC for the disabled. Guide Dogs allowed.
£ **Adult:** £5.30. **Child:** £2.70 **Other:** £13.80 (family).

## REGAN HOUSE

**23 Lansdowne Terrace, Cheltenham, Gloucestershire**

Regency house, now flats. Richly detailed stone façade with portico. Mews arch between No. 22 and Regan House.
**Grant Recipient:** Abel Developments/Forward Construction
**Access contact:** Mr Mark Davis ARICS
**T:** 01242 260266
**Open:** January–27 September: access to the exterior only at all times.
**Heritage Open Days:** No.
P Spaces: 2
 No wheelchair access. No WC for the disabled. Guide Dogs allowed.
£ No.

## STANCOMBE PARK TEMPLE

**Dursley, Gloucestershire GL11 6AU**

One in a series of buildings in the folly gardens at Stancombe Park, in the form of a Greek temple. Built in approximately 1815.
**www.thetemple.info**
**Grant Recipient:** Mr N D Barlow
**Access contact:** Mrs G T Barlow
**T:** 01453 542815
**E-mail:** nick@nicbarlow.com
**Open:** All year by prior telephone arrangement. To the exterior only during Heritage Open Days.
**Heritage Open Days:** Yes
P Spaces: 50
 No wheelchair access. No WC for the disabled. Guide Dogs allowed.
£ **Adult:** £3.00 (charity donation for visits to garden). **Other:** No charge is made for anyone specifically wishing to see the temple only.

## STANLEY MILL

**King's Stanley, Stonehouse, Gloucestershire GL10 3HQ**

Built 1813, with large addition c1825, of Flemish bond red brick with ashlar dressings and Welsh slate roof. Early example of fireproof construction (which survived a major fire in 1884).
**Grant Recipient:** Stanley Mills Ltd
**Access contact:** Mr Mark Griffiths/ Jill May
**T:** 01453 821800   **F:** 01453 791 167
**E-mail:** jill@marlings.co.uk
**Open:** By prior written arrangement as the Mill is used by various manufacturing companies.
**Heritage Open Days:** No.
P Spaces: 30. By prior written arrangement as the Mill is used by various manufacturing companies.
 No wheelchair access. No WC for the disabled. No Guide Dogs allowed.
£ No.

## TANHOUSE FARM TITHE BARN

**Frampton-on-Severn, Gloucestershire GL2 7EH**

17th century Tithe Barn with cattle Byre.
**Grant Recipient:** M R & C R Williams
**Access contact:** M R & C A Williams
**T:** 01452 741 072
**E-mail:** tanhouse.farm@lineone.net
**Open:** By prior arrangement with M R or C R Williams (tel: 01452 741072).
**Heritage Open Days:** No.
P Spaces: 20
Parking within 100 metres.
 Partial. Wheelchair access to main areas. No WC for the disabled. Guide Dogs allowed.
£ No.

## WEST BANQUETING HOUSE

**Chipping Campden, Gloucestershire**

The West Banqueting House stands opposite the East Banqueting House across a broad terrace. It is elaborately

decorated with spiral chimney stacks, finials and strapwork parapets.
**www.landmarktrust.org.uk**
**Grant Recipient:** The Landmark Trust
**Access contact:** Mrs Victoria O'Keeffe
**T:** 01628 825920   **F:** 01628 825417
**E-mail:** vokeeffe@landmarktrust.org.uk
**Open:** The Landmark Trust is an independent charity, which rescues small buildings of historic or architectural importance from decay or unsympathetic improvement. Landmark's aim is to promote the enjoyment of these historic buildings by making them available to stay in for holidays. West Banqueting House can be rented by anyone, at all times of the year, for periods ranging from a weekend to three weeks. Bookings can be made by telephoning the Booking Office on 01628 825925. The public can also view the building on eight Open Days throughout the year (dates to be set) or by prior arrangement; telephone the access contact Victoria O'Keeffe on 01628 825920 to make an appointment. Potential visitors will be asked to write to confirm the details of their visit.
**Heritage Open Days:** Yes
🅿 Parking available in town only.
♿ No wheelchair access. No WC for the disabled. Guide Dogs allowed.
£ No.

## WICK COURT

**Overton Lane, Arlingham, Gloucestershire GL2 7JJ**
Medieval, 16th and 17th century Grade II* listed manor house with a range of farm buildings enclosed by a moat. The house is now a Farms for City Children centre.
**www.farmsforcitychildren.co.uk**
**Grant Recipient:** Farms for City Children
**Access contact:** Ms Heather Tarplee
**T:** 01452 741023   **F:** 01452 741366
**E-mail:** wickcourt@yahoo.co.uk
**Open:** 4–20 January, 17–28 February, 31 March–20 April and 21 July–3 September. At other times by prior arrangement with Heather Tarplee, Farm School Manager (tel: 01452 741023).
**Heritage Open Days:** No.
🅿 Spaces: 20
♿ Partial. Wheelchair access to ground floor of manor house only. WC for the disabled. Guide Dogs allowed.
£ Adult: £2.50 (guided tour).

## WOODCHESTER PARK MANSION

**Nympsfield, Stonehouse, Gloucestershire GL10 3TS**
Grade I listed Victorian mansion, abandoned incomplete in 1870. One of the most remarkable houses of its period and uniquely exhibiting its construction process. Set in a large landscaped park (possibly by 'Capability' Brown). The building is also a Site of Special Scientific Interest housing two nationally important populations of endangered bats.
**www.woodchestermansion.org.uk**
**Grant Recipient:** Woodchester Mansion Trust
**Access contact:** Mr Steven Woodman
**T:** 01453 861541   **F:** 01453 861337
**E-mail:** office@woodchestermansion.org.uk
**Open:** Easter–End of October: every Sunday, first Saturday in month and Bank Holiday weekends; July–August: Saturday and Sunday, and 6 April, 11am–5.00pm (last admission to house at 4.00pm). Groups and private visits by prior arrangement.
**Heritage Open Days:** Yes
🅿 Spaces: 60. Parking is 1 mile from Mansion, access via woodland walk. Minibus service available.
♿ Partial. Wheelchair access to ground floor only. No WC for the disabled. Guide Dogs allowed.
£ Adult: £5.00. Child: Free with parents. Other: £4.00 (English Heritage & National Trust members, senior citizens & NUS card holders).

## GREATER MANCHESTER

### 1830 WAREHOUSE

**The Museum of Science & Industry in Manchester, Liverpool Road, Castlefield, Manchester, Greater Manchester M3 4FP**
Former railway warehouse, c1830, originally part of the Liverpool Road Railway Station (the oldest surviving passenger railway station in the world) which was the terminus of the Liverpool and Manchester Railway built by George Stephenson and his son Robert. Now part of The Museum of Science and Industry in Manchester.

**www.msim.org.uk**
**Grant Recipient:** The Museum of Science & Industry in Manchester
**Access contact:** Mr Robin Holgate
**T:** 0161 832 2244   **F:** 0161 606 0186
**E-mail:** collections@msim.org.uk
**Open:** Daily (except 24/25/26 December and 1 January), 10am–5pm.
**Heritage Open Days:** No.
🅿 Spaces: 50
♿ Full. WC for the disabled. Guide Dogs allowed.
£ Free entry to all to main museum building. Charge for special exhibitions.

### DAM HOUSE

**Astley Hall Drive, Astley, Tyldesley, Greater Manchester M29 7TX**
17th century house with extensive additions in the 19th century. Formerly a hospital, now a community facility. Retains many original and Regency features.
**www.damhouse.net**
**Grant Recipient:** Morts Astley Heritage Trust
**Access contact:** Mrs Helen Bolton
**T:** 01942 876417   **F:** 01942 876417
**E-mail:** info@damhouse.net
**Open:** Daily, 9am–5pm.
**Heritage Open Days:** Yes
🅿 Spaces: 50. Parking at rear/front of building
♿ Full. WC for the disabled. Guide Dogs allowed.
£ No.

### HALL I' TH' WOOD MUSEUM

**Green Way, Bolton, Greater Manchester BL1 8UA**
Grade I listed manor house, early 16th century, where Samuel Crompton invented and built his spinning mule in 1779. Part of the Hall is timber-framed and shows the development of a house in the 16th and 17th centuries. Now a museum.
**www.boltonmuseums.org.uk**
**Grant Recipient:** Bolton Council
**Access contact:** Miss Elizabeth Shaw
**T:** 01204 332370   **F:** 01204 332215
**E-mail:** hallithwood@bolton.gov.uk
**Open:** 8 January–9 April: Saturday and Sunday, 11am–5pm. 12 April–30 October: Wednesday–Sunday, 11am–5pm (last admission 4.15pm). 31 October–end March 2008: Saturday & Sunday, 11am–5pm (last admission 4.15pm).
**Heritage Open Days:** Yes
🅿 Spaces: 10
♿ No wheelchair access. No WC for the disabled. No Guide Dogs allowed.
£ Adult: £2.00. Child: £1.00. Other: £1.00 (senior citizens).

### HEATON PARK TEMPLE

**Prestwich, Greater Manchester M25 2SW**
Grade II* listed ornamental temple. Probably late 18th century, by James Wyatt. Situated on a hill in Heaton Park near Heaton Hall. The form is a simple, small rotunda of Tuscan columns with domed roof and lantern. It is said that Sir Thomas Egerton may have used the structure as an observatory.
**www.heatonpark.org.uk**
**Grant Recipient:** Manchester City Council
**Access contact:** Mr Graham Wightman, General Manager
**T:** 0161 773 1085   **F:** 0161 798 0107
**E-mail:** g.wightman@manchester.gov.uk
**Open:** The temple can be viewed externally 365 days a year. Access to the interior by prior arrangement or when local artist is in residence (usually during summer months). Internal access also available in the winter through the park warden's team: please phone for details (tel: 0161 773 1085 x207).
**Heritage Open Days:** Yes
🅿 Spaces: 500
♿ Partial. External viewing only possible: pathway to the temple on a steep incline. WC for the disabled. Guide Dogs allowed.
£ No.

### MANCHESTER LAW LIBRARY

**14 Kennedy Street, Manchester M2 4BY**
Built in Venetian Gothic style in 1885 to a design by Manchester architect, Thomas Hartas. Has stained glass windows by Evans of Birmingham.
**www.manchester-law-library.co.uk**

**Grant Recipient:** The Manchester Incorporated Law Library Society
**Access contact:** Mrs Jane Riley
**T:** 0161 236 6312   **F:** 0161 236 6119
**E-mail:** librarian@manchester-law-library.co.uk
**Open:** January–1 September: by prior telephone or written arrangement, Monday–Friday, 9am–5pm.
**Heritage Open Days:** Yes
🅿 No.
♿ No wheelchair access. No WC for the disabled. Guide Dogs allowed.
£ No.

### OLD GRAMMAR SCHOOL

**Boarshaw Road, Middleton, Greater Manchester M24 6BR**
Endowed by Elizabeth I in 1572, completed in 1584 with house added 1830s. Restored in 1998. Grade II* listed building with fine original oak beams and items of historical and local interest. An important early example of a building type for which there was little architectural precedent.
**Grant Recipient:** The Old Grammar School Trust
**Access contact:** Mr David Brenan, Trustee
**T:** 0161 643 2693   **F:** 0161 643 2693
**E-mail:** davebrennan@tinyworld.co.uk
**Open:** All year except Christmas/New Year period: Tuesday, Wednesday and Thursday, 2–4pm. Parties by arrangement on 0161 643 7442 or 0161 653 4526. Regular programme of events and use by community groups.
**Heritage Open Days:** Yes
🅿 Spaces: 17
♿ Full. WC for the disabled. Guide Dogs allowed.
£ No.

### STAIRCASE HOUSE

**30a/31 Market Place, Stockport, Greater Manchester SK1 3XE**
Timber framed town house. Dating from 1460, enlarged in 16th and 17th centuries and altered in 18th, 19th and 20th centuries. Early panelled rooms and an important 17th century caged newel staircase from which the house takes its name. Damaged by fire, but restored by Stockport Council. Interpretation charts the history of the house and its evaluation to WWII. The house is fully interactive with visitors invited to touch all objects and furniture.
**www.staircasehouse.org.uk**
**Grant Recipient:** Stockport Metropolitan Borough Council
**Access contact:** Mr Scott Manton
**T:** 0161 480 1731   **F:** 0161 474 0312
**E-mail:** scott.manton@stockport.gov.uk
**Open:** Daily 1–5pm, closed Christmas Day, Boxing Day and New Years Day.
**Heritage Open Days:** Yes
🅿 Town centre car parks and street parking.
♿ Full. WC for the disabled. Guide Dogs allowed.
£ Adult: £3.50. Child: Free to under 5s. Other: £1.75 with leisure key.

### VICTORIA BATHS

**Hathersage Road, Manchester, Greater Manchester M13 0FE**
An ornate and complete municipal swimming pool complex built 1903–1906, with 2 pools, Turkish and Russian Bath suite, Aeratone and extensive stained glass and tile work. Restoration work will commence in 2007 on the Turkish Baths and the front block of the building.
**www.victoriabaths.org.uk**
**Grant Recipient:** The Manchester Victoria Baths Trust
**Access contact:** Ms Gill Wright
**T:** 0161 224 2020   **F:** 0161 224 0707
**E-mail:** info@victoriabaths.org.uk
**Open:** April–October: first Sunday in each month, 12–4pm. Additional opening days include Heritage Open Days in September, but please ring to confirm. At other times by prior arrangement with Ms Gill Wright of the Manchester Victoria Baths Trust, Studio 20, Longsight Business Park, Hamilton Road, Longsight, Manchester M13 0PD (tel: 0161 224 2020). Group visits welcome.
**Heritage Open Days:** Yes
🅿 Spaces: 100. On-street parking during the week. Use of large adjacent car park at weekends.
♿ Partial. Wheelchair access to ground floor with assistance. Most of the building can be seen from the ground floor. No WC for the disabled. Guide Dogs allowed.
£ Adult: £1.00. Child: Free.

# HAMPSHIRE

## AVINGTON PARK

**Winchester, Hampshire SO21 1DB**
Palladian mansion dating back to the 11th century, enlarged in 1670 by the addition of two wings and a classical Portico surmounted by three statues. Visited by Charles II and George IV. Has highly decorated State rooms and a Georgian church in the grounds.
**www.avingtonpark.co.uk**
**Grant Recipient:** Mrs Sarah Bullen
**Access contact:** Mrs Sarah Bullen
**T:** 01962 779260    **F:** 01962 779202
**E-mail:** enquiries@avingtonpark.co.uk
**Open:** May–September: Sundays and Bank Holidays and Mondays in August, 2.30–5.30pm. Group booking and other times by prior arrangement.
**Heritage Open Days:** Yes
**P** Spaces: 150
**占** Partial. Wheelchair access to ground floor only. Church with assistance (one step to interior). WC for the disabled. Guide Dogs allowed.
**£** Adult: £4.50. Child: £2.00.

## BOATHOUSE NO. 6

**Portsmouth Naval Base, Portsmouth PO1 3LJ**
Large Victorian naval boathouse constructed 1845. Designed by Captain James Beatson of the Royal Engineers, it is one of the first examples of a brick building constructed around a metal frame. Its massive cast iron beams are inscribed with their load-bearing capacity.
**www.actionstations.org**
**Grant Recipient:** Portsmouth Naval Base Property Trust
**Access contact:** Mr Mark Meacher
**T:** 023 9282 0921    **F:** 023 9286 2437
**E-mail:** mm@pnbpt.com
**Open:** All year except Christmas Eve, Christmas Day and Boxing Day, 10am–5.30pm (April–October) and 10am–5pm (November–March). Groups by prior arrangement.
**Heritage Open Days:** Yes
**P** Spaces: 150. Additional parking 500 metres from the site.
**占** Full. WC for the disabled. Guide Dogs allowed.
**£** Adult: £11.50. Child: £9.00. Other: £32.00 (family).

## BREAMORE HOME FARM TITHE BARN

**Breamore, nr. Fordingbridge, Hampshire SP6 2DF**
Late 16th century tithe barn with dwarf walls supporting a timber-frame and external cladding under a tiled roof with massive timber aisle posts, double doors in the centre of each side and an area of threshing boards.
**Grant Recipient:** Breamore Ancient Buildings Conservation Trust
**Access contact:** Mr Michael Hulse
**T:** 01725 512858    **F:** 01725 512858
**Open:** Weekdays by prior arrangement with Mr Michael Hulse of Breamore House.
**Heritage Open Days:** No.
**P** Spaces: 10
**占** Full. No WC for the disabled. Guide Dogs allowed.
**£** No.

## CALSHOT

**(Activities Main Hanger, Games Hanger & FFF Hanger), Calshot, Fawley, Hampshire SO45 1BR**
Part of the most outstanding group of early aircraft structures of this type in Britain and the largest hanger built for use by fixed-wing aircraft during World War 1. Now an activities centre.
**www.calshot.com**
**Grant Recipient:** Hampshire County Council
**Access contact:** Mr Peter Davies
**T:** 01962 841841    **F:** 01962 841326
**E-mail:** arccpd@pbrs.hants.gov.uk
**Open:** Daily except Christmas Day, Boxing Day and New Year's Day.
**Heritage Open Days:** No.
**P** Spaces: 150. Ample free parking on-site.
**占** Full. WC for the disabled. Guide Dogs allowed.
**£** No.

## HIGHCLERE CASTLE & PARK

**Highclere, Newbury, Hampshire RG20 9RN**
Early Victorian mansion rebuilt by Sir Charles Barry in 1842, surrounded by 'Capability' Brown parkland with numerous listed follies including Heavens Gate, an 18th century eye-catching hill-top landscape feature and The Temple, c1760, altered by Barry in mid 19th century, a regular classical circular structure. Family home of the 8th Earl and Countess of Carnarvon.
**www.highclerecastle.co.uk**
**Grant Recipient:** Executors of the 7th Earl of Carnarvon & Lord Carnarvon
**Access contact:** Mr Alec Tompson
**T:** 01223 236996    **F:** 01223 3234859
**E-mail:** agent@hwdean.co.uk
**Open:** 1-5 & 8-12 April, 6,7, 28 & 29 May, 1 July–30 August Sunday–Thursday and 2 September: 11am–4pm (gates open 10am). Last admission 3pm. Temple: permissive path on days when Castle is open. At all other times by prior arrangement with Estate Office, Highclere Park (Tel: 01635 255401).
**Heritage Open Days:** No.
**P** Spaces: 200. Unlimited parking.
**占** Partial. Wheelchair access to ground floor only. WC for the disabled. Guide Dogs allowed.
**£** Adult: £7.50 (provisional). Child: £4.00 (provisional). Other: £6.00 (senior citizens, provisional).

## HOUGHTON LODGE GARDENS

**Stockbridge, Hampshire SO20 6LQ**
Landscaped pleasure grounds and a park laid out c1800 with views from higher ground over informal landscape (Grade II*) surrounding the 18th century Cottage Ornee (Grade II*). Chalk cob walls enclose ancient espaliers, greenhouses and herb garden. Formal topiary 'Peacock' Garden, snorting topiary dragon and wild flowers. A popular TV Film location. 14 acres of Meadow Walks through river valley.
**www.houghtonlodge.co.uk**
**Grant Recipient:** Captain M W Busk
**Access contact:** Capt. M W Busk
**T:** 01264 810502    **F:** 01264 810063
**E-mail:** info@houghtonlodge.co.uk
**Open:** 1 March–30 September: daily, 10am–5pm. Closed Wednesdays.
**Heritage Open Days:** No.
**P** Spaces: 100
**占** Partial. WC for the disabled. Guide Dogs allowed.
**£** Adult: £5.00. Child: Free. Other: £4.50 (group rate).

## MANOR FARMHOUSE

**Hambledon, Hampshire PO7 4RW**
12th century stone built house with later medieval wing. 17th and 18th century re-fronting of part and minor renovation.
**Grant Recipient:** Mr Stuart Mason
**Access contact:** Lt. Col. Neil Mason
**T:** 01929 462559
**Open:** By prior arrangement only.
**Heritage Open Days:** No.
**P** Spaces: 2
**占** Partial. No WC for the disabled. Guide Dogs allowed.
**£** No.

## ST MICHAEL'S ABBEY

**Farnborough, Hampshire GU14 7NQ**
Grade I listed church and Imperial Mausoleum crypt of Napoleon III and his family. Abbey Church also built for the Empress Eugenie so the monks could act as custodians of the tombs. Initially a Benedictine priory, raised to Abbey status in 1903.
**www.farnboroughabbey.org**
**Grant Recipient:** Empress Eugenie Memorial Trust
**Access contact:** Fr Magnus Wilson
**T:** 01252 894211/546105    **F:** 01252 372822
**E-mail:** abbot@farnboroughabbey.org
**Open:** Daily: 6am–7.30pm. Saturdays and Public Holidays guided tours at 3.30pm. Contact Fr Magnus Wilson, Bursar, or Fr D C Brogan, Abbot, for further information.
**Heritage Open Days:** No.
**P** Spaces: 10
**占** No wheelchair access. No WC for the disabled. No Guide Dogs allowed.
**£** No.

## THE VYNE

**Sherborne St John, Basingstoke, Hampshire RG24 9HL**
Built in the early 16th century for Henry VIII's Lord Chamberlain. The house acquired a classical portico mid 17th century (the first of its kind in England). Tudor chapel with Renaissance glass, Palladian staircase, old panelling and fine furniture. Grounds, containing wild garden, lakes and woodland walks.
**www.nationaltrust.org.uk**
**Grant Recipient:** The National Trust
**Access contact:** The Property Manager
**T:** 01256 883858    **F:** 01256 881720
**E-mail:** thevyne@nationaltrust.org.uk
**Open:** House: 24 March–28 October: daily except Thursday and Friday (but open Good Friday and Bank Holidays) Saturday and Sunday, 11am–5pm; Monday–Wednesday, 1–5pm (11am–1pm pre-booked groups only for guided tours). Grounds: 3 February–18 March, weekends only, 11am–5pm; 24 March–28 October, as house, 11am–5pm.
**Heritage Open Days:** No.
**P** No.
**占** Partial. Wheelchair access to ground floor, stairs to other floors. No WC for the disabled. No Guide Dogs allowed.
**£** Adult: £8.00, £5.00 (grounds only). Child: £4.00, £2.50 (grounds only). Other: £20.00 (family). Free to National Trust members.

## WHITCHURCH SILK MILL

**28 Winchester Street, Whitchurch, Hampshire RG28 7AL**
Grade II* watermill built c1800 and has been in continuous use as a silk weaving mill since the 1820s. Now a working museum, the winding, warping and weaving machinery installed between 1890 and 1927 produces traditional silks for theatrical costume, historic houses, fashion and artworks.
**www.whitchurchsilkmill.org.uk**
**Grant Recipient:** Hampshire Buildings Preservation Trust
**Access contact:** General Manager
**T:** 01256 892065    **F:** 01256 893882
**E-mail:** silkmill@btinternet.com
**Open:** Mill and shop: Tuesday–Sunday, 10.30am–5pm (last admission 4.15pm). Mill and shop closed Mondays (except Bank Holidays) and between Christmas and New Year.
**Heritage Open Days:** Yes
**P** Spaces: 20. Adjacent to Mill and additional parking in the town.
**占** Partial. Wheelchair access to ground floor, shop and gardens. Stairlift to first floor and two steps to tea room. WC for the disabled. Guide Dogs allowed.
**£** Adult: £3.50. Child: £1.75 Other: £3.00, £8.75 (family).

# HEREFORDSHIRE

## CHANDOS MANOR

**Rushall, Ledbury, Herefordshire HR8 2PA**
Farmhouse, probably late 16th century with 18th century extensions. Timber-frame, partly rendered.
**Grant Recipient:** Mr Richard White
**Access contact:** Mr Richard White
**T:** 01531 660208
**Open:** Easter–1 July: Sundays by prior arrangement.
**Heritage Open Days:** No.
**P** Spaces: 12
**占** No wheelchair access. No WC for the disabled. Guide Dogs allowed.
**£** Donations to charity welcome.

## EASTNOR CASTLE

**nr. Ledbury, Herefordshire HR8 1RL**
Norman-style castellated mansion set in the western slopes of the Malvern Hills. Constructed 1812–1820 and designed by Sir Robert Smirke, the castle has 15 state and other rooms fully-furnished and open to visitors. The decoration includes tapestries, paintings, armour and a drawing room by Augustus Pugin.
**www.eastnorcastle.com**
**Grant Recipient:** Mr J Hervey-Bathurst
**Access contact:** Mr S Foster
**T:** 01531 633160    **F:** 01531 631776
**E-mail:** enquiries@eastnorcastle.com
**Open:** Easter–end September: Sundays and Bank Holiday Mondays, 11am–5pm. 17 July–31 August: Sunday–Friday, 11am–5pm.
**Heritage Open Days:** Yes
**P** Spaces: 150

Partial. Wheelchair access to grounds and ground and first floor with assistance (always available). WC for the disabled. Guide Dogs allowed.
**Adult:** £7.00. **Child:** £4.00. **Other:** £6.00 (senior citizens).

## HERGEST COURT

**Kington, Herefordshire HR5 3EG**
House dates back to 1267 and was the ancestral home of the Clanvowe and Vaughan families. It is an unusual example of a fortified manor in the Welsh Marches. It has literary associations with Sir John Clanvowe and Lewis Glyn Cothi.
**Grant Recipient:** Mr W L Banks
**Access contact:** Mr W L Banks
**T:** 01544 230160   **F:** 01544 232031
**E-mail:** gardens@hergest.co.uk
**Open:** By prior arrangement with the Hergest Estate Office, Kington, Herefordshire HR5 3EG. Bookings by phone or fax with five days' notice.
**Heritage Open Days:** No.
Spaces: 5
Partial. Wheelchair access to ground floor only. No WC for the disabled. Guide Dogs allowed.
**Adult:** £5.00. **Child:** Free. **Other:** £3.50 (groups).

## THE PAINTED ROOM

**Town Council Offices, Church Street, Ledbury, Herefordshire HR8 1DH**
The wall paintings, discovered here in 1989, are a unique example of domestic wall painting dating from the Tudor period. They are clearly the work of a commoner, created to imitate the rich tapestries or hangings that would have been found in the homes of the gentry.
**Grant Recipient:** Ledbury Town Council
**Access contact:** Ms T Wildermoth
**T:** 01531 632306   **F:** 01531 631193
**E-mail:** ledburytowncouncil@ledbury.net
**Open:** Easter–end September: guided tours Monday–Friday, 11.00am–1pm and 2–4pm. Mid July–mid September: Sundays, 2–5pm. Rest of year: Monday, Tuesday, Wednesday and Friday, 10am–2pm, if member of staff available. Tours may be arranged out of these hours at a cost of £1.00 per adult (minimum 10 persons). Children's parties are free.
**Heritage Open Days:** Yes
Town centre car parks nearby.
No wheelchair access. Guides are aware of the location of the nearest WC for the disabled. Guide Dogs allowed.
No charge when open normally (£1.00 for adults on out of hours tours) but donations welcome.

## THE WATERWORKS MUSEUM–HEREFORD

**(formerly Broomy Hill Pumping Station), Broomy Hill, Hereford, Herefordshire**
Set in the Victorian water pumping station of Hereford with working pumping engines telling the story of drinking water. Oldest triple-expansion steam engine working in Britain plus beam, gas and diesel engines and overshot waterwheel.
**www.waterworksmuseum.org.uk**
**Grant Recipient:** Herefordshire Waterworks Museum Ltd
**Access contact:** Dr Noel Meeke
**T:** 01600 890 118   **F:** 01600 890 009
**E-mail:** info@waterworksmuseum.org.uk
**Open:** Easter–October: every Tuesday, 11am–4pm. Engines working on second and last Sundays in month. Plus Easter, Spring and August Bank Holidays, 1–4pm.
**Heritage Open Days:** Yes
Spaces: 30. Additional 50 spaces nearby, disabled parking in courtyard. Space for one full size coach.
Full. WC for the disabled. Guide Dogs allowed.
**Adult:** £3.00. **Child:** £1.00. **Other:** £2.00 (senior citizens).

## WILTON CASTLE

**Bridstow, nr. Ross on Wye, Herefordshire HR9 6AD**
12th century castle, partly demolished for 16th century house which in turn became ruinous. A dry moat surrounds restored curtain walls which include three fortified accommodation towers.
**Grant Recipient:** Mr & Mrs A K Parslow
**Access contact:** A K Parslow
**T:** 07836 386317
**Open:** 9 April, 17 June, 19 July and 1 September, 11am–6pm.
**Heritage Open Days:** Yes

---

Spaces: 25
Partial. Wheelchair access to the Towers only. WC for the disabled. Guide Dogs allowed.
**Adult:** £3.50. **Child:** £1.75. **Other:** English Heritage members free.

# HERTFORDSHIRE

## ALL SAINTS PASTORAL CENTRE

**Shenley Lane, London Colney, St Albans, Hertfordshire AL2 1AF**
Grade II* listed building, designed by architect Leonard Stokes. Chapel begun in 1927 by Ninian Comper and finished in 1964 by his son Sebastian Comper.
**www.allsaintspc.org.uk**
**Grant Recipient:** Diocese of Westminster
**Access contact:** Mr Alan Johnstone
**T:** 01727 829306   **F:** 01 727 822 880
**E-mail:** conf.office@allsaintspc.org.uk
**Open:** Daily, 9am–5pm except last week of December.
**Heritage Open Days:** No.
Spaces: 130
Full. WC for the disabled. Guide Dogs allowed.
No.

## BERKHAMSTED TOWN HALL

**196 High Street, Berkhamsted, Hertfordshire HP4 3AP**
Berkhamsted Town Hall and Market House, built in 1859, also housed the Mechanics' Institute. It has a gothic façade and retains much of the original stonework. There are three rooms: the Great Hall, Clock Room, Sessions Hall. In the Great Hall many of the original features have been preserved, including the fireplace and barrel vaulted ceiling.
**www.berkhamstedtownhall.com**
**Grant Recipient:** Berkhamsted Town Hall Trust
**Access contact:** Mrs Angela Smith
**T:** 01442 862288
**E-mail:** bthtmanager@tiscali.co.uk
**Open:** Monday–Friday, 10am–1pm. At other times the Town Hall is let for functions. Additional opening by arrangement with the Town Hall Manager (tel: 01442 862288).
**Heritage Open Days:** Yes
Parking in nearby public car parks.
Full. WC for the disabled. Guide Dogs allowed.
No.

## BRIDGEWATER MONUMENT

**Ashbridge Estate, Aldbury, Hertfordshire HP4 1LT**
The monument was erected in 1832 to commemorate the Duke of Bridgewater. It is the focal point of Ashridge Estate which runs across the borders of Hertfordshire and Buckinghamshire along the main ridge of the Chilterns.
**www.nationaltrust.org.uk**
**Grant Recipient:** The National Trust
**Access contact:** Property Manager
**T:** 01442 851227   **F:** 01442 850000
**E-mail:** ashridge@nationaltrust.org.uk
**Open:** Monument: 17 March–28 October: Saturday, Sunday and Bank Holiday Mondays, 12 noon–5pm. Monday–Friday by prior arrangement, weather permitting. Estate: open all year. Visitor Centre: 17 March–16 December, daily Monday–Friday, 12–5pm. Saturday, Sunday, Bank Holiday Mondays and Good Friday, 12 noon–5pm.
**Heritage Open Days:** No.
Spaces: 100
Partial. Wheelchair access to monument area, monument drive and visitor centre. Map of accessible route available. WC for the disabled. Guide Dogs allowed.
**Adult:** £1.40. **Child:** 70p. **Other:** Free to National Trust and Countryside members.

## CROMER WINDMILL

**Ardeley, Stevenage, Hertfordshire SG2 7QA**
Grade II* postmill dated 1674, last surviving postmill in Hertfordshire. Restored to working order (but not actually working). Houses displays about Hertfordshire's lost windmills, television and video display on the history of Cromer Mill and audio sound effects of a working mill.
**www.hertsmuseums.org.uk**
**Grant Recipient:** Hertfordshire Building Preservation Trust
**Access contact:** Ms Cristina Harrison
**T:** 01279 843301/07949 577760   **F:** 01279 843301

---

**E-mail:** cristinaharrison@btopenworld.com
**Open:** 12 May–9 September, open Saturday before National Mill Day, i.e. second Sunday in May. Thereafter Sundays and Bank Holidays, and second and fourth Saturdays, until Heritage Open Days. 2.30–5pm. 30 minute video available for schools and other groups. Guided tours. Special parties by prior arrangement with Ms Cristina Harrison, The Forge Museum, High Street, Much Hadham, Hertfordshire SG10 6BS. Refreshments available.
**Heritage Open Days:** Yes
Spaces: 20
Partial. No WC for the disabled. Guide Dogs allowed.
**Adult:** £1.50. **Child:** 25p.

## DUCKLAKE HOUSE WALLPAINTING

**Springhead, Ashwell, Baldock, Hertfordshire SG7 5LL**
16th century wall painting, located on the ground floor, containing classical grotesques holding cartouches.
**Grant Recipient:** Mr P W H Saxton
**Access contact:** Mr P W H Saxton
**T:** 01462 742 491
**Open:** January–14 July: by prior written arrangement to view the wall painting only.
**Heritage Open Days:** No.
Spaces: 1
No wheelchair access. No WC for the disabled. No Guide Dogs allowed.
No.

## FOLLY ARCH

**Hawkshead Road, Little Heath, Potters Bar, Hertfordshire EN6 1NN**
Grade II* listed gateway and folly, once the entrance to Gobions estate. Circa 1740 for Sir Jeremy Sambrooke, probably by James Gibbs. Red brick with large round-headed arch and thin square turrets.
**Grant Recipient:** Mr RJ Nicholas
**Access contact:** Mr and Mrs Nicholas
**T:** 01707 663553
**E-mail:** robnic@mac.com
**Open:** The Arch is on the boundary between public open space and a private garden and can be viewed from public ground at any time.
**Heritage Open Days:** No.
On-street parking.
Full. No WC for the disabled. Guide Dogs allowed.
No.

## KNEBWORTH HOUSE

**Knebworth, nr. Stevenage, Hertfordshire SG3 6PY**
Originally a Tudor manor house, rebuilt in gothic style in 1843. Contains rooms in various styles, which include a Jacobean banqueting hall. Set in 250 acres of parkland with 25 acres of formal gardens. Home of the Lytton family since 1490.
**www.knebworthhouse.com**
**Grant Recipient:** Knebworth House Education & Preservation Trust
**Access contact:** Mrs Christine Smith
**T:** 01438 812661   **F:** 01438 811908
**E-mail:** info@knebworthhouse.com
**Open:** Daily: 31 March–15 April, 26 May–3 June, 30 June–5 September. Weekends and Bank Holidays: 24–25 March, 21 April–20 May, 9–24 June, 8–30 September. Gardens, Park and Playground: 11.00am–5.30pm. House: 12 noon- 5.00pm (last admission 4.15pm).
**Heritage Open Days:** No.
Spaces: 75. 50–75 parking spaces on gravel, unlimited space on grass.
Partial. Wheelchair access to ground floor of House only. Gravel paths around gardens and House but level route from car park to House entrance. WC for the disabled. Guide Dogs allowed.
**Adult:** £9.00 (£8.00 group). **Child:** £8.50 (£7.50 group). **Other:** £8.50 (senior citizens, £7.50 group).

## THE OLD CHURCH TOWER OF ALL SAINTS

**Chapel Lane, Long Marston, Hertfordshire HP23 4QT**
Grade II* listed 15th century tower set in small churchyard with ancient yew trees. The only remnant of a Chapel of Ease dating back to the 12th century, the rest of the church was demolished in 1883.
**Grant Recipient:** Tring PCC Tower Conservation
**Access contact:** Dr Noakes

**T:** 01296 660 072
**Open:** Exterior (churchyard) open at all times. Interior by prior arrangement and under supervision only.
**Heritage Open Days:** No.
**P** Parking in nearby village, 200 metre walk.
**&** Partial. Wheelchair access to churchyard only. No WC for the disabled. Guide Dogs allowed.
**£** No.

### THE OLD CLOCKHOUSE

**Cappell Lane, Stanstead Abbots, Hertfordshire SG12 8BU**
Grammar school, now private residence, c1636 also used for Sunday services in 17th century.
**Grant Recipient:** Mr Michael Hannon
**Access contact:** Mr Michael Hannon
**T:** 01920 871495
**Open:** Access to exterior at all times; Bell Tower can only be viewed from High Street.
**Heritage Open Days:** No.
**P** Public car park in Stansted Abbots High Street.
**&** No wheelchair access. No WC for the disabled. No Guide Dogs allowed.
**£** No.

### TORILLA

**11 Wilkins Green Lane, Nast Hyde, Hatfield, Hertfordshire AL10 9RT**
'Torilla' (house at Nast Hyde) was built by F R S Yorke in 1935 in the international style and features a flat roof, 2 balconies and a large double height living room. Constructed of concrete with large steel framed windows. F R S Yorke was a key figure in the evolution of modern architecture in Britain.
**Grant Recipient:** Mr Alan Charlton
**Access contact:** Mr Alan Charlton
**T:** 01707 259582
**Open:** By prior arrangement (written or telephone), 11am–5pm on Sunday 13 May and Sunday 12 August. At other times by prior written arrangement.
**Heritage Open Days:** No.
**P** Spaces: 5
**&** Partial. Wheelchair access to ground floor only. No WC for the disabled. Guide Dogs allowed.
**£** No.

### WOODHALL PARK

**Watton-at-Stone, Hertfordshire SG14 3NF**
Country house, now school. Designed and built by Thomas Leverton in 1785 in neo-Classical style. Normally associated with London houses, this is one of his few country houses. Highly decorated interiors which include the Print Room with walls covered in engraved paper, reproductions of paintings with frames, ribbons, chains, busts, candelabra and piers with vases.
**Grant Recipient:** The Trustees of R M Abel Smith 1991 Settlement
**Access contact:** The Trustees of R M Abel Smith 1991 Settlement
**T:** 01920 830286   **F:** 01920 830162
**E-mail:** rmas@woodhallestate.co.uk
**Open:** At all reasonable times, preferably school holidays, by prior arrangement with the Trustees.
**Heritage Open Days:** No.
**P** Spaces: 30. Parking limited to 10 spaces during school terms.
**&** Partial. Wheelchair access to ground floor only. No WC for the disabled. Guide Dogs allowed.
**£** No.

## KENT

### ALL SAINTS REDUNDANT CHURCH

**Waldershare, Dover, Kent**
Redundant Norman church with later chapels containing examples of classical funerary monuments, Victorian murals and stained glass. Still a consecrated building although not used for regular worship.
**www.visitchurches.org.uk**
**Grant Recipient:** Diocese of Canterbury
**Access contact:** Wendy Drummer
**T:** 07958 409336
**E-mail:** jvigar@tcct.org.uk
**Open:** All year: daily, 10.30am–3.30pm.
**Heritage Open Days:** No.
**P** Spaces: 4
**&** Partial. Assistance needed at lychgate, thereafter

church is accessible. No WC for the disabled. Guide Dogs allowed.
**£** No.

### AYLESFORD PRIORY

**The Friars, Aylesford, Kent ME20 7BX**
Home of a community of Carmelite Friars and a popular centre of pilgrimage. Chapels contain modern religious art created by Adam Kossowski and other notable artists.
**www.thefriars.org.uk**
**Grant Recipient:** The Carmelite Friars
**Access contact:** Father Prior
**T:** 01622 717272   **F:** 01622 715575
**E-mail:** jkemsley@carmelnet.org
**Open:** At all times.
**Heritage Open Days:** Yes
**P** Spaces: 1500
**&** Full. WC for the disabled. Guide Dogs allowed.
**£** No.

### BARN AT HOWBURY FARM

**Moat Lane, Slade Green, Kent DA8 2NE**
Tithe barn, 17th century or earlier. In agricultural use. Situated in an urban area of Bexley.
**Grant Recipient:** Trustees of The Russell Stoneham Estate
**Access contact:** Mr C Stoneham
**T:** 01322 333111   **F:** 01322 330347
**E-mail:** russellstoneham@aol.com
**Open:** By prior arrangement throughout the year, plus London Open House weekend.
**London Open House:** Yes
**P** Spaces: 10
**&** Full. No WC for the disabled. Guide Dogs allowed.
**£** No.

### CHURCH HOUSE

**72 High Street, Edenbridge, Kent TN8 5AR**
Late 14th century timber-framed farmhouse. Tudor additions include fireplace and 18th century brick frontage. Now houses the Eden Valley Museum which illustrates economic and social changes during the 14th to 20th centuries.
**www.evmt.org.uk**
**Grant Recipient:** Edenbridge Town Council
**Access contact:** Mrs Jane Higgs
**T:** 01732 868102   **F:** 01732 867866
**E-mail:** curator@evmt.org.uk
**Open:** February–December (until Christmas): Wednesday and Friday, 2–4.30pm, Thursday and Saturday, 10am–4.30pm. April–September: Sundays, 2–4.30pm. Closed Good Friday and Easter Sunday.
**Heritage Open Days:** Yes
**P** Spaces: 150. Free parking in town centre car park, 200 yards from House.
**&** Partial. Wheelchair access to ground floor only (visual computer link to upstairs). WC for the disabled. Guide Dogs allowed.
**£** No. **Other:** Except for out of hours pre-arranged visits.

### COBHAM HALL AND DAIRY

**Cobham, Kent DA12 3BL**
Gothic-style dairy in grounds of Cobham Hall, built by James Wyatt c1790.
**www.cobhamhall.com**
**Grant Recipient:** Cobham Hall Heritage Trust
**Access contact:** Mr N G Powell
**T:** 01474 823371   **F:** 01474 825904
**E-mail:** enquiries@cobhamhall.com
**Open:** Easter–July / August: Hall open Wednesday and Sunday, 2–5pm (last tour 4.30pm). Please telephone to confirm opening times. At other times (and coach parties) by prior arrangement. Self-guided tour of Gardens and Parkland (historical/conservation tour by prior arrangement).
**Heritage Open Days:** No.
**P** Spaces: 100
**&** Partial. Wheelchair access to ground floor, manual assistance required for first floor access. WC for the disabled. Guide Dogs allowed.
**£** Adult: £4.50. Child: £3.50. Other: £3.50 (senior citizens & groups).

### CRABBLE CORN MILL

**Lower Road, River, nr. Dover, Kent CT17 0UY**
Georgian watermill with millpond, cottages and gardens. Guided and non-guided tours and demonstrations of milling techniques. Flour produced and sold on site.

Cafeteria and art gallery. Available for group tours, functions and events.
**www.ccmt.org.uk**
**Grant Recipient:** Crabble Corn Mill Trust
**Access contact:** Mr Anthony Skaveley
**T:** 01304 823292   **F:** 01304 823292
**E-mail:** info@crabblecornmill.org.uk
**Open:** February–April: Weekends, 11am–5pm. April–September: Tuesday–Sunday, 11am–5pm. October–December: Weekends. Open to group visits all year round by prior arrangement (contact Alan Davis, Tony Staveley, Anne Collins or Anthony Reid, tel: 01304 823292).
**Heritage Open Days:** No.
**P** Spaces: 32. Parking in recreation ground opposite site.
**&** Partial. Wheelchair access to ground and first floor, art gallery, cafeteria and milling floor. No WC for the disabled. Guide Dogs allowed.
**£** Adult: £4.00 (mill tour). Child: £3.00 (age 5-15, mill tour). Other: £3.00 (seniors & students, mill tour), £9.00 (family, mill tour).

### DOVER TOWN HALL

**Biggin Street, Dover, Kent CT16 1DL**
The Town Hall incorporates the remains of a medieval hospital, 14th century chapel tower, 19th century prison, town hall and assembly rooms. The Maison Dieu Hall of c1325 was originally part of a hospital founded by Hubert de Burgh in the early 13th century. The Town Hall designed by Victorian Gothic architect William Burges was built in 1881 on the site of the hospital.
**Grant Recipient:** Dover District Council
**Access contact:** Mr Steve Davis
**T:** 01843 296111 (Admin)
**E-mail:** dover@leisureforce.co.uk
**Open:** Normally open during the week for functions and other bookings. Open on Wednesdays throughout the year. Guided tours can be arranged.
**Heritage Open Days:** No.
**P** Parking at the rear of the building.
**&** Full. WC for the disabled. Guide Dogs allowed.
**£** No.

### HERNE WINDMILL

**Mill Lane, Herne Bay, Kent CT6 7DR**
Kentish smock mill built 1789, worked by wind until 1952 and then by electricity until 1980. Bought by Kent County Council in 1985, which carried out some restoration. Now managed by Friends of Herne Mill on behalf of the County Council. Much of the original machinery is in place, some is run for demonstration and the sails used when the wind conditions permit.
**www.kentwindmills.co.uk**
**Grant Recipient:** Kent County Council
**Access contact:** Mr Ken Cole
**T:** 01227 361326
**Open:** Easter–end September: Sunday and Bank Holidays, plus Thursdays in August, 2–5pm. National Mills Weekend, Saturday and Sunday, 2–5pm. For further information contact Ken Cole, Secretary, Friends of Herne Mill (tel: 01227 361326) or John Fishpool (Chairman, tel: 01227 366863).
**Heritage Open Days:** Yes
**P** Spaces: 6. Six parking spaces in Mill grounds. Free on-street parking (Windmill Road).
**&** Partial. Wheelchair and guide dog access to ground floor of Mill and meeting room. WC for the disabled. Guide Dogs allowed.
**£** Adult: £1.00. Child: 25p (accompanied by an adult).

### IGHTHAM MOTE

**Ivy Hatch, Sevenoaks, Kent TN15 0NT**
Moated manor house covering nearly 700 years of history from medieval times to 1960s. Extended visitor route now includes the refurbished north-west quarter with Tudor Chapel, Billiards Room and Drawing Room, South West Quarter and apartments of Charles Henry Robinson, the American donor of Ightham Mote to the National Trust. Interpretation displays and special exhibition featuring conservation in action.
**www.nationaltrust.org.uk/ightammote**
**Grant Recipient:** The National Trust
**Access contact:** Property Manager
**T:** 01732 810378   **F:** 01732 811 029
**E-mail:** ighthammote@nationaltrust.org.uk
**Open:** 4 March–28 October, daily except Tuesday and Saturday. House, 10.30am–5.30pm; Garden, 10.00am–5.30pm. Estate open all year Dawn–Dusk.

**Heritage Open Days:** Yes
P Spaces: 420
Partial. Wheelchair access to ground floor with assistance and part of the exterior only. WC for the disabled. Guide Dogs allowed.
£ **Adult:** £9.50. **Child:** £4.75. **Other:** £23.75 (family), £7.50 (groups).

## PENSHURST PLACE PARK

**Tonbridge, Kent TN11 8DG**
Open parkland, formerly a medieval deer park, circa 80 hectares. Scattered mature trees, lake with a small island and Lime Avenue originally planted in 1730s.
**www.penshurstplace.com**
**Grant Recipient:** Lord De L'Isle
**Access contact:** Mr Ian R Scott
**T:** 01892 870307 **F:** 01892 870866
**E-mail:** ianscott@penshurstplace.com
**Open:** Footpaths through parkland open 365 days a year.
**Heritage Open Days:** No.
P Spaces: 50
No wheelchair access. No WC for the disabled. Guide Dogs allowed.
£ No.

## PROVENDER

**Provender Lane, Faversham, Swale, Kent ME13 0ST**
A grade II* listed timber framed country house dating from 14th century with later additions. The north east range has been restored. Further restoration work is in progress.
**Grant Recipient:** Princess Olga Romanoff
**Access contact:** Princess Olga Romanoff
**T:** 01795 521300
**Open:** Due to open from end of July although, restoration work will restrict access, please check the English Heritage website or with the access contact for opening arrangements.
**Heritage Open Days:** No.
P Spaces: 7
Partial. Wheelchair access to the entrance hall, dining room, and ground floor of north east range. No WC for the disabled. No Guide Dogs allowed.
£ **Adult:** Will depend on extent of completed restoration work, but will be in the order of £6.50. **Child:** £2.50. **Other:** £3.50.

## THE ARCHBISHOPS' PALACE

**Mill Street, Maidstone, Kent ME15 6YE**
14th century Palace built by the Archbishops of Canterbury. Much altered and extended over the centuries, the interior contains 16th century panelling and fine wood or stone fireplaces. Now used as Kent County Council's Register Office.
**www.tour-maidstone.com**
**Grant Recipient:** Mr John Williams, Maidstone Borough Council
**Access contact:** Mr Christopher Finch
**T:** 01622 602720 **F:** 01622 602586
**E-mail:** christopherfinch@maidstone.gov.uk
**Open:** Throughout the year for weddings and at other times by prior arrangement with the Registrar.
**Heritage Open Days:** Yes
P Spaces: 100. Public parking in town centre car parks (pay and display).
Partial. Wheelchair access to ground floor via lift. WC for the disabled. Guide Dogs allowed.
£ No.

## THE GRANGE

**St Augustine's Road, Ramsgate, Kent CT11 9PA**
The Grange is a Grade I listed building that was designed and lived in by Augustus Pugin, an influential 19th century architect. The building fell into a state of severe disrepair in the 1990s and was acquired and restored by the Landmark Trust.
**Grant Recipient:** The Landmark Trust
**Access contact:** Mrs Victoria O'Keeffe
**T:** 01628 825920 **F:** 01628 825417
**E-mail:** vokeeffe@landmarktrust.org.uk
**Open:** The Landmark Trust is an independent charity, which rescues small buildings of historic or architectural importance from decay or unsympathetic improvement. Landmark's aim is to promote the enjoyment of these historic buildings by making them available to stay in for holidays. [Name of property] can be rented by anyone, at all times of the year, for periods ranging from a weekend to three weeks. Bookings can be made by telephoning the Booking Office on 01628 825925. As the building is in full-time use for holiday accommodation, it is not normally open to the public. However, the public view the building by prior arrangement by telephoning the access contact (Victoria O'Keeffe on 01628 825920) to make an appointment. Potential visitors will be asked to write to confirm the details of their visit. In addition, the main rooms will be open every Wednesday afternoon by appointment. There is a small exhibition in the Cartoon Room (a separate building next to The Grange) which provides information about the building, its history and the Pugin family. Open on Wednesday afternoons (2–4pm), on Open Days and by appointment.
**Heritage Open Days:** Yes
P Parking on Royal Esplanade nearby.
Partial. Wheelchair access to ground floor. WC for the disabled. Guide Dogs allowed.
£ No.

# LANCASHIRE

## BROWSHOLME HALL

**nr. Clitheroe, Lancashire BB7 3DE**
Browsholme Hall, pronounced 'Brewsom', was built in 1507 and the ancestral home of the Parker Family who have lived there since it was built. Listed Grade I. The house contains a collection of oak furniture, portraits and stained glass.
**www.browsholme.co.uk**
**Grant Recipient:** Mr R R Parker
**Access contact:** Mr Robert Redmayne Parker
**T:** 01254 826719
**E-mail:** rrp@browsholme.co.uk
**Open:** 9 April, 20 May and 26–28 May; 30 June–6 July (except Mondays); 11–31 August (except Mondays, but including Bank Holiday Monday), 2–5pm.
**Heritage Open Days:** No.
P Spaces: 30
Partial. Wheelchair access to ground floor. WC for disabled. Guide Dogs allowed.
£ **Adult:** £5.00 (provisional). **Child:** £1.00 (provisional). **Other:** £4.50 (senior citizens & groups), £2.50 (grounds only).

## GAWTHORPE HALL

**Padiham, nr. Burnley, Lancashire BB12 8UA**
An Elizabethan property in the heart of industrial Lancashire. Restored and refurbished in the mid 19th century by Sir Charles Barry. There are many notable paintings on display loaned to the National Trust by the National Portrait Gallery, and a collection of needlework, assembled by the last family member to live there, Rachel Kay-Shuttleworth.
**www.nationaltrust.org.uk**
**Grant Recipient:** The National Trust
**Access contact:** Property Manager
**T:** 01282 771004 **F:** 01282 770178
**E-mail:** gawthorpehall@nationaltrust.org.uk
**Open:** Hall: 1 April–29 October, daily except Monday and Friday (but open Good Friday and Bank Holiday Mondays), 1–5pm. Garden: all year, 10am–6pm.
**Heritage Open Days:** No.
P Spaces: 50
Partial. Wheelchair access to garden only. WC for the disabled. Guide Dogs allowed.
£ **Adult:** £4.00 (provisional). **Child:** Free when accompanied by an adult. **Other:** £1.50 (concessions), garden free (provisional).

## GRAND THEATRE

**33 Church Street, Blackpool, Lancashire FY1 1HT**
Grade II* 1200-seat theatre designed by Frank Matcham, 1894. Major restoration ongoing.
**www.blackpoolgrand.co.uk**
**Grant Recipient:** Blackpool Grand Theatre Trust Ltd
**Access contact:** Mr David Fletcher
**T:** 01253 290111 **F:** 01253 751767
**E-mail:** geninfo@blackpoolgrand.co.uk
**Open:** Daily. Tours take place on a semi-regular basis. Shows in the auditorium once or twice a day. Contact David Fletcher (tel: 01253 290111) for more information.
**Heritage Open Days:** Yes
P Spaces: 200. Parking in West Street car park (2 minute walk).

Partial. Wheelchair access to stalls and bar. WC for the disabled. Guide Dogs allowed.
£ **Adult:** £5.00 (guided tour). **Child:** £3.50. **Other:** Charges made for performances. Free on open days.

## INDIA MILL CHIMNEY

**Bolton Road, Darwen, Blackburn, Lancashire BB3 1AE**
Chimney, 1867, built as part of cotton spinning mill. Brick with ashlar base. Square section, 300 feet high, in the style of an Italian campanile. Rests on foundation stone said to have been the largest single block quarried since Cleopatra's Needle. Listed Grade II*.
**www.indiamill.com**
**Grant Recipient:** Brookhouse Managed Properties Ltd
**Access contact:** Ms Pamela Blackwell
**T:** 01254 777 788 **F:** 01254 777 799
**E-mail:** pam.blackwell@indiamill.com
**Open:** Chimney visible from public highway (no interior access).
**Heritage Open Days:** No.
P On-street parking.
Full. No WC for the disabled. Guide Dogs allowed.
£ No.

## LATHOM HOUSE

**Lathom, Lancashire L40 5UQ**
Grade II* listed wing of former country house built c1730 with an addition of c1862. Various outbuildings arranged around a double courtyard to the rear.
**Grant Recipient:** TRU Ltd
**Access contact:** Mr Arthur Edwardson
**T:** 01942 707 000 **F:** 01942 707 030
**E-mail:** truerehab@aol.com
**Open:** By prior arrangement to the exterior (subject to building work).
**Heritage Open Days:** No.
P Spaces: 2
No wheelchair access. No WC for the disabled. Guide Dogs allowed.
£ No.

## LEIGHTON HALL

**Carnforth, Lancashire LA5 9ST**
Country House, 1765, probably by Richard Gillow, with earlier remains. Gothic south-east front early 19th century, possibly by Thomas Harrison. Tower at west end of the façade 1870 by Paley and Austin. Ancestral home of the Gillow family with fine furniture, paintings and objects d'art.
**www.leightonhall.co.uk**
**Grant Recipient:** Mr Richard Reynolds
**Access contact:** Richard Reynolds
**T:** 01524 734474 **F:** 01524 720357
**E-mail:** leightonhall@yahoo.co.uk
**Open:** May–September: Tuesday–Friday (also Bank Holiday Sundays and Mondays), 2–5pm. August only: Tuesday–Friday and Sunday (also Bank Holiday Monday), 12.30–5pm. Groups of 25+ all year by prior arrangement. The owner reserves the right to close or restrict access to the Hall and grounds for special events (please see our website for up to date information).
**Heritage Open Days:** No.
P Spaces: 100
Partial. Wheelchair access to ground floor, shop and tea rooms. WC for the disabled. Guide Dogs allowed.
£ **Adult:** £6.00. **Child:** £4.00 (age 5-12). **Other:** £5.00 (senior citizen/student), £18.00 (family), £4.50 (adult group of 25+), £3.50 (child group).

## QUEEN STREET MILL

**Harle Syke, Burnley, Lancashire BB10 2HX**
Built in 1894, containing much of its original 19th century equipment including over 300 Lancashire looms and steam engine.
**www.lancsmuseums.gov.uk**
**Grant Recipient:** Lancashire County Council
**Access contact:** Ms Catherine Pearson, Acting Assistant Keeper
**T:** 01282 412555 **F:** 01282 430220
**E-mail:** queenstreet.mill@mus.lancscc.gov.uk
**Open:** March and November: Tuesday–Thursday, 12–4pm. April and October: Tuesday–Friday, 12–5pm. May–September: Tuesday–Saturday, 12–5pm. Open Sunday and Mondays on bank holiday weekends only. Closed December, January and February.
**Heritage Open Days:** Yes

**P** Spaces: 40. Free parking.
**&** Full. WC for the disabled. Guide Dogs allowed.
**£** Adult: £3.00. Child: Free if accompanied. **Other:**
£2.00 (concessions).

## SAMLESBURY HALL

**Preston New Road, Samlesbury, Preston,**
**Lancashire PR5 0UP**
Built in 1325, the hall is an attractive black and white
timbered manor house set in extensive grounds.
Independently owned and administered since 1925 by The
Samlesbury Hall Trust whose primary aim is to maintain
and preserve the property for the enjoyment and pleasure
of the public. Currently open to the public as an
antiques/craft centre.
**www.samlesburyhall.co.uk**
**Grant Recipient:** Samlesbury Hall Trust
**Access contact:** Ms Sharon Jones
**T:** 01254 812010/01254 812229  **F:** 01254 812174
**E-mail:** samlesburyhall@btconnect.com
**Open:** Daily except Saturdays, 11am–4.30pm. Open Bank
Holidays. For Christmas closing times please contact the
Hall.
**Heritage Open Days:** No.
**P** Spaces: 70. Additional parking for 100 cars in overflow
car park.
**&** Partial. Wheelchair access to ground floor of historical
part of Hall. WC for the disabled. Guide Dogs allowed.
**£** Adult: £3.00. Child: £1.00 (ages 4-16).

## STONYHURST COLLEGE

**Stonyhurst, Clitheroe, Lancashire BB7 9PZ**
16th century manor house, now home to a Catholic
independent co-educational boarding and day school.
Contains dormitories, library, chapels, school-rooms and
historical apartments.
**www.stonyhurst.ac.uk**
**Grant Recipient:** Stonyhurst College
**Access contact:** Miss Frances Ahearne
**T:** 01254 826345  **F:** 01254 827040
**E-mail:** domestic-bursar@stonyhurst.ac.uk
**Open:** House: 23 July–27 August daily (except Friday), plus
August Bank Holiday Monday, 1–5pm. Gardens: 1 July–27
August daily (except Friday), plus August Bank Holiday
Monday, 1–5pm. Coach parties by prior arrangement.
**Heritage Open Days:** No.
**P** Spaces: 200
**&** Partial. WC for the disabled. Guide Dogs allowed.
**£** Adult: £6.00. Child: £5.00. **Other:** £5.00.

## TODMORDEN UNITARIAN CHURCH

**Honey Hole Road, Todmorden, Lancashire OL14 6LE**
Grade I church with a large wooded burial ground and
ornamental gardens designed by John Gibson, 1865-69.
Victorian Gothic style with tall tower and spire. Detached
smaller burial ground nearby and listed lodge in
churchyard. Lavish interior with highly decorated fittings
and furnishings. One of the most elaborate Non
conformist churches of the High Gothic Revival.
**www.hct.org.uk**
**Grant Recipient:** Historic Chapels Trust
**Access contact:** Mr Rob Goldthorpe
**T:** 01706 815648
**E-mail:** rob.goldthorpe@btinternet.com
**Open:** At all reasonable times by application to the
keyholder, Mr Rob Goldthorpe, 14 Honey Hole Close,
Todmorden, Lancashire OL14 6LH or by calling at the
caretaker's house, Todmorden Lodge, at the entrance to
the churchyard.
**Heritage Open Days:** Yes
**P** Spaces: 10. Parking in local industrial estate is possible
out of hours.
**&** Full. WC for the disabled. Guide Dogs allowed.
**£** Donations invited.

## LEICESTERSHIRE

### 7 KING STREET

**Melton Mowbray, Leicestershire  LE13 1XA**
Dating from 1330, this is the oldest secular building in
Melton Mowbray. The building has Medieval roof timbers,
a 16th century timber-framed extension and has been
modified and gentrified through the centuries. Listed
Grade II*, the building was at risk for many years.
Restoration by Melton Mowbray Borough Council was
completed in 2004 and is the Council's Tourist Information

Centre.
**Grant Recipient:** Mellton Borough Council
**Access contact:** Mr Richard Spooner MA IHBC
**T:** 01664 502387  **F:** 01664 410283
**E-mail:** rspooner@melton.gov.uk
**Open:** Monday–Saturday (hours to be determined). Access
to the upper floors by prior arrangement.
**Heritage Open Days:** No.
**P** Public car park adjacent (Pay and Display).
**&** Partial. Wheelchair access to ground floor rooms. WC
for the disabled. Guide Dogs allowed.
**£** No.

### REARSBY PACKHORSE BRIDGE

**Rearsby, Leicestershire LE7 4YE**
Low narrow medieval bridge, perhaps 16th century,
comprising seven arches of random granite masonry and
brick coping. On the upstream side there are four
cutwaters, three of granite and one of brick. The bridge
has recently been restored.
**Grant Recipient:** Leicestershire County Council
**Access contact:** Mr C Waterfield
**T:** 0116 265 7167  **F:** 0116 265 7135
**E-mail:** cwaterfield@leics.gov.uk
**Open:** Always: in use as a public highway.
**Heritage Open Days:** No.
**P** Street parking.
**&** Full. No WC for the disabled. Guide Dogs allowed.
**£** No.

### TOMB OF ANDREW LORD ROLLO

**St Margaret's Church, Canning Place, Leicester**
Grade II* listed tomb of 1765. Each face has a large
rectangular plaque with ornate carved pilaster panels. The
west front has a long inscription on the slate plaque
recording the life and exploits of Andrew Lord Rollo, who
died in 1765. The remaining three fronts each have a
shallow carved relief of Lord Rollo's arms and military
trophies.
**Grant Recipient:** The Abbey Parish PCC
**Access contact:** Mr Jack Adams
**T:** 0116 2897432
**Open:** The churchyard is open at all times.
**Heritage Open Days:** No.
**P** Spaces: 3. Additional street parking adjacent.
**&** Full. No WC for the disabled. Guide Dogs allowed.
**£** No.

## LINCOLNSHIRE

### 13/13A MINSTER YARD

**Lincoln, Lincolnshire LN2 1PW**
Houses, mid-18th century, with late 18th and 19th century
alterations.
**Grant Recipient:** Dean & Chapter of Lincoln Cathedral
**Access contact:** Mrs Carol Heidschuster
**T:** 01522 527637  **F:** 01522 575 688
**E-mail:** worksmanager@lincolncathedral.com
**Open:** January–15 May: by prior written arrangement with
the Works Manager, Lincoln Cathedral, 28 Eastgate,
Lincoln LN2 4AA.
**Heritage Open Days:** No.
**P** No.
**&** No wheelchair access. No WC for the disabled. Guide
Dogs allowed.
**£** No.

### ARABELLA AUFRERE TEMPLE

**Brocklesby Park, Grimsby, Lincolnshire DN41 8PN**
Garden Temple of ashlar and red brick with coupled doric
columns on either side of a central arch leading to a rear
chamber. Built c1787 and attributed to James Wyatt.
Inscription above inner door: "Dedicated by veneration
and affection to the memory of Arabella Aufrere."
**Grant Recipient:** The Earl of Yarborough
**Access contact:** Mr H A Rayment
**T:** 01469 560214  **F:** 01469 561346
**E-mail:** office@brocklesby-estate.co.uk
**Open:** 1 April–31 August: viewable from permissive paths
through Mausoleum Woods at all reasonable times.
**Heritage Open Days:** No.
**P** Spaces: 10. Free parking in village or walks car park, ¼
mile from site.
**&** No wheelchair access. No WC for the disabled. Guide
Dogs allowed.
**£** No.

## BROCKLESBY MAUSOLEUM

**Brocklesby Park, Grimsby, Lincolnshire DN41 8PN**
Family Mausoleum designed by James Wyatt and built
between 1787 and 1794 by Charles Anderson Pelham,
who subsequently became Lord Yarborough, as a
memorial to his wife Sophia who died at the age of 33.
The classical design is based on the Temples of Vesta at
Rome and Tivoli.
**Grant Recipient:** The Earl of Yarborough
**Access contact:** Mr H A Rayment
**T:** 01469 560214  **F:** 01469 561346
**E-mail:** office@brocklesby-estate.co.uk
**Open:** Exterior: 1 April–31 August: viewable from
permissive paths through Mausoleum Woods at all
reasonable times. Interior (excluding private crypt) by prior
arrangement with the Estate Office. Admission charge for
interior.
**Heritage Open Days:** No.
**P** Spaces: 10. Free parking in village or walks car park, ¼
mile from site.
**&** No wheelchair access. No WC for the disabled. No
Guide Dogs allowed.
**£** Adult: £2.00 (charge for interior). Child: £2.00 (charge
for interior). **Other:** £2.00 (charge for interior).

## BURGHLEY HOUSE

**Stamford, Lincolnshire PE9 3JY**
Large country house built by William Cecil, Lord High
Treasurer of England, between 1555 and 1587, and still
lived in by descendants of his family. Eighteen State
Rooms, many decorated by Antonio Verrio in the 17th
century, housing a collection of artworks including 17th
century Italian paintings, Japanese ceramics, European
porcelain and wood carvings by Grinling Gibbons and his
followers. There are also four State Beds, English and
continental furniture, and tapestries and textiles.
'Capability' Brown parkland.
**www.burghley.co.uk**
**Grant Recipient:** Burghley House Preservation Trust Ltd
**Access contact:** Mr Philip Gompertz
**T:** 01780 761 974  **F:** 01780 480125
**E-mail:** philip.gompertz@burghley.co.uk
**Open:** 31 March–28 October: daily (except  Fridays and 2
September), 11am–4.30pm. Guided tours available at
certain times.
**Heritage Open Days:** No.
**P** Spaces: 500. Parking for the disabled available close to
visitors' entrance.
**&** Full. Please telephone the Property Manager for
information on wheelchair access. WC for the disabled.
Guide Dogs allowed.
**£** Adult: £9.00. Child: £4.00. **Other:** £8.00 (senior
citizens & students), £7.80 (per person for groups 20+),
£22.00 (family).

## FYDELL HOUSE GATES, PIERS AND RAILINGS

**South Street, Boston, Lincolnshire PE21 6HU**
Fronted by renewed, grant-aided gate, gate piers and
railings, Fydell House was built in 1726 with minor 19th
century alterations. Example of a small 18th century stately
home. It contains links between Boston England and
Boston Mass and houses the Fydell House Centre Ltd, a
provider of educational and cultural facilities.
**Grant Recipient:** Boston Preservation Trust Ltd
**Access contact:** Mr Ronald Ernest Coley
**T:** 01205 351520
**Open:** Access to the exterior at all reasonable times. Open
throughout the year (except Bank Holidays) but in term-
time access to rooms is limited.
**Heritage Open Days:** No.
**P** Public car park nearby.
**&** Full. WC for the disabled. Guide Dogs allowed.
**£** No.

## HARDING HOUSE

**48-54 Steep Hill, Lincoln, Lincolnshire LN2**
Grade II listed house of the 16th century, remodelled in
the 18th and restored in the 20th. Built of coursed rubble
and brick with a pantile roof. The building is divided up
into several studios predominantly used for a variety of
craft uses.
**Grant Recipient:** Lincoln City Council
**Access contact:** Mr Mark Wheater
**T:** 01522 873464  **F:** 01522 542589
**E-mail:** mark.wheater@lincoln.gov.uk
**Open:** During normal shop opening hours.
**Heritage Open Days:** No.

P No.

🦽 No wheelchair access. No WC for the disabled. Guide Dogs allowed.

£ No.

## HARLAXTON MANOR RAILWAY TUNNEL

**Harlaxton, Grantham, Lincolnshire NG32 1AG**

Curved brick viaduct with buttresses and slate roof containing a narrow gauge railway for supplying the service courtyard of Harlaxton Manor. The entrance vestibule has at the north end two 3-bay arcades with heavily rusticated round arches adorned with enormous ashlar trophies. Constructed between 1838-1844. The Elizabethan, Revival style Manor is now a university.

**www.ueharlax.ac.uk**

**Grant Recipient:** University of Evansville-Harlaxton College

**Access contact:** Mr Ian Welsh

**T:** 01476 403000    **F:** 01476 403030

**E-mail:** iwelsh@ueharlax.ac.uk

**Open:** Guided tours (for approx. 20 plus) by prior arrangement. 12 August, 11am–5pm open house.

**Heritage Open Days:** Yes

P Spaces: 150

🦽 Full. WC for the disabled. Guide Dogs allowed.

£ **Adult:** £5.50. **Child:** £2.25. **Other:** £4.50 (concessions), £8.00 (guided tours, including refreshments).

## HEGGY'S COTTAGE

**Hall Road, Haconby, nr. Bourne, Lincolnshire PE10 0UY**

Built c1500 of mud and stud construction, a good example of early conversion to two storeys. Restored to its original state in 1995.

**Grant Recipient:** J E Atkinson & Son

**Access contact:** Mrs J F Atkinson

**T:** 01778 570790

**Open:** By prior written arrangement with Mrs J F Atkinson, Haconby Hall, nr. Bourne, Lincolnshire PE10 0UY.

**Heritage Open Days:** No.

P Spaces: 1

🦽 No wheelchair access. No WC for the disabled. No Guide Dogs allowed.

£ No.

## JEWS COURT

**(the Society for Lincolnshire History & Archaeology), 2/3 Steep Hill, Lincoln, Lincolnshire LN2 1LS**

Grade I two storey stone building, c12th century, with cellar and attic. Traditionally the medieval synagogue. Now used by the Society for Lincolnshire History & Archaeology and for worship.

**www.lincolnshirepast.org.uk**

**Grant Recipient:** Jews' Court Trust

**Access contact:** Ms Pearl Wheatley

**T:** 01522 521337    **F:** 01522 521337

**E-mail:** slha@lincolnshirepast.org.uk

**Open:** Daily except Sundays, 10am–4pm. Also closed over the Christmas period.

**Heritage Open Days:** No.

P Ample public parking within 300 yards.

🦽 Access for wheelchairs is not possible. Electric stair-lift is available for access to first floor. Several days notice is required as two trained staff members need to be in attendance. No WC for the disabled. Guide Dogs allowed.

£ No.

## KYME TOWER

**Manor Farm, South Kyme, Lincoln, Lincolnshire LN4 4JN**

23.5m high tower with one storey and a stair turret. Remainder of a fortified medieval manor house, built on the site of an Augustinian priory, itself built on an Anglo-Saxon religious establishment. There are also visible earthworks of the former moat and fishponds.

**Grant Recipient:** The Crown Estate Commissioners

**Access contact:** Mr W B Lamyman

**T:** 01526 860603

**Open:** By prior telephone arrangement with Mr W B Lamyman of Manor Farm (tel: 01526 860603). At least one week's notice required.

**Heritage Open Days:** No.

P Spaces: 3

🦽 No wheelchair access. No WC for the disabled. No Guide Dogs allowed.

£ No.

## LINCOLN CASTLE

**Castle Hill, Lincoln, Lincolnshire LN1 3AA**

Lincoln Castle was begun by William the Conqueror in 1068. For 900 years the castle has been used as a court and prison. Many original features still stand and the wall walks provide magnificent views of the cathedral, city and surrounding countryside.

**www.lincolnshire.gov.uk/lincolncastle**

**Grant Recipient:** Lincolnshire County Council

**Access contact:** Mr Peter Allen

**T:** 01522 511068    **F:** 01522 512150

**E-mail:** allenp@lincolnshire.gov.uk

**Open:** Monday–Saturday: 9.30am–5.30pm. Sunday 11am–5.30pm. Winter closing at 4pm. Also closed 24–26 December, 31 December and 1 January.

**Heritage Open Days:** No.

P Paid parking available in the Castle / Cathedral area.

🦽 Partial. Wheelchair access to grounds, Magna Carta exhibition, audio visual presentation, Victorian Prison Experience and café. WC for the disabled. Guide Dogs allowed.

£ **Adult:** £3.80. **Child:** £2.50 (under 5s free) **Other:** £2.50 (concessions), £9.90 (family).

## MONKSTHORPE CHAPEL

**Spilsby, East Lindsey, Lincolnshire**

Resembling a brick barn, this remote chapel with outdoor baptistery was used by local Baptists as a secluded place of worship and is one of the two best surviving examples in England. It was substantially altered to its present appearance in the early 19th century.

**Grant Recipient:** The National Trust

**Access contact:** The National Trust

**T:** 01909 486411    **F:** 01909 486377

**Open:** 5 May, 2 June, 30 June (craft fair), 4 August, 1 September. Services at 3pm on 21 April, 19 May, 16 June, 14 July, 18 August, 15 September, 6 October, 15 December. At other times access by key, please contact The National Trust East Midlands Regional Office (Tel: 01909 486411) for further details. £10.00 returnable deposit required for the key.

**Heritage Open Days:** No.

P No.

🦽 No wheelchair access. No WC for the disabled. No Guide Dogs allowed.

£ No.

## ST PETER

**Sotby, Lincolnshire**

Grade II* listed church dating from early 12th and 13th centuries.

**Grant Recipient:** Mr B F Cotton

**Access contact:** Ms Sandra Meakin

**T:** 01507 343662 (evenings)

**Open:** Key available by prior arrangement with Sandra Meakin, Chapel Cottage, Moor Lane, Sotby, Lincolnshire (Tel: 01507 343662).

**Heritage Open Days:** No.

P Roadside parking.

🦽 Partial. Grass entry to building and small step. No WC for the disabled. Guide Dogs allowed.

£ No.

## TATTERSHALL CASTLE

**Tattershall, Lincoln, Lincolnshire LN4 4LR**

A vast fortified and moated red-brick tower, built c1440 for Ralph Cromwell, Treasurer of England. The building was rescued from becoming derelict by Lord Curzon 1911-14 and contains four great chambers with enormous Gothic fireplaces, tapestries and brick vaulting. Gatehouse with museum room.

**www.nationaltrust.org.uk**

**Grant Recipient:** The National Trust

**Access contact:** Property Manager

**T:** 01526 342543    **F:** 01526 342543

**E-mail:** tattershallcastle@nationaltrust.org.uk

**Open:** 3 March–18 March and 3 November–9 December: Saturday and Sunday, 12 noon–4pm; 24 March–26 September: Saturday–Wednesday and Good Friday, 11am–5.30pm. 29 September–31 October: Saturday–Wednesday, 11am–4pm. Castle opens at 1pm on Saturdays except during July and August.

**Heritage Open Days:** No.

P Spaces: 40

🦽 Partial. Wheelchair access to ground floor via ramp. Photograph album of inaccessible parts of Castle. WC for the disabled. Guide Dogs allowed.

£ **Adult:** £4.50. **Child:** £2.30. **Other:** £11.30 (family). Admission price includes voluntary gift aid donation.

## WESTGATE HOUSE

**Westgate, Louth, Lincolnshire LN11 9YQ**

Grade II* Georgian town house in brick and stone, with 1775 neo-classical additions and proto-Regency remodelling c1799 on the Westgate façade. Interior contains fine plasterwork, mahogany doors, Carrara fireplaces and other fine details. Used as a school 1937-1980s but now in course of restoration as a residence by the present owners, after dereliction.

**Grant Recipient:** Professor P Byrne

**Access contact:** Professor Byrne & Mrs Byrne

**T:** 01507 354388

**Open:** Ground floor only. Guided visits between, 11.30am–4pm, by prior arrangement. Evening group visits for societies, etc., by prior arrangement throughout the year.

**Heritage Open Days:** Yes

P Public parking in town centre (5 minutes walk).

🦽 No wheelchair access. No WC for the disabled. Guide Dogs allowed.

£ **Adult:** £3.00. **Child:** Free (when accompanied by an adult). **Other:** Evening group visits: £5.00 per person (maximum 30) including wine and canapés.

# LIVERPOOL

## WEST DERBY COURTHOUSE

**Almonds Green, Liverpool L12 5HP**

Mid 17th century sandstone Courthouse. Its interior, lit by four mullioned windows contains original court furniture such as stewards and jury benches as well as muniment cupboards for rolls of parchment documents produced by the Manor and Hundred Courts.

**Grant Recipient:** Liverpool City Council

**Access contact:** Ms Irene Vickers

**T:** 0151 233 6910    **F:** 0151 228 2817

**E-mail:** croxtethcountrypark@liverpool.gov.uk

**Open:** 1 April–31 October: Sundays, 2–4pm. All other times by prior arrangement, seven days notice required.

**Heritage Open Days:** Yes

P No.

🦽 No wheelchair access. No WC for the disabled. Guide Dogs allowed.

£ No.

# LONDON

## BENJAMIN FRANKLIN'S HOUSE

**36 Craven Street, London WC2N 5NF**

A 1730s terraced house with c1792 alterations. Part of the Craven family's 18th century development of their Brewhouse estate, laid out by Flitcroft. Listed Graded I for historical associations, retaining a majority of original features (central staircase; lathing; 18th century panelling; stoves; windows; fittings; beams; brick, etc) 'unimproved' over time. The world's only remaining home of the diplomat, scientist, inventor, writer, and philosopher Benjamin Franklin. The house is a museum and educational facility.

**www.benjaminfranklinhouse.org**

**Grant Recipient:** Friends of Benjamin Franklin House

**Access contact:** Dr Marcia Balisciano.

**T:** 020 7839 2006    **F:** 020 7930 9124

**E-mail:** info@benjaminfranklinhouse.org

**Open:** October–May: Wednesday–Sunday, 9.45am–6pm. June–September: Wednesday–Monday, 9.45am–6pm. Friday late night shows 6.30pm and 8pm (pre-booked only).

**London Open House:** No.

P No.

🦽 No wheelchair access. No WC for the disabled. Guide Dogs allowed.

£ **Adult:** £9.00 (summer), £8.00 (winter). **Child:** £6.00 (summer), £5.00 (winter). **Other:** Concessions: £6.00 (summer), £5.00 (winter).

## BRIXTON ACADEMY

**211 Stockwell Road, Lambeth, London SW9 9SL**
Built in 1929 as the largest of the four "Astoria" theatres. Retains many original features including elaborate presenium arch over stage and art deco interior. Presently used as a music venue.
www.brixton-academy.co.uk
**Grant Recipient:** McKenzie Group Ltd (Ex Magstack Ltd)
**Access contact:** Mr Nigel Downs
**T:** 020 7787 3131    **F:** 020 7738 4427
**E-mail:** nigel@brixton-academy.co.uk
**Open:** Academy Open Day: 15 September, 10am–4pm. Performances throughout the year.
**London Open House:** Yes
**P** Spaces: 300. NCP car park located on Popes Road. Restricted parking around Brixton Academy.
**&** Partial. Wheelchair access to ground floor and auditorium. WC for the disabled. Guide Dogs allowed.
**£** No. **Other:** Charge applies to events at the venue.

## BROMLEY HALL

**Gillender Street, Tower Hamlets, London E14 6RN**
A rare surviving 15th century house and one of the oldest brick built houses in London. Tree ring analysis has established that the Hall was constructed around 1485 and it retains features from all periods dating back to Tudor times. The house has been used as a private residence, calico printing works and offices. The building now provides the new home for the London Voluntary Sector Training Consortium.
www.leasideregeneration.com
**Grant Recipient:** Leaside Regeneration
**Access contact:** Mr John Hills/ Mr Helen James
**T:** 0845 262 0846    **F:** 0845 262 0847
**E-mail:** jhills@leasideregeneration.co.uk
**Open:** By prior arrangement during working hours.
**London Open House:** Yes
**P** Spaces: 4
**&** Full. WC for the disabled. Guide Dogs allowed.
**£** No.

## BRUCE CASTLE MUSEUM

**(Haringey Libraries Archives & Museum Service), Lordship Lane, London N17 8NU**
Once a 16th century manor house, Bruce Castle has been modified over the 17th, 18th and 19th centuries. Past owners include Sir Rowland Hill, the postal reformer, who ran a school here. Now a museum, set in parkland, it houses displays about the building, local history & art, and an archive.
www.haringey.gov.uk/brucecastlemuseum
**Grant Recipient:** London Borough of Haringey
**Access contact:** Ms Deborah Hedgecock
**T:** 020 8808 8772    **F:** 020 8808 4118
**E-mail:** museum.services@haringey.gov.uk
**Open:** Museum: Wednesday–Sunday, 1–5pm plus Easter Monday, May Day, late May Bank Holiday and August Bank Holiday. Closed Good Friday, Christmas Day, Boxing Day and New Year's Day. Groups at other times by prior arrangement. Archive: Wednesday and Saturday, 1–5pm, Thursday and Friday, 9am–5pm. Visitors to the archive are advised to book an appointment.
**London Open House:** Yes
**P** Spaces: 15
**&** Full. WC for the disabled. Guide Dogs allowed.
**£** No.

## BRUNSWICK SQUARE GARDENS

**Brunswick Square, London WC1**
A public park originally part of the grounds of the Foundling Hospital, founded by Sir Thomas Coram.
www.camden.gov.uk
**Grant Recipient:** London Borough of Camden
**Access contact:** Mr Martin Stanton
**T:** 020 7974 1693    **F:** 020 7974 1543
**E-mail:** martin.stanton@camden.gov.uk
**Open:** From 7.30am until dusk throughout the year.
**London Open House:** No.
**P** On-street parking.
**&** Full. No WC for the disabled. Guide Dogs allowed.
**£** No.

## BUILDING 40

**Royal Military Academy, Woolwich, London SE18 6ST**
Building 40 is a Grade II* listed building on the historic Royal Arsenal site. Constructed in 1718 and 1723 of red brown stock brick with a slate roof, attributed to Nicholas Hawsmoor. One of four buildings now housing the Royal Artillery Museum called Firepower.
www.firepower.org.uk
**Grant Recipient:** Royal Artillery Museums Ltd
**Access contact:** Mrs Eileen Noon
**T:** 020 8855 7755    **F:** 020 88557100
**E-mail:** eileen@firepower.org.uk
**Open:** Building 40: used for corporate events and temporary exhibitions. Museum: Wednesday–Sunday, 10:30am–5pm, closed Monday and Tuesday.
**London Open House:** Yes
**P** Spaces: 400
**&** Partial. Wheelchair access through the rear of the building to the ground floor only. WC for the disabled. Guide Dogs allowed.
**£** **Adult:** £5.00. **Child:** £2.50. **Other:** £12.00 (family), £4.50 (concessions).

## CATHEDRAL FOOTBRIDGE

**Borough High Street, Southwark, London SE1 9DA**
Victorian footbridge providing access from Borough High Street to the Cathedral churchyard.
www.southwark.anglican.org/cathedral
**Grant Recipient:** Dean and Chapter of Southwark Cathedral
**Access contact:** Mr Matthew Knight
**T:** 020 7367 6726    **F:** 020 7367 6725
**E-mail:** matthew.knight@southwark.anglican.org
**Open:** At all times.
**London Open House:** Yes
**P** No.
**&** Partial. Wheelchair access to footbridge but steps down to churchyard. Step-free access available via Borough Market. WC for the disabled. Guide Dogs allowed.
**£** No.

## CHURCH OF THE HOSPITAL OF ST JOHN AND ST ELIZABETH

**60 Grove End Road, London NW8 9NH**
Built in 1864 and designed by George Goldie, a leading Catholic architect of the day in the Italian Baroque style.
**Grant Recipient:** Trustees fo the Hospital Church
**Access contact:** Ms Christine Malcolmson, Matron
**T:** 0207 806 4000 (ext.4294)    **F:** 0207 806 4001
**E-mail:** christine.malcolmson@hje.org
**Open:** All year. Mass said in Church on Sundays between, 11am–12pm and other times during the week, most Wednesdays 12.15pm.
**London Open House:** No.
**P** NCP Car Park.
**&** Partial. Wheelchair access is via the balconies on the first floor. WC for the disabled. Guide Dogs allowed.
**£** No.

## CLISSOLD HOUSE

**Stoke Newington Church Street, London N16**
House built c1770 for Jonathan Hoare, a Quaker banker. Located in middle of Clissold park, a late 18th Century park, developed in 1880s into a public park.
**Grant Recipient:** London Borough of Hackney
**Access contact:** Ms Carole Stewart
**T:** 020 8356 7476    **F:** 020 8356 7575
**E-mail:** carole.stewart@hackney.gov.uk
**Open:** Café is open throughout the year, daily 9am–half an hour before park closing at dusk. London Open House: guided tours for small groups.
**London Open House:** Yes
**P** On street parking.
**&** No wheelchair access. WC for the disabled is outside the house. Guide Dogs allowed.
**£** No.

## COLLEGE OF ARMS

**Queen Victoria Street, London EC4V 4BT**
Built in 1670s/1680s to the design of Francis Sandford and Morris Emmett to house the Heralds' offices, on the site of their earlier building, Derby Place, which was destroyed in the Great Fire of 1666. The principal room is Earl Marshal's Court, which is two floors high with gallery, panelling and throne. New record room added 1842 and portico and terrace in 1867.
www.college-of-arms.gov.uk
**Grant Recipient:** College of Arms
**Access contact:** The Bursar
**T:** 020 7248 2762    **F:** 020 7248 6448
**E-mail:** enquiries@college-of-arms.gov.uk
**Open:** Earl Marshal's Court only: all year (except Public Holidays and State and Special Occasions), Monday–Friday, 10am–4pm. Group tours of Record Room (max 20) and lecture in evenings after 6pm by prior arrangement with Officer-in -Waiting (tel. 020 7248 2762).
**London Open House:** Yes
**P** National Car Park nearby.
**&** No wheelchair access. No WC for the disabled. Guide Dogs allowed.
**£** No.

## DISSENTERS' CHAPEL

**Kensal Green Cemetery, Harrow Road, London W10 4RA**
Grade II* listed building within Grade II* Registered cemetery. Cemetery dates from 1832 and is London's oldest. The Chapel was designed in Greek Revival style by John Griffith in 1834. It is now used by the Friends of Kensal Green Cemetery as a headquarters, exhibition space and art gallery and as a centre for their guided walks, lectures and special events.
www.hct.org.uk or www.kensalgreen.co.uk
**Grant Recipient:** Historic Chapels Trust
**Access contact:** Mr Henry Vivian-Neal
**T:** 020 8960 1030
**E-mail:** henry.vivianneal@btinternet.com
**Open:** Cemetery: daily: Dissenters' Chapel: Sunday afternoons and at other times by prior arrangement. Guided tours of chapels and cemetery for modest charge, also tours of the Catacombs 1st and 3rd Sunday in every month.
**London Open House:** Yes
**P** Parking in adjacent streets, parking for the disabled in cemetery.
**&** Full. WC for the disabled. Guide Dogs allowed.
**£** **Other:** £5.00 (donation requested for guided tours only).

## DR JOHNSON'S HOUSE

**17 Gough Square, London EC4A 3DE**
Fine 18th century town house in the heart of the City of London. Here Dr Johnson compiled his dictionary (published 1755). Original staircase and woodwork throughout and collection of prints, paintings and Johnson memorabilia.
www.drjohnsonshouse.org
**Grant Recipient:** Dr Johnson's House Trust
**Access contact:** The Curator Dr Johnson's House Trust
**T:** 020 7353 3745    **F:** 020 7353 3745
**E-mail:** curator@drjohnsonshouse.org
**Open:** Monday–Saturday: May–September, 11am–5.30pm, October–April, 11am–5pm. Closed Sundays and Bank Holidays.
**London Open House:** Yes
**P** On-street meter parking.
**&** No wheelchair access. WC for the disabled. Guide Dogs allowed.
**£** **Adult:** £4.50. **Child:** £1.50. **Other:** £3.50 (student/senior citizens).

## DULWICH COLLEGE

**College Road, Dulwich, London SE21 7LD**
Dulwich College was founded in 1619; the main buildings date from 1866-70 by the younger Charles Barry and are listed Grade II*. Three blocks lined by arcades in ornate Northern Italian Renaissance style. Close to Dulwich Village.
www.dulwich.org.uk
**Grant Recipient:** Dulwich College
**Access contact:** Ms Julia Field
**T:** 020 8299 9296    **F:** 020 8299 9262
**E-mail:** fieldjg@dulwich.org.uk
**Open:** Exterior visible from South Circular. Interior by prior arrangement with the Bursar.
**London Open House:** Yes
**P** Spaces: 50. 200 parking spaces during school holidays.
**&** Partial. Wheelchair access with assistance (a few steps at entrance). WC for the disabled. Guide Dogs allowed.
**£** **Adult:** £5.50, £7.50 (tour and archives). **Child:** £5.50, £7.50 (tour and archives). **Other:** £5.50, £7.50 (tour and archives).

## FULHAM PALACE STABLEYARD WALL

**Bishop's Avenue, London SW6**
Home to the Bishops of London for over a thousand years to 1973. The two storey medieval west court is red brick with terracotta roof tiles. The mainly three storey Georgian east court is brown and yellow brick with parapets and slate roofs. Set in historic grounds near the river.
**www.fulhampalace.org**
**Grant Recipient:** London Borough of Hammersmith & Fulham
**Access contact:** Dr Scott Cooper
**T:** 020 7736 8140   **F:** 020 7751 0164
**E-mail:** scott.cooper@lbhf.gov.uk
**Open:** The Palace grounds are open daily throughout the year during daylight hours. Tours of principal rooms and gardens every 2nd and 4th Sunday. Please check for current information.
**London Open House:** Yes
P Pay parking on Bishop's Avenue, next to Palace.
Partial. Prior notice is required for wheelchair users wishing to visit the ground floor rooms to enable the ramp to be installed. Gardens accessible. WC for the disabled. Guide Dogs allowed.
£ No.

## GARRICK'S TEMPLE

**Hampton Court Road, Hampton, London TW12 2EN**
The actor-manager David Garrick built the Temple in 1756 to celebrate the genius of William Shakespeare. The Temple was restored between 1997-1999 and now houses an exhibition of Garrick's acting career and life at Hampton, while the grounds have been landscaped to echo their original 18th century layout.
**www.garrickstemple.org.uk**
**Grant Recipient:** London Borough of Richmond-upon-Thames
**Access contact:** Mark De Novellis
**T:** 020 8831 6000   **F:** 020 8744 0501
**E-mail:** m.denovellis@richmond.gov.uk
**Open:** Temple: Beginning of April–end of September, Sundays 2–5pm. Also pre-arranged visits for small groups throughout the year (tel: 020 8831 6000). Lawn: open all year 7.30am–dusk.
**London Open House:** Yes
P Public parking in various locations near the Temple and large car park in Molesey Hurst from where Temple access is via Ferry which runs all day throughout the summer.
Partial. Wheelchair access to lawn gardens only. WC for the disabled. Guide Dogs allowed.
£ No.

## GUNNERSBURY PARK TEMPLE

**Gunnersbury Park, Popes Lane, Acton, London W3 8LQ**
Grade II* listed temple. Built before 1760. Red brick with stone Doric portico. Situated in Gunnersbury Park, the estate of Princess Amelia in the 18th century. The 185 acre park became a public park in 1926.
**www.hounslow.info/gunnersburypark**
**Grant Recipient:** London Borough of Hounslow
**Access contact:** Ms Vanda Foster
**T:** 020 8992 1612   **F:** 020 8752 0686
**E-mail:** gp-museum@cip.org.uk
**Open:** Park open daily, 8am–dusk. The interior will be open for London Open House and at other times by prior arrangement. The Temple is used for events throughout the year and is available for hire.
**London Open House:** Yes
P Spaces: 120
Partial. Wheelchair access to the exterior only. There are two toilets for the disabled within the park, but not in close proximity to the Temple. Guide Dogs allowed.
£ No.

## HACKNEY EMPIRE

**291 Mare Street, London E8 1EJ**
Hackney Empire, designed and built by Frank Matcham in 1901, is one of the finest surviving variety theatres in Britain. Restoration and renovation completed 2004, providing modern facilities and access for all.
**www.hackneyempire.co.uk**
**Grant Recipient:** Hackney Empire Ltd
**Access contact:** Mr S Thomsett
**T:** 020 8510 4500   **F:** 020 8510 4530
**E-mail:** info@hackneyempire.co.uk
**Open:** Performances throughout the year.
**London Open House:** Yes

---

P On-street parking.
Full. WC for the disabled. Guide Dogs allowed.
£ **Other:** Charges are made for performances and some organised tours.

## HIGHPOINT

**North Hill, Highgate, London N6 4BA**
Two blocks of flats built in 1935 and 1938 by Lubetkin and Tecton. Constructed of reinforced concrete with decorative features.
**Grant Recipient:** Mantra Ltd
**Access contact:** Mr Stephen Ellman
**T:** 0870 702 2700   **F:** 0870 702 2701
**E-mail:** stephen.ellman@grossfine.com
**Open:** By prior arrangement with Mr Stephen Ellman of Gross Fine, Saffron House, Saffron Way, London EC1N 8YB
**London Open House:** Yes
P No.
No wheelchair access. No WC for the disabled. Guide Dogs allowed.
£ No.

## HIMALAYA PALACE CINEMA

**(formerly Liberty Cinema), 14 South Road, Southall, London UB1 1RT**
Former cinema, later market hall. 1928. An early work by George Coles; the only known example of cinema built in the Chinese style. Street elevation faced with coloured glazed tiles with red pantiled pagoda roofs. Interior badly fire damaged. Repaired and returned to use as a three screen cinema showing Bollywood, Tamil, Telugu and Afghanistan movies.
**www.himalayapalacecinema.co.uk**
**Grant Recipient:** Himalaya Carpets Ltd
**Access contact:** Mr S Pandher
**T:** 020 8574 6193   **F:** 020 8574 2317
**E-mail:** himalayacarpets@tiscali.co.uk
**Open:** Daily 10.30am–11.30pm. Non-public areas by prior arrangement.
**London Open House:** Yes
P Council car park at rear of cinema.
Full. WC for the disabled. No Guide Dogs allowed.
£ **Adult:** £3.95 (before 2pm), £5.95 other times. **Child:** £4.95 (all times). **Other:** £4.95 (senior citizens).

## KEW BRIDGE STEAM MUSEUM

**Kew Bridge Pumping Station, Green Dragon Lane, Brentford, London TW8 0EN**
19th century Victorian waterworks with original steam pumping engines which are operated every weekend. "Water for Life" gallery exploring 2000 years of London's water.
**www.kbsm.org**
**Grant Recipient:** Kew Bridge Engines Trust & Water Supply Museum Ltd
**Access contact:** Kew Bridge Engines Trust & Water Supply Museum Ltd
**T:** 020 8568 4757   **F:** 020 8569 9978
**E-mail:** info@kbsm.org
**Open:** Daily (except Mondays), 11am–5pm. Closed Good Friday and Christmas. Contact the Museum or website for up-to-date information.
**London Open House:** Yes
P Spaces: 45
Partial. Wheelchair access to all areas except upper floors of Pump Houses. WC for the disabled. Guide Dogs allowed.
£ **Adult:** £4.25 (weekdays), £6.50 (weekends,) £7.50 (Cornish weekend). **Child:** Free. **Other:** £3.25 (weekdays), £5.50 (weekends), £6.50 (Cornish weekends).

## LANDMARK ARTS CENTRE

**Ferry Road, Teddington, London TW11 9NN**
Grade II* former church, c1889, in French-Gothic style by architect William Niven. A number of intended architectural features were never in the end built, due to insufficient funds (hence the incomplete flying buttresses for example). Redundant as a church in 1977. Following renovation now used as an Arts Centre with a variety of arts events, classes and private events.
**www.landmarkartscentre.org**
**Grant Recipient:** London Diocesan Fund
**Access contact:** Mr Graham Watson
**T:** 020 8614 8036   **F:** 020 8614 8080
**E-mail:** grahamgwatson@aol.com
**Open:** Normally open Monday–Friday, 10am–5pm (shorter hours at weekends when public events are held), visitors

---

are advised to contact the Arts Centre Manager at the Landmark Arts Centre (tel: 020 8977 7558, fax: 020 8977 4830, email: info@landmarkartscentre.org) to check. Visits at other times by prior arrangement with the Arts Centre Manager, subject to staff availability.
**London Open House:** No.
P Spaces: 4. Additional on-street parking nearby.
Full. WC for the disabled. Guide Dogs allowed.
£ No. **Other:** Admission charges for some public events.

## LSO ST LUKE'S

**161 Old Street, London EC1V 9NG**
Former Church of St Luke, 1727-33. The west tower, spire and flanking staircase wings by Nicholas Hawksmoor. Listed Grade I. Restored to become the home of the London Symphony Orchestra's music education and community programme. Its conversion began in 2000 and the building combines external restoration with a contemporary interior.
**www.lso.co.uk/lsostlukes**
**Grant Recipient:** St Luke Centre Management Company Ltd
**Access contact:** Ms Alison Thompson
**T:** 020 7490 3939   **F:** 020 7566 2881
**E-mail:** lsostlukes@lso.co.uk
**Open:** By prior arrangement only.
**London Open House:** Yes
P Spaces: 5. Strictly limited to people attending events at the site, by prior arrangement only.
Full. WC for the disabled. Guide Dogs allowed.
£ No. **Other:** Admission charges for events.

## MAPPIN TERRACE CAFÉ

**London Zoo, Regents Park, London NW1 4RY**
The café was designed by John James Joass and built between 1914-20. It was funded by John Newton Mappin. It is a single story red-brick building with a pantiled roof. It is characterised by paired Tuscan columns, French windows, bracketed eaves and pavilion towers at three angles.
**Grant Recipient:** Zoological Society of London
**Access contact:** Ms Philippa Roberts
**T:** 020 7449 6226   **F:** 020 7586 6177
**E-mail:** philippa.roberts@zsl.org
**Open:** On view to visitors to London Zoo which is open daily except 25 December.
**London Open House:** No.
P Spaces: 300. Car park £9.00 and 250 yards away.
Full. Guide Dogs are housed and a personal guide provided. WC for the disabled.
£ **Adult:** £13.00. **Child:** £10.00 (under 3s free). **Other:** £11.20 (concessions).

## ORLEANS HOUSE GALLERY

**Riverside, Twickenham, London TW1 3DJ**
Orleans House Gallery comprises the Octagon Room (1721) with its fine Baroque interior, and the surviving wing/Orangery of the 18th century Orleans House, the rest having been demolished in 1926. Overlooking the Thames and residing in preserved natural woodland, the Gallery presents a programme of temporary exhibitions, organises educational projects/activities and is responsible for the Richmond Borough Art Collection.
**www.richmond.gov.uk/orleanshouse**
**Grant Recipient:** London Borough of Richmond-upon-Thames
**Access contact:** Mr Mark De Novellis
**T:** 020 8831 6000   **F:** 020 8744 0501
**E-mail:** m.denovellis@richmond.gov.uk
**Open:** All year: Tuesday–Saturday, 1–5.30pm. Sundays 2–5.30pm. October–March, closes 4.30pm. Grounds open every day from 9am until dusk. For Bank Holiday and Christmas opening hours please call in advance.
**London Open House:** Yes
P Spaces: 60
Partial. Wheelchair access to ground floor only. WC for the disabled. Guide Dogs allowed.
£ No.

## PITZHANGER MANOR HOUSE AND GALLERY

**Walpole Park, Mattock Lane, London W5 5EQ**
Pitzhanger Manor House is set in Walpole Park, Ealing and was owned and rebuilt by architect and surveyor Sir John Soane (1753-1837). Much of the house has been restored to its early 19th century style and a Victorian wing houses a collection of Martinware Pottery (1877-1923). Pitzhanger Manor Gallery opened in 1996 in a 1940s extension and

exhibitions of professional contemporary art in all media are shown in both the House and Gallery.
www.ealing.gov.uk/pmgalleryandhouse
**Grant Recipient:** London Borough of Ealing
**Access contact:** Ms Helen Walker
**T:** 020 8567 1227    **F:** 020 8567 0596
**E-mail:** pmgallery&house@ealing.gov.uk
**Open:** Tuesday–Friday 1pm–5pm, Saturday 11am–5pm. Summer Sunday openings (ring for details). Closed Bank Holidays, Christmas and Easter.
**London Open House:** Yes
**P** Parking meters in Mattock Lane.
**占** Partial. Access for certain types of wheelchair only with assistance (domestic lift and some steps), please phone in advance for further information. WC for the disabled. Guide Dogs allowed.
**£** No.

### PRIORY CHURCH OF THE ORDER OF ST JOHN
**St John's Square, Clerkenwell, London EC1M**
Remains of the Priory Church of the Knights Hospitallers' London headquarters, including choir and 12th century crypt. Museum in adjacent St John's Gate presents information on the Order of St John and conducts guided tours.
www.sja.org.uk/history
**Grant Recipient:** The Order of St John of Jerusalem
**Access contact:** Ms Pamela Willis
**T:** 020 7324 4071    **F:** 020 7336 0587
**E-mail:** museum@nhq.sja.org.uk.
**Open:** Guided tours: Tuesday, Friday and Saturday, 11am and 2.30pm. Other days and times by arrangement with the Museum.
**London Open House:** Yes
**P** Metered parking available in St John's Square.
**占** Partial. Wheelchair access to Church with assistance, but not the crypt. WC for the disabled at St John's Gate. Guide Dogs allowed.
**£** Other: Donations requested for guided tours.

### RAINHAM HALL
**The Broadway, Rainham, Havering, London RM13 9YN**
Georgian house built in 1729 to a symmetrical plan and with fine wrought iron gates, carved porch and interior panelling plasterwork.
www.nationaltrust.org.uk
**Grant Recipient:** The National Trust
**Access contact:** Property Manager
**T:** 020 7799 4552
**E-mail:** rainhamhall@nationaltrust.org.uk
**Open:** 7 April–27 October: Saturdays and Bank Holiday Mondays, 2- 5pm.
**London Open House:** No.
**P** On-street pay-and-display parking nearby.
**占** Partial. Wheelchair access to ground floor only via external steps. Guide dogs by prior arrangement. No WC for the disabled. Guide Dogs allowed.
**£** Adult: £2.50. Child: £1.30. Other: Family £6.30. Free to National Trust members.

### RICHMOND WEIR & LOCK
**Riverside, Richmond-upon-Thames, London**
The lock and weir are important examples in the history of hydraulic engineering. Constructed in 1894 to control river levels between Richmond and Teddington at half-tide level, the weir was engineered to ensure that the river remained navigable at all times. Operated and maintained by the Port of London Authority since its establishment in 1909, the machinery was designed and built by Ransomes & Rapier.
www.portoflondon.co.uk
**Grant Recipient:** Port of London Authority
**Access contact:** Mr James Trimmer
**T:** 01474 562200    **F:** 01474 562398
**E-mail:** james.trimmer@pola.co.uk
**Open:** The lock and weir are open at all times for passage by river except for 3 weeks in November/December for major maintenance undertaken by the Port of London Authority. The footbridge over the lock is open 6.30am–9.30pm British Summer Time and 6.30am–7.30pm GMT.
**London Open House:** Yes
**P** No.
**占** No wheelchair access. No WC for the disabled. No Guide Dogs allowed.
**£** No.

### ST ANDREWS OLD CHURCH
**Old Church Lane, Kingsbury, Brent, London**
Possibly of Saxon origin, now of 15th century appearance with 19th century restoration work. Considered to be the oldest building in Brent. Contains brasses and memorials to well-known local families dating from the 16th to the 19th centuries.
**Grant Recipient:** The Churches Conservation Trust
**Access contact:** Ms Chloe Cockerill
**T:** 020 7213 0660    **F:** 020 7213 0678
**Open:** 28 May (Welsh Harp Day) and London Open House, at other times by prior arrangement.
**London Open House:** Yes
**P** On-street parking.
**占** Full. No WC for the disabled. Guide Dogs allowed.
**£** No.

### ST ETHELBURGA'S CENTRE FOR RECONCILIATION AND PEACE
**78 Bishopgate, London EC2N 4AG**
Church of St Ethelburga the Virgin built in the late 14th and early 15th centuries. Devastated by a terrorist bomb in April 1993 and re-opened in November 2002, after restoration, for use as a Centre for Reconciliation and Peace.
www.stethelburgas.org
**Grant Recipient:** St Ethelburga's Centre for Reconciliation & Peace
**Access contact:** Mr Simon Keyes
**T:** 020 7496 1610    **F:** 020 7638 1440
**E-mail:** enquiries@stethelburgas.org
**Open:** Every Friday, 11am–3pm. Groups may visit at other times by arrangement. Details of services, public lectures and other events available from the website or by telephone.
**London Open House:** Yes
**P** No.
**占** Full. WC for the disabled. Guide Dogs allowed.
**£** No.

### ST MATTHIAS OLD CHURCH COMMUNITY CENTRE
**113 Poplar High Street, Poplar, London E14 0AE**
Built by in 1650-54 by the East India Company, St Matthias Old Church is the oldest building in Docklands. Declared redundant in 1977, the building became derelict. In 1990 the building was restored and is now used as a community arts/cultural centre.
**Grant Recipient:** London Diocesan Fund
**Access contact:** Mr Nizam Uddin
**T:** 020 7987 0459    **F:** 020 7531 9973
**E-mail:** niz_68@hotmail.com
**Open:** Monday–Friday: 10am–3pm.
**London Open House:** Yes
**P** Car park for limited number of cars.
**占** Full. WC for the disabled. Guide Dogs allowed.
**£** No.

### ST PAUL'S STEINER PROJECT
**1 St Paul's Road, London N1 2QH**
Grade II* listed church, 1826-28 by Sir Charles Barry. Perpendicular in style. Converted to a 'cradle to grave' education and cultural centre, including a Steiner school, multi use community performance space, adult education and information centre.
www.stpaulssteinerproject.org
**Grant Recipient:** St Paul's Steiner Project
**Access contact:** Ms Jane Gerhard
**T:** 020 7226 4454    **F:** 102 7226 2062
**E-mail:** st.pauls.school@btinternet.com
**Open:** 16 January, 6 March, 15 May, 12 June, 26 September and 14 November. At other times by prior arrangement with 2 days notice.
**London Open House:** No.
**P** Pay and display.
**占** Partial. Wheelchair access to ground floor. WC for the disabled. Guide Dogs allowed.
**£** No.

### THE HOUSE MILL
**Three Mill Lane, Bromley-by-Bow, London E3 3DU**
Industrial water mill, originally built 1776 as part of a distillery. Contains four floors with remains of un-restored machinery, four water wheels and gearing. Originally had 12 pairs of millstones and has unique survival of Fairbairn-style "silent millstone machinery".

**Grant Recipient:** River Lea Tidal Mill Trust
**Access contact:** Ms Patricia Wilkinson
**T:** 020 8539 6726    **F:** 020 8539 2317
**E-mail:** RLTMT@bcos.demon.co.uk
**Open:** Sunday of National Mills Week, Heritage Open Days and the first Sunday of each month April–December: 11am–4pm. Other Sundays May–October: 2–4pm. Groups by prior arrangement with Ms Patricia Wilkinson, 1B Forest Drive East, Leytonstone, London E11 1JX. For further information tel. 020 8539 6726.
**London Open House:** Yes
**P** Car park nearby.
**占** Full. WC for the disabled. Guide Dogs allowed.
**£** Adult: £3.00. Child: Free. Other: £1.50.

### THE QUEEN'S CHAPEL OF THE SAVOY
**Savoy Hill, Strand, London WC2R 0DA**
Originally part of a hospital founded in 1512 by Henry VII. Rebuilt by Robert Smirke after a fire in 1864, from which time the ceiling covered with heraldic emblems dates. Recently restored.
**Grant Recipient:** Duchy of Lancaster
**Access contact:** Mr Phillip Chancellor
**T:** 020 7836 7221
**E-mail:** pdc46@mailcity.com
**Open:** All year except August and September: Tuesday–Friday, 11.30am–3.30pm; Sunday for Morning Service only. Closed the week after Christmas Day and the week after Easter Day.
**London Open House:** No.
**P** No.
**占** Full. No WC for the disabled. Guide Dogs allowed.
**£** No.

### THE ROUND CHAPEL
**(Clapton Park United Reformed Church), 1d Glenarm Road, London E5 0LY**
Grade II* listed United Reformed Church, c1871. Horseshoe-shaped plan with roof and gallery supported by iron pillars. Detailed columns form a continuous iron arcade at roof level with latticework effects. Contemporary pulpit with double flight of stairs, organ and organ case.
**Grant Recipient:** Hackney Historic Buildings Trust
**Access contact:** Dr Ann Robey
**T:** 020 8525 0706    **F:** 020 8986 0029
**E-mail:** roundchapel@pop3.poptel.org.uk
**Open:** Many public/community events take place in the Round Chapel which the public can attend, it is also available to hire for private events, otherwise access by arrangement.
**London Open House:** Yes
**P** Spaces: 3
**占** Partial. Wheelchair access to ground floor only. WC for the disabled. Guide Dogs allowed.
**£** No.

### THE ROUNDHOUSE
**Chalk Farm Road, London NW1 8EH**
The Roundhouse is a grade II* listed engine maintenance and turning shed built in 1846 for the London and North Western railway. By the 1860s engines had become too long to be turned and stored there so it was leased to W&A Gilbey Ltd as a liquor store until its conversion into a theatre in the 1960s. The Roundhouse re-opened in 2006 and houses an international performance venue and creative centre for young people, The Roundhouse Studios.
www.roundhouse.org.uk
**Grant Recipient:** The Roundhouse Trust
**Access contact:** Ms Emily Hahn, Development Manager
**T:** 020 7424 9991    **F:** 020 7424 9992
**E-mail:** info@roundhouse.org.uk
**Open:** All year, excluding some public holidays.
**London Open House:** No.
**P** 7 spaces for disabled parking only.
**占** Full. WC for the disabled. Guide Dogs allowed.
**£** No. Other: Charges apply for most events.

### WALPOLE'S HOUSE
**St Mary's College, Strawberry Hill, Waldegrave Road, Twickenham, London TW1 4SX**
Bought by Horace Walpole in 1749 and over the next half century converted into his own vision of a 'gothic' fantasy with 14 rooms open to the public containing chimneypieces based on Medieval tombs and a collection of 16th century painted glass roundels. Reputedly the first substantial building of the Gothic Revival.
**Grant Recipient:** St Mary's, Strawberry Hill

**Access contact:** Head of Catering and Conference Services
**T:** 020 8240 4044   **F:** 020 8255 4255
**E-mail:** gallaghs@smuc.ac.uk
**Open:** 7 May–24 September: Sunday only, 2–3.30pm. Guided group tours (minimum 10 people) by prior arrangement on any day except Saturday. Please check opening arrangements prior to visit.
**London Open House:** No.
🅿 Spaces: 60. Parking available at weekends only.
♿ Partial. Wheelchair access to ground floor and grounds with difficulty–doorways are small. WC for the disabled. Guide Dogs allowed.
💷 **Adult:** £5.50. **Child:** £4.75. **Other:** £4.75 (senior citizen) Admission charges subject to annual review.

## WAPPING HYDRAULIC POWER PUMPING STATION
### Wapping Wall, London E1W 3ST
The Wapping Hydraulic Power Station was built by the London Hydraulic Power Company in 1890. One of the five London Stations of its kind, it harnessed Thames water to provide power throughout the central London area. The showcase building of the LHPC, it was used as a model for power stations in Argentina, Australia, New York and Europe. Now houses an art gallery and restaurant.
**www.thewappingproject.com**
**Grant Recipient:** Women's Playhouse Trust
**Access contact:** Women's Playhouse Trust
**T:** 020 7680 2080   **F:** 020 7680 2081
**E-mail:** jules@wapping-wpt.com
**Open:** Throughout the year except 23 December–4 January: Monday–Friday: 12 noon–Midnight. Saturday 10am–Midnight and Sunday 10am–6pm.
**London Open House:** No.
🅿 Spaces: 30
♿ Full. WC for the disabled. Guide Dogs allowed.
💷 No.

## WHITECHAPEL ART GALLERY
### Whitechapel High Street, London E1 7QX
Grade II* listed Arts and Crafts building constructed in the late 1890s by C H Townsend. Occupied by the Whitechapel Art Gallery, which was founded in 1901 by the Revd Canon Barnett 'to bring great art to the people of the East End'.
**www.whitechapel.org**
**Grant Recipient:** Trustees of the Whitechapel Art Gallery
**Access contact:** Mr Tom Wilcox
**T:** 020 7522 7865   **F:** 020 7377 1685
**E-mail:** TomWilcox@whitechapel.org
**Open:** All year: Tuesday–Sunday 11am–6pm, Thursday 11am–9pm. Various exhibitions (5–6 per year).
**London Open House:** No.
🅿 Paid parking in Spreadeagle Yard to the left of the gallery off Whitechapel High Street.
♿ Full. WC for the disabled. Guide Dogs allowed.
💷 No. **Other:** One exhibition per year will have entrance fee.

## WILTONS MUSIC HALL
### Graces Alley, Tower Hamlets, London E1 8JB
The world's oldest surviving grand Victorian music hall listed Grade II*. John Wilton built the theatre behind his public house 'The Prince of Denmark' in 1858, in Graces Alley and it continued as a music hall until 1884. Hall open for regular performances, shows and private events.
**www.wiltons.org.uk**
**Grant Recipient:** Wiltons Music Hall Trust
**Access contact:** Frances Mayhew, House Manager
**T:** 020 7702 9555   **F:** 0871 2532424
**E-mail:** info@wiltons.org.uk
**Open:** Monday–Friday 10am–4pm, pre-booked guided tours only. Other public events/productions in evenings.
**London Open House:** Yes
🅿 Parking facilities nearby.
♿ Full. Wheelchair access to main building and auditorium. WC for the disabled. Guide Dogs allowed.
💷 **Other:** £4.00 (guided tour).

# MERSEYSIDE

## BROUGHTON HALL CONSERVATORY
### Convent of Mercy, Yew Tree Lane, West Derby, Liverpool, Merseyside L12 9HH
Victorian conservatory of rectangular shape with an entrance porch at one end and an access bay to main building, at the other. The cast iron structure is mounted on a stone plinth. The elevations are divided into a series of panels with decorated cast iron circular columns. From the capitols spring semi-circular arches. These form the bases of the frieze moulding which runs round the periphery of the building. The flooring is of quarry tiles.
**Grant Recipient:** The Institute of Our Lady of Mercy
**Access contact:** Sister Josephine Davies
**T:** 01132 500253   **F:** 01132 500 241
**Open:** January–3 April: by prior written arrangement only, Monday–Saturday, 10am–4pm. No access on Sundays or Bank Holidays.
**Heritage Open Days:** No.
🅿 Spaces: 4
♿ Full. WC for the disabled. Guide Dogs allowed.
💷 No.

## FORMBY HALL
### Southport Old Road, Formby, Merseyside L37 0AB
Built c1620 with 18th century extensions and later alterations.
**Grant Recipient:** Mr Michael McComb
**Access contact:** Mr Michael McComb
**T:** 01704 878 999   **F:** 01704 572 436
**Open:** Access to the exterior by prior arrangement with Mr McComb, 8 Victoria Road, Formby, Liverpool L37 7AG. Telephone: 01704 878 999.
**Heritage Open Days:** No.
🅿 Spaces: 1
♿ No wheelchair access. No WC for the disabled. No Guide Dogs allowed.
💷 No.

## LIVERPOOL COLLEGIATE APARTMENTS
### Shaw Street, Liverpool, Merseyside L6 1NR
Grade II* former school built 1843 of red sandstone in Tudor Gothic style, gutted by fire and now converted into residential block.
**Grant Recipient:** Urban Splash Ltd
**Access contact:** Mr Bill Maynard
**T:** 0161 839 2999   **F:** 0161 839 8999
**E-mail:** billmaynard@urbansplash.co.uk
**Open:** Exterior only, visible from Shaw Street.
**Heritage Open Days:** No.
🅿 No.
♿ Full. No WC for the disabled. No Guide Dogs allowed.
💷 No.

## SEFTON PARK
### Liverpool, Merseyside L18 3JD
108 hectare public park, designed in 1867, the first to introduce French influence to the design of parks through the designer Edouard André who had worked on the design of major Parisian parks. Sefton Park is Grade II* registered and contains several listed statues and other features. The Grade II* listed Palm House, 1896 by Mackenzie and Moncur, is an octagonal iron frame structure which appears as 3 domed roofs, one above the other.
**www.palmhouse.org.uk**
**Grant Recipient:** Liverpool City Council
**Access contact:** Ms Emma Reid
**T:** 0151 726 9304   **F:** 0151 726 2419
**E-mail:** info@palmhouse.org.uk
**Open:** Park open at all times. Palm House: 1 April–31 October: Monday–Saturday 10.30am–5pm, Sunday 10.30am–4pm, may be closed on Tuesdays and Thursdays and from 4pm for events; 1 November–31 March: Monday–Sunday 10.30am–4pm, may be closed on Tuesdays and Thursdays for events. The Trust reserves the right to shut the Palm House on other occasions and will endeavour to give as much notice as possible on the website and information line (tel:0151 726 2415).
**Heritage Open Days:** Yes
🅿 On-street parking available on edge of park.
♿ Full. No WC for the disabled. Guide Dogs allowed.
💷 No.

## SPEKE HALL
### The Walk, Liverpool, Merseyside L24 1XD
One of the most important timber framed manor houses in the country, dating from 1530. The interior spans many periods: the Great Hall and priest holes evoke Tudor times, the Oak Parlour and smaller rooms, some with William Morris wallpapers, show the Victorian desire for privacy and comfort. There is some Jacobean plasterwork and intricately carved furniture. Restored garden and woodland walks.

**www.nationaltrust.org.uk**
**Grant Recipient:** The National Trust
**Access contact:** Mr Simon Osbourne, Property Manager
**T:** 0151 427 7231   **F:** 0151 427 9860
**E-mail:** spekehall@nationaltrust.org.uk
**Open:** House: 17 March–28 October, Wednesday–Sunday (open Bank Holidays); November and December, Saturday and Sunday only. March–mid October, 1–5.30pm; mid October–December, 1–4.30pm. Woodland and garden: open daily throughout the year, closed 24–26 and 31 December, 1 January. Times: March–mid October, 11am–5.30pm; mid October–mid March, 11am–dusk.
**Heritage Open Days:** Yes
🅿 Spaces: 400. Car park is 500 yards from the property. Courtesy shuttle service available.
♿ Partial. Wheelchair access to ground floor of house. WC for the disabled. Guide Dogs allowed.
💷 **Adult:** £6.70, £4.00 (grounds only). **Child:** £3.70, £1.90 (grounds only). **Other:** £20.50 (family), £11.00 (family, grounds only).

## WALLASEY UNITARIAN CHURCH
### Manor Road, Liscard, Wallasey, Merseyside CH44 1BU
'Arts & Crafts' chapel interior dating from 1899 with fittings by Bernard Sleigh and craftsmen associated with Bromsgrove Guild.
**www.hct.org.uk**
**Grant Recipient:** Historic Chapels Trust
**Access contact:** Mr Terry Edgar
**T:** 0151 639 9707
**E-mail:** terryedgar@hotmail.com
**Open:** At all reasonable times by prior arrangement with key holder, Terry Edgar, 5 Mere Lane, Wallasey Village, Wirral CH45 3HY.
**Heritage Open Days:** Yes
🅿 Restricted on-street parking.
♿ Full. WC for the disabled. Guide Dogs allowed.
💷 Donations invited.

# NORFOLK

## CHURCH OF ST MARY THE VIRGIN
### Houghton-on-the-Hill, Norfolk PE37 8DP
Ancient church at least 900 years old. Many original features remain including double splay windows, keyhole chancel, Roman brick arch, 12th century North door and early wall paintings. All areas open.
**www.saintmaryschurch.org.uk**
**Grant Recipient:** Norfolk County Council
**Access contact:** Mr Davey
**T:** 01760 440470
**Open:** All year at any reasonable time.
**Heritage Open Days:** Yes
🅿 Spaces: 40
♿ Full. No WC for the disabled. Guide Dogs allowed.
💷 No.

## FELBRIGG HALL
### Felbrigg, Norwich, Norfolk NR11 8PR
17th century house containing its original 18th century furniture and paintings. The walled garden has been restored and features a working dovecote, small orchard and the national collection of Colchicum. The park is renowned for its fine and aged trees.
**www.nationaltrust.org.uk**
**Grant Recipient:** The National Trust
**Access contact:** Property Manager
**T:** 01263 837444   **F:** 01263 837032
**E-mail:** felbrigg@nationaltrust.org.uk
**Open:** House: 17 March–28 October: Saturday–Wednesday, 1–5pm. Garden: 17 March–21 October: Wednesday–Saturday, 28 May–3 June: daily, 23 July–31 August: daily, 22–28 October: daily, 11am–4pm; 27 -31 December: Thursday–Monday, 11am–4pm. Open Bank Holidays and Good Friday. Estate walks: All year, dawn to dusk.
**Heritage Open Days:** No.
🅿 Spaces: 200. Separate parking for disabled and drop-off point.
♿ Partial. Wheelchair access to ground floor, photograph album of first floor. Garden, shop and bookshop (ramp), tea room and restaurant accessible. WC for the disabled. Guide Dogs allowed.
💷 **Adult:** £7.50 (house), £3.50 (garden). **Child:** £3.50 (house, £1.50 (garden). **Other:** £18.50 (family). Groups: £6.50 (adult), £3.00 (child).

## HALES HALL BARN

**Loddon, Norfolk NR14 6QW**

Late 15th century brick and thatch barn 180ft long, built by James Hobart, Henry VII's Attorney General. Queen post roof, and crown post roof to living accommodation, and richly patterned brickwork. The Barn and similar sized gatehouse, ranged around defended courtyards, are all that remains of the house that stood on this site. Large garden with topiary and yew hedges, and national collections of citrus, grapes and figs.

www.haleshall.com

**Grant Recipient:** Mr & Mrs Terence Read

**Access contact:** Mr & Mrs Terence Read

**T:** 01508 548507   **F:** 01508 548040

**E-mail:** judy@haleshall.com

**Open:** All year, Tuesday–Saturday, 10am–5pm (or dusk if earlier); plus Easter–October, Sunday afternoons and Bank Holiday Mondays, 11am–4pm. Closed 25 December–5 January and Good Friday. Garden with yew and box topiary included in admission charge. Parties and guided tours by prior arrangement with Mr or Mrs Terence Read, Hales Hall, Loddon, Norfolk NR14 6QW (tel. 01508 548507). Barn and garden may be used for wedding receptions, particularly Saturday afternoon: telephone to ensure access.

**Heritage Open Days:** Yes

P Spaces: 40

 Full. First floor accessible by new staircase. WC for the disabled. Guide Dogs allowed.

£ **Adult:** £2.00 (including guide). **Child:** Free. **Other:** £1.50, £3.00 (guided tours by arrangement).

## HOLKHAM HALL VINERY

**Wells-next-the-Sea, Norfolk NR23 1AB**

Range of late 19th century Glasshouses. Six houses in the range, four of which have been repaired.

www.holkham.co.uk

**Grant Recipient:** Coke Estates Ltd

**Access contact:** Mr Richard Gledston

**T:** 01328 710227   **F:** 01328 711707

**E-mail:** enquiries@holkham.co.uk

**Open:** Exterior can be viewed when the gardens are open to the public during the summer months. Access to the interior by appointment.

**Heritage Open Days:** No.

P Spaces: 25

 No wheelchair access. No WC for the disabled. No Guide Dogs allowed.

£ No.

## KING'S LYNN CUSTOM HOUSE

**Purfleet Quay, King's Lynn, Norfolk PE30 1HP**

Built 1683 as a merchants exchange, became official Custom House in 1703. Building purchased by the Crown in 1717 for £800 and was used by HM Customs until 1989. The Borough Council of King's Lynn and West Norfolk obtained a lease of the building in 1995 and restored it.

**Grant Recipient:** King's Lynn & West Norfolk Council

**Access contact:** Mrs Karen Cooke

**T:** 01553 763044   **F:** 01553 819441

**E-mail:** kings-lynn.tic@west-norfolk.gov.uk

**Open:** Monday–Saturday, 10.30am–4pm and Sundays, 12–4pm. Opening times likely to be longer during summer months, check with the access contact for current information.

**Heritage Open Days:** Yes

P Parking in public car parks, plus many pay and display spaces within 10 minute walk.

 Partial. Wheelchair access to ground floor only. No WC for the disabled. Guide Dogs allowed.

£ No.

## OLD BUCKENHAM CORNMILL

**Green Lane, Old Buckenham, Norfolk NR17**

Mill with the largest diameter tower in England, which had five sets of stones when it was working. Once owned by the Colmans of Norwich and Prince Duleep Singh. Built by John Burlingham in 1818.

www.norfolkwindmills.co.uk

**Grant Recipient:** Norfolk Windmills Trust

**Access contact:** Mrs A L Rix

**T:** 01603 222708   **F:** 01603 224413

**E-mail:** amanda.rix@norfolk.gov.uk

**Open:** April–September: second Sunday of each month, 2–5pm. Groups at other times by prior arrangement with Mrs A L Rix, Conservation Officer, Building Conservation

Section, Dept of Planning & Transportation, Norfolk County Council, County Hall, Martineau Lane, Norwich, Norfolk NR1 2SG.

**Heritage Open Days:** No.

P Spaces: 6

 No wheelchair access. No WC for the disabled. No Guide Dogs allowed.

£ **Adult:** £2.00. **Child:** Free.

## OLD HALL

**Norwich Road, South Burlingham, Norfolk NR13 4EY**

Small Elizabethan manor house with a painted stucco fireplace, painted stucco mermaids and scrollwork on the front porch, and a long gallery of hunting scenes in grisaille, c1600.

**Grant Recipient:** Mr P Scupham

**Access contact:** Mr P Scupham

**T:** 01493 750804

**E-mail:** margaret@moonshinecat.fsnet.co.uk

**Open:** By prior telephone arrangement with Mr P Scupham or Ms M Steward. No access for guide dogs to the Long Gallery.

**Heritage Open Days:** Yes

P Spaces: 8. 12 extra parking spaces available in small attached meadow.

 Partial. Wheelchair access to ground floor and garden, painted gallery inaccessible. No WC for the disabled. Guide Dogs allowed.

£ No.

## OXBURGH HALL

**Oxborough, King's Lynn, Norfolk PE33 9PS**

Moated manor house with Tudor gatehouse, was built in 1482 by the Bedingfeld family who still live there. The rooms show the development from medieval austerity to Victorian comfort, and include a display of embroidery by Mary, Queen of Scots and Bess of Hardwick. Gardens include a French Parterre and woodland walks, as well as a Catholic chapel.

www.nationaltrust.org.uk

**Grant Recipient:** The National Trust

**Access contact:** Property Manager

**T:** 01366 328258   **F:** 01366 328066

**E-mail:** oxburghhall@nationaltrust.org.uk

**Open:** House: 17 March–31 July and 1–30 September: Saturday–Wednesday 1–5pm. 1–31 August: daily, 1–5 pm. 1–28 October: Saturday–Wednesday, 1–4pm. Garden: 6 January–11 March, 3 November–23 December and 5 January–24 February: Saturday and Sunday, 11am–4pm. 17 March–31 July and 1–30 September: Saturday–Wednesday, 11am–5.30pm. August: daily, 11am–5.30pm.

**Heritage Open Days:** No.

P Spaces: 100

 Partial. Wheelchair access to 4 ground floor rooms (shallow ramp), difficult stairs to upper floors. Garden largely accessible, restaurant and shop accessible. WC for the disabled. Guide Dogs allowed.

£ **Adult:** £6.75 (house & garden), £3.50 (garden). **Child:** £3.50 (house & garden), £2.00 (garden). **Other:** £17.00 (family: house & garden).

## RUINED CHURCH OF ST PETER

**Wiggenhall St Peter with Wigge, Norfolk**

Former parish church, largely 15th century, now ruined. South aisle was demolished in 1840.

**Grant Recipient:** Wiggenhall St Peter PCC

**Access contact:** Mrs A Yeoman

**T:** 01553 617518

**Open:** To the exterior at all reasonable times.

**Heritage Open Days:** No.

P Spaces: 2

 No wheelchair access. No WC for the disabled. No Guide Dogs allowed.

£ No.

## ST ANDREW'S CHURCH

**Illington, Norfolk**

Medieval Church, restored 1887. Listed Grade II*.

**Grant Recipient:** Norfolk Churches Trust Ltd

**Access contact:** Mrs Shaw

**T:** 01953 498546

**Open:** Three services a year. At other times, key is available from Mrs Shaw (tel: 01953 498546).

**Heritage Open Days:** No.

P Spaces: 12. Parking in the farmyard.

 Partial. Steps into the Church. No WC for the disabled. Guide Dogs allowed.

£ No.

## ST ANDREW'S HALL

**St Andrew's Plain, Norwich, Norfolk NR3 1AU**

Remains of medieval friary, including the nave (St Andrew's Hall), choir (Blackfriars Hall), crypt, cloisters, private chapel (Beckets) and chapter house. Hammerbeam roof in nave, medieval bosses in choir and a 13th century 7-light East Window. A civic hall in use since 1540.

www.norwich.gov.uk

**Grant Recipient:** Norwich City Council

**Access contact:** Mr Richard Sapiano

**T:** 01603 628477   **F:** 01603 762182

**E-mail:** richardsapiano@norwich.gov.uk

**Open:** January–25 June 2007: Monday–Saturday, 9am–4pm. Subject to events.

**Heritage Open Days:** Yes

P Parking in multi-storey car park in city centre. Blue Badge on site, Orange Badge if space is available.

 Partial. Wheelchair access to ground floor only. WC for the disabled. Guide Dogs allowed.

£ No.

## ST BENET'S ABBEY

**Horning, Norfolk**

Site of the medieval abbey beside the River Bure. Parts of the gatehouse remain attached to an 18th century brick windmill. Within the whole monastic precinct are the foundations of the abbey church, monastic fishponds and other earthworks, all surrounded by a ditch.

www.norfarchtrust.org.uk

**Grant Recipient:** Norfolk Archaeological Trust

**Access contact:** Norfolk Archaeological Trust

**Open:** At all times.

**Heritage Open Days:** No.

P Spaces: 4

 No WC for the disabled. Guide Dogs allowed.

£ No.

## ST BENET'S LEVEL MILL

**Ludham, Norfolk**

Typical example of a Broadland drainage mill with tapering red brick tower, white boat shaped cap, sails and fantail. Built in 18th century and altered over the years, it became redundant in the 1940s. Ground and first floors accessible. Information boards on site.

**Grant Recipient:** Crown Estates Commissioners

**Access contact:** Mrs Alison Ritchie

**T:** 01692 678232

**E-mail:** alison@ludhamhall.co.uk

**Open:** Second Sunday in May and first Sunday in August. At other times by prior arrangement with Mrs Alison Ritchie at Hall Farm, Ludham, Great Yarmouth, Norfolk NR29 5NU (tel: 01692 678232) or Mrs Jenny Scaff, Carter Jonas, 6-8 Hills Road, Cambridge CB2 1NH (tel: 01223 346628).

**Heritage Open Days:** Yes

P No.

 No wheelchair access. Guide dog access possible to ground floor only. No WC for the disabled. Guide Dogs allowed.

£ No.

## ST CLEMENT

**Colegate, Norwich, Norfolk NR3 1BQ**

15th century church, now a pastoral care and counselling centre. Has a slender tower decorated with lozenges of flushwork (patterns made from flint and stone).

**Grant Recipient:** Norwich Historic Churches Trust

**Access contact:** Reverend Jack Burton

**T:** 01603 622747

**Open:** Daily, 10am–4pm (sometimes longer). Occasionally closed when steward on leave.

**Heritage Open Days:** Yes

P In city centre car parks.

 Partial. Wheelchair access to Nave at street level. No WC for the disabled. Guide Dogs allowed.

£ No.

## ST LAWRENCE

**The Street, South Walsham, Norfolk NR13 6DQ**

Medieval church destroyed by fire and rebuilt in 1832 as a parish church and used for worship until c1890. Formerly redundant but now re-licensed for worship. Now houses St Lawrence Centre for Training and the Arts, open to the public and used for exhibitions, classes and concerts. Access to Sacristans Garden.

**www.st-lawrence.org.uk**
**Grant Recipient:** South Walsham Parochial Church Council
**Access contact:** Mrs Caroline Linsdell
**T:** 01603 270522
**Open:** Daily, 9am–6pm or dusk in winter.
**Heritage Open Days:** No.
**P** Spaces: 8
**⬤** Full. WC for the disabled. Guide Dogs allowed.
**£** No.

## ST MARGARET-DE-WESTWICK
**St Benedict's Street, Norwich, Norfolk**
Medieval church, now redundant. Used for art exhibitions.
**Grant Recipient:** Norwich Historic Churches Trust
**Access contact:** Ms Jane Jones
**T:** 07867 801 995
**E-mail:** norhistch.trust@btinternet.com
**Open:** By prior arrangement with Jane Jones (tel: 07867 801 995). Also open for art exhibitions during the summer months.
**Heritage Open Days:** Yes
**P** No.
**⬤** Full. No WC for the disabled. Guide Dogs allowed.
**£** No.

## ST MARTIN AT OAK
**Oak Street, Norwich, Norfolk**
15th century former church, now redundant.
**Grant Recipient:** Norwich Historic Churches Trust
**Access contact:** Mrs J Jones
**T:** 07867 801995  **F:** 01603 722008
**E-mail:** norhistch.trust@btinternet.com
**Open:** By arrangement with the tenant. Please telephone 07867 801995 for details.
**Heritage Open Days:** Yes
**P** Parking metres in St Martin Lane and city centre car parks.
**⬤** No wheelchair access. No WC for the disabled. No Guide Dogs allowed.
**£** No.

## ST MARTIN AT PALACE PLAIN
**(Norfolk ACRO), Norwich, Norfolk NR3 1RW**
Medieval former church, now housing the Norfolk Association for the Care and Resettlement of Offenders. Has a fine 16th century tomb for Lady Elizabeth Calthorpe.
**Grant Recipient:** Norwich Historic Churches Trust
**Access contact:** Ms Amanda Payne
**T:** 01603 763555  **F:** 01603 230524
**E-mail:** amanda@norfolkacro.org
**Open:** By prior written arrangement.
**Heritage Open Days:** No.
**P** In city centre car parks.
**⬤** Partial. Wheelchair access to ground floor only, by prior arrangement. WC for the disabled. Guide Dogs allowed.
**£** No.

## ST MARY
**Fordham, Downham Market, Norfolk**
Medieval aisleless church in rural landscape, now redundant. Listed Grade II*.
**Grant Recipient:** Fordham St Mary Preservation Trust
**Access contact:** Mr Robert Bateson
**T:** 01366 388399  **F:** 01366 385859
**E-mail:** bateson@rannerlow.org
**Open:** By prior arrangement or key may be available from farm opposite church.
**Heritage Open Days:** No.
**P** Spaces: 12
**⬤** No wheelchair access. No WC for the disabled. Guide Dogs allowed.
**£** No.

## ST MARY'S ABBEY
**West Dereham, Norfolk**
The present six bay house is the remains of the service block of Sir Thomas Dereham's Renaissance style mansion, which he built after 1689 incorporating the surviving parts of a Premonstratensian Abbey founded in 1188 by Hubert Walter. Had become a ruin and was only recently restored, with the building re-roofed, re-fenestrated and a first floor and stair tower added. The house is now a private residence.
**Grant Recipient:** Mr G Shropshire

**Access contact:** Mrs Ann King
**T:** 01353 727200  **F:** 01353 727325
**E-mail:** ann.king@gs-marketing.com
**Open:** January–8 October: by prior arrangement with Mrs Ann King, G's Marketing Ltd, Barway, Ely, Cambridgeshire CB7 5TZ (tel: 01353 727200, Monday-Friday only). Up to one month's notice may be required.
**Heritage Open Days:** No.
**P** Spaces: 20
**⬤** Full. WC for the disabled is available on request, although it is not specifically designed for such use. Guide Dogs allowed.
**£** No.

## ST PETER & ST PAUL
**Tunstall, Norfolk**
Chancel and ruined nave and tower of medieval church.
**Grant Recipient:** Tunstall (Norfolk) Church Preservation Trust
**Access contact:** The Secretary
**T:** 01493 700279  **F:** 01493 700279
**Open:** Normally all year. If locked, it is due to severe weather. Key available at the Manor House in Tunstall.
**Heritage Open Days:** No.
**P** Spaces: 6
**⬤** Full. Wheelchair access is across uneven path. No WC for the disabled. Guide Dogs allowed.
**£** No.

## THE DEANERY
**56 The Close, Norwich, Norfolk NR1 4EG**
13th century with later additions, originally the Prior's lodgings. It remains the residence of the Dean of Norwich. The interior is closed to the public.
**www.cathedral.org.uk**
**Grant Recipient:** The Chapter of Norwich Cathedral
**Access contact:** The Chapter Steward
**T:** 01603 218300  **F:** 01603 766032
**E-mail:** chapter@cathedral.org.uk
**Open:** Exterior visible from The Close which is open to visitors during daylight hours throughout the year.
**Heritage Open Days:** No.
**P** No.
**⬤** Full. No WC for the disabled. No Guide Dogs allowed.
**£** No.

## THURNE DYKE DRAINAGE MILL
**Thurne Staithe, Thurne, Norfolk**
Broadland drainage mill c1820 with classic 'hained' appearance and turbine pump. Originally 2 storey tapering circular whitewashed brick tower but raised to 3 storeys in mid 19th century, with timber weatherboarded boat shaped cap, sails and fan.
**www.norfolkwindmills.co.uk**
**Grant Recipient:** Norfolk Windmills Trust
**Access contact:** Mrs Amanda Rix
**T:** 01603 222705  **F:** 01603 224413
**E-mail:** amanda.rix@norfolk.gov.uk
**Open:** April–September: second and forth Sunday of each month; National Mills weekend (second weekend in May), 2–5pm and at other times by arrangement.
**Heritage Open Days:** No.
**P** Spaces: 4. Parking at parish staithe, approx. 100 yards. Pub also allows parking for visitors.
**⬤** No wheelchair access. No WC for the disabled. No Guide Dogs allowed.
**£** Donations invited.

## WAXHAM GREAT BARN
**Sea Palling, Norfolk NR1 2DH**
Grade I listed barn, 1570s-80s, with later additions. Flint with ashlar dressings and thatched roof. Much of its fabric is reused material from dissolved monasteries.
**Grant Recipient:** Norfolk County Council
**Access contact:** Ms Caroline Davison
**T:** 01603 222706  **F:** 01603 224413
**E-mail:** caroline.davison@norfolk.gov.uk
**Open:** Provisional: 5 May–28 October, daily, 10.30am–4.30pm. Visitors should ring nearer the time to confirm opening times.
**Heritage Open Days:** No.
**P** Spaces: 100. Free parking.
**⬤** Partial. Wheelchair access with assistance (gravel path from car park to Barn). WC for the disabled. Guide Dogs allowed.
**£** Adult: £3.00. Child: Free. Other: £2.50 concessions.

# NORTH YORKSHIRE

## AISKEW WATER CORNMILL
**Bedale, North Yorkshire DL8 1AW**
Grade II* watermill, late 18th and early 19th century. Sold in 1918 in a major dispersal of estate properties. Roof and main structure restored. Restoration of interior with original wooden machinery is planned.
**www.farmattraction.co.uk**
**Grant Recipient:** David Clark
**Access contact:** Jared, Duncan & Carol Clark
**T:** 01677 422125  **F:** 01677 425205
**E-mail:** enquiries@farmattraction.co.uk
**Open:** Access to the exterior at all reasonable times. Guided tours available by prior arrangement.
**Heritage Open Days:** Yes
**P** Spaces: 40
**⬤** Full. WC for the disabled. Guide Dogs allowed.
**£** No.

## BENINGBROUGH HALL
**Shipton-by-Beningbrough, North Yorkshire YO30 1DD**
Country house, c1716, contains an impressive Baroque interior exhibiting over one hundred 18th century portraits in partnership with the National Portrait Gallery. A very high standard of craftsmanship is displayed throughout, most of the original work surviving with extremely fine woodcarving and other ornate decoration, and an unusual central corridor running the full length of the house. There is a fully equipped Victorian laundry and walled garden.
**www.nationaltrust.org.uk**
**Grant Recipient:** The National Trust
**Access contact:** Property Manager
**T:** 01904 470666  **F:** 01904 470002
**E-mail:** beningbrough@nationaltrust.org.uk
**Open:** House: 17 March–31 October: daily except Thursday and Friday, 12 noon–5pm. Grounds and shop: 17 March–28 June: daily except Thursday and Friday, 11am–5.30pm. 1 July–1 September: daily except Thursday and Friday, 11am–5.30pm. 4 November–17 December: Saturdays and Sundays, 11am–3.30pm. Restaurant: as grounds.
**Heritage Open Days:** No.
**P** Spaces: 250
**⬤** Partial. Wheelchairs available on all floors, as well as seating. Steps to entrance with handrail or lift available as well as alternative entrance. Access to ground floor and stairs with handrail or lift to other floors. WC for the disabled. Guide Dogs allowed.
**£** Adult: £7.70 (house & grounds). Child: £3.90 (house & grounds). Other: £17.60 (Family: 2 Adults & 3 Children/1 Adult & 4 Children). Group: £6.50 (adult), £4.00 (child). Reduced rate when arriving by cycle.

## CASTLE HOWARD
**York, North Yorkshire YO60 7DA**
Large stately home dating from the beginning of the 18th century and designed by Sir John Vanbrugh. Situated in 10,000 acres of landscaped grounds, which includes numerous monuments.
**www.castlehoward.co.uk**
**Grant Recipient:** The Hon. Simon Howard
**Access contact:** Mr D N Peake
**T:** 01653 648444  **F:** 01653 648529
**E-mail:** estatemanager@castlehoward.co.uk
**Open:** 1 March–5 November: daily, 11am–4.00pm (Grounds only from 10am); November–mid-March: grounds open most days but please telephone for confirmation in November, December and January. Access to interior of Temple of the Four Winds by prior arrangement only.
**Heritage Open Days:** No.
**P** Spaces: 300
**⬤** Partial. Wheelchair access to all but chapel and first floor of exhibition wing. WC for the disabled. Guide Dogs allowed.
**£** Adult: £9.50 (provisional). Child: £7.00 (provisional). Other: £8.50 (provisional).

## CONSTABLE MAUSOLEUM
**Halsham, nr. Kingston-upon-Hull, East Riding of Yorkshire**
The Constable Mausoleum was commissioned by Edward Constable in 1792, built by Atkinson and York and completed in 1802 at a cost of £3,300. It comprises a central domed rotunda of stone, internally lined with black

marble and surrounded by heraldic shields. The external raised and railed podium is part of a vaulted ceiling to the crypt below, in which various generation of the Constable family are interned.
**Grant Recipient:** Mr John Chichester-Constable
**Access contact:** Mr John Chichester-Constable
**T:** 01964 562316    **F:** 01964 563283
**E-mail:** info@burtonconstable.co.uk
**Open:** By prior written arrangement with Mr John Chichester-Constable, South Wing-Estate Office, Burton Constable Hall, nr Kingston-upon-Hull, East Riding of Yorkshire HU11 4LN.
**Heritage Open Days:** No.
P Spaces: 1. On street parking.
No wheelchair access. WC for the disabled at Halsham Arms approximately 300 metres. No Guide Dogs allowed.
£ No.

## DUNCOMBE PARK

**Helmsley, York, North Yorkshire YO62 5EB**
Recently restored family home of Lord and Lady Feversham. Originally built in 1713 and then rebuilt after a fire in 1879 largely to the original design. Early 18th century gardens.
www.duncombepark.com
**Grant Recipient:** Lord Feversham
**Access contact:** Duncombe Park Estate Office
**T:** 01439 770213    **F:** 01439 771114
**E-mail:** liz@duncombepark.com
**Open:** 6 May–28 October: Sunday–Thursday, house: tours hourly, 12.30pm–3.30pm lasting 1¼ hours. Garden: 11am–5.30pm (last admission to gardens and parkland 4.30pm). Special Events throughout the year. Duncombe Park reserve the right to alter opening arrangements without prior notice–please telephone to check.
**Heritage Open Days:** No.
P Spaces: 200
Partial. Wheelchair access to ground and first floor only. WC for the disabled. Guide Dogs allowed.
£ **Adult:** £7.25 (house & gardens), £4.00 (gardens & parkland), £2.00 (parkland). **Child:** £3.25 (10-16, house & garden), £2.00 (10-16, gardens & parkland), £1.00 (10-16, parkland). **Other:** £5.50 (concessions, house & garden), £15.00 (family, house & garden), £5.25 (groups, house & garden), £30.00 (family season ticket).

## FOUNTAINS HALL

**Ripon, North Yorkshire HG4 3DY**
Elizabethan mansion, built between 1589 and 1604 for Stephen Proctor. Three rooms; the Stone Hall, the Arkell Room, and the Reading Room, all unfurnished, are open to the public. The conservation of a fourth room, the Great Chamber, has recently been completed. This upper room features an ornate chimney piece depicting the Biblical story of the Judgement of Solomon. The mansion is situated within a World Heritage Site which also includes the ruins of a 12th century Cistercian Abbey, monastic water mill and Georgian water garden.
www.fountainsabbey.org.uk
**Grant Recipient:** The National Trust
**Access contact:** Property Manager
**T:** 01765 608888    **F:** 01765 601002
**E-mail:** fountainsenquiries@nationaltrust.org.uk
**Open:** As part of the Fountain's Abbey and Studley Royal Estate. January–February: 10am–4pm. March–October, 10am–5pm. November–December, 10am–4pm. Estate closed 24, 25 December and Fridays in January, November and December. Deer Park: open all year, dawn to dusk.
**Heritage Open Days:** No.
P Spaces: 500
Full. WC for the disabled. Guide Dogs allowed.
£ **Adult:** £7.50. **Child:** £4.00. **Other:** £20.00 (family). £6.50 (adult, groups 15–30), £3.50 (child, groups 15-30). £6.00 (adult, groups 31+), £3.00 (child, 31+). EH Members free.

## GIGGLESWICK SCHOOL CHAPEL

**Giggleswick, Settle, North Yorkshire BD24 0DE**
Built 1897-1901 by T G Jackson for Walter Morrison as a gift to the school to commemorate the Diamond Jubilee of Queen Victoria. Constructed of Gothic banded rockfaced millstone grit sandstone and limestone, with lead hipped roof to nave and copper covered terracotta dome to chancel. Contains Italian sgraffito work throughout.
www.giggleswick.org.uk
**Grant Recipient:** The Governors of Giggleswick School
**Access contact:** The Bursar and Clerk to the Governors

**T:** 01729 893000/893012    **F:** 01729 893150
**E-mail:** bursar@giggleswick.org.uk
**Open:** Monday–Friday, 9am–5pm, closed Bank Holidays. Other times by arrangement. Visitors must report to reception to obtain the key to the Chapel.
**Heritage Open Days:** Yes
P Spaces: 40
Partial. Wheelchair access to ground floor only. WC for the disabled in main school premises. No Guide Dogs allowed.
£ No.

## HOVINGHAM HALL

**Hovingham, York, North Yorkshire YO62 4LU**
Palladian house built c1760 by Thomas Worsley to his own design. Unique entry through huge riding school. Extensive gardens in a parkland setting. The private cricket ground in front of the house is reported to be the oldest in England.
www.hovingham.co.uk
**Grant Recipient:** Mr William Worsley
**Access contact:** Mrs Kathryn Lamprey
**T:** 01653 628771    **F:** 01653 628668
**E-mail:** office @hovingham.co.uk
**Open:** 4 June–7 July: Monday–Saturday, 1.15–4.30pm (closed Sunday). Last tour 3.30pm.
**Heritage Open Days:** No.
P Spaces: 80
Partial. Wheelchair access to ground floor. WC for the disabled in adjacent village hall. Guide Dogs allowed.
£ **Adult:** £6.00. **Child:** £3.00. **Other:** £5.50 (concessions), £3.50 (gardens).

## JERVAULX ABBEY

**Ripon, North Yorkshire HG4 4PH**
Ruins of Cistercian Abbey moved to this site in 1156, built of sandstone ashlar in Early English style. Remains of nave, transepts and choir, with a cloister on the south side of the nave, flanked by a chapter house to the east and a kitchen and dorter to the south.
**Grant Recipient:** Mr Ian Burdon
**Access contact:** Mr Ian Burdon
**T:** 01677 460391/01677 460226
**E-mail:** ba123@btopenworld.com
**Open:** At any reasonable time throughout the year.
**Heritage Open Days:** No.
P Spaces: 55
Partial. Wheelchair access to church, infirmary, frater and cloisters. Uneven terrain and steps on other parts of site. WC for the disabled. Guide Dogs allowed.
£ **Adult:** £2.00 (honesty box). **Child:** £1.50 (honesty box).

## MAISTER HOUSE

**160 High Street, Kingston-upon-Hull,**
**East Riding of Yorkshire HU1 1NL**
Rebuilt in 1743 during Hull's heyday as an affluent trading centre, this house is a typical but rare survivor of a contemporary merchant's residence. The restrained exterior belies the spectacular plasterwork staircase inside. The house is now let as offices.
www.nationaltrust.org.uk
**Grant Recipient:** The National Trust
**Access contact:** Property Manager
**T:** 01482 324114/ 01723 870423    **F:** 01482 227003
**Open:** Daily except Saturday and Sunday (closed Good Friday and all Bank Holidays), 10am–4pm. Access is to entrance hall and staircase only. Unsuitable for groups.
**Heritage Open Days:** No.
P No.
No wheelchair access. No WC for the disabled. Guide Dogs allowed.
£ Donations welcome.

## MARKENFIELD HALL

**Ripon, North Yorkshire HG4 3AD**
Fortified moated manor house, built 1310-1323 for John de Markenfield (Chancellor of the Exchequer to Edward II), with further additions and alterations in the 16th, 18th and 19th centuries. Restored 1981-4 and 2001-3.
www.markenfield.com
**Grant Recipient:** Lady Deirdre Curteis
**Access contact:** Mrs Sarah Robson
**T:** 01765 692303    **F:** 01765 607195
**E-mail:** markenfieldhall@btinternet.com
**Open:** 29 April–12 May and 17–30 June 2–5pm (last entry 4.30pm). Groups with guided tour by appointment all year round.

**Heritage Open Days:** No.
P Spaces: 25
Partial. Wheelchair access to ground floor only. No WC for the disabled. Guide Dogs allowed.
£ **Adult:** £4.00. **Child:** £3.00. **Other:** £3.00 (senior citizens), £80.00 (minimum charge groups out of opening times).

## MARSKE HALL

**Marske by the Sea, Redcar and Cleveland TS11 6AA**
Country house built by Sir William Pennyman in 1625. 2 storeys with 3-storey projecting towers in a 9-bay range forming a symmetrical front approx. 115ft long. Altered in the late 19th and 20th centuries. Varied uses during 20th century include as quarters for the Royal Flying Corps in WWI, Army quarters in WWII, school 1948-58 and since 1963 a Cheshire Foundation nursing home.
**Grant Recipient:** Teesside Cheshire Homes
**Access contact:** Mrs Sue O'Brien
**T:** 01642 482672    **F:** 01642 759973
**E-mail:** marske@ney.leonard-cheshire.org.uk
**Open:** Hall by prior arrangement only. Grounds open to public at all fund raising events such as the Summer Fete (one Saturday in June).
**Heritage Open Days:** No.
P Spaces: 20
Full. WC for the disabled. Guide Dogs allowed.
£ No.

## MOWBRAY POINT

**The Ruin, Hackfall, Harrogate, North Yorkshire**
Folly, built c1750, standing in the Grade I registered remains of the 18th century garden at Hackfall. It is a small pavilion above a steep wooded gorge.
www.landmarktrust.org.uk
**Grant Recipient:** The Landmark Trust
**Access contact:** Ms Victoria O'Keeffe
**T:** 01628 825920    **F:** 01628 825417
**E-mail:** vokeeffe@landmarktrust.org.uk
**Open:** The Landmark Trust is an independent charity, which rescues small buildings of historic or architectural importance from decay or unsympathetic improvement. Landmark's aim is to promote the enjoyment of these historic buildings by making them available to stay in for holidays. Mowbray Point can be rented by anyone, at all times of the year, for periods ranging from a weekend to three weeks. Bookings can be made by telephoning the Booking Office on 01628 825925. As the building is in full-time use for holiday accommodation, it is not normally open to the public. However, the public have access to and across the terrace all year 11am–4pm and to the interior by prior arrangement by telephoning the access contact (Victoria O'Keeffe on 01628 825920) to make an appointment. Potential visitors will be asked to write to confirm the details of their visit.
**Heritage Open Days:** Yes
P Spaces: 2
No wheelchair access. No WC for the disabled. Guide Dogs allowed.
£ No.

## NATIONAL CENTRE FOR EARLY MUSIC

**St Margaret's Church, Walmgate,**
**York, North Yorkshire YO1 9TL**
14th century church with highly decorated 12th century Romanesque doorway (removed from chapel of the ruined hospital of St Nicholas, probably during 1684-5 rebuilding of church (orange-red brick tower of same date) occasioned by Civil War damage). Now houses the National Centre for Early Music and used for concerts, music educational activities, conferences, recordings and events.
www.ncem.co.uk
**Grant Recipient:** York Early Music Foundation
**Access contact:** Mrs G Baldwin
**T:** 01904 632220    **F:** 01904 612631
**E-mail:** info@ncem.co.uk
**Open:** All year: Monday–Friday, 10am–4pm. Also by prior arrangement. Access is necessarily restricted when events are taking place.
**Heritage Open Days:** No.
P Spaces: 9. 2 parking places for the disabled.
Full. WC for the disabled. Guide Dogs allowed.
£ No.

## NORTON CONYERS

**nr. Ripon, North Yorkshire HG4 5EQ**

Medieval house with Stuart and Georgian additions. Listed Grade II*. Family pictures, furniture and costumes. Visited by Charlotte Bronte in 1839; a family legend of a mad woman confined in an attic room contributed towards the mad Mrs Rochester in 'Jane Eyre' and the house was a model for 'Thornfield Hall'. Located within the walled garden to the west of the house, the 18th century Orangery is a five bay arcaded sandstone building, flanked by Victorian glasshouses. The Orangery is listed at Grade II.
**Grant Recipient:** Sir James Graham Bt
**Access contact:** Sir James Graham Bt
**T:** 01765 640333    **F:** 01765 640333
**E-mail:** norton.conyers@bronco.co.uk
**Open:** Garden and Orangery: 8 & 9 April; 6 & 7, 27 & 28 May; 3 June–30 July Sundays and Mondays; 4–7 July daily; 26 & 27 August: 2–5pm (last admission 4.40pm). House: building work will be taking place during 2007 and opening dates for the house uncertain at time of publication. Please contact Sir James Graham Bt for further information before planning a visit.
**Heritage Open Days:** No.
P Spaces: 60. Free car park approx. 50m from the house; disabled parking available near front door by arrangement.
Partial. Wheelchair access to ground floor of house only. Some gravelled paths in garden may be difficult. WC for the disabled. Guide Dogs allowed.
£ **Adult:** Charge is made on charity open days. At other times, donations are welcome. **Child:** Free (16 and under).

## ORMESBY HALL

**Church Lane, Ormesby, Middlesbrough, North Yorkshire TS7 9AS**

A mid-18th century Palladian mansion, notable for its fine plasterwork and carved wood decoration. The Victorian laundry and kitchen with scullery and game larder are interesting. 18th century stable block, attributed to Carr of York, is leased to the Cleveland Mounted Police. Large model railway and garden with holly walk.
**www.nationaltrust.org.uk**
**Grant Recipient:** The National Trust
**Access contact:** Property Manager
**T:** 01642 324188    **F:** 01642 300937
**E-mail:** ormesbyhall@nationaltrust.org.uk
**Open:** Hall: 31 March–4 November, Saturdays and Sundays only (and Bank Holiday Mondays), 1.30–5pm (last admission 4.30pm). Tea room: as Hall, 12.30–5pm.
**Heritage Open Days:** No.
P Spaces: 100. Car park 100 metres from House.
Partial. Wheelchair access to ground floor of Hall (shallow step at entrance), shop, tea room and garden. No WC for the disabled. Guide Dogs allowed.
£ **Adult:** £4.40. **Child:** £2.80. **Other:** £11.50 (family), £3.50 (groups).

## RIBBLEHEAD VIADUCT

**Ribblehead, North Yorkshire**

Railway viaduct, 1870-74, rockfaced stone and brick. 104 feet high at highest point. Largest and most impressive of the viaducts of the Settle–Carlisle line of the Midland Railway.
**Grant Recipient:** British Rail
**Access contact:** Mr Simon Brooks
**T:** 0161 228 8574    **F:** 0161 228 4958
**E-mail:** simon.brooks@networkrail.co.uk
**Open:** Viewing from ground level only. Strictly no access from Network Rail property.
**Heritage Open Days:** No.
P On-street parking in Cave.
No wheelchair access. No WC for the disabled. No Guide Dogs allowed.
£ No.

## SCAMPSTON HALL

**Scampston, Malton, North Yorkshire, YO17 8NG**

Late 17th century country house, extensively remodelled in 1801 by Thomas Leverton. Contains Regency interiors and an art collection. Set in a parkland designed by 'Capability' Brown with 10 acres of lakes and a Palladian bridge.
**www.scampston.co.uk**
**Grant Recipient:** Sir Charles Legard Bt
**Access contact:** Sir Charles Legard Bt
**T:** 01944 758224    **F:** 01944 758700
**E-mail:** info@scampston.co.uk
**Open:** 22 May–21 June (closed Mondays), 1.30–5.00pm.
**Heritage Open Days:** No.

P Spaces: 50.
Partial. WC for the disabled. Guide Dogs allowed.
£ **Adult:** £6.00 (house, garden & park). **Child:** £3.00 (age 12-16). Free for 11 & under.

## ST MARY'S CHURCH STAIRS

**Whitby, North Yorkshire**

Flight of steps originally built of wood in 14th century, replaced now largely 18th and 19th century. Flight of 199 stone steps leading up to the parish church. Listed Grade I.
**Grant Recipient:** PCC of St Mary's Whitby
**Access contact:** Canon Edwyn Newlyn
**T:** 01947 606578    **F:** 01974 602798
**E-mail:** whitbyparishoffice@biscit.co.uk
**Open:** At all times.
**Heritage Open Days:** No.
P Pay and display parking.
Partial. Wheelchair access for viewing only. WC for the disabled in the church. Guide Dogs allowed.
£ No.

## ST PAULINUS

**Brough Park**

Richmond, North Yorkshire DL10 7PJ
Catholic neo-Gothic chapel designed by Bonomi with priest's accommodation and school room in undercroft.
**Grant Recipient:** Mr Greville Worthington
**Access contact:** Mr Greville Worthington
**T:** 01748 812127
**E-mail:** grev@saintpaulinus.co.uk
**Open:** By prior arrangement.
**Heritage Open Days:** No.
P Spaces: 2
Partial. Wheelchair access to downstairs. No WC for the disabled. Guide Dogs allowed.
£ No.

## ST SAVIOUR'S CHURCH (DIG)

**St Saviourgate, York, North Yorkshire YO1 8NN**

Church on site by late 11th century, present building dates from the 15th and extensively remodelled in 1845. Refurbished 2005/06 as DIG–An archaeological centre introduces the visitor to exploration, scientific study and conservation.
**www.digyork.co.uk**
**Grant Recipient:** York Archaeological Trust
**Access contact:** Mrs Christine McDonnell
**T:** 01904 654324    **F:** 01904 671756
**E-mail:** cmcdonnell@yorkarchaeology.co.uk
**Open:** By prior arrangement (tel: 01904 543403). Or alternatively archaeological centre all year: daily, 10am–5pm.
**Heritage Open Days:** No.
P No.
No wheelchair access. No WC for the disabled. No Guide Dogs allowed.
£ **Adult:** £5.00. **Child:** £5.00 (under 5s free). **Other:** £16.00 (family), £19.60 (family of five). Carers/enablers free when helping disabled person.

## STAMFORD BRIDGE VIADUCT

**Stamford Bridge, East Riding of Yorkshire**

Built 1847 for the York & North Midland Railway Company, East Riding lines. Mainly red brick with 10 unadorned round brick arches. The railway line was closed in the mid 1960s and is now repaired as part of a circular pedestrian walkway around the village.
**Grant Recipient:** East Riding of Yorkshire Council
**Access contact:** Mr Patrick Wharam
**T:** 01482 395201
**E-mail:** patrick.wharam@eastriding.gov.uk
**Open:** The site is permanently open as a footpath.
**Heritage Open Days:** No.
P Spaces: 20. Informal parking for approximately 20 cars near sports hall.
Partial. Access to viaduct, but some large wheelchairs may be restricted. No WC for the disabled. Guide Dogs allowed.
£ No.

## THE MOUNT SCHOOL LINDLEY MURRAY SUMMERHOUSE

**Dalton Terrace, York, North Yorkshire YO24 4DD**

Grade II* listed summerhouse built c1774, formerly situated in the grounds of Holgate House, York. Octagonal timber structure on raised stepped circular base with lead

ogee roof and decorated with Doric columns. Restored in 1997.
**Grant Recipient:** The Mount School
**Access contact:** Mrs Julie Davis
**T:** 01904 667500    **F:** 01904 667524
**E-mail:** bursar@mount.n-yorks.sch.uk
**Open:** By prior arrangement Monday–Friday all year (except Bank Holidays) 9am–4.30pm.
**Heritage Open Days:** No.
P Spaces: 3
Full. WC for the disabled. Guide Dogs allowed.
£ Donations welcome.

## THOMPSON MAUSOLEUM

**Little Ouseburn Churchyard, Little Ouseburn, North Yorkshire YO26 9TS**

18th century Mausoleum in magnesian limestone. It is a rotunda encircled by 13 Tuscan columns, above which a frieze and cornice support a plain drum and ribbed domed roof. Listed Grade II*. Built for the use of the Thompson family of Kirby Hall.
**Grant Recipient:** Little Ouseburn Mausoleum Ltd
**Access contact:** Mr H Hibbs
**T:** 01423 330414
**E-mail:** helier@talktalk.net
**Open:** Always available to view from the outside, interior visible through a replica of the original wrought iron gate. Access to interior by arrangement. Contact Mr Hibbs, Little Ouseburn Mausoleum Ltd, Hilltop Cottage, Little Ouseburn, North Yorks YO26 9TD (tel:01423 330414) for current information.
**Heritage Open Days:** Yes
P Spaces: 8
Partial. Wheelchair access with assistance (gravel path and grass). No WC for the disabled. Guide Dogs allowed.
£ No.

## THORPE PREBEND HOUSE

**High St. Agnesgate, Ripon, North Yorkshire HG4 1QR**

Late medieval house with 17th century alterations. Restored 2002-4 to form a heritage interpretation centre for the region. The house also has facilities for small scale public events and meetings.
**Grant Recipient:** Chapter of Ripon Cathedral
**Access contact:** The Administrator
**T:** 01765 603462/ 01765 609076
**E-mail:** ianhorsford@riponcathedral .org.uk
**Open:** April–end of October: daily except Sunday, 10.30am- 4pm. Occasionally closed for special events, please telephone to check before visiting.
**Heritage Open Days:** No.
P Parking available for the disabled.
Full. WC for the disabled. Guide Dogs allowed.
£ **Adult:** £2.00. **Child:** £1.00. **Other:** £1.00 (students).

## TRINITY CHURCH TOWER

**Market Place, Richmond, North Yorkshire DL10 4QN**

Church clock tower to the former castle church, now in the centre of Richmond Market Place.
**Grant Recipient:** Richmond Town Council
**Access contact:** Richmond Town Council
**Open:** Access to the exterior at all times from Richmond Market Place.
**Heritage Open Days:** No.
P Spaces: 120
Full. WC for the disabled available in Town Hall opposite. Guide Dogs allowed.
£ No.

# NORTHAMPTONSHIRE

## BOUGHTON PARK

**Boughton, Northamptonshire NN16 9UP**

Extensive remains of formal gardens of late 17th and early 18th century around a country house rebuilt at the same time, set in a park developed from a late medieval deer park. Beyond the park are avenues and rides, also part of the landscape of the late 17th and early 18th centuries. The grant aided Lily pool is approximately 100 meters south of the House.
**www.boughtonhouse.org.uk**
**Grant Recipient:** Boughton Estates Ltd
**Access contact:** Mr Christopher B Sparrow MRICS
**T:** 01536 482308    **F:** 01536 410 452
**E-mail:** csparrow@boughtonestate.co.uk
**Open:** 1 May–1 September daily (except Fridays in

May–July), 1–5pm.
**Heritage Open Days:** No.
**P** Spaces: 100
**&** Partial. Wheelchair access to ground floor fully accessible, first floor viewable on virtual tour in gift shop. No WC for the disabled. Guide Dogs allowed.
**£ Adult:** £1.50 (grounds), £6.00 (house and grounds).
**Child:** £1.00 (grounds), £5.00 (house and grounds).
**Other:** £1.00 (grounds), £5.00 (house and grounds).

### HARROWDEN HALL GARDEN STATUES
**Wellingborough, Northamptonshire NN9 5AD**
Early 18th century Harrowden Hall retains its surprisingly unaltered contemporary garden containing a number of garden features, including statues by the Dutch sculptor Van Nost, of which one has recently been repaired.
**Grant Recipient:** Wellingborough Golf Club
**Access contact:** Mr David Waite
**T:** 01933 677234   **F:** 01933 67937
**E-mail:** secretary@wellingboroughgolfclub.com
**Open:** 27 March to 2 October: Mondays.
**Heritage Open Days:** No.
**P** Spaces: 100
**&** Full. WC for the disabled. Guide Dogs allowed.
**£** No.

### LAXTON HALL
**Corby, Northamptonshire NN17 3AU**
Stone built 18th century manor house, enlarged and modified in 19th century and set in 60 acres of parkland. Stable block by Repton. Formerly a boys school, now a residential home for elderly Poles.
**Grant Recipient:** Polish Benevolent Housing Association Ltd
**Access contact:** Sister Teresa Sabok
**T:** 01780 444 292   **F:** 01780 444 574
**E-mail:** Teresa@pbfgroup.co.uk
**Open:** By prior written arrangement with Sister Teresa at Laxton Hall.
**Heritage Open Days:** No.
**P** Spaces: 10
**&** Partial. Wheelchair access to ground floor only. WC for the disabled. Guide Dogs allowed.
**£** No.

## NORTHUMBERLAND

### ALNWICK TOWN HALL
**Market Place, Alnwick, Northumberland NE66 1HS**
Situated in Alnwick Market Place. Property includes the Hall, the Freemens Council Room and the Clock Tower. The 18th century building houses the Freemen's Shields and various items of Freemens History.
**Grant Recipient:** The Freemens' Common Council
**Access contact:** Mr Dennis Nixon, Clerk to the Freemen
**T:** 01665 603 517   **F:** 01665 603 517
**Open:** To the exterior at all times and to the interior by prior arrangement.
**Heritage Open Days:** Yes
**P** No.
**&** No wheelchair access. No WC for the disabled. No Guide Dogs allowed.
**£** No.

### BELFORD HALL
**Belford, Northumberland NE70 7EY**
Palladian Country House by James Paine, 1754-56, Wings & North Front added 1818 by John Dobson. Derelict for 40 years until restored and converted into private apartments by North East Civic Trust and Monument Trust, 1984-87. The Saloon, Staircase, Portico and Wine Cellar are open to the public.
**Grant Recipient:** North East Civic Trust
**Access contact:** Mr John Harris
**T:** 01668 219 716
**E-mail:** jhharris@dircon.co.uk
**Open:** Interior and exterior: any day, excluding Christmas and Easter, 10am–4.30pm (3pm in winter months) by prior arrangement with Mr JH Harris (tel: 01668 219716) or Lady Graham (tel: 01668 213140). No public toilets.
**Heritage Open Days:** Yes
**P** Spaces: 8. Free parking.
**&** Partial. Wheelchair access to ground floor by ramp (or three steps to main entrance). No WC for the disabled. No Guide Dogs allowed.
**£** No.

### COANWOOD FRIENDS MEETING HOUSE
**Coanwood nr. Haltwhistle, Northumberland NE49**
Built in 1760, remaining relatively unchanged. Located in a remote valley south of Hadrian's Wall.
**www.hct.org.uk**
**Grant Recipient:** Historic Chapels Trust
**Access contact:** Dr Jennifer Freeman
**T:** 020 7481 0533   **F:** 020 7488 3756
**E-mail:** chapels@hct.org.uk
**Open:** At all reasonable times.
**Heritage Open Days:** Yes
**P** Spaces: 20
**&** Full. No WC for the disabled. Guide Dogs allowed.
**£** Donations invited.

### HIGH STAWARD FARM
**Langley-on-Tyne, Hexham, Northumberland NE47 5NS**
Georgian farmhouse standing inside a walled garden surrounded by the farm steading. Has a ging gang, threshing machine, pig stys with stone troughs and a blacksmiths shop. Most of the house and buildings are of dressed stone and the house has flagged floors, ceiling hooks, cheeseboard and rail, large pantry and servants staircase. Still a working hill farm.
**Grant Recipient:** Mr R J Coulson
**Access contact:** Mr R J Coulson
**T:** 01434 683619
**Open:** January–23 September: by prior arrangement.
**Heritage Open Days:** No.
**P** Spaces: 2
**&** No wheelchair access. No WC for the disabled. Guide Dogs allowed.
**£** No.

### LADY'S WELL
**Holystone, Harbbottle, Northumberland**
The Lady's Holy Well is considered to be of Roman origin and is located on a halting place along the Roman road. The main feature of the well today is a rectangular stone tank which is fed by a natural spring.
**www.nationaltrust.org.uk**
**Grant Recipient:** The National Trust
**Access contact:** Mr John O'Brien
**T:** 01669 620333 ext. 101   **F:** 01669 620066
**Open:** At all times.
**Heritage Open Days:** No.
**P** No.
**&** No wheelchair access. No WC for the disabled. Guide Dogs allowed.
**£** No.

### LAMBLEY VIADUCT
**Lambley, Tynedale, Northumberland**
17 arch stone viaduct, 100ft high and 1650ft long, spanning the South Tyne river. Originally carried single track, now used as a footpath.
**www.npht.com**
**Grant Recipient:** British Rail Property Board/North Pennines Heritage Trust
**Access contact:** Mr David Flush, Chief Executive
**T:** 01434 382 294   **F:** 01434 382 294
**E-mail:** trust@npht.com
**Open:** At all times as part of the South Tyne Trail between Featherstone Park and Alston.
**Heritage Open Days:** No.
**P** Spaces: 30
**&** Full. No WC for the disabled. Guide Dogs allowed.
**£** No.

### LINDISFARNE CASTLE
**Holy Island, Berwick-upon-Tweed, Northumberland TD15 2SH**
Built in 1550 to protect Holy Island harbour from attack, the castle was converted into a private house for Edward Hudson by Sir Edwin Luytens in 1903. Small walled garden was designed by Gertrude Jekyll. 19th century lime kilns in field by the castle.
**www.nationaltrust.org.uk**
**Grant Recipient:** The National Trust
**Access contact:** Property Manager
**T:** 01289 389244   **F:** 01289 389349
**E-mail:** lindisfarne@nationaltrust.org.uk
**Open:** Castle: 17 February–25 February daily. 17 March–28 October: daily except Monday (open Scottish and English Bank Holiday Mondays). 27, 28, 29 & 30 December. Open for 4½ hours either 10.30am–3pm or 12

noon–4.30pm, depending on the tide. Garden: all year, 10am–dusk.
**Heritage Open Days:** No.
**P** No.
**&** No wheelchair access. No WC for the disabled. Guide Dogs allowed.
**£ Adult:** £5.20 (castle), £1.00 (garden only). **Child:** £2.90 **Other:** £14.50 (family), NT members free, £6.00 (groups 10+ out-of-hours by prior arrangement).

### LITTLE HARLE TOWER
**Kirkwhelpington, Newcastle-upon-Tyne, Northumberland NE19 2PD**
Medieval tower with 17th century range and a Victorian wing which contains a recently restored 1740s drawing room. It has been one family's home since 1830 though part is now let.
**Grant Recipient:** Mr J P P Anderson
**Access contact:** Mr Simon Rowarth
**T:** 01434 609000   **F:** 01434 606900
**E-mail:** simon.rowarth@youngscs.com
**Open:** By prior arrangement (at least two weeks notice required) with Mr Simon Rowarth of Youngs, 3 Wentworth Place, Hexham, Northumberland NE46 1XB.
**Heritage Open Days:** No.
**P** Spaces: 6
**&** Partial. Wheelchair access to the ground floor only. No WC for the disabled. Guide Dogs allowed.
**£** Donations to the church requested.

### MITFORD HALL CAMELLIA HOUSE
**Morpeth, Northumberland NE61 3PZ**
East wing and conservatory of country house built c1820 by John Dobson, detached from main house by demolition of north-east wing in the 20th century. The conservatory houses a superb specimen of a red flowering camellia dating to c1826.
**Grant Recipient:** Shepherd Offshore plc
**Access contact:** Mr B Shepherd
**T:** 01670 512637   **F:** 0191 2639872
**Open:** By prior written arrangement during the summer.
**Heritage Open Days:** No.
**P** Spaces: 3
**&** Full. Wheelchair access by prior arrangement. Ordinary toilet on site may be accessible for some disabled persons, please contact Hall for further information. Guide Dogs allowed.
**£** No.

### NETHERWITTON HALL
**Morpeth, Northumberland NE61 4NW**
Grade I listed mansion house built c1685 by Robert Trollope for Sir Nicholas Thornton. Access to main ground floor rooms and external elevations. Built as a family home and remains the current family home.
**Grant Recipient:** Mr J H T Trevelyan
**Access contact:** Mr J H T Trevelyan
**T:** 01670 772 249   **F:** 01670 772 510
**Open:** By prior arrangement at least 24 hours in advance. 30 April–28 May and 4–12 June: Monday–Friday, 11am–2pm by compulsory tour. Groups at other times by prior arrangement.
**Heritage Open Days:** No.
**P** Spaces: 20
**&** Full. Use of ramps up external steps. WC for the disabled available at village hall. Guide Dogs allowed.
**£ Adult:** £5.00. **Child:** £1.00.

### SEATON DELAVAL HALL
**Seaton Sluice, Whitley Bay, Northumberland NE26 4QR**
Country house, 1718-29 by Sir John Vanbrugh for Admiral George Delaval. Listed Grade I. The house comprises a centre block between two arcaded pedimented wings. In 1822 the centre block was gutted by fire and was partially restored in 1862-63, and again in 1959-62 and 1999-2000. Extensive gardens with statues and also a Norman church.
**Grant Recipient:** The Lord Hastings
**Access contact:** Mrs Mills
**T:** 0191 2371493
**E-mail:** lordhastings@onetel.com
**Open:** 1 June–30 September: May and August Bank Holiday Mondays, Wednesdays and Sundays, 2–6pm.
**Heritage Open Days:** No.
**P** Spaces: 50
**&** Partial. Wheelchair access to Stables, Tea Room, Coach

House, Ice House, Norman Church and gardens WC for the disabled. Guide Dogs allowed.
**£** **Adult:** £4.00. **Child:** £1.00. **Other:** £3.50 (senior citizens), £1.00 (students), £3.00 (groups 20+ adults).

## ST CUTHBERT'S CHAPEL
### Farne Islands, Northumberland

St Cuthbert's Chapel was completed in 1370. By the early 19th century it was in a ruinous condition. Restored in 1840 by Archdeacon Thorp it includes some fine 17th century woodwork from Durham Cathedral and a memorial to Grace Darling. Remains of an original window.
**www.nationaltrust.org.uk**
**Grant Recipient:** The National Trust
**Access contact:** Mr John Walton
**T:** 01665 720651  **F:** 01665 720651
**E-mail:** john.walton@nationaltrust.org.uk
**Open:** 1–30 April and 1 August–30 September: daily, 10.30am–6pm. 1 May–31 July (breeding season) daily Staple Island, 10.30am–1.30pm, Inner Farne, 1.30–5pm.
**Heritage Open Days:** No.
**P** Public parking in Seahouses (nearest mainland village).
**&** Partial. Inner Farne is accessible for wheelchairs (telephone the Property Manager in advance). Staple Island is not accessible. WC for the disabled on Inner Farne. Guide dogs are allowed on boat but not on islands.
**£** **Adult:** £5.40 (breeding season), £4.40 (outside breeding season). **Child:** £2.70 (breeding season), £2.20 (outside breeding season). **Other:** £2.60 (booked school parties, breeding season, per island), £2.10 (outside breeding season, per island). Admission fees do not include boatmen's charges.

## ST MICHAEL'S PANT
### Alnwick, Northumberland

St Michael's Pant (drinking fountain) was built in 1765 by Matthew Mills, designed by Mr Bell. St Michael and Dragon (the symbol of the Town) on top of an octagonal drum, gargoyle for the water spout with large square trough which measures approximately ten square metres. Listed Grade II*.
**Grant Recipient:** The Freemen of Alnwick
**Access contact:** Mr D Nixon
**T:** 01665 603517  **F:** 01665 603517
**Open:** To the exterior at all times.
**Heritage Open Days:** Yes
**P** No.
**&** Full. No WC for the disabled. Guide Dogs allowed.
**£** No.

## SWINBURNE CASTLE
### Hexham, Northumberland NE48 4DQ

Kitchen range 1600-1650, incorporating earlier fabric and with later alterations, stands at right angles to the footprint of the now demolished (1966) mid 18th century house which stood on the site of the medieval castle. East (laundry) wing 1770, restored in 2000. Orangery early 19th century.
**Grant Recipient:** Trustees of R W Murphy
**Access contact:** Major R P Murphy
**T:** 01434 681610
**Open:** 3–6, 9–13, 16–20, 23–27, 30 April; 1–4, 7–9, 28 May; 27 August: 12 noon–4.30pm.
**Heritage Open Days:** No.
**P** Spaces: 6
**&** Partial. Wheelchair access to East Wing ground floor only. No WC for the disabled. No Guide Dogs allowed.
**£** No.

## THE TOWER
### Elsdon, Northumberland NE19 1AA

14th century Tower House, residence of the Rector until 1961 and originally used as a refuge from the Border Reivers. Fine example of a medieval tower house and listed Grade I.
**Grant Recipient:** Dr J F Wollaston
**Access contact:** Dr J F Wollaston
**F:** 01830 520904
**Open:** 1 April–30 October: by previously arranged guided visit, weekends only.
**Heritage Open Days:** No.
**P** Spaces: 30
**&** No wheelchair access. No WC for the disabled. Guide Dogs allowed.
**£** **Adult:** £5.00.

## VINDOLANDA ROMAN FORT
### Bardon Mill, Hexham, Northumberland, NE47 7NJ

Roman Fort and civilian settlement in central sector of Hadrian's Wall with active excavation and education programmes. The site is owned and administered by the Vindolanda Charitable Trust and has an on-site museum, with full visitor services, reconstructed Roman buildings and gardens.
**www.vindolanda.com**
**Grant Recipient:** Vindolanda Trust
**Access contact:** Mrs Patricia Birley
**T:** 01434 344277  **F:** 01434 344060
**E-mail:** info@vindolanda.com
**Open:** 14 February–14 November. February–March and October–November: daily, 10am–5pm. April–September: daily, 10am–6pm. Winter opening to be decided.
**Heritage Open Days:** No.
**P** Spaces: 60. Coach parking available on-site.
**&** Partial. Wheelchair access to parts of the archaeological site and all of the museums, gardens and open air museum. WC for the disabled. Guide Dogs allowed.
**£** **Adult:** £4.95 (10% reduction for EH members). **Child:** £3.00 (10% reduction for EH members). **Other:** £4.10 (10% reduction for EH members).

## WALLINGTON HALL & CLOCK TOWER
### Cambo, Morpeth, Northumberland NE61 4AR

Dating from 1688, the house was home to many generations of the Blackett and Trevelyan family. Contains Rococo plasterwork, fine ceramics, paintings and a doll's house collection. Pre-Raphaelite central hall with scenes from Northumbrian history. Hall, Clock Tower and stable buildings set among lawns, lakes and woodland with walled garden.
**www.nationaltrust.org.uk**
**Grant Recipient:** The National Trust
**Access contact:** Property Manager
**T:** 01670 773600  **F:** 01670 774420
**E-mail:** wallington@nationaltrust.org.uk
**Open:** House: daily except Tuesday. 17 March–2 September, 1–5.30pm. 4 September–4 November, 1-4.30pm. Walled garden: daily, 1 April–30 September, 10am–7pm. 1 October–31 October, 10am–6pm. 1 November–31 March, 10am–4pm. Grounds: daily in daylight hours.
**Heritage Open Days:** No.
**P** Spaces: 500
**&** Partial. Lift to first floor for visitors with mobility problems. WC for the disabled. Guide Dogs allowed.
**£** **Adult:** £8.80 (house & gardens), £5.50 (gardens only). **Child:** £4.40 (house & gardens), £2.75 (gardens only). **Other:** £22.00 (family, house & gardens), £15.40 (family, gardens only), £6.80 (groups 15+ house & gardens), £4.70 (groups 15+ gardens only).

# NOTTINGHAMSHIRE

## CHURCH OF ST MARY
### New Road, Colston Bassett, Rushcliffe, Nottinghamshire NG12 3FP

Grade I listed and scheduled monument dating from 1130, now ruined in isolated hill-top position.
**Grant Recipient:** St Mary's Church Repair Fund Committee
**Access contact:** Mr A J M Alcock
**T:** 01949 81248
**Open:** Access at all times.
**Heritage Open Days:** No.
**P** Spaces: 7. Additional unlimited on street parking on New Road.
**&** Full. No WC for the disabled. Guide Dogs allowed.
**£** No.

## KILN WAREHOUSE
### Mather Road, Newark, Nottinghamshire NG24 1FB

Grade II* former warehouse. Early example of the use of massed concrete construction. Interior completely destroyed by fire in the early 1990s, the exterior walls have been restored and warehouse converted into offices.
**Grant Recipient:** British Waterways Midlands & South West
**Access contact:** Mrs Karen Tivey
**T:** 0115 950 7577  **F:** 0115 950 7688
**E-mail:** karen@fhp.co.uk
**Open:** The exterior walls for which the property is notable can be viewed without arrangement. Access to the

internal courtyard is by prior arrangement with Karen Tivey of Fisher Hargreaves Proctor, Chartered Surveyors, 10 Oxford Street, Nottingham NG1 5BG (tel: 0115 950 7577).
**Heritage Open Days:** No.
**P** Parking is available on adjacent land.
**&** Full. WC for the disabled. Guide Dogs allowed.
**£** No.

## PLEASLEY COLLIERY
### Pit Lane, Pleasley, nr. Mansfield, Nottinghamshire

Victorian winding engine house and associated buildings. Engine house contains two steam winding engines under restoration, one turns on electronic motor and work to dismantle the second engine has started.
**Grant Recipient:** Pleasley Pit Trust
**Access contact:** Mr Peter Chambers
**T:** 01623 811231
**Open:** All year: Thursdays, 10am–1pm and Sundays, 9am–3pm. Open weekend 8th and 9th September. Group visits by prior arrangement.
**Heritage Open Days:** No.
**P** Spaces: 50. Free parking.
**&** No wheelchair access. No WC for the disabled. No Guide Dogs allowed.
**£** No.

## UPTON HALL
### (the British Horological Institute), Upton, Newark, Nottinghamshire NG23 5TE

Grade II* listed house in Greek revival style, 1832, incorporating the earlier 17th century house. Large addition and interior remodelled in 1895. During the Second World War the house was a school for partially-sighted children. Now houses the British Horological Institute watch and clock museum featuring clocks from the 17th–20th centuries.
**www.bhi.co.uk/tour/start.htm**
**Grant Recipient:** British Horological Institute
**Access contact:** British Horological Institute
**T:** 01636 813795  **F:** 01636 812258
**E-mail:** clocks@bhi.co.uk
**Open:** Museum: 25 March, 11am–5pm. At other times groups and guided tours by prior appointment.
**Heritage Open Days:** No.
**P** Spaces: 50. Coach parking available.
**&** Partial. No WC for the disabled. Guide Dogs allowed.
**£** **Adult:** £3.50, (guided tours £5.00 per person). **Child:** £2.00 (under 10s free). **Other:** £3.00 (seniors), £10.00 (family).

# OXFORDSHIRE

## ASTON MARTIN HERITAGE TRUST
### Drayton St Leonard, Wallingford, Oxfordshire OX10 7BG

15th century tithe barn, 6 bays. Constructed of elm with hipped roof. Listed Grade II*.
**www.amheritrust.org**
**Grant Recipient:** Aston Martin Owners Club
**Access contact:** Mr Robert Ellis
**T:** 01865 400414  **F:** 01865 400200
**E-mail:** secretary@amheritrust.org
**Open:** Wednesday afternoons: 2–5pm. At other times by prior arrangement.
**Heritage Open Days:** No.
**P** Spaces: 30
**&** Partial. Wheelchair access to ground floor only. WC for the disabled. Guide Dogs allowed.
**£** No.

## BAPTIST CHAPEL
### Shifford Road, Cote, Oxfordshire OX18 2EG

Built around 1739-40 on earlier site and enlarged in 1756.
**www.hct.org.uk**
**Grant Recipient:** Historic Chapels Trust
**Access contact:** Mr Ray Sale
**T:** 01993 850 421
**Open:** At all reasonable times by prior arrangement with key holder, Ray Sale, Elm Barn, Shilford Road, Cote, Oxon OX18 2EG.
**Heritage Open Days:** Yes
**P** Spaces: 30. On-street parking.
**&** Full. WC for the disabled. Guide Dogs allowed.
**£** Donations invited.

## BLENHEIM PALACE & PARK
### Woodstock, Oxfordshire OX20 1PX

Ancestral home of the Dukes of Marlborough and

birthplace of Winston Churchill. Built between 1705-22 for John Churchill, the 1st Duke, in recognition of his victory at the Battle of Blenheim in 1704. Designed by Sir John Vanbrugh, the house contains in its many state rooms a collection of paintings, furniture, bronzes and the Marlborough Victories tapestries. A five-room Churchill Exhibition includes his birth room. 'Capability' Brown park and gardens.
**www.blenheimpalace.com**
**Grant Recipient:** Duke of Marlborough
**Access contact:** Mrs Heather Carter
**T:** 01993 810531   **F:** 01993 813527
**E-mail:** hcarter@blenheimpalace.com
**Open:** Palace: 11 February–10 December, daily, 10.30am–5.30pm (last admission 4.45pm). November and December closed Monday & Tuesday. Park: daily (except Christmas Day), 9am–6pm (last admission 4.45pm).
**Heritage Open Days:** No.
**P** Spaces: 10000
**&#x267F;** Partial. WC for the disabled. Guide Dogs allowed.
**£** Adult: £12.00 off peak, £14.00 peak. Child: £6.50 off peak, £8.50 peak. Other: £9.50 off peak, £11.50 peak (senior citizens).

## CLATTERCOTE PRIORY FARM
**Claydon, Banbury, Oxfordshire OX17 1QB**
Founded c1150, the Priory is now a family house–part farmhouse, part tenanted. A rare example of a Gilbertine Priory with cellars and 'chapel', probably medieval.
**Grant Recipient:** Mr Adrian Taylor
**Access contact:** Mr Adrian Taylor
**T:** 01295 690476   **F:** 01295 690476
**E-mail:** clattercote1@aol.com
**Open:** By prior written arrangement.
**Heritage Open Days:** No.
**P** Spaces: 4
**&#x267F;** No wheelchair access. No WC for the disabled. Guide Dogs allowed.
**£** Adult: £5.00 (to cancer charity).

## CORNBURY PARK
**Charlbury, Oxford, Oxfordshire OX7 3EH**
400 acre deer park adjacent to Wychwood Forest containing newly restored/replanted beech avenues, ancient English oak trees and several ancient monuments.
**www.cornburypark.co.uk**
**Grant Recipient:** The Lord Rotherwick
**Access contact:** Ms Helen Spearman
**T:** 01608 811276   **F:** 01608 811252
**E-mail:** estate@cpark.co.uk
**Open:** 1 March–31 October: Tuesdays and Thursdays, 10am–4pm. Please note that a permit is required for access to the Park; permit must be applied for in advance. Organised educational access walks for groups by prior arrangement.
**Heritage Open Days:** No.
**P** Spaces: 20
**&#x267F;** No wheelchair access. No WC for the disabled. No Guide Dogs allowed.
**£** No.

## CULHAM MANOR DOVECOTE
**The Green, Culham, Oxfordshire OX14 4LZ**
Dovecote constructed from brick and stone, with a date stone above the door of 1685. Reputed to be the second largest dovecote in England, formed of two large cells each with an entry lantern for dove access. In total, it has over 3,000 nesting boxes.
**Grant Recipient:** Mr James Wilson MacDonald
**Access contact:** Mr James Wilson MacDonald
**T:** 01235 527009   **F:** 01865 744520
**E-mail:** wil.mac@virgin.net
**Open:** By prior arrangement (telephone: evenings, fax/e-mail: anytime).
**Heritage Open Days:** No.
**P** Spaces: 20. On Green by Church.
**&#x267F;** No wheelchair access. No WC for the disabled. Guide Dogs allowed.
**£** No.

## FARNBOROUGH HALL, FARNBOROUGH
**Banbury, Oxfordshire OX17 1DU**
Mid-18th century honey-coloured stone built home of the Holbech family for over 300 years, contains impressive plasterwork. Set in grounds with 18th century temples, a terrace walk and an obelisk.
**www.nationaltrust.org.uk**

**Grant Recipient:** The National Trust
**Access contact:** Mrs Julie Smith
**T:** 01295 670266   **F:** 01295 671144
**E-mail:** julie.smith@nationaltrust.org.uk
**Open:** House and garden: 7 April–29 September, Wednesday and Saturday, 2–5.30pm. 6–7 May: Sunday and Monday, 2–5.30pm.
**Heritage Open Days:** No.
**P** Spaces: 10. Additional free parking, 200 yds.
**&#x267F;** Partial. Wheelchair access to ground floor of house and garden. Terrace walk may be difficult as it is very steep. No WC for the disabled. Guide Dogs allowed.
**£** Adult: £4.50. Child: £2.25. Other: £11.75 (family).

## FREEMAN MAUSOLEUM
**St Mary's Churchyard, Fawley, nr Henley-on-Thames, Oxfordshire RG9 6HZ**
Built in 1752 for the Freeman family who owned the Fawley Estate. Design by John Freeman based on the mausoleum of Cecilia Metella on the Appian Way in Rome, which he visited while on his Grand Tour. It contains 30 coffin slots with 12 being filled by the Freemans before they sold the Estate in 1850.
**Grant Recipient:** St Mary's Parochial Church Council
**Access contact:** Mrs Dorothea Giddy
**T:** 01491 572686
**Open:** By prior arrangement with the key holder, Mrs D Giddy (tel:01491 572686).
**Heritage Open Days:** No.
**P** Spaces: 10. On-street parking adjacent to church.
**&#x267F;** Full. No WC for the disabled. Guide Dogs allowed.
**£** No.

## MARTYRS' MEMORIAL
**St. Giles, Oxford, Oxfordshire OX1**
Erected in 1841-3 and designed by Sir George Gilbert Scott, in commemoration of Protestant martyrs, Archbishop Cranmer, Bishops Ridley and Latimer who were burnt to death in 1555 and 1556. The memorial is hexagonal in plan and takes the form of a steeple of three stages reaching a height of 21 metres.
**Grant Recipient:** Oxford City Council
**Access contact:** Mr Nick Worlledge
**T:** 01865 252147   **F:** 01865 252144
**E-mail:** nworlledge@oxford.gov.uk
**Open:** Accessible at all times.
**Heritage Open Days:** No.
**P** No.
**&#x267F;** Full. No WC for the disabled. Guide Dogs allowed.
**£** No.

## SHOTOVER PARK GOTHIC TEMPLE
**Wheatley, Oxfordshire OX33 1QS**
Early 18th century garden folly. The Gothic Temple/ eyecatcher (designer unknown) lies east of the house at the end of a long canal vista. Has a battlemented gable with a central pinnacle and a rose-window, below which is an open loggia of three pointed arches.
**Grant Recipient:** Shotover Estate Company
**Access contact:** Beville Stanier Bt
**T:** 07778 305419   **F:** 01865 875838
**Open:** Access to Temple at all reasonable times (lies close to public rights of way).
**Heritage Open Days:** No.
**P** Spaces: 50. Parking for a few cars at the Gothic Temple, otherwise other arrangements can be made in advance with Sir Beville Stanier on 07778 305419.
**&#x267F;** Partial. Wheelchair access to the Gothic Temple with assistance. No WC for the disabled. Guide Dogs allowed.
**£** No.

## SWALCLIFFE TITHE BARN
**Shipston Road, Swalcliffe, nr. Banbury, Oxfordshire OX15 5DR**
15th century barn built for the Rectorial Manor of Swalcliffe by New College, who owned the Manor. Constructed between 1400 and 1409, much of the medieval timber half-cruck roof remains intact. It is now a museum.
**www.oxfordshire.gov.uk**
**Grant Recipient:** Oxfordshire Historic Building Trust Ltd
**Access contact:** Mr Raj Pal
**T:** 01993 814114   **F:** 01993 813239
**E-mail:** raj.pal@oxfordshire.gov.uk
**Open:** Easter–end of September: Sunday and Bank Holidays, 2–5pm. At other times by prior arrangement (contact Jeff Demmar tel: 01295 788278).

**Heritage Open Days:** No.
**P** Spaces: 10
**&#x267F;** Full. WC for the disabled. Guide Dogs allowed.
**£** No.

## THE OLD RECTORY DOVECOTE
**Mill Street, Kidlington, Oxford, Oxfordshire OX5 2EE**
Large round medieval dovecote.
**Grant Recipient:** Ms Felicity Duncan
**Access contact:** Ms Felicity Duncan
**T:** 01865 513816
**Open:** Daily: 10am–5.30pm.
**Heritage Open Days:** No.
**P** No.
**&#x267F;** No wheelchair access. No WC for the disabled. Guide Dogs allowed.
**£** No.

# SHROPSHIRE

## 2/3 MILK STREET
**Shrewsbury, Shropshire SY1 1SZ**
Timber-framed two and a half storey building dating from the 15th century with later alterations and additions. Medieval shop front to rear. Still a shop.
**Grant Recipient:** Mr M J Cockle
**Access contact:** Mr H Carter
**T:** 01743 276633   **F:** 01743 242140
**E-mail:** htc@pooks.co.uk
**Open:** Ground floor shop open 6 days a week all year. Monday–Saturday, 9.30am–5.30pm. Upper floor flats can be visited only by prior arrangement with Mr H Carter, Pooks, 26 Claremont Hill, Shrewsbury, Shropshire SY1 1RE.
**Heritage Open Days:** No.
**P** No.
**&#x267F;** Partial. Wheelchair access to ground floor only. No WC for the disabled. Guide Dogs allowed.
**£** No.

## ATTINGHAM PARK
**Atcham, Shrewsbury, Shropshire SY4 4TP**
Built 1785 by George Steuart for the 1st Lord Berwick, with a picture gallery by John Nash. Contains Regency interiors, Italian neo-classical furniture and Grand Tour paintings. Park landscaped by Humphrey Repton in 1797.
**www.nationaltrust.org.uk**
**Grant Recipient:** The National Trust
**Access contact:** The Property Manager
**T:** 01743 708162/708123   **F:** 01743 708155
**E-mail:** attingham.park@nationaltrust.org.uk
**Open:** House: 3–25 March, Saturday and Sunday, 1–4.30pm. 26 March–30 October daily except Wednesday and Thursday, 1–5pm (last admission 4.30pm). Guided tours, 12 noon–1pm only. Park: 1 March–31 October, 10am–5pm, 1 November–29 February 2008: daily, 9am–4pm, closed Christmas Day.
**Heritage Open Days:** No.
**P** Spaces: 150
**&#x267F;** Partial. Wheelchair access: to lower ground and ground floors only (house), drives and paths (grounds), and shop. WC for the disabled. Guide Dogs allowed.
**£** Adult: £7.00, £3.50 (house & grounds) £4.00, £2.00 (park & grounds). Other: £17.50 (family: house & grounds), £10.00 (family: grounds only), £5.50 (booked parties 15+).

## BENTHALL HALL
**Broseley, Shropshire TF12 5RX**
16th century stone house situated on a plateau above the gorge of the River Severn, with mullioned and transomed windows, carved oak staircase, decorated plaster ceilings and oak panelling. Also has a restored plantsman's garden, old kitchen garden and a Restoration church.
**www.nationaltrust.org.uk**
**Grant Recipient:** The National Trust
**Access contact:** The Custodian
**T:** 01952 882159
**E-mail:** benthall@nationaltrust.org.uk
**Open:** 3 April–27 June: Tuesday and Wednesday, 2–5.30pm. 1 July–30 September: Tuesday, Wednesday and Sunday, 2–5.30pm. Open Bank Holiday Sundays and Mondays. Groups by prior arrangement with the custodian.
**Heritage Open Days:** No.
**P** Spaces: 50
**&#x267F;** Partial. Wheelchair access to ground floor of Hall and part of garden only. No WC for the disabled. Guide Dogs

allowed.

£ **Adult:** £4.80. **Child:** £2.40. **Other:** Admission price includes voluntary gift aid donation.

### BROSELEY PIPEWORKS

**King Street, Broseley, Shropshire TF8 7AW**

19th century clay pipe factory comprising a three storey factory range, bottle kiln, workers cottage and school room. Contents include pipe-making machinery and collection of smoking pipes. Main rooms contain the original equipment installed in the 1880s and used until the site was abandoned at the end of the 1950s.

**www.ironbridge.org.uk**

**Grant Recipient:** Ironbridge Gorge Museum Trust

**Access contact:** Tourist Information Centre Manager

**T:** 01952 884 391   **F:** 01952 884 391

**E-mail:** tic@ironbridge.org.uk

**Open:** Late May–end of October: 1–5pm.

**Heritage Open Days:** No.

P Spaces: 10. Overflow car park at adjacent site for 20.

♿ Partial. Wheelchair access to ground floor and yard. WC for the disabled. Guide Dogs allowed.

£ **Adult:** £3.50. **Child:** £2.00. **Other:** £2.30 (senior citizens) £2.50.

### COMBERMERE ABBEY

**Whitchurch, Shropshire SY13 4AJ**

Originally founded in 1133 as a Cistercian Abbey, and it has now evolved into a complex medieval and 16th century building with extensive pasteboard Gothic enveloping dating from the early 19th century.

**www.combermereabbey.co.uk**

**Grant Recipient:** Mrs S Callander Beckett

**Access contact:** Mrs Sarah Callander Beckett

**T:** 01948 662880   **F:** 01948 871 604

**E-mail:** estate@combermereabbey.co.uk

**Open:** 10 April–8 June: Tuesday, Wednesday and Thursday afternoon, guided tours only at midday, 2pm and 4pm. Please telephone in advance. Plus Heritage Open Days in September.

**Heritage Open Days:** Yes

P Spaces: 50. Weather dependent.

♿ No wheelchair access. No WC for the disabled. Guide Dogs allowed.

£ **Adult:** £5.00. **Child:** £3.00 (16 and under).

### DORTER HOUSE

**15 Barrow Street, Much Wenlock, Shropshire TF13 6EN**

A detached portion of the former Wenlock Priory Guesten hall, comprising solar chamber and ground floor service accommodation, of early 14th century origin. Some medieval window openings exist. Converted to residential use.

**Grant Recipient:** Mr and Mrs L de Wet

**Access contact:** L de Wet

**T:** 01952 727911

**Open:** Access to exterior only, 14–18 May and 17–21 September (inclusive), 12 noon–4pm.

**Heritage Open Days:** No.

P Spaces: 35. Public car park off Barrow Street, within 200 meters of Dorter House.

♿ No wheelchair access. No WC for the disabled. Guide Dogs allowed.

£ **Adult:** £1.00. **Child:** £1.00. **Other:** £1.00.

### DUDMASTON

**Quatt, Bridgnorth, Shropshire WV15 6QN**

Queen Anne mansion of red brick with stone dressings, situated in parkland overlooking the Severn. Contains furniture, Dutch flower paintings, contemporary paintings and sculpture. Gardens, wooded valley and estate walks starting from Hampton Loade.

**www.nationaltrust.org.uk**

**Grant Recipient:** The National Trust

**Access contact:** The Administrator

**T:** 01746 780866   **F:** 01746 780744

**E-mail:** dudmaston@nationaltrust.org.uk

**Open:** 1 April–30 September: House: Tuesday, Wednesday and Sunday, 2–5.30pm. Garden: Monday, Tuesday, Wednesday and Sunday, 12 noon–6pm. Shop: open same days as house, 1–5.30pm. Tea Room: open same days as garden, 11.30am–5.30pm.

**Heritage Open Days:** No.

P Spaces: 150.

♿ Partial. Wheelchair access to main and inner halls, Library, oak room, No 1 and Derby galleries, old kitchen,

garden and grounds (some estate walks), shop and tea room. WC for the disabled. Guide Dogs allowed.

£ **Adult:** £5.80 (admission price includes voluntary gift aid donation). **Child:** £2.90. **Other:** £14.50 (family), £4.60 (garden only), £4.50 (booked groups of 15+).

### HALSTON CHAPEL

**Ellesmere Road, Halston, nr. Whittington, Shropshire**

Timber framed chapel dating from mid 16th century with alter additions including west tower of circa 1725. The Chapel stands across the fields from Halston Hall and remains a private chapel. Listed Grade I.

**Grant Recipient:** Major and Mrs J L Harvey

**Access contact:** Mrs P V T Harvey

**T:** 01691 662 335

**Open:** By prior arrangement with Mrs Harvey (tel: 01691 662 335). Further public access under review at time of publication, please check the English Heritage website or with the access contact for current information.

**Heritage Open Days:** No.

P Spaces: 20

♿ No wheelchair access. No WC for the disabled. Guide Dogs allowed.

£ No.

### HOSPITAL OF THE HOLY AND UNDIVIDED TRINITY

**Hospital Lane, Clun, Shropshire SY7 8LE**

Founded in 1607 by Henry Howard, Earl of Northampton and built in 1618 with alterations of 1857. Dwellings and other rooms arranged around a square courtyard. A well preserved example of a courtyard-plan almshouses.

**Grant Recipient:** The Trustees of Trinity Hospital

**Access contact:** Mrs JS Woodroffe

**T:** 01588 672303

**Open:** Gardens and chapel open each day apart from Christmas Day. The Dining Hall and quadrangle: 22, 23 and 24 June, 2–6pm. At other time by prior arrangement.

**Heritage Open Days:** No.

P Spaces: 70

♿ Full. No WC for the disabled. Guide Dogs allowed.

£ No.

### JACKFIELD TILE MUSEUM & FACTORY

**Jackfield, Telford, Shropshire TF8 7LJ**

Home to the Craven Dunnill factory, where decorative tiles were mass-produced from 1874 until just after the Second World War. Surviving example of a purpose-built Victorian tile factory and continues to manufacture products today.

**www.ironbridge.org.uk**

**Grant Recipient:** Ironbridge Gorge Museum Trust

**Access contact:** Tourist Information Centre Manager

**T:** 01952 884 391   **F:** 01952 884 391

**E-mail:** tic@ironbridge.org.uk

**Open:** Daily 10am–5pm. Closed 24 and 25 December and 1 January 2007.

**Heritage Open Days:** No.

P Spaces: 30. Free car park.

♿ Full. WC for the disabled. Guide Dogs allowed.

£ **Adult:** £5.00. **Child:** £3.50. **Other:** £4.60 (senior citizens).

### JOHN ROSE BUILDING

**High Street, Coalport, Telford, Shropshire TF8 7HT**

A range of china painting workshops, centre part dating from late 18th century, outer wings rebuilt early 20th century. Restored and converted to a Youth Hostel, craft workshops and shop. Main entrance is paved with mosaic celebrating the amalgamation of Coalport, Swansea and Nantgarw brands. Coalbrookdale cast iron windows of large dimension line both major elevations.

**www.ironbridge.org.uk**

**Grant Recipient:** Ironbridge Gorge Museum Trust

**Access contact:** Mr Andrew Grant

**T:** 01952 588 755   **F:** 01952 588 722

**E-mail:** tic@ironbridge.org.uk

**Open:** Access to exterior at all times. Shop: March–October, 11.30am–5pm. October–March, 11am–4.30pm. At all other times by prior arrangement.

**Heritage Open Days:** No.

P Spaces: 65. Museum car park.

♿ Partial. Youth Hostel: wheelchair access to ground and first floor (stair lift) with WC and shower facilities for the disabled. China Museum: majority accessible, visiting guide available on arrival. Guide Dogs allowed.

£ No.

### LANGLEY GATEHOUSE

**Acton Burnell, Shropshire SY5 7PE**

This gatehouse has two quite different faces: one is of plain dressed stone; the other, which once looked inwards to long demolished Langley Hall, is timber-framed. It was probably used for the Steward or important guests. It was rescued from a point of near collapse and shows repair work of an exemplary quality.

**www.landmarktrust.org.uk**

**Grant Recipient:** The Landmark Trust

**Access contact:** Mrs Victoria O'Keeffe

**T:** 01628 825920   **F:** 01628 825417

**E-mail:** vokeeffe@landmarktrust.org.uk

**Open:** The Landmark Trust is an independent charity, which rescues small buildings of historic or architectural importance from decay or unsympathetic improvement. Landmark's aim is to promote the enjoyment of these historic buildings by making them available to stay in for holidays. Langley Gatehouse can be rented by anyone, at all times of the year, for periods ranging from a weekend to three weeks. Bookings can be made by telephoning the Booking Office on 01628 825925. As the building is in full-time use for holiday accommodation, it is not normally open to the public. However, the public can view the building by prior arrangement by telephoning the access contact (Vicky O'Keeffe on 01628 825920) to make an appointment. Potential visitors will be asked to write to confirm the details of their visit.

**Heritage Open Days:** No.

P Spaces: 2

♿ No wheelchair access. No WC for the disabled. Guide Dogs allowed.

£ No.

### LOTON HALL

**Alberbury, Shropshire SY5 9AJ**

Country house, c1670, but extensively altered and enlarged in the early 18th and 19th centuries. Set in parkland which includes the ruins of the early 13th century Alberbury Castle. Home of the Leighton family since the 14th century.

**Grant Recipient:** Sir Michael Leighton

**Access contact:** Mr Mark Williams

**T:** 01691 655334   **F:** 01691 657798

**Open:** House: 8 January–16 April, Mondays and Thursdays by guided tour only at 10am or 12 noon. Garden and castle can also be viewed at the same times.

**Heritage Open Days:** No.

P Spaces: 30

♿ Partial. Wheelchair access to ground floor only. 5 steps at front door–ramp can be put in place for wheelchair access. No WC for the disabled. Guide Dogs allowed.

£ **Adult:** £5.00. **Child:** Free. **Other:** £5.00 (senior citizens).

### OLD MARKET HALL

**The Square, Shrewsbury, Shropshire SY1 1HJ**

Old market hall and court house, dated 1596 and listed Grade I. Recently repaired and refurbished to accommodate a Film and Digital Media Centre, including auditorium and cafe / bar.

**www.oldmarkethall.co.uk**

**Grant Recipient:** Shrewsbury & Atcham Borough Council

**Access contact:** Mr David Jack

**T:** 01743 281250   **F:** 01743 281283

**E-mail:** davidjack@musichall.co.uk

**Open:** Daily, 10am–11pm. Auditorium closed to public when film being screened. Current screening times: Monday–Sunday evening films. Matinee films on most days.

**Heritage Open Days:** Yes

P No.

♿ Full. WC for the disabled. Guide Dogs allowed.

£ No. **Other:** Charges for performances only (Adult £5.00, Child £4.00).

### PRADOE

**West Felton, Oswestry, Shropshire SY11 4ER**

Georgian country house set in park and garden designed by John Webb. Grade II* listed house contains furniture dating from 1803–1812 during initial occupation by the Kenyon family. Attached service ranges, walled kitchen garden and outbuildings including dairy, brewhouse and carpenter's shop, contain original early 19th century features, recently restored.

**Grant Recipient:** Colonel John F Kenyon

**Access contact:** Col. John F Kenyon

T: 01691 610218   F: 01691 610913
**Open:** 1 June–end of September: Mondays and Tuesdays, 10am–12pm or 1- 3pm, by prior arrangement.
**Heritage Open Days:** No.
**P** Spaces: 50
**&#9855;** Partial. No WC for the disabled. Guide Dogs allowed.
**£** **Adult:** £5.00 (groups of not more than 30). **Child:** £2.00.

### THE LYTH
**Ellesmere, Shropshire SY12 0HR**
Grade II* listed small country house, c1820, with minor later additions. Cast-iron verandah with trellised supports, one of the earliest and largest examples in the country. Birthplace of E & D Jebb, founders of Save the Children.
**Grant Recipient:** Mr L R Jebb
**Access contact:** Mr L R Jebb
**T:** 01691 622339   **F:** 01691 624134
**Open:** To the exterior: 25 March, 20 May, 16 September, 7 October, 2–6pm. At other times by arrangement with Mr Lionel Jebb.
**Heritage Open Days:** No.
**P** Spaces: 40
**&#9855;** Full. No WC for the disabled. Guide Dogs allowed.
**£** **Adult:** £2.00 (charity donation for visits to garden). **Child:** £1.00 (charity donation for visits to garden).

### THE OLD MANSION
**St Mary's Street, Shrewsbury, Shropshire SY1 1UQ**
Early 17th century house with original staircase. The building was renovated in 1997 and now provides 4 bedroom suites for the Prince Rupert Hotel.
**Grant Recipient:** Mr A Humphreys
**Access contact:** Mr A Humphreys
**T:** 01291 672 563
**Open:** By prior arrangement with the Prince Rupert Hotel (tel: 01743 499 955).
**Heritage Open Days:** No.
**P** No.
**&#9855;** Partial. WC for the disabled. Guide Dogs allowed.
**£** No.

### YEATON PEVEREY HALL
**Yeaton Peverey, Shrewsbury, Shropshire SY4 3AT**
Mock Jacobean country house, 1890-2 by Aston Webb. Previously a school, now reinstated as a family home. Principal rooms on the ground floor open to visitors.
**Grant Recipient:** Mr Martin Ebelis
**Access contact:** Mr Martin Ebelis
**T:** 01743 851185   **F:** 01743 851186
**E-mail:** mae@earlstone.co.uk
**Open:** 19 and 20 March, 13 and 24 April, 7 and 8 May, 4 June:12 noon–5pm. When family is in residence by prior arrangement with written confirmation or introduction through known contact.
**Heritage Open Days:** No.
**P** Spaces: 6. Parking adjacent to the property for the disabled.
**&#9855;** Full. No WC for the disabled. Guide Dogs allowed.
**£** **Adult:** £5.00. **Child:** £2.00. **Other:** £5.00.

## SOMERSET

### BATH ASSEMBLY ROOMS
**Bennett Street, Bath, Somerset BA1 2QH**
Built in 1771 by John Wood the Younger, now owned by the National Trust and administered by Bath and North East Somerset District Council. Each of the rooms has a complete set of original chandeliers. The Museum of Costume is located on the lower ground floor.
**www.museumofcostume.co.uk**
**Grant Recipient:** Bath City Council/National Trust
**Access contact:** Mr Iain Johnston
**T:** 01225 477752   **F:** 01225 444793
**E-mail:** costume_enquiries@bathnes.gov.uk
**Open:** Daily: January, February, November and December, 11am–5pm; March–October, 11am–6pm when not in use for pre-booked functions. Last admission is one hour before closing. Telephone in advance (01225 477789) to check availability. There are no pre-booked functions during the day during August. Closed Christmas Day and Boxing Day.
**Heritage Open Days:** No.
**P** On-street car parking (pay and display).
**&#9855;** Full. WC for the disabled. Guide Dogs allowed.
**£** No. **Other:** But charge for Museum of. Costume.

### CHARD GUILDHALL
**Fore Street, Chard, Somerset TA20 2PP**
Grade II* listed building dating to 1834. Former Corn Exchange and Guildhall, now Town Hall.
**www.chard.gov.uk**
**Grant Recipient:** Chard Town Council
**Access contact:** Guildhall Manager
**T:** 01460 260 371   **F:** 01460 260 372
**E-mail:** sandra.hutchings@chard.gov.uk
**Open:** Public events throughout the year. Also available for hire and the Tourist Information Centre is based in the Guildhall. Access at any other time by prior arrangement.
**Heritage Open Days:** No.
**P** No.
**&#9855;** Full. WC for the disabled. Guide Dogs allowed.
**£** No.

### CLEVEDON PIER
**The Beach, Clevedon, Somerset BS21 7QU**
Pier with attached toll house built c1860s to serve steamers bound for South Wales. Wrought and cast iron structure and shelters consisting of eight 100ft arched spans leading to a landing stage. The exceptionally slender spans are constructed from riveted broad-gauge railway track as designed by W H Barlow for the Great Western Railway. Scottish baronial style toll house contains shop and art gallery. Pier restored in 1999 after partial collapse 30 years earlier and is one of only two Grade I listed piers. This pier is of outstanding importance for its delicate engineering and the relationship of pier to landward buildings, which creates an exceptionally picturesque ensemble.
**www.clevedonpier.com**
**Grant Recipient:** The Clevedon Pier and Heritage Trust
**Access contact:** Mrs Linda Strong
**T:** 01275 878846   **F:** 01275 790077
**E-mail:** clevedonpier@zoom.co.uk
**Open:** All year except Christmas Day: Monday–Wednesday, 10am–5pm, Thursday–Sunday, 9am–5pm. Please check opening times prior to visit.
**Heritage Open Days:** No.
**P** Car parking on seafront.
**&#9855;** Partial. No wheelchair access to art gallery. No WC for the disabled. No Guide Dogs allowed.
**£** **Adult:** £1.00. **Child:** 50p. **Other:** 75p (concession).

### ENGLISHCOMBE TITHE BARN
**Rectory Farmhouse, Englishcombe, Bath, Somerset BA2 9DU**
Early 14th century cruck framed tithe barn. Recently restored with new crucks, masonry and straw lining to the roof, and filigree windows unblocked. There are masons and other markings on the walls.
**Grant Recipient:** Mrs Jennie Walker
**Access contact:** Mrs Jennie Walker
**T:** 01225 425073
**E-mail:** jennie.walker@ukonline.co.uk
**Open:** Bank Holidays, 2–6pm; all other times by arrangement with Mrs Walker (tel:01225 425073).
**Heritage Open Days:** Yes
**P** Spaces: 34
**&#9855;** Full. WC for the disabled. Guide Dogs allowed.
**£** Donations invited.

### FAIRFIELD, STOGURSEY
**nr. Bridgwater, Somerset TA5 1PU**
Elizabethan and medieval house and Grade II* listed. Undergoing repairs. Occupied by the same family (Acland-Hoods and their ancestors) for over 800 years. Woodland garden with views of the Quantocks and the sea.
**Grant Recipient:** Lady Gass
**Access contact:** Mr D W Barke
**T:** 01722 555131 or 01278 732251
**Open:** House: 25 April–28 May and 6 June–6 July: Wednesday, Thursday, Friday and Bank Holiday Mondays by guided tour at 2.30pm and 3.30pm. Groups at other times by prior arrangement. Garden: open for NGS and other charities on dates advertised in Spring. No inside photography. No dogs except Guide Dogs.
**Heritage Open Days:** No.
**P** Spaces: 30. No parking for coaches.
**&#9855;** Full. WC for the disabled. Guide Dogs allowed.
**£** **Adult:** £4.00. **Child:** £1.00. **Other:** Admission charges in aid of Stogursey Church.

### FORDE ABBEY
**Chard, Somerset TA20 4LU**
Cistercian monastery founded in 1140 and dissolved in 1539 when the church was demolished. The monks quarters were converted in 1640 into an Italian style "palazzo" by Sir Edmund Prideaux. Interior has plaster ceilings and Mortlake tapestries.
**www.fordeabbey.co.uk**
**Grant Recipient:** Trustees of the Roper Settlement
**Access contact:** Mrs Clay
**T:** 01460 220231
**E-mail:** info@fordeabbey.co.uk
**Open:** Gardens: daily, 10am–4.30pm. House: April–October; Tuesday–Friday, Sunday and Bank Holidays, 12 noon–4pm.
**Heritage Open Days:** No.
**P** Spaces: 500
**&#9855;** Partial. Wheelchair access to ground floor and garden. WC for the disabled. Guide Dogs allowed.
**£** **Adult:** £7.80. **Child:** Free. **Other:** £7.30 (senior citizen)

### GREAT HOUSE FARM
**Theale, Wedmore, Somerset BS28 4SJ**
17th century farmhouse with Welsh slate roof, oak doors and some original diamond paned windows. Inside is a carved well staircase with two murals on the walls. There are four servants rooms at the top, three of which are dark and occupied by Lesser Horseshoe bats.
**Grant Recipient:** Mr A R Millard
**Access contact:** Mr A R Millard
**T:** 01934 713133
**Open:** April–August: Tuesdays and Thursdays, 2–6pm by prior telephone arrangement.
**Heritage Open Days:** No.
**P** Spaces: 6
**&#9855;** No wheelchair access. No WC for the disabled. Guide Dogs allowed.
**£** **Adult:** £2.00. **Child:** Free. **Other:** £1.00 (senior citizens).

### HALL FARM HIGH BARN
**Stogumber, Taunton, Somerset TA4 3TQ**
17th century Grade II* listed building with seven bays of red local sandstone rubble with jointed cruck roof. South wall supported by four buttresses but there are none on the North wall. There are blocked windows on the South wall and two stub walls extend north. Lines of joist holes were provided for internal flooring and the two main entrances were to the north and south.
**Grant Recipient:** CM & R Hayes
**Access contact:** CM & R Hayes
**T:** 01984 656321
**Open:** By prior arrangement with CM & R Hayes. at Hall Farm.
**Heritage Open Days:** No.
**P** Spaces: 4
**&#9855;** Full. No WC for the disabled. Guide Dogs allowed.
**£** No.

### HIGHER FLAX MILLS
**(John Boyd Textiles Ltd), Torbay Road, Castle Cary, Somerset BA7 7DY**
Listed Grade II*, Higher Flax Mills is one of the largest and unusually complete examples of an integrated rope and twine works in the West Country, a significant regional industry in the 19th century. Part of the site is used by John Boyd Textiles, Horsehair fabric manufacturer established in 1837 and still using the original looms of 1870. The company is unique in being the only horsehair weaving factory in the world which uses power looms.
**www.johnboydtextiles.co.uk**
**Grant Recipient:** South Somerset District Council
**Access contact:** John Boyd Textiles Ltd
**T:** 01963 350 451   **F:** 01963 351 078
**Open:** By prior arrangement only: Monday–Friday, 8am–5pm.
**Heritage Open Days:** No.
**P** Spaces: 7. Parking for cars or 3 coaches.
**&#9855;** Partial. WC for the disabled. Guide Dogs allowed.
**£** **Other:** Small charge agreed with trip organisers.

## LANCIN FARMHOUSE

**Wambrook, Chard, Somerset TA20 3EG**

14th century farmhouse with old oak beams, fireplaces with the original smoking thatch, flagstone floors and breadoven.

**Grant Recipient:** Mr S J Smith
**Access contact:** Mrs R A Smith
**T:** 01460 62290
**Open:** 10 April, 8 and 29 May, 5, 13, 21 and 27 June, 13 and 27 September and 24 October, 10am–3.00pm. At other times Tuesday, Wednesday or Thursday, 10am–5pm by prior arrangement.
**Heritage Open Days:** No.
**P** Spaces: 5
No wheelchair access. No WC for the disabled. No Guide Dogs allowed.
**£** Adult: £2.00.

## PRIOR PARK COLLEGE OLD GYMNASIUM

**Ralph Allen Drive, Bath, Somerset BA2 5AH**

Built for Ralph Allen in the mid-18th century as an early and successful demonstration of the quality of Bath stone. The Chapel and Old Gymnasium are part of the mid-19th century additions to adapt the property as a Catholic seminary for Bishop Baines. Now a boarding and day school.

**www.priorpark.co.uk**
**Grant Recipient:** Governors of Prior Park College
**Access contact:** C J Freeman
**T:** 01225 837491    **F:** 01225 835753
**E-mail:** bursar@priorpark.co.uk
**Open:** 21–25 August: daily, 10.30am–4pm. Group tours during school holidays, otherwise by prior arrangement. Please telephone in advance.
**Heritage Open Days:** No.
**P** No.
No wheelchair access. No WC for the disabled. No Guide Dogs allowed.
**£** No.

## ROWLANDS MILL, ROWLANDS

**Ilminster, Somerset TA19 9LE**

Grade II* stone and brick 3-storey millhouse and machinery, c1620, with a mill pond, mill race, overshooting wheel and waterfall. The millhouse is now a holiday let but the machinery has separate access and is in working condition.

**Grant Recipient:** Mr P G H Speke
**Access contact:** Mr P G H Speke
**T:** 01460 52623    **F:** 01460 52623
**Open:** Millhouse Fridays and machinery Monday–Friday, 10am–4pm by prior written arrangement (at least 1 week's notice required). Heritage Open Days machinery only unless a Friday, then whole building.
**Heritage Open Days:** Yes
**P** Spaces: 7
Partial. Wheelchair access to ground floor only. No WC for the disabled. Guide Dogs allowed.
**£** Adult: £3.00. Child: Free.

## ST ANDREWS

**Stogursey, Somerset**

Benedictine priory church, now parish church. Listed Grade I.

**Grant Recipient:** St Andrews PCC, Church of England
**Access contact:** Mr Graham McLeod
**T:** 01278 733 206
**Open:** Daily during daylight hours.
**Heritage Open Days:** Yes
**P** Spaces: 6
Partial. Wheelchair access to most areas except the High Altar, ramp available on request. No WC for the disabled. Guide Dogs allowed.
**£** No.

## ST GEORGE'S BRISTOL

**Great George Street, Bristol, Somerset BS1 5RR**

Grade II* listed Georgian former church, c1821-3, by Robert Smirke in Greek Revival style, now 550 seater concert hall. A Waterloo church, built as a chapel-of-ease to Cathedral of St Augustine, and converted to a concert hall in 1987. The crypt now houses a café and art gallery.

**www.stgeorgesbristol.co.uk**
**Grant Recipient:** St George's Bristol
**Access contact:** Ms Jillian Wilson
**T:** 0117 929 4929    **F:** 0117 927 6537

**E-mail:** j.wilson@stgeorgesbristol.co.uk
**Open:** For seasonal concert programmes–mainly evenings, some lunchtimes and Sunday afternoons, contact Box Office on 0845 40 24 001 for brochure. Free access to crypt and art gallery from 1 hour before concerts. Tours can be arranged if dates comply with events schedule.
**Heritage Open Days:** No.
**P** Spaces: 3
Partial. Wheelchair access via Charlotte Street. The auditorium stalls, crypt, café, gallery and Box Office are accessible but preferable if you ring in advance as entry is not straightforward. WC for the disabled. Guide Dogs allowed.
**£** No. **Other:** Tickets required for concerts.

## TEMPLE OF HARMONY

**Halswell Park, Goathurst, nr. Bridgwater, Somerset TA5 2DH**

18th century folly, a copy of the Temple of Verilis, forms part of the 18th century Pleasure Gardens at Halswell House. Restored in 1994.

**www.somersite.co.uk/temple.htm**
**Grant Recipient:** Somerset Buildings Preservation Trust
**Access contact:** Mrs Tessa Howard
**T:** 01278 662167
**E-mail:** tessa.howard@virgin.net
**Open:** 27 May–end September: Saturday and Sunday, 2–5pm. Any other day by prior arrangement with Mrs Tessa Howard (tel: 01278 662167)
**Heritage Open Days:** Yes
**P** Spaces: 4
No wheelchair access. No WC for the disabled. Guide Dogs allowed.
**£** Adult: £1.00. Child: 50p. Other: 50p (senior citizens).

# SOUTH YORKSHIRE

## HICKLETON HALL

**Hickleton, South Yorkshire DN5 7BB**

Georgian Mansion, Grade II* listed, built in the 1740s to a design by James Paine with later additions. The interior is noted for its plasterwork ceilings. Set in 15 acres of formal gardens laid out in the early 1900s, the Hall is now a residential care home.

**Grant Recipient:** Sue Ryder Care
**Access contact:** The Administrator
**T:** 01709 892070    **F:** 01709 890140
**Open:** By prior arrangement with the administrator at Sue Ryder Care, Monday–Friday, 2–4pm.
**Heritage Open Days:** No.
**P** Parking available.
Partial. Wheelchair access to Hall only; no access to gardens. WC for the disabled. Guide Dogs allowed.
**£** No.

## THE LYCEUM THEATRE

**Tudor Square, Sheffield, South Yorkshire S1 1DA**

Grade II* listed theatre built 1897. The only surviving example of the work of WGR Sprague outside London. Its special features include a domed corner tower, a lavish Rococo auditorium (1097 seats) and a proscenium arch with a rare open-work valance in gilded plasterwork. A notable example of a theatre of the period, with a largely unaltered interior.

**www.sheffieldtheatres.co.uk**
**Grant Recipient:** The Lyceum Theatre Trust
**Access contact:** Ms Angela Galvin, Chief Executive
**T:** 0114 249 5999    **F:** 0114 249 6003
**E-mail:** info@sheffieldtheatres.co.uk
**Open:** Performances throughout the year. 21 scheduled backstage tours per year. All tours commence at 10.30am. Group guided tours by prior arrangement. Contact the Box Office (tel: 0114 249 6000) or check the website for further information.
**Heritage Open Days:** No.
**P** Spaces: 600. National Car Park adjacent to the theatre.
Partial. Wheelchair access to all areas except two private entertaining rooms. WC for the disabled. Guide Dogs allowed.
**£** Adult: £3.00 (backstage tour). **Other:** Admission charge for performances.

# STAFFORDSHIRE

## 10 THE CLOSE

**Lichfield, Staffordshire WS13 7LD**

Early 15th century timber-framed house, originally one-up one-down and part of a five-dwelling range in the Vicar's Close. Notable doors and solid tread staircase remains in attic.

**Grant Recipient:** Dean & Chapter of Lichfield Cathedral
**Access contact:** Administrator
**T:** 01543 306100    **F:** 01543 306109
**E-mail:** enquiries@lichfield-cathedral.org
**Open:** By prior written arrangement with Cathedral Chapter Office.
**Heritage Open Days:** No.
**P** Public car parks nearby.
No wheelchair access. No WC for the disabled. Guide Dogs allowed.
**£** No.

## BARLASTON HALL

**Barlaston, nr. Stoke-on-Trent, Staffordshire ST12 9AT**

Mid-18th century Palladian villa attributed to Sir Robert Taylor, with public rooms containing some fine examples of 18th century plasterwork. Extensively restored during the 1990s.

**Grant Recipient:** Mr James Hall
**Access contact:** Mr James Hall
**F:** 01782 372391
**E-mail:** wadey54@mac.com
**Open:** 6 March–11 September: Tuesdays, 2–5pm. No groups.
**Heritage Open Days:** No.
**P** Spaces: 3
No wheelchair access. No WC for the disabled. No Guide Dogs allowed.
**£** Adult: £2.50. Child: £1.50. **Other:** No charge for Historic Houses Association members.

## BIDDULPH GRANGE GARDEN

**Biddulph, Staffordshire ST8 7SD**

Garden with series of connected compartments designed to display specimens from James Bateman's extensive and wide ranging plant collection. Visitors are taken on a miniature tour of the world featuring the Egyptian court, China, a Scottish glen, as well as a pinetum and rock areas.

**www.nationaltrust.org.uk**
**Grant Recipient:** The National Trust
**Access contact:** Property Manager
**T:** 01782 517999    **F:** 01782 510624
**E-mail:** biddulphgrange@nationaltrust.org.uk
**Open:** 17 March–28 October: Wednesday–Sunday 11.30am–5.30pm (High Season). 3 November–16 December: Saturday and Sunday, 11am–3pm (Low Season).
**Heritage Open Days:** No.
**P** Spaces: 100
Partial. Wheelchair access to Lime Avenue, Lake, Pinetum, Cheshire Cottage, Egypt and East Terrace. Steps and undulating terrain throughout the garden. WC for the disabled. Guide Dogs allowed.
**£** Adult: £6.00 (High Season), £2.30 (Low Season). Child: £3.00(High Season), £1.10 (Low Season). **Other:** £14.00 (family, High Season), £5.50 (family, Low Season).

## BISHTON HALL DORIC SCREEN

**Woseley Bridge, Staffordshire ST17 0XN**

1840s screen with a summerhouse at the centre, in the form of a Greek Doric temple, with flanking porticos and terrace. Listed Grade II*. The screen might have been built to screen the gardens from the nearby Trent Valley Railway Line, which was built in 1845-7.

**Grant Recipient:** St Bede's School Limited
**Access contact:** St Bede's School Limited
**Open:** 26–30 March, 16–20 April, 9–13 and 16–20 July, 3–5 September, 16–22 December: 10am–2pm. Please report to the School Office on arrival.
**Heritage Open Days:** No.
**P** Spaces: 5
Partial. Steps up to the screen. No WC for the disabled. No Guide Dogs allowed.
**£** No.

### CHEDDLETON FLINT MILL

**Cheddleton, Leek, nr. Stoke-on-Trent, Staffordshire ST13 7HL**

18th century complex for grinding flint comprising two working watermills. South Mill modified in 19th century and now contains displays relating to the pottery industry.

**www.ex.ac.uk/~akoutram/cheddleton-mill**

**Grant Recipient:** Cheddleton Flint Mill Industrial Heritage Trust

**Access contact:** Mr E E Royle, MBE

**T:** 01782 502907

**Open:** April–September (including Bank Holidays), Saturday–Sunday 1pm–5pm. Weekdays by arrangement (tel: 01782 502907).

**Heritage Open Days:** No.

P Spaces: 18

 Partial. Wheelchair access to ground floor only. WC for the disabled. Guide Dogs allowed.

£ No.

### CHILLINGTON HALL

**Codsall Wood, nr. Wolverhampton, Staffordshire WV8 1RE**

House by Sir John Soane with earlier wing by Francis Smith (1724). Home of the Giffard family for over 800 years. Extensive grounds with gardens landscaped by Capability Brown.

**www.chillingtonhall.co.uk**

**Grant Recipient:** Mr J W Giffard

**Access contact:** Mr J W Giffard

**T:** 01902 850236    **F:** 01902 850 768

**E-mail:** mrsplod@chillingtonhall.co.uk

**Open:** Hall: Easter, May and August Bank Holiday Sunday and Monday. July: Sundays. August: Wednesday, Thursday, Friday and Sunday, 2–5pm. Parties at other times by prior arrangement. Grounds only: Easter–1 June: Sundays only.

**Heritage Open Days:** No.

P Spaces: 100. Unlimited parking.

 Full. No WC for the disabled. Guide Dogs allowed.

£ Adult: £4.00, (£2.00 grounds only). Child: £2.00. Other: Free to HHA members.

### CLAYMILLS PUMPING ENGINES

**The Victorian Pumping Station, Meadow Lane, Stretton, Burton-on-Trent, Staffordshire DE13 0DA**

Large Victorian steam-operated sewage pumping station built in 1885. Four beam engines in two Italianate engine houses, two operational on steaming weekends. Boiler house with range of five Lancashire boilers, large Victorian steam-operated workshop with blacksmith's forge, steam hammer, and steam driven machinery. 1930s dynamo house with very early D.C. generating equipment, earliest dynamo 1889 (all operational). The site houses the largest number of steam engines in Britain still working in their original state (19).

**www.claymills.org.uk**

**Grant Recipient:** Severn Trent Water Ltd

**Access contact:** Mr Roy Barratt

**T:** 01283 534960    **F:** 07092 275534

**E-mail:** webmaster@claymills.org.uk

**Open:** Every Thursday and Saturday for static viewing. Easter 8 & 9 April, Early May Bank Holiday 6 & 7 May, End of May Bank Holiday 27 & 28 May, 26 & 27 August, 15 & 16 September, 20 & 21 October, 31 December & 1 January.

**Heritage Open Days:** Yes

P Spaces: 100. Parking for the disabled adjacent to site. Parking available for 1 coach.

 Partial. Wheelchair access to ground floor only (boiler house, workshop, refreshment area, engine house). Interactive video link to Engine House. WC for the disabled. Guide Dogs allowed.

£ Other: Charges apply on steaming days, at other times donation invited.

### CLIFTON HALL

**Clifton Campville, Staffordshire B79 0BE**

Small country house built in 1705, perhaps by Francis Smith of Warwick for Sir Charles Pye. Two monumental wings flanking a courtyard, the intention being to link them with a central main building which was never constructed. This strange history explains why the Hall unusually developed out of what would have been the servants wing.

**Grant Recipient:** Mr Richard Blunt

**Access contact:** Mr Richard Blunt

**T:** 01827 373681    **F:** 01827 373681

**E-mail:** richard@stauntonharoldhall.co.uk

---

**Open:** By prior arrangement only, any weekday, 9am–5pm all year.

**Heritage Open Days:** No.

P Spaces: 10

 Full. No WC for the disabled. Guide Dogs allowed.

£ Adult: £4.50. Child: £2.00. Other: £2.00.

### HAMSTALL HALL

**Hamstall Ridware, Staffordshire WS15 3RS**

Small scheduled ancient monument known as 'The Porch', with stone balcony, now restored and two stone fireplaces. Restored oak doors and windows. Some carvings on the stone balcony. Interior is made up of two rooms.

**Grant Recipient:** Mr and Mrs Shore

**Access contact:** Shore

**T:** 0121 382 6540 office hrs only

**Open:** By prior arrangement with Mr and Mrs Shore.

**Heritage Open Days:** No.

P No.

 No wheelchair access. No WC for the disabled. Guide Dogs allowed.

£ No.

### MALTHOUSE

**Malthouse Road, Alton, Staffordshire ST10 4AG**

Rare underground malthouse. Brick vaulted cellars and network of tunnels. Listed Grade II*. Used to produce malt for brewing from late 17th century.

**Grant Recipient:** Owen John Venables

**Access contact:** Mr Owen John Venables

**T:** 01538 703 273

**E-mail:** enquiries@the-malthouse.com

**Open:** April, May, June, July, September and October: every Saturday; Heritage Open Days in September (Thursday to Sunday), 12 noon–4pm (last admittance at 3.30pm).

**Heritage Open Days:** Yes

P On-street parking.

 No wheelchair access. No WC for the disabled. Guide Dogs allowed.

£ No.

### MIDDLEPORT POTTERY

**Port Street, Middleport, Stoke on Trent, Staffordshire ST6 3PE**

Grade II* listed pottery works built 1888-9 in brick and terracotta. The site includes a Burgundy bottle oven, the largest now standing in Stoke-on-Trent. In use by Burleigh–a family pottery business established in 1851 and still manufacturing using Victorian methods and machinery.

**www.burleigh.co.uk**

**Grant Recipient:** Burgess Dorling & Leigh

**Access contact:** Mrs Rosemary Dorling

**T:** 01782 577 866    **F:** 01782 575 529

**E-mail:** sales@burleigh.co.uk

**Open:** All year: Wednesdays 10am guided tour only, except during Potters holidays (usually last week of June, first week of July, last week of August and 2 weeks over Easter). At all other times by prior arrangement. Due to hazardous nature of the site, minimum age for children is 10 years.

**Heritage Open Days:** Yes

P Weekday parking, 6 spaces. Weekend parking, 24 spaces. Additional on street parking available.

 Partial. Wheelchair access to shop only. No WC for the disabled. Guide Dogs allowed.

£ Adult: £5.00.

### SHUGBOROUGH

**Milford, Stafford, Staffordshire ST17 0XB**

The present house was begun c1695. Between 1760 and 1770 it was enlarged and again partly remodelled by Samuel Wyatt at end of 18th century. The interior is particularly notable for its plaster work and other decorations. Ancestral home of the Earls of Lichfield. Houses the Staffordshire County Museum, Georgian working farm and Rare Livestock Breed project.

**www.shugborough.org.uk**

**Grant Recipient:** The National Trust

**Access contact:** Ms Louise Jones, Property Manager

**T:** 01889 881388    **F:** 01889 881323

**E-mail:** shugborough.promotions@staffordshire.gov.uk

**Open:** House, servants' quarters, farm and gardens: 16 March–26 October, daily, 11am–5pm (last admission 4.30pm). Tours for booked groups daily from 10.30am.

---

Evening tours also available.

**Heritage Open Days:** No.

P Spaces: 150

 Partial. Wheelchair access to ground floor of house and museum only. WC for the disabled. Guide Dogs allowed.

£ Adult: £10.00. Child: £6.00. Other: £25.00 (family), £8.00 (concessions), Free to house for NT members.

### SINAI HOUSE

**Shobnall Road, Burton on Trent, Staffordshire DE14 2BB**

Timber-framed E-shaped house, two-thirds derelict, on moated hill-top site, dating from the 13th century. House built variously during 15th, 16th and 17th centuries with later additions, including wall paintings and carpenters marks. 18th century bridge and plunge pool in the grounds.

**Grant Recipient:** Ms C A Newton

**Access contact:** Ms C A Newton

**T:** 01283 544161/01283 840732

**E-mail:** knewton@brookesvernons.co.uk

**Open:** By prior arrangement only. Minimum of one week's notice required.

**Heritage Open Days:** No.

P Spaces: 10

 Partial. Temporary ramps to internal steps can be arranged. No WC for the disabled. Guide Dogs allowed.

£ Other: Donations requested.

## SUFFOLK

### ABBEY FARM BARN

**Snape, Saxmundham, Suffolk IP17 1RQ**

Grade II* listed Aisled barn. Circa 1300. Built by resident monks living in adjacent Priory (no remains standing above ground). Refurbished and still used by farmer for storage.

**Grant Recipient:** Mr & Mrs Raynor

**Access contact:** Mr and Mrs Raynor

**T:** 01728 688088    **F:** 01728 688989

**E-mail:** thecartshed@onetel.net.uk

**Open:** By prior arrangement.

**Heritage Open Days:** No.

P Spaces: 10

 Full. No WC for the disabled. Guide Dogs allowed.

£ No.

### CHRISTCHURCH MANSION

**Christchurch Park, Soane Street, Ipswich, Suffolk IP4 2BE**

16th century red brick mansion with some blue brick diapering, set in fine parkland in the centre of town. The Mansion and its collections trace the lives of the three wealthy families who made it their home. Paintings, English domestic furniture, kitchen and servants' area.

**www.ipswichmuseum.co.uk**

**Grant Recipient:** Ipswich Borough Council

**Access contact:** Mr Tim Heyburn

**T:** 01473 433 543    **F:** 01473 433558

**E-mail:** museums.service@ipswich.gov.uk

**Open:** November–March: Tuesday–Saturday 10am–4pm, Sunday 2.30pm–4pm. April–October: Monday–Saturday 10am–4pm, Sunday 10–4.30pm. For further information please contact Tim Heyburn, or the Mansion (Tel: 01473 433543, fax: 01473 433558)

**Heritage Open Days:** No.

P Spaces: 1200. Public parking within 400 metres. Parking for the disabled adjacent to the Mansion.

 Partial. Wheelchair access to most of ground floor and Wolsey Art Gallery. WC for the disabled. Guide Dogs allowed.

£ No.

### CULFORD SCHOOL IRON BRIDGE

**Culford, Bury St Edmunds, Suffolk IP28 6TX**

Constructed for the second Marquis Cornwallis in the late 1790s by Samuel Wyatt, brother of James, to a design patented by Samuel Wyatt. The bridge, in Culford Park, is one of the earliest surviving bridges with an unmodified cast-iron structure, being the earliest known example with hollow ribs.

**Grant Recipient:** Methodist Colleges and Schools

**Access contact:** Michael Woolley

**T:** 01284 729318    **F:** 01284 729077

**E-mail:** bursar@culford.co.uk

**Open:** Access to the iron bridge and Culford Park is available at any time throughout the year.

**Heritage Open Days:** No.

P Spaces: 100

⌖ Partial. Access for the disabled may be difficult as over grass and rough track. Toilet facilities are only available when Culford School is open and ramps in place. No WC for the disabled. Guide Dogs allowed.
💷 No.

## FLATFORD MILL, WILLY LOTT'S HOUSE AND FLATFORD BRIDGE COTTAGE

**Flatford, East Bergholt, Colchester, Suffolk CO7 6UL**
Flatford watermill, 1733 date stone, incorporating possibly earlier but altered former granary range to rear and further 19th century range adjoining granary. The mill was in the possession of the Constable family from the mid 18th century. Willy Lott's farmhouse, late 16th century–17th century. Grade I listing of both buildings reflects their significance in the life and work of John Constable. Both buildings are leased by the National Trust to the Field Studies Council. Flatford Bridge Cottage 16th century thatched cottage, upstream from Flatford Mill houses an exhibition on John Constable.
**www.nationaltrust.org.uk**
**Grant Recipient:** The National Trust
**Access contact:** Property Manager
**T:** 01206 298260    **F:** 01206 299193
**E-mail:** flatfordbridgecottage@nationaltrust.org.uk
**Open:** Flatford Mill and Willy Lott's House are owned by the National Trust and leased to the Field Studies Council which runs arts-based courses for all age groups (for information on courses tel: 01206 298283). There is no general public access to these buildings, but the Field Studies Council will arrange tours for groups. Flatford Bridge Cottage: 1 March–29 April and 31 October–22 December: Wednesday–Sunday, 11am–5pm; 30 April–30 September: daily, 10.30am–5.30pm; 1–28 October daily, 11am–4pm; 5 January 2008–24 February: Saturday and Sunday, 11am–3.30pm. For further information contact the Property Manager on 01206 298260.
**Heritage Open Days:** No.
🅿 Spaces: 2000. Private pay car park 200 meters from Flatford Bridge Cottage. Parking near the Cottage is available for disabled visitors.
⌖ Partial. Wheelchair access to tea-garden and shop. Lavatory for the disabled available in car park owned by Babergh DC, 23 metres from the Cottage. WC for the disabled. Guide Dogs allowed.
💷 Other: £2.50 (Adult guided walks (when available)).

## FRESTON TOWER

**Freston, Babergh, Suffolk IP9 1AD**
Elizabethan six-storey tower built in 1578 by Thomas Gooding, an Ipswich Merchant, to demonstrate his wealth and status and probably used as a look-out tower. Overlooks the estuary of the River Orwell.
**www.landmarktrust.org.uk**
**Grant Recipient:** The Landmark Trust
**Access contact:** Mrs Victoria O'Keeffe
**T:** 01628 825920    **F:** 01628 825417
**E-mail:** vokeeffe@landmarktrust.org.uk
**Open:** The Landmark Trust is an independent charity, which rescues small buildings of historic or architectural importance from decay or unsympathetic improvement. Landmark's aim is to promote the enjoyment of these historic buildings by making them available to stay in for holidays. Freston Tower can be rented by anyone, at all times of the year, for periods ranging from a weekend to three weeks. Bookings can be made by telephoning the Booking Office on 01628 825925. The public can also view the building on eight Open Days throughout the year (dates to be set) or by prior arrangement; telephone the access contact Victoria O'Keeffe on 01628 825920 to make an appointment. Potential visitors will be asked to write to confirm the details of their visit.
**Heritage Open Days:** Yes
🅿 Spaces: 2
⌖ No wheelchair access. No WC for the disabled. Guide Dogs allowed.
💷 No.

## FRISTON MILL

**Friston, Suffolk IP17 1NW**
A Suffolk post windmill, one of the tallest of its type built in Britain. Built in 1812 and operational until 1956. Listed Grade II*. In a semi-derelict condition but many of the original components can still be seen. Suffolk once had 250 mills. Today there are fewer than a dozen.
**Grant Recipient:** Mr Piers Hartley
**Access contact:** Mr Piers Hartley

**T:** 01728 688 650
**E-mail:** piersh@rtley.com
**Open:** By prior arrangement. Due to building being in a semi-derelict state, it may not be suitable for people with mobility difficulties and very young children. Sensible footwear essential.
**Heritage Open Days:** No.
🅿 No.
⌖ No wheelchair access. No WC for the disabled. No Guide Dogs allowed.
💷 No.

## ICKWORTH HOUSE

**Park and Garden, Horringer,**
**Bury St Edmunds, Suffolk IP29 5QE**
The Earl of Bristol created this eccentric house, with its central rotunda and curved corridors, in 1795 to display his collections. These include paintings by Titian, Gainsborough and Velazquez and a Georgian silver collection. The house is surrounded by an Italianate garden set in a 'Capability' Brown park with woodland walks, deer enclosure, vineyard, Georgian summerhouse, church, canal and lake.
**www.nationaltrust.org.uk**
**Grant Recipient:** The National Trust
**Access contact:** Property Manager
**T:** 01284 735270    **F:** 01284 735175
**E-mail:** ickworth@nationaltrust.org.uk
**Open:** House & Gardens: 17 March–30 September: Friday–Tuesday, 1–5pm (gardens open 10am). 1 October–4 November: Friday–Tuesday, 1–4.30pm (gardens open at 11am–4pm until 17 March 2008). Park open daily, 8am–8pm, but closed Christmas Day.
**Heritage Open Days:** No.
🅿 Spaces: 200
⌖ Partial. Wheelchair access to House: ramped access (restricted access in House for large powered vehicles/chairs); lift to first floor; stair-lift to basement (shop and restaurant) suitable for wheelchair users able to transfer; wheelchair on each floor. Garden largely accessible, some changes of level, gravel drive and paths. West Wing: all floors accessible. Separate parking in visitor car park (200 yards). WC for the disabled. Guide Dogs allowed.
💷 **Adult:** £7.50 (House & garden), £3.50 (garden). **Child:** £3.00 (House & garden), £1.00 (garden). **Other:** £18.00 (family, house & garden), £8.00 (family, garden).

## MORETON HALL

**Mount Road, Bury St Edmunds, Suffolk IP32 7BJ**
White brick residence designed by Robert Adam in 1773 for Dr. Symonds, noted Cambridge professor and author. The design was inspired by the ruins of Emporor Diocletian's palace and many of the original Adam features remain on the ground and first floors. It is now the home of Moreton Hall Preparatory School.
**www.moretonhall.net**
**Grant Recipient:** Moreton Hall School Trust Ltc
**Access contact:** Ms Doreen Young
**T:** 01284 753 532    **F:** 01284 769 197
**E-mail:** office@moretonhall.net
**Open:** By prior arrangement at any reasonable time, plus the Saturday of Heritage Open Days weekend.
**Heritage Open Days:** Yes
🅿 Spaces: 20. Free parking.
⌖ Partial. Wheelchair access to ground floor only. WC for the disabled. Guide Dogs allowed.
💷 No.

## RUINED CHURCH TOWER

**Fornham St Genevieve, St Edmundsbury, Suffolk**
Only the tower remains of the 15th century church. Church destroyed by fire in 1782.
**Grant Recipient:** Rossfleet Investments Ltd
**Access contact:** Mr Steve Stuteley
**T:** 01953 717176    **F:** 01953 717173
**Open:** By prior arrangement with Steve Stuteley (Rossfleet Investments, Manor Farm, Bridgham, Norfolk).
**Heritage Open Days:** No.
🅿 No.
⌖ No wheelchair access. No WC for the disabled. Guide Dogs allowed.
💷 No.

## SOMERLEYTON HALL & GARDENS

**Somerleyton, Lowestoft, Suffolk NR32 5QQ**
Early Victorian stately home, built in Anglo-Italian style for Sir Morton Peto by John Thomas upon former Jacobean mansion. Contains fine furnishings, paintings, ornate carved stonework and wood carving, and state rooms. Set in twelve acres of historic gardens including a yew hedge maze.
**www.somerleyton.co.uk**
**Grant Recipient:** The Rt Hon Lord Somerleyton GCVO
**Access contact:** Mr Edward Knowles
**T:** 01502 730224    **F:** 01502 732143
**E-mail:** enquiries@somerleyton.co.uk
**Open:** 1 April–28 October: Thursday, Sunday and Bank Holidays, plus Tuesday and Wednesday in July and August, 10am–5pm.
**Heritage Open Days:** No.
🅿 Spaces: 200
⌖ Full. WC for the disabled. Guide Dogs allowed.
💷 **Adult:** £4.75 (gardens only), £8.00 (Hall & gardens). **Child:** £2.75 (gardens only), £4.00 (Hall & gardens). **Other:** Senior citizens: £3.75 (gardens only), £7.00 (Hall & gardens).

## ST LAWRENCE

**Dial Lane, Ipswich, Suffolk IP1 1DL**
15th century aisleless church with a 97 foot west tower, enlarged in the 19th century and recently restored. Declared redundant in 1975. Owned by Ipswich Borough Council.
**Grant Recipient:** Ipswich Historic Churches Trust
**Access contact:** Mr J S Hall
**T:** 01473 232300/406270    **F:** 01473 406385
**E-mail:** james-hall@birketts.co.uk
**Open:** By prior arrangement with Mr Hall (tel: 01473 406270), office hours and weekdays only. At least 24 hours notice required. At other times and days subject to longer notice.
**Heritage Open Days:** No.
🅿 Public parking in town centre car parks (10 minute walk).
⌖ No wheelchair access. No WC for the disabled. No Guide Dogs allowed.
💷 No.

## ST PETER, COLLEGE STREET

**Ipswich, Suffolk IP4 1DD**
Large medieval church near the docks, owned by Ipswich Borough Council and redundant since the 1970s. Noted for a Tournai font and adjacent to Thomas Wolsey's gateway.
**Grant Recipient:** Ipswich Historic Churches Trust
**Access contact:** Mr J S Hall
**T:** 01473 232300/406270    **F:** 01473 406385
**E-mail:** james-hall@birketts.co.uk
**Open:** May–September: most Thursdays, 1.30–3.30pm (advisable to check in advance). Otherwise by prior arrangement with Mr Hall (tel: 01473 406270), office hours and weekdays only. 24 hours notice required. At other times and days subject to longer notice.
**Heritage Open Days:** Yes
🅿 Car parks in town centre (½ mile).
⌖ Partial. Wheelchair access to all of church apart from the vestry and parts of the chancel. No WC for the disabled. Guide Dogs allowed.
💷 No.

## WALTON OLD HALL

**Felixstowe, Suffolk**
Remains of 13th century Manor House built by the Bigod family c1292.
**Grant Recipient:** Suffolk Coastal District Council
**Access contact:** Mrs Chris Robinson
**T:** 01394 444 518    **F:** 01394 385 100
**E-mail:** chris.robinson@suffolkcoastal.gov.uk
**Open:** Monday–Friday, 8am–4pm, at all other times by prior arrangement.
**Heritage Open Days:** No.
🅿 On-street parking.
⌖ Partial. Wheelchair access to all areas but grass surfaces may limit access in poor weather conditions. No WC for the disabled. Guide Dogs allowed.
💷 No.

# SURREY

## CAREW MANOR DOVECOTE

**Beddington Park, Church Road,
Beddington, Wallington, Surrey SM6 7NH**
Early 18th century large octagonal brick dovecote with
c1200 interior nesting boxes and original potence (circular
ladder).
www.sutton.gov.uk
**Grant Recipient:** London Borough of Sutton
**Access contact:** Ms Valary Murphy
**T:** 020 8770 4781   **F:** 020 8770 4777
**E-mail:** valary.murphy@sutton.gov.uk
**Open:** 22 April, 20 May, 15 July and 23 September,
2–5pm. Guided tours of Carew Manor at 2pm and
3.30pm. 17 June: Wandle Valley Festival Day (no guided
tours, free access to Dovecote). Groups at other times by
prior arrangement with Valary Murphy, The Heritage
Service, Central Library, St Nicholas Way, Sutton, Surrey
SM1 1EA (tel: 020 8770 4781).
**Heritage Open Days:** No.
**P** Spaces: 30
**&** No wheelchair access. No WC for the disabled. Guide
Dogs allowed.
**£** Adult: £3.75. Child: £2.00. Other: Admission charges
for guided tours of dovecote and Carew Manor, otherwise
dovecote is free.

## CLANDON PARK

**West Clandon, Guildford, Surrey GU4 7RQ**
Palladian mansion, built c1730 by Venetian architect
Giacomo Leoni with a two-storeyed Marble Hall, collection
of 18th century furniture, porcelain, textiles, carpets, the
Ivo Forde Meissen collection of Italian comedy figures and
a series of Mortlake tapestries. Grounds contain grotto,
sunken Dutch garden, Maori Meeting House and Museum
of the Queen's Royal Surrey Regiment.
www.nationaltrust.org.uk
**Grant Recipient:** The National Trust
**Access contact:** Property Manager
**T:** 01483 222482   **F:** 01483 223479
**E-mail:** clandonpark@nationaltrust.org.uk
**Open:** House: 18 March–28 October, daily except Monday,
Friday and Saturday (but open Good Friday, Easter
Saturday and Bank Holiday Mondays), 11am–4.30pm (last
admission as house, 12 noon–5pm). Museum: as house,
Garden: as house, 11am–5pm.
**Heritage Open Days:** No.
**P** Spaces: 200
**&** Partial. Lift provides access to all areas of the house
open to the public, some restrictions apply; please
telephone for details. Grounds partially accessible, with
some slopes and uneven terrain. WC for the disabled.
Guide Dogs allowed.
**£** Adult: £7.20. Child: £3.60. Other: £18.00 (family),
£5.69 (groups).

## GREAT HALL

**Virginia Park, Christchurch Road, Virginia Water,
Surrey GU25 4BH**
By W H Crossland for Thomas Holloway and opened 1884.
Built of red brick with Portland stone dressings and slate
roofs in Franco-Flemish Gothic style. Formerly part of the
Royal Holloway Sanatorium.
**Grant Recipient:** Virginia Park Management Co Ltd
**Access contact:** Ms Liz Adams
**T:** 01344 845276   **F:** 01344 842428
**E-mail:** virginia.park@btinternet.com
**Open:** Entrance Hall, Staircase and Great Hall of former
Sanatorium: February 14 & 25, March 21 & 25, April 11,
18 & 22, May 9, 23 & 29, June 13, 20 & 24, July 11, 18 &
22, August 8, 15 & 19, September 9 & 23, October
10, 17 & 21, November 7, 21 & 25, 10am–4pm. At other
times by prior telephone arrangement with the Estate
Office.
**Heritage Open Days:** No.
**P** Public car park nearby at Virginia Water Station.
**&** Partial. Wheelchair access with assistance (steps into
building to be negotiated). Downstairs entrance Hall but
not the Great Hall (no lift). WC for the disabled. Guide
Dogs allowed.
**£** Adult: £3.00.

## IVY CONDUIT

**Holy Cross Preparatory School, George Road,
Kingston, Surrey KT2 7NU**
Conduit house built c1514, part of an elaborate water
system built in 16th century to provide water to Hampton
Court Palace situated over 5km away. Scheduled Ancient
Monument.
**Grant Recipient:** Holy Cross Preparatory School
**Access contact:** Mr Michael Harrison
**T:** 020 8942 0729   **F:** 020 8336 0764
**E-mail:** michael@holycrossprep.co.uk
**Open:** By prior arrangement on weekdays, with 24 hours
notice.
**Heritage Open Days:** No.
**P** Spaces: 20
**&** Partial. Steep gradient through gardens, about 150m
from car park. No WC for the disabled. Guide Dogs
allowed.
**£** No.

## PAINSHILL PARK

**Portsmouth Road, Cobham, Surrey KT11 1JE**
Restored Grade I Registered 18th century landscape
garden of 150 acres, created by Charles Hamilton between
1738 and 1773. Contains a Gothic temple, Chinese
bridge, ruined abbey, Turkish tent, grotto and 14 acre
serpentine lake fed by a large waterwheel. Europa Nostra
medal winner for 'Exemplary Restoration'.
www.painshill.co.uk
**Grant Recipient:** Painshill Park Trust Ltd
**Access contact:** Miss Sarah AM Hallett
**T:** 01932 868113   **F:** 01932 868001
**E-mail:** info@painshill.co.uk
**Open:** Throughout the year: 10.30am–6pm (last admission
4.30pm) or dusk if earlier. Closed Christmas Day and
Boxing Day. Guided tours by prior arrangement at
additional cost.
**Heritage Open Days:** Yes
**P** Spaces: 400. Parking for 8 coaches.
**&** Partial. Wheelchair access to most of the site, apart
from the Grotto and Alpine Valley. Wheelchairs and
electric buggies available on request. Pre-book one week
in advance. WC for the disabled. Guide Dogs allowed.
**£** Adult: £6.60. Child: £3.85 (under 5s free). Other:
£5.80; £22.00 (family–2 adults and 4 children).

# SUSSEX

## DE LA WARR PAVILION

**The Marina, Bexhill-on-Sea, East Sussex TN40 1DP**
Built in 1935 by architects Erich Mendholson and Serge
Chermayeff was the first welded steel-framed building in
this country. Its circular staircase and sweeping sea views
make it unique as an iconic building of the Modernist
movement.
www.dlwp.com
**Grant Recipient:** De La Warr Pavilion Trust
**Access contact:** Ms Emma Morris
**T:** 01424 229134   **F:** 01424 229101
**E-mail:** info@dlwp.com
**Open:** Daily 10am–6pm. Closed Christmas Day.
**Heritage Open Days:** Yes
**P** Spaces: 100. Pay car park.
**&** Full. WC for the disabled. Guide Dogs allowed.
**£** No.

## GLYNDE PLACE

**Glynde, nr. Lewes, East Sussex BN8 6SX**
Elizabethan manor house built in 1589 from local flint and
stone from Normandy, then extensively added to in the
18th century. Contains a collection of Old Masters, family
portraits, furniture, embroidery and silver belonging to the
family who have lived there for over 400 years.
**Grant Recipient:** Viscount Hampden
**Access contact:** Viscount Hampden
**T:** 01273 858224   **F:** 01273 858224
**E-mail:** info@glyndeplace.co.uk
**Open:** May: Sundays and Bank Holidays. June–August:
Sundays, Wednesdays and Bank Holidays, 2–5pm (last
admission 4.45pm). House open at other times by prior
arrangement. Admission prices for groups if booked in
advance. Refreshments available.
**Heritage Open Days:** No.
**P** Spaces: 150
**&** Partial. Wheelchair access to tearoom and gardens. WC
for the disabled. Guide Dogs allowed.
**£** Adult: £5.50. Child: £2.75. Other: £4.50 (groups of
25+ on open days), £7.50 (groups of 25+ at other times).

## GREAT DIXTER HOUSE & GARDENS

**Northiam, nr. Rye, East Sussex TN31 6PH**
Original medieval hall house built c1450 comprising three
rooms, the Great Hall, Parlour and Solar. Bought by
Nathanial Lloyd in 1910 who employed Lutyens to restore
and extend the property. A Yeoman's hall, originally
located in Benenden, was dismantled and re-erected at
Great Dixter.
www.greatdixter.co.uk
**Grant Recipient:** Ms O Eller
**Access contact:** Mr Perry Rodriguez
**T:** 01797 252878   **F:** 01797 252878
**E-mail:** office@greatdixter.co.uk
**Open:** 1 May–30 September: Tuesday–Sunday, 2pm–5pm.
Gardens open from 11am.
**Heritage Open Days:** No.
**P** Spaces: 100
**&** Partial. Wheelchair access to most areas. Map of routes
available. WC for the disabled. Guide Dogs allowed.
**£** Adult: £7.50 (house and garden), £6.00 (garden only).
Child: £3.00 (house and garden), £2.50 (garden only).

## HIGH BEECHES WOODLAND & WATER GARDENS

**High Beeches, Handcross,
Haywards Heath, West Sussex RH17 6HQ**
Twenty five acre garden with woodland, open glades,
natural wildflower meadows and water gardens. Many
rare plants to be seen in all seasons. National collection of
Stewartia Trees. Tree and walking trails. Restaurant in
restored Victorian farm buildings and tea room/garden.
www.highbeeches.com
**Grant Recipient:** The Trustees of High Beeches Gardens
Conservation Trust
**Access contact:** Mrs Sarah Bray
**T:** 01444 400589   **F:** 01444 401543
**E-mail:** gardens@highbeeches.com
**Open:** 17 March–31 October: 1–5pm (last admission
4.30pm), closed Wednesdays. All coaches and Guided
Tours by prior arrangement. Tea room open all year except
Wednesdays.
**Heritage Open Days:** No.
**P** Spaces: 100. Free parking, coaches by prior
arrangement, disabled parking adjacent to tea room.
**&** Partial. Wheelchair access to tea room and tea garden
only. WC for the disabled. Guide Dogs allowed.
**£** Adult: £5.50. Child: Free. Other: Concessions for
groups. Guided tours £10.00 per person.

## LAMB HOUSE (COROMANDEL LACQUER PANELS)

**3 Chapel Hill, Lewes, East Sussex, BN7 2BB**
The incised lacquer panels in the study of Lamb House are
a unique surviving example of imported late 17th century
Chinese lacquer work that remains as decorative wall
panelling. Recently restored.
**Grant Recipient:** Professor Paul Benjamin
**Access contact:** Professor Paul Benjamin
**T:** 01273 475657
**E-mail:** p.r.benjamin@sussex.ac.uk
**Open:** Weekends only by prior telephone or e-mail
arrangement.
**Heritage Open Days:** Yes
**P** On-street parking.
**&** Partial. Steps to front door. Wheelchair access to
ground floor only. No WC for the disabled. No Guide Dogs
allowed.
**£** No.

## OUSE VALLEY VIADUCT

**Balcombe, West Sussex**
The most important surviving architectural feature of the
original layout of the London–Brighton railway, the grade
II* Ouse Valley Viaduct has 37 circular arches, is 492 yards
long and 92 feet high. Designed by John Rastrick with
stonework accredited to David Mocatta, it is known for its
pierced piers, ornate limestone parapets and pavilions.
Built 1839-1841.
**Grant Recipient:** Railtrack plc (now Network Rail)
**Open:** Public access at all times on the footpath running
underneath the viaduct. It is possible to view the viaduct
from Borde Hill Lane without walking across the field.
**Heritage Open Days:** No.
**P** Limited on-street parking.
**&** Partial. Wheelchair users can view viaduct form Borde
Hill Lane. No WC for the disabled. Guide Dogs allowed.
**£** No.

## PARHAM HOUSE

**Parham Park, Storrington, nr. Pulborough, West Sussex RH20 4HS**

Granted to the Palmer family in 1540 by Henry VIII, the foundation stone of this grey-stone Elizabethan house was laid in 1577. From the panelled Great Hall to the Long Gallery running the length of the roof-space, the house contains a collection of paintings, furniture and needlework.

**www.parhaminsussex.co.uk**
**Grant Recipient:** Parham Park Ltd
**Access contact:** Ms Patricia Kennedy
**T:** 01903 742021   **F:** 01903 743260
**E-mail:** pat@parhaminsussex.co.uk
**Open:** Easter–End of September: Wednesday, Thursday, Sunday and Bank Holiday Mondays. Tuesdays and Fridays during August (also Saturday 7 July). Gardens open at 12 noon, House at 2pm with last entry at 4.30pm.
**Heritage Open Days:** No.
**P** Spaces: 300. Parking for the disabled close to the house.
**&** Partial. Wheelchair access to ground floor only by prior arrangement, there is a reduced admission charge for wheelchair users and carers. Free loan of recorded tour tape. WC for the disabled. Guide Dogs allowed.
**£** **Adult:** £6.50 (provisional). **Child:** £2.50 (age 5 -15) (provisional). **Other:** £5.50 (senior citizens), £15.50 (family) (provisional).

## PETWORTH HOUSE

**Petworth, West Sussex GU28 0AE**

Late 17th century mansion in 'Capability' Brown landscaped park. The house contains the Trust's largest collection of pictures including Turners and Van Dycks, as well as sculpture, furniture and Grinling Gibbons' carvings. Also there are the Servants' Quarters with interesting kitchens and other service rooms. Extra rooms open Monday, Tuesday and Wednesday afternoon by kind permission of Lord and Lady Egremont.

**www.nationaltrust.org.uk/petworth**
**Grant Recipient:** The National Trust
**Access contact:** Property Manager
**T:** 01798 342207   **F:** 01798 342963
**E-mail:** petworth@nationaltrust.org.uk
**Open:** House and Servants' Quarters: 31 March–31 October, daily except Thursday and Friday (but open Good Friday), 11am–5pm (last admission to house 4.30pm). Extra rooms shown weekday afternoons (but not Bank Holiday Mondays) as follows: Monday: White and Gold Room and White Library; Tuesday and Wednesday: three bedrooms on first floor. Park: All year, daily and afternoons of open-air concerts in July.
**Heritage Open Days:** Yes
**P** Spaces: 150. Car park for house and park on A283, 800 yards from property.
**&** Partial. Wheelchair access to ground floor of house, shop and tea room. WC for the disabled. Guide Dogs allowed.
**£** **Adult:** £9.00. **Child:** £4.50. **Other:** £22.50 (family), £7.11 (booked groups of 15+).

## ROTUNDA TEMPLE

**Brightling Park, nr. Rotherbridge, East Sussex**

Built c1812 as an eyecatcher by Sir Robert Smirke for John Fuller, wealthy philanthropist and eccentric. Small circular building with colonnade and dome: the centre-piece of Brightling Park.
**Grant Recipient:** Mr H C Grissell
**Access contact:** Mr H C Grissell
**T:** 01424 838207   **F:** 01424 838467
**E-mail:** henrygrissell@hotmail.co.uk
**Open:** By prior arrangement only. Otherwise Temple can be viewed from public footpaths and other permitted access routes through Park.
**Heritage Open Days:** No.
**P** Parking in surrounding roads.
**&** No wheelchair access. No WC for the disabled. Guide Dogs allowed.
**£** No.

## SHIPLEY WINDMILL

**Shipley, nr. Horsham, West Sussex RH13 8PL**

Grade II* listed smock mill with five floors, built 1879 and restored in 1990 to full working order. Once owned by the Sussex writer and poet, Hilaire Belloc, who lived nearby. The milling process is demonstrated on open days for the benefit of visitors.

**www.shipleywindmill.org.uk**
**Grant Recipient:** Shipley Windmill Charitable Trust
**Access contact:** Ms Penny Murray
**T:** 01243 777642   **F:** 01243 777848
**E-mail:** penny.murray@westsussex.gov.uk
**Open:** April–October: first, second and third Sunday of each month, plus Bank Holiday Mondays. Also National Mills Day, Shipley Festival (May) and the Sunday of the Heritage Open Days weekend.
**Heritage Open Days:** Yes
**P** Spaces: 10
**&** Partial. Wheelchair access to ground floor of mill and engine shed. No WC for the disabled. No Guide Dogs allowed.
**£** **Adult:** £2.00. **Child:** £1.00. **Other:** £1.50 (senior citizens).

## ST HUGH'S CHARTERHOUSE

**Henfield Road, Partridge Green, Horsham, West Sussex RH13 8EB**

Large monastery covering 10 acres. One large cloister of over 100 square yards comprising 34 four-room hermitages where the monks live. The fore part is a smaller cloister about 200ft square which contains the cells of the Brothers and their work places. There is also a large church, library, refectory, Brothers Chapel and other monastic buildings. The large quad encloses a cemetery. The spire is 203ft high and has a five-bell chime.

**www.parkminster.org.uk**
**Grant Recipient:** St Hugh's Charterhouse
**Access contact:** John Babeau
**T:** 01403 864231   **F:** 01403 864231
**Open:** By prior arrangement, with due respect for the rules of the Charterhouse monastery. For further details please contact the monastery.
**Heritage Open Days:** No.
**P** Spaces: 20
**&** Partial. Wheelchair access to ground level only. No WC for the disabled. Guide Dogs allowed.
**£** No.

## ST MARY-IN-THE-CASTLE

**Pelham Crescent, Hastings, East Sussex TN34 3AF**

Built in 1828, architect Joseph Kay, forming an integral part of the design of Pelham Crescent. The Church has a horseshoe-shaped auditorium with gallery and is now used as an arts centre.

**www.hastings.gov.uk**
**Grant Recipient:** Friends of St Mary in the Castle
**Access contact:** Ms Penny Precious
**T:** 01424 781154/01424 781122   **F:** 01424 781133
**E-mail:** pprecious@hastings.gov.uk
**Open:** Guided tours Tuesday–Saturday by prior arrangement. Arts activities run throughout the year. Contact the Bookings Office (01424 781072 or 781154), the access contacts or check the website for further information.
**Heritage Open Days:** Yes
**P** Spaces: 400. Pay and Display parking opposite.
**&** Full. WC for the disabled. Guide Dogs allowed.
**£** No. **Other:** Tours free but donations accepted. Events individually priced.

## THE DOVECOTE

**Alciston, East Sussex BN8 6NS**

14th century dovecote of flint facings with green sand stone dressings on a chalk rubble core with chalk blocks and nesting boxes internally.

**www.firleplace.co.uk**
**Grant Recipient:** Trustees of the Firle Estate Settlement
**Access contact:** Mr Jamie Evans-Freke
**T:** 01273 858567   **F:** 01273 858570
**E-mail:** jamie@firleplace.co.uk
**Open:** Access to the dovecote is by prior arrangement with the Estate Office.
**Heritage Open Days:** No.
**P** No.
**&** Partial. No WC for the disabled. Guide Dogs allowed.
**£** No.

## THE FLUSHING INN

**4 Market Street, Rye, East Sussex TN31 7LA**

15th century timber-framed building, now a restaurant, with large recently restored 16th century wall painting.

**www.theflushinginn.com**
**Grant Recipient:** Mr Flynn
**Access contact:** Mr Flynn
**T:** 01797 223292   **F:** 01797 229748
**E-mail:** j.e.flynn@btconnect.com
**Open:** Restaurant open Wednesday–Sunday for lunches and dinners, Mondays lunch only and Tuesdays closed. Closed first two weeks in January and June. Unless dining, visiting to view the Fresco is restricted to 10.30am–12 noon.
**Heritage Open Days:** No.
**P** Parking on-street but restricted to 1 hour, otherwise public parking elsewhere in Rye.
**&** Partial. Wheelchair access to Fresco with assistance (entrance steps to be negotiated). No WC for the disabled. Guide Dogs allowed.
**£** No.

## THE ROYAL PAVILION

**Brighton, East Sussex BN1 1EE**

Former seaside residence of George IV in Indian style with Chinese-inspired interiors. Originally a neo-classical villa by Henry Holland was built on the site in 1787, but this was subsequently replaced by the current John Nash building constructed between 1815-23.

**www.royalpavilion.org.uk**
**Grant Recipient:** Brighton & Hove City Council
**Access contact:** Mr Andrew Barlow
**T:** 01273 292746   **F:** 01273 292871
**E-mail:** andrew.barlow@brighton-hove.gov.uk
**Open:** April–September: daily 9.30am–5.45pm (last admission 5pm). October–March, daily, 10am–5.15pm (last admission 4.30pm). Closed 25 and 26 December. Admission charges are valid until 31 March 2007, for rates after that date please check with the Royal Pavilion for current information.
**Heritage Open Days:** No.
**P** NCP car park on Church Street. Parking for the disabled is available in the grounds of the Pavilion by prior arrangement.
**&** Partial. Wheelchair access to ground floor only, reduced rate of admission is payable. WC for the disabled. Guide Dogs allowed.
**£** **Adult:** £6.10, £2.35 (local residents, Oct–Feb only). Prices valid until 31.3.07 **Child:** £3.60 under 16 (Oct–Feb, local residents free with paying adult). Prices valid until 31.3.07. **Other:** £5.75 (seniors/students/unemployed), £19.00 (family of 2 adults, 4 children), £11.50 (1 adult, 4 children). Prices valid until 31.3.07.

## TITHE BARN

**Court Farm, East Street, Brighton, West Sussex BN1 9PB**

Grade II* listed medieval tithe barn. Mainly of timber construction with thatched roof.
**Grant Recipient:** Brighton and Hove County Council
**Access contact:** Mr Richard Butler
**T:** 01273 291440   **F:** 01273 291467
**E-mail:** richard.butler@brighton-hove.gov.uk
**Open:** By prior arrangement with Richard Butler, Brighton and Hove County Council (or Thomas Stanley at Smiths Gore 01798 345983) and Eric Huxham–tenant at Court Farm (07802 453842).
**Heritage Open Days:** No.
**P** On-street parking within Falmer village.
**&** Partial. Barn within working farm so access can be muddy. Guide dogs are welcome but as a working farm care is requested. No WC for the disabled.
**£** No.

## WINDMILL HILL WINDMILL

**Herstmonceux, Hailsham, East Sussex BN27 4RT**

Grade II* listed, dating from 1815, the second tallest and largest post mill in body size. The mill last worked by wind in 1894 and has recently been authentically restored.

**www.windmillhillwindmill.co.uk**
**Grant Recipient:** Windmill Hill Windmill Trust
**Access contact:** Mrs B Frost
**T:** 01323 833033   **F:** 01323 833744
**E-mail:** admin@windmillhillwindmill.co.uk
**Open:** All year: First and third Sunday of the month and Bank Holidays, 2.30–5pm. School parties and groups by prior arrangement.
**Heritage Open Days:** Yes
**P** Spaces: 4
**&** Partial. Wheelchair access to visitor centre. Film enables full visitor experience without physically going up mill body. WC for the disabled. Guide Dogs allowed.
**£** No.

## TYNE AND WEAR

### FREEMASONS HALL

**Queen Street East, Sunderland, Tyne and Wear SR1 2HT**
Grade I listed oldest purpose-built Masonic meeting place in the world, c1785. Contains an ornate Lodge Room which remains virtually unaltered with elaborate thrones from 1735. Also has a cellar is in its original condition and the last remaining example of a Donaldson organ which was specially constructed for the building in 1785.
**Grant Recipient:** Queen Street Masonic Temple Ltd
**Access contact:** Mr Colin Meddes
**T:** 0191 522 0115  **F:** 0191 522 0115
**E-mail:** colinmeddes@tiscali.co.uk
**Open:** Guided tours throughout the year by prior arrangement. Heritage Open Days Sunday, 11am-3pm.
**Heritage Open Days:** Yes
**P** Spaces: 80
**&** Full. Five external steps to main entrance: guides available to assist wheelchair users. Access ramp for the disabled due to be installed. WC for the disabled. Guide Dogs allowed.
**£** No.

### HIGH LEVEL BRIDGE

**linking Newcastle & Gateshead, Tyne and Wear**
Grade I listed railway and road bridge of ashlar and cast iron, 1849, designed by Robert Stephenson. One of the finest pieces of architectural iron work in the world.
**Grant Recipient:** Network Rail
**Access contact:** Mr Richard Bell
**T:** 01904389 876  **F:** 01904 389 802
**E-mail:** richard.bell@networkrail.co.uk
**Open:** Best viewed from adjacent riverbanks or via access road/footpath under bridge. Also may be viewed from the footways which cross the lower deck of the bridge. Access to the lower deck is not available during 2007 as major refurbishment will be taking place. No access to the upper deck of the bridge.
**Heritage Open Days:** No.
**P** On-street parking.
**&** Partial. Footways across the lower deck of the bridge are accessible for wheelchairs but the lower deck is not available during 2007 due to major refurbishment. No WC for the disabled. Guide Dogs allowed.
**£** No.

## WARWICKSHIRE

### CHARLECOTE PARK

**Wellesbourne, Warwick, Warwickshire CV35 9ER**
Owned by the Lucy family since 1247, Sir Thomas built the house in 1558. Now much altered, it is shown as it would have been a century ago. The balustraded formal garden gives onto a deer park landscaped by 'Capability' Brown.
**www.nationaltrust.org.uk**
**Grant Recipient:** The National Trust
**Access contact:** Glen Sutton, Property Manager
**T:** 01789 470277  **F:** 01789 470544
**E-mail:** charlecote.park@nationaltrust.org.uk
**Open:** House: 3 March–28 October: Friday–Tuesday, 12 noon–5pm; 3 November–23 December, Saturday and Sunday, 12 noon–4pm. Gardens: 3 March–28 October, Friday–Tuesday, 10.30am–6pm; 3 November–23 December, Saturday and Sunday, 11am–4pm. Park: 3 March–29 February, Friday–Tuesday, dawn to dusk.
**Heritage Open Days:** Yes
**P** Spaces: 200. Overflow car park available.
**&** Partial. Wheelchair access to ground floor of house, restaurant and shop. WC for the disabled. Guide Dogs allowed.
**£** Adult: £7.90. Child: £4.00. Other: £19.00 (family), £6.20 (group).

### LORD LEYCESTER HOSPITAL

**High Street, Warwick, Warwickshire CV34 4BH**
14th century chantry chapel, Great Hall, galleried courtyard and Guildhall. Acquired by Robert Dudley, Earl of Leicester in 1571 as a home for his old soldiers. Still operating as a home for ex-servicemen.
**www.lordleycester.com**
**Grant Recipient:** Patron & Governors of Lord Leycester Hospital
**Access contact:** Lieut. Colonel G F Lesinski
**T:** 01926 491422
**E-mail:** lordleycester@btinternet.com

**Open:** Tuesday–Sunday, 10am–4pm (winter), 10am–5pm (summer), plus Bank Holiday Mondays. Closed Good Friday and Christmas Day.
**Heritage Open Days:** No.
**P** Spaces: 10
**&** Partial. Wheelchair access to ground floor only. WC for the disabled. Guide Dogs allowed.
**£** Adult: Summer: £4.90, £2.00 (garden only), Winter: £3.40. Child: Summer: £3.90, free (garden only), Winter: £2.40. Other: Summer: £4.40, £2.00 (garden only), Winter £2.90.

### POLESWORTH NUNNERY GATEWAY

**22-24 High Street, Polesworth, nr. Tamworth, Warwickshire B78 1DU**
Abbey gatehouse, late 14th century with later alterations. Upper floors now in residential use.
**www.polesworthabbey.co.uk**
**Grant Recipient:** Polesworth PCC
**Access contact:** Reverend Philip Wells
**T:** 01827 892340  **F:** 01827 892770
**E-mail:** polesworthabbey@aol.com
**Open:** Exterior at all reasonable times, ground floor interior by prior arrangement with The Revd Philip Wells, Polesworth Vicarage, High Street, Polesworth B78 1DU (tel 01827 892 340).
**Heritage Open Days:** No.
**P** Spaces: 20. Parking in Abbey driveway.
**&** Partial. Wheelchair access to ground floor only. WC located in the nearby Abbey Refectory. No WC for the disabled. Guide Dogs allowed.
**£** No.

### RAGLEY HALL

**Alcester, Warwickshire B49 5NJ**
Family home of the Marquess and Marchioness of Hertford. Built in 1680 to a design by Robert Hooke in the Palladian style, with portico added by Wyatt in 1780. Contents include baroque plasterwork by James Gibb, family portraits by Sir Joshua Reynolds and a mural by Graham Rust completed in 1983. Surrounding park designed by 'Capability' Brown.
**www.ragleyhall.com**
**Grant Recipient:** Hugh Edward Conway Seymour The 8th Marquess of Hertford & Earl of Yarmouth
**Access contact:** Mr Richard Webb
**T:** 01789 762090  **F:** 01789 764791
**E-mail:** richardwebb@ragleyhall.com
**Open:** State Rooms: 22 March–30 September: Thursday, Friday, Sunday, Bank Holiday Mondays, 11am–4pm; Saturday, 11am–1pm. Times and dates may vary subject to events and functions, please phone 01789 762 090 to confirm. Park and gardens: Thursday–Sunday, Bank Holiday Mondays; daily in school holidays, 11am–6pm (last admission 4.30pm).
**Heritage Open Days:** No.
**P** Spaces: 4000
**&** Full. Wheelchair access via lift to first floor. WC for the disabled. Guide Dogs allowed.
**£** Adult: £8.00. Child: £4.50 (age 5-16). Other: £6.50 (seniors & Orange/Blue Badge), £25.00 (family). Groups 20+ £6.00 (adult/seniors), £4.00 (child). Season: £85.00 (family), £30.00 (single).

### STONELEIGH ABBEY

**Kenilworth, Warwickshire CV8 2LF**
16th century house built on site and incorporating remains of Cistercian Abbey founded in 1155. West wing designed by Francis Smith of Warwick between 1714-26 and northern wing reconstructed in 19th century by Charles S Smith of Warwick. South wing c1820. West wing contains a range of State Apartments. Also has restored Regency riding stables, 19th century conservatory and Humphrey Repton landscaped riverside gardens.
**www.stoneleighabbey.org**
**Grant Recipient:** Stoneleigh Abbey Preservation Trust (1996) Ltd
**Access contact:** Estate Office
**T:** 01926 858535  **F:** 01926 850274
**E-mail:** enquire@stoneleighabbey.org
**Open:** Good Friday–end of October: Tuesday, Wednesday, Thursday and Sunday, plus Bank Holidays. Opening arrangements may change, please check with the Preservation Trust for current information.
**Heritage Open Days:** No.
**P** Spaces: 400
**&** Full. WC for the disabled. Guide Dogs allowed.

**£** Adult: £6.50. Child: £3.00 Other: £5.00 (senior citizens), £3.00 grounds only.

## WEST MIDLANDS

### MOLINEUX HOTEL

**Whitmore Hill, Wolverhampton, West Midlands**
Grade II* listed house of c1720 with mid 18th century additions. Used as an hotel from 1860 onwards. Vacant since 1979 and acquired by Wolverhampton City Council in 2004. The first stage of repairs was undertaken during 2004-2005. Restoration and conversion to house the City's Archives and Local Studies service will take place during 2007.
**www.wolverhampton.gov.uk**
**Grant Recipient:** Wolverhampton City Council
**Access contact:** Mr Nigel Brown
**T:** 01902 556 556  **F:** 01902 555 637
**E-mail:** nigel.brown@wolverhampton.gov.uk
**Open:** Guided tours for groups by prior arrangement (subject to building work).
**Heritage Open Days:** No.
**P** Spaces: 80. Parking available evenings and most weekends.
**&** Partial. Wheelchair access to ground floor and most of the site. No WC for the disabled. Guide Dogs allowed.
**£** No.

### PERROTT'S FOLLY

**Edgbaston, Birmingham, West Midlands**
Built in 1758 by John Perrott as folly adjacent to his house (long demolished). The tower or folly is 94 feet high with circular stair tower attached. In 1884 the Birmingham glass-maker and meteorologist Abraham Follet Osler began using the building for weather observations. As the Edgbaston Observatory it became part of one of the world's first regular weather forecasting services–keeping up that work until 1979, at which time it fell into disuse. First phase of repair completed.
**Grant Recipient:** The Perrott's Folly Company
**Access contact:** Mr Dennis Minnis
**T:** 0121 454 4152
**E-mail:** dennis.minnis@linone.net
**Open:** By prior arrangement.
**Heritage Open Days:** Yes
**P** No.
**&** No wheelchair access. No WC for the disabled. No Guide Dogs allowed.
**£** No.

### RED HOUSE GLASSCONE

**Wordsley, Stourbridge, West Midlands DY8 4AZ**
Built around 1790, the Cone was used for the manufacture of glass until 1936 and is now one of only four left in the Country. Reaching 100ft into the sky, the Cone enclosed a furnace where glass was made for 140 years. In its 200 year history, the site has remained virtually unaltered and therefore provides an interesting insight into the history and tradition of glassmaking. Glassmaking and exhibitions tell the story of glassmaking in the area and the history of the glassworks.
**www.dudley.gov.uk/redhousecone**
**Grant Recipient:** Dudley Metropolitan Borough Council
**Access contact:** Ms Sarah Hall
**T:** 01384 812752  **F:** 01384 812751
**E-mail:** sarah.hall@dudley.gov.uk
**Open:** January–31 March: daily, 10am–4pm. 1 April–31 October: Monday–Saturday, 10am–5pm, Sunday, 10am–4pm.
**Heritage Open Days:** Yes
**P** Spaces: 40
**&** Partial. Full wheelchair access to the Cone, glassmaking area and all display areas. Lift to upper floor and galleries. Some studios are inaccessible. WC for the disabled. Guide Dogs allowed.
**£** No. Other: £1.50 (audio guide).

### SOHO HOUSE MUSEUM

**Soho Avenue, Handsworth, Birmingham, West Midlands B18 5LB**
Soho House Museum is the former home of Matthew Boulton, Birmingham industrialist, entrepreneur and partner of James Watt. Designed by James and Samuel Wyatt, the house was once a meeting place of the Lunar Society and contains period rooms and displays on Boulton's manufacturing activities. The visitor centre houses a temporary exhibition gallery, shop and tearoom.

**www.bmag.org.uk**
**Grant Recipient:** Birmingham Museums & Art Gallery
**Access contact:** Curator/Manager
**T:** 0121 554 9122   **F:** 0121 554 5929
**Open:** 31 March–28 October: Tuesday–Sunday,
11.30am–4pm, also open Bank Holiday Mondays.
**Heritage Open Days:** Yes
P Spaces: 23
Full. WC for the disabled. Guide Dogs allowed.
£ No.

## ST JAMES

**Great Packington, Meriden,**
**nr. Coventry, West Midlands CV7 7HF**
Red brick building with four domes topped by finials in
neo-classical style. Built to celebrate the return to sanity of
King George III. The organ was designed by Handel for his
librettist, Charles Jennens, who was the cousin of the 4th
Earl of Aylesford, who built the church.
**Grant Recipient:** St James Great Packington Trust
**Access contact:** Packington Estate Office
**T:** 01676 522020   **F:** 01676 523399
**E-mail:** jameschurch@packingtonestate.co.uk
**Open:** Monday–Friday, 9am–5pm: key can be obtained
from the Estate Office at Packington Hall, preferably by
phoning in advance (01676 522020). At other times by
prior arrangement with Lord Guernsey (tel: 01676
522274).
**Heritage Open Days:** No.
P Spaces: 10
Partial. Wheelchair access with assistance (entrance
steps and heavy door to be negotiated). No WC for the
disabled. Guide Dogs allowed.
£ Donations towards restoration welcomed.

## THE BIG HOUSE

**44 Church Street, Oldbury, West Midlands B69 3DE**
Grade II* 3-storey house dating from c1730. Originally
with agricultural land and later the house and officers of a
solicitor in 1857 when the land was sold. Restored and
reopened in 2002 as Civic offices.
**www.sandwell.gov.uk**
**Grant Recipient:** Sandwell Metropolitan Borough Council
**Access contact:** Civic Affairs Officer
**T:** 0121 569 3041   **F:** 0121 569 3050
**E-mail:** ann_oneill@sandwell.gov.uk
**Open:** By arrangement with the Mayor's office via the
Civic Affairs officer (tel: 0121 569 3041). The Mayor will
also hold "Open House" at various times throughout the
year.
**Heritage Open Days:** No.
P Market Street Public Car Park (30 spaces). Parking for
the disabled (4 spaces) adjacent to property.
Full. WC for the disabled. Guide Dogs allowed.
£ No.

## WIGHTWICK MANOR

**Wightwick Bank, Wolverhampton,**
**West Midlands WV6 8EE**
Built 1887, the house is a notable example of a late
Victorian manor house. Contains original William Morris
wallpapers and fabrics, Pre-Raphaelite paintings, Kempe
glass and de Morgan ware. Also has a 17 acre
Victorian/Edwardian garden designed by Thomas Mawson.
**www.nationaltrust.org.uk**
**Grant Recipient:** The National Trust
**Access contact:** Property Manager
**T:** 01902 761400/01902 760100   **F:** 01902 764663
**E-mail:** wightwickmanor@nationaltrust.org.uk
**Open:** By guided tour only 1 March–22 December:
Thursday, Friday and Saturday (also Bank Holiday Sunday
and Monday to ground floor only), 12.30–5pm. Also
family open days Wednesdays in August, 12.30–5pm.
Admission by timed ticket issued from 11am at Visitor
Reception. Other days by prior arrangement. Garden:
Wednesday–Saturday and Bank Holiday Sunday and
Monday, 11am–6pm. First Thursday and Saturday of each
month: no guided tours, free flow only.
**Heritage Open Days:** Yes
P Spaces: 50. For coach parking please telephone 01902
760100.
Partial. Wheelchair access to ground floor only, two
steps. WC for the disabled. Guide Dogs allowed.
£ **Adult:** £7.50, £3.70 (garden only). Admission price
includes voluntary gift aid donation. **Child:** £3.70 (children
free for garden only). **Other:** £3.70 (students), £19.00
(family).

## WEST YORKSHIRE

### BOLLING HALL MUSEUM

**Bowling Hall Road, Bradford,**
**West Yorkshire BD4 7LP**
Furnished house, mainly 17th and 18th centuries with
some earlier parts. Large stained glass window with
armorial glass, fine collection of 16th century oak
furniture. Now a free public museum with temporary
exhibition space.
**www.bradfordmuseums.org**
**Grant Recipient:** Bradford Metropolitan District Council
**Access contact:** Miss Liz McIvor
**T:** 01274 431826   **F:** 01274 726220
**E-mail:** liz.mcivor@bradford.gov.uk
**Open:** January–9 June: Wednesday, Thursday and Friday,
11am–4pm; Saturday, 10am–5pm; Sunday, 12 noon–5pm.
Closed on Mondays (except Bank Holidays) and Christmas
Day, Boxing Day and Good Friday.
**Heritage Open Days:** No.
P Spaces: 75. Free parking 100 metres from Museum.
Partial. Wheelchair access to ground floor only. WC for
the disabled. Guide Dogs allowed.
£ No.

### BRAMHAM PARK LEAD LADS TEMPLE

**Wetherby, West Yorkshire LS23 6ND**
Park folly, in the form of an open temple in the classical
style, built in the 1750s by local craftsmen on the
instructions of Harriet Benson (about a mile from the
house in woodland called Black Fen, close to a public
footpath). The 'Lead Lads' were classical lead figures that
stood on the three small blocks at the apex and base of
the front pediment, and were lost to vandals many years
ago.
**www.bramhampark.co.uk**
**Grant Recipient:** Trustees of the Bramham Settled Estate
**Access contact:** The Estate Office
**T:** 01937 846000   **F:** 01937 846007
**E-mail:** enquiries@bramhampark.co.uk
**Open:** 1 April–30 September. Closed 4–10 June and 13
August–1 September.
**Heritage Open Days:** No.
P Spaces: 50. Car park for visitors to Bramham Park (1
mile).
Partial. WC for the disabled is not on site, but in
visitors car park (1 mile). WC for the disabled. Guide Dogs
allowed.
£ **Adult:** £4.50. **Child:** £2.50 (under 5s free). **Other:**
£2.50 (senior citizens). No charge made for visitors via the
footpath but charge made for visitors to the house and
gardens.

### CROSSLEY PAVILION

**The People's Park, King Cross Road, Halifax,**
**West Yorkshire HX1 1EB**
Grade II* listed building, designed by Sir Joseph Paxton
and constructed in 1857. Contains seating and a statue of
the park's benefactor, Sir Francis Crossley (1860), by
Joseph Durham. Four gargoyle fountains supply pools
flanking each side of the pavilion, set on formal terrace,
balustrades and steps.
**www.calderdale.gov.uk/tourism/parks/peoples.html**
**Grant Recipient:** Calderdale Metropolitan Borough
Council
**Access contact:** People's Park Development Officer
**T:** 01422 323824   **F:** 01422 323824
**Open:** Park: daily, 8am–dusk. Pavilion: visits by prior
arrangement with Calderdale Metropolitan Borough
Council Leisure Services, 25 Bedford Street North, Halifax,
West Yorkshire HX1 5BH. Public toilets open during park
hours. Information Centre open by prior arrangement as
above.
**Heritage Open Days:** Yes
P On-street parking in Park Road (up to 10 spaces).
Limited spaces in adjacent college.
Partial. There is one step into the pavilion, otherwise
full wheelchair access. WC for the disabled. Guide Dogs
allowed.
£ No.

### FARFIELD FRIENDS MEETING HOUSE

**off Bolton Road, Addingham, nr. Ilkley,**
**West Yorkshire LS29**
Land for burial ground purchased in 1666, followed by
construction of Meeting House in 1669. A simple single

cell building with rubblestone walls, mullioned windows,
stone-slated roof and stone-flagged floor. Contains loose
benches and an oak minister's stand of an unusual
panelled design with turned balusters.
**www.hct.org.uk**
**Grant Recipient:** Historic Chapels Trust
**Access contact:** Barry Cody
**T:** 01756 710587
**Open:** At all reasonable times by application to key
holders Mr & Mrs Barry Cody, Riverview Cottage, Farfield,
nr Addingham, West Yorks LS29 0RQ. Burial ground open
for viewing and picnics.
**Heritage Open Days:** No.
P Spaces: 2
No wheelchair access. No WC for the disabled. Guide
Dogs allowed.
£ Donations box.

### HAREWOOD HOUSE

**Harewood, Leeds, West Yorkshire LS17 9LQ**
Designed in neo-classical style by John Carr and completed
in 1772. Contains Adam interiors, Chippendale furniture,
an art collection and museum. Home of the Earl and
Countess of Harewood.
**www.harewood.org**
**Grant Recipient:** The Trustees of Harewood House Trust
Ltd
**Access contact:** Mr Terence Suthers
**T:** 0113 218 1010   **F:** 0113 218 1002
**E-mail:** business@harewood.org
**Open:** Daily 24 March–29 October: Grounds and Bird
Garden open 10am–6pm (last admission 4pm). House
11am–4.30pm (last admission 4pm). Grounds close at
6pm. Grounds and Bird Garden also open weekends
between 4 November and 10 December. Guide dogs are
not allowed in the Bird Garden but a free sound guide is
available for the partially sighted visitor and a minder for
the dog.
**Heritage Open Days:** Yes
P Spaces: 200. Unlimited overflow parking on grass.
Full. WC for the disabled. Guide Dogs allowed.
£ **Adult:** £11.30 (weekdays), £13.15 Saturdays, Sundays
and Bank Holidays. **Child:** £6.50 (Mon-Fri), £8.15 (Sat &
Sun). **Other:** £10.00 (senior), £37.50 (family), season
tickets & concessions for disabled groups, 50% reduction
for arrivals by public transport, students free Wednesday

### HUDDERSFIELD STATION

**St George's Square, Huddersfield,**
**West Yorkshire HD1 1JF**
Designed by J P Pritchett of York and built by local builder
Joseph Kaye using local ashlar sandstone, the station is the
oldest of the seven Grade I listed station buildings in use
for railway passengers having opened on 3 August 1847.
When the foundation stone was laid the year before a
public holiday was declared and church bells were rung
from dawn till dusk. The grandeur of the station is the
result of it having been built at the joint expense of the
Huddersfield & Manchester Rail & Canal Company and the
Manchester & Leeds Railway Company.
**Grant Recipient:** Kirklees Metropolitan Council
**Access contact:** Head of Design & Property Service
**T:** 01484 226174   **F:** 01484 226086
**Open:** Operational building open to the public every day
except Christmas Day and Boxing Day. Please note that the
building may also be closed on other days specified by
Network Rail or other railway operators.
**Heritage Open Days:** No.
P Spaces: 20. One hour stay maximum in station car
park.
Full wheelchair access to main buildings. Access with
assistance to inner platforms. No WC for the disabled.
Guide Dogs allowed.
£ No.

### KIRKSTALL ABBEY

**Leeds, West Yorkshire LS5 3EH**
One of the best preserved examples of a ruined Medieval
Cistercian Monastery in the country. Founded by monks
from Fountains and the primary building work was
completed in 1182. The Reredorter has been restored as a
Visitor Centre.
**www.leeds.gov.uk/kirkstallabbey**
**Grant Recipient:** Leeds City Council
**Access contact:** Ms Katherine Baxter
**T:** 0113 230 5492   **F:** 0113 230 5499
**E-mail:** katherine.baxter@leeds.gov.uk

**Open:** 1 October–31 March: Tuesday, Wednesday, Thursday, Saturday, Sunday (closed Mondays and Fridays), 11am–3pm. Free Tours (booked groups) Thursdays. 1 April–30 September: Tuesday–Sunday (closed Mondays), 11am–4pm. Schools/tours can book for Tuesdays–Friday all year.
**Heritage Open Days:** Yes
P Spaces: 70. Parking for 3 coaches and for the disabled.
Full. WC for the disabled. Guide Dogs allowed.
£ No.

## NATIONAL COAL MINING MUSEUM FOR ENGLAND

### Caphouse Colliery, New Road, Wakefield, West Yorkshire WF4 4RH

A colliery complex dating back to the 18th century with an underground tour into authentic coal workings and major galleries covering social history, science and technology within mining. Most of the historic buildings are open to the public. Facilities include a research library, restaurant, shop and education services.
**www.ncm.org.uk**
**Grant Recipient:** The National Coal Mining Museum for England Trust Ltd
**Access contact:** Dr M Faull
**T:** 01924 848806    **F:** 01924 840694
**E-mail:** info@ncm.org.uk
**Open:** All year: daily, 10am–5pm except 24–26 December and 1 January.
**Heritage Open Days:** Yes
P Spaces: 200
Partial. Wheelchair access to all galleries and historic buildings and underground (limited tour) but not the screens. WC for the disabled. Guide Dogs allowed.
£ No.

## NOSTELL PRIORY

### Doncaster Road, Nostell, Wakefield, West Yorkshire WF4 1QE

Country house, c1736-1750, by James Paine for Sir Rowland Winn 4th baronet. Later Robert Adam was commissioned to complete the State Rooms. On display is a collection of Chippendale furniture, designed especially for the house, an art collection with works by Pieter Breughel the Younger and Angelica Kauffmann, an 18th century dolls house, complete with its original fittings and Chippendale furniture and an un-restored 18th century Muniments Room. Other attractions include lakeside walks, historic park, family croquet, giant chess set and open day for cabinets.
**www.nationaltrust.org.uk**
**Grant Recipient:** The National Trust
**Access contact:** Property Manager
**T:** 01924 863892    **F:** 01924 866846
**E-mail:** nostellpriory@nationaltrust.org.uk
**Open:** House: 17 March–4 November, daily except Monday and Tuesday (open Good Friday and Bank Holidays) 1–5pm. 9 December–17 December: daily, 12 noon–4pm. Grounds, shop and tea room: 13–19 February: daily 11am–4pm. 4–26 March: weekend only, 11am–6pm. 1 April–5 November, 11am–6pm.
**Heritage Open Days:** No.
P Spaces: 120
Partial. Wheelchair access to ground floor of house with lift to first floor, tea room, children's playground and shop. No WC for the disabled. Guide Dogs allowed.
£ **Adult:** £7.20. **Child:** £3.60. **Other:** £17.50 (family).

## PONTEFRACT OLD TOWN HALL AND ASSEMBLY ROOMS

### Bridge Street, Pontefract, West Yorkshire WF8 1PG

Grade II and II* Listed buildings. Old Town Hall built in 1785 and designed by Bernard Hartlley. Assembly Rooms later added in 1882 and designed by Perkin & Bulmer. Currently used for productions, concerts and dance.
**Grant Recipient:** Wakefield Metropolitan District Council
**Access contact:** Mrs Olive Rendell
**T:** 01924 305 573    **F:** 01924 306 963
**E-mail:** orendell@wakefield.gov.uk
**Open:** Monday–Thursday, 9–11.30am. Friday, 9–10.30am. All other times by prior arrangement.
**Heritage Open Days:** Yes
P Car park nearby, disabled parking adjacent to property.
Full. WC for the disabled. Guide Dogs allowed.
£ No.

## TEMPLE NEWSAM HOUSE

### Leeds Museums and Galleries, Leeds, West Yorkshire LS15 0AE

Tudor-Jacobean mansion in 1200 acre park. Birthplace of Henry Lord Darnley, husband of Mary Queen of Scots, and later the home of the Ingram family, Viscounts Irwin. Over 30 rooms open to the public with pre-eminent collections of paintings, furniture, metalwork, ceramics, textiles and wallpapers.
**www.leeds.gov.co.uk/templenewsam**
**Grant Recipient:** Leeds City Council
**Access contact:** Mr Anthony Wells-Cole
**T:** 0113 264 7321    **F:** 0113 260 2285
**E-mail:** temple.newsam@leeds.gov.uk
**Open:** January–December: daily except Monday (open Bank Holiday Mondays), 10.30am–5.00pm (4pm in winter). Last admission 45 minutes before closing.
**Heritage Open Days:** Yes
P Spaces: 200
Partial. Wheelchair access to all public areas except the first floor of the south wing. WC for the disabled. Guide Dogs allowed.
£ **Adult:** £3.50 (includes audio tour). **Child:** £2.50 (5-16). Free (under 5). **Other:** £8.00 (family) Admission charges subject to change.

## THE ROUNDHOUSE

### Wellington Road, Leeds, West Yorkshire LS12 1DR

Grade II* railway roundhouse built in 1847 for the Leeds and Thirsk Railway by Thomas Granger. In full use by the North-Eastern Railway until 1904, now home to Leeds Commercial Van and Truck Hire.
**Grant Recipient:** Wellbridge Properties Ltd
**Access contact:** Mr J D Miller
**T:** 0113 2435964    **F:** 0113 246 1142
**E-mail:** sales@leedscommercial.co.uk
**Open:** By prior written arrangement with the occupiers, Leeds Commercial, who manage the property as a working garage, or call in during office hours.
**Heritage Open Days:** Yes
P Spaces: 100. Free parking
Full. WC for the disabled. Guide Dogs allowed.
£ No.

# WILTSHIRE

## AVONCLIFFE AQUEDUCT

### Kennet & Avon Canal, Westwood, Wiltshire

19th century limestone aqueduct carrying the Kennet and Avon Canal over the River Avon and the railway line. The canal towpath crosses alongside the canal providing a foot link to Bradford-on-Avon or Bath.
**www.britishwaterways.co.uk/southwest**
**Grant Recipient:** British Waterways
**Access contact:** Mrs Eliza Botham
**T:** 01452 318000    **F:** 01452 318062
**E-mail:** eliza.botham@britishwaterways.co.uk
**Open:** At all times.
**Heritage Open Days:** No.
P Spaces: 12
Partial. Wheelchair access to top of aqueduct from the small car park beside the canal. No WC for the disabled. Guide Dogs allowed.
£ No.

## BARTON GRANGE FARM WEST BARN

### Bradford on Avon, Wiltshire

Part of Barton Farm, once a grange of Shaftesbury Abbey (the richest nunnery in England), which includes the adjacent 14th century Tithe Barn. The West Barn was destroyed by fire in 1982 but has subsequently been rebuilt by the Preservation Trust and is now used as an 'Interpretation Centre'.
**www.bradfordheritage.co.uk/PAGES/project.htm**
**Grant Recipient:** Bradford on Avon Preservation Trust Limited
**Access contact:** Mr Chris Penny
**T:** 01225 866551
**E-mail:** chrispenny@lineone.net
**Open:** May–September: weekends and Bank Holidays, 12 noon–4pm. Also open at other times throughout the year, please check with Mr Penny for further details.
**Heritage Open Days:** Yes
P Pay parking (15 spaces) near the site. Pay parking (200 spaces) at railway station.
Partial. Wheelchair access to main building but not

galleries. Entrance pathways are loose gravel. WC for the disabled. Guide Dogs allowed.
£ No.

## HEMINGSBY

### 56 The Close, Salisbury, Wiltshire SP1 2EL

14th century canonical residence with spacious 18th century rooms and medieval Great Hall. Contains 15th century linenfold panelling. Large and interesting garden. Home of Canon William Fideon, a Greek scholar who escaped from Constantinople in 1453, and Canon Edward Powell, advocate of Catherine of Aragon and later hanged for denying the Act of Supremacy.
**Grant Recipient:** The Dean & Chapter of Salisbury Cathedral
**Access contact:** Mr Peter Edds
**T:** 01722 555115    **F:** 01722 555140
**E-mail:** p.edds@salcath.co.uk
**Open:** By prior arrangement only. Exterior can be viewed at all times.
**Heritage Open Days:** No.
P No.
No wheelchair access. No WC for the disabled. Guide Dogs allowed.
£ Donations invited.

## LACOCK ABBEY

### Lacock, nr. Chippenham, Wiltshire SN15 2LG

Founded in 1232 and converted into a country house c1540, the fine medieval cloisters, sacristy, chapter house and monastic rooms of the Abbey have survived largely intact. The handsome 16th century stable courtyard has half timbered gables, a clockhouse, brewery and bakehouse. Victorian woodland garden. Former residents include William Fox Talbot 'the father of modern photography'.
**www.nationaltrust.org.uk**
**Grant Recipient:** The National Trust
**Access contact:** Property Manager
**T:** 01249 730459/730227    **F:** 01249 730501
**E-mail:** lacock.estate@nationaltrust.org.uk
**Open:** Abbey: 17 March–28 October: daily, 1–5.30pm (closed Tuesdays and Good Friday). Museum, cloisters and garden: 24 February–28 October, daily 11am–5.30pm (closed Good Friday). Museum also open 3 November–16 December & 5 January–17 February, 11am–4pm.
**Heritage Open Days:** Yes
P Spaces: 300
Partial. Wheelchair access to Abbey is difficult as four sets of stairs. Garden, cloisters and museum are accessible (non-wheelchair stairlift in museum). Limited parking in Abbey courtyard by arrangement. WC for the disabled at Red Lion car park, High Street, and abbey courtyard, RADAR lock. WC for the disabled. Guide Dogs allowed.
£ **Adult:** £8.30 (Abbey, museum, cloisters & garden), £6.70 (Abbey & garden), £5.10 (garden, cloisters & museum). **Child:** £4.10 (Abbey, museum, cloisters & garden), £3.40 (Abbey & garden), £2.50 (garden, cloisters & museum). **Other:** £21.20 (family: Abbey, museum, cloisters & garden), £17.10 (family: Abbey & garden), £12.90 (family: garden, cloisters & museum). Group rates.

## LADY MARGARET HUNGERFORD ALMSHOUSES

### Pound Pill, Corsham, Wiltshire SN13 9HT

Fine complex of Grade I listed 17th Almshouses, Schoolroom, Warden's House and Stables. Schoolroom with original 17th century furniture and Exhibition Room. Recently restored. Lady Margaret Hungerford founded the Almshouses for the care of six poor people and the schoolroom for educating poor children. Arms of the foundress are well displayed.
**Grant Recipient:** Trustees Of The Lady Margaret Hunderford Charity
**Access contact:** Mr R L Tonge
**T:** 01225 742471    **F:** 01225 742471
**E-mail:** rtonge@northwilts.gov.uk
**Open:** 4 April–30 September: Tuesday, Wednesday, Friday and Saturday, 1.30–4.00pm. October, November, February & March: Saturdays, 1.30pm–4.00pm. Closed December and January and Bank Holidays. Groups welcome by appointment.
**Heritage Open Days:** No.
P Spaces: 100. Parking in the town within 100 yards.
Partial. Wheelchair access to ground floor only. WC for the disabled. Guide Dogs allowed.
£ **Adult:** £2.00. **Child:** 50p. **Other:** £1.75 (senior citizens and concessions).

## LARMER TREE GARDENS

**nr Tollard Royal, Salisbury, Wiltshire SP5 5PY**

Created by General Pitt Rivers in 1880 as a pleasure grounds for 'public enlightenment and entertainment', the Larmer Tree Gardens are set high on the Cranbourne Chase providing exceptional views of the surrounding countryside. One of the most unusual gardens in England containing an extraordinary collection of colonial and oriental buildings, a Roman Temple and an Open Air Theatre.
**www.larmertree.co.uk**
**Grant Recipient:** Trustees of MALF Pitt-Rivers No. 1 Discretionary Settlement
**Access contact:** Estate Secretary
**T:** 01725 516225   **F:** 01725 516321
**E-mail:** enquiries@larmertree.co.uk
**Open:** Summer opening: Easter Sunday–End of September: Sunday–Thursday, 11am–5pm. Closed July, Fridays and Saturdays for private hire. Winter opening: October, November, February and March: Monday–Friday, 11am–4pm. Tea rooms: Sundays & Bank Holidays. Please check opening arrangements on website.
**Heritage Open Days:** No.
P Spaces: 500
Partial. Wheelchair access to the sunken dell is difficult. WC for the disabled. Guide Dogs allowed.
£ **Adult:** £3.75. **Child:** £2.50 (over 5 yrs). **Other:** £3.00 (Admission charges apply on Sundays only, other times donations invited).

## LYDIARD PARK

**Lydiard Tregoze, Swindon, Wiltshire SN5 3PA**

Ancestral home of the Bolingbrokes, the restored Palladian mansion contains family furnishings and portraits, plasterwork, rare 17th century painted window and room dedicated to 18th century society artist Lady Diana Spencer. Parkland, walled garden and lake being restored.
**www.lydiardpark.org**
**Grant Recipient:** Swindon Borough Council
**Access contact:** Mrs Sarah Finch-Crisp
**T:** 01793 770401   **F:** 01793 770968
**Open:** Provisional: House: Monday–Saturday, 10am–5pm and Sunday, 2–5pm. November–February early closing at 4pm. Grounds: all day, closing at dusk.
**Heritage Open Days:** Yes
P Spaces: 400
Full. WC for the disabled. Guide Dogs allowed.
£ **Adult:** £2.20 (price valid until 31.04.2007). **Child:** £1.00 (price valid until 31.04.2007). **Other:** £1.00 (Swindon Card Holders) (price valid until 31.04.2007).

## MERCHANT'S HOUSE

**132 High Street, Marlborough, Wiltshire SN8 1HN**

17th century town house built by the Bayly family, mercers between 1653 and c1700. Situated prominently in the High Street it contains a unique stripe-painted dining room c1665, painted balustrading to the oak staircase and a panelled chamber of the Commonwealth period.
**www.merchantshouse.co.uk**
**Grant Recipient:** Merchant's House (Marlborough) Trust
**Access contact:** Mr Michael Gray
**T:** 01672 511491   **F:** 01672 511491
**E-mail:** manager@merchantshouse.co.uk
**Open:** Easter–end September: Fridays and Saturdays, 11am–4pm. Other times by arrangement with the Secretary at Merchant's House.
**Heritage Open Days:** No.
P Parking for the disabled outside the building. Public parking in High Street.
Works to provide wheelchair access scheduled to finish in 2007. No WC for the disabled. Guide Dogs allowed.
£ **Adult:** £4.00. **Child:** 50p.

## OLD BISHOP'S PALACE

**Salisbury Cathedral School, 1 The Close, Salisbury, Wiltshire SP1 2EQ**

13th century building, much altered over the centuries, with 13th century undercroft, Georgian drawing room and a chapel.
**www.salisburycathedralschool.com**
**Grant Recipient:** Salisbury Diocesan Board of Finance
**Access contact:** Mr Neil Parsons
**T:** 01722 555302   **F:** 01722 410910
**E-mail:** bursar@salisburycathedralschool.com
**Open:** Guided tours on 10 days in July/August. Details can be obtained from the Visitors' Office at Salisbury Cathedral (tel: Jan Leniston: 01722 555124).

---

**Heritage Open Days:** No.
P No.
No wheelchair access. There is a WC for the disabled in the cloister (100 yards). No Guide Dogs allowed.
£ **Adult:** £2.50.

## SALISBURY CATHEDRAL EDUCATION CENTRE

**(Wren Hall), 56c The Close, Salisbury, Wiltshire SP1 2EL**

Originally north wing of adjacent Braybrook House, early 18th century. Former choristers' school (founded 13th century). Many of the original fixtures and fittings are still present. Items of particular interest are the teacher's and head teacher's desks, original wood panelling and various photographs and artefacts from the history of the schoolroom.
**www.salisburycathedral.org.uk/education.php**
**Grant Recipient:** The Dean & Chapter of Salisbury Cathedral
**Access contact:** Mr Peter Edds
**T:** 01722 555115   **F:** 01722 555 140
**E-mail:** p.edds@salcath.co.uk
**Open:** By prior arrangement.
**Heritage Open Days:** No.
P As part of Close parking arrangements for members of the public.
No wheelchair access. WC for the disabled available within the Close. Guide Dogs allowed.
£ No.

## THE CLOISTERS

**Iford Manor, Bradford-on-Avon, Wiltshire BA15 2BA**

Small stone-built cloister in gardens of Manor, completed 1914 by Harold Peto and based on 13th century Italian style. Interesting early contents. Used for concerts and opera evenings during the summer.
**www.ifordmanor.co.uk**
**Grant Recipient:** Mrs E Cartwright-Hignett
**Access contact:** Mrs E Cartwright-Hignett
**T:** 01225 863146   **F:** 01225 862364
**Open:** Gardens only: April and October, Sundays and Easter Monday, 2–5pm; May–September, daily (except Mondays and Fridays), 2–5pm. Children under 10 not encouraged at weekends. Coaches and groups by prior arrangement only outside normal opening hours.
**Heritage Open Days:** No.
P Spaces: 100. Free parking.
Partial. Wheelchair access by prior arrangement to Cloisters and part of the gardens. WC for the disabled. Guide Dogs allowed.
£ **Adult:** £4.50. **Child:** £4.00 (10-16, under 10 free). **Other:** £4.00 (concessions).

## WILTON HOUSE

**Wilton, Salisbury, Wiltshire SP2 0BJ**

Ancestral home of the Earls of Pembroke for over 450 years, rebuilt by Inigo Jones and John Webb in the Palladian style with further alterations by James Wyatt c1801. Contains 17th century state rooms and an art collection including works by Van Dyck, Rubens, Joshua Reynolds and Brueghel. Surrounded by landscaped parkland.
**www.wiltonhouse.com**
**Grant Recipient:** Wilton House Charitable Trust
**Access contact:** Mr Duncan Leslie
**T:** 01722 746720   **F:** 01722 744447
**E-mail:** tourism@wiltonhouse.com
**Open:** House: 1 April–15 April, 5 May–31 August, 10.30am–5.30pm (last admission 4.30pm). House closed on Saturdays except bank holiday weekends. Grounds: 1 April–30 September, 10.30am–5.30pm.
**Heritage Open Days:** Yes
P Spaces: 200
Full. WC for the disabled. Guide Dogs allowed.
£ **Adult:** £12.00. **Child:** £6.50. **Other:** £9.75 (senior citizens), £29.50 (family); Group rates on application.

# WORCESTERSHIRE

## ABBERLEY HALL CLOCK TOWER

**Great Witley, Worcester, Worcestershire, WR6 6DD**

Victorian folly, built 1883-4, by J P St Aubyn in a fantastic mixture of 13th and 14th century Gothic styles. 161ft tall, it can be seen from six counties.
**Grant Recipient:** Abberley Hall Ltd
**Access contact:** Mr John G W Walker
**T:** 01299 896275   **F:** 01299 896875

---

**E-mail:** johnwalker@abberleyhall.co.uk
**Open:** 19 and 20 July; other times by prior arrangement.
**Heritage Open Days:** No.
P Spaces: 20
No wheelchair access. No WC for the disabled. No Guide Dogs allowed.
£ **Adult:** £3.00. **Child:** £1.50.

## HANBURY HALL

**Hanbury, Droitwich, Worcestershire WR9 7EA**

Built in 1701, this William and Mary-style house contains painted ceilings and staircase. It has an orangery, ice house and Moorish gazebos. The re-created 18th century garden is surrounded by parkland and has a parterre, wilderness, fruit garden, open grove and bowling green pavilions.
**www.nationaltrust.org.uk**
**Grant Recipient:** The National Trust
**Access contact:** Property Manager
**T:** 01527 821214   **F:** 01527 821251
**E-mail:** hanburyhall@nationaltrust.org.uk
**Open:** House: 3–18 March, Saturday and Sunday; 19 March–31 October, Saturday–Wednesday, 1–5pm. Garden, grounds, tea room and shop: 3 -18 March, Saturday and Sunday; 19 March–31 October, Saturday–Wednesday (except July & August, daily); 3 November–16 December, weekends only, 11am–5.30pm.
**Heritage Open Days:** No.
P Spaces: 150. Car parking 200 metres from house. Buggy transfer available.
Partial. Wheelchair access to ground floor, gardens, tea room and shop. WC for the disabled. Guide Dogs allowed.
£ **Adult:** £6.80, £4.50 (garden only). **Child:** £3.40, £2.25 (garden only). **Other:** £17.00 (family), £5.30 (group) Admission price includes voluntary gift aid donation.

## HAWFORD GRANGE DOVECOTE

**Hawford, Worcestershire**

16th century dovecote restored by The National Trust in 1978.
**Grant Recipient:** National Trust
**Access contact:** Property Manager
**T:** 01527 821 214
**Open:** All year: daily, 9am–6pm.
**Heritage Open Days:** No.
P Spaces: 3
Partial. View from exterior. No WC for the disabled. Guide Dogs allowed.
£ **Adult:** £1.00

## HOPTON COURT CONSERVATORY

**Cleobury Mortimer, Kidderminster, Worcestershire DY14 0EF**

Grade II* listed conservatory, c1830, of cast iron with a rounded archway leading to a rear room roofed with curved glass. Two rooms either side, one housing the boiler beneath to supply heat by way of cast iron grilles running around the floor of the interior.
**www.hoptoncourt.co.uk**
**Grant Recipient:** Mr C R D Woodward
**Access contact:** Mr Christopher Woodward
**T:** 01299 270734   **F:** 01299 271132
**E-mail:** chris@hoptoncourt.fsnet.co.uk
**Open:** Weekends of 12/13 May and 1/2 September, 10am–4.30pm. At other times by prior arrangement.
**Heritage Open Days:** No.
P Spaces: 150
Full. WC for the disabled. Guide Dogs allowed.
£ **Adult:** £3.50.

## LOWER BROCKHAMPTON

**Bringsty, Worcestershire WR6 5UH**

A late 14th century moated manor house with a detached half-timbered 15th century gatehouse. Also, the ruins of a 12th century chapel. Woodland walks.
**www.nationaltrust.org.uk**
**Grant Recipient:** The National Trust
**Access contact:** Property Manager
**T:** 01885 488099   **F:** 01885 482151
**E-mail:** brockhampton@nationaltrust.org.uk
**Open:** House: 3 March–1 April, Saturday and Sunday (open Bank Holiday Mondays and Good Friday), 12 noon–4pm. 4 April–28 October: Wednesday–Sunday, 12 noon–5pm (until 4pm in October) & Bank Holiday, 12–5pm.
**Heritage Open Days:** No.
P Spaces: 60. Parking for the disabled near house. Car parking free when visiting house.

**&** Partial. WC for the disabled in estate car park. WC for the disabled. Guide Dogs allowed.
**£** **Adult:** £4.50 (admission price includes voluntary gift aid donation). **Child:** £2.50. **Other:** £11.50 (family).

### ST MICHAEL'S RUINED NAVE & WEST TOWER
**Abberley, Worcestershire**
Ruins of tower, nave (both 12th century) and south aisle (c1260). Walls standing approximately 4ft high with many surviving features from Medieval church. 12th century chancel and south chapel, c1260, repaired in 1908 and still used for services.
**Grant Recipient:** Abberley Parochial Church Council
**Access contact:** Mrs M A Nott
**T:** 01299 896392
**Open:** At all times.
**Heritage Open Days:** Yes
**P** Spaces: 7. Also parking at Manor Arms Hotel.
**&** Full. Full wheelchair access to ruins but assistance required to visit interior of church. No WC for the disabled. Guide Dogs allowed.
**£** Donations welcome (place in Green Box).

### WALKER HALL
**Market Square, Evesham,**
**Worcestershire WR11 4RW**
16th century timber-framed building adjoining Norman gateway, much altered. In the late 19th century the floor was removed and it became an open hall. In 1999 it was repaired and refitted to form offices (first floor) and a retail unit (ground floor).
**Grant Recipient:** Saggers & Rhodes
**Access contact:** Messrs Saggers & Rhodes
**T:** 01386 446623    **F:** 01386 48215
**E-mail:** wds@ricsonline.org
**Open:** Access to interior by prior arrangement only.
**Heritage Open Days:** No.
**P** Spaces: 500. Parking in town centre car parks.
**&** Partial. Wheelchair and guide dog access to ground floor only. WC for the disabled. Guide Dogs allowed.
**£** Charitable donation only.

### WHITBOURNE HALL AND PALM HOUSE
**Whitbourne, Worcester, Worcestershire WR6 5SE**
Victorian Greek Revival style country house with large palm house built later (circa 1865–77) in the space between main block and service wing. The south front has an imposing Ionic portico. The main hall, with Maw and Co. mosaic tiled floor, is lit entirely by glazed blue-glass ceiling and surrounded by a gallery accessed by a white marble staircase with limestone balustrade.
**www.whitbournehall.co.uk**
**Grant Recipient:** Whitbourne Hall Community Ltd
**Access contact:** Ms Heather Coley
**T:** 01886 821165
**Open:** 29 April 12 noon–5pm; 3, 10, 17, 24, 31 May, 4, 11, 18, 25 June, 11am–4pm.
**Heritage Open Days:** No.
**P** Spaces: 150
**&** Partial. Wheelchair access to garden. Mobile ramps available for access to the house (three steps). No WC for the disabled. Guide Dogs allowed.
**£** **Adult:** £5.00. **Child:** £1.50. **Other:** £2.50 (senior citizens and students).

---

**Heritage Open Days:** is an annual event over four days in September which aims to increase opportunities for access to properties outside London which are predominately inaccessible to the general public or usually charge an admission fee. English Heritage funds the Civic Trust to co-ordinate Heritage Open Days.

**London Open House:** a similar annual event, co-ordinated by London Open House, for buildings in the Capital over one weekend in September.

© Bryan McDonald

Ragley Hall, West Midlands

# Indexes

**Plant Sales**     **564**

Properties and gardens offering collections of rare and unusual plants not generally available.

**Corporate Hospitality**     **567**

Properties able to accommodate corporate functions, wedding receptions and events.

**Education**     **571**

Properties providing facilities for schools / educational groups.

**Accommodation**     **575**

Historic properties which offer accommodation - from basic comfort to ultimate luxury.

**Civil Wedding Venues**     **577**

Places where the ceremony itself can take place and may also provide facilities for reception.

**Open All Year**     **580**

Properties and/or their grounds included in this list are open for all or most of the year.

**Special Events**     **585**

Historical re-enactments, festivals, country & craft fairs, concerts, fireworks, car & steam rallies.

# Plant Sales

Properties where plants are offered for sale.

# ENGLAND

## LONDON

Chelsea Physic Garden ............................................ 81
Ham House & Garden ............................................. 83
Myddelton House Gardens ....................................... 87
Syon Park ............................................................. 78

## SOUTH EAST

Belmont House & Gardens, Kent .............................. 139
Borde Hill Garden, Park & Woodland, Sussex ........... 171
Broughton Castle, Oxfordshire ............................... 153
Charleston, Sussex ............................................... 182
Chenies Manor House, Buckinghamshire ................. 102
Denmans Garden, Sussex ...................................... 182
Dorney Court, Berkshire ......................................... 98
Exbury Gardens & Steam Railway, Hampshire .........114
Finchcocks, Kent .................................................. 141
Fishbourne Roman Palace, Sussex .......................... 183
Gilbert White's House & The Oates Museum, Hampshire ......... 114
Glynde Place, Sussex ............................................ 183
Goodnestone Park Gardens, Kent ........................... 142
Great Comp Garden, Kent ..................................... 142
Great Dixter House & Gardens, Sussex ................... 184
Groombridge Place Gardens, Kent .......................... 130
Hall Place & Gardens, Kent ................................... 131
Hever Castle & Gardens, Kent ................................ 132
High Beeches Woodland & Water Gardens, Sussex ........ 185
Hole Park Gardens, Kent ....................................... 143
Kingston Bagpuize House, Oxfordshire ................... 157
Knole, Kent ........................................................ 134
Leonardslee Lakes & Gardens, Sussex .................... 173
Loseley Park, Surrey ............................................ 162
Lullingstone Castle, Kent ...................................... 143
Merriments Gardens, Sussex .................................. 186
Michelham Priory, Sussex ...................................... 186
Mottistone Manor Garden, Isle of Wight ................. 193
Parham House & Gardens, Sussex .......................... 187
Pashley Manor Gardens, Sussex ............................ 174
Polesden Lacey, Surrey ......................................... 167
Priest House, The, Sussex ..................................... 188
RHS Garden Wisley, Surrey ................................... 167
Ramster Gardens, Surrey ...................................... 168
Sackville College, Sussex ...................................... 189
Savill Garden, Berkshire ......................................... 98
Scotney Castle, Kent ............................................ 147
Sheffield Park Garden, Sussex ............................... 178
Sissinghurst Castle Garden, Kent ........................... 148
Smallhythe Place, Kent ......................................... 148
Standen, Sussex .................................................. 190
Stansted Park, Sussex .......................................... 190
Uppark, Sussex ................................................... 190
Vyne, The, Hampshire ........................................... 119
Waddesdon Manor, Buckinghamshire .....................101
Weald & Downland Open Air Museum, Sussex .........191
West Dean Gardens, Sussex ................................... 191

## SOUTH WEST

A La Ronde, Devon .............................................. 212
Abbotsbury Subtropical Gardens, Dorset ................. 224
American Museum & Gardens, Somerset ................. 248
Arlington Court, Devon ......................................... 212
Athelhampton House & Gardens, Dorset ................. 225
Barrington Court, Somerset ................................... 249
Batsford Arboretum, Gloucestershire ...................... 238
Berkeley Castle, Gloucestershire ............................ 235
Bicton Park Botanical Gardens, Devon .................... 210
Bourton House Garden, Gloucestershire .................. 238
Buckland Abbey, Devon ........................................ 213
Burncoose Nurseries & Garden, Cornwall ............... 202
Cadhay, Devon .................................................... 214
Caerhays Castle & Garden, Cornwall ...................... 203
Castle Drogo, Devon ............................................ 214
Clovelly, Devon ................................................... 211
Coleton Fishacre House & Garden, Devon ............... 215
Cotehele, Cornwall .............................................. 200
Cothay Manor, Somerset ...................................... 250
Deans Court, Dorset ............................................ 229
Dunster Castle, Somerset ...................................... 251
Dyrham Park, Gloucestershire ................................ 239
Edmondsham House & Gardens, Dorset .................. 229
Escot, Devon ...................................................... 217
Forde Abbey & Gardens, Dorset ............................ 226
Frampton Court, Gloucestershire ............................ 239
Garden House, The, Devon .................................... 217
Glendurgan Garden, Cornwall ............................... 203
Godolphin, Cornwall ............................................ 203
Greenway, Devon ................................................ 218
Hailes Abbey, Gloucestershire ............................... 239
Hartland Abbey, Devon ........................................ 218
Hestercombe Gardens, Somerset ........................... 253
Hidcote Manor Garden, Gloucestershire .................. 240
Kiftsgate Court Gardens, Gloucestershire ................ 241
Killerton House & Garden, Devon ........................... 219
Kingston Lacy, Dorset .......................................... 227
Kingston Maurward Garden, Dorset ........................ 230
Knightshayes Court, Devon ................................... 219
Lanhydrock, Cornwall .......................................... 201
Lost Gardens of Heligan, Cornwall ......................... 204
Mapperton, Dorset .............................................. 231
Milton Lodge Gardens, Somerset ........................... 254
Montacute House, Somerset .................................. 254
Mount Edgcumbe House & Country Park, Cornwall ... 204
Muchelney Abbey, Somerset ................................. 254
Overbeck's, Devon ...............................................220
Painswick Rococo Garden, Gloucestershire ..............242
Pencarrow, Cornwall ............................................ 205
Pine Lodge Gardens & Nursery, Cornwall ............... 205
Powderham Castle, Devon ..................................... 221
RHS Garden Rosemoor, Devon .............................. 221
St Michael's Mount, Cornwall ................................ 207
Saltram, Devon ................................................... 222
Stourhead, Wiltshire ............................................ 260
Sudeley Castle & Exhibitions, Gloucestershire .......... 237
Trebah Garden, Cornwall ...................................... 208

Trelissick Garden, Cornwall ....................... 208
Trengwainton Garden, Cornwall.................. 209
Trerice, Cornwall ....................................... 209
Trewithen, Cornwall ................................... 209
Tyntesfield, Somerset ................................. 256
Wilton House, Wiltshire .............................. 261

## EASTERN REGION

Anglesey Abbey, Gardens &
   Lode Mill, Cambridgeshire ...................... 273
Blickling Hall, Norfolk ................................ 289
Bradenham Hall Gardens, Norfolk ............... 289
East Bergholt Place Garden, Suffolk ............. 295
Elton Hall, Cambridgeshire ......................... 274
Felbrigg Hall, Norfolk ................................. 291
Gardens of Easton Lodge, Essex .................. 280
Haughley Park, Suffolk ............................... 296
Helmingham Hall Gardens, Suffolk ............... 297
Houghton Hall, Norfolk .............................. 292
Hylands House, Essex ................................. 280
Ickworth House & Park, Suffolk ................... 297
Ingatestone Hall, Essex .............................. 280
Knebworth House, Hertfordshire .................. 284
Layer Marney Tower, Essex ......................... 281
Mannington Gardens & Countryside, Norfolk .. 293
Manor, Hemingford Grey, Cambridgeshire ..... 275
Marks Hall Gardens & Arboretum, Essex ....... 281
Melford Hall, Suffolk .................................. 298
Peckover House & Garden, Cambridgeshire .....275
RHS Garden Hyde Hall, Essex ..................... 282
Sandringham, Norfolk ................................ 288
Shaw's Corner, Hertfordshire ...................... 286
Somerleyton Hall & Gardens, Suffolk ............ 300
Sutton Hoo, Suffolk ................................... 300
Swiss Garden, Bedfordshire ........................ 271
Walsingham Abbey Grounds & Shirehall Museum, Norfolk ...... 294
Wimpole Hall & Home Farm, Cambridgeshire ......... 276
Wyken Hall Gardens, Suffolk ...................... 301

## EAST MIDLANDS

Boughton House, Northamptonshire ............. 324
Carnfield Hall, Derbyshire .......................... 309
Clumber Park, Nottinghamshire ................... 334
Coton Manor Garden, Northamptonshire ....... 329
Cottesbrooke Hall & Gardens, Northamptonshire ...... 330
Easton Walled Gardens, Lincolnshire ............ 321
Hodsock Priory Gardens, Nottinghamshire ..... 334
Holdenby House, Northamptonshire ............. 331
Kedleston Hall, Derbyshire .........................306
Kelmarsh Hall, Northamptonshire ................ 326
Renishaw Hall Gardens, Derbyshire .............. 312
Sulgrave Manor, Northamptonshire .............. 328
Wartnaby Gardens, Leics & Rutland ............. 316

## WEST MIDLANDS

Baddesley Clinton, Warwickshire .................. 355
Biddulph Grange Garden, Staffordshire .......... 350
Birmingham Botanical Gardens & Glasshouses, West Midlands  367
Coughton Court, Warwickshire ..................... 363
Croft Castle & Parkland, Herefordshire ........... 340
Croome Park, Worcestershire ....................... 369
Erasmus Darwin House, Staffordshire ............. 350
Greyfriars, The, Worcestershire ....................369
Hanbury Hall, Worcestershire ...................... 370
Hergest Croft Gardens, Herefordshire ............ 341
Longner Hall, Shropshire ............................ 346

Lord Leycester Hospital, Warwickshire ........... 365
Moseley Old Hall, Staffordshire .................... 351
Packwood House, Warwickshire .................... 356
Trentham Gardens, Staffordshire .................. 353
Upton House & Gardens, Warwickshire ........... 360
Witley Court & Gardens, Worcestershire .......... 372

## YORKSHIRE & THE HUMBER

Beningbrough Hall & Gardens ...................... 385
Brodsworth Hall & Gardens ......................... 377
Burton Agnes Hall & Gardens ...................... 387
Castle Howard ......................................... 379
Constable Burton Hall Gardens .................... 388
Harewood House ...................................... 381
Mount Grace Priory ................................... 391
Newby Hall & Gardens ............................... 382
Norton Conyers ....................................... 392
RHS Garden Harlow Carr ............................ 393
Rievaulx Abbey ........................................ 394
Ripley Castle ........................................... 383
Scampston Hall, The Walled Garden .............. 395
Shandy Hall ............................................ 395
Skipton Castle ......................................... 384
Sledmere House ....................................... 396
Thorp Perrow Arboretum, Woodland Garden,
   Birds of Prey & Mammal Centre ............... 397
York Gate Garden ..................................... 399

## NORTH WEST

Acorn Bank Garden & Watermill, Cumbria ...... 414
Adlington Hall, Cheshire ............................. 402
Arley Hall & Gardens, Cheshire .................... 403
Brantwood, Cumbria .................................. 414
Cholmondeley Castle Garden, Cheshire .......... 405
Dalemain, Cumbria .................................... 415
Dunham Massey, Cheshire ........................... 406
Holker Hall & Gardens, Cumbria ................... 417
Leighton Hall, Lancashire ............................ 420
Levens Hall, Cumbria ................................. 412
Little Moreton Hall, Cheshire ....................... 407
Norton Priory Museum & Gardens, Cheshire .... 407
Rode Hall, Cheshire ................................... 408
Sizergh Castle & Garden, Cumbria ................ 418
Tatton Park, Cheshire ................................ 409

## NORTH EAST

Belsay Hall, Castle & Gardens, Northumberland ...... 436
Chillingham Castle, Northumberland .............. 434
Herterton House Gardens, Northumberland ...... 438
Raby Castle, Co Durham ............................. 429
Souter Lighthouse, Tyne & Wear .................. 442
Wallington, Northumberland ........................ 440

# SCOTLAND

Ardkinglas Estate, West Highlands & Islands ............................ 480
Bowhill House & Country Park, Borders ..................................... 446
Castle Kennedy Gardens, South West Scotland .........................457
Castle of Mey, Highlands & Skye ............................................ 490
Drumlanrig, SW Scotland ...................................................... 455
Dunninald, Perthshire/Fife .................................................... 475
Floors Castle, Borders ........................................................... 447
Glamis Castle, Perthshire/Fife ............................................... 472
Mellerstain House, Borders ................................................... 452
Monteviot House Gardens, Borders ......................................... 453
Mount Stuart, West Highlands & Islands ................................. 482
Paxton House, Gallery & Country Park, Borders ........................ 453
Torosay Castle & Gardens, West Highlands & Islands ............... 483

# WALES

## NORTH WALES

Bodnant Garden.................................................................... 496
Chirk Castle ........................................................................ 497
Erddig ................................................................................ 498
Plas yn Rhiw....................................................................... 500
Powis Castle & Garden.......................................................... 500

## SOUTH WALES

Aberglasney Gardens ........................................................... 502
Dyffryn Gardens and Arboretum ........................................... 505
National Botanic Garden of Wales, The .................................. 507
Picton Castle ...................................................................... 508

# NORTHERN IRELAND

Mount Stewart ................................................................... 516
Seaforde Gardens ............................................................... 516

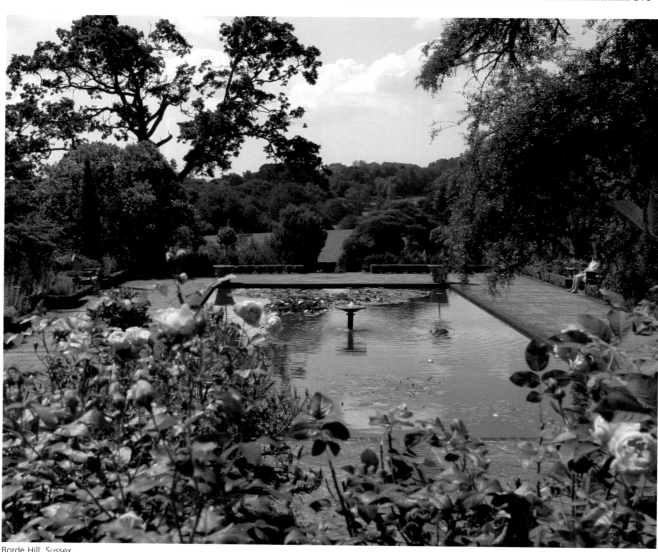

Borde Hill, Sussex

**visit hudsons guide online**

# Corporate Hospitality

Properties which are able to accommodate corporate functions, wedding receptions and events. Some properties specialise in corporate hospitality and are open, only rarely, if ever, to day visitors. Others do both. See entry for details.

## ENGLAND

### LONDON

Banqueting House .................................................... 79
Burgh House ........................................................... 80
Chelsea Physic Garden .............................................. 81
Chiswick House ....................................................... 71
Eltham Palace ......................................................... 72
Geffrye Museum, The ............................................... 83
Ham House & Garden ............................................... 83
Handel House Museum ............................................. 84
Kensington Palace ................................................... 85
Kenwood ............................................................... 73
Leighton House Museum ........................................... 86
Marble Hill House .................................................... 87
Osterley Park & House .............................................. 88
Royal Observatory, National Maritime Museum
    & Queen's House .................................................. 74
St Paul's Cathedral ................................................... 75
Somerset House ...................................................... 76
Southwark Cathedral ................................................ 90
Spencer House ........................................................ 77
Syon Park .............................................................. 78
Tower of London, The ............................................... 91
Wellington Arch ...................................................... 92

### SOUTH EAST

Ardington House, Oxfordshire ................................... 151
Avington Park, Hampshire ......................................... 112
Beaulieu, Hampshire ........................................ 108/109
Belmont House & Gardens, Kent ............................... 139
Blenheim Palace, Oxfordshire ................................... 152
Borde Hill Garden, Park & Woodland, Sussex ............... 171
Boughton Monchelsea Place, Kent ............................. 122
Broadlands, Hampshire ............................................ 113
Buscot Park, Oxfordshire .......................................... 155
Charleston, Sussex .................................................. 182
Chartwell, Kent ...................................................... 123
Chichester Cathedral, Sussex .................................... 182
Chiddingstone Castle, Kent ............................... 124/125
Clandon Park, Surrey ............................................... 160
Claydon House, Buckinghamshire .............................. 103
Cobham Hall, Kent .................................................. 126
Danson House, Kent ................................................ 127
Deal Castle, Kent .................................................... 140
Dorney Court, Berkshire ............................................ 98
Dover Castle & The Secret Wartime Tunnels, Kent ........ 129
Eton College, Berkshire ............................................. 98
Exbury Gardens & Steam Railway, Hampshire .............. 114
Finchcocks, Kent ..................................................... 141
Firle Place, Sussex ................................................... 183
Fort Brockhurst, Hampshire ...................................... 114
Friars, The, Kent ..................................................... 142
Glynde Place, Sussex ............................................... 183
Goodwood House, Sussex ........................................ 172
Great Fosters, Surrey .............................................. 165
Groombridge Place Gardens, Kent ............................. 130
Hall Place & Gardens, Kent ....................................... 131
Hammerwood Park, Sussex ...................................... 184
Hampton Court Palace, Surrey .................................. 165
Hever Castle & Gardens, Kent ................................... 132
Highclere Castle & Gardens, Hampshire ..................... 110
Houghton Lodge Gardens, Hampshire ........................ 116
Kew Gardens, Surrey ............................................... 166
King John's House & Heritage Centre, Hampshire .......... 117
King's Head, The, Buckinghamshire ............................ 105
Kingston Bagpuize House, Oxfordshire ....................... 157
Leeds Castle, Kent .................................................. 135
Leonardslee Lakes & Gardens, Sussex ........................ 173
Loseley Park, Surrey ................................................ 162
Mapledurham House & Watermill, Oxfordshire ............. 157
Michelham Priory, Sussex ........................................ 186
Nurstead Court, Kent ............................................... 144
Osborne House, Isle of Wight .................................... 192
Painshill Park, Surrey .............................................. 163
Pashley Manor Gardens, Sussex ................................ 174
Penshurst Place & Gardens, Kent .............................. 136
Petworth House & Park, Sussex ................................. 175
Portsmouth Heritage (Buckingham House &
    Wymering Manor), Hampshire ............................... 111
Preston Manor, Sussex ............................................ 188
Royal Pavilion, Sussex ............................................. 176
St Mary's House & Gardens, Sussex ........................... 189
Sackville College, Sussex ......................................... 189
Saint Hill Manor, Sussex .......................................... 177
Savill Garden, Berkshire ............................................ 98
Squerryes Court, Kent ............................................. 137
Standen, Sussex ..................................................... 190
Stansted Park, Sussex ............................................. 190
Stonor, Oxfordshire ................................................ 154
Stowe House, Buckinghamshire ................................ 100
Turkey Mill, Kent .................................................... 138
Vyne, The, Hampshire .............................................. 119
Waddesdon Manor, Buckinghamshire ........................ 101
Walmer Castle and Gardens, Kent ............................. 149
West Dean Gardens, Sussex ..................................... 191
Westenhanger Castle and Barns, Kent ........................ 150
Winchester Cathedral, Hampshire ............................. 120

### SOUTH WEST

1 Royal Crescent, Somerset ...................................... 248
Abbotsbury Subtropical Gardens, Dorset .................... 224
American Museum & Gardens, Somerset ..................... 248
Athelhampton House & Gardens, Dorset ..................... 225
Berkeley Castle, Gloucestershire ............................... 235
Bicton Park Botanical Gardens, Devon ....................... 210
Boconnoc, Cornwall ................................................ 202
Buckland Abbey, Devon ........................................... 213

Cadhay, Devon ............................................. 214
Chavenage, Gloucestershire ....................... 236
Chettle House, Dorset ................................. 228
Cotehele, Cornwall ...................................... 200
Cothay Manor, Somerset ............................ 250
Culver House, Devon ................................... 216
Escot, Devon ............................................... 217
Frampton Court, Gloucestershire ............... 239
Fursdon House, Devon ................................ 217
Gloucester Cathedral, Gloucestershire ....... 239
Greenway, Devon ........................................ 218
Haldon Belvedere/Lawrence Castle, Devon .... 218
Halswell House, Somerset ........................... 252
Hartland Abbey, Devon ............................... 218
Highcliffe Castle, Dorset ............................. 230
Holst Birthplace Museum, Gloucestershire .... 240
Killerton House & Garden, Devon .............. 219
Kingston Maurward Garden, Dorset ........... 230
Knightshayes Court, Devon ........................ 219
Lanhydrock, Cornwall ................................. 201
Larmer Tree Gardens, Wiltshire .................. 263
Lodge Park & Sherborne Estate, Gloucestershire .... 241
Longleat, Wiltshire ...................................... 259
Lulworth Castle & Park, Dorset .................. 231
Maunsel House, Somerset ........................... 254
Minterne Gardens, Dorset .......................... 232
Mount Edgcumbe House & Country Park, Cornwall .... 204
Museum of Costume & Assembly Rooms, Somerset .... 246
Newhouse, Wiltshire ................................... 264
Owlpen Manor, Gloucestershire ................. 242
Pencarrow, Cornwall ................................... 205
Pendennis Castle, Cornwall ........................ 205
Portland Castle, Dorset ............................... 232
Powderham Castle, Devon .......................... 221
Prideaux Place, Cornwall ............................ 206
Prior Park Landscape Garden, Somerset ..... 255
Roman Baths & Pump Room, Somerset ...... 247
St Mawes Castle, Cornwall .......................... 206
Salisbury Cathedral, Wiltshire .................... 266
Saltram, Devon ........................................... 222
Sausmarez Manor, Channel Islands ............ 199
Sherborne Castle, Dorset ............................ 233
Stanway House & Water Garden, Gloucestershire ....244
Sudeley Castle & Exhibitions, Gloucestershire .... 237
Trelissick Garden, Cornwall ........................ 208
Wilton House, Wiltshire .............................. 261
Wolfeton House, Dorset .............................. 234

## EASTERN REGION

Audley End House & Gardens, Essex .......... 278
Belchamp Hall, Suffolk ............................... 295
Blickling Hall, Norfolk ................................ 289
Cecil Higgins Art Gallery, Bedfordshire ...... 271
Dragon Hall, Norfolk .................................. 290
Elton Hall, Cambridgeshire ......................... 274
Felbrigg Hall, Norfolk ................................. 291
Gardens of Easton Lodge, Essex ................. 280
Hatfield House, Hertfordshire ..................... 283
Haughley Park, Suffolk ............................... 296
Helmingham Hall Gardens, Suffolk ............. 297
Holkham Hall, Norfolk ................................ 287
Hylands House, Essex .................................. 280
Ingatestone Hall, Essex ............................... 280
Kentwell Hall & Gardens, Suffolk ............... 297
Kimberley Hall, Norfolk .............................. 292
Kimbolton Castle, Cambridgeshire .............. 275
Knebworth House, Hertfordshire ................. 284
Layer Marney Tower, Essex ......................... 281
Mannington Gardens & Countryside, Norfolk .... 293

Marks Hall Gardens & Arboretum, Essex .... 281
Moggerhanger Park, Bedfordshire .............. 271
Otley Hall, Suffolk ...................................... 299
Sandringham, Norfolk ................................ 288
Somerleyton Hall & Gardens, Suffolk ......... 300
South Elmham Hall, Suffolk ........................ 300
Sutton Hoo, Suffolk .................................... 300
Swiss Garden, Bedfordshire ........................ 271
Walkern Hall, Hertfordshire ........................ 286
Wimpole Hall & Home Farm, Cambridgeshire .... 276
Woburn Abbey, Bedfordshire ...................... 270
Wolterton Park, Norfolk .............................. 294

## EAST MIDLANDS

78 Derngate, Northamptonshire .................. 329
Ayscoughfee Hall Museum & Gardens, Lincolnshire .... 319
Belvoir Castle, Leics & Rutland ................... 313
Bolsover Castle, Derbyshire ........................ 308
Carlton Hall, Nottinghamshire .................... 334
Catton Hall, Derbyshire .............................. 309
Chatsworth, Derbyshire .............................. 304
Clumber Park, Nottinghamshire .................. 334
Cottesbrooke Hall & Gardens, Northamptonshire .... 330
Deene Park, Northamptonshire .................... 325
Doddington Hall & Gardens, Lincolnshire ... 320
Easton Walled Gardens, Lincolnshire .......... 321
Eyam Hall, Derbyshire ................................ 310
Grimsthorpe Castle, Park & Gardens, Lincolnshire .... 318
Holdenby House, Northamptonshire ............ 331
Holme Pierrepont Hall, Nottinghamshire .... 334
Kedleston Hall, Derbyshire ......................... 306
Kelmarsh Hall, Northamptonshire ............... 326
Lamport Hall & Gardens, Northamptonshire .... 332
Lawrence Heritage, D H, Nottinghamshire ... 334
Newstead Abbey, Nottinghamshire ............. 335
Nottingham Castle, Nottinghamshire .......... 335
Pavilion Gardens, Derbyshire ..................... 307
Prebendal Manor, The, Northamptonshire ... 332
Quenby Hall, Leics & Rutland ..................... 314
Renishaw Hall Gardens, Derbyshire ............ 312
Rockingham Castle, Northamptonshire ........ 327
Stanford Hall, Leics & Rutland ................... 315
Sulgrave Manor, Northamptonshire ............. 328
Thrumpton Hall, Nottinghamshire .............. 335
Tissington Hall, Derbyshire ........................ 312
Wollaton Hall & Park, Nottinghamshire ...... 335

## WEST MIDLANDS

Arbury Hall, Warwickshire .......................... 354
Baddesley Clinton, Warwickshire ................ 355
Charlecote Park, Warwickshire ................... 362
Combermere Abbey, Shropshire .................. 345
Compton Verney, Warwickshire .................. 362
Coughton Court, Warwickshire ................... 363
Eastnor Castle, Herefordshire ..................... 339
Erasmus Darwin House, Staffordshire .......... 350
Hagley Hall, West Midlands ........................ 366
Hanbury Hall, Worcestershire ..................... 370
Harvington Hall, Worcestershire ................. 371
Hereford Cathedral, Herefordshire .............. 341
Hodnet Hall Gardens, Shropshire ............... 346
Kenilworth Castle, Warwickshire ................ 365
Lord Leycester Hospital, Warwickshire ........ 365
Ludlow Castle, Shropshire ...........................347
Oakley Hall, Shropshire .............................. 342
Ragley Hall & Gardens, Warwickshire ......... 357
Sandon Hall, Staffordshire .......................... 352
Shakespeare Houses, The, Warwickshire ...... 358

Shugborough Estate, Staffordshire ............................ 352
Stoneleigh Abbey, Warwickshire ............................... 359
Trentham Gardens, Staffordshire ............................... 353
Upton House & Gardens, Warwickshire ..................... 360
Warwick Castle, Warwickshire ................................... 361
Weston Park, Shropshire ........................................... 343

## YORKSHIRE & THE HUMBER

Bolton Abbey ........................................................... 385
Bolton Castle ........................................................... 385
Bramham Park .......................................................... 376
Broughton Hall ......................................................... 386
Cannon Hall Museum, Park & Gardens ...................... 387
Castle Howard .......................................................... 379
Duncombe Park ........................................................ 388
East Riddlesden Hall .................................................. 388
Fairfax House ............................................................ 389
Fountains Abbey & Studley Royal ............................... 380
Harewood House ....................................................... 381
Hovingham Hall ........................................................ 390
Markenfield Hall ....................................................... 391
Newby Hall & Gardens .............................................. 382
Nostell Priory & Parklands ......................................... 392
RAF Holmpton – Bunker Tours ................................... 393
Ripley Castle ............................................................ 383
Scampston Hall, The Walled Garden ........................... 395
Skipton Castle .......................................................... 384
Sledmere House ........................................................ 396
Sutton Park .............................................................. 397
Temple Newsam ........................................................ 397
Treasurer's House ...................................................... 397
Walcot Hall .............................................................. 397

## NORTH WEST

Adlington Hall, Cheshire ............................................ 402
Arley Hall & Gardens, Cheshire .................................. 403
Blackwell – The Arts & Crafts House, Cumbria ............ 411
Capesthorne Hall, Cheshire ....................................... 404
Cholmondeley Castle Garden, Cheshire ....................... 405
Dalemain, Cumbria ................................................... 415
Heaton Hall, Lancashire ............................................ 421
Hoghton Tower, Lancashire ....................................... 422
Holker Hall & Gardens, Cumbria ................................ 417
Hutton-in-the-Forest, Cumbria ................................... 417
Leighton Hall, Lancashire .......................................... 420
Meols Hall, Merseyside .............................................. 424
Muncaster Castle, Gardens, Owl Centre
    & MeadowVole Maze, Cumbria ............................... 413
Quarry Bank Mill & Styal Estate, Cheshire ..................408
Rufford Old Hall, Lancashire ...................................... 422
Tatton Park, Cheshire ................................................ 409

## NORTH EAST

Alnwick Castle, Northumberland ................................. 432
Auckland Castle, Co Durham ...................................... 430
Belsay Hall, Castle & Gardens, Northumberland .......... 436
Bowes Museum, The, Co Durham ............................... 428
Brinkburn Priory, Northumberland .............................. 437
Chillingham Castle, Northumberland ........................... 434
Gibside, Tyne & Wear ................................................ 442
Raby Castle, Co Durham ............................................ 429
Souter Lighthouse, Tyne & Wear ................................ 442
Tynemouth Priory & Castle, Tyne & Wear ................... 442
Wallington, Northumberland ...................................... 440
Washington Old Hall, Tyne & Wear ............................ 442

# SCOTLAND

Ardkinglas Estate, West Highlands & Islands .............. 480
Argyll's Lodging, West Highland & Islands .................. 478
Ayton Castle, Borders ............................................... 450
Blair Castle, Perthshire/Fife ....................................... 470
Bowhill House & Country Park, Borders ...................... 446
Castle Leod, Highlands & Skye ................................... 490
Cawdor Castle, Highlands & Skye ............................... 488
Craig Castle, Grampian Highlands .............................. 485
Dalmeny House, Edinburgh City, Coast & Countryside ............. 460
Delgatie Castle, Grampian Highlands .......................... 485
Duart Castle, West Highlands & Islands ...................... 481
Dumbarton Castle, West Highlands & Islands .............. 481
Dunrobin Castle, Highlands & Skye ............................ 490
Edinburgh Castle, Edinburgh City, Coast & Countryside ......... 464
Floors Castle, Borders ............................................... 447
Fort George, Highlands & Skye ................................... 491
Glamis Castle, Perthshire/Fife .................................... 472
Greywalls, Edinburgh City, Coast & Countryside ......... 465
Hopetoun House, Edinburgh City, Coast & Countryside .......... 461
Kelburn Castle & Country Centre, SW Scotland ........... 458
Lennoxlove House, Edinburgh City, Coast & Countryside ......... 465
Linlithgow Palace, Edinburgh City, Coast & Countryside ......... 466
Manderston, Borders ................................................. 448
Megginch Castle Gardens, Perthshire/Fife ................... 476
Mellerstain House, Borders ........................................ 452
Mount Stuart, West Highlands & Islands ..................... 482
New Lanark World Heritage Centre,
    Greater Glasgow & Clyde Valley ............................. 468
Paxton House, Gallery & Country Park, Borders ........... 453
Scone Palace & Grounds, Perthshire/Fife ..................... 473
Stirling Castle, West Highlands & Islands ................... 483
Thirlestane Castle, Borders ........................................ 454
Torosay Castle & Gardens, West Highlands & Islands .............. 483
Traquair, Borders ...................................................... 449
Urquhart Castle, Highlands & Skye ............................. 491

# WALES

## NORTH WALES

Bodelwyddan Castle .................................................. 496
Gwydir Castle ........................................................... 498
Iscoyd Park .............................................................. 499

## SOUTH WALES

Caldicot Castle & Country Park .................................. 503
Fonmon Castle .......................................................... 506
Judge's Lodging, The ................................................ 506
National Botanic Garden of Wales, The ...................... 507
Picton Castle ........................................................... 508
Tredegar House & Park .............................................. 509
Treowen ................................................................... 509
Tythegston Court ...................................................... 510
Usk Castle ............................................................... 510

# NORTHERN IRELAND

Argory, The ............................................................ 514
Ballywalter Park ..................................................... 514
Castle Coole .......................................................... 514
Castle Ward & Strangford Loch Wildlife Centre ......................... 515
Crom ................................................................ 515
Florence Court ...................................................... 515
Giant's Causeway .................................................... 515
Killyleagh Castle .................................................... 516
Mount Stewart ....................................................... 516
Mussenden Temple & Downhill Demesne ................................. 516
Seaforde Gardens .................................................... 516
Springhill House & Costume Collection ............................... 516

Dining Room – Belvoir Castle, Grantham, Leicestershire

# Education

The properties listed below provide special facilities for schools' groups. The range of these services varies, so it is vital that you contact the property directly when preparing to arrange a school trip. English Heritage offers free admission for pre-booked educational groups. For a free teacher's information pack: tel: 020 7973 3385 or e-mail: education@english-heritage.org.uk or visit the website www.english-heritage.org.uk/education

## ENGLAND

### LONDON

Banqueting House, The ................................................. 79
Buckingham Palace, The State Rooms,
   The Queen's Gallery, The Royal Mews ...................... 70
Burgh House .............................................................. 80
Chelsea Physic Garden .............................................. 81
Chiswick House .......................................................... 71
Church Farmhouse Museum ....................................... 81
Eastbury Manor House ............................................... 81
Forty Hall .................................................................. 82
Geffrye Museum, The ................................................ 83
Ham House & Garden ................................................ 83
Handel House Museum ............................................... 84
Honeywood Heritage Centre ...................................... 84
Keats House ............................................................... 84
Kensington Palace ..................................................... 85
Kenwood .................................................................... 73
LSO St Luke's UBS and LSO Music Education Centre ..... 85
Leighton House Museum ............................................ 86
Linley Sambourne House ............................................ 86
Osterley Park & Park .................................................. 88
Pitzhanger Manor-House ............................................ 88
Royal Observatory, National Maritime Museum
   & Queen's House ................................................... 74
St John's Gate, Museum of the Order of St John .......... 89
Somerset House .......................................................... 76
Southside House ......................................................... 89
Southwark Cathedral .................................................. 90
Sutton House ............................................................. 90
Syon Park .................................................................. 78
Tower of London, The ................................................ 91
'Wernher Collection', The, at Ranger's House ............. 92
Westminster Cathedral ............................................... 92
Whitehall ................................................................... 92

### SOUTH EAST

Anne of Cleves House, Sussex ..................................... 179
Ardington House, Oxfordshire .................................... 151
Arundel Castle, Sussex ............................................... 169
Beaulieu, Hampshire ........................................... 108/109
Bembridge Windmill, Isle of Wight ............................. 193
Bignor Roman Villa, Sussex ........................................ 180
Blenheim Palace, Oxfordshire ..................................... 152
Boarstall Duck Decoy, Buckinghamshire ..................... 102
Bodiam Castle, Sussex ............................................... 181
Borde Hill Garden, Park & Woodland, Sussex ............. 171
Broughton Castle, Oxfordshire ................................... 153
Charleston, Sussex ..................................................... 182

Chiddingstone Castle, Kent .......................... 124/125
Clandon Park/Hatchlands Park, Surrey ....................... 160
Cobbe Collection at Hatchlands, The, Surrey .............. 161
Cobham Hall, Kent .................................................... 126
Danson House, Kent ................................................... 127
Darwin, The Home of Charles, Kent ........................... 128
Dorney Court, Berkshire .............................................. 98
Dover Castle & The Secret Wartime Tunnels, Kent ...... 129
Exbury Gardens & Steam Railway, Hampshire ............. 114
Finchcocks, Kent ....................................................... 141
Fishbourne Roman Palace, Sussex .............................. 183
Friars, The, Kent ....................................................... 142
Goodwood House, Sussex .......................................... 172
Groombridge Place Gardens, Kent .............................. 130
Hall Place & Gardens, Kent ........................................ 131
Hammerwood Park, Sussex ........................................ 184
Hampton Court Palace, Surrey ................................... 165
Hever Castle & Gardens, Kent .................................... 132
Highclere Castle & Gardens, Hampshire ..................... 110
Ightham Mote, Kent .................................................. 133
Kew Gardens, Surrey ................................................. 166
King John's House & Heritage Centre, Hampshire ....... 117
King's Head, The, Buckinghamshire ........................... 105
Knole, Kent ............................................................... 134
Leeds Castle, Kent ..................................................... 135
Lewes Castle & Barbican House Museum, Sussex ........ 185
Michelham Priory, Sussex ........................................... 186
Needles Old Battery, Isle of Wight ............................. 194
Osborne House, Isle of Wight .................................... 192
Painshill Park, Surrey ................................................. 163
Parham House & Gardens, Sussex .............................. 187
Penshurst Place & Gardens, Kent ............................... 136
Petworth House & Park, Sussex .................................. 175
Portsmouth Heritage (Buckingham House &
   Wymering Manor), Hampshire ............................... 111
Preston Manor, Sussex ............................................... 188
Priest House, The, Sussex ........................................... 188
RHS Garden Wisley, Surrey ........................................ 167
Rochester Cathedral, Kent .......................................... 146
Royal Pavilion, Sussex ............................................... 176
St Agatha's Church, Hampshire .................................. 118
St Mary's House & Gardens, Sussex ........................... 189
Sackville College, Sussex ............................................ 189
Sandham Memorial Chapel, Hampshire ...................... 118
Standen, Sussex ......................................................... 190
Stansted Park, Sussex ................................................. 190
Stowe House, Buckinghamshire .................................. 100
Stowe Landscape Gardens & Park, Buckinghamshire ... 106
Taplow Court, Berkshire .............................................. 98
Vyne, The, Hampshire ................................................ 119
Weald & Downland Open Air Museum, Sussex ........... 191
West Dean Gardens, Sussex ........................................ 191
Westenhanger Castle and Barns, Kent ........................ 150

Winchester Cathedral, Hampshire ............................................. 120
Winchester City Mill, Hampshire ............................................. 120
Windsor Castle, St George's Chapel
    & Frogmore House, Berkshire ..................................... 97

## SOUTH WEST

1 Royal Crescent, Somerset ..................................................... 248
Abbotsbury Subtropical Gardens, Dorset ............................... 224
American Museum & Gardens, Somerset ............................... 248
Arlington Court, Devon .......................................................... 212
Athelhampton House & Gardens, Dorset ............................... 225
Avebury Manor & Garden, Avebury Stone Circle
    & Alexander Keiller Museum, Wiltshire ............................ 262
Barrington Court, Somerset .................................................... 249
Batsford Arboretum, Gloucestershire ..................................... 238
Berkeley Castle, Gloucestershire ............................................ 235
Bicton Park Botanical Gardens, Devon .................................. 210
Boconnoc, Cornwall .............................................................. 202
Bowood House & Gardens, Wiltshire ..................................... 257
Brean Down, Somerset .......................................................... 249
Brownsea Island, Dorset ....................................................... 228
Buckland Abbey, Devon ......................................................... 213
Chalice Well & Gardens, The, Somerset ................................. 249
Chambercombe Manor, Devon .............................................. 215
Chavenage, Gloucestershire ................................................... 236
Chedworth Roman Villa, Gloucestershire ............................... 238
Clouds Hill, Dorset ............................................................... 228
Clovelly, Devon ..................................................................... 211
Corfe Castle, Dorset .............................................................. 228
Corsham Court, Wiltshire ...................................................... 258
Custom House, Devon ........................................................... 216
Dunster Castle, Somerset ...................................................... 251
Dyrham Park, Gloucestershire ............................................... 239
Escot, Devon ......................................................................... 217
Finch Foundry, Devon ........................................................... 217
Glastonbury Abbey, Somerset ............................................... 252
Gloucester Cathedral, Gloucestershire ................................... 239
Godolphin Blowinghouse, Cornwall ...................................... 204
Haldon Belvedere/Lawrence Castle, Devon ........................... 218
Halswell House, Somerset ...................................................... 252
Hardy's Cottage, Dorset ........................................................ 229
Hidcote Manor Garden, Gloucestershire ................................ 240
Highcliffe Castle, Dorset ....................................................... 230
Holnicote Estate, Somerset .................................................... 253
Holst Birthplace Museum, Gloucestershire ............................ 240
Kelmscott Manor, Gloucestershire ......................................... 240
King John's Hunting Lodge, Somerset .................................... 253
Kingston Lacy, Dorset ........................................................... 227
Kingston Maurward Garden, Dorset ...................................... 230
Lacock Abbey, Fox Talbot Museum & Village, Wiltshire .......... 263
Lanhydrock, Cornwall ........................................................... 201
Larmer Tree Gardens, Wiltshire ............................................. 263
Lodge Park & Sherborne Estate, Gloucestershire .................... 241
Longleat, Wiltshire ................................................................ 259
Lost Gardens of Heligan, The, Cornwall ................................. 204
Lulworth Castle & Park, Dorset .............................................. 231
Lydiard Park, Wiltshire .......................................................... 264
Mapperton, Dorset ................................................................ 231
Max Gate, Dorset .................................................................. 231
Mompesson House, Wiltshire ................................................ 264
Montacute House, Somerset .................................................. 254
Museum of Costume & Assembly Rooms, Somerset ............... 246
Newark Park, Gloucestershire ................................................ 241
Overbeck's, Devon ................................................................ 220
Painswick Rococo Garden, Gloucestershire ............................ 242
Pencarrow, Cornwall ............................................................. 205
Pendennis Castle, Cornwall ................................................... 205
Pine Lodge Gardens & Nursery, Cornwall .............................. 205
Powderham Castle, Devon ..................................................... 221

Prideaux Place, Cornwall ...................................................... 206
Prior Park Landscape Garden, Somerset ................................ 255
Rodmarton Manor, Gloucestershire ....................................... 242
Roman Baths & Pump Room, Somerset ................................. 247
Salisbury Cathedral, Wiltshire ............................................... 266
Sausmarez Manor, Channel Islands ....................................... 199
Sherborne Castle, Dorset ...................................................... 233
Snowshill Manor, Gloucestershire .......................................... 243
Stembridge Tower Mill, Somerset .......................................... 255
Stourhead, Wiltshire ............................................................. 260
Tiverton Castle, Devon .......................................................... 223
Trebah Garden, Cornwall ...................................................... 208
Wilton House, Wiltshire ........................................................ 261

## EASTERN REGION

Ashridge, Hertfordshire ......................................................... 285
Audley End House & Gardens, Essex ..................................... 278
Blickling Hall, Norfolk ........................................................... 289
Cambridge University Botanic Garden, Cambridgeshire .......... 273
Castle Acre Priory, Norfolk .................................................... 290
Cecil Higgins Art Gallery, Bedfordshire .................................. 271
Copped Hall, Essex ............................................................... 279
Dragon Hall, Norfolk ............................................................. 290
Elton Hall, Cambridgeshire .................................................... 274
Gainsborough's House, Suffolk .............................................. 296
Gardens of Easton Lodge, Essex ............................................ 280
Hatfield House, Hertfordshire ................................................ 283
Holkham Hall, Norfolk ........................................................... 287
Houghton Hall, Norfolk ......................................................... 292
Hylands House, Essex ............................................................ 280
Ickworth House & Park, Suffolk ............................................. 297
Ingatestone Hall, Essex ......................................................... 280
Kentwell Hall & Gardens, Suffolk .......................................... 297
Kimbolton Castle, Cambridgeshire ........................................ 275
Knebworth House, Hertfordshire ........................................... 284
Layer Marney Tower, Essex ................................................... 281
Mannington Gardens & Countryside, Norfolk ........................ 293
Manor, Hemingford Grey, Cambridgeshire ............................ 275
Oxburgh Hall & Estate, Norfolk ............................................. 293
Peterborough Cathedral, Cambridgeshire .............................. 275
RHS Garden Hyde Hall, Essex ................................................ 282
St Edmundsbury Cathedral, Suffolk ....................................... 299
St George's Guildhall, Norfolk ............................................... 294
Shaw's Corner, Hertfordshire ................................................ 286
Sheringham Park, Norfolk ...................................................... 294
Somerleyton Hall & Gardens, Suffolk ..................................... 300
South Elmham Hall, Suffolk ................................................... 300
Sutton Hoo, Suffolk ............................................................... 300
Tilbury Fort, Essex ................................................................. 282
Walkern Hall, Hertfordshire ................................................... 286
Walsingham Abbey Grounds
    & Shirehall Museum, Norfolk .......................................... 294
Wimpole Hall & Home Farm, Cambridgeshire ........................ 276
Woburn Abbey, Bedfordshire ................................................ 270
Wolterton Park, Norfolk ........................................................ 294
Yaxley Hall, Suffolk ............................................................... 301

## EAST MIDLANDS

78 Derngate, Northamptonshire ............................................ 329
Ashby de la Zouch Castle, Leics & Rutland ............................ 316
Ayscoughfee Hall Museum & Gardens, Lincolnshire ............... 319
Belton House, Lincolnshire .................................................... 320
Belvoir Castle, Leics & Rutland .............................................. 313
Bolsover Castle, Derbyshire ................................................... 308
Boughton House, Northamptonshire ...................................... 324
Burghley House, Lincolnshire ................................................. 317
Chatsworth, Derbyshire ......................................................... 304
Clumber Park, Nottinghamshire ............................................ 334

Doddington Hall & Gardens, Lincolnshire ............................... 320
Easton Walled Gardens, Lincolnshire ................................... 321
Elvaston Castle Country Park, Derbyshire ............................. 309
Eyam Hall, Derbyshire ....................................................... 310
Grimsthorpe Castle, Park & Gardens, Lincolnshire .................... 318
Haddon Hall, Derbyshire .................................................... 305
Hardwick Hall, Gardens, Park & Stainsby Mill, Derbyshire ......... 310
Hardwick Old Hall, Derbyshire ............................................ 311
Holdenby House, Northamptonshire ..................................... 331
Kedleston Hall, Derbyshire ................................................. 306
Kelmarsh Hall, Northamptonshire ........................................ 326
Kirby Hall, Northamptonshire .............................................. 331
Lamport Hall & Gardens, Northamptonshire ........................... 332
Lawrence Heritage, D H, Nottinghamshire ............................. 334
Lyddington Bede House, Leics & Rutland ............................... 316
Newstead Abbey, Nottinghamshire ...................................... 335
Nottingham Castle, Nottinghamshire .................................... 335
Oakham Castle, Leics & Rutland .......................................... 316
Peveril Castle, Derbyshire .................................................. 311
Rockingham Castle, Northamptonshire .................................. 327
Sulgrave Manor, Northamptonshire ...................................... 328
Tissington Hall, Derbyshire ................................................ 312

## WEST MIDLANDS

Ancient High House, Staffordshire ....................................... 350
Arbury Hall, Warwickshire ................................................. 354
Attingham Park, Shropshire ................................................ 344
Back to Backs, West Midlands .............................................367
Baddesley Clinton, Warwickshire ......................................... 355
Berrington Hall, Herefordshire ............................................ 338
Boscobel House & The Royal Oak, Shropshire ........................ 345
Broadway Tower, Worcestershire ......................................... 369
Casterne Hall, Derbyshire .................................................. 350
Charlecote Park, Warwickshire ............................................ 362
Coleham Pumping Station, Shropshire .................................. 345
Compton Verney, Warwickshire ........................................... 362
Eastnor Castle, Herefordshire ............................................. 339
Erasmus Darwin House, Staffordshire ................................... 350
Hagley Hall, West Midlands ................................................ 366
Hartlebury Castle, Worcestershire ....................................... 370
Harvington Hall, Worcestershire .......................................... 371
Hereford Cathedral, Herefordshire ....................................... 341
Hodnet Hall & Gardens, Shropshire ..................................... 346
Kenilworth Castle, Warwickshire ......................................... 365
Longner Hall, Shropshire ................................................... 346
Lord Leycester Hospital, Warwickshire ................................. 365
Ludlow Castle, Shropshire .................................................. 347
Mawley Hall, Shropshire .................................................... 347
Moseley Old Hall, Staffordshire .......................................... 351
Old Sufton, Herefordshire .................................................. 341
Packwood House, Warwickshire ........................................... 356
Ragley Hall & Gardens, Warwickshire ................................... 357
Selly Manor, West Midlands ............................................... 368
Shakespeare Houses, The, Warwickshire ............................... 358
Shrewsbury Castle & The Shropshire
    Regimental Museum, Shropshire ..................................... 348
Shugborough Estate, Staffordshire ...................................... 352
Spetchley Park Gardens, Worcestershire ............................... 372
Stoneleigh Abbey, Warwickshire ......................................... 359
Sufton Court, Herefordshire ............................................... 341
Tamworth Castle, Staffordshire ...........................................352
Trentham Gardens, Staffordshire ......................................... 353
Warwick Castle, Warwickshire ............................................ 361
Weston Park, Shropshire .................................................... 343
Witley Court & Gardens, Worcestershire ............................... 372
Wroxeter Roman City, Shropshire ....................................... 349

## YORKSHIRE & THE HUMBER

Aldborough Roman Site ..................................................... 385
Beningbrough Hall & Gardens ............................................. 385
Bolton Abbey .................................................................. 385
Bolton Castle .................................................................. 385
Brodsworth Hall & Gardens ................................................ 377
Brontë Parsonage Museum ................................................. 386
Burton Constable Hall ...................................................... 378
Byland Abbey .................................................................. 387
Cannon Hall Museum, Park & Gardens .................................. 387
Castle Howard ................................................................. 379
Duncombe Park ............................................................... 388
East Riddlesden Hall ......................................................... 388
Harewood House .............................................................. 381
Helmsley Castle ............................................................... 389
Kiplin Hall ..................................................................... 390
Kirkham Priory ................................................................ 390
Lotherton Hall & Gardens .................................................. 391
Mount Grace Priory .......................................................... 391
National Centre For Early Music, Yorks ................................. 391
Newby Hall & Gardens ...................................................... 382
Nostell Priory & Parklands ................................................. 392
Pickering Castle ............................................................... 392
Plumpton Rocks ............................................................... 393
RAF Holmpton – Bunker Tours ........................................... 393
RHS Garden Harlow Carr.................................................... 393
Richmond Castle .............................................................. 393
Rievaulx Abbey ............................................................... 394
Ripley Castle .................................................................. 383
Roche Abbey ................................................................... 394
Scarborough Castle ........................................................... 395
Shibden Hall ................................................................... 396
Skipton Castle ................................................................ 384
Sledmere House ............................................................... 396
Temple Newsam .............................................................. 397
Thorp Perrow Arboretum, Woodland Garden,
    Birds of Prey & Mammal Centre ..................................... 397
Treasurer's House ............................................................ 397
Whitby Abbey ................................................................. 398

## NORTH WEST

Abbot Hall Art Gallery, Cumbria .......................................... 410
Adlington Hall, Cheshire ................................................... 402
Arley Hall & Gardens, Cheshire ........................................... 403
Beeston Castle, Cheshire ................................................... 405
Blackwell – The Arts & Crafts House, Cumbria ........................ 411
Brantwood, Cumbria ........................................................ 414
Brougham Castle, Cumbria ................................................. 414
Carlisle Castle, Cumbria .................................................... 414
Dove Cottage & The Wordsworth Museum, Cumbria ................. 415
Dunham Massey, Cheshire .................................................. 406
Furness Abbey, Cumbria .................................................... 416
Heaton Hall, Lancashire ..................................................... 421
Hoghton Tower, Lancashire ................................................ 422
Holker Hall & Gardens, Cumbria .......................................... 417
Hutton-in-the-Forest, Cumbria ........................................... 417
Lanercost Priory, Cumbria .................................................. 417
Leighton Hall, Lancashire .................................................. 420
Levens Hall, Cumbria ........................................................ 412
Little Moreton Hall, Cheshire ............................................. 407
Liverpool Metropolitan Cathedral of
    Christ the King, Merseyside .......................................... 424
Lyme Park, Cheshire ......................................................... 407
Mirehouse, Cumbria ......................................................... 417
Muncaster Castle Gardens, Owl Centre
    & MeadowVole Maze, Cumbria ...................................... 413
Nether Alderley Mill, Cheshire ........................................... 407
Norton Priory Museum & Gardens, Cheshire ......................... 407

Quarry Bank Mill & Styal Estate, Cheshire ................................ 408
Rufford Old Hall, Lancashire ................................................ 422
Rydal Mount & Gardens, Cumbria ......................................... 418
Stott Park Bobbin Mill, Cumbria ........................................... 419
Tatton Park, Cheshire ......................................................... 409
Wordsworth House, Cumbria ...............................................419

## NORTH EAST

Alnwick Castle, Northumberland ........................................... 432
Auckland Castle, Co Durham ............................................... 430
Aydon Castle, Northumberland ............................................ 436
Bamburgh Castle, Northumberland ....................................... 433
Belsay Hall, Castle & Gardens, Northumberland ..................... 436
Berwick Barracks, Northumberland ....................................... 436
Bessie Surtees House, Tyne & Wear ...................................... 442
Bowes Museum, The, Co Durham ......................................... 428
Brinkburn Priory, Northumberland ........................................ 437
Chesters Roman Fort & Museum, Northumberland .................. 437
Chillingham Castle, Northumberland ..................................... 434
Corbridge Roman Town, Northumberland .............................. 437
Cragside, Northumberland ................................................... 437
Dunstanburgh Castle, Northumberland .................................. 437
Etal Castle, Northumberland ................................................ 438
Gibside, Tyne & Wear ......................................................... 442
Herterton House Gardens, Northumberland ........................... 438
Housesteads Roman Fort, Northumberland ............................ 438
Lindisfarne Priory, Northumberland ...................................... 439
Prudhoe Castle, Northumberland .......................................... 439
Raby Castle, Co Durham ..................................................... 429
St Paul's Monastery, Tyne & Wear ........................................ 442
Seaton Delaval Hall, Northumberland ................................... 440
Souter Lighthouse, Tyne & Wear .......................................... 442
Tynemouth Priory & Castle, Tyne & Wear .............................. 442
Wallington, Northumberland ................................................ 440
Warkworth Castle, Northumberland ...................................... 441
Warkworth Hermitage, Northumberland ................................ 441
Washington Old Hall, Tyne & Wear ....................................... 442

## SCOTLAND

Argyll's Lodging, West Highlands & Islands ............................. 478
Blair Castle, Perthshire/Fife .................................................. 470
Bowhill House & Country Park, Borders .................................. 446
Caerlaverock Castle, SW Scotland ......................................... 456
Castle of Mey, Highlands & Skye .......................................... 490
Cawdor Castle, Highlands & Skye ......................................... 488
Delgatie Castle, Grampian Highlands ..................................... 485
Dirleton Castle & Garden, Edinburgh City,
   Coast & Countryside ....................................................... 464
Drumlanrig Castle, SW Scotland ........................................... 455
Dunninald, Perthshire/Fife ................................................... 475
Dunstaffnage Castle, West Highlands & Islands ....................... 481
Dunvegan Castle, Highlands & Skye ...................................... 489
Edinburgh Castle, Edinburgh City, Coast & Countryside .......... 464
Edzell Castle & Garden, Perthshire/Fife ................................. 475
Floors Castle, Borders ......................................................... 447
Fort George, Highlands & Skye ............................................. 491
Glamis Castle, Perthshire/Fife .............................................. 472
Glenluce Abbey, SW Scotland .............................................. 457
Hopetoun House, Edinburgh City, Coast & Countryside .......... 461
Inveraray Castle, West Highlands & Islands ............................ 479
Inveraray Jail, West Highlands & Islands ................................ 482
Iona Abbey & Nunnery, West Highlands & Islands .................. 482
Jedburgh Abbey, Borders .................................................... 452
Kelburn Castle & Country Centre, SW Scotland ...................... 458
Lochleven Castle, Perthshire/Fife .......................................... 476
Manderston, Borders .......................................................... 448
MacLellan's Castle, SW Scotland .......................................... 458

Melrose Abbey, Borders ...................................................... 452
Mount Stuart, West Highlands & Islands ................................ 482
New Abbey Corn Mill, South West Scotland ........................... 458
New Lanark World Heritage Site, Greater Glasgow
   & Clyde Valley ............................................................... 468
Palace of Holyroodhouse & The Queen's Gallery,
   Edinburgh City, Coast & Countryside ................................ 462
Paxton House, Gallery & Country Park, Borders ...................... 453
St Andrews Castle, Perthshire/Fife ........................................ 476
Scone Palace & Grounds, Perthshire/Fife ............................... 473
Skara Brae & Skaill House, Outer Islands ............................... 493
Stirling Castle, West Highlands & Islands ............................... 483
Tantallon Castle, Edinburgh City, Coast & Countryside ............ 467
Thirlestane Castle, Borders .................................................. 454
Tullibole Castle, Perthshire/Fife ........................................... 477
Urquhart Castle, Highlands & Skye ....................................... 491

# WALES

## NORTH WALES

Aberconwy House .............................................................. 496
Bodelwyddan Castle ........................................................... 496
Chirk Castle ...................................................................... 497
Erddig ............................................................................. 498
Hafod .............................................................................. 498
Penrhyn Castle .................................................................. 499
Plas Newydd ..................................................................... 499

## SOUTH WALES

Aberdulais Falls ................................................................. 503
Aberglasney Gardens .......................................................... 502
Caldicot Castle & Country Park ............................................ 503
Dinefwr ........................................................................... 505
Dyffryn Gardens and Arboretum .......................................... 505
Judge's Lodging, The .......................................................... 506
National Botanic Garden of Wales, The ................................. 507
Pembroke Castle ................................................................ 507
Tredegar House & Park ....................................................... 509
Tudor Merchant's House ..................................................... 510
Usk Castle ........................................................................ 510

# NORTHERN IRELAND

Barons Court .................................................................... 514
Mount Stewart .................................................................. 516
Patterson's Spade Mill ........................................................ 516
Seaforde Gardens ............................................................... 516

# Accommodation

The historic properties listed below are not hotels. Their inclusion indicates that accommodation can be arranged, often for groups only. The type and standard of rooms offered vary widely – from the luxurious to the utilitarian. Full details can be obtained from each individual property.

# ENGLAND

## SOUTH EAST

Ardington House, Oxfordshire ................................... 151
Cobham Hall, Kent .................................................. 126
Friars, The, Kent .................................................... 142
Goddards, Surrey ................................................... 165
Grange, The, Kent .................................................. 142
Great Fosters, Surrey .............................................. 165
Hammerwood Park, Sussex ....................................... 184
Mapledurham House & Watermill, Oxfordshire ............... 157
Portsmouth Heritage (Buckingham House & Wymering Manor), Hampshire .............................. 111
Stowe House, Buckinghamshire .................................. 100
Wilmington Priory, Sussex ........................................ 191

## SOUTH WEST

Anderton House, Devon ........................................... 212
Athelhampton House & Gardens, Dorset ....................... 225
Boconnoc, Cornwall ................................................ 202
Cadhay, Devon ...................................................... 214
Clovelly, Devon ..................................................... 211
Frampton Court, Gloucestershire ................................ 239
Fursdon House, Devon ............................................ 217
Haldon Belvedere/Lawrence Castle, Devon ................... 218
Halswell House, Somerset ........................................ 252
Hartland Abbey, Devon ........................................... 218
Lulworth Castle & Park, Dorset .................................. 231
Maunsel House, Somerset ........................................ 254
Old Campden House, Gloucestershire ........................... 241
Owlpen Manor, Gloucestershire ................................. 242
Robin Hood's Hut, Somerset ..................................... 255
Sausmarez Manor, Channel Islands ............................. 199
Sudeley Castle & Exhibitions, Gloucestershire ............... 237
Tiverton Castle, Devon ............................................ 223

## EASTERN REGION

Ancient House, The, Suffolk ...................................... 295
Freston Tower, Suffolk ............................................ 296
Layer Marney Tower, Essex ....................................... 281
Peckover House & Garden, Cambridgeshire .................... 275
South Elmham Hall, Suffolk ...................................... 300
Sutton Hoo, Suffolk ............................................... 300

## EAST MIDLANDS

Catton Hall, Derbyshire ........................................... 309
Deene Park, Northamptonshire ................................... 325
Quenby Hall, Leics & Rutland .................................... 314
Stanford Hall, Leics & Rutland ...................................315

## WEST MIDLANDS

Combermere Abbey, Shropshire .................................. 345
Eastnor Castle, Herefordshire .................................... 339
Ludlow Castle, Shropshire ........................................ 347
Oakley Hall, Shropshire ........................................... 342
Weston Park, Shropshire .......................................... 343

## YORKSHIRE & THE HUMBER

Bolton Abbey ....................................................... 385
Ripley Castle ....................................................... 383

## NORTH WEST

Heaton Hall, Lancashire ........................................... 421
Muncaster Castle, Gardens, Owl Centre & MeadowVole Maze, Cumbria ............................... 413

Weston Park, Shropshire

## NORTH EAST

Chillingham Castle, Northumberland ...................................... 434
Eshott Hall, Northumberland .................................................. 435

## SCOTLAND

Auchinleck House, SW Scotland ............................................. 456
Balfluig Castle, Grampian Highlands ..................................... 484
Balmoral Castle (Grounds & Exhibitions),
   Grampian Highlands ........................................................ 484
Delgatie Castle, Grampian Highlands ................................... 485
Duns Castle, Borders ............................................................ 450
Dunvegan Castle, Highlands & Skye ..................................... 489
Greywalls, Edinburgh City, Coast & Countryside ...................... 465
Lennoxlove House, Edinburgh City, Coast & Countryside ........ 465
Manderston, Borders ............................................................ 448
New Lanark World Heritage Site,
   Greater Glasgow & Clyde Valley .......................................... 468
Torosay Castle & Gardens, West Highlands & Islands .............. 483
Tower of Hallbar, Greater Glasgow & Clyde Valley ................... 469
Traquair, Borders ................................................................. 449
Tullibole Castle, Perthshire/Fife ............................................ 477

## WALES

### NORTH WALES

Bryn Bras Castle ................................................................... 496
Dolbelydr ............................................................................ 498
Gwydir Castle ....................................................................... 498
Tower ................................................................................. 500

### SOUTH WALES

Aberglasney Gardens ............................................................ 502
Cresselly ............................................................................. 504
Treowen .............................................................................. 509

## NORTHERN IRELAND

Castle Ward & Strangford Lough Wildlife Centre ..................... 515
Crom ................................................................................... 515
Florence Court ..................................................................... 515
Killyleagh Castle ................................................................... 516

Eastnor Castle, Herefordshire

# Civil Wedding Venues

**Places at which the marriage or Civil partnership ceremonies can take place – many will also be able to provide facilities for wedding receptions.**

Full details about each property are available in the regional listings. There are numerous other properties included within Hudson's which do not have a Civil Wedding Licence but which can accommodate wedding receptions. In Scotland religious wedding ceremonies can take place anywhere, subject to the Minister being prepared to perform them.

# ENGLAND

## LONDON

Burgh House .......... 80
Chiswick House .......... 71
Eastbury Manor House .......... 81
Eltham Palace .......... 72
Ham House & Garden .......... 83
Marble Hill House .......... 87
Osterley Park & Park .......... 88
Pitzhanger Manor-House .......... 88
Royal Observatory, National Maritime Museum
  & Queen's House .......... 74
Spencer House .......... 77
Sutton House .......... 90
Syon Park .......... 78

## SOUTH EAST

Anne of Cleves House, Sussex .......... 179
Ardington House, Oxfordshire .......... 151
Avington Park, Hampshire .......... 112
Basildon Park, Berkshire .......... 96
Blenheim Palace, Oxfordshire .......... 152
Boughton Monchelsea Place, Kent .......... 122
Chiddingstone Castle, Kent .......... 124/125
Clandon Park, Surrey .......... 160
Cobham Hall, Kent .......... 126
Danson House, Kent .......... 127
Exbury Gardens & Steam Railway, Hampshire .......... 114
Finchcocks, Kent .......... 141
Goodwood House, Sussex .......... 172
Great Fosters, Surrey .......... 165
Groombridge Place Gardens, Kent .......... 130
Hall Place & Gardens, Kent .......... 131
Herstmonceux Castle Gardens, Sussex .......... 184
Highclere Castle & Gardens, Hampshire .......... 110
Houghton Lodge Gardens, Hampshire .......... 116
Kew Gardens, Surrey .......... 166
Kingston Bagpuize House, Oxfordshire .......... 157
Leeds Castle, Kent .......... 135
Loseley Park, Surrey .......... 162
Michelham Priory, Sussex .......... 186
Mottisfont Abbey & Garden, Hampshire .......... 117
Nurstead Court, Kent .......... 144
Penshurst Place & Gardens, Kent .......... 136
Ramster Gardens, Surrey .......... 168
Royal Pavilion, Sussex .......... 176
St Mary's House & Gardens, Sussex .......... 189
Stansted Park, Sussex .......... 190
Stowe House, Buckinghamshire .......... 100
Stowe Landscape Gardens & Park, Buckinghamshire .......... 106
Turkey Mill, Kent .......... 138
Vyne, The, Hampshire .......... 119
Waddesdon Manor, Buckinghamshire .......... 101
Weald & Downland Open Air Museum, Sussex .......... 191
Westenhanger Castle and Barns, Kent .......... 150

## SOUTH WEST

Arlington Court, Devon .......... 212
Athelhampton House & Gardens, Dorset .......... 225
Bicton Park Botanical Gardens, Devon .......... 210
Boconnoc, Cornwall .......... 202
Clovelly, Devon .......... 211
Cadhay, Devon .......... 214
Edmondsham House & Gardens, Dorset .......... 229
Escot, Devon .......... 217
Forde Abbey & Gardens, Dorset .......... 226
Haldon Belvedere/Lawrence Castle, Devon .......... 218
Halswell House, Somerset .......... 252
Hartland Abbey, Devon .......... 218
Highcliffe Castle, Dorset .......... 230
Kingston Maurward Garden, Dorset .......... 230
Larmer Tree Gardens, Wiltshire .......... 263
Lodge Park & Sherborne Estate, Gloucestershire .......... 241
Longleat, Wiltshire .......... 259
Lulworth Castle & Park, Dorset .......... 231
Mapperton, Dorset .......... 231
Maunsel House, Somerset .......... 254
Minterne Gardens, Dorset .......... 232
Mount Edgcumbe House & Country Park, Cornwall .......... 204
Museum of Costume & Assembly Rooms, Somerset .......... 246
Newhouse, Wiltshire .......... 264
Old Wardour Castle, Wiltshire .......... 265
Painswick Rococo Garden, Gloucestershire .......... 242
Pencarrow, Cornwall .......... 205
Pendennis Castle, Cornwall .......... 205
Portland Castle, Dorset .......... 232
Powderham Castle, Devon .......... 221
Prideaux Place, Cornwall .......... 206
Roman Baths & Pump Room, Somerset .......... 247
St Mawes Castle, Cornwall .......... 206
Sausmarez Manor, Channel Islands .......... 199
Sherborne Castle, Dorset .......... 233
Stourhead, Wiltshire .......... 260
Sudeley Castle & Exhibitions, Gloucestershire .......... 237
Trerice, Cornwall .......... 209
Wilton House, Wiltshire .......... 261

## EASTERN REGION

Audley End House & Gardens, Essex ........................................ 278
Blickling Hall, Norfolk ...................................................... 289
Dragon Hall, Norfolk ....................................................... 290
Hatfield House, Hertfordshire ............................................. 283
Haughley Park, Suffolk ..................................................... 296
Hylands House, Essex ...................................................... 280
Kentwell Hall & Gardens, Suffolk ......................................... 297
Kimberley Hall, Norfolk .................................................... 292
Kimbolton Castle, Cambridgeshire ........................................ 275
Knebworth House, Hertfordshire .......................................... 284
Layer Marney Tower, Essex ................................................ 281
Peckover House & Garden, Cambridgeshire ............................... 275
Somerleyton Hall & Gardens, Suffolk ..................................... 300
South Elmham Hall, Suffolk ............................................... 300
Swiss Garden, Bedfordshire ............................................... 271
Wimpole Hall & Home Farm, Cambridgeshire .............................. 276
Woburn Abbey, Bedfordshire .............................................. 270
Wolterton Park, Norfolk ................................................... 294
Yaxley Hall, Suffolk ....................................................... 301

## EAST MIDLANDS

Belton House, Lincolnshire ................................................ 320
Belvoir Castle, Leics & Rutland ........................................... 313
Bolsover Castle, Derbyshire ............................................... 308
Burghley House, Lincolnshire .............................................. 317
Chatsworth, Derbyshire .................................................... 304
Doddington Hall & Gardens, Lincolnshire ................................. 320
Elvaston Castle Country Park, Derbyshire ................................. 309
Eyam Hall, Derbyshire ..................................................... 310
Holdenby House, Northamptonshire......................................... 331
Holme Pierrepont Hall, Nottinghamshire .................................. 334
Kedleston Hall, Derbyshire ................................................ 306
Kelmarsh Hall, Northamptonshire ......................................... 326
Lamport Hall & Gardens, Northamptonshire ............................... 332
Lawrence Heritage, D H, Nottinghamshire ................................ 334
Newstead Abbey, Nottinghamshire ........................................ 335
Oakham Castle, Leics & Rutland .......................................... 316
Pavilion Gardens, Derbyshire ............................................. 307
Quenby Hall, Leics & Rutland ............................................. 314
Renishaw Hall Gardens, Derbyshire ....................................... 312
Rockingham Castle, Northamptonshire ..................................... 327
Sulgrave Manor, Northamptonshire ........................................ 328
Tattershall Castle, Lincolnshire .......................................... 322
Tissington Hall, Derbyshire ............................................... 312

## WEST MIDLANDS

Birmingham Botanical Gardens & Glasshouses,
    West Midlands .......................................................... 367
Casterne Hall, Derbyshire ................................................. 350
Combermere Abbey, Shropshire ............................................ 345
Eastnor Castle, Herefordshire ............................................ 339
Greyfriars, The, Worcestershire .......................................... 369
Hagley Hall, West Midlands ............................................... 366
Hanbury Hall, Worcestershire ............................................. 370
Heath House, The, Staffordshire .......................................... 351
Izaak Walton's Cottage, Staffordshire .................................... 351
Kenilworth Castle, Warwickshire .......................................... 365
Ludlow Castle, Shropshire ................................................. 347
Moseley Old Hall, Staffordshire .......................................... 351
Oakley Hall, Shropshire ................................................... 342
Ragley Hall & Gardens, Warwickshire ..................................... 357
Sandon Hall, Staffordshire ................................................ 352
Selly Manor, West Midlands ............................................... 368
Shakespeare Houses (Hall's Croft), Warwickshire ......................... 358
Shrewsbury Castle & The Shropshire Regimental Museum,
    Shropshire ............................................................. 348
Shugborough Estate, Staffordshire ........................................ 352
Stoneleigh Abbey, Warwickshire ........................................... 359
Tamworth Castle, Staffordshire ........................................... 352
Upton House & Gardens, Warwickshire ..................................... 360
Weston Park, Shropshire .................................................. 343

## YORKSHIRE & THE HUMBER

Beningbrough Hall & Gardens ............................................. 385
Bolton Castle ............................................................. 385
Cannon Hall Museum, Park & Gardens .................................... 387
Duncombe Park ........................................................... 388

Loseley Park, Surrey

East Riddlesden Hall ........................................ 388
Fountains Abbey & Studley Royal ............................ 380
Harewood House ............................................. 381
Kiplin Hall ................................................ 390
Markenfield Hall ........................................... 391
Newburgh Priory ............................................ 392
Newby Hall & Gardens ....................................... 382
Nostell Priory & Parklands ................................. 392
Ripley Castle .............................................. 383
Sledmere House ............................................. 396
Treasurer's House .......................................... 397
Walcot Hall ................................................ 397

## NORTH WEST

Adlington Hall, Cheshire ................................... 402
Arley Hall & Gardens, Cheshire ............................. 403
Brantwood, Cumbria ......................................... 414
Capesthorne Hall, Cheshire ................................. 404
Gawsworth Hall, Cheshire ................................... 406
Heaton Hall, Lancashire .................................... 421
Leighton Hall, Lancashire .................................. 420
Meols Hall, Merseyside ..................................... 424
Muncaster Castle Gardens, Owl Centre &
   MeadowVole Maze, Cumbria ................................ 413
Quarry Bank Mill & Styal Estate, Cheshire .................. 408
Rufford Old Hall, Lancashire ............................... 422
Tabley House, Cheshire ..................................... 408
Tatton Park, Cheshire ...................................... 409

## NORTH EAST

Bamburgh Castle, Northumberland ............................ 433
Bowes Museum, The, Co Durham ............................... 428
Chillingham Castle, Northumberland ......................... 434
Cragside, Northumberland ................................... 437
Eshott Hall, Northumberland ................................ 435
Gibside, Tyne & Wear ....................................... 442
Wallington, Northumberland ................................. 440
Washington Old Hall, Tyne & Wear ........................... 442

# WALES

## NORTH WALES

Bodelwyddan Castle ......................................... 496
Bodrhyddan ................................................. 496
Chirk Castle ............................................... 497
Gwydir Castle .............................................. 498

## SOUTH WALES

Caerphilly Castle .......................................... 503
Caldicot Castle & Country Park ............................. 503
Castell Coch ............................................... 504
Dyffryn Gardens and Arboretum .............................. 505
Fonmon Castle .............................................. 506
Judge's Lodging, The ....................................... 506
Llanvihangel Court ......................................... 506
National Botanic Garden of Wales, The ...................... 507
Picton Castle .............................................. 508
Tredegar House & Park ...................................... 509
Treowen .................................................... 509

# NORTHERN IRELAND

Argory, The ................................................ 514
Castle Coole ............................................... 514
Castle Ward & Strangford Lough Wildlife Centre ............. 515
Crom ....................................................... 515
Florence Court ............................................. 515
Killyleagh Castle .......................................... 516
Mount Stewart .............................................. 516
Mussenden Temple & Downhill Demesne ........................ 516
Springhill House & Costume Collection ...................... 516

Chiswick House, London

# Open All Year

Properties included in this list are open to some extent for all or most of the year.
See individual entries for details.

## ENGLAND

### LONDON

18 Folgate Street ............................................ 79
Apsley House ................................................. 69
Banqueting House ........................................... 79
Burgh House ................................................. 80
Capel Manor Gardens ...................................... 80
Church Farmhouse Museum .............................. 81
Eastbury Manor House ..................................... 81
Forty Hall .................................................... 82
Franklin House, Benjamin .................................. 82
Geffrye Museum, The ...................................... 83
Handel House Museum ..................................... 84
Hogarth's House ............................................. 84
Honeywood Heritage Centre .............................. 84
Jewel Tower ................................................. 84
Keats House ................................................. 84
Kensington Palace .......................................... 85
Kenwood ..................................................... 73
Leighton House Museum ................................... 86
Linley Sambourne House ................................... 86
Little Holland House ........................................ 87
Myddelton House Gardens ................................. 87
Osterley Park & Park ....................................... 88
Pitzhanger Manor-House ................................... 88
Royal Observatory, National Maritime Museum
    & Queen's House ........................................ 74
St John's Gate, Museum of the Order of St John ..... 89
St Paul's Cathedral ......................................... 75
Somerset House ............................................. 76
Southwark Cathedral ....................................... 90
Sutton House ................................................ 90
Syon Park .................................................... 78
Tower of London, The ...................................... 91
Wellington Arch ............................................. 92
Westminster Cathedral ..................................... 92
Whitehall ..................................................... 92

### SOUTH EAST

1066 Battle of Hastings Abbey and Battlefield, Sussex ............. 180
Anne of Cleves House, Sussex ............................. 179
Arundel Castle, Sussex ..................................... 169
Austen's House, Jane, Hampshire ......................... 112
Beaulieu, Hampshire ................................. 108/109
Belmont House & Gardens, Kent .......................... 139
Blenheim Palace, Oxfordshire ............................. 152
Bodiam Castle, Sussex ..................................... 181
Boughton Monchelsea Place, Kent ....................... 122
Box Hill, Surrey ............................................. 164
Boxgrove Priory, Sussex ................................... 181
Bramber Castle, Sussex .................................... 181
Brighstone Shop & Museum, Isle of Wight ............. 193
Broughton Castle, Oxfordshire ............................ 153
Buckingham Chantry Chapel, Buckinghamshire ........ 102
Carisbrooke Castle, Isle of Wight ........................ 193
Chenies Manor House, Buckinghamshire ................ 102
Chichester Cathedral, Sussex ............................. 182
Cliveden, Buckinghamshire ................................ 104
Danson House, Kent ....................................... 127
Deddington Castle, Oxfordshire ........................... 156
Denmans Garden, Sussex .................................. 182
Ditchley Park, Oxfordshire ................................ 156
Donnington Castle, Berkshire .............................. 98
Dorney Court, Berkshire .................................... 98
Dover Castle & The Secret Wartime Tunnels, Kent ... 129
Eton College, Berkshire ..................................... 98
Fishbourne Roman Palace, Sussex ....................... 183
Friars, The, Kent ........................................... 142
Gilbert White's House & The Oates Museum, Hampshire ........ 114
Great Coxwell Barn, Oxfordshire ......................... 156
Great Fosters, Surrey ...................................... 165
Great Hall & Queen Eleanor's Garden, Hampshire .... 115
Guildford House Gallery, Surrey .......................... 165
Guildhall Gallery, Hampshire .............................. 115
Hall Place & Gardens, Kent ............................... 131
Hammerwood Park, Sussex ................................ 184
Hampton Court Palace, Surrey ............................ 165
Hever Castle & Gardens, Kent ............................ 132
Hughenden Manor, Buckinghamshire ..................... 105
Kew Gardens, Surrey ...................................... 166
King John's House & Heritage Centre, Hampshire ..... 117
King's Head, The, Buckinghamshire ...................... 105
Kingston Bagpuize House, Oxfordshire .................. 157
Knole, Kent ................................................. 134
Leeds Castle, Kent ......................................... 135
Leith Hill, Surrey ........................................... 166
Lewes Castle & Barbican House Museum, Sussex ..... 185
Loseley Park, Surrey ....................................... 162
Lullingstone Roman Villa, Kent ........................... 143
Milton Manor House, Oxfordshire ........................ 157
Minster Lovell Hall & Dovecote, Oxfordshire ........... 158
Nether Winchendon House, Buckinghamshire ........... 105
Netley Abbey, Hampshire .................................. 117
Nunwell House & Gardens, Isle of Wight ............... 194
Nurstead Court, Kent ...................................... 144
Osborne House, Isle of Wight ............................. 192
Painshill Park, Surrey ...................................... 163
Penshurst Place & Gardens, Kent ........................ 136
Petworth House & Park, Sussex .......................... 175
Pevensey Castle, Sussex ................................... 188
Polesden Lacey, Surrey .................................... 167
Portchester Castle, Hampshire ............................ 118
Portsmouth Heritage (Buckingham House &
    Wymering Manor), Hampshire .......................... 111
RHS Garden Wisley, Surrey ............................... 167
Reculver Towers & Roman Fort, Kent .................... 145
Rochester Castle, Kent ..................................... 146
Rochester Cathedral, Kent ................................. 146
Rousham House, Oxfordshire .............................. 158
Royal Pavilion, Sussex ..................................... 176
Runnymede, Surrey ........................................ 168
St Agatha's Church, Hampshire ........................... 118

**visit hudsons guide online**

St Augustine's Abbey, Kent ...................... 147
St John's Commandery, Kent ...................... 147
Sackville College, Sussex ...................... 189
Saint Hill Manor, Sussex ...................... 177
Sandham Memorial Chapel, Hampshire ...................... 118
Savill Garden, Berkshire ...................... 98
Scotney Castle, Kent ...................... 147
Sheffield Park Garden, Sussex ...................... 178
Stansted Park, Sussex ...................... 190
Stowe House, Buckinghamshire ...................... 100
Stowe Landscape Gardens & Park, Buckinghamshire ...................... 106
Titchfield Abbey, Hampshire ...................... 119
Tonbridge Castle, Kent ...................... 149
Turkey Mill, Kent ...................... 138
Weald & Downland Open Air Museum, Sussex ...................... 191
Westenhanger Castle and Barns, Kent ...................... 150
White Cliffs of Dover, Kent ...................... 150
Winchester Cathedral, Hampshire ...................... 120
Windsor Castle, St George's Chapel &
   Frogmore House, Berkshire ...................... 97
Winkworth Arboretum, Surrey ...................... 168

# SOUTH WEST

Abbotsbury Subtropical Gardens, Dorset ...................... 224
Arlington Court, Devon ...................... 212
Athelhampton House & Gardens, Dorset ...................... 225
Avebury Manor & Garden, Avebury Stone Circle, Wiltshire ...... 262
Batsford Arboretum, Gloucestershire ......................238
Bayard's Cove Fort, Devon ...................... 212
Bicton Park Botanical Gardens, Devon ...................... 210
Boconnoc, Cornwall ...................... 202
Bradford-on-Avon Tithe Barn, Wiltshire ...................... 262
Brean Down, Somerset ...................... 249
Buckland Abbey, Devon ...................... 213
Burncoose Nurseries & Garden, Cornwall ...................... 202
Castle Drogo, Devon ...................... 214
Chalice Well & Gardens, The, Somerset ...................... 249
Chavenage, Gloucestershire ...................... 236
Church of Our Lady & St Ignatius, Dorset ...................... 228
Clovelly, Devon ...................... 211
Corfe Castle, Dorset ...................... 228
Corsham Court, Wiltshire ...................... 258
Cotehele, Cornwall ...................... 200
Dartmouth Castle, Devon ...................... 216
Dyrham Park, Gloucestershire ...................... 239
Escot, Devon ...................... 217
Farleigh Hungerford Castle, Somerset ...................... 251
Forde Abbey & Gardens, Dorset ...................... 226
Frampton Court, Gloucestershire ...................... 239
Gatcombe Court, Somerset ...................... 251
Glastonbury Abbey, Somerset ...................... 252
Glastonbury Tor, Somerset ...................... 252
Glastonbury Tribunal, Somerset ...................... 252
Halswell House, Somerset ...................... 252
Hestercombe Gardens, Somerset ...................... 253
Highcliffe Castle, Dorset ...................... 230
Holnicote Estate, Somerset ...................... 253
Hound Tor Deserted Medieval Village, Devon ...................... 218
Kentsford, Somerset ...................... 253
King's House, The, Wiltshire ...................... 263
Kingston Maurward Garden, Dorset ...................... 230
Lacock Abbey, Fox Talbot Museum & Village, Wiltshire ...................... 263
Lanhydrock, Cornwall ...................... 201
Longleat, Wiltshire ...................... 259
Lost Gardens of Heligan, Cornwall ...................... 204
Loughwood Meeting House, Devon ...................... 220
Lulworth Castle & Park, Dorset ...................... 231
Lydford Castle & Saxon Town, Devon ...................... 220
Lydiard Park, Wiltshire ...................... 264

Maunsel House, Somerset ...................... 254
Montacute House, Somerset ...................... 254
Mount Edgcumbe House & Country Park, Cornwall ...................... 204
Museum of Costume & Assembly Rooms, Somerset ...................... 246
Norrington Manor, Wiltshire ...................... 265
Old Sarum, Wiltshire ...................... 265
Old Wardour Castle, Wiltshire ...................... 265
Overbeck's, Devon ...................... 220
Painswick Rococo Garden, Gloucestershire ...................... 242
Pencarrow, Cornwall ...................... 205
Pendennis Castle, Cornwall ...................... 205
Pine Lodge Gardens & Nursery, Cornwall ...................... 205
Powderham Castle, Devon ...................... 221
Prideaux Place, Cornwall ...................... 206
Prior Park Landscape Garden, Somerset ...................... 255
Puslinch, Devon ...................... 221
RHS Garden Rosemoor, Devon ...................... 221
Robin Hood's Hut, Somerset ...................... 255
Rodmarton Manor, Gloucestershire ...................... 242
Roman Baths & Pump Room, Somerset ...................... 247
St Catherine's Castle, Cornwall ...................... 206
St Mawes Castle, Cornwall ...................... 206
Salisbury Cathedral, Wiltshire ...................... 266
Saltram, Devon ...................... 222
Sand, Devon ...................... 222
Sausmarez Manor, Channel Islands ...................... 199
Sezincote, Gloucestershire ...................... 243
Stanway House & Water Garden, Gloucestershire ...................... 244
Stonehenge, Wiltshire ...................... 266
Stourhead, Wiltshire ...................... 260
Tintagel Castle, Cornwall ...................... 207
Tiverton Castle, Devon ...................... 223
Trebah Garden, Cornwall ...................... 208
Trelissick Garden, Cornwall ...................... 208
Tythe Barn, Gloucestershire ...................... 244
Wolfeton House, Dorset ...................... 234

# EASTERN REGION

Anglesey Abbey, Gardens & Lode Mill, Cambridgeshire ...................... 273
Berkhamsted Castle, Hertfordshire ...................... 285
Binham Priory, Norfolk ...................... 289
Blickling Hall, Norfolk ...................... 289
Brentwood Cathedral, Essex ...................... 279
Burgh Castle, Norfolk ...................... 289
Cambridge University Botanic Garden, Cambridgeshire ...................... 273
Castle Acre Priory, Norfolk ...................... 290
Castle Rising Castle, Norfolk ...................... 290
Cecil Higgins Art Gallery, Bedfordshire ...................... 271
Copped Hall, Essex ...................... 279
Dragon Hall, Norfolk ...................... 290
Ely Cathedral, Cambridgeshire ...................... 274
Framlingham Castle, Suffolk ...................... 296
Gainsborough's House, Suffolk ...................... 296
Gardens of Easton Lodge, Essex ...................... 280
Harwich Redoubt Fort, Essex ...................... 280
Haughley Park, Suffolk ...................... 296
Holkham Hall, Norfolk ...................... 287
Houghton House, Bedfordshire ...................... 271
Hylands House, Essex ...................... 280
Kimbolton Castle, Cambridgeshire ...................... 275
Layer Marney Tower, Essex ...................... 281
Leiston Abbey, Suffolk ...................... 298
Mannington Gardens & Countryside, Norfolk ...................... 293
Manor, Hemingford Grey, Cambridgeshire ...................... 275
Marks Hall Gardens & Arboretum, Essex ...................... 281
Moggerhanger Park, Bedfordshire ...................... 271
Old Gorhambury House, Hertfordshire ...................... 285
Orford Castle, Suffolk ...................... 299
Otley Hall, Suffolk ...................... 299

Peterborough Cathedral, Cambridgeshire ............................... 275
RHS Garden Hyde Hall, Essex ............................................... 282
St Edmundsbury Cathedral, Suffolk ...................................... 299
St George's Guildhall, Norfolk .............................................. 294
Sheringham Park, Norfolk ................................................... 294
Somerleyton Hall & Gardens, Suffolk ................................... 300
South Elmham Hall, Suffolk ................................................ 300
Sutton Hoo, Suffolk ........................................................... 300
Swiss Garden, Bedfordshire ................................................ 271
Tilbury Fort, Essex ............................................................. 282
Walkern Hall, Hertfordshire ................................................ 286
Walsingham Abbey Grounds & Shirehall
  Museum, Norfolk ............................................................ 294
Waltham Abbey Gatehouse & Bridge, Essex ......................... 282
Wimpole Hall & Home Farm, Cambridgeshire ....................... 276
Woburn Abbey, Bedfordshire .............................................. 270
Wolterton Park, Norfolk ..................................................... 294
Wyken Hall Gardens, Suffolk ............................................... 301
Yaxley Hall, Suffolk ............................................................ 301

## EAST MIDLANDS

Ashby de la Zouch Castle, Leics & Rutland ........................... 316
Ayscoughfee Hall Museum & Gardens, Lincolnshire ............... 319
Belvoir Castle, Leics & Rutland ........................................... 313
Bolsover Castle, Derbyshire ................................................ 308
Boughton House, Northamptonshire .................................... 324
Calke Abbey, Derbyshire .................................................... 308
Carlton Hall, Nottinghamshire ............................................ 334
Chatsworth, Derbyshire ..................................................... 304
Clumber Park, Nottinghamshire .......................................... 334
Deene Park, Northamptonshire ........................................... 325
Eleanor Cross, Northamptonshire ........................................ 330
Elvaston Castle Country Park, Derbyshire ............................. 309
Eyam Hall, Derbyshire ....................................................... 310
Fulbeck Manor, Lincolnshire ............................................... 321
Holme Pierrepont Hall, Nottinghamshire .............................. 334
Kelmarsh Hall, Northamptonshire ....................................... 326
Kirby Hall, Northamptonshire ............................................. 331
Lamport Hall & Gardens, Northamptonshire .......................... 332
Lawrence Heritage, D H, Nottinghamshire ............................ 334
Lincoln Medieval Bishops' Palace, Lincolnshire ..................... 322
Lyveden New Bield, Northamptonshire ................................. 332
Nottingham Castle, Nottinghamshire ................................... 335
Oakham Castle, Leics & Rutland .......................................... 316
Papplewick Hall, Nottinghamshire ....................................... 335
Pavilion Gardens, Derbyshire .............................................. 307
Peveril Castle, Derbyshire .................................................. 311
Quenby Hall, Leics & Rutland ............................................. 314
Rufford Abbey, Nottinghamshire ......................................... 335
Sulgrave Manor, Northamptonshire ..................................... 328
Sutton Scarsdale Hall, Derbyshire ....................................... 312
Thrumpton Hall, Nottinghamshire ....................................... 335
Tissington Hall, Derbyshire ................................................ 312
Wartnaby Gardens, Leics & Rutland ..................................... 316
Wollaton Hall & Park, Nottinghamshire ................................ 335

## WEST MIDLANDS

Acton Burnell Castle, Shropshire ......................................... 344
Ancient High House, Staffordshire ....................................... 350
Arbury Hall, Warwickshire .................................................. 354
Attingham Park, Shropshire ................................................ 344
Birmingham Botanical Gardens
  & Glasshouses, West Midlands ....................................... 367
Broadway Tower, Worcestershire ......................................... 369
Brockhampton Estate, Herefordshire .................................... 340
Clun Castle, Shropshire ...................................................... 345
Combermere Abbey, Shropshire .......................................... 345
Compton Verney, Warwickshire ........................................... 362

Erasmus Darwin House, Staffordshire ................................... 350
Goodrich Castle, Worcestershire .......................................... 369
Harvington Hall, Worcestershire .......................................... 371
Hereford Cathedral, Herefordshire ....................................... 341
Hergest Court, Herefordshire .............................................. 341
Hergest Croft Gardens, Herefordshire .................................. 341
Iron Bridge, Shropshire ...................................................... 346
Kenilworth Castle, Warwickshire .......................................... 365
Kinver Edge and the Rockhouses, West Midlands ................... 368
Langley Chapel, Shropshire ................................................ 346
Longner Hall, Shropshire .................................................... 346
Longtown Castle, Herefordshire ........................................... 341
Lord Leycester Hospital, Warwickshire .................................. 365
Ludlow Castle, Shropshire ................................................... 347
Mawley Hall, Shropshire ..................................................... 347
Moreton Corbet Castle, Shropshire ...................................... 347
Oakley Hall, Shropshire ...................................................... 342
Old Sufton, Herefordshire ................................................... 341
Packwood House, Warwickshire ........................................... 356
Rotherwas Chapel, Herefordshire ......................................... 341
Sandon Hall, Staffordshire .................................................. 352
Selly Manor, West Midlands ................................................ 368
Shakespeare Houses, The, Warwickshire ............................... 358
Stafford Castle & Visitor Centre, Staffordshire ...................... 352
Stokesay Castle, Shropshire ................................................ 348
Tamworth Castle, Staffordshire ........................................... 352
Trentham Gardens, Staffordshire ......................................... 353
Upton House & Gardens, Warwickshire ................................. 360
Warwick Castle, Warwickshire ............................................. 361
Wenlock Priory, Shropshire ................................................. 349
Witley Court & Gardens, Worcestershire ............................... 372
Wroxeter Roman City, Shropshire ........................................ 349

## YORKSHIRE & THE HUMBER

Bolton Abbey ................................................................... 385
Bolton Castle ................................................................... 385
Brodsworth Hall & Gardens ................................................ 377
Brontë Parsonage Museum ................................................. 386
Broughton Hall ................................................................. 386
Cannon Hall Museum, Park & Gardens ................................. 387
Castle Howard .................................................................. 379
Clifford's Tower ................................................................ 387
Conisbrough Castle ........................................................... 387
Fairfax House ................................................................... 389
Fountains Abbey & Studley Royal ........................................ 380
Helmsley Castle ............................................................... 389
Lindley Murray Summerhouse, The ...................................... 391
Longley Old Hall .............................................................. 391
Markenfield Hall ............................................................... 391
Middleham Castle ............................................................. 391
Mount Grace Priory ........................................................... 391
National Centre for Early Music .......................................... 391
RHS Garden Harlow Carr .................................................... 393
Richmond Castle ............................................................... 393
Rievaulx Abbey ................................................................ 394
Ripley Castle ................................................................... 383
Scarborough Castle ........................................................... 395
Shibden Hall .................................................................... 396
Skipton Castle .................................................................. 384
Thorp Perrow Arboretum, Woodland Garden,
  Birds of Prey & Mammal Centre ..................................... 397
Whitby Abbey ................................................................... 398

## NORTH WEST

Abbot Hall Art Gallery, Cumbria .......................................... 410
Adlington Hall, Cheshire ..................................................... 402
Beeston Castle, Cheshire .................................................... 405
Blackwell – The Arts & Crafts House, Cumbria ....................... 411

Brantwood, Cumbria ............................................. 414
Brough Castle, Cumbria ....................................... 414
Carlisle Castle, Cumbria ...................................... 414
Chester Roman Amphitheatre, Cheshire .................. 405
Dove Cottage & The Wordsworth Museum, Cumbria ............. 415
Dunham Massey, Cheshire ..................................... 406
Fell Foot Park, Cumbria ....................................... 416
Furness Abbey, Cumbria ....................................... 416
Gawthorpe Hall, Lancashire .................................. 421
Hardknott Roman Fort, Cumbria ............................. 416
Heaton Hall, Lancashire ....................................... 421
Hoghton Tower, Lancashire ................................... 422
Holmston Hall Barn, Cheshire ............................... 406
Leighton Hall, Lancashire ..................................... 420
Liverpool Metropolitan Cathedral of Christ
    the King, Merseyside ....................................... 424
Lyme Park, Cheshire ........................................... 407
Manchester Cathedral, Lancashire .......................... 422
Norton Priory Museum & Gardens, Cheshire ............. 407
Quarry Bank Mill & Styal Estate, Cheshire ............. 408
Rydal Mount & Gardens, Cumbria .......................... 418
Tatton Park, Cheshire .......................................... 409
Towneley Hall Art Gallery & Museums, Lancashire .... 422
Warton Old Rectory, Lancashire ............................ 423

## NORTH EAST

Bamburgh Castle, Northumberland .......................... 433
Barnard Castle, Co Durham .................................. 430
Belsay Hall, Castle & Gardens, Northumberland ........ 436
Berwick Barracks, Northumberland ......................... 436
Berwick Ramparts, Northumberland ........................ 436
Bessie Surtees House, Tyne & Wear ....................... 442
Bowes Museum, The, Co Durham ........................... 428
Capheaton Hall, Northumberland ........................... 437
Chesters Roman Fort & Museum, Northumberland ...... 437
Chillingham Castle, Northumberland ....................... 434
Corbridge Roman Town, Northumberland ................. 437
Dunstanburgh Castle, Northumberland .................... 437
Edlingham Castle, Northumberland ......................... 438
Eshott Hall, Northumberland ................................. 435
Gibside, Tyne & Wear .......................................... 442
Housesteads Roman Fort, Northumberland ............... 438
Lindisfarne Priory, Northumberland ........................ 439
Preston Tower, Northumberland ............................. 439
St Paul's Monastery, Tyne & Wear ......................... 442
Tynemouth Priory & Castle, Tyne & Wear ............... 442
Wallington, Northumberland .................................. 440
Warkworth Castle, Northumberland ........................ 441

# SCOTLAND

Aberdour Castle, Perthshire/Fife ........................... 474
Arbroath Abbey, Perthshire/Fife ............................ 474
Arbuthnott House, Grampian Highlands ................... 484
Ardkinglas Estate, West Highlands & Islands ........... 480
Argyll's Lodging, West Highlands & Islands ............. 478
Arniston House, Edinburgh City, Coast & Countryside ........... 463
Ayton Castle, Borders ......................................... 450
Balfluig Castle, Grampian Highlands ...................... 484
Black House, Outer Islands .................................. 492
Blackness Castle, Edinburgh City, Coast & Countryside ........... 463
Blair Castle, Perthshire/Fife ................................ 470
Bowhill House & Country Park, Borders .................. 446
Caerlaverock Castle, SW Scotland ......................... 456
Cairness House, Grampian Highlands ...................... 484
Cardoness Castle, SW Scotland ............................. 456
Castle Campbell, Perthshire/Fife ........................... 474
Castle of Old Wick, Highlands & Skye .................... 490

Colzium House & Walled Garden, Greater Glasgow
    & Clyde Valley .............................................. 468
Corgarff Castle, Grampian Highlands ..................... 484
Cortachy Estate, Perthshire/Fife ........................... 474
Craigmillar Castle, Edinburgh City, Coast & Countryside .......... 463
Craignethan Castle, Greater Glasgow & Clyde Valley .............. 468
Craigston Castle, Grampian Highlands .................... 485
Dallas Dhu Distillery, Grampian Highlands ............. 485
Dalmeny House, Edinburgh City, Coast & Countryside ............. 460
Delgatie Castle, Grampian Highlands ...................... 485
Dirleton Castle & Garden, Edinburgh City,
    Coast & Countryside ....................................... 464
Doune Castle, West Highlands & Islands ................. 480
Drumlanrig Castle, SW Scotland ........................... 455
Dumbarton Castle, West Highlands & Islands ........... 481
Dunblane Cathedral, West Highlands & Islands ........ 481
Dundrennan Abbey, SW Scotland .......................... 457
Dunfermline Abbey & Palace, Perthshire/Fife .......... 475
Dunglass Collegiate Church, Edinburgh City,
    Coast & Countryside ....................................... 464
Duns Castle, Borders .......................................... 450
Dunstaffnage Castle, West Highlands & Islands ....... 481
Dunvegan Castle, Highlands & Skye ....................... 489
Edinburgh Castle, Edinburgh City, Coast & Countryside .......... 464
Edzell Castle & Garden, Perthshire/Fife .................. 475
Elgin Cathedral, Grampian Highlands ..................... 486
Fort George, Highlands & Skye ............................. 491
Glamis Castle, Perthshire/Fife .............................. 472
Glasgow Cathedral, Greater Glasgow & Clyde Valley .............. 468
Gleneagles, Perthshire/Fife .................................. 475
Glenluce Abbey, SW Scotland .............................. 457
Hailes Castle, Edinburgh City, Coast & Countryside ............... 465
Hirsel Gardens, Country Park
    & Homestead Museum, The, Borders .................. 451
Hopetoun House, Edinburgh City, Coast & Countryside ........... 461
Huntingtower Castle, Perthshire/Fife ..................... 475
Huntly Castle, Grampian Highlands ....................... 486
Inveraray Jail, West Highlands & Islands ................ 482
Iona Abbey & Nunnery, West Highlands & Islands ..... 482
Jedburgh Abbey, Borders ..................................... 452
Kelburn Castle & Country Centre, SW Scotland ....... 458
Linlithgow Palace, Edinburgh City, Coast & Countryside ......... 466
Maeshowe, Outer Islands ..................................... 492
Manderston, Borders ........................................... 448
Melrose Abbey, Borders ....................................... 452
Monzie Castle, Perthshire/Fife .............................. 476
Motherwell Heritage Centre, Greater Glasgow
    & Clyde Valley .............................................. 468
New Abbey Corn Mill, SW Scotland ...................... 458
New Lanark World Heritage Site, Greater Glasgow
    & Clyde Valley .............................................. 468
Newliston, Edinburgh City, Coast & Countryside ...... 466
Palace of Holyroodhouse & Queen's Gallery,
    Edinburgh City, Coast & Countryside ................. 462
Paxton House, Gallery & Country Park, Borders ....... 453
Ring of Brodgar Stone Circle & Henge, Outer Islands ............ 492
Rothesay Castle, West Highlands & Islands ............. 482
St Andrews Castle, Perthshire/Fife ........................ 476
St Andrews Cathedral, Perthshire/Fife .................... 476
St Blane's Church, West Highlands & Islands ........... 482
St Machar's Cathedral Transepts, Grampian Highlands ........... 487
Scone Palace & Grounds, Perthshire/Fife ................ 473
Skara Brae & Skaill House, Outer Islands ............... 493
Smailholm Tower, Borders .................................... 453
Spynie Palace, Grampian Highlands ....................... 487
Stirling Castle, West Highlands & Islands ............... 483
Sweetheart Abbey, SW Scotland ........................... 459
Tantallon Castle, Edinburgh City, Coast & Countryside .......... 467
Tolquhon Castle, Grampian Highlands .................... 487
Torosay Castle & Gardens, West Highlands & Islands ............ 483

Tower of Hallbar, Greater Glasgow & Clyde Valley ................... 469
Urquhart Castle, Highlands & Skye ........................................... 491
Welch Winter Gardens, David – Duthie Park,
    Grampian Highlands ............................................................. 487

# WALES

## NORTH WALES

Beaumaris Castle ................................................................. 496
Bodelwyddan Castle ........................................................... 496
Bryn Bras Castle ................................................................. 496
Caernarfon Castle ............................................................... 497
Cochwillan Old Hall ............................................................ 497
Conwy Castle ..................................................................... 497
Criccieth Castle .................................................................. 497
Denbigh Castle ................................................................... 498
Dolwyddelan Castle ............................................................ 498
Fferm ................................................................................ 498
Hafod ................................................................................ 498
Harlech Castle .................................................................... 499
Hartsheath ........................................................................ 499
Iscoyd Park ........................................................................ 499
St Asaph Cathedral ............................................................ 500
Valle Crucis Abbey ............................................................. 501

## SOUTH WALES

Aberglasney Gardens .......................................................... 502
Caerleon Roman Baths & Amphitheatre ................................ 503
Caerphilly Castle ................................................................ 503
Carreg Cennen Castle .......................................................... 504
Castell Coch ....................................................................... 504
Chepstow Castle ................................................................. 504
Cilgerran Castle .................................................................. 504
Dyffryn Gardens and Arboretum .......................................... 505
Fonmon Castle ................................................................... 506
Kidwelly Castle ................................................................... 506
Lamphey Bishop's Palace ..................................................... 506
National Botanic Garden of Wales, The ................................. 507
Pembroke Castle ................................................................. 507
Raglan Castle ..................................................................... 508
St Davids Bishop's Palace .................................................... 508
Strata Florida Abbey ........................................................... 508
Tintern Abbey .................................................................... 509
Usk Castle .......................................................................... 510
Weobley Castle ................................................................... 510
White Castle ...................................................................... 510

# NORTHERN IRELAND

Antrim Castle Gardens ........................................................ 514
Barons Court ...................................................................... 514
Castle Coole ....................................................................... 514
Castle Ward & Strangford Lough Wildlife Centre .................... 515
Crown Bar, The ................................................................... 515
Divis & The Black Mountain ................................................. 515
Killyleagh Castle ................................................................. 516
Mount Stewart ................................................................... 516
Rowallane Garden ............................................................... 516
Seaforde Gardens ............................................................... 516

© National Maritime Museum

Meridian Line & Observatory – National Maritime Museum, London

**visit hudsons guide online**

# Special Events

This is merely a selection of special events being staged in 2007 – more information can be obtained from individual property websites – for quick access to these sites visit: www.hudsonsguide.co.uk (this information is intended only as a guide, please check with individual properties before travelling).

## JANUARY

### 21
Weston Park, Shropshire
Albrighton Point-to-Point.

### 26-28
Sandon Hall, Staffordshire
Antiques Fair.

### 27-28
Tatton Park, Cheshire
Wedding Show (tel 01625 262800).

## FEBRUARY

### 10
Easton Walled Gardens, Lincolnshire
Snowdrop Connoisseurs' Day. Private tours of the snowdrop displays with Lady Cholmeley. Rare snowdrops will be available for sale (tel 01476 530063).

### 11
Kelmarsh Hall, Northamptonshire
Snowdrop Sunday.

Weston Park, Shropshire
Meynell & South Staffs Point-to-Point.

### 11-23
Easton Walled Gardens, Lincolnshire
Snowdrop Spectacular. Fantastic snowdrop banks and display of Amaryllis. Refreshments. Open 11am-4pm. £4 adults, children free. Tel 01476 530063 for further details.

### 12
Holme Pierrepont Hall, Nottinghamshire
Snowdrop Sunday.

### 14
Weston Park, Shropshire
St Valentine's Day Dining in the House.

### 15
Floors Castle, Borders
Snowdrop Festival.

### 19-23
Weald & Downland Open Air Museum, Sussex
February Fun Half Term Activities.

### 24-25
Great Dixter House & Gardens, Sussex
Snowdrop and Crocus Weekend, £6 (Annual Ticket Holders Free).

### 25
Wartnaby Gardens, Leicestershire & Rutland
Spring Plant Fair, 11am-3pm.

### 26
Great Dixter House & Gardens, Sussex
Study Day: 'Preparing your border for Spring and Summer – the practicalities' (tel 01797 252878).

## MARCH

### 2-4
Scone Palace & Grounds, Perthshire
Galloway Antiques Fair.

Tatton Park, Cheshire 38th Cheshire Spring Fine Art & Antiques Fair (tel 01277 214677).

Wilton House, Wiltshire
30th Annual Antiques Fair.

### 3-4
Great Dixter House & Gardens, Sussex
Snowdrop and Crocus Weekend, £6 (Annual Ticket Holders Free).

### 4
Kelmarsh Hall, Northamptonshire
Marie Curie Daffodil Run.

Weston Park, Shropshire
Springtime Walk and Lunch in the Stables.

### 11
Sandon Hall, Staffordshire
Spring Wedding Fayre.

### 18
Exbury Gardens & Steam Railway, Hampshire
Mothering Sunday Daffodils and Spring Train.

Weald & Downland Open Air Museum, Sussex
Open House on Mothering Sunday.

Weston Park, Shropshire
Mothering Sunday Lunch in the House. Mothering Sunday Walk and Lunch in the Stables.

### 19
Holme Pierrepont Hall, Nottinghamshire
Daffodil Sunday.

### 23-24
Boconnoc, Cornwall
Tour of Cornwall Rally weekend.

### 24-25
Exbury Gardens & Steam Railway, Hampshire
Steam Railway Open Weekend.

### 24-31
Compton Verney, Warwickshire Opulence and Anxiety – Landscape Paintings from the Royal Academy of Arts.

### 26
Great Dixter House & Gardens, Sussex
Study Day: 'Nursery Propagation Day' (tel 01797 252878).

### 31 March
Boconnoc, Cornwall
Cornwall Garden Society Spring Flower Show.

### 31 March
Exbury Gardens & Steam Railway, Hampshire
Spring New Forest Breakfast Walk.

# APRIL

**1**

Boconnoc, Cornwall
Cornwall Garden Society Spring Flower Show.

Cobham Hall, Kent
British Red Cross (+ House open 2-5pm).

Exbury Gardens & Steam Railway, Hampshire
Spring New Forest Breakfast Walk.

**1-13**

Borde Hill Garden, Park & Woodland, Sussex
Eggmazingly Easter.

**1-30**

Compton Verney, Warwickshire
Opulence and Anxiety – Landscape Paintings from the Royal Academy of Arts.

**6-9**

Arley Hall & Gardens, Cheshire
Easter with Winnie the Pooh.

Groombridge Place Gardens, Kent
Easter Eggstravaganza.

Scone Palace & Grounds, Perthshire
Easter Extravaganza Weekend.

Weald & Downland Open Air Museum, Sussex
Easter Festivities.

**6-15**

Hampton Court Palace, Surrey
Tudor Cookery.

**7**

The Ancient High House, Staffordshire
Easter Eggcentrics.

Sandon Hall, Staffordshire
Point-to-Point Races.

Weston Park, Shropshire
Easter Trail.

**7-9**

Burton Constable Hall, Yorkshire
Easter Egg Parkland Trail.

Exbury Gardens & Steam Railway, Hampshire
Easter Bunny Train.

Tatton Park, Cheshire
Easter Festival at Tatton Park incorporating Crafts and Country Shopping Fair (tel 01509 217444).

**8**

Floors Castle, Borders
Easter Eggstravaganza.

Stafford Castle & Visitor Centre, Staffordshire
Easter Eggscapades.

Traquair, Borders
Easter Egg Extravaganza.

**8-9**

Arundel Castle, Sussex
Medieval Tournament.

Eastnor Castle, Herefordshire
Egg-citing Easter Chicken Hunt.

Kelmarsh Hall, Northamptonshire
Country Fair.

Rockingham Castle, Northamptonshire
Children's Easter Egg Hunt and family fun quiz.

Tamworth Castle, Staffordshire
'Fashion through the ages'. Fun catwalk presentation in Great Hall.

Weston Park, Shropshire
Midlands Festival of Transport.

**9**

Chenies Manor House, Buckinghamshire
Easter Fun for Children, 2-5pm.

Holme Pierrepont Hall, Nottinghamshire
Tulip Sunday.

**10-13**

Exbury Gardens & Steam Railway, Hampshire
Plant Explorer Trails.

**13-15**

Weston Park, Shropshire
Spring Horse Trials.

**14-15**

Borde Hill Garden, Park & Woodland, Sussex
Spring Plant Fair.

Tatton Park, Cheshire
Lambing Weekend.

**15**

Cobham Hall, Kent
National Garden Scheme (+ House open 2-5pm).

**16**

Great Dixter House & Gardens, Sussex
Study Day: 'Good Planting and Border Management' (tel 01797 252878).

**20-30**

Ramster Gardens, Surrey
Embroidery Exhibition.

**21**

Weston Park, Shropshire
Head Gardener's "Handy Hints" and Lunch in the Stables.

**21-30**

Exbury Gardens & Steam Railway, Hampshire
'4 Seasons' Art at Exbury.

**26-30**

Renishaw Hall Gardens, Derbyshire
Bluebell Fortnight.

**29**

Beaulieu, Hampshire
Boatjumble & Boatworld.

Hole Park Gardens, Kent
NCCPG Plant Fair, 11am-6pm.

Weston Park, Shropshire
Jazz Sunday, Roast Lunch in the Stables.

# MAY

**1**

Ramster Gardens, Surrey
Embroidery Exhibition.

**1-13**

Renishaw Hall Gardens, Derbyshire
Bluebell Fortnight.

**1-22**

Exbury Gardens & Steam Railway, Hampshire
'4 Seasons' Art at Exbury.

**1-31**

Borde Hill Garden, Park & Woodland, Sussex
Sculptural Art in the Garden.

Compton Verney, Warwickshire
Opulence and Anxiety – Landscape Paintings from the Royal Academy of Arts.

**5**

Scone Palace & Grounds, Perthshire
MG Car Club Classic Tour – start point.

**5-7**

Exbury Gardens & Steam Railway, Hampshire
Spring Fair.

Hampton Court Palace, Surrey
Tudor Cookery.

**5-7**

Leonardslee Lakes & Gardens, Sussex
Bonsai Weekend.

Mapledurham House & Watermill,
Oxfordshire
Annual Craft Fair.

Raby Castle, Co Durham
Raby Castle Annual Orchid Show.

Tatton Park, Cheshire
The Design Weekend incorporating the Food
and Drink Festival (tel 01244 346347).

**6**

Athelhampton House & Gardens, Dorset
NCCPG Plant Sale.

Hole Park Gardens, Kent
Rolls Royce Enthusiast Club Rally,
11am-6pm.

Weston Park, Shropshire
Bluebell Walks and Lunch in the Stables.

**6-7**

Eastnor Castle, Herefordshire
'Armouritis' – Arms and Armour.

Easton Walled Gardens, Lincolnshire
The Easton Spring Plant & Gardening Fair
(tel 01476 530063).

Kelmarsh Hall, Northamptonshire
Hardy Plant Fair.

Kelmarsh Hall, Northamptonshire
Facets Textile Show.

Tamworth Castle, Staffordshire
World War I Re-enactment with the
Birmingham Pals.

Weald & Downland Open Air Museum,
Sussex
'Celebrate the Taste'.

**7**

Chenies Manor House, Buckinghamshire
Tulip Festival, 2-5pm.

Sandon Hall, Staffordshire
Garden/Plants Show.

**9-10**

Boconnoc, Cornwall
Spring Interiors Fair.

**10 May**

Kelmarsh Hall, Northamptonshire
Facets Textile Show.

**10-13**

Hatfield House, Hertfordshire
Living Crafts.

**12**

Weston Park, Shropshire
Dawn Chorus and Breakfast in the Stables.
Watercolour Painting 'Taster' Workshop.

**12-13**

Beaulieu, Hampshire
Spring Motormart & Autojumble.

Exbury Gardens & Steam Railway, Hampshire
Exbury at its Best New Forest Breakfast Walk.

Leonardslee Lakes & Gardens, Sussex
Centenary Weekend.

**14**

Great Dixter House & Gardens, Sussex
Study Day: 'Meadow Gardening' (tel 01797
252878).

**14-18**

Exbury Gardens & Steam Railway, Hampshire
Exbury evenings.

**19**

Weston Park, Shropshire
'Parkland Landscape' Watercolour Painting
Workshop.

**19-20**

Floors Castle, Borders
Floors Castle Horse Trials.

**20**

Boconnoc, Cornwall
St John Ambulance Mini Marathon.

Weston Park, Shropshire
Jazz Sunday Roast Lunch in the Stables.

**20-21**

Weald & Downland Open Air Museum,
Sussex
Sustainability Event.

**26**

Kingston Bagpuize House, Oxfordshire
Rare Plants Fair.

**26-27**

Arley Hall & Gardens, Cheshire
Arley Horse Trials & Country Fair.

Traquair, Borders
Traquair Medieval Fayre.

**27**

Scone Palace & Grounds, Perthshire
History with Puppets – Puppet Theatre.

**27-28**

Arundel Castle, Sussex
Jousting & Medieval Tournament.

Eastnor Castle, Herefordshire
Country & Steam Fair – 'Made in
Herefordshire'.

Holdenby House, Northamptonshire
Plant Fair, 11am-6pm.

Tamworth Castle, Staffordshire
Period Dancing Workshops.

Weston Park, Shropshire
The Midlands Pets and People Show.

**28**

Chenies Manor House, Buckinghamshire
Special Entertainment, 2-5pm.

**28-29**

Borde Hill Garden, Park & Woodland, Sussex
Borde Hill Horse Trials.

**28-31**

Weald & Downland Open Air Museum,
Sussex
Countryside Adventures Half Term Activities.

**28**

Wartnaby Gardens, Leicestershire & Rutland
Spring Plant Fair, 11am-4pm.

# JUNE

**1**

Weald & Downland Open Air Museum,
Sussex
Countryside Adventures Half Term Activities.

Weston Park, Shropshire
'Making A Face!' Lecture and Lunch in the
Stables.

**1-10**

Compton Verney, Warwickshire
Opulence and Anxiety – Landscape Paintings
from the Royal Academy of Arts.

**2-3**

Tatton Park, Cheshire
Classic and Performance Car Spectacular &
Giant Autojumble (tel 01565 723991).

## JUNE cont.

**3 June**

Borde Hill Garden, Park & Woodland, Sussex
Classic Car Show.

Burton Constable Hall, Yorkshire
Classic Car Rally.

Sandon Hall, Staffordshire
Illyrium – Open Air Theatre – "Wind in the Willows".

Stonor, Oxfordshire
VW Owners' Rally.

Weald & Downland Open Air Museum, Sussex
Heavy Horse Spectacular.

**7-10**

Bramham Park, Yorkshire
Bramham International Horse Trials.

Ripley Castle, Yorkshire
Grand Summer Sale.

Scone Palace & Grounds, Perthshire
Spirit of the Horse.

**8**

Kelmarsh Hall, Northamptonshire
Elgar Concert.

**9-10**

Cawdor Castle, Highlands & Skye
Special Gardens Weekend: guided tours of gardens.

Eastnor Castle, Herefordshire
Land Rover World Show (Deer Park).

Exbury Gardens & Steam Railway, Hampshire
Petal Fall Weekend (children free).

**10**

Rockingham Castle, Northamptonshire
Medieval Jousting.

Tatton Park, Cheshire
Orchid Show (tel 0113 289 3933).

**10-14**

Athelhampton House & Gardens, Dorset
Flower Festival.

**12-30**

Ripley Castle, Yorkshire
"Much Ado About Nothing."

**13**

Hole Park Gardens, Kent
Wine in the Garden, 5-8pm.

**15**

Kelmarsh Hall, Northamptonshire
Hot Air Balloons & Jazz.

**16**

Weston Park, Shropshire
Watercolour Painting 'Taster' Workshop.

**16-17**

Exbury Gardens & Steam Railway, Hampshire
Narrow Gauge in the Gardens.

Hatfield House, Hertfordshire
Rose Weekend.

Kelmarsh Hall, Northamptonshire
Rolls Royce Enthusiasts Annual Concours.

Tatton Park, Cheshire
Medieval Fayre.

Weston Park, Shropshire
International Model Air Show.

**17**

Wartnaby Gardens, Leicestershire & Rutland
Summer Plant Fair, 11am-4pm.

Weald & Downland Open Air Museum, Sussex
Fathers' Day 'Toys for the Boys!'.

Weston Park, Shropshire
Fathers' Day Sunday Roast Lunch in the Stables.

**20**

Weston Park, Shropshire
'Flowers' Watercolour Painting Workshop.

**21**

Tatton Park, Cheshire
"Comedy of Errors" produced by Theatre Set-Up.

**22-24**

Goodwood House, Sussex
Festival of Speed.

Kelmarsh Hall, Northamptonshire
Homes & Gardens Show.

**23**

Lamport Hall & Gardens, Northamptonshire
Theatre in the garden.

**23-24**

Arley Hall & Gardens, Cheshire
Arley Garden Festival.

Beaulieu, Hampshire
Motorcycle World.

**23-24**

Eastnor Castle, Herefordshire
Mountain Mayhem (Deer Park).

**24**

The Friars, Kent
Summer Fayre.

Lamport Hall & Gardens, Northamptonshire
Traditional jazz in the garden.

Weston Park, Shropshire
Staffordshire Healthy Living Walk. Jazz Sunday, Roast Lunch in the Stables.

**24-29**

Easton Walled Gardens, Lincolnshire
Sweet Pea Week (tel 01476 530063).

**27**

Weston Park, Shropshire
'Buildings' Watercolour Painting Workshop.

**28**

Kelmarsh Hall, Northamptonshire
RHS Garden Tour.

**28-30**

Stafford Castle & Visitor Centre, Staffordshire
Stafford Festival Shakespeare.

**29-30**

The Friars, Kent
Potters' Fayre.

Scone Palace & Grounds, Perthshire
Game Conservancy Scottish Fair.

**30**

Exbury Gardens & Steam Railway, Hampshire
Hampshire Food Festival Breakfast Walk.

Leonardslee Lakes & Gardens, Sussex
Vintage Engine Show.

Tatton Park, Cheshire
Stars and Stripes Classic American Car Show.

# JULY

## 1

Borde Hill Garden, Park & Woodland, Sussex
Borde Hill Plant Fair.

The Bowes Museum, Co Durham
Teesdale Brass Band Contest.

Exbury Gardens & Steam Railway, Hampshire
Hampshire Food Festival Breakfast Walk.

The Friars, Kent
Potters' Fayre.

Leonardslee Lakes & Gardens, Sussex
Vintage Engine Show.

Ripley Castle, Yorkshire
"Much Ado About Nothing."

Scone Palace & Grounds, Perthshire
Game Conservancy Scottish Fair.

Tatton Park, Cheshire
Stars and Stripes Classic American Car Show.

Weald & Downland Open Air Museum, Sussex
Early Music Afternoon.

## 1-14

Stafford Castle & Visitor Centre, Staffordshire
Stafford Festival Shakespeare.

## 3-4

Weston Park, Shropshire
'Trees & Water' Two Day Watercolour Painting Workshop.

## 4-5

Peckover House & Garden, Cambridgeshire
Wisbech Rose Fair.

## 6

Weston Park, Shropshire
'Weston and the Grand Tour' Lecture and Lunch in the Stables.

## 6-8

Tatton Park, Cheshire
13th Cheshire Summer Fine Art & Antiques Fair (tel 01277 214677).

## 7-8

Exbury Gardens & Steam Railway, Hampshire
1940s Weekend.

Floors Castle, Borders
Gardeners' Festival.

Tatton Park, Cheshire
1940s Day.

## 7-8

Weston Park, Shropshire
Midlands Gardeners' Weekend.

## 8

Burton Constable Hall, Yorkshire
Open Air Theatre – "Far from the Madding Crowd".

Weston Park, Shropshire
Cycling Fun Day – Le Tour de Weston 'London'.

## 8-9

Parham House & Gardens, Sussex
14th Annual Garden Weekend.

## 9

Great Dixter House & Gardens, Sussex
Study Day: 'Succession Planting in the Mixed Border' (tel 01797 252878).

## 11

Weston Park, Shropshire
Evening Gardens Tour with Wine.

## 12

Mapledurham House & Watermill, Oxfordshire
Open Air Theatre – "Much Ado About Nothing".

Weston Park, Shropshire
Watercolour Painting 'Taster' Workshop.

## 14

Arley Hall & Gardens, Cheshire
Concert on the Park.

Tatton Park, Cheshire
"Robin Hood" – open air theatre by Illyria.

Weston Park, Shropshire
'Buildings' Pen & Ink Drawing Workshop.

Wilton House, Wiltshire
BSO Fireworks Concert.

## 14-15

Leonardslee Lakes & Gardens, Sussex
Model Boat Regatta.

Tatton Park, Cheshire
Rare Breeds Weekend.

## 15

Burton Constable Hall, Yorkshire
Country Fair.

Chenies Manor House, Buckinghamshire
Plant & Garden Fair, 2-5pm (the Manor House opens 2pm).

## 15

Cobham Hall, Kent
National Garden Scheme (+ House open 2-5pm). Ellenor Foundation Charity Walk.

Sandon Hall, Staffordshire
Classic Car Show (admission includes gardens with access to Hall at extra cost).

Wassand Hall, Yorkshire
Afternoon Concert.

## 18-22

Tatton Park, Cheshire
RHS Flower Show.

## 19

Arley Hall & Gardens, Cheshire
Romeo and Juliet.

## 19-21

Kelmarsh Hall, Northamptonshire
Land Rover Enthusiasts Annual Show.

## 20

Eastnor Castle, Herefordshire
'Romeo & Juliet' performed by The Lord Chamberlain's Men.

## 21

Ripley Castle, Yorkshire
Last Night of the Proms.

## 20-22

Boconnoc, Cornwall
Liskeard Steam & Vintage Club Rally.

## 21

Hatfield House, Hertfordshire
Battle Proms Concert.

## 21-22

The Bowes Museum, Co Durham
Teesdale Food & Craft Festival.

Clovelly, Devon
Clovelly Maritime Festival – street entertainment and sailing trips in the "Kathleen & May", a vintage trading sailing vessel.

## 21-31

Exbury Gardens & Steam Railway, Hampshire
Summer Holiday Children's Trail.

## 22

Arundel Castle, Sussex
Siege of Arundel Castle 1643.

Eastnor Castle, Herefordshire
Totally Natural – Bug Hunts & Nature Trails.

## JULY cont.

**22**

Groombridge Place Gardens, Kent
Wings, Wheels & Steam.

Weald & Downland Open Air Museum, Sussex
Rare Breeds Show.

**28**

Exbury Gardens & Steam Railway, Hampshire
Chapterhouse Theatre Company – "Much Ado About Nothing".

Tatton Park, Cheshire
Hallé Fireworks and Light Spectacular – open air concert with the Hallé Orchestra.

Weston Park, Shropshire
Proms Spectacular.

**29**

Eastnor Castle, Herefordshire
Teddy Bears' Picnic.

Glynde Place, Sussex
Jaguar Cars Enthusiasts' Club.

Hopetoun House, Edinburgh City, Coast & Countryside
Summer Fair.

Tatton Park, Cheshire
Tatton Park Picnic Concert.

Weston Park, Shropshire
Cycling Fun Day – Le Tour de Weston 'Paris'. Jazz Sunday, Roast Lunch in the Stables.

**31**

Goodwood House, Sussex
Glorious Goodwood Races.

Tamworth Castle, Staffordshire
Children's Art Workshop.

# AUGUST

**1**

Cobham Hall, Kent
Summer Stroll at 7pm (guidebook tour and glass of wine, £5 pp – tel to book).

**1-2**

Tamworth Castle, Staffordshire
Butter Making Demonstrations.

**1-4**

Goodwood House, Sussex
Glorious Goodwood Races.

**1-31**

Borde Hill Garden, Park & Woodland, Sussex
Summer Fun for Children (Mon-Fri pm).

Exbury Gardens & Steam Railway, Hampshire
Summer Holiday Children's Trail.

Goodwood House, Sussex
'Scotland in Sussex' Exhibition.

**3**

Weston Park, Shropshire
'Restoration! From Civil War to Civilisation' Lecture and Lunch in the Stables.

**3-5**

Eastnor Castle, Herefordshire
The Big Chill Festival (Deer Park).

Hatfield House, Hertfordshire
Art in Clay.

**4**

Borde Hill Garden, Park & Woodland, Sussex
Proms.

Stonor, Oxfordshire
Classic Concert in the Park.

**4-5**

Arundel Castle, Sussex
Jousting & Medieval Tournament.

Exbury Gardens & Steam Railway, Hampshire
Teddy on the Train.

Traquair, Borders
Traquair Fair.

**5**

Athelhampton House & Gardens, Dorset
MG Car Club Rally.

The Friars, Kent
West Kent Classic Bike Show.

Groombridge Place Gardens, Kent
Hot Air Balloons & Ferraris.

Helmingham Hall Gardens, Suffolk
Festival of Classic and Sports Cars, 10am-5pm (tel 01473 890799).

Tatton Park, Cheshire
Fun Dog Show.

**7**

Tamworth Castle, Staffordshire
Children's Art Workshop.

**7-9**

Eastnor Castle, Herefordshire
Children's Summer Fun Days.

**8-9**

Tamworth Castle, Staffordshire
The Medieval Wise Woman.

**9**

Arley Hall & Gardens, Cheshire
"Little Women".

Eastnor Castle, Herefordshire
'The Wizard of Oz' – Children's Theatre, The Heartbreak Theatre Company.

**10**

Tatton Park, Cheshire
"The Hound of the Baskervilles" – Illyria open air theatre.

**11**

Wassand Hall, Yorkshire
Music & Mirth Review Evening.

**11-12**

Kelmarsh Hall, Northamptonshire
English Heritage 'Festival of History'.

**12**

Sandon Hall, Staffordshire
TVR Rally.

Tatton Park, Cheshire
VW North-West Car Show.

**12-17**

Arley Hall & Gardens, Cheshire
Children's Fun Week.

**14**

Tamworth Castle, Staffordshire
Children's Art Workshop.

**15-16**

Tamworth Castle, Staffordshire
Tea Making.

**16**

Arundel Castle, Sussex
Living History Day.

**17**

Tatton Park, Cheshire
"Much Ado About Nothing" – Illyria open air theatre.

**17-19**

Hatfield House, Hertfordshire
Hatfield House Country Show.

**18-19**

Borde Hill Garden, Park & Woodland, Sussex
Borde Hill Country Fair.

Eastnor Castle, Herefordshire
The Model & Hobby Spectacular (Deer Park).

Leonardslee Lakes & Gardens, Sussex
Model Boat Regatta.

Tatton Park, Cheshire
20th Vintage, Classic and Sports Car show
with Autojumble (tel 01565 723863).

Weston Park, Shropshire
V Festival.

**19**

Kelmarsh Hall, Northamptonshire
Cut Flower Day.

**21**

Arundel Castle, Sussex
Living History Day.

Tamworth Castle, Staffordshire
Children's Art Workshop.

**22**

Mapledurham House & Watermill,
Oxfordshire
Open Air Theatre – "Hansel and Gretel" and
"Jack and the Beanstalk".

**22-23**

Tamworth Castle, Staffordshire
Free guided tours.

**24-26**

Bramham Park, Yorkshire
Leeds Festival.

**24-27**

Stonor, Oxfordshire
Chilterns Craft Fair.

**25-26**

Borde Hill Garden, Park & Woodland, Sussex
Outdoor Theatre.

**25-27**

Exbury Gardens & Steam Railway, Hampshire
Exbury Scarecrow Festival.

Tatton Park, Cheshire
Tatton Park Country Show.

Weston Park, Shropshire
The Noddy Tour.

**26**

Exbury Gardens & Steam Railway, Hampshire
Chapterhouse Theatre Company – "A
Midsummer Night's Dream".

Floors Castle, Borders
Massed Pipe Band Day.

Weston Park, Shropshire
Jazz Sunday, Roast Lunch in the Stables.

**26-27**

Eastnor Castle, Herefordshire
Ghostly Ghoul Hunt.

Rockingham Castle, Northamptonshire
Vikings! Of Middle England.

Tamworth Castle, Staffordshire
14th Century Re-enactment.

**27**

Chenies Manor House, Buckinghamshire
Special Entertainment, 2-5pm.

**31**

Goodwood House, Sussex
Goodwood Revival.

# SEPTEMBER

**1-2**

Exbury Gardens & Steam Railway, Hampshire
Summer Holiday Children's Trail.

Goodwood House, Sussex
Goodwood Revival.

**1-30**

Goodwood House, Sussex
'Scotland in Sussex' Exhibition.

**2**

Sandon Hall, Staffordshire
British Mini Day Car Show (admission
includes gardens with access to Hall at extra
cost).

Weston Park, Shropshire
Jazz Sunday Roast Lunch in the Stables.

**3**

Great Dixter House & Gardens, Sussex
Study Day: 'Nursery Propagation Day'
(tel 01797 252878).

**8-9**

Beaulieu, Hampshire
International Autojumble.

**9**

Arundel Castle, Sussex
Living History Day.

Kelmarsh Hall, Northamptonshire
Kettering Rotary Club Country Fair.

Scone Palace & Grounds, Perthshire
Scottish Vintage Tractor and Engine Club
Show.

**10**

Great Dixter House & Gardens, Sussex
Study Day: 'Exotic Gardening' (tel 01797
252878).

**12**

Stonor, Oxfordshire
Evening Demonstration – Historical Dress.

**15-16**

Weston Park, Shropshire
Midland Game & Country Sports Fair.

**16**

Helmingham Hall Gardens, Suffolk
NCCPG Plant Sale, 10am-4pm.

**17**

Great Dixter House & Gardens, Sussex
Study Day: 'Good Planting and Border
Management' (tel 01797 252878).

**21-23**

Stonor, Oxfordshire
Stonor Flower Festival.

Tatton Park, Cheshire
38th Cheshire Autumn Fine Art & Antiques
Fair (tel 01277 214677).

**22-23**

Glynde Place, Sussex
Glynde Fine Food Festival.

Tatton Park, Cheshire
Harvest Festival at the Farm.

**23**

Kelmarsh Hall, Northamptonshire
2:09 Run.

**29**

Cawdor Castle, Highlands & Skye
'Living Food at Cawdor Castle', 10am-5pm.

**29-30**

Compton Verney, Warwickshire
The Naked Portrait in the 20th Century.

**30**

Hole Park Gardens, Kent
HPS Plant Fair, 2-6pm.

# OCTOBER

**1-31**

Compton Verney, Warwickshire
The Naked Portrait in the 20th Century.

Exbury Gardens & Steam Railway, Hampshire
Nerine (Jewel Lily) Display.

Leonardslee Lakes & Gardens, Sussex
Autumn Colours.

**4-7**

Weston Park, Shropshire
International Autumn Horse Trials.

**6-7**

Exbury Gardens & Steam Railway, Hampshire
Steam in the Gardens.

Weald & Downland Open Air Museum,
Sussex
Autumn Countryside Show.

**7**

Hole Park Gardens, Kent
Meet the Gardener, 2.30pm prompt
(£3 supplement payable).

**12**

Weston Park, Shropshire
'Staffordshire's Vanished Country Houses'
Lecture and Dinner in the Stables.

**13-14**

Exbury Gardens & Steam Railway, Hampshire
Big Draw Weekend (children free).

Tatton Park, Cheshire
Cheshire Crafts & Gifts Fair (tel 01509
217444).

**14**

Weston Park, Shropshire
Fungi Walks and Lunch in the Stables.

**15**

Weston Park, Shropshire
Silver Study Day and Lunch in the House.

**20-21**

Exbury Gardens & Steam Railway, Hampshire
New Forest Breakfast Walk and Fungi
Foray Events.

Tatton Park, Cheshire
Christmas Gift Fair (tel 01509 217444).

**21**

Exbury Gardens & Steam Railway, Hampshire
Fungi Foray.

Hole Park Gardens, Kent
Meet the Gardener, 2.30pm prompt
(£3 supplement payable).

Weston Park, Shropshire
Cancer Research UK 10.

**22-26**

Weald & Downland Open Air Museum,
Sussex
Autumn Action Half Term Activities.

**23-28**

Exbury Gardens & Steam Railway, Hampshire
Exbury Ghost Train.

Tatton Park, Cheshire
Halloween Hauntings at the Old Hall.

**24-25**

Arundel Castle, Sussex
Living History Day.

**26-27**

Groombridge Place Gardens, Kent
Halloween in the Spooky Forest.

**26-28**

Traquair, Borders
Traquair Halloween Experience.

**27**

Beaulieu, Hampshire
Fireworks Spectacular.

Weston Park, Shropshire
'Autumn Colour' Watercolour Painting
Workshop.

**27-28**

Arley Hall & Gardens, Cheshire
Pumpkin and Halloween Festival.

Scone Palace & Grounds, Perthshire
Halloween Weekend.

Tatton Park, Cheshire
North West Food Lovers' Festival.

**31**

Burton Constable Hall, Yorkshire
Halloween Ghost Tours.

# NOVEMBER

**1-30**

Compton Verney, Warwickshire
The Naked Portrait in the 20th Century.

**3**

Groombridge Place Gardens, Kent
Spectacular Fireworks.

**3-4**

Tatton Park, Cheshire
Christmas Shopping Fair (tel 01509 217444).

**4**

Weston Park, Shropshire
Bonfire & Firework Extravaganza.

**9-11**

Galloway Antiques Fair.

**10-11**

Weald & Downland Open Air Museum,
Sussex
'Pig to Pork'. Learn about jointing, salting
and using pork.

**11**

Sandon Hall, Staffordshire
Autumn Wedding Fayre.

**19-23**

Rockingham Castle, Northamptonshire
Victorian Christmas.

**23-25**

Hopetoun House, Edinburgh City, Coast &
Countryside
Christmas Fair.

**24-25**

Traquair, Borders
Christmas Opening.

# DECEMBER

### 1-2
Eastnor Castle, Herefordshire
Christmas at Eastnor.

### 1-9
Compton Verney, Warwickshire
The Naked Portrait in the 20th Century.

### 1-10
Arley Hall & Gardens, Cheshire
Christmas Floral Extravaganza.

### 2
Weald & Downland Open Air Museum, Sussex
Tree Dressing. Make a lantern (bring a jam jar) and join the procession to dress the trees as darkness falls.

Weston Park, Shropshire
Christmas Flowers Workshop and Lunch in the House.

### 6
Weston Park, Shropshire
Christmas Traditional Dining in the House.
Christmas Party Night in the Stables.

### 7
Weston Park, Shropshire
Christmas Dinner Dance in the House.
Christmas Party Night in the Stables.

### 8
Weston Park, Shropshire
Christmas Traditional Dining in the House.
Christmas Party Night in the Stables.

### 8-9
Exbury Gardens & Steam Railway, Hampshire
Exbury Santa Steam Specials.

Floors Castle, Borders
Christmas Winter Wonderland.

Scone Palace & Grounds, Perthshire
Christmas Weekend.

### 13-14
Weston Park, Shropshire
Christmas Traditional Dining in the House.
Christmas Party Night in the Stables.

### 15
Weston Park, Shropshire
Christmas Dinner Dance in the House.
Christmas Party Night in the Stables.

### 15-16
Exbury Gardens & Steam Railway, Hampshire
Exbury Santa Steam Specials.

### 20
Weston Park, Shropshire
Christmas Traditional Dining in the House.
Christmas Party Night in the Stables.

### 20-21
Kelmarsh Hall, Northamptonshire
Kelmarsh Christmas Fair.

### 21
Weston Park, Shropshire
Christmas Dinner Dance in the House.
Christmas Party Night in the Stables.

### 22
Weston Park, Shropshire
Christmas Traditional Dining in the House.
Christmas Party Night in the Stables.

### 23
The Bowes Museum, Co Durham
Victorian Christmas Market.

### 26-31
Weald & Downland Open Air Museum, Sussex
A Sussex Christmas.

Exbury Gardens & Steam Railway, Hampshire

MAP 15

MAP 16

MAP 17
SHETLAND ISLANDS

MAP 19
Greater London

MAP 20
Central London

MAP 21
Edinburgh & York

WESTERN ISLES

HIGHLANDS & SKYE

GRAMPIAN
HIGHLANDS

MAP 12

MAP 13

MAP 14

PERTHSHIRE / FIFE

WEST HIGHLANDS
& ISLANDS

ORKNEY ISLANDS

EDINBURGH

GREATER
GLASGOW

BORDERS

MAP 18

MAP 9

MAP 10

MAP 11

SOUTH WEST
SCOTLAND

NORTHUMBERLAND

TYNE & WEAR

NORTHERN
IRELAND

DURHAM

CUMBRIA

ISLE OF MAN

YORKSHIRE

REPUBLIC OF
IRELAND

LANCASHIRE

MAP 5

MAP 6

MAP 7

MAP 8

CHESHIRE

DERBYSHIRE

LINCOLNSHIRE

NORTH
WALES

NOTTINGHAMSHIRE

STAFFORDSHIRE

LEICESTERSHIRE

RUTLAND

NORFOLK

SHROPSHIRE

WEST
MIDLANDS

NORTHAMPTONSHIRE

CAMBRIDGESHIRE

SUFFOLK

WORCESTERSHIRE

WARWICKSHIRE

BEDFORDSHIRE

HEREFORDSHIRE

BUCKINGHAMSHIRE

HERTFORDSHIRE

ESSEX

SOUTH
WALES

GLOUCESTERSHIRE

OXFORDSHIRE

MAP 1

MAP 2

MAP 3

MAP 4

BERKSHIRE

GREATER
LONDON

WILTSHIRE

SURREY

SOMERSET

HAMPSHIRE

KENT

DEVON

DORSET

SUSSEX

ISLE OF WIGHT

CORNWALL

GUERNSEY

ISLES OF SCILLY

**Left:** Hafod Estate, Wales © Phil Smith

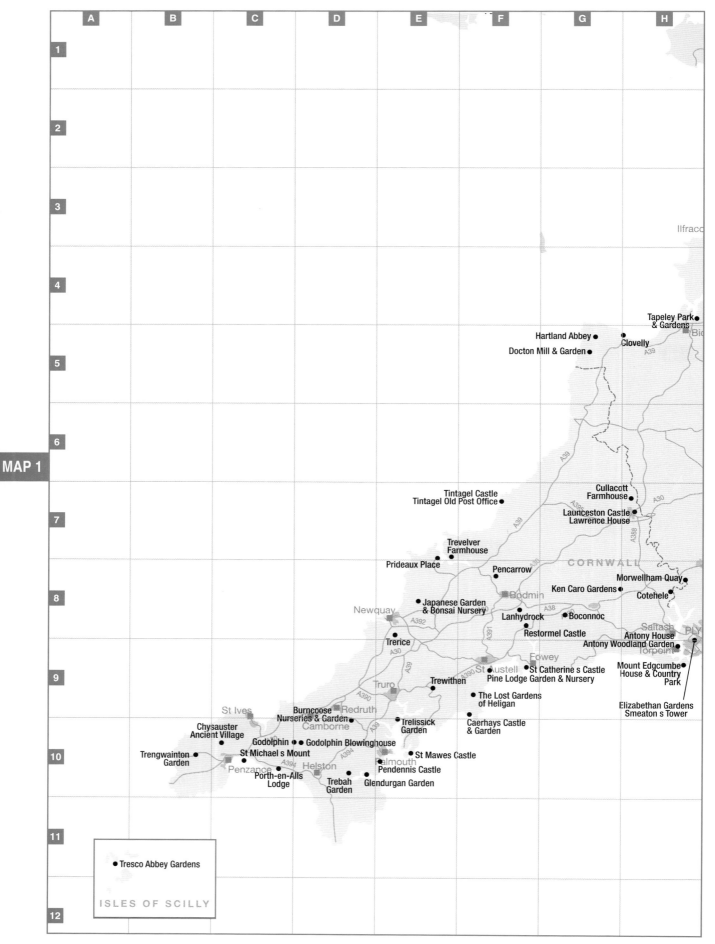

**MAP 1**

| | A | B | C | D | E | F | G | H |
|---|---|---|---|---|---|---|---|---|
| 1 | | | | | | | | |
| 2 | | | | | | | | |
| 3 | | | | | | | | Ilfraco |
| 4 | | | | | | | | |

Tapeley Park & Gardens ●

Hartland Abbey ● Clovelly ●

Docton Mill & Garden ● Bic

Tintagel Castle ●
Tintagel Old Post Office ●

Cullacott Farmhouse ●

Launceston Castle ●
Lawrence House

CORNWALL

Trevelver Farmhouse

Prideaux Place ● Pencarrow ● Morwellham Quay ●

Ken Caro Gardens ● Cotehele ●

Bodmin

Japanese Garden & Bonsai Nursery ●

Newquay

Lanhydrock ● Boconnoc ●

Restormel Castle ● Antony House ●
Antony Woodland Garden ●

Trerice ● Saltash PLY

Fowey Torpoint

St austell Mount Edgcumbe House & Country Park ●

Trewithen ● St Catherine s Castle ●
Pine Lodge Garden & Nursery

Truro

The Lost Gardens of Heligan ●

Elizabethan Gardens
Smeaton s Tower

St Ives

Burncoose Nurseries & Garden ● Redruth

Chysauster Ancient Village ● Camborne Trelissick Garden ●

Godolphin ● ● Godolphin Blowinghouse Caerhays Castle & Garden ●

Trengwainton Garden ● St Michael s Mount ●

St Mawes Castle ●

Penzance almouth
Helston Pendennis Castle ●

Porth-en-Alls Lodge Trebah Garden ● Glendurgan Garden ●

● Tresco Abbey Gardens

ISLES OF SCILLY

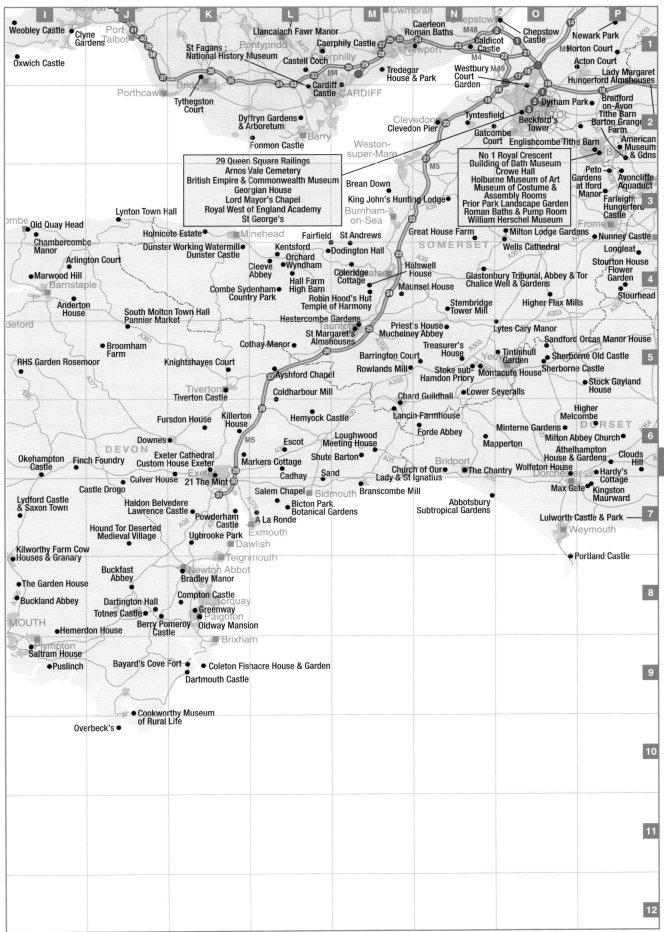

MAP 2

Weobley Castle • Clyne Gardens • Port Talbot
Oxwich Castle •

Llancaiach Fawr Manor •
St Fagans : National History Museum •
Castell Coch •
Caerphilly Castle •
Cardiff Castle • CARDIFF
Tythegston Court •

Caerleon Roman Baths •
Caldicot Castle •
Chepstow Castle •
Newark Park •
Horton Court •
Acton Court •
Lady Margaret Hungerford Almshouses •
Westbury Court Garden •
Tredegar House & Park •

Dyffryn Gardens & Arboretum •
Fonmon Castle •

Clevedon
Clevedon Pier •
Tyntesfield •
Beckford's Tower •
Gatcombe Court •
Englishcombe Tithe Barn •
Dyrham Park •
Bradford on-Avon
Tithe Barn
Barton Grange Farm •
American Museum & Gdns •
Peto Gardens at Iford Manor •
Avoncliffe Aquaduct •
Farleigh Hungerford Castle •

Weston-super-Mare

29 Queen Square Railings
Arnos Vale Cemetery
British Empire & Commonwealth Museum
Georgian House
Lord Mayor's Chapel
Royal West of England Academy
St George's

No 1 Royal Crescent
Building of Bath Museum
Crowe Hall
Holburne Museum of Art
Museum of Costume & Assembly Rooms
Prior Park Landscape Garden
Roman Baths & Pump Room
William Herschel Museum

Brean Down •
King John's Hunting Lodge •
Burnham-on-Sea

Lynton Town Hall •
Old Quay Head •
Chambercombe Manor •
Arlington Court •
Marwood Hill •
Anderton House •
Broomham Farm •
RHS Garden Rosemoor •

Holnicote Estate •
Minehead
Dunster Working Watermill •
Dunster Castle •
Cleeve Abbey •
Combe Sydenham Country Park •
South Molton Town Hall Pannier Market •
Cothay Manor •

Fairfield •
St Andrews •
Kentsford •
Orchard Wyndham •
Dodington Hall •
Coleridge Cottage •
Hall Farm •
High Barn •
Robin Hood's Hut •
Temple of Harmony •
Hestercombe Gardens •
Taunton
St Margaret's Almshouses •

Great House Farm •
Milton Lodge Gardens •
Nunney Castle •
Wells Cathedral •
Longleat •
Stourton House Flower Garden •
Halswell House •
Glastonbury Tribunal, Abbey & Tor •
Chalice Well & Gardens •
Maunsel House •
Stembridge Tower Mill •
Higher Flax Mills •
Stourhead •
Priest's House •
Muchelney Abbey •
Lytes Cary Manor •
SOMERSET

Knightshayes Court •
Ayshford Chapel •
Coldharbour Mill •
Tiverton
Tiverton Castle •
Fursdon House •
Killerton House •
Downes •
DEVON
Okehampton Castle •
Finch Foundry •
Exeter Cathedral •
Custom House Exeter •
Culver House •
Castle Drogo •
Haldon Belvedere •
Lawrence Castle •
Lydford Castle & Saxon Town •
Powderham Castle •
Hound Tor Deserted Medieval Village •
Ugbrooke Park •
Kilworthy Farm Cow Houses & Granary •

Barrington Court •
Treasurer's House •
Rowlands Mill •
Stoke sub-Hamdon Priory •
Montacute House •
Tintinhull Garden •
Sherborne Old Castle •
Sherborne Castle •
Sandford Orcas Manor House •
Stock Gayland House •
Chard Guildhall •
Lower Severalls •
Hemyock Castle •
Lancin Farmhouse •
Forde Abbey •
Escot •
Loughwood Meeting House •
Shute Barton •
Markers Cottage •
Cadhay •
Sand •
Salem Chapel •
Bicton Park Botanical Gardens •
A La Ronde •
Sidmouth
Branscombe Mill •
Church of Our Lady & St Ignatius •
The Chantry •
Mapperton •
Minterne Gardens •
Milton Abbey Church •
Athelhampton House & Gardens •
Wolfeton House •
Hardy's Cottage •
Max Gate •
Kingston Maurward •
Abbotsbury Subtropical Gardens •
Higher Melcombe •
DORSET
Clouds Hill •
Dorchester
Lulworth Castle & Park •
Weymouth
Portland Castle •

The Garden House •
Buckfast Abbey •
Bradley Manor •
Compton Castle •
Dartington Hall •
Greenway •
Buckland Abbey •
Totnes Castle •
Hemerdon House •
Berry Pomeroy Castle •
Oldway Mansion •
Paignton
Torquay
Brixham
PLYMOUTH
Saltram House •
Plympton
Puslinch •
Bayard's Cove Fort •
Coleton Fishacre House & Garden •
Dartmouth Castle •
Cookworthy Museum of Rural Life •
Overbeck's •

1
2
3
4
5
6
7
8
9
10
11
12

I J K L M N O P

MAP 3

MAP 4

MAP 5

A B C D E F G H

1

2
Holyhead
Beaumaris Castle
Plas Mawr
Conwy Castle
Aberconwy House
Llandudno
Colwyn Bay
Conwy
Abergele
Wern Isaf
Bangor
Penrhyn Castle
Cochwillan Old Hall
Bodnant Garden
Plas Newydd

3
Caernarfon Castle
Bryn Bras Castle
Gwydir Castle
Dolwyddelan Castle
Ty Mawr Wybrnant

4
Plas Brondanw Gardens
Criccieth Castle
Portmeirion
NORTH WALES
Plas yn Rhiw
Harlech Castle

5

6

7
Aberystwyth
Hafod

8
Strata Florida Abbey
Llanerchaeron

9
Cae Hir Gardens
SOUTH WALES

10
Cilgerran Castle

11
St Davids Cathedral
St Davids Bishops Palace
Carmarthen
Aberglasney Gardens
Carreg Cennen Castle
Carmarthen Castle
Dinefwr Park
Picton Castle
National Botanic Gardens of Wales
Ammanford
Laugharne Castle
Cresselly
Colby Woodland Garden
Kidwelly Castle
Milford Haven
Llanelli
Pembroke Castle
Tudor Merchant's House
Lamphey Bishop's Palace
Swansea
Aberdulais Falls
Neath

12

**MAP 6**

Croxteth Hall
Liverpool Cathedral
Liverpool Metropolitan
Cathedral of Christ the King
Liverpool Collegiate Apartments
West Derby Courthouse

1830 Warehouse
Heaton Hall
Law Library
Manchester Cathedral
Victoria Baths

2/3 Milk Street
Coleham Pumping Station
Old Mansion
Old Market Hall
Shrewsbury Abbey
Shrewsbury Castle
Shrewsbury Museum & Art Gallery

10 The Close
Erasmus Darwin House
St Mary's

MAP 7

A  B  C  D  E  F  G  H

1  A1(M)
Rotherham
Lyceum Theatre  Roche Abbey
Hodsock Priory
Gainsborough Old Hall
Louth
Westgate House
St Peter

2  Renishaw Hall Gardens
Drsomden
Barlborough Hall
Clumber Park
Worksop  Retford
Lincoln Medieval Bishop's Palace
Monksthorpe Chapel
Lincoln
Chesterfield
Sutton Scarsdale Hall
Bolsover Castle
Doddington Hall & Gardens
LINCOLNSHIRE
Gunby Hall
Staveley

3  Pleasley Colliery
Hardstoft Herb Garden
Hardwick Hall
Stainsby Mill
Hardwick Old Hall
Rufford Abbey
Carlton Hall
Auburn Hall
Tattershall Castle
Ashfield
NOTTINGHAMSHIRE
Winkburn Hall
Newark-on-Trent
arnfield Hall
Newstead Abbey
Papplewick Hall
Upton Hall
Newark Townhall
Kiln Warehouse
Leadenham House
Kyme Tower
Sibsey Trader Windmill
Ripley
Fulbeck Manor

4  D H Lawrence Heritage
Bennerley Viaduct
Ilkeston
NOTTINGHAM
Nottingham Castle
Holme Pierrepont Hall
Wollaton Hall & Park
Bridgford
Marston Hall
Belton House
Heckington Windmill
Boston
Fydell House Gates, Piers & Railings

5  Elvaston Castle Country Park
Church of St Mary
Grantham
Thrumpton Hall
Melbourne Hall
Staunton Harold Church
Calke Abbey
Ashby de La Zouch Castle
Belvoir Castle
Wartnaby Gardens
Melton Mowbray
7 King Street
Harlaxton Manor
Easton Walled Gardens
Woolsthorpe Manor
Grimsthorpe Castle Park & Gardens
Heggy's Cottage
Spalding
Ayscoughfee Hall Museum & Gardens
Sandringham
Castle Rising Castle
King's Lynn Custom House
St George's Guildhall
King's Lynn
Ruined Chapel of St Peter

6  Donington le Heath Manor House
Bradgate Park
LEICESTERSHIRE
Kirby Muxloe Castle
LEICESTER
Tomb of Andrew Lord Rollo
Rearsby Packhorse Bridge
Quenby Hall
Oakham Castle
RUTLAND
Stamford
Burghley House
Longthorpe Tower
Peterborough
Peterborough Cathedral
Minster Precincts
Thorpe Hall Hospice
Peckover House & Garden
Sulehay House
Wisbech
Downham Market
St Mary's Abbey

7  Arbury Hall
Lyddington Bede House
Laxton Hall
Prebendal Manor
Elton Hall
Rushton Triangular Lodge
Rockingham Castle
Kirby Hall
Deene Park
Southwick Hall
Lyveden New Bield
Eleanor Cross
Boughton House
CAMBRIDGESHIRE
Ely
Black Hostelry
Chapter House
Ely Cathedral
Old Palace
Oliver Cromwell's House
Prior Crauden's Chapel
Queen's Hall

8  Stanford Hall
Market Harborough
Kelmarsh Hall
Cottesbrooke
Lamport Hall
Coton Manor Garden
Haddonstone Show Gardens
Holdenby House
Harrowden Hall Gardens
Rushden
Kimbolton Castle
Buckden Towers
St Neots
Island Hall
The Manor, Hemingford Grey
Denny Abbey & Farmland Museum
Anglesey Abbey
Cambridge
Newmarket
University Botanic Garden
Madingley Post Mill
Huntingdon
St Ives

9  Compton Verney
Farnborough Hall
Clattercote Priory Farm
Sulgrave Manor
Upton House
Banbury
NORTHAMPTONSHIRE
Canons Ashby
Stoke Park Pavilions
Wakefield Lodge
Althorp
Northampton Cathedral
78 Derngate
Turvey House
Cowper & Newton Museum
Bedford
Sir John Jacob's Almshouse Chapel
Cecil Higgins Art Gallery
Bromham Mill
Moggerhanger Park
Swiss Garden
Wimpole Hall
Docwra's Manor Garden
Saffron
Haver

10  Brook Cottage
Broughton Castle
Swalcliffe Barn
Deddington Castle
Rousham House
BEDFORDSHIRE
Buckingham Chantry Chapel
BUCKINGHAMSHIRE
Stowe House
Stowe Landscape Gardens
Houghton House
Grey Mausoleum
Wrest Park Gardens
Letchworth Garden City
Cromer Windmill
Prior's Hall Barn
Audley End House & Gardens
John Webb's Windmill
Ditchley Park
Cornbury Park
Bicester
Boarstall Duck Decoy
Waddesdon Manor
Wotton House
Ashott
Claydon House
Old Church Tower of All Saints
Ford End Windmill
Pitstone Windmill
Woburn Abbey
Hitchin
Stevenage
Walkern Hall
Benington Lordship Gardens
Old Friends Meeting House
Saling Hall
Braintree

11  Blenheim Palace
Old Rectory Dovecote
Kidlington
Boarstall Tower
Shotover Park
Oxford
King's Head
Nether Winchendon House
Berkhamsted Castle
Walter Rothschild Zoological Museum
Ashridge Bridgewater Monument
Shaw's Corner
Knebworth
Woodhall Park
Welwyn
Hertford Museum
Forge Museum
Scott's Grotto
HERTFORDSHIRE
Gorhambury
St Albans
Hatfield House
Old Clockhouse
Chelmsford Cathedral
Gardens of Easton Lodge
Great Dunmow Maltings

12  Corpus Christi College
Christ Church Cathedral
Martyrs' Memorial
Kingston Bagpuize
26A East St Helen Street
Aston Martin Club
Long Crendon Courthouse
Rycote Chapel
Wheatley
Hughenden Manor
Amersham
Redbournbury Mill
Berkhamsted Castle & Town Hall
All Saints Pastoral Centre
Chenies Manor House
Tring
Folly Arch
Capel Manor Gardens
Copped Hall
Myddelton House Gardens
Forty Hall
Waltham Abbey Gatehouse & Bridge
Ingatestone Hall
Hylands House
Brentwood
Cathedral & Abbey Church of St Albans
Redbourn
Hoddesdon

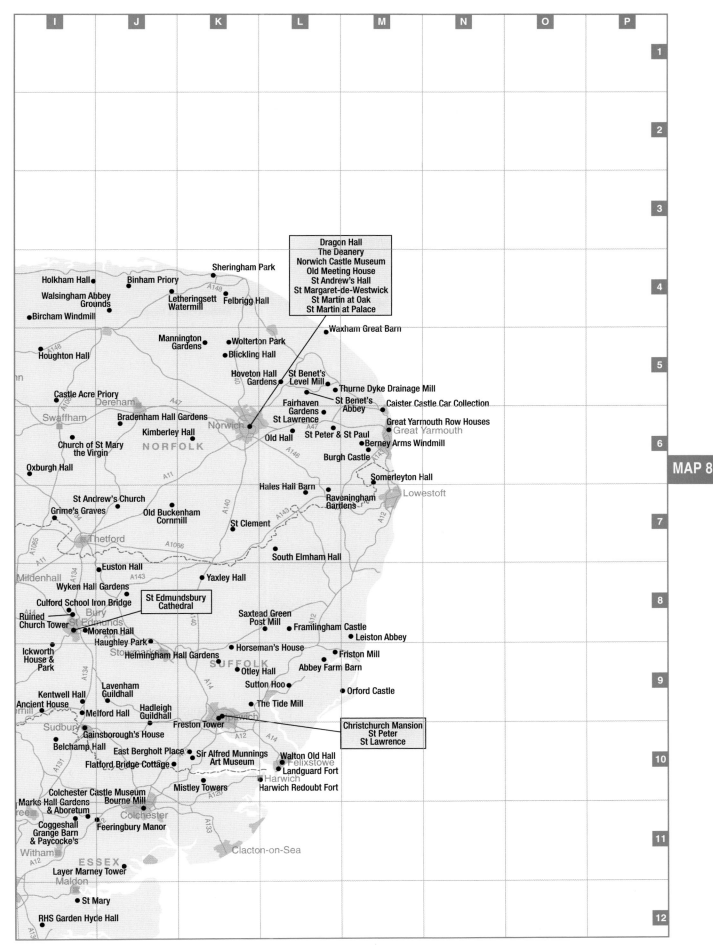

I   J   K   L   M   N   O   P

1
2
3
4
5
6
7
8
9
10
11
12

**MAP 8**

Holkham Hall
Binham Priory
Sheringham Park
Walsingham Abbey Grounds
Letheringsett Watermill
Felbrigg Hall
Bircham Windmill
A148

Dragon Hall
The Deanery
Norwich Castle Museum
Old Meeting House
St Andrew's Hall
St Margaret-de-Westwick
St Martin at Oak
St Martin at Palace

Mannington Gardens
Wolterton Park
Houghton Hall
Blickling Hall
Waxham Great Barn

Castle Acre Priory
Dereham
A47
Hoveton Hall Gardens
St Benet's Level Mill
Thurne Dyke Drainage Mill
Swaffham
Bradenham Hall Gardens
Fairhaven Gardens
St Benet's Abbey
Caister Castle Car Collection
Kimberley Hall
Norwich
St Lawrence
Great Yarmouth Row Houses
Church of St Mary the Virgin
NORFOLK
Old Hall
St Peter & St Paul
Great Yarmouth
Oxburgh Hall
A11
A146
Berney Arms Windmill
Burgh Castle
A143

Somerleyton Hall
St Andrew's Church
Lowestoft
Grime's Graves
Old Buckenham Cornmill
A140
Hales Hall Barn
Raveningham Gardens
A12
Thetford
A1066
St Clement
A143

South Elmham Hall

Euston Hall
Yaxley Hall
A143
Mildenhall
A134
Wyken Hall Gardens
Culford School Iron Bridge
St Edmundsbury Cathedral
Ruined Church Tower
Bury St Edmunds
Saxtead Green Post Mill
A12
Moreton Hall
Framlingham Castle
Haughley Park
Leiston Abbey
Ickworth House & Park
Stowmarket
Helmingham Hall Gardens
Horseman's House
Friston Mill
SUFFOLK
Abbey Farm Barn
Otley Hall
Kentwell Hall
Lavenham Guildhall
Sutton Hoo
A14
Ancient House
Orford Castle
Melford Hall
Hadleigh Guildhall
The Tide Mill
Sudbury
Freston Tower
Ipswich
Christchurch Mansion
St Peter
St Lawrence
Gainsborough's House
A12
A14
Belchamp Hall
East Bergholt Place
Sir Alfred Munnings Art Museum
Walton Old Hall
Felixstowe
Flatford Bridge Cottage
Landguard Fort
A131
Mistley Towers
Harwich
Colchester Castle Museum
A120
Harwich Redoubt Fort
Bourne Mill
Marks Hall Gardens & Aboretum
Tree
Colchester
Coggeshall Grange Barn & Paycocke's
Feeringbury Manor
A133
Witham
A12
ESSEX
Clacton-on-Sea
Layer Marney Tower
Maldon
St Mary
RHS Garden Hyde Hall
A13

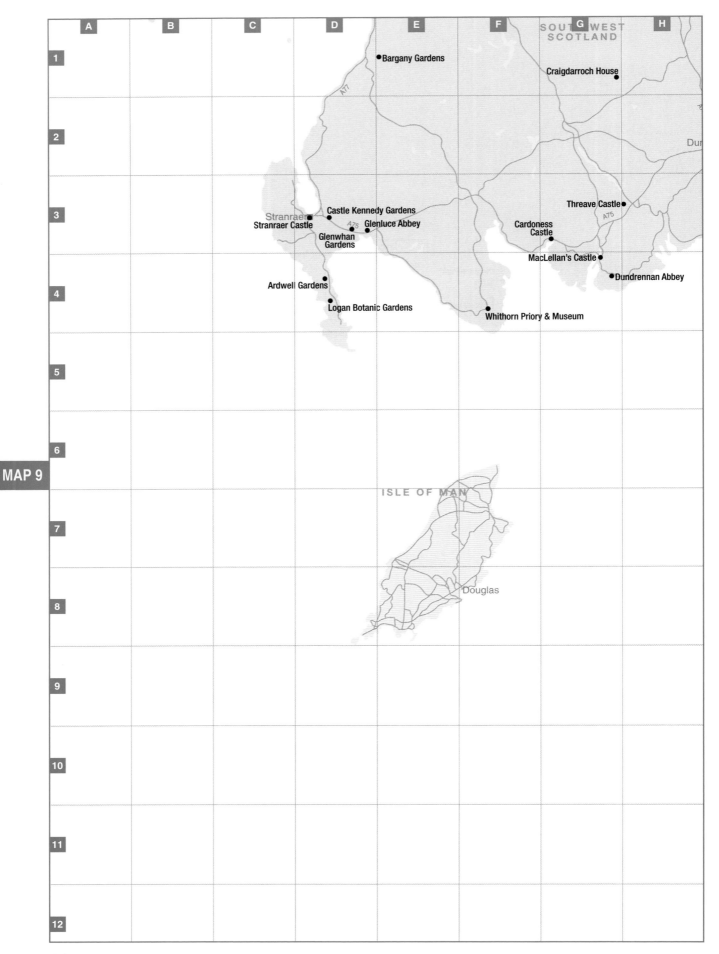

Bargany Gardens

Craigdarroch House

Dur

Threave Castle

Castle Kennedy Gardens

Stranraer
Stranraer Castle

Glenluce Abbey

Cardoness
Castle

Glenwhan
Gardens

MacLellan's Castle

Dundrennan Abbey

Ardwell Gardens

Logan Botanic Gardens

Whithorn Priory & Museum

MAP 9

ISLE OF MAN

Douglas

MAP 10

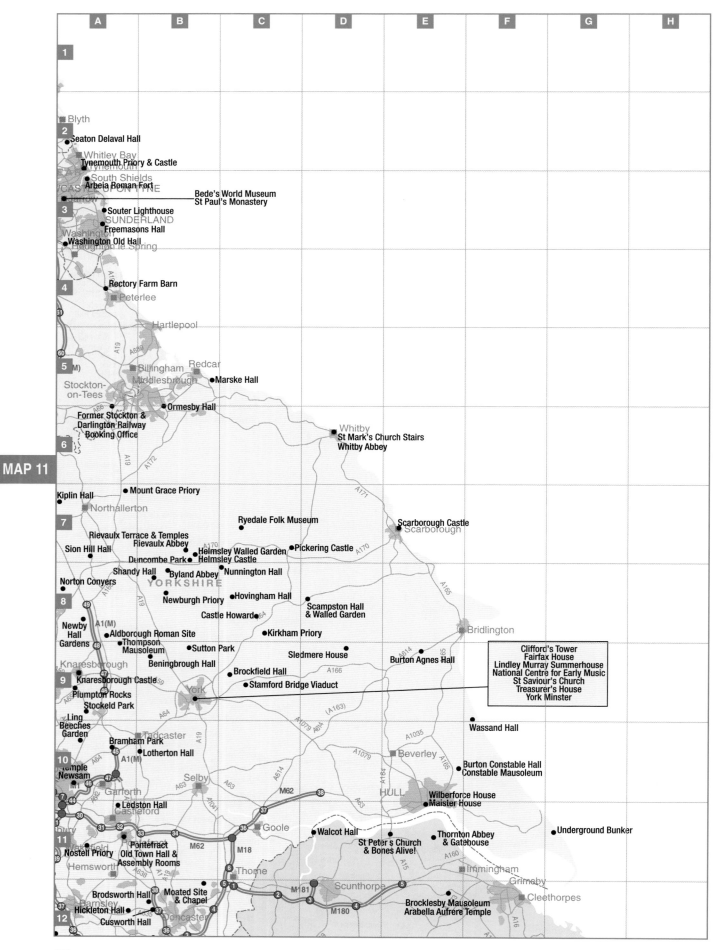

MAP 11

A · B · C · D · E · F · G · H

Blyth
Seaton Delaval Hall
Whitley Bay
Tynemouth Priory & Castle
Tynemouth
South Shields
Arbeia Roman Fort
NEWCASTLE UPON TYNE
Jarrow
Bede's World Museum
St Paul's Monastery
SUNDERLAND
Souter Lighthouse
Freemasons Hall
Washington
Washington Old Hall
Houghton le Spring

Rectory Farm Barn
Peterlee

Hartlepool

Billingham
Middlesbrough
Redcar
Stockton-on-Tees
Marske Hall
Ormesby Hall
Former Stockton &
Darlington Railway
Booking Office

Whitby
St Mark's Church Stairs
Whitby Abbey

Kiplin Hall
Mount Grace Priory
Northallerton

Ryedale Folk Museum
Scarborough Castle
Scarborough

Rievaulx Terrace & Temples
Rievaulx Abbey
Sion Hill Hall
Helmsley Walled Garden
Pickering Castle
Duncombe Park
Helmsley Castle
Shandy Hall
Byland Abbey
Nunnington Hall
Norton Conyers
YORKSHIRE
Newburgh Priory
Hovingham Hall
Scampston Hall
& Walled Garden

Newby
Hall
Gardens
Aldborough Roman Site
Castle Howard
Bridlington
Thompson
Mausoleum
Sutton Park
Kirkham Priory
Knaresborough
Beningbrough Hall
Sledmere House
Burton Agnes Hall
Knaresborough Castle
Brockfield Hall
York
Stamford Bridge Viaduct
Plumpton Rocks
Stockeld Park

Clifford's Tower
Fairfax House
Lindley Murray Summerhouse
National Centre for Early Music
St Saviour's Church
Treasurer's House
York Minster

Ling
Beeches
Garden
Tadcaster
Wassand Hall
Bramham Park
Lotherton Hall
Beverley
Temple
Newsam
Selby
Burton Constable Hall
Constable Mausoleum
Garforth
HULL
Wilberforce House
Maister House
Ledston Hall
Castleford
Underground Bunker
Goole
Walcot Hall
Pontefract
Old Town Hall &
Assembly Rooms
Thorne
St Peter's Church
& Bones Alive!
Thornton Abbey
& Gatehouse
Nostell Priory
Hemsworth
Immingham
Grimsby
Scunthorpe
Cleethorpes
Brodsworth Hall
Moated Site
& Chapel
Hickleton Hall
Doncaster
Brocklesby Mausoleum
Arabella Aufrère Temple
Cusworth Hall

1

A830

2

3

A828

Castle Stalker

Barcaldine Castle

4

Torosay Castle
Dunstaffnage Castle
Duart Castle

Bonawe Iron Furnace

Angus's Garden

Iona Abbey

A816

5

6

**MAP 12**

A83

7

8

9

A83

Brodick Castle

10

11

12

MAP 13

I   J   K   L   M   N   O   P

1

● Dunnottar Castle

Arbuthnott
House ●

Edzell Castle
& Garden ●

2

House of Dun ●
Brechin Castle ●          ■ Montrose

Forfar ■          ● Dunninald

ORKNEY ISLANDS    Carrick House ●

Hollandstoun ●

Lady
Village ●

3

Arbroath Abbey ●
Arbroath

Twatt ●          ● Broch of Gurness

Whitehall ●

4

Broughty Castle ●

Skaill House ●
Skara Brae ●
Ring of Brodgar Stone ●          ● Maeshowe
Circle & Henge

Balfour
Balfour Castle ●

5

Strathtyrum House ●
St Andrews ●
St Andrews Castle ●
St Andrews Cathedral ●
● Cambo Gardens
Balcarres ●
● Kellie Castle & Garden
● Charleton House

Stromness ●

Tankerness House ●    Kirkwall ●
Bishop's Palace
Earl's Palace

Gritley ●

6

MAP 14

Red Row ●
Dirleton Castle ●
Tantallon Castle ●
Greywalls ●          Gosford House
Harelaw Farmhouse
Preston Mill
Amisfield ● Beanston
Mains    ● Hailes Castle
Lennoxlove
House ●

St Margaret's
Hope ●

Longhope ●

7

EDINBURGH

● Dunglass Collegiate Church

8

● Ayton Castle ●

Duns Castle ●     ● Paxton House
Manderston ●

Berwick Barracks
Berwick Ramparts
Berwick-upon-Tweed

9

Thirlestane Castle ●

Norham Castle ●

Melrose Abbey ●
Old Gala
House ●
Galashiels
Mellerstain
House ●
Hirsel
Gardens ●
● Etal Castle
Lindisfarne Priory ●
● Lindisfarne Castle

Smailholm Tower ●
● Floors Castle
● Mertoun Gardens
Lady Waterford Hall
& Murals ●
Belford Hall ●

St Cuthbert's Chapel ●
Bamburgh Castle ●

10

Abbotsford ●  Dryburgh
Abbey ●
Halliwell's House
Museum ●
Monteviot House Gardens ●

Chillingham Castle ●

Preston Tower ●

Dunstanburgh Castle ●

Ferniehurst Castle ●  ● Jedburgh Abbey

Alnwick Castle ●
Alnwick Town Hall
St Michael's Pant ●

11

Drumlanrig's Tower ●

Edlingham Castle ●

Warkworth Hermitage
Warkworth Castle ●

BORDERS

Cragside ●

Lady's Well ●
NORTHUMBERLAND

● Brinkburn Priory

Eshott Hall ●

12

The Tower ●

609

MAP 15

WESTERN ISLES

Black House

Dunvegan Castle

Kisimul Castle

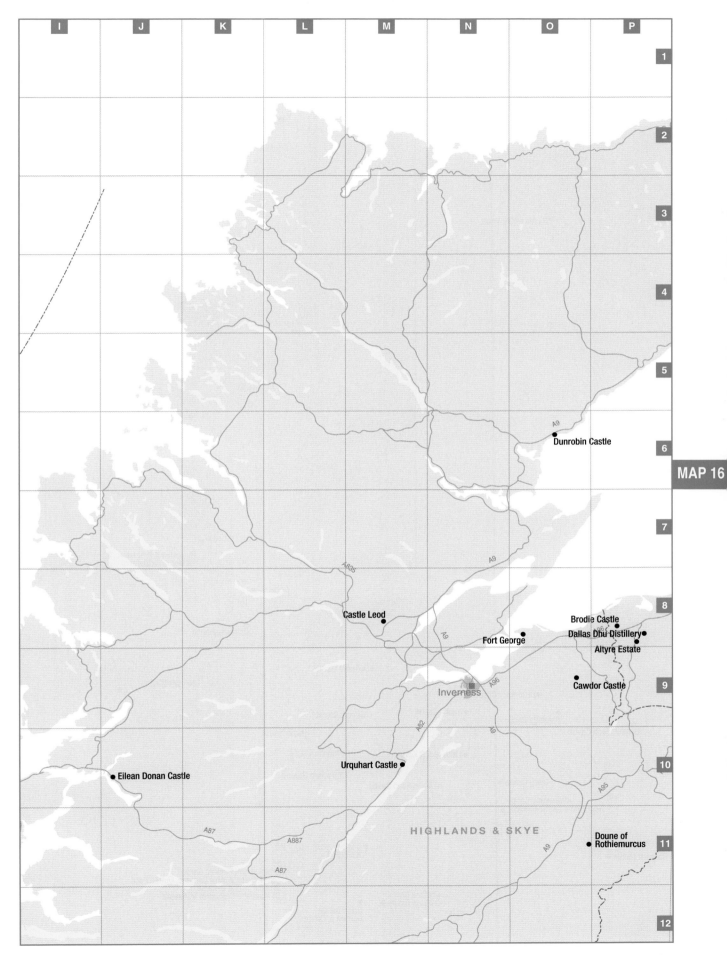

I    J    K    L    M    N    O    P

1
2
3
4
5

Dunrobin Castle

6

MAP 16

7

Castle Leod

Brodie Castle
Dallas Dhu Distillery

Fort George

Aityre Estate

8

Cawdor Castle

9

Inverness

Eilean Donan Castle

Urquhart Castle

10

A87

A887

HIGHLANDS & SKYE

Doune of
Rothiemurcus

11

A87

12

MAP 17

**Castle of Mey**

**Castle of Old Wick**

SHETLAND ISLANDS

Norwick
Haroldswick
Baltasound

Horra

Tresta

Mid
Yell

Burravoe

Voe
Symbister

Sandness

Girlsta
Walls

Garderhouse

Hillwell

Jarlshof Prehistoric &
Norse Settlement

Fraserburgh

Spynie Palace
Elgin
Elgin Cathedral

Duff House

Cairness House

Pluscarden Abbey

Craigston Castle

Delgatie Castle

Peterhead

Drummuir Castle

Huntly Castle

Fyvie Castle

Balvenie Castle

Haddo House

Ballindalloch Castle

Leith Hall & Garden

Tolquhon Castle

GRAMPIAN
HIGHLANDS

Pitmedden Garden

Craig Castle

Lickleyhead Castle

Kildrummy Castle
Kildrummy Castle Gardens

Corgarff Castle

Castle Fraser
& Garden

Aberdeen
Cruickshank Botanic Garden
David Welch Winter Gardens, Duthie Park
Provost Skene's House
St Machar's Cathedral Transepts

Crathes Castle
Garden & Estate

Drum Castle
Garden & Estate

Giant's
Causeway

Mussenden Temple ●● Hezlett House & Farmyard

Coleraine

LONDONDERRY

NORTHERN
IRELAND

Ballymena

Larne

Gray's Printing Press

Antrim Castle
Gardens

Patterson's
Spade Mill

Carrickfergus

Newtownabbey

Bangor

Barons Court

Springhill House &
Costume Collection

Cookstown

Divis & The Black Mountain
Crown Liqour Saloon

Ballywalter Park

Newtownards

Wellbrook
Beetling Mill

Mount Stewart

The Argory

Craigavon

Rowallane
Garden

Ardress House

Portadown

Templetown
Mausoleum

Castle Coole

Armagh

Killyleagh Castle

Castle Ward
Seaforde Gardens

Florence Court

Crom

Derrymore

Newry

Sligo

Cavan

Dundalk

Drogheda

Navan

REPUBLIC OF
IRELAND

DUBLIN

Dun Laoghaire

Galway

Bray

Portlaoise

LIMERICK

Carlow

Kilkenny

Tipperary

Clonmel

WATERFORD

CORK

MAP 18

# GREATER LONGON

**MAP 19**

D — Benington Lordship Gardens

E F G H

1 — St Pauls Walden Bury
Knebworth
Woodhall Park
Forge Museum
Gardens of Easton Lodge

2 — Shaw's Corner
Scott's Grotto

Gorhambury
Hatfield House
Old Clockhouse

3 — Cathedral & Abbey Church of St Albans
Torilla
Copped Hall
Waltham Abbey Gatehouse & Bridge

4 — Capel Manor Gardens
Myddelton House
Forty Hall

5 — Bruce Castle Museum
Valentines Mansion
William Morris Gallery
Brentwood Cathedral

6 — St Andrews Old Church

7 — Pitzhanger Manor-House
Dissenters' Chapel
Wapping Hydraulic Power Pumping Station
The House Mill
Bromley Hall
Rainham Hall
Himalaya Palace Cinema
Boston Manor House
Gunnersbury Park Museum
St Matthias
Eastbury Manor House
Lesnes Abbey
Osterley Park
Kew Bridge Steam Museum
Kew Gardens
Kew Palace
Hogarth s House
Royal Observatory
Queen s House
Building 40 Royal Military Academy
Syon Park

8 — The Octagon
Marble Hill House
Chiswick House
Richmond Weir & Lock
Strawberry Hill
Ham House
Dulwich College
Eltham Palace
Danson House
Hall Place
Red House

9 — Pope's Grotto
Landmark Arts Centre
Garricks Temple
Southside House
Morden Hall Park
Hampton Court Palace
Carew Manor Dovecote
Lullingstone Roman Villa
Lullingstone Castle
Claremont Landscape Garden
Whitehall
Honeywood Heritage Centre
Little Holland House
Home of Charles Darwin

10 — Painshill Park
RHS Garden Wisley
Titsey Place
Quebec House
Knole
Hatchlands Park
The Cobbe Collection
Squerryes Court
Emmetts Garden
Riverhill House
Chartwell
Ightham Mote

11 — Clandon
Polesden Lacey
Box Hill
Church House
Tonbridge Castle
Hever Castle
Chiddingstone Castle

12 — Goddards
Leith Hill
Penshurst Place

SURREY

614

CENTRAL LONDON

MAP 20

I J K L M

Highgate
Archway
Kenwood House
Highpoint
Upper Holloway
Finsbury Park

1

Fenton House
Burgh House
2 Willow Road
Hampstead
Keats House
Stoke Newington
Clissold House

2

The Round Chapel
St Paul's Steiner Project
Hackney Empire
Sutton House
Islington
Shoreditch

3

Swiss Cottage
The Roundhouse
Camden Town
Geffrye Museum

4

St John's Wood
Mappin Terrace Caf
King's Cross
Angel
City Rd
Bethnal Green

5

Kilburn
Chapel of the Hospital of St John & St Elizabeth
Regent's Park
Euston
Priory Church
Old St

Maida Vale
Brunswick Square Gardens
St John's Gate
LSO St Luke's
18 Folgate St

6

Marylebone
Foundling Museum
Bloomsbury

Paddington
Sir John Soane's Museum
Dr Johnson's House
St Paul's Cathedral
Whitechapel Art Gallery

Handel House Museum
College of Arms
Wiltons Music Hall
St Ethelburga's Centre

7

Oxford St
Mayfair
Queen's Chapel
Somerset House
Benjamin Franklin's House
Tower of London

Hyde Park
Bayswater Rd
Park Lane
Banqueting House
Southwark Cathedral & Footbridge
Tower Bridge Exhibition

Spencer House
Wellington Arch

Kensington Palace
Albert Memorial
Apsley House
Palace of Westminster
Kensington
Linley Sambourne House
Queen's Gallery
Buckingham Palace
Chapter House
Jewel Tower

8

Leighton House Museum
Royal Mews
Blewcoat School
St George's Cathedral
Bermondse

Westminster Cathedral
Elephant & Castle

9

Sloane Sq
Earls Court
Carlyle's House
Pimlico
Vauxhall
Kennington

Chelsea
Chelsea Physic Garden
Oval
Camberwell

10

Nine Elms
Brixton Academy

Fulham
Battersea
Stockwell

11

Fulham Palace & Museum
Clapham

12

MAP 21

# EDINBURGH

Royal Botanic Garden

A90
Queensferry Road

Charlotte Square

Scottish National Portrait Gallery

St Andrews Square

York Place

Broughton Street

Leith Walk

A1

Regent Road

The Georgian House

Queen Street

George Street

Hanover St

Dean Bridge

Princes Street

The Mound

GPO

Waverley Station

Palace of Holyroodhouse

Canongate

A702

Melville Street

Shandwick Place

Gladstone's Land

High Street

(Royal Mile)

St Mary's Episcopal Cathedral

Edinburgh Castle

Lawnmarket

Lothian Road

Johnston Terrace

George IV Bridge

Nicolson Street

A7/A68

A8

Haymarket Terrace

Dalry Road

Morrison Street

Lauriston Place

A702

Glasgow

Carlisle

# YORK

A19 Thirsk

Bootham

Gillygate

Lord Mayors Walk

A1036 (A64) Scarborough

Bootham Bar

Treasurer's House

Monkgate

St Maurice's Rd

St Leonards Place

York Minster

Museum Street

Duncombe Place

Deangate

Aldwark

CITY CENTRE

Railway Station

Station Road

River Ouse

Stonebow

Foss Islands Road

Micklegate

Ousegate

Piccadilly

Fossgate

Fairfax House

National Centre for Early Music

Walmgate

City Wall

Micklegate Bar

City Wall

Tower Street

Clifford's Tower

City Wall

A166 & A1079

A59

The Mount

A1036 (A64) Blossom St Leeds

Nunnery Lane

Mount School – Lindley Murray Summerhouse

Fisher-gate

Paragon Street

Bishopgate Street

# A

1 Royal Crescent, Bath, Somerset .................. 248
2 Willow Road, London ....................................... 79
2/3 Milk Street, Shropshire ............................ 549
7 Hammersmith Terrace –
      Home of Emery Walker, London ................. 79
7 King Street, Leicestershire ........................... 537
10 The Close, Staffordshire ............................ 552
13-13A Minster Yard, Lincolnshire ............... 537
18 Folgate Street, London ................................ 79
21 The Mint, Devon ........................................ 527
26A East St Helen Street, Oxfordshire ....... 155
29 Queen Square Railings, Somerset ........... 521
78 Derngate, Northamptonshire ..................... 329
1830 Warehouse, Greater Manchester .......... 532
A La Ronde, Devon ........................................ 212
Abberley Hall Clock Tower, Worcestershire ..... 560
Abbey Dore Court Garden, Herefordshire ...... 340
Abbey Farm Barn, Suffolk ............................ 553
Abbot Hall Art Gallery, Cumbria .................... 410
Abbotsbury Subtropical Gardens, Dorset ....... 224
Abbotsford, Borders ....................................... 450
Abercamlais, South Wales ............................. 503
Aberconwy House, North Wales ..................... 496
Aberdour Castle, Perthshire/Fife ................... 474
Aberdulais Falls, South Wales ...................... 503
Aberglasney Gardens, South Wales .............. 502
Acorn Bank Garden & Watermill, Cumbria .... 414
Acton Burnell Castle, Shropshire .................. 344
Acton Court, Gloucestershire ........................ 530
Adlington Hall, Cheshire .................... 402 & 523
Aiskew Water Cornmill, Yorkshire ................. 544
Albert Memorial, London ................................. 79
Aldborough Roman Site, Yorkshire ............... 385
Alfriston Clergy House, Sussex ..................... 179
All Saints Pastoral Centre, Hertfordshire ....... 534
All Saints Redundant Church, Kent ............... 535
Alnwick Castle, Northumberland .................... 432
Alnwick Town Hall, Northumberland .............. 547
Althorp, Northamptonshire ............................ 323
Altyre Estate, Grampian Highlands ............... 484
American Museum & Gardens, Somerset ....... 248
Amisfield Mains, Edinburgh City,
      Coast & Countryside ................................ 463
Ancient High House, The, Staffordshire ......... 350
Ancient House, The, Suffolk .......................... 295
Anderton House, Devon ...................... 212 & 527
Anglesey Abbey, Gardens
      & Lode Mill, Cambridgeshire ................... 273
Angus's Garden, West Highlands & Islands ... 480
Anne of Cleves House, Sussex ...................... 179
Antony House & Garden and
      Antony Woodland Garden, Cornwall ........ 202
Antrim Castle Gardens, Ireland ..................... 514
Apsley House, London ..................................... 69
Arabella Aufrere Temple, Lincolnshire ........... 537
Arbeia Roman Fort, Tyne & Wear .................. 442
Arbroath Abbey, Perthshire/Fife ................... 474
Arbury Hall, Warwickshire ............................ 354
Arbuthnott House, Grampian Highlands ......... 484
Archbishop's Palace, The, Kent ..................... 536
Ardencraig Gardens, West Highlands
      & Islands ................................................ 480
Ardkinglas Estate, West Highlands & Islands ... 480
Ardington House, Oxfordshire ........................ 151
Ardress House, Ireland .................................. 514
Ardwell Gardens, SW Scotland ..................... 456
Argory, The, Ireland ..................................... 514
Argyll's Lodging, West Highlands & Islands .... 478
Arley Hall & Gardens, Cheshire .................... 403
Arlington Court, Devon .................................. 212
Arniston House, Edinburgh City,
      Coast & Countryside ................................ 463
Arnos Vale Cemetery, Somerset .................... 521
Arundel Castle, Sussex ................................. 169
Arundel Cathedral, Sussex ............................ 179
Ascott, Buckinghamshire ............................... 102
Ashby de la Zouch Castle,
      Leics & Rutland ...................................... 316
Ashdown House, Oxfordshire ......................... 155
Ashridge, Hertfordshire ................................. 285
Aske Hall, Yorkshire ..................................... 385

Assembly Rooms, Derbyshire ........................ 526
Aston Martin Heritage Trust, Oxfordshire ....... 548
Athelhampton House & Gardens, Dorset ........ 225
Attingham Park, Shropshire ................. 344 & 549
Aubourn Hall, Lincolnshire ............................ 319
Auchinleck House, SW Scotland .................... 456
Auckland Castle, Co Durham ........................ 430
Auckland Castle Deer House, Co Durham ..... 430
Audley End House & Gardens, Essex ........... 278
Austen's House, Jane, Hampshire .................. 112
Avebury Manor & Garden, Avebury Stone Circle
      & Alexander Keiller Museum, Wiltshire ..... 262
Avington Park, Hampshire .................. 112 & 533
Avoncliffe Aqueduct, Wiltshire ...................... 559
Aydon Castle, Northumberland ...................... 436
Aylesford Priory, Kent .................................. 535
Ayscoughfee Hall Museum & Gardens,
      Lincolnshire ........................................... 319
Ayshford Chapel, Devon ............................... 527
Ayton Castle, Borders ................................... 450

# B

1066 Battle of Hastings Abbey
      and Battlefield, Sussex .............................180
Bache House Farm, Cheshire .........................523
Back to Backs, West Midlands .......................367
Baddesley Clinton, Warwickshire ................... 355
Bagshaw Museum, Yorkshire .......................... 385
Balcarres, Perthshire/Fife ............................. 474
Balfluig Castle, Grampian Highlands............... 484
Balfour Castle, Outer Islands ........................ 492
Balgonie Castle, Perthshire/Fife .................... 474
Balhousie Castle (Black Watch Museum),
      Perthshire/Fife ....................................... 474
Ballindalloch Castle, Highlands & Skye .......... 490
Balloch Castle Country Park, West Highlands
      & Islands ................................................ 480
Ballywalter Park, Ireland .............................. 514
Balmoral Castle (Grounds & Exhibitions),
      Grampian Highlands................................. 484
Balvenie Castle, Grampian Highlands ............. 484
Bamburgh Castle, Northumberland ................. 433
Banqueting House, The, London ...................... 79
Baptist Chapel, Oxfordshire .......................... 548
Bargany Gardens, SW Scotland ..................... 456
Barlaston Hall, Staffordshire ......................... 552
Barlborough Hall, Derbyshire ........................ 526
Barn at Howbury Farm, Kent ........................ 535
Barnard Castle, Co Durham .......................... 430
Barnard Castle Market Cross, Co Durham ...... 529
Barons Court, Ireland ................................... 514
Barrington Court, Somerset ........................... 249
Barton Grange Farm West Barn, Wiltshire ...... 559
Basildon Park, Berkshire......................... 96 & 521
Basing House, Hampshire............................... 113
Bateman's, Sussex ....................................... 170
Bath Assembly Rooms, Somerset ................... 551
Batsford Arboretum, Gloucestershire.............. 238
Bayard's Cove Fort, Devon ........................... 212
Bayham Old Abbey, Sussex .......................... 180
Beanston, Edinburgh City,
      Coast & Countryside ................................ 463
Beatrix Potter Gallery, Cumbria .................... 414
Beaulieu, Hampshire ............................. 108/109
Beaumaris Castle, North Wales ..................... 496
Beckford's Tower & Museum, Somerset ......... 249
Bede's World Museum, Tyne & Wear ............. 442
Bedgebury National Pinetum, Kent ................ 139
Beeston Castle, Cheshire .............................. 405
Belchamp Hall, Suffolk ................................. 295
Belford Hall, Northumberland ........................ 547
Belmont House & Gardens, Kent ................... 139
Belmont Hall, Cheshire ................................. 523
Belsay Hall, Castle & Gardens,
      Northumberland ...................................... 436
Belton House, Lincolnshire ............................ 320
Belvoir Castle, Leics & Rutland ..................... 313
Bembridge Windmill, Isle of Wight ............... 193
Beningbrough Hall & Gardens,
      Yorkshire ....................................... 385 & 544
Benington Lordship Gardens, Hertfordshire .... 285
Benmore Botanic Garden,
      West Highlands & Islands ........................ 480

Bennerley Viaduct, Derbyshire ...................... 526
Benthall Hall, Shropshire ..................... 344 & 549
Berkeley Castle, Gloucestershire ................... 235
Berkhamsted Castle, Hertfordshire ................ 285
Berkhamsted Town Hall, Hertfordshire .......... 534
Berney Arms Windmill, Norfolk ..................... 289
Berrington Hall, Herefordshire ...................... 338
Berry Pomeroy Castle, Devon ....................... 212
Berwick Barracks, Northumberland ............... 436
Berwick Ramparts, Northumberland .............. 436
Bessie Surtees House, Tyne & Wear ............. 442
Bicton Park Botanical Gardens, Devon .......... 210
Biddulph Grange Garden,
      Staffordshire .................................. 350 & 552
Big House, The, West Midlands ..................... 558
Bignor Roman Villa, Sussex .......................... 180
Binchester Roman Fort, Co Durham .............. 430
Binham Priory, Norfolk .................................. 289
Bircham Windmill, Norfolk ............................ 289
Birmingham Botanical Gardens
      & Glasshouses, The, West Midlands .......... 367
Bishop's & Earl's Palaces, Outer Islands .......... 492
Bishop's Waltham Palace, Hampshire ............ 113
Bishton Hall Doric Screen, Staffordshire ....... 552
Black Hostelry, The, Cambridgeshire ............. 522
Black House, Outer Islands ........................... 492
Blackburn Cathedral, Lancashire ................... 421
Blackfriars Priory, Gloucestershire ................ 238
Blackness Castle, Edinburgh City,
      Coast & Countryside ................................ 463
Blackwell – The Arts & Crafts House,
      Cumbria ................................................. 411
Blaenavon Ironworks, South Wales ................ 503
Blair Castle, Perthshire/Fife ......................... 470
Blandford Forum Town Hall
      & Corn Exchange, Dorset ........................ 529
Blenheim Palace, Oxfordshire .............. 152 & 548
Blewcoat School, London ................................ 80
Blickling Hall, Norfolk ................................... 289
Boarstall Duck Decoy, Buckinghamshire ......... 102
Boarstall Tower, Buckinghamshire ................. 102
Boathouse No. 6, Hampshire ......................... 533
Boconnoc, Cornwall ...................................... 202
Bodelwyddan Castle, North Wales ................. 496
Bodiam Castle, Sussex .................................. 181
Bodnant Garden, North Wales ....................... 496
Bodrhyddan, North Wales .............................. 496
Bolling Hall Museum, Yorkshire ..................... 558
Bolsover Castle, Derbyshire .......................... 308
Bolton Abbey, Yorkshire ............................... 385
Bolton Castle, Yorkshire ............................... 385
Bonawe Iron Furnace, West Highlands
      & Islands ................................................ 480
Borde Hill Garden, Park & Woodland,
      Sussex ................................................... 171
Boscobel House & The Royal Oak,
      Shropshire .............................................. 345
Boston Manor House, London .......................... 80
Boughton House, Northamptonshire ... 324 & 546
Boughton Monchelsea Place, Kent ................. 122
Bourne Mill, Essex ....................................... 279
Bourton House Garden, Gloucestershire ......... 238
Bowes Museum, The, Co Durham .................. 428
Bowhill House & Country Park, Borders ......... 446
Bowood House & Gardens, Wiltshire ............. 257
Box Hill, Surrey ........................................... 164
Boxgrove Priory, Sussex ............................... 181
Bradenham Hall Gardens, Norfolk .................. 289
Bradford-on-Avon Tithe Barn, Wiltshire ......... 262
Bradgate Park & Swithland Wood
      Country Park, Leics & Rutland .................. 316
Bradley Manor, Devon ................................... 213
Bramall Hall, Cheshire .................................. 523
Bramber Castle, Sussex ................................ 181
Bramham Park, Yorkshire .............................. 376
Bramham Park Lead Lads Temple, Yorkshire ... 558
Branklyn Garden, Perthshire/Fife .................. 474
Branscombe Manor Mill, The Old Bakery
      & Forge, Devon ...................................... 213
Brantwood, Cumbria ..................................... 414
Breamore Home Farm Tithe Barn, Hampshire . 533
Breamore House & Museum, Hampshire ........ 113
Brean Down, Somerset .................................. 249
Brechin Castle, Perthshire/Fife ...................... 474

Brentwood Cathedral, Essex ........................... 279
Bridgewater Monument, Hertfordshire ........... 534
Brighstone Shop & Museum, Isle of Wight ..... 193
Brinkburn Priory, Northumberland .................. 437
British Empire & Commonwealth
    Museum, Somerset ..................................... 521
Brixton Academy, London ............................... 539
Broadlands, Hampshire .................................. 113
Broadleas Gardens, Wiltshire .......................... 262
Broadway Tower, Worcestershire ..................... 369
Broch of Gurness, Outer Islands ..................... 492
Brockfield Hall, Yorkshire .............................. 386
Brockhampton Estate, Herefordshire .............. 340
Brocklesby Mausoleum, Lincolnshire ............... 537
Brodick Castle, SW Scotland .......................... 456
Brodie Castle, Grampian Highlands ................. 484
Brodsworth Hall & Gardens, Yorkshire ........... 377
Bromham Mill & Gallery, Bedfordshire ............ 271
Bromley Hall, London ................................... 539
Brontë Parsonage Museum, Yorkshire ............. 386
Brook Cottage, Oxfordshire ............................ 155
Broomham Farm, Devon ................................ 527
Broseley Pipeworks, Shropshire ...................... 550
Brough Castle, Cumbria ................................ 414
Brougham Castle, Cumbria ............................. 414
Broughton Castle, Oxfordshire ....................... 153
Broughton Hall, Yorkshire ............................. 386
Broughton Hall Conservatory, Merseyside ....... 542
Broughty Castle, Perthshire/Fife ..................... 474
Brownsea Island, Dorset ............................... 228
Browsholme Hall, Lancashire .............. 421 & 536
Bruce Castle Museum, London ............. 80 & 539
Brunswick Square Gardens, London ................ 539
Bryn Bras Castle, North Wales ....................... 496
Buckden Towers, Cambridgeshire .................... 522
Buckfast Abbey, Devon .................................. 213
Buckingham Chantry Chapel,
    Buckinghamshire ......................................... 102
Buckingham Palace, The State Rooms,
    The Queen's Gallery, The Royal Mews,
    London ......................................................... 70
Buckland Abbey, Devon.................................. 213
Building 40, London ...................................... 539
Building of Bath Museum,
    The, Somerset ............................................ 249
Buildwas Abbey, Shropshire ........................... 345
Burgh Castle, Norfolk ................................... 289
Burgh House, London .................................... 80
Burghley House, Lincolnshire ............... 317 & 537
Burncoose Nurseries & Garden, Cornwall ....... 202
Burns' Cottage, SW Scotland ......................... 456
Burrell Collection, Greater Glasgow
    & Clyde Valley .......................................... 468
Burton Agnes Hall & Gardens, Yorkshire ........ 387
Burton Constable Hall, Yorkshire ................... 378
Buscot Old Parsonage, Oxfordshire ................. 155
Buscot Park, Oxfordshire ............................... 155
Bushmead Priory, Bedfordshire ...................... 271
Byland Abbey, Yorkshire ................................ 387

## C

Cadhay, Devon .............................................. 214
Cae Hir Gardens, South Wales ....................... 503
Caerhays Castle & Garden, Cornwall ... 203 & 524
Caerlaverock Castle, SW Scotland .................. 456
Caerleon Roman Baths
    & Amphitheatre, South Wales ..................... 503
Caernarfon Castle, North Wales ..................... 497
Caerphilly Castle, South Wales ....................... 503
Cage, The, Cheshire ...................................... 523
Cairness House, Grampian Highlands ............... 484
Caister Castle Car Collection, Norfolk ............ 290
Caldicot Castle & Country Park, South Wales . 503
Calke Abbey, Derbyshire ..................... 308 & 526
Calshot, Hampshire ....................................... 533
Calshot Castle, Hampshire.............................. 113
Camber Castle, Sussex ................................... 181
Cambridge University Botanic Garden,
    Cambridgeshire ........................................... 273
Cannon Hall Museum, Park & Gardens,
    Yorkshire .................................................... 387
Canons Ashby, Northamptonshire ................... 329
Capel Manor Gardens, London ....................... 80

Capesthorne Hall, Cheshire ................. 404 & 523
Capheaton Hall, Northumberland .................... 437
Cardiff Castle, South Wales ........................... 503
Cardoness Castle, SW Scotland ...................... 456
Carew Manor Dovecote, London .......... 80 & 555
Carisbrooke Castle, Isle of Wight ................... 193
Carlisle Castle, Cumbria ................................ 414
Carlisle Cathedral, Cumbria ........................... 414
Carlton Hall, Nottinghamshire ........................ 334
Carlyle's House, London ................................ 80
Carmarthen Castle, South Wales ..................... 503
Carnfield Hall, Derbyshire ............................. 309
Carreg Cennen Castle, South Wales ............... 504
Carrick House, Outer Islands .......................... 492
Castell Coch, South Wales ............................. 504
Casterne Hall, Derbyshire .................... 350 & 526
Castle Acre Priory, Norfolk ........................... 290
Castle Bromwich Hall Gardens,
    West Midlands ............................................ 367
Castle Campbell, Perthshire/Fife ..................... 474
Castle Coole, Ireland ..................................... 514
Castle Drogo, Devon ..................................... 214
Castle Fraser & Garden, Grampian Highlands .. 484
Castle Howard, Yorkshire .................... 379 & 544
Castle Kennedy Gardens, SW Scotland ........... 457
Castle Leod, Highlands & Skye ....................... 490
Castle of Mey, Highlands & Skye .................... 490
Castle of Old Wick, Highlands & Skye ........... 490
Castle Rising Castle, Norfolk .......................... 290
Castle Stalker, West Highlands & Islands ........ 480
Castle Ward & Strangford Lough
    Wildlife Centre, Ireland .............................. 515
Cathedral & Abbey Church of St Alban,
    Hertfordshire .............................................. 285
Cathedral Footbridge, London ........................ 539
Catton Hall, Derbyshire ...................... 309 & 526
Cawdor Castle, Highlands & Skye ................... 488
Cawthorne Victoria Jubilee Museum,
    Yorkshire .................................................... 387
Cecil Higgins Art Gallery, Bedfordshire........... 271
Chalice Well & Gardens, The, Somerset .......... 249
Chambercombe Manor, Devon ....................... 215
Chandos Manor, Herefordshire ....................... 533
Chantry, The, Dorset ..................................... 529
Chapter House, The, Cambridgeshire .............. 522
Chapter House, London ................................. 81
Chard Guildhall, Somerset ............................. 551
Charlecote Park, Warwickshire ............. 362 & 557
Charleston, Sussex ........................................ 182
Charleton House, Perthshire/Fife .................... 474
Chart Gunpowder Mills, Kent ........................ 139
Chartwell, Kent ............................................ 123
Chastleton House, Oxfordshire ............. 156 & 531
Chatsworth, Derbyshire ................................. 304
Chavenage, Gloucestershire ................. 236 & 531
Cheddleton Flint Mill, Staffordshire ................ 553
Chedworth Roman Villa, Gloucestershire ........ 238
Chelmsford Cathedral, Essex .......................... 279
Chelsea Physic Garden, London ...................... 81
Chenies Manor House, Buckinghamshire.......... 102
Chepstow Castle, South Wales ....................... 504
Cherryburn – Thomas Bewick
    Birthplace, Northumberland ........................ 437
Chester Cathedral, Cheshire ........................... 405
Chester Roman Amphitheatre, Cheshire .......... 405
Chesters Roman Fort & Museum,
    Northumberland .......................................... 437
Chettle House, Dorset ................................... 228
Chichester Cathedral, Sussex .......................... 182
Chiddingstone Castle, Kent...................... 124/125
Chillingham Castle, Northumberland ............... 434
Chillington Hall, Staffordshire ............. 350 & 553
Chiltern Open Air Museum,
    Buckinghamshire ......................................... 103
Chipchase Castle, Northumberland ................. 437
Chirk Castle, North Wales ............................. 497
Chiswick House, London ................................ 71
Cholmondeley Castle Garden, Cheshire ......... 405
Christ Church Cathedral, Oxfordshire ............. 156
Christchurch Mansion, Suffolk ............. 295 & 553
Church Farmhouse Museum, London .............. 81
Church House, Kent ...................................... 535
Church of Our Lady & St Ignatius, Dorset ....... 228
Church of St Mary, Nottinghamshire ............... 548

Church of St Mary the Virgin, Norfolk ........... 542
Church of the Hospital of St John
    and St Elizabeth, London ............................ 539
Chysauster Ancient Village, Cornwall .............. 203
Cilgerran Castle, South Wales ........................ 504
Clandon Park/Hatchlands Park,
    Surrey ............................................... 160 & 555
Claremont Landscape Garden, Surrey ............. 164
Clattercote Priory Farm, Oxfordshire .............. 549
Claydon House, Buckinghamshire.................... 103
Claymills Pumping Engines, Staffordshire ........ 553
Cleeve Abbey, Somerset ................................ 249
Clevedon Pier, Somerset ................................ 551
Cliffe Castle, Yorkshire .................................. 387
Clifford's Tower, Yorkshire ............................. 387
Clifton Hall, Staffordshire .............................. 553
Clissold House, London ................................. 539
Clive Garden, The, Dorothy, Shropshire .......... 350
Cliveden, Buckinghamshire .................. 104 & 521
Cloisters, The, Wiltshire ................................ 560
Clouds Hill, Dorset ....................................... 228
Clovelly, Devon ............................................ 211
Clumber Park, Nottinghamshire ...................... 334
Clun Castle, Shropshire ................................. 345
Clyne Gardens, South Wales .......................... 504
Coanwood Friends Meeting House,
    Northumberland .......................................... 547
Cobbe Collection at Hatchlands, The, Surrey .. 161
Cobham Hall, Kent ....................................... 126
Cobham Hall & Dairy, Kent ........................... 535
Cochwillan Old Hall, North Wales .................. 497
Coggeshall Grange Barn, Essex ...................... 279
Colby Woodland Garden, South Wales ........... 504
Colchester Castle Museum, Essex ................... 279
Coleham Pumping Station, Shropshire ............. 345
Coldharbour Mill, Devon ............................... 528
Coleridge Cottage, Somerset .......................... 250
Coleton Fishacre House & Garden,
    Devon ........................................................ 215
College of Arms, London ...................... 81 & 539
Colzium House & Walled Garden,
    Greater Glasgow & Clyde Valley ................. 468
Combe Sydenham Country Park, Somerset .... 250
Combermere Abbey, Shropshire ........... 345 & 550
Compton Castle, Devon ................................. 216
Compton Verney, Warwickshire ...................... 362
Conisbrough Castle, Yorkshire ........................ 387
Conishead Priory & Buddhist Temple,
    Cumbria ..................................................... 414
Constable Burton Hall Gardens, Yorkshire ...... 388
Constable Mausoleum, Yorkshire .................... 544
Conwy Castle, North Wales ........................... 497
Cookworthy Museum of Rural Life
    in South Devon, Devon .............................. 528
Copped Hall, Essex ....................................... 279
Corbridge Roman Town, Northumberland ........ 437
Corehouse, Greater Glasgow & Clyde Valley ... 468
Corfe Castle, Dorset ..................................... 228
Corgarff Castle, Grampian Highlands .............. 484
Cornbury Park, Oxfordshire ........................... 549
Cornwall House, South Wales ........................ 504
Corsham Court, Wiltshire............................... 258
Cortachy Estate, Perthshire/Fife ..................... 474
Cotehele, Cornwall ............................. 200 & 524
Cothay Manor, Somerset ............................... 250
Coton Manor Garden, Northamptonshire ........ 329
Cottesbrooke Hall & Gardens,
    Northamptonshire ....................................... 330
Coughton Court, Warwickshire ....................... 363
Cound Hall, Shropshire ................................. 345
Coventry Cathedral, West Midlands ................ 367
Cowper & Newton Museum, Buckinghamshire 104
Crabble Corn Mill, Kent ................................ 535
Cragside, Northumberland ............................. 437
Craig Castle, Grampian Highlands ................... 485
Craigdarroch House, SW Scotland .................. 457
Craigieburn Garden, SW Scotland .................. 457
Craigmillar Castle, Edinburgh City,
    Coast & Countryside ................................... 463
Craignethan Castle, Greater Glasgow
    & Clyde Valley .......................................... 468
Craigston Castle, Grampian Highlands ............. 485
Crathes Castle & Garden,
    Grampian Highlands .................................... 485

Cresselly, South Wales .................................. 504
Criccieth Castle, North Wales .................... 497
Crichton Castle, Edinburgh City,
 Coast & Countryside .............................. 463
Croft Castle & Parkland, Herefordshire .......... 340
Crom, Ireland ............................................ 515
Cromer Windmill, Hertfordshire .......... 285 & 534
Cromford Mill, Derbyshire .......................... 526
Cromwell's House, Oliver, Cambridgeshire ...... 273
Crook Hall & Gardens, Co Durham .............. 430
Croome Park, Worcestershire ...................... 369
Crossley Pavilion, Yorkshire ...................... 558
Crossraguel Abbey, SW Scotland .................. 457
Crowe Hall, Somerset .............................. 250
Crown & Nisi Prius Court, Cumbria .............. 524
Crown Bar, The, Ireland ............................ 515
Croxdale Hall, Co Durham ........................ 529
Croxteth Hall & Country Park, Merseyside ...... 424
Cruickshank Botanic Garden,
 Grampian Highlands .............................. 485
Culford School Iron Bridge, Suffolk ..............553
Culham Manor Dovecote, Oxfordshire .......... 549
Cullacott Farmhouse, Cornwall .................... 524
Culross Palace, Perthshire/Fife .................... 475
Culver House, Devon ................................ 216
Culzean Castle, SW Scotland ...................... 457
Custom House, Devon .................... 216 & 528
Cusworth Hall & Park, Yorkshire .................. 388
Cyfarthfa Castle Museum, South Wales .......... 505

## D

Dalemain, Cumbria .................................. 415
Dalgarven Mill Museum, SW Scotland .......... 457
Dallas Dhu Distillery, Grampian Highlands ...... 485
Dalmeny House, Edinburgh City,
 Coast & Countryside .............................. 460
Dam House, Greater Manchester .................. 532
Danson House, Kent ................................ 127
Dartington Hall, Devon ............................ 528
Dartmouth Castle, Devon .......................... 216
Darwin, The Home of Charles, Kent .............. 128
Dawyck Botanic Garden, Borders ................ 450
De Grey Mausoleum, Bedfordshire ................ 271
De la Warr Pavilion, Sussex ........................555
Deal Castle, Kent .................................... 140
Dean Castle Country Park, SW Scotland ........ 457
Deanery, The, Norfolk .............................. 544
Deans Court, Dorset ................................ 229
Deddington Castle, Oxfordshire .................. 156
Deene Park, Northamptonshire .................... 325
Deer Park, Gloucestershire ........................ 531
Delgatie Castle, Grampian Highlands ............ 485
Denbigh Castle, North Wales ...................... 498
Denmans Garden, Sussex .......................... 182
Denny Abbey & The Farmland Museum,
 Cambridgeshire .................................... 273
Derrymore, Ireland .................................. 515
Derwentcote Steel Furnace, Co Durham ........ 430
Devonshire Royal Hospital, Derbyshire .......... 526
Dinefwr, South Wales ................................505
Dirleton Castle & Garden, Edinburgh City,
 Coast & Countryside .............................. 464
Dissenters' Chapel, London ........................ 539
Ditchley Park, Oxfordshire ........................ 156
Divis & The Black Mountain, Ireland .............. 515
Dixon's Chimney, Cumbria ........................ 525
Docton Mill & Garden, Devon .................... 217
Docwra's Manor Garden, Cambridgeshire ...... 273
Doddington Hall & Gardens, Lincolnshire ...... 320
Doddington Place Gardens, Kent.................. 140
Dodington Hall, Somerset .......................... 250
Dolbelydr, North Wales ............................ 498
Dolwyddelan Castle, North Wales ................ 498
Donington-le-Heath Manor House,
 Leics & Rutland .................................... 316
Donnington Castle, Berkshire ...................... 98
Dorfold Hall, Cheshire .............................. 406
Dorney Court, Berkshire ............................ 98
Dorter House, Shropshire .......................... 550
Doune Castle, West Highlands & Islands ........ 480
Doune of Rothiemurchus, The,
 Highlands & Skye .................................. 490

Dove Cottage & The Wordsworth Museum,
 Cumbria ............................................ 415
Dovecote, The, Sussex .............................. 556
Dover Castle & The Secret Wartime
 Tunnels, Kent ...................................... 129
Dover Town Hall, Kent .............................. 535
Downes, Devon ...................................... 217
Dragon Hall, Norfolk ................................ 290
Drawdykes Castle, Cumbria ........................ 525
Drayton House, Northamptonshire ................ 330
Drum Castle & Garden,
 Grampian Highlands .............................. 485
Drumlanrig Castle, SW Scotland .................. 455
Drummond Castle Gardens, Perthshire/Fife .... 471
Drummuir Castle, Grampian Highlands .......... 485
Dryburgh Abbey, Borders .......................... 450
Duart Castle, West Highlands & Islands .......... 481
Ducklake House Wallpainting,
 Hertfordshire ...................................... 534
Dudmaston, Shropshire .................... 346 & 550
Duff House, Grampian Highlands .................. 485
Dulwich College, London .......................... 539
Dumbarton Castle, West Highlands
 & Islands ............................................ 481
Dunblane Cathedral, West Highlands
 & Islands............................................ 481
Duncombe Park, Yorkshire ................ 388 & 545
Dundrennan Abbey, SW Scotland ................ 457
Dunfermline Abbey & Palace,
 Perthshire/Fife .................................... 475
Dunglass Collegiate Church, Edinburgh City,
 Coast & Countryside .............................. 464
Dunham Massey, Cheshire .......................... 406
Dunninald, Perthshire/Fife ..........................475
Dunnottar Castle, Grampian Highlands .......... 486
Dunrobin Castle, Highlands & Skye .............. 490
Duns Castle, Borders ................................ 450
Dunstaffnage Castle, West Highlands
 & Islands ............................................ 481
Dunstanburgh Castle, Northumberland .......... 437
Dunster Castle, Somerset .......................... 251
Dunster Working Watermill, Somerset ............ 251
Dunvegan Castle, Highlands & Skye .............. 489
Durham Castle, Co Durham .............. 431 & 529
Durham Cathedral, Co Durham .................... 431
Dyffryn Gardens and Arboretum,
 South Wales ........................................ 505
Dymchurch Martello Tower, Kent.................. 140
Dyrham Park, Gloucestershire ............ 239 & 531

## E

East Bergholt Place Garden, Suffolk .............. 295
East Riddlesden Hall, Yorkshire .................... 388
Eastbridge Hospital of St Thomas, Kent .......... 140
Eastbury Manor House, London .................... 81
Eastnor Castle, Herefordshire ............ 339 & 533
Easton Walled Gardens, Lincolnshire ............ 321
Ebley Mill, Gloucestershire ........................ 531
Edinburgh Castle, Edinburgh City,
 Coast & Countryside .............................. 464
Edlingham Castle, Northumberland .............. 438
Edmondsham House & Gardens, Dorset ........ 229
Edzell Castle & Garden, Perthshire/Fife .......... 475
Egglestone Abbey, Co Durham .................... 431
Eilean Donan Castle, Highlands & Skye .......... 491
Elcho Castle, Perthshire/Fife ...................... 475
Eleanor Cross, Northamptonshire ................ 330
Elgin Cathedral, Grampian Highlands ............ 486
Eling Tide Mill, Hampshire ........................ 113
Elizabethan Gardens, The, Devon ................ 217
Elmore Court Entrance Gates, Gloucestershire 531
Elton Hall, Cambridgeshire ................ 274 & 522
Elvaston Castle Country Park, Derbyshire ...... 309
Ely Cathedral, Cambridgeshire .................... 274
Emmetts Garden, Kent .............................. 141
Englishcombe Tithe Barn, Somerset ..... 251 & 551
Erasmus Darwin House, Staffordshire ............ 350
Erddig, North Wales ................................ 498
Escomb Church, Co Durham ...................... 431
Escot, Devon .......................................... 217
Eshott Hall, Northumberland ...................... 435
Etal Castle, Northumberland ...................... 438

Eton College, Berkshire .............................. 98
Euston Hall, Suffolk .................................. 295
Exbury Gardens & Steam Railway,
 Hampshire .......................................... 114
Exeter Cathedral, Devon ............................ 217
Eyam Hall, Derbyshire .............................. 310

## F

Fairfax House, Yorkshire ............................ 389
Fairfield, Somerset .......................... 251 & 551
Fairhaven Woodland & Water Garden, Norfolk 290
Falkland Palace, Perthshire/Fife .................... 475
Farfield Friends Meeting House, Yorkshire ...... 558
Farleigh Hungerford Castle, Somerset ............ 251
Farnborough Hall, Warwickshire .......... 364 & 549
Farnham Castle, Surrey .............................. 164
Farnham Castle Keep, Surrey ...................... 164
Feeringbury Manor, Essex .......................... 279
Felbrigg Hall, Norfolk ...................... 291 & 542
Fell Foot Park, Cumbria ............................ 416
Fenton House, London .............................. 82
Ferniehirst Castle, Borders ........................ 451
Fferm, North Wales .................................. 498
Finch Foundry, Devon ...................... 217 & 528
Finchale Priory, Co Durham ........................ 431
Finchcocks, Kent .................................... 141
Firle Place, Sussex .................................. 183
Fishbourne Roman Palace, Sussex ................ 183
Flatford Bridge Cottage, Suffolk .................. 295
Flatford Mill, Willy Lott's House and Flatford
 Bridge Cottage, Suffolk .......................... 554
Floors Castle, Borders .............................. 447
Florence Court, Ireland ............................ 515
Flushing Inn, The, Sussex .......................... 556
Folly Arch, Hertfordshire .......................... 534
Fonmon Castle, South Wales ...................... 506
Ford End Watermill, Buckinghamshire .......... 104
Forde Abbey & Gardens, Dorset .......... 226 & 551
Forge Museum & Victorian Cottage Garden,
 Hertfordshire ...................................... 285
Formby Hall, Merseyside ............................ 542
Former Stockton & Darlington
 Railway Booking Office, Co Durham .......... 529
Fort Brockhurst, Hampshire ........................ 114
Fort George, Highlands & Skye .................... 491
Forty Hall, London .................................. 82
Foundling Museum, The, London .................. 82
Fountains Abbey & Studley Royal, Yorkshire .... 380
Fountains Hall, Yorkshire .......................... 545
Framlingham Castle, Suffolk ...................... 296
Frampton Court, Gloucestershire .................. 239
Frampton Manor, Gloucestershire ................ 239
Frampton Manor Barn, Gloucestershire .......... 531
Franklin House, Benjamin, London ........ 82 & 538
Freeman Mausoleum, Oxfordshire ................ 549
Freemasons Hall, Tyne & Wear .................... 557
Freston Tower, Suffolk ...................... 296 & 554
Friars, The, Kent .................................... 142
Friston Mill, Suffolk ................................ 554
Fulbeck Manor, Lincolnshire ...................... 321
Fulham Palace & Museum, London ................ 82
Fulham Palace Stableyard Wall, London .......... 540
Furness Abbey, Cumbria ............................ 416
Fursdon House, Devon .............................. 217
Furzey Gardens, Hampshire ........................ 114
Fydell House Gates, Piers & Railings,
 Lincolnshire ........................................ 537
Fyvie Castle, Grampian Highlands ................ 486

## G

Gainsborough Old Hall, Lincolnshire .............. 321
Gainsborough's House, Suffolk .................... 296
Garden House, The, Devon ........................ 217
Gardens of Easton Lodge, Essex .................. 280
Garrick's Temple, London .......................... 540
Gatcombe Court, Somerset ........................ 251
Gawsworth Hall, Cheshire .......................... 406
Gawthorpe Hall, Lancashire .............. 421 & 536
Geffrye Museum, The, London .................... 83
Georgian House, The, Edinburgh City,
 Coast & Countryside .............................. 464
Georgian House, The, Somerset .................... 251
Georgian Theatre Royal, The, Yorkshire .......... 389

Giant's Causeway, Ireland ..................... 515
Gibside, Tyne & Wear ........................... 442
Giggleswick School Chapel, Yorkshire ........... 545
Gilbert White's House & The Oates Museum,
    Hampshire ..................................... 114
Gilnockie Tower, SW Scotland ................... 457
Gladstone's Land, Edinburgh City,
    Coast & Countryside .......................... 464
Glamis Castle, Perthshire/Fife ................. 472
Glasgow Cathedral, Greater
    Glasgow & Clyde Valley ....................... 468
Glastonbury Abbey, Somerset .................... 252
Glastonbury Tor, Somerset ...................... 252
Glastonbury Tribunal, Somerset ................. 252
Glendurgan Garden, Cornwall .................... 203
Gleneagles, Perthshire/Fife .................... 475
Glenluce Abbey, SW Scotland .................... 457
Glenwhan Gardens, SW Scotland .................. 457
Gloucester Cathedral, Gloucestershire .......... 239
Glynde Place, Sussex ..................... 183 & 555
Goddards, Surrey ............................... 165
Godolphin, Cornwall ...................... 203 & 524
Godolphin Blowinghouse, Cornwall ............... 204
Goodnestone Park Gardens, Kent ................. 142
Goodrich Castle, Worcestershire ................ 369
Goodwood House, Sussex ......................... 172
Gorhambury, Hertfordshire ...................... 285
Gosford House, Edinburgh City,
    Coast & Countryside .......................... 465
Grand Theatre, Lancashire ...................... 536
Grange, The, Kent ...................... 142 & 536
Gray's Printing Press, Ireland ................. 515
Great Chalfield Manor & Gardens, Wiltshire ... 262
Great Comp Garden, Kent ........................ 142
Great Coxwell Barn, Oxfordshire ................ 156
Great Dixter House & Gardens, Sussex . 184 & 555
Great Dunmow Maltings, Essex ................... 530
Great Fosters, Surrey .......................... 165
Great Hall, Surrey ............................. 555
Great Hall & Queen Eleanor's Garden,
    Hampshire .................................... 115
Great House Farm, Somerset ..................... 551
Great Yarmouth Row Houses
    & Greyfriars' Cloisters, Norfolk ............. 291
Greenway, Devon ................................ 218
Greyfriars, The, Worcestershire ................ 369
Greys Court, Oxfordshire ....................... 156
Greywalls, Edinburgh City,
    Coast & Countryside .......................... 465
Grime's Graves, Norfolk ........................ 291
Grimsthorpe Castle, Park & Gardens, Lincs ..... 318
Groombridge Place Gardens, Kent ................ 130
Guildford House Gallery, Surrey ................ 165
Guildhall Gallery, Hampshire ................... 115
Gunby Hall, Lincolnshire ....................... 321
Gunnersbury Park & Museum, London ............. 83
Gunnersbury Park Temple, London ................ 540
Gwydir Castle, North Wales ..................... 498

# H

Hackney Empire, London ......................... 540
Haddo House, Grampian Highlands ................ 486
Haddon Hall, Derbyshire ........................ 305
Haddonstone Show Gardens,
    Northamptonshire ............................. 330
Hadleigh Guildhall, Suffolk .................... 296
Hafod, North Wales ............................. 498
Hagley Hall, West Midlands ..................... 366
Hailes Abbey, Gloucestershire .................. 239
Hailes Castle, Edinburgh City,
    Coast & Countryside .......................... 465
Haldon Belvedere/Lawrence Castle,
    Devon .................................. 218 & 528
Hales Hall Barn, Norfolk ....................... 543
Hall Barn Gothic Temple, Buckinghamshire ..... 521
Hall Farm High Barn, Somerset .................. 551
Hall i'th'Wood, Lancashire ............... 421 & 532
Hall Place & Gardens, Kent...................... 131
Halliwell's House Museum, Borders .............. 451
Halston Chapel, Shropshire ..................... 550
Halswell House, Somerset ....................... 252
Ham House & Garden, London ..................... 83
Hammerwood Park, Sussex ........................ 184

Hampton Court Palace, Surrey ................... 165
Hamptworth Lodge, Wiltshire .................... 263
Hamstall Hall, Staffordshire ................... 553
Hamsteels Hall, Co Durham ...................... 529
Hanbury Hall, Worcestershire ............. 370 & 560
Handel House Museum, London .................... 84
Harding House, Lincolnshire .................... 537
Hardknott Roman Fort, Cumbria .................. 416
Hardstoft Herb Garden, Derbyshire .............. 310
Hardwick Hall, Gardens, Park
    & Stainsby Mill, Derbyshire ........... 310 & 526
Hardwick Old Hall, Derbyshire .................. 311
Hardy's Cottage, Dorset ........................ 229
Hare Hill, Cheshire ............................ 406
Harelaw Farmhouse, Edinburgh City,
    Coast & Countryside .......................... 465
Harewood House, Yorkshire ............... 381 & 558
Harlaxton Manor, Lincolnshire .................. 538
Harlech Castle, North Wales .................... 499
Harrowden Hall Garden Statues,
    Northamptonshire ............................. 547
Hartland Abbey, Devon .......................... 218
Hartlebury Castle, Worcestershire .............. 370
Hartsheath, North Wales ........................ 499
Harvington Hall, Worcestershire ................ 371
Harwich Redoubt Fort, Essex ..............280 & 530
Hatchlands Park/Clandon Park, Surrey ........... 160
Hatfield House, Hertfordshire .................. 283
Haughley Park, Suffolk ......................... 296
Haughmond Abbey, Shropshire .................... 346
Hawford Dovecote, Worcestershire ...... 371 & 560
Hawkstone Hall & Gardens, Shropshire .......... 346
Heath House, The, Staffordshire ................ 351
Heaton Hall, Lancashire ........................ 421
Heaton Park Temple, Greater Manchester ........ 532
Heckington Windmill, Lincolnshire .............. 321
Heggy's Cottage, Lincolnshire .................. 538
Hellens, Herefordshire ......................... 340
Helmingham Hall Gardens, Suffolk ............... 297
Helmsley Castle, Yorkshire ..................... 389
Helmsley Walled Garden, Yorkshire .............. 390
Hemerdon House, Devon .......................... 218
Hemingsby, Wiltshire ........................... 559
Hemyock Castle, Devon .......................... 218
Hereford Cathedral, Herefordshire .............. 341
Hergest Court, Herefordshire ............. 341 & 534
Hergest Croft Gardens, Herefordshire........... 341
Hermitage Castle, Borders ...................... 451
Herne Windmill, Kent ........................... 535
Heron Corn Mill & Museum
    of Papermaking, Cumbria ...................... 416
Herstmonceux Castle Gardens, Sussex ........... 184
Herterton House Gardens, Northumberland ... 438
Hertford Museum, Hertfordshire ................. 285
Hestercombe Gardens, Somerset .................. 253
Hever Castle & Gardens, Kent ................... 132
Hezlett House & Farmyard, Ireland .............. 516
Hickleton Hall, Yorkshire ...................... 552
Hidcote Manor Garden, Gloucestershire ......... 240
High Beeches Woodland & Water Gardens,
    Sussex .................................. 185 & 555
High Level Bridge, Tyne & Wear ................. 557
High Staward Farm, Northumberland .............. 547
Highclere Castle & Gardens, Hampshire.......... 110
Highcliffe Castle, Dorset ............... 230 & 529
Highdown Gardens, Sussex ....................... 185
Higher Flax Mills, Somerset .................... 551
Higher Melcombe, Dorset ........................ 230
Highfields, Cheshire ........................... 523
Highpoint, London .............................. 540
Hill House, The, West Highlands & Islands ..... 482
Hill of Tarvit Mansionhouse, Perthshire/Fife ... 475
Hill Top, Cumbria .............................. 416
Hiller Garden, The, Warwickshire ............... 364
Himalaya Palace Cinema
    (formerly Liberty Cinema), London ............ 540
Hinton Ampner, Hampshire ....................... 116
Hirsel Gardens, Country Park
    & Homestead Museum, The, Borders ......... 451
Historic Dockyard, Chatham, The, Kent .......... 143
Hodnet Hall Gardens, Shropshire ................ 346
Hodsock Priory Gardens, Nottinghamshire ...... 334
Hogarth's House, London ........................ 84
Hoghton Tower, Lancashire ...................... 422

Holburne Museum of Art, Somerset .............. 253
Holdenby House, Northamptonshire ............... 331
Hole Park Gardens, Kent ........................ 143
Holehird Gardens, Cumbria ...................... 416
Holker Hall & Gardens, Cumbria ................. 417
Holkham Hall, Norfolk .......................... 287
Holkham Hall Vinery, Norfolk ................... 543
Holme Pierrepont Hall, Nottinghamshire ........ 334
Holmston Hall Barn, Cheshire ................... 406
Holnicote Estate, Somerset ..................... 253
Holst Birthplace Museum, Gloucestershire ...... 240
Honeywood Heritage Centre, London ............. 84
Honington Hall, Warwickshire ................... 364
Hopetoun House, Edinburgh City,
    Coast & Countryside .......................... 461
Hopton Court Conservatory, Worcestershire ... 560
Horton Court, Gloucestershire .................. 240
Hospital of the Holy and Undivided
    Trinity, Shropshire .......................... 550
Houghton Hall, Norfolk ......................... 292
Houghton House, Bedfordshire ................... 271
Houghton Lodge Gardens, Hampshire .. 116 & 533
Hound Tor Deserted Medieval
    Village, Devon ............................... 218
House Mill, The, London ........................ 541
House of Dun, Perthshire/Fife .................. 475
House of the Binns, Edinburgh City,
    Coast & Countryside .......................... 465
Housesteads Roman Fort, Northumberland ... 438
Hoveton Hall Gardens, Norfolk .................. 292
Hovingham Hall, Yorkshire ............... 390 & 545
Huddersfield Station, Yorkshire ................ 558
Hughenden Manor, Buckinghamshire.............. 105
Huntingtower Castle, Perthshire/Fife ........... 475
Huntly Castle, Grampian Highlands .............. 486
Hurst Castle, Hampshire ........................ 116
Hutton-in-the-Forest, Cumbria .................. 417
Hylands House, Essex .................... 280 & 530

# I

Ickworth House & Park, Suffolk .......... 297 & 554
Ightham Mote, Kent........................ 133 & 535
Inchcolm Abbey, Perthshire/Fife ................ 475
Inchmahome Priory, West Highlands & Islands . 482
India Mill Chimney, Lancashire ................. 536
Ingatestone Hall, Essex ........................ 280
Inveraray Castle, West Highlands & Islands ..... 479
Inveraray Jail, West Highlands & Islands........... 482
Iona Abbey & Nunnery, West Highlands
    & Islands .................................... 482
Iron Bridge, Shropshire ........................ 346
Iscoyd Park, North Wales ....................... 499
Island Hall, Cambridgeshire .................... 274
Ivy Conduit, Surrey ............................ 555
Izaak Walton's Cottage, Staffordshire ..........351

# J

Jackfield Tile Museum & Factory, Shropshire ... 550
Jacob's Almshouse Chapel,
    Sir John, Cambridgeshire ..................... 522
Japanese Garden & Bonsai Nursery, The,
    Cornwall ..................................... 204
Jarlshof Prehistoric & Norse
    Settlement, Outer Islands .................... 492
Jedburgh Abbey, Borders ........................ 452
Jefferies Farmhouse and Museum,
    Richard, Oxfordshire ......................... 156
Jervaulx Abbey, Yorkshire ............... 390 & 545
Jewel Tower, London ............................ 84
Jews' Court, Lincolnshire ...................... 538
Johnson's House, Dr, London ............. 84 & 539
Judge's Lodging, The, South Wales .............. 506

# K

Keats House, London ............................ 84
Kedleston Hall, Derbyshire .............. 306 & 526
Kelburn Castle & Country Centre,
    South West Scotland .......................... 458
Kellie Castle & Garden, Perthshire/Fife ........ 476
Kelmarsh Hall, Northamptonshire ............... 326
Kelmscott Manor, Gloucestershire ............... 240
Ken Caro Gardens, Cornwall..................... 204

Kenilworth Castle, Warwickshire ...................... 365
Kensington Palace, London .............................. 85
Kentsford, Somerset ......................................... 253
Kentwell Hall & Gardens, Suffolk .................... 297
Kenwood, London ............................................. 73
Kew Bridge Steam Museum, London ............ 540
Kew Gardens, Surrey ....................................... 166
Kew Palace, Surrey .......................................... 166
Kidwelly Castle, South Wales .......................... 506
Kiftsgate Court Gardens, Gloucestershire ....... 241
Kilchurn Castle, West Highlands & Islands ...... 482
Kildrummy Castle, Grampian Highlands ......... 486
Kildrummy Castle Garden,
         Grampian Highlands .................................. 486
Killerton House & Garden, Devon ................... 219
Killyleagh Castle, Ireland ................................. 516
Kiln Warehouse, Nottinghamshire ................... 548
Kilworthy Farm Cow Houses & Granary,
         Devon ...................................................... 528
Kimberley Hall, Norfolk ................................... 292
Kimbolton Castle, Cambridgeshire .................. 275
King John's House & Heritage Centre,
         Hampshire ............................................... 117
King John's Hunting Lodge, Somerset ............ 253
King's Head, The, Buckinghamshire ............... 105
King's House, The, Wiltshire ........................... 263
King's Lynn Custom House, Norfolk ............... 543
Kingston Bagpuize House, Oxfordshire ........... 157
Kingston Lacy, Dorset ..................................... 227
Kingston Maurward Garden, Dorset .............. 230
Kinver Edge and the Rockhouses,
         West Midlands .......................................... 368
Kiplin Hall, Yorkshire ...................................... 390
Kirby Hall, Northamptonshire .......................... 331
Kirby Muxloe Castle, Leics & Rutland ............. 316
Kirkby Hall Wallpaintings, Cumbria ................ 525
Kirkham Priory, Yorkshire ............................... 390
Kirkstall Abbey, Yorkshire ............................... 558
Kisimul Castle, Outer Islands .......................... 492
Knaresborough Castle & Museum,
         Yorkshire .................................................. 390
Knebworth House, Hertfordshire .......... 284 & 534
Knightshayes Court, Devon ............................. 219
Knole, Kent .................................................... 134
Knoll Gardens & Nursery, Dorset ................... 231
Kyme Tower, Lincolnshire ............................... 538

**L**

LSO St Luke's UBS & LSO
         Music Education Centre, London ...... 85 & 540
Lacock Abbey, Fox Talbot Museum
         & Village, Wiltshire ......................... 263 & 559
Lady Margaret Hungerford Almshouses,
         Wiltshire .................................................. 559
Lady Waterford Hall & Murals,
         Northumberland ........................................ 438
Lady's Well, Northumberland ........................... 547
Lamb House, Sussex .......................... 185 & 555
Lambley Viaduct, Northumberland ................... 547
Lamphey Bishop's Palace, South Wales .......... 506
Lamport Hall & Gardens, Northamptonshire ... 332
Lancin Farmhouse, Somerset .......................... 552
Landguard Fort, Suffolk ................................... 298
Landmark Arts Centre, London ....................... 540
Lanercost Priory, Cumbria .............................. 417
Langley Chapel, Shropshire ............................. 346
Langley Gatehouse, Shropshire ....................... 550
Langstone Court, Herefordshire ...................... 341
Lanhydrock, Cornwall ...................................... 201
Larmer Tree Gardens, Wiltshire ........... 263 & 560
Lathom House, Lancashire .............................. 536
Laugharne Castle, South Wales ...................... 506
Launceston Castle, Cornwall ........................... 204
Lavenham: The Guildhall of Corpus Christi,
         Suffolk ..................................................... 298
Lawrence Castle/Haldon Belvedere,
         Devon .............................................. 218 & 528
Lawrence Heritage, D H, Nottinghamshire ...... 334
Lawrence House, Cornwall .............................. 204
Laxton Hall, Northamptonshire ....................... 547
Layer Marney Tower, Essex ............................ 281
Leadenham House, Lincolnshire ...................... 321
Ledston Hall, Yorkshire ................................... 390

Leeds Castle, Kent ......................................... 135
Leigh Court Barn, Worcestershire ................... 371
Leighton Hall, Lancashire ..................... 420 & 536
Leighton House Museum, London .................... 86
Leiston Abbey, Suffolk .................................... 298
Leith Hall & Garden, Grampian Highlands ...... 486
Leith Hill, Surrey ............................................ 166
Lennoxlove House, Edinburgh City,
         Coast & Countryside ................................ 465
Leonardslee Lakes & Gardens, Sussex ........... 173
Lesnes Abbey, Kent ....................................... 143
Letheringsett Watermill, Norfolk ..................... 293
Levens Hall, Cumbria .......................... 412 & 525
Lewes Castle & Barbican House Museum,
         Sussex ..................................................... 185
Liberton House, Edinburgh City,
         Coast & Countryside ................................ 466
Lickleyhead Castle, Grampian Highlands ........ 486
Lilleshall Abbey, Shropshire ............................ 346
Lincoln Castle, Lincolnshire .................. 321 & 538
Lincoln Cathedral, Lincolnshire ....................... 321
Lincoln Medieval Bishops' Palace, Lincolnshire  322
Lindisfarne Castle, Northumberland ..... 438 & 547
Lindisfarne Priory, Northumberland ................ 439
Lindley Murray Summerhouse, The,
         Yorkshire ......................................... 391 & 546
Ling Beeches Garden, Yorkshire ..................... 391
Linley Sambourne House, London ................... 86
Linlithgow Palace, Edinburgh City,
         Coast & Countryside ................................ 466
Little Harle Tower, Northumberland ................ 547
Little Holland House, London .......................... 87
Little Malvern Court, Worcestershire .............. 371
Little Moreton Hall, Cheshire ......................... 407
Liverpool Cathedral, Merseyside ..................... 424
Liverpool Collegiate Apartments,
         Merseyside .............................................. 542
Liverpool Metropolitan Cathedral of Christ
         the King, Merseyside ............................... 424
Llancaiach Fawr Manor, South Wales ............ 506
Llanerchaeron, South Wales ........................... 506
Llanvihangel Court, South Wales .................... 506
Lochleven Castle, Perthshire/Fife ................... 476
Lodge Park & Sherborne Estate,
         Gloucestershire ....................................... 241
Logan Botanic Garden, SW Scotland .............. 458
Long Crendon Courthouse, Buckinghamshire . 105
Longleat, Wiltshire ......................................... 259
Longley Old Hall, Yorkshire ............................ 391
Longner Hall, Shropshire ................................ 346
Longthorpe Tower, Cambridgeshire ................ 275
Longtown Castle, Herefordshire ...................... 341
Lord Leycester Hospital, Warwickshire .. 365 & 557
Lord Mayor's Chapel, Somerset ...................... 521
Loseley Park, Surrey ...................................... 162
Lost Gardens of Heligan, The, Cornwall ......... 204
Lotherton Hall & Gardens, Yorkshire .............. 391
Loton Hall, Shropshire ................................... 550
Loughwood Meeting House, Devon ................. 220
Low Butterby Farmhouse, Co Durham ........... 530
Lower Brockhampton, Worcestershire ............. 560
Lower Severalls, Somerset .............................. 254
Ludlow Castle, Shropshire .............................. 347
Lullingstone Castle, Kent ............................... 143
Lullingstone Roman Villa, Kent ...................... 143
Lulworth Castle & Park, Dorset ...................... 231
Lyddington Bede House, Leics & Rutland ........ 316
Lyceum Theatre, The, Yorkshire ..................... 552
Lydford Castle & Saxon Town, Devon ............. 220
Lydiard Park, Wiltshire ........................ 264 & 560
Lyme Park, Cheshire ...................................... 407
Lynton Town Hall, Devon ............................... 528
Lytes Cary Manor, Somerset .......................... 254
Lyth, The, Shropshire .................................... 551
Lyveden New Bield, Northamptonshire ........... 332

**M**

MacLellan's Castle, SW Scotland .................... 458
Madingley Post Mill, Cambridgeshire .............. 522
Madresfield Court, Worcestershire .................. 371
Maeshowe, Outer Islands ............................... 492
Maison Dieu, Kent.......................................... 144
Maister House, Yorkshire ................................ 545

Malthouse, Staffordshire ................................ 553
Manchester Cathedral, Lancashire .................. 422
Manchester Law Library,
         Greater Manchester ................................. 532
Manderston, Borders ...................................... 448
Mannington Gardens & Countryside,
         Norfolk .................................................... 293
Manor Farmhouse, Hampshire ....................... 533
Manor, Hemingford Grey,
         Cambridgeshire ............................... 275 & 523
Mapledurham House & Watermill,
         Oxfordshire ............................................. 157
Mapperton, Dorset ........................................ 231
Mappin Terrace Café, London ........................ 540
Marble Hill House, London ............................. 87
Markenfield Hall, Yorkshire ................... 391 & 545
Marker's Cottage, Devon ............................... 220
Marks Hall Gardens & Arboretum, Essex ........ 281
Marlipins Museum, Sussex ............................. 185
Marske Hall, Cleveland ................................... 545
Marston Hall, Lincolnshire .............................. 322
Martholme, Lancashire ................................... 422
Martyrs' Memorial, Oxfordshire ...................... 549
Marwood Hill, Devon ...................................... 220
Masson Mills, Derbyshire ............................... 527
Maunsel House, Somerset .............................. 254
Mawley Hall, Shropshire ................................ 347
Max Gate, Dorset .......................................... 231
Medieval Merchants House, Hampshire........... 117
Megginch Castle Gardens, Perthshire/Fife ...... 476
Melbourne Hall & Gardens, Derbyshire .......... 311
Melford Hall, Suffolk ...................................... 298
Mellerstain House, Borders ............................ 452
Melrose Abbey, Borders ................................. 452
Meols Hall, Merseyside .................................. 424
Merchant's House, Wiltshire .............. 264 & 560
Merriments Gardens, Sussex .......................... 186
Mertoun House, Borders ................................ 453
Michelham Priory, Sussex .............................. 186
Middleham Castle, Yorkshire .......................... 391
Middleport Pottery, Staffordshire ................... 553
Middleton Hall, Warwickshire ......................... 365
Milton Abbey Church, Dorset ......................... 232
Milton Chantry, Kent ..................................... 144
Milton Lodge Gardens, Somerset .................... 254
Milton Manor House, Oxfordshire ................... 157
Milton's Cottage, John, Buckinghamshire ....... 105
Minster Lovell Hall & Dovecote, Oxfordshire ... 158
Minster Precincts, Cambridgeshire .................. 522
Minterne Gardens, Dorset .............................. 232
Mirehouse, Cumbria ...................................... 417
Mistley Towers, Essex .................................... 281
Mitford Hall Camellia House,
         Northumberland ....................................... 547
Moggerhanger Park, Bedfordshire .................. 271
Molineux Hotel, West Midlands ...................... 557
Mompesson House, Wiltshire ......................... 264
Monk's House, Sussex .................................... 186
Monksthorpe Chapel, Lincolnshire .................. 538
Montacute House, Somerset .......................... 254
Monteviot House Gardens, Borders ................ 453
Monzie Castle, Perthshire/Fife ....................... 476
Morden Hall Park, London .............................. 87
Moreton Corbet Castle, Shropshire ................ 347
Moreton Hall, Suffolk ..................................... 554
Morris Gallery, William, London ...................... 87
Morton Manor, Isle of Wight .......................... 193
Morville Hall, Shropshire ................................ 347
Morwellham Quay, Devon ............................... 220
Moseley Old Hall, Staffordshire ...................... 351
Motherwell Heritage Centre, Greater Glasgow
         & Clyde Valley .......................................... 468
Mottisfont Abbey & Garden, Hampshire.......... 117
Mottistone Manor Garden, Isle of Wight ........ 193
Mount Edgcumbe House & Country Park,
         Cornwall .................................................. 204
Mount Ephraim Gardens, Kent ....................... 144
Mount Grace Priory, Yorkshire ....................... 391
Mount Stewart, Ireland .................................. 516
Mount Stuart, West Highlands & Islands ........ 482
Mowbray Point, Yorkshire .............................. 545
Muchelney Abbey, Somerset .......................... 254
Muncaster Castle Gardens, Owl Centre
         & MeadowVole Maze, Cumbria ...... 413 & 525

Munnings Art Museum, Sir Alfred, Essex ........ 281
Museum of Costume & Assembly Rooms,
    Somerset ............................................. 246
Mussenden Temple & Downhill Demesne,
    Ireland ............................................... 516
Myddelton House Gardens, London ............... 87

## N

National Botanic Garden of Wales, The,
    South Wales ....................................... 507
National Centre for Early Music,
    Yorkshire ................................. 391 & 545
National Coal Mining Museum for England,
    Yorkshire ............................................ 559
Needles Old Battery, Isle of Wight ............... 194
Ness Botanic Gardens, Cheshire ................... 407
Nether Alderley Mill, Cheshire ..................... 407
Nether Winchendon House, Buckinghamshire .. 105
Netherwitton Hall, Northumberland .............. 547
Netley Abbey, Hampshire ............................. 117
New Abbey Corn Mill, SW Scotland .............. 458
New Lanark World Heritage Site,
    Greater Glasgow & Clyde Valley .............. 468
Newark Castle, Greater Glasgow
    & Clyde Valley ................................... 468
Newark Park, Gloucestershire ............. 241 & 531
Newark Town Hall, Nottinghamshire ............. 335
Newburgh Priory, Yorkshire ......................... 392
Newby Hall & Gardens, Yorkshire ................. 382
Newcastle Castle Keep, Tyne & Wear ........... 442
Newhouse, Wiltshire ................................... 264
Newliston, Edinburgh City,
    Coast & Countryside ............................ 466
Newstead Abbey, Nottinghamshire ................ 335
Newtown Old Town Hall, Isle of Wight ......... 194
Niddry Castle, Edinburgh City,
    Coast & Countryside ............................ 466
Norham Castle, Northumberland ................... 439
Norrington Manor, Wiltshire ........................ 265
North Lees Hall, Derbyshire ......................... 527
Northampton Cathedral, Northamptonshire ... 332
Northington Grange, Hampshire .................... 117
Norton Conyers, Yorkshire ................. 392 & 546
Norton Priory Museum & Gardens, Cheshire .. 407
Norwich Castle Museum & Art Gallery,
    Norfolk .............................................. 293
Nostell Priory & Parklands, Yorkshire .... 392 & 559
Nottingham Castle, Nottinghamshire ............. 335
Nunney Castle, Somerset ............................. 255
Nunnington Hall, Yorkshire .......................... 392
Nunwell House & Gardens, Isle of Wight ...... 194
Nurstead Court, Kent ................................. 144
Nymans Garden, Sussex .............................. 186

## O

Oakham Castle, Leics & Rutland ................... 316
Oakhurst Cottage, Surrey ............................ 166
Oakley Hall, Shropshire .............................. 342
Octagon, The, Orleans House Gallery,
    London ....................................... 87 & 540
Okehampton Castle, Devon ......................... 220
Old Bishop's Palace, The, Wiltshire .............. 560
Old Buckenham Cornmill, Norfolk ................. 543
Old Campden House, Gloucestershire ............ 241
Old Church Tower of All Saints, The,
    Hertfordshire ...................................... 534
Old Clockhouse, Hertfordshire ..................... 535
Old Friends Meeting House, Essex ................ 530
Old Gala House, Borders .............................. 453
Old Gorhambury House, Hertfordshire ........... 285
Old Grammar School, Greater Manchester .... 532
Old Hall, Norfolk ....................................... 543
Old Mansion, The, Shropshire ...................... 551
Old Market Hall, Shropshire ........................ 550
Old Palace, The, Cambridgeshire .................. 523
Old Quay Head, Devon ............................... 528
Old Rectory Dovecote, The, Oxfordshire ....... 549
Old Sarum, Wiltshire .................................. 265
Old Soar Manor, Kent ................................ 144
Old Sufton, Herefordshire ........................... 341
Old Warden Park, Bedfordshire .................... 521
Old Wardour Castle, Wiltshire ..................... 265

Oldway Mansion, Devon .............................. 220
Orchard Wyndham, Somerset ....................... 255
Orford Castle, Suffolk ................................. 299
Ormesby Hall, Yorkshire ..................... 392 & 546
Orthwaite Hall Barn, Cumbria ...................... 525
Osborne House, Isle of Wight ...................... 192
Osterley Park & House, London ..................... 88
Otley Hall, Suffolk ..................................... 299
Ouse Valley Viaduct, Sussex ........................ 555
Overbeck's, Devon ..................................... 220
Owletts, Kent ........................................... 144
Owlpen Manor, Gloucestershire .................... 242
Oxburgh Hall & Estate, Norfolk ............. 293 & 543
Oxwich Castle, South Wales ......................... 507

## P

Packwood House, Warwickshire ..................... 356
Painshill Park, Surrey ........................ 163 & 555
Painswick Rococo Garden, Gloucestershire ..... 242
Painted Room, The, Herefordshire ................ 534
Palace of Holyroodhouse & The Queen's Gallery,
    Edinburgh City, Coast & Countryside ........ 462
Palace of Westminster, London ...................... 88
Pallant House Gallery, Sussex ....................... 187
Papplewick Hall, Nottinghamshire ................. 335
Parcevall Hall Gardens, Yorkshire ................. 392
Parham House & Gardens, Sussex ........ 187 & 556
Pashley Manor Gardens, Sussex .................... 174
Patterson's Spade Mill, Ireland ..................... 516
Pavilion Gardens, Derbyshire ....................... 307
Paxton House, Gallery & Country Park,
    Borders .............................................. 453
Paycocke's, Essex ...................................... 281
Peckover House & Garden, Cambridgeshire .... 275
Pembroke Castle, South Wales ..................... 507
Pencarrow, Cornwall ......................... 205 & 524
Pendennis Castle, Cornwall .......................... 205
Penrhyn Castle, North Wales ....................... 499
Penrith Castle, Cumbria .............................. 418
Penshurst Place & Gardens, Kent ........ 136 & 536
Peover Hall, Cheshire ................................. 407
Percy House, Cumbria ................................. 525
Perrott's Folly, West Midlands ...................... 557
Peterborough Cathedral, Cambridgeshire ....... 275
Peto Garden at Iford Manor, The, Wiltshire .... 265
Petworth Cottage Museum, Sussex ............... 187
Petworth House & Park, Sussex ........... 175 & 556
Pevensey Castle, Sussex .............................. 188
Peveril Castle, Derbyshire ........................... 311
Pickering Castle, Yorkshire .......................... 392
Picton Castle, South Wales .......................... 508
Pine Lodge Gardens & Nursery, Cornwall ...... 205
Pitmedden Garden, Grampian Highlands ........ 486
Pitstone Windmill, Buckinghamshire .............. 106
Pitzhanger Manor-House, London .......... 88 & 540
Plas Brondanw Gardens, North Wales ........... 499
Plas Mawr, North Wales .............................. 499
Plas Newydd, North Wales .......................... 499
Plas yn Rhiw, North Wales .......................... 500
Pleasley Colliery, Nottinghamshire ................ 548
Plumpton Rocks, Yorkshire .......................... 393
Pluscarden Abbey, Grampian Highlands ......... 486
Polesden Lacey, Surrey ............................... 167
Polesworth Nunnery Gateway, Warwickshire .. 557
Pollok House, Greater Glasgow & Clyde Valley 469
Pontefract Old Town Hall & Assembly Rooms,
    Yorkshire ............................................ 559
Portchester Castle, Hampshire ..................... 118
Porth-en-Alls Lodge, Cornwall ..................... 524
Portland Castle, Dorset ............................... 232
Portmeirion, North Wales ............................ 500
Portsmouth Cathedral, Hampshire ................. 118
Portsmouth Heritage (Buckingham House
    & Wymering Manor), Hampshire .............. 111
Powderham Castle, Devon ........................... 221
Powis Castle & Garden, North Wales ............. 500
Pradoe, Shropshire .................................... 550
Prebendal Manor, The, Northamptonshire ...... 332
Preen Manor Gardens, Shropshire ................. 348
Preston Manor, Sussex ............................... 188
Preston Mill, Edinburgh City,
    Coast & Countryside ............................ 466
Preston Tower, Northumberland ................... 439

Prideaux Place, Cornwall ............................. 206
Priest House, The, Sussex ........................... 188
Priest's House, Somerset ............................. 255
Prior Crauden's Chapel, Cambridgeshire ........ 522
Prior Park College Old Gymnasium,
    Somerset ............................................ 552
Prior Park Landscape Garden, Somerset ........ 255
Prior Slee Gatehouse, Cumbria .................... 525
Prior's Hall Barn, Essex .............................. 282
Prior's Tower, Cumbria ............................... 525
Priory Church of the Order of St John,
    London .............................................. 541
Priory Cottages, Oxfordshire ....................... 158
Provender, Kent ........................................ 536
Provost Skene's House, Grampian Highlands .. 487
Prudhoe Castle, Northumberland .................. 439
Puslinch, Devon ........................................ 221

## Q

Quarry Bank Mill & Styal Estate, Cheshire ....... 408
Quebec House, Kent ................................... 145
Queen Street Mill, Lancashire ...................... 536
Queen's Chapel of the Savoy, London ........... 541
Queen's Hall, Cambridgeshire ...................... 522
Quenby Hall, Leicestershire & Rutland .......... 314
Quex Museum, House & Gardens,
    The Powell-Cotton Collection, Kent........... 145

## R

RAF Holmpton – Bunker Tours, Yorkshire ........ 393
RHS Garden Harlow Carr, Yorkshire .............. 393
RHS Garden Hyde Hall, Essex ...................... 282
RHS Garden Rosemoor, Devon ..................... 221
RHS Garden Wisley, Surrey ......................... 167
Raby Castle, Co Durham ............................. 429
Raglan Castle, South Wales ......................... 508
Ragley Hall & Gardens, Warwickshire ... 357 & 557
Rainham Hall, London ................................. 541
Rammerscales, SW Scotland ........................ 458
Ramster Gardens, Surrey ............................ 168
Raveningham Gardens, Norfolk .................... 294
Rearsby Packhorse Bridge, Lancashire ........... 537
Rectory Farm Barn, Co Durham .................... 530
Reculver Towers & Roman Fort, Kent ............ 145
Red House, London ...................................... 88
Red House Glasscone, West Midlands ............ 557
Red Row, Edinburgh City,
    Coast & Countryside ............................ 466
Regan House, Gloucestershire ...................... 531
Renishaw Hall Gardens, Derbyshire ............... 312
Restoration House, Kent .............................. 146
Restormel Castle, Cornwall ......................... 206
Rhuddlan Castle, North Wales ...................... 500
Ribblehead Viaduct, Yorkshire ..................... 546
Richborough Roman Fort, Kent ..................... 146
Richmond Castle, Yorkshire ......................... 393
Richmond Weir & Lock, London .................... 541
Rievaulx Abbey, Yorkshire ........................... 394
Rievaulx Terrace & Temples, Yorkshire ........... 394
Ring of Brodgar Stone Circle & Henge,
    Outer Islands ...................................... 492
Ripley Castle, Yorkshire .............................. 383
Ripon Cathedral, Yorkshire .......................... 394
Riverhill House, Kent .................................. 146
Robin Hood's Hut, Somerset ........................ 255
Roche Abbey, Yorkshire .............................. 394
Rochester Castle, Kent ................................ 146
Rochester Cathedral, Kent ........................... 146
Rockingham Castle, Northamptonshire ........... 327
Rode Hall, Cheshire ........................... 408 & 523
Rodmarton Manor, Gloucestershire ............... 242
Rokeby Park, Co Durham ............................ 431
Roman Baths & Pump Room, Somerset .......... 247
Roman Painted House, Kent ......................... 146
Rose Building, John, Shropshire .................... 550
Rotherwas Chapel, Herefordshire .................. 341
Rothesay Castle, West Highlands & Islands ..... 482
Rothschild Zoological Museum,
    The Walter, Herts ................................ 285
Rotunda Temple, Sussex ............................. 556
Round Chapel, The (Clapton Park United
    Reformed Church), London ..................... 541